Short Story Criticism

Guide to Gale Literary Criticism Series

For criticism on	Consult these Gale series
Authors now living or who died after December 31, 1999	*CONTEMPORARY LITERARY CRITICISM (CLC)*
Authors who died between 1900 and 1999	*TWENTIETH-CENTURY LITERARY CRITICISM (TCLC)*
Authors who died between 1800 and 1899	*NINETEENTH-CENTURY LITERATURE CRITICISM (NCLC)*
Authors who died between 1400 and 1799	*LITERATURE CRITICISM FROM 1400 TO 1800 (LC)* *SHAKESPEAREAN CRITICISM (SC)*
Authors who died before 1400	*CLASSICAL AND MEDIEVAL LITERATURE CRITICISM (CMLC)*
Authors of books for children and young adults	*CHILDREN'S LITERATURE REVIEW (CLR)*
Dramatists	*DRAMA CRITICISM (DC)*
Poets	*POETRY CRITICISM (PC)*
Short story writers	*SHORT STORY CRITICISM (SSC)*
Literary topics and movements	*HARLEM RENAISSANCE: A GALE CRITICAL COMPANION (HR)* *THE BEAT GENERATION: A GALE CRITICAL COMPANION (BG)*
Asian American writers of the last two hundred years	*ASIAN AMERICAN LITERATURE (AAL)*
Black writers of the past two hundred years	*BLACK LITERATURE CRITICISM (BLC)* *BLACK LITERATURE CRITICISM SUPPLEMENT (BLCS)*
Hispanic writers of the late nineteenth and twentieth centuries	*HISPANIC LITERATURE CRITICISM (HLC)* *HISPANIC LITERATURE CRITICISM SUPPLEMENT (HLCS)*
Native North American writers and orators of the eighteenth, nineteenth, and twentieth centuries	*NATIVE NORTH AMERICAN LITERATURE (NNAL)*
Major authors from the Renaissance to the present	*WORLD LITERATURE CRITICISM, 1500 TO THE PRESENT (WLC)* *WORLD LITERATURE CRITICISM SUPPLEMENT (WLCS)*

ISSN 0895-9439

Volume 85

Short Story Criticism

Criticism of the
Works of Short Fiction Writers

DISCARD

Thomas J. Schoenberg
Lawrence J. Trudeau
Project Editors

GALE®

THOMSON
™
GALE

THOMSON
GALE

Short Story Criticism, Vol. 85

Project Editors
Thomas J. Schoenberg and Lawrence J. Trudeau

Editorial
Jessica Bomarito, Kathy D. Darrow, Jeffrey W. Hunter, Jelena O. Krstović, Michelle Lee, Rachelle Mucha, Russel Whitaker

Data Capture
Francis Monroe, Gwen Tucker

Indexing Services
Factiva®, a Dow Jones and Reuters Company

Rights and Acquisitions
Ronald Montgomery, Sue Rudolph, Andrew Specht

Imaging and Multimedia
Dean Dauphinais, Leitha Etheridge-Sims, Lezlie Light, Mike Logusz, Dan Newell, Christine O'Bryan, Kelly A. Quin, Denay Wilding, Robyn Young

Composition and Electronic Capture
Kathy Sauer

Manufacturing
Rhonda Dover

Associate Product Manager
Marc Cormier

LIBRARY OF CONGRESS CATALOG CARD NUMBER 88-641014

ISBN 0-7876-8882-7
ISSN 0895-9439

Printed in the United States of America
10 9 8 7 6 5 4 3 2 1

Contents

Preface

Short Story Criticism (*SSC*) presents significant criticism of the world's greatest short-story writers and provides supplementary biographical and bibliographical materials to guide the interested reader to a greater understanding of the authors of short fiction. This series was developed in response to suggestions from librarians serving high school, college, and public library patrons, who had noted a considerable number of requests for critical material on short-story writers. Although major short-story writers are covered in such Thomson Gale series as *Contemporary Literary Criticism* (*CLC*), *Twentieth-Century Literary Criticism* (*TCLC*), *Nineteenth-Century Literature Criticism* (*NCLC*), and *Literature Criticism from 1400 to 1800* (*LC*), librarians perceived the need for a series devoted solely to writers of the short-story genre.

Scope of the Series

SSC is designed to serve as an introduction to major short-story writers of all eras and nationalities. Since these authors have inspired a great deal of relevant critical material, *SSC* is necessarily selective, and the editors have chosen the most important published criticism to aid readers and students in their research.

Approximately eight to ten authors are included in each volume, and each entry presents a historical survey of the critical response to that author's work. The length of an entry is intended to reflect the amount of critical attention the author has received from critics writing in English and from foreign critics in translation. Every attempt has been made to identify and include the most significant essays on each author's work. In order to provide these important critical pieces, the editors sometimes reprint essays that have appeared elsewhere in Thomson Gale's Literary Criticism Series. Such duplication, however, never exceeds twenty percent of an *SSC* volume.

Organization of the Book

An *SSC* entry consists of the following elements:

- The **Author Heading** cites the name under which the author most commonly wrote, followed by birth and death dates. Also located here are any name variations under which an author wrote, including transliterated forms for authors whose native languages use nonroman alphabets. If the author wrote consistently under a pseudonym, the pseudonym will be listed in the author heading and the author's actual name given in parentheses on the first line of the biographical and critical introduction. Uncertain birth or death dates are indicated by question marks. Single-work entries are preceded by the title of the work and its date of publication.

- The **Introduction** contains background information that introduces the reader to the author and the critical debates surrounding his or her work.

- A **Portrait of the Author** is included when available.

- The list of **Principal Works** is ordered chronologically by date of first publication and lists the most important works by the author. The first section comprises short-story collections, novellas, and novella collections. The second section gives information on other major works by the author. For foreign authors, the editors have provided original foreign-language publication information and have selected what are considered the best and most complete English-language editions of their works.

- Reprinted **Criticism** is arranged chronologically in each entry to provide a useful perspective on changes in critical evaluation over time. All short-story, novella, and collection titles by the author featured in the entry are printed in boldface type. The critic's name and the date of composition or publication of the critical work are given at the beginning of each piece of criticism. Unsigned criticism is preceded by the title of the source in which it appeared. Footnotes are reprinted at the end of each essay or excerpt. In the case of excerpted criticism, only those footnotes that pertain to the excerpted texts are included.

- Critical essays are prefaced by brief **Annotations** explicating each piece.

- A complete **Bibliographical Citation** of the original essay or book precedes each piece of criticism. Source citations in the Literary Criticism Series follow University of Chicago Press style, as outlined in *The Chicago Manual of Style,* 14th ed. (Chicago: The University of Chicago Press, 1993).

- An annotated bibliography of **Further Reading** appears at the end of each entry and suggests resources for additional study. In some cases, significant essays for which the editors could not obtain reprint rights are included here. Boxed material following the further reading list provides references to other biographical and critical sources on the author in series published by Thomson Gale.

Indexes

A **Cumulative Author Index** lists all of the authors that appear in a wide variety of reference sources published by Thomson Gale, including *SSC*. A complete list of these sources is found facing the first page of the Author Index. The index also includes birth and death dates and cross references between pseudonyms and actual names.

A **Cumulative Nationality Index** lists all authors featured in *SSC* by nationality, followed by the number of the *SSC* volume in which their entry appears.

An alphabetical **Title Index** lists all short-story, novella, and collection titles contained in the *SSC* series. Titles of short-story collections, separately published novellas, and novella collections are printed in italics, while titles of individual short stories are printed in roman type with quotation marks. Each title is followed by the author's last name and corresponding volume and page numbers where commentary on the work is located. English-language translations of original foreign-language titles are cross-referenced to the foreign titles so that all references to discussion of a work are combined in one listing.

In response to numerous suggestions from librarians, Thomson Gale also produces an annual paperbound edition of the SSC cumulative title index. This annual cumulation, which alphabetically lists all titles reviewed in the series, is available to all customers. Additional copies of this index are available upon request. Librarians and patrons will welcome this separate index; it saves shelf space, is easy to use, and is recyclable upon receipt of the next edition.

Citing *Short Story Criticism*

When citing criticism reprinted in the Literary Criticism Series, students should provide complete bibliographic information so that the cited essay can be located in the original print or electronic source. Students who quote directly from reprinted criticism may use any accepted bibliographic format, such as University of Chicago Press style or Modern Language Association (MLA) style. Both the MLA and the University of Chicago formats are acceptable and recognized as being the current standards for citations. It is important, however, to choose one format for all citations; do not mix the two formats within a list of citations.

The examples below follow recommendations for preparing a bibliography set forth in *The Chicago Manual of Style,* 14th ed. (Chicago: The University of Chicago Press, 1993); the first example pertains to material drawn from periodicals, the second to material reprinted from books:

Morrison, Jago. "Narration and Unease in Ian McEwan's Later Fiction." *Critique* 42, no. 3 (spring 2001): 253-68. Reprinted in *Short Story Criticism.* Vol. 57, edited by Janet Witalec, 212-20. Detroit: Gale, 2003.

Brossard, Nicole. "Poetic Politics." In *The Politics of Poetic Form: Poetry and Public Policy,* edited by Charles Bernstein, 73-82. New York: Roof Books, 1990. Reprinted in *Short Story Criticism.* Vol. 57, edited by Janet Witalec, 3-8. Detroit: Gale, 2003.

The examples below follow recommendations for preparing a works cited list set forth in the *MLA Handbook for Writers of Research Papers,* 5th ed. (New York: The Modern Language Association of America, 1999); the first example pertains to material drawn from periodicals, the second to material reprinted from books:

Morrison, Jago. "Narration and Unease in Ian McEwan's Later Fiction." *Critique* 42.3 (spring 2001): 253-68. Reprinted in *Short Story Criticism.* Ed. Janet Witalec. Vol. 57. Detroit: Gale, 2003. 212-20.

Brossard, Nicole. "Poetic Politics." *The Politics of Poetic Form: Poetry and Public Policy.* Ed. Charles Bernstein. New York: Roof Books, 1990. 73-82. Reprinted in *Short Story Criticism.* Ed. Janet Witalec. Vol. 57. Detroit: Gale, 2003. 3-8.

Suggestions are Welcome

Readers who wish to suggest new features, topics, or authors to appear in future volumes, or who have other suggestions or comments are cordially invited to call, write, or fax the Associate Product Manager:

Associate Product Manager, Literary Criticism Series
Thomson Gale
27500 Drake Road
Farmington Hills, MI 48331-3535
1-800-347-4253 (GALE)
Fax: 248-699-8054

Acknowledgments

The editors wish to thank the copyright holders of the excerpted criticism included in this volume and the permissions managers of many book and magazine publishing companies for assisting us in securing reproduction rights. Following is a list of the copyright holders who have granted us permission to reproduce material in this volume of *SSC*. Every effort has been made to trace copyright, but if omissions have been made, please let us know.

COPYRIGHTED MATERIAL IN *SSC*, VOLUME 85, WAS REPRODUCED FROM THE FOLLOWING PERIODICALS:

Atlantic Monthly, v. 289, January, 2002 for "Incomparable Naturalism" by Philip Hensher. Reproduced by permission of A P Watt Ltd on behalf of Philip Hensher.—*Canadian Slavonic Papers,* v. XXXV, September-December, 1993; v. XLII, September, 2000. Copyright © Canadian Slavonic Papers, Canada, 1993, 2000. Both reproduced by permission.—*College Literature,* v. XII, fall, 1985. Copyright © 1985 by West Chester University. Reproduced by permission.—*The Comparatist,* v. XXI, May, 1997. Copyright © 1997 by the Southern Comparative Literature Association. Used by permission of the University of North Carolina Press.—*Dalhousie French Studies,* v. 56, fall, 2001. Reproduced by permission.—*European Journal of English Studies,* v. 2, 1998 for "Angela Carter's Pronominal Acrobatics: Language in 'The Erl-King' and 'The Company of Wolves'" by Monika Fludernik. © Swets & Zeitlinger. Reproduced by permission of the author and Taylor & Francis, Ltd at http//:www.tandf.co.uk/journals.—*Hungarian Journal of English and American Studies,* v. 5, 1999. Copyright © by HJEAS. All rights reserved. Reproduced by permission.—*Journal of the Utah Academy of Sciences, Arts, and Letters,* v. 76, 1999. Copyright © Gary Godfrey. All rights reserved. Reproduced by permission.—*Kenyon Review,* v. 19, summer-fall, 1997 for "In Olden Times, When Wishing Was Having … Classic and Contemporary Fairy Tales" by Joyce Carol Oates. Copyright © 1997 Ontario Review. All rights reserved. Reprinted by permission of John Hawkins & Associates, Inc.—*Marvels & Tales,* v. 17, 2003. Copyright © 2003 Wayne State University Press. Reproduced with permission of the Wayne State University Press.—*Mediaevalia: An Interdisciplinary Journal of Medieval Studies Worldwide,* v. 22, Special Issue, 1999. Copyright © 1999 by CEMERS. Reproduced by permission.—*Neophilologus,* v. LXXI, April, 1987 for "Chekhov and the Modern Short Story in English" by David W. Martin. © 1987 Wolters-Noordhoff, Groningen, The Netherlands. Reproduced by permission of the author.—*North Dakota Quarterly,* v. 59, summer, 1991. Copyright 1991 by The University of North Dakota. Reproduced by permission.—*Review of Contemporary Fiction,* v. 14, fall, 1994. Copyright © 1994 The Review of Contemporary Fiction. Reproduced by permission.—*Romance Quarterly,* v. 39, August, 1992; v. 48, winter, 2001; v. 51, winter, 2004. Copyright © 1992, 2001, 2004 by Helen Dwight Reid Educational Foundation. All reproduced with permission of the Helen Dwight Reid Educational Foundation, published by Heldref Publications, 1319 18th Street, NW, Washington, DC 20036-1802.—*Romanic Review,* v. 86, March, 1995. Copyright © 1995 by the Trustees of Columbia University in the City of New York. Reproduced by permission.—*Russian Literature,* v. XXXV, February 15, 1994; v. 44, November 15, 1998; v. XLVIII, November 15, 2000. © 1994, 1998, 2000, Elsevier Science B.V. All reproduced with permission from Elsevier.—*Russian Review,* v. 53, January, 1994; v. 58, July, 1999. Copyright © 1994, 1999 Basil Blackwell Ltd. Both reproduced by permission of Blackwell Publishers.—*Scottish Slavonic Review,* spring, 1991. Copyright © Scottish Slavonic Review and contributors 1991. Reproduced by permission.—*Sixteenth Century Journal ,* v. XXXI, summer, 2000; v. XXXIV, summer, 2003. Copyright © 2000, 2003 by the Sixteenth Century Journal Publishers, Inc., Kirksville, Missouri 63501-0828 U. S. A. All rights reserved. Both reproduced by permission.—*Slavic and East European Journal,* v. 44, autumn, 2000; v. 47, fall, 2003. Copyright © 2000, 2003 by AATSEEL of the U.S., Inc. Both reproduced by permission.—*Slavic Review,* v. 62, summer, 2003. Copyright © 2003 by the American Association for the Advancement of Slavic Studies, Inc. Reproduced by permission.—*Studies in Short Fiction,* v. 27, spring, 1990; v. 33, summer, 1996. Copyright © 1990, 1996 by Studies in Short Fiction. Both reproduced by permission.—*Style,* v. 29, fall, 1995. Copyright © Style, 1995. All rights reserved. Reproduced by permission of the publisher.—*Women's Studies,* v. 25, 1996, for "'Seeing is believing, but touching is the truth': Female Spectatorship and Sexuality in The Company of Wolves" by Catherine Lappas. © 1996 OPA (Overseas Publishers Association). Reproduced by permission of the author and Taylor & Francis, Ltd at http//:www.tandf.co.uk/journals.—*World Literature Today,* v. 70, spring, 1996. Copyright © 1996 by World Literature Today. Reproduced by permission of the publisher.

COPYRIGHTED MATERIAL IN *SSC*, VOLUME 85, WAS REPRODUCED FROM THE FOLLOWING BOOKS:

Clive, H. P. From an Introduction to *Marguerite de Navarre: Tales from the* **Heptaméron.** Edited by H. P. Clive. The Athlone Press, 1970. Copyright © H. P. Clive, 1970. Reproduced by permission of Continuum International Publishing Com-

Thomson Gale Literature Product Advisory Board

The members of the Thomson Gale Literature Product Advisory Board—reference librarians from public and academic library systems—represent a cross-section of our customer base and offer a variety of informed perspectives on both the presentation and content of our literature products. Advisory board members assess and define such quality issues as the relevance, currency, and usefulness of the author coverage, critical content, and literary topics included in our series; evaluate the layout, presentation, and general quality of our printed volumes; provide feedback on the criteria used for selecting authors and topics covered in our series; provide suggestions for potential enhancements to our series; identify any gaps in our coverage of authors or literary topics, recommending authors or topics for inclusion; analyze the appropriateness of our content and presentation for various user audiences, such as high school students, undergraduates, graduate students, librarians, and educators; and offer feedback on any proposed changes/enhancements to our series. We wish to thank the following advisors for their advice throughout the year.

Angela Carter
1940-1992

(Born Angela Olive Alexander) English short story writer, novelist, essayist, playwright, screenwriter, and editor.

The following entry provides an overview of Carter's short fiction. For additional information on her short fiction career, see *SSC,* Volume 13.

INTRODUCTION

Carter is best known for award-winning fiction that successfully combines postmodern literary theories and feminist politics. Often interrogating culturally accepted views of sexuality, the stories in *The Bloody Chamber* (1979), *Black Venus* (1985), and Carter's other collections are distinguished by sensual prose, eroticism, irony, violence, and gothic themes. Her protagonists frequently confront grotesque characters and macabre situations that underscore such issues as gender roles and identity formation. Carter's short stories are also characterzed by the use of the language and motifs of the fairy-tale and fantasy genres. By exploiting societal anxieties inherent in the motifs of many popular fairy tales, Carter's stories undertake feminist revisions of the Freudian concept of the unconscious and the cultural foundations of gender roles. Although some commentators have found her preoccupation with psychosexual deviance disturbing, most critics have acknowledged Carter as one of England's most notable practitioners of magical realism.

BIOGRAPHICAL INFORMATION

The daughter of a Scottish journalist, Carter was born in London on May 7, 1940. During World War II she lived in Wath-upon-Deare with her grandmother, whose suffragist activities and radical political views would later influence Carter's literary themes and characters. After reuniting with her parents Carter suffered from anorexia. Prior to entering the University of Bristol in 1962, where she studied medieval literature, she wrote features and record reviews for the *Croydon Advertiser* and married Paul Carter. After graduating in 1965 Carter published her first novel, *Shadow Dance* (1966), and contributed cultural criticism and observation pieces to the *Guardian* newspaper and *New Society* magazine. During the late 1960s Carter published two more novels, *The Magic Toyshop* (1967)—which received the John Llewellyn Rhys prize—and *Several Perceptions* (1968), which won the Somerset Maugham Award. In 1969, after separating from her husband, Carter went to live in Japan until her divorce was finalized. She returned to England in 1972. Her immersion in a foreign culture marked a professional and personal turning point for Carter, who subsequently found her voice both as a woman and as a social radical, as evidenced by such novels as *The Infernal Desire Machines of Doctor Hoffmann* (1972) and *The Passion of New Eve* (1977), as well as in her first short story collection, *Fireworks* (1974). In 1978 Carter received the Cheltenham Festival Literary Prize for *The Bloody Chamber.*

In 1982 Carter settled in Clapham, South London, with Mark Pearce, a potter, and gave birth to a son the following year. During the early 1980s Carter served as an Arts Council fellow at Sheffield University as well as a visiting professor of creative writing at both Brown University in Rhode Island and Adelaide University in

South Australia. While teaching creative writing at the University of East Anglia from 1984 to 1987, she wrote the novel *Nights at the Circus* (1984), which won the James Tait Black Memorial Prize, and co-wrote the screenplay for the film *The Company of Wolves* (1984), which is based on her short story of the same title from *The Bloody Chamber*. She also published her third short story collection, *Black Venus,* in 1985. During the early 1990s Carter edited *The Virago Book of Fairy Tales* (1990) and published her last novel, *Wise Children* (1991). Carter died of cancer on February 16, 1992.

MAJOR WORKS OF SHORT FICTION

The narratives in *Fireworks* display many of the fantastic, surreal elements that mark all of Carter's work and reflect the cultural experiences of her life in Japan. In this collection, "A Souvenir of Japan" lucidly describes Japan from the perspective of a woman in a failing relationship, while "Flesh and the Mirror" features a life-size female puppet with a lust for life who tours the world. *The Bloody Chamber* contains Carter's most critically acclaimed fiction. Based on the classic fairy tales of Charles Perrault and the Brothers Grimm, these narratives re-imagine several of Western culture's most famous tales and fables to suit wry, modern sensibilities. The resulting stories emphasize the gender-based power and violence only hinted at in the source materials. For example, "The Courtship of Mr. Lyon," a retelling of "Beauty and the Beast," interrogates patriarchal norms and the role of women as objects of men's desire. In a similar investigation of cultural constructions in "The Tiger's Bride," a man loses his daughter on a bet with the Beast. The story concludes with the young girl falling in love with the Beast and rejecting her father. In "The Company of Wolves," a revision of "Little Red Riding Hood," a young girl conquers the wolf by asserting her sexuality. Based on "Snow White," "Snow Child" introduces an Oedipal subtext as a jealous Countess curses a child her husband has created from a series of wishes. "The Bloody Chamber" heavily borrows from Perrault's "Bluebeard," but substitutes the original story's titular wife-killer with a character reminiscent of the Marquis de Sade. Other stories from this collection build upon archetypes of the horror genre. In "Wolf-Alice," a girl who is raised by wolves fails to act civilized after being rescued from the wilderness, and subsequently discovers that the reclusive duke with whom she lives is a werewolf. Other works in *The Bloody Chamber* include "The Lady of the House of Love," which details a female vampire's failed attempt to seduce a young soldier, and "The Erl-King," in which the title character entices young women with his mysterious music so that he may trap them in cages like songbirds. The stories of *Black Venus* recount "everyday life among the mythic classes," which number such literary figures as *A Midsummer Night's Dream*'s Puck, Edgar Allan Poe, and Charles Baudelaire as members. The title story of the collection refers to Baudelaire's Creole mistress who represents dual senses of "otherness": as woman and as dark-skinned. Other tales in this collection include "The Fall River Axe Murders," which examines the events leading up to the infamous murder of Lizzie Borden's parents, and "The Kiss," which imagines the homecoming of the fabled conqueror Tamburlaine from the perspective of his wife. The posthumously published *Burning Your Boats* (1995) gathers all of Carter's short fiction in one volume, including a parody of Disneyland and its artificial fantasies entitled "In Pantoland."

CRITICAL RECEPTION

Although authors as diverse as Salman Rushdie, Margaret Atwood, and Anthony Burgess have praised Carter's tales and fables, other critics have come away from her writings unimpressed, confused, or repulsed. Feminist scholars have debated the merits of Carter's revised fairy tales, either admiring their deft subversion of patriarchal values or lamenting their perpetuation of misogynistic ideology. In addition, other feminists have either celebrated or condemned the alternatives proposed by Carter for her heroines. Literary scholars have studied many of Carter's stories for insights into her concept of literary genres, investigating the connection between romance narratology and ideology. On the other hand, critics have also observed several links on different levels between the Marquis de Sade's pornographic literature and Carter's writing. Furthermore, the irony, dark wit, and bleak humor that characterize much of Carter's writing have prompted scholarship on the postmodern aesthetics of her work. Most critics have recognized her capacity for creating challenging narratives within seemingly simple storylines, yet some reviewers feel that a fully exhaustive study of Carter's stories has yet to be conducted.

PRINCIPAL WORKS

Short Fiction

Fireworks: Nine Profane Pieces 1974; also published in the United States as *Fireworks: Nine Stories in Various Disguises,* 1981
The Bloody Chamber and Other Stories 1979
Black Venus 1985; also published in the United States as *Saints and Strangers,* 1986
Wayward Girls & Wicked Women: An Anthology of Stories [editor] 1986

The Virago Book of Fairy Tales [editor] 1990
The Second Virago Book of Fairy Tales [editor] 1992
American Ghosts and Old World Wonders 1993
Burning Your Boats: Stories 1995

Other Major Works

Shadow Dance (novel) 1966
The Magic Toyshop (novel) 1967
Several Perceptions (novel) 1968
The Infernal Desire Machines of Doctor Hoffman
    (novel) 1972; also published in the United States as
    The War of Dreams, 1974
The Passion of New Eve (novel) 1977
The Sadeian Woman and the Ideology of Pornography
    (nonfiction) 1978; also published in the United States
    as *The Sadeian Woman: An Exercise in Cultural History,* 1979
The Company of Wolves [with Neil Jordan] (screenplay)
    1984
Nights at the Circus (novel) 1984
Come Unto These Yellow Sands (radio plays) 1985
Wise Children (novel) 1991
Expletives Deleted: Selected Writings (essays) 1992
The Curious Room: Plays, Film Scripts and an Opera
    (plays) 1996
Shaking a Leg: Collected Journalism and Writings
    (nonfiction) 1997

CRITICISM

Merja Makinen (essay date 1992)

SOURCE: Makinen, Merja. "Angela Carter's *The Bloody Chamber* and the Decolonisation of Feminine Sexuality." In *Angela Carter,* edited by Alison Easton, pp. 20-36. Basingstoke, England: Macmillan, 2000.

[*In the following essay, originally published in 1992, Makinen studies Carter's textual uses of violence as a feminist literary strategy in* The Bloody Chamber, *assessing the impact of this strategy on readers' responses.*]

The last thing you'd ever need to do with an Angela Carter text is to send it on an assertiveness training course. With her death (and no one has spoken more effectively on that than her last novel, *Wise Children,* 'a broken heart is never a tragedy. Only untimely death is a tragedy') the obituaries have started to evoke her as the gentle, wonderful white witch of the north. But far from being gentle, Carter's texts were known for the excessiveness of their violence and, latterly, the almost violent exuberance of their excess. Many a reader has found the savagery with which she can attack cultural stereotypes disturbing, even alienating. Personally I found (and find) it exhilarating—you never knew what was coming next from the avant-garde literary terrorist of feminism.

Margaret Atwood's memorial in the *Observer* opens with Carter's 'intelligence and kindness' and goes on to construct her as a mythical fairy-tale figure: 'The amazing thing about her, for me, was that someone who looked so much like the Fairy Godmother . . . should actually *be* so much like the Fairy Godmother. She seemed always on the verge of bestowing something— some talisman, some magic token . . .' Lorna Sage's obituary in the *Guardian* talked of her 'powers of enchantment and hilarity, her generous inventiveness' while the *Late Show*'s memorial on BBC2 had the presenter calling her the 'white witch of English literature', J. G. Ballard a 'friendly witch', and Salman Rushdie claimed 'English literature has lost its high sorceress, its benevolent witch queen . . . deprived of the fairy queen we cannot find the magic that will heal us' and finished by describing her as 'a very good wizard, perhaps the first wizard de-luxe'.[1] But this concurrence of white witch/fairy godmother mythologising needs watching; it is always the dangerously problematic that are mythologised in order to make them less dangerous. As Carter herself argued strongly in *Sadeian Woman,* 'if women allow themselves to be consoled for their culturally determined lack of access to the modes of intellectual debate by the invocation of hypothetical great goddesses, they are simply flattering themselves into submission (a technique often used on them by men).'

The books are not by some benign magician. The strengths and the dangers of her texts lie in a much more aggressive subversiveness and a much more active eroticism than perhaps the decorum around death can allow. For me, the problematics of Carter's writing were captured with more frankness when *New Socialist* dubbed her—wrongly, I think, but wittily—the 'high-priestess of post-graduate porn' in 1987. For Carter's work has consistently dealt with representations of the physical abuse of women in phallocentric cultures, of women alienated from themselves within the male gaze, and conversely of women who grab their sexuality and fight back, of women troubled by and even powered by their own violence.

Clearly, Angela Carter was best known for her feminist re-writing of fairy-tales; the memorials blurring stories with storyteller stand testimony to that. ***The Bloody Chamber and Other Stories,*** published in 1979, is also midway between the disquietingly savage analyses of patriarchy of the 1960s and 1970s, such as *The Magic Toyshop, Heroes and Villains, Passion of New Eve*; and the exuberant novels of the 1980s and early 1990s,

Nights at the Circus and *Wise Children.* This is not to argue that the latter novels are not also feminist, but their strategy is different. The violence in the events depicted in the earlier novels (the rapes, the physical and mental abuse of women) and the aggression implicit in the representations, are no longer foregrounded. While similar events may occur in these two last texts, the focus is on mocking and exploding the constrictive cultural stereotypes and in celebrating the sheer ability of the female protagonists to survive, unscathed by the sexist ideologies. The tales in *The Bloody Chamber* still foreground the violence and the abuse, but the narrative itself provides an exuberant re-writing of the fairy-tales that actively engages the reader in a feminist deconstruction. I am therefore focusing my discussion on Carter's fairy-tales to allow a specific analysis of Carter's textual uses of violence as a feminist strategy, alongside a case study assessing the relationship of such a strategy to an assessment of her readership.

Fairy-tale elements had been present in Carter's work as early as *The Magic Toyshop* in 1967, but she didn't come to consider them as a specific genre of European literature until the late seventies. In 1977 she translated for Gollancz a series of Perrault's seventeenth-century tales, and in 1979 published *The Bloody Chamber,* her re-writing of the fairy-tales of Perrault and Madame Leprince de Beaumont. In 1982 she translated another edition, which included the two extra stories by Madame de Beaumont, 'Beauty and the Beast' and 'Sweetheart'. Three of the stories from *Bloody Chamber* were rewritten for Radio 3,[2] and she took part in adapting one of them, **'Company of Wolves'**, into the film by Neil Jordan (1984). Finally, she edited the *Virago Book of Fairy Tales* in 1990, and the *Second Virago Book of Fairy Tales* for 1992.

Carter saw fairy-tales as the oral literature of the poor, a literature that spanned Europe and one that encoded the dark and mysterious elements of the psyche. She argued that even though the seventeenth- and eighteenth-century aristocratic writers 'fixed' these tales by writing them down and added moral tags to adapt them into parables of instruction for children, they could not erase the darkness and the magic of the content.[3] She argued that both literature and folklore were 'vast repositories of outmoded lies, where you can check out what lies used to be a la mode and find the old lies on which new lies are based'. But folk-tales, unlike the more dangerous myths (which she tackled in *Passion of New Eve*), were straightforward devices whose structures could easily be re-written with an informing, feminist tag, where the curiosity of the women protagonists is rewarded (rather than punished) and their sexuality is active (rather than passive or suppressed altogether). Carter's Red Riding Hood in **'Company of Wolves'** is more than a match for her werewolf:

> What big teeth you have . . .
>
> All the better to eat you with.
>
> The girl burst out laughing; she knew she was nobody's meat. She laughed at him full in the face, she ripped off his shirt for him and flung it into the fire, in the fiery wake of her own discarded clothing.[4]

Feminist critics who have written on *Bloody Chamber* argue that the old fairy-tales were a reactionary form that inscribed a misogynistic ideology, without questioning whether women readers would always and necessarily identify with the female figures (an assumption that Carter too shares in). They argue that Carter, in using the form, gets locked into the conservative sexism, despite her good intentions. Patricia Duncker uses Andrea Dworkin's *Pornography: Men Possessing Women* to argue that Carter is 're-writing the tales within the strait-jacket of their original structures' and therefore reproducing the 'rigidly sexist psychology of the erotic'. Avis Lewallen agrees, Carter has been unable adequately to revision the conservative form for a feminist politics, and so her attempts at constructing an active female erotic are badly compromised—if not a reproduction of male pornography.[5]

I would argue that, conversely, it is the critics who cannot see beyond the sexist binary opposition. In order to do this, two issues need to be addressed: whether a 'reactionary' form can be re-written; and the potential perversity of women's sexuality. The discussion of the first issue will lead to an argument for a feminist strategy of writing and also of reading, and hence throw some light on Carter's potential audiences.

Firstly, the question of the form of the fairy-tale: is it some universal, unchangeable given or does it change according to its specific historic rendition? Narrative genres clearly do inscribe ideologies (though that can never fix the readings), but later re-writings that take the genre and adapt it will not necessarily encode the same ideological assumptions. Otherwise, one would have to argue that the African novels that have sought to decolonise the European cultural stereotypes of themselves, must always fail. One would need to argue that Ngugi's or Achebe's novels, for example, reinforce the colonial legacy because they use the novel format. This is clearly not true. When the form is used to critique the inscribed ideology, I would argue, then the form is subtly adapted to inscribe a new set of assumptions. Carter argued that *Bloody Chamber* was 'a book of stories *about* fairy stories' (my emphasis) and this ironic strategy needs to be acknowledged. Lewallen complains that Duncker is insensitive to the irony in Carter's tales, but then agrees with her assessment of the patriarchal inscriptions, seeing the irony as merely 'blurring the boundaries' of binary thinking. Now I want to push the claim for irony a lot further than Lewallen, and argue that rather than a blurring, it enacts an oscillation that is itself deconstructive.

Naomi Schor, in an essay on Flaubert's ironic use of Romanticism, states that irony allows the author to reject and at the same time re-appropriate the discourse that s/he is referring to, (i.e., Romanticism is both present and simultaneously discredited in Flaubert's texts).[6] Schor historicises the continuity between nineteenth-century and modernist irony as inherently misogynistic (because linked to the fetishisation of women) and calls for a feminist irony that incorporates the destabilising effects, while rejecting the misogyny. She cites Donna Haraway's opening paragraph from 'A manifesto for cyborgs': 'Irony . . . is a rhetorical strategy and political method, one I would like to see more honoured within socialist feminism.' Utilising this model of an ironic oscillation, I want to argue that Carter's tales do not simply 'rewrite' the old tales by fixing roles of active sexuality for their female protagonists—they 're-write' them by playing with and upon (if not preying upon) the earlier misogynistic version. Look again at the quote from **'Company of Wolves'** given earlier. It is not read as a story read for the first time, with a positively imaged heroine. It is read, with the original story encoded within it, so that one reads of *both* texts, aware of how the new one refers back to and implicitly critiques the old. We read 'The girl burst out laughing; she knew she was nobody's meat' as referring to the earlier Little Red Riding Hood's passive terror of being eaten, before she is saved by the male woodman. We recognise the author's feminist turning of the tables and, simultaneously, the damage done by the old inscriptions of femininity as passive. 'I am all for putting new wine in old bottles, especially if the pressure of the new wine makes the old bottles explode.'[7]

What should also not be overlooked, alongside this ironic deconstructive technique, is the role of the reader; the question of *who* is reading these tales. These are late twentieth-century adult fairy-tales conscious of their own fictive status and so questioning the very constructions of roles while asserting them. When a young girl resolutely chops off the paws of the wolf threatening her, and we read 'the wolf let out a gulp, almost a sob . . . wolves are less brave than they seem'—we are participating in the re-writing of a wolf's characteristics and participating not only in the humour but also the arbitrariness. 'Nature' is not fixed but fluid within fiction.

Carter was insistent that her texts were open-ended, written with a space for the reader's activity in mind. She disliked novels that were closed worlds and described most realist novels as etiquette manuals. And she placed Marilyn French's *The Women's Room* in such a category, as well as the novels of Jane Austen. The fact that the former was feminist didn't let it off the protocol hook. Books written to show the reader how she should behave, were not only an insult to the

reader but also a bore to write. Carter's own fiction seems always aware of its playful interactions with the reader's assumptions and recognitions.[8] *The Bloody Chamber* is clearly engaging with a reader historically situated in the early 1980s (and beyond), informed by feminism, and raising questions about the cultural constructions of femininity. Rather than carrying the heavy burden of instruction, Carter often explained that for her 'a narrative is an argument stated in fictional terms'. And the two things needed for any argument are, something to argue *against* (something to be overturned) and someone to make that argument *to* (a reader).

The question therefore arises of whether this deconstructive irony is activated if the reader is uninformed by feminism. The answer must be, on the whole, no. *Bloody Chamber* draws on a feminist discourse—or at least an awareness that feminism is challenging sexist constructions. Mary Kelly, the feminist artist, when challenged on the same question of the accessibility of her *Post Partum Document* to a wider audience, cogently argued, 'there is no such thing as a homogeneous mass-audience. You can't make art for everyone. And if you're enjoyed within a particular movement or organisation, then the work is going to participate in its debates.' Lucy Lippard goes on to suggest that Kelly's art 'extends the level of discourse within the art audience for all those who see the art experience as an *exchange,* a collaboration between artist and audience—the active audience an active art deserves'.[9] I would argue that Carter's tales evoke a similar active engagement with feminist discourse.

At first sight, such a conclusion may sound odd, because if anyone has taken feminist fiction into the mainstream, it is Carter. But if a feminist writer is to remain a feminist writer (rather than a writer about women) then the texts must engage, on some level, with feminist thinking. There is a wide constituency of potential readers who satisfy the minimum requirement of having an awareness that feminism challenges sexist constructions. One does not need to be a feminist to read the texts, far from it, but if the reader does not appreciate the attack on the stereotypes then the payback for that level of engagement, the sheer cerebral pleasure and the enjoyment of the iconoclasm, will be missing. And without the humour or the interest in deconstructing cultural gender stereotypes, the textual anger against the abuse of women in previous decades can prove very disquieting, even uncomfortable, to read. To enjoy the humour—the payback with many of Carter's texts—readers need to position themselves outside phallocentric culture (at least for the process of reading). The last two novels, with their lighter tone and more exuberant construction of interrelationships, probably have the widest readership of all. This mellowing of textual aggression is not the only explanation for the increasing popularity of Carter's later texts. Helen Carr notes that the mid-eighties saw the arrival of South American magic realism on the British scene.[10] From that moment, Carter's readers could assign her anarchic fusion of fantasy and realism to an intelligible genre, and so feel more secure.

However, a fuller explanation of Carter's popularity needs to take account of marketing and distribution: not just accessibility of ideology, but accessibility of purchase. Is the text on the general bookshop shelves? Is it marketed under a feminist imprint, thus signalling to the potential reader, for feminist eyes only? Nicci Gerrard in her examination of how feminist fiction has impacted on mainstream publishing, argues that Carter, along with Toni Morrison and Keri Hulme, have been more widely read because while still remaining explicitly feminist, they have brought feminism out of its 'narrow self-consciousness'.[11] Narrow is always a difficult adjective to quantify. In Britain, Angela Carter—like Morrison and Hulme—has been published by mainstream publishers from the beginning. The publishing history for her hardback fiction runs: Heinemann 1966-70, Hart Davis 1971-2, Gollancz 1977-84, Chatto & Windus 1984-92. As far as marketing and distribution are concerned, Carter has always been presented directly to mainstream audiences.

Both *Passion of New Eve* (1977) and ***Bloody Chamber*** (1979) initially came out under Gollancz's 'Fantasy' series, placing them within a specific genre, and the former was the first into paperback—being issued by Arrow in 1978. In 1981 Penguin issued ***Bloody Chamber*** along with *Heroes and Villains* and *The Infernal Desire Machine of Doctor Hoffman*. In the same year Virago published the paperback of *Magic Toyshop*, followed by *Passion of New Eve* the year after, and ***Fireworks*** in 1987. The covers of both publishing houses initially focused on the surreal, vaguely sci-fi elements, Penguin doing a nice line in suggestive plants, designed by James Marsh. (Thankfully, Virago has scrapped the original tawdry cover of the sci-fi couple embracing, on ***Fireworks,*** for the more tasteful modernist depiction of a Japanese urban environment.) Virago also published Carter's non-fiction and commissioned her to edit collections of stories.

Nights at the Circus reached a very large audience, in paperback. Picador published it in 1985 and it was taken up as a major lead title for Pan to promote and distribute. Gerrard cites Virago's average fiction print-run as 5000-7000 in the second half of the eighties. By the early nineties, *Nights at the Circus* had achieved sales which exceeded this figure ten times over. But even this success needs to be placed in context. It still only reaches about 20 per cent of the sales for a number one best seller, such as Martin Amis's *London Fields* or Julian Barnes's *History of the World in 10½ Chapters*.[12]

So Carter's involvement with feminist publishers came relatively late in the day and seems to have stemmed from Virago's publishing of her first piece of non-fiction, *Sadeian Woman: An Exercise in Cultural History* (1979). Her fiction's reputation was made from mainstream publishing houses and was reinforced by the awards of mainstream literary prizes: the John Llewellyn Rhys Prize for *Magic Toyshop*; Somerset Maugham Award for *Several Perceptions*; Cheltenham Festival of Literature Award for ***Bloody Chamber***; and the James Tait Black Award for *Nights at the Circus*. The shortlisting of the 1984 Booker Prize caused a minor furore when *Nights at the Circus* was not included (it was won that year by Anita Brookner's *Hotel du Lac*). Even many of the individual tales from ***The Bloody Chamber*** first saw the light of day in small but fairly prestigious literature reviews such as *Bananas, Stand, Northern Arts Review,* and *Iowa Review* (the only academic journal), none of them notably feminist in their editorial policy. And '**The Courtship of Mr Lyon**' was first published in the British edition of *Vogue*.

Clearly I am arguing that texts that employ a feminist irony, that engage activity with a feminist discourse, do not automatically confine themselves to a feminist ghetto. There is a wide and growing audience for at least some kinds of feminist fiction. But I am also arguing that exuberance sells better than discomfort. The more textually savage books are published by Virago in paperback; the more magical by Penguin; and two celebratory ones by the big-money bidders, Picador and Vantage.

But what also sells in this commodified age of ours, as everyone knows, is sex, and Carter's texts have always engaged with eroticism. The quotes included by Penguin on the book covers invariably make reference to 'the stylish erotic prose', 'erotic, exotic and bizarre romance'. And this clearly also has a lot to do with her popularity. In order to counter Lewallen and Duncker's perception of her work as pornographic, I need to examine the feminist strategies of her representations of sexuality, particularly the debate surrounding the construction of sexuality within the ***Bloody Chamber*** stories. I believe Carter is going some way towards constructing a complex vision of female psychosexuality, through her invoking of violence as well as the erotic. But that women can be violent as well as active sexually, that women can choose to be perverse, is clearly not something allowed for in the calculations of such readers as Duncker, Palmer and Lewallen.[13] Carter's strength is precisely in exploding the stereotypes of women as passive, demure cyphers. That she therefore evokes the gamut of violence and perversity is certainly troubling, but to deny their existence is surely to incarcerate women back within a partial, sanitised image only slightly less constricted than the Victorian angel in the house.

Carter was certainly fascinated by the incidence of 'beast marriage' stories, in the original fairy-tales, and she claimed they were international. In discussing how the wolves subtly changed their meaning in the film of the story, she comments that nevertheless they still signified libido. Fairy-tales are often seen as dealing with the 'uncanny', the distorted fictions of the unconscious revisited through homely images—and beasts can easily stand for the projected desires, the drive for pleasure of women. Particularly when such desires are discountenanced by a patriarchal culture concerned to restrict its women to being property (without a libido of their own, let alone a mind or a room).[14]

In all of the tales, not only is femininity constructed as active, sensual, desiring and unruly—but successful sexual transactions are founded on an equality and the transforming powers of recognising the reciprocal claims of the other. The ten tales divide up into the first, **'The Bloody Chamber'**, a re-writing of the Bluebeard story; three tales around cats: lion/tiger/puss in boots; three tales of magical beings: erl-king/snow-child/vampire; and finally three tales of werewolves. Each tale takes up the theme of the earlier one and comments on a different aspect of it, to present a complex variation of female desire and sexuality.

In the Finale to *Sadeian Woman* Carter discusses the word flesh in its various meanings:

> the pleasures of the flesh are vulgar and unrefined, even with an element of beastliness about them, although flesh tints have the sumptuous succulence of peaches because flesh plus skin equals sensuality.

> But, if flesh plus skin equals sensuality, then flesh minus skin equals meat.[15]

This motif of skin and flesh as signifying pleasure, and of meat as signifying economic objectification, recurs throughout the ten tales, and stands as an internal evaluation of the relationship shown. The other recurring motif is that of the gaze, but it is not always simply the objectification of the woman by male desire, as we shall discover.

In each of the first three tales, Carter stresses the relationship between women's subjective sexuality and their objective role as property: young girls get bought by wealth, one way or another. But in the feminist re-write, Bluebeard's victimisation of women is overturned and he himself is vanquished by the mother and daughter.

> The puppet master, open-mouthed, wide eyed, impotent at the last, saw his dolls break free of their strings, abandon the rituals he had ordained for them since time began and start to live for themselves.

> (p. 39)

In the two versions of the beauty-and-the-beast theme, the lion and the tiger signify something other than man. 'For a lion is a lion and a man is a man' argues the first tale. In the first, Beauty is adored by her father, in the second, gambled away by a profligate drunkard. The felines signify otherness, a savage and magnificent power, outside of humanity. In one story, women are pampered, in the other treated as property, but in both cases the protagonists chose to explore the dangerous, exhilarating change that comes from choosing the beast. Both stories are careful to show a reciprocal awe and fear in the beasts, as well as in the beauty, and the reversal theme reinforces the equality of the transactions: lion kisses Beauty's hand, Beauty kisses lion's; tiger strips naked and so Beauty chooses to show him 'the fleshly nature of women'. In both cases the beasts signify a sensuality that the women have been taught might devour them, but which, when embraced, gives them power, strength and a new awareness of both self and other. The tiger's bride has her 'skins of a life in the world' licked off to reveal her own magnificent fur beneath the surface.

Each of the three adolescent protagonists has been progressively stronger and more aggressive, and each has embraced a sensuality both sumptuous and unrefined. With the fourth story, **'Puss in Boots'**, the cynical puss viewing human love and desire in a light-hearted *commedia dell'arte* rendition, demythologises sex with humour and gusto.

If the wild felines have signified the sensual desires that women need to acknowledge within themselves, the three fictive figures signify the problematics of desire itself. **'Erl-king'** is a complex rendering of a subjective collusion with objectivity and entrapment within the male gaze. The woman narrator both fears and desires entrapment within the birdcage. The erl-king, we are told, does not exist in nature, but in a void of her own making (hence his calling her 'mother' at the end). The disquieting shifts between the two voices of the narrator, first and third person, represent the two competing desires for freedom and engulfment, in a tale that delineates the very ambivalence of desire. **'Snowchild'** presents the unattainability of desire, which will always melt away before possession. No real person can ever satisfy desire's constant deferral. **'Lady of the House of Love'**, with its lady vampire, inverts the gender roles of Bluebeard, with the woman constructed as an aggressor with a man as the virgin victim. But with this construction of aggressor, comes the question of whether sadists are trapped within their nature: 'can a bird sing only the song it knows or can it learn a new song?' And, through love and the reciprocal theme—he kisses her bloody finger, rather than her sucking his blood—this aggressor is able to vanquish ancestral desires, but at a cost. In this tale the overwhelming fear of the cat tales, that the protagonist might be consumed by the otherness of desire, is given a new twist.

The three wolf stories also deal with women's relationship to the unruly libido, but the werewolf signifies a stranger, more alienated otherness than the cats, despite the half-human manifestations. Old Granny is the werewolf in the first tale, and the girl's vanquishing of her is seen as a triumph of the complaisant society (the symbolic) that hounds the uncanny. The tiger's bride had been a rebellious child and chooses desire over conventional wealth; now we have a 'good' child who sacrifices the uncanny for bourgeois prosperity. In the second tale, **'Company of Wolves'**, the list of manifestations of werewolves, the amalgam of human and wolf, symbolic and imaginary, concludes with the second Red Riding Hood story. This time the wolf does consume the granny, but is outfaced by Red Riding Hood's awareness that in freely meeting his sensuality, the libido will transform 'meat' into 'flesh'. After the fulfilment of their mutual desire, he is transformed into a 'tender' wolf, and she sleeps safe between his paws. The final tale is of a girl raised by wolves, outside of the social training of the symbolic. Alluding to Truffaut's *L'Enfant sauvage*, Lewis Carroll and Lacan, the young girl grows up outside the cultural inscriptions and learns a new sense of self from her encounters with the mirror and from the rhythms of her body. She learns a sense of time and routine. Finally her pity begins to transform the werewolf Duke into the world of the rational, where he too can be symbolised.

Reading Carter's fairy-tales as her female protagonists' confrontations with desire, in all its unruly 'animalness', yields rich rewards. However, Patricia Duncker simplistically reads the tales as 'all men are beasts to women' and so sees the female protagonists as inevitably enacting the roles of victims of male violence. Red Riding Hood of the twice mentioned quotation, according to her 'sees that rape is inevitable . . . and decides to strip off, lie back and enjoy it. She wants it really, they all do.' Reading **'The Tiger's Bride'** Duncker claims the stripping of the girl's skin 'beautifully packaged and unveiled, is the ritual disrobing of the willing victims of pornography'. Because she reads the beasts as men in furry clothing, Duncker argues Carter has been unable to paint an 'alternative anti-sexist language of the erotic' because there is no conception of women as having autonomous desire. But Carter is doing that. Read the beasts as the projections of a feminine libido, and they become exactly that autonomous desire which the female characters need to recognise and reappropriate as a part of themselves (denied by the phallocentric culture). Isn't that why at the end of **'Tiger's Bride'** the tiger's licking reveals the tiger in the woman protagonist, beneath the cultural construction of the demure? Looked at again, this is not read as woman re-

enacting pornography for the male gaze, but as woman reappropriating libido:

> And each stroke of his tongue ripped off skin after successive skin, all the skins of a life in the world, and left behind a nascent patina of shining hairs. My earrings turned back to water and trickled down my shoulders; I shrugged the drops off my beautiful fur.
>
> (p. 67)

Lewallen does read the beasts as female desire, but argues that the female protagonists are still locked within a binary prescription of either 'fuck or be fucked'. However, I would argue she too brings this binary division into the discussion with her, when she asserts 'Sade's dualism is simple: sadist or masochist, fuck or be fucked, victim or aggressor'. She uses a reading of Carter's reading of Sade, in *Sadeian Woman,* to inform the stories and argues, wrongly I think, that Carter is putting forward woman as sexual aggressor (Sade's Juliette), rather than victim (Sade's Justine). I would suggest that Carter is using de Sade to argue for a wider incorporation of female sexuality, to argue that it too contains a whole gamut of 'perversions' alongside 'normal' sex. My main problem with Lewallen's dualism is that it incorporates no sense of the dangerous pleasures of sexuality and that is not necessarily simply a choice between being aggressor or victim. Her 'fuck or be fucked' interpretation ignores the notion of consent within the sado-masochistic transaction, and the question of who is fucking whom. Pat Califia's novel of lesbian S& M illustrates how it is usually the masochist who has the real control, who has the power to call 'enough'.[16] While asking for a more mutual sexual transaction, Lewallen dismisses the masochism in **'The Bloody Chamber'**, as too disturbing, 'my unease at being manipulated by the narrative to sympathise with masochism'.

Now I don't deny that it is disturbing (except, perhaps, for the reader who is a masochist). And if it was the only representation of female sexuality, I would be up in arms against its reinforcement of Freudian views. But it is only one of ten tales, ten variant representations. Moreover, the protagonist retracts her consent halfway through the narrative, when she realises her husband, Bluebeard, is planning to involve her in real torture and a 'snuff' denouement. Up until then, the adolescent protagonist has not denied her own interest in the sado-masochist transaction:

> I caught myself, suddenly, as he saw me, my pale face, the way the muscles in my neck stuck out like thin wire. I saw how much that cruel necklace became me. And, for the first time in my innocent and confined life, I sensed in myself a potentiality for corruption that took my breath away.
>
> (p. 11)

Throughout the narrative, this 'queasy craving' for the sexual encounters ('like the cravings of pregnant women for the taste of coal or chalk or tainted food') is admitted by the narrator, until she discovers the torture chamber and the three dead previous wives. Then she removes her consent and, with the help of an ineffectual blind piano-tuner[17] and her avenging mother, Bluebeard is defeated. Of course I would not deny that the tale, through its oscillation with the original fable, also comments on male sexual objectification and denigration of women. Clearly much of its representation draws on this—but the male violator is also portrayed as captured within the construction of masculinity (just as the female vampire was trapped within hers). The protagonist can recognise his 'stench of absolute despair . . . the atrocious loneliness of that monster'. Carter's representations of sexuality are more complex than many of her critics have allowed.

Maggie Anwell, in an excellent analysis of how the film *The Company of Wolves* was unable to get past the binary divide of victim/aggressor, does argue for a more complex psychic reading of female sexuality represented in the tale.[18] She suggests that the confrontation between 'repressed desire' (wolf) and the 'ego' (Red Riding Hood) ends with the ego's ability to accept the pleasurable aspects of desire, while controlling its less pleasurable aspects:

> The story, with its subversion of the familiar and its structure of story-telling within a story, suggests an ambiguity and plurality of interpretations which reminds us of our own capacity to dream . . . Not only does the material world shift its laws; we experience our own capacity for abnormal behaviour.
>
> (p. 82)

Are we to call only for constructions of sexuality with which we feel at ease, at this point in time, still within a phallocentric society? Especially when all we have to inscribe our own sexual identities from are cultural constructions? I would argue that just as it is the debates around the marginalised and pathologised 'perversities' that are breaking up the phallocentric construction of sexuality, so Carter's texts are beginning to sketch the polymorphous potentialities of female desire. These new representations may not fit into comfortable notions of sisterhood, but they may well prove liberating all the same. And Carter clearly knew what she was doing. In her foreword to her edition of the Perrault stories, she caricatures the seventeenth-century rationalistic response:

> The wolf consumes Red Riding Hood; what else can you expect if you talk to strange men, comments Perrault briskly. Let's not bother our heads with the mysteries of sado-masochistic attraction.
>
> (pp. 17-18)

Until we can take on board the disturbing and even violent elements of female sexuality, we will not be able to decode the full feminist agenda of these fairy-tales. We will be unable to recognise the representations of drives so far suppressed by our culture:

> Yet this, of course, is why it is so enormously important for women to write fiction *as* women—it is part of the slow process of decolonising our language and our basic habits of thought. I really do believe this . . . it has to do with the creation of a means of expression for an infinitely greater variety of experience than has been possible heretofore, to say things for which no language previously existed.[19]

With the death of Angela Carter we have lost an important feminist writer who was able to critique phallocentrism with ironic gusto and to develop a wider and more complex representation of femininity. Neither the mystification of her gentleness, nor the assumption that representations of sexuality are locked into pornography, should blind us to Carter's works' attempts to decolonise our habits of thought. If we need to expand our criteria to encompass her achievements, then so much the better.

Notes

[The above essay was originally published in the *Feminist Review,* 42 (1992), 2-15.]

[Merja Makinen's essay on *The Bloody Chamber and Other Stories,* one of Carter's most discussed texts, engages directly with material issues which have been central to recent feminist politics, in particular its debates about sexuality, violence and pornography. Makinen also participates in an early but already heated debate about Carter's work in relation to the politics of women's rewriting of the patriarchal literary tradition. In Makinen's hands the focus of this debate is moved to the politics of reading and the textual positioning of the reader. Her insistence on a historically specific analysis of readers leads to a sense of a reading process which is productive of irony, destabilisation and the opening up of meaning. This brings about fresh thinking on the question of whether Carter's texts only reproduce what they intend to attack. Makinen argues that, in order to comprehend Carter's deliberately disturbing text, critics, specifically feminist critics, need both to move beyond an overly simple opposition of masculine and feminine (the binary of victim/aggressor), and to expand their criteria of what constitutes a feminist text. Makinen's essay is also illuminating on formal matters in that it reads *The Bloody Chamber* as a set of interacting rather than separate stories. Ed.]

1. Margaret Atwood, 'Magic Token Through the Dark Forest', *Observer,* 23 February 1992, p. 61; Lorna Sage, 'The Soaring Imagination', *Guardian,* 17 February 1992, p. 37; *The Late Show,* presented by Tracy McLeod, BBC2, 18 February 1992.

2. Later published with another of her radio plays, as *Come Unto These Yellow Sands: Four Radio Plays* (Newcastle, 1985).

3. For all that I will go on to question Patricia Duncker's reading of Carter's representation of female sexuality in 'Re-Imagining the Fairy Tales: Angela Carter's Bloody Chambers', *Literature and History,* 10:1 (1984), 3-14, she does give a good historical reading of fairy-tales, with much more analysis than Carter's version.

4. Angela Carter, *The Bloody Chamber and Other Stories* (London, 1979), p. 118. All subsequent quotations are from this edition.

5. Avis Lewallen, 'Wayward Girls But Wicked Women?', in *Perspectives on Pornography,* ed. Gary Day and Clive Bloom (Basingstoke, 1988).

6. Naomi Schor, 'Fetishism and its Ironies', *Nineteenth-Century French Studies,* 17:1-2 (1988-89), 89-97.

7. Carter, 'Notes from the Front Line', in *On Gender and Writing,* ed. Michelene Wandor (London, 1983), p. 69.

8. 'I try when I write fiction, to think on my feet—to present a number of propositions in a variety of different ways, and to leave the reader to construct her own fiction for herself from the elements of my fiction' (Carter, 'Notes from the Front Line').

9. Mary Kelly, *Post Partum Document* (London, 1984), p. xiii.

10. Helen Carr, ed. *From My Guy to Sci-Fi* (London, 1989).

11. Nicci Gerrard, *Into the Mainstream* (London, 1989).

12. I am indebted to Helena Blakemore's forthcoming doctoral thesis, 'Reading Strategies: Problems in the Study of Contemporary British Fiction' (Middlesex University).

13. Paulina Palmer, 'From Coded Mannequin to Bird Woman: Angela Carter's Magic Flight', in *Women Reading Women Writing,* ed. Sue Roe (Brighton, 1987), pp. 177-205.

14. Arguably Christina Rossetti's poetry, especially the notorious *Goblin Market,* employed a similar device in the nineteenth century and Ellen Moers in *Literary Women* (London, 1978) argued for a tradition of 'female gothic' tales that such strategies could belong to.

15. Carter, *The Sadeian Woman: An Exercise in Cultural History* (London, 1979).

16. Pat Califia, *Macho Sluts* (Boston, MA, 1989).

17. That Duncker argues the blind piano-tuner represents castrated male sexuality, referring to Rochester in *Jane Eyre,* situates her feminist strategy. She does not incorporate later psychoanalytic feminist readings, that could allow Carter's protagonist to elect for a man with whom she will not be the object of the male gaze, as she was with her husband.

18. Maggie Anwell, 'Lolita Meets the Werewolf', in *The Female Gaze: Women As Viewers of Popular Culture,* ed. Lorraine Gamman and Margaret Marshment (London, 1988), pp. 76-85.

19. Carter, 'Notes from the Front Line', p. 75.

Rikki Ducornet (essay date fall 1994)

SOURCE: Ducornet, Rikki. "A Scatological and Cannibal Clock: Angela Carter's 'The Fall River Axe Murders.'" *Review of Contemporary Fiction* 14, no. 3 (fall 1994): 37-41.

[*In the following essay, Ducornet details the narrative significance of various bodily symbols and metaphors in "The Fall River Axe Murders."*]

At the story's ["**The Fall River Axe Murders**"] center, the sun's vortex gyres; it is, turn by turn: a Catherine's wheel, the unstoppable face of a clock, the mouth of Moloch, of an ogress, a furnace, an anus, and a vexing mirror which, like a hangman's noose, mercilessly distorts the features.

Automatons, the Bordens—all freaks, extremes of nature, the sins of avarice, gluttony, and anger personified—ambulate within the abridged universe of a clockwork house. Wound to a frenzy, they rotate about the dark hole of Lizzie's rage in an ever-diminishing orbit.

Like Saint Catherine, Lizzie is emblematic and exemplary; she is reduced to sign—the ax she carries within her grinding madly. In fact, Lizzie is the other side of Catherine's coin, the dark face of the moon: she is the Saint's negative. Her raptures lead not to Heaven but to Hell. In place of a halo Lizzie Borden wears a chamber pot. And like that other emblematic female, Red Riding Hood ("**A Company of Wolves**"), Lizzie is bleeding. The menstrual cycle, the ticking clock, the factory siren, the sun, the moon, and the chamber pot are all incontournable reminders of mortality.

Upon her room's revolving stage, Lizzie makes a *planetary round.* (And here I cannot help but recall a possible pun on *axis* and *axes* uncovered in *Alice* [*Alice's*

Adventures in Wonderland]; i.e., the Red Queen's viciously cycled obsession with axing off heads.) An infernal teetotum spelled upon a wheeling stage, Lizzie keeps herself indoors as if she were a piece of photosensitive paper; she would remain white, unimpressed by the dark man she has conjured and who she believes circles the house relentlessly. (Lizzie is much like that other murderous puppet of Carter's—Lady Purple. Part Kali, part Erzsebet Bathory, Lady Purple, too, has been made monstrous by the voracity of others. She, too, is *all twang, all tension.*)

Infernal machine, a circus ring which offers the devil's own dancing dogs (Sirius, along with sun and moon, blazes down upon this cosmical theater), Spindle City and the Borden homestead are contained within a magic circle, transmogrified into things so small as to fit in Old Borden's pocket. Lizzie has been *spelled,* reduced to dead. Self-repeating, her soul in bandages, she paces the coffin house like a perambulating mummy. (So coffinlike is the house, that *the maid lies on her back . . . in case she dies during the night. . . .*) And this *spelling* refers to Morse code, to the coded messages that tattoo murderous demands upon Lizzie's brain—perhaps the ghostly drumming of those vanished aborigines who have cursed the land with madness and death. Finally, Lizzie's stepmother *oppressed her like a spell.* If Lizzie escapes briefly to Europe, the trip is but a *round trip,* and any news of abroad ripped into squares *so that they can wipe their arses. . . .*

Lizzie suffers *peculiar spells when her mind misses a beat.* Curious *lapses of consciousness . . . which often . . . come at the time of her menses.* The *sputtering radiance* which *emanates from everything* recalls the sputtering City Hall clock. At such moments, the very birds that sit in the trees are reduced to clockwork: *whirring, clicking and chucking like no birds known before.* And we are given the marvelous image of time halved like an apple: *time opened in two.* Time's halved apple affords a species of fractured gnosis, an *over-clarity.* Within the fracture, when the world stutters and Lizzie's brain misses a beat, a burglary takes place and a safe is assaulted with a pair of scissors. Old Borden confuses private property with private parts and is *a man raped.* To break the spell of evil fortune, he locks his rooms for luck and expands his holdings by constructing a brick building the size of a city block (but this will not prevent his own block from being knocked off in the end. He will lie in his coffin headless, Lizzie's gold ring orbiting his little finger.)[1]

Emperor of the City of Spindles, Old Borden is Capital as Coffin Maker, Grim Reaper, Time's Passing. He is both undertaker and hearse. The only thing Edenic in

the wasteland of his making is a pear tree laden with fruit and which he *waters with his own urine.* Time is money, and both spell Death. Like salmonella, emblems proliferate, and suddenly Old Borden and his fat wife embody Appetite; the gingerbread house and all within it are threatened by that bottomless pit: Mrs. Borden's mouth. If Time and Heat have thus far ruled the day, Meat joins in at noon creating a diabolic trinity whose holy of holies is the chamber pot—a necromancer's mirror of *merde* which reflects a flux of apocalyptic associations. Household objects rise to the surface of a *queasy water*; the master bedroom is a *wunderkammer* of domestic horrors which includes the mystic implements of Mrs. Borden's *toilette: a bone comb missing three teeth and lightly threaded with grey hairs* and *a hairpiece curled up like a dead squirrel.*

Consider for a moment that squirrel and that comb. Skull-like, the comb is missing teeth, just as Lizzie's mind misses beats. The comb represents mortality (comb and hairpiece comprising an impoverished *Vanitas*); a comb *sans* teeth could be an emblem of stuttering time. Curled up, the squirrel is simultaneously fetal and dead (Lizzie's own menses are all for naught); it creates a snarling vortex, a cingulum of sorts, a noose. (This *nature morte* prefigures the list of burgled objects which include Mrs. Borden's *collar* necklace and her watch!)

And now, the house, an architectural infamy—built like a squirrel cage or a revolving door, spelled, smelling of menstrual blood and sweat—is reduced by the rotary mouth of the ogress stepmother to a prodigious body of mortal evidence: it fumes.

If at the house's center an anus rages and a mouth, an inventory of sound, like so many gaseous bodies in orbit, will return as inevitably as sun, moon, and mutton (like the cow of nursery rhyme, the mutton, quite *high* enough to jump over the moon, will return to the table morning, noon, and night): *hot, fire, sputter, stutter* (Lizzie's hair, cracking with static, stutters too); *heat, meat, eat.*[2]

Excessive appetite and *copious purges,* gyre and gimble until Lizzie cuts loose and *the eaters become the meal.* Within the house of gingerbread, appetite is the only thing *not kept within confinement.* Not only is Mrs. Borden's appetite prodigious, Old Borden *would gobble up the city of Fall River.*

A constant confusion is sustained between mentally and physically ingesting and digesting, between mouth and anus, coffin and house, pockets, chamber pots and clocks. The Bordens are likened to the Sprats who, as you will recall, licked the platter clean. In other words, they left Lizzie nothing with which to satisfy her hunger. She is not an eater but is instead eaten away by anger and the gnashing of her bleeding womb. This anger has made her supernatural; if she has *the jaws of a concentration camp attendant* and the eyes of Red Riding Hood's wolf, she is in fact a werewolf ruled by the moon. We even catch a glimpse of her howling.

Clocks are central to the tale, and the Borden dining room contains a very special clock intriguingly silent. Recall what Lewis Carroll had to say about stopped clocks: *they are right twice a day.* Even when time stands still, history repeats itself: *A stopped clock of black marble, shaped like a Greek mausoleum, stood on the sideboard, becalmed. Father stood at the head of the table and shaved the meat.*

The father standing at the head of the Greek table is Jupiter who, because he feared his offspring with Metis would be more exalted than he, devoured her. After, he suffered such acute pain he told Vulcan to split his head open. Armed and fully grown, Minerva leaped from her father's brain.

The story is revelatory. Children of Freud, we know that Lizzie, motherless and eaten, is Old Borden's brain child. By cleaving her father's head, she gives birth to her full-grown self. And we know, without being told, that Lizzie's *dark man* is a figment of her mind; that the scatalogical burglar who fouls Old Borden's bed is none other than Lizzie herself. (We can appreciate, also, that Borden's factory chimney was the tallest for its time in the United States!)

Finally, to return to Saint Catharine: Catharine's wheel was set with razors. Just as her body was placed upon it and made to spin, the wheel broke apart with such violence the razors reeled into the crowd hacking limbs and slitting throats.[3]

The coloring of this domestic apocalypse must be crude and the *design profoundly simplified for the maximum emblematic effect.*

Notes

1. The Bordens' skulls were sent to Harvard for examination.

2. Again, I think of Alice: that tea party in orbit. The Bordens are a syzygy—sun, earth, and moon in alignment.

3. If the Palladium—the clockwork statue of Pallas Athena (Minerva)—did not carry an ax or a wheel, she did carry a pike and a *spindle.*

Becky McLaughlin (essay date fall 1995)

SOURCE: McLaughlin, Becky. "Perverse Pleasure and Fetishized Text: The Deathly Erotics of Carter's 'The Bloody Chamber.'" *Style* 29, no. 3 (fall 1995): 404-22.

[*In the following essay, McLaughlin analyzes the psychosexual implications of the narrator's "perverted" point of view in "The Bloody Chamber."*]

> It takes an iron nerve to perceive the connection between the promise of life implicit in eroticism and the sensuous aspect of death. Mankind conspires to ignore the fact that death is also the youth of things. Blindfolded, we refuse to see that only death guarantees the fresh upsurging without which life would be blind.
>
> —Georges Bataille, *Death and Sensuality*

Angela Carter shows through her collection of short stories, ***The Bloody Chamber,*** that she has just such a nerve of iron as Georges Bataille suggests is needed for perceiving the connection between life and death. Even the illustration on the front cover of this slim volume suggests the eroticism of life and the sensuality of death: a dewy, white lily with a phallic stamen jutting from its hidden center emerges through a rupture in dry, flat ground. Around the base of the lily, thick black cords of stem wrap themselves in vertiginous, maze-like coils. Like the book itself, the lily is a kind of bloody chamber, for it has droplets of blood on its interior and exterior walls where the stem's sharp thorns have pricked it.[1]

What makes this illustration interesting is its kaleidoscopic quality. One moment the lily represents life and the next moment, death. Because of the lily's lush, white petals, it seems bloated with fecund vegetable vitality, and yet lilies are known as burial flowers, funeral decor, the stuff of a dead man's nosegay. Even the blood that trickles down the sides of the lily and splashes onto its leaves has an ambiguous quality, for it suggests both the vitality of the circulatory system and the mortality of flesh. One moment the lily looks female and the next moment, male. At first glance, for example, the lily appears to be a female receptacle, its stamen a clitoris, and the serpentine stem a phallus. On second glance, however, the penile shape of the lily begins to suggest the contours of the phallus and the coiled stem an all-encompassing vaginal "maw." This vaginal "maw" doubles as the mysterious place from which life emerges and that dark abyss into which man fears falling and from which he fears never to return: eros and thanatos, the life force and the death drive.

In a discussion of the partial drive and its circuit, Jacques Lacan makes reference to a fragment of Heraclitus: "to *the bow is given the name of life . . . and its work is death*" (177). The dialectic of the bow, says Lacan, is integrated in the drive. This bow or the curve of sexual fulfillment in the living being is represented by Lacan in the form of an inverted lily:

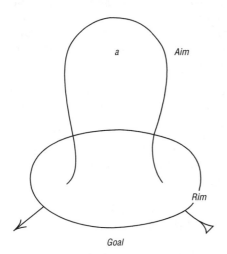

It is appropriate that the cover of Carter's collection evokes life and death, sexuality and aggression, female and male, the *jouissance* of the real and the dry cracked ground of the symbolic. For all of these elements are present in Carter's stories, overlapping and intertwining with one another just as they do in the best of fantasies. I do not, however, intend to discuss these intersections in each story. Instead, I intend to economize or, more accurately, to metonymize by allowing one story, **"The Bloody Chamber,"** to stand in for the entire collection. Obviously, this casts me into the position of fetishist or pervert, as I realize but at the same time disavow Carter's symbolic castration, her inability to say it all. I take this perverted position because I am not entirely sure that it is possible to read Carter's story from any other. In fact, as I will argue in this paper, Carter herself writes from the position of pervert and thus forces her reader into perverse collaboration. But, then, perhaps this is as it should be, for in fantastic literature, says Rosemary Jackson, "[m]ovement and stillness, life and death, subject and object, mind and matter, become as one" (80). The impossible structures around which fantastic narratives are woven, she says, are "related to this drive towards a realization of contradictory elements merging together in the desire for undifferentiation" (80), a desire for that which is beyond the pleasure principle. This fantastic movement "towards an imaginary zero condition, without time or space, a condition of entropy" (79), produces an "other" region, one described by Maurice Blanchot as "the result of pure transgression" (qtd. in Jackson 79).[2] It is into this "other" region of perversion that Carter's first-person narrator goes when she travels by train to the "faery solitude" of her husband's castle, which is "at home neither on the land

nor on the water, a mysterious, amphibious place, contravening the materiality of both earth and waves" (**"Chamber"** [**"The Bloody Chamber"**] 13).

I. Mirror Images: Paranoia's Delusion and Perversion's Fetish

The story of "Blue Beard" has been around a long time—at least since 1697, when it appeared in Charles Perrault's book of fairy tales. Although Carter renames the story, calling it **"The Bloody Chamber,"** we know almost immediately who the rich marquis really is and the violent end he has in mind for his innocent young wife. Because his wife is the narrator of the story, however, we know that the marquis's murderous plot will be interrupted and his wife spared. What we do not know, until the end of the story, is who will get the credit for this heroic intervention. As we read along, we think perhaps that it will be the blind piano-tuner who befriends the hapless narrator. But as adept as he may be at keeping the narrator's piano in tune, he is useless as an opponent to the marquis. No, Carter's hero turns out to be none other than the narrator's mother, a woman who brandishes a gun and gallops up on a horse in a manner not unlike the cavalry at the end of a Cowboy-and-Indian movie. Except for its rather startling ending, Carter's story has much in common with gothic fiction and its celluloid offspring: the paranoid woman's film and the horror flick. I mention the gothic tradition because Carter seems to have drawn on it in her rewriting of "Blue Beard" and because its paranoid aspect is reflected in the perversion of **"The Bloody Chamber."**

In the paranoid woman's film—recall, for example, Hitchcock's *Rebecca*—a young woman marries a man many years her senior, a man who is still virtually a stranger to her, a man with a past that he is unable or unwilling to talk about. Paranoia sets in once the newlyweds arrive at what Mary Ann Doane describes as the genre's "large and forbidding house, mansion, or castle" (124).[3] There the new wife is introduced to the staff, which usually includes a hostile housekeeper who views the new wife with dislike or disdain. Before long, the husband's business begins to occupy most of his time, and the lonely wife becomes unsure of his love for her. It does not help matters that the husband generally has been married before to a beautiful woman. With very little to keep her busy, the naive young wife begins an investigation in order to learn more about her distant husband, and this investigation always leads to the very room that has been put off limits. What the wife finds behind the locked door either clears away all doubts about her husband or renders him absolutely monstrous. Whichever the case may be, what the wife finds is, according to Doane, always an element of herself.

Obviously, this narrative could be Carter's, for in **"The Bloody Chamber"** the narrator describes herself as a seventeen-year-old girl with "pointed breasts and shoul-

ders" (8) and her husband as a man much older than
she is, a fact to which attest the "streaks of pure silver
in his dark mane" (9). We know that he is very much a
stranger to her when she says that his face sometimes
appeared to her as a mask that concealed his "real"
face. Upon arrival at his castle "with its turrets of misty
blue, its courtyard, its spiked gate" (13), the young
bride, like the young bride in *Rebecca,* is introduced to
the housekeeper, a woman with a "bland, pale, impas-
sive, dislikeable face" (14) whose "correct but lifeless"
(14) greeting chills her to the bone. Worse yet is the
fact that even before the marriage is properly consummated, the marquis announces that he has business to
attend to in connection with his estates and his companies. Later in the story, the marquis's business takes
him away from the castle, and during his absence, his
young wife finds herself riven by jealous speculations:
"Might he have left me, not for Wall Street but for an
importunate mistress tucked away God knows where
who knew how to pleasure him far better than a girl
whose fingers had been exercised, hitherto, only by the
practice of scales and arpeggios?" (22). Soon after begins the search for her husband's "true nature." After
ransacking his desk and discovering a file marked "Personal" that contains letters from his former wives, she
makes her way to the one room the marquis has asked
her not to enter, a room that contains the remains of his
three murdered wives.

Like the female character at the center of the paranoid
woman's film, Carter's heroine encounters the residue
of some other woman (other *women,* in this case) who
once occupied her position as wife. This encounter,
says Doane, occasions the "collapse of the subject/
object distinction," for the "woman sees herself slowly
becoming another, duplicating an earlier identity as
though history, particularly in the case of women, were
bound to repeat itself" (142). Although this collapse
represents two aspects of the paranoid structure—what
Doane refers to as "a destabilization of the oppositions
between internal and external, subject and object" and
"the foreclosure of the paternal signifier and corresponding fusion with the maternal" (134)—it might just as
well represent the perverse structure. For perversion,
too, upsets these defining limits. Or, as Louise Kaplan
says, "perversion is an attempt to unsettle the boundaries between the real and the not-real" (119).

What I wish to illustrate, in drawing a parallel between
paranoia and perversion, is the similarity of the positions out of which Carter's narrator and the marquis
function. In other words, the narrator's paranoia is the
mirror image of the marquis's perversion. The fact that
both characters have been reared by powerful mother
figures and that both are fatherless is of the utmost importance, for the pathology of paranoia and perversion
arises out of a problematic relationship to the father or
the paternal signifier. As we know from the beginning

of the story, because the narrator loses her father when
she is just a child, she thus grows up in an entirely female household, one that consists of herself, her mother,
and her nurse. In a passage during which she describes
her mother as "eagle-featured" and "indomitable," she
says that her mother had "gladly, scandalously, defiantly
beggared herself for love; and, one fine day, her gallant
soldier never returned from the wars, leaving his wife
and child a legacy of tears that never quite dried" (7-8).
And although the marquis is old enough to have witnessed the death of both parents, his mother's influence
lives on in the form of the opal ring that he gives to his
new bride, of which I will have more to say later. As if
one mother is not enough for the marquis, the housekeeper he employs has once been his foster mother;
consequently, when he introduces her to his young
bride, any vague hope the bride has of unseating the
housekeeper or undermining her authority is immediately crushed, for, as the marquis says, she is "as much
part of the house as I am, my dear" (14).

Because the intervention of the father disturbs the dyadic, narcissistic bond between mother and child,
thereby creating difference, introducing lack, and setting desire in motion, his function is crucial. For the
seventeen-year-old bride and her silver-maned husband,
however, this intervention appears not to have occurred.
Thus, both characters are involved in a "drama of seeing" that is related, in one way or another, to castration
anxiety. In paranoia, on the one hand, the Name-of-the-
Father is foreclosed, resulting in a disturbance of the relation between subject and object or an inability to distinguish between the two. In perversion, on the other
hand, the Name-of-the-Father is disavowed rather than
foreclosed, but the end result is virtually the same: the
perverse subject refuses to acknowledge the difference
between mother and father, insisting as he does that the
mother, too, possesses a penis. In paranoia, the same
mechanism that suggests a destabilization of oppositions is the same mechanism with which the paranoiac
attempts to re-establish the opposition between subject
and object—the mechanism of projection.[4] Similarly, in
perversion the very thing the fetishist uses to avow the
maternal penis is also the thing he uses to defend against
psychosis by re-establishing the field of illusion necessary to a desiring or "normal" subject. In other words,
it is only through projection and the fetish that desire
and fantasy come into play.

According to Doane, "The delusion of paranoia is built
up to . . . take the place of the missing paternal signifier, the Name of the Father, hence the Law. There is a
sense, then, in which the paranoid delusion is a simulacrum of the law" (145). In gothic films, as well as in
Carter's narrative, "this simulacrum of legality is constituted by a hyperbolization of the image of the aggressive, punishing, castrating Father—an image which
compensates for a precise lack of castration anxiety on

the part of the paranoid subject" (145). Needless to say, the marquis functions as this "simulacrum of legality" for the seventeen-year-old narrator, since he is *precisely* a hyperbolic version of the father image Doane describes. For the pervert, by contrast, the simulacrum of the law is constituted by an other who is securely situated within the respectability of the social order—by a priest or policeman, for example, or in the case of Carter's story by an innocent young classical pianist straight from her mother's nurturing bosom.[5] The pervert must recreate the place of the Law in order to transgress it, for no sense of debauchery can be achieved unless the other is wrenched out of his or her system by accepting the *jouissance* that the pervert has succumbed to.

Thus, the narrator's paranoid delusion functions in much the same way as the marquis's fetish does. Both serve as substitutes for something that is missing in the symbolic register—that is, the parental signifiers. While the narrator uses the marquis as the castrating father in order to compensate for her lack of castration anxiety, the marquis uses the narrator as his fetish (the thing that allows him to believe in the existence of his mother's penis) to mask his overwhelming fear of castration. Paradoxically, then, the narrator and the marquis are situated in positions of protection and threat to each other. What I mean by this is that a simulacrum is just that—a simulacrum. There is always the possibility that this counterfeit image will crumble and the traumatic truth reassert itself.

Although Doane suggests that the image of "a potentially murderous father-like husband" actually conceals a far more acute fear, one "concerning the maternal figure and the annihilation of subjectivity" (145), I am not convinced that Carter's story bears this out. According to Doane, the female fears the sameness of the mother because of its threat to her subjectivity, while the male fears the difference of the mother because of its threat to his bodily integrity. And yet Carter uses the figure of the mother to protect both the marquis and his wife. For the marquis, the opal ring and the housekeeper function to keep his young wife from upsetting the apple cart or changing the status quo—that is, from asserting her difference, a difference against which the marquis must protect himself at all costs. For the narrator, the galloping mother on horseback functions as her rescuer and as a part of the new household established at the end of the story. In fact, the marital bliss of the narrator and her new husband, the blind piano-tuner, is made triangular by the presence of the narrator's mother, who moves in with the newly weds on the outskirts of Paris. Apparently, Carter's narrator has no fear of losing her subjectivity. In any event, she appears to have recovered from her bout with paranoia by the end of the story, for she no longer has need of the castrating, voyeuristic gaze of a man such as the marquis. Once she escapes the clutches of her murderous husband, she

gives herself to the blind piano-tuner, a man whose blindness signifies him as castrated. Though a man who could offer emotional support to her at the castle, he is completely ineffectual in saving her from the marquis.

II. DIEGETIC PERVERSION: THE MARQUIS AND HIS WIFE

According to Jean Clavreul, author of "The Perverse Couple," a child first becomes a desiring subject (that is, first enters language) when it realizes that the mother has no penis. Formerly, the child has not known that there is a difference between mother and father, thinking incorrectly as it does that both are equipped with the same bodily accoutrements. The new discovery forces a reinterpretation that situates the child as the one who did not know. Its new knowledge is thus lodged in a previous not-knowing: to wit, there is a before and an after, a past, present, and future. The past involves not knowing; the present involves both a wish to know and the subsequent discovery; and the future entails a relationship between these events or positions with respect to knowledge. The child must learn that someone else knew more about the object of its desire (the mother) than it did. This place of non-knowledge with regard to sex and desire is the place at which the subject locates itself in the signifying chain, a place marked by the desire of the Other, the father.

In the perverse subject, however, this discovery is rejected or disavowed. The child refuses to be the one who did not know, refuses to acknowledge that someone else—namely, the father—had prior knowledge. And so the perverse subject's understanding of the human condition, conceived as the truth, becomes rigid and unmovable. He or she refuses to believe in the illusions or disillusions to which the "normal" subject submits, refuses to believe that the thing loved most was first unknown, then known and lost in one and the same moment. What this means in more concrete terms is that the perverse subject refuses to recognize that the mother does not have a penis. By refusing to recognize this absence or lack, the subject may then avow its existence elsewhere—in some other part of the body or in some external object. The material object that represents or initiates this disavowal is the fetish. The problem with perversion, however, is that it always hovers near the edge of psychosis, which entails an absolute knowledge outside of time and the field of illusion. Because the field of illusion is constitutive of the symbolic order, a knowledge that makes no place for it is a psychotic knowledge. For the psychotic, there is no field of illusion because nothing is thought to lie beneath the surface. Nothing is thought to be missing, nothing creates desire or curiosity. And without curiosity, there is no questioning spirit and little possibility of exchange within the symbolic community.

Although Parveen Adams argues in "Of Female Bondage" that the field of perversion is not a homogeneous one, pointing out differences not only among fetishism, masochism, and sadism but also among various sub-categories of masochism, she does mention a single characteristic from which all perversions derive: disavowal. While I think Adams is right to make a distinction between one form of perversion and another, I believe that all forms of perversion also include fantasy, the factor of suspense or deferral, and transgression of the Oedipal law. Because Carter's marquis is a virtual grab-bag of the perversions—fetishism, masochism, sadism, and voyeurism, to name a few—I will not spend time making the case that the marquis is one type of pervert or another. I will simply assert that he is a pervert *par excellence,* hovering as he does in that precarious border-land between the "normal" and the psychotic. For example, through the use of the fetish and the fantasy screen, the marquis reconstructs the missing field of illusion just long enough to consummate his marriage. But once the sexual act has been completed—a genital consummation that satisfies desire and restores the symbolic order of difference—the marquis's wife must be murdered. For it is she who threatens the entire structure of disavowal upon which the marquis's being rests. Once she is strangled, decapitated, or pierced by a hundred spikes, her dead body becomes the fetishized object that allows the drive to continue its circuit.

Carter's text shows how these features operate. In the account the narrator gives of her courtship and marriage to the marquis, she mentions deferral time and time again. As she recounts the night spent in transit to the marquis's castle, she recalls his kiss and the nightdress he had given her, both of which hint at the wedding night "voluptuously deferred" until their installation "in his great ancestral bed" (8). While the young bride restlessly tosses and turns in her travel compartment aboard the train, wishing no doubt that her husband would take her maidenhead as the great pistons of the train thrust its powerful bulk along the tracks, he instead calmly smokes a cigar, rising up only once to look at his new wife in the adjoining compartment. Once they arrive at the castle, though the marquis strips his bride for inspection, he again delays genital consummation. As the narrator tells it, "he closed my legs like a book" and said, "Not yet. Later. Anticipation is the greater part of pleasure, my little love" (15). If what Adams says is accurate, that "disavowal . . . extends to sexual pleasure itself which is postponed through waiting and suspense" (252), then the marquis's words are certainly in keeping with the pervert's disavowal of difference. Like the masochist of which Gaylyn Studlar speaks, the marquis compulsively replays a moment that hesitates between concealment and disclosure, absence and presence, seduction and rejection—a moment that embodies the "Yes, I know, but . . ." of disavowal.

It is not until the marquis finds his wife looking at a pornographic book that he is able to perform the sexual act. What the fascinated young bride sees in that "slim volume with no title" is a picture of "a girl with tears hanging on her cheeks like stuck pearls, her cunt a split fig below the great globes of her buttocks on which the knotted tails of the cat were about to descend, while a man in a black mask fingered with his free hand his prick" (16-17). The caption beneath this picture reads, "Reproof of curiosity." Until now the marquis's wife has been an obstacle to his fantasy, but when her curiosity lures her into innocent prurience, she is projected into his fantasy.[6] She becomes the girl whose curiosity must be reproved and he the masked man. It is not surprising that the pervert would perceive curiosity as something that requires punishment, for it was his own original curiosity, his own initial desire to see or to know, that led to the horrifying discovery that must forever after be disavowed. In this structure, the pages of the girl's book function as his fantasy screen. Though this time he kisses his wife with no reticence, he requests before impaling her with his connubial prick that she put on the ruby choker. Because the marquis's desire is based on presence rather than absence or lack, he must use an object—in this case, the choker—as the symbolic replacement of the mother's missing penis. So important is this fetish that, indeed, the marquis kisses "those blazing rubies" before kissing his wife. "Rapt, he intoned: 'Of her apparel she retains / Only her sonorous jewellery'" (17).[7]

The real reproof of curiosity comes after Carter's heroine has discovered "a door of worm-eaten oak" behind which lie the remains of the marquis's three former wives. In her fright at discovering the mutilated bodies of her predecessors, she drops the door's key into a pool of blood. No amount of scrubbing can remove the bloody stain that proves to the marquis his wife's guilt. And once the marquis has evidence of her guilt (the blood on the key suggests a knowledge that contravenes innocence), he can no longer use her as part of the perverse contract, for the disparity between them of innocence and corruption no longer exists. But the stain is more than evidence of a desire to see that must be punished. Because blood stains are often associated with menstruation and loss of maidenhead, the blood on the key is a reminder to the marquis of the mother's difference from the father. What has been repressed, through disavowal, is "the vision of the female body as the signifier of castration and hence disunity" (Doane 140), but for the marquis the repressed returns in the uncanny form of the red stain.

III. EXTRA-DIEGETIC PERVERSION: CARTER AND HER READER

Is it not patent, asks Clavreul, "that on the whole, erotic literature has been made up of writings by perverts?" (216). Perhaps it would be intemperate to say that the eroticism of **"The Bloody Chamber"** suggests the perversion of its writer. But, like the best of perverts, Carter knows that from the standpoint of eroticism, the so-called "normal" individual is "an inept yokel unable to elevate his love above a routine. The sexual good health that he brags about appears to derive from a lack of imagination" (Clavreul 216). Think, for example, of how Carter represents Jean-Yves, the young piano-tuner who falls in love with the narrator. He is described as a "slight, stooping figure" with "singularly sweet" eyes. Next to the sadistic and perverted marquis, he is pretty dull fare. Let us say, then, that Carter successfully employs the marquis's perversion in order to create an erotic narrative. The question is where this places her reader with respect to the field of perversion. As Clavreul argues, the fetishist's wife, the nymphomaniac's husband, and the pederast's protective older woman are even more in question than the fetishist, the nymphomaniac, or the pederast. What Clavreul seems to be suggesting is that the partner of a perverse subject is even more perverse than the perverse subject him- or herself. Perhaps it would not be inappropriate to conclude that part of the pleasure or bliss of reading Carter's narrative stems from the fact that writer and reader are caught up together in a perverse dynamic.

But wherein lies the eroticism of **"The Bloody Chamber"**? In order to answer this question, we must return to the fantasy that Freud refers to in his study of the origin of sexual perversion, "A Child Is Being Beaten." What I would like to suggest is that Carter's story recreates the child's fantasy of being beaten by the father. The original story of "Blue Beard," told through a third-person narrator, can be thought of as the first and third phases of the fantasy, in which the patient is merely the observer of another child's beating. Carter's rewriting, on the other hand, which is told through a first-person narrator, represents the repressed second phase of the fantasy, in which the patient herself is being beaten by her father. According to Freud,

> This being beaten is now a meeting-place between the sense of guilt and sexual love. It *is not only the punishment for the forbidden genital relation, but also the regressive substitute for it,* and from this latter source it derives the libidinal excitation which is from this time forward attached to it. . . . Here for the first time we have masochism.

> (117-18; Freud's italics)

Of course, in **"The Bloody Chamber"** no actual beatings take place, but there are metaphorical substitutes. When the marquis and the narrator are having cognac and cointreau in the library, for example, he takes her "to perch on his knee in a leather armchair beside the flickering log fire" (19).[8] The image, here, is one of father and chaste little daughter in a "shift of white muslin." As they sit together, he twines his fingers in the narrator's hair until she winces, and he insists that she continue wearing the ruby choker even though she tells him that it is growing very uncomfortable. What we have, in short, is a father figure punishing his young daughter.

Because the reader identifies with the first-person narrator, the point of view from which Carter writes the story places the reader in the position of the child who is being beaten. Does this, perchance, make Carter a sadist and the reader a masochist? Hardly. According to Slavoj Zizek, the usual notion of sadism places the sadist in "the position of an absolute subject usurping the right to enjoy, without restraint, the body of the other, reducing him/her to an object-instrument for the satisfaction of his own will" (*Looking Awry* 108). But this is not the way a Lacanian defines the sadist. As Zizek explains it, the sadist occupies "the position of the object-instrument, while the split subject is precisely his other (the victim). The pervert does not pursue his activity for his own pleasure, but for the enjoyment of the Other—he finds enjoyment precisely in this instrumentalization, in working for the enjoyment of the Other" (108-09). Since Carter is the author of the story, we might be tempted to place her in the position of absolute subject, but we must not allow ourselves to make this mistake. The position she occupies is that of object-instrument, while the reader represents her victim, or the split subject. In providing a story for the reader's consumption, Carter is pursuing not her own pleasure, but that of the Other. She is the reader's instrument, the means through which the reader achieves enjoyment.

IV. CARTER'S MARQUIS: THE OBSCENE FIGURE OF THE ANAL FATHER

It is appropriate to think of the marquis in terms of the punishing father, for he is what Mladen Dolar refers to as "the bad father, the castrater, the menacing and jealous figure that evokes the father of the primal horde, the father linked with *jouissance*" (10). In a discussion of Gaston Leroux's *The Phantom of the Opera*, Zizek refers to the same figure as the "anal father." According to Zizek, the phantom-like object that hinders a "normal" sexual relationship is not the "dead" symbolic father, but the father who is still alive, the father who has not been transformed into a symbolic function, but remains a partial object: "the obscene little man who is the clearest embodiment of the phenomenon of the 'uncanny'" ("Grimaces" 54). Although it may seem odd to conflate the handsome marquis with the phantom of the opera, both wear masks that conceal their place among the living dead. That is not to say that they inhabit a place between life and death, but that "as the dead . . . they are 'more alive than life itself,' having access to the life-substance prior to its symbolic mortification" ("Grimaces" 47). According to the narrator, the marquis's waxen face is "perfectly smooth, like a stone on a beach whose fissures have been eroded by successive tides" (9). And it is this very smoothness that suggests the mask, for as the narrator says,

> sometimes that face, in stillness when he listened to me playing, with the heavy eyelids folded over eyes that always disturbed me by their absolute absence of light, seemed to me like a mask, as if his real face, the face that truly reflected all the life he had led in the world before he met me, before, even, I was born, as though that face lay underneath this mask.
>
> (9)

Even the absence of light in the marquis's eyes is reminiscent of Leroux's phantom. For, as is said of the phantom, his "eyes are so deep that you can hardly see the fixed pupils. All you can see is two big black holes, as in a dead man's skull" (12).

Of course, what the marquis hides beneath his "waxen stillness" are centuries of sadism and murder. Although the narrator knows that her husband is far older than she is, what she does not know is that he has survived for eons—like the figure of the vampire—on the bloody murder of young women. As the blind piano-tuner tells Carter's heroine, there once lived a marquis who hunted "young girls on the mainland; he hunted them with dogs, as though they were foxes. My grandfather had it from his grandfather, how the Marquis pulled a head out of his saddle bag and showed it to the blacksmith. . . . And it was the head of the blacksmith's wife" (33). In his naivete, the blind piano-tuner assumes that this is mere legend, but as both he and the marquis's hapless bride soon discover, the marquis of yore is none other than the narrator's new husband, still "alive" after all these years, but forced to find a new hunting ground, the salons of Paris.

Like any figure of the living dead, including Leroux's phantom and Bram Stoker's vampire, Carter's marquis confronts those who get too close with what Joan Copjec calls "an absence of absence—an Other—who threatens to asphyxiate [them]" ("Vampires" 33). Although the narrator of **"The Bloody Chamber"** does not refer to the affect of anxiety by name, her references to the oppressive heaviness that imbues the marquis suggest the anxiety that accompanies the surplus body of the real. Early in the story, for example, the narrator describes the marquis as older, much older than she. And yet, she says, "his strange, heavy, almost waxen face was not lined by experience" (9). Later in the story, when describing how her new husband's embraces affect her, she says that he creates in her both arousal and a repugnance "for his white, heavy flesh that had too much in common with the armful of arum lilies . . . , those undertakers' lilies with the heavy pollen" (15).

The lily, with which I began my discussion of Carter's story, turns up here in all its ambiguous glory, functioning as part of the cloying, claustrophobic atmosphere into which the narrator is thrust after her marriage to the marquis. These lilies "that are white. And stain you," says the narrator, "I always associated with him [the marquis]" (15). In fact, the lilies, which sit in a tall jar, their stems distorted by the thick glass into dismembered arms, represent that massive, oppressive presence Žižek refers to as the stain of the real—that is, a dramatic surplus of the real—a mute object of enjoyment. Still later, the narrator refers to the marquis's "monstrous presence, heavy as if he had been gifted at birth with more specific gravity than the rest of us" (20)—a presence that always subtly oppresses her, even when she believes herself most in love with him. Finally, at the end of the story, the young bride finds her husband's proximity almost too much to bear. "The chthonic gravity of his presence," she tells us, "exerted a tremendous pressure on the room, so that the blood pounded in my ears as if we had been precipitated to the bottom of the sea" (35). The suffocating surplus that the narrator encounters in each of these moments with the marquis suggests a moment of anxiety, in which there is a doubling of the subject's self. In fact, what Žižek refers to as the "anal father" is the subject's double, a figure who follows him or her like a shadow and embodies a particular surplus. What the double gives body to is, as Žižek says, "the phantom-like Thing in me" ("Grimaces" 55): "In my double, I don't simply encounter myself (my mirror image), but first of all what is 'in me more than myself,' yet . . . conceived under another modality, that of the other, sublime, ethereal body, pure substance of enjoyment" (55).

It would seem, then, that though the marquis functions as the narrator's double, what she sees when she looks into his eyes is not so much her mirror image as the non-specular *objet petit a* (the surplus or what is "in her more than herself"). One might think, here, of Henry James's "The Jolly Corner," in which Spencer Brydon pursues his double only to be overcome with horror upon actually confronting it. What he sees in his double is himself, but also a monstrous surplus of himself. In each new encounter with the marquis, then, the narrator recognizes more and more of herself in the radical otherness of her double. Recall, for example, her revelation the night of the opera. She is wearing the ruby choker the marquis has given her, and when she sees the "sheer carnal avarice" of his regard, she drops her eyes only to lift them to her own lust-filled gaze seen in the gilded mirrors of the opera house: "I saw how much that cruel necklace became me. And, for the first time in my innocent and confined life, I sensed in myself a potentiality for corruption that took my breath away" (11). That is to say, she recognizes in herself the same excessive "sprout of enjoyment" that shows itself in the marquis. Recall, too, the scene in which he gives her the keys to the house. The narrator expresses fear, not of the marquis but of herself: "I seemed reborn in his unreflective eyes, reborn in unfamiliar shapes. I hardly recognized myself from his descriptions of me and yet, and yet—might there not be a grain of beastly truth in them?" (20). Until the end of the story, Carter's heroine is in fascinated pursuit of this double, but, just as Spencer Brydon does, when she realizes what the hunt is leading to—her own immolation—she wants out of the chase.

What is this phantom-like Thing, asks Žižek, "if not the so-called 'pregenital' (anal) object that must be surmounted for the 'normal' sexual relationship to realize itself?" (57). Because enjoyment and the symbolic order are thoroughly incompatible, one must renounce, sacrifice, or murder this surplus in order to become a member of the community. And that is exactly what the narrator in **"The Bloody Chamber"** must do—get rid of that impediment (that is, the marquis *qua* "anal father") to the "normal" sexual relationship. Because of the perverse nature of their relationship—because the third term has been excluded—the narrator and the marquis are transgressors of the Law and as such remain outside the symbolic, on the margins of meaning, beyond the beautiful, which Frances Ferguson defines as "the world of society under the aegis of women and children" (7). In fact, their alienation is attested to, metaphorically, by the very position of the castle, which is for a portion of each day literally "cut off by the tide from land."

It is only symbolic authority, or the Name-of-the-Father, that can save the narrator from the horror of the real. And this symbolic authority arrives, not a minute too soon, in the person of the narrator's mother, who carries an antique service revolver that originally belonged to the narrator's father. What this revolver represents, of course, is the phallus. One might say, therefore, that in being hit by that "single, irreproachable bullet," the marquis has been submitted to the phallic function. At last he is truly "dead." And the narrator is able to join the world of generation that operates by way of habit, custom, and familiarity. All that remains of her life with the marquis is a blood-red reminder lodged between her eyes: a heart-shaped stain, the residue of the real, the *objet petit a*. The marquis is dead and gone, yes, but he has left his mark, for in pressing the blood-stained key to his disobedient wife's forehead, he has left there the tell-tale sign of her desire branded on her face for all to see.

V. THE OPAL RING: GAZE AS THE MATERNAL SUPEREGO

The opal ring is first mentioned when the narrator recounts the marquis's marriage proposal: "He had the ring ready in a leather box lined with crimson velvet, a fire opal the size of a pigeon's egg set in a complicated circle of dark antique gold" (9). But the narrator is not the first woman to wear the marquis's ring. In fact, says

the narrator, it "had been his own mother's ring, and his grandmother's, and her mother's before that, given to an ancestor by Catherine de Medici" (9). Not only is the ring's history matrilineal, but also, time out of mind, every bride that has come to the castle has worn it. Like the blot or the stain in a Hitchcock film, the fire opal in Carter's text is the strange detail that stands out, that does not entirely mesh with the symbolic network of reality—and, ultimately, it is this strange detail which indicates in the story that something is not quite right. Perhaps one might argue that the ring belongs with the rites of marriage, that institutional "fiction" within the symbolic order of exchange. But the fact that the ring is an opal rather than a diamond suggests a corruption of the institutional signifiers. A diamond is forever, but opals mean bad luck. A testament to this superstition is that the marquis's wives, each of whom has worn the ring, have suffered fatal accidents. The wives, who are corporeal, die; but the ring, which is real in the Lacanian sense, remains very much alive.

As if to exaggerate the ring's obscenely large size and the perversity of its precious stone, the marquis demands that his wife wear it on the outside of her kid glove. There it glimmers "like a gypsy's magic ball." So described, the ring, like the Hitchcockian stain of which Žižek speaks, evokes the threatening gaze of the Other—the gaze, that is, of the mother or the maternal superego. Even words used to describe the ring such as "sultry" and "witchy" invest it with a powerful female sexuality. What I would like to suggest, therefore, is that the ring, in Žižek's words, is an "embodiment in the real of a discord, an unresolved tension in intersubjective relations" (*Looking Awry* 99). This unresolved tension relates, of course, to the marquis's perversion and his mother's complicity in it. Because it is through the eye that the pervert makes the discovery of his mother's castration, the eye will continue to play an important role in his life. For the pervert, says Clavreul, the eye will hold the problematic position that the phallus and the beloved object hold for the normal or neurotic subject. Naturally, the mother's look occupies a place of particular importance to the pervert. Because she is his spectator at the important moment of the discovery and the subsequent disavowal, it is her look that participates or assists in the formation of the young pervert's sexuality. But how does this formation occur? When Piera Aulagnier asks, "With what eye does the mother see her child, who looks at her?" (qtd. in Clavreul 226), the question points to the more primary question of the scopophilic drive: "Can the mother," asks Clavreul, "believe that her child is looking at her innocently?" He answers by asserting that the relation between the look and the eye is one cloaked in mystery:

> This eye, which did not consent to recognize itself as deceived or tricked, discovers itself and lets itself be discovered as deceiving. Is the eye there to see, to

look, to *jouir,* or better yet, to seduce? It is always there that the pervert will have to employ his charms [or spells]. From the side of this "seeing" that proposes itself as true, he will have to reconstitute the illusory.

(226)

What Clavreul is talking about in this discussion of the relation between the eye and the look is the dialectic that exists between the rim-structure of the eye and what Lacan refers to as the gaze, one of the many manifestations of the *objet petit a.* Because the perverse subject has been "wounded" through the eye—he sees, at some horrific moment, that there is a difference between mother and father—it will be through the eye that he protects himself from further traumatic discoveries. But his eye will operate as the lure or the *fascinum,* of which Lacan speaks in his chapter on the gaze in *The Four Fundamental Concepts of Psycho-Analysis,* and *not* as the desiring eye. The reverse of Lacan's formula for fantasy, $ \$ \diamond a $, is the formula for perversion, $ a \diamond \$ $. In fantasy, the split subject takes up some position in relation to the *objet petit a* as cause of desire. In perversion, on the other hand, by taking up the opposite position in the formula, the subject offers "itself" to the other as *objet petit a* or the object-instrument of enjoyment. Because the gaze arrests movement, freezing it through fascination, it is associated with the evil eye or the *fascinum.* And this arrested movement, or suspension, is precisely what the perverse subject seeks in order to keep disavowal in play. If the *fascinum* is antimovement, the moment of seeing is its corrective. As Lacan says, it "can intervene here only as a suture . . . , and it is taken up again in a dialectic, that sort of temporal progress that is called haste, thrust, forward movement" (118).

It is also important to understand that the mother plays the role of accomplice to the young pervert. She turns a blind or *unseeing* eye to the way in which her child's disavowal manifests itself and at the same time allows her look to "be seduced by the charm of the fetishes, by the child's gifts" (Clavreul 227). Although we can only speculate as to what gifts the young marquis might have offered his mother, we know exactly what form the gifts of the adult marquis take: the murders of his beautiful young wives. The murders that have taken place in **"The Bloody Chamber"** operate in much the same way they do in a Hitchcock movie. According to Žižek, murder does not involve a binary relationship, but a ternary one. That is to say, murder is always committed for the benefit of a third party. In the case of **"The Bloody Chamber,"** the third party is the marquis's dead but still very present mother.[9] In the story, the fire opal stands in for the marquis's mother or, more accurately, her complicitous look. Like the birds in Hitchcock's movie, *The Birds,* the ring is an incarnation of what Žižek describes as "a fundamental disorder in family relationships—the father is absent, the paternal

function . . . is suspended[,] and that vacuum is filled by the 'irrational' maternal superego, arbitrary, wicked, blocking 'normal' sexual relationships" (*Looking Awry* 99).

That the ring is the Lacanian object-gaze seems proven by the fact that each time the narrator looks at the ring, it seems to be gazing back at her. For example, when she enters the forbidden room where the marquis's dead wives are on display, the ring flashes what might be called a baleful look at the narrator, "as if to tell [her] the eye of God—his eye—was upon [her]" (29). Through most of the story, during which time the young bride has the ring in her possession, the ring is said to "glimmer" or "flash" or "simmer." At the end of the story, however, when the ring makes its way back into the marquis's possession, it loses all its fire. Because its insistent demand has been (or is about to be) answered, the ring shuts up, as it were. While the marquis's new wife manages to deny the horrifying demands of the "superegoical imperative," the marquis himself does not. He has ceded his desire and given in to the drive. And that is why he says, near the end of the story, that the fire opal will serve him "for a dozen more fiancées" (38). It must, for he is compelled to repeat, over and over again, the same bloody scenario—if he is not stopped somehow.

VI. From Bataille to Carter and Back Again: The Circuit of the Drive

The moment we identify Carter's story as a repeat performance of "Blue Beard," we know that we are in the field of the drives, for Freud believed repetition to be their key ingredient. In fact, says Copjec, the "being of the drives . . . *is* the compulsion to repeat. The aim of life is not evolution but regression, or, in its most seemingly contradictory form, the aim of life is death" ("Cutting Up" 232). To put it another way, if the drive is seen as pure life force, or *lamella,* then it is like the amoeba, immortal in its ability to survive any division. This division, which occurs spatially, is a splitting of one into two, two into four, four into eight, and so on. In other words, it is an endless and timeless proliferation of life that cannot be understood in the temporal terms of desire. There is no before or after, there are no markers of time in the field of the drives. And although no one likes to contemplate one's demise, perhaps more horrific still is the contemplation of living on forever. Regression can be thought of, then, as an endless loop or a return to that mythical place where no movement occurs, that place where progress is not the name of the game. But what has this to do with Carter? Her attempt to rewrite "Blue Beard" is not an evolution, but a regression that includes disavowal. Carter seems to say, "Yes, this is 'Blue Beard,' but. . . ." Her work is a renunciation of the old narrative, a throwing away of the cotton reel, an enunciation of the unary signifier, *fort,* that is meaningless in itself. And yet the old narrative reappears from "without" like the uncanny return of the repressed. This return is an utterance of the *da* that confers meaning onto the story. As in psychosis, the thing that gets thrown out—"only to return from 'without'—is, Lacan tells us, none other than the original (both desired and feared, loved and hated) signifier of the phallus" (McCauley 53). This circular movement is a rough adumbration of the drive, the purpose of which manifests itself in the aim rather than in the goal. According to Žižek, "the drive's ultimate aim is simply to reproduce itself as drive, to return to its circular path, to continue its path to and from the goal" (*Looking Awry* 5).

Although any narrative is by definition a kind of repetition, Carter's story engages writer and reader in the perverse act of telling or hearing a story whose end they already know. Or they both know and don't know. As Roland Barthes would say, they act toward themselves as if they do not know. The effect? A kind of literary disavowal. What is produced by this disavowal is a text that splits these subjects twice over, partaking as they do in both the field of bliss and that of pleasure. The text of bliss, on the one hand, says Barthes, "imposes a state of loss" (14). It is "the text that discomforts . . . , unsettles the reader's historical, cultural, psychological assumptions, the consistency of his tastes, values, memories, brings to a crisis his relation with language" (14). The text of pleasure, on the other hand, "contents, fills, grants euphoria" (14). It is "the text that comes from culture and does not break with it, is linked to a *comfortable* practice of reading" (14). The fact that Carter chooses to retell an old and familiar tale is a comfort to the reader. Like a child who requests that her or his parent read and re-read the same story over and over again, we are happy to encounter a story that we know, one that we have long ago mastered. And yet, by allowing what has been repressed in the original version to return full-force in the rewriting, Carter turns this familiar world upside down, upsetting our expectations and unsettling our assumptions about the nature of eroticism. If she offers us pleasure, she also offers us bliss. The sublime and the beautiful, the death drive and the life force: **"The Bloody Chamber"** contains them all. Carter's story is, as Bataille might say, an attempt to tear off the blindfold, to see that the body's "sewers" are also its sexual channels, to understand therein the connection between death and eroticism.

Notes

1. My references, here, are to the cover of the 1979 Penguin edition. In later years, the cover changed, depicting a young woman in the foreground and a castle in the background.

2. See Rosemary Jackson's discussion of Blanchot's *Le pas au-dela* in *Fantasy: The Literature of Subversion* (79).

3. This structure is the first in a long list of what Mary Ann Doane refers to as the usual elements of gothic fiction, the others being "a secret, often related to a family history, which the heroine must work to disclose; storms incarnating psychical torment; portraits; and locked doors" (124).

4. As Freudian theory explains projection, the infant expels and projects into the external world those things in itself that it finds unpleasurable. What it finds pleasurable, on the other hand, it incorporates or retains. It is through projection and introjection that the subject constructs the external and internal spaces that will make up its world.

5. See Clavreul's discussion (227) of "The Perverse Couple."

6. According to Clavreul, what creates erotic excitement in the pervert is the other's innocence. And, certainly, at this point in the story the narrator is still "innocent."

7. The marquis's fetish object is, I think, an interesting choice. The ruby choker had belonged to his grandmother, who lived through the Reign of Terror and into the days of the Directory. The origin of the choker, as the narrator explains, is thus: "the aristos who'd escaped the guillotine had an ironic fad of tying a red ribbon round their necks at just the point where the blade would have sliced it through, a red ribbon like the memory of a wound. And his grandmother, taken with the notion, had her ribbon made up in rubies; such a gesture of luxurious defiance!" (11). Most striking about this fetish is its paradoxical potential for castrating (death by strangulation) and at the same time concealing castration (a cover for the mark of the guillotine—or, perhaps, for a vampire bite).

8. The mere mention of *leather,* by metonymic association, suggests the boots and whip of the sadist.

9. It is important to mention the presence of the housekeeper in this connection, since she has been the marquis's foster mother and thus remains "bound to his family in the utmost feudal complicity" (14). What I am suggesting, of course, is that the housekeeper is yet another manifestation of the maternal superego. Although the narrator refers to the house as "this extraordinary machine," she might as well be referring to the housekeeper, for there is something machine-like and implacable in her demeanor, something that suggests the cruelty of Kant's moral law or the superego. As I have already suggested, so long as the housekeeper remains, the narrator will never become mistress of her own home.

Works Cited

Adams, Parveen. "Of Female Bondage." *Between Feminism and Psychoanalysis.* Ed. Teresa Brennan. London: Routledge, 1989. 247-65.

Barthes, Roland. *The Pleasure of the Text.* Trans. Richard Miller. New York: Hill and Wang, 1975.

Bataille, Georges. *Death and Sensuality: A Study of Eroticism and the Taboo.* New York: Walker, 1962.

Carter, Angela. "The Bloody Chamber." *The Bloody Chamber and Other Stories.* New York: Penguin, 1979. 7-41.

Clavreul, Jean. "The Perverse Couple." *Returning to Freud: Clinical Psychoanalysis in the School of Lacan.* Ed. and trans. Stuart Schneiderman. New Haven: Yale UP, 1980. 215-33.

Copiec, Joan. "Cutting Up." *Between Feminism and Psychoanalysis.* Ed. Teresa Brennan. London: Routledge, 1989. 227-46.

———. "Vampires, Breast-Feeding, and Anxiety." *October* 58 (1991): 24-43.

Doane, Mary Ann. "Paranoia and the Specular." *The Desire to Desire.* Bloomington: Indiana UP, 1987. 123-54.

Dolar, Mladen. "'I Shall Be with You on Your Wedding-Night': Lacan and the Uncanny." *October* 58 (1991): 5-23.

Ferguson, Frances. "The Nuclear Sublime." *Diacritics* 14 (1984): 4-10.

Freud, Sigmund. "A Child Is Being Beaten." *Sexuality and the Psychology of Love.* Ed. Philip Rieff. New York: Collier, 1963. 107-32.

Jackson, Rosemary. *Fantasy: The Literature of Subversion.* London: Methuen, 1981.

Kaplan, Louise J. *Female Perversions.* New York: Doubleday, 1991.

Lacan, Jacques. *The Four Fundamental Concepts of Psycho-Analysis.* Ed. Jacques-Alain Miller. Trans. Alan Sheridan. New York: Norton, 1973.

Leroux, Gaston. *The Phantom of the Opera.* New York: Hippocrene, 1990.

McCauley, Karen A. "Lacan and Questions of Desire in Psychosis and Feminine Sexuality." *Literature and Psychology* 37 (1992): 47-62.

Studlar, Gaylyn. "Masochism, Masquerade, and the Erotic Metamorphoses of Marlene Dietrich." *Fabrications: Costume and the Female Body.* Ed. Jane Gaines and Charlotte Herzog. New York: Routledge, 1990. 229-49.

Žižek, Slavoj. "Grimaces of the Real, or When the Phallus Appears." *October* 58 (1991): 44-68.

———. *Looking Awry: An Introduction to Jacques Lacan through Popular Culture.* Cambridge: MIT P, 1991.

Elín Elgaard (review date spring 1996)

SOURCE: Elgaard, Elín. Review of *Burning Your Boats,* by Angela Carter. *World Literature Today* 70, no. 2 (spring 1996): 404-05.

[*In the following review, Elgaard focuses on Carter's depiction of female characters in her short stories.*]

"If there's a beast in man," quoth the late Angela Carter, "there's one in women, too." An equality point she elaborated when editing **Wayward Girls & Wicked Women**: "Most—in these stories contrive to evade the victim's role—share a certain cussedness, a bloodymindedness" *not* to be confused with the sexual (im)morality usually women's only share in so-called ethics!

Typically, as in the volume of collected stories **Burning Your Boats,** the Carter definition of sin is not indulgence but rather failure to give in to it. Vicarious lives, whether in a double-bass player or a puppeteer (i.e., from very first story on), lead only to destruction, literally to a splintered instrument and marionette. Suppressed or perverted, the beast when caged (consider corseted Lizzie Borden "howling to the moon") will become murderous, as evidenced by our first glimpse of it (story two): "The woman's beauty was so intense that it seemed to have the quality of deformity, so far was it from the human norm." Significantly, Carter's most atrocious characters—Erl King, Executioner, Bluebeard of **"The Bloody Chamber"**—*stay* human, their self-denial demanding annihilation in the sexual act: "What big eyes you have—a preservative, like a green liquid amber—I am afraid I will be trapped in it forever—I shall become so small you can keep me in one of your osier cages and mock my loss of liberty."

Conversely, should one of Carter's "wise children" survive adolescence intact and penetrate into "the dark country where desire is objectified and lives," what beauty awaits! Whether Wolf-Girl, Tiger Bride, or the beloved of Mr Lyon (the ending to *Beauty and the Beast* I've wanted since a child!), erotic "extinction" turns liberation as beast meets beast: "He was far more frightened of me than I of him.—He snuffled the air as if to smell my fear; he could not.—A tremendous throbbing, as of the engine that makes the earth turn, filled the little room; he had begun to purr." As in **"The Com-**

pany of Wolves" (film version included), a demasking ensues: "My earrings turned back to water and trickled down my shoulders; I shrugged the drops off my beautiful fur."

In his affectionate introduction Salman Rushdie, while admiring Carter's *un*dying wit (and bringing to mind Timothy Findley's tribute to Marian Engel, who also died and did not die of cancer, sparkling to the painful last), admits to her excesses of language. I would add to those a certain mean streak, essayistically: accusing D. H. Lawrence of cross-dressing *because* he conjures up the feel of a stocking, an earring, is surely indefensible! But then, in all the above, and as sensually, Carter cross-dresses with a will from skin to fur, opposing "victim art" as trenchantly as did Lawrence before her. To borrow her phrase, they're "nobody's meat"—which, regardless of any pungency, is so refreshing!

Wendy Swyt (essay date summer 1996)

SOURCE: Swyt, Wendy. "'Wolfings': Angela Carter's Becoming-Narrative." *Studies in Short Fiction* 33, no. 3 (summer 1996): 315-23.

[*In the following essay, Swyt discusses how "The Company of Wolves" subverts patriarchal assumptions about female psychosexual development by the deconstruction of the sexual socialization implicit in the Red Riding Hood fairy tale.*]

> Who has not known the violence of these animal sequences, which uproot one from humanity, if only for an instant, making one scrape at one's bread like a rodent or giving one the yellow eyes of a feline? A fearsome involution calling us toward unheard-of becomings.
>
> —Gilles Deleuze and Felix Guattari, *A Thousand Plateaus* (240)

> The wolfsong is the sound of the rendering you will suffer, in itself a murdering.
>
> —Angela Carter, **"The Company of Wolves"** (110)

In his essay "Angela Carter's Desire Machine" Robert Clark claims that Carter's reworking of the Little Red Riding Hood story plays out "the standard patriarchal opposition between a feral domineering male and gentle submissive female" (149). In Carter's **"The Company of Wolves"** Red Riding Hood ends up in the wolf's arms instead of his stomach, significantly, as the wolf pack's howls rise around them on the night of the solstice. What I will argue in this essay is that, contrary to Clark's interpretation, the components of this peculiar alliance challenge the narrative of masculine desire rather than reinforce it. Because he overlooks the dimensions and determinations of this bond, Clark's read-

ing remains on the Oedipal path in a psychosexual forest, a path that I believe Carter's version actually foregrounds and critiques.

When the beast and his prey lie down in each other's arms, consumption is narrativized in **"The Company of Wolves"** as a metamorphosis, what Gilles Deleuze and Felix Guattari term "the becoming-woman." Although Carter's Red Riding Hood might be interpreted as the modern heterosexual woman "out on the town" (Clark describes her as a woman "enjoying her own sexuality and using it to tenderize the wolf"), the girl's alliance with the wolf attests to more than just a rewritten feminist ending. Instead of reinscribing the full meal deal, Carter's narrative performs a deconstruction of "the virgin function" (what Vladimir Propp might term the "minimal unit" of wolf-o-centric desire). It is a tale of girl becoming . . . more than just meat or nourishment for the quest.

With his interpretation of the wolf as "sexual threat metaphorized . . . literally," Clark reads Carter's version as a typical story of sadistic male dominance without closely examining the terms of this metamorphosis (148). He most obviously overlooks this transformation with his failure to consider the significance of the werewolf legends that begin the narrative. In Carter's version, a sampling of folk wisdom about wolves and three distinct werewolf legends precede the actual Red Riding Hood tale. The move from these old wives' tales to the "tamed" nursery fable challenges the oppositions of purity and danger that Clark insists upon reading the story through. Carter deliberately saturates the tale with a proliferation of genres and thus, in a sense, reframes the sexual socialization that the nursery tale implies. These narrative transformations, or "becomings" as Deleuze and Guattari term them, suggest a (dis)ordering that explodes the "natural" sublimation of civilized glances and table manners that hold the binaries of purity/evil, subject/object, and beast/girl.

THE PATH

The legends and old wives' tales that open **"The Company of Wolves"** encode an ideology of borders and the human subject, a dialectics of safety and dissolution of the self. "[S]tep between the gateposts of the forest with greatest trepidation and infinite precautions," the narrator warns, "for if you stray from the path for one instant, the wolves will eat you" (111). The warnings, a pack of wolf tails, suggest a narrative multiplicity, a proliferation of the tale within its own variations that indicates the metonymic dislocation of old wives' tales into folk legends into a child's nursery fable.[1] This multitude of stories mimics tales told round the fire, blessed by the dark circumference of forest. As stories that welcome the darkness with the pleasure of the telling, they are tales of ambiguous origin: "They say there's an ointment the Devil gives you that turns you into a wolf the minute you rub it on" (113). Suggesting secret negotiations with the night and an old wife's recipe for wolf stew, legendary invectives draw the narratee into the circle of the fire, pupils dilated to the encroaching night.

The implied narrator of Carter's story is the old wife herself, a widow who both mourns and celebrates the demise of social order as she mutters 'round the cook fire. Because her lore reveals the process by which the village stakes its borders, her stories and invectives inscribe local customs of common sense, morality and religion: "If you spy a naked man among the pines, you must run as if the Devil were after you" (113). Yet with the violation of generic boundaries—the bleeding of folk wisdom into nursery rhyme—the interpretive context is thrown askew and common sense is destabilized.

The old wife-narrator pulls the narratee close to the fire with three of the werewolf legends that make up local lore: "There was a hunter once, near here, that trapped a wolf in a pit . . ." (111). In these stories, social contracts are twisted and broken so that a wedding party becomes a pack of wolves and serenades an abandoned bride, while a long lost husband turned werewolf returns to eat his remarried wife. This narrative proliferation suggests a promiscuity of telling that exceeds and infiltrates the mob of self-righteous villagers that would contain the wolf and the forest in traditional versions. Even in a place where "the blades are sharpened daily," the legends cannot tame the threat, and the narrator's tales become irreverent, a midnight romp at the grotesque feast that the narrator describes: "the teeming perils of the night and the forest, ghost, hobgoblins, ogres that grill babies upon gridirons, witches that fatten their captives in cages for cannibal feasts" (111). While this generic contamination violates the borders of meaning—the subject of the narrative, the wolf inscribed in these tales, challenges the configuration of the social subject.

THE WOLF

> A becoming-animal always involves a pack, a band, a population, a peopling, in short, a multiplicity.

> —Deleuze and Guattari, *A Thousand Plateaus* (239)

The legends of the wolf have always addressed the borders between the woods and the village, the path the becoming-victim, becoming-undead should have stayed on. At the beginning of Carter's story, the old wife-narrator cautions, "Fear and flee the wolf; for, worst of all, the wolf may be more than he seems" (111). These warnings signal the attempted schematization of the wolf into a teleological order, the struggle to place transformations within a structural, mythic system of explanation: "old wives hereabouts think it some protection

to throw a hat or apron at the werewolf, as if clothes made the man" (111). But the unreason of the wolf indicates that there is no stable border between the village and the forest: "wolves have ways of arriving at your own hearthside. We try and try but sometimes we cannot keep them out" (111). The wolf exploits the interstices and threatens the safety of village life with its "lean, grey, famished snout questing under the door" (111). Its howl articulates lack, lacunae in the symbolic, "irremediable appetites" (110). The beast is not easily tamed by fables and moral tales because, as Deleuze and Guattari claim, the werewolf "is not fundamentally a characteristic or a certain number of characteristics; it is a wolfing" (239).

In *A Thousand Plateaus* Deleuze and Guattari describe these "wolfings" as part of an order of animals:

1. Oedipal animals each with its own petty history—"my" cat "my" dog.

2. mythic animals with assigned "characteristics" or "attributes"

3. demonic animals, pack or affect animals [werewolves] that form a multiplicity, a becoming, a population, a tale.

(241)

As a "demonic animal," the werewolf serves as a challenge to the fixed traits and social definitions that establish boundaries between self and Other, the stable community and the depths of the forest. The becoming-wolf exists in the ruptures of social order, implying illegal alliances, strange couplings and pacts that "threaten the very category of body" (Sansom 167). The "wolfing"— its metamorphosis—suggests the carnivalistic misalliances that Bakhtin describes as "a body in the act of becoming" (312). With its transformation of ordered boundaries into mobile flesh, the becoming-wolf threatens the programmed social body with dissolution and formlessness so that the "affects" of the Beast, the werewolf, the witch, inscribe "the effectuation of a power of the pack that throws the self into upheaval and makes it reel" (Deleuze and Guattari 240).[2] The "wolfings" that the old wife describes violate the social and physical body; a wolf trapped by a hunter becomes "the bloody trunk of a man, headless, footless, dying, dead" (111).

THE GIRL

> Nursery fears made of flesh and sinew; earliest and most archaic of fears, fear of devourment.

> —Carter, **"The Tiger's Bride"** (67)

From these wolfings, legends, warnings, the girl in Carter's version, a "strong minded child," begins her journey. But what significance do these "becomings" hold for Red Riding Hood? Is she as limited to her part as Clark claims, always the wolf's victim, carried in body parts through eerie moonlit forests? According to Deleuze and Guattari, the girl's body has been stolen and fed into "the great dualism machines" of male subjectivity and female objectivity, and thus her position in traditional narrative is that of a typical second order animal, a mythic characteristic within the Oedipal system of desire (277). The traditional fairy tales that preserve the integrity of this second order animal suggest that order will prevail—the virgin is saved, the beast is exorcised, the village rejoices. In the Grimm version where she is birthed from the belly of the wolf by a kindly hunter, Red Riding Hood's uneaten body bears the weight of this Oedipal conclusion.

But in **"The Company of Wolves,"** I believe Carter's irreverent narrative elides these constructions of Woman-as-signifier. The narrative reframing that begins her story indicates a transformation from bounded generic domains to contaminated forms, and with this contamination, Carter challenges the traditional logic of narrative possibilities for women. Throughout the story discursive play on the tropes of meat, flesh, virgin, and beast creates a radical twist on eating out. Becoming "more than she seems," Carter's Red Riding Hood challenges the binary fields of purity and danger and escapes the path.

After her cautions and legends about the wolves, the narrator begins what we might identify as the story of Little Red Riding Hood. True to the legends of the werewolf, when the girl sets out on the path to her grandmother's house, it is the night of the solstice, "the hinge of the year when things do not fit together as well as they should" (112). The excessively sensual diction signals an attempt to hold back the forest, to stake out the claims of village life with its pots of jam and "stout wooden shoes" (113). In Grandmother's house the details suggest a security and order that will hold back the wolf, "Two china spaniels with liver-colored blotches on their coats and black noses sit on either side of the fireplace. There is a bright rug of woven rags on the pantiles" (115). As the old wife-narrator tells us, "We keep the wolves outside by living well" (115). But the narrative is so saturated with details that the description becomes an ironic display, rather than a reification of domestic order.

This sense of exaggerated materiality organizes the coding of Red Riding Hood as a symbol of female sexuality: "Her breasts have just begun to swell; her hair is like lint, so fair it hardly makes a shadow on her pale forehead; her cheeks are an emblematic scarlet and white" (113). In Carter's story, Red Riding Hood is not named as such; instead she remains "the girl" while her cloak is foregrounded as a sign, a key element in the semiotic system that encodes her in the story. As "red as the blood she must spill," the cloak that has named her in other versions of the tale glows against the snow,

"the color of poppies, the color of sacrifices, the color of her menses" (117). She has just entered the cycle of time, "her woman's bleeding, the clock inside her that will strike, hence forward, once a month" (113).

As in the traditional narrative the "invisible pentacle of her own virginity" promises both salvation and sacrifice in this system. The tropes of the sacrificial lamb surround her: warm oatcakes in a basket, the path away from mother, illicit companions. Like a sleeping princess, she is orphaned by circumstance and her own agency, her father not home, her mother too indulgent to forbid her.

But this narrative proliferation of symbols only foregrounds the mythic signifier of female objectivity, "the sealed vessel," and empties the meaning by reiteration. The order that her purity encodes is overplayed in a repetition of the sign: "an unbroken egg . . . she has inside her a magic space the entrance to which is shut tight with a plug of membrane; she is a closed system; she does not know how to shiver" (114). The meaning of these signs is not secure; rather they are reconstituted, in the context of the traditional fairy tales, as parodic nostalgia. Thus the girl's innocence defines her as a sacrifice, yet it also affords her a strange detachment from this system: "she does not know how to shiver. She has her knife and she is afraid of nothing" (114).

In this proliferation of the sign, the logical time of the grandfather clock collapses into the uneven cycles of the moon. As the old wife reminds the listener, "the malign door of the solstice still swings on its hinges" (113). Designs and impressions pitch and sway; token symbols are jumbled, the legends not quite right. When the fine fellow "in the green coat and the wide awake hat of a hunter" approaches the girl on the path, there is "no sign of a wolf at all, nor of a naked man neither" (114). With a compass to direct him away from the path, the becoming-wolf tells the girl that he does not need a path and bets her that he will arrive first at her grandmother's house. This man-wolf-hunter eliminates the distinctions that the Brothers Grimm make in their version. Who will save Red Riding Hood?

When the becoming-wolf reaches the grandmother's house, the traditional means of protection against these beasts disintegrate. The narrator's lewd voice mocks the grandmother's struggles:

> you can heave your Bible at him and your apron after, granny, you thought that was a sure prophylactic against these infernal vermin—now call on Christ and his mother and all the angels in heaven to protect you but it won't do any good.
>
> (116)

But no amount of civility will suppress the beast because "the forest has come into the kitchen" (116). Here the narrative gaze is multiply identified, a coven of lecherous old wives siding with the wolf, the granny, the moonlight on clean bones.[3] As the wolf approaches the grandmother, the promiscuous narrative eye / I whirls around the room so that it is unclear who—lecherous old wife or innocent granny—exclaims, "his genitals, huge. Ah! huge." The naked man, stained sheets: desire is everywhere.

When the girl faces the wolf at her grandmother's cottage, the scene holds all of the "commonplaces of rustic seduction," as the narrator confides (115). In line with the narrative's generic proliferation, discursive forms are read through each other so that nursery tale refrains suggest dangerous appetites:

> She wanted her knife from her basket but she did not dare reach for it because his eyes were fixed upon her—huge eyes that now seemed to shine with a unique, interior light, eyes the size of saucers, saucers full of Greek fire, diabolic phosphorescence.
>
> What big eyes you have.
>
> All the better to see you with.
>
> (117)

The dialogue exaggerates the sexual tension behind the fairy tale's traditional prohibition of social and sexual misconduct: "There's nobody here but we two, my darling" (115). As the girl confronts the becoming-wolf, gothic details hint at both desire and consumption, "He laughed at her again; gleaming trails of spittle clung to his teeth" (114).

Ignoring the old wives' warnings, the girl embraces this devourment, a willed loss that thwarts the "closed system." Because she is a "wise child" that knows what she wants, she fulfills her part of the bet "freely" and gives the wolf his kiss (118). The sights and sounds of the room signal the rendering of the traditional ending, "The flames danced like the dead souls on Walpurgisnacht and the old bones under the bed set up a terrible clattering but she did not pay them any heed" (118). To the sound of the wolves' "threnody" outside the cottage, she burns the scarlet shawl and ceases to be afraid, leaving the symbolic economy that claims her by her red cloak, the sacrifice. (To pun on another wolf tale, straw houses don't hold up to heavy huffing and puffing.)

At the climax of the tale—in a gruff voice to titillate the child—"All the better to eat you with" becomes a release of sexual tension instead of the typical sacrificial virgin vs. contagion binary. Laughing with the knowledge that she is "nobody's meat," but instead an economy of flesh and skin reflecting the becoming moon, the girl ruptures what Teresa de Lauretis terms the "nexus of image and narrative" (151). When she disrobes and throws her clothes into the fire she transcends the symbols that would contain her in the story

and embraces the becoming-woman.[4] The dimensions and determinations of the Oedipal animal, the 'closed system,' dissolve to the sound of Granny's jumpin' bones. "Into the fire with it, too, my pet," the becoming-wolf tells her as she leaves social domestication.

As she undresses, a wolf pack's howls perform a canticle of desire outside the house, a "prothalamion" that celebrates the murder of sense and order and signals the encroachment of darkness and dissolution (118). Laughing at the wolf, the man and the beast, the girl strips him into his own becoming in a "savage marriage ceremony" (118). At the end of Carter's story, the rhythm of the becoming-wolf matches the pulse of the becoming-woman as they lie down together. The cyclical force of the moon, menses, and the wolf's becomings join: "It is Christmas Day, the werewolves' birthday, the door of the solstice stands wide open; let them all sink through" (118). The becoming-wolf replaces the Christ child as the savior—a joke on the path.

THE BECOMING NARRATIVE

> What if there were lodged within the heart of the law itself, a law of impurity, a principle of contamination?
>
> —Jacques Derrida, "On Genre" (53)

In the village archives, the wolf is excised from the narrative to insure the stability of female sexuality as signifier. As de Lauretis explains, in these traditional narrative structures the girl is "not susceptible to transformation, to life or death; she (it) is an element of plot space, a topos, a resistance" (119). But in the company of wolves, when the wolf and the girl lie down together, this sacrificial contract is broken. In Carter's version "Snowlight, moonlight, a confusion of pawprints" (118) mark the heterogeneous desire that escapes the system, what D. L. Simmons terms "the slippages of the sacrificial machine" (218). The old wife's telling of the wolf performs a rendering of the subject so that the lamb and the beast lie together as witness to "an inhuman connivance with the animal, rather that an Oedipal symbolic community" (Deleuze and Guattari 281).

In **"The Company of Wolves"** Carter seeks a new conceptual framework, a place in narrative that does not punish women for leaving the path. As Nora in Djuna Barnes's novel *Nightwood* realizes, "children know something they can't tell; they like Red Riding Hood and the wolf in bed!" (79). And in her story of the becoming narrative, Carter tells us what we have known all along: genre does not hold to the boundaries of the path. At the crossroads of legend and nursery tale, the werewolf meets the becoming-woman. It is a story that bids us to "unheard of becomings," to the undressing of the social subject in the Oedipal transaction.

Notes

1. Which is how the monsters got under the bed.

2. The transformation of the becoming-wolf holds much fascination as evidenced by popular were-wolf movies. In his essay "Fangoric Horrality," Gareth Sansom claims that "the crux of the onto-logical horror" in these films "is encapsulated in the dynamic of the body to flesh transformation" (167). According to Sansom, werewolf movies il-lustrate the "indices of a subjectivity being dis-placed as the integral body is transformed into something else by 'flesh' (including bones, hair, etc.) which has acquired either its own agency or has become the repository of one or many other agencies" (167). Because in Western metaphysical tradition the body is the exclusive property of the subject, the monster movie focuses on the "propri-ety of the 'body' being somehow violated" (166).

3. Clark interprets the tale as encoding the gaze of the "male voyeur," but this reading discounts the multiple positionings of the narrator in this scene.

4. This undermines Clark's reading in which the wolf is "essentially coercing her" to perform a "strip tease" for him which she agrees to with "*surprising* readiness," an interpretation that re-veals *his own* unwillingness to abandon the "closed system" of the virtuous maid (149; em-phasis added).

Works Cited

Bakhtin, Mikhail. *Rabelais and His World*. Trans. Helene Ismolsky. Cambridge: MIT P, 1968.

Barnes, Djuna. *Nightwood*. New York: New Directions, 1961.

Carter, Angela. "The Tiger's Bride" and "The Company of Wolves." *Bloody Chamber and Other Stories*. Lon-don: Penguin, 1979.

Clark, Robert. "Angela Carter's Desire Machine." *Wom-en's Studies* 14 (1987): 147-61.

De Lauretis, Teresa. *Alice Doesn't: Feminism, Semiot-ics, Cinema*. Bloomington: Indiana UP, 1984.

Deleuze, Gilles and Felix Guattari. *A Thousand Pla-teaus: Capitalism and Schizophrenia*. Trans. Brian Mas-sumi. Minneapolis: U of Minnesota P, 1987.

Derrida, Jacques. "The Law of Genre." Trans. Avital Ronell. *On Narrative*. Ed. W. J. T. Mitchell. Chicago: U of Chicago P, 1981.

Sansom, Gareth. "Fangoric Horrality: The Subject and Ontological Horror in a Contemporary Cinematic Sub-genre." *Discours Social/Social Discourse* 2 (1989): 163-73.

Simmons, D. L. "Sacrifice and Revolt: René Girard and the Return of the Other(s)." *Discours Social/Social Dis-course* 2 (1989): 213-19.

Catherine Lappas (essay date 1996)

SOURCE: Lappas, Catherine. "'Seeing is believing, but touching is the truth': Female Spectatorship and Sexu-ality in *The Company of Wolves*." *Women's Studies* 25, no. 2 (1996): 115-35.

[*In the following essay, Lappas examines the thematic significance of the female gaze and "feminine touch" in the literary and cinematic texts of "The Company of Wolves."*]

> In passing through a wood she met an old neighbor wolf, who had a great desire to eat her. . . . He asked her where she was going. The poor child, who did not know that it is dangerous to stop and listen to a wolf, said to him: "I am going to see my grandmother. . . ."
>
> —"Little Red Riding Hood," 1697

> And as soon as Little Red Cap entered the woods, she encountered the wolf. However, Little Red Cap did not know what a wicked sort of animal he was and was not afraid of him.
>
> "Good day, Little Red Cap."
>
> "Thank you kindly, wolf."
>
> "Where are you going so early, Little Red Cap?"
>
> "To grandmother's."
>
> "What are you carrying under your apron?"
>
> . . . The wolf thought to himself, this is a good morsel for me. How are you going to manage to get her?
>
> —"Little Red Cap," 1812

> The girl burst out laughing; she knew she was nobody's meat. She laughed at him full in the face, she ripped off his shirt for him and flung it into the fire, in the fi-ery wake of her own discarded clothing.
>
> —**"The Company of Wolves,"** 1979

In reworking the 17th and 19th century versions of "Little Red Riding Hood"[1] into her contemporary short story **"The Company of Wolves,"**[2] Angela Carter bold-ly transforms themes of victimization and voyeurism into opportunities for female empowerment. In rework-ing **"The Company of Wolves"** for the screen, her transformation of these same themes becomes even more apparent. I argue that instead of the gaze being solely initiated and possessed by the male, Carter's re-writing of Red Riding Hood's and the wolf's encounter in the woods and in grandmother's house, in her short story and more so in her film, signals an important mo-ment for female spectatorship—a pleasurable moment in which woman acts as a distinct subject with agency and identity. For Carter, furthermore, it is sight in com-bination with touch, rather than sight alone, which most accurately reflects the complex and polymorphous po-tential of female desire. Challenging psychoanalysis' privileging of sight as the supreme form of knowledge, she reveals the radical potential of touch. For it is *touch* that acts as ultimate metaphor for Carter's incorporation of the patriarchal into herself.

In "A Second Gaze at Little Red Riding Hood's Trials and Tribulations," a comprehensive study of the structuring of the gaze in illustrations of "Little Red Riding Hood," Jack Zipes writes that "the origins of the literary fairy tale can be traced to male phantasies about women and sexuality."[3] Zipes explores how key illustrations of the standard "Little Red Riding Hood" texts reinforce the perception of a complicit female protagonist. Perrault's and the Grimm's "Little Red Riding Hood," he adds, "is *not* an ancient and anonymous folk tale reflecting 'universal' psychic operations of men and women, but rather it is the product of gifted male European writers, who projected their needs and values onto the actions of fictitious characters within a socially conventionalized genre."[4]

In quoting Susan Brownmiller's influential interpretation of the tale, Zipes finds further support for the argument of female agency's denial. "'Red Riding Hood' is a parable of rape" quotes Zipes: "1) [it makes] women willing participants in their own defeat; 2) [it obscures] the true nature of rape by implying that women *want* to be raped; 3) [it asserts] the supreme rightness of male power either as offender or protector."[5] This also seems to be the belief of some critics of the film, who read Rosaleen's transformation into a wolf at the end of the film as a "duplication of the symbol for repressed desire."[6] But it is important not to misread Carter's intentions. For the revelation of unpalatable truths about sexual relations within our culture is feminism's most powerful condemnation of violence directed at women; it is "a critique of the current relations between the sexes."[7]

The industry of illustration has long been controlled by men, argues Zipes, and those "male illustrators were interpreters and mediators of the fairy-tale texts, and they projected their sexual phantasies through the images they composed."[8] Exactly the same logic is reflected in the work of male film directors like Alfred Hitchcock and Brian De Palma, who regard female violence as requisite to visual pleasure.[9] Zipes emphasizes the crucial influence of illustration on the sexual politics of filmic gazing: "[T]he underlying question in the images depicting the male/female encounter, whether it be in magazines, books, films, advertisements, or cartoons concerns women's use of their sexual powers to attain supreme gratification through male sexual prowess."[10] Furthermore, Zipes is convinced that the important signifiers of the traditional tale—the seductive look of Red Riding Hood, the size of the wolf, and the proximity of the two characters—confirm the same meaning in many illustrations: that "Little Red Riding Hood" is a tale about "seduction, intimacy, and power," a tale which

"suggests that it is primarily she who is asking for it."[11] However, he also points out the ambivalence of *male* desire in the tale:

> [I]t is possible to interpret Little Red Riding Hood's desire for the wolf as a desire for the other, or a general quest for self-identification. She seeks to know herself in a social context, gazes into the wolf's eyes to see a mirror reflection of who she might be, a confirmation for her feelings. . . . The self can explore its possibilities and undergo symbolic exchanges with nature inside and outside the self.[12]

And further complicating matters,

> the gaze or look of Little Red Riding Hood appears to invite the gaze/desire, and, therefore, she incriminates herself in his act. Implicit in her gaze is that she may be leading him on—to granny's house, to a bed, to be dominated. She tells him the way, the path to the house. But where is she actually leading him? Why?[13]

Provocative though these questions seem, they are not as provocative as Carter's answer: because she *wants* to. Rather than falling into the old trap of punishing her protagonists for feeling and expressing their desire, Carter subverts the Grimm and Perrault tales by suggesting an alternative ending: Little Red Riding Hood and the wolf fall in love. Zipes, on the other hand, rehearses a phallocentric reading of the tale:

> [T]he girl in the encounter with the wolf gazes but really does not gaze, for she is the image of male desire. She is projected by the authors Perrault and Grimm and generally by male illustrators as an object without a will of her own. The gaze of the wolf will consume her and is intended to dominate and eliminate her. The gaze of the wolf is a phallic mode of interpreting the world and is an attempt to gain what is lacking through imposition and force. . . . [H]er role is basically one intended to mirror his desire. . . . Her identity will be violated and fully absorbed by male desire either as wolf or as gamekeeper.[14]

Zipes' comments about the illustration of "Little Red Riding Hood" acknowledge a striking misogyny in the 17th and 19th century versions of the tale as well as an effort to maintain that misogyny in subsequent renditions of the tale. In both the 17th and the 19th century versions, moreover, Red Riding Hood's ignorance inevitably leads to a fatal or near-fatal encounter in grandmother's house, just punishment for her disregard of patriarchal authority. While Carter's provocative rewriting of the story gives Red Riding Hood the upper hand ("The girl burst out laughing; she knew she was nobody's meat"[15]), it achieves more than mere plot reversal. Carter's rewrite delves into "the complexity of the inner world of the protagonist."[16] In the film, too, more than mere plot reversal occurs, for Rosaleen's and the wolf's *transformations* offer an exploration of psychic repression and doubling.

Zipes is not alone of course in invoking the "gaze" to expose misogyny. Theories of spectatorship have appeared steadily since Laura Mulvey's landmark work, "Visual Pleasure and Narrative Cinema,"[17] which first established the relationship between gender representation in cinema and patriarchal ideology. While recent writings on the subject have maintained the importance of Mulvey's observation—that "woman" is constructed to reflect patriarchal desires and anxieties—they have also bemoaned the female spectator's absence as agent giving and receiving pleasure. Because, according to Mulvey, spectatorship is "incontrovertibly masculine," writers like Mary Ann Doane, Teresa de Lauretis, Christine Gledhill, and E. Ann Kaplan[18] have all pondered the opportunities and limitations of the gendered gaze for feminism. Despite all attempts to appropriate the gaze, however, their theories have not argued convincingly for the existence of an autonomous female spectator. As Jackie Stacey aptly remarks, for such theorists woman is at best "offered only three rather frustrating options of *masculinization, masochism* or *marginality*."[19] [emphasis added]

Maggie Humm's "Is the Gaze Feminist?" provides an interesting antithesis to the conclusions cited above by suggesting a feminist reading of the gaze that is both empowering and distinct from the psychoanalytic model.[20] Humm's interest is in generating new notions of female sexuality by introducing "*avant-garde* practices of spectator-film relationships in order to deconstruct the scopic gaze."[21] For Humm,

> many women directors are taking the problematic of voyeurism as the *content* of their own films. If one of the most important areas of feminist criticism is the critique of the 'gaze,' an equally crucial aspect of women and cinema . . . concerns the representation of discourse[22]

and "the reconstitution of a more diverse female sexuality."[23] Carter exposes this relationship between visual and verbal discourses, through first the written version and then the film version of *The Company of Wolves,* and in the process critiques the inherent sexism of all traditional narratives: they are systems of structuring and making meaning, and they are concerned with subjectivity, the process of looking and image formation, and questions about sexual difference.[24]

Much as Humm does, Jackie Stacey envisions a feminist gaze which subverts the "masculine"/dominance "feminine"/submission pattern inherent in the scopics of cinema. For Stacey, female pleasure is situated within a female referential frame of experience that disdains a sexual exchange in which women participate only as objects of circulation and fetishism. Stacey's conclusion: existing theories of differences fail to provide a theoretical space in which desire and identification are interwoven. Like de Lauretis, Stacey sees as one of the central themes of feminine subjectivity "the construction and reproduction of feminine identities" wherein "the activity of looking is highlighted as an important part of these processes."[25] Included among the possible pleasures of female spectatorship are, according to Stacey, "representation of woman's desire for another woman which constitutes a re-enactment of an experience common to all women in their relationship with the mother" and "representation of woman's desire to identify with a female ideal."[26] Carter's text and film rewrites give embodiment to Stacey's and Humm's observations about a feminist gaze—namely, that it is *not* an impossible sign. An examination of female desire in *The Company of Wolves,* a film informed by and at the same time posing a challenge to feminist ideology, reveals Carter's call for a feminist irony which simultaneously rejects misogynist assumptions *and* inscribes a new set of assumptions.

Proceeding from the assumption that Oedipal processes are central to the production of all art works, the film *The Company of Wolves* shows Rosaleen (the Red Riding Hood character) recognizing herself as other in the figure of her mother throughout the film. Mother and daughter share a bond beyond words, a bond which poignantly reveals itself when, at the end of the film, Rosaleen's mother recognizes the wolf in Granny's house as her transformed daughter and prevents the father/huntsman from shooting her. This immediate recognition of mother in daughter/wolf intensifies the association between woman and beast as well as their shared status as outsiders in patriarchal culture. Similarly Carter's iconoclastic story **"The Company of Wolves"** can be read as a critique of dominant cultural inscriptions of sexual difference and desire. In the film, Granny's repeated injunctions against treading through the forest as well as her persistent attempts at linking sexual appetite with male violence set up the protagonist as willing victim of the ensuing wolf attack, just as the Perrault and Grimm versions do. Furthermore, Granny clearly states her belief that men *are* beasts "all of them beasts," and that sexual violence against women is solicited, thus reinscribing Perrault's and the Grimm's infamous moral about female sexual curiosity.

While the story **"The Company of Wolves"** seemingly privileges the male point-of-view, male desire and authority implicitly controlling all fairy tale narratives, as Susan Suleiman discovers, Carter's fiction suggests

> a direction for postmodern feminist fiction, based on parody and the multiplication of narrative possibilities rather than on their outright refusal . . . ; it expands our notions of what it is possible to dream in the domain of sexuality, criticizing all dreams that are too narrow. . . . It is the desire, or dream, of going beyond old dichotomies.[27]

In the film this control is intensified, as the omniscient look of the camera conspires with the inherent voyeurism of the narrative to render the viewer passive during the wolf's manipulation of the protagonist. The wolf disguised as a "fine gentleman" constantly captures Rosaleen in his gaze, for it is primarily through his eyes that her story is filmed. As a red spot against an otherwise dark and monochromatic backdrop Rosaleen is strikingly visible to the audience and to the wolf, both of whom share a fetishizing perspective of the protagonist. Rosaleen's climbing of the tree invites a voyeuristic perspective which underscores the entire film. The camera's eye unlike the narrator's voice is "always *there*," controlling the viewer's scope, order, and duration of perceiving.[28]

Indeed, the camera presents little else of Little Red Riding Hood besides her physical appearance: virtually every shot fetishizes her wide-eyed, smooth-skinned face, and parted lips. Rosaleen is thus transformed into a fetish, her face and form becoming a reassuring rather than threatening image to the audience. Her female form is indeed her essence, her totality. In the film *The Company of Wolves* the narrative tradition which inscribed and which subsequently is inscribed by the classic fairy tale is highly conscious of itself as such, encoding the original story within it, so that one reads *both* texts, the literary and the film, as referring back to and implicitly critiquing the "old." The film, furthermore, draws attention to the mechanism behind the gendered gaze and connects this to the sexism inherent in traditional illustrations of Little Red Riding Hood. Carter's screen heroine is neither as naive nor as helpless as her storybook predecessors. She asks daring questions about human sexuality ("Mummy." "Yes, pet?" "Does he hurt you? . . ." "Who?" "Daddy." "No . . . If there's a beast in men it meets its match in women, too. Do you understand?") and equipped with this knowledge consciously seduces the wolf:

ROSALEEN:

"Are you our kind or their kind?"

WOLF:

"Not one nor the other—both."

ROSALEEN:

"Then where do you live, in our world or theirs?"

WOLF:

"I come and go between them. My home is nowhere."

ROSALEEN:

"Are you a man only when you dress like one, like Granny said? . . . My what big arms you have!"

WOLF:

"All the better to hug you with."

In drawing conclusions from her experiences, in resisting the stories which literary and cultural traditions have patterned for her, most notably through Granny, Rosaleen's narrative becomes an alternative model for the female subject's desire, constructing what de Lauretis says feminist cinematic and written narrative must: "the terms of reference of another measure of desire and the conditions of visibility for a different social subject."[29] Furthermore, the terms of looking are significantly altered, for Rosaleen is subject of *her own* gaze as well as the object of the wolf's. The desires of both are in an ambivalent and unexplored state. Actively initiating herself into the dominant discourse, Rosaleen bargains with the dominant narrative to redeem her story and subjectivity on her own terms. She tells the story—which acts as filmic subtext—of a girl who casts a spell on an old lover for forsaking her, and thus releases the repressed anger of women who are denied their own desire, such as they are in Granny's tales.

In another story Rosaleen narrates, the story about the she-wolf, Carter visualizes Rosaleen's subconscious. Both Rosaleen and the she-wolf are trapped in a hostile and unfamiliar land, encased in unfamiliar skins, illfitted for traditional gender roles, and shunned because of their differences. Indeed, throughout the film Carter make obvious that the wolf's very otherness is what intrigues Rosaleen. Her sympathy and inclination toward other than what society has dictated, signals her own difference and surfaces explicitly in her natural affection for the wolf and for other reviled beasts of the forest. In both bearing her gaze and forcing her to look upon his natural nakedness, especially during the transformation scene, the wolf brings Rosaleen to a clearer vision of herself, that is, into a position of better seeing her desire and of exploring herself. We witness Rosaleen's reaction to the transformation as a commingling of desire and disgust; she cannot avert her attention from the abject spectacle.

Sylvia Bryant argues that the reciprocal relationship of desire and trust, not with words, but with the equal, non-differentiating, illuminating gaze makes Rosaleen subject of the gaze, not just object, and makes a place for her desire—a multiple sexual subjectivity which she has freely experienced and embraced.[30] And she adds about Carter's practice of rewriting:

> To tell a different story, to imagine and construct otherness as positive not negative difference, and to offer positive positionalities for identification within that otherness, to disrupt the ideological *status quo* enough to disturb the heretofore complacent acceptance it has met among readers and viewers; such is precisely the work of Carter's fairy tale narratives.[31]

In "When a Woman Looks," Linda Williams evaluates "gazing" in classical narrative cinema and shows how the heroine is often represented as blind. Williams also tries to theorize female sexual difference as a positive condition. But in the instances she cites, Williams, following Doane, observes woman's recurrent punishment for gazing: "curiosity and desire," she writes, are repeatedly transformed into "masochistic fantasy."[32] She then describes the kind of punishment peculiar to horror films. Her insights are especially relevant to a discussion of the film *The Company of Wolves,* which can be read as a parody of horror.

In the horror film, Carter identifies a dangerous and seductive area for exploring female sexuality. Often in horror, female gazing is synonymous with her own victimization: "The woman's gaze is punished . . . by narrative processes that transform curiosity and desire into masochistic fantasy."[33] She is punished, that is, for gazing at "the horrible body of the monster."[34] At the same time, however, there is a "subversive affinity between monster and woman, the sense in which her look at the monster recognizes their similar status within patriarchal structures of seeing."[35] But the woman's look at the monster differs from the man's in that the woman's

> paralyzes her in such a way that [specular] distance is overcome; the monster or the freak's own spectacular appearance holds her originally active, curious look in a trance-like passivity that allows him to master her through *her* look. At the same time, this look momentarily shifts the iconic center of the spectacle away from the woman to the monster.[36]

Not only is woman erased as a subject, according to Williams, but her object position is usurped as well. For Carter reading the monster as the embodiment of male sexuality alone is too limiting. She focuses instead on the similarity and solidarity between monster and woman and sees the source of the monster's difference and power as sexual. Indeed, woman and monster both differ from the "normal" male in that their gaze does not carry within themselves "the power of action and possession."[37]

Williams argues that the monster's difference is often revealed as a lack or absence—similar to woman's—and that this difference renders *him* (monsters are usually gendered male) a freak under patriarchy, just as it does woman. As a result,

> the power and potency of the monster in many classic horror films . . . should not be interpreted as an eruption of the normally repressed animal sexuality of the civilized male (the monster as a double for the male viewer and characters in the film), but as the feared power and potency of a different kind of sexuality (the monster as double for the woman).[38]

Mastery over the mutilated (castrated) body of the monster is signified in many horror films by his destruction. In the film *The Company of Wolves* the destruction of the monster is more powerfully represented than in the

written text, since in the film Granny narrates "The Travelling Man," a story in which a werewolf is decapitated in order for the rightful husband to restore his position as head of the household. According to Williams, at the "key moment" of the monster's castration, often signified by his dismemberment or decapitation, the woman is displaced by the monster "as site of the spectacle." Finally,

> displaying the freakish difference of the monster's body [elicits] reactions of fear and awe in audiences that can be compared to the Freudian hypothesis of the reaction of the male child in his first encounter with the "mutilated" body of his mother.[39]

When the woman looks at the monster, then, there is a "potentially subversive recognition of the power and potency of a non-phallic sexuality," and because of this potential to harm patriarchy, she must be punished.[40] Thus, telling a story reenacts gazing. And when the wife in "The Travelling Man" allows a stranger into her house, who she quickly recognizes as her ex-husband, she is beaten by her current husband, by coincidence also a huntsman.

Williams examines films she calls "psychological horrors," whose plots often revolve around a threatening male who stalks his female victim, endangering and often killing her, a direct result, according to Williams, of female protagonist's "desiring look." In recent horror films, furthermore, there has been a trend toward blaming the woman for her victimization, especially where she identifies with the monster: there, she becomes the monster and her mutilated body is the only visible horror.[41] This trend is apparent and can be traced consistently through *The Company of Wolves* in Granny's stories.

The two stories she narrates are rife with sexual prohibitions and punishments for sexual transgression. "The Travelling Man" warns against trusting strangers and reinforces control over women's sexuality:

ROSALEEN:

> "I'd never let a man strike me."

GRANNY:

> "Oh, they're nice as pie until they've had their way with you, but once the bloom is gone, the beast comes out."

ROSALEEN:

> "When the wolves though, the *real* wolves, when the real wolves mate, do the dogs beat the bitches afterwards?"

GRANNY:

> "Animals, all wild animals!"

Similarly, in "The Priest's Bastard Son" Granny overtly links sexual curiosity with the devil:

GRANNY:

"They say the priest's bastards often turn into wolves as they grow older."

ROSALEEN:

"What do you mean?"

GRANNY:

"If the child is born on Christmas Day, if the child is born feet first, he'll be the one. If he's born feet first and his eyebrows meet in the middle, one day he'll meet the devil in the wood."

In both stories narrated by Granny in the film, Carter parodies the voices of literature and folklore which represent "vast repositories of outmoded lies, where you can check what lies used to be *à la mode* and find the old lies on which new lies are based."[42]

While interesting in its application of horror to highlight sexual difference as a construction of patriarchal ideology, Williams' article finally offers rather ambivalent sentiments towards horror and its potential to act as a liberating genre for women:

The horror film may be a rare example of a genre that permits the expression of women's sexual potency and desire, and which associates this desire with the autonomous act of looking, but it does so in these more recent examples only to punish her for this very act, only to demonstrate how monstrous female desire can be.[43]

Williams' ambivalence is perhaps a function of the films she chooses to analyze—*Psycho* and *Peeping Tom* from the 1960s, and more recently, *Halloween, Dressed to Kill, The Texas Chainsaw Massacre,* and *Friday the 13th*—all of which portray women as "non-existent fantasies" of the male imagination.[44] *The Company of Wolves,* however, consciously places issues of female imagination at the epicenter of the film's plot. Just as in her written story, **"The Company of Wolves,"** the traditionally frightful encounter is refigured as a highly erotic and loving scene between Rosaleen, the precocious Little Red Riding Hood character, and the wolf. Here, as in the original story, Carter juxtaposes myths of female sexuality against women's real dreams and desires: the girl and the wolf become one, not as a result of a vicious attack but of mutual consent.

Carter foregrounds the relationship between fairy tales and reality, both of which prescribe action for females within similar ideological parameters. She has written that the fairy tale is an "orally transmitted narrative with a relaxed attitude to the reality principle and plots constantly refurbished in the retelling."[45] From its inception

the story was put together in the form we have it, more or less, out of all sorts of bits of other stories long ago and far away, and has been tinkered with, had bits added to it, lost other bits, got mixed up with other stories, until our informant *herself* has tailored the story personally, to suit an audience of, say, children, or drunks at a wedding, or bawdy old ladies, or mourners at a wake—or, simply, to suit *herself*. [emphasis added][46]

Carter deliberately invokes the archetype of the female storyteller to reassign woman her lost power as "tale spinner." What is interesting in Carter's fiction is her awareness of the mechanisms behind the construction of subject positions in literary and filmic discourse, as well as her awareness that fairy tales and reality, like the conscious and unconscious, are not easily separable.

According to John Collick, *The Company of Wolves* is a film that tries to "recreate" and "imitate" the processes of dreaming.[47] The film is heavily laden with sexual symbols and metaphors which are offered as "a parody of the Freudian dream work in which the dream symbols, instead of being scrambled images or 'puzzles' that represent unconscious wishes, turn out to be familiar literary symbols."[48] Structured like a dream *The Company of Wolves* undercuts "the narrative coherence of cinema, simultaneously alienating the viewer from the image while underscoring film's similarity with the process of dreaming itself. No analysis is offered, the viewer is merely presented with absurd images that probably mean something else, but meaning is elusive."[49]

The capacity of the fairy tale to transform itself in story and shape is what draws Carter to it again and again. As Marina Warner writes in the introduction to *Strange Things Sometimes Still Happen,* a collection of fairy tales Carter was preparing just before her death in 1992, "Carter's partisan feeling for women, which burns in all her work, never led her to any conventional form of feminism; but she continues here one of her original and effective strategies, snatching out of the jaws of misogyny itself, 'useful stories' for women."[50] In both the written and the film narrative, this is precisely Carter's strategy: to invoke and then weave together misogynist conventions of the fairy tale and dream narrative to create a story to "suit herself," as storyteller and as feminist.

Even while operating out of patriarchy, the literary and cinematic texts of *The Company of Wolves* simultaneously and powerfully subvert it. In both texts, "other," signified by the wolf, is seen and recognized by Red Riding Hood as the "other" she represents. By the end of the film, this transformation is made literal when Little Red Riding Hood becomes a wolf. As an outsider, Little Red Riding Hood looks at the wolf not with fear, as traditional readings would hold, but with compassion and identification—both are manipulated to reflect long-held Christian—patriarchal values:

The entire period from 1480 to 1650 can be seen as an historical transition in which the Catholic Church and the reform movement of Protestantism combined efforts with the support of the rising mercantile and industrial classes to rationalize society and literally to exterminate social deviates who are associated with the devil such as female witches, male werewolves, Jews and gypsies. . . . Hundreds of thousands if not millions of people . . . were executed to arouse fear and anxiety while new models of male and female behavior were created to exalt a more ascetic way of life.[51]

The potential for such a bond between the heroine and the "villain" problematizes the apparent truth of the traditional moral quoted at the end of the film: "Never stop upon your way. / Never trust a strange-friend; / No one knows how it will end." Female sexual behavior is at once prescribed by the invocation of the authority of the proverbial word at the end of the narrative, but throughout female sexuality, primarily in the character of Rosaleen, asserts its struggle to free itself from this word.

"The Company of Wolves" together with **"The Werewolf"** and **"Wolf Alice,"** which constitute the sources for the film drawn from Carter's collection *The Bloody Chamber,* foreground the folk origins of various lycanthrope myths and then turn these into a narrative with a *new* message. Carter begins **"The Company of Wolves"** by focusing on the wolves' eyes, their peculiar gaze:

At night, the eyes of wolves shine like candle flames, yellowish, reddish, but that is because the pupils of their eyes fatten on darkness and catch the light from your lantern to flash it back to you—red for danger; if a wolf's eyes reflect only moonlight, then they gleam a cold and unnatural green, a mineral, a piercing colour.[52]

She chooses to narrate in the second person in order to identify the female audience with Red Riding Hood. The colors of the wolves eyes are reminiscent of lights from a camera, creating a kind of cinematic effect, which draws attention to the illusory nature of all films including the 1984 film *The Company of Wolves.* Carter adds: "But those eyes are all you will be able to glimpse of the forest assassins as they cluster invisibly round your smell of meat as you go through the wood unwisely late."[53] The linking of desire to sight and language is clear here. Carter associates Red Riding Hood metonymically with "meat," an object of consumption, which also doubles as a vulgar and sexist allusion to women.

In this way throughout the written narrative, Carter's speaker shifts between authority and parody; in the film the shift is played out between Rosaleen and Granny. All the stories the teller conjures have occurred within familiar territory—"up the valley" or "in our village"—invoking a narrative folk convention. But at the same time, their self-consciousness as "old wives' tales" is also apparent. For example, Carter offers a subversive rewriting of the significance of the cloak. It is red not because it signifies vanity or sin, but because it is emblematic of Little Red Riding Hood's burgeoning sexuality, "her cheeks are . . . scarlet and white and she has just started her woman's bleeding."[54] In the film Rosaleen, acting as literary critic, perfectly understands the unspoken symbolism of the cloak:

ROSALEEN:

"Soft as snow."

GRANNY:

"Red as a berry."

ROSALEEN:

"Red as blood."

The textual emphasis on blood makes Rosaleen's virginity another powerful and dangerous signifier of her sexuality. In "The Taboo of Virginity," Freud writes that woman represents the physical and psychical danger of castration, "woman is also looked upon as a source of such dangers and the first sexual act with a woman stands out as a specially perilous one."[55] Carter exploits this threatening image of the virgin Little Red Riding Hood, when she writes:

She stands and moves within the invisible pentacle of her own virginity. She is an unbroken egg; she is a sealed vessel; she has inside her a magic space the entrance to which is shut tight with a plug of membrane; she is a closed system; she does not know how to shiver. She has her knife and she is afraid of nothing.[56]

The image of Carter's Red Riding Hood is loaded with contradictions—she is both "pure" and phallic, both virginal and aggressive—in order to illustrate the inadequacies of existing theories of spectatorship which do not help theorize the presence of woman as active agent in the cinematic text, or her relationship to the characters in the narrative. Carter's/Jordan's rendition of the gaze between Rosaleen and the "Gentleman" recalls traditional fairy tale iconography. The significant difference however is that Rosaleen stands armed with a knife (phallus), hardly the image of frailty and innocence suggested by Perrault's and the Grimm's tales. Juxtaposed against recent illustrations of "Little Red Riding Hood" found in children's books, Carter's film provides ironic commentary on the gaze between the protagonist and the wolf. Traditionally, Red Riding Hood is depicted as naive and culpable; she is innocently disposed toward the wolf and the woods and hence must be "eaten."

If Carter's Rosaleen is actually a phallicized heroine (a reconstituted male), then male spectators derive pleasure by having castration anxieties allayed and women by being contaminated by the aggressive and violent values of patriarchy.[57] However, such a perception

. . . appears to be based on the argument that only phallic masculinity is violent and that femininity is never violent—not even in the imagination. This argument is essentialist. . . . This is the very argument that patriarchal ideology has used for the past 2,000 years to control women—it is precisely because women by definition are "pure" creatures that they need to "guide" them through life's stormy passage.[58]

Carter regards essentialist arguments circumspectly precisely for the reasons mentioned above: they trap women into definitions which are used against them. But Carter is equally troubled by remaining within the strictures of any one genre, for narrative determinism has *its* potential dangers. Carter's solution is to adopt an ironic tone in order to blur and to attack the boundaries which purport to fix reality one way or another—whether in the direction of feminist tract, or "splatter" film:[59]

Yet this, of course, is why it is so enormously important for women to write fiction *as* women—it is part of the slow process of decolonizing our language and our basic habits of thought. I really do believe this . . . it has to do with the creation of a means of expression for an infinitely greater variety of experience than has been possible heretofore, to say things for which no language previously existed.[60]

In her story **"The Werewolf"** Carter again draws on existing language to create a new language for women, bringing together the folklore surrounding wolves and their transformative powers into the narrative's foreground. Structured like "Little Red Riding Hood," Carter's anonymous narration, here taking on the authority of cultural anthropology, begins with a description of the origins of all werewolf stories and how these are linked to cultural setting:

It is a northern country; they have cold weather, they have cold hearts. . . . To these upland woodsmen, the Devil is as real as you or I. More so; . . . At midnight, especially on Walpurgisnacht, the Devil holds picnics in the graveyards and invites the witches; they dig up fresh corpses, and eat them. Anyone will tell you that.[61]

Warning of the evil that lurks in dark winter woods, Carter's narrator, much like Granny in *The Company of Wolves,* is at once engaged in the storytelling and distant from it. She at once warns against going into the woods and tempts Rosaleen into going. Carter's intervention becomes obvious when she inverts conventional narrative structure by giving Red Riding Hood, and not the woodsman, the power to fight off the wolf, and finally, by gendering the wolf female, as the grandmother's secret identity, giving the moral "The wolf may be more than he seems"[62] an added irony. This change in the traditional Grimm narrative is more than mere gender reversal; it signifies Carter's interest in gender-identity games.

Carol Clover speaks of the distinction between "sex" and "gender," which is frequently and mistakenly con-

flated into one category, a distinction that Carter is fond of calling attention to:

The idea that appearance and behaviour do not necessarily indicate sex—indeed, can misindicate sex—is predicated on the understanding that sex is one thing and gender another; in practice, that sex is life, a less-than-interesting given, but that gender is theatre.[63]

In *The Company of Wolves,* with characteristic wit and subversiveness, Carter occupies the male voice of narrative authority while impersonating it to the point of parody. Her writing is high theatre and masquerade. She adopts the literary and cinematic conventions of gender representation in order to transform traditional gender stereotypes. Carter excels at masquerade, as Mary Ann Doane defines it, but goes far beyond it. According to Doane,

The masquerade's resistance to patriarchal positioning [lies] in its denial of the production of femininity as closeness, as presence-to-itself, as, precisely imagistic. The transvestite adopts the sexuality of the other—the woman becomes the man in order to attain the necessary distance from the image. Masquerade, on the other hand, involves a realignment of femininity, the recovery, or more accurately, simulation, of the missing gap or distance. *To masquerade is to manufacture a lack in the form of a certain distance between oneself and one's image.*[64]

[emphasis added]

Masquerade involves wearing a mask which has been constructed to conceal a lack of subjecthood: "By destabilizing the image [of femininity], the masquerade confounds this masculine structure of the look. It effects a defamiliarization of female iconography."[65] Carter inscribes scenarios of voyeurism—Rosaleen's beauty and desirability—makes these functions of the cinematic apparatus—framing, lighting, camera movement, angle. She thus associates Rosaleen with the surface of the image and constructs a two-dimensional illusion which the spectator is forced to inhabit and hence control. Carter thus points out not only the constructedness of the feminine mask but also the constructedness of the cinematic process itself.

When at the end of **"The Werewolf"** Carter's protagonist drives the grandmother/werewolf/witch into the arms of the angry droves and usurps her position in the house, this is unmistakably a reworking of the Oedipal myth, which, according to Teresa de Lauretis, inscribes narrative desire in such a way as to make it paradigmatic of all narratives:

. . . and though its object may be woman (or Truth or knowledge or power), its term of reference and address is man: man as social being and mythical subject, founder of the social order, and source of mimetic violence.[66]

Furthermore, the curt ending and the refusal to add "happily ever after" to the story serve as critiques of the rewarding of male violence inherent in most fairy tales:

> They knew the wart on the hand at once for a witch's nipple; they drove the old woman, in her shift as she was, out into the snow with sticks, beating her old carcass as far as the edge of the forest, and pelted her with stones until she fell down dead. Now the child lived in her grandmother's house; she prospered.[67]

The obvious understated tone ("she prospered") reinforces the notion that violence begets violence, and that the brutal treatment of the grandmother signifies the granddaughter's unquestioning acceptance of the Oedipal myth and of the symbolic order. The girl structures her consciousness around the sadism which allows the stoning of her grandmother to occur. Finally, in **"Wolf Alice,"** Carter offers a tale

> of a girl raised by wolves, outside the social training of the symbolic. Alluding to Truffaut's *L'Enfant sauvage*, Lewis Carroll and Lacan, the young girl grows up outside the cultural inscriptions and learns a new sense of self from her encounters with the mirror and from the rhythms of her body. She learns a sense of time and routine. Finally her pity begins to transform the werewolf Duke into the world of the rational, where he too can be symbolized.[68]

In *The Company of Wolves,* the story is framed within the larger frame of the film's narrative. Rosaleen is the narrator of the tale, which is told in maternal fashion to the transformed Gentleman. As in the original tale from ***The Bloody Chamber,*** the she-wolf is an outsider, but in Rosaleen's version the ambivalent nature of the girl makes her ill-suited for life in the symbolic. She must return to her world through the well, metaphorically a repression of her libidinal drive and rejection of the mirror metaphor suggested by Carroll and Lacan: woman *cannot* locate herself in the patriarchal symbolic.

In psychoanalysis, sexual difference is always established during the "mirror-phase," which Elizabeth Grosz explains depends on the primacy of vision:

> Vision performs a distancing function, leaving the looker unimplicated in or uncontaminated by its object. With all of the other senses, there is a contiguity between subject and object, if not an internationalization and incorporation of the object by the subject. The tactile, for example, keeps the toucher in direct contact with the object touched; taste further implicates the subject, for the object must be ingested, internalized in order for it to be accessible to taste.[69]

Touch acts as metaphor for Carter's incorporation of the patriarchal into herself. For some, this involvement signifies a disturbing entrapment within the "ideological parameters" which as feminist Carter is trying to escape.[70] By virtue of its ability to distance, vision and viewing have achieved the position of "domain and mastery"[71]; indeed, everything becomes "subordinate to the primacy of sight."[72] With respect to sexual pleasure, vision achieves primacy in the male psyche, while touching achieves primacy in the female. Indeed, Mary Ann Doane sees this difference as key to articulating gender differences in the experience of filmic viewing. Because of the daughter's pre-oedipal relationship with the mother, she is unable in adulthood to separate from the maternal body and thus is unable to achieve a distance from the text, or from the image on the cinema screen. Carter, as well, implies that truth is constituted for women differently than it is for men. For if under patriarchy sight is the privileged way of knowing, when appropriated by the female subject, knowing becomes equated with touching. But for Carter, this difference is not equated with inferiority—touching is an alternative way of knowing that has been repressed by patriarchal ideology.

Donald Haase echoes this argument in "Is Seeing Believing? Proverbs and Film Adaptations of a Fairy Tale." With respect to Carter's reworking of the old proverb, "Seeing is believing," which serves as a leitmotif throughout *The Company of Wolves,* Haase writes:

> The film's depiction of touching (or feeling) as a radical alternative to the limited experience of sight clearly suggests that the filmmakers understand the cultural primacy of sight and seek to subvert its narrative power by embracing other experience—especially touch.[73]

Although Haase does not see the potential subversion in expressly feminist terms, when viewed in light of psychoanalytic theory's privileging of sight and its equation of sight with male subjectivity, Carter's reformulation is indeed worthy of exploration. The recurring motif of the gaze in *The Company of Wolves*—signified by the father's/huntman's proverb "Seeing is believing"—is not simply the objectification of women by male desire, but rather the competing desire for freedom and engulfment, which delineates the very ambivalence of desire: "She knew the worst of wolves are hairy on the inside and she shivered, in spite of the scarlet shawl she pulled more closely round herself as if it could protect her although it was as red as the blood she must spill."[74] Red is the color both of Rosaleen's burgeoning sexuality and her "sacrifice" in becoming a woman. She cannot have one without the other, but the choice is still hers.

Appropriated by western-bourgeois-male interests, "Little Red Riding Hood" offers no hope of reducing "the possibility for violence and brutality" toward women; "if anything, it perpetuates sexual notions which contribute to our frustration and aggressiveness."[75] But Zipes' article nonetheless raises interesting possibilities for reading a text such as Carter's *The Company of Wolves*. He shows the connection between two signifying systems—the literary text and the illustration—and how these work to perpetuate misogyny. As has been suggested, Red Riding Hood's curiosity is traditionally punished by her consumption. The wolf having succeeded in outwitting his victim erupts from his disguise to engulf her. Carter, on the other hand, offers an iconoclastic version of the events. She uses two similar signifying systems—the literary text and the filmic text—to show how these can work to promote feminist ideology. At the end of *The Company of Wolves*, the story and the film, Rosaleen domesticates the wolf. Rather than engulfing her in his arms, it is *she* who initiates the amorous embrace, clearly a reversal and subversion of the familiar tale.

Carter forges out of the traditional fairy story a tale of horror, borrowing many conventions of the classical narrative cinema only to turn around and flout them. Her approach to screen writing strongly resembles her approach to storytelling: she takes "all sorts of bits" and pieces from many sources and turns these into her "own" stories about female desire. She "shakes out the fear and dislike of women [some folktales] expressed to create a new set of values, about strong, outspoken, zestful, sexual women who can't be kept down."[76]

Notes

1. Carter's tale is an adaptation of the Perrault and Grimm versions of "Little Red Riding Hood." See *The Trials and Tribulations of Little Red Riding Hood: Versions of the Tale in Sociocultural Context*, ed. Jack Zipes (South Hadley, MA: Bergin and Garvey, 1984, pp. 70-71 and pp. 124-26).

2. See rewrites of other Perrault and Grimm fairy tales in Carter's collection *The Bloody Chamber and Other Stories* (London: Penguin, 1979).

3. Zipes, "A Second Gaze at Little Red Riding Hood's Trials and Tribulations," in *Don't Bet on the Prince: Contemporary Fairy Tales in North America and England*, ed. Jack Zipes (New York: Routledge, 1989), p. 227.

4. Ibid., p. 231.

5. Brownmiller quoted in Zipes, *Don't Bet*, p. 232.

6. Maggie Anwell, "Lolita Meets the Werewolf," in *The Female Gaze: Women as Viewers of Popular Culture*, eds. Loraine Gamman and Margaret Marshment (London: The Women's P, 1988), p. 83.

7. Angela Carter, *The Sadeian Woman: An Exercise in Cultural History*. (London: Virago, 1979), p. 19.

8. Zipes, *Don't Bet*, p. 232.

9. While cinema can hardly claim to have invented the "art" of female victimization, it does perpetuate it. As Brian De Palma is quoted as saying in Carol J. Clover's "Her Body, Himself: Gender and the Slasher Film" (*Gender, Language, and Myth: Essays on Popular Narrative*. Toronto: U of Toronto P, 1992): "'Women in peril work better in the suspense genre. It all goes back to the *Perils of Pauline* . . . If you have a haunted house and you have a woman walking around with a candelabrum, you fear more for her than you would for a husky man. Or Hitchcock, during the filming of *The Birds*: "I always believe in following the advice of the playwright, Sardou. He said 'Torture the women!' The trouble today is that we don't torture women enough"'" (p. 271).

10. Zipes, *Don't Bet*, p. 237.

11. Ibid., p. 242.

12. Ibid., p. 243.

13. Ibid., p. 243.

14. Ibid., p. 248.

15. Angela Carter, "The Company of Wolves," in *The Bloody Chamber*, p. 118.

16. Anwell, p. 78.

17. In *Visual and Other Pleasures*, ed. Laura Mulvey (Bloomington: Indiana UP), pp. 16-28. See also, Laura Mulvey, "Afterthoughts on 'Visual Pleasure and Narrative Cinema' Inspired by *Duel in the Sun*," in *Visual and Other Pleasures*, pp. 29-38.

18. See Doane's important articles "Film and the Masquerade: Theorizing the Female Spectator," in *Femmes Fatales: Feminism, Film Theory, Psychoanalysis* (New York: Routledge, 1991) pp. 17-32, and "Masquerade Reconsidered: Further Thoughts on the Female Spectator," in *Femmes Fatales*, pp. 33-43; Teresa de Lauretis, *Alice Doesn't: Feminism, Semiotics, Cinema* (Bloomington: Indiana UP, 1984) and "Aesthetic and Feminist Theory: Rethinking Women's Cinema" in *Female Spectators: Looking at Film and Television*, ed. E. Deidre Pribram (London: Verso, 1988), pp. 174-95; Gledhill's "Pleasurable Negotiations," in *Female Spectators*, pp. 64-89; Kaplan's "Is the Gaze Male?" in *Women and Film: Both Sides of the Camera* (New York: Methuen, 1983), pp. 23-35.

19. "Desperately Seeking Difference," in *The Sexual Subject: A Screen Reader in Sexuality* (London: Routledge, 1992), pp. 223-57.

20. "Is the Gaze Feminist? Pornography, Film and Feminism," in *Perspectives on Pornography: Sexuality in Film and Literature*, eds. Gary Day and Clive Bloom (New York: St. Martin's P, 1988), pp. 69-82.

21. Ibid., p. 73.

22. Ibid., p. 77.

23. Ibid., p. 81.

24. Janet Bergstrom and Mary Ann Doane, "The Female Spectator: Contexts and Directions." *Camera Obscura* 20/21 (Sept 1989), pp. 5-27.

25. Stacey, p. 250.

26. Ibid., p. 225.

27. *Subversive Intent: Gender, Politics, and the Avant-Garde* (Cambridge, MA.: Harvard UP, 1990), pp. 139-40.

28. Seymour Chatman, "What Novels Can Do That Films Can't (and Vice Versa)." *Critical Inquiry* 7.1 (Autumn 1980), p. 132.

29. de Lauretis, *Alice Doesn't*, p. 155.

30. "Re-Constructing Oedipus Through 'Beauty and the Beast.'" *Criticism: A Quarterly for Literature and the Arts* 31.4 (Fall 1989), pp. 439-53.

31. Ibid., p. 452.

32. Linda Williams, "When a Woman Looks," in *Re-Vision: Essays in Feminist Film Criticism,* eds. Mary Ann Doane et al. (New York: U Publications of America, 1984), pp. 83-99.

33. Williams, p. 85.

34. Ibid., p. 85.

35. Ibid., p. 85.

36. Ibid., p. 86.

37. Kaplan, p. 31.

38. Williams, p. 87.

39. Ibid., p. 89.

40. Ibid., p. 90.

41. Ibid., p. 96.

42. Carter quoted in Merja Makinen, "Angela Carter's *The Bloody Chamber* and the Decolonialization of Feminine Sexuality." *Feminist Review* 42 (Autumn 1992), p. 4.

43. Williams, p. 97.

44. Ibid., p. 97.

45. Carter, ed. *Old Wives' Fairy Tale Book,* intro. Angela Carter (New York: Pantheon, 1990), p. xvii.

46. Ibid., p. x.

47. John Collick. "Wolves Through the Window: Writing Dreams/Dreaming Films/Filming Dreams." *Critical Survey* 3.3 (1991), p. 288.

48. Ibid., p. 286.

49. Ibid., p. 288.

50. Carter, ed. *Strange Things Sometimes Still Happen: Fairy Tales From Around the World,* intro. Marina Warner (Boston: Faber and Faber, 1993), p. x.

51. Jack Zipes, *Fairy Tales and the Art of Subversion: The Classical Genre for Children and the Process of Civilization* (London: Heinemann, 1983), p. 22.

52. Carter, "The Company of Wolves," p. 110.

53. Ibid., p. 110.

54. Ibid., p. 113.

55. In *Sigmund Freud: Collected Papers,* trans. James Strachey (New York: Basic Books, 1959), vol. 4., p. 226.

56. Carter, "The Company of Wolves," p. 114.

57. Barbara Creed has recently drawn attention to the feminine in horror in *The Monstrous Feminine: Film, Feminism, Psychoanalysis* (New York: Routledge, 1993). She writes: "the notion of the monstrous feminine challenges the view that femininity, by definition, constitutes passivity," that is, she acts not as castrated victim but as "agent of castration." At the same time, however, Creed believes, "those images which define woman as monstrous in relation to her reproductive functions [as archaic mother, monstrous womb, vampire, possessed monster, femme castratrice, witch, and castrating mother] work to reinforce the phallocentric notion that female sexuality is abject," pp. 151, 55.

58. Ibid., pp. 155-56.

59. For a lively albeit disturbing defense of the slasher film and its "progressive [feminist] claims," see Carol J. Clover, "Her Body, Himself: Gender in the Slasher Film" in *Gender, Language, and Myth: Essays on Popular Narrative,* ed. Glenwood Irons (Toronto: U of Toronto P, 1992, pp. 252-302); see also Harold Schechter's "The Bloody Chamber: Terror Films, Fairy Tale, and Taboo" (*Gender, Language, and Myth,* pp. 233-51) which explores the connection between horror films and folk stories more explicitly. Schechter argues that both films and folk tales deal with primitive taboo and ritual. Both appeal to a side of the human psyche which has been suppressed by rationalizing tendencies, and in addition to offering entertainment, both communicate in the primordial "picture-language of myth" (Campbell qtd. in Schechter, p. 249). As a Jungian, Schechter maintains that "myths can only appear clothed in the cultural

trappings of a particular time and place," and thus, "the superficial details of the story have changed. . . . [even while] the archetypal essence of the story" remains the same (p. 248). The major weakness of his article is exposed at the end when he conveniently blames society for not providing the "key" to unlocking the "meaning of myth" (p. 249), thus suggesting only a tenuous link between "terror films, fairy tales, and taboo." *The Company of Wolves* also has aspects of the "splatter" film in it. According to John McCarty, "splatter" film aims "not to scare . . . audiences necessarily, nor to drive them to the edge of their seats in suspense, but to mortify them with scenes of explicit gore. In splatter movies, mutilation is . . . the message" (qtd. in Schechter, p. 240). Two scenes in *The Company of Wolves* are overtly gory—both involve the horrifying physicality of transformation, the excruciating pain of giving birth to oneself.

60. Carter, "Notes from the Frontline," in *On Gender and Writing,* ed. Michelene Wandor (London: Pandora, 1983), p. 75.

61. Carter, "The Werewolf," in *The Bloody Chamber,* p. 108.

62. Carter, "The Company of Wolves," p. 111.

63. Clover, pp. 287-88.

64. Mary Ann Doane, "Film and the Masquerade: Theorizing the Female Spectator" in *Femmes Fatales,* pp. 25-26.

65. Ibid., p. 26.

66. de Lauretis, *Alice Doesn't,* p. 112.

67. Carter, "The Werewolf," pp. 109-10.

68. Makinen, p. 11.

69. *Jacques Lacan: A Feminist Introduction* (New York: Routledge, 1990), p. 38.

70. Avis Lewallen, "Wayward Girls but Wicked Women? Female Sexuality in Angela Carter's *The Bloody Chamber,*" in *Perspectives on Pornography: Sexuality in Film and Literature,* eds. Gary Day and Clive Bloom (New York: St. Martin's P, 1988), p. 157.

71. Grosz, p. 38.

72. Ibid., p. 38.

73. "Is Seeing Believing? Proverbs and Film Adaptation of a Fairy Tale." *Proverbium* 7 (1990), p. 98.

74. Carter, "The Company of Wolves," p. 117.

75. Zipes, *Don't Bet,* 259.

76. Warner, *Strange Things,* p. x.

Linda C. Middleton (essay date 1996)

SOURCE: Middleton, Linda C. "A Consummation Devourly To Be Wished: Representations of Anorexia in Angela Carter's 'The Lady of the House of Love.'" In *Constructions and Confrontations: Changing Representations of Women and Feminisms, East and West: Selected Essays,* edited by Cristina Bacchilega and Cornelia N. Moore, pp. 140-45. Honolulu: University of Hawai'i Press, 1996.

[*In the following essay, Middleton explores the anorexic subtext of "The Lady of the House of Love," demonstrating the story's subversive use of patriarchal clinical discourse on the eating disorder.*]

In Angela Carter's anthology of retold folktales, **The Bloody Chamber,** "The Lady of the House of Love" follows **"The Snow Child"** and precedes **"The Werewolf"**—two stories which share its theme of unnatural consummation, as manifested in aberrant sexuality and distorted appetite. These issues are treated in **"The Lady"** [**"The Lady of the House of Love"**] within the convention of the vampire tale. But this vampire plot is supported by another narrative of sexual, appetitive distortion: an anorexic subtext which alerts us, as do many of the other stories in **The Bloody Chamber,** to the feminist implications of Carter's postmodern "fairy tales."

The anorexic subtext of **"The Lady"** is introduced in **"The Snow Child,"** a variant on the traditional "Snow White" story, which itself suggests the dangers of ingestion when a Wicked Stepmother Queen tempts the heroine with a poisonous apple. The stepmother figure in **"The Snow Child"** is a Countess, jealous of a girl her husband, the Count, has constructed for himself, with a series of wishes. The "child of his desire" has snow-white skin, raven-black hair and blood-red lips (91-2); and the Countess, like the "Snow White" stepmother prototype wants the girl killed, but does it with a rose instead of an apple. The story ends in Oedipal retaliation, as the dead snow child, in the guise of a rose herself, bites the hand of the mother who would not feed her.

"The Snow Child" sets the patriarchal scene for the story it precedes, **"The Lady of the House of Love."** As the first heroine is narratively-constructed by her father, so also, though perhaps not so magically, The Lady of the House of Love is patriarchally determined. She is the last Countess of the Vampires, descendant of Vlad the Impaler, who "picnicked on corpses in the forests of Transylvania" (94). Here we note an echo of **"The Snow Child,"** where the Count rapes the dead daughter of his desires, "picnicking" in his own way on a corpse, though he "weeps" as he does so (92).

The Lady of the House of Love often also weeps as she participates in the imperative appetite of her blood: after her nocturnal feasts in the forests surrounding "the castle of her inheritance," the Lady "creep[s] home, whimpering, with blood smeared on her cheeks" (95). Along with the patriarchal "inheritance" of the castle which "incarcerates her," the Lady's additional legacy is this savage appetite.[1] When viewed in context of *The Bloody Chamber*'s other heroines, The Countess's bizarre appetite reflects Carter's shift from the feline-like heroines featured in the early stories to less conventionally seductive bestial metamorphoses: a shift made more explicit in **"The Werewolf,"** which as mentioned above follows **"The Lady"**; and a shift of the House of Love, though, is the first in the sequence of *Bloody Chamber* heroines to assume a wolf's form, and hunt down the "crunch of the fragile bones of rabbits and small, furry things" (95). This feline-to-wolf shift allows Carter to suggest one of the key elements in the anorexic subtext: a compulsory diet the heroine rejects. Whether her prey is a baby rabbit, a field mouse or a man, the Lady of the House of Love "loathes the food she eats" (96).

Though the feral diet of the Lady of the House of Love is not literally that of most anorexics, the "loathing of food" is similar, as well as the motive of that loathing. As the story indicates, the heroine is "incarcerated" and trapped by her vampire legacy, which is patriarchally determined. Anorexia is defined as a failed attempt by a daughter to "separate herself" from parental determination. In The Lady's case, in detesting the vampire diet, she attempts to create a "space" beyond the "desires" of her dead father (Mahbobah 88). Angela Carter herself concurred with this notion of anorexia as "a means of asserting control" (Clapp 26). Carter suffered from anorexia when she was in her teens. While contemplating her "A-level" exams, and an application to Oxford, Carter lost "six stone [84 lbs.] in six months." She remembered the dislocating experience of "looking at myself in the mirror and not recognis[ing] myself— except that I still looked big" (Clapp 26). This is consistent with the "highly elaborated visual distortion" of clinical anorexia (Caskey 181). And it is also an aspect of the theme of afflicted specularity in **"The Lady of the House of Love."**

For example, this vampiress's château is, according to vampire convention, replete with mirrors that return no reflection of its mistress. And, of course, the Lady cannot bear sunlight, so she must be securely coffined during the day and exposed only to the lamplight at night. Carter uses these elements of the vampire tale to suit her obvious narrative, but also to illumine her subtext. The empty mirrors hint at the denied body-image of the anorexic, but they also mock one of the anorexic's main fascinations. Though out of touch with her "realistic" image, the anorexic uses her emaciated body as a "spectacle," a kind of "body theater," which "enunciates, simultaneously, an exhibitionistic joy and the agony of starvation" (Mahbobah 91). This ambiguous enunciation is both a source of confusion and a means of con-

trol for real-life anorexics; but in **"The Lady of the House of Love,"** the main witness of the heroine's body theater—the young British soldier—succumbs only briefly to confusion, and seems to escape control.

The soldier's arrival, itself, is an element in the tale that falls in the realm of that which is *out of* control. His presence follows the amazingly chance appearance in the Lady's endless deal of the Tarot cards, of *"Les Amoureux"*—"The Lovers." This game of Tarot, though seemingly a vicious cycle in itself, is in fact the way "The Lady" has elected to try and "evade" her "destiny" (94). The "arcana" of the Tarot as a means of self-determination correspond to what psychologists have noted about anorexic strategies, which rely on "magical effectiveness" rather than logical planning (Caskey 182).[2] Counterpointing "The Lady's" oracle, the soldier provides an opposing narrative of his arrival which is the epitome of *logos* and rationality. Even his means of transportation, a bicycle, is touted as "the product of pure reason applied to motion" (97).

The soldier conveys *logos* into The Lady's realm in several other ways. For one, he brings language— something The Lady is challenged by, as she explains of her mute servant: "'my one companion . . . cannot speak. Often I am so silent that I think I, too, will soon forget how to do so and nobody here will ever talk any more'" (102). As a secondary harbinger of *logos,* the soldier brings "time," for his arrival is marked in the story by the first historical reference, to a "hot, ripe summer in the pubescent years of the present century" (97). But most importantly, the soldier brings light: light which dazzles the visually-challenged Lady, and light which dazzles us. For we, obeying the authority of the soldier's logical narrative, imagine that by the light of his vision we finally see the heroine. However, the image the soldier offers us of the Lady—the one that does not achieve the "control" of anorexic "body theater"—is also an image that Carter's narrative finally leads us to question.

We are told that a "lack of imagination is what gives . . . heroism to the hero" (104). The root word "image" in "imagination" cues us to aporias in his vision due to his "lack of imagination." Undoubtedly the soldier's vision, narrated so logically, seems to reduce the gesture of the Lady's "body theater" from a sign of her vampirism to a hysterical symptom. When the soldier refers to the Lady as a "bedizened scarecrow" (100), we suddenly *see* an "image" of the heroine stripped of the imaginative *puissance* (a kind of empowered *jouissance*) of her vampire narrative. The Lady's previous "threat" is represented now as ritualistic limitation: "She only knows of one kind of consummation" (103) we are told, as if in preview of the soldier's deeper consummatory knowledge. The Lady's narrative tells us that, "The bridegroom bleeds on my inverted marriage bed" (105), but we come to doubt this the moment the Lady's protective glasses are knocked off and their shattering leaves her vulnerable, at a loss to "invent" a new route to *her* traditional consummation, and confronted for the first time with the image of her own blood instead of her victim's.

The sight of her own blood radically alters the nature of this heroine's "bloody chamber" (in keeping with the motif of the title of Carter's collection) from a vampire's chamber, stained with the blood of past victims, to a much more intimate construct. As she registers that she herself bleeds, the heroine must come to terms with "the pain of becoming human" (106). In terms of the anorexic subtext, the signification here refers to one symptom of anorexia—amenorrhea, caused by a low body fat ratio, which clinical discourse sees as the anorexic's goal rather than the consequence of her disorder. The loss of her period is seen as the anorexic's "attempt to defer her maturation indefinitely" (Mahbobah 89). In one sense, then, The Lady's bleeding can be seen as the onset of her deferred maturation, stimulated by the soldier's presence. In a related sense, it might also signify the blood of defloration, which this scene suggests will displace The Lady's ritual "consummation" of her victim. However, signification in **"The Lady of the House of Love"** must not be so neatly conflated with logical representation. As one critic has put it, representation, in *The Bloody Chamber*'s stories, "can be confused with validation" (Bacchilega 78); but the way Carter's stories are "consciously mediated by other texts" makes a "mimetic approach" to them "narrow as well as potentially misleading" (Bacchilega 84, n2).

Thus, the mediations of the anorexic subtext provide a disruption of the overt narrative that should make us question its representations: such as the Countess's[3] blood-stained negligé, and whether this blood corresponds, as the soldier tells us, to the menses which would validate the psychoanalytic discourse of anorexia; or whether the blood signals a consummation that undoes the Countess's vampirism and baptizes her into human sexuality.[4] The confusion of significations here is captured in the image of the rose which the soldier notices on the floor of the sunlit bedroom, and which he supposes the Countess rose early to "gather" for him (106). But the Countess's narrative tells us differently: "I leave you as a souvenir the dark, fanged rose I plucked from between my thighs, like a flower laid on a grave" (107). The Countess's narrative implies an agency on her part that negates the soldier's role as seducer. The identification of the rose as having come from between her thighs instead of blowing in from her mother's rose bushes also suggests that the Countess, though inspired by the mother's emblem, has engendered her own maturity—has appropriated her mother's power for her own use as a woman.

The representation of this rose provides further narrative disruptions when the soldier, back at his quarters, "decided to try and resurrect" it (107). It revives from its faded, post-defloration wilt to "a glowing, velvet, monstrous flower" of "corrupt, brilliant, baleful splendour" (108). The resurrection has taken place in, of all things, the soldier's "tooth glass" (107)—a ludicrous echo of the vampire narrative conventions. For the tooth glass is afloat with what the soldier has consumed orally, evoking the carnivorous vampirism of the Countess's ancestry. The rose's revival thus refutes the soldier's triumph over the superstitious legacy of the vampire text. But the rose's vivid florescence also refigures the psychoanalytic aspects of the anorexic subtext. For the rose in the tooth glass is also a "vagina dentata," refuting the Countess's death into time and sexuality—the anorexic's main terrors—by affirming a post-mortem *puissance*.[5]

Earlier in the story, we were told of the Countess's impotence to frighten the soldier with her emaciated image: "He will learn to shudder in the trenches. But this girl cannot make him shudder" (104). The last image of the rose, though, and the line following ("Next day, his [the soldier's] regiment embarked for France," (108)) achieve the link of fear with the anorexic image. The anorexic's "body theater," designed to induce fear, only provoked the soldier's pity. But the resurrected "fanged rose" is hardly a pitiful image. In this way, Carter represents and symbolically validates the rebellion anorexia poses to the representations of that most patriarchal of discourses: the psychoanalytic. While the Countess's story is subtextually representative of anorexia, thus, it does not validate the psychoanalytic representations of this disorder, but, instead, is—like the anorexic's body itself—"a response to the misogyny of [psychoanalytic] discourses" (Mahbobah 95). Though the Lady may seem to move through the steps of "loathing," "body-denial," "body-acceptance," and sexual maturity evocative of the clinical narrative of anorexic diagnosis and recovery, we are in fact being shown that "anorexia" both "as spectacle and voice" is not a mere "stance" to be cured, but a "defacement of many culturally endorsed signifiers" (Mahbobah 95).

Thus, the blatant rose at the close of **"The Lady of the House of Love"** thrives not *on,* but in spite of the culture of the soldier's tooth glass, and mocks his refusal to shudder at the body theater of rebellion to culturally-determined femininity which is anorexia. Also, in keeping with Carter's post-modernity, this image of the unreal rose also mocks the Western European culture of the modernist period: an era evocative of those trenches where the soldier is heading, and where he will finally be consumed by a violence much more treacherous than the consummation he seemingly escaped in "The House of Love."

Notes

1. The patriarchal imperative of the heroine's vampire appetite is complicated by the seeming complicity of her mother in her fate. After all, it is the "roses her dead mother planted" which have become "a huge, spiked wall that incarcerates her in the castle of her inheritance" (95). In this story, as in most other anorexic narratives, the mother's role is hardly a minor one. One critic notes that the anorexic's thinness is a signal directed *specifically* to the mother for help (Caskey 188). And the theme of a mother responding to her daughter's need for help is crucial to the title story in *The Bloody Chamber,* and less central but still relevant in several others. Whether The Countess's mother is a rescuer or a contributor in her daughter's imprisonment is ambiguous. But the association of roses with the mother, and the triumphant rose image at the conclusion of the story suggest that, indeed, the Lady's mother does—despite those ominous rose bushes—somehow come to her daughter's aid in providing an emblematic escape from her patriarchal imperatives.

2. The references to The Lady's unexpected "deal" of Les Amoureux in her Tarot game interestingly parallels how Carter referred to her own anorexic bout: "It all got completely out of hand," she reflected on her quest for thinness (Clapp 26). The Lady, turning up Les Amoureux, "shakes" and "trembles" at the unprecedented card: the game of Tarot would seem to have gotten "out of hand." However, Carter does not seem to be suggesting that The Lady deludes herself in connecting her deal with the soldier's arrival. Such a suggestion would be consistent with a criticism of the faulty logic of anorexic strategies of "magical effectiveness." The logic of the opposing soldier's narrative would consequently be validated. But Carter's remarks about fiction making are more supportive of serendipity-like occasions, such as the Countess's Tarot deal. "Chance . . . is the mother of invention," Carter has written (Clapp 27), and the Tarot dealing heroine is one image of the author visited by "chance"—an illogical phenomenon also invoked in the "magically effective" devices of the anorexic.

3. References to the heroine alternate between "the Lady" and "the Countess" throughout this essay.

4. This interpretation is supported by the soldier's observation the next morning, of The Lady's "lace negligé lightly soiled with blood, as it might be from a woman's menses" (106). It is important to note, however, that this is the *soldier's* observation, further qualified by the words "might be." There is no real evidence that the blood is either menstrual or the result of sexual consummation.

Though one critic has suggested that the Countess of the Vampires has bled and died in "giving birth" to a new vampire—the soldier (Fowl 78)—this is unsubstantiated. The soldier is not transformed during his night with the Countess. He remains naively convinced of her hysteria, and, in fact, plans to take her to a "specialist" (sounding suspiciously Freudian) to "cure her" (107). The soldier thus remains firmly entrenched in the psychoanalytic discourse the story is questioning. And even the supposed defloration which yields the rose is, as my discussion suggests, effected by the Countess herself—not the soldier. It is a gesture *for* him, but not of surrender. Certainly the "fanged" quality of the proffered rose suggests this is not a complacent surrender of virginity on the Countess's part. (I am grateful to Sylvia Spalding for calling this important distinction, and Fowl's essay to my attention.)

5. The connection of anorexia with not simply a resistance to mature female sexuality, but to the passage of time and death itself is connected to one of the vampire tale conventions discussed earlier: the absence of mirror reflections. The recognition of one's mirror image, one critic writes of the girl/woman's maturation process, is a "fall into division, the birth of self-consciousness. . . . Such an experience is the end of childhood. The mirror destroys the Edenic absence of self-cognizance" (La Belle 50). Although it seems blasphemous to connect an "Edenic" longing with vampirism, it is fairly obvious that the resistance to time's ravages and to natural death are central perquisites of the vampire's unusual existence.

Works Cited

Bacchilega, Cristina. "Sex Slaves and ? Resisting Masochism in *The Bloody Chamber." Across the Oceans, Studies from East to West in Honor of Richard K. Seymour.* Ed. Irmengard Rauch and Cornelia Moore. Honolulu University of Hawaii Press, 1995: 77-86.

Carter, Angela. *The Bloody Chamber and Other Stories.* London: Penguin Books, 1979.

Caskey, Noelle. "Interpreting Anorexia Nervosa." *The Female Body in Western Culture: Contemporary Perspectives.* Ed. Susan Rubin Suleiman. Cambridge: Harvard UP, 1985. 174-89.

Clapp, Susannah. "On Madness, Men and Fairy-tales." *The Independent on Sunday.* 9 June 1991: 26-27.

Fowl, Melinda. "Angela Carter's *The Bloody Chamber* Revisited." *Critical Survey.* 3.1 (1991): 71-79.

La Belle, Jenijoy. *Herself Beheld: The Literature of the Looking Glass.* Ithaca: Cornell UP, 1988.

Mahbobah, Albaraq. "Reading the Anorexic Maze." *Genders.* No. 14 (Fall, 1992): 87-97.

Nicoletta Pireddu (essay date May 1997)

SOURCE: Pireddu, Nicoletta. "Carterbury Tales: Romances of Disenchantment in Geoffrey Chaucer and Angela Carter." *The Comparatist* 21 (May 1997): 117-48.

[*In the following essay, Pireddu compares Geoffrey Chaucer's and Carter's tales with respect to the "revisionary" tradition of romance narratives, examining the transitional ideologies implicit in both authors' works.*]

To associate romance with the illusion-breaking strategy of post-modernism may at first seem paradoxical, yet, in fact, romance is being increasingly taken as the privileged mode, staging the hybridity and openness of contemporary critical discourse. Associated with excess, impurity, and self-difference, romance shares the aesthetic and political agenda of postmodern literature and theory: through textual dispersion and playfulness, it provides a counternarrative to the project of knowledge as deployment of authority and conquest of certainty.[1] Beyond periodization and formal categories, romance can thus indicate a state, a certain attitude towards the cultural and historical heritage and its representation which is at work whenever a straightforward *quest for meaning* in fact becomes *questioning of meaning*—whenever, instead of offering a pleasurable escape to a freer world, narrative crosses the conceptual and aesthetic boundaries between referentiality and representation, disputing the neutrality of both.

The works of Angela Carter suitably illustrate such a destabilizing approach to enthralling fantasies. With her blend of literary tradition and mass-culture stereotypes, this British contemporary writer creates a sophisticated fictional world that investigates our knowledge of reality, exposing the degree to which culture and power inform such knowledge. Romance is particularly suitable to this purpose because of the highly codified ideology that is sedimented within its structure, namely, the anticipation of a utopian idyll.[2] The more conventional and crystallized Carter's target is, the more provocative her reinscription turns out to be. That's why her imaginary territory mainly takes over the magical realm of children's fables. Disfigured by gothic and macabre motifs, dreams become indistinguishable from nightmares. Interrogated by gender, the apparently naive genre of romance reveals that its wish-fulfilling mechanism can not only perpetuate but also subvert the cultural values embedded in narrative form. Carter is all for "putting new wine in old bottles, especially if the pressure of the new wine makes the old bottles ex-

plode" ("Notes" ["Notes from the Front Line"] 69). It is by writing as an analyst of mythologies and as a skeptical female fantasist that she can explode the practices and roles imposed by male tradition. Thus, romance for Angela Carter—like myth for Roland Barthes—can be either oppressive or liberatory depending on how it is appropriated. It is never innocent, always an alibi.

Although Angela Carter's revision of romance is receiving considerable attention, most studies concentrate on her reinscription of modern literature—for instance, her parody of Perrault's and Grimm's stories, or her appropriation of the gothic tradition, of symbolism and surrealism, of Hollywood myths and of the culture of consumerism. In fact, however, Carter's own statements, as well as the observations of her friend, scholar Lorna Sage, emphasize the equally pivotal role played by medieval literature in her education at Bristol (*Carter* ix): medieval texts allowed her to cheer up "the leftover Leavisite canon" (*Flesh and the Mirror* 4), leading her "into the territory of romance and folk tale" (5). Carter's journey towards the roots of storytelling, however, is anything but a search for an *ur*-text: rather, it brings to the foreground the notion of a communal literary patrimony, belonging to nobody and being constantly disseminated and manipulated by everyone. "Who first invented meatballs?"—Carter asks in her much-quoted Introduction to *The Virago Book of Fairy Tales* (x). "In what country? Is there a definitive recipe for potato soup?" (x). Romance invites us to think of literature "in terms of the domestic arts" (x): just as in cooking I can only tell "how *I* make potato soup" (x), narratives of myth and magic become each time what our craft makes of them. Literature, like folklore, is not so much created as re-used, taken as raw material for new stories and contingent truths.

Walking along Carter's road from the ghosts of modern fiction back to the old wonders of yarn-spinning, we find another pivotal author who adopts romance to negotiate between repetition and reinterpretation of his literary and cultural heritage beyond stable meanings and values—Geoffrey Chaucer. For its enactment of chivalric models and simultaneous questioning of their authority, Chaucer's literary operation prefigures what in Carter's terms becomes "speculative fiction," that is, storytelling as "a system of continuing inquiry" (Katsavos 14). Actually, in the post-feudal world of *The Canterbury Tales,* where such tellers as the clerk, the miller, the cook, and the merchant outnumber the figure of the knight, "th'olde dayes of the Kyng Arthour" (*Canterbury Tales* III, 857) appear as unquestionably remote. By reducing the themes of the quest and courtly love respectively to pilgrimage and marriage, Chaucer domesticates the dangerous adventures and the sense of mystery that shape Arthurian literature, thus deeply revising medieval romance.[3] *The Canterbury Tales* can be said to stand at a crossroads: they are indebted to knightly and courtly culture, yet, at the same time, they portray and address a late 14th-century social structure in which the spreading mercantile class challenges precisely the ethics of feudal aristocracy. Far from accidental, the role played by romance in such an ambivalent context has significant effects. On the one hand, the insertion of bourgeois threads in an idealized texture decrees the inadequacy of a narrative mode of the past vis-à-vis the more complex society of Chaucer's time, and hence betrays a polemical reception of such daydreaming fantasies because of their conservative impulse. On the other hand, Chaucer's allegiance to the fundamental components of romance in spite of his attempts at experimentation reveals that the very "pastness" of this genre can play a significant role in his narrative world. As they reenact the feudal order, *The Canterbury Tales* problematize those conditions for imaginary excitement represented in the Middle Ages as natural.[4] The ultimate aim of romance in *The Canterbury Tales* may well be that of making us dream once more—an aspect with which Auerbach would agree—yet not without passing through the "earthly contingencies" (136) of their time, not before grounding such dreams into "the practical business" (137) of Chaucer's world. Thus, Chaucer rechannels desire from the sexual adventures of medieval aristocracy to the institutionalized husband-wife liaison within domestic walls; he appropriates the convention of *gentillesse* but he derives it not so much from lineage as from individual virtue; he does not repudiate the prodigies of the marvelous but now he associates them with the rationality of science and the power of money.

Janus-like, romance hence looks both backwards and forwards, according to a dialectical process that recalls—but only to a certain extent—the tension proposed by Fredric Jameson between ideological and Utopian impulses in literature (105; 286-92). Chaucer's retrieval of romance could at first correspond to what Jameson describes as an ideological standpoint: by adopting romance as a form for some of his tales, Chaucer may also be said to be reinscribing its originary "socio-symbolic message" (141). *The Canterbury Tales* would thus appear as an example of utopian, positive hermeneutics *à la* Frye, one which treats the text as a compensatory space with the aim of strengthening the link between the mythical patterns of romance and a post-feudal social and cultural reality. In fact—as I will try to show—there is no innocent displacement in *The Canterbury Tales*. The irony underlying Chaucer's experiments with romance breaks the sense of continuity with the feudal code in a significant way. Not only does it point at that fall into history which for Jameson determines the secularization and the reinvention of romance, it also challenges the presence of those "magical categories of Otherness" (131) that medieval romance allegedly "found ready to hand in its socio-economic environment" (131). Chaucer reads the cel-

ebration of the golden age of Arthurian romance as a nostalgia for a mythical organic society which was a myth even before the collapse of feudalism, or before what Jameson describes as the commodification of desire brought about by capitalism. As he resurrects the dead language of romance, the author of the *Canterbury Tales* also employs the *topos* of the Middle Ages as a dream fabricated by the rationalized world—a utilitarian bricolage, as Eco would say, in the service of the fantasies of the modern era (61-72).[5]

As a functional example of the historicity of romance, Chaucer's collection of stories can be located at the beginning of a line of "magical narratives" (Jameson 103) which traverses all subsequent cultural manifestations down to contemporary ones. Nevertheless, starting from the *Canterbury Tales,* I would like to enrich the analysis of the transformations of romance in Jameson's *Political Unconscious* by calling attention to *ironic* reinscriptions of such a mode. Jameson seems to leave open the possibility of irony, but only in his brief discussion of romance in our century,[6] when the desacralization of good and evil replaces the reinvention of mystery through secular equivalents like theology or psychology (134-5). In fact, however, Chaucer himself already questions both the raw materials and the substitute codes of the older magical contents. Therefore, on the one hand, as an enclave of freedom from the oppression of the reality principle, the fairy-tale atmosphere can accommodate social and ethical conflicts, and even restore the prospect of salvation. On the other hand, *The Canterbury Tales* show that the *topoi* of romance can also be employed to thwart the expectations of freedom and reconciliation they seem to encourage. The dreamlike aura of a tale may prove inadequate to recontain antinomies; it may be unable to absorb an unappealing or problematic present into the oblivion of immemorial time.

Through a comparative reading of Chaucer and Carter, I propose a supplement to Jameson's genealogy of redeeming romances—a trajectory of magical narratives at least equally conscious of the historical discontinuity between mythical past and prosaic present, but also increasingly *self-conscious* to the point of shattering any promise of delusory re-enchantment. The authors chosen for this parallel are not the only options, but they occupy significant positions in this revisionary tradition of romance, being almost its chronological alpha and omega.[7] Furthermore, extraordinary analogies emerge from their repertories of narrative situations, besides a common adhesion to the form of the tale. With these observations I do not mean to suggest that Angela Carter wants to rewrite precisely *The Canterbury Tales,* although, as previously stated, the literature of Chaucer's time had considerable weight in her eclectic education. In any case, the two authors can be legitimately treated as *bricoleurs* of a mythical patrimony they share: in

The Canterbury Tales and in such collections of stories as **BC** [*The Bloody Chamber*] and *and Strangers,* Chaucer and Carter stage the textual nature of romance and make it inseparable from a critical examination of the ideology it transmits.

"Can a bird sing only the song it knows, or can it learn a new song?" (**BC** 103) asks Carter in **"The Lady of the House of Love,"**[8] that is, can romance be renovated in such a way as to raise new issues, as to become an effective means of investigation of a new reality? Both authors answer in the affirmative. Nevertheless, a comparison of some of their tales highlights the qualitatively different solutions provided by Chaucer and Carter to the questions of good and evil, innocence and experience, fact and fancy, in line with the paramount epistemological changes that separate the postmodern condition from the late Middle Ages. Romance's critique of the medieval world in *The Canterbury Tales* is the literary correlative of a transitional moment in which conflicting social forces and ethical principles overlap as a result of an institutional and ideological shift. Those clashes are reflected in the form of romance, with its dychotomy of masculine and feminine, "authority and submission, familiarity and exoticism, justice and mercy, public and private" (Crane 12). Although Chaucer depicts binary oppositions as precarious and questionable, he is still faithful to a clear-cut and hierarchical system of distinction. In the paradoxical universe of Carter's fables, such contrasts become chronic. Carter's romance, in other words, rethinks history as "an ironic coexistence of temporalities" (Elam 3): the only reality that romance reinvents is itself contaminated by the blurring of the values, classes, codes, and styles it is expected to clarify.

PICKING THE WITHERING "FLOUR OF CHIVALRY"

On his way to Canterbury, Chaucer the pilgrim tells the most rigorously parodic romance of the whole collection: "The Tale of Sir Thopas." The story of the "fair and gent" (VII, 715) knight riding out into the "contree of Fairye" (VII, 802) in search of the "elf-queene" (VII, 795) at once displays and undermines all canonical components of medieval chivalric poetry. We owe to Angela Carter's imagination another epigone of Sir Perceval, namely, the intrepid officer of **"The Lady of the House of Love,"** a short story in which the topoi of romance already parodied by Chaucer are subject to an additional twist, and charged with a new message.

Young, blond, "blue-eyed" and "heavy-muscled" (**BC** 97), Carter's officer rivals in beauty and strength Chaucer's "doghty swayn" (VII, 724), whose hair and beard are "lyk saffroun" (VII, 730) and whose skills are unequalled in "wrastlyng" (VII, 740), "in bataille and in tournayment" (VII, 716). However, each of them only seems to possess the qualities of the perfect knight. The

allusions to Sir Thopas's lips as "rede as rose" (VII, 726), to his "rode . . . lyk scarlet in grayn" (VII, 727), and to his "sydes smale" (VII, 836) ridicules the chivalric topos of youth by reducing it to images of childhood, chastity and effeminacy.[9] Also, the officer in **"The Lady of the House of Love"** is virgin and inexperienced, and needs to remind himself that he is "no child, now, to be frightened of his own fancies" (**BC** 99). Yet Carter's way of commenting on her character's features endows parody with more subtle and more complex effects than the ones in "Sir Thopas." Carter's protagonist "has the special quality of virginity, most and least ambiguous of states: ignorance, yet at the same time, power in potentia, and, furthermore, unknowingness, which is not the same as ignorance" (**BC** 97). With this openness to the future, with this promise of achievement, the story seems to adhere to the motif of a challenging vocation which in medieval romances engages youthful aspirations (Stevens 24). However, not unlike the "*ripe summer in the pubescent* years of the present century" (**BC** 97; my emphasis) when the story takes place, the officer has already used up all his potential sense of mystery and excitement for the new: when he "quixotically" (**BC** 97) decides to explore the uplands of Romania by bicycle, he mainly sees "all the humour of it" (**BC** 97), and it is a cynical laughter that accompanies his departure.

Therefore the adventure in **"The Lady of the House of Love"** begins under the aegis of irony, one which the character shares with his creator. Being "rooted in change and time" (**BC** 97), the officer is aware of his own historicity, which makes him "collide with the timeless Gothic eternity of the vampires" (**BC** 97) he is about to join. Ready to step into the world of romance, he remains a prisoner of self-consciousness and disenchantment, and is therefore unable to suspend his disbelief. Quite the opposite can be said about the tale of Sir Thopas, where the analogy of the child reinforces the protagonist's naïvete and his excessive enthusiasm for the quest. Chaucer's literary *jeu d'esprit* against medieval romance finds not so much an accomplice as a scapegoat in the "knyght auntrous" (VII, 909): through the exemplary parody of Sir Thopas's gullibility and uncritical loyalty to the Arthurian tradition, the tale mocks those 14th-century English poems which persist in representing a chivalric world by then considered old-fashioned. A substantial difference already emerges from the ways in which our two story(re)tellers tackle the relationship between the reality of their time and the fictional world of romance. If Sir Thopas's weakness is that of believing too much in the possibility of performing heroic deeds and of pursuing noble ideals in a bourgeois milieu, the British officer of **"The Lady of the House of Love,"** the son of an industrialized world on the verge of the Great War, is affected by skepticism towards illusions, as the progression of the each tale further clarifies.[10]

As 20th-century analogues of the details with which Chaucer exhibits Sir Thopas's bourgeois extraction—his blatantly comic name, his attire and his taste for exotic spices—Carter's story provides the officer's bicycle—a technological surrogate for the knight's horse—and his commodification of time and space through tourism—a by-product of modern capitalistic societies. It is upon this commercial and rationalized substratum that the two characters revive and revise the adventures of the hero in love. Chaucer literalizes the motif of the mysterious, desirable and inaccessible lady of medieval romances by merging it with the dream-vision theme of French oneiric poems: the object of Sir Thopas's "love longynge" (VII, 772)—the elf-queen he "dremed al this nyght" (VII, 787)—is by definition unattainable, since she is a figment of his delusory imagination. However, Chaucer's parody further plays with the dialectics of heroism and desire. Actually, the development of Sir Thopas's quest does not even outlast its first phase, the *agon* (Frye 192), in which the hero of romances struggles with the enemy. The encounter with "sire Olifaunt" (VII, 808), "a greet geaunt" (VII, 807) marks not so much the beginning of a sequence of glorious adventures as the endless deferral of them: the ritual of the "armynge" (VII, 846) before the challenge with the "perilous man of dede" (VII, 809) in fact fills in the space left empty by Sir Thopas's lack of courage.

Angela Carter's character, in this respect, behaves in a less predictable way and thus more deeply defamiliarizes the quest pattern. Instead of the "geaunt with hevedes three" (VII, 842) who hinders Chaucer's protagonist from attaining the object of his desire, the young officer of **"The Lady of the House of Love"** meets "an old woman who smile[s] eagerly, almost conciliatorily at him" (*BC* 98). As the key ring at her waist suggests, she literally opens the realm of romance to him: after bobbing a curtsy and beckoning him to follow her, the old woman unlocks the door of the mansion, where the officer finds supper and a bed ready for him. The magic of Carter's story paradoxically fulfills wishes before they are actually expressed, but it does not create a *Pays de Cocagne*. If, on the one hand, there are no more material obstacles to the object of desire, on the other hand, the officer's persisting cynicism remains the main threat to his romantic quest. Stepping unemotionally over the threshold of the castle, he does "not shiver in the blast of cold air" (*BC* 99), nor does he overcome "his own childish lack of enthusiasm" (*BC* 99) for the uncanny atmosphere of the place, although "he sharply reprimanded himself" (*BC* 99).

"[I]f one were sufficiently imaginative" (*BC* 98)—Carter comments—one could transfigure the landscape by seeing apparitions and envisioning secrets. This—we can add—would make the officer a new Sir Thopas, since it would restore precisely the promise of heroic enterprises, although only of temporary and hallucinatory ones. In fact, however, the protagonist of Carter's story dismisses even this extreme possibility, as can be inferred from other textual details. When Sir Thopas "priketh thrugh a fair forest" (VII, 754), Chaucer initially stirs in the reader the expectation of "many a wilde best" (VII, 755), even though he soon tames it with the reference to "bukke and hare" (VII, 756) in the following line. More radically, Carter transforms a dangerous wild animal into a merely decorative item: the lion that in many medieval romances offers the pretext for the knight's demonstration of courage is here aestheticized and reduced to "the lion's mouth" (*BC* 98) of a fountain where the officer can quench his thirst. There is nothing to fight for or to embellish through daydreaming fantasies in the House of Love. Significantly, the name of the mansion recalls the medieval motif of the allegorical house that Chaucer himself elaborates in *The House of Fame* to explore dream visions and the nature of love. Yet from its "sombre visage" (*BC* 98) to its "worm-eaten" (*BC* 100) and collapsing interior, its cobwebs, its "rotted away" (*BC* 101) carpet, the manor rather discards its literary antecedent, and becomes the objective correlative of the decay of romance. Whereas Sir Thopas "nolde slepen in noon hous" (VII, 910) and "drank water of the well" (VII, 915) in order to reproduce the efforts of the knight's quest, the officer does not need to struggle for anything. All the romance situations are generously lavished on him, but as he experiences them he cannot but acknowledge their degradation and shabbiness: they are as "tawdry," "thin and cheap" (*BC* 106) as the satin and the catafalque in the mansion's bedroom.

His encounter with the Lady of the House of Love is no exception to such general feeling: she turns out to be the appropriate "châtelaine of all this decay" (*BC* 101). The excitement that seemed to be aroused in the officer by "the most seductively caressing voice he had ever heard in his life" (100) promptly peters out on facing "the hectic, unhealthy beauty of a consumptive" (101). In her "dress fifty or sixty years out of fashion but once, obviously, intended for a wedding" (100) the woman looks "like a shipwrecked bride" (101) and occupies a middle ground that denies both the courtly code of adulterous love typical of medieval aristocracy and the institutionalization of sexuality through the bourgeois ethos of marriage. Ultimately, the tarnished values of Carter's story also affect the protagonist's desire. Those very "wide, full, prominent lips of a vibrant purplish-crimson" (*BC* 101) that should convey feminine sensuality are disturbing and repellent to him. They do not even seem to belong to the body of a living woman: they are rather perceived as a self-contained mechanism grafted on an automaton. Therefore, while the Lady of the House of Love lets her real identity as Countess Nosferatu gradually emerge through a macabre ritual of seduction made of an announced "succession of mysteries" (*BC* 104), the officer reacts to his increasing "sense of strangeness" by clinging to his "fundamental disbelief in what he sees before him" (103).

Significantly, Carter's story no longer grants the clear-cut separation that we find in "The Tale of Sir Thopas" between Chaucer's ironic lucidity and his character's fantasies. On the one hand, Sir Thopas opposes no resistance to the spell of pure passion for the queen of his dreams, and merely wonders "What eyleth this love at me / to bynde me so soore?" (VII, 785-86). On the other hand, it is thanks to a paradoxical sort of heroism born of a "lack of imagination" (*BC* 104)—and not of too much of it, as in the case of Sir Thopas—that Carter's young man can avoid being ensnared by the plot that the Tarot card of "Les Amoureux" (*BC* 103) has weaved for his future. This plot blends idealized love with blood and death, thus tainting romance with gothic tones: after a night of "embraces [and] kisses" with the Countess, he would be "stark and dead" (*BC* 105). The officer will be safe only by refusing "to shudder" (106), either with fear or with lust; he will be protected from the pains of romance by being insensitive to its pleasures. In the Lady who is alluring him with the erotic promise of a strip-tease he only sees "a disordered girl" (105) in need of the "innocent remedies of the nursery" (106). Thus when the Lady cuts her thumb on her broken glasses and is fascinated by the sight of her own blood, the officer maternally kisses the wound. He himself is the "exorcism" (106) which domesticates the female vampire by turning her into a human being. With the aid of medical science, he will "cure her of all these nightmares" (107): in a Swiss clinic she can be treated "for nervous hysteria" (107), while an eye specialist, a dentist and a manicurist will provide the finishing touch. It is sufficient to normalize all her eccentricities, and the vampire will become "the lovely girl she is" (107).

Paradoxically, by resorting to psychoanalysis, medicine, and beauty-culture—new positivities that should substitute for the loss of magical content in modern society (Jameson 134)—the officer does not reinvent romance: he destroys it. "The end of exile is the end of being" (*BC* 107) Carter remarks: romance is killed as soon as the rationalized, secular world appropriates Otherness, although unwittingly, in the name of goodness and sanity. The officer finds symbolic appeasement at the price of immolating enchantment on the "sacrificial altar" (*BC* 104) of common sense—a twist that has pivotal implications not only for narrative form but also for the representation of gender relationships. By turning the female vampire into a human being, the officer prevents her from sucking his blood, that is, from annihilating his humanity. The bridegroom, who in the Lady's plans was supposed to bleed on her "inverted marriage bed" (*BC* 105), does not succumb to the spell of a predatory woman, and with his lack of imagination he restores the clichés of female fragility and of male supremacy.

So far it would seem that **"The Lady of the House of Love"** had come full circle without bringing about any development in its world or any growth in its protagonist's psyche. The story would then be a mere reenactment of Frye's fourth phase of romance, which aims at maintaining "the integrity of the innocent world against the assault of experience" (Frye 201). Carter, it is true, turns these two categories upside down—since she associates reason with prelapsarian bliss, and fantasy with degeneration—but she preserves their binary opposition, which she resolves precisely in favor of innocence . . . that is, of rationality. As if to offset the mysterious influence of "the cards of destiny" (*BC* 107) with which the lady-vampire wants to put his life *en jeu,* the officer clings to his bicycle, "the product of pure reason applied to motion" (97), and joins his regiment. Ultimately, it is the horror of the war that occupies the vacant space of magic.

Yet Carter's story would not be postmodern enough without a further turning point that destabilizes the facile conclusions previously fostered. Not even with the last bicycle ride back to the real world is the officer at a safe distance from the bizarre occurrences of the enchanted mansion. Just when geographical displacement seems to substantiate the split between the logic of ordinariness and the code of a disturbing elsewhere, he discovers in his pocket the rose that the Lady of the House of Love had given him as a souvenir. Working as a synecdoche for the whole realm of romance that the officer has so far duly shunned with the aid of common sense, the rose—"withered" (*BC* 107) but far from dead—regains its original fragrance and contaminates the austere corridors of the barracks with a "corrupt, brilliant, baleful splendour" (108). "Vous serez ma proie" (104), the Lady had proclaimed: these words, that the events in the castle had apparently invalidated, now reinstate their disquieting prophetic value. Indeed, the officer ultimately capitulates to the enthrallment of romance. He becomes its prey precisely by yielding to the very "rich, faintly corrupt sweetness" (98) that he had previously rejected as the loathsome fruit of a perverted Garden of Love:

> Too many roses bloomed on enormous thickets . . . bristling with thorns, and the flowers themselves were almost too luxuriant, their huge congregations of plush petals somehow obscene in their excess, their whorled, tightly budded cores outrageous in their implications.
>
> (*BC* 98)

Well before the officer's sensuous intoxication in the garden of "obese roses" (*BC* 102), "love-longynge" (VII, 772) overwhelmed Sir Thopas in an equally suggestive *locus amoenus,* rich in "herbes grete and smale" (VII, 760) and vibrating with the songs of the "sparhauk and the papejay" (VII, 767), the "thrustelcok" (VII, 769) and the "wodedowve" (VII, 770). However, while through such visionary infatuation Chaucer's gullible knight wants to transfigure the world according to his desire and is precisely ridiculed for this, Carter's officer tests the romance topos of the *locus amoenus* in order to exorcise its dangers, yet he is not immune to them.

"The Lady of the House of Love" thus stages a quest in order to parody blind faith in rationality, yet simultaneously refuses to present romance as a consolatory alternative universe, as an innocent surrogate of ordinary reality. Facts and fancy overlap but not completely: a travel into the extratemporal dimension of a Romanian enchanted castle does not efface the painful actuality of World War I, that the final sentence of the story brings once more to the foreground despite the resurrection of the rose: "Next day the regiment embarked for France" (**BC** 108). Furthermore, if it is true that there is room for surprises even in the coherent and predictable life of the officer, the nature of such wonder can be far from reassuring. In the face of a barren world of common sense and rationality, **"The Lady of the House of Love"** fosters a kind of longing for the world of romance, yet ultimately it exhibits its disturbing duplicity, its tawdriness and vampiric deadliness. In Carter's hands, "the flour of roial chivalry" (VII, 901-2) that Sir Thopas in vain tried to pick becomes a "glowing, velvet, monstrous flower" (**BC** 108)—no longer a dream, not simply a nightmare, perhaps a bit real.

ON THE "WYNGES" OF LOVE TOWARD
DECEPTION

With respect to its blatant parodic disfiguration in "The Tale of Sir Thopas" and in **"The Lady of the House of Love,"** romance seems to play a constructive role in Chaucer's "The Franklin's Tale" and in Carter's **"The Kiss."** Both stories open with an emphasis on their textual nature by situating themselves in relation to idealized literary worlds. However, they encourage and prolong illusions only to make the reader's awakening more disturbing.

The Franklin explicitly acknowledges the authority of the Breton *lai* form, which he adopts for his narration. He thus creates the expectation of "delicate and delightful absurdity, hyperbole of pathos and sentiment, refinement rather than power" (Stevens 66) by extolling "the qualities of *gentillesse* and *franchyse*."[11] In the Prologue, his sense of inadequacy emerging from his excuses for his "rude speeche" (V, 718) and for his ignorance of the "colours of rethoryk" (V, 726) even reinforces the superiority of the romance model over the realistic paradigm: the Franklin strives to recollect the "diverse aventures" (V, 710) of the "olde gentil Britouns" (709), although—despite his "good wyl" (V, 715)—he can offer only a simplified reproduction. With the beginning of the actual tale, moreover, the stylistic

simplification at which the Prologue hints blends with a conceptual one:[12] the love between Dorigen and Arveragus is introduced as a happy, mutual and balanced relationship, a "wys accord" (V, 791) between a lady and a knight that harmonizes "lordshipe and servage" (V, 794), "maistrie" (V, 765) and "libertee" (V, 768), beyond any psychological, social or historical modification.

Carter's **"The Kiss"** resorts to the romance paradigm to promise an analogous re-enchantment. The magic of the April air makes "an authentically fabulous city" blossom from the squalid topography of the story, with its "bleak winters" and its "sweating, foetid summers," bringing "cholera, dysentery and mosquitoes" (**Saints** [**Saints and Strangers**] 35). Significantly, the narrator asks us to imagine this city by appealing to the naïve creativity of "a child's colouring box" (**Saints** 35): like the "bare and pleyn" (V, 720) talking with which the Franklin depicts an equally plain and unproblematic human union, the "straightforward, geometric shapes" (**Saints** 35) traced by the crayons replace the intricacy and the ambiguity of the real world with a serene coexistence of nature and civilization. We are carried away to a city as "beautiful as an illusion," where inhabitants appear "as extraordinary to the foreign eye as a unicorn" and where "irises grow in the gutters" (**Saints** 36). Not merely space but also time functions "in direct contradiction to history" (**Saints** 36): if, paradoxically, the peasant women can overcome the dreamlike aura of the place only by pretending they do "not live in an imaginary city" (35), the lily-seller at the marketplace "scarcely seems to inhabit time" (36). The mystery surrounding her identity and her origin—"When she has sold her lilies, she will go back to the place where they are growing"—suggests her fable-like nature, which is soon accentuated by her alleged role in the domain of storytelling: she "might vanish" as a fictional character "waiting for Scheherezahde to perceive a final dawn had come and, the last tale of all concluded, fall silent" (**Saints** 36).

It is within this frame of "glittering and innocent exoticism" (**Saints** 36) that the narration evokes the legendary figure of Tamburlaine and further entangles the lily-seller into textuality by insinuating a connection between her and Tamburlaine's wife. The connection becomes more evident at the end of the narrative, where Tamburlaine's wife steps out of her story and back into the frame: "After she ran away from him perhaps she made her living in the market. Perhaps she sold lilies there" (**Saints** 37). Not unlike the Franklin's *imperfect* rehearsal of the Breton *lai*, the objective correlative that kindles the romantic imagination in Carter's story is a *flawed* building: the mosque that Tamburlaine's wife had built to celebrate his return is now a heap of ruins. However, the disfiguration caused by time does not shake the original integrity of that remote world of romance, which, as in Chaucer's tale, is introduced precisely as a viable epistemological model for reality: in line with Dorigen's and Arveragus's idyll, Carter's story opens under the sign of love, which the title itself—**"The Kiss"**—brings to the foreground. Nevertheless, as soon as the premises of their respective plots have titillated us with the wonders of passion, Chaucer and Carter adopt an illusion-breaking strategy which dissipates all traces of nostalgia for the idealized world of romance. Significantly, it is not simply a sense of belatedness that prevents them from identifying with such innocent, fantastic province. More radically, they want to challenge the very myth of a Golden Age, to demystify romance at its roots by calling into question the values upon which it is founded. We can follow such a process by examining the way Chaucer and Carter employ and undermine two topoi of romance: the love triangle and the marvelous.

After painting married life with the nuances of medieval courtly love, "The Franklin's Tale" soon separates domesticity from the knight's lust for "worshipe and honour" in arms (V, 811). Actually, Arveragus's chivalric enterprises occupy just two lines of the tale, and remain peripheral throughout the plot (Burrow 117). Moreover, it is not accidental that the "General Prologue" defines the Franklin "a vavasour" (I, 360). By ascribing to the narrator of this tale the character traits and the role that vavasors played in Arthurian literature, Chaucer confirms precisely the marginal status of traditional romantic concerns in his work. Among the features of such a low feudal rank in romance episodes are old age, loose contacts with the royal court and a settled, sedentary life, in clear contrast with the young age, "mobility and nobility of the knight errant" (Pearcy 45). With "his berd" (I, 332) as white "as is the dayesye" (I, 332) and his household in a "contree" (I, 340) the Franklin fits this stereotype. Furthermore, a parallel is thus established between Chaucer's vavasor and the female protagonist of his tale: both the Franklin and Dorigen belong to the domain of the household rather than to the world of heroic actions. Hence, they share a subordinate position vis-à-vis the centrality of the knight (Crane 244).

Actually, the power that Dorigen exerts on Arveragus as an arbiter of gentility and of virtue throughout his courtship is only temporary. With marriage, she loses the elevated status that characterizes romance heroines as objects of male devotion. Arveragus's absence even deprives Dorigen of her own identity. She is not able either to define herself as an autonomous being or to interact with society until her husband is back: "Desir of his presence hire so destreyneth / That al this wyde world she sette at noght" (V, 820-1). However, it is significant that the romantic topos of the love triangle does not serve as an escape from the yoke of married life. On the contrary, it is exploited as a strategy to restore

precisely the routine of the conjugal union and to decree the superiority of the marriage covenant over courtly love. On discovering Aurelius's secret passion for her, Dorigen at first drastically rejects even the hypothesis of betraying her husband, but then, as if blunt seriousness were not convincing enough, she resorts to a hyperbolic request, "an inpossible" (V, 1009), which in her mind should definitely crush her lover's hopes: she will yield to Aurelius if "endelong Britayne" (V, 992) he manages to "remoeve all the rokkes, stoon by stoon, / That they ne lette ship ne boot to goon" (V, 993-4), namely, if he eliminates the obstacles that may endanger Arveragus's return. Ultimately, Dorigen adopts the romance motif of the love trial with the aim of simply denying its feasibility: "For wel I woot that it shal never bityde. / Lat swiche folies out of youre herte slyde" (V, 1001-2). However, she remains prisoner of her own rash promise, since she is now confronted with the following dilemma: either the rocks do not disappear—which saves her from adultery but simultaneously does not eliminate the threat to her husband's life—or Aurelius succeeds in his enterprise, thus granting Arveragus a safe return home but only to make him face her wife's infidelity. As we will see below, the clerk of Orleans offers a way out of such an impasse through an equally paradoxical kind of magic, which problematizes the serene intermingling of mystery and rationality accepted by romance.

The female protagonist of Carter's story cannot avoid Dorigen's contradictory ethos. In **"The Kiss,"** too, the love triangle is initially introduced in the service of the marriage union, in an attempt to reconcile the code of an institutionalized relationship with the "gospel of leisure and pleasure" (Stevens 51) typical of courtly love. Tamburlaine's wife resorts to the architect's aid in order to complete the mosque, since the accomplishment of the building would be her surprise for her husband's return. However, she has to pay a price for this favor: "One kiss, one single kiss" (*Saints* 36). As in Chaucer's tale, the woman is at a crossroads: in order to give Tamburlaine a tangible demonstration of her affection, she has to yield to the architect. Her immediate reaction is a defense of her marriage through a rhetoric that figuratively reproduces Dorigen's apostrophe to Aurelius: "What deyntee sholde a man han in his lyf / For to go love another mannes wyf, / That hath hir body whan so that hym liketh?" (V, 1003-5). Indeed Tamburlaine's wife tries to outwit the architect and to divert his desire towards someone else by showing him how different appearances conceal an identical nature: "Each of these eggs looks different to the rest but they all taste the same. So you may kiss any one of my serving women that you like but you must leave me alone" (*Saints* 37). Nevertheless, the impulse to preserve the husband-wife bond to the detriment of adultery is based upon opposite logics in the two stories: the law of the supernatural and the marvelous in the case of Dorigen, and the cause-

and-effect principle in the case of Tamburlaine's wife. Precisely such a gap reveals the distinct message that each episode conveys about the role of romance.

Dorigen exorcises the specter of unfaithfulness by asking her would-be lover to accomplish a deed that both of them consider nothing less than miraculous, hence unachievable. The supernatural and the marvelous are consciously introduced as mere literary topoi, with no actual effect upon the lives of Chaucer's characters, as the evolution of the plot confirms. It is significant that Arveragus "is comen hoom" (V, 1089) while Aurelius is still "Dispreyed in . . . torment and . . . thoght" (V, 1084), that is, Dorigen's husband is safely back despite the peril of the rocks, and long before Aurelius is even aware of the existence of the clerk of Orléans. Furthermore—and this is the most intriguing detail of the story—the clerk can merely *pretend* to get rid of the rocks "by . . . an apparence or jogelrye" (V, 1265). His power, which consists of "japes and . . . wrecchedness / of . . . a supersticious cursednesse" (V, 1271-2), makes him a craftsman of ephemeral illusions. The fact that, thanks to the clerk's "magik" (V, 1295), it "semed that alle the rokkes were awaye" (V, 1296) only "for a wyke or tweye" (V, 1295) decrees the extinction of that medieval wonderland of knights and fairies where enchantments were a component of everyday life. Chaucer repudiates precisely those irrational and mysterious situations in which romance characters surrender to superhuman forces. He retrieves supernatural events from an earlier literary tradition and reduces them to the special effects that the magician displays in front of Aurelius and his brothers: "Forestes, parkes ful of wilde deer" (V, 1190), "Thise fauconer upon a fair ryver" (V, 1196), "knyghtes justyng in a playn" (V, 1198), a whole Arthurian repertory that can materialize and evaporate by simply clapping hands within the walls of a study.

Significantly, Chaucer's attack on the improbable and the occult is here even more decisive than in "The Squire's Tale." In the latter the "strange knyght" (V, 89) distrusts the marvelous by giving king Cambyuskan a flying "steede of bras" (V, 115) with specific mechanical properties: their explanation, however, remains a secret shared only by the two characters. "The Franklin's Tale," for its part, condemns even this residue of mystery as a source of dangerous lies precisely because their nature is beyond everyone's grasp: "I ne kan no termes of astrologye" (V, 1266), says the Franklin—the clerk's scientific readings lead only to "swiche illusiouns and swiche meschaunces" (V, 1292) as the fallacious disappearance of those material obstacles. Taken as a metaphor, such an image suggests the aesthetic and moral concerns of the tale. Indeed, we can still see the artificially benign vision of romance as an ideal for Chaucer only if we treat it like the fantasy of temporarily invisible, yet existing, rocks—only if we choose to overlook the complexity of his world. Similarly, the

merely delusive intervention of the marvelous casts a polemical shadow on the wish-fulfilling mechanism. In order to have dreams and desires easily realized, as in romances, Chaucer's characters should reinstate the private dimension of romance adventures, that is, ignore the moral concerns required by a social context. This is precisely what emerges from the last sequence of the clerk's deceptive show, where Dorigen appears in a dance "[o]n which . . . [Aurelius] daunced, as hym thoughte" (V, 1201). Under the impulse of his desire Aurelius projects himself into the hallucinatory scene but significantly excludes all the impediments of real life—Arveragus, the rocks, the social consequences of his transgression (Kolve 190-91).

As hinted above, contrary to Chaucer's "inpossible" (V, 1009), Carter resolves the dispute between the faithful wife and her insidious lover in rational terms. Tamburlaine's wife, who is "not only very beautiful and very virtuous but also very clever" (*Saints* 36), uses her wit and her rhetorical skills in order to resist the architect's harassment. However, he retaliates with the same strategy by retorting the message of the parable of the eggs against the woman herself: a vodka and a water bowl "both look alike but each tastes quite different. . . . And it is the same with love" (*Saints* 37). A new Dorigen, Carter's female protagonist thus remains caught in the trap of *logos*—the male domain *par excellence,* which she has illegally invaded when trying to rival with the opposite sex. Yet, unlike "The Franklin's Tale," no magician's art reconciles the architect's appetite with the lady's commitment to integrity, any more than no "franchise and . . . gentillesse" (V, 1524) allows the woman to overcome the deadlock. The kiss on the architect's mouth accomplishes the rash promise that Tamburlaine's wife is obliged to make and keep all at once. Unwilling to embellish the potentially romantic topos of the love triangle with the utopian hues of courtly sentiment, and simultaneously skeptical about reciprocal love in marriage, Carter uses cynicism to unmask all the squalor underlying man-woman relationships. The plot does not question romance by thwarting desires. It rather satisfies them easily—too easily, as in **"The Lady of the House of Love"**—thus showing the uselessness of wish fulfillment in the absence of freedom, and its destructiveness whenever in the service of power. Actually, just as the disappearance of the rocks has no influence upon Arveragus's trip home, the surprise of the completed mosque—the reason why the woman yielded to the architect—plays no role in the scene of Tamburlaine's return. It is violence that dominates the encounter between husband and wife: a taste of vodka on the woman's lips is automatically taken as a confession of betrayal, which Tamburlaine finally extorts from her by beating her "with a knout" (*Saints* 37).

However, precisely when the realistic tones of the story have dissolved the dreamlike atmosphere of the "authentically fabulous city" (*Saints* 35) by bringing to the foreground the suffering and oppression involved in sexual relations, Carter once again violates our expectations by introducing the marvelous. In the light of a comparison with Chaucer it is significant that here we are not confronted with the *illusion* of the marvelous, as provided by the clerk of Orléans's sleight of hand. Rather, we are puzzled by an example of pure marvelous, an event which—as in the best romance tradition—is inexplicable according to the law of cause-and-effect that has so far prevailed in Carter's story: when the architect heard Tamburlaine's executioners approaching, "he grew wings and flew away to Persia" (*Saints* 37). In the light of our genealogy of self-conscious magical narratives, what is the gist of Carter's move? Is it one step back with respect to Chaucer's speculative revision of romance? By no means. **"The Kiss"** exploits supernatural prodigies but subverts their redeeming function. Actually, far from reinstating innocence in Carter's fictional world, the mystery of the wings is in the service of the rogue's rescue, which leaves the woman as the only scapegoat of the love triangle, an even weaker and more deceived character, although not a blameless one. With the architect's flight away from a realistic and morally binding situation, Carter's romance may well "revive our sense of our own omnipotence" (Beer 3), yet it does not grant us the cathartic epilogue which should distribute rewards and punishments through a clear-cut distinction between heroes and villains.[13]

"The Franklin's Tale" itself has a great deal to say about the moral scope of romance conventions in the lives of its protagonists. The initial courtly belief that should grant sovereignty in marriage—"Love wol nat been constreyned by maistrye. / Whan maistrie cometh, the God of Love anon / Beteth his wynges, and farewel, he is gon!" (V, 764-6)—in fact collapses under the violence of Arveragus's threat to Dorigen when he forces her to submit to Aurelius: "I now forbede, up peyne of deeth, / That nevere, whil thee lasteth lyf ne breeth, / To no wight telle thou of this aventure" (V, 1481-3). Dorigen, on her part, is guilty of flirting with her rash promise, even though she does not want to behave like a romance heroine but only to be Arveragus's "humble trewe wyf" (V, 758). As for Aurelius, his fault lies in the stubbornness with which he pursues the fantasy of a liaison with Dorigen, despite his awareness of her unromantic nature (Hamel 327). Ultimately, the obstacles that in a chivalric-courtly situation would stimulate desire and strengthen the love bond have become dangerous interferences leading to the degeneration of marital happiness. Therefore, on the one hand, Aurelius finally behaves like those noble characters of medieval romances who release their adversary from a binding vow; on the other hand, however, such demonstration of com-

passion has above all the flavor of a compromise. It accommodates events but does not efface all signs of clash between a literary code of ideal behavior and the deviation from it that actual life entails. As we have seen, Arveragus's search for adventure and honor is incompatible with Dorigen's cult of domesticity; Aurelius manipulates Dorigen before surrendering to *gentillesse*; and, last but not least, he needs to pay a fee for a touch of marvelous in an increasingly utilitarian and bourgeois society. All things considered, to ride on horseback does not automatically make one a knight. In the light of the traditional romance ethos, Chaucer's implicit answer to the Franklin's *demande d'amour* is that no character in the tale is really "fre" (V, 1622), although the expectation of a happy ending is met.

As is probably clear by now, Carter accepts Chaucer's transmutation of romance and pushes it forward towards higher conceptual complexity. "The Franklin's Tale" expresses a dialectical truth (Kolve 193): throughout the plot it tests romantic illusions against human realities, but it finally provides reconciliation by mediating between these two well-defined poles. **"The Kiss"** goes beyond such either/or logic. A repulsive referentiality shades off into wonderland as mysteriously as the "throbbing blue of Islam transforms itself to green while you look at it" (*Saints* 35). Yet even the candor and purity of the lilies in the imaginary market-place conceal "flowers like blown bubbles of blood" (36): the beauty and innocence of Carter's Samarkand "dazzle like an optical illusion" (35) which in fact disguises the violence of "Tamburlaine, the scourge of Asia" (35). Indeed, here Carter strategically exploits intertextuality so that all the violence concealed below the surface of romance can explode. The phrase "Tamburlaine, the scourge of Asia" obviously summons the protagonist of Christopher Marlowe's play, which—well before Carter's **"The Kiss"**—defines Tamburlaine not only as the scourge of Asia but also as the "scourge of the world," "Scourge of Jove," and "scourge of God" (*Tamburlaine* 105; 136; 64). Along with the reference to Marlowe, Carter's story inherits all the horrible deeds of his Tamburlaine, including the massacre of the virgins and his insensitivity toward his wife Zenocrate. Further evidence of Carter's intentional allusions to the cruelty of Marlowe's character is offered by her observations in *The Sadeian Woman,* where she compares the life of Sade's Juliette to "the reign of Tamburlaine the Great, an arithmetical progression of atrocities" (*Sadeian* [*The Sadeian Woman*] 80).

"The Kiss" tells a story of defamiliarization and hybridization. It romanticizes reality only to mar romance with the stigmas of evil, to denounce its hypocrisy and intrinsic corruption, ultimately, to destroy the myth of a happy ending as an escape from the dismal tones of everyday life. Carter refuses to tell us exactly what happens to Tamburlaine's wife after being beaten, but any prospected outcome is bleak: "After she ran away from him perhaps she made her living in the market. Perhaps she sold lilies there" (*Saints* 37). With this hypothetical turning point, the woman's painful vicissitudes pierce through her verisimilar love story as well as through the idealized life in the "glittering and innocent" city (*Saints* 36). These two mutually exclusive worlds thus blend into each other, being contaminated by the same all-encompassing desolation.

In **"The Kiss,"** the "either/or" logic of "The Franklin's Tale" has become "both/and"; Chaucer's final compromise between poetic fable and truth has turned into undecidability. "What is a world?" Angela Carter implicitly asks in her works. Chaucer does not get so far as to pose such a question. His tale ends with interpretive openness, yet still within the order of his own world. Chaucer always aims at a critical appraisal of a reality which, although no longer so simple as the cosmos of romance, is knowable by definition, and can be described through a specific set of parameters. Therefore, the dominant in "The Franklin's Tale" is epistemological.[14] **"The Kiss,"** on the other hand, precisely by shaking even such reference points, raises ontological concerns. What is romance? What is realism? What is reality? The ambiguous and impenetrable world of Carter's fiction stands in the way of the reader's heuristic quest with all its richness and thickness, but without an answer.

LIONS, WIVES AND LIES

My analysis has emphasized the distinction between romance and referentiality on Chaucer's side, and the inseparability of the two on Carter's side. Such a difference in the formal and aesthetic strategies that Chaucer and Carter adopt in their use of romance can help us delineate the two authors' respective attitudes towards the cultural and social values of their times. Among the *Canterbury Tales,* the episode of the Wife of Bath is particularly effective for this purpose. Chaucer here links the prologue and the tale through a continuity of issues—marriage, desire, beauty, and violence in an early modern world in which human relationships are already commodified. However, he fosters two remarkably different conclusions depending on the realistic tones of the Wife's first-person speech or on the romantic atmosphere of her fable. Uncanny echoes of the Chaucerian Alisoun of Bath can be found in **"The Courtship of Mr. Lyon"** and **"The Tiger's Bride,"** two stories in which Carter—like the author of *The Canterbury Tales*—revises the beauty-and-the-beast archetype in order to uncover the patriarchal ideology it perpetrates with its representation of women as instrumental to male desire. Nevertheless, although the two authors build their anecdotes upon the same truth about the female status, the quantum leap from Chaucer to Carter endows romance with far more disturbing impli-

cations. The marvelous sneaks into even the most polemical portions of **"The Courtship of Mr. Lyon"** and **"The Tiger's Bride,"** while, simultaneously, a de-idealizing strategy chokes illusions. Carter accepts and rejects the reality pact at her whim, but ultimately she ends both stories with skepticism—with the woman's metamorphosis into an animal, that is, with a female identity in the likeness of man. Neither fact nor fancy offers a privileged, external position from which the submissive role imposed upon women can be overturned.

Probably the best known character in Chaucer's collection of tales, the Wife of Bath has been attributed all kinds of labels, from that of radical feminist *ante litteram* to that of mere pawn in the grips of male power. I believe the most significant way of dealing with this episode of *The Canterbury Tales* is to consider both extremes, that is, to concentrate on the interaction of these two antithetical portraits. I thus propose a combined reading of the prologue and the tale according to which the tale temporarily sublimates the issues tackled in the prologue,[15] yet without encouraging withdrawal from actuality.

Alisoun opens her speech by highlighting the gap between a ponderous legacy of texts on matrimony and her lived experience "of wo that is in mariage" (III, 3). She wants to proclaim *her* truth about feminine will and desire—a truth ignored by antifeminist written "auctoritee" (III, 1)—and she achieves her goal by mimicking the stereotype of the married woman. Throughout the prologue the Wife stages the parts she had to perform in life. It is precisely in the parody of herself that she lays bare the violence and the exploitation of which her category is the target. The account of her five marriages are based on a series of stock situations and models of feminine behavior which she appropriates from masculine representation of women and reenacts with critical distance, either by pushing them to the limit or by turning them upside down.

From the static locus where men inscribe the prowess of their virility, the female body becomes an active, insatiable desiring machine. After an invective against "virginitee" (III, 82) and monogamy, Alisoun even welcomes the prospect of a sixth husband. She challenges the morality of restraint by showing that—far from disciplining sexuality—lack and prohibition in fact intensify lust: "Wayte what thyng we may nat lightly have, / Thereafter wol we crie al day and crave. / Forbede us thyng, and that desiren we" (III, 517-9). Thus, in contrast with the ineptitude of her first three husbands, whom she in vain "a-nyght made . . . swynke" (III, 202), the Wife boasts an appetite which knows "no discrecioun" (III, 622) and which requires no discrimination in the choice of a partner: "Al were he short, or long, or blak, or whit; / I took no kep, so that he liked me" (III, 624-5). In line with the mercantile logic of her time, the Wife treats sexual relationships as economic transactions in which, however, she wants also to be the dealer, not only the commodity endowed with exchange value. Paradoxically, it is from Christ that Alisoun draws the justification for a utilitarian ethics, according to which profit must compensate for the expenditure of human capital involved in feelings and intercourses: Christ "[b]ad nat every wight he sholde go sell / Al that he hadde, and gyve it to the poore" (III, 108-9), but he rather spoke only "to hem that wolde lyve parfitly" (III, 111). Happy not to partake of those holy few, the Wife manipulates the alliance between matrimony and patrimony to her advantage in order to enjoy the "fruyt of mariage" (III, 114), picking the best of her husbands' "nether purs and . . . cheste" (III, 44b). A good entrepreneur in a society for which "al is for to selle" (III, 414), Alisoun thus reads the Scriptures as an account book which records men's sexual "dette" (III, 130) and "paiement" (III, 131) to their wives. However, this wife who allegedly has the power upon her husband's "propre body" (III, 159), so as to render him her "dettour and [her] thral" (III, 155), is by no means left untouched by the economy of possession and traffic in which she now participates as a manager. In fact Alisoun herself is on the market, as precisely *the* object of exchange around which patriarchal society and culture are organized.[16] In her own words, she locates wives on almost the same level as animals and objects on sale, with the only difference that—unlike what happens for "hors, and houndes" (III, 285), "[b]acyns, lavours" (III, 287), "pottes, clothes, and array" (III, 289)—women undergo "noon assay" (III, 290) before being purchased through the marriage contract. If women cannot be appreciated other than in economic terms, it becomes crucial for them to know and master the laws of the market, so that they can at least increase the only kind of value they can still aspire to—the pecuniary one. Not accidentally, Alisoun calls attention to the fact that scarcity renders any merchandise precious, a mechanism that women—by making virtue of necessity—slyly exploit for their own promotion: "With daunger oute we al oure chaffare; / Greet prees at market maketh deere ware, / And to greet cheep is holde at litel prys: / This knoweth every womman that is wys" (III, 521-4).

The double bind that ties the Wife of Bath to the misogynous cultural system she contests renders her transgression something other than an unconditional celebration of excess for its own sake. Alisoun soon reveals that if she were more docile she would be annihilated: "Whoso that first to mille comth, first grynt" (III, 389); hence she has to be constantly vigilant and remind men with her domineering manner that they are not masters of "[her] body and of [her] good" (III, 314). Following this very first-come-first-served logic, as if trying to ward off her husband's oppression, Alisoun aggresses him by retorting against him the crystallized identities

in which men have imprisoned women. Before her husband judges her according to clichés, the Wife takes hold of them and lavishes them all on him in one long tirade: female vanity, falsity, jealousy, fickleness, seductiveness, debauchery. She thus accuses her potential accuser: as a man, he should feel guilty of having created stifling female images and of persisting in using them as the only guidelines in his relationship with Alisoun. This is the "wo that is in mariage" (II, 303): the Wife of Bath's "tirbulacion" (III, 156) lies in the necessity of using "the whippe" (III, 175) to offset male violence, of bestowing sexual favors on the best bidder as if her "*bele chose*" (III, 447) were on sale. She would renounce "sleighte [and] force" (III, 405), together with the ethos of trade and profit, if she could get love in some other way. Therefore, her desire is not so much intrinsically insatiable as temporarily unfulfilled: it will find closure as soon as Alisoun finds affection and tolerance in a mutually respectful marital relationship, one which—unlike her union with Jankyn—does not attain reciprocity at the price of blows and offenses, nor at the price of the woman's renunciation to "lond and fee" (III, 630) in favor of her husband. Despite the happily-ever-after conclusion of the prologue, not even the fifth marriage is consolatory enough to efface the permanent injuries inflicted upon the Wife. Indeed, the way in which Chaucer introduces the Wife of Bath in the General Prologue suggests that the violence Alisoun received from Jankyn has left a deeper mark on her than the harmony they have conquered later in their married life; her permanent deafness appears as her distinctive feature: "A good WIF was ther OF biside BATHE, / But she was somdel deef, and that was scathe" ("General Prologue" 445-6).

It is precisely in the tale she narrates that Alisoun fully articulates and ultimately satisfies her wish: "Wommen desiren to have sovereynetee / As wel over hir housbond as hir love" (III, 1038-9).[17] The romance of the knight and the old hag thus seems to liberate from everyday reality through representation, through an individual fantasy. In and of itself, such a polarization could be interpreted—in the light of Jameson's *Political Unconscious*—as Chaucer's attempt to rechannel the Wife's subversive impulses in the kingdom of enchantment, so as to grant her symbolic appeasement and to retrain her for an unchangeable social and cultural order. Alisoun, in other words, would merely be free to *imagine* a different reality, but would simultaneously subject her dream to repression by acknowledging the absolute and eternal nature of her world. Yet, in my view, the blunt return to the fabliau register through the harshness of Alisoun's final curse against unyielding husbands reinstates the question of the male power of exclusion, and, along with it, the urgency of a yet-to-come solution for women. Significantly, in her prologue, the Wife warns her audience that in her tale she will "speke after [her] fantasye" (III, 190): whereas she means to "seye sooth" (III, 195) about her married life, her "entente" (III, 192) as a storyteller "nys but for to pleye" (III, 192). In proposing a romance which tackles the very issues she has to face in everyday life, Alisoun is perfectly conscious of the gap between fancy and fact, and furthermore reveals that the utopian, sentimental simplicity of the former is no longer adequate to explain the latter. Thus, the Wife resorts to romance as to a rhetorical strategy which may still be aesthetically effective to illustrate her problems and her wishes; however, she also knows that the answer must be found neither in fairy magic nor in any other prodigy of the unexplained marvelous, but rather back in the realm of "[e]xperience" (III, 1).

The two main characters in Alisoun's tale are actually too stylized and too idealized to offer a wishful and viable alternative to the marriage relationships depicted in the Wife's Prologue. Although the Wife pursues the very "parfit joye" (III, 1258) that gladdens the knight's and the old hag's lives, the values that sustain such harmony belong to an irretrievable feudal past that she evokes with a great deal of irony and without nostalgia. Confronted with the obligation of marrying a "foul, and oold, and poore" (III, 1063) woman, the knight clings to his class-based notion of gentility: one of his "nacioun" (III, 1068) cannot choose a wife "of so lough a kynde" (III, 1101). The hag, on her part, replies to her companion's anachronistic ethics with an equally abstract view of "gentillesse" as moral worth which derives neither from "old richesse" (III, 1118) nor from "oure place" (III, 1164), but rather from "bountee" (III, 1160) and "grace" (III, 1163): in her view, one becomes noble by beginning to "lyven vertuously and weyve synne" (III, 1176). She thus embodies the ethereal and submissive figure advocated as a model of femininity in medieval conduct books (Carruthers 213)—a product of what Georges Duby defines as rigorously male Middle Ages, yet already at odds with the reality of medieval marriages, and all the more unfeasible for the practical bourgeois wife. The dismissal of "possesioun" (III, 1147) in the hag's sermon cannot but widen the gap between feudal past and proto-capitalist present: whereas for the female protagonist of romance "Whoso that halt hym payd of his poverte" (III, 1185) is "riche" (III, 1186), in the society of Alisoun of Bath, a loathly lady cannot be loved as a "fair" (III, 1241), "good and trewe" (III, 1243) wife without first securing her own economic independence. Paradoxically, the tale itself points to the limits of its own sentimental idealization. Magic and *gentillesse* may well have promoted the knight's reformation, but they have not at all uprooted rape: with the shift from "fayeryes" (III, 872) to "dayeryes" (III, 871), the elf (or the knight) who in "th'olde dayes of the Kyng Arthour" (III, 857) assaulted women is simply replaced by another "incubus" (III, 880), the "lymytour" (III, 874).

If with her question, "Who peyntede the leon, tel me who?" (III, 692), the Wife of Bath calls attention to the arbitrariness of male representation of women, the tale she tells does not denounce "of men moore wikkednesse" (III, 695) than "clerkes han withinne hire oratories" (III, 694), but rather stages an idyll which once again honors male pleasure. With its stereotypical and normative portrayal of women, "The Wife of Bath's Tale" appears as ideological as Jankyn's "book of wikked wyves" (III, 685). Alisoun's female letter can challenge the glosses of patriarchal hermeneutics (Dinshaw 113-31) only if the tale interacts with the prologue: in this way, Chaucer's romance functions not simply as a regressive fantasy but, more subtly, as a demystification of regressive fantasies. Alisoun looks for the man of her dreams not in the ranks of reformed knights[18] but rather in her social and historical *milieu*, among "Housbondes meeke, yonge, . . . fressh abedde" (III, 125) and not "nygardes of dispence" (III, 1263), that is, still within the domain of masculine "auctoritee" (III, 1) but with room for feminine will and choice. Nevertheless, the potential female sovereignty that Alisoun celebrates with her rebellious transvestism is not sanctioned by the social hierarchy (Crane 130-31): it has to be seized.

I would assert that Angela Carter had clearly in mind all the motifs and the ironic twists of this Chaucerian episode. The surprising textual affinities with Alisoun's life and story invite us to read **"The Courtship of Mr. Lyon"** and **"The Tiger's Bride"** as Carter's postmodern replies to, respectively, "The Wife of Bath's Tale" and "The Wife of Bath's Prologue," which she distorts so as to deprive Chaucer's *Weltanschauung* of its glimpse of hope. Unlike the fairy-tale of the old hag, Carter's romance never puts reason to sleep: it never departs from the inhibitions and preoccupations of everyday life to absorb us into an otherwise unattainable experience. At the same time, Carter's reality effects do not mean to shelter her story from the truth that lies in fables. As a feminist anatomist of a culture made of a tangle of imagination and reality, Carter travels to fantasy land not in search of "consolatory nonsenses," as myths and archetypes are defined in *The Sadeian Woman* (5; 106) but rather—as in the idyll of Mr. and Mrs. Lyon—in search of evidence of the archetypical objectification of women. Furthermore, unlike Alisoun of Bath's confessional prologue in support of the female voice, the girl's magical metamorphosis into a beast in **"The Tiger's Bride"** reveals, despite her initial first-person denunciation of female oppression, that the ideology of male power embodied in myths and tales is well rooted and systematically exploited even in an apparently rational and commonsensical context. Neither in the timeless and placeless world of romance nor in history and institutions can women find a place as protagonists of their own actions and desires.

The opening of **"The Courtship of Mr. Lyon"** reproduces the enchanted atmosphere in which Alisoun sets her tale. Carter's landscape—just as Chaucer's "land fulfild of fayerye" (III, 859) dancing in "many a grene mede" (III, 861)—has a dreamlike quality: the snow has "a light of its own," the same "unearthly, reflected pallor" envelopes the falling flakes as well as the girl's skin, so that "you would have thought she, too was made all of snow" (*BC* 41). However, the mystery and openness of the Wife of Bath's Arthurian romance soon dissolve with Carter's subsequent simile: the snowy country road the girl sees is "white and unmarked as a spilled bolt of bridal satin" (*BC* 41). A girl's destiny is marriage—an everlasting, universal truth that is inscribed not only into culture but even into nature. It is significant that the reference to marriage in Carter's story occupies the same position as rape in Chaucer's tale: they both produce the first blunt tear in the fabric of illusions. Where, however, the hag works against female "oppressioun" (III, 889) by knotting once again the threads of an idyll, the girl's subsequent adventures reinforce the image of marriage as a metaphorical rape.

"What thyng is it that wommen moost desiren" (III, 905) in **"The Courtship of Mr. Lyon"**? Nothing more than "one white, perfect rose" (*BC* 44), Carter answers—that is, a non-utilitarian, non-practical object, hence the perfect expression of self-reflexive, *autonomous* desire. The development of the story reveals precisely that such autonomous female desire cannot eschew masculine jurisdiction. The father figure who at first tries to fulfill the girl's wish soon surrenders his daughter to a Beast, who symbolically rapes her by snatching her photograph, and who also appropriates her physically by making her promise she will live with him. Carter alerts us against thinking that the girl "had no will of her own" (*BC* 45); in fact, it is her "sense of obligation" towards paternal authority that induces her to stay and smile to the Beast, "because her father wanted her to do so" (*BC* 45). The girl's imposed passivity thus quickly dismisses the possibility of that female "maistrie" (III, 1236) which the old hag barters with beauty and honesty. But **"The Courtship of Mr. Lyon"** offers an even bleaker point of view about the connection of love and "possessioun" (III, 147) that "The Wife of Bath's Tale" deliberately ignores when it sentimentally celebrates "Glad poverte" (III, 1183). Not only is the girl's liaison with the Beast fully entangled with economic concerns, more sadly, she is not even the beneficiary of the deal. The female body and feelings given as a pledge to a man favor the profit of another man: "her visit to the Beast must be, on some magically reciprocal scale, the price of her father's good fortune" (*BC* 45). The inexplicable prodigy that in Alisoun's romance can turn an old hag into an attractive, good, and loyal woman is here unmasked by the author as the power of money in disguise—a discovery that in Chaucer, as we have seen, is made possible only

if the Wife's comic prologue interacts with the idealizing aura of the tale. Precisely the cynicism that makes Carter suspicious about "the black and white ethical world" (*Sadeian* 82) of fables leads her to contaminate the mysteries of her fairyland with the brutal principles of practical reality, while simultaneously she lures us into believing that we—like the female protagonist of the story—are entering "a place of privilege" (*BC* 42) where "the natural laws of the world [are] held in suspension" (47).

With sovereignty over her husband, the Chaucerian hag loses her ugliness and acquires all the quintessential features of the ideal woman. With submissiveness, the girl in Carter's story loses personality and discernment, but paradoxically this is how she can be accepted by and accept patriarchy in her turn. In other words, this is how she can begin to see "no longer a lion in her arms but a man" (*BC* 51). Therefore, Carter's final, ironic response to the Chaucerian question about women's desire is that both tales and human institutions represent women as wishing to yield to men: they can get happiness in exchange for their individual will. The girl's efforts to overcome the sense of "bewildering difference" (*BC* 45) between the lion and herself conceal the necessity for women to suppress their own specificity, to relinquish their own identity and adopt the one that men choose for them. Only with her nominal metamorphosis into the patronymic "Mrs. Lyon" through marriage can the girl find Beauty in a Beast. Significantly, whereas Chaucer's knight is "certeyn . . . deed" (III, 1005-6) if he does not acknowledge the existence and the nature of female longing, Carter's lion blackmails the girl with his impending death if she does not satisfy his appetite. Therefore, the knight's reformation from rapist to perfect husband in "The Wife of Bath's Tale" has become for Carter the woman's reformation from the master of her own desires to the object of male desire. With its unexciting and predictable happy ending—"Mr. and Mrs. Lyon walk in the garden; the old spaniel drowses on the grass, in a drift of fallen petals" (*BC* 51)—**"The Courtship of Mr. Lyon"** confirms that the truth of the female protagonist lies in the only label chosen by the girl to designate her own status. She remains "Miss Lamb," the "spotless, sacrificial" (*BC* 45) victim of a legalized system of violence against women that has replaced the knight's rape—a deed which, as Chaucer tells us, was frequent in feudal times but was at least declared illegal and condemned by "cours of lawe" (III, 892).

It is precisely this essentialized opposition between feminine meekness and masculine strength that the opening of **"The Tiger's Bride"** seems to denounce. Here, Carter lets her own Alisoun of Bath speak of all the woe that accompanies sexual relationships. As in the case of "The Wife of Bath's Prologue," a female first-person confession breaks the spell of the newly-acquired harmony in the romance of Mr. and Mrs. Lyon: "ah! you think you've come to the blessed plot where the lion lies down with the lamb" (*BC* 51). The female protagonist is no longer as naive as in **"The Courtship of Mr. Lyon"**: she now filters her sentimentality and imaginary excitement through the "furious cynicism peculiar to women whom circumstances force mutely to witness folly" (52). She herself produces the metanarrative interferences with which Carter in the previous story kept us at a distance from the idealization of marriage.

With the same lucidity with which Alisoun claims that no man is the master "of [her] body and of [her] good" (III, 314), the girl admits her father lost her "to the Beast at cards" (*BC* 51). For a moment, the girl seems to rival Alisoun of Bath for entrepreneurial skills: "my own skin was my sole capital in the world and today I'd make my first investment" (*BC* 56). However, when she meditates on her status she realizes that—unlike the Wife of Bath—she will never be able to decide whether and how "to selle [her] *bele chose*" (III, 447): her experience has taught her that women are nothing more than men's "ransom" (*BC* 54). Just as her mother has been "bartered for her dowry" (52), she too has been "bought and sold, passed from hand to hand" (63). The capitalistic philosophy of her father teaches that "if you have enough money, anything is possible" (62), yet the magic of such a formula is ineffective whenever applied to the female world. Far from being the queen of the marriage-mart as in Chaucer's prologue, Carter's woman is a mere commodity. Far from representing passion made flesh like Alisoun's body, she incarnates the "cold, white meat of contract": she is inert and lifeless, just as she has to be according to the laws of "the market place, where the eyes that watch you take no account of your existence" (*BC* 66). And when she thinks she can jump outside the exploitative circle of exchange and utility maximization by finding a shelter within the disinterested realm of feelings, the specter of objectification still haunts her. In fact—not unlike the profit-oriented nature of sexual relationships—the *voyeurism* of the Beast, whose only desire is "to see the lady unclothed" (*BC* 58), denies the woman's humanity, and simply treats her as a catalyst for male narcissism. In any case, even if Carter's female protagonist made an effort to wrap such squalid moments of intimacy up with bliss, the inflexible rules of the marketplace would soon break the spell: after being on display, she would "be returned to her father undamaged with bankers' orders for the sum which he lost to [her] master at cards and also a number of fine presents such as furs, jewels and horses" (*BC* 58).

"The lamb must learn to run with the tigers" (*BC* 64): in the light of Chaucer's prologue, this statement by Carter's female protagonist might sound like an invitation to women to use "sleighte [and] force" (III, 405),

as the Wife of Bath successfully does—that is, to resort to typical strategies of male power to avoid being overpowered by men. Nevertheless, the conclusion of the tale suggests a more debasing interpretation of such a moral, one which reinforces female acquiescence instead of overcoming it. As **"The Courtship of Mr. Lyon"** has shown, when Carter's female lamb runs with the tigers, she agrees to give up her selfhood and her ability to choose. From "the los of al mankynde" (III, 720) she can thus be redeemed to the tigers' eyes and be flattered as "a woman of honour" (*BC* 59). In worse conditions than the battered and deafened Alisoun, she must be immolated on the beast's "carnivorous bed of bone"—thus also literally performing the part of Miss Lamb, "white, shaking [and] raw" (*BC* 67) like the scapegoat of tribal sacrifices. The woman as *pharmakos*—ready to execute *her*self to be reborn as *his* self—is the way to "a peaceable kingdom" in which male "appetite" does not entail female "extinction" (*BC* 67). Carter's protagonist ultimately expels her accursed share through a metamorphosis, this time a physical (therefore real?) one: the beast's tongue rips off, layer after layer, the girl's skin—that very skin through which she hoped she could gain her independence—and bares a "beautiful fur" (*BC* 67).[19] Thus, there is still surprise in store for us. Wonder finally shakes the disenchanted and delegitimized magic kingdom of **"The Tiger's Bride"**: it springs from the all-but-comforting touch of a postmodern fairy who renders women's nursery "fear of devourment" nothing less than "flesh and sinews" (*BC* 67). This final brush of unexplained marvelousness repaints not only "the leon" (III, 692) of The Wife of Bath's prologue and tale but also the Mr. and Mrs. Lyon of Carter's previous romance.

CONCLUSION: CAN DREAMS COME TRUE?

The stories I have chosen from Chaucer's and Carter's archives by no means exhaust the variety of situations and issues tackled by the two authors. However, they are particularly appropriate to illustrate how romance affects the representation of reality when we switch from the early sparks of modernity to its last embers. In *The Canterbury Tales*, romance is taken as the expression of a stylized, simplified view of the world which has become inadequate to contain Chaucer's heterogeneous society and its new values: reason over emotion, science over the marvelous, the power of money over heroism in battle. On the level of form, as well, romance narratives contradict the cause-and-effect perspective required by Chaucer's proto-realistic description: their most typical device—interlace—abandons one knightly adventure and juxtaposes it to another one without establishing any evident reciprocal link (Vinaver 68). Chaucer, who on the whole wants to save something of the optimistic *Weltanschauung* of romance, also understands the need for adapting to the spirit of his time, and hence reduces romance to one of the many interacting components of a secularized and materialized context.

At the other extreme of our chronological sequence, Angela Carter recuperates romance in order to tell us that reason itself is no longer sufficient to the depiction of reality. However, her revisionary operation does not go back toward higher simplicity: it rather entrusts to romance in order to stage the intricacy of desire, of sexuality, of our psyche—of all that the censorship of reason and of power does not allow to surface. Where Chaucer presents romance as a subset of reason, Carter makes reason shrink to an appendix of romance; where in *The Canterbury Tales* the reality principle includes the pleasure principle, in Carter's stories the pleasure principle spreads so much as to envelope the reality principle. With her fiction Carter has taken us a long way from "the suspicion that the romance world is essentially a lie . . . because it is not equivalent to the actual world and not realizable within it" (Beer 32): she actually reveals that this very lie is to be found in the reality of realism, and that it is precisely romance which tells the most hidden truth. With a final twist, in any case, Carter prevents her fictional world from becoming a magic land where wishes are fulfilled and anxieties exorcized. Significantly, she *does not* offer a locus of freedom from the reality principle. If, on the one hand, she urges us to flee from realism because it has been telling us stories, on the other hand the embrace of romances is no cozy shelter, either. Beyond good and evil, beyond any possible sublimation or symbolic appeasement, we plunge into the unconscious still burdened with our common sense, and we reemerge bringing back disquieting and irrational elements that deconstruct everyday, allegedly "real," life. The structural endlessness for which Chaucer indicts Arthurian romance returns in Carter's postmodern fiction in the form of a conceptual openness. Precisely the deferred reconciliation of irreconcilable but paradoxically intertwined orders of reality makes Carter's romance rigorously "inescapable."[20]

Notes

1. Two significant works about the interrelation of romance and postmodern/poststructuralist theory are Parker's *Inescapable Romance* and Elam's *Romancing the Postmodern*. Elam further elaborates on the romance-postmodern connection by taking postmodern romance as the privileged woman's genre, feminism being the political question *par excellence* posed by romance. I would like to take a wider stance on the self-excessive nature of romance, one which sees the politics of female fantasy as one possible form of postmodern discourse. For instance, in my view, magical realism is an equally effective instance of postmodern romance, without being necessarily in the service of an exclusively female or feminist agenda. Unquestionably, if we endorse a less biologically-gendered conception of female discourse and think of the latter as a mode, the two positions can be reconciled.

2. The reference to the more "traditional" notion of romance as a literary genre opposed to realism is not incompatible with the notion of romance as a postmodern discourse. As I will try to show throughout this paper, it is interesting to see how the very *topoi* of romance as a narrative of the extraordinary can substantiate the more sophisticated view of romance as self-excessive discourse.

3. Given the very broad range of narrative traditions encompassed by "medieval romance"—such as saints' lives, knightly adventures, fabliaux, and dream visions—and the purpose of this paper, I would like to narrow down my discussion of romance in Chaucer to tales that show the intrusion of bourgeois values into a usually aristocratic genre. Indeed, as Burrow observes (109), among the various kinds of romance narratives, chivalric material is what makes Chaucer particularly uncomfortable.

4. In this respect, Chaucer's use of romance answers to a more articulated logic than the one emerging, for instance, from the critical appraisals of Auerbach (138-39), Beer (2-3), and Finlayson (58-9)—who all tend to see romance as devoid of any practical purposes.

5. A passage from "The Wife of Bath's Tale"—which will be dealt with in the third section of this essay—explicitly shows Chaucer's disenchantment towards the feudal past. After extolling the knight's reformation thanks to magic and *gentillesse,* the tale points at the limits of its own sentimental idealization: both the prosaic present time of "dayeryes" (III, 871) and the allegedly idyllic past of "fayeryes" (III, 872) are afflicted by rape. The "lymytour" (III, 874) assaults women in Alisoun's world just as the elf (or the knight) did in "th'olde dayes of the Kyng Arthour" (III, 857).

6. In relation to the role of romance in contemporary literature, a reference to Jonathan Goldberg's poststructuralist revision of Jameson can be useful (*Endlesse Worke* 76-77, note 1). In a note dealing with magical narratives, Goldberg summarizes Jameson's interpretation of romance as a confrontation with Otherness which is resolved with the recognition of the Other as a mirror, that is, with a reconciliation of differences into sameness. Goldberg, on his part, sees romance's confrontation with Otherness as an occasion to raise "the ques-

tion of differences, not as solutions, but as problematic, and as generative of further narration." This is precisely the agenda of postmodern literature.

7. *The Faerie Queene* of course represents an equally decisive step in the revisionary tradition of romance. In Book IV, Canto II (32-34), Spenser explicitly declares his intention to revive and prolong Chaucer's literary enterprise: since "Wicked Time" has "quite defaste" the monumental work of "*Chaucer,* well of English vndefyled," and "robd the world of threasure endlesse deare," Spenser thus invokes the spirit of his predecessor:

> Then pardon, O most sacred happie spirit, / That I thy labours lost may thus reuiue, / And steale from thee the meede of thy due merit, / That none durst euer whilest thou wast aliue, / And being dead in vaine yet many striue: / Ne dare I like, but through infusion sweete / Of thine owne spirit, which doth in me surviue, / I follow here the footing of thy feete, / That with thy meaning so I may the rather meete.

(The Faerie Queene 587)

In fact, however, the effect of Spenser's revisionary operation in the steps of Chaucer is far more "medieval" than his predecessor's. On the one hand it is true that, with respect to Chaucer, Spenser further removes romance from accommodation and closure. Spenser can thus inspire poststructuralist readings such as that of J. Goldberg and become "the poet of deferred endings" (*Endlesse Worke* 10). On the other hand, the princes, the queens, the knights, the Muses, and the Gods in *The Faerie Queene* reconstruct the aristocratic and idealized world of old romances. Therefore, Chaucer not only occupies a more "originary" position than Spenser in our lines of magical narratives, but is also more critical towards the values that romance conveys.

8. In an interview with A. Katsavos, Carter reveals the feminist politics of form underlying this sentence. She took it from a movie version of a story by Dostoyevsky, in which the passive female protagonist—a metonymy for women and women writers in general—posits the need for women to speak and act without paying lip service to the ideology of male culture (Katsavos 16).

9. These qualities are also explicitly mentioned in the course of the tale: "he was chaast and no lechour" (VII, 745); "the child seyde" (VII, 817); "child Thopas" (VII, 830). As Susan Crane observes, Sir Thopas's femininity and the parodic tones of the narration suggest that, despite the extolment of masculinity in romance, male characters in fact undergo "crossgendering." In this way,

romance leaves room for intimacy between two genders initially defined in opposition to each other (*Gender and Romance* 193-94). Significantly, as we will soon see, Carter indicts precisely male fear of crossgendering, which leads the officer of "The Lady of the House of Love" to destroy romance situations.

10. On the other hand, see Wilson ("SLIP PAGE" 108) for an interpretation of Carter's protagonist as substantially innocent.

11. These are the main qualities that John Stevens attributes to the Breton lai, while emphasizing its close relation to romance (see Stevens 66). Joanne Rice confirms such a link between lai and romance by describing the former as a variety of brief romance characterized by "simplicity, idealism, and concern with love and the supernatural" (see *Riverside Chaucer,* Notes: 895).

12. It is precisely this conceptual simplicity in characterization which reinstates romance. See, for instance, Beer 10.

13. *Heroes and Villains* is precisely the title of an earlier novel by Carter in which the seemingly neat division between a "good," rational civilization and "bad" primitive tribes falls apart. The female protagonist of this post-apocalyptic romance blurs the contrast between heroic Professors and contemptible Barbarians by choosing the jungle. Marianne—a Professor's daughter—ultimately becomes the bride of a tribe's leader. However, with her exotic adventure she experiences anything but the noble savage's benign innocence. More subtly, Carter produces a further crack in the heroes/villains dialectic by introducing a third group of "non-connoted" characters—significantly designated as "the Out People" and described as mutilated and marginalized creatures. They effectively stand for a residual, radical Otherness that hinders the reconstitution or the overturning of the binary opposition.

14. We adopt the distinction proposed by McHale in *Postmodernist Fiction* between an epistemological dominant, typical of modernist fiction, and an ontological dominant characterizing postmodernist fiction. The latter does not merely try to interpret the world that it projects; it rather foregrounds questions on the status of the literary text when the boundary between world and words is violated.

15. As I concentrate on the ideological significance entailed by the structure of the Wife of Bath episode, I intentionally overlook the debate about the Wife's characterization which has engaged contemporary critics. Even if we treat Alisoun as an

allegory, as a fictional figure without psychological depth rather than as the verisimilar protagonist of the prologue and maker of the tale, the interaction between the prologue and the tale, that is, between the concrete details of a fabliau and the idealizing stance of romance, does not lose its effectiveness for the representation of the social position of women. For an interpretation of the Wife of Bath as allegorical and fictional, see for instance Disbrow 59-71; Fleming 151-61.

16. At once the embodiment and the severe judge of the woman-on-the-market figure, Alisoun anticipates the *leitmotif* in the thought of the French feminist Luce Irigaray. It is worth calling attention to such a parallel not so much in the attempt to superimpose a 20th-century frame of mind upon a literary creation which belongs to the late Middle Ages, but rather as evidence of the persistence of a number of questions about the female status in Western culture and in its representation. Irigaray's essay "Women on the Market" (*This Sex* 170-91) raises precisely the issues hinted at in Alisoun's speech: women's exchange value in patriarchal society, the need for women to be scarce commodities so as to be desirable, the exclusively male control of the market. Also the Wife of Bath's discourse on polygamy is surprisingly attuned with Irigaray's standpoint. In contrast to anthropologists like Claude Lévy-Strauss, who take the male polygamous tendency as absolutely natural, Irigaray discloses the exploitative logic at its foundation. The consumption and circulation of the female body has created Western society and culture. In positing a role reversal, with a woman as entrepreneur and a plurality of men as objects of her desire, Alisoun already problematizes such cultural norms. On the other hand, we cannot expect the Wife of Bath to propose a 20th-century alternative organizing principle. Actually, where Chaucer's prologue still contemplates the possibility of love between husband and wife, for Irigaray the end of male transactions is offered by a female economy of abundance, an alternative kind of commerce that women maintain among themselves.

17. I accept the interpretation of these lines given by Richman ("Rape and Desire"), who rejects the more frequent gloss, "Women desire to have sovereignty / As well over their husband as [over] their love[r]," and proposes, "As well over their husband as *their [husband's] love.*" I believe the latter gloss is far more faithful to the development and conclusion of a tale in which the pivotal issue is precisely the tension between sovereignty and love.

18. Fradenburg, on the other hand, maintains that the knight *is* the man of Alisoun's dreams—dreams which she fulfills within the private and interiorized dimension of a fantasy.

19. Indeed, by taking on a bestial look, the woman goes beyond the binary opposition between the traditional monolithic categories of male and female identity, and may be seen to replace an ideological construction of the feminine *subject* with a notion of femininity as multiple and protean *subjectivity.* Yet transvestism makes her like the male figure of the story, in a way which is anything but deliberate: her choice rather seems the lesser evil in the face of patriarchy's violent threat.

20. For the notion of romance as deferral of presence and truth, and for its implications in terms of Derrida's and Barthes's theories, see Parker.

Works Cited

Auerbach, Erich. *Mimesis: The Representation of Reality in Western Literature.* Princeton: Princeton UP, 1968.

Beer, Gillian. *The Romance.* London and New York: Methuen, 1970.

Burrow, John Anthony. "The *Canterbury Tales* I: Romance." *The Cambridge Chaucer Companion.* Ed. Pierro Boitani and Jill Mann. Cambridge (UK): Cambridge UP, 1986.

Carruthers, Mary. "The Wife of Bath and the Painting of Lions," *PMLA* 94.2 (March 1979): 209-22.

Carter, Angela. *The Bloody Chamber and Other Stories.* Harmondsworth: Penguin, 1979.

————. *Heroes and Villains.* Harmondsworth: Penguin, 1969.

————. "Notes from the Front Line." *On Gender and Writing.* Ed. M. Wandor. London: Pandora Press, 1983.

————. *The Sadeian Woman.* New York: Pantheon Books, 1979.

————. *Saints and Strangers.* Harmondsworth: Penguin, 1985.

————, ed. *The Virago Book of Fairy Tales.* London: Virago, 1990.

Chaucer, Geoffrey. *The Canterbury Tales.* In *The Riverside Chaucer.* Ed. Larry D. Benson. Boston: Houghton Mifflin Co., 1987. 3-328. Explanatory notes, 795-965.

————. *The House of Fame.* In *The Riverside Chaucer.* 347-73. Explanatory notes, 977-90.

Crane, Susan. *Gender and Romance in Chaucer's Canterbury Tales.* Princeton: Princeton UP, 1994.

———. "The Franklin as Dorigen." *The Chaucer Review* 24.3 (1990): 236-52.

Dinshaw, Carolyn. *Chaucer's Sexual Poetics.* Madison: U of Wisconsin P, 1989.

Disbrow, S. "The Wife of Bath's Old Wives' Tale." *Studies in the Age of Chaucer* 8 (1986): 59-71.

Duby, Georges. *Mâle Moyen Age.* Paris: Flammarion, 1988.

Eco, Umberto. *Travels in Hyperreality: Essays.* Trans. William Weaver. New York: Harcourt Brace Jovanovich, 1986.

Elam, Diane. *Romancing the Postmodern.* London and NY: Routledge, 1992.

Finlayson, John. "Definitions of Middle English Romance." *The Chaucer Review,* 15 (1980-1). 44-62, 168-81.

Fleming, Martha H. "Repetition and Design in the *Wife of Bath's Tale.*" *Chaucer in the Eighties.* Ed. Julian N. Wasserman and Robert J. Blanch. Syracuse: Syracuse UP, 1986: 151-61.

Fradenburg, Louise O. "The Wife of Bath's Passing Fancy." *Studies in the Age of Chaucer* 8 (1986): 31-58.

Frye, Northrop. *The Anatomy of Criticism.* Princeton: Princeton UP. 1957.

Goldberg, Jonathan. *Endlesse Worke: Spenser and the Structures of Discourse.* Baltimore: The Johns Hopkins UP, 1981.

Hamel, Mary. "The Franklin's Tale and Chrétien de Troyes." *The Chaucer Review* 17.4 (1983): 316-31.

Irigaray, Luce. *This Sex Which is not One.* Ithaca: Cornell UP, 1985.

Jameson, Fredric. *The Political Unconscious.* Ithaca: Cornell UP, 1981.

Katsavos, Anna. "An Interview with Angela Carter." *The Review of Contemporary Fiction* 14.3 (Fall 1994): 11-17.

Kolve, V. A. "Rocky Shores and Pleasure Gardens: Poetry vs. Magic in Chaucer's *Franklin's Tale.*" In *Poetics: Theory and Practice in Medieval English Literature.* Eds. Pierro Boitani and Anna Torti. Cambridge: D. S. Brewer, 1991.

Marlowe, Christopher. *Tamburlaine.* London: New Mermaids, 1971.

McHale, Brian. *Postmodernist Fiction.* New York: Methuen, 1987.

Parker, Patricia A. *Inescapable Romance: Studies in the Poetics of a Mode.* Princeton: Princeton UP, 1987.

Pearcy, Roy J. "Chaucer's Franklin and the Literary Vavasour." *The Chaucer Review* 8.1 (1973): 33-59.

Richman, G. "Rape and Desire in *The Wife of Bath's Tale.*" *Studia Neophilologica* 61 (1989): 161-165.

Sage, Lorna. *Angela Carter.* Plymouth, UK: Northcote House, 1994.

———. ed. *Flesh and the Mirror. Essays on the Art of Angela Carter.* London: Virago Press, 1994.

Spenser, Edmund. *The Faerie Queene.* Ed. T. P. Roche, Jr. New Haven: Yale UP, 1981.

Stevens, John. *Medieval Romance: Themes and Approaches.* London: Hutchinson U Library, 1973.

Vinaver, Eugene. *The Rise of Romance.* New Jersey: Barnes and Noble, 1971.

Wilson, R. Rawdon. "SLIP PAGE: Angela Carter, In/Out/In the Postmodern Nexus." *Ariel,* 20.4 (1989): 96-114.

Joyce Carol Oates (essay date summer-fall 1997)

SOURCE: Oates, Joyce Carol. "In Olden Times, When Wishing Was Having . . . : Classic and Contemporary Fairy Tales." *Kenyon Review* n.s. 19, nos. 3-4 (summer-fall 1997): 98-110.

[*In the following excerpt, Oates focuses on Carter's characterization of the fairy-tale virgin in* The Bloody Chamber.]

In Angela Carter's similarly iconoclastic collection of stories, **The Bloody Chamber** (in **Burning Your Boats**), a lush, fevered prose style expresses the exoticism of the fairy-tale world in a way that, ironically, the pedestrian, serviceable prose of the fairy tales themselves did not. (Angela Carter, a scholar/translator of Perrault's *Histoires ou contes du temps passé,* defined their essence as "heroic optimism," the principle that makes possible "happy" endings.) A postmodernist fantasist, an experimenter in form and voice, Carter created for her tales a florid, self-conscious, overwrought prose, as in these musings of the seventeen-year-old virgin bride of Bluebeard:

> I felt so giddy as if I were on the edge of a precipice; I was afraid, not so much of him, of his monstrous presence, heavy as if he had been gifted at birth with more specific *gravity* than the rest of us, the presence that, even when I thought myself most in love with him, always subtly oppressed me. . . . No. I was not afraid of him; but of myself. I seemed reborn in his unreflective eyes, reborn in unfamiliar shapes. I hardly recognized myself from his description of me and yet, and yet—might there not be a grain of beastly truth in

them? And, in the red firelight, I blushed again, unnoticed, to think he might have chosen me because, in my innocence, he sensed a rare talent for corruption.

(115)

The "talent for corruption" in fairy-tale virgins is one of Carter's most provocative revisionist-feminist themes, often equated with food, drink, perfumes, and flowers, in sensuous prose: "The reeling odor of a glowing, velvet, monstrous [rose] whose petals had regained all their former bloom and elasticity, their corrupt, brilliant, baleful splendor" (**"The Lady of the House of Love"** 209).

In Carter's revision of the Bluebeard legend, the collection's title story, the virgin-bride of the murderous marquis is saved, in an unexpected ending, by her own mother, a huntswoman who arrives at just the right moment: "You never saw such a wild thing as my mother, with her hat seized by the winds and blown out to sea so that her hair was her white mane, her black lisle legs exposed to the thigh, her skirts tucked around her waist, one hand on the reins of the rearing horse while the other clasped my father's service revolver. . . . And my husband stood stock-still, as if she had been Medusa, the sword still raised over his head as in those clockwork tableaux of Bluebeard you see in glass cases at fairs" (142)—to fire a single bullet through his forehead. (A ridiculous ending, perhaps, but no more ridiculous than any other fairy-tale ending, the feminist Carter seems to be saying. And why not, for once, feminist wish-fulfillment?) In Carter's similarly lush, sensuous revision of "Beauty and the Beast," titled **"The Courtship of Mr. Lyon,"** the mythical marriage of innocent virgin and good, decent beast evolves into ordinary domestic marital happiness: "Mr. and Mrs. Lyon walk in the garden; the old spaniel drowses on the grass, in a drift of fallen petals" (153). (How welcome, for once, a fairy-tale ending that subverts the fantastic altogether.) In an artful variant of this marriage tale, **"The Tiger's Bride,"** a female sexuality emerges passionately from a lifetime of repression, conquering "nursery fears made flesh and sinew; earliest and most archaic of fears, fear of devourment. The beast and his carnivorous bed of bone and I, white, shaking, raw, approaching him as if offering, in myself, the key to a peaceable kingdom in which his appetite need not be my extinction" (168). Beauty craves Beast as Beast craves Beauty; in erotic union, female and male are perfectly conjoined: "And each stroke of his tongue ripped off skin after successive skin, all the skins of a life in the world, and I left behind a nascent patina of shiny hairs. My earrings turned back to water and trickled down my shoulders; I shrugged the drops off my beautiful fur" (169).

Carter's females are hardly "good" girls but complex, morally ambiguous individuals, not to be defined or predicted by gender, as in **"The Company of Wolves"**:

"See! sweet and sound she sleeps in granny's bed, between the paws of the tender wolf" (220). And females can be as cruelly rapacious as males, in **"The Snow Child"** (in which a decadent nobleman's wife conspires in his brutal rape and murder of a young girl, the "child of his desire"); and **"The Werewolf,"** in which, unexpectedly, the grandmother herself is the wolf against whom the shrewd young virgin must defend herself with her father's knife and a public denunciation of her grandmother to neighbors: "They knew the wart on the hand at once for a witch's nipple; they drove the old woman, in her shift as she was, out into the snow with sticks, beating her old carcass as far as the edge of the forest, and pelted her with stones until she fell down dead" (211). The tale ends abruptly with the girl (never identified as Red Riding Hood) moving into her grandmother's house and "prospering." *The Bloody Chamber* revels in such startling reversals, dramatic surprises that suggest the tales' schematic intentions rather more than they evolve from a graceful conjunction of character and tale itself.

Like Sexton's more slapdash, idiomatic poems, Carter's prose fictions recapitulate familiar fairy-tale forms radical angles of perspective. Sexton's women are trapped in their legends like puppets on strings, while Carter's are more realized as protagonists, willful and often perverse creations who define themselves against their seemingly prescribed fates. Not "heroic optimism" after all but "defiant self-dramatization" most accurately describes the mood of *The Bloody Chamber*.

Note

This essay will appear, in a slightly different form, in *Into the Mirror: An Anthology of Women on Fairy Tales*, edited by Kate Bernheimer (Anchor, Doubleday; forthcoming in 1998).

Works Cited

Carter, Angela. *Burning Your Boats: The Collected Short Stories*. New York: Holt, 1995.

Sexton, Anne. *Transformations*. Boston: Houghton, 1972.

Sarah Gamble (essay date 1997)

SOURCE: Gamble, Sarah. "*The Bloody Chamber* (1979)." In *Angela Carter: Writing from the Front Line*, pp. 130-41. Edinburgh: Edinburgh University Press, 1997.

[*In the following essay, Gamble investigates the thematic relationship between metamorphosis and predation represented in* The Bloody Chamber *with respect to the fairy tale genre.*]

Having thoroughly debunked myth in *The Passion of New Eve,* Carter's interests returned to a literary genre she had long been fascinated by, and whose subversive potential she had already explored in *The Magic Toyshop*—fairy tale. Lest one might be mistaken in thinking that myth and fairy tale are merely different sides of the same coin, Carter elaborated on the distinction she drew between mythology and folklore (which she uses here as a term synonymous with fairy tale) in 'Notes from the Front Line'. The relationship between the radical writer and myth, she implies, has necessarily to be contentious because, as 'extraordinary lies designed to make people unfree', myths have to be argued with, dismantled through the act of writing. Folklore, however, is an ideal tool for an author 'in the demythologizing business', because it is 'a much more straightforward set of devices for making real life more exciting and is much easier to infiltrate with other kinds of consciousness'.[1]

Precisely why fairy tale is so suitable for this task is, as I have already observed, something that Carter began to engage with in her fiction as early on as *The Magic Toyshop,* and she outlined her views in a more theoretical form in the introduction to the first collection of frailties she edited for Virago Press in 1990. Here she argued that, while the novel is always tied to the figure of the author, whose name legitimises its status as a unique, original work of art, fairy tale is a more democratic art form. Originally transmitted orally, it was passed from teller to teller, all of whom freely modified it to suit the specific requirements of their audience. For Carter, this willingness to accommodate is what makes the fairy tale indispensable for, as Marina Warner similarly argues, the form's innate flexibility thus allows it to

> illuminate experiences embedded in social and material conditions . . . [and] reveal . . . how human behaviour is embedded in material circumstances, in the laws of dowry, land tenure, feudal obedience, domestic hierarchies and marital dispositions, and that when these pass and change, behaviour may change with them.[2]

In a modern period where 'the mythologies of advanced industrialized countries'[3] are disseminated through a global media, fairy tale's willingness to adapt to suit the specific circumstance has never been more valuable.

For both Carter and Warner, another important attribute of the fairy tale is that, precisely because it is regarded as a domestic and personal narrative form, 'a medium for gossip, anecdote, rumour',[4] it has always been identified with women, who have played a large part in its development both as tellers and as writers. In rewriting such traditional tales as 'Bluebeard', 'Beauty and the Beast' and 'Puss-in-Boots', Carter was not only exploiting the potential inherent in fairy tale for demonstrating how experiences are 'embedded in material and social

conditions', but also doing so through a specifically feminist sensibility which consciously recovered a female tradition of storytelling obscured by the popularity of such male adapters as Charles Perrault, the Brothers Grimm and Hans Christian Andersen. The fact that Carter had herself published a translation of Perrault's collection in 1977 adds another pleasing twist to this scenario, so that *The Bloody Chamber* can be regarded as a gleeful, subversive, commentary on her own earlier work.

The steady growth of Carter's popularity throughout the 1980s can to a large extent be traced back to the publication of this collection of stories, most particularly because they provided her with material that could be transposed into other media, thus bringing her name to the attention of people who might not necessarily read her books. She adapted 'Puss-in-Boots' and **'The Lady of the House of Love'** (re-entitled *Vampirella*) for radio,[5] while the **'The Company of Wolves'** was not only made into a radio play, but also into a film.[6] Shortly before her death, Carter edited two collections of frailties for Virago (the latter, ***The Second Virago Book of Fairy Tales,*** was published posthumously with an introduction by Marina Warner).[7]

Merja Makinen has argued that the public perception of Carter as a writer owed a great deal to the success of ***The Bloody Chamber*** and its adaptations, and backs up the point with references to Carter's obituaries, many of which characterised her as a 'Fairy Godmother' (Margaret Atwood), 'friendly witch' (J. G. Ballard), 'very good wizard' (Salman Rushdie).[8] Makinen, however, is suspicious of 'this concurrence of white witch/ fairy godmother mythologizing'[9] for, however sincerely meant, it smacks of the very process of false universalisation that Carter spent most of her career protesting against and thus runs the risk of fatally misrepresenting her work. As Makinen says, 'the books are not by some benign magician. The strengths and the dangers of her texts lie in a much more aggressive subversiveness and a much more active eroticism than perhaps the decorum around death can allow'.[10]

The idea of Angela Carter as Mother Goose also misrepresents ***The Bloody Chamber*** itself, for it's not nearly as straightforward a rewriting of the traditional fairy tale collection as such an image might suggest. Firstly, as recent critics have begun to realise, all the stories are interconnected. Rather than being a series of segregated little narratives, therefore, each tale 'bleeds' into the other to form an intricately inter-linked whole. Makinen, for example, observes that 'each tale takes up the theme of the earlier one and comments on a different aspect of it';[11] while Lucie Armitt argues that the collection 'functions less as a collection of individual short stories and more as a single narrative which uses the short story medium to work and rework compulsive repetitions'.[12] Armitt, indeed, speculates that this refusal to remain enclosed within the parameters of the short-story form is encoded in the book's title, observing that the 'bloody chamber' of the title need not necessarily be read as 'room' but as 'vase or vessel'. 'In this case the blood is the liquid with which the vessel is filled. . . . The associated excesses are those of over-spill, not those which threaten containment'.[13]

Exactly what Carter is so compulsively circling and re-working within the blurred boundaries of these stories constitutes another departure from the traditional image of the fairy tale narrative, for these are no children's bedtime stories or cosy fireside flights into fabulation. On the contrary, they are fierce, dark, erotic, gothic and, as the title itself suggests, frequently dripping with gore. Margaret Atwood argues, I think very percep-tively, that *The Bloody Chamber* is best understood as a kind of fictionalised companion volume to *The Sade-ian Woman,* for it constitutes an exploration of the same predator/prey equation that preoccupies the de Sade study. In a description that could equally as well be ap-plied to the latter text, Atwood reads *The Bloody Cham-ber* as 'a "writing against" de Sade, a talking-back to him',[14] and sees this as informing the organising prin-ciple underlying the book as a whole:

> *The Bloody Chamber* is arranged according to catego-ries of meat-eater; three cat family stories at the begin-ning, followed by 'Puss-in-Boots' as a kind of comic coda; three wolf family stories at the end; and three ambiguous supernatural creatures—erl-king, snow-child, female vampire—in the middle.[15]

Such parallels aren't that surprising when one considers that Carter was working on *The Sadeian Woman* at the same time as writing the stories that make up *The Bloody Chamber.* Indeed, in her interview with Les Bedford it is obvious that she considered the writing of the latter light relief from the monumental task of sort-ing out her thoughts on de Sade. His influence is par-ticularly apparent in the collection's title story **'The Bloody Chamber'**, of which Carter said with evident satisfaction that it 'did manage to get in most of de Sade, which pleased me'.[16]

However, while all these stories share a Sadeian interest in predation, which is why they're populated with car-nivores, they also convey Carter's concern with renego-tiating the relationship between predator and prey, which is why metamorphosis is such a prevalent theme within the collection as a whole. A good example of how Carter utilises these elements within a fairy tale setting is provided by her two Beauty and the Beast stories, **'The Courtship of Mr Lyon'** and **'The Tiger's Bride'**. The first contains most of the elements of the familiar tale, although brought up-to-date—the Beast is a country squire, while Beauty is a modish, cigarette-smoking, debutante. In fact, in many ways this is a rela-tively tame rewrite. Beauty is another of Carter's dad-dy's girls, who 'would have gone to the ends of the earth for her father, whom she loved dearly' (p. 58);[17] and the story ends, as all good traditional frailties should, in marriage and the promise of future domestic-ity: 'Mr and Mrs Lyon walk in the garden; the old span-iel drowses on the grass, in a drift of fallen petals' (p. 66).

Ellen Cronan Rose's observation that this story shows Beauty 'simply chang[ing] masters—from a beastly fa-ther to a fatherly beast'[18] has a certain validity in this context, but I think there's more to the issue here than she allows. In the context of Carter's fiction as a whole, Beauty and the Beast's mutual avowal of love is a re-markable achievement, for it is the very first time a couple have succeeded in meeting on terms which are founded on genuine affection on both sides. It is an en-counter which changes both of them, for it is not only the Beast, as he always traditionally does in this story, who gains humanity thorough the love of another; Beauty, too, is saved from a not-quite-human fate. The spoiled, petulant daughter of an indulgent father before she takes the step of commitment to the Beast, she hov-ers on the verge of becoming a kind of automaton born of the stasis of privilege, 'acquiring, instead of beauty, a lacquer of the invincible prettiness that characterizes certain pampered, exquisite expensive cats' (p. 63).

The motif of metamorphosis, therefore, works both ways, for these are not just stories where the once so submissive, so passive, fairy tale heroine gets her own back. On the contrary, by giving as good as she gets, the heroine works towards a utopian space where both male and female benefit from the transformation of the old power relations. This is shown even more clearly in Carter's second reworking of 'Beauty and the Beast', where the same themes are explored on a far more ex-plicitly radical level. The Beauty of **'The Tiger's Bride'** has a negligent father who loses her to the Beast in a game of cards, while the Beast himself is a grotesque enigma awkwardly disguised as a man, 'a carnival fig-ure made of papier mâché and fake hair' (p. 70). Beauty herself is a spiky, astute character who looks at the world with the eyes of a shrewd accountant. Having de-cided that the withdrawal of her father's support leaves her only 'my skin . . . [as] my sole capital in the world' (p. 74), she is determined to get as much out of the deal as she possibly can when the Beast tells her the price of her freedom is to allow him to see her naked. Beauty's mercenary ethics are severely shaken, however, when she sees the Beast in the magnificence of his true feline form. Realising that 'the tiger will never lie down with the lamb; he acknowledges no pact that is not reciprocal' (p. 84), Beauty gives herself freely to the Beast, 'white, shaking, raw, approaching him as if offering, in myself, the key to a peaceable kingdom in which his appetite need not be my extinction' (p. 88). And it isn't, for instead of devouring Beauty the tiger licks her into her proper shape, which is the mirror of his: 'each stroke of his tongue ripped off skin after successive skin, all the skins of a life in the world, and left behind a nascent patina of shining hairs' (p. 89). Both Beauty and Beast in this story thus shrug off the disguises that society forces them to assume, and in this way the predator/prey dichotomy is shattered with the establishment of a harmonic and mutually beneficial relationship between man and woman.

However, Carter's exploration of this relationship between the carnivore and his victim is carried to its most disturbing, and potentially problematic extreme in **'The Company of Wolves'**. Here, the beast takes the form of a wolf, and his metaphorical function within the text is barely disguised. As a lycanthrope, he represents the threatened destruction of the means by which human society differentiates itself from nature; in particular, as the story clearly conveys, its own animal nature. Through his metamorphosis into wolf and back again, he escapes the social regulations by which human society is structured, with the concomitant threat that he might bring the law of the (primitive) forest back into the (civilised) village upon his return. And according to the prim and censorial voice which dominates the first part of the narrative, the law of the forest is not only predatory—'if you stray from the path for one instant, the wolves will eat you' (p. 149)—but also specifically sexual: 'Before he can become a wolf, the lycanthrope strips stark naked. If you spy a naked man among the pines, you must run as if the Devil were after you' (p. 152). In this context, therefore, the wolf's hunger for flesh has an acknowledged double meaning.

This Red Riding Hood, however, is more than a match for the wolf when she meets him, and little resembles the shrinking violet of Perrault's version of the tale. For a start, she's not a small girl, but an adolescent who has just reached sexual maturity: 'Her breasts have just begun to swell . . . her cheeks are an emblematic scarlet and white and she has just started her woman's bleeding' (p. 152). In other words, the girl is in herself a variation on the 'bloody chamber' trope, with all the connotations of the risk of overspill already discussed by Armitt. But although the heroine's menstrual blood is already flowing, she is still a virgin, 'inside her a magic space the entrance to which is shut tight with a plug of membrane' (p. 153); and this is what constitutes both her particular vulnerablity and her peculiar defence. It is what marks her out as the lycanthrope's prey, for the shedding of her hymeneal blood is what he specifically desires. However, Carter's description of the heroine as 'a closed system' (p. 153) is reminiscent of the Sadeian subject's willed invulnerability; like them, 'she does not know how to shiver' (p. 153).

This heroine, therefore, is trapped in a double bind, precariously secure in the closed circle of her virginal

state, but unable to progress without becoming prey. Unlike the Count and Tristessa, however, whose intense preoccupation with self she to a great extent shares, the girl finds her way out of this conundrum by running towards, rather than away from, the sexual threat of the lycanthrope. In her assertion that she is 'nobody's meat' (p. 158), she refuses to confirm his own perceptions of her as his natural victim, and thus ends the story sleeping 'sweet and sound . . . in granny's bed, between the paws of the tender wolf' (p. 159). In opening out the closed circle of her self (represented here by the spilling of her blood beyond her body's boundaries), and by giving it 'freely' (p. 158), the implication is that she and the wolf enter into a relationship of complete equality. As Atwood says:

> [This may be a] consolatory nonsense perhaps—don't try this technique on a street mugger—but at least [it is] a different kind of consolatory nonsense, one that tries for the kind of synthesis Carter suggested in *The Sadeian Woman*: 'neither submissive nor aggressive'.[19]

Yet this story is more explicit than most in the disturbing echoes it arouses, and it is therefore not surprising, perhaps, that it has become a focus for those critics who regard this collection as less liberatory than it obviously purports to be, for how much choice, in actuality, does the poor child have? Patricia Duncker, for example, says the ending of **'The Company of Wolves'** shows Red Riding Hood realising 'that rape is inevitable . . . and decides to strip off, lie back and enjoy it. They want it really. They all do'.[20] Her views are closely echoed by Robert Clark who argues that although the story finally 'represents the woman enjoying her own sexuality and using this as a power which tenderizes the wolf', such

> positive aspects are achieved at the cost of accepting patriarchal limits to women's power . . . the implication may be that the girl has her own sexual power, but this meaning lies perilously close to the idea that all women want it really and only need forcing to overcome their scruples.[21]

The opinions of Duncker and Clark are distinctly reminiscent of the concerns voiced by critics of *The Sadeian Woman,* in that none of them see Carter as able to transcend the limitations of her chosen medium. In spite of Carter's best efforts to radicalise such forms, they argue, pornography and fairy tale are literary modes whose conventions will always lean towards the status quo: compare, for example, Patricia Duncker's argument that 'the infernal trap inherent in the fairy tale, which fits the form to its purpose, to be the carrier of ideology, proves too complex and pervasive to avoid'.[22] with Susanne Kappeler's view of *The Sadeian Woman*:

> Sade is more subtle than Carter gives him credit for. He does not rattle her chains in order for her to escape them, and she should suspect his 'liberating spirit' bred

from hatred. . . . While his options are strictly binary—to suffer or to cause suffering, to belong to one half of 'mankind' or the other—these are not for her to choose from: they are gender specific.[23]

It is interesting in this context to note that Carter changed the ending of **'The Company of Wolves'** slightly but significantly on each of its subsequent rewrites. In the radio play, the heroine's increased assertiveness robs the ending of much of the hidden connotations of rape that Duncker and Clark read into the original version. Whereas there the lycanthrope loses none of his threatening connotations, and it is entirely up to the girl to rise to the challenge he represents, here the predator is left thoroughly nonplussed by the heroine's unexpected enthusiasm for her defloration:

RED RIDING HOOD.

> I do believe, since you got here before me, that you owe me a kiss.
>
> What big teeth you have!

WEREWOLF.

> (*Choking—grabbing at straws.*) All the better . . . to eat you with.

RED RIDING HOOD.

> Oh, I say!
>
> *She goes into peals of laughter.*
>
> Well, each to his meat but I am meat for no man! Now I shall burn your clothes, just like I burned my own.
>
> . . . . .

WAREWOLF.

> Not that!

RED RIDING HOOD.

> Why, anybody would think you were scared of being a good wolf all the time . . .[24]

Carter's destabilising of the power relationship between girl and werewolf in the heroine's favour is taken still further, although I would argue with less success, in her screenplay for the film of **'The Company of Wolves'**. The heroine (here named Rosaleen) burns the lycanthrope's discarded clothing in the fire along with her own, thus trapping him in his wolfish form; an aspect of the narrative which is entirely absent in the original story, although, as the above quotation demonstrates, it is hinted at in the radio play. Completely outmanoeuvred in this version, the lycanthrope grovels and howls, his head in Rosaleen's lap, who addresses him as if he were a pet: 'Come on, old fellow, old dog. Good boy, good. . . .'[25] Although the notion of an equal relationship between the two is belatedly (re)established with Rosaleen's final implied metamorphosis into wolf, as Maggie Anwell says, this does nothing to reinstate the

overtly expressed sexuality of the original story. Instead of the disruptive, implicitly taboo, image of the girl asleep in the arms of the wolf, we are left with two wolves running off into the forest together; a manifestation of the film's 'coy reluctance . . . to allow an image of successful sexual initiation',[26] Carter would have it that one of the things that so attracted her to fairy tale was the anonymity of the teller, who acts only as a vehicle for the transmission of stories that both pre-and post-date her literary intervention. It is distinctly ironic, therefore, that the publication of **The Bloody Chamber** contributed to the formation of a popular identity which brought her, if not exactly into the mainstream of British fiction writing—she still remained rather too contentious for that—at least an established and distinctive literary voice. Indeed, what fairy tale did was to offer Carter a way to be *more herself,* which is, perhaps, why she always claimed to have 'relaxed' into it.[27] As a rather kitsch fantastic form with, nevertheless, a subversive past, it provided her with a model that corresponded exactly to what she was already doing in novels such as *The Infernal Desire Machines of Doctor Hoffman* and *The Passion of New Eve*—the interrogation of master narratives and, particularly, of the divergence between the roles male and female are permitted to play within them. Such a demythologizing impulse is doubly shocking when applied to cherished traditional fairy stories, yet Carter would argue that it is only bringing them back in line with their original function. As she said to Helen Cagney Watts, 'The tales in my volume **The Bloody Chamber** are part of the oral history of Europe, but what has happened is that these stories have gone into the bourgeois nursery and therefore lost their origins'.[28] While there was a side of the oral fairy tale tradition that Perrault considered unsuitable for bourgeois consumption, Carter's aim is to reintroduce her readers to such discomforting aspects—with a vengeance.

Notes

1. Angela Carter, 'Notes from the Front Line', p. 71.

2. Marina Warner, *From the Beast to the Blonde: On Fairytales and Their Tellers* (London: Chatto & Windus, 1994), pp. xviii-xix.

3. Angela Carter, Introduction to *The Virago Book of Fairy Tales* (London: Virago Press, 1991), p. xxi.

4. ibid.

5. The radio plays are collected in *Come Unto These Yellow Sands: Four Radio Plays by Angela Carter* (Newcastle upon Tyne: Bloodaxe Books, 1985), and also in *The Curious Room: Collected Dramatic Works* (London: Chatto & Windus, 1996).

6. *The Company of Wolves,* directed by Nell Jordan (ITC Entertainment Palace Production, 1984). Carter's screenplay is collected in *The Curious Room.*

7. Angela Carter (ed.), *The Second Virago Book of Fairy Tales* (London: Virago, 1992).

8. Merja Makinen, 'Angela Carter's *The Bloody Chamber* and the Decolonization of Feminine Sexuality', *Feminist Review* 42 (Autumn 1992), pp. 2-15 (p. 2).

9. ibid.

10. ibid., p. 3.

11. ibid., p. 10.

12. Lucie Armitt, 'The Fragile Frames of *The Bloody Chamber*', unpublished manuscript, forthcoming in Treva Broughton and Joe Bristow (eds), *The Infernal Desires of Angela Carter* (London: Longman, 1997).

13. ibid.

14. Margaret Atwood, 'Running with the Tigers', in Lorna Sage (ed.), *Flesh and the Mirror: Essays on the Art of Angela Carter* (London: Virago Press, 1994), pp. 117-35 (p. 120).

15. ibid., p. 122.

16. Les Bedford, 'Angela Carter: An Interview' (Sheffield University Television, February 1977).

17. Angela Carter, *The Bloody Chamber* (Harmondsworth: Penguin Books, 1981). All subsequent references in the text are from this edition.

18. Ellen Cronan Rose, 'Through the Looking Glass: When Women Tell Fairy Tales', in Elizabeth Abel, Marianne Hirsch and Elizabeth Langland (eds), *The Voyage In: Fictions of Female Development* (University Press of New England, 1983), pp. 209-27 (p. 223).

19. Atwood, 'Running with the Tigers', p. 130.

20. Patricia Duncker, 'Re-Imagining the Fairy Tales: Angela Carter's Bloody Chambers', *Literature and History* X:I (Spring 1984), pp. 3-14 (p. 7).

21. Robert Clark, 'Angela Carter's Desire Machine', *Women's Studies* 14 (1987), pp. 147-61 (p. 149).

22. Duncker, 'Re-Imagining the Fairy Tales', p. 6.

23. Susanne Kappeler, *The Pornography of Representation* (Cambridge: Polity Press, 1986), p. 135.

24. Angela Carter, *The Company of Wolves*, in *Come Unto These Yellow Sands*, p. 80.

25. Angela Carter, screenplay for *The Company of Wolves*, in *The Curious Room: Collected Dramatic Works*, p. 241.

26. Maggie Anwell, 'Lolita Meets the Werewolf: *The Company of Wolves*', in Lorraine Gamman and Margaret Marshment (eds), *The Female Gaze: Women as Viewers of Popular Culture* (London: The Women's Press, 1988), pp. 76-85 (p. 81).

27. Angela Carter, 'Notes from the Front Line', p. 71. It was a phrase she reiterated in interview with Olga Kenyon, in *The Writer's Imagination* (University of Bradford Print Unit, 1992), p. 29.

28. Cagney Watts, 'Angela Carter: An Interview', p. 170.

Select Bibliography

Anwell, Maggie, 'Lolita Meets the Werewolf: *The Company of Wolves*', in Lorraine Gamman and Margaret Marshment (eds), *The Female Gaze: Women as Viewers of Popular Culture* (London: The Women's Press, 1988), pp. 76-85

Armitt, Lucie, 'The Fragile Frames of *The Bloody Chamber*', unpublished manuscript, forthcoming in Treva Broughton and Joe Bristow (eds), *The Infernal Desires of Angela Carter* (London: Longman, 1997)

Bedford, Les, 'Angela Carter: An Interview' (Sheffield: Sheffield University Television, February 1977)

Cagney Watts, Helen, 'Angela Carter: An Interview', *Bête Noir* 8 (August 1985), pp. 161-76

Carter, Angela, *The Magic Toyshop* [1967] (London: Virago Press, 1981)

Carter, Angela, *The Infernal Desire Machines of Doctor Hoffman* [1972] (Harmondsworth: Penguin, 1982)

Carter, Angela, *The Passion of New Eve* (London: Virago Press, 1977)

Carter, Angela, *The Sadeian Woman: An Exercise in Cultural History* (London: Virago Press, 1979)

Carter, Angela, *The Bloody Chamber* [1979] (Harmondsworth: Penguin, 1981)

Carter, Angela, *Come Unto These Yellow Sands: Four Radio Plays by Angela Carter* (Newcastle upon Tyne: Bloodaxe Books, 1985)

Carter, Angela (ed.), *The Virago Book of Fairy Tales* (London: Virago Press, 1991)

Carter, Angela (ed), *The Second Virago Book of Fairy Tales* (London: Virago Press, 1992)

Carter, Angela, *Burning Your Boats: Collected Short Stories* (London: Chatto & Windus, 1995)

Carter, Angela, *The Curious Room: Collected Dramatic Works* (London: Chatto & Windus, 1996)

Carter, Angela, 'Notes from the Front Line', in Michelene Wandor (ed), *On Gender and Writing* (London: Pandora Press, 1983), pp. 69-77

Clark, Robert, 'Angela Carter's Desire Machine', *Women's Studies* 14 (1987), pp. 147-61

Cronan Rose, Ellen, 'Through the Looking Glass: When Women Tell Fairy Tales', in Elizabeth Abel, Marianne Hirsch and Elizabeth Langland (eds), *The Voyage In: Fictions of Female Development* (University Press of New England, 1983), pp. 209-27

Duncker, Patricia, 'Re-Imagining the Fairy Tales: Angela Carter's Bloody Chambers', *Literature and History* X/1 (Spring 1984), pp. 3-14

Kappeler, Susanne, *The Pornography of Representation* (Cambridge: Polity Press, 1986)

Kenyon, Olga, *The Writer's Imagination* (University of Bradford Print Unit, 1992)

Makinen, Merja, 'Angela Carter's *The Bloody Chamber* and the Decolonization of Feminine Sexuality', *Feminist Review* 42 (Autumn 1992), pp. 2-15

Sage, Lorna (ed), *Flesh and the Mirror: Essays on the Art of Angela Carter* (London: Virago Press, 1994)

Warner, Marina, *From the Beast to the Blonde: On Fairytales and Their Tellers* (London: Chatto & Windus, 1994)

Monika Fludernik (essay date 1998)

SOURCE: Fludernik, Monika. "Angela Carter's Pronominal Acrobatics: Language in 'The Erl-King' and 'The Company of Wolves.'"[1] *European Journal of English Studies* 2, no. 2 (1998): 215-37.

[*In the following essay, Fludernik highlights Carter's use of pronouns in "The Erl-King" and "The Company of Wolves" as it affects other grammatical constructs, narrative points of view, and thematic concerns in the stories.*]

Unaccountably, Angela Carter's short fiction has received comparatively little attention in the criticism of her work. Most of the short stories are analysed in the pastiche mode, as an imitation and rewriting of the genre of the fairy tale.[2] Perhaps the recent publication of Carter's collected short fiction, **Burning Your Boats**,[3] will help amend this situation soon. Carter's linguistic mastery and stunning use of metaphor are most clearly on display in her short stories—a fact that has so far been little appreciated in the criticism.

In this article, I will focus on Carter's sophisticated use of pronouns in two stories from the collection **The Bloody Chamber,** and I will attempt to link the linguistic data to other linguistic items (the use of tense), to narratological frames (first-person vs. third-person vs. second-person narrative), and to the thematic concerns of the two stories. No definitive true textual 'meaning' or function can ultimately be attributed to a change of

pronoun; as I will argue, such a formal shift correlates with a cognitive category, that of defamiliarisation, and with a subsequent need to step out of the grooves of one's reading experience. This triggering of the need for additional processing leads to an intensification of the reader's interpretative engagement with the text, and it also enhances the sophistication of the textual analysis. Temporal and pronominal changes such as those employed by Carter in the two stories therefore ultimately serve as shifters and as metatextual clues to the need for interpretative sophistication.

Several of Carter's short stories refuse to abide by a consistent deployment of the narratological category *person*—first-person, third-person or second-person fiction. They additionally 'play' with personal pronouns in a more general way, in particular by resorting to the gnomic or generic *you* or *we,* which interact with the authorial *I* and with impersonal constructions. In what follows, I will concentrate on **'The Erl-King'** and **'The Company of Wolves'** with a brief glance at **'The Cabinet of Edgar Allan Poe'** (from the **Black Venus** collection). All three texts accompany their manipulation of pronominal and referential forms, in particular their strategic deployment of the second person, with a concomitant shifting of temporal forms (past tense/present tense system alternation) and with deictic vacillation in spatial reference (proximal deictics vs. adeictic expressions and reference). Many of these features suggest, and they do so particularly in their *constellation,* that Carter presents the story from a figural perspective, i.e., that these deictic features signal internal focalization.[4] On closer inspection, however, a large percentage of the same phenomena, it turns out, function in the employ of authorial discourse, even if they hypostatize an illusionary identification with a character position. Conversely, other passages appear to be unambiguously authorial, but insidiously transmute into subjective, figural narrative.

I

'The Erl-King' is a first-person narrative which has an authorial beginning and a third-person ending. The inappropriateness of such a merely formal categorization becomes apparent immediately when one starts to analyse the text in detail, scrutinizing the seams of the presumptive first or third person segments. Such a regard for detail pays off in disclosing a web of intricate deictic shifts and moves that refuse to congeal into a stable surface structure. The opening lines of **'The Erl-King'** are as follows:

> The lucidity, the clarity of the light *that* afternoon was sufficient to itself; perfect transparency must be penetrable, *these* vertical bars of a brass-coloured distillation of light coming down from sulphur-yellow interstices in a sky hunkered with grey clouds that bulge with more rain. It struck the wood with nicotine-stained

fingers, the leaves glittered. A cold day of late October, when the withered blackberries dangled like their own dour spooks on the discoloured brambles. There were crisp husks of beechmast and cast acorn cups underfoot in the russet slime of dead bracken where the rains of the equinox had so soaked the earth that the cold oozed up through the soles of *the* shoes, lancinating cold of the approaching of winter that *grips* hold of *your* belly and *squeezed* it tight. *Now* the stark elders have an anorexic look; there is not much in the autumn wood to make *you* smile but it is not yet, not quite yet, the saddest time of the year. Only, there is a haunting sense of the imminent cessation of being; the year, in turning, turns in on itself. Introspective weather, a sickroom hush.

The woods enclose. You step between the fir trees and then you are no longer in the open air; the wood swallows you up. There is no way through the wood any more, this wood has reverted to its original privacy. Once you are inside it, you must stay there until it lets you out again for there is no clue to guide you through in perfect safety. [. . .]

(*BC* [*The Bloody Chamber*], p. 84 / *BB* [*Burning Your Boats*], p. 186)[5]

The past tense *was* in the first line and the apodictic tone of the opening statement ('must be') as well as the highly metaphorical quality of the passage seem to indicate an authorial source for the language. Even in this first sentence, however, the seemingly adeictic, gnomic mould of the diction is being subtly undermined by the deictics *that* ('that afternoon') and *these* ('these vertical bars [. . .] of light') which insinuate a subjective (deictic) position on the story level into the objective discourse of evaluative pronouncements *on* or *about* the story world. Initially, these 'non-sequential sequence signals' (Backus)[6] can be aligned with the expressivity of the authorial narrator, who starts the story *medias in res*. The same is true for the following sentences in which the clipped syntax can be read as the expressive rhetoric of the authorial speaker. That speaker increasingly invokes the experience of a virtual on-the-scene experiencer whose shoes fail to keep out the cold ('*the* shoes') and whose sensations physically affect his/her stomach: 'grips hold of *your* belly and squeezed it tight'. This is also the first instance in the text of a gnomic or generic *you* (*you* as 'everyone'), and it serves to maximize empathy with the experiential position in the story world. Note also the tense shift at this point ('grip*s* hold'), an anticipation of the subsequent lines in which the present tense installs itself for good. Only 'squeezed' has a preterite form, and it belongs to the only narrative clause (Labov) in the entire first paragraph since it is the only verb denoting a narrative event. (The tenuousness of that 'event' in the sequence is underlined by the impersonal agent of this 'action'—it is the cold that grips the belly of an unspecified [generic] 'you'.) The passage continues with a proximal deictic 'now' which posits a specific action time on the story level and introduces a description of subjective quality: 'Now the

stark elders have an anorexic look', which is as much as to say, the elders acquire an anorexic look in the mind of the 'you' gripped by cold. The second instance of 'you' in this first paragraph proposes a virtual action (or, really, reaction) on the part of the experiencer: virtual since negated ('there is not much') and part of an intentional clause ('to make you smile')—there is no definite indication whether or not the 'you' actually *did* smile.

The second paragraph now turns into second-person narrative, though of a pronounced generic quality. The forest closes round the experiencer. A sequence of three narrative events ('enclose', 'you step', 'swallows') is followed by narrative comment which, initially, can be read as the impressions of the 'you': 'There is no way through the wood any more'. The final sentence as quoted, however, quite clearly reverts to the opening apodictiveness—'you must stay here'—and thereby reinstates the communicative, authorial level of the text. Indeed, the final pronouncement can be read as a metafictional statement: you-the-reader will be lost in the fictional woods without a clue until the narrative ejects you from the text in its own good time. The fictional woods (in the mimetic and the metafictional senses of the term) therefore function as a kind of prison to the experiencer and/or reader. This links with a consistent metaphorics of imprisonment in '**The Erl-King**', which is already adumbrated in the 'vertical bars of brass-coloured distillation', an image for slanting rain that suggests that the very sun beams bar the observer from direct access to the sunlight. (The comparison with a downpour is invoked metonymically by reference to the 'gray clouds that bulge with rain.'[7])

There follows a description of the woods which can be read in authorial or figural terms, that is to say, either as the narrator's evaluation of the landscape or as a rendering of the character's impressions of it. In the subsequent paragraphs, the text undergoes a major sea change and shifts into first-person narrative:

A young girl would go into the wood as trustingly as Red Riding Hood to her granny's house but *this* light admits no ambiguities and, *here,* she will be trapped in her own illusion because everything in the wood is exactly as it seems.

The woods enclose and then enclose again, like a system of Chinese boxes opening one into another; the intimate perspectives of the wood *changed* endlessly around *the interloper, the imaginary traveller* walking towards an invented distance that perpetually *receded* before *me*. It is easy to lose *yourself* in these woods.

The two notes of the song of a bird rose on the still air, as if *my* girlish and delicious loneliness had been made into a sound.

(*BC,* p. 85 / *BB,* pp. 186-7)

At the beginning of this section, the authorial narrator seems to reassert her/himself by means of a speculative *would*-clause which compares the virtual 'you'-

protagonist's fictional experience to that of Little Red Riding Hood; 'but' the text immediately withdraws that analogy of trustingness and proposes that 'here' and in 'this light' (again proximal deictics referring to the story level) contain no ambiguities; the woods are ineluctably illusionistic: 'everything in the wood is exactly as it seems'. In contrast to ordinary fiction of the fairy-tale variety, perhaps, this virtual traveller will be 'trapped in her own illusion' if she ventures into the fictional woods of **'The Erl-King'**. This dictum of a prophetic cast must be attributed to the narrator exclusively, as also the beginning of the next sentence. From the present tense of the opening of this second paragraph ('enclose and then enclose again') the sentence continues after the semi-colon with the past-tense verbs ('changed', 'receded'), thus reverting to the style of the story opening quoted above. Only this time there is an agent in full view; the indefinite 'a young girl' and the generic 'you' have metamorphosed into 'the interloper, the imaginary traveller', and that traveller 'perpetually receded before *me*'. In the next but one sentence the story line (if one can use the word at all) continues with 'rose on the still air' and comes to a stop in another comparison: 'as if *my* girlish [. . .] loneliness had been made into a sound'. The intermediate clause ('It is easy to lose yourself in these woods') can be read as a gnomic statement, as a metafictional commentary, or as the imaginary traveller's (or I's?) thought.

What we have here, first of all formally, is therefore a brisk shift from a hypothetical young girl to an 'imaginary traveller' of unknown identity and gender (the young girl? the hypothetical 'you' of unspecified gender from above? the female first-person protagonist?) and then to a first-person pronoun—the very first in the story!—which appears to be co-referential with the noun phrase 'the imaginary traveller'. There are three possible explanations that may be proffered for this extraordinary set-up:

(1) the 'narratological' solution: shift from third-person to first-person text within one sentence (the first-person protagonist is identical to the imaginary traveller).

(2) the 'authorial' solution: the 'me' refers to the narrator persona who has imaginatively projected herself into the figure of 'a young girl' who is or is not Red Riding Hood. In this version, the authorial narrator had already anticipated this identificatory strategy in the earlier incipient you-narrative, and now continues the hypothetical story of Little Red Riding Hood by hypostatizing a fictional 'I' which is the projection of the narrator's invention and imagination. The story, as we will get it, therefore also carries a metafictional load.

(3) the 'authorial first-person narrator': the 'real' quality of the story is that of a first-person narrative; in the opening section, however, the narrator arrogates to herself the liberties of an authorial voice. She distances herself from her own experience, and she does so by means of a series of hypothetical roles—'you', the 'interloper', 'a young girl'—all of which are objectifications of her own situation in the forest and therefore meta-narrative (but not meta*fictional*) figurations.

Options two and three, it will be appreciated, subvert a neat shift from third to first-person narrative in favour of positing a *continuity* of narrative situation, but they have to pay for this assumption of consistency with the invocation of narrative acrobatics that have few precedents in their present shape. Although quasi-authorial features of first-person narrative have been commented on in narratology,[8] these comments usually concern the extent of the first-person narrator's knowledge (access to information beyond the protagonist's scope) rather than the stylistic, pronominal and structural features involved in the present case. (Note, for instance, that whereas the protagonist is a young girl, the *style* of the writing certainly belongs to a mature and practised rhetorician.) As regards the second proposed solution, the authorial narrator here 'becomes' a fictional persona; this constitutes a most unheard-of metamorphosis in classical narratology, although it might be regarded as less scandalous if seen from the point of view of natural narratology—for instance, as a radical development of the technique of figuralization.[9] At this stage of the essay, it is too early to weigh these three options against each other; I will do so later after completing my analysis of the entire story.

After the preliminaries which I have discussed above, Carter's story continues for some time as a first-person narrative in the past tense. However, this consistency is again broken up by the introduction of a second-person pronoun and by an alternation of present-tense passages and past-tense passages with a concomitant alternation of you-forms and he-forms, both in reference to the Erl-King. (The protagonist is consistently first-person.) The four following passages illustrate this alternation:

> The trees threaded a cat's cradle of half-stripped branches over me so that I felt I was in a house of nets and though the cold wind that always heralds *your* presence, had I but known it then, blew gently around me, I thought that nobody was in the wood but me.
>
> Erl-King will do *you* grievous harm.
>
> Piercingly, now, there came again the call of the bird, as desolate as if it came from the throat of the last bird left alive. That call, with all the melancholy of the failing year in it, went directly to my heart.
>
> (*BC*, p. 85 / *BB*, p. 187)

Here, in a past-tense passage, the 'I' refers to the Erl-King as 'you' ('your presence'), obviously from a latter-day perspective ('had I but known it then'). The following one-line paragraph ('Erl-King will do you grievous harm') is open to multiple interpretations. It could be read as a thought articulated by the first-person protagonist, echoing a saying she has been taught by her elders (in parallel to the warnings about wolves that reverberate in **'The Company of Wolves'**); the Erl-King then appears to be a kind of wolf. Like Gretel from 'Babes in the Wood', the female protagonist is in mortal danger of captivity. She finds herself affected by the call of a bird, presumably uttered by one of the Erl-King's victims, who has turned all his lovers into birds and keeps them imprisoned in bird cages in his hut. At this early point in the narrative the 'you' can also, quite falsely, be read as co-referential with 'your presence'. This second option would need to find a referent for 'you' different from the Erl-King, for instance a reference to the narratee. Third, both instances of 'you'/'your presence' could be interpreted as co-referential with the earlier generic 'you' from the beginning of the tale. Owing to the later unambiguous clarification of 'your presence' as referring to the Erl-King, this co-reference equation does not work either. Fourth, the 'you' in the one-line paragraph can be attributed to an address by the narrator to the first-person protagonist (whether as the narrating self warning her earlier incarnation, or as an authorial narrator warning the protagonist). Finally, the paragraph could also be argued to relapse into the pronominal distribution of the beginning of the tale—the 'you' is then read as generic, but as applicable to the protagonist; the speaker as the narratorial voice. It goes without saying that not a few of the named options depend on a prior decision of what, precisely, is the referential structure at the beginning of the story—a question that, as we have seen, is still very much unresolved at this point in the story. As a consequence, the one-line paragraph evinces a radical indeterminacy, and it could be symbolically interpreted as the protagonist's entry into the realm of magic in which appearances are no longer transparent, because 'everything in the wood is [no longer] exactly as it seems' (***BC,*** p. 85 / ***BB*** p. 186).

In the next two cited passages the protagonist's first meeting with the Erl-King is related *twice*: once in the static present tense and with a *he* reference to the Erl-King; the other time, explicitly with the noun phrase and in past tense narration.

> He smiles. He lays down his pipe, his elder bird-call. He lays upon me his irrevocable hand.
>
> (***BC,*** p. 86 / ***BB,*** p. 187)
>
> I found the Erl-King sitting on an ivy-covered stump winding all the birds in the wood to him on a diatonic spool of sound, one rising note, one falling note; such a sweet piercing call that down there came a soft, chirruping jostle of birds.
>
> (***BC,*** p. 88 / ***BB,*** p. 189)

In the first passage, internal focalization prevails: it is the protagonist's feelings that are rendered. The en-counter is symbolically loaded: the smile, the pipe, the irrevocable hold on the protagonist. Note that the pronoun *he* is a referentless pronoun; the anaphor has no explicit antecedents except in the 'your' of 'your presence' (a noun phrase the narrative position of which, as we have seen, is more than indeterminate), or in the title of the story **'The Erl-King'**.

> And now—ach! I feel *your* sharp teeth in the subaqueous depths of your kisses. The equinotical [sic ***BB***: i.e., equinoctial] gales seize the bare elms and make them whizz and whirl like dervishes; you sink your teeth into my throat and make me scream.
>
> (***BC,*** p. 88 / ***BB,*** p. 190)

This passage is a typical example of internal focalization—again rendered by the present tense of immediacy. The second-person pronoun in reference to the Erl-King operates in an intimate, almost incantatory manner. Here one can no longer easily align these second-person forms with a situation of address or communication after the fact, and the presumable retrospective nature of the writing is in any case exploded in the last lines of the tale, as we will see. The quoted passage continues with the protagonist's thoughts about her situation, even speculations about her future: 'If I strung that old fiddle with your hair, *we* could waltz together to the music as the exhausted daylight founders among the trees [. . .]' (***BC,*** p. 89 / ***BB,*** p. 190). Note, incidentally, the *we* ('I' plus 'you') in this sentence. This immediacy of emotional surrender is played out for another few paragraphs, and the chirping of the birds in their cages subtly hints at the real meaning of the Erl-King's embraces: sexual incorporation as a prelude (the musical pun is intended) to life imprisonment as a bird. The old witch from 'Babes in the Wood' plans to eat the children she has caught; the Erl-King turns the victims of his musical arts of seduction into instruments of that very art: an allegory on the insidious dangers of art such as it is also articulated by Carter in **'The Loves of Lady Purple'**.

Let me now turn to the ending of the story, which presents another surprising metamorphosis. The protagonist's experience of complete surrender, at first portrayed in very positive terms, acquires increasingly threatening overtones. Thus, towards the end of the long present-tense second-person passage the beginning of which I quoted above, the protagonist feels that she is going to be swallowed up by the Erl-King: 'What big eyes you have' (***BC,*** p. 90 / ***BB,*** p. 191) invokes the ending of 'Little Red Riding Hood' (compare **'The Company of Wolves'**). She becomes afraid of falling into the 'black hole in the middle of both your eyes' which operates as 'a reducing chamber', and she realizes that she is scheduled to be kept in the cage 'you are weaving for me' (***BC,*** p. 90 / ***BB,*** p. 191).

At this point the distancing past-tense narrative reasserts itself, as does the third-person reference to the Erl-King:

> When I realised what the Erl-King meant to do to me, I was shaken with a terrible fear [. . .] But in his innocence he never knew he might be the death of me, although I knew from the first moment I saw him how Erl-King would do me grievous harm.
>
> (*BC,* p. 90 / *BB,* pp. 191—2)

Here the reference of *you* in the earlier inexplicable clause ('**The Erl-King** will do you grievous harm'— *BC,* p. 85 / *BB,* p. 187) is finally relieved of ambiguity: the 'you' referred to the first-person protagonist, the sentence rendered her realization of impending danger. The text continues with a longer present-tense passage of internal focalization in which the protagonist comes to realize that the birds in the cages do not sing, 'they only cry because they can't find their way out of the wood, have lost their flesh when they were dipped in the corrosive pools of *his* regard [. . .]' (*BC,* p. 90 / *BB,* p. 192). Losing oneself in the wood, therefore, is tantamount to being drowned in the pool of Erl-King's eyes. The 'you' in reference to the Erl-King has turned into a 'he' ('his'), and the 'you' returns only briefly in the final passage of the text, in an invocation, an address to the protagonist's victim-to-be:

> Lay your head on my knee so that I can't see the greenish inward-turning suns of your eyes any more.
>
> My hands shake.
>
> I shall take two huge handfuls of his rustling hair as he lies half dreaming, half waking, and wind them into ropes, very softly, so he will not wake up, and softly, with hands as gentle as rain, I will strangle him with them.
>
> Then *she* will open all the cages and let the birds free; they will change back into young girls, every one, each with the crimson imprint of his love-bite on their throats.
>
> She will carve off his great mane with the knife he uses to skin the rabbits; she will string the old fiddle with five single strings of ash-brown hair.
>
> (*BC,* p. 91 / *BB,* p. 192)

In this passage, the first-person protagonist metamorphoses back to a third-person referent. The outcome of her liberation is rendered in the *future tense* which, unlike the previous 'I shall' has no intentional quality but the quality of prognosis or prophecy. This is what the imaginary traveller *will do*—she will free the birds and restore the Erl-King's Orphic fiddle to its original musical purpose, unperverted art perhaps?

The Orphic parallel, incidentally, lends itself to extensive interpretative recuperation. The Erl-King has been luring the girls to his net by means of a pipe or flute (another fairy-tale motif from the Grimm Brothers—only, there, it is rats that are drawn by the piper). The broken strings on the Erl-King's fiddle (*BC,* p. 90 / *BB,* p. 192) seem to allude to the cessation of Orphic song—no longer is music used to appease the Gods and regain Eurydice; it has been perverted into an instrument of entrapment. The Erl-King therefore duly falls prey to the revenge of the woman he has harmed—in intertextual allusion to Orpheus' assassination by the Bacchic celebrants.[10]

Let us return to the pronominal and temporal shift in the last paragraphs. This shift clearly disproves a retrospective reading of the narrative (the latter-day wise first-person-narrator evaluating her past experiences); it proposes the ending of the 'story' as a future, or perhaps, rather: *hypothetical,* setting, and by these means closes the circle. We are back at the beginning of an imaginary hypostatized traveller, a persona projected from the metafictional speculations of the narrator. The final passage, therefore, it seems to me, clinches the metafictional reading of the tale, and it additionally suggests that the first-person protagonist must be of a hypothetical character, *not* constitutive of the basic narrative situation in the story. Of course, the suggestion that the first-person narrator acquires authorial faculties still remains in force: one can also read the story as a first-person narrative in which the first-person narrator 'authorializes' herself at the beginning of the tale and then distances herself from her own aims and purposes in a *medias in res* ending which leaves the accomplishments of the protagonist's intentions quite open. Such a non-retrospective behaviour of a first-person narrator is odd to start with, although to be encountered increasingly in present-tense fiction;[11] however, with the quasi-authorial opening of the tale such a solution looks much less convincing, although it remains available as a remote interpretative possibility, I would say.

II

Before coming to any general conclusions, I would first like to turn to my second example story, '**The Company of Wolves**'.

'**The Company of Wolves**' starts with a clearly gnomic comment by the authorial narrator: 'One beast and only one howls in the woods by night' (*BC,* p. 110 / *BB,* p. 212). This is followed by a quasi-definitional characterization of 'the wolf' and a paragraph of even more non-scientific folk-lore about wolves which provides instructions to a generic 'you' travelling through the forest at night—a 'benighted traveller' in two senses of the word: 'At night, the eyes of wolves shine like candle flames, yellowish, reddish, but that is because the pupils of their eyes fatten on darkness and catch the light from *your* lantern to flash it back to *you*—red for danger [. . .]' (*BC,* p. 110 / *BB,* p. 212).

In the continuation of the text, the scene is set in winter ('It is winter') and 'now' (*BC,* p. 110 / *BB,* p. 212), and the hypothetical encounter of the 'you' with the wolves becomes more generic with 'You could count [their] ribs [. . .] if they gave you time before they pounced' (*BC,* p. 110 / *BB,* p. 212)—a phrasing that employs the conditional to good generic purpose. A comparison of wolves that 'cannot listen to reason' (*BC,* p. 111 / *BB,* p. 212) with fairy-tale characters such as ogres grilling babies on grid-irons or witches fattening their captives for subsequent consumption underlines the generic reference which also returns to a more authorial mode.

In the subsequent paragraph the text moulds itself on the example of an instruction manual or guidebook, dispensing standard advice on how to proceed in dangerous forests: 'You are always in danger in the forest [. . .] step between the gateposts of the forest with [. . .] infinite precautions, for if you stray from the path for one instant, the wolves will eat you' (*BC,* p. 111 / *BB,* p. 212). This series of imperatives of ostensibly good advice is undercut stylistically by the poetic comparisons of the passage ('as if the vegetation itself were in a plot with the wolves', 'as though the wicked trees go fishing', 'unkind as plague').

From the alignment of the generic 'you' with a traveller through the forest at night—the Red Riding Hood scenario to which the story will return—the text now shifts into a second section in which the potential victims of the wolves (and, as we will see in a minute, the werewolf) are 'we', the householders at the margins of the forest. These margins of the forest, the endangered circumference of the dark realm of evil and the unknown, to be entered 'with the greatest trepidation' through 'portals' or 'gateposts' (and note the implicit allusion to wickets in 'wicked trees'—all *BC,* p. 111 / *BB,* p. 213), symbolize the realm of the sexual, as the conclusion of the story clarifies, but can be interpreted as thresholds from various other perspectives (the transcendental, for instance) as well. That these margins are meant to be generally relevant to the narratee is indicated by the close collocation of 'at your own hearthside', 'we' and 'the cottager'. The sequence also forms a kind of link to the injunction 'Fear and flee the wolf; for, worst of all, the wolf may be more than he seems' (*BC,* p. 111 / *BB,* p. 213)—the introductory paragraph to the 'wolf as werewolf' theme.

The narrator, previously classified as 'authorial', now slips into the role of a narrator within the fictional world, though situated at the periphery of the action—in analogy with oral storytelling traditions[12] the narrator 'outs' himself as a member of the village community ('There was a hunter once, *near here*'; 'A witch from *up* the valley;' 'a young woman in *our* village'—*BC,* pp. 111—12 / *BB,* p. 213) in which the following events

supposedly occurred. These references to the speaker's deictic origo[13] locate the speaker on the level of the story world of these three anecdotes. The third, longest anecdote (the three stories in a sense iconically reproduce the three sections of the story as a whole) also anticipates the move into third-person narrative, and introduces the possibility of a love relationship with the wolf—a concept to be realized in the climax of **'The Company of Wolves'**.

The third anecdote has a brief epilogue by the narrator who has donned his authorial trappings again and relates more folklore about wolves, directly addressing the narratee in his/her generic aspect. The passage is particularly interesting from the point of view of gender attribution. Whereas the 'you' had so far been gender-nonspecific, it here invokes gender roles and moves from an implicitly male to an implicitly female attribution. Since the werewolves in the three anecdotes have been male, the ointment that the 'Devil gives *you* that turns *you* into a wolf' (*BC,* p. 113 / *BB,* p. 214) appears to address a male reader persona; in the middle section the person who, by burning the werewolf's clothes, condemns him to life-long wolfishness can be of either sex; but in the final paragraph the addressee—if one assumes a heterosexual default reading—is cast in a female gender role: 'If *you* spy a naked man among the pines, *you* must run as if the Devil were after *you*' (*BC,* p. 113 / *BB,* p. 214). This last sentence not only beautifully manages to attune the reader to the shift back to Little Red Riding Hood, but it also explicitly invokes the puritanical satanization of sexuality, and it alludes to the earlier sexual overtones of the text in reference to the wood as a realm of (sexual) endangerment.

The story of the protagonist in the following pages is, indeed, one of sexual initiation, with starkly Freudian overtones (the relinquishment by the girl of her big knife). Not only has she just started her period; the impending loss of her virginity is prefigured also in the 'red shawl that, today, has the ominous brilliant look of blood on snow' (*BC,* p. 113 / *BB,* p. 215). Her strong-headed insistence to go visit her grandmother on Christmas Eve constitutes an infraction, a trans*gression* of cultural boundaries, and her passing into the forest (we remember the portals from earlier on) is figured in terms of ingestion ('The forest closed upon her like a pair of jaws'—*BC,* p. 114 / *BB,* p. 215).[14] The forest, however, also mirrors the 'magic space' of her own physiology: her blood has issued from the 'unbroken' shell of her 'sealed vessel' (*BC,* p. 114 / *BB,* p. 215), and just as she forces her entrance into the forest, the hitherto denied 'entrance' into her 'magic space' (*BC,* p. 114 / *BB,* p. 215) will be accomplished by the end of the story. It will be figured, precisely, in terms of ingestion as she lies between the 'paws' (*BC,* p. 118 / *BB,* p. 220: cf. jaws) of 'the tender wolf' when 'the door of the solstice stands wide open' and the werewolves on their birthday are allowed to 'all sink through' (**BC**, p. 118 / **BB**, p. 220).

At this point of the story when the narrator embarks on Red Riding Hood's story (although the prospective bride of the wolf has a red scarf, not a red hat), the narrative also refers back to the hypothetical scenario from the first page of the story by repeating the description of the setting provided earlier ('It is winter and cold weather'—**BC**, p. 110 / **BB**, p. 212): 'It is midwinter [. . .]' (**BC**, p. 113 / **BB**, p. 215). The presentation of the scene, again in parallel fashion, employs the present tense—a present tense that initially may be read as referring back to the generic scenario of 'the benighted traveller' / 'you', but now solidifies into narration proper by the establishment of a new deictic centre (note the proximal deictic *this* in 'this strong-minded child'—**BC**, p. 113 / **BB**, p. 215), that of the girl. The 'freezing' of the narrative action in this extended present-tense description of the protagonist obviously resembles the technique in **'The Erl-King'**, although it does not correlate with internal focalization but, on the contrary, with a pronounced 'authorial' presentation of the heroine's situation, with a psychological analysis of her mindset, of whose content she is presumably quite unconscious. As in **'The Erl-King'**, here, too, the plotline verbs come (for the most part) in the past tense ('The forest *closed* upon her [. . .]'; 'When she *heard* [. . .]'—**BC**, p. 114 / **BB**, p. 215), and the interspersed present-tense passages after the onset of the story at least sometimes lend themselves to a figuralized interpretation. (Thus, the very first present-tense passage after the past tense 'closed'—'There is always something to look at'—describes the motives for the heroine's dawdling, but it can be read both from an omniscient-authorial and from an internally focalized point of view.)

When the young man, the wolf, arrives at the grandmother's house, another succession of three present-tense passages alternating with the action report ensues (cf. 'He rapped upon the panels with his knuckle'—**BC**, p. 115 / **BB**, p. 217, twice). All three again freeze the action in a descriptive interlude. In the first and briefest, the young man is said to have a faint trace of blood on his chin (**BC**, p. 115 / **BB**, p. 216)—this inset mirrors the earlier symbolic anticipation of Red Riding Hood's loss of virginity in a nearly equivalent symbol of the young man's impending cannibalistic spree. In the second passage, granny is described in her natural habitat of cosy snug homeliness ('We keep the wolves outside by living well' [**BC**, p. 115 / **BB**, p. 217], interjects the authorial narrator). The third passage, however, departs from this descriptive mode; it can be read, rather, as a continuation of the pseudo-instructional discourse from the beginning of the short story, only this time the piece of advice is directed at the grandmother: '[. . .] you

can hurl your Bible at him and your apron after, granny, you thought that was a sure prophylactic against these infernal vermin . . . now call on Christ and his mother and all the angels in heaven to protect you but it won't do you any good'. (**BC**, pp. 115—6 / **BB**, p. 217)

There follows an extended present-tense passage which definitely employs internal focalization (note the interior monologue—'Oh, my God, what have you done with her'—in which the *her* takes the *you* of 'your dear girl's basket' [**BC**, p. 116 / **BB**, p. 217] as an antecedent) and intermittently refers to the grandmother by means of the second-person pronoun. The conclusion of this present-tense interlude is worth quoting in full:

> He strips off his shirt [. . .] but he's so thin *you* could count the ribs under his skin if only he gave *you* the time. He strips off his trousers and *she* can see how hairy his legs are. His genitals, huge. Ah! huge.
>
> The last thing *the old lady saw* in all this world was a young man, eyes like cinders, naked as a stone, approaching her bed.
>
> The wolf is carnivore incarnate.
>
> When he had finished with her, he licked his chops. [. . .]
>
> (**BC**, p. 116 / **BB**, p. 217)

There are two near-verbatim repetitions in this sequence that relate back to the authorial opening of the story: the hypothetical counting of the ribs of the wolf(man), and the 'definition' of the wolf as 'carnivore incarnate'. This repetition suggests one possible non-focalized reading of the passage, namely that in which the authorial narrator figure not merely addresses the grandmother but, in addition to this, starts to mime her reactions. In narratological terms, this would therefore constitute a radical instance of reflectorization[15] in parallel to the figuralization posited for the beginning of **'The Erl-King'**. On a more prosaic level, one can note that the 'you' which had first been generic, was then implicitly associated with the granddaughter, is now used to refer to the grandmother, just as the opening of the story had moved from a generic victim of wolves to the narratee as hypothetical victim on to the (female) villager as a more specific victim. Granny's story is therefore to be seen as a counterpoint to the young woman's in the third anecdote (in contrast to that tale, the wolf here enters rather than disappears), just as the conclusion of the story with Red Riding Hood as the Wolf's lover reflects (on) the third anecdote: would the werewolf have returned to his bride and would she have securely turned him back into a man if she had remained 'immaculate flesh', the only thing that can 'appease' the 'carnivore incarnate' (**BC**, p. 118 / **BB**, p. 219)?

The heroine's near-devourment is rendered in consistent past-tense narration but is interspersed with snatches of dialogue (a fraction of which echo the fairy-tale dialogue). There are two important departures from this pattern: the onset of this final section of the story ('Rat-a-tap-tap. / Who's there, he *quavers* in granny's antique falsetto. [. . .] / So she *came* in [. . .]'), and secondly, the conclusion of the story. In a near-echo of the penultimate paragraph from **'The Erl-King'**, the text there reads:

> She *will* lay his fearful head on her lap [. . .] The blizzard *will* die down.
>
> The blizzard died down, leaving the mountains as randomly covered with snow as if a blind woman had thrown a sheet over them, the upper branches of the forest pines limed, creaking, swollen with the fall.
>
> Snowlight, moonlight, a confusion of paw-prints.
>
> All silent, all still.
>
> Midnight; and the clock strikes. It is Christmas Day, the werewolves' birthday, the door of the solstice stands wide open; let them all sink through.
>
> See! sweet and sound she sleeps in granny's bed, between the paws of the tender wolf.
>
> (*BC*, p. 118 / *BB*, pp. 219-20)

The non-violent thought-projection on the part of the heroine in 'She *will* lay his fearful head on her lap' (but there is no real proof of internal focalization in contrast to the ending of **'The Erl-King'**) is finalized in the plot of the story by the echo of 'will die down' in 'died down'. The forest is reestablished in the pristine purity of the snow that covers it like a sheet, and Christmas Day breaks to the implicit chime of the Christmas carol ('All silent, all still'). The door of the solstice, earlier swinging on its hinges ('The malign door of the solstice still swings upon its hinges'—*BC*, p. 113 / *BB*, p. 215), 'stands wide open' (*BC*, p. 118 / *BB*, p. 220). The sweet sound of the carol reverberates in the heroine's 'sweet and sound' sleep in between the paws of the wolf. From the past-tense endpoint 'died down' the text moves on to a present-tense vignette in which time, and therefore mortality, seem to come to a standstill. In this vignette the impossible—the taming of the beast, the pacification of man's worst fears—is realized in the mythical time of the fictional present, in the 'magic space' of the white 'sheet' of 'immaculate' paper.

III

From the above analysis, several conclusions can be drawn regarding Carter's use of personal pronouns and of the past-tense/present-tense alternation. For one, the shift from first to third-person reference in **'The Erl-King'** and the use of the second-person pronoun in both stories appear to be strategic even if no specific *uniform* function can be attributed to these phenomena. Second, the change from past tense to present tense in both stories correlates with a 'freezing' of the action,[16] and this sometimes (but not consistently) lends itself to a pre-

sentation of a protagonist's perceptions, impressions or feelings at a given moment in the story. Additional occurrences of the present tense, specifically at the *opening* of the two stories, link with the authorial mode of Carter's text and its gnomic aspects: the present-tense of narration (narrative present[17]) develops out of the gnomic present of the authorial disquisitions, with an intermediate stage of hypothetical discourse which, likewise, comes in the present tense.

Despite these insights, one cannot help noticing, however, that there is no explanatory model that could ascribe *a (definitive)* meaning to the temporal or pronominal forms. Thus, the present tense operates almost like a floating signifier that modulates from generic uses in gnomic utterances to narratorial commentary, from its use in hypothetical propositions to the deployment as a narrative tense, and it additionally acquires secondary interpretations when juxtaposed with past-tense segments. This constellation correlates with the fact that the present tense constitutes the default within the discourse system so that it is open to future, hypothetical (modal), generic and relational (simultaneity) uses in addition to its purely deictic (speaker's 'here-and-now') reference. Indeed, in the absence of a definite communicative context, and in the absence of a past tense to which the present can be opposed, the present tense, like Weinrich's narrating tenses, immediately induces a relaxed attitude on the part of the reader and is therefore qualified to replace the narrative past tense (or epic preterite).[18]

The situation is even more complex with reference to the personal pronouns. There are two major issues relevant for the texts which I have discussed. For one, there is the shift from first to third-person reference and from third to first-person reference in designating the protagonist (*she, I* in **'The Erl-King'**). This alternation gave rise to serious interpretative problems in our analysis, but these problems did not relate to the *she/I* alternation on the story line but to the opening and concluding sections of the story and the possible relationship between protagonist and the authorial-narrator persona. In the body of the tale the pronominal alternation, indeed, affected the textual reference to the Erl-King (*he* vs. *you*) and was partly explained as coinciding with focalizational aspects of the narrative, and it also correlated with temporal alternation.

The distribution of personal pronouns in **'The Erl-King'** is, however, additionally dependent on the use of the second-person pronoun, and in **'The Company of Wolves'** the shift from second-person to third-person references took pride of place in our discussion of that story. I will now attempt to place these uses of the second-person pronoun within a larger functional frame. *You*, as a pronoun of address, like the present tense in its default reading, displays a marked flexibility and a wide variety of quite disparate applications.[19]

The address-pronoun *you* has a basic *deictic* function by means of which it designates the current interlocutor in a communicational exchange. Within a narrative, the current interlocutor of the narrator is the narratee or the persona of a projected listener or reader. Since empiric readers are reading the text, addresses by the narrator to his or her narratees lend themselves to a reading in which the actual, empirical reader feels personally addressed. The *you* is then taken to have immediate relevance to the real author-real reader circuit of communication. Real readers will feel immediately affected by second-person pronouns in literary texts if the projected role of the narratee coincides with the reader role which they have assumed or see themselves as occupying. Likewise, explicitly metafictional statements by the narrator (as frequently in John Barth) trigger identificational or distancing moves on the reader's part. Fictional address pronouns, however, cannot be said to *refer* to empirical readers—they only 'refer to' projected reader personae. If actual readers do feel addressed, they do so because they allow themselves to be interpellated by the text.

An example of a second-person pronoun which functions as an address to the persona of the current reader of the story occurs in Carter's **'The Fall River Axe Murders'** (from the collection *Black Venus*):

> If *you* were sorting through a box of old photographs in a junk shop and came across this particular, sepia, faded face above the choked collars of the 1890s, you might murmur when you saw her: 'Oh, what big eyes you have!' as Red Riding Hood said to the wolf, but then you might not even pause to pick her out and look at her more closely, for hers is not, in itself, a striking face.
>
> But as soon as the face has a name, once you recognise her, when you know who she is and what it was she did, the face becomes as if of one possessed, and now it haunts you, you look at it again and again, it secretes mystery.
>
> (*BV* [*Black Venus*], p. 119 / *BB*, p. 315)

Here the *you* at first appears to refer to 'anyone'—a generic figure—but as soon as the narratee's experiences are outlined ('you recognise her'), the current reader may or may not take up this challenge and actually remember Lizzi Borden, and imaginatively transport her/himself into the 'frame' of sorting through newspaper clippings.

Besides this deictic use of the second-person pronoun on the narratorial level of the text, *intra*textual deictic uses also abound. This is true, most obviously, in the characters' dialogue. A more sophisticated kind of deictic usage concerns that of the (first-person) narrator's address to a fictional persona. The apostrophe by Red Riding Hood to the Erl-King constitutes such a case. In this particular instance, the passages either suggest that

the address is one of interior monologue (the girl is only mentally focussing on the Erl-King) or that there is an inexplicit situation of address that *frames* the story: the girl as first-person narrator invokes the (now dead?) Erl-King as her virtual interlocutor or apostrophizes the image of her former lover. In the second case, the apostrophe can be compared to authorial narrators' empathetic apostrophe to their characters, a case which, as I argued, might apply in the case of Granny in **'The Company of Wolves'**.

In my analysis, I have noted the generic *you* throughout. As we saw, the generic *you* in both tales functions as an intermediary ploy to provide a transition from authorial to more subjective (first-person or second-person) narrative strategies. I have noted elsewhere[20] that *you*, like *one*, is eminently suited to the purposes of polite non-commitment. Generic second-person pronouns allow potential addressees to take up the roles they prescribe for them, or to distance themselves at their discretion. Conversely, *you* (again like *one*) provides a mask for the speaker behind which he or she may hide: since 'you' do, or anyone does, these things, I myself can legitimately do them.

You is also frequently used in self-address in the exchange between ego and super ego or virtual alter ego in people's and fictional characters' internal speech. We noted such an example in **'The Erl-King'** when the young girl realizes that the Erl-King 'will do you grievous harm' as one possible reading of that passage.

The most unusual deployment of the second-person pronoun, however, is in narrative texts where it designates the protagonist within the recently discovered 'second-person narrative'.[21] In Carter's two stories only brief incipient second-person narrative can be posited—Carter's oeuvre does not have a consistent second-person text on the lines of Frederick Barthelme's or Joyce Carol Oates's stories; nor did she write any second-person novels like Butor, Duras, McInerney or Tom Robbins.[22] There is, however, at least one story in which second-person fiction briefly appears in the text. In Carter's **'The Cabinet of Edgar Allan Poe'** (from the *Black Venus* collection) the generic *you* modulates into a reader address in which 'you yourself' at first evokes readers' identificational strategies but then narrows the possible reference down to 'a child'—an indication that only Edgar Allan could be the referent:

> Here he will find a painted backdrop of, say, an antique castle—a castle! such as they don't build here; a Gothic castle all complete with owls and ivy. The flies are painted with segments of trees, massy oaks or something like that, all in two dimensions. Artificial shadows fall in all the wrong places. Nothing is what it seems. *You* knock against a gilded throne or horrid rack that looks perfectly solid, thick, immovable, and *you* kick it sideways, it turns out to be made of papier

mâché, it is as light as air—*a child, you yourself,* could pick it up and carry it off with *you* and sit in it and be a king or lie in it and be in pain.

(*BV,* p. 57 / *BB,* p. 267)

Further on the generic *you* clearly develops into a narrative *you* as the reader is transported into the fiction and into the mind of Edgar Allan:

A creaking, an ominous rattling scares the little wits out of you; when you jump round to see what is going on behind your back, why the very castle is in mid-air! Heave-ho and up she rises, amid the inarticulate cries and muttered oaths of the stagehands, and down comes Juliet's tomb or Ophelia's sepulchre, and a super scuttles in, clutching Yorrick's skull.

(*BV,* p. 57 / *BB,* p. 268)

This strategy of drawing in the reader by means of his/her projective identification with a narrative role is here employed to place the reader directly in the mind of little Edgar Allan. This specification of a *you* qua character emerges either in strong figural contexts, where internal focalization prepares the way for an empathetic you=I=he/she equation; alternatively, such a second person develops in strongly generic contexts where the authorial voice foregrounds its appellative (conative) and persuasional rhetoric. *You* therefore correlates with the presence of heightened experientiality and serves to either draw the addressee into the experientiality of the character, or—alternatively—to draw the addressee into a personal involvement with the fictional world, as at the beginning of **'The Erl-King'** where the reader 'becomes' a virtual Red Riding Hood.

Carter's pronominal acrobatics, one can therefore conclude, make use of a large variety of fairly sophisticated pronominal strategies, and exploit the available ambiguities and the potential for eliciting reader involvement to the hilt. However, Carter's meaningful deployment of the second-person pronoun and of referential alternation does not allow for a uniform explanation, since a panoply of features—temporal, narratological, intertextual—interconnect and result in a variegated application of the various pronominal options and strategies.

Such a scenario runs counter to the Formalist and Structuralist explication of linguistic devices in their deviational significance. Not only is there little foregrounding or deviation in Carter's tales—or, one can also say, there is nothing but deviation in some respects—; none of the techniques seem to be alignable with *a* specific *function* on the interpretative level. On the contrary, narratological and interpretative concerns clearly pattern the analysis (a shift in pronouns is odd, primarily, because of a set of traditional generic expectations), and possible meanings or functions of textual features feed back onto the narratological plane, resulting in re-

vised frames. Although some of these have been proposed here in the attempt to explain the linguistic surface structure of the two tales, these explanations are merely adumbrations of possible interpretative moves and cannot lay claim to unequivocal validity. Nevertheless, whatever may be said about the oddities that I have discussed, they do need to be accounted for on the basis of certain well-established deictic givens within the linguistic system and in reference to proven textual strategies and functions in narrative texts. Interpretations of the linguistic data are therefore constrained from the outset and do not lend themselves to illimitable poetic and interpretative licence. It will therefore be best to talk of textual *effects* and interpretative *moves* rather than insisting on the underlying positivistic framework that the terms *functions* and *meanings, devices* and *systems* invoke. Besides these specifically theoretical concerns, I also hope to have created some appreciation for Carter's non-novelistic oeuvre for its stylistic brilliance and linguistic sophistication. Carter's short fiction deserves a wide-ranging and exhaustive critical effort.

Notes

1. This essay is a revised version of a paper read at IALS II in Freiburg in September 1997.

2. See Sylvia Bryant, 'Re-Constructing Oedipus Through "Beauty and the Beast"', *Criticism* 31.4 (1989), 439-53; Patricia Duncker, 'Re-Imagining the Fairy Tales: Angela Carter's Bloody Chambers', *Literature and History* 10.1 (1984), 3-14; Melinda G. Fowl, 'Angela Carter's *The Bloody Chamber* Revisited', *Critical Survey* 3.1 (1991), 71-79; Mary Kaiser, 'Fairy Tale as Sexual Allegory: Intertextuality in Angela Carter's *The Bloody Chamber*', *The Review of Contemporary Fiction* 14.3 (1994), 30-36; and Avis Lewallen, 'Wayward Girls but Wicked Women? Female Sexuality in Angela Carter's *The Bloody Chamber*', in *Perspectives on Pornography Sexuality in Fiction and Literature* (New York: St. Martin's, 1988), pp. 144-58.

3. Angela Carter, *Burning Your Boats. Collected Short Stories* (London: Virago, 1995).

4. On the narratological terminology see Franz Karl Stanzel, *A Theory of Narrative* (Cambridge: Cambridge University Press, 1984); and Gérard Genette, *Narrative Discourse. An Essay in Method* (Ithaca, NY: Cornell University Press, 1980).

5. My emphases in italics throughout. All quotations from Carter's texts are given a double citation to the individual collection and the *Collected Short Stories.* See Angela Carter, *The Bloody Chamber* (London: Penguin, [1979] 1981), henceforth *BC*; *Black Venus* (London: Picador, 1986) henceforth

BV; *American Ghosts & Old World Wonders* (London: Vintage, [1993] 1994), henceforth *AG*; and *Burning Your Boats,* henceforth *BB* (cp. footnote 3).

6. See Joseph M. Backus, '"He Came into her Line of Vision Walking Backward": Non-sequential Sequence Signals in Short Story Openings', *Language Learning* 15 (1965), 67-83.

7. Carter's obsessive use of prison settings and prison metaphors in her fiction is the subject of work in progress.

8. See, most prominently, Mieke Bal's external first-person narrator. (Compare Mieke Bal, *Narratology. Introduction to the Theory of Narrative,* trans. Christine van Boheemen [Toronto: University of Toronto Press, 1985].) Genette treats the authorial behaviour of a first-person narrator as an infraction of homodiegesis (Genette, *Narrative Discourse,* pp. 251-2), but one that is adequate for Proust. See also Stanzel (*A Theory,* pp. 214-18) for the inherent violation of fictional verisimilitude in such cases.

9. See Monika Fludernik, *Towards a 'Natural' Narratology* (London: Routledge, 1996), esp. pp. 178-222.

10. This is borne out by the final paragraph of the story following the quoted passage in which the strings accuse the 'Mother' of having murdered them.

11. See Dorrit Cohn, '"I Doze and I Wake": The Deviance of Simultaneous Narration in *Tales and "Their Telling Difference"*', in *Zur Theorie und Geschichte der Narrativik. Festschrift zum 70. Geburtstag von Franz K. Stanzel,* eds. Herbert Foltinek, Wolfgang Riehle, and Waldemar Zacharasiewicz (Heidelberg: Winter, 1993), pp. 9-23.

12. See similar constellations in Sherwood Anderson's *Winesburg, Ohio* (Harmondsworth: Penguin, [1919] 1983). (Cp. Fludernik, *Natural Narratology,* pp. 73-4; for the theoretical notation of this peripheral first-person narrator see Stanzel, *A Theory,* pp. 204-9).

13. On the term *deictic origo* referring to the speaker's here-and-now, see Karl Bühler, *Sprachtheorie. Die Darstellungsfunktionen der Sprache* (Jena: Gustav Fischer, 1934).

14. Note the ogres and witches referred to above.

15. For this term see Fludernik, *Natural Narratology,* ch. 5.

16. See W. J. M. Bronzwaer, *Tense in the Novel. An Investigation of Some Potentialities of Linguistic Criticism* (Groningen: Wolters-Noordhoff, 1970);

Christian Paul Casparis, *Tense Without Time. The Present Tense in Narration,* Schweizer Anglistische Arbeiten 84 (Berne: Francke, 1975).

17. On the narrative present see Cohn (*Zur Theorie*) and Fludernik (*Natural Narratology,* ch. 6). The term *narrative present* refers to the consistent use of the present tense for plot-line narrative clauses. It replaces the 'epic preterite' in traditional past-tense narratives.

18. For these formulations see Harald Weinrich, 'Tempus. Besprochene und erzählte Welt', *Sprache und Literatur 16* (Stuttgart: Kohlhammer, [1964] 1985). Fourth edition based on the second, extensively modified edition of 1971.

19. Compare Monika Fludernik, 'Introduction: Second-Person Narrative and Related Issues', *Style* 28.3 (1994), 281-311; Monika Fludernik, 'Second-Person Narrative as a Test Case for Narratology: The Limits of Realism', *Style* 28.3 (1994), 445-79; and Vimala Herman, *Deictic projections and conceptual blending in epistolarity,* Paper read at IALS II in Freiburg, Germany, 1 Sept 1997.

20. See Monika Fludernik, 'Pronouns of Address and "Odd" Third Person Forms: The Mechanics of Involvement in Narrative', in *New Essays on Deixis,* ed. Keith Green (Amsterdam: Rodopi, 1995), pp. 99-129.

21. See Monika Fludernik, 'Second Person Fiction: Narrative YOU as Addressee and/or Protagonist. Typological and Functional Notes on an Increasingly Popular Genre', *Arbeiten aus Anglistik und Amerikanistik* [*AAA*] 18.2 (1993), 217-47, and Fludernik *Style,* 28.3, pp. 281-311, pp. 445-479 (cf. note 19).

22. For a complete bibliography of second-person texts see Monika Fludernik, 'Second Person Narrative: A Bibliography', *Style* 28.4 (1994), 525-48.

Andrew Teverson (essay date 1999)

SOURCE: Teverson, Andrew. "'Mr. Fox' and 'The White Cat': The Forgotten Voices in Angela Carter's Fiction." *Hungarian Journal of English and American Studies* 5, no. 2 (1999): 209-22.

[*In the following essay, Teverson analyzes "The Courtship of Mr. Lyon" and "The Bloody Chamber" to demonstrate that Carter's short fiction privileges non-canonical fairy tale devices over canonical ones and reveals the ideological biases implicit in the literary tradition and feminist revisions.*]

Angela Carter is not a forgotten voice; if anything, she is more likely to be numbered amongst those voices that have defined and shaped the literature of late twentieth century Britain. Her fiction, however—somewhat ironically—is deeply concerned with that which is neglected in literature; with the rags, the junk, the jumble of the past that is not to be found in any canon, but must be sought out in the back streets and avenues of literary marginalia. In this essay, I would like to consider Carter's exploration of some of these back streets in detail with the intention of showing how a study of her engagement with literary amnesia can illuminate certain crucial features of her work. In the process, I would also like to offer some more general responses to the questions that were central to the conference that generated this collection of papers: questions concerning our reasons and motives for remembering one thing but forgetting another, and questions concerning the importance of recollecting things that have suffered neglect. In particular, I would like to focus upon a specific area of Carter's engagement with "the forgotten," and consider the ways in which she plays non-canonical (forgotten) fairy tales off against canonical (remembered) fairy tales in order to challenge the ideological biases implicit in the accepted canon. This will involve a brief consideration of the ways in which feminist writers have responded to fairy tales and an exploration of the ways in which Carter conforms with (or fights against) the feminist critique.

FEMINISM AND THE FAIRY TALE

The early feminist consensus on fairy tales, established by writers such as Andrea Dworkin, Kay Stone and Ruth Bottigheimer, is now familiar enough to have become a literary commonplace. They all suggest that the fairy tales canonised in western culture (that is the fairy tales of Charles Perrault, The Brothers Grimm and Hans Christian Andersen) assign asymmetric gender roles to girls and boys, masculinity being represented as the active principle, femininity as the passive. In Patricia Duncker's pithy formula: "Princes act, Princesses react" (*Sisters* 153).

There has been some resistance to this view from feminist quarters. Margaret Atwood—acting both as critic and rewriter—reacts to the view that the *Grimms' Tales* are sexist with surprise, and suggests that

> various traits were quite evenly spread. There were wicked wizards as well as wicked witches, stupid women as well as stupid men, slovenly husbands as well as slovenly wives. . . . When people say "sexist fairy tales," they probably mean the anthologies that concentrate on "The Sleeping Beauty," "Cinderella," and "Little Red Riding Hood" and leave out everything else.
>
> (291-92)

Maria Tatar similarly qualifies the feminist critique by pointing out that the hero, as well as being competitive and authoritarian, is also "'[i]nnocent,' 'silly,' 'useless,'

'foolish,' 'simple' and 'guileless.'" "If the female protagonists of fairy tales are often as good as they are beautiful," she adds, "their male counterparts generally appear to be as young and naive as they are stupid" (86, 87). Despite these points of resistance, however, the weight of evidence does tend to suggest that sexual inequality is the rule in canonical tales. Ruth Bottigheimer has conducted a thorough study of all 210 tales in the *Kinder und Hausmärchen* (7th ed. 1857) and has argued convincingly, contrary to Atwood's speculation, that it is not just the anthologised fairy tales that can be seen as "sexist" but that sexism operates consistently throughout the collection (168-71). Furthermore, whilst the passivity and lack of autonomy of the female characters is represented as "inevitable" and "natural," the "silliness" and naivety of the male character is invariably represented as a "lack" that it is the function of the fairy tale to correct. The female's lack of autonomy is part of what she is, the male's lack of autonomy is temporary and will be remedied in the course of the tale. Such double standards are operative on every level of the Grimms' tales. The girl is represented as a possession of the male character, passed on from father to prince and defined almost exclusively in terms of her appearance. The boy, however idiotic, is the one who sets out to forge his own destiny.

These critical ideas have generated, and in turn are generated by, a considerable body of re-written fairy tales in literature. In the 1970s and 1980s, a large number of anthologies, short story collections, poems and novels were published which attempted to change the gender representations on offer in traditional fairy tales and suggest new symbolic paradigms for identity construction. The fairy tale had rarely been so popular, but since many of these writings were predominantly critical of the traditional values expressed in the genre it was a kind of popularity through notoriety. This notoriety has led to a widespread belief that fairy tales are, in some way, inherently repressive. Andrea Dworkin, for instance, has argued that the fairy tale form is indigestible; that, given the role models it offers and the ideologies it encodes, women "never did have much of a chance" to escape from the gender stereotypes that confine them (33). Similarly, Patricia Duncker has argued, in response to Angela Carter's uses of fairy tale, that their "original structures" are straitjackets that it is impossible to escape from. "[T]he tale, especially the fairy tale," she writes,

> is the vessel of false knowledge, or more bluntly, interested propaganda . . . fairy tales are, in fact, about power, and about the struggle for possession, by fair or magical means, of kingdoms, goods, children, money, land, and—naturally, specifically,—the possession of women.
>
> ("Re-Imagining" 3-4)

The fact, however, that there were feminist writers such as Angela Carter attempting to reutilise fairy tales as early as the 1970s without necessarily having a hostile attitude towards them, has led, more recently, to several attempts at a critical reconsideration of the genre. Jack Zipes and Marina Warner, both directly influenced by Carter's work, have consistently argued that the fairy tale is not inherently antithetical to feminist concerns, but can, on the contrary, be used in a way that is positively empowering for women (Warner, *From the Beast* 193-97; Zipes, *Trials* xiii). This recuperation rests upon the realisation that it is not fairy tales in themselves that are pernicious, but the uses to which they have been put at specific historical moments, for specific sociopolitical reasons. Both Perrault and Grimm, in their respective periods, adapted traditional fairy tales considerably so that they would prove acceptable to the middle class, patriarchal households for which they wrote. They converted what was, effectively, a diverse and non-homogenous body of narratives into what Zipes has called "a type of literary discourse about mores, values and manners so that children would be civilised according to the social code of that time" (*Subversion* 3). This meant, of course, that these fairy tales found fruitful soil and flourished—becoming so ubiquitous that one commentator has even defined the fairy tale as "a story like the ones collected in the *Kinder und Hausmärchen* of the brothers Grimm" (A. Jolles qtd. in Gerhardt 277). But Perrault and Grimm, although they in practice comprise the western canon of fairy tale, do not represent the only examples of the genre available. Even as they were writing, in fact, a considerable body of narratives was being produced that were written by women, for women, and represented values that were antagonistic towards patriarchy. Just at the time when Grimms' tales were becoming firmly established in German culture, for instance—as Shawn Jarvis's research has shown—members of the Kaffeterkreis, a "female association" that was formed as a response to exclusive male literary cliques, were writing and collecting tales that were breaking open "the traditional parameters of the Märchen as found in the Grimms' collection." Jarvis writes:

> Grimm model females were passive, silent, industrious, and rewarded with riches and a man to support them, while male models were destined to seek out adventure and take as their reward passive, silent, industrious females. Kaffeter fairy tales reversed these roles and presented heroines who found happiness in being educated and single rather than married and brain dead.
>
> (106)

This type of women's storytelling, claims Jarvis, was prolific in France and Germany at this time but, because of its failure to agree with dominant ideologies, has been entirely excluded from the canon of the classical fairy tale. The same is true of Perrault's contemporaries. Before and after Perrault published his Contes de ma Mère L'Oye in 1697, his compatriot and fellow salon-writer Marie Catherine d'Aulnoy was publishing

tales that offer far more sprightly, active and intelligent role models for women. Again, however, because of "the canonical principles governing [the genre] . . . which [magnify] the male role while diminishing the female contribution" the tales "have hardly been received in critical literature." The fact that these tales did not make the dominant canon does not mean that they are not fairy tales. On the contrary, as Jarvis points out, the literary products of writers like Madame d'Aulnoy and Madame de Murat "actually constituted the genre of the contes de fées" (Jarvis 119).

In the stories of *The Bloody Chamber* (1979) Angela Carter shows a full awareness of this tension between the canonical and non-canonical and exploits it with interesting effects. On the surface, the fairy tales she is dealing with are the familiar ones that comprise the bulk of most anthologies. But there are moments, brief interruptions in her texts, in which the less common voices intrude. In the remainder of this essay I want to look at two instances of such intrusion, one in the short story **"The Courtship of Mr Lyon,"** one in the title story of the collection—**"The Bloody Chamber"**—in order to show how Carter employs these voices to subtly question the androcentric bias of her primary sources.

"THE WHITE CAT" AND "MR FOX"

It is generally accepted that the source of Carter's tale **"The Courtship of Mr Lyon"** is Jeanne-Marie Leprince de Beaumont's "La Belle et la Bête" published in 1757. This is the Beauty and the Beast story that most Europeans are familiar with, and Carter's story actually follows the plot very closely. It is interesting, however, that, although Carter's overt narrative source is de Beaumont's version, the one *direct* reference within the short story is to another writer of fairy stories altogether. This reference comes when Beauty, in **"Mr Lyon,"** [**"The Courtship of Mr Lyon"**] finds and begins to read "a collection of courtly and elegant French fairy tales about white cats who were transformed princesses and fairies who were birds" (*Bloody Chamber* 46). This passage refers *not* to a collection by de Beaumont, but to one of the several collections of tales by Marie Catherine d'Aulnoy published between 1696 and 1698, considerably earlier than either Villeneuve or de Beaumont, and pre-dating the time when these narratives were, as David Buchan puts it, "prettified and rewritten into children's fairy tales" (977). There are no attempts at facile moralising in the tales, courtly, elegant and mannered though they may be, the humour is fiercer and more bizarre, and the female characters are far more spirited and independent-minded than most of their generic kinsfolk.[1]

Jack Zipes, uncharacteristically insensitive to the universalising gesture, attempts to homogenise the canon of fairy tale by suggesting that d'Aulnoy was engaged in the same pursuit as Perrault, rewriting fairy tales so that they would conform to bourgeois patriarchal codes. All d'Aulnoy's fairy tales, he writes, "provide moral lessons, and the ones that involve Beauty and the Beast reiterate the message of Perrault's tales. The woman must be constantly chastened for her curiosity, unreliability and whimsy" (*Subversion* 37). He argues that particularly the d'Aulnoy tale entitled "The Ram" carries the message that "women must be placed under constant surveillance even when they are endowed with reason to temper their appetites" (36). A close reading of the tale, however, shows this criticism to be ill-considered and unjust. For "The Ram" is openly critical of attempts by a king to impose his patriarchal whim on an intelligent and active young woman, and shows how she escapes his tyranny, using her own wit and the loyalty of her companions, in order to discover a more just and equal society where she will not be coerced by violent and cruel male figures.

One of the particular d'Aulnoy tales that Beauty reads in **"The Courtship of Mr Lyon,"** "The White Cat," carries a similar message. The principal female character is presented a figure of considerable self-sufficiency: a "smart politician" who "since she never said anything but what she chose . . . never gave answers that did not wholly suit her" (d'Aulnoy 529), and when the prince arrives, it is she that actively assists him in fulfilling various tasks, whilst he himself does next to nothing. In the denouement, moreover, it is she that condescends to the king, rather than, as is more traditionally the case, the king condescending to her:

> The king . . . was so overcome by this wondrous appearance that he could not resist exclaiming, "Behold the incomparable beauty who deserves the crown!"
>
> "My liege," she announced, "I come not to deprive you of a throne you fill so worthily, for I was born heiress to six kingdoms. Permit me to offer one to you and one to each of your elder sons. . . ."
>
> (d'Aulnoy 544)

De Beaumont's story, Carter's apparent source, expounds a far more conservative moral than this. As Carter indicates elsewhere the French, eighteenth-century Beauty is designed more to "house-train the id" than to liberate it ("Beauty" [Review of *Beauty and the Beast: Visions and Revisions*] 124). She is a perfect example of how to be morally beautiful, modest, self-effacing, considerate, and of how to sacrifice oneself for the good of others. When her sisters are cruel to Beauty, for instance, de Beaumont shows us a self-martyring, self-deprecating character who is "so good that she loved and pardoned them with all her heart" (23, my trans.) and when her father tells her about his pact with the beast she is only too willing to sacrifice herself for his benefit.

This message—that a young woman must be prepared to reconcile herself to the beastliness of a husband if it improves her father's financial standing—is frequently cited as the principal message of all beauty and the beast myths—from Cupid and Psyche, through to the Disney musical on London's west-end. As the "Greatest Living Poet" explains to Salman Rushdie's narrator in *Shame*: "the classic fable *Beauty and the Beast* is simply the story of an arranged marriage" (158). The idea that this marriage is somehow essential to the tale is illusory, however, for the message of d'Aulnoy's beauty-beast tales is diametrically, and categorically, opposite. In "The White Cat," for example, when the trope appears as a sub-plot in which the fairies attempt to force the princess to marry King Migonnet, "a frightful monkey" who has "talons like an eagle" (d'Aulnoy 538, 539), d'Aulnoy gives the princess the right to thwart and confound the proposed union with the monster using all the means and ingenuity at her disposal. She tricks the fairies into letting her make a rope ladder, attempts to elope with a charming prince, and finally, when the prince is devoured by a dragon, elects to be transformed into a magic cat, rather than lose her liberty.

Rather than being a tale that upholds the patriarchal institution of arranged marriage, therefore, "The White Cat" operates more as a parable of feminine independence. It is this sleight of hand on Carter's part—the introduction of a tale that is radically opposed to enforced unions into the rewrite of one that is meant to recommend them—that is her most ingenious revisionary stroke, and constitutes a subtle subversion of de Beaumont's narrative. This subversion, furthermore, does not come from a source external to the fairy tale—Carter is not revising the fairy tale from outside. She is pitting fairy tale against fairy tale, using one variant to modify a later bowdlerised variant, and thus insisting that the fairy tale is wider, more diverse, less reactionary than is suggested by a reading of de Beaumont, Perrault, or Grimm alone.

This backward glance at d'Aulnoy's "White Cat" is not the only example of Carter using non-canonical sources to undermine the authority of more traditional variants. She also, I believe, indicates a subversive approach to Perrault's "Bluebeard" in her adaptation by selecting, as the title for the story, a phrase taken, not, as one might expect, from "Bluebeard" but from a more obscure English tale called "Mr Fox."

The phrase appears when the heroine of the tale, Lady Mary, has followed Mr Fox, her affianced, to his Manor, and witnesses him cutting off the hand of an unconscious victim in order to get her ring:

> Mr Fox cursed and swore and drew his sword, raised it, and brought it down upon the hand of the poor lady. The sword cut off the hand, which jumped up into the air, and fell of all places in the world into Lady Mary's

lap. Mr Fox looked about a bit, but did not think of looking behind the cask, so at last he went on dragging the young lady up the stairs into the Bloody Chamber.

(Carter, *Virago* [*The Virago Book of Fairy Tales*] 9)

"The Bloody Chamber," it is hardly necessary to add, not only appears in the first and last tales of Carter's collection, but also provides the title of the collection's longest tale and, consequently, the title of the work as a whole.[2] It is possible to argue, therefore, that, even though the tales are re-writings of canonical works such as Perrault, Grimm and de Beaumont, the actual inspiration for the whole, the actual model for the sort of fairy tale that Carter was trying to reproduce is, in fact, this alternative non-canonical source "Mr Fox." Carter wants to reproduce this kind of tale, I would further argue, because Lady Mary, the heroine, is not a victim, or a model of self-abnegation, but—as the title of the section in *The Virago Book of Fairy Tales* under which Carter later includes the tale suggests—is "brave, bold and wilful." When she is due to marry Mr Fox she persists in discovering his secret, ignoring all the blood-curdling injunctions warning her not to, and when all are assembled for the wedding she outwits Mr Fox, despite his cunningly ambiguous replies, by producing the severed hand as evidence.

Even if Lady Mary doesn't deal the actual death blow herself, and male companions must do the deed, she still reveals considerably more spirit than her French counterpart, Bluebeard's nameless wife. She does not tremble, become flustered or quaver, neither does she fling "herself at her husband's feet, weeping and begging his pardon" (Zipes, *Beauties* 33); instead, she is forthright, cunning and unruffled. Unlike Perrault's heroine, furthermore, she is not blamed in the "Moral" for the curiosity that led her to discover the tyrant's crime. Neither is Mr Fox, the violent man, the ogre, shown to have the moral upper hand: on the contrary, he is shown to be guilty of crimes against women, and Mary's bravery in putting a stop to these crimes is represented as something to be commended.

Although **"The Bloody Chamber"** is modelled, in narrative terms, upon Perrault's "Bluebeard," then, I would suggest that it also recalls, in its title, this more "feminist" source "Mr Fox" and that in the background of the tale, as an ironic comment, as a utopian suggestion, or even as a reminder of what fairy tale women can be, lurks the spirit of Lady Mary.

Jacqueline Simpson, in an essay from a volume of *Folklore* to which Carter later contributed, approaches "Mr Fox" in a very similar fashion. There are tales such as "Mr Fox," she argues, that have "spirited and inquisitive" [19] heroines, that should be used to encourage a revision of the "gloomy picture" [16] created by the feminist critique of fairy tales. Fairy tales, she goes on

to say, can only be assessed fully, in ideological terms, if examples "from outside the Perrault-Grimm canon, or even versions of the 'classic' ones drawn directly from oral tradition" [16] are also taken into account. Twelve years prior to the publication of this essay, in *The Bloody Chamber,* Carter is illustrating just this: there are tales which do not quite fit into the canon, tales which do not quite conform to Dworkin's stereotype of the "indigestible" tale, which can be used to regenerate the fairy tale tradition from within.

Angela Carter's use of both these tales—"The White Cat" and "Mr Fox"—provides evidence that the revisionary process that she engages in is not, solely, one of reaction; it is also one of remembering. She is not simply responding to the genre of fairy tales by rejecting canonical ones or creating radical new ones; she is reviving lost, forgotten, repressed fairy tales that have been excluded from the canon because they do not conform with its ideological biases.

Carter's use of fairy tales in this way makes it possible to identify a shift in the feminist appropriation of the fairy tale more generally; away from those critiques, such as Dworkin's, which involve an outright rejection of the mythologies of the past, towards a recognition that the politics of remembering mythologies can be just as potent, if not more potent, than the politics of erasing them. This recent rethinking of fairy tale can be neatly represented by Marina Warner's Reith Lectures, *Managing Monsters: Six Myths of our Time,* broadcast on BBC Radio in 1994. Her primary models for these lectures were—as she notes—"Roland Barthes's famous essays of 1957, *Mythologies,*" but her intention was to update Barthes' project for the 1990s (xiii). Warner thus begins by noting the validity of the fundamental principle of *Mythologies*: "that myths are not eternal verities, but historical compounds, which successfully conceal their own contingency, changes and transitoriness so that the story they tell looks as if it cannot be told otherwise" (xiii). But she develops Barthes' idea by going on to argue that

> myths are not always delusions, that deconstructing them does not necessarily mean wiping them, but that they can represent ways of making sense of universal matters, like sexual identity and family relations, and that they enjoy a more vigorous life than we perhaps acknowledge, and exert more of an inspiration and influence than we think.
>
> (xiii)

This reworking of Barthes seems to reflect the transformation in the way that creative writers are using the fairy tale in the manner initiated by Angela Carter. The primary aim is no longer to attack the fairy tale, demystifying it and forcibly revising it against the grain of the source, but to recuperate it, appropriating it as a genre that is broad enough and rich enough to be used as a powerful expression of identity in its own right. Whereas the previous model of the re-written fairy tale presents the source as an enchantment that has to be broken, a pernicious magic spell, the new approach recognises the fairy tale's capacity for enchantment and attempts to appropriate the mechanism for its own ends. If, in this pursuit, the agenda expressed in any given fairy tale seems unacceptable to the writer who is re-utilising it, the fictional procedure followed is not to blatantly contradict and demystify the enchantment, but to mobilise equally potent enchantments, that express different agendas, against it. "Replying to one story with another which unravels the former," as Marina Warner goes on to add, "has become central to contemporary thought and art" (4).

To be able to approach fairy tales in this way, as Cristina Bacchilega reminds us, is a privilege earned for us by deconstructive writers such as Dworkin and Duncker. "We fortunately do not need to reject fairy tales as inherently sexist narratives which offer 'narrow and damaging role-models for young readers,'" she says, because the work has already been done for us; and we are now free to "view the fairy tale as a powerful discourse" [9-10] that can be used to define and shape new kinds of gender identity. It was necessary to understand the limitations of fairy tale before it was possible to understand its potential; but now that those limitations *have* been understood it has become possible to recuperate the genre, and revivify the muted tradition. Angela Carter, I believe, exemplifies this approach to the fairy tale. She shows, on the one hand, how fairy tales have been used to express models of identity formation that exclude or marginalise other possibilities, and on the other, how fairy tales also exist that formulate powerful alternative conceptions of identity that are inclusive of difference and variation.

These observations on Carter's uses of fairy tale need not be limited to the field of fairy tale, or even to feminist literary criticism. Angela Carter's treatment of fairy tale, and the changing approach to "mythologies" that it reflects, can enable us to formulate an argument about the re-appropriation of discourses by writers and thinkers in much broader terms. In all cases of marginalisation, theorists with an interest in identity politics are finding that a key element in the suppression of one form of identity, or one way of life, is the suppression, the "forgetting," of voices that have represented that form of identity or way of life in the past. As a result, writers have realised that the most effective and powerful means of counteracting discrimination lie not only in an abandonment of the past, and a commitment to make things new, but also in a desire to remember the past, and to recall the "voices" that have been submerged and suppressed because they did not conform to dominant ideas of what is normal or acceptable. This is the case in many different disciplines—not just in literature—but also in the study of history, or the study of languages; and it has been used to offer alternative forms of identity in many different contexts—whether it be identity related to class, gender, race or sexuality. In conclusion then, and in confirmation of this idea, I would like to end with a quotation from David Palumbo-Liu, discussing the ideological importance of memory from an entirely different perspective: the historical memory of the ethnic subject. "The ethnic narrative presents an occasion for a subversive revision of the dominant version of history," writes Palumbo-Liu,

> it gives voice to a text muted by dominant historical referents; and it makes possible an imaginative invention of a self beyond the limits of the historical representations available to the ethnic subject . . . [I]t is through memory alone, as the repository of things left out of history, that the ethnic subject can challenge history.

(211)

Notes

1. For a more detailed discussion of d'Aulnoy's tales see Warner, *Beast* 284-91.

2. That Carter was already familiar with "Mr Fox" at the time of writing "The Bloody Chamber" is evident from her use of the tale in *The Magic Toyshop* (1967). Melanie, exploring her uncle's house, wonders whether it is "Bluebeard's castle" or "Mr Fox's manor house" with "'Be bold, be bold but not too bold' written up over every lintel and chopped up corpses neatly piled in all the wardrobes" (83). Having read "Mr Fox" it also becomes apparent where the hand that Melanie finds in the knife drawer comes from. It is the hand, with ring, that Mr Fox severs off in the quotation above. The hand, soft, plump and tidy, clearly symbolises Melanie's old adolescent self, now mutilated by Uncle Philip, a twentieth century version of the fairy tale tyrant.

Works Cited

Atwood, Margaret. "Grimms' Remembered." Haase 290-92.

Aulnoy, Marie Catherine d'. "The White Cat." *Beauties, Beasts and Enchantments: Classic French Fairy Tales.* Ed. Jack Zipes. London: Meridian, 1991. 515-44.

Bacchilega, Cristina. *Postmodern Fairy Tales: Gender and Narrative Strategies.* Philadelphia: U of Pennsylvania P, 1997.

Barthes, Roland. *Mythologies.* Trans. Annette Lavers. London: Paladin, 1973.

Beaumont, Mme. Leprince de. *Les Contes de Fées.* Paris: Librairie Centrale, 1865.

Bottigheimer, Ruth B. *Grimms' Bad Girls and Bold Boys: The Moral and Social Vision of the Tales.* New Haven: Yale UP, 1987.

Buchan, David. "Folk Literature." *Encyclopedia of Literature and Criticism.* Ed. Martin Coyle et al. London: Routledge, 1990. 976-90.

Carter, Angela. Rev. of *Beauty and the Beast: Visions and Revisions of an Old Tale,* by Betsy Hearne. *Folklore* 102.1 (1991): 123-24.

———. *The Bloody Chamber.* 1979. London: Penguin, 1981.

———. *The Magic Toyshop.* 1967. London: Virago, 1981.

———. ed. *The Virago Book of Fairy Tales.* London: Virago, 1990.

Duncker, Patricia. "Re-Imagining the Fairy Tales: Angela Carter's Bloody Chambers." *Literature and History* 10.1 (1984): 3-14.

———. *Sisters and Strangers: An Introduction to Contemporary Feminist Fiction.* Oxford: Blackwell, 1992.

Dworkin, Andrea. *Woman Hating.* New York: Dutton, 1974.

Gerhardt, Mia I. *The Art of Storytelling: A Literary Study of the Thousand and One Nights.* Leiden: Brill, 1963.

Haase, Donald, ed. *The Reception of Grimms' Fairy Tales: Responses, Reactions, Revisions.* Detroit: Wayne State UP, 1993.

Jarvis, Shawn. "Trivial Pursuit?: Women Deconstructing the Grimmian Model in the 'Kaffeterkreis.'" Haase 102-26.

Palumbo-Liu, David. "The Politics of Memory: Remembering History in Alice Walker and Joy Kogawa." *Memory and Cultural Politics.* Ed. Amritjit Singh, Joseph T. Skerrett, and Robert E. Hogan. Boston: Northeastern UP, 1996. 211-26.

Rushdie, Salman. *Shame.* 1983. London: Picador, 1984.

Simpson, Jacqueline. "'Be Bold, But not too Bold': Female Courage in some British and Scandinavian Legends." *Folklore* 102.1 (1991): 16-30.

Stone, Kay. "Things Walt Disney Never Told Us." *Women and Folklore.* Ed. Claire R. Farrer. Austin: U of Texas P, 1975. 42-50.

Tatar, Maria. *The Hard Facts of the Grimms' Fairy Tales.* Princeton: Princeton UP, 1987.

Warner, Marina. *From the Beast to the Blonde: On Fairy Tales and Their Tellers.* London: Vintage, 1995.

———. *Managing Monsters: Six Myths of Our Time.* The Reith Lectures. London: Vintage, 1994.

Zipes, Jack, ed. and trans. *Beauties, Beasts and Enchantments: Classic French Fairy Tales.* London: Meridian, 1991.

———, ed. and trans. *The Complete Fairy Tales of the Brothers Grimm.* New York: Bantam, 1987.

———. *Fairy Tales and the Art of Subversion: The Classical Genre for Children and the Process of Civilisation.* London: Heinemann, 1983.

———. *The Trials and Tribulations of Little Red Riding Hood.* 2nd ed. New York: Routledge, 1993.

Soman Chainani (essay date 2003)

SOURCE: Chainani, Soman. "Sadeian Tragedy: The Politics of Content Revision in Angela Carter's 'Snow Child.'" *Marvels & Tales* 17, no. 2 (2003): 212-35.

[*In the following essay, Chainani concentrates on the narrative significance of the wicked woman figure in "The Snow Child" and the Snow White fairy tale, illustrating how in each the villainess both determines and completes the cultural context for the heroine's self-realization.*]

After considering archetypal representations of women in her study *The Feminine in Fairy Tales,* M. L. von Franz concludes: "With women it is important to go into things in detail, to see, for instance, how and where a misunderstanding began, for this is frequently caused by a lack of clarity" (156). And yet, it would seem that clarity is a distinctive feature of the fairy-tale genre. The genre has a clearly defined canon; any reference instantly conjures images of "classic" stories like "Snow White," "Cinderella," and "Red Riding Hood." In the analyses of narratological critics, the array of versions and variations is streamlined into a simple sequence of motifs, fragments, and stereotypes—poisoned apples, fairy godmothers, resuscitating kisses. The prose style of fairy tales is one of clear and "artless simplicity" (Tatar xi). And the archetypes of the genre—the innocent heroine, the charming prince, the terrorizing witch—offer clearly drawn, unnuanced gender roles. But Cristina Bacchilega considers the ideological dimension of this clarity fundamental to the genre's façade and a trap for the complacent reader: "What distinguishes the tale of magic or fairy tale as a genre [. . .] is its effort to conceal its work systematically—to naturalize its artifice, to make everything so clear that it works magic, no questions asked" (8). By relentlessly questioning, deconstructing, and posing alternatives to this "naturalized artifice," postmodern fairy tales rigorously hold these transparent stories up to the light.

Two kinds of compositional choices determine the relationship of a postmodern revision to its fairy-tale original. First, the original stories can either be replicated for effect or completely disassembled. For instance, a postmodern revision might stay within the boundaries of the familiar plot but filter the story through an ironic narrator; or it might reconceive the storyline, developing a "backstory" for the villain or divulging the real ending to the original tale, beyond the "happily ever after." Second, these postmodern stories arrive in a variety of forms—a revised fairy tale, a poem, a novel, a play, even a film or television series. Even so, the few critical studies of the postmodern fairy-tale genre gloss over these differences and isolate the portrayal of the heroine as the key to evaluating these revisions. Cristina Bacchilega's *Postmodern Fairy Tales* does a remarkable job of laying out the issues at stake for the genre, but her close readings privilege the heroine archetype. Her analysis of the postmodern Snow White stories, for instance, forgoes a discussion of the revised stepmother figure and generalizes: "Snow White is a constructed child woman whose snow-white features and attitudes are assumed to conform to nature in a powerfully metaphoric way [. . .] Postmodern revisions of 'Snow White' acknowledge the power that such a metaphor has had" (Bacchilega 35). Jack Zipes also sees the heroine's archetypal development at the center of these tellings; of Anne Sexton's *Transformations,* he concludes, "Each one of Sexton's transformed fairy tales is a foreboding of that fate which awaits the young woman as she matures" (21). If all the other revisions to content and form in a given postmodern tale are interpreted in the context of the heroine's discovery, then not only do we lack the full context to evaluate whether the new story revises the passive/good, active/evil female archetypes, but we also presume that only the heroine's "self-definition determines the plot" (Zipes 14). Moreover, this type of interpretation fails to question the active/evil association, leaving the villainess archetype intact. As a result, the "self-defining" heroine does not "reconstruct sexual arrangements and aesthetics," but rather inverts the archetypal schema—the conventionally passive woman, the heroine, now claims the "active" role (Zipes 11).

Angela Carter's short story **"Snow Child"** gives us the opportunity to address the glossed-over divergences in form and content and incomplete conclusions of heroine-focused analyses. In close-reading her revision of the Snow White tale, this study combines two analytic approaches. First, I propose that we approach this story—and indeed all postmodern tales—not by isolating the heroine's self-creation and new course of development, but rather by focusing on the figure of the wicked woman and the revised account of her motivations. If we begin by evaluating the author's explanation for the villainess' downfall in the source tales, then we can position the heroine's self-realization in this context and determine what allows her to succeed. Is the villainess wicked because she fails to see the alternatives to patriarchy and thus comes to serve it? How

does the heroine come to pursue these potential alternatives? Another reason for concentrating on the wicked woman involves the fact that evil is given more room for interpretation of character in the original stories. These perverse women not only embody the seven deadly sins (like the gluttonous witch in "Hansel and Gretel" or the envious Queen in "Snow White"), but they also project sexual deviance (like the grotesquely sensual witch in "The Little Mermaid" or the possessive crone in "Rapunzel"). But why is evil associated with sexual deviance? Do the postmodern authors disavow this perversity or do they connect deviance with the subversion of patriarchy? Finally, whereas the heroine remains stagnant across the original stories, the wicked woman is a product of both content *and* form. Devoid of agency, the heroine waits for the evil woman's temptation, waits to be rescued, and waits to be rewarded. The villainess, meanwhile, determines the thrust of the original storylines and tends to account for most of the variation in the multiplicity of versions for each tale type. Thus, the form and content revisions of the postmodern story should be viewed not only in terms of the heroine's role reversal, but also as functions of the villainess's explained motivations and particular brand of evil.

Second, we will look closely at the model of revision for **"Snow Child"** as a way of understanding the complications between form and content that (re)writers must reconcile. Though Carter's story retains the fairy-tale form, it attempts to revamp the content to suggest a new context for understanding the rivalry between stepmother and child. But can the "classic" fairy-tale structure support the weight of a self-conscious revision? Or more tellingly, can it disguise its subtext so as to still appear that it "works magic"?

WHAT A STEPMOTHER WANTS: A SNOW WHITE PRIMER

Magic mirrors that cannot lie. Juicy red apples drenched in poison. The hapless ebony-haired maiden darting through a haunted forest. The resuscitating kiss of a handsome prince. Reproduced almost recklessly in popular culture, these are the images that we have readily come to associate with the "definitive" tale of Snow White. Yet, the popularization of this particular narrative and the imprinting of these motifs in our cultural consciousness is ironic considering that the Snow White story has perhaps the most historical variations and incarnations of any fairy tale. Indeed, the 1937 Disney film which has become so inescapable is itself a pastiche of different versions—versions of the rivalry between a young girl and her (step)mother, scattered over time, continents, languages, and cultures. As expected, the monstrous female drives most of this variation. In 'The Young Slave," one of the earliest versions of Snow White, the evil aunt eschews mirrors for simple intuition; she pummels her young niece into submission after suspecting her of sleeping with her husband. In a Spanish variation, the queen does not ask the hunter for the girl's heart, but rather a bottle of blood stoppered with the girl's toe. In the Gaelic "Lasair Gheug," the queen is spurred to action by a second villainess, a malicious old woman who warns of her daughter's plans to steal her inheritance. The Disney film has the heroine poisoned by an apple, but other versions favor toxic corsets, combs, cakes, and braids (Tatar 74). With the overwhelming number of variations in the relationship of the wicked woman and her young rival, folklorists have tried valiantly to include Snow White in the collection of episodic "tale types," which define each collective myth in terms of sequential plot moments. But whereas other fairy tales might see their versions fall neatly into structural analyses like the Aarne-Thompson index, the Snow White story has always been problematic; its consistency comes not from a common set of images or motifs in the tale, but rather from a stable thematic core. Indeed, the essence of Snow White cannot be diluted into motifs like mirrors, apples, or dwarves because its cultural staying power comes from its place as the prototypal story of female jealousy. With this understanding of Snow White's significance, Angela Carter believes that a successful retelling delicately re-imagines the story's content while preserving the boundaries of a form that led to such remarkable narrative stability.

Suggesting that the anomaly of Snow White calls for a new and less stringent form of folktale classification, Steven Swann Jones believes current typologies unsuitable because they not only dilute the plethora of variations, but also ignore the significance of the fairy tale's thematic core. In the particular case of Snow White, the Aarne-Thompson index privileges details of imagery over fundamental themes, implying that "motifs such as red as blood/white as snow, the magic mirror, the compassionate executioner, the dwarfs, the poisoned lace, comb, and apple, the glass coffin, and the red hot shoes are a crucial part of the narrative. This is generally not the case—there are versions that include none of these motifs" (Jones 22). Moreover, the AT index for Snow White remains incomplete because it relies on a listing of specific motifs; thus some versions are not included in the resulting taxonomy, while other variations have some of their most crucial episodes ignored. To refine the Aarne-Thompson system, Swann Jones identifies nine "essential dramatic events common to different versions of this narrative: origin, jealousy, expulsion, adoption, renewed jealousy, death, exhibition, resuscitation, and resolution" (22). Jones' approach is less a taxonomic system than a broad narrative typology meant to "show us the heart of the folktale operating beneath its abundant corpus of versions" (38). In order for this modified typological description to have significance, then, he must successfully isolate this "heart" as

the thematic core around which the nine dramatic moments revolve. Indeed, only by making this final extrapolation, suggests Maria Tatar, can Swann Jones actually account for the "staying power of this cultural story" (74). Unfortunately, Swann Jones' cautious hypothesis is not only vague, but also appears grounded outside the text: "What we find in our overall assessment of the broad range of versions of 'Snow White' is that this folktale essentially traces a child's personal development and that the tale acts as a kind of psychological and sociological primer, a basic childhood text, designed to anticipate and alleviate anxieties, fears, and difficulties that typically accompany the complex process of maturation" (38-39). Because Jones not only sees "a child's personal development" at the heart of the fairy tale, but also focuses on the story's therapeutic role in this development instead of its potential to *heighten* childhood anxieties, the nine episodes he outlines in his typology are appropriately skewed towards the heroine's point of view. Furthermore, if Snow White occupies the center of all these stories, then his typology reduces the villainess to nothing more than a narrative device for this "complex process of maturation," a stock agent that deserves no typology of her own. But if the wicked woman drives most of the variation in the Snow White tale type, can we ignore the possibility that she might, in fact, be the true center of the narrative—or more plausibly, a divergent center that merits equal attention to psychology?

Dispensing with the typologies in favor of a general explanation for the myth's narrative stability, Sandra Gilbert and Susan Gubar argue that the fairy tale should actually be entitled "Snow White and Her Wicked Stepmother" since the "central action of the tale—indeed, its only real action—arises from the relationship between these two women" (36). In addition to the plotline conflict that has the stepmother relentlessly persecute and ultimately issue a death warrant for the heroine, the Snow White tale type relies on textual binaries in their female-female relationship: "the one fair, young, pale, the other just as fair, but older, fiercer; the one a daughter, the other a mother; the one sweet, ignorant passive, the other both artful and active; the one a sort of angel, the other an undeniable witch" (Gilbert and Gubar 36). Yet, the existence of these oppositions cannot itself explain the stepmother's vehement hatred of her stepdaughter; as a result, folklorists consistently locate the queen's motivation outside the text. The most popular rationale for the conflict is "that the mother is as threatened by her daughter's 'budding sexuality' as the daughter is by the mother's 'possession' of the father," but this collapses once we consider "the depth and ferocity of the Queen's rage" (Gilbert and Gubar 39). Bettleheim declares that "it is reasonable to assume that it is competition for [the father] which sets mother against daughter," even though the father/king is, for all intents and purposes, *absent* from the story (203). Gilbert and Gubar propose that the relationship between a stepmother and stepdaughter is doomed because "female bonding is extraordinarily difficult in patriarchy: women almost inevitably turn against women because the voice of the looking glass sets them against each other" (39). Yet, why then are many Snow White versions conspicuously devoid of this patriarchal "voice of the looking glass"? The mirror might have become a catch-all patriarchal voice of judgment in many critics' eyes, but if we accept this vague, transcultural notion of patriarchy, we will lose sight of the context that will be crucial in rewriting the tales. Judith Butler cautions: "The very notion of 'patriarchy' has threatened to become a universalizing concept that overrides or reduces distinct articulations of gender asymmetry in different cultural contexts" (*Gender* 9). Instead of blindly accepting entrenched patriarchy as key to understanding the Queen's motivation, we should consider another suggestion by Gilbert and Gubar—namely, that the Queen is marked by an intense desperation that produces ritualized acts of self-absorption. The two feminists critics conclude: "Innocent, passive and self-lessly free of the mirror madness that consumes the Queen, Snow White represents the ideal of renunciation that the Queen has already renounced at the beginning of the story—free of the mirror, innocent, passive. Thus, Snow White is destined to replace the Queen because the Queen hates her, rather than vice versa. The Queen's hatred of Snow White, in other words, exists before the looking glass has provided an obvious reason for the hatred" (39-40). But this hypothesis is also fatally grounded outside the text. Gilbert and Gubar argue at once that the hatred preexists the story, and yet the ultimate significance of this hatred will manifest itself in Snow White's replacement of the Queen *after* the story ends. This "ideal of renunciation" is a comforting but unsatisfactory etiology since it demands further justification: without a source for her own self-hatred, the Queen's dementia remains unexplained.

For Angela Carter, revision provides an opportunity to ground the stepmother's hatred in a larger social context. From the outset, Carter does not reject the fairy-tale form itself as incapable of sustaining this context. Her first step involves finding a version of Snow White that eschews all the popularized, supposedly indispensable elements of the tale (i.e. the mirror, the apple, the prince) in order to reclaim the story's original meaning—a meaning about which Gilbert and Gubar could venture speculation but could not precisely locate in the Grimms' published version. Carter's **"Snow Child"** is inspired by one of the many Snow White stories that the Grimms collected but never chose to print. This version portrays the young girl's birth in terms of the *father*'s desire. Instead of the mother pleading for a daughter before her death, a count is the agent of creation in this story; he and his wife are traveling by sled when they pass three mounds of snow, three pools of

blood and three ravens. The count wishes aloud for a daughter made of these three colors and they immediately come upon a girl who fits the description. The count then takes her into the sled but it is quite clear from the outset that the countess is not particularly fond of the girl. She drops her glove and asks the snow child to get it. The driver is commanded to leave and the girl eventually makes her way to the home of the dwarves (Jones 12).

Motivated by the presence of the male arbitrator in this particular Grimms' version, Carter's revision of Snow White creates a complex triangle of desire between the father, mother, and child that fills in the gaps in Gilbert and Gubar's hypothesis. Indeed, once the stepmother and young girl are engaged in a battle for the count's affection, Carter can rewrite Snow White's conclusion, dispensing with dwarves, princes, and resuscitating kisses in order to produce a socially engaged story that maintains the ritualized action of the fairy-tale form, but also has an eye to the ultimate significance of the female-female rivalry.

DEATHLY EROTIC: CARTER'S MODEL OF REVISION

After deciding on a version that can potentially achieve the level of social critique, Carter's next step is to build a model of revision which functions within the structural parameters of the fairy-tale form. Because most of the stories in *The Bloody Chamber* are inspired by the same genre, critical analyses of the anthology tend to generalize interpretation in order to locate a single purpose of revision. Most of these generalized explanations try to identify a common feminist goal in the stories; Merja Mankinen believes that the tales systematically eradicate all traces of misogyny from the originals, while Robert Clark criticizes Carter for not fulfilling "feminist definitions based upon a radical deconstruction and reconstruction of women's history" (Mankinen 5; Clark 158). Other critics attempt to group the stories on the basis of common structural features. Patricia Duncker, for instance, faults the anthology for "rewriting the stories within the strait-jacket of their original structures" (6). Because these types of interpretations "lay a grid across [Carter's] work" and "read off meaning from it," **"Snow Child"** has been lumped together with the other stories as an example of "Carter rewrit[ing] fairy tales from a feminist perspective" (Benson 38, 41). Indeed, even though each story in *The Bloody Chamber* has its own system of revision, **"Snow Child"** stands apart because of two crucial differences in form and context.

Unique in form among the stories in *The Bloody Chamber*, **"Snow Child"** retains and even exaggerates the fairy-tale milieu. By contrast, the rest of the anthology's selections all rely on a hybridization of forms where the "fairy tale mixes with other fantasy modes (gothic, romantic)" to give Carter space for using style as a transformative strategy (Fowl 71). We can explain the apparent incompleteness of revision in **"Snow Child"** by analyzing the revised villainess in the context of the companion work to *The Bloody Chamber*—Carter's own *The Sadeian Woman,* published in the same year. To see *The Bloody Chamber* as a collection of feminist fairy tales is to ignore the other half of Carter's source material. During the 1970s, Carter had been re-reading fairy tales and Sade in tandem; thus, her essay on Sade provides "the prime historical and critical context within which the tale collection has subsequently been read" (Benson 30). Though Carter believes Sade complicates the reductionism of pornographic archetypes, she still sees a fundamental connection between fairy tales and the Marquis's work. In its simplest form, Justine is a "black inverted fairy-tale" while Sade's larger body of work often resonates with the "black and white ethical world of fairy tale and fable" (Benson 30). The clearest link between the two genres appears in Carter's "polemical preface" which condemns portrayals of women that reinforce sexual archetypes because each new portrayal "denies, or doesn't have time for, or can't find room for, or, because of its underlying ideology, ignores the social context in which sexual activity takes place, that modifies the very nature of that activity. Therefore pornography must always have the false simplicity of fable" (*Sadeian* [*The Sadeian Woman*] 16). If pornography and fairy tales do not "have time for, or can't find room for" true social context, how can the story operate within the confines of the fairy-tale form and still propose a legitimate context for the stepmother's psychology?

The second major difference between **"Snow Child"** and the other stories in *The Bloody Chamber* involves the form in which revised content serves as feminist critique of the original plot. **"The Bloody Chamber"** re-imagines the Bluebeard tale as a gothic romance and female revenge story, the Beauty and the Beast revisions suggest an animalistic rebirth for the passive heroine, and **"The Company of Wolves"** envisions an explosive carnal relationship between Red Riding Hood and the Wolf. **"Snow Child,"** however, empowers neither the heroine nor the villainess and instead simply depicts the power imbalance of the patriarchal status quo. If Gilbert and Gubar lack the textual basis to explain the stepmother's hatred, then Carter brings back the absent King/father figure to imply that an unflinching depiction of current sexual relations provides sufficient context for a meaningful revision of the original story. But what is the significance of this replication of the status quo within the confines of the fairy-tale form? According to Stephen Benson, this technique brings up a fundamental question involving the aforementioned link between pornography and fairy tales and the status of female representation: "It was around this subject [pornography] that conflicting camps of feminist thought arranged themselves in the late 1970s and 1980s [. . .]. [W]hile it was accepted that pornography reflected a sort of distilled essence of the entrenched binaries of patriarchal gender relations, the conflict revolved around the extent to which pornographic representations could be appropriated as a critique of the status quo and as a medium for the speculative imagining of alternatives. Thus the debate was, and to an extent still is, a test case for a conception of feminism and feminist cultural production and given that fairy tales underwent a concerted feminist critique in the 1970s, the parallels are self-evident" (30). With **"Snow Child,"** Carter herself produces a test case for this debate. Not only is **"Snow Child"** operating within the fairy-tale framework that "underwent a concerted feminist critique," but it also employs pornographic representations as a critique of the status quo. But if neither form nor content carries an explicit critique, can fairy tales, "as traditionally miniature carriers of a conservative ideology of gender be appropriated to critique, and imagine alternatives to, traditional conceptions of gender" given the history of their role in entrenching these traditions (Benson 30)? Just as we embark on our analysis of **"Snow Child,"** we realize that the shortest story in Carter's anthology s the key to understanding the relationship between fairy-tale form and content. Built into this harsh, simple fable is a dangerously subversive experiment testing the limits of appropriation.

We can best understand Carter's methodology of revision if we consider her rewrites in terms of a two-part model: an "above-ground" text and an "underground" motivating subtext. In most of the stories in the anthology, the above ground text reproduces the set pieces and character interactions of the *pornographic,* not the fairy-tale, genre. Carter reduces the original stories to a set of themes that inspire these new sexual fantasies; indeed, the fairy-tale milieu and themes ultimately become inconsequential because the homogeneity of those stories is replaced with a "style of literary telling [. . .] which disrupts any suggestion of genetic purity" (Benson 37). The purpose of the underground subtext is to expose this above—ground fantasy as a façade. In order to rupture the "sexy, tricky, surface gloss and shimmer" of the new plotline, the subtext must swell the narrative from below and deny a "straight-forward engagement of the [reader] at a non-intellectual level" (Benson 15). This model thus inverts the more common narrative that has its intellectual/rational content on the surface and the mythical/sexual subtext beneath it. If the actual text of the stories is dominated by enticing pornographic archetypes, how can the undercurrent engage the reader "intellectually"?

In *The Sadeian Woman,* Carter condemns pornography for subsisting on the same false universals that Jack Zipes discovers at the heart of the fairy-tale genre (Zipes

19). Produced by men for male audiences, pornography "denies the social fact of reality" because it "serves to defuse the explosive potential of all sexuality"; Carter decries pornography as one of the great bastions of repression since it continues to keep "sex in its place" outside "everyday human intercourse" (*Sadeian* 18). Though revising pornography to reflect the social context in which sex actually operates might seem like a Sisyphian task, Carter ventures a practical solution: because sexuality is at its heart a "social fact," it will "change its nature according to changes in social conditions. If we could restore the context of the world to the embraces of these shadows then, perhaps, we could utilize their activities to obtain a fresh perception of the world and, in some sense, transform it" (17). When the act of sexual intercourse is juxtaposed against the realities of patriarchal authority, then it is expelled from "the kitsch area of timeless, placeless fantasy and into the real world [where] it loses its function of safety valve" (18).

To make pornography "moral," or responsible in its reflection of true sexual relations, the pornographer replicates the "techniques of real literature, of real art" in accordance with the theory that "art disinfects eroticism of its latent subversiveness, and pornography that is also art loses its shock and its magnetism, becomes 'safe'" (*Sadeian* 19). Accordingly, most of the revisions in Carter's anthology have the above-ground pornographic archetypes swimming in stylistic excess. As literary techniques like "plotting and characterization are used to shape the material" of fairy-tale inspired pornography and "comment on real relations in the real world," the reader eventually comes to a chasm between pleasure and justice because he "faces the moral contradictions inherent in real sexual encounters" (*Sadeian* 18). These moral contradictions slowly amass, swelling the erotic façade until the reader faces a climactic dilemma: "To opt for the world or to opt for the wet dream?" (*Sadeian* 18) Regardless of the path chosen, the text ruptures because flesh is demystified and the sexual act itself becomes a critique of "the real relations of man and his kind" (*Sadeian* 18).

"Snow Child," however, builds a different model because it never takes the first step of separating the fairy tale and pornographic milieus; the two genres coalesce so that the Snow White story becomes an erotic fable. The above-ground portion of the model, then, is an experimental, hybrid construction—a pornographic fairy tale that conjoins the stepmother and child in a triangle of desire. Thematically, the change of role from villainess to victim directly reflects Carter's source of inspiration for *The Sadeian Woman* since Sade's moral pornography consistently presents a schema where "male means tyrannous and female means martyrised" (24). Structurally, this above-ground hybrid construction comes together because both genres "rely on repeated motifs, multiple versions and inversions, and the hole in the text where the readers insert themselves" (*Sadeian* 56). This "hole in the text" refers to the power of both genres to elicit identification responses from the reader; fairy tales provoke an empathetic experience of the protagonist's anxieties while pornography "has a gap left in it on purpose so that the reader may, in imagination, step inside it" (*Sadeian* 14). In all the other stories, Carter swells the pornography and the reader's ejaculatory experience with the didactic quality and "stamp of elitist culture" that accompanies "real art" (*Sadeian* 19). Now that the hybrid construction relies on the false simplicity of a fable and the ability of sexual archetypes to reproduce Sade's schema of gender relations, what runs beneath the text as the complicating undercurrent?

To explain the "psychology" of Snow White, N. J. Girardot suggests that the young girl makes the "necessary move from the egocentric self-love of the child to the other directed love" required for marriage (280). Judith Brown, meanwhile, asserts that Snow White endures the "conflict of social identity" that comes from childhood identification with the mother (843). And Sheldon Cashdan sees the heroine's maturation as a product of "normal apprehensions about abandonment" (42). Certainly more than other fairy tales, Snow White has spawned a substantial range of theories determined to explain the central character's psychological development. Since most of these interpretations focus on the education of the heroine in the published Grimms' story, Bruno Bettleheim argues that the version Carter chooses to retell is unique because of its psychoanalytic implications for the villainess; in positioning the mother as the determining figure in the father-daughter, the "oedipal desires of a father and daughter, and how these arouse the mother's jealousy which makes her wish to get rid of the daughter, are much more clearly stated here than in more common versions" (200). While the other stories in *The Bloody Chamber* forego development of the fairy tales' concealed subtexts in favor of the productive complication of literariness, **"Snow Child"** "forces these ideas into our consciousness" by exploring the psychological potential of Sade's women—Justine and Juliette—in relation to the stepmother-daughter conflict (*Sadeian* 200). In other words, rather than simply replicating Sade's stylistic methodology in her own pornographic stories (as stated before, the fairy-tale sources becomes inconsequential to this methodology), now Carter must refine and then apply Sade's psychoanalytic subtext to a pornographic fairy tale. This final piece of the model makes Carter's experiment all the more daring—the same psychoanalytic approach that has not only produced wildly disparate interpretations of character psychology but also has been associated almost exclusively with the heroine must now both reposition the villainess as the story's center and appropriate Sade's archetypal women in order to suggest potential feminist recourse. Success, says

Helene Cixous, would mean straddling the razor-thin boundary between mourning and laughter. Once a monolithic story like Snow White has been exposed for what it is and "tears are shed" for the tragic Sadeian women, there will be "endless laughter instead. Laughter that breaks out, overflows, humor no one would expect to find in women—because it's a humor that sees man much further away than he has ever been" (Cixous 54).

We need not concern ourselves with the tediousness of the debate over the inherent validity of Freudian theory since Carter's model lets us concentrate on a specific theoretical complication: Just as literary techniques problematized pornography, how can psychoanalysis illuminate the false universals of fairy tales? More specifically, how can psychological subtext modify the Justine/Juliette relationship to force the reader into a similar confrontation with the "moral contradictions inherent in real sexual encounters" (*Sadeian* 19)? This question becomes more troublesome when we consider that the most prevalent form of psychoanalytic subtext is wholly inadequate for this purpose. According to Shoshana Feldman, this common subtext systematically conceals its work by making "sexuality, valorized as both the foundation and the guidepost of the critical interpretation [. . .] the *answer* to the *question* of the text" (105). Sexuality can effectively lie *beneath* the text because "the question comes to be articulated only by virtue of the fact that the answer is as such *concealed*. Indeed, the question is itself but an answer in disguise: the question is the answer's hiding place" (Felman 105). Because the Freudian critic's job is "to pull the answer out of its hiding place—not so much to give an answer *to* the text as to answer *for* the text, it is only natural that virtually all the psychoanalytic readings of the classic Grimm version have isolated the heroine" (Felman 105, 117). Unlike the stepmother who must die because of her inability to develop, Snow White both survives her ordeal and is subject to the moralizing question, "What does she learn?" Because her psychology and sexuality can be evaluated in this framework, Snow White can occupy the center of the text and all the other characters/elements of the fairy tale can be interpreted in the context of her discovery. She effectively becomes the answer to the question of the text. Yet, because of the stability of this answer, the question becomes naggingly unspecific; our fundamental, motivating question of "What does the stepmother want?" can now be substituted with "What does Snow White want?" or virtually any other open-ended inquiry since the model of the heroine's development, the purported answer to the text, becomes a convenient metonym for the mother/daughter relationship. As a result, these readings tend to reduce both Snow White and the stepmother to archetypes that not only ignore the sexual context that Carter believes a psychoanalytic reading must expose in order to be productive, but also reinscribe the totalizing view of gender relations that Judith Butler warned would ultimately derail feminist appropriations. Girardot's psychoanalytic initiation theory encapsulates these problems. In evaluating the heroine's rite of passage, he perceives the stepmother "in functional terms as introducing the main problem to be dealt with by Snow White in her development [. . .]. The stepmother is the one that prompts a real life crisis for the child in that she is the one who represents the dangers of retarded development" (288). Instead of identifying the stepmother's own unique sexuality, this type of reading bundles up the villainess' motivation with the archetypal development of the heroine. Thus, the answer to the text does not change with context since the *question* of context is ultimately irrelevant. How can Carter's rendition avoid these false universals to produce a subtext swelling with ambiguity?

To evaluate the efficacy of this subtext in re-imagining social context for these revised Sadeian women, we must systematically uncover the answers hidden beneath the surface narrative. Almost like stage directions, Carter orients the reader with a descriptive fragment: "Midwinter—invincible, immaculate" (**"Snow Child"** 91). Most versions of Snow White begin with the birth of the heroine in midwinter, but Carter uses the setting here to create a *tabula rasa* for her revision of the child's origin. According to Girardot's theory of seasons, midwinter is "the transitional period in the cosmic round of the year; a period during the season of death but at the same time, the moment, marked ritually in many traditions, which turns toward the coming of spring and new life" (274). The words "invincible, immaculate" suggest both the qualities of the virgin child about to be born and the power of this moment between life and death. Not only is the canvas for the story literally blank ("Fresh snow fell on snow already fallen; when it ceased the whole world was white") but the use of the present tense to initiate the narrative action ("The Count and his wife go riding") also intensifies this effect (91). Against this white background, the two figures are introduced with immediate attention to color symbolism; the Count rides "on a grey mare and she on a black one, she wrapped in the glittering pelts of black foxes" (**"Snow Child"** 91). The Countess is the black antithesis of her white surroundings, the surroundings that will spawn a child of nature, while the Count represents the "grey" arbiter between these two extremes. In suggesting both the wild, animalistic aspects of human nature and the demeanor of a wily predator, the "pelts of black foxes" that adorn the Countess reinforce the classic image of the evil stepmother popularized by the published Grimms' story. Indeed, early on in her revision, Carter seems determined to perpetuate the archetypal rivalry. If the fox furs have the added effect of intimating sexual predation, then the Countess' "high, black shining boots with scarlet heels, and spurs" explicitly link her with the women of Sader Masoch and

Sade; she is positioned in the role of sadist before the masochist is even born (**"Snow Child"** 91). The Countess, it seems, is Sade's Juliette, the "sexual terrorist" who "acts according to the precepts and also the practice of a man's world and so she does not suffer. Instead, she causes suffering" (*Sadeian Woman* 79). As Juliette, the Countess must function in a "dialectical relationship" with a Justine figure since Sade's opposing heroines "mutually reflect and complement one another, like a pair of mirrors" (*Sadeian* 79). In the first departure from the traditional Grimm story, the Count—not the Countess—steps in to wish for this antithetical martyr: "I wish I had a child as white as snow" (91). Having the father utter these words instead of the mother creates a startling ambiguity absent from other versions since the word "had" acquires the doubled meaning of possession as a father and possession as a lover. Riding on, the couple comes to "a hole in the snow; this hole is filled with blood" (91). While in most versions the blood drops onto the snow when the mother pricks herself sewing, here it preexists the story without explanation and thus instantly rises to the level of abstraction. When the father wishes he "had a child as red as blood," not only is the word "had" ambiguous once more, but the impossibility of distinguishing between child and sex object is reinforced by our inability to attribute the blood to the symbolically dead mother or the deflowered child.

The black feather of the raven on the bough provides the third and final seed, but tellingly, the father, unlike the classic Grimm mother, does not have to die for Snow Child to come to life. The girl appears beside the road, "white skin, red mouth, black hair and stark naked" and in describing her, the narrator adds his first omniscient claim: "she was the child of his desire and the Countess hated her" (92). The statement deserves attention for several reasons. For one thing, the phrase "child of his desire" echoes the ambiguity of the word "had" in the wish constructions since it can refer either to the literal outcome of his three conditions or the manifestation of his lust for a young girl. Moreover, to use the conjunction "and" instead of "so" leaves open the possibility that the Countess' hatred preexists the appearance of the child (and indeed, even the Count's *desire* for the child). Born as a combination of human desire and nature's ingredients, the Snow Child is obviously not the product of a sexual union as in other versions that have the mother physically give birth to the girl before dying. Yet because the child is *only* the outcome of the father's desire, the Countess still retains the stepmother role. Indeed, the Count putting the girl on his saddle yields the exact same reaction that the Queen has after hearing the magic mirror's fateful words in the classic Grimm story: "How shall I be rid of her?" (92).

At this point in the story, then, we are faced again with the task of explaining the stepmother's inherent hatred for the father's child. But whereas before we had to settle for vague hypotheses like Gilbert and Gubar's, Carter's Sadeian subtext already gives us a new framework in which to evaluate the villainess' motivation. First, the spontaneous birth of Snow Child explicitly renders Sade's attitudes towards the physical mother. In *The Sadeian Woman,* Carter argues that Sade divorces sexuality from reproduction in order to "deny any significance to the activity of the physical mother beyond the fact of the ripening of the embryo in her body" (121). Because there is "no value in physical mothering at all," the relationship between mother and child—and to an even greater degree, stepmother and stepchild—is rooted in conflict: "The existence of the child is essential to the notion of motherhood but the child has had even less choice in the matter than its mother has. In this enforced and involuntary relationship, how can mother and child be anything but enemies?" (*Sadeian* 121) Moreover, this rivalry intensifies "when a girl child grasps the fact of her mother's passive acquiescence in her conception, and in, Freudian terms, realizes that her mother is castrated" (*Sadeian* 121). As a result, a female-female alliance against a male arbitrator will never take hold because both mother and child have only an artificial investment in each other and thus will instinctively compete for their own survival first.

As a second possibility, we can eliminate the Count from this triangular schema involving mother and child and position the Countess and Snow Child as Sadeian sisters in a binary, *complementary* relationship. Before her fateful midwinter ride, the Countess survives and prospers as an aristocrat because, like Juliette, she identifies her interests with the "hangman" in a country "where the hangman rules. The hangman is god, the king and the law itself; the hangman is the representative of a patriarchal order which is unjust not because such an order specifically oppresses women but because it is oppressive in itself" (*Sadeian* 99). When Snow Child appears in the role of the martyred Justine, however, the Countess must inhabit this role as hangman in order to execute her rival. Yet, why are Snow Child and the Countess rivals here if Justine and Juliette can successfully co-exist? According to Sade, the two sisters survive in the same world because they "mutually reflect and complement one another, like a pair of mirrors," both living examples of the reality that "the comfort of one class depends on the misery of another class" (*Sadeian* 78). Though both are subject to the patriarchal order, Juliette thrives because Justine exists; to avoid suffering a man's world, she *causes* suffering. However, when Snow Child and the Countess are forced into battle for the same male, these Justine and Juliette figures compete for the survival of their kind—one of the paired mirrors will shatter. Thus, the Countess assumes her role as sexual terrorist against the child martyr in a critical death match: "If Justine is a pawn because she is a woman, Juliette transforms herself from pawn to queen in a single move and henceforward goes wherever she pleases on the chess board" (*Sadeian* 79-80). In Carter's world, however, we must determine who makes the first move—and more importantly, who triumphs.

Just as in other versions of the tale, the Countess drops her glove in the snow and tells the child to look for it, fully intending to gallop off without her. From this point on, however, Carter substantially rewrites content in order to tell her particular story. This revision begins with the Count's intervention: "I'll buy you new gloves," he tells his wife, and with these words, "the furs sprang off the Countess' shoulders and twined round the naked girl" (92). The Count's first arbitration in the mother-child conflict is significant for three reasons. First, it disrupts the trajectory of the Justine-Juliette war. Because the Countess has carried herself as the Juliette figure that willingly trades status for sex, the Count attempts to buy her continued submission with the promise of new gloves. At the same time, he still has every intention of raping the virginal child. Ironically, then, the Count tries to keep both women in their archetypal roles just as they begin competing under the assumption that only one of them can survive. Second, the transferring of the furs brings up the issue of agency—who causes the Countess to lose her possessions? The possibility of the child wielding magical powers is inconsistent with the rest of the story and the Count surely is not responsible since his wife's loss of status undermines his attempts to keep both girls under control. More probable is the symbolic use of the trade-off to suggest the gradual reversal of roles in the struggle for survival; as the Count prevents his wife from terrorizing the martyr, the Countess degenerates into a martyr herself. Yet, there cannot be two Justines—and as such, the Snow Child acquires the symbolic furs of the sexual terrorist. Third, the Count's intervention begins the three-episode ritualized action that is a defining feature of the Snow White tale type. In the classic Grimm story, the stepmother visits the cottage in the woods three times. Even though it seems that the *last* thing she would want to give the child is greater beauty, the Queen's first two attempts to kill Snow White involve tempting her with beauty *accessories*—a suffocating corset, a poisoned comb; both times, the girl is saved by the timely arrival of the dwarves. On the third trip, the stepmother lures Snow White's senses with an apple—a simple product of nature—and a bite into the fruit effectively poisons the heroine. Though Carter might appear to be freely rewriting the heroine and villainess' fate once she departs from the plotline of the original, her revision faithfully retains the tripartite encounter between Snow White and the stepmother. Like the lace and the comb, the gloves and the diamond brooch threaten the heroine's life, but a male figure in-

tervenes. Only when the stepmother appeals to nature on the third attempt—in this case, she sees the murderous possibilities of a rose bush—can she avoid the meddling hand of an arbitrator: "'Pick me one,' said the Countess to the girl. 'I can't deny you that,' said the Count." The girl "picks a rose; pricks her finger on the thorn; bleeds; screams; falls" (92). Interestingly, though Carter is principally concerned with the stepmother's motivation and tells an especially brief fairy tale to emphasize this, she also clearly operates within the thematic structure of the Snow White tale type; **"Snow Child"** progresses through Steven Swann Jones's proposed sequence of origin, jealousy, expulsion, adoption, renewed jealousy, and death just like the popularized version that the Grimms chose to publish. But instead of a prince coming to the girl's rescue, the Count and the Countess alone are left to complete the myth's last three requirements—exhibition, resuscitation, and resolution (22).

Instead of the heroine being put on display to be claimed (and ultimately deflowered) by a passing prince, Carter's revised "exhibition" scene has the Count rape the dead child in front of his wife. After the girl collapses in the snow, the Count "got off his horse, unfastened his breeches and thrust his virile member into the dead girl"; we are not privy to the omniscient thoughts of the Countess, however, who "reined in her stamping mare and watched him narrowly" (92). Thus, the Count makes the final move to decide the metaphorical chess match between Justine and Juliette. Even though the Countess succeeds in destroying her rival, the Count will not relinquish possession of either body; he asserts his right to the ownership of the terrorized by deflowering her even after her suffering has supposedly ended, and he asserts his right to the ownership of the terrorist by making her watch the vile deed. The Count seems to have two different ways of defining a "wife"—as a subservient, loyal companion and as a disposable fantasy. Even when the two women play according to their own rules whereby one will survive and the other die, the chess match is ultimately determined by the "presence of the king, who remains the lord of the game"; when the queen calls check mate, the Count simply moves out of turn (*Sadeian* 79).

Snow Child begins to dissolve into her natural elements—the feather of the raven, a bloodstain "like the trace of a fox's kill on the snow," and the rose she had pulled off the bush (**"Snow Child"** 92). With the death and dissolution of the child, the Countess finds herself furred and booted once more as the "fox" that has vanquished her "kill." The Count, now heavy with postcoital languor, realizes he must win back the loyalty of his wife in order to ensure future sexual fulfillment; after eyeing the rose and picking it up, he "bowed and handed it to his wife" (92). By this point, however, the rose has lost its power as the romantic symbol *par ex-*

cellence. Ordinarily, a rose is inexhaustible as a symbol since it is an "irreplaceable literary device, that suggest[s] a direction, or a broad area of significance rather than, like an item in an allegorical narrative, a relatively determinate reference" (Abrams 184). But in **"Snow Child,"** the rose's symbolic power is stifled by the allegorical nature of the narrative. In attempting to reassert the romantic capability of the plucked rose after the child is raped, the Count effectively asks his wife to renew her position as his Juliette, as his sexual partner that trades intercourse for class benefits. But in hastily offering it to the Countess and in her acceptance of the gesture, neither of them recognize that the rose not only still carries the stigma of a murder weapon, but its symbolic power has been replaced with the allegorical, metonymic power of the martyred child. The countess drops the rose in shock: "It bites!" she exclaims (92).

In order for us to evaluate potential resolution, we can interpret this momentary "resuscitation" image in terms of three different frameworks for the Snow Child-Countess relationship. If we consider the two women as Sadeian sisters, the reinitiation of conflict exposes the futility, the sheer impossibility of Justine's death at the hands of Juliette. In killing her sister, the Countess tries to eradicate her mirror image, her natural "complement" (78). But by responding to the Count's bait and following this artificial rivalry to its violent end, the Countess reinforces the legitimacy of Justine's existence—the Snow Child is now the *ultimate* martyr. After all, Justine subsists on "a self-regarding female masochism," as "a woman with no place in the world, no status" (57). Yet, ironically, only in this suffering does she ever have a "sense of being," a sense of *why* she exists (74). And thus, when Snow Child/Justine finds herself pitted as the archetypal masochist against the Countess/Juliette as the archetypal sadist, the martyr awakens with a fleeting glimpse of transcendent power. To protect these archetypal roles, to effectively reset the conflict, she bites back—and the war resumes. Second, the relationship between the heroine and the villainess can be understood in terms of virgin-wife binaries. If Justine is the "holy virgin" and Juliette the "profane whore"/wife, then the rose can also represent the fatal power of the phallus—it can only kill the unstained (101). The Countess can survive the prick, the figurative "thrust," but the virgin cannot, and her stain is left against the snow as a symbol of the both metaphorical and literal deflowering. Third, the association of the rose with the *vagina dentata* motif recalls the Freudian conflict between mother and child discussed previously. Psychoanalytic theory explains the *vagina dentata,* or the vagina that "bites," as a motif that represents "the fear of castration inside the vagina" (Otero 269). This fear in a female child normally leads to the experience of "the castration complex" and the realization that "her only hope of happiness is to desire a baby from the father" (Otero 277). But sometimes "this transition does not go

smoothly" and penis envy causes intense anger. In literature, this resentment is expressed in "folkloric manifestations of the vagina dentata [that] represent the 'castrated' penis of a woman." Thus Snow Child "bites" her mother in a jealous rage, the "rage" that a woman feels in being born "castrated" (Otero 277).

Looking at Swann Jones' progression, **"Snow Child"** fulfills the first eight themes, but resolution is noticeably absent after the heroine's resuscitation. Indeed, all three interpretations of the Countess-child relationship suggest the artificiality of any conclusion to this parable. Returning to Gilbert and Gubar's motivating question, we now see how Carter's subtext illuminates the stepmother's hatred for the child as a natural consequence of the "lording" male's intervention—regardless of how direct or indirect this intervention actually is. With our account of Carter's model of revision in **"Snow Child"** complete, we can ask our last but most important question: How effective is this subtext in moving the fairy tale "out of the kitsch area of timeless placeless fantasy and into the real world" (*Sadeian* 19)?

FEMINISM AS TREASON: EVALUATING THE MODEL'S SUBTEXT

Carter's model for **"Snow Child"** attempts to deconstruct fairy-tale and pornographic archetypes simultaneously by tracing their origin to the same source. By exposing the surface falsity of both constructions, she can open up the possibility of revealing sexuality at an unconscious level, of creating a reading experience designed to replace pleasure with discomfort. Still, even if we accept the model as perfectly constructed, our close-reading of the subtext yields three problems with its functioning that prevent the reader from having a productive "moral dilemma" (*Sadeian* 19).

The first involves the objective of replacing the Snow White and stepmother archetypes with depictions of women that reflect "real relations in the real world" (*Sadeian* 19). In analyzing their relationship from the perspectives of sister-sister, wife-virgin, and mother-child, we have seen how the re-imagined subtext for the Snow White myth effectively complicates the universality of the good, passive heroine and evil, active villainess archetypes. The problem, however, is that instead of deconstructing these character templates, **"Snow Child"** substitutes them with three *more* archetypal relationships. Accepting the exchange of the (step)mother myth for the histories of Sade's sister characters, for instance, ignores the reality that Justine and Juliette are themselves reductive molds; as Susannah Kaeppler writes in *The Pornography of Representation*: "Sade's pornographic assault on one particular patriarchal representation of woman—the Mother—renders him, in the eyes of Carter, a provider of a service to women [. . .] Women, of course, neither produced nor sanctified the mothering aspect of their patriarchal representation, but it is doubtful whether they would thank Sade for replacing the myth of the Mother with that of the victim or the inverted sadist" (134). Kaeppler rightly points out that even if the mother's previously unexplained hatred for the child is framed in terms of Juliette's dialectical relationship with Justine, the "inverted sadist" to "victim" story offers no more of a challenge to patriarchal representation than the myth of the Mother. Attacking Kaeppler head on, Lorna Sage retorts: "She is wrong to suggest that Carter's Sade replaces Mother with her suffering and sadist daughters Justine and Juliette. All three, Carter argues, belong to the same mythology [. . .] it's Mother who makes her daughters this way, though this whole family of women is of course also formed by patriarchal society" (58). Besides ignoring the fact that the Mother must fit into either the Justine or Juliette role and consequently either mold or destroy her daughter, Sage's response fails to see the larger significance of Kaeppler's case—that regardless of how the myths interlock, an archetypal presentation of women will *always* reinforce the status quo. Indeed, the sisters' respective histories are defined by the same "categorical and fictive universality of the structure of domination" that Judith Butler cautioned against and thus come to perpetuate the seminal myth of the "blameless woman" (Butler 4). Ironically, this is the same myth that Sage insists Carter dismantles: "Carter's reading of Sade, and of fairy tales, is precisely an attack on this version of women as blameless, as having no part in the construction of their world and of themselves [. . .] The blameless woman is for Carter also the unimaginative woman" (Butler 4; Sage 58). The argument could also be made that Carter begins with the portrayal of an individuated female, but no matter how unique this character or particularized the circumstances, the woman will eventually be classified into one of these archetypal binaries; thus, woman cannot be anything but a Justine or Juliette, a wife or a virgin, a mother or a child. Perhaps the fairy-tale form is the best place to represent this inevitability, but no matter what the purpose behind the archetypes, false universals within the confines of a pornographic fairy tale cannot do anything else but reinforce the set pieces of a reductive genre. Unlike "literary arts" which "disinfect eroticism" by creating unconscious discomfort in the reader, using archetypes to deconstruct other archetypes is a futile task since, as Carter puts it, "an archetype is only an image that has got too big for its boots and bears, at best, a fantasy relation to reality. All archetypes are spurious [. . .]" (*Sadeian* 6). As a result, **"Snow Child,"** no matter how noble its intentions, cannot do anything but "assist the process of false universalizing" (*Sadeian* 12).

A second concern involves Carter's insistence that pornography can in fact be "moral" if it "uses pornographic material as part of the acceptance of the logic of a world of absolute sexual license for all the genders, and projects a model of the way such a world might work" (*Sadeian* 19). Though **"Snow Child"** uses a different route to achieve this logic than the rest of *The Bloody Chamber* stories, the story still uses pornographic sex—specifically the rape of the child by the father—to critique current relations between the sexes. But what if this idea of moral pornography itself is flawed, preventing the rape from ever discomforting the reader at all? Patricia Duncker finds the whole theory to be "utter nonsense":

> Pornography, indeed, the representation of all sexual relations between men and women, will 'necessarily render explicit the nature of social relations in the society in which they take place.' That is why most bourgeois fiction concentrates upon the choices surrounding courtship and marriage, for it is there that the values and realities upon which a society is based will be most sharply revealed. The realities of power perhaps, but not the imagined experience of desire. Pornography, heightened, stylized, remote, mirrors precisely these socially constructed realities. The realities of male desire, aggression, force; the reality of women, compliant and submissive.
>
> (8)

Though the rape might "mirror these socially constructed realities," **"Snow Child"** tries to challenge Duncker's assertion that "the realities of power" and "the imagined experience of desire" are mutually exclusive. As Cixous proposes, Carter wants her subtext to both mourn the real fates of her two subjugated women while opening up the possibilities for the endless laughter that erupts once this mourning gives way to a reimagination of feminine desire. But a text cannot satisfy both these requirements if female sexuality is confined to a heterosexual, sadomasochistic framework—at the very least, there has to be a glimpse or ironic suggestion "of women's sexuality as autonomous desire" (*Sadeian* 9). True, Carter recognizes the limitations of a Sadeian framework, but **"Snow Child,"** in particular, falls into the trap of only depicting "women's sensuality simply as a response to male arousal" (*Sadeian* 9). Avis Leewallen sees the Sadeian boundaries as a curious limitation for Carter: "One wonders why, given her recognition of what she sees as Sade's failure, there is no attempt to address the question of these ideologically defined parameters" (146). As a result of her investment of feminist politics in a Sadeian framework, Carter cannot challenge Duncker's concept of mutual exclusivity; she inevitably falls under what Benson terms the "either/or scenario: either we see the representation of some form of alternative to or merely the replication of traditionally sanctioned roles" (31). **"Snow Child,"** regardless of how intricate its psychoanalytic undercurrent, only concerns itself with the latter. Moreover, in its appropriation of the status quo for its revisionary agenda, Robin Sheets can only see stories like **"Snow Child"** as alluring—perhaps even satisfying—but ultimately restrictive *"aesthetic* sado-masochism" (347; italics added). And indeed, the potential for **"Snow Child"** to actually be aesthetically satisfying, possibly even *erotic,* dangles dangerously over the text like a sword of Damocles. For if the pornographic set pieces embedded in the fairy-tale form are still titillating even after the presentation of contextualized realities of power, then the first step in the progression toward laughter—the mourning of woman—is preempted and Carter finds herself with the same sort of text she so vehemently condemns: "If the world has been lost, the world may not be reassessed. Libidinous fantasy in a vacuum is the purest, but most affectless, form of day-dreaming" (*Sadeian* 18). If, in fact, the subtext of **"Snow Child"** *never actually swells* the narrative from below, then it morphs from an experimental disruption of the complacent reader to a literal—perhaps too literal—exercise in ejaculatory pleasure.

But deconstructing pornographic models involves only one half of the "above-ground" text—we must also consider the possibility that the form for **"Snow Child"** also prevents the revision of fairy-tale archetypes. A classic tale like "Snow White" has become so integral to acculturation that some folklorists even believe that these stories mold conscious and unconscious perceptions of gender. "Millions of women must surely have formed their psycho-sexual concepts, and their ideas of what they could or could not accomplish, what sort of behavior would be rewarded, and of the nature of reward itself, in part from their favorite fairy tales" (Lieberman 189). Though located in the realm of fantasy, these stories are thus impinging on the reader's reality and unconsciously expose the "raw nerves of real conflicts between classes, families, men and women, mothers and daughters, fathers, and sons" (Lieberman 390). But if hundreds of years of passive heroines and evil stepmothers have infected the fairy-tale form and consequently distorted the reader's reality, can **"Snow Child"** still operate within the same paradigm to propose a new psycho-sexual concept? Duncker admires the attempt, but concludes that by rewriting the stories "within the strait-jacket of their original structure," Carter's rewritings are crushed under the burden of an ideology "too complex and pervasive to avoid" (Duncker 6). But Duncker also makes the mistake of lumping all the revisions together instead of beginning with the painstaking but necessary task of comparing models for each story. As a result, she misses the significance of **"Snow Child"** as the *only* story that functions "within the strait-jacket" of the fairy-tale milieu—the others transfer the tales' themes to pornography—to become the crucial text in determining whether fairy-tale form and ideology are forever inextricable. Consequently, her textual analysis of **"Snow Child,"** which only sees the revision in terms of its Oedipal tensions, cannot even begin to support her categorical conclusion

about the efficacy of Carter's supposed objective for the entire collection. But if we evaluate Duncker's analysis away from the slippery notion of authorial intention, we see that her extrapolation of the mother-daughter conflict potentially has Carter's model imploding with ideology instead of swelling with ambiguity. Duncker believes that **"Snow Child"** never "questions the ideology implicit in the story," that "Mother and Daughter will—necessarily—become rivals for the Father's love" (7). This Freudian schism between "Mother and Daughter" offers up one of the cornerstones of patriarchy and thus is fundamental to any revisions that want to dismantle patriarchal structures. At the same time, unless the ideology behind it is clearly presented as its own subject for revision, how can we unconsciously distinguish between the rewritten text and the original since the fact that "so many tales suggest and endorse these old enmities is both sinister and predictable" (Duncker 7)? But Carter is more concerned with surface adjustments, not penetrating to the root of the contaminating ideology. As we discussed in our evaluation of her handling of pornographic archetypes, Carter might add new dimensions to the relationship between the Countess and the child, but she "still leaves the central taboos unspoken" (Duncker 8). By keeping her revision grounded in a critique of the status quo, Carter leaves the possibility that her new fairy tale will never take flight in the face of unconscious prejudices.

Perhaps, as Andrea Dworkin suggests, we have to obliterate these entrenched forms, these long-standing structures of patriarchal culture, in order to build a "new culture—nonhierarchical, nonsexist, noncoercive, non-exploitative—in other words, a culture which is not based on dominance and submission in any way" (62). The call to action is vague—and certainly a tall order—but Carter approaches the task with the added burden of trying to create this new culture within the restrictive parameters of existing structures. But what if the revision were to operate in reverse, boldly relocating fairy-tale culture—the characters, relationships, and themes—to a new, untested form?

Works Cited

Aarne, Antii and Stith Thompson. "The Types of the Folktale: A Classification and Bibliography." *FF Communications* 184. Helsinki: Academia Scientarum Fennica, 1961.

Bacchilega, Cristina. *Postmodern Fairy Tales: Gender and Narrative Strategies.* Philadelphia: U of Pennsylvania P, 1997.

Benson, Stephen. "Angela Carter and the Literary Marchen: A Review Essay." *Marvels & Tales* 12.1 (1998): 23-51.

Bettleheim, Bruno. *The Uses of Enchantment: The Meaning and Importance of Fairy Tales.* New York: Random House, 1977.

Brown, Judith K. "A Cross-Cultural Study of Female Initiation Rites." *American Anthropologist* 65 (1963): 837-53.

Butler, Judith. *Gender Trouble: Feminism and the Subversion of Identity.* New York: Routledge, 1990.

————. "Gender Trouble, Feminist Theory, and Psychoanalytic Discourse." *Feminism/Postmodernism.* Ed. Linda Nicholson. London: Routledge, 1990. 324-341.

Carter, Angela. *The Bloody Chamber and Other Stories.* Hammondsworth: Penguin, 1981.

————. *The Sadeian Woman and the Ideology of Pornography.* New York: Pantheon, 1979.

Cashdan, Sheldon. *The Witch Must Die.* New York: Basic, 1999.

Cixous, Helene. "Castration or Decapitation?" Trans. Annette Kuhn. *Signs* 1 (1981): 41-55.

————. "The Laugh of the Medusa." *Critical Theory Since 1965.* Ed. Hazard Adams. Tallahassee: Florida State UP, 1986. 309-320.

Clark, Robert. "Angela Carter's Desire Machine." *Women's Studies* 14 (1987): 147-61.

Duncker, Patricia. "Re-Imagining the Fairy Tale: Angela Carter's Bloody Chambers." *Literature and History* 10 (1984): 3-12.

Dworkin, Andrea. *Woman Hating.* New York: Dutton, 1974.

Feldman, Shoshana. "Turning the Screw of Interpretation." *Literature and Psychoanalysis: The Question of Reading Otherwise.* Baltimore: Johns Hopkins UP, 1977. 94-208.

Fowl, Melinda. "The Bloody Chamber Revisited." *Critical Survey* 31 (1991): 71-79.

Franz, M. L. von. *The Feminine in Fairy Tales.* Dallas: Spring Publications, 1972.

Gilbert, Sandra, and Susan Gubar. *The Madwoman in the Attic: The Woman Writer and the Nineteenth Century Literary Imagination.* New Haven: Yale UP, 1979.

Girardot, N. J. "Initiation and Meaning in the Tale of Snow White and the Seven Dwarfs." *Journal of American Folklore* 90 (1977): 274-300.

Jones, Steven Swann. *The New Comparative Method: Structural and Symbolic Analyses of the Allomotifs of "Snow White."* Helsinki: Academia Scientiarum Fennica, 1990.

Kaeppler, Susannah. *The Pornography of Representation.* Minneapolis: Minnesota UP, 1986.

Lewallen, Avis. "Wayward Girls But Wicked Women? Female Sexuality in Angela Carter's The Bloody Chamber." *Perspectives on Pornography: Sexuality in Film and Literature.* Ed. Gary Day and Clive Bloom. New York: St. Martin's Press, 1998. 144-157.

Lieberman, Marcia K. "Some Day My Prince Will Come: Female Acculturation through the Fairy Tale." Zipes 185-200.

Mankinen, Merja. "Angela Carter's *The Bloody Chamber* and the Decolonization of Feminine Sexuality." *Feminist Review* 42 (1992): 2-15.

Otero, Solimar. "'Fearing Our Mothers?' An Overview of the Psychoanalytic Theories Concerning the Vagina Dentata Motif." *American Journal of Psychoanalysis* 56.3 (1996): 269-99.

Sage, Lorna. "Angela Carter: The Fairy Tale." *Marvels & Tales* 12 (1998): 52-68.

Sexton, Anne. *Transformations.* Boston: Houghton Mifflin, 1971.

Sheets, Robin. "Pornography, Fairy Tales, and Feminism: Angela Carter's 'The Bloody Chamber.'" *Journal of the History of Sexuality* 1 (1991): 633-57.

Tatar, Maria, ed. *The Classic Fairy Tales: Text, Criticism.* New York: Norton, 1998.

Zipes, Jack, ed. *Don't Bet on the Prince: Contemporary Feminist Fairy Tales in North America and England.* New York: Methun, 1986.

FURTHER READING

Criticism

Atwood, Margaret. "Running with the Tigers." In *Flesh and the Mirror: Essays on the Art of Angela Carter,* edited by Lorna Sage, pp. 117-35. London: Virago Press, 1994.

> Delineates Carter's different approaches to the "nature" of woman in the fictional *The Bloody Chamber* and the theoretical *The Sadeian Woman.*

Crunelle-Vanrigh, Anny. "The Logic of the Same and Différance: 'The Courtship of Mr Lyon.'" *Marvels & Tales* 12, no. 1 (1998): 116-32.

> Traces various ways that Carter retells and revises the traditional structure and interpretation of fairy tales within the context of "The Courtship of Mr. Lyon."

Day, Aidan. "*The Bloody Chamber and Other Stories* (1979)." In *Angela Carter: The Rational Glass,* pp. 132-66. Manchester, England: Manchester University Press, 1998.

> Outlines themes of gender and class politics in Carter's short fiction.

Deszcz, Justyna. "Beyond the Disney Spell, or Escape into Pantoland." *Folklore* 113, no. 1 (April 2002): 83-91.

> Discusses political parallels between narrative elements of "In Pantoland" and Disneyland.

Kaiser, Mary. "Fairy Tale as Sexual Allegory: Intertextuality in Angela Carter's *The Bloody Chamber*." *Review of Contemporary Fiction* 14, no. 3 (fall 1994): 30-6.

> Examines "The Bloody Chamber" and "The Snow Child" in terms of Carter's use of intertextuality and her manipulation of the cultural contexts surrounding gender relations and sexuality.

Matus, Jill. "Blonde, Black and Hottentot Venus: Context and Critique in Angela Carter's 'Black Venus.'" *Studies in Short Fiction* 28, no. 4 (fall 1991): 467-76.

> Investigates how "Black Venus" develops the anthropological, physiological, and aesthetic contexts that linked "blackness," primitive sexuality, prostitution, and disease in the nineteenth century.

Additional coverage of Carter's life and career is contained in the following sources published by Thomson Gale: *British Writers Supplement*, Vol. 3; *Contemporary Authors*, Vols. 53-56, 136; *Contemporary Authors New Revision Series*, Vols. 12, 36, 61, 106; *Contemporary Literary Criticism*, Vols. 5, 41, 76; *Dictionary of Literary Biography*, Vols. 14, 207, 261; *DISCovering Authors 3.0*; *Exploring Short Stories*; *Feminist Writers*; *Literature Resource Center*; *Major 20th-Century Writers*, Eds. 1, 2; *Major 21st-Century Writers*; *Reference Guide to Short Fiction*, Ed. 2; *St. James Guide to Fantasy Writers*; *St. James Guide to Science Fiction Writers*, Ed. 4; *Short Stories for Students*, Vols. 4, 12; *Short Story Criticism*, Vol. 13; *Something about the Author*, Vols. 66, 70; *Supernatural Fiction Writers*, Vol. 2; *Twentieth-Century Literary Criticism*, Vol. 139; and *World Literature and Its Times*, Vol. 4.

Anton Chekhov
1860-1904

(Full name Anton Pavlovich Chekhov; transliterated as Čexov, Čeckov, Chekov, Tchehov, Tchekhov, Cechov, Cexov, Cekov, Cecov, Chikhoff, and Chehov; also wrote under the pseudonym Antosha Chekhonte) Russian short story writer, playwright, and essayist.

The following entry presents an overview of Chekhov's short fiction. For additional information on his short fiction career, see *SSC,* Volumes 2 and 51; for discussion of the short story "Kryžovnik" (1898; "Gooseberries"), see *SSC,* Volume 28; for discussion of the short story "Duél'" (1891; "The Duel"), see *SSC,* Volume 41.

INTRODUCTION

Chekhov is widely acknowledged as one of the most important short story writers of all time. A prolific author, he wrote hundreds of tales, from humorous, "slice-of-life" vignettes to complex stories that explore social and political issues. Critics often trace his development as a writer, contrasting his early works—often objective observations on the human condition—with his later stories, which are characterized by an assured subjectivity and are among his most highly regarded. Scholars identify Chekhov as the quintessential writer of a generation that ended the age of realism—known as the Golden Age—in nineteenth-century Russian literature, and discuss his stylistic innovations in the short fiction genre. Chekhov's fiction has influenced myriad celebrated authors, including Katherine Mansfield, James Joyce, Sherwood Anderson, Franz Kafka, and Raymond Carver.

BIOGRAPHICAL INFORMATION

Chekhov was born on January 17, 1860, in Taganrog, Russia. When he was sixteen years old, his family went bankrupt and subsequently moved to Moscow to escape creditors. Chekhov, however, remained in Taganrog until 1879, when he completed his education and earned a scholarship to Moscow University to study medicine. After receiving his degree in 1884, he formed a medical practice. His experiences as a physician would later become a recurring element of his fiction. While establishing his practice, Chekhov began to publish sketches in popular magazines to help support his family. His

output was prodigious and consisted mainly of light fare such as anecdotes, extended jokes, and potboilers. These short pieces exhibit several of Chekhov's defining short story characteristics, such as his impressionistic narrative style and surprise endings, and form what critics generally consider to be his first major literary period. In 1884 his first collection of short stories, *Skazki Mel'pomeny* was published. That same year he became acquainted with Aleksey S. Suvorin, editor of the conservative Moscow daily journal *Novow vremja,* in which many of Chekhov's later stories would appear. Critics agree that Chekhov's second major literary period began in 1888, at which point he began to show the influence of Leo Tolstoy, evinced by the emphasis on morality and altruism in his fiction. In this significant era of Chekhov's literary development, he experimented with lyricism and thematic contrasts—beauty over ugliness, sensitivity over banality, and life over death. Yet after his trip to the eastern Siberian penal colony at Sakhalin in 1890, he rejected Tolstoy's ideas and underwent a spiritual crisis. These philosophical and spiritual reevaluations signaled the start of Chekhov's third creative era. Critics contend that during this period he composed his most complex and distinctive short stories and dramas. His literary output was cut short, however, when a recurring bout of pulmonary tuberculosis ended his life on July 2, 1904.

MAJOR WORKS OF SHORT FICTION

Among the jokes and light anecdotes that characterize Chekhov's earliest phase of productivity, critics have found many of the author's central thematic concerns: the sufferings of the poor; the petty tyranny of government officials; and the vulgarity and insensitivity of the peasant class. Indeed, in the mid-1880s a few of his stories explored very serious themes, such as starvation in "Ustricy" ("Oysters") and abandonment in "Eger" ("The Huntsman"). In addition, several stories demonstrate his ability to portray life from within the minds of his characters through the utilization of well-chosen details. A number of his stories are satires of the adult world from the perspective of children. Chekhov's objectivity and lack of moral perspective in these early stories garnered censure from reviewers at the time. The 1888 publication of his story "Step" ("The Steppe"), an impressionistic account of a young boy's voyage across the plains of southern Russia with his uncle and a priest, is thought to signal Chekhov's maturity as a writer and his entry into the ranks of the great Russian authors. Another important story from Chekhov's early period, "Spat' khochetsya" ("Sleepy"), depicts an exploited, young nursemaid, who, while watching her employers' infant, strangles the baby out of desperation and weariness. In "Supruga" ("His Wife"), a cuckolded husband reflects on his troubled marriage and his own capacity for self-deception. At the end of the 1880s Chekhov abandoned his pen name, Antosha Chekhonte, and his work began to reflect the literary philosophy of Tolstoy. In particular, he adopted Tolstoy's doctrine of nonresistance to evil, which led to such stories as "Pripadok" ("The Nervous Breakdown"), about the immorality of prostitution, and "Khoroshie lyudi" ("Good People"), a moralizing tale that celebrates the benefits of physical labor. In other stories, Chekhov explored Tolstoy's belief in the futility of violence and anger.

By the end of the 1890s Chekhov had abandoned Tolstoy's strict moral dogma in favor of a deepened concern for social matters, such as the injustice, corruption, and violence of Russian society. His new commitment to social issues is evident in stories such as "Baby" ("Peasant Wives"), which depicts the oppression of women in a patriarchal peasant society, and "Zhena" ("The Wife"), which explores the disastrous effects of famine on the Russian peasantry and portrays the aris-

tocracy as cruel and ineffectual. Chekhov was not only concerned with social problems but also sought to establish his own individual philosophy toward the world. Specific philosophical questions are explored in stories such as "Skuchnaya istoriya" ("A Dreary Story"), "Duél'" ("The Duel"), and "Palata No. 6" ("Ward No. 6"). In "A Dreary Story," a dying medical professor, Nicolai Stepanovich, describes his night fears and insomnia, his impatience with colleagues, and his indifference to family affairs. Commentators have detected numerous parallels between Chekhov and Stepanovich, particularly relating to the professor's cynical perspective on life and academia. Chekhov's longest story, "The Duel," is set in the Caucasus region and portrays the conflict between Layevsky, a young bohemian idealist, and von Koren, a cold-blooded, ambitious zoologist, who is consumed with the Nietzschean concept of a superman. In "Ward No. 6," the director of a decrepit insane asylum allows rampant corruption and eventually ends up committed to his own ward. The third category of Chekhov's short stories, spanning the years 1894 to 1904, are unified by his concern about the growing divide between the privileged class and village peasantry in Russia, as well as an intensified interest in social justice. In "Bab'e carstvo" ("A Woman's Kingdom"), a newly rich woman who has inherited a factory fails to uphold her philanthropic endeavors; instead, she abandons her ethical and societal obligations on a whim. Chekhov's controversial story "Muzhiki" ("Peasants") is an unsentimental look at the condition and future of the Russian peasantry. The short story trilogy of "Chelovek v futlyare" ("The Man in a Shell"), "Kryžovnik" ("Gooseberries"), and "O lyubvi" ("About Love") explores man's spirituality and failure to communicate. Near the end of his life, Chekhov demonstrated further philosophical and intellectual growth through his short fiction. The stories from this last period retain a tenuous optimism, allowing the characters sympathy and hope for spiritual fulfillment. Viewed as one of his finest pieces, "Dama s sobachkoy" ("The Lady with the Dog") is the story of an adulterous summer tryst that deepens into a profound romantic and spiritual attachment. Critics have found parallels between the love affair in the story and Chekhov's romance and marriage to the actress Olga Knipper in 1901.

CRITICAL RECEPTION

Although today he is regarded as one of the world's greatest short story writers, the critical response to Chekhov's short fiction varied widely during his lifetime. Some reviewers derided his seeming indifference to social and political concerns in his early stories and asserted that his fiction lacked plot and action. Others argued that his focus on fragments of everyday reality and the interior life of his characters, his impressionistic narrative style, and his rejection of the formalized short story signaled the emergence of a new kind of short fiction. Today his influence on the short story form is widely acknowledged. In recent years critics have focused on Chekhov's use of the realistic and the poetic in his stories and have investigated parallels between the author's life and his work; they note that although Chekhov has been perceived as a cynic and pessimist—largely due to his realistic and detached portrayal of a divided and unsettled Russian society—he was personally somewhat optimistic with regard to social progress and scientific advancement. The influence of Tolstoy and Fyodor Dostoevsky on Chekhov's fiction has long been a topic of critical discussion. Recent studies of Chekhov's short fiction have concentrated on the link between Chekhov and modern art, the relationship between his medical stories and his experiences as a physician, the use of the "descent" motif in his work, and the reasons for his enduring appeal to readers and scholars alike. Critics concur that Chekhov's innovative narrative approach to storytelling and his insight into the human condition altered the narrative standards for an entire literary form.

PRINCIPAL WORKS

Short Fiction

Skazki Mel'pomeny [as Antosha Chekhonte] 1884
Pestrye rasskazy [as Antosha Chekhonte] 1886
Nevinnye rechi [as Antosha Chekhonte] 1887
V sumerkakh: Ocherki i rasskazy 1887
Rasskazy 1888
The Black Monk, and Other Stories 1903
The Kiss, and Other Stories 1908
The Darling, and Other Stories 1916
The Duel, and Other Stories 1916
The Tales of Tchehov. 13 vols. 1916-22
Collected Works. 5 vols. 1987
Anton Chekhov: Later Short Stories, 1888-1903 1999
The Comic Stories 1999
The Complete Early Short Stories of Anton Chekhov 2001
The Undiscovered Chekhov: Fifty-One New Stories 2001

Other Major Works

Ivanov (play) 1887
Leshii [*The Wood Demon*] (play) 1889
Ostrov Sakhalin (essay) 1895
Chaika [*The Seagull*] (play) 1896

Diadia Vania [*Uncle Vania*] (play) 1898
Tri sestry [*Three Sisters*] (play) 1901
Vishnevyi sad [*The Cherry Orchard*] (play) 1904
The Selected Letters of Anton Chekhov (letters) 1955

CRITICISM

Lawrence Jay Dessner (essay date fall 1985)

SOURCE: Dessner, Lawrence Jay. "Head, Heart, and Snout: Narrative and Theme in Chekhov's 'Misery.'" *College Literature* 12, no. 3 (fall 1985): 246-57.

[*In the following essay, Dessner examines Chekhov's narrative technique and the central thematic concerns of "Misery."*]

At the penultimate paragraph of Chekhov's early short story **"Misery,"** Iona Potapov, an old sledge-driver who has been unable to find anyone to talk to about his son, dead for almost a week, begins to tell his horse "all about it."[1] It is a shocking moment, very touching, perhaps, as an eminent student of Chekhov has found it, "too directly moving."[2] It is surely a clear example of what Chekhov told his brother was his practice when writing plays: "I end each act like a story: I conduct the entire action peacefully and quietly, but at the end I bash the viewer in the snout."[3] Surprised as we are by the rude blow administered to us, the story's extraordinary structure—"tailored with superb skill"[4]—is such that on reflection we realize that the fist that delivered it to us had been raised and on its way to us from the very start. A careful examination of the text can reveal something of the narrative practice and thematic management with which this inevitable blow was prepared, disguised, and ultimately delivered. The blow itself is remarkable for the tonal ambiguity which lets heart-rending pathos quiver on the edge of something very like pleasantly mild good humor.[5] It is an example of what Tolstoy and others have described as Chekhov's practice of depicting the ridiculous in such a light that it turns out to be "not ridiculous but wonderful and holy,"[6] not a coarse and rather obvious joke but "a horrifying and heartbreaking revelation."[7] The effect has been called, on the pattern of "comic relief" no doubt, "a kind of pathetic relief": Chekhov starts with a broadly comic situation, even with a cheap and sentimental comic anecdote, and sees the pathos in it. "The absurd . . . no longer amuses us. In a sense, the punch line falls flat; in another, it stirs a pang in our hearts."[8] But it is also typical of Chekhov's way that some flavor of the "ridiculous" or the comically "absurd" lingers through the epiphany and provides the reader with some literal "relief" from a revelation of otherwise unbearable pathos.

This very short story, some 2,100 words long, lets us see how these effects may be prepared for and achieved and also suggests something of the relationship of this method to a central interest of Chekhov criticism, the narrator's relationship to his materials and the author's relationship to his narrator. We recall Chekhov's famous remark to Ivan Bunin that "one had to be ice cold before sitting down to write."[9] Chekhov's "aloofness, a kind of principled objectivity, a deliberate restraint,"[10] is expressed through his narrator's tendency to see the ridiculous in the pathetic at the same time that he is seeing the pathetic in the ridiculous. The drama of the narrator's approach to and withdrawal from the misery of Iona Potapov culminates here not in the typical Chekhovian stalled perpetual motion around an ever decreasing orbit, but in the narrator's eventual unconditional surrender to what we might ordinarily call sentimentality. Perhaps it is this surrender that lets one think that the story is "too directly moving."

The sense of inevitability that hangs over the story and its conclusion is not merely a function of its subtitle or headnote—"To Whom Shall I Tell My Grief?"—which points directly toward the ending, but of a system of reiterated comparisons and connections that runs throughout the story and suggests that human life is bound to animal life; that suffering is bound to suffering even across the line that separates man from beast; and that speech, the need for it and the ability to produce it, is the distinctive human attribute and therefore the essential human need. Images of these themes make up such a large part of the story and are so interrelated that the guidance provided by the headnote, and by the story's plot—Iona's several failed attempts to find a willing ear for his tale of woe—turn out to have been superfluous or at least superficial components of the story's meaning. With its last one-sentence paragraph, the story surprises us again with another shock at what we will realize was inevitable also: the collapse of the narrator's ability to maintain his seeming composure and objectivity in the face of misery such as Iona's.

The story opens with a description of Iona sitting on the box of his sledge, "without stirring" despite the falling snow which has made him "all white as a ghost." He looks as though he would not move even if the snow had been "a regular snowdrift."[11] His mare is "white and motionless too." The narrator notices from the start and directs us to this living image of that grandfather of jokes, the seeming similarity or equality of man and beast. The snow falls and collects equally on the backs of each. The man is as unconcerned with the weather as if he had a beast's coat and its minimal consciousness. We shall soon see what the narrator knows already, that Iona's lack of concern for the weather and for his bodily comfort is due to his preoccupation with his son's death, not to any sub-human moral or intellectual characteristics. But the narrator subtly deflects such

awareness of the pathos of Iona's plight into the channel of the harmless old joke. Iona sits "bent as double as the living body can be bent." At this point, the story's first paragraph, the reader has only the story's motto to suggest that Iona's posture is related to his "grief" rather than to the weather, and the narrator, protecting us, as he protects himself, from full awareness of **"Misery,"** allows us to reach the bland conclusion that the weather is Iona's problem.[12] But to be "bent"—as Iona is now and the mare is always—and to be "motionless" long enough for snow to gather on one, is to be as potentially pathetic as comic. As if aware of this tendency in his words, the narrator immediately de-animates the mare, reduces her, as it were, to the domain of the insensate image: "Her stillness, the angularity of her lines and the stick-like straightness of her legs makes her look like a halfpenny gingerbread horse." But this distancing maneuver is not without its sentimental coloration, to the degree that the coldness of the inanimate, square, stiff and two-dimensional cookie is displaced by the warmth of associations of the halfpenny gingerbread with such things as holiday treats, children's allowances, and their imaginative games. The narrator's next words, however, mark his retreat from the suggestion that the mare is a mere two-dimensional token or plaything, for with his very next sentence he startles us with the tacit assumption that this manufactured thing of flour and sugar is possessed of a human's self-consciousness: "She is probably lost in thought." The broad irony of this mocks the horse's inability to think and therefore the sentimental notion that it ever could be "lost in thought." On the other hand, the less obvious target of irony is Iona. The horse needs no excuse for standing out in the snowfall, but Iona might well seem to need one. The narrator's coldly ironic imputation is that Iona's consciousness is similar to that of a beast's, that is, minuscule or non-existent. If *he* were to be "lost in thought," his excuse, which is suggested by the parallels already made between Iona and the mare, would be at hand. The narrator's next sentence provides a reason why such a one might be so preoccupied as to ignore the accumulating snow: "Anyone who has been torn from the plough, from the familiar gray landscapes, and cast into this slough, full of monstrous lights, of unceasing uproar and hurrying people, is bound to think." The word "anyone" pleads for sympathy while it emphasizes the painfulness of the forced exile. The experience is such that no imaginable victim of it would not be led to "think"—a protective euphenism—about it. The narrator, ironically, invites us to exercise our imagination. The irony is that he is sure our attempts to discover "one" who would endure the ordeal unshaken will be in vain. The case is universal, including by implication both the narrator and the author. But while the "any" insists on its universality of reference, the "one" can only refer to a human, to Iona among those in the foreground. But the legitimate grammatical antecedent of the pronoun can only be the mare. The explanation itself might apply to either being, or both. Both are indeed natives of an agricultural milieu who have been transported to the bewildering bustle of the alien metropolis. Both have been cruelly "torn" and "cast." Both have had their "familiar gray landscapes" replaced by unaccustomed noise and glare. Iona has suddenly re-emerged as a figure of pathos, but only for an instant. The narrator's expression of his sensitivity to that pathos is undercut, not to say undermined, by the absurdity of the sentence which contains these invitations to sympathize. The logical skeleton of that sentence is: "Any horse, or person like a horse . . . is bound to think." But horses, of course, do not think. And the man who is the horse's equivalent in this is the country bumpkin who doesn't know enough, as one says, to come in out of the rain. The pathos of his ridiculous case is whirled away by the endless play of recursive ironies. Iona Potapov is again a passive, somnolent, barely sentient figure of easy fun.

That is the attitude of the military officer who appears at this point and orders Iona to drive him to Vyborgskaya. In response, Iona "cranes his neck like a swan, rises in his seat, and more from habit than necessity brandishes his whip." The animal-like peasant thoughtlessly whips his mare, although the animal he is compared to is, of all things, the stately swan! (The motif which connects Iona with animal life is not confined to comparisons with his mare. Iona's various passengers call him or refer to him as a "dog," a "devil," a "brute," a "louse" or flea, and a "dragon." At the end, Iona himself compares his own ability to experience grief over the loss of a child with the mare's ability to do the same.) Whereupon the beast of burden "cranes her neck, too." The narrator is conscious that man and beast are two of a kind and insistently brings that fact to our attention: there is that emphatic "too," and the syntactical similarity—Iona and the mare are each subjects of a string of verbs—in the consecutive sentences which describe the actions of first Iona, then the mare.

Iona's entrance into the stream of traffic produces an immediate and vociferous barrage of complaint. Whereupon his passenger, with broad irony, pretends to take Iona's part: "They are simply doing their best to run up against you or fall under the horse's feet. They must be doing it on purpose." The jest means nothing to Iona who "turns his eyes as one possessed, as though he did not know where he was or why he was there." He is too preoccupied or too dense to understand the joke or to resent it. But he has turned around and is face to face with another human being. Hesitantly but without prologue and not at all as if it were in excuse for his bad driving—the complaints on that score don't seem to have registered on his consciousness—Iona announces to his passenger that "my son died this week." The officer is trapped, physically, by his position in the back

of Iona's dangerously moving sledge. And he is at Iona's mercy in a moral sense at well, stunned by the suddenness with which Iona's terrible words have been uttered and by the rudeness with which Iona has enforced his will—or is it his need?—on this total stranger. Under such duress, his freedom of response is drastically if temporarily limited. Like a well-intentioned but nervous mourner, the officer can only voice his feelings in inanity. He asks: "What did he die of?" Iona has found a sounding board, pinned down and squirming, and he pounces on his chance: "Who can tell! It must have been from fever. He lay three days in the hospital and then he died. God's will." And surely Iona would have continued, to the merciless discomfort of his passenger, had not a voice burst out of the darkness complaining heatedly of Iona's dangerous driving. The officer, taking his chance as it comes, joins in with his own words of abuse, and Iona's opportunity is over. "Several times he looks round at the officer, but the latter keeps his eyes shut and is apparently disinclined to listen." (We may pause to notice the high formal diction of that "apparently disinclined" and the ironic understatement of "apparently," which emphasizes not only the officer's disinclination but the narrator's emotionally charged apprehension of it. The formality of the language is ironic in its contrast with the squalor of the signified. It also tends to distance the narrator from Iona. Just when the latter stands in need of sympathy, the narrator pointedly refuses him the sympathy which would be signaled, and which Chekhov's narrators, including this one, often do signal by imitated speech habits and the use of a shared lexicon.)[13] And who will blame this narrator, our representative at the scene, for seizing *his* chance as the officer did, and avoiding further discourse with this tiresome old bore, this selfish and imperceptive fool, this embarrassing reminder?

So ends the first act, as it were, of Iona's story, his first attempt, before our eyes, to find someone to tell "all about it." And it has been the first act too of the narrator's story, of *his* attempt to find a point of rest between the oscillations of approach and rejection, between ridicule of the absurd and sympathetic approach to the pathetic. It ends with Iona's rejection, by the officer and by the narrator too. But when the repulsed Iona raises his whip again, the narrator sees that he swings it "with heavy grace." The irony in which the narration has been swimming is noticeably absent from that phrase. It is an omen of the shifting of the narrator's balance. And in its light one can say that "apparently disinclined" conveys the narrator's disappointment at the officer's response and even a desire, or a hope, against reason and common sense, that in this case appearances deceive.

The second act begins as did the first. While Iona waits for his next fare, we are reminded of the apparent equivalence of man and beast by "Again the wet snow paints him and the horse white." ("Again" reminds us that we are being reminded.) Iona, desperate for any chance to tell his tale, accepts an unfairly low offer from three boisterous young men, one a hunchback, who want a ride. Even before his attempts to engage them in conversation about his dead son, the young men mock Iona's cap and his driving. His anguish is so great, the narrator tells us entering Iona's consciousness directly for the first time, that this mockery itself, because it is addressed to himself, lessens the "loneliness . . . [weighing] on his heart." Earlier the narrator had noticed that Iona looked "as though he were sitting on thorns." Here the narrator overleaps the distancing "as though," plunges to an unmitigated acceptance of his own awareness of Iona's suffering. The passengers return to boasting to each other about their triumphs with drink and women and Iona interrupts with his announcement of his son's death. The hunchback's initial response is a sighing "We shall all die," but this is immediately followed by severe criticism of Iona's slow driving. As if he were a slow-moving beast of burden, Iona is offered "encouragement" in the form of a "slap in the back of his neck." "Iona hears rather than feels" the blow. With a terribly pathetic forced joviality, Iona laughs at the high spirits of his "Merry gentlemen" and takes their mocking question about whether he is married or not as an invitation to pontificate to them about his late wife, his late son, and the oddities of fate. But they have arrived at their destination, and Iona is, once more, left alone with his grief. This is something of a relief to the reader and not merely because Iona is separated from him and we from the spectacle of the hunchback transferring his own pain to Iona's back. For Iona these passengers are potential sharers of his grief. He has forgotten, or surrendered, his dignity to his need so that his fawning attempts at comraderie are painfully embarrassing. His jovial laughter is as close to the speech he yearns for as his situation allows. Before the story's next act or episode begins, the narrator notices the external marks of Iona's suffering—his long silent act of "gaz[ing]"—and plunges again, but not as briefly, into the sympathetic identification with that suffering that allows him to say, "The misery which has been for a brief space eased comes back again and tears his heart more cruelly than ever." (Is this Iona's point of view, his words in the narrator's mouth, or does the narrator know enough about the case to make the comparative judgment himself?) The narrator retreats to an external, objective view of Iona's eyes again, which now "stray relentlessly," and now the narrator unhesitatingly interprets their movements in an extended lyric, an aria which begins with, "can he not find among the crowds moving to and fro on both sides of the street?" and ends, bursting and then declining as Iona's heart threatens to do, with this: "If Iona's heart were to burst and his misery to flow out, it would flood the whole world, it seems, but yet it is not seen. It has found a hiding-

place in such an insignificant shell that one would not have found it with a candle by daylight." Iona's insignificance, for which he has been ridiculed, is now offered as an aspect of the pathos of his condition. The narrator's elaborate literary metaphor draws on Iona's peasant idiom for its completion. It seems as if the narrator's elevated, even poetic, diction and imagery do not imply here a distance between narrator and hero nor does the concluding drop into the colloquial imply ironic condescension. Iona's loneliness has intensified. Knowing him as we have been led to do, we realize that his prospects for finding a sympathetic ear are not good. Indeed, the only potential listener in sight—the mare having recently disappeared from the field of notice—is the narrator himself.

The interlude between acts two and three ends with that rhapsodic outburst. The structure of the third act differs from its predecessors. There is no introductory description of Iona's animal-like posture and pace. He approaches, without success, a porter and, back at the cab stables, a young driver, and finally, his mare. The narrator continues to notice Iona's visible condition and to interpret with increasing regularity and insistence its subjective cause: Iona "bends himself double, and gives himself up to his misery. He feels it is no good to appeal to people." Iona "shakes his head as though he feels a sharp pain, and tugs at the reins." The narrator confidently explains what these external signs signify: "He can bear it no longer."

The narrator's confidence extends, remarkably, to Iona's mare. After his first rejection in this act, Iona thinks of returning "to the yard," "and his little mare, as though she knew his thoughts, falls to trotting." Of course horses do not know the unspoken thoughts of others any more than they, mourning exile from familiar fields, "are bound to think." The contrast between the ironic charge of the narrator's two ventures into imaginative animal psychology trace his evolving identification with Iona. Does the narrator believe that the semblance of a preternatural bond between Iona and his mare is anything other than coincidental? Is he raising the absurd and comic possibility that a horse can read a man's mind in order to scoff at it or hope for it? (At this point, Iona's mare is "little" for the first time since the opening paragraph in which it was likened to a gingerbread horse. One might be tempted to see in this Chekhov's rather easy and sentimental use of the affectionate diminutive. But "little colt" is Iona's phrase at the story's end when he repeatedly compares his own lost son to his mare's hypothetical lost offspring. And it is the epithet the narrator himself applies to the mare in the last paragraph.)

Back at the stables and rejected again, Iona thinks about his dead son and his own loneliness, and thanks to the narrator who lends Iona the language he lacks, we listen in at length: "To talk about him with someone is possible, but to think of him and picture him is insufferable anguish." At the end of his soliloquy, Iona decides that while his story should be sympathetically received by anyone, "it would be even better to talk to women." (His horse, of course, is a mare.) "Though they are silly creatures, they blubber at the first word." Moving as the story is, near as we may be moving to unguarded sympathy with it, neither reader nor narrator wants to deserve Iona's censure for blubbering. Chekhov, here, in effect, warns his reader and his narrator; he dares them to "blubber at the first word."

Iona walks outside to where the mare is tethered and proceeds to feed it. Talking to the mare about its diet, Iona refers to himself and the mare as "we." And it is a mere step from that to telling the mare "all about it." It is a breathtaking moment, and the pressure on us to "blubber" is very soon intensified when Iona drops into an appalling baby-talk, mawkishly and unpardonably sentimental in any imaginable context, except, perhaps, the present one: Iona asks the mare to "suppose you had a little colt, and you were own mother to that little colt. And all at once that same little colt went and died. You'd be sorry, wouldn't you?" Here at the story's end we have the culmination of its intense pathos as well as of its thematic linkage of man and animal. But Iona, who had been repeatedly linked with animal life, now credits an animal with a human's sensitivity to personal anguish.

What are we to do in the face of this assault on our sensibilities? What can the narrator, our surrogate, do? He has no choice but to surrender, to overcome his scruples, and to agree with Iona that the mare has a human's consciousness and sensitivity. So he says that "the little mare munches, listens, and breathes on her master's hands." The horse does not *seem* to listen, or chew *as if* she were listening. The narrator's aloofness, and objectivity, not to mention his mockery of this vulgar and ridiculous man has been swept away. The narrator withholds nothing from the "sudden tragic illumination,"[14] not even the flimsy shield of the "as if." "Carried away," he gives himself to Iona as freely and completely as Iona gives himself to his mare.

It may be well to briefly sketch two aspects of the story's thematic development which broaden its pertinence. Iona is not the only suffering character in the story; there is the young hunchback, who, in his own misery, although ostensibly at the urging of one of his impatient companions, strikes Iona "on the back of his neck." The fashionable young men who make up his party, "shoving each other and using bad language, go up to the sledge, and all three try to sit down at once. The question remains to be settled: Which are to sit down and which one is to stand? After a long altercation, ill-temper, and abuse, they come to the conclusion that the

hunchback must stand *because* he is the shortest" (emphasis added). The irony is almost painfully blunt. We cannot assent, nor does the narrator ask us to assent, to the suggestion that the long and loud altercation reaches a rational conclusion or that there is any logic at all to the allotting of seats to those who are tall. Of course, the hunchback stands because he is the weakest. He joins his back to those of our other sufferers, Iona and the mare, and requires us to reconsider whether Iona's back is indeed "bent as double as the living body can be bent."[15] The hunchback's response to the abuse of his companions is very much like Iona's response to their abuse of him, fawning officiousness. A word of encouragement is all it takes for him to change his verbal abuse of Iona to physical abuse. The hunchback beats Iona's back so that he in turn will beat the mare's back! We are as embarrassed by this revelation of what we assume to be the depths of the hunchback's misery as we are by our insight into Iona's distress. Here, without the Shakespearean theatrical context and language, is "the thing itself; unaccommodated man." Edgar, like Iona, "is no more but such a poor, bare, forked animal," "unaccommodated," in Lear's fancy (3.4. 110-12) in that he has not been provided with clothing and scent made from animals.

Perhaps the hunchback's plight is even worse than Edgar's or Iona's, for, other than in striking Iona, he finds no outlet for his grief, no "one" at all to whom to tell his grief. The importance of telling is a theme suggested throughout the story. Iona is so deeply anguished that his response to his first passenger is silent: "In token of assent Iona gives a tug at the reins. . . ." In response to the officer's sarcasm about Iona's driving, Iona first looks around and "moves his lips. Apparently he means to say something, but nothing comes but a sniff," an animal-like, meaningless, vocalization. The hunchback's speech production also shows signs of struggle and inadequacy. Ordering Iona's cab on behalf of his party of three, he "cries in a cracked voice." He abuses Iona in a "quivering voice," "swears at him, till he chokes over some elaborately whimsical string of epithets."[16] Iona's announcement of his loss is invariably offered in a hesitant, halting manner: "This week . . . er . . . my . . . er . . . son died!" His attempts at fawning and smiling his way into the young men's conversation distort his language: "Me-er-ry gentlemen" he calls them. This motif, in which the physical production of speech is a metaphor for moral, invisible, communication, is made explicit when Iona fails to catch the attention of the young cabman who arises from sleep to drink from the water bucket. He brushes off Iona's advance and is very quickly asleep again. The narrator tells us that "just as the young man had been thirsty for water, he [Iona] thirsts for speech." This is followed by Iona's soliloquy—in the narrator's indirect discourse—in which, in effect, Iona finds an outlet for his speech within himself. His sentences repeat and elaborate on the kernel sentence: "He wants to talk." "He wants to talk of it properly, with deliberation." He also "wants to tell," "wants to describe," "to talk about," and "to talk to." And what he wants to tell to others includes the last words his son had told to him.

Iona is fully self-conscious now. He knows of his need for speech. He has found and used the speech which defines his need. He knows that he cannot tolerate thinking about his son while alone. He knows that "to talk" is to make it bearable. With the restoration or recovery of such self-consciousness comes the restoration of Iona's full and unquestioned dignity, his status as man, not beast. He goes out to the stables. When the mare offers no resistance to Iona's approach and to his first references to his son, "Iona is silent for a while, and then he goes on." In that uninterpreted silence, we know what Iona is thinking: he will be permitted to tell "her all about it." What an extraordinary twist of irony it is that allows the beast to be the man's salvation, if the term is not too strong. Critics' reminders that **"Misery"** comes almost at the start of Chekhov's literary career, that it is perhaps "too directly moving," or too close to sentimentality, need not be refuted. The rudeness of its emotional blows, its bashing in our snout, cannot be denied. But perhaps it is this very immaturity of the work to which we owe our ability to trace with unwonted confidence and unseemly ease the narrative and thematic practices through which our hearts have been enthralled.

Notes

1. I use the Constance Garnett translation which first appeared in *The Schoolmistress and Other Stories,* New York: Macmillan, 1921: 57-65. As this text is quite short and has been reprinted in numerous collections, I do not supply page references. The story may be conveniently found in the Norton Critical Edition of Chekhov's short stories (New York, 1979). Among the college textbook anthologies which reprint it are *The Modern Tradition: An Anthology of Short Stories,* ed. Daniel F. Howard, 4th ed. (Boston: Little, 1979) and various versions of *Elements of Literature,* ed. Robert Scholes et al (Oxford UP, 1978-82). In this last textbook, the story is titled "Heartache." More than one of Chekhov's stories bears the translated title "Misery." The text being considered here was published in *Petersburgskaya gazeta,* No. 26, and bore the title "Toska." The text often uses a series of three or four periods to indicate pauses. In all but one instance, my quotations silently remove these periods in the interest of clarity. I am aware of the dangers of close reading of a translated text, the dangers that the translator, not the author, might be the one responsible for a given effect. I have had the good fortune of having the gracious

cooperation of Professor Zenon M. Kuk, Professor of Russian and German at the University of Toledo. Professor Kuk read my text against Chekhov's story in its original tongue and advised me of instances in which my innocence of the Russian language might have led me astray. For a thoughtful and informed discussion of the "limitations and difficulties" of close critical readings in translated literary texts, see Beverly Hahn. *Chekhov: A Study of the Major Stories and Plays.* Cambridge: Cambridge UP, 1977: ix-xi. Hahn finds that "in Chekhov's case there are some special factors to help mitigate the difficulties." These are the "highly structured" nature of his art and his preference for simile over metaphor. Her treatment of "Misery" concentrates on "the falling snow and the lights of the impersonal city, unheedful of Iona, [which] insist imaginatively upon the transience of life and the loneliness of sorrow" (69).

2. Ronald Hingley. *A New Life of Anton Chekhov.* London: Oxford UP, 1976: 58. Hahn (62) implies a similar judgment, finding "overdone" the episode of Iona's second fare. She also states that "whole paragraphs, though bordering on ["Dickens"ian] sentimentality, . . . are intensely moving."

3. Quoted by A. B. Derman. *O Masterstve Chekhova,* Moscow, 1959, portions of which, translated by Ralph E. Matlaw, appear in *Anton Chekhov's Short Stories.* Ed. Ralph E. Matlaw. New York: Norton, 1979: 304.

4. Hingley, 58.

5. Renato Poggioli. *The Phoenix and the Spider: A Book of Essays about some Russian Writers and their View of the Self.* Cambridge, Mass.: Harvard UP, 1957: 119.

6. Poggioli, 126, quoting Tolstoy.

7. Edmund Wilson. *A Window on Russia.* New York: Farrar, 1972: 54-55.

8. Poggioli, 111.

9. Quoted by Robert Louis Jackson, "Introduction: Perspectives on Chekhov," in *Chekhov: A Collection of Critical Essays.* Ed. Robert Lewis Jackson. Englewood Cliffs, N.J.: Prentice, 1967: 4.

10. Jackson, 4.

11. "Even if a whole snowdrift had fallen on him" is the translation of Robert Payne. *The Image of Chekhov.* New York: Knopf, 1971: 99.

12. Poggioli, 119, errs here where he says that Iona bends in response to the extreme cold. The text says nothing of the temperature. The snow is "wet," falls "lazily," and lies "in a thin soft layer." By implication, the weather is relatively mild.

13. A. P. Chudakov. *Chekhov's Poetics*. Trans. Edwina Jannie Cruise and Donald Dragt. Ann Arbor: Ardis, 1983: 33.

14. Derman, 305.

15. Poggioli, 119, notices the connection between Iona's back and that of the unnamed hunchback.

16. Professor Kuk thinks the translator's "whimsical" here misses the point of the original which is that the hunchback cursed Iona with particularly strong obscenities.

David W. Martin (essay date April 1987)

SOURCE: Martin, David W. "Chekhov and the Modern Short Story in English." *Neophilologus* 71, no. 2 (April 1987): 129-43.

[*In the following essay, Martin assesses Chekhov's influence on modern English literature and considers his place within the tradition of the short story genre.*]

The purpose of this essay is to discuss Chekhov's place as a major figure in the art of the short story as it has developed in modern times, with particular regard to his reception and appreciation by people of letters in the English-speaking world. Attention will therefore be paid to some of those comments made on the subject of Chekhov by critics whose background and experience are associated in the main with English literature and whose viewpoint is for this reason different from that of Russian writers on Chekhov and indeed from that of English-speaking slavists.

Apart from this and more importantly there will be an examination of the impact made by Chekhov's stories upon modern writers in English and of his role as an initiator of a new approach to the short story, an approach which was to be developed and broadened by a number of writers of fiction in the West.

Here the main emphasis will be upon the presentation of this new approach in terms of a loosely interrelated school but not upon the specific notion of influence. To talk of the influence of one writer upon another is often misleading and can be wrong, especially where there are no reliable means to distinguish between coincidence of expression and influence. However, in a number of cases critics and other writers do refer specifically to Chekhov's influence as a short-story writer and mention will be made of them when the occasion presents itself.

First and foremost there arises the question of what exactly is meant by the term "modern short story". Although forms of the story as a genre have existed for centuries, its popularity increased markedly at the beginning of the nineteenth century in response to the requirements of a growing number of literary magazines. The magazine has remained the chief outlet for stories, upon which it has necessarily imposed the stricture of brevity, something of no small importance in the overall composition of a periodical. However, as not infrequently happens, this practical necessity was to become an aesthetic virtue; and even before the first half of the nineteenth century was out, economy of design had come to be regarded as a prime quality of the short story. This we may see from Edgar Allan Poe's writing on the subject.

Allied to the notion of brevity came the concept of singleness of effect. The short story should not digress or involve itself in a multiplicity of plots like the novel, but should rather take for its subject a single occasion or an integral series of occasions, and for its goal an overall effect to which all aspects of action and characterization must be subjugated. Thus, in his review of Hawthorne's *Twice-Told Tales,* Poe writes:

> A skilful literary artist has constructed a tale. If wise, he has not fashioned his thoughts to accommodate his incidents; but having conceived, with deliberate care, a certain unique or single *effect* to be wrought out, he then invents such incidents—he then combines such events as may best aid him in establishing this preconceived effect. If his very initial sentence tend not to the outbringing of this effect, then he has failed in his first step. In the whole composition there should be no word written, of which the tendency, direct or indirect, is not to the one pre-established design. And by such means, with such care and skill, a picture is at length painted which leaves in the mind of him who contemplates it with a kindred art, a sense of the fullest satisfaction. The idea of the tale has been presented unblemished, because undisturbed; and this is an end unattainable by the novel. Undue brevity is just as exceptionable here as in the poem; but undue length is yet more to be avoided.[1]

In the above Poe lays the foundation for a school of writing, developed by Chekhov and others, which was to oust the corner-stone of Poe's own art: the tale of drama and adventure. His attention to form, singleness of purpose and overall effect helped win for them a position superior to that of outward content in the short story.

This is not to imply that content became unimportant but rather that writers in more recent years have had less regard for the dramatic, suspenseful, perhaps frightening, certainly unique quality of their themes, and more for the inventiveness and skill with which devices of style and tone are employed to achieve the desired general effect. For this reason it is not impossible nowadays, and has been for some time, for two stories by different writers to be identical in theme but totally dissimilar in the aesthetic impression they create simply because of their individual styles of composition. It is this trait which most clearly distinguishes the specifically modern short story from the genre as a whole.

In the case of Chekhov this feature is strongly felt in a number of statements he made which even go so far as to suggest a total disinterest on his part in the subject of any given composition. To Teleshov he remarked: "You can even write well about the moon, and that's a worn-out theme alright. And it will be interesting. Only you must just the same see something of your own in the moon and not something already seen or exhausted."[2] To Bunin he said: "It is immaterial whether you write about love or not about love, the main thing is that it should be talented."[3] And Avilova records him as saying: "I can write about anything you like. Tell me to write about a bottle and there will be a story entitled "The Bottle". Living images create thought, it is not the thought which creates the image."[4]

Thus, for Chekhov, the image, the literary vehicle, is the living matter of which thought is born; and thought, the supreme act and goal of creativity, is diametrically opposed by him to the initial stage of composition: its basic, often incidental theme or scheme of events. Poe used the term "thought" in a similar sense above. He also referred to this final aim of a work as "effect", "design", "idea"; and from the statements of both writers a certain hierarchy emerges, that of, in ascending order, incident, image, idea.

It is not at all difficult to find stories in Chekhov where the emphasis of the work is placed on the artistic means of expression employed to a certain end, rather than on action, the chain of events, or indeed abstract ideas for their own sake alone. One of the first people to draw attention to this fact in the West was Somerset Maugham, who commented that Chekhov's stories, unlike his own, cannot be recounted after dinner, something which made them inferior; for in Chekhov, Maugham maintained, there is "nothing to tell".[5] Here he alludes to that apparent lack of content which characterizes Chekhov's art, where poetic vision and strength of expression take precedence over outward movement.

We would argue that the unique personality of Chekhov's writing chiefly lies in his formal innovations and characteristics of style, from which come the "idea" and overall effect of a work: yet his stories possess personality not only by dint of the peculiarities of his formal techniques but also because they are essentially lyrical, having a thinking and feeling narrator, rather than syllogistic and removed. E. Baldeshwiler has written interestingly on this general topic;[6] and E. Taylor comments specifically on the personality, the "signature", contained in the manner in which a writer chooses to bring a short story to its close.[7]

Virginia Woolf was among the first to recognize an organic connection between Chekhov's compositional methods and his role as lyrical and philosophic mentor:

> There is an originality in his choice of the elements which make up a story which sometimes produces an arrangement so unlike any we have met with before that it is necessary to consider whether he is not hinting at some order hitherto unguessed at, though perhaps never fully stated by him.[8]

It is, then, in these areas of composition and tone, as opposed to the outward show of action and event, that we will begin to look for evidence of a creative experience shared by Chekhov and major writers in the West. Avrom Fleishman in his article, "Forms of the Woolfian Short Story", takes us to the heart of the question when he writes: "Though it has long been recognized that the stories of Chekhov, Joyce, Mansfield, Woolf, and a variable number of later writers constitute a loose but inevitable grouping, this critical commonplace remains untested by the usual historical and stylistic evidence for generic developments".[9]

It would be difficult to say which of the two writers, Virginia Woolf or Katherine Mansfield, has been the most regularly associated with Chekhov as close followers if not imitators of his style. Certainly, we are indebted to Virginia Woolf for her championing of Russian writers in the West, including Chekhov, whom she held in particular esteem. In her essay, "The Russian Point of View", she refers to that same lack of content which struck Somerset Maugham and which has since become characteristic of our western view of Chekhov. "Our first impressions of Tchekov", she writes, "are . . . of bewilderment. What is the point of it, and why does he make a story out of this?" Woolf goes on to point out the astonishing novelty of Chekhov, in whom one finds an approach very different from that of "most Victorian fiction" where, in her words, "the tune is familiar and the end emphatic—lovers united, villains discomfited, intrigues exposed", for in Chekhov nothing is settled, nothing completed. However, Woolf underlines that it is only these less subtle aspects of the popular short story which are absent in the Russian writer. The public ear, she says, is used to "louder music" and "fiercer measures" than Chekhov's. Yet it is apparent to her that Chekhov's works do indeed have content, that their emptiness is only seeming, for an activity of the mind and character has replaced the interest of earlier fiction in the surface movements of human life. "These stories", she comments on Chekhov, "are always showing us some affectation, pose, insincerity. Some woman has got into a false relation; some man has been perverted by the inhumanity of his circumstances. The soul is ill; the soul is cured; the soul is not cured. These are the emphatic points in his stories."[10]

Woolf goes on to indicate a correlation between this, the underlying and real content of Chekhov's stories, and his method of composition, both of which stand in contrast to previous concepts of the genre:

> Once the eye is used to these shades, half the "conclusions" of fiction fade into thin air; they show like transparencies with a light behind them—gaudy, glaring, superficial. The general tidying up of the last chapter, the marriage, the death, the statement of values so sonorously trumpeted forth, so heavily underlined, become of the most rudimentary kind . . . On the other hand, the method which at first seemed so casual, inconclusive, and occupied with trifles, now appears the result of an exquisitely original and fastidious taste, choosing boldly, arranging infallibly, and controlled by an honesty for which we can find no match save among the Russians themselves.[11]

Particular attention should be paid to the two phrases used here by Woolf, "choosing boldly" and "arranging infallibly", for here she underscores the importance in Chekhov of composition and the degree to which the two authorial domains of choice and arrangement are refined in his works. This was a topic she had written about more elaborately in a review of 1919. Chekhov's stories, she observed,

> provide a resting point for the mind—a solid object casting its shade of reflection and speculation. The fragments of which it is composed may have the air of having come together by chance. Certainly it often seems as if Tchehov made up his stories rather in the way that a hen picks up grain. Why should she pick here and there, from side to side, when, so far as we can see, there is no reason to prefer one grain to another! His choice is strange, and yet there is no longer any doubt that whatever Tchehov chooses he chooses with the finest insight.[12]

The fastidiousness, to modify Woolf's own word, with which Chekhov defended, developed, propagated and employed those techniques of choice and arrangement which are the primary generic hall-mark of the modern short story is unsurpassed; and of all the qualities of the short story the one most vociferously and zealously guarded by Chekhov was that it should actually be short, a quality which naturally required a discerning exercise of choice. Chekhov had in his own words a mania for everything short; new writers just acquiring their skills should, he said, tear up the first half of each of their stories, which generally contained unnecessary introductory material; the art of writing, he remarked, really consists in the art of crossing out everything that is badly written.

T. O. Beachcroft, in his book on the short story, *The Modest Art,* writes of Chekhov's comment to the effect that there had been a great deal of talk about the development of the short story as an art form, but that all that had really happened was that "Maupassant in France and I in Russia began writing very short stories. There's your new movement in literature." Beachcroft then points out that "We have to remember that it was Chekhov and Maupassant who were writing the short stories that were really short."[13]

In the search for brevity not only does the right of authorial choice, fastidiousness, perhaps, become particularly important, but it naturally follows that a maximum power of expression can only be achieved through the correct arrangement of that material which has passed scrutiny. The Chekovian story is a composite of quite deliberately arranged sections and subsections, assembled like the bricks and beams of a house, where every small brick adds to the strength of the whole and every beam carries weight.

J. B. Priestly, discussing a neatly handled scene in **"The Bishop,"** writes:

> Chekhov has a genius—and it *is* genius, not simply an experienced writer's trick—for this power of suggestion, this maximum of effect created by the smallest possible means. (And here his influence on later writers throughout the world has been all to the good). He can do it with people, with situations, with backgrounds. He could do more with fifty words than most of his contemporaries could do with five hundred. He is the master in language of the swift impressionistic sketch or the powerful drawing with most of the lines left out.[14]

What lines, then, are in fact left out of this powerful drawing of Chekhov's, as Priestly puts it? The answer is clear enough: everything that has no bearing on the purpose of the work, and this is to depict the characters' inner life. Thus we shall search in vain in Chekhov for what we take for granted in other fiction—a detailed account of a hero's forbears and family, of his environment, his house, his dress, his education, the less meaningful aspects of conversation, marriage, death—all these things, unless they have radical importance in the revelation of inner life, are either not mentioned by the writer at all or dismissed with a perfunctoriness befitting their actual insignificance.

In short, Chekhov does not dwell on social background or incidental environment, but Beachcroft is right when he comments that Chekhov's "care for the inner truth of the individual makes the people in his stories points of irradiation which shed light on the conditions of their lives and of other people around them. The discursive background is contained in the truth with which the individual is seen."[15] In other words, depth of vision removes any necessity for superficial narrative scope.

Let us compare here two stories, one Chekhov's **"Teacher of Literature,"** the other, **"Lappin and Lapinova"** by Virginia Woolf. In the first, the hero, Nikitin, falls in love and marries, only to realize that his wife is unthinking, unfeeling and interested in little other than jars of sour cream. And it is to this superficiality and domestic vegetation on the part of the wife, because it bears so strongly upon the hero's view of things, that Chekhov devotes a major part of his attention. There is a wealth of detail about the heroine's petty cares, about her time-wasting, her lazy existence, even her cat. By the end of the story the marriage is in effect over, with Nikitin shouting that he must leave or go mad. But the actual end of the marriage is not described, Nikitin's departure is not presented to us; perhaps he never went, perhaps he stayed, we are simply not told. Yet the story is complete, the point has been made, the tragic clash of personalities revealed. There is nothing left for Chekhov to write.

In Virginia Woolf's story, again there is a marriage and again it ends because of the sudden revelation of an inner incompatibility and, as in Chekhov, this is conveyed to us by means of a seemingly unimportant scheme of events. This time it is the heroine who is disillusioned, but she maintains her resolve to save the marriage by playing a game with her husband, in which he pretends to be a rabbit called Lappin, and she a hare called Lapinova. This game holds them together, it is their shield against the world. Yet they both know it is an artifice. For him it is simply a game, soon to be forgotten amid the serious activities of life; for her, it is the saving of their marriage. But this is too much to ask of any game, and in the end she despairs. These are the final lines of the story:

> "Oh Ernest, Ernest!" she cried, starting up in her chair.
>
> "Well, what's up, now?" He asked briskly, warming his hands at the fire.
>
> "It's Lapinova . . ." she faltered, glancing wildly at him out of her great startled eyes. "She's gone, Ernest. I've lost her!"
>
> Ernest frowned. He pressed his lips tight together. "Oh, that's what's up, is it?" he said, smiling rather grimly at his wife. For ten seconds he stood there, silent; and she waited, feeling hands tightening at the back of her neck.
>
> "Yes", he said at length. "Poor Lapinova . . ." He straightened his tie at the looking-glass over the mantelpiece.
>
> "Caught in a trap", he said, "killed" and sat down and read the newspaper.

And these are the very last words of the story: "So that was the end of that marriage."[16]

Clearly, both Chekhov's and Woolf's stories are of one type, for here again no words are wasted on the actual depiction of the end of the marriage. That—the important thing—is missing. In its place we have a succession of incidentals, but of telling incidentals. And there is something else missing from the two works, Woolf being here in fact more consistent than Chekhov, and that is any probing examination of the characters' feelings. Certainly, both writers successfully convey their heroes' inner experience to the reader, but they do so by means of actions which are symbolic. And it is to Chekhov and now, as we see, to Woolf, that we owe the development of this technique of symbolism, one which is central to the laconicism exacted of the modern short story.

William Gerhardi, one of Chekhov's earliest commentators in English, remarked that Chekhov showed us the importance of the "little things".[17] Now this observation on its own is misleading, for it implies that Chekhov somehow reveals to us the innate importance of everyday phenomena which we have hitherto looked upon as more or less insignificant. Of course he did not do that, but rather he invested with symbolic significance things which of themselves remain of little import. The symbol points to a wider whole; moreover the concrete object in its symbolic role may contain pent up within itself the whole explosive force of the emotion of the moment. And this, too, is of fundamental importance to the short story writer who, instead of attempting to convey emotion—something amorphous and abstract—in its own terms or by means of direct and drawn-out description, can wrap it up in a concrete symbol and present it to the reader in a form much more readily assimilated by the imagination.

Chekhov's story, **"The Murder,"** contains an instance of this. It is a story of fratricide. Yakov kills his brother Matvei by hitting him with an iron, partly because Matvei has insisted on having oil with his boiled potatoes, something which offends Yakov's religious sensitivities. There follows the quarrel at the end of which Matvei is killed. Yakov takes fright, but Chekhov does not at this point enter upon any direct description of Yakov's state of mind. Such abstractions would have a debilitating effect on the immediacy of the narrative, and in place of them he writes simply: "Nothing was as frightening for Yakov as the blood-soaked boiled potatoes, upon which he was afraid to tread".[18]

In this way something incidental, essentially unimportant, is made to bear the whole emotional weight of the scene; and this symbolic concretization is one method by which Chekhov is able to combine verbal economy with fullness of expression. There is also a certain dynamism in the device, where abstractions, ideas, feelings and other intangible emotive forces are conveyed in terms of a concrete reality. Among later writers, Sherwood Anderson employs the technique to good effect in, for example, "His Chest of Drawers," where the fate of the article of furniture mirrors that of the hero and becomes the vehicle of its expression.

A development of this technique is found when emotions and abstractions are not conveyed by means of concrete symbols, but are treated as if they were themselves concrete. This conversation takes place between Sof'ia L'vovna and Vladimir Mikhailych in Chekhov's **"Big Volodia and Little Volodia,"** the context is immaterial:

> And when he made ready to go, she asked him agitatedly:
>
> "When? Today? Where?"
>
> And she reached up with both arms to his mouth, as if trying to grasp his answer even with her hands.[19]

Here, then, then aesthetic effect is encapsulated in the implied concretization of the awaited answer. And in this field we find similarities in the style of Katherine Mansfield. These words occur in her story, "The Daughters of the Late Colonel":

> A perfect fountain of bubbling notes shook from the barrel-organ, round, bright notes, carelessly scattered.
>
> Constantia lifted her big, cold hands as if to catch them . . .[20]

This device of concretization is also one of visualization; and it is employed in both Chekhov and Mansfield in any number of ways. Nor is it absent from the literary style of more recent practioners of the art of the short story. The following is from "The Comforts of Home" by F. O'Connor, whose work possesses a number of features of structure and tone which may be traced back to Chekhov. In this passage the reference to Sarah Ham's laugh exemplifies both concrete visualization and personification of an intangible entity: "Thomas . . . lunged back to the car and sped off. The other door was still hanging open and her laugh, bodiless but real, bounded up the street as if it were about to jump in the open side of the car and ride away with him".[21]

The same visual technique may be used to convey not a simple, single abstraction or emotion but a whole complex of ideas; and again, the vehicle used to convey it may take the form not of a single object or action, but of a more wide-ranging pictorial representation. The morbid imaginings and indeed the whole psychological condition of the dying professor in Chekhov's **"A Boring Story"** are made immediate and real to us when he comments succinctly that it seems to him that the whole of nature is waiting, its ear cocked, for him to die.[22]

The economy of style present here, where involved psychological analysis gives way to visual immediacy, is, then, characteristic of the modern short story. As Beachcroft concludes, "Not until the stories are really short do the especial insights of the form truly show themselves."[23]

Thus the very necessity for brevity has given birth to such dynamic creative devices. In the story by Mansfield mentioned previously, "The Daughters of the Late Colonel," the whole atmosphere of life as it had been during the colonel's lifetime—the oppression, the authoritarianism of his house, the abject state of subjugation and intimidation in which he kept his daughters—is given to us in an imaginative picture. In Chapter V we read:

> Neither of them could possibly believe that father was never coming back. Josephine had had a moment of absolute terror at the cemetery, while the coffin was lowered, to think that she and Constantia had done this thing without asking his permission. What would father say when he found out? For he was bound to find out sooner or later. "Buried. You two girls had me *burried*!" She heard his stick thumping. Oh, what would they say? What possible excuse could they make?[24]

In this way the overbearing manner of the father is presented in an imaginary moment of domestic drama. The hidden, the abstract is made visible, audible. Yet this instance serves to highlight a distinction between Chekhov and Mansfield and reveals in the latter a lesser sense of compositional balance and stylistic nicety. For a writer cannot necessarily prolong an aesthetic effect by prolonging the stylistic means by which it is achieved. This is certainly true in the present case. The essence of Mansfield's effect lies in its pithiness, its succinct depiction of the episode and its anecdotal character. In fact the amusing nature of the instance heightens our understanding of the sisters' tragic psychological inadequacy. The scene thus seems to be complete, yet Mansfield continues:

> It sounded such an appallingly heartless thing to do. Such a wicked advantage to take of a person because he happened to be helpless at the moment. The other people seemed to treat it as a matter of course. They were strangers; they couldn't be expected to understand that father was the very last person for such a thing to happen to. No, the entire blame for it all would fall on her and Constantia. And the expense, she thought, stepping into the tight-buttoned cab. When she had to show him the bills. What would he say then?
>
> She heard him absolutely roaring. "And do you expect me to pay for this gimcrack excursion of yours?"
>
> "Oh", groaned poor Josephine aloud, "we shouldn't have done it, Con!"
>
> And Constantia, pale as a lemon in all that blackness, said in a frightened whisper, "Done what, Jug?"
>
> "Let them bu- bury father like that", said Josephine, breaking down and crying into her new, queer-smelling mourning handkerchief.
>
> "But what else could we have done?" asked Constantia wonderingly. "We couldn't have kept him, Jug—we couldn't have kept him unburied. At any rate, not in a flat that size."
>
> Josephine blew her nose; the cab was dreadfully stuffy.
>
> "I don't know", she said forlornly. "It is all so dreadful. I feel we ought to have tried to, just for a time at least. To make perfectly sure. One thing's certain"— and her tears sprang out again—"father will never forgive us for this—never!"[25]

So ends Chapter V of the story. Chapter VI begins: "Father would never forgive them. That was what they felt more than ever when, two mornings later, they went into his room to go through his things".[26]

Thus a fine narrative idea is impossibly diluted by more being demanded of it than it is able to give; and the present writer contends that Chekhov would have avoided such an excess. The term "flash of insight" is not infrequently encountered in critical writing on the modern short story. In the quoted passage from Mansfield, the insight may be present, but the flash is lost.

This "flash" only occurs when a statement on the human condition—or, perhaps, on the life of nature—is made with the maximum economy of form. The fewer the words, the greater the power of expression invested in each and the greater the explosion, the flash. Now economy of form can never be greater than when the statement and its means of expression in the terms of the story are identical. Beachcroft writes:

> It may be possible for a novelist to create his images in a novel, and also to step aside and discuss their significance. The two elements can be separated, or may even complement each other. But within the smaller limits of the short story the comment and the vision cannot appear separately. The vision arises at that moment when the symbolic image corresponds with the natural image.[27]

The vision, the flash, is found, then, when the chosen form stands in a closer relationship, if not one of total identity, to authorial statement (the idea, the overall purpose), than is contained in the plain meaning of the words.

Whereas, however, image and idea tend to merge in the story into a single productive whole, they together militate against grand developments on the level of incident and background narrative. Saying "what happened" in a short story is not sufficient and is often of less importance than the manner of expression. The following conversation is recorded as taking place between Chekhov and Korolenko, when Chekhov asked:

> Do you find that this happens: when you are writing, between two episodes which you can see clearly in your imagination there is suddenly an empty space?

> Across which . . . you have to build little bridges not with your imagination any more, but with logic?

> Yes, yes.[28]

Here "logic", those routine verbal perambulations by which gaps between artistically conceived scenes are bridged, is not only seen as opposed to imagination, but actually as inferior to it. That is to say, the short story writer strives for the creative vision, for "living images" in Chekhov's phrase, not for a dogged relation of circumstantial events chronologically set out. E. Taylor has commented perceptively on the topic, beginning with how a work should start:

> The moment of arrival into a story—the reader's arrival—must be carefully chosen. Guy de Maupassant's *Boule-de-Suif* opens with a sense of occasion, of action continuing. "For several days in succession remnants of a defeated army had been passing through the town." This filling-in by narrative is necessary to the story, and it continues for a page or two. Rereading it, I long impatiently for the author to be writing in scenes—to get into the coach, and begin the real story; for this seems to me to be one of the great charms of the short story—to be able to write in scenes, without the tedious repetition of how time has gone on, and with what effects, of the cumbrous moving about of characters from one place to another. We all know those banal links and explanations—getting from A to B: "Many years had passed, and the pretty little girl had grown into a beautiful woman." Not for me, I think; for unity is broken, and the magic gone.[29]

Chekhov, Woolf and Mansfield's stories are comparatively bereft of incident; for the charge that "nothing happens" can be levelled at the work of all three. Yet the art of the modern story does not require incident or action in time in order to be significant, because it strives to capture what humanity is rather than what it does. There is a story by Virginia Woolf called "The Mark on the Wall." The first sentence reads: "Perhaps it was the middle of January in the present year that I first looked up and saw the mark on the wall".[30] Having seen it, the author begins to wonder what the mark might be, but her imagination takes over and the story branches into a series of philosophic reflections, occasionally returning to the subject of the mark, only to leave it again. There is certainly nothing Chekhovian in these reflections, they have a strangely contrived air, but here is a sample which illustrates the subordination of the incident—the appearance of the mark—to the inner life of the subject, which in this case is of course Woolf herself:

> But for that mark, I'm not sure about it; I don't believe it was made by a nail; it's too big, too round, for that. I might get up, but if I got up and looked at it, ten to one I shouldn't be able to say for certain; because once a thing's done, no one ever knows how it happened. Oh! dear me, the mystery of life; the inaccuracy of thought! The ignorance of humanity! To show how very little control of our possessions we have—what an accidental affair this living is after all our civilization—let me just count over a few of the things lost in one lifetime, beginning, for that seems always the most mysterious of losses—what cat would gnaw, what rat would nibble—three pale blue canisters of book-binding tools?[31]

The story proceeds in this vein, with the mark losing importance as the reflections gain it, until an unnamed person at the end of the work happens to comment, "I don't see why we should have a snail on our wall", and Woolf adds, "Ah, the mark on the wall! It was a snail."[32]

Here we have a story which is almost totally without incident, but which is rich in imagination and invention. Indeed a natural extension of this narrative method is the story where the motivating event behind the whole does not actually form part of the story at all. There is a well-known story by Chekhov about a coachman whose son has died and who wants to tell his passengers about it. No one listens and he finishes by confiding in his horse. But the main event—the death of the son—does not figure anywhere in the work on the level of incident; for the story is concerned only with the experience of the coachman, his anguish and frustration.[33] In this respect we may compare it to Mansfield's "The Voyage," where the emotive event—the death of a small girl's mother—does not form part of the story, but nevertheless colours the entire narrative.

The modern short story, then, describes inner experience, not superficial activities or the logical sequence of events for their own sake. C. K. Stead in his essay "Katherine Mansfield and the Art of Fiction", writes of Mansfield's realization that:

> fiction did not have to be shaped towards a conclusion, a climax, a dénouement; or . . . that a fiction [by which Stead means a *modern* short story] is not quite the same thing as a story. A fiction survives, not by leading us anywhere, but by being at every point authentic, a recreation of life, so that we experience it and remember it as we experience and remember actual life itself.[34]

Later Stead comments in this way on two of Mansfield's stories: "The items of "Prelude" and "At the Bay" cohere without narrative linking. And individually they are most successful when they are not forced to make a point."[35]

Narrative linking is absent or reduced to a minimum in Mansfield as in Chekhov again because both writers omit what happens outwardly to their characters, except where it contributes to their characters' life experience. This accent on life experience is particularly evident in passages of description. The eyes and ears of the hero observer or narrator are, we may suppose, open to everything, but we are not presented with this "everything" in the work of fiction, but only with that which reaches the conscious mind and forms part of its experience. On the simplest level this is demonstrated in the especial attention paid by both Chekhov and Mansfield to the recording of salient sensory perceptions: a sudden noise amidst silence, a source of brightness against a dark background.

Chekhov writes: "The bell slowly and lingeringly, sharply disturbing the quiet of the evening, struck ten."[36] Mansfield has: "There was . . . something else—what was it?—a faint stirring and shaking, the snapping of a twig and then such silence that it seemed someone was

listening."[37] Chekhov describes a "village on the far bank [of the lake], with a tall, narrow bell-tower on which the cross was burning in the reflected rays of the setting sun."[38] Mansfield says: "Little faint winds were playing chase, in at the tops of the windows, out at the doors. And there were two tiny spots of sun, one on the inkpot, one on a silver photograph frame, playing too."[39] In Chekhov we read: "Finally the train appeared. From the smoke-stack completely pink steam poured out and rose over the woods, and two windows in the last carriage suddenly flashed in the sun so brightly that it was painful to look."[40] In Mansfield we find: "The far away sky—a bright, pure blue—was reflected in the puddles, and the drops, swimming along the telegraph poles, flashed into points of light. Now the leaping, glittering sea was so bright it made one's eyes ache to look at it."[41]

In these instances, particularly the latter where eyes are said to suffer because of bright light, we feel the presence of a subjective hero, of a lyrical observer, and it is his experience which is crystallized in this method of narrative.

The crystallization of experience, the flash of vision, the insight which comes from the casual, seemingly unimportant event, all these things are found in various forms in the modern short story and form its character. James Joyce invented the succinct term "epiphany" to describe this technique, which is frequently manifest in his collection of stories, *Dubliners*. Harry Levin, in his preface to the 1950 edition of the *Essential James Joyce*, comments:

> The older technique of short-story writing, with Maupassant and O. Henry, attempted to make daily life more eventful by unscrupulous manipulation of surprises and coincidences. Joyce—with Chekhov—discarded such contrivances, introducing a genre which has been so widely imitated that nowadays its originality is not readily detected. The open structure, which casually adapts itself to the flow of experience, and the close texture, which gives precise notation to sensitive observation, are characteristic of Joycean narrative. The fact that so little happens, apart form expected routines, connects form with theme: the paralysed uneventfulness to which the modern city reduces the lives of its citizens. Little of the actual story need be told: the romance of "Two Gallants" is painfully implicit in conversations before and after. Not one but many of these sketches might be titled "An Encounter." In calling his original jottings "epiphanies", Joyce underscored the ironic contrast between the manifestation that dazzled the Magi and the apparitions that manifest themselves on the streets of Dublin; he also suggested that these pathetic and sordid glimpses, to the sentient observer, offer a kind of revelation. As the part, significantly chosen, reveals the whole, a word or detail may be enough to exhibit a character or convey a situation.[42]

This lengthy but fruitful passage from Levin's preface extends to Joyce a number of points to which attention has already been drawn in relation to other modern short-story writers: "the flow of experience", "precise notation", "sensitive observation"—no formula does justice to the phenomenon and Sherwood Anderson's phrase, "the thing", is really no worse than any.[43] In Levin's remarks, however, there is the added question of theme. The paralysed uneventfulness of Joycean stories certainly corresponds to the renowned "philistinism" depicted in a number of Chekhov's stories, **"The Pecheneg,"** for example, as well as to the banality on which some of Mansfield's characters flounder: her "Marriage à la Mode" is a devastating indictment of a life of ineptitude and stupidity. And when we read the ending of Joyce's "Eveline" we are reminded again of Nikitin in **"A Teacher of Literature,"** who had to escape from the emptiness of his life or else go mad. Joyce writes:

> As she mused the pitiful vision of her mother's life laid its spell on the very quick of her being—that life of commonplace sacrifices closing in final craziness. She trembled as she heard again her mother's voice saying constantly with foolish insistence:
>
> "Derevaun Seraun! Derevaun Seraun!"
>
> She stood up in a sudden impulse of terror. Escape! She must escape! Frank would save her. He would give her life, perhaps love, too. But she wanted to live. Why should she be unhappy? She had a right to happiness. Frank would take her in his arms, fold her in his arms. He would save her.[44]

And then there is this passage in "A Little Cloud," again reminiscent of Chekhov, perhaps **"The Betrothed,"** with its depiction of the frustrations of a closed domestic world. Joyce puts it like this:

> He found something mean in the pretty furniture which he had bought for his house on the hire system. Annie had chosen it herself and it reminded him of her. It too was prim and pretty. A dull resentment against his life awoke within him. Could he not escape from his little house?[45]

Gabriel Conroy in "The Dead" talks of his fear that "this new generation, educated or hypereducated as it is, will lack those qualities of humanity, of hospitality, of kindly humour which belonged to an older day." He feels that they were living in a "less spacious age".[46]

Chekhov, Mansfield, Joyce and, indeed, Woolf all wrote stories which display the emptiness and aimlessness of the age, its paralysis of spirit. This is in part exemplified in that love of anti-climax and fruitlessness which Chekhov shared with others, from Mansfield to Anderson (see his "A Walk in the Moonlight," for example). Yet the real point to be made here—and with it this essay is concluded—is that it became possible to choose such themes only with the discovery by writers from Chekhov on of those stimulating and incisive techniques of style which have been the subject of discussion

above. For how else can one write a viable story depicting banality without being banal? How else can one describe boredom without being boring, or weakness of will without feebleness of expression? The old short story took its strength from the robustness of its theme; the new, from the dynamics of its style, a style which, it might be argued, actually required a certain lack of superficial incident in order to throw its properties into starker relief and by so doing deepen the insight, make keener the vision, more revelatory the epiphany.

Notes

1. Review of Nathaniel Hawthorne's *Twice-Told Tales,* in E. A. Poe, *Selected Prose and Poetry,* revised edition by W. H. Auden, New York, 1955, p. 450. Poe's italics.

2. *A. P. Chekhov o literature* (*A. P. Chekhov on Literature*), edited by L. Pokrovskaia, Moscow, 1955, p. 300.

3. Ibid., p. 301.

4. Ibid., p. 281.

5. Quoted in T. O. Beachcroft, *The Modest Art: A Survey of the Short Story in English,* London, 1968 p. 5.

6. See Eileen Baldeshwiler, "The Lyric Short Story: The Sketch of a History", *Studies in Short Fiction,* 6, 1968-9, 443-53.

7. Elizabeth Taylor, "England", in "The International Symposium of the Short Story: Part Three", *Kenyon Review,* 31, 1969, 469-73 (p. 472).

8. Virginia Woolf, "Tchehov's Questions", *The Times Literary Supplement,* 16 May 1918, p. 231.

9. Avrom Fleishman, "Forms of the Woolfian Short Story", in *Virginia Woolf: Revaluation and Continuity,* edited by Ralph Freedman, Berkeley, 1980, pp. 44-5.

10. "The Russian Point of View", in Virginia Woolf, *The Common Reader,* fifth edition, London, 1945, p. 224.

11. Ibid., pp. 224-5. Woolf's remarks are based on her review, "Tchehov's Questions".

12. Virginia Woolf, "The Russian Background", *The Times Literary Supplement,* 14 August 1919, p. 435.

13. Beachcroft, *The Modest Art,* p. 123.

14. J. B. Priestly, *Anton Chekhov,* International Profiles, London, 1970, pp. 67-8. His italics.

15. Beachcroft, *The Modest Art,* p. 123.

16. "Lappin and Lapinova," in Virginia Woolf, *A Haunted House and Other Short Stories,* fourth impression, London, 1947, p. 69.

17. See A. C. Ward, *Aspects of the Modern Short Story: English and American,* London, 1924, p. 282.

18. "The Murder," in A. P. Chekhov, Polnoe sobranie sochinenii i pisem, Moscow, 1974-82, Sochineniia IX, p. 154.

19. "Big Volodia and Little Volodia," in *Polnoe sobranie sochinenii i pisem,* Sochineniia VIII, p. 224.

20. "The Daughters of the Late Colonel," in Katherine Mansfield, *The Garden-Party and Other Stories,* London, 1922, pp. 123-4.

21. "The Comforts of Home," in Flannery O'Connor, *Everything that Rises Must Converge,* thirteenth printing, New York, 1973, p. 126.

22. See "A Boring Story," in *Polnoe sobranie sochinenii i pisem,* Sochineniia VII, p. 301.

23. Beachcroft, *The Modest Art,* p. 123.

24. Katherine Mansfield, *The Daughters of the Late Colonel, The Garden-Party and Other Stories,* p. 104. Her italics.

25. Ibid., pp. 104-5.

26. Ibid., p. 105.

27. Beachcroft, *The Modest Art,* pp. 259-60.

28. *Chekhov o literature,* edited by L. Pokrovskaia, p. 302.

29. Taylor, "England", p. 472.

30. Virginia Woolf, "The Mark on the Wall," in *A Haunted House and Other Short Stories,* p. 35.

31. Ibid., p. 36.

32. Ibid., p. 43.

33. See "Anguish," in *Polnoe sobranie sochinenii i pisem,* Sochineniia IV, pp. 326-30.

34. Quoted in W. Allen, *The Short Story in English,* Oxford, 1981, p. 173.

35. Quoted ibid., p. 173.

36. "Fear," in *Polnoe sobranie sochinenii i pisem,* Sochineniia VIII, p. 132.

37. Katherine Mansfield, "At the Bay," in *The Garden-Party and Other Stories,* p. 8.

38. "The House with the Mezzanine," in *Polnoe sobranie sochinenii i pisem,* Sochineniia IX, p. 175.

39. Katherine Mansfield, "The Garden-Party," in *The Garden-Party and Other Stories,* p. 74.

40. "Three Years," in *Polnoe sobranie sochinenii i pisem,* Sochineniia IX, p. 68.

41. Katherine Mansfield, "At the Bay," in *The Garden-Party and Other Stories,* pp. 9-10.

42. *The Essential James Joyce,* with an introduction and notes by Harry Levin, London, 1950, pp. 21-2.

43. See "The Lost Novel," in Sherwood Anderson, *Short Stories,* edited by Maxwell Geismar, New York, 1962, p. 144.

44. *The Essential James Joyce,* p. 43.

45. Ibid., p. 73.

46. Ibid., p. 160.

Boyd Creasman (essay date spring 1990)

SOURCE: Creasman, Boyd. "Gurov's Flights of Emotion in Chekhov's 'The Lady with the Dog.'" *Studies in Short Fiction* 27, no. 2 (spring 1990): 257-60.

[*In the following essay, Creasman contends that Gurov's two moments of intense feeling in "The Lady with the Dog" are crucial to understanding the character's motivations and demonstrate the significance of emotional flight in Chekhov's short fiction.*]

In 1921, Conrad Aiken made the following assessment of Anton Chekhov's work: "This, after all, is Chekhov's genius—he was a master of mood" (151). Indeed Aiken's statement is a good starting point for a discussion of the structure of Chekhov's short fiction. Many of Chekhov's short stories—the later ones in particular—are structured around the main character's moments of strong emotion, a feature of the author's short fiction that has never been fully explored, even in discussions of individual stories. For example, much of the criticism of **"The Lady with the Dog,"** one of Chekhov's most revered short stories, has focused on its parallels with his real life love for Olga Knipper, the influence of Tolstoy's *Anna Karenina,* the story's similarities with Chekhov's later plays, and its exemplification of the author's realism and modernity, which have greatly influenced twentieth-century short fiction. In tracing the story's biographical and literary influences and its relation to other literature, though, Chekhov critics have generally ignored an important feature of **"The Lady with the Dog"**—namely, the significance of Gurov's two flights of emotion, the first with Anna at Oreanda, the second outside the Medical Club at Moscow.[1] These two moments of intense feeling are crucial to understanding Gurov's motivations and illustrate the importance of this kind of emotional flight to the structure of Chekhov's short fiction.

In the first of his two flights of emotion, Gurov contemplates the transcendence of love as he sits quietly on a bench with Anna at Oreanda:

Not a leaf stirred, the grasshoppers chirruped, and the monotonous hollow roar of the sea came up to them, speaking of peace, of the eternal sleep lying in wait for us all. The sea had roared like this before there was any Yalta or Oreanda, it was roaring now, and it would go on roaring, just as indifferently and hollowly, when we had passed away. And it may be that in this continuity, this utter indifference to life and death, lies the secret of our ultimate salvation, of the stream of life on our planet, and of its never-ceasing movement toward perfection.

Side by side with a young woman, who looked so exquisite in the early light, soothed and enchanted by the sight of all this magical beauty—sea, mountains, clouds and the vast expanse of the sky—Gurov told himself that, when you came to think of it, everything in the world is beautiful really, everything but our own thoughts and actions, when we lose sight of the higher aims of life, and of our dignity as human beings.

(226)

This passage reveals one of the strengths of Chekhov's writing, his superb handling of the theme of transcendence through love. In *Anton Chekhov and the Lady with the Dog,* Virginia Llewellyn Smith discusses the importance of this theme: "In Chekhov's later work, this ideal of love was to become increasingly associated with the concept of something above and beyond the transient, or more precisely, with a quasi-philosophical speculative interest, and a quasi-mystical faith in the future of mankind" (138). Another critic, Beverly Hahn, makes a similar point, finding in some of Chekhov's work a "mysterious transcendence . . . of the great moral and philosophical issues of existence" (253). Finding the eternal in a particular moment, Chekhov's characters can turn away mortality and meaninglessness, if only briefly, by turning to each other. However, it is important to remember that at this point in the story, Gurov clearly has not fallen in love with Anna. At first it is not Anna in particular whom he desires, but rather a pretty woman in general, and the reader is told that Gurov, who refers to women as "the lower race," actually "could not have existed a single day" without them (222). Indeed, Gurov enjoys Anna's company at Yalta but is at first surprised, then bored and annoyed with her sense of having sinned. And when Anna must leave Yalta and return to her husband, Gurov does not seem greatly to regret that the affair has apparently ended: "And he told himself that this had been just one more of the many adventures in his life, and that it, too, was over, leaving nothing but a memory . . ." (227). However, when he returns home, he cannot seem to forget the lady with the dog.

Gurov's second flight of emotion results from his sudden awareness of the grossness and banality of life in Moscow, and the way it pales in comparison to the time he spent with Anna in Yalta. When Gurov starts to tell one of his companions at the Medical Club about her,

his friend interrupts him with a comment about dinner, "the sturgeon was just a *leetle* off." At this moment, all of Gurov's pent-up frustrations with his life in Moscow find release in the quintessential Chekhovian flight:

> These words, in themselves so commonplace, for some reason infuriated Gurov, seemed to him humiliating, gross. What savage manners, what people! What wasted evenings, what tedious, empty days! Frantic card-playing, gluttony, drunkenness, perpetual talk always about the same thing. The greater part of one's time and energy went on business that was no use to anyone, and on discussing the same thing over and over again, and there was nothing to show for all of it but a stunted, earth-bound existence and a round of trivialities, and there was nowhere to escape to, you might as well be in a madhouse or a convict settlement.

(229)

In some ways, this passage represents the climax of the story, for after Gurov resolves to go to Anna's town, the remainder of the story, in which the characters are forced to keep up appearances by not telling anyone about the affair, has an aura of inevitability about it. In addition to this structural importance, this intense burst of emotion is also very important to an understanding of Gurov's motivations for renewing the affair and thus raises an interesting question: is his decision to find Anna motivated more by love for her or by his desire to escape the tedium of life in Moscow? Certainly the Gurov in the first two sections of the story does not seem like the kind of man who is capable of falling in love with Anna. He becomes bored and uncomfortable, rather than concerned or sensitive, when she gets upset. Does Gurov truly love Anna, or is she simply the natural person for him to turn to in his time of depression?

In his excellent "Chekhov and the Modern Short Story," Charles E. May argues that the question is unanswerable:

> It is never clear in the story whether Gurov truly loves Anna Sergeyevna or whether it is only the romantic fantasy that he wishes to maintain. What makes the story so subtle and complex is that Chekhov presents the romance in such a limited and objective way that we realize that there is no way to determine whether it is love or romance, for there is no way to distinguish between them.

(151)

May's otherwise good interpretation is slightly off the mark on this point. While it is true that throughout most of the story it is difficult—because of the objectivity to which May alludes—to determine whether Gurov loves Anna, the reader is directly told just before the conclusion of the story that the two main characters do indeed love each other and that Gurov has "fallen in love properly, thoroughly, for the first time in his life" (234). It is crucial to recognize that the Gurov at the end of the story is not the same as the one at the beginning, and the difference is not merely that he now needs love, but that he has clearly found the woman he loves. Certainly, Gurov does not love less simply because he feels a need for love in his life; in fact, it is precisely this yearning that causes his love for Anna to awaken and grow. And again the key to understanding Gurov's motivations for leaving Moscow and going to Anna is his flights of emotion in which he recognizes the essential truth of the story: his love for Anna is far more noble than his banal, socially acceptable life in Moscow.

Still, at the end of the story, the couple's problem—how to keep their love for each other alive while hiding the relationship from society—remains unresolved. Moreover, neither character seems to have the courage to reveal the truth of their love to anyone else, and therefore, the characters find themselves in a kind of limbo:

> And it seemed to them that they were within an inch of arriving at a decision, and that then a new, beautiful life would begin. And they both realized that the end was still far, far away, and that the hardest, the most complicated part was only just beginning.
>
> (235)

Gurov and Anna find themselves in a desperate situation, but as Beverly Hahn suggests, "desperation is not the dominant note of the story, nor is its outcome really tragic, because the hardship of Anna's and Gurov's love cannot be separated from the *fact* of that love and from the fact that it brings each a degree of fulfilment not known before" (253).

With its elegant language, complex main characters, and realistic detail, **"The Lady with the Dog"** is indeed a masterful story of many moods and, therefore, an illustration of the validity of Conrad Aiken's judgment that Chekhov is a master of mood. Gurov's two intense moments of emotion are important to the structure of the story and demonstrate an important feature of the author's style, for similar Chekhovian flights can be found in many of his other stories, especially his later ones, such as **"About Love,"** **"A Visit to Friends,"** **"The Bishop,"** and **"The Betrothed,"** just to name a few. These flights of emotion are as important in Chekhov's stories as epiphanies are in Joyce's and therefore merit further exploration by those interested in the study of Chekhov's short fiction.

Note

1. A. P. Chudakov, in *Chekhov's Poetics* (Ann Arbor: Ardis, 1983), comes closest to recognizing the structural importance of such scenes in his discussion of how characters' emotional states affect the presentation of physical detail. See chapter 3, "Narrative from 1895-1904," of Chudakov's book.

Works Cited

Aiken, Conrad. *Collected Criticism*. London: Oxford UP, 1968.

Chekhov, Anton. "The Lady with the Dog." Trans. Ivy Litvinov. *Anton Chekhov's Short Stories*. Norton Critical Edition. Ed. Ralph E. Matlaw. New York: Norton, 1979. 221-35.

Chudakov, A. P. *Chekhov's Poetics*. Ann Arbor: Ardis, 1983.

Hahn, Beverly. *Chekhov: A Study of the Major Stories and Plays*. Cambridge: Cambridge UP, 1977.

May, Charles E. "Chekhov and the Modern Short Story." *A Chekhov Companion*. Ed. Toby W. Clyman. Westport, CT: Greenwood, 1985. 147-63.

Smith, Virginia Llewellyn. *Anton Chekhov and the Lady with the Dog*. London: Oxford UP, 1973.

Joseph L. Conrad (essay date spring 1991)

SOURCE: Conrad, Joseph L. "Studies in Deception: Anton Chekhov's Short Story 'His Wife.'" *Scottish Slavonic Review*, no. 16 (spring 1991): 47-63.

[*In the following essay, Conrad views "His Wife" as an insightful portrayal of human behavior and investigates a possible inspiration for the story in Chekhov's life.*]

I

Despite its brevity (under seven pages) Chekhov's **'His Wife'** ("Supruga"; 1895)[1] presents a number of intriguing questions. To begin with, the least complicated: why did Chekhov write, at this stage in his career, a story more like those he had written ten years earlier than the major works surrounding it? By the same token: why did it take him almost four months to compose the tale?

In contrast to the wealth of knowledge available about most of Chekhov's stories written during his mature period (between ca. 1891 and 1904), little is known about the conception of **'His Wife'**.[2] Neither N. I. Gitovich's chronicle of Chekhov's life nor the notes to Volume Nine of the definitive Russian edition offer much information.[3]

What little do we know about the origin of this story? On 1 October 1894, Chekhov was asked to contribute to the first issue of *Pochin* (*New Enterprise*), a journal initiated by the Society of Lovers of Russian Literature; but at that time he was preoccupied with the composition of the much longer **'Three Years'** ("Tri goda"; 1895), which he did not immediately finish. There were to be other interruptions between October and December of that year. For example, he penned a short work, the **'Tale of a Senior Gardener'** (**"Rasskaz starshego sadovnika"**), which was sent to the printer on 23 December 1894. And the onset of the Christmas-New Year's holiday period brought a succession of guests, including the arrival of, and his reconciliation with, I. I. Levitan, the pre-Impressionist landscape artist from whom he had been estranged since the publication of **'The Grasshopper'** (**"Poprygun'ya"**) in 1892.

There was yet another factor which must certainly have delayed Chekhov's completion of the tale. His health was poor: he was having respiratory problems and, as he complained in a letter of 21 January 1895 to his friend and publisher A. S. Suvorin, his haemorrhoids were painful.

There is no mention of the story in Chekhov's published correspondence until 3 February 1895, when he mailed the manuscript to N. I. Storozhenko, the editor of *New Enterprise,* with an apology for its being late and a comment that he might change the title when he received the page proofs. It is not known whether the original title was «Супруга», or if indeed this title resulted from his or an editor's change. Thus the reason why the story was not completed sooner would seem to stem from a combination of factors: Chekhov's poor health, his other authorial obligations, and the extraordinary level of social activity at the end of the year. The story's brevity remains almost anomalous when considered in light of the many longer tales written during the remainder of 1895.[4]

Yet a much more complicated question arises: just what did Chekhov intend the story to demonstrate? Written before the general European wave of Freudian analysis, **'His Wife'** succeeds admirably in exposing the psychological foundations of destructive failure in human communication. Answers to certain final questions may be reserved, at least for the moment, e.g.: what might have been the stimulus for this stark tale of a marital relationship gone sour? And: what prompted Chekhov, who was as yet unmarried, to present such a negative picture of what is otherwise, but often ironically, termed 'wedded bliss'?

First let us examine Chekhov's, or the narrator's, presentation of the story's content (in German literary criticism, its *Gehalt*). Upon first reading, **'His Wife'** seems to be a minor anecdote such as many written by Chekhov in the early stages of his literary career (1883-85). In it he focuses the reader's attention on an evening in the life of a married couple.[5] But, by describing the events of that one evening, he demonstrates the couple's mode of existence: their mutual frustration with and deception of one another, and ultimately, their self-deception. It is no exaggeration to say that Chekhov's

depiction of the wife's callous treatment of her husband offers one of the most forceful presentations of human manipulation to be found in his mature prose.

The story's narrative voice is relatively uncomplicated. **'His Wife'** is told primarily by an omniscient narrator; yet several passages border on interior monologues: at a number of places the colloquial syntax and vocabulary suggest the doctor's own interpretation of his situation, not that of the narrator. This was not a new feature in Chekhov's narrative style; it was already present in his **'Heartache'** (**"Toska"**; 1886) and **'Sleepy'** (**"Spat' khochetsya"**; 1888); in fact, by 1888 the technique of mixing narrative voices was well-established in Chekhov's prose.

As was common in Chekhov's short stories, the structure is temporally straightforward, and it is comprised of three parts: the first concentrates on the husband, Nikolay Evgrafych, a doctor, and his reaction to discovering a telegram from his wife's lover. The second shifts the focus to his wife, Olga Dmitrievna, and centres around their confrontation (a meeting which ends in a mutual challenge). The third section, which describes the man's bewildered state on the next morning, shows him desperately reviewing the extent of his own self-deception. But—and with an undeniable finality—the last sentence reveals that his wife is in complete control, not only of her own life, but of his as well. Thus he is a victim both of her manipulation and of his own self-deception.

Judged from a psychoanalytical point of view, Chekhov's presentation seems typical of confrontations resulting from marital infidelity where one spouse is betrayed and mistreated, while the other seems to be not only inconsiderate, but calculating. He creates a situation which reveals the commonness of the characters' psychology. And, in doing so, he leads us to understand the primary source for this couple's incompatibility: the emotional immaturity which characterizes *both* the wife *and* the husband. When other factors frequently found in such discordant unions are added, e.g., concern over money, mutual suspicion, and a marked lack of honesty, the result is the bleakest picture of marriage in all of Chekhov's *oeuvre*.

As the reader begins to see, each partner in **'His Wife'** is engaged in role-playing, both to justify his or her own behaviour and to bring pressure on the other. Chekhov's tale demonstrates his intuitive perception of the motives of human interaction. It not only anticipates Freudian analysis, but well illustrates types of interpersonal behaviour as treated much later in Eric Berne's *Games People Play. The Psychology of Human Relationships.*[6] While it is not at first clear that, however unconsciously, the husband is playing a role, it is clear that he suspects his wife is deceiving him. The basis for his suspicion is immediately apparent. His distrust is introduced at the outset: beginning *in medias res,* the narrator shows him, sometime after midnight, reproaching a tired (and surprisingly) indifferent maid for straightening the papers on his desk. In response, she hands him a basket of local telegrams; but he is so preoccupied with searching for a congratulatory cable from his brother that the urgent messages from his patients are left unattended. Thus his irritation makes him neglect his professional duty in an unpardonable way and suggests to the reader some measure of personal guilt even before we learn of his wife's infidelity. The doctor's irritation is explained as follows:

> Nikolay Evgrafych knew that his wife would not be home soon, at least not until about five in the morning. He did not trust her and felt depressed and could not sleep when she stayed out late. And at the same time he despised his wife, her bed, her mirror, her boxes of chocolates and those lilies-of-the-valley and hyacinths which someone was sending to her every day and which made the whole house smell as sickly-sweet as a florist's shop. On nights like this he grew irritable, moody and snappish . . .[7]

From the information given, the reader easily pictures the doctor's wife as one of those vain and vulgar creatures representative of *poshlost'* in Chekhov's early stories, a memorable example being Susanna in **'Slime'** (**"Tina"**, 1886). This interpretation is reinforced by the items which are associated with her—her bed, mirror, chocolates, and the overly fragrant flowers, representing in turn her laziness, vanity, gluttony, and excessive luxury. By contrast, the doctor seems to be a maligned husband and, possibly, an unwitting cuckold.[8]

The atmosphere becomes tense when the doctor discovers an intimate telegram in English from his wife's lover. Curiously enough, this material evidence of her infidelity at first presents more of a challenge to his intelligence than a personal insult. A note of smug satisfaction can be detected in his reaction:

> In the seven years of married life he had grown accustomed to suspicion, guessing, understanding the evidence, and more than once it had occurred to him that because of this practice at home, he could have become an excellent detective.

(92-94)

The reader, however, might question the accuracy of his understanding of the situation: if his wife is frequently out late and receives flowers every day, why has he not previously asked for an explanation? Thus we have an early indication that he is deceiving himself by thinking that his powers of perception are greater than they actually are.

Recognizing that the signatory of the telegram is a young man from Monte Carlo whom they met recently, the doctor now begins to understand why his wife had discounted his colleagues' recommendation that he go to the Crimea for his newly diagnosed tuberculosis. She had strongly suggested the south of France instead. With utmost irony, Chekhov lets Nikolay Evgrafych recall that

> hearing about it [his illness], she acted as if it frightened her terribly; she began making up to her husband and kept assuring him that it was cold and boring in the Crimea, that it would be better in Nice, and that she would go with him and take care of him, and protect him, give him some peace and quiet.

(94)

Of course, his life with her is anything but peaceful and quiet, and it is soon to reach a crescendo of mutual recrimination.

It is already a commonplace in nineteenth-century literature that the onset of incurable disease brings clearer and heightened perception. But Chekhov's presentation of this development was relatively new for his time in Russian literature. Tolstoy's 'Death of Ivan Ilyich' (1886) had preceded Chekhov's story by only a few years. Nikolay Evgrafych's response to his discovery is, in fact, characteristic. His immediate thought is that he would have played a 'ridiculous and pitiful role', had he agreed to go to Nice. Chekhov's underlying ironic touch is again apparent: it does not yet occur to the doctor to examine the current role he is playing. That role is equally ridiculous and pitiful. All the more so since he is deceiving only himself. Nevertheless, he begins to recognize that he has allowed her to take advantage of him. His thoughts are presented as follows:

> His pride, his sense of common decency were aroused. Clenching his fists and wincing from disgust, he asked himself how it was that he, the son of a village priest, brought up in a seminary, a plain, unsophisticated man and a surgeon by profession,—how it was that he could have let himself be enslaved, that he so shamefully submitted to this feeble, mean-spirited, dishonest and base creature?

(94)

This passage suggests an interesting combination of contrasting formative experiences: early religous education and seminary schooling and a presumed lack of sophistication (which, in the context of the nineteenth-century Russian background, was normal). But these are combined with his pride in surgical training. One must ask: with the advanced schooling in medicine he had had in order to become a surgeon, how is it that he remained so oblivious to his wife's extra-marital activity? Should not a man intelligent enough to reach such heights of education have noticed his wife's infidelity sooner? Chekhov leaves it to the reader to understand the resolution of this combination. The last lines of the passage also show Nikolay Evgrafych's rueful self-condemnation for weakness *and* his misconception that his wife is 'feeble'. As it turns out, she is much stronger than he suspects.

The plot line quickly reaches an *impasse*: Nikolay Evgrafych is overcome by a surge of self-pity. Here Chekhov shows his genius for psycholoanalytical insight: Nikolay Evgrafych now regrets his marriage; but, at the same time, he has an unexpectedly positive memory of her first impression on him seven years ago, an impression made on him when he was younger and, certainly, more naive, of her 'long, fragrant hair, masses of lace, and her tiny foot (*malen'kaya nozhka*)'. Somewhat belatedly, he had now come to the realization that, far from the expected romantic bliss at the onset of his marriage, his life is contaminated by her 'hysterics, shrieks, responses, and barefaced, deceitful lying'. But his realization is accompanied by a certain penchant for poetic imagination in which he likens his wife to a bird caught in a house, frantically trying to escape through a window and all the while knocking things over. However, he is no longer the young innocent of his earlier days: he now understands that his wife has created for him a life of utter defeat (*razgrom*). It is with considerable lamentation that he now reviews his situation. 'The best years of his life had passed as if in Hell; his hopes of happiness had been dashed and mocked, his health had gone, and his rooms were full of the paraphernalia of a vulgar coquette' (95). Clearly, Chekhov has shown that Nikolay Evgrafych, true to the commonplace of seven years of marriage reaching its nadir, has awakened from his sleep of self-deception.

The husband's perceived existential agony casts him in the self-appointed role of martyr: he blames himself and thinks that he, 'who could not understand women', was a bad match for Olga Dmitrievna, whereas another might have had a good influence on her. One wonders whether this thought represents Chekhov's subtle mockery of Tolstoy's views. Magnanimously, the doctor resolves to give her a divorce so that she may go off with her lover. But the reader sees that his self-righteous pity, his wounded pride and indignation, even his exaggerated magnanimity despite contempt for his wife, well mark his personality as emotionally immature.

The second section begins as his wife returns, just as he expected, some time before five in the morning. Only her attire is described, her physical features are not. This is unusual for Chekhov at this stage of his writing career; likewise, there has been no physical description of Nikolay Evgrafych. But his purpose is clear: he wishes to concentrate the reader's attention on her essential vanity. We are told only that she is dressed in a white coat (ironically, perhaps sarcastically, suggesting purity?), a hat (which is, after all, a form of protective covering), and galoshes (which may be intended to keep her not only out of foul weather, but even out of the filth of life).

Her emotional state, like that of Nikolay Evgrafych at the beginning of the story, is one of furious frustration, and it is marked by the childish gesture of foot-stamping. When we remember that her 'tiny foot' connotes fragility, even delicacy, Chekhov's irony becomes quite obvious: she is stamping that 'tiny foot' in aggressive rage. Another example of Chekhov's skilled use of detail is evident: she has been crying effusively because not only is her handkerchief wet with tears, but her gloves are soaked as well.

While Nikolay Evgrafych tries in vain to discuss their future, she is concerned only with an accidental loss of fifteen rubles. Desperately and, as it turns out, foolishly, he promises to give her twenty-five if she will hear him out. Again, and in a very human touch, Chekhov lets us see that, despite his jealousy and anger at her infidelity, Nikolay Evgrafych is reminded of the little things which bind them together. For example, as he takes her coat he notices the smell of 'white wine, the very same with which she liked to eat oysters (in spite of her ethereal nature, she ate and drank very much)' (96). His recollection of this detail and his parenthetical remark not only reveal his human vulnerability but—and more importantly—reinforce our perception of Olga Dmitrievna's vanity and her gluttony; the reader's impression of her is indeed justified. The three items which Nikolay Evgrafych associates with her are mentioned again: her lace, her hair, and her 'tiny foot'; thus they become leitmotifs which recall the emotions that he experienced while awaiting her return, and they prepare us for the battle of wits which is to follow.

The reader quickly sees that Olga Dmitrievna is anything but refined and dainty. For example, she immediately seizes the initiative by asking in a commanding tone: 'Well, what of it?' Her insistent stance demonstrates that she is very much in control of herself, and of her husband as well. When he, in his extreme agitation, tells her that he knows of her extra-marital affair, she coolly tries to explain the telegram as an insignificant New-Year's greeting; thereby does she reveal how accustomed she is to lying and to manipulation. The ensuing scene is a masterful demonstration of the psychological warfare that embittered couples sometimes wage with one another.

As noted above, in this second section the focus shifts to Olga Dmitrievna: her role-playing in earnest becomes evident as she quietly begins to cry. When Nikolay Evgrafych insists that she is free, she immediately suspects his motives. Having at last overcome his earlier self-deception, he now sees her nature more clearly: as she approaches to examine his face, he finds in her eyes 'a green fire like that of a cat's eyes' (97). Chekhov's villainesses are regularly depicted or perceived as having green eyes, and feline allusions are frequent. This assessment is in striking contrast to his earlier association likening her to a helpless bird. Leaving no time for additional reflection on his part, her response that she is not interested in a divorce reaffirms her commanding posture. The narrator indicates her calculating nature in a speech which remarkably demonstrates her self-control.

> 'I understand you,' she said, moving away from him. Her face took on an evil, vindictive expression. 'I understand you very well. You're fed up with me and you just want to get rid of me, to hang this divorce on me. I'll not accept a divorce and I'm not leaving you, not leaving you! In the first place, I don't want to lose my social position,' she went on quickly as though afraid he might stop her. 'In the second, I'm already twenty-seven and [he] is only twenty-three. In a year's time he'll get fed up and drop me. And in the third place, if you want to know, I won't guarantee that my attraction can last long. So there! I will not leave you!'
>
> (98)

By its arrogant delivery this speech effectively reveals the characteristic features of her personality: inherent suspicion and a sense of personal insult and concomitant revenge; plus an insecure fear of social disgrace and realistic recognition of her true situation as the (very likely) temporary mistress of a younger man. At the same time it demonstrates her independence and self-reliance, which are easily more than a match for the impotent Nikolay Evgrafych. In a last and futile gesture, the doctor responds by stamping his foot and threatening to evict her, but she welcomes the challenge: 'We'll see about that!' She leaves him in frustration, as he absently pens the phrases 'Dear Sir' and 'tiny foot' (98). It may be noted that their angry gestures of foot-stamping not only mark each partner's emotional immaturity, but maintain distance between the reader and the event.

The third and final scene consists primarily of an interior monologue in which Nikolay Evgrafych must face his previous self-deception. Unable to sleep, he re-examines a family portrait made seven years earlier, when he was a happy newly-wed. Now he recognizes his father-in-law as 'cunning and lusting after money' (*khitryy i zhadnyy do deneg*; 98); in his mother-in-law's face he reads 'petty and predatory features' (*melkie i khishchnye cherty*), like those of a ferret. And he discovers in his wife's expression 'those same petty and predatory features, but more pronounced . . .'. Yet, still unable to admit the possibility of his culpability in the failure of his marriage, he sees in his own likeness

> . . . such a straightforward fellow . . . such a terribly nice chap; a good-natured seminarian's smile lit up his whole face. He looked as if he believed in his simple way that this brood of predators, into which fate had accidentally thrust him, was going to bring him poetry, happiness and all that he had dreamed of when he was a student. . . .
>
> (99)

A prisoner of self-deception, Nikolay Evgrafych again asks himself despairingly how he could have 'surrendered so abjectly to that contemptible, lying, vulgar, mean-spirited, wholly alien creature'. He now understands the degree of his wife's habitual deception and considers himself wiser; finally, he has recognized the full extent of his own previous self-deception.

But no relief is to come from the tension created by the strained relationship of this mismatched couple.[9] The dénouement presents a forceful surprise: at about eleven the next morning Nikolay Evgrafych's despairing bewilderment is shattered when, in the story's last sentence, the maid informs him that his wife is demanding twenty-five rubles. After carefully noting the time-frame (from midnight to five and then to eleven in the morning) and by chronicling the doctor's emotions from the evening before and skilfully using them as leitmotifs—the perceptions of her lace, her hair, and that little foot—Chekhov has now brought the events to a complete standstill. The reader sees that the lives of this couple will continue to be marked by childish petulance, spiteful bitterness, and deep unhappiness. It is clear that they are locked together in a mutually intolerable situation but, as it also seems, in a state of mutual need as well. The reader may justly conclude: they deserve each other.

Chekhov has presented this exemplary instance of devastating married interaction with considerable insight: at the base of the couple's tragedy are both mutual distrust and conscious deception. The husband's previously unwitting self-deception, now exposed, leaves him in a state of despair. His wife's self-composure in rejecting his position and her demand that he give even more, show her to be the stronger. The opposition of a strong woman and a weak man is, of course, not uncommon in nineteenth-century Russian fiction; but here Chekhov has made the theme almost grotesque as we see the helpless husband being drawn ever more tightly into her web. To the perceptive reader their mutual suspicion of ulterior motives and their addiction to role-playing to gain ends are immediately evident. But it is Nikolay Evgrafych's and Olga Dmitrievna's inability to assess correctly their own motives and their emotional immaturity which are at the core of the matter. As in so many of his stories, Chekhov has here created a vignette which is at once particular and near-universal, for this couple's mode of existence is regrettably common.

II

Let us now return to the question of the possible stimulus for **'His Wife'**. Given the absence of contrary information, one might conclude that it was written quickly and without much thought. But still we must ask: just what might have led Chekhov to present such a damning character sketch of a man and a woman and such a depressing view of married life?

While there is no indication of a model for Olga Dmitrievna in Chekhov's published correspondence, a possible literary source for her personality is that of Turgenev's adulterous Irina Litvinova (*Smoke/Dym*; 1867). In Turgenev's novel, Irina's husband remembers that she wore perfume which was 'persistent, importunate, sweet, and heavy', which 'did not give him any peace, and ever more strongly spilled over into the darkness, and ever more insistently reminded him of something which he couldn't quite fathom . . .'.[10] This attitude towards his spouse sounds very like that of Chekhov's Nikolay Evgrafych.

What is more, Turgenev's Irina is highly-strung and self-willed; she is proud and secretive; and she has passionate dark grey-and-green eyes and is primarily interested in fashion. She has an unpleasant smile when she is moody, and her behaviour is marked by an almost contemptuous harshness and chilliness. Finally, she stamps her foot in vexation when things do not go her way. In short, Turgenev's characterization of Irina seems to foreshadow Chekhov's Olga Dmitrievna—and even more so, the eponymous heroine of **'Ariadna'**, which he completed soon after **'His Wife'**.[11]

But a more probable stimulus has been curiously neglected: it may be that the negative personality of the wife in this story came to Chekhov from his short affair (between January and April 1895) with Lidiya Yavorskaya (1872-1921), a rising young actress of the day. His opinion of her was at first very positive. Soon after the beginning of their affair Chekhov described Yavorskaya in a letter to Suvorin (21 January 1895) as follows: 'She's a very kind woman and actress who might go far, if she hadn't been spoiled by her training'. But then he added: 'She is a bit of a hussy, but that doesn't matter.'[12] Still more significantly, in the same letter he described a negative reaction to women in general—a reaction, incidentally, which he experienced after seeing Yavorskaya in a play:

> Women take away one's youth, but not in my case. In the course of my life I've been steward, not master, and fate hasn't exactly spoiled me. I've had a few affairs. . . . Silk gowns only spell pleasure to me in that they are soft to the touch. Comfort has its appeal to me, but debauchery has no allure.[13]

Was this also a reaction to the probable sexual encounter they had in Room Five of the Grand Moscow Hotel? Yavorskaya was noted for her lively sexuality and for her demanding vanity.

It is not known just how long their affair lasted, but it was probably not more than a few months. Yavorskaya's star began to fade as the reviews of her performances

that spring grew more and more critical; they cited in particular her affected manner, and the 'falseness' (*fal'sh'*) of her acting.[14] Judging by his subsequent letters to Suvorin in which she is mentioned, Chekhov seems also to have cooled towards Yavorskaya rather quickly. On 30 March he wrote:

> She's intelligent and dresses nicely, and sometimes can be smart. She's the daughter of Kiev police chief Giubennet, so that in her arteries there flows the blood of an actress, but a policeman's blood in her veins . . . The Moscow critics have poisoned her all winter like a rabbit [?], but she doesn't deserve it. If it were not for her loudness and a certain affectation (posturing), she would be a real actress. In any case she's a curious one.[15]

In this letter he seemed to sympathize with her because of the critics' perhaps unfair reports, but then he added the mildly condescending remark about her behaviour. His next mention of her came some two weeks later when he wrote (18 April 1895) to Suvorin, who had reportedly criticized her soundly: 'Your opinion of Yavorskaya did not seem to me to be harsh.'[16] We can only speculate whether indeed she was a real-life model for Olga Dmitrievna, or whether Chekhov was merely venting his vexation with her or some other woman. In fact, the early months of 1895 were marked by Chekhov's association not only with Yavorskaya, but with her friend Tatyana Shchepkina-Kupernik (1874-1953), a literary prodigy of the period whose work was liked by the reading public despite a certain triteness. Simon Karlinsky has pointed out that her verse contained 'facile doggerel, full of obvious pseudo-poetic clichés'. He continues: 'With her actress friend Lidiya Yavorskaya, Tatyana formed something like a two-woman sexual-freedom league, which numbered among its joint conquests both Chekhov and the old Suvorin.'[17]

This statement is made without substantiation; nevertheless it does provide an interesting perspective. Chekhov alluded to such a situation when he wrote (2 November 1895) to Suvorin: 'Rumours are going around . . . that you arrived in Moscow in October together with Yavorskaya. You were seen.'[18]

In this connection a final question should also be posed: to what extent was Chekhov studiously deceiving his friends—and himself? Mikhail Chekhov recalled that in addition to his persistent cough and haemorrhoids, his brother was experiencing heart irregularity, nightmares, and a serious pain in his left temple which caused a flashing sensation in his eyes.[19] He also noted that, having recognized the seriousness of his condition, Anton Pavlovich 'didn't complain to anyone, tried to hide it from others and, it seems, to deceive even himself' (*staralsya . . . obmanut' i samogo sebya*).[20] Did his penchant for deception during this period lead to a major theme of **'His Wife'**? He apparently did not discuss the tale, and there does not seem to be extant any documentary evidence to answer this question conclusively.

Among the reviews of **'His Wife'**, which were generally positive, an anonymous critic praised Chekhov for his depiction of 'living truth and sketching a base and greedy woman and a husband, a man broken by life and eternal jealousy, suspicion, terrible insults, and wounded male pride'. Soon after its publication, Tolstoy was reported to have been enthusiastic about the story, and to have considered it one of Chekhov's best. But Tolstoy's worldview had changed by 1905, when he said of the tale: 'It's morally scandalous. That's the way life is sometimes, but an artist should not depict it.'[21] It may also be noted here that Chekhov's younger contemporary, Ivan Bunin, considered **'His Wife'** among Chekhov's best works.[22] Of course, it must be left to present-day readers to value the story for its analytical portrayal of both husband and wife, whatever the stimulus or desire of its author might have been.

In short, this brief tale presents highly revealing insights into certain motivations of human behaviour, and that fact alone makes **'His Wife'** one of Chekhov's more worthwhile contributions to Russian—and world—literature.

Notes

1. The story's ironic Russian title, "Supruga", has been translated as 'The Helpmate' by Constance B. Garnett, and as 'His Wife' by Ronald Hingley (see Note 5, below). But the Russian title connotes respect, and translates literally as '[feminine] Spouse', so neither English title is perfectly apt. 'The Helpmate' is not on the same, somewhat elevated level as the Russian, and English 'The Spouse' does not reflect Chekhov's irony (nor the feminine gender). Hingley's 'His Wife' shifts the point of view closer to that found in the story, both of the third-person narrator and of the interior monologues of the husband. It also maintains the distinction between this story and Chekhov's earlier (1892), and longer (ca 43pp.) story *Zhena* (*The Wife*).

2. Recent major bibliographies of works about Chekhov list no studies specifically devoted to this story. They are—The 'Selected Bibliography' compiled by Leonard Polakiewicz, in: Toby Clyman (ed.), *A Chekhov Companion* (Greenwood Press, Westport, CT, and London, 1985), pp. 311-31; Edgar H. Lehrman, *A Handbook to Eighty-six of Chekhov's Stories in Russian* (Slavica, Columbus, 1985), pp. 292-314; K. A. Lantz, *Anton Chekhov. A Reference Guide to Literature* (G. K. Hall & Co., Boston, 1985); and Munir Sendich, 'Anton Chekhov in English: A Comprehensive Bibliography of Works about and by Him (1889-1984', in Savely Senderovich and Munir Sendich (eds.), *Anton Chekhov Rediscovered: A Collection of New Studies with a Comprehensive Bibliography*, publ.

by the *Russian Language Journal* (East Lansing, Michigan, 1987), pp. 189-349.

3. In her *Letopis' zhizni i tvorchestva A. P. Chekhova* (Khudozhestvennaya literatura, M., 1955), N. I. Gitovich is usually very informative, but not in this case. In fact, her brief notations of his meetings with, among others, Lidiya Yavorskaya engender more curiosity than comfort. The notes to the story in A. P. Chekhov, *Polnoe sobranie sochineniy i pisem* (*PSSP*; 1974-83), *Sochineniya* 9 (Nauka, M., 1977): 465-67, offer almost two pages of commentary, but still do not illuminate the circumstances of the story's creation or any events in Chekhov's personal life which might have been its stimulus.

4. Written in the autumn of 1894, 'Three Years' is some eighty-five pages long. Following 'The Wife' in 1895 are: 'Ariadna', which was begun in March and sent to the printer in April; this tale numbers twenty-six pages; 'Murder' ("Ubiystvo"), begun soon thereafter but not completed until the autumn, has twenty-eight pages; and 'Anna on the Neck' ("Anna na shee"), which was completed in mid-October, has approximately thirteen printed pages. While his 'Tale of a Senior Gardener' comprises six pages, and his children's story about a dog, 'Whitebrow' ("Belolobyy"; finished in April 1895), is equally short, these do not make such a powerful impression as 'His Wife', nor are they considered among the more significant stories of this period.

5. Chekhov's brother, Mikhail, wrote in *Anton Chekhov and His Subjects* (*Anton Chekhov i ego syuzhety*, "9-e yanvarya", M., 1923) that he had suggested this subject to Chekhov, a subject which was based on the personal experience of a certain A. A. Sablin, a former district official in Yaroslavl Province, and that it was virtually 'the biography of the late Sablin' (p. 124). Whether Mikhail's suggestion was the sole stimulus is open to debate; see below. 'His Wife' was first published in the journal *Pochin* (*New Enterprise*, M., 1895, pp. 279-85). References to the text are taken from A. P. Chekhov, *PSSP, Sochineniya* 9 (M., 1977). An accessible English translation is that of Ronald Hingley in Volume 8 of *The Oxford Chekhov* (OUP, 1965), which I have used as the basis for the English passages cited here, but I have felt it sometimes necessary to retranslate certain passages to make them correspond more closely to the original. Also available are various reprints of Constant Garnett's *The Darling and Other Stories*, which contains 'The Helpmate'.

6. Grove Press, N.Y., 1964.

7. *PSSP, Sochineniya* 9:92. Hereafter, page references to the Russian text will be included in parentheses following the passage quoted.

8. Such an assessment is not necessarily correct, however, for the information is presented from the husband's point of view. The word 'those' (эти) before 'lilies', etc., shifts the focus away from the doctor. While normally эти is translated as 'these', the distance between English 'these' and 'those' is not identical to that between эти and те; in some contexts, this one included, эти seems better rendered as 'those'.

9. For early establishment of this technique in Chekhov's prose, see my 'Unresolved Tension in Chekhov's Stories, 1886-1888', in *Slavic and East European Journal*, 16, 1 (Spring 1972), pp. 55-64.

10. I. S. Turgenev, *Polnoe sobranie sochineniy i pisem v 28 tt., Sochineniya* 9 (Nauka, M.-L. 1965): 178. The translation is my own. Chekhov had written to Suvorin some two years earlier (24 February 1893) his assessment of Turgenev, which included, among other remarks: 'I don't like *Smoke* at all' ("Dym" *mne ne nravitsya sovsem; PSSP, Pis'ma* 5:174); for the English translation, see *Letters of Anton Chekhov,* tr. Michael Heim (in collaboration with Simon Karlinsky, Harper & Row, N.Y., 1973—hereafter abbreviated as *Letters*), p. 251. Chekhov continued: '. . . Irina in *Smoke,* Odintsova in *Fathers and Sons* and all those lionesses, the torrid, appetizing, insatiable seekers, they are all so much nonsense.' The negative view expressed in this letter has widely been accepted as a rejection of Turgenev's influence on Chekhov. In fact, that influence has been greatly underestimated in Western criticism of Chekhov's prose and, to a somewhat lesser degree, even in Soviet Russian criticism. For arguments that Turgenev's influence was indeed important for much of Chekhov's writing, see my 'Chekhov's "Verochka": a Polemical Parody', in *Slavic and East European Journal* 14 (4, Winter 1970): 465-74, and 'Chekhov's "The House with the Attic": Echoes of Turgenev', in *Russian Literature,* 26 (1989): 373-95.

11. Chekhov was to develop this situation in several other stories written soon after he completed 'His Wife'. His opinion in 1901 was that he considered this story to be 'of the same tone as "Ariadna"' (printed in *Russkaya Mysl',* 12/1895; the quotation is from *PSSP, Pis'ma* 10:94). In 'Ariadna' he expanded the theme into a much deeper examination of the heroine's negative psychology. Along with Lika Mizinova, Lidiya Yavorskaya has been identified as a possible model for Ariadna (se E. A. Polotskaya's notes to the story in *Sochineniya* 9:472-74). Yet despite her wilfulness and un-

Victorian morals, Chekhov's Ariadna has a certain vulnerable quality, which may or may not have been a characteristic of Yavorskaya. In 'Anna on the Neck' (published in *Russkie Vedomosti,* 1895, No. 292 (22 October), which has several elements in common with the heroine's life in Tolstoy's *Anna Karenina,* Chekhov's almost Gogolian treatment of a wife's domination of a foolish, bureaucratic husband is at first comic but, ultimately, pathetic.

12. *PSSP, Pis'ma,* 6 (1978):17.

13. The quotation is from *PSSP, Pis'ma,* 6:18. See Virginia Llewellyn Smith, *Anton Chekhov and the Lady with the Pet Dog,* OUP, 1973, pp. 56-59, for additional details.

14. See the notes to Chekhov's letter to Suvorin of 30 March, 1895 (*PSSP, Pis'ma,* 6:405).

15. *PSSP, Pis'ma,* 6:44.

16. *PSSP, Pis'ma,* 6:55. Unfortunately, Yavorskaya destroyed Chekhov's letters to her before her marriage in 1896 to a certain Prince Vladimir Vladimirovich Baratinsky.

17. *PSSP, Pis'ma,* 6:84. For further information on Shchepkina-Kupernik and Yavorskaya, see Karlinsky's commentary to Chekhov's letter to Suvorin of 21 January 1895, in *Letters,* pp. 266-67. See also Llewellyn Smith, pp. 56-59.

18. [Note not present in original source].

19. M. P. Chekhov, p. 118.

20. ibid. p. 124.

21. Cited in *PSSP, Sochineniya* 9:466.

22. For more detailed information, see *PSSP, Sochineniya* 9:466-67. Bunin's list of his favourite works by Chekhov is published in *Literaturnoe nasledstvo,* Vol. 69 (Nauka, M., 1960), p. 677.

Priscilla Long (essay date summer 1991)

SOURCE: Long, Priscilla. "Fiction as Biography: The Character as a Window on the Human Condition." *North Dakota Quarterly* 59, no. 3 (summer 1991): 201-07.

[*In the following essay, Long compares the depth and complexity of Mavis Gallant's "Overhead in a Balloon" and Chekhov's "The Darling."*]

Fiction can function as a kind of biography. A short story can reveal the texture of a character's life, and underneath the texture, the whole shape of the life. The fictional person thus revealed stands as a case study of a human life in society. His or her condition represents the human condition, at least in one form. To see lives revealed in such depth and with such focus is certainly one of the fundamental reasons we read fiction.

A nonfiction biographer can do much the same thing. But the biographer is confined by the documents (letters, etc.) from which he or she works. Individuals who have not left substantial documentation of their lives cannot become subjects of biographies. Further, the documentation left by a real-life individual, no matter how famous, tends to give a somewhat random picture of a life. Certain critical turning points or relationships may not be documented at all. For years I worked on a biography of the labor organizer, "Mother" Mary Jones, which I never finished. The documentation on her life proved to be limited and fragmented. For this and other reasons, I ended up writing a history of coal mining in the United States instead.

Fiction has the ability to reveal the life of an ordinary (rather than famous) human being and to reveal the inner as well as the outer shape of a life in powerful ways inaccessible to the historical biography. Nevertheless, fiction writers are increasingly withholding the kind of revelatory depth possible in a fictional portrayal. At the same time biographers are claiming the ground on which fiction writers once stood, and perhaps this explains why biography has become, as James Atlas writes, "the dominant literary genre of our time." As the novel has become "more limited in scope, more introspective and autobiographical, readers have looked increasingly to biography to provide what fiction did in the era of Joyce and Proust, Fitzgerald and Hemingway: details about the way we live and the way we used to live." Readers are turning to biography because that is where a rich and meaningful portrait of a human life may still be found. In too much modern fiction, the characters have diminished to the point of flatness. They do not interest us much and it is hard to feel for them.

A case in point is Mavis Gallant's Walter, the protagonist of "Overhead in a Balloon."[1] Walter is a sad, irritating character who hates his life, his employer, and art (he works in an art gallery), but he is too passive to do anything about it. His dilemma is surely worth a story, but instead we are given flat, summarizing description of his problems: "These were, in order, that for nine years his employer had been exploiting him; that he had his foot caught in the steel teeth of his native Calvinism and was hoping to ease it free without resorting to a knife . . ." (Gallant 51). We see Walter and his problems in an external way, as if we were observing a miscellaneous passerby in a train station. We are not given anything to like about him. Neither is he genuinely repulsive. We simply have difficulty feeling anything at all for him. It is illuminating to compare him to Anton Chekhov's Olenka, the protagonist of **"The Darling."**

Olenka is no more heroine than Walter is hero. She too is frozen into a neurotic pattern. She is a woman who can't live without love; she has no center within herself. But we feel for her and we feel the world with her. It is possible for us to see ourselves in her, to see her predicament as part of the human condition.

Gallant is a writer of our own time who, according to one reviewer, has "a Chekhovian eye for the intricacies of human relationships" (Cunningham). But in comparing these two stories at any rate, Chekhov emerges as the greater artist by far. Both are fine writers with an eye for the acute observation, the telling detail. But the surface of a story, the texture of the writing, is not a substitute for a memorable character. Chekhov has something that Gallant lacks: a depth of vision which enables him to portray a character in rich and compassionate terms. He gives us not only Olenka, but Olenka's experience of the world.

Each of the stories tells the life of an ordinary person afflicted with a neurotic compulsion which dominates everything. Gallant's Walter chronically becomes entangled with people who are indifferent to him or who wish him actual harm. His passivity precludes his gaining control over the events in his life. Chekhov's Olenka is dependent and "addicted to love." She has no center in her own self. She takes on the life and opinions of the one she loves. So dependent is she on having someone (anyone) to love that when her first husband dies she misses him terribly for only three months, until a new man comes along to replace him. At that point she quickly becomes happy again, substituting the new husband's opinions and way of life for those of the old. Both Walter and Olenka repeat neurotic behavior patterns. Their stories function to reveal these patterns, which they do not overcome. Neither Walter nor Olenka have changed by the end of their respective stories. Nevertheless, their lives revealed have the potential to illuminate the human condition.

The problem is that we never quite understand Walter's condition. He is introduced thus: "Walter, assistant manager of the gallery, was immediately attracted to Aymeric, as to a new religion—this time, one that might work" (Gallant 49). In our first meeting we are told what is the matter with him in a summarizing, conclusive statement. Apparently he adheres to new people with religious fervor, deluding himself about them and chronically setting himself up for disappointment. Yet Gallant never tells us what this feels like: Walter's initial characterization is slipped into a long passage about Aymeric. Because it is told from such a distance, as from a psychiatrist's notes, we get no insight into the way it feels to relate to the world the way Walter does.

Compare this with the way in which Chekhov first characterizes Olenka in **"The Darling."** She is sitting on her back porch listening to Kukin, the director of the theatre, complaining, as he does day after day. "Olenka listened to Kukin with silent gravity, and sometimes tears came into her eyes. In the end his misfortunes touched her; she grew to love him. . . . She was always fond of someone, and could not exist without loving. In the early days she had loved her Papa . . ." (Chekhov 210). Tears have come to Olenka's eyes before we know anything about her. She empathizes with an *other* and in turn we can empathize with her. Moreover, as Olenka's life unfolds in the story, her condition is revealed to us far beyond its initial description. We come to know what it means to be unable to exist without love.

From the beginning we feel distant from Walter and close to Olenka. Walter's condition is reported as in a newspaper. He is sad, but we do not feel sad for him or with him. "The mysterious sadness he felt on waking he had until now blamed on remoteness from God" (Gallant 58). This is pathetic, but difficult to empathize with. We can see Walter's behavior and even his thoughts, but we can't experience his affliction. The summarizing and external manner in which even his thoughts are reported, and the cynical tone of the narration, blocks whatever insights we might gain from really understanding Walter's world.

Walter hates his employer, the gallery owner, whom he calls Trout Face. He and Aymeric are sitting at a café when Trout Face (otherwise unnamed in this story) walks by. "'I hate him,' he told Aymeric. 'I *hate* him. I dream he is in danger. A police car drives up and the execution squad takes him away. . . .' Aymeric wondered what bound Walter to that particular dealer. There were other employers in Paris, just as dedicated to art" (Gallant 54). Thereupon, Walter states that he hates art as well. Later we learn that once Walter and his employer were on good terms, that, apparently long ago, Walter's employer had given him a dressing gown as a gift, and that he used to send him off to museums "with a list of things to examine and ponder." But now "virtually anything portrayed as art turned his stomach. There was hardly anything he could look at without feeling sick" (Gallant 66). Walter stays on at the gallery for the sole reason that if he does so for eleven more years he will get the full benefit of his pension fund.

In the above passage I reveal everything Gallant tells us about Walter's relationship with his employer. Something has happened: what was once good has gone sour and hateful. But Gallant leaves out what did happen. She gives us the outer story, the outline, the plot, but leaves the inner story vacant.

What function, it is important to ask, does this spareness, so fashionable in the 1980s, serve? Spareness (or any other technique, such as the richness of language that is its opposite) is by itself valueless. Any technique

or style should serve the story it holds in its mesh. A technique is a means to an end. If the technique itself becomes the end, the story becomes shallow, of mainly technical interest.

I can think of two artistic situations (and there may be others) that seem to call for spareness. One is in the portrayal of events so horrendous that they essentially exceed our human ability to understand them. Such would be portrayals of massacres, such as the Nazi genocide during World War II (portrayed by Jona Obersky in *Childhood*), the massacre of Palestinians at Sabra and Shatila (portrayed by Zakaria al-Shaikh in an account published in *Journal of Palestine Studies*), or the 1890 massacre of Indians at Wounded Knee (portrayed in *Black Elk Speaks*). These three accounts have in common an extreme spareness of style. One is simply asked to experience the events as the authors (each of whom is a survivor) have experienced them. These events were so horrendous in themselves that opinions about them expressed by the narrator would be like adding to the text the ineffectual comment, "It was just awful!" The challenge of such material is to render it in such a way that the reader can share in the experience, as fearful as it was.

Another reason for using a stripped down, spare style is to bring into sharp relief that which remains. The famous example is Hemingway's "Hills Like White Elephants" in which the lack of miscellaneous and characterizing details (and the use of the landscape) bring into sharp relief the woman's dreamlike and organic notion of the hills (like white elephants) in contrast to the man's *reasonableness,* expressed in one of the two adverbs in the piece. It is worth noting that the conflict this story brings into relief is one that is central to human existence—the conflict between passion and reason. To elaborate the details of the story would have been to bring in the inessential.

Gallant's spareness, on the other hand, moves the story forward in no way that I can see. Not knowing enough about Walter makes it hard to care about him. For the same reason, it is difficult to care about most of the people we read about in the newspaper. We may see the events of their lives but we don't see the world through their eyes; we don't know how it feels to be in their shoes. The same is true of Walter. He gets a remarkably small amount of space in his own story. He is buried among details about the two other main characters, Aymeric, who doesn't much like him, and Aymeric's cousin Robert, who doesn't much like him either. Walter moves into their house and is suddenly paying them for all kinds of extras; using the elevator, for instance. They are using him; they are small-minded, manipulative people. But so is Walter, for he ends up stealing from them just as they are stealing from him. Indeed, these three pathetic beings seem to deserve one another.

Walter, like his two "friends," has few if any redeeming qualities. No wonder we don't warm up. Who needs these people? And by the end of the story, we just don't understand them sufficiently well to empathize with their humanity.

In contrast Chekhov conveys Olenka's positive qualities, as well as her character defect. He piles on details of all kinds, with the result of a fully round character. As our understanding of Olenka's inner emptiness develops, so does our understanding of her positive ability to "love." Although this is a flawed sort of love, based entirely on her own needs, Chekhov portrays it in a warm rather than cynical way. "She was a gentle, soft-hearted, compassionate girl, with mild, tender eyes and very good health." People were drawn to her warmth. The men would say, "Yes, not half bad," while "lady visitors could not refrain from seizing her hand in the middle of a conversation, exclaiming in a gush of delight, 'You darling!'" (Chekhov 211). A reader, too, can feel her basic goodness, her warmth, and this in turn makes her inner emptiness tragic rather than irritating or boring.

Not only does Chekhov portray Olenka as a complex character, warm and good as well as empty inside. He also paints her daily life in an intricately textured way, leaving no doubt as to its quality. For instance, when she is married to the theater director (and has assumed his opinions), her life becomes his:

> They got on very well together. She used to sit in his office, to look after things in the Tivoli [theatre], to put down the accounts and pay the wages. And her rosy cheeks, her sweet, naive, radiant smile, were to be seen now at the office window, now in the refreshment bar or behind the scenes of the theatre. And already she used to say to her acquaintances that the theatre was the chief and most important thing in life, and that it was only through the drama that one could derive true enjoyment and become cultivated and humane. . . . And what Kukin said about the theatre and the actors she repeated.
>
> (Chekhov 211)

Three months after her first husband's death, she marries a man in the lumber business; immediately the day to day quality of her life, again fully rendered, becomes the lumber business. She forgets the theater utterly. Worse, she now considers it trivial. Thus Chekhov bares her flawed character. But because he renders her daily life so explicitly, we are also able to empathize with her. Her world, and her experience of it, has become part of our experience.

In contrast, Gallant gives us precious few details of Walter's day. We can't relate to his life because we can't experience it. We don't know what it's like to work in the gallery. We learn nothing (in this story)

about his employer.[2] The story is set mostly in the house in which the three "friends" live, and the house is drawn in vivid detail. But the texture of Walter's day is absent. We want to say to Walter: "Gee whiz! Stop complaining! Just quit your job!" Or we want to say, "Why don't you wait to see whether or not people care for you before you fall down on your face before them?" Because his compulsions are available to us only from the outside, we are out of sympathy with him. We see the surface of his life, but not its inner quality.

With Olenka, it is different: we feel sad for her. The whole cloth of her life is stitched from her husband's experience, and when her second husband dies she spends some years in total and desperate sorrow. "She looked into her yard without interest, thought of nothing, wished for nothing, and afterwards, when night came on she went to bed and dreamed of her empty yard. . . . And what was worst of all, she had no opinions of any sort. She saw the objects about her and understood what she saw, but could not form any opinion about them, and did not know what to talk about. And how awful it is not to have any opinions!" (Chekhov 216). How awful indeed. We feel how awful it is. We feel her tragedy. We feel it because we identify with it. This is familiar, and no less awful because familiar. This could be ourselves.

Olenka is a damaged creature, but a noble one. Walter is a damaged creature too, but small in every way, perhaps too small to quite deserve a story.

An important function of the artist in society is to illuminate the human condition. The writer ought to scrutinize a character to the point of achieving a mature understanding of his or her condition. (In fairness to Gallant, she achieves this in other stories, for example, in her marvelous "Lena.") The artist ought to push the materials of a story as far as they will go. The process of writing a story is one of discovering, through twists and turns, false starts, dead ends, and sudden insight, a vision of a character's life, of his or her story. And we read for the vision. We read to enter the utterly different world of any character not ourselves, and to thereby enlarge our own world.

Every human being, every character, represents one form or another of the human condition. To read **"The Darling"** by Anton Chekhov is to deepen our understanding of our own humanity. To read "Overhead in a Balloon" by Mavis Gallant is to remain in the dark.

Notes

This essay originated in an excellent class on literary genres given by Lois Phillips Hudson at the University of Washington. To her warm thanks are due.

1. This is the title story in the volume of the same name.

2. The employer's story is related elsewhere in this collection in "Speck's Idea." Gallant 1-48.

Works Cited

al-Shaikh, Zakaria. "Sabra and Shatila, 1982: Resisting the Massacre." *Journal of Palestine Studies* 14, No. 1 (Fall 1984): 57-91.

Atlas, James. "Speaking Ill of the Dead." *New York Times,* Nov. 6, 1988, Sec. 6 40-50.

Chekhov, Anton. "The Darling" in *The Norton Anthology of Short Fiction.* Ed. R. V. Cassill. New York: Norton, 1986. 210-20.

Cunningham, John. *Pittsburgh Press.* Quoted on the cover of Gallant.

Gallant, Mavis. *Overhead in a Balloon.* New York: Norton, 1985.

Neihardt, John G. *Black Elk Speaks.* 1932. Lincoln: U of Nebraska P, 1972.

Obersky, Jona. *Childhood.* New York: Doubleday, 1983.

C. J. G. Turner (essay date September-December 1993)

SOURCE: Turner, C. J. G. "Chekhov's Story without a Title: Chronotope and Genre." *Canadian Slavonic Papers* 35, nos. 3-4 (September-December 1993): 329-34.

[*In the following essay, Turner considers the unique place of "Without a Title" within Chekhov's short story oeuvre.*]

The story in question ["**Without a Title**"] was written at the end of December 1887 and published in *Novoe Vremia* (*New Time*) on 1 January 1888 under the title of "**Skazka.**"[1] This term is often translated "fairy-tale" but, at least in this instance, I should prefer to translate simply "A Tale," since it is not a fairy-tale and "tale" (although often used to translate *povest'*) of itself bears the required connotations of something archaic, perhaps childish, perhaps fantastic. It was, however, removed and replaced by "**Bez zaglaviia**" ("**Without a Title**") when the story was republished in a charitable miscellany, *Pomoshch' postradavshim ot neurazhaia* (*Aid for the Victims of the Failed Harvest,* Moscow, 1899).

It covers about four pages of text and its plot may be seen as having four phases plus a coda: first comes a relatively lengthy description of life in a fifth-century monastery; then a townsman arrives, apparently by accident, and, again apparently without forethought, challenges the monks to do something about the sinful life of the nearest town; thirdly, the Abbot of the monastery responds to the challenge by going on a mission to the town; and, fourthly, he returns and reports to the monks on what he had found there. The coda reads: "When he came out of his cell on the following morning there was not a single monk left in the monastery. They had all run off to the town."

If we consider its setting in time and place, what Bakhtin calls the chronotope of the work, then we soon realise that this story is unique in Chekhov's works in being a regular Chekhovian story but set back chronologically to long before Chekhov's lifetime. Few writers have so consistently as Chekhov set their works in their own time and country. Thomas Eekman has called Chekhov "a writer primarily concerned with contemporary and Russian themes [who] never delved into the past."[2] E. A. Polotskaia claims that he wrote only three stories whose action takes place outside Russia or outside his own time: "**Without a Title**" is set in an Eastern monastery of the fifth century; "**Pari**" ("**The Bet**") is set in an unnamed, "obviously European" city (she does not suggest that the title could be a pun!); and "**Rasskaz starshego sadovnika**" ("**The Head Gardener's Story**") is a frame-story for an old Swedish legend.[3] And A. P. Chudakov writes that, with the exception of "**Greshnik iz Toledo**" ("**The Sinner from Toledo**") and "**Without a Title,**" Chekhov has no works in the genre of historical prose and that "neither of these stylizations can pretend to being historical."[4] Of the other titles offered here, however, "**The Bet**" may be alien to Chekhov in location ("**Gusev**" could also have been adduced, set as it is at sea in the Far East; Ariadna and the Anonymous Man too, in their respective stories, spend time in some of the capitals and resorts of Western Europe, like Mme Ranevskaia of *Vishnevyi sad* [*The Cherry Orchard*] and Chekhov himself) but certainly is not alien in time; "**The Head Gardener's Story**" has an extended contemporary frame such that the legend could almost be called an "inserted narrative" within a contemporary story (nor is it necessarily set back in time by more than a few generations); and "**The Sinner from Toledo**" is indeed a parodic stylization of another time and place, as is intimated by its subtitle "Translated from the Spanish." But there is no reason for calling "**Without a Title**" a "stylization": it is merely set in the fifth century, and this fact makes it unique in Chekhov.

There are some surprising features of this story that one is tempted to attribute to Chekhov's haste or negligence (he expended no great time or care on its composition), perhaps sheer ignorance. One surprise is that Polotskaia should set it so positively in an *Eastern* monastery, just as the poet Ia. P. Polonskii should, on its first publication, call it an "Eastern Tale."[5] For the Abbot is said to write Latin verses and, at least in the first edition, it is clear that the monastery is Latin-speaking, although the surrounding populace is Arabic-speaking. Latin-speakers were by no means unknown in Eastern monasteries (witness St. Jerome), but a whole Latin-speaking community would be exceptional. Presumably the claim that it is set in the East is based on the reference to a tiger's having been sighted in the vicinity, since tigers are purely Asiatic and were never found west of Armenia. Strictly speaking the tiger is incompatible with an Arabic-speaking populace in the fifth century, since Arabic was not spoken outside the Arabian peninsula before the spread of Islam in the seventh century. Nevertheless, tigers are clearly depicted in a fine fourth-century mosaic from Algeria,[6] so that one can say at least that they were known further west. Alternatively, it is just possible to suppose that the monk who claimed to have seen one was, through fear or for some other reason, mistaken. If a real locale has to be found for the story, it has also to be on a coast since the monks are said to be able to hear the sea. The first edition mentioned also palms and fig-trees.

A second surprise is the organ that is played by the Abbot. One immediately thinks of large organs in western churches, but that plainly cannot be what Chekhov has in mind if he knows what he is talking about. Both hydraulic and bellows-driven organs had been known since Hellenistic times and were widespread in the later Roman Empire. Nero numbered organ-playing among his skills! But they were used primarily at secular celebrations and never have been used in the Eastern Church. There are, in fact, few written references to them from the fifth century (perhaps as a result of the barbarian invasions), except for some Church Fathers (particularly from the south or east coasts of the Mediterranean) who use the organ as a symbol.[7] It is noticeable, however, that the Abbot plays the organ not in the monastery church (to which there is no reference) but in his cell, which is, of course, remotely possible.

The story is, then, in principle, a highly unusual one for Chekhov with an ill-defined setting; and from this there follow a number of peculiarities. Its opening words tell us that, although set in the fifth century, it is told from a modern point of view ("In the fifth century, *as now,* every morning the sun rose . . ." [emphasis added—C. J. G. Turner]). This merely formalizes and makes explicit what, according to A. A. Mendilow, is normal and perhaps inevitable: that the sensibilities of historical fiction should be those of the writer's time.[8] Not only the point of view, but also the lightly ironical tone and the style (with scarcely an archaism in sight) are those of a modern Chekhovian narrator. While this modern narrator allows his imagination to go a little way towards individualizing the characters of the Abbot and the visitor, he is noticeably reticent and vague about the realia of his story: trees, animals, birds, flowers are mentioned, but only once is a tiger specified; and the monastery has cells and gates, but seems devoid of furnishings, and the monks have food and wine for themselves

and their visitor, but what they eat we are not told. Chekhov, who knew his trees and birds, as well as monastic fare, normally tells us more; and he was normally careful and accurate about his realia, as D. W. Martin has shown while indicating at the same time that he was not infallible.[9]

The structure of the story is simple. Its opening paragraphs stress repetition, with their imperfective aspects and phrases such as "every day and night went on being just like every preceding day and night" (*vse den' pokhodil na den', noch' na noch'*). This continuum is broken by a one-time (*odnazhdy*) event, the arrival at night of a visitor to the "surprise of the monks." He is an outsider, a foreign body (in the first edition he even spoke only Arabic while "here one can save one's soul only in Latin"[10]), whose visit culminates in a challenging harangue that is reproduced in direct speech. Having completed this task, he is forgotten by the narrator who neglects to tell us anything about his departure. But his challenge has reached home to the Abbot who, in an almost symmetrical action, leaves the monastery for three months, but returns and also makes a speech (rendered, however, in reported speech). The consequence is given cynically in two lines, with "no comment."[11]

It is noticeable that the realia of the story suddenly become more specific in the Abbot's speech. A table is mentioned for the first time, and on the table is a harlot, the first character in the story whose appearance is described. She is wearing silk and brocade. And when the Abbot leaves the brothel he discovers that the town has also "horse-races, bullfights, theatres, and artists' workshops." The impression is given of a Hellenistic or perhaps a North African city in the later Roman Empire. Bullfighting, for instance, was practised in ancient Thessaly, from where it was imported to Rome as an innovation by Julius Caesar. It became especially popular in the Greek cities of the Empire. While gladiatorial contests in which men took part were ended in theory under Constantine and in practice by the early fifth century, the more common *venationes* (in which animals fought against animals—and the more exotic the species the better) continued into the sixth century; artistic representations of them include North African mosaics and a Constantinopolitan ivory from the beginning of the sixth century.[12] Chekhov probably envisaged something more like modern Spanish bullfighting and would have been hard put to it to provide evidence of its existence in the fifth century. The relative richness of concrete detail in the Abbot's account may ultimately be due to the fact that he found it easier to imagine a fifth-century town than a fifth-century monastery, but it does at the same time fulfil a function of inciting the monks' nocturnal imaginations.

There are, however, also a few further incongruities that are more probably attributable to Chekhov's haste than to the deficiencies of the modern narrator. The Abbot is called an "old man" when he is first mentioned but, after "tens of years have passed," he is still the same vigorous old man. The isolation of the monastery is stressed (perhaps in order to justify the extraordinary degree of ignorance and naiveté on the monks' part about city-life) by there being a hundred versts of wilderness between it and the nearest human habitation; yet the wilderness cannot be an absolute desert because the visitor is able to hunt there and because the Abbot, as he crosses it, is encouraged by the babbling brooks and, on his return, he can use the "fresh verdure of spring" for a simile. And whence, incidentally, comes the monastery's supply of food and wine? Either it has more contact with the outside world than we are led to suppose (for years, we are told, the only living souls to show themselves near the monastery were those who were taking refuge from the world) or the desert is indeed blooming.

Although I have rejected "fairy-tale" as an appropriate designation for this story, it is susceptible of the kind of analysis that is reminiscent of Propp's work on fairy-tales[13]: an established and ritual status quo in which a hero-figure is identified in the person of the Abbot is invaded by an intruder from the town who sets the hero a task; the hero goes forth to fulfil the task by doing battle with the dragon of evil; the account of the battle is retarded by seven days before we learn that the prize has eluded the hero, since the princess has remained in the power of the dragon—the town remains unconverted and the harlot has failed to follow in the footsteps of Mary of Egypt or even of Makovkina/Mother Agnes in Tolstoi's *Otets Sergii* (*Father Sergius*). But in regard to its chronotope the story is further from the genre of the fairy-tale, which typically is totally unlocated in space and time, than it is from the kind of romance or *gistoriia* that was popular from Hellenistic times to early-modern Russia and that normally has an ostensible location (perhaps more often in place than in time) but not always one that avoids incompatibilities and inconsistencies.

The story ends with a cynical twist forcibly reminding us of what we had learnt at the start: that it is being told by a modern man. This modern man, unlike his predecessors in folklore and literature, will avoid any implication of a moral beyond the cynical intimations that a cloistered naiveté is dangerous or that the will to convert is hubristic. He is sophisticated enough to laugh at a bunch of fifth-century monks but not sophisticated enough to avoid some incongruities in the telling of his tale. He is, I suggest, a regular Chekhovian narrator, standing apart from his heroes in order to poke gentle fun at their weaknesses but, having once strayed beyond his accustomed milieu, he is just a little out of his depth; and this is what makes it not a stylization, nor a fairy-tale nor a romance, but a regular Chekhovian story.

The fable and its chronotope are unique in Chekhov, but the style, manner and narratorial stance are typical of his early and only too often hastily composed stories. But such an anomalous combination was an experiment that he did not repeat, preferring generally to keep his feet firmly on his home turf of late nineteenth-century Russia, which is where even that hallucinatory visitant from a ninth-century Eastern monastery, the Black Monk, makes himself at home.

Notes

1. A. P. Chekhov, *Polnoe sobranie sochinenii i pisem: Sochineniia* (Moscow, 1974-82; in future references *PSSP*) vol. 6: 455-58.

2. In *Slavia* 40 (1971): 49.

3. E. A. Polotskaia, *A. P. Chekhov: dvizhenie khudozhestvennoi mysli* (Moscow, 1979) 55.

4. A. P. Chudakov, *Mir Chekhova* (Moscow, 1986) 321.

5. Chekhov, *PSSP* vol. 6: 703.

6. Reproduced in the *Grande Dictionnaire Encyclopédique Larousse* (1982) under "Tigre."

7. J. Perrot, *L'Orgue de ses origines hellénistiques à la fin du XIIIe siècle* (Paris, 1965) 95-97.

8. A. A. Mendilow, *Time and the Novel* (New York, 1965) 87-89.

9. D. W. Martin, "Realia and Chekhov's 'The Student'" in *Canadian-American Slavic Studies* 12 (1978): 266-73.

10. Chekhov, *PSSP* vol. 6: 608.

11. This is the rendering of the title given in *Chekhov: The Early Stories, 1883-88,* chosen and translated by P. Miles and H. Pitcher (London, 1982).

12. L. Friedländer, *Roman Life and Manners under the Early Empire* (London and New York, 1908-13) vol. 2: 81; G. Jennison, *Animals for Show and Pleasure in Ancient Rome* (Manchester, 1937) 26-27, 98; J. M. C. Toynbee, *Animals in Roman Life and Art* (London, 1973) 150.

13. See V. Ia. Propp, *Morfologiia skazki* (Leningrad, 1928).

Ronald L. Johnson (essay date 1993)

SOURCE: Johnson, Ronald L. "The Short Fiction: The Master, 1895-1903." In *Anton Chekhov: A Study of the Short Fiction,* pp. 76-103. New York: Twayne Publishers, 1993.

[*In the following essay, Johnson surveys prominent motifs in Chekhov's later short fiction, categorizing the stories into four thematic groups.*]

Raymond Carver believed an agreement might be reached among "thoughtful" readers that Chekhov was the greatest short story writer who ever lived, not only because of the "immense number" of stories he wrote, but the "awesome frequency" with which he produced masterpieces.[1] That frequency is most apparent in this last period, from 1895 through 1903, when Chekhov treated the same subjects, but with a shift in point of view technique to include a narrating author persona in many stories. In general, this persona is disembodied, commenting on the characters and action as do the narrators in Henry James and George Eliot. A. P. Chudakov remarks that his characteristic manner of "depicting the world through a *concrete, perceiving consciousness*" has not been replaced. Rather the "old manner remains and a new one is added to it" (99-100).

Chekhov's contemporaries noticed this shift in point of view. One critic commented in 1898 that Chekhov was no longer the "objective artist" he had been earlier; that same year, another critic perceived that Chekhov's "added subjectivity" would deepen the content of his creative work (Chudakov, 73). The modern critic Nicholas Moravcevich traces the evolution of Chekhov's earlier artistic creed of strict objectivity to the new "persuasiveness" of his "artistic aims," a transformation that gradually occurred over a five-year span from 1887 to 1892; Moravcevich believes this different approach marked the end of Chekhov's formative period and the beginning of his "transcendence of the aesthetic dictates of naturalism" (225).

Stories of Love and the Authentic Life

"A Lady with a Dog" (Hingley) beautifully illustrates Chekhov's use of a shift in point of view, for in addition to the perceiving consciousness of the protagonist, comment is presented directly to the reader through Chekhov's disembodied narrating persona. Like many of Chekhov's middle-class protagonists, the bank employee Gurov does not have a satisfactory relationship with his wife. He fears her because she is outspoken and intellectual. Any happiness he finds with women occurs in a series of affairs, and while on vacation in Yalta, he engages in what appears to be another such affair. The woman, the "lady with the dog," is named Anne, and on an outing to a church at Oreanda, the couple sit on a bench, entranced by the view. Shifting beyond Gurov's conscious mind, Chekhov adopts a narrating persona who relates that "borne up from below, the sea's monotonous, muffled boom spoke of peace, of the everlasting sleep awaiting us" (IX, 132). This passage has a mystical dimension that recalls the last section of **"Gusev,"** also narrated beyond the conscious mind of the protagonist. The comment becomes more lyrical as it develops in a passage on eternity and the indifference of the universe, which measures not only Gurov but the reader against its endless vastness. It

concludes with an optimistic comment on the eternal nature of life—not on the individual, who is mortal, but on life itself which is immortal and constantly progressing, a recurring motif in Chekhov's stories from this period.

The paragraph closes with a return to Gurov's mind as he reflects that "everything on earth is beautiful, really, when you consider it—everything but what we think and do ourselves when we forget the lofty goals of being and our human dignity" (IX, 132). This thought, mirroring Chekhov's own sensibilities, makes Gurov a more sympathetic character. Although he lives an inauthentic life—in which he speaks disparagingly of women, calling them the "inferior species"—he is capable of this insightful observation when sitting beside Anne. The couple takes a number of excursions which invariably leave an impression of "majesty and beauty," while a subtle transformation begins to occur in each of them. Anne articulates her desire for that transformation when she voices her yearning for a different life—in Chekhov, such a desire is usually the telltale sign of a character's living an inauthentic life. Like Gurov, she does not love her spouse, but her adulterous relationship with Gurov disturbs her because she wants to live a "decent, moral life."

Gurov on the other hand easily dismisses the affair until he returns to his inauthentic life in Moscow. There he resumes his boring life of "futile activities," realizing such meaningless activities "engross most of your time, your best efforts, and you end up with a sort of botched, pedestrian life: a form of imbecility from which there's no way out, no escape" (IX, 135). Gurov's thought recalls the final comments of Nikitin on his domestic life in **"The Russian Master"**: "You might as well be in jail or in a madhouse" (IX, 135). Gurov feels the same desperation Anne felt before her vacation in Yalta, a desperation marked by the feeling she could not control herself. He now flees Moscow to seek out Anne, because their affair has become the most important aspect of his life. This transformation in Gurov's attitude constitutes the dramatic climax of the plot.

After Gurov finds Anne, their situation develops into a prolonged affair, and Gurov begins to live two lives. One is the false life he has been living, full of "stereotyped truths and stereotyped untruth," identical to the life of his friends and acquaintances. He despises this inauthentic life, and feels that "everything vital, interesting and crucial to him, everything which called his sincerity and integrity into play, everything which made up the core of his life" (IX, 139) occurs in his other, secret life with Anne. In contrast to those protagonists from earlier stories such as **"Lights"** and **"The Duel"** who undergo a transformation and throw off their inauthentic lives, Gurov retains his old life in the form of a facade that satisfies the decorum of the age. This compromise makes him a more complex character, a typical modern hero unable to integrate his multiple lives into one.

As the story closes, both Anne and he feel their love has "transformed" them, but the most difficult part of their lives is "only just beginning" (IX, 141). Chekhov's method of ending a story with the suggestion that the lives of his characters will go on developing becomes one of his most effective closures during this period. This conclusion reinforces the theme that through love—one of Chekhov's favorite topics—the characters have been transformed, making them better people.

Chekhov approaches the power of love with a different tone, achieved partially through a shift in point of view, in **"Angel"** (Hingley). Chekhov has a tongue-in-cheek attitude toward the protagonist, Olga, who is "always in love with someone—couldn't help it" (IX, 82). She is a "quiet, good-hearted, sentimental, very healthy young lady with a tender, melting expression" (IX, 82) to whom men are attracted and to whom women respond openly and kindly. At first Chekhov conveys his criticism through light satire as Olga marries a theater manager and adopts his opinions in all matters, especially on the importance of the theater. When the theater manager dies a few years later, she marries a lumberyard manager and in turn adopts his opinions in all matters, including the idea that the theater is a "trifle." Olga is not consciously insincere, merely naive and shallow.

When the lumberyard manager dies after six years—during which the couple prayed for children but had none—Olga falls in love with an army veterinarian who is estranged from his wife, and, in turn, takes up his opinions. But when he is transferred, Olga goes through a crisis because "she no longer had views on anything"—she cannot form her own opinions. She feels she needs a love "to possess her whole being, all her mind and soul: a love to equip her with ideas, with a sense of purpose, a love to warm her ageing blood" (IX, 88). This function of love is the object of Chekhov's satire. Although Chekhov presents some of Olga's experiences from her perspective, he also addresses much of the action directly to the reader. In earlier works, **"Ward Number Six"** and **"Three Years,"** for example, the passages outside the consciousness of the characters are almost always pure exposition, unmediated by the assertive voice of a separate, vital narrating persona.

To this point in the action, **"Angel"** satirizes Olga's sensibility in an amusing series of events without a focused form, reading more like a character sketch than a story. What makes the work a masterpiece is the last episode, in which the tone shifts to one of compassion for the protagonist, much as it does for Jacob in **"Rothschild's Fiddle."** With this shift, the character is re-deemed in the reader's eye, becoming worthy of respect and sympathy. After a half-dozen years, the veterinarian returns as a civilian with his wife and son, and Olga emotionally adopts the child, a nine-year-old boy named Sasha. Olga cares for all his needs as her love for him becomes boundless, eclipsing her earlier loves. Olga's desire to love, which Chekhov has been satirizing, now becomes meaningful by its very compassion: "For this boy—no relative at all—for his dimpled cheeks, for his cap she would give her whole life, give it gladly, with tears of ecstasy. Why? Who knows?" The satire is absent from this statement, which is as straightforward as the closing passage of **"A Lady with a Dog."** The question "Why? Who knows?"—Chekhov directly addressing the reader—deftly deepens the reader's involvement in the action.

"Angel" has generated a number of widely different critical interpretations. One of the more insightful comes from an anonymous reviewer in 1916 who notes Chekhov possessed the "subtlest sympathy," which enables him to "understand and reveal" his characters; this critic maintains that the effect of reading Chekhov's tales is to be "washed free of petty impatience and acerbity of judgement."[2]

In **"Ariadne"** (Hingley), the character of Olga in **"The Butterfly"** is recast into a colder, more calculating young woman, and in place of the virtuous Dr. Dymov is a sensitive, idealistic young landowner, Shamokhin, who must resolve his feelings for the woman who makes him a victim of his love. Dr. Dymov escapes his situation with Olga through death, but in this later story, Chekhov develops the situation to its more complex, more logical, and more realistic conclusion.

Shamokhin narrates his story to a first-person character. As in the earlier stories, **"Easter Eve"** and **"Uprooted,"** this first-person character is a writer. The difference between this character and the persona identified in **"A Lady with a Dog"** and **"Angel"** is that in **"Ariadne"** the narrator is an actual character who interacts with another character, Shamokhin, not simply a narrating voice. The setting of the frame of **"Ariadne"** provides a backdrop for the telling of Shamokhin's story: the two men are on the passenger deck of a Black Sea steamer when Shamokhin makes some general comments on the nature of women and love, comments that recall the initial attitude of Gurov in **"A Lady with a Dog"**: because of disappointing love affairs, he looks upon women as "mean, restless, lying, unfair, primitive, cruel creatures" (VIII, 74). Shamokhin then relates his specific story to illustrate this opinion.

A few years previously, in his mid twenties, Shamokhin fell very much in love with a neighbor's sister, Ariadne, a beautiful woman whose selfish demands for luxurious items were bringing her brother's estate to ruin. Like many of Chekhov's landowners, Shamokhin is an idealist who "romanticizes" love, but he is wise enough to realize Ariadne is so self-centered, so taken with her own beauty and charm, that she is incapable of really loving another person. However, Shamokhin cannot resist her, so he follows her to Europe and eventually becomes her lover. There they live at resorts with the money Shamokhin obtains from his father, who must mortgage their estate to pay for the extravagance. Like Olga in **"The Butterfly,"** Ariadne begins painting, but her real interest is "to attract": she must "bewitch, captivate, drive people out of their minds" (VIII, 90). Although Ariadne is without much taste, she is "diabolically sharp and cunning, and in company she had the knack of passing as educated and progressive" (VIII, 91). She is one of Chekhov's least likeable characters, a hypocrite whose behavior causes some critics to condemn her, and others to find in her an attack upon the marriage customs and lack of opportunities for women of the day.

After a short while, Shamokhin falls out of love and yearns to return to Russia, "to work and earn my bread by the sweat of my brow and make good my mistakes" (VIII, 92). This desire is a common goal for Chekhov's idealistic heroes—the same salvation through work the engineer espouses in **"Lights"** and Vanya clings to in the play *Uncle Vanya.* The story closes with a return to the frame, where the author character argues against Shamokhin's attitude toward women, maintaining one cannot generalize from Ariadne on the nature of women, but Shamokhin remains unconvinced. In contrast to Olga and Dymov in **"The Butterfly,"** the relationship between Shamokhin and Ariadne is portrayed over the entire course of its development and decline in a remarkable illustration of Chekhov's mastery of point-of-view technique.

The situation of a person trapped in a frustrating, harmful relationship is also the subject of **"The Order of St. Anne"** (Hingley). The narrative is often at a considerable distance from the heroine, but at times, shifts into her mind. In contrast to Ariadne, the young woman is a sympathetic character, and her husband takes advantage of her. Chekhov begins the story outside the consciousness of the heroine, commenting on people's response to a government official of fifty-two marrying an eighteen-year-old girl. Anne, the daughter of a recent widower, marries the wealthy official for independence and security, hoping to help her family, but in Chekhov, marrying for such reasons is inviting trouble.

Once married, Anne realizes she doesn't even like Modeste, her husband, and soon discovers she now has less money than before since Modeste will give her nothing. But, afraid to protest, she forces herself "to smile and pretend to be pleased when defiled by clumsy caresses and embraces that sickened her" (VIII, 36).

Anne's position suddenly changes, however, when Modeste has her attend a ball to impress his supervisor and colleagues, where she dazzles the dignitaries in Cinderella-like fashion. The next day, after Modeste's supervisor visits the house to thank her for her attendance, Modeste appears before her with the "crawling, sugary, slavish, deferential look" (VIII, 41) he keeps for powerful people. With her newly won power, Anne now gains the upper hand, and begins spending his money freely, cavorting with other men in an ironic reversal of her situation: she is now the one who orders Modeste about. However, Modeste is not dissatisfied, for he receives a medal—the Order of St. Anne, Second Class—from his supervisor. Ronald Hingley observes that this story is one of the many by Chekhov that are only a "mere dozen pages" but seem to have the content of full-length novels because of Chekhov's ability to "conjure up a whole milieu by suggestion without needing to fill in every detail" (VIII, 7). The government official's desiring the medal, his fawning before a superior, and the ironic reversal recall Chekhov's early humorous period.

In contrast to the coarse, philistine Modeste is the idealistic, sensitive artist in **"The Artist's Story"** (Hingley). A landscape painter, his idealism resembles that of Shamokhin in **"Ariadne."** In commenting on first-person stories from this period, A. P. Chudakov notes a shift in narrative technique away from the "individualized features" of the protagonist's speech toward a conventional literary narrator, similar to the use of the persona in such third-person stories as **"A Lady with a Dog," "Angel,"** and **"The Order of St. Anne."** (69). In both instances, strict objectivity is replaced by the author's presence. Because the pretext in **"Ariadne"** is that the author himself is a character, the conventional literary narration is justified; but in **"An Artist's Story,"** the narrative suggests a written manuscript although the story mentions none. Like Shamokhin, the narrator—he remains unnamed in the story—falls in love with a young woman from a neighboring estate, but unlike Ariadne, this girl, Zhenya, is sensitive and caring. Only seventeen or eighteen, Zhenya is five years younger than her sister, Lydia, who dominates the family, even their mother.

Lydia is an idealist, like the narrator, but her ideals have led her in a different, more practical direction: she builds schools and hospitals for the local peasants and teaches them herself. The artist, on the other hand, believes such efforts actually are keeping the peasants in poverty. He maintains a radical transformation of society is required for any real change. In one of the arguments between the narrator and Lydia, he declares that the peasants must be freed from their manual labor so that they can develop meaningful, spiritual lives. Otherwise, he believes work has no meaning, and thus refuses to do any. Lydia rejects his position, accusing him of simply saying "charming things" to excuse his laziness, for she believes "rejecting hospitals and schools is easier than healing or teaching" (VIII, 108). She believes such work is more valuable than "all the landscapes ever painted" (VIII, 109). This exchange of ideas is effective as fiction because Chekhov is portraying characters whose ideas are an integral part of their individuality.

But the artist finally is no match for Lydia with her practical sense. Lydia forbids Zhenya to ever see the narrator again, ordering Zhenya and her mother to leave the district. The story closes as the narrator relates that several years after his departure from the district he learned that Lydia continues to teach, struggling to improve the life of the peasants, and Zhenya no longer lives in the district. Now when he paints, he recalls their love, and it seems to him as if soon they shall meet again. Chekhov poignantly evokes a sense of expectation in the character that the reader is aware can never be realized.

The complexity of the story evolves from the ambiguity of the characters' situations. The narrator and Zhenya are both sensitive and sympathetic, and their love is obviously a beautiful, desirable emotion. The hardworking idealist Lydia, although a valuable member of her community, is the very person who makes the further development of that love impossible. Once again, Chekhov presents no solutions to his characters' problems in life.

Love is the subject of another landowner's story in **"Concerning Love"** (Hingley), which shares characters and a narrative approach with **"A Hard Case"** and **"Gooseberries."** Because of these similarities, critics refer to these stories as the "Little Trilogy." One function of the frame setting for the story—the opening and closing sections are in the third person—is to set the atmosphere for the landowner's inner story. Two sportsmen—Ivan Ivanovich, a veterinarian, and Burkin, a teacher—have been caught in a rainstorm while out hunting, so they must spend the night at the estate of Alyokhin, a landowner. The next day at lunch, Alyokhin comments on the general "mystery" of love in a metaphor that is not only particularly appropriate for Chekhov as a doctor, but can be applied to his poetics in short fiction: "What seems to fit one instance doesn't fit a dozen others. It's best to interpret each instance separately in my view, without trying to generalize. We must isolate each individual case, as doctors say" (IX, 41). The comparison to a case history is an apt one for many of Chekhov's stories, and Alyokhin's further comment on a lack of a solution in love suggests Chekhov's own position.

In Alyokhin's particular case, he took up farming his estate—"not without a certain repugnance"—to pay off the mortgage, and over the course of several years, he

and a married woman who lived in town fell in love. However, because of her family duties, and because of Alyokhin's sense of responsibility to her household, they did not declare their love to each other. She eventually became depressed, feeling that her life was unfulfilled and wasted. When her husband secures a judgeship in a different province, the family moves away. As they part for the last time, Alyokhin realizes how inessential, how trivial, and how deceptive and unnecessary everything that frustrated their love was. As the story closes, the narrating persona returns to comment on how the two listeners—Ivan and Burkin—feel compassion for Alyokhin, and regret he has nothing to make his life more pleasant. This sense of regret, of love unfulfilled, of wasted opportunities and unlived lives, is the essence of the popular Chekhovian mood.

Stories of the Authentic Life

These aspects of the Chekhovian mood also are present in another story published in 1898, **"All Friends Together"** (Hingley). The structure does not resemble **"Concerning Love"** as much as a more complex **"Verotchka,"** published eleven years earlier in 1887. As in **"Verotchka,"** a professional man from the city travels to the provinces where he has the opportunity for a life of love, but like the protagonist in **"Verotchka,"** he rejects that opportunity. The story is filtered through the consciousness of Podgorin, a successful lawyer who visits the estate of some old friends, where he had served as a tutor when a poor student. Both the types of characters and the estate's atmosphere resemble the characters and setting of Chekhov's later plays: because of mismanagement, the estate is to be sold, as in *The Cherry Orchard*; and the three women and Sergy are similar in many ways to the family in *The Three Sisters*. The story should not be confused with the earlier prose plays where the structure is composed of dialogue, for the interior, psychological action in Podgorin's consciousness is the structural center of this story.

The dramatic line of development involves Podgorin's relationship with Nadya. Ten years before, Podgorin had tutored her, and later, fallen in love with her. Now Nadya, an attractive twenty-three-year-old, desires to marry, and the plot revolves around whether Podgorin will propose. One moonlit summer night, when Podgorin is sitting out on the grounds, Nadya appears. She senses his presence, but since she cannot see him in the shadows, she asks if someone is there. Podgorin knows that now is the time to speak, if he wishes to propose, but like the protagonist in **"Verotchka,"** he feels strangely indifferent. His emotions remain disengaged from this "poetic vision" of the woman in the moonlight. Podgorin remains silent, and Nadya turns away with the comment, "There's no one there" (IX, 242). On one level, her "no one" suggests Podgorin's lack of substance as a human being, for he has rejected the opportunity to become part of this "poetic vision," the chance for a life of love. In his action, Podgorin on a deeper level rejects himself: "this Podgorin with his apathy, his boredom, his perpetual bad temper, his inability to adapt to real life" (IX, 241). Shortly afterward, Podgorin leaves for Moscow, feeling "indifferent," not sad.

In **"Verotchka,"** the protagonist's rejection is a clearcut turning away from a vital life experience, but Podgorin's choice is more ambiguous. He does not wish to become entangled in the web of problems in Nadya's family, and more importantly, he yearns for a "new, lofty, rational mode of existence" (IX, 241), which he senses this marriage could not provide. The desire to change one's life is a common trait of the Chekhov protagonist who senses he is living an inauthentic life.

A story published later in 1898, **"Dr. Startsev"** (Hingley), is similar to **"All Friends Together"** in subject, but where **"All Friends Together"** has the tight dramatic focus of a play, **"Dr. Startsev"** suggests a novel that has been marvelously telescoped into a short story. Instead of the highly focused time span of one day, which lends itself to remaining exclusively in the consciousness of the protagonist, the time in **"Dr. Startsev"** spans several years, during which the protagonist ages considerably and his position in society changes. The story provides a good example of Chekhov's narrating persona, with several shifts into the consciousness of the protagonist during key dramatic moments.

In the opening, the narrator provides a general introduction to a provincial town and to the Turkins, the town's most cultivated and accomplished family. Dr. Startsev, a young doctor recently appointed to the area, falls in love with an aspiring pianist named Catherine Turkin, but when he proposes, Catherine rejects him. Although she believes he is kind and intelligent, she is determined to escape the provincial town with its "empty, futile existence" (IX, 60). In the four years that pass after Catherine leaves for Moscow, Startsev settles into a middle-class existence: he grows to resent the limited views of the provincial townspeople, gains a great amount of weight, and becomes a nightly bridge player. When Catherine returns after her discovery that she will never become a great pianist, she desires Startsev's company, but he rejects her request to call upon her.

The story closes after a few more years in which Startsev has built a vast practice, and has gained even more weight. Now a dedicated materialist primarily interested in acquiring property, he lives a dreary life without other interests. Like Podgorin, he has rejected the opportunity for a different life, and the narrator describes him as a rather pathetic figure. In commenting on the artistic merit of the story, Ronald Hingley observes that although **"Dr. Startsev"** has been comparatively neglected by the critics, the story holds its own with any rival (IX, 1).

Life in the provinces takes a different turn in **"The Savage"** (Hingley), in which the protagonist is not Chekhov's typical middle-class hero but an elderly, retired Cossack officer who invites a lawyer to his farm. At the farmhouse, the lawyer discovers the Cossack's wife is still young and pretty, although the couple has two full-grown sons. But the Cossack treats her with indifference: "She wasn't a wife, she wasn't the mistress of the house or even a servant, she was more of a dependent—an unwanted poor relation, a nobody" (VIII, 232). This deplorable condition is dramatized not only by the manner in which the Cossack orders his wife about, but when the Cossack says that "women aren't really human to my way of thinking" (VIII, 231).

The Cossack's treatment of his wife is but one form of his behavior that the lawyer finds objectionable, and Chekhov's achievement in the story is in portraying this very unsympathetic character in human terms. Because of a recent stroke, the Cossack is searching for "something to hold on to in his old age," some belief so he will not be afraid of dying. For all his callous behavior, the old Cossack knows that for the "good of his soul" he should shake off "the laziness" that causes "day after day and year after year to be engulfed unnoticed, leaving no trace" (VIII, 232). Despite his cultural difference, the Cossack displays the same search for individual meaning exhibited by Chekhov's common middle-class protagonists.

Another character like Dr. Startsev who becomes confined to a life in the provinces is the heroine of **"Home"** (Hingley). Vera, a sensitive, educated, young woman, returns to her grandfather's farm after ten years in Moscow. At first, she is excited about her life in the country, although the wide-open landscape with its "boundless plain" is "so monotonous, so empty" it frightens her, and although she has reservations about her grandfather, who before emancipation had his peasants flogged and who still terrorizes his servants. But as Vera discovers the limited nature of the provincial society—she had never met people so "casual and indifferent"—her feelings about her life and future begin to change to uncertainty, and like so many Chekhov characters, she yearns for something to give her life meaning, a situation which will enable her to "love and have a family of her own" (VIII, 244).

Vera's aunt suggests that Vera marry Dr. Neshchapov, who is attracted to Vera. In his materialism, this doctor shares characteristics with Dr. Startsev: the director of a factory, he considers his medical practice his secondary profession. Vera is not attracted to him, but her other

possibilities seem even more limiting, for the "vast ex-
panses, the long winters, the monotony and tedium
make you feel so helpless" (VIII, 246). She fears that
disabling boredom so many Chekhov protagonists experience, but "there seemed to be no way out. Why do
anything when nothing does any good?" (VIII, 246).
One day Vera vents her frustration on her servant. Realizing the inappropriateness of her action—she detests
such behavior in her grandfather—she agrees to marry
Dr. Neshchapov, and thus resigns herself to her own
"perpetual discontent with herself and others" (VIII,
247), the same discontent that Podgorin displays. Defeated, she accepts that "happiness and truth have nothing to do with ordinary life" (VIII, 247). In surrendering her aspirations and dreams for a better life, Vera
knows she will now "expect nothing better." The provincial social reality will overcome her desire for a better, richer life.

Chekhov had a special place in his heart for schoolteachers, and it shows in **"In the Cart"** (Hingley), published five weeks after **"Home"** in 1897. The events are
structured around the journey of a rural schoolmistress.
As in **"All Friends Together"** and **"Home,"** the story
is centered in the consciousness of the protagonist,
Marya, who has taught at the same school for thirteen
years, although to her, the constant hardship makes it
seem a "hundred years or more." During Marya's journey, a local landowner, an alcoholic about her age,
passes Marya's cart in his carriage. She feels attracted
to him, but knows to fall in love would be a "disaster."
Although she desires a husband and wants "love and
happiness," she feels her job has made her unattractive,
and so her love would not be returned.

Through her thoughts, Chekhov details the hardships of
her position. All winter she must endure the cold school-
house, and she must struggle constantly against the attitudes of the janitor and the school manager. She realizes that no one finds her attractive, for the job is
wearing her out, making her a drudge ashamed of her
timid behavior. Her salary is low, and she is so worried
about finances that she misses the satisfaction of serving an ideal in her work.

As Marya enters her home village, she sees a woman
on a train who resembles her dead mother, reminding
Marya of her life before teaching. This experience gives
her a sudden surge of happiness and joy, a form of rap-
ture. When the landowner again appears, she imagines
"such happiness as has never been on earth" (VIII, 258).
She feels the sky and trees and building windows are
"aglow with her triumphant happiness" (VIII, 258).
This mystical experience, which resembles the happiness of Gusev, is the climax of the story.

But this wonderful experience vanishes as Marya's cart
continues into the village, leaving her "shivering, numb
with cold." She realizes she will continue her joyless

life as before. She is trapped as firmly in her barren,
provincial environment as Vera or Dr. Startsev. In commenting on her character, however, Kenneth Lantz notes
that she is not "fixed, limited, easily defined," but a
character in flux: he compares her to Nadya Shimin in
"A Marriageable Girl," contending that characters
such as these are "alive"—they are "unpredictable, and
they can develop."[3]

In many ways **"A Marriageable Girl"** (Hingley), the
last short story Chekhov wrote, stands in opposition to
such stories as **"Dr. Startsev," "Home,"** and **"In the
Cart."** Unlike Vera, who decides that marriage is the
only available option, or Marya, who desires the opportunity for a suitor, the protagonist Nadya escapes her
inauthentic life by a brave decision. When the story
opens, Nadya has a fiancé whom she will marry in a
few weeks, but she becomes depressed. Nadya attempts
to tell her mother about this depression, but her widowed mother does not understand. A friend of the family, Sasha, encourages Nadya to flee the engagement
and her home. He is one of those revolutionary students
in Chekhov who advocates radical change—Trofimov
in *The Cherry Orchard,* written immediately after **"A
Marriageable Girl,"** is another example. Sasha accuses
the whole family, including Nadya, of being "sordid
and immoral" in their idleness. Although Nadya agrees
with Sasha's criticism, she feels trapped in her situation
and unable to change it.

A critical point comes a few weeks before the marriage,
when her fiancé takes her to inspect their luxurious future house. Nadya hates it. She realizes she also hates
her fiancé's "sheer complacency," and "sheer stupid,
mindless, intolerable smugness" (IX, 214-15). Afterwards Nadya explains to her mother that she cannot
marry the man, and declares that their lives are "petty
and degrading" and that she despises herself and "this
idle, pointless existence" (IX, 217). In contrast to Vera
in **"Home,"** Nadya does not submit to the objective,
social reality of her circumstances, but begins a transformation of her life that affirms her subjective view of
the world. The next day she runs away to St. Petersburg
to go to school, "on her way to freedom." Ronald Hingley notes that in the story's own time, Nadya would
have been readily identified as a revolutionary figure
(IX, 10); she feels a "new life opening before her, with
its broad horizons" (IX, 223). In contrast to Vera in
"Home," Nadya does not settle for a life she knows
will eventually defeat her. The last of Chekhov's great
fiction protagonists, Nadya is a heroine in a most positive manner, a final tribute to Chekhov's ability to view
each story as a fresh effort in his search for artistic integrity.

If the character of Nadya represents a challenge to the
restrictions imposed by society, then Belikov, the protagonist of **"A Hard Case"** (Hingley), represents the

other extreme. Belikov demands that everyone rigidly conform to the restrictions and rules of the objective, social reality. Like the others in the informal trilogy, **"Concerning Love"** and **"Gooseberries,"** there is a story within a story. Burkin, a schoolteacher, relates the inner story of Belikov to Ivan, the veterinarian surgeon, in a village barn after a day of hunting. Belikov, who died a few months before, was a classics teacher who had taught at the local school for fifteen years. He had terrorized not only other schoolteachers and students, but the whole town with his strict adherence to the rules. Out of fear of Belikov's disapproval, the townspeople gave up their amateur theatricals, and the clergy would not eat meat or play cards in his presence. Instead of directly bullying the townspeople like Sergeant Prishibeyev, Belikov, also one of Chekhov's more famous characters, intimidates them with the authority of his position.

Chekhov's portrayal of Belikov's personal life gives the character credibility. Belikov was afraid of life: he feared "repercussions" in his job, feared his throat would be cut by his servant, feared burglars; and the crowded school itself "terrified him, revolted his whole being" (IX, 18). Belikov's undoing begins when a Ukrainian woman moves to town, and the townspeople decide the two of them should marry. When Belikov sees the Ukrainian woman riding a bicycle, he goes to her brother to protest what he feels is a lack of decorum. But the brother—a robust, new teacher—tosses Belikov out of his lodgings, and he falls down the stairs. Although he is unhurt, the Ukrainian woman and some other ladies laugh at his ludicrous expression. Greatly upset, Belikov returns home where he goes to bed for a month, until he dies. Burkin remembers that after the funeral everyone enjoyed an hour or two of "absolute freedom," but within a week, life was back to its "old rut. It was just as austere, wearisome, and pointless as before" (IX, 25).

Burkin closes his inner story with the comment that Belikov left behind a lot of other men in "shells" who will continue to be a force in the future. In contrast to Nadya from **"A Marriageable Girl,"** such men have a fixed response to life, and in their rigidity are living inauthentic lives, incapable of change or growth. Ivan believes everyone in the provincial town is living in a "shell," like Belikov, and expresses the desire to tell an "extremely edifying" story himself, but since Burkin is tired and soon falls asleep, Ivan is left pondering the story he wanted to tell. On one level, this ending is an effective closure to the story, for Burkin's story strikes a moral chord in Ivan that makes him want to relate his own tale. On another level, it sets the stage for the next story in the trilogy.

Ivan relates his "edifying" story, **"Gooseberries"** (Hingley), on another hunting trip. Again Chekhov uses his narrator persona to establish the frame setting for Ivan's story: it begins raining, so the two men seek shelter on the estate of Alyokhin, who later will narrate **"Concerning Love,"** the last story in the trilogy. Over tea, Ivan begins his tale of his brother Nicholas, who spent much of his life saving for a small estate like the one on which the brothers spent their childhood. The dramatic section of Ivan's inner story occurs a year before his present narration, when he first visited Nicholas' estate. Nicholas, like Dr. Startsev, had gained weight; in describing him, his dog, and his cook, Ivan employs imagery that recalls pigs, so that Nicholas himself seems "all set to grunt." Nicholas has undergone a great change, and behaves like "a real squire, a man of property." Ivan believes he has become blatantly arrogant, with a typical landowner's attitude toward his peasants; he believes education is not right for "the lower orders," and corporal punishment is "in certain cases useful and indispensible" (IX, 34).

The important change in the story, however, occurs in Ivan himself, which is appropriate since he is the point-of-view character. During the long years of saving, Nicholas dreamed of eating gooseberries from his estate, and his first action as owner was to order twenty bushes and plant them himself. A few hours after Ivan's arrival, when Nicholas picks his first gooseberries and, in silence and tears, eats them, Ivan realizes Nicholas is a happy man. But that realization plunges Ivan into a "despondency akin to despair." Later that night Ivan realizes what a crushing force the happy people of the world are, for among the "grotesque poverty everywhere, the overcrowding, degeneracy, drunkenness and hypocrisy" (IX, 35), there is the impudence and idleness of the strong. Ivan believes happy people have "no eyes or ears" for those who suffer, and the "silent happiness" of a community is a collective hypnosis that allows such suffering to continue simply as "mute statistics" (IX, 35-36). Because of this system, Ivan believes at the door of every contented man should be someone standing with a little hammer, someone to keep "dinning into his head" that unhappy people do exist, and that, happy though he may be, life "will round on him sooner or later" (IX, 36).

In presenting this idea, Ivan becomes a voice advocating a moral position that underlies much of Chekhov's work in the last decade of his life, from the character of the earlier Ivan in **"Ward Number Six"** in 1892 to the revolutionary Sasha in **"A Marriageable Girl"** in 1903. In **"Gooseberries,"** Ivan relates this realization has worked a change in him, a kind of moral conversion, so now he finds the peace and quiet of town life unbearable, and no spectacle more depressing than a happy family having tea around a table. Ivan's search for meaning and authenticity in life becomes the focus for the larger moral content of the story.

When the story returns to the frame setting, the dissatisfaction of the listeners with Ivan's story is portrayed with Chekhov's tongue-in-cheek tone as they wish for a different kind of story, one about elegant persons that does not bore them. With this comment, Chekhov makes a light, ironic statement about the stereotypical concept of the function of fiction. To add to the irony, the listeners watch a pretty young maid clearing the table of their teacups, and believe watching her is "better than any story" (IX, 37).

In commenting on this masterpiece, Thomas Gullason states that nothing is solved, but the story is like "a delayed fuse" that depends on "after-effects on the reader via the poetic technique of suggestion and implication."[4] In Chekhov's own comments on **"Thieves,"** he maintained he would allow "the jury" to decide the "guilt" of the characters and would avoid "sermonizing" (Yarmolinsky, 133), but in **"Gooseberries,"** the character of Ivan seems to occupy the role of the prosecuting attorney. The idea that Chekhov could use the character of Ivan in this manner, and yet avoid didacticism, is implied in Gullason's further comment that the story seems "as artless, as unplanned, as unmechanical as any story can be; it seems to be going nowhere, but it is going everywhere" (27). Chekhov achieves the effect of the master artist in creating the illusion that the story is artless, as episodic as life itself, while presenting a moral content as well-defined and as detailed as in any story he wrote.

That search for meaning in life is the subject of Chekhov's most complex and accomplished novella written in the first person: **"My Life—A Provincial's Story"** (Hingley). The narrating protagonist Misail Poloznev, one of Chekhov's most compelling characters, embodies that search for the authentic life with his honesty and his integrity. As the subtitle suggests, the story is a portrayal of provincial life, Chekhov's most extensive effort in prose in that direction, and the limiting nature of that life is explored in depth. One situation involves the tension that family relationships generate. The twenty-five-year old son of the town architect, Misail is considered a failure because he cannot retain a clerk's position, although it requires no "mental effort, talent, special ability or creative drive" (VIII, 118). Since he despises the work, he has been fired nine times. Chekhov's characters frequently turn to work in their search for an authentic life, but that work must be meaningful labor. After his last dismissal, Misail wishes to find such meaning through manual labor, but his typically middle-class father is ashamed that Misail would do such work, believing it is the "hallmark of slaves and barbarians" (VIII, 116). In the ensuing argument, the father beats Misail with an umbrella, causing a permanent break between them. The tension involves more than manual labor, for Misail believes his father is an incompetent architect because his imagination is "muddled, chaotic, stunted"—another example of the limiting nature of provincial life. Not only does Misail

rebel, but when his sister Cleopatra discovers her provincial, middle-class life to be inauthentic, she does also.

Misail finds manual labor as a house painter, working for a Dickens-like character named Radish. Chekhov's portrayal of the laboring men and their attitudes toward life, each other, and the townspeople illustrates a broad knowledge of life. Misail's ideas on the meaning of life are articulated in a dialogue with another of Chekhov's doctor figures, Dr. Blagovo, whom Misail believes to be the "best and most cultivated" man in town. Like the dialogues in **"In Exile"** and **"Ward Number Six,"** the philosophic positions of both characters are dramatized in lengthy conversations. Where Blagovo believes the "gray and commonplace" concerns of present life are not worth one's effort, Misail is committed to improving society. He is afraid "the art of enslavement" is gradually being perfected in the modern world, and believes although serfdom has been abolished, capitalism is spreading, so that "the majority still feeds, clothes and protects the minority, while remaining hungry, unclothed and unprotected itself" (VIII, 139). Misail also believes every man should do manual work, a belief similar to the artist's in **"An Artist's Story,"** published earlier in the same year of 1896. Like in **"An Artist's Story,"** Chekhov's artistic achievement in **"My Life"** lies not in articulating such ideas, but in creating emotionally complex characters capable of thinking deeply and passionately about the nature of man and society.

One aspect of the search for an authentic life in **"My Life"** involves love. Masha Dolzhikov, the daughter of a wealthy railway builder, falls in love with and marries Misail. Masha, who in contrast to the other provincials has lived in St. Petersburg, is an idealist who shares Misail's belief that rich and educated people should work like everyone else. She and Misail occupy one of her father's estates, where she attempts to live a meaningful life by farming. Misail knows Masha is not committed to a laboring life, for she has other choices with her wealth, but against his better judgment, he falls unequivocally in love with her. Chekhov's portrayal of the suffering this love causes Misail is one of the great accomplishments of the novella. The love between Misail and Masha is complemented by the love between Cleopatra and Dr. Blagovo, who has left his estranged wife and children in St. Petersburg. Cleopatra's love for the doctor incites her to seek an authentic life. In typical Chekhovian fashion, neither of these love relationships endure.

The relationship between Misail and Masha becomes dependent on her success with the estate. In contrast to Lydia in **"An Artist's Story,"** Masha becomes disillusioned in attempting to build a school for the peasants. Chekhov's portrayal of her efforts and the peasants' response illustrate the immense difficulty of effecting change in society; one of Chekhov's many achievements in this novella is presenting that complex relationship between landowner and peasant. The peasant is presented sympathetically through the attitudes of Misail, for through plowing, harrowing, and sowing, he develops some sense of the "barbarous, brute force" that both confronts the peasant and is a part of him. Misail, drawn to the peasants, concludes they are a "highly strung, irritable people" who have had a raw deal and whose imaginations have been "crushed" (VIII, 170). For all the limitations of the peasants, Misail sees something vital and significant in them, something that is "lacking in Masha and the doctor for instance" (VIII, 170). That element is the belief in the truth, and the power of the truth to save not only the peasant himself, but all mankind. Misail believes the peasant "loves justice more than anything else in the world" (VIII, 170), a belief that connects Misail directly to Leo Tolstoy. As Ronald Hingley notes, no contemporary Russian reader would have missed the connection. (VIII, 5).

As the love relationship between Misail and Masha dissolves, she leaves for St. Petersburg, and then, before leaving for America, she requests a divorce. The other love relationship ends as Cleopatra dies shortly after giving birth to the doctor's child out of wedlock. In their last days, the suffering that Cleopatra and Misail endure in their poverty recalls the novels of Charles Dickens and Fyodor Dostoevsky. Like characters in those novels tried by circumstances, Misail experiences a mental breakdown from the emotional strain, and wanders the streets out of his mind.

After his recovery, in the final, expository chapter, Misail continues to work as a painter in town as he cares for his sister's child, like the narrator in **"An Anonymous Story."** In Misail's final comments, he declares the townspeople have been "reading and hearing about truth, mercy and freedom for generations" but "their entire progress from cradle to grave is one long lie"; they torment each other, "fearing and hating freedom as if it were their worst enemy" (VIII, 181). Chekhov thus links the relationship between the lie and freedom in this masterpiece. In commenting on **"My Life,"** D. S. Mirsky states only one other story by Chekhov, entitled **"In the Hollow,"** can rival it in terms of "poetical grasp" and significance (363).

The search for meaning in life in the provinces is also the subject of **"On Official Business"** (Hingley). The protagonist is a young coroner Lyzhin, who accompanies a doctor to a small village to investigate a suicide, the "official business" of the title. Once again, the limitations of provincial life are a theme. Because of a blizzard, Lyzhin must remain with the body for a number of hours in a hut, where he visits, with the local constable, an old peasant who tells him about the dead man. After the peasant retires to another room, Lyzhin

considers his life in this provincial outpost, contrasting it with the excitement of Moscow where he lived as a student, and decides "here you want nothing, you easily come to terms with your own insignificance, and you expect only one thing in life: just let it hurry up and go away" (IX, 117). If he could escape to Moscow in five or ten years, it still would not be too late to have a "whole life" ahead of him. To this point in the action, the events seem typical of many of Chekhov's stories about the limitations of provincial life, but events take a different direction when the doctor returns and invites Lyzhin to a local estate.

Lyzhin contrasts the gay happenings on the estate with the dismal peasant hut, feeling the difference between them is "magical." That night he dreams of the suicide and the old peasant marching together through the freezing cold and the deep snow, singing, "We know no peace, no joy. We bear all the burdens of this life, our own and yours" (IX, 122). When Lyzhin wakes, he realizes "some link—invisible, but significant and essential" (IX, 122) exists not only between the suicide and the old peasant, but between all men. Such a thought recalls **"The Student,"** another story deceptively simple in its events, but in **"On Official Business,"** the moral context of the idea is based in a secular humanism, without a Christian holiday as backdrop for the vision. Even in this remote backwater, Lyzhin realizes nothing is arbitrary, for "everything is imbued with a single common idea, everything has one spirit, one purpose" (IX, 122). This mystical thought occurs to an ordinary coroner, an undistinguished protagonist, and it suggests even ordinary man is capable of profound experiences. Lyzhin realizes reasoning is not enough to furnish these insights, but the gift of penetrating "life's essence" is required, and that gift is available to him who "sees and understands his own life as part of the common whole" (IX, 122). This vision of the individual's relationship to mankind serves as Chekhov's own moral position. The idea that the sense of man's responsibility to his fellow man could occur to such an ordinary man in such a remote backwater does not refute the limitations of provincial life, but illustrates the possibility that even here, man can exercise his human responsibility.

Chekhov's vision of mankind has a sociological dimension in **"A Case History"** (Hingley) written shortly before **"On Official Business."** The events are narrated through the consciousness of Dr. Korolyov, an assistant to a professor of medicine in Moscow, one of Chekhov's scientist doctors with a well-developed moral vision of the relationship between the individual and society. Society is represented by the setting of a factory town, similar to that in **"A Woman's Kingdom,"** written four years previously; the stories share other similarities as well, one being the burden of social responsibility felt by the future heiress.

When Korolyov is summoned from Moscow to treat the owner's daughter, he ascertains her primary problem is not physiological but "nerves." Her symptoms are an indication of her inauthentic life, for like Anne in **"A Woman's Kingdom,"** this young woman will inherit the vast mill with all its responsibility and she is "worried and scared" without understanding the reason. Her problem is she does not believe she has "the right" to be a mill owner and rich heiress, and Korolyov tells her that her insomnia is a good sign because it shows concern about right and wrong. Korolyov has a moral vision of the age: the previous generation was not bothered by such moral questions, and future generations will have solved them. In his belief in the future—"Life will be good in fifty years' time" (IX,77)—he resembles other optimistic doctors in Chekhov's work.

Korolyov's most profound thoughts on the nature of man and society develop as he strolls around the mill that evening. He had never visited a factory before, and previously had compared improvements in the workers' lives to the treatment of incurable diseases. The situation is so hopeless for the worker and/or the patient that he can only be made as comfortable as possible and never really healthy or cured. But now Korolyov realizes not only the workers, but the supervisors and the "bosses" are all involved in a labor in which the "principal, the main beneficiary, is the devil" (IX, 75).

Korolyov actually does not believe in the devil, but the image comes to mind because of the appearance of the mill fires at night. He imagines in the chaos of everyday life, some malevolent, mysterious force has forged the relationship between weak and strong so that both are "equal victims." Like the mutually harmful relationship between master and slave, the strong as well as the weak are victims of the "primitive mindless force" (IX, 75) that rules mankind.

With this vision, Korolyov functions as a metaphor for a spiritual doctor, "accustomed to forming accurate diagnoses of incurable chronic ailments deriving from some unknown ultimate cause" (IX, 74), with society as the sick patient, suffering from the malevolent, mysterious force that creates the illness in man's relationship to his fellow man. On one level, **"On Official Business"** complements this earlier story, for the coroner's vision of the common bond among men with its "one spirit, one purpose" becomes an answer, a cure, to the metaphoric illness that Korolyov diagnoses.

STORIES OF THE PEASANT

During this last period Chekhov wrote two masterpieces with peasant village life as his primary subject, **"Peasants"** and **"In the Hollow."** After appearing in 1897 in a literary journal, **"Peasants"** was printed as a separate volume with **"My Life"** and became very popular, with seven reprints in the following few years. Where the narrator in **"My Life"** is from the middle class and views the peasant in an objective, but sympathetic manner, in **"Peasants"** Chekhov mainly presents the peasants' experiences directly to the reader. The second masterpiece, **"In the Hollow,"** resembles **"Peasants"** in that the characters and events also are presented directly through Chekhov's narrator. **"The New Villa"** (Hingley) is an important, chronologically intermediate story that gives the landowner and the peasant equal weight. The landowners in this story are a railway engineer and his compassionate wife who have recently moved to the area and built a new villa. They attempt to forge a relationship of integrity with the peasants in a neighboring village, but some of the peasants constantly take advantage of the engineer. In disgust, the engineer leaves the villa with his family and sells the estate.

The events provide insight into the difficulties of communication between both individuals and social groups. The goodwill efforts of two sets of characters—the engineer and his family, and a peasant blacksmith and his family—are defeated by the attitudes and actions of other hostile peasants. A new owner of the villa behaves much worse toward the peasants than the original compassionate owners, but the peasants get along with him much better. In one scene, the peasants pass the villa and wonder why they get along so well with the new owner, but knowing no answer, they "trudge on silently, heads bowed" (IX, 107). This image, when well-meaning people are defeated by some powerful force that operates against the betterment of human relations, is a powerful comment on the mysteriousness of human affairs.

If the portrait of peasant conditions that emerges from **"The New Villa"** is not encouraging, then the portrait in **"Peasants"** (Hingley) is a downright bleak naturalistic picture of unrelenting poverty that grinds down the human spirit. The portrayal is so unrelenting that Leo Tolstoy is reported to have termed it "a sin against the common people,"[5] but in Russia during Chekhov's own lifetime, **"Peasants"** was the most famous of all his stories. Ronald Hingley believes the story clearly is "a great work of art," and "a work of genius" (VIII, 3).

Brutal violence and indignities characterize life in a small peasant village of some forty huts. The narrative is a succession of hardship scenes with only an occasional experience to relieve the bleakness. A terminally ill waiter, Nicholas, returns from Moscow with his wife Olga and their ten-year-old daughter to live with his parents and his brother's families, all in one hut. When they arrive, Nicholas "actually took fright" as he sees how dark, cramped and dirty the hut is, recognizing the "real poverty and no mistake" (VIII, 196).

Later that first day, Nicholas and Olga have the opportunity to enjoy the beauty in the natural surroundings, but then Nicholas' drunk brother Kiryak comes to the hut and punches his wife Marya in the face. Pleased at the fear he causes, Kiryak drags Marya out of the hut "bellowing like a wild animal to make himself more frightening still" (VIII, 198). As usual in cases of domestic violence, Kiryak's beatings increase in intensity, and later are so severe that Marya has to be doused with water to bring her back to consciousness. Another instance of violence occurs as Kiryak himself is taken off to be flogged by the authorities.

The characters experience other disheartening indignities. Fyokla, another sister-in-law whose husband is away in the army, also lives in the hut with her children. One night she is stripped naked by the neighboring estate's servants, with many of whom she has been having sexual relations, and is left to wander home alone. When she returns, she weeps for her debasement. Another moving scene occurs when Nicholas' mother, Gran, who works hard to provide for the family, verbally abuses Nicholas. The samovar, their pot for heating tea water and symbol of the household, has been taken to pay taxes. Although she loves Nicholas, she feels so degraded and insulted when this happens she unfairly blames his family's presence for the misfortune. Since the members of the family have no one to turn to for help, they are completely vulnerable to these sufferings and hardships.

Although the events of the novella are narrated primarily through Chekhov's persona, certain passages are presented through the sensibility of Nicholas' wife Olga. As a newcomer, she notices behavior and detail that would not consciously register with the other characters. After a few months, Olga realizes life in the village is such a struggle that little time or effort is allowed for people to behave with anything but "mutual disrespect, fear and suspicion." But for all the hardship, Olga learns these people have a sense of community. When Kiryak is taken off to be flogged, Olga remembers "how pitiful and crushed the old people had looked" (VIII, 221).

During the middle of winter, Nicholas dies, and that spring Olga decides to return to Moscow, to secure a position as housemaid. As the novella closes, she and her daughter are walking to Moscow, begging for alms. Chekhov employs his objective technique in this scene so that the effect paradoxically provides the reader with a sense of intimacy with these destitute characters.

The sociological information contained in "Peasants" created a political uproar among parts of society, generating the kind of public response that recalled the appearance of a new novel by Ivan Turgenev or Fyodor Dostoevksy in previous times (Simmons, 393). The artistic value of the novella, however, derives from the validity of the characters and from the experience of village life that Chekhov depicts. Chekhov's portrayal of Fyokla's sensibility and motivation is superb, and there are a number of powerful, lyrical descriptions. One is a fire scene when one of the village huts burns; another is the peasants' response to the visit of a traveling religious procession and another is the simple experience of attempting to sleep in the crowded hut. Since there is no sharp dramatic conflict, the narrative becomes a succession of mosaics that remains etched in the reader's mind.

Since the characters of "In the Hollow" (Hingley) are engaged in a dramatic conflict, the form is more traditional. In contrast to the beautiful natural surroundings in "Peasants," the setting for this village is, as the title suggests, in the bottom of a ravine. Chekhov's environmental concerns are evident here where the village water is polluted by a tannery factory and the air always smells of factory waste, as if it were "clogged by a dense miasma of sin" (IX, 155). Unlike "Peasants," which focuses on a poor family, the subject for "In the Hollow" is the members of the family that operate the village store, the Tsybukins, the wealthiest family in the village. The head of the family is a clever old man who has built up his business by constantly cheating his peasant customers. In addition to illegal vodka, Tsybukin sells putrid salt beef before feast days, "stuff with so vile a stench you could hardly go near the barrel" (IX, 155). But Tsybukin does love his family, especially his eldest son Anisim, now a police detective in Moscow, and his daughter-in-law Aksinya, a "beautiful, well-built" peasant married to his younger son, a mentally impaired deaf man. The basic family situation in this novella recalls "Peasant Women," and in many ways "In the Hollow" develops from where the earlier story ends: the tensions in the family relationships, unresolved in "Peasant Women," are worked dramatically through in "In the Hollow" until the dissatisfied daughter-in-law controls the family.

Aksinya is one of Chekhov's most sinister characters, an ambitious woman with an unusual head for business. She operates the store as effectively and dishonestly as her father-in-law. Chekhov often uses the image of the snake in describing her; like a viper, she is physically dangerous, eventually killing her sister-in-law's baby in a fit of rage. In contrast to her dishonesty is the goodness of Barbara, Tsybukin's second wife; cheerful and lighthearted, she freely gives alms to beggars and various pilgrims who stop at the store. Another sister-in-law, Lipa, is a poor, self-effacing, but physically attractive peasant girl whom the eldest son Anisim marries on a return trip to the village. While the guests at this major event are feasting at table, a crowd of poor peasants gathers in the store yard. Occasionally when the band is not playing, one village woman's cry carries clearly to the table: "Rotten swine, grinding the faces of the poor. May you rot in hell!" (IX, 163). This cry of protest recalls Misail's comment in **"My Life"** on the desire of the peasant for justice. By the end of the novella, Lipa emerges as a symbol of the peasant. Both a victim and an endurer of wrongdoing, she joins that mosaic of suffering depicted in **"Peasants."**

The novella's key dramatic event occurs several months after Anisim is arrested for counterfeiting money. Ironically, Anisim's dishonest behavior was learned from his father. When Tsybukin returns from the sentencing of his son to Siberia, he wills some land to his grandson, the baby of Lipa and Anisim, but Aksinya is operating a brick factory on this land, and flies into a rage. In one of the most memorable scenes in Chekhov's work, she scalds the baby with boiling wash water. Once again, Chekhov uses irony: the action taken to help the baby instead destroys it. As Lipa attempts to come to terms with her grief, she wanders the countryside with the dead baby in her arms and questions the meaning of suffering in her simple, eloquent language.

In the final section, which occurs three years later, Lipa's character is once again juxtaposed against the members of the family. Aksinya has become the head of the house since Tsybukin is becoming feeble-minded, in part from grief. Aksinya is now a force in the community because of her brick factory; her power attracts the ardor of a local landowner. As Lipa passes through the village with a group of peasants who work in Aksinya's brickyard, she gives Tsybukin something to eat. This act, symbolic of her human compassion, is juxtaposed against the thriving dishonesty of the very family that threw her out, and is Chekhov's final use of irony in the novella. In commenting on the complexity and power of **"In the Hollow,"** V. S. Pritchett pairs it with **"The Bishop"** as one of Chekhov's two "surpassing masterpieces" (178).

Stories of Religion

During this period Chekhov wrote two stories about characters committed to a religious life, stories in many ways diametrically opposed and indicative of Chekhov's great range as a writer. The characters in **"Murder"** (Hingley), Chekhov's most sensational story, are members of a fundamentalist religion who, in a frenzy of rage generated by frustration, beat a member of their household to death. The narrative begins in the consciousness of the victim, Matthew Terekhov, a laborer whose primary pleasures are attending church and singing in the choir. The element that makes his character so appropriate for the events that befall him is Matthew himself is a former religious fanatic, reared in a fundamentalist family like his cousin Jacob. After Matthew left home as a youth, he became increasingly devoted until he crossed over into fanaticism, doing penance

such as going barefoot in the snow, wearing irons, and dragging around heavy stones. He established his own church where members went into "crazy fits" of shouting and dancing until they dropped. In one such service, Matthew committed fornication and when he requested forgiveness from his landlord, the man admonished Matthew to be an "ordinary man," for "overdoing things is devil's work" (VIII, 52). Matthew eventually responded to that guidance, and now does everything— "eat, drink *and* worship"—like everyone else.

Because of this experience, Matthew criticizes his cousin Jacob's religious practices. Jacob believes the churches are observing the rites incorrectly, and spends his time in special fasts and prayer sessions. In describing Jacob, Chekhov employs one key detail that resembles his later description of Belikov in **"A Hard Case"**: both men wear galoshes all the time. Like Belikov, Jacob desperately clings to the "rules" because of his fear of life. Jacob's devotion is not to receive benefits from God, but for "form's sake"—upholding decorum, the same motivation of Belikov. During Easter week, when Jacob feels his faith leaving him and cannot worship as before, the stage is set for confrontation. Matthew implores Jacob to reform and accuses him of evil because he maintains a tavern at the inn where they live.

The murder is related with clever use of detail, revealing that Chekhov could be a superb writer of physical action, a fact often overlooked because so many of his stories are concerned with psychological action. One reason the scene is so effective is the unpremeditated manner in which the event unfolds. Like so much domestic violence, an argument simply gets out of hand. Jacob's sister engages Matthew in an argument about the use of oil on his food, forbidden during Lent, and Jacob joins the argument. Ironically, this day of religious observance becomes the scene for a deadly disagreement. Growing increasingly angry, Jacob grabs Matthew to drag him from the table, and in the confusion, the sister believes Matthew is attacking Jacob; she slams the bottle of oil down on Matthew's head, rendering him semiconscious. Jacob, who is "very worked up," props Matthew up and, pointing to the flat iron beside the table, directs his sister to hit him again. In their fury, they beat Matthew to death, not realizing what is happening until it is too late.

A year later, after the trial, Jacob is disgusted at his former religion—"it seemed irrational and primitive" (VIII, 67). But in a situation that recalls the events in "God Sees the Truth, But Waits" (1872) by Leo Tolstoy, Jacob, while in prison, eventually turns to God and the "true faith" once again. Like many of Chekhov's characters, Jacob now wants "to live." His heart aches with longing for his home, and he wants to return to tell people about his new faith.[6] Ivan Bunin, a short story writer especially sensitive to technique, thought this story the best of Chekhov's later work because the "objective narrator lets the shocking conduct make a great impact upon the reader" (Meister, 117).

Another masterpiece involving a character's commitment to religion is **"The Bishop"** (Hingley). Part of the power of the narrative derives from the subtle portrayal of an intelligent man's perceptions, his mind and emotions. In contrast to the characters in **"Murder,"** the bishop is a reasonable and learned man with a good grasp of humankind who becomes annoyed during service by "the occasional shrieks of some religious maniac in the gallery" (IX, 191). Born into relative poverty, the bishop worked his way up to a position of power and influence and is now a distinguished figure, one of Chekhov's most elevated characters. The events are structured around his final struggle and test, typhoid fever. Appropriately enough, given the spiritual nature of the protagonist, the time is Easter week: the passions of the traditional religious ceremony are an effective backdrop for the protagonist's own emotional experiences. This story and **"Easter Eve"** are the crowning achievements of the Easter stories Chekhov had written since early in his career.

The focus is the bishop's evaluation of his life, a process initiated by the visit of his mother when she appears unexpectedly on the eve of Palm Sunday during his service. That evening his mind is filled with delight in recalling his poor native village and happy childhood, memories that his mother's appearance has triggered. The sheer delight with which the details are remembered—"the wheels creaking, sheep bleating, church bells pealing on bright summer mornings" (IX, 193)—recalls the thoughts of the character Gusev in his feverish state. The bishop is unknowingly developing typhoid fever, and like **"Gusev"** (1890), where the mind of the ill character is filled with memories before he eventually dies, the bishop's mind increasingly alters with his feverish state. The impressionistic prose is a development from those earlier depictions of altered states of consciousness in **"Typhus"** and **"Sleepy."**

During the next few days, as the bishop performs his administrative duties, he reflects on the "pettiness and pointlessness" of his tasks. The church ladies seem "tiresomely stupid," the peasants rough, the theological students ill-educated, and the paperwork overwhelming. The bishop is experiencing that particularly modern day Chekhovian test: instead of fire or sword, he must fight the trifles of everyday life, the "sheer weight" of which is dragging him down.

During the week, the bishop's illness progresses until he experiences the desire to escape and become a simple priest or ordinary monk, for his position seems to "crush" him. After he suffers an intestinal hemorrhage,

he is diagnosed with typhoid fever, and in his weakness, he feels his past has escaped from him "to some infinitely remote place beyond all chance of repetition or continuation" (IX, 203). A sense of past provides a sense of identity, and so as the bishop desires, his identity is now dissolving. At this moment, his mother kisses him like a "dearly beloved child," and with her soothing presence, he feels like an "ordinary simple man walking quickly and cheerfully through a field," as "free as a bird" so he can go where he likes (IX, 203-204). Released at last from his worldly responsibilities, the bishop dies, symbolically just before dawn on Holy Saturday. The lyrical description of that joyful Easter Sunday captures the traditional rising of the spirit in Christian ritual as the continuity of the life process is thus assured. Chekhov relates in the closing paragraph no one remembered the bishop anymore except his mother, who lives in a remote province. His desire to become "ordinary" is fulfilled.

The subject of this masterpiece seems particularly appropriate for Chekhov at this stage in his life, when he himself was dying and confined to Yalta. That he should convert such personal materials into this work of art when writing itself was becoming an increasingly physically demanding task marks his great dedication as an artist.

Notes

1. Quoted in the Ecco Press fall catalog for 1990, 13.

2. *Times Literary Supplement,* 9 November 1916, 537a, quoted in Charles W. Meister, *Chekhov Criticism: 1880 Through 1986* (Jefferson, North Carolina: McFarland, 1988), 143; hereafter cited in text.

3. "Chekhov's Cast of Characters," in *A Chekhov Companion,* ed. Toby W. Clyman (Westport, Conn.: Greenwood Press, 1985), 83.

4. "The Short Story," *Short Story Theories,* ed. Charles May (Athens, Ohio: Ohio University Press, 1976), 27. Hereafter references will be cited with "Gullason" and page number.

5. Quoted in Meister, 123. Gleb Struve notes this opinion is not, however, documented in Tolstoy's own writing. *Chekhov: Seven Short Novels,* trans. Barbara Makanowitzky; introduction and prefaces by Gleb Struve (New York: Norton, 1971), 365-6. Hingley uses the quote in his introduction (VIII, 5), with the source from N. I. Gitovich, *Letopis zhizni i tvorchestva A. P. Chekhov* [Chronicle of the Life and Literary Activity of A. P. Chekhov] (Moscow, 1955), 821. In 1962, Ernest Simmons termed this Gitovich book "the most indispensible reference work for all aspects of Chekhov's life and writings" (642), but unfortunately, the book remains untranslated.

6. The closing events of "Murder" contain Chekhov's most realized portrait of Sakhalin Island in fiction. Some of Chekhov's prose non-fiction narratives such as "Yegor's Story," in *The Island: A Journey to Sakhalin,* trans. Luba and Michael Terpak; introduction by Robert Payne (New York: Washington Square Press, 1967), suggest the origins for characters such as Anisim from "In the Hollow," Yergunov in "Thieves" and Jacob Terekhov in "Murder." In his introduction to this translation, Robert Payne terms *The Island* "a strange work, brilliant and wayward, scrupulously honest and unpretentious, lit by a flame of quiet indignation and furious sorrow" (xxxvi).

Selected Bibliography

Primary Works

Translations of Short Fiction

Note: I have listed the translations cited in this book. For a more complete list of translations, with 36 entries by 26 translators noted in chronological order, see Constance Garnett's *Tales of Chekhov,* vol. 13, 339-341.

Chertok, I. C., and Jean Gardner, trans. *Late-Blooming Flowers and Other Stories.* New York: Carroll and Graf, 1964.

Dunnigan, Ann, trans. *Selected Stories.* New York: New American Library, 1960.

FitzLyon, April, and Kyril Zinovieff, trans. *The Woman in the Case and Other Stories.* London: Spearman and Calder, 1953.

Garnett, Constance, trans. *The Tales of Chekhov.* 13 vols. New York: Macmillan, 1917-23; rpt. New York: Ecco Press, 1984-87. Vol. 13 includes a title index.

Hinchcliffe, Arnold, trans. *The Sinner from Toledo and Other Stories.* Rutherford, New Jersey: Fairleigh Dickinson University Press, 1972.

Hingley, Ronald, trans. and ed. *The Oxford Chekhov.* Vol. 4-9. London: Oxford University Press, 1965-1980.

Jones. *St. Peter's Day and Other Tales.* Translated by Frances H. Jones. New York: Capricorn Books (Copyright: G. P. Putnam's Sons), 1959.

Miles. *Chekhov: The Early Stories, 1883-1888.* Translated by Patrick Miles and Harvey Pitcher. New York: Macmillan Publishing Co., 1982.

Miller. *Anton Chekhov: Collected Works in Five Volumes: Volume One: Stories 1880-1885.* Translated by Alex Miller and Ivy Litvinov (other translators listed at the end of some stories). Edited by Raissa Bobrova. Moscow: Raduga Publishers, 1967.

Payne. *The Image of Chekhov: Forty Stories by Anton Chekhov in the Order in Which They Were Written.* Translated by Robert Payne. New York: Vintage, 1966. Reprinted by arrangement with Alfred A. Knopf; copyright 1963 by Alfred A. Knopf.

Smith. *The Thief and Other Tales.* Translated by Ursula Smith. New York: The Vantage Press, 1964.

Yarmolinsky 1947. *The Portable Chekhov.* (Stories used in this text translated by Yarmolinsky.) Edited by Avrahm Yarmolinsky. New York: The Viking Press, 1947. (Note: reference to Chekhov's letters are not from this source, but from *Letters of Anton Chekhov,* ed. Avrahm Yarmolinsky. See Bibliography, "Letters" below.)

Yarmolinsky 1954. *The Unknown Chekhov: Stories and Other Writings hitherto Untranslated.* Translated with an Introduction by Avrahm Yarmolinsky. New York: The Noonday Press, 1954. (Note: references to Chekhov's letters are not from this source, but from *Letters of Anton Chekhov,* ed. Avrahm Yarmolinsky. See Bibliography, "Letters" below.)

Collected Works in Russian

Belchikov, N. F., et al, eds. *Polnoye sobraniye sochineny i pisem v tridsati tomakh.* 30 vols. Moscow, 1974-83.

Balukhaty, S. D., et al, eds. *Polnoye sobraniye sochineny i pisem v dvenadtsati tomakh.* 20 vols. Moscow, 1944-51.

Letters

Anton Chekhov's Life and Thought: Selected Letters and Commentary. Translated by Michael Heim with Simon Karlinsky; selection, commentary and introduction by Simon Karlinsky. Originally published as *Letters of Anton Chekhov.* New York: Harper and Row, 1973. Rpt. Berkeley: University of California Press, 1975.

Letters of Anton Chekhov. Selected and edited by Avrahm Yarmolinsky. New York: Viking Press, 1973.

Letters of Anton Chekhov to His Family and Friends with Biographical Sketch. Trans. Constance Garnett. New York: Macmillan, 1920.

Letters on the Short Story, the Drama, and Other Literary Topics. Selected and ed. Louis S. Friedland, with a Preface by Ernest Simmons. New York: Minto Beach, 1924; rpt. New York: Benjamin Blom, 1964.

The Life and Letters of Anton Tchekhov. Trans. and ed. S. S. Koteliansky and Philip Tomlinson. Cassell & Co. Ltd., London, 1925; rpt: New York: Benjamin Blom, 1965.

The Selected Letters of Anton Chekhov. Translated by Sidonie K. Lederer; edited with an Introduction by Lillian Hellman. New York: Farrar, Straus and Giroux, Inc., 1984.

Plays

The Oxford Chekhov. Vol. 1-3. Edited and translated by Ronald Hingley. London: Oxford University Press, 1964-1967. Vol. 1: *Short Plays.* Vol. 2: *Uncle Vanya, Three Sisters, The Cherry Orchard,* and *The Wood-Demon.* Vol. 3: *Platonov, Ivanov,* and *The Seagull.*

NONFICTION

The Island: A Journey to Sakhalin. Translated by Luba and Michael Terpak. Introduction by Robert Payne. New York: Washington Square Press, 1967.

SECONDARY WORKS

Buford, Walter H. *Chekhov and His Russia: A Sociological Study.* 2d. ed., London: Routledge and Kegan Paul, 1948; rpt. Hamden, Conn.: Archon Books, 1971.

Chudakov, A. P. *Chekhov's Poetics.* Translated by Edwina Cruise and Donald Dragt. Ann Arbor: Ardis, 1983.

Clyman, Toby W., ed. *A Chekhov Companion.* Westport, Conn.: Greenwood Press, 1985.

Eekman, Thomas, ed. *Anton Cechov 1860-1960: Some Essays.* Leiden: Brill, 1960.

Eekman, Thomas, ed. *Critical Essays on Anton Chekhov.* Boston: G. K. Hall, 1989.

Halunciski, Leo and David Savignac, trans. and eds. *Anton Chekhov as a Master of Story-Writing: Essays in Modern Soviet Literary Criticism.* The Hague: Mouton, 1976.

Hahn, Beverly. *Chekhov: A Study of the Major Stories and Plays.* Cambridge: Cambridge University Press, 1977.

Hingley, Ronald. *A New Life of Anton Chekhov.* New York: Knopf, 1976.

Jackson, Robert Louis, ed. *Chekhov: A Collection of Critical Essays.* Englewood Cliffs, New Jersey: Prentice-Hall, 1967.

Kirk, Irina. *Anton Chekhov.* Boston: Twayne, 1981.

Kramer, Karl. *The Chameleon and the Dream: The Image of Reality in Cexov's Stories.* The Hague: Mouton, 1970.

Meister, Charles W. *Chekhov Criticism: 1880 Through 1986.* Jefferson, North Carolina: McFarland and Company, Inc., 1988.

McConkey, James, ed. *Chekhov and Our Age.* Ithaca, New York: Cornell University, n.d.

Rayfield, Donald. *Chekhov: The Evolution of His Art.* New York: Barnes and Noble, 1975.

Simmons, Ernest J. *Chekhov: A Biography.* Boston: Little Brown, 1962.

Stowell, H. Peter. *Literary Impressionism, James and Chekhov.* Athens, Ga.: University of Georgia Press, 1980.

Tulloch, John. *Chekhov: A Structuralist Study.* New York: Harper & Row, 1980.

Welleck, Rene and Nonna D. Welleck, eds. *Chekhov: New Perspectives.* Englewood Cliffs, New Jersey: Prentice-Hall, 1984.

Williames, Lee J. *Anton Chekhov: The Iconoclast.* Scranton, Pa.: University of Scranton Press, 1989.

Winner, Thomas. *Chekhov and His Prose.* New York: Holt, Rhinehart and Winston, 1966.

Yermilov, Vladimir. *Anton Pavlovich Chekhov, 1860-1904.* Trans. Ivy Litvinov. Moscow: Foreign Language Publishing House, n.d.[1956]. (Russian original: Moscow, 1953.)

BIBLIOGRAPHIES

"Bibliographical Index to the Complete Works of Anton Chekhov." In David Magarshack, *Chekhov: A Life.* New York: Grove Press, 1953; rpt. Westport, Conn.: Greenwood Press, 1970. 393-423.

"Chekhov's Stories: A Chronology." *Tales of Chekhov,* vol. 13, 345-350.

Leighton, Lauren. "Chekhov's Works in English: Selective Collections and Editions." In *A Chekhov Companion,* edited by Toby W. Clyman. 306-309.

Lantz, Kennth. *Anton Chekhov: A Reference Guide to Literature.* Boston: Mass.: G. K. Hall, 1985.

Heifitz, Anna. *Chekhov in English: A List of Works By and About Him.* Ed. with a foreword by Avrahm Yarmolinsky. New York: New York Public Library, 1948.

Yachnin, Rissa. *Chekhov in English: A Selective List of Works By and About Him 1949-1960.* New York: New York Public Library, 1960.

Michael Finke (essay date January 1994)

SOURCE: Finke, Michael. "The Hero's Descent to the Underworld in Chekhov." *Russian Review* 53, no. 1 (January 1994): 67-80.

[*In the following essay, Finke analyzes Chekhov's use of the archetypal motif of the descent, known as katabasis, throughout his writings, particularly his short fiction.*]

The distant twang occurring twice in *The Cherry Orchard* is one of the most overtly symbolic moments in Anton Chekhov's oeuvre: here the surface of an artistic structure begs to be understood through an appeal to depth. Lopakhin's explanation of the uncanny sound's source—that a cable has snapped in a nearby mine shaft—evokes a frightening image of plutonic depths, an underworld of wealth-producing mines. In the most literal sense, Lopakhin's mention of mines adds an unseen subterranean dimension to the play's setting; and this opens up the space necessary for a descent into the earth, a descent into hell. Although a number of scholars have drawn attention to imagery of the underworld in individual works, it has somehow escaped notice that Chekhov made repeated use of the archetypal motif of the hero's descent—katabasis—throughout his writing career. This article will lay the groundwork for the study of this phenomenon.

The topic, like most descents to hell, is fraught with danger. The very power and pervasiveness of the katabatic masterplot threatens to impoverish the treatment of its appearance in Chekhov, for to register the formal presence of descent motifs and subtexts in stories, letters, and plays is unsatisfactory as a research goal: what one wants is a conceptualization of the descent motif's general significance in Chekhov. The insights of archetypal critics and mythologists do offer attractive resolutions to this problem of semantics; but in demonstrating that an archetypal pattern with a universal and timeless deep symbolic meaning instantiates itself in Chekhov and his literary works, what is really learned about *Chekhov*? After all, he lived and wrote in the context of a personal and cultural history. And there is yet another risk: the equation of difficult circumstances and personal crisis with "being in hell," a "hellish life," is more often than not far from profound, indeed, a cliché meaning little more than "highly unpleasant."

First I will establish a representative set of texts in which the descent motif is both rather manifest and central. Only works where several features of the masterplot are present will be considered here; moreover, the journey to hell must serve—though not necessarily overtly—as an overarching structural feature of the work where it appears. This should suffice to provide a sense of the scope of the phenomenon. I will then take up the derivations of these hellish visions, their complicity with certain other remarkable features of Chekhov's poetics, and their potential for revealing some fixation or node of concerns in their author's psyche.

A number of descent models from disparate arenas of discourse were available to Chekhov, and Chekhov was catholic in his borrowings. His descents echo those of Russian folklore, the myths of the Ancients, canonical and apocryphal Orthodox Christianity, and contemporary popular culture.[1] The following assumes the reader is familiar with a variety of geographies of hell, the characters typically populating them, and the typical plot functions or purposes for the hero's descent.[2]

The most striking katabatic journey in both Chekhov's life and his writings is surely his epic project of visiting the prison colony of Sakhalin. "I was in hell, represented by Sakhalin, and in heaven, that is, on the island of Ceylon," Chekhov wrote to the author I. L. Leont'ev on returning from the east (10 December 1890).[3] Here

is indeed a case where the analogy with hell is expected, even a cliché; but there was precedent for Chekhov's more profound usage in Dostoevsky's treatment of the prison camp in *Notes from the House of the Dead* (1860), where descent is associated with rebirth on a higher plane of being. And Chekhov does follow Dostoevsky: in *Sakhalin Island,* as in the travel sketches Chekhov wrote en route and in his letters, the penal-colony-as-hell is more than an apt metaphor, more than a means of charging social critique with effective imagery. Chekhov conceived of this journey *from the start* along the lines found in paradigmatic katabatic journeys. He did not travel to a place so horrible it could only be described as hell; he planned a trip to hell.

It follows that surfacings of the katabatic subtext in Chekhov's writings on Sakhalin acquire special interest to the reader less interested in the social and natural history of Sakhalin than in Chekhov. The equation of this place with hell tends to shift the focus of Chekhov's narrative from the object of his pseudoscientific study to himself. Thus, those moments when the hell metaphor is most apparent are always characterized by the strange, uncanny effect the sights have on their reporter: as when, for instance, it appears to him "as if all of Sakhalin is burning" and "everything is in smoke, as in hell"; when he describes a spot where "judging by sight, only toads and the souls of great sinners can live"; or when, during the visit of the area's governor-general, "people wandered the streets like shades, and they remain silent like shades" (14-15:54, 19, 65), and he witnesses a "dreadful picture," it is "oppressive" (*skuchno*) on the streets, and music arouses "deathly melancholy" (*smertnaia toska*; ibid., 54, 65).

These highly emotive moments occur repeatedly in conjunction with crossing a body of water. Such crossings, sometimes on ferries operated by hostile ferrymen and always with great forebodings about what will be found on the other side, are the central events of the travel sketches Chekhov wrote *en route,* that is, *before* he had experienced the Russian Devil's Island. When Chekhov departed from Sakhalin, he apparently had in mind as models for the feat he was about to accomplish not only the explorers and scientists whose works on the island he had studied, but also Aeneas and Dante. The blank information cards Chekhov had printed in advance testify to his intentions to gather empirical evidence as a social scientist; the katabatic imagery in his travel sketches suggest that the "hard journey" there and back was preconceived in mythopoetic terms.[4]

Of all the underworlds offered to Chekhov by the katabatic tradition, Dante's seems to have been most important for the Sakhalin book. This is no surprise, since the hell of Dante and of Christian mythology is, unlike the underworld of classical paradigms, tightly connected with notions of sin, crime, and punishment.[5] Given the parallel these connections establish, the ending of *Sakhalin Island* becomes particularly significant. Chekhov devotes this highly marked structural position to a description of the appalling conditions at the infirmary at Aleksandrovsk. It is a kind of last circle of hell.[6]

In certain other works the demonic underworld of Slavic folklore appears key. This is signaled in the very title of Chekhov's ill-fated play of the year preceding his journey, *The Wood Demon* (*Leshii*, 1889), for the wood demon is a Russian folkloric spirit who lives in the forest and is master of all other creatures living there.[7] In the play's context the appellation of "wood demon" belongs to the doctor-environmentalist hero, Khrushchov. The underworld motifs associated with Khrushchov's nickname are compounded in the scene where the hero first appears on the stage: he declares he has a "hellish appetite" (12:137). Later the mill Khrushchov owns is described by Diadin as "a secluded and poetic corner of the earth where you can hear water-nymphs (*rusalki*) splashing at night," and there is even a Gogolian, devilish black piglet poking around where it does not belong (12:174).[8] Both the water-nymph and the piglet belong to the other-worldly and demonic of folklore.

Chekhov's deployment of these underworld motifs in *The Wood Demon* is entirely different from that in *Sakhalin Island*. The folkloric other-world of woods and waters evoked by the play's title acquires a very positive value, and is set in opposition to the everyday social life of the play's characters. "No," remarks Khrushchov, "it's the earth itself that's crazy for still supporting us" (12:178). In this comment the folkloric otherworld is conceived as the center of its own values—it is *rodnoe*—while the world of human society is, from its perspective, alien or other, *chuzhoe*.

What is more, this alien human world is in turn associated with the underworld of Classical and canonical Christian mythologies, as reflected in "high" literature; the character Elena, married to a famous scholar but in love with Khrushchov, is its prisoner. "It's as if you all arranged to make my life hell," she complains (12:177). Meanwhile a neighbor and would-be seducer, who speaks publicly of his love for a married woman, obliquely offers to make Elena queen of his underworld through his repeated citation of Anton Rubenshtein's operatic version of Lermontov's "Demon": "And you will be queen of the world, my faithful mistress" (12:138, 143). This character owns two estates in the Caucasus—here the southern geographical location also represents the downwards direction of the typical katabatic journey—to which he gallops back and forth "like one possessed" (*kak ugorelyi*; 12:137).

A life organized around the obsessive, useless scholarship of Elena's husband becomes associated with the hell of high culture and canonical literary tradition; life organized around ecology and ethical concerns, on the other hand, is associated with the other-world of Slavic folklore (in which demons are traditionally quite ambivalent, often harmful, but sometimes helpful). Elena's choices thus amount to two different types of underworlds. She eventually escapes to the mill, where she hides from both the wood demon (Khrushchov) and her husband. But when her husband and the others gather at the mill for a picnic, she reveals herself, declaring: "I'm ready. Well, take me, like the statue of the Commendatore [from *Don Giovanni*], and disappear with me down into your twenty-six gloomy rooms!" (12:197-98). This denouement is punctuated by an alarm indicating a huge forest fire in neighboring lands—hell bursting up to the surface of this world, as in stagings of Mozart's opera. Khrushchov announces: "I'll grow myself eagle's wings, and neither that glow nor the devil himself will frighten me! Let the woods burn—I'll plant new ones!" (12:197).

This hellish subtext was greatly attenuated when, seven years later, Chekhov reworked *The Wood Demon* into *Uncle Vania*, but hell burst into the foreground in Chekhov's major story of that same year, **"Peasants."** The story's apocalyptic imagery has been noted by previous readers,[9] but it is fair to say that all tend to view the descent imagery as indexical signs of chaos and poverty: these motifs are construed as illustrating "the hellish element in the peasants' lives," rather than as part of a deep symbolic structure.[10]

Nevertheless, the whole of **"Peasants"** is structured as a descent to hell: it is an instance of psychopomps, escorting the soul of the dead (the dying Nikolai) to the underworld.[11] And the family returning to its native village *really does* go to hell, for the metaphoric association of the peasant village with hell becomes concretized during the catastrophic fire at the start of chapter 5. The whole of chapter 4 had dealt with Sasha's thoughts of God, church and religious cosmology, especially hell and "the end of the world." In the same chapter Fëkla tells her dying brother-in-law that "the devil brought you here," and Granny curses Motka and Sasha. At the chapter's end Sasha is beaten by her grandmother and comforts herself with the thought that the old woman is surely bound for hell. She then dreams: "A huge stove, like a kiln, was burning, and the unclean spirit, with horns like a cow's, all black, was driving granny into the fire with a long stick, like she herself had just been driving the geese" (9:294). Over the space of the chapter break which follows Sasha's dream materializes. The fire described in the next chapter breaks out during the Feast of the Assumption, that is, on the festival marking the day when the mother of God was *bodily* taken from this world to heaven. In Chekhov's text the figurative has also materialized, this village is bodily carried down to hell.

Chekhov's 1895 story, **"Ariadne,"** is associated by its title with the descent of Theseus and his slaying of the Minotaur. The invocation of this mythological subtext is highly ironic: here the self-centered and sensuous Ariadne, who summons the narrator to southern lands to rescue her, is herself a devourer of men. The far-off southern lands to which the narrator travels are, like the Caucasus in *The Wood Demon,* a substitution for the notion of lower lands, a projection of the vertically organized space of katabic myths onto the horizontal plane of geography. Instead of assisting the narrator in his task, on the model of the innocent and trusting mythological Ariadne, this debauched heroine ruins him entirely. Ariadne's thread is a leash, or the strings of a marionette, by which her miserable lover is manipulated. In Chekhov's story hell is the erotic charms of a captivating woman.

Like **"Ariadne,"** the very early **"Sinner from Toledo"** (1881) treats the traditional descent pattern ironically. The story is set in Barcelona during the Inquisition. A woman accused of practicing witchcraft is hidden by her husband. Although he is an educated man and knows his beautiful wife is no witch, an insurmountable fear of hell possesses him, and he expects to be condemned to hell for studying the "black arts" of medicine and mathematics. The inquisitors' promise of absolution of all sins and an escape from hell in return for handing over his wife proves too great to resist: "He was ready to give up everything" (1:114). He poisons his wife and hands over her corpse to men he recognizes as "ravens," that is, black creatures of hell, so as to be cleansed of his own sins. (There is a similar case in Canto 27 of Dante's *Inferno*: Guido, a warrior turned repentant monk, is promised absolution by the Pope for help in waging war; that is, past sins are absolved in exchange for committing further, perhaps greater sins in the service of the church.) Thus, what began as a chivalric rescue of the beloved—one typical purpose behind the hero's descent—has ended in betraying the beloved, delivering her to be burned, in order to avoid the katabatic journey altogether. The story turns on the co-presence in this young, skeptical man of science—an *intelligent* projected back in time—of contempt for the priests and what they are doing, and terror of the hell in the name of which they act.

A simultaneous intellectual rejection of the devil and hell, and yet what can only be understood as a vision of them, appears in **"A Doctor's Visit"** (**"Sluchai iz prak-tiki,"** 1898). This story features the journey there and back of an *intelligent* of Chekhov's time. A physician named Korolev—the name derives from *korol'*, "king," a princely title appropriate for a hero summoned to do battle in the other world—is sent to attend to the daughter of a factory-owning family in the provinces in response to a "long, incoherently composed telegram" (10:75). This incoherence initiates a series of diabolic

motifs which culminates in the doctor's vision of the factory as the devil himself. After examining the patient and finding "nothing special" wrong with her, the doctor agrees to spend the night with the family (10:78). Unable to sleep, he wanders about the grounds of the factory complex, like a shaman wandering the underworld in search of the soul of his subject, and concludes that the whole factory is arranged to the advantage of one being only—the devil. This thought is repeated (via free indirect discourse) three times, the last and most emphatic of which follows:

> And he thought about the devil, in whom he did not believe, and looked back at the two windows in which lights were shining. It seemed to him that it was the devil himself watching him with those crimson eyes, that mysterious force which had established the relations between the strong and the weak, a gross blunder which is beyond correction by any means.
>
> (10:82)

It subsequently emerges that the suffering girl makes sense of her situation through a similar operation in mythopoesis: she tells him that "Lermontov's Tamara was alone and saw the devil" (10:84). For the first time, Liza has found an interlocutor with whom she can speak the idiom of her soul. Their successful communication, a distinctive combination of psycho-socioeconomic analysis and overt myth-making, has a therapeutic, rejuvenating effect on them both.

The next day all are returned to the realm of the sun, that is, to "this" world. Church bells are ringing, the patient is dressed festively, in white with a flower in her hair, and the same "windows in the factory complex glistened gaily"; the doctor "thought about how pleasant it was on such spring mornings to ride in a troika, in a good carriage, and to be warmed by the sun." Nevertheless, the doctor notices the same sadness in his patient, who "talked with an expression as if she wanted to tell him something special, something important, something for him alone" (10:85). However uplifting the rhetoric of the story's ending, the doctor's departure constitutes an ironic twist on the expected ending of a katabatic journey undertaken to rescue a beloved from the underworld: Korolev—married and a professional—abandons his patient, now adorned as a bride, to the sufferings that are sure to return as the sun sets.

An earlier story treating the same theme of a woman imprisoned by her patrimony of industrial wealth, **"A Woman's Kingdom"** (1894), also makes use of the descent motif. Robert Louis Jackson has shown that "On the mythopoetic plane of the story . . . Chekhov opposes the 'kingdom of Christ,' with its doctrine of freedom, responsibility and sacrifice, to the pagan 'woman's kingdom' with its superstition, lottery tickets, fortune-telling and slavery to fate." The woman's kingdom, a pagan underworld, is located on the lower floor of the heroine's manor. As in *Wood Demon,* however, the upper region of the house, where she receives the lawyer Lyseich, is only another kind of hell. This can be seen in the sameness of the advice she receives from the witchy Spirodonovna and the lawyer Lyseich and in the diabolic motifs associated with the latter, which Jackson has pointed out.[12]

"The Student" (1894), one of Chekhov's own favorite stories, is explicitly structured as a descent and ascent. Echoing Dante's *Inferno,* it opens with the student suddenly finding himself in a dark wood. The hero moves in spirit and space from cheerfulness in the thick woods before the onset of darkness, to despondency with the onset of night and bitter cold in a low, marshy place, and then to euphoria with the crossing of a river and ascent in space. The cold winds are repeatedly associated with an untimely return of winter, in mythological terms the periodic descent of Persephone (8:306-7).

The story takes place at sunset on Good Friday and turns on the student's retelling of Peter's denial, one segment of the myth of Christ's death and resurrection. In its general trajectory the story parallels **"A Doctor's Visit"**: in both cases a transformation in the mood of the central hero occurs as the result of mythopoetic storytelling; in both cases, the stories are told to a woman or women trapped in unhappy situations, captives in the underworld. The student's descent occurs during the same interval—between crucifixion and resurrection—when in the apocryphal tradition Christ made his own descent: the "harrowing of hell."

The preceding selection of works by Chekhov displaying katabatic masterplots is doubly inadequate: the list needs to be extended, and each individual work deserves treatment in greater depth. But the task here is to make some generalizations. Is there one consistent, or a set of consistent meanings associable with the descent in Chekhov? Why was he so attracted to the motif, and how does it fit in with other features of his poetics?

To begin with the obvious, the descent into hell, always an ordeal, is something that a certain kind of hero does. For Lord Raglan, Joseph Campbell, and many others, it is in fact the paradigm of heroic activity; as Northrop Frye writes, the hero's descent "is not a good plot, but *the* good plot."[13] Among heroes who make the descent, it has become traditional to distinguish between the active hero and the passive, suffering hero: the former, who gets through his ordeal by martial feats or trickery, conquers the beast of hell and brings back a boon or his beloved, while the latter's initiatory journey—often of death and rebirth—provides him with esoteric knowledge and an elevated state of being.[14]

Both paradigms are exploited in Chekhov's works, though always in a deeply ambivalent fashion. In the travel sketches "From Siberia" and *Sakhalin Island* the hell subtext emerges most notably when the narrative is focusing on the narrator, that is, on Chekhov himself. If the hero's descent was a masterplot for the journey to Sakhalin, then it would appear that one purpose for the journey was to cast the traveling author as hero; Chekhov was setting himself a hero's task, a *podvig.* There is nothing new about such an interpretation: the taxing and dangerous journey has often been understood as the act of a socially committed physician risking his life and bucking the regime.[15] In an uncharacteristic emotional outburst, just before leaving for Sakhalin Chekhov played up this aspect of his impending voyage in a letter to V. M. Lavrov, who had published the criticism that Chekhov's writing was "unprincipled." Chekhov would not have responded to this charge, he wrote on 10 April 1890, except for the fact that "very soon I am departing Russia for a long time, perhaps never to return." Chekhov researched the explorers who preceded him, and their exploits were prominent in his consciousness before he departed. On 9 March 1890 he wrote to Suvorin that "not more than twenty-five or thirty years ago our own Russians, exploring Sakhalin, performed feats amazing enough to deify man." As Lord Raglan remarked, "Heroes visit the underworld, the dwelling place of the dead . . . in order that they may return from the dead as gods."[16]

The active descent pattern involving the rescue of a beloved from the underworld and the conquering of hell—in its paradigmatic versions often requiring the slaying of a monster—intersects with another persistent mythologem in Chekhov's writings, recently disclosed by Savely Senderovich: that of St. George the Dragon Slayer.[17] This is evident in **"Peasants,"** for instance, where the young student who rides over to the village from the other side and extinguishes the fire—conquers hell—is named *Zhorzh,* or George (note that once finished with the fire, he turns his weapon [a hose] on the peasants themselves). How striking, in this context, that the most prized souvenirs Chekhov brought back from his trip to the Far East were mongooses, creatures whose serpent-killing abilities he touted on his return![18]

As the mongooses would suggest, Chekhov was by nature apt to poke fun at his own deepest aspirations. His letters anticipating the Sakhalin journey often joke about the risk of being eaten by bears or tigers, or murdered by escaped convicts: "I've bought myself a sheepskin coat, an officer's leather waterproof, big boots and a big knife for cutting sausage and hunting tigers. I'm armed from head to foot."[19] And several years later, when Chekhov learned how G. I. Rossolimo's inquiries regarding the possibility of Chekhov's receiving a doctoral degree in medicine for his work on Sakhalin had been rebuffed by the Dean, his response was to burst out laughing.[20]

Heroism of the active, triumphant sort is consistently travestied in Chekhov's poetic world, too.[21] In this respect **"Ariadne"** and **"The Sinner from Toledo,"** in which the active heroic possibilities associated with katabasis are invoked only in order to be treated ironically, are characteristic. The impossibility of heroic action in the present-day Russian milieu is also a prominent theme in *The Wood Demon*. Shortly before the appearance of Elena at the picnic, Khrushchov declares:

> The whole district—all the women—see a hero in me, a progressive man, and you are famous throughout Russia. And if they seriously consider people like me heroes, and if people like you are seriously famous, that means that for lack of people even a dumb peasant is a nobleman, that there are no true heroes, no talents, no people who would lead us out of this dark forest, who would fix what we spoil, no real eagles who deserve the honor of fame.
>
> (12:194)

If the "dark forest" is another allusion to Dante, then the way out must involve a journey through hell. When Elena reveals herself in the play's denouement, the old man with whom she has been hiding, Diadin, echoes Khrushchov's discourse on heroism and confesses to having "kidnapped" her, as Paris did Helen of Troy; he then immediately undermines the parodistic allusion: "Although there are no pock-marked Parises, but, my friend Horatio, there is much in this world of which our philosophers have not dreamt" (12:195). Diadin, a man of the old school, constantly couches his speech in such allusions to classical literature. Here he underlines the nonheroicalness of his milieu by combining a reference to Homer's *Iliad* with a quotation from Prince Hamlet, whose very name evokes decades of Russian socioliterary criticism regarding the nature of the hero in Russian literature. Indeed, one suspects that the name "Diadin" is derived from the "diadia" (old man) of Lermontov's poem, "Borodino"; there the contrast between an elder, heroic generation, and a younger, nonheroic one, received one of its paradigmatic articulations in Russian literature.

In Chekhov little separates such ironic treatments of the "active" descent pattern from the passive pattern. Chekhov departed for the Far East in a state of spiritual and physical exhaustion: he had lost his brother a short time before taking the journey, and his own blood-spitting and palpitations had already given ample reason to contemplate, however quietly, his own mortality. There is nothing new in adducing the search for spiritual and creative rebirth as a reason for Chekhov's journey to Sakhalin; but Chekhov himself linked this search with the archetypal descent pattern, he sought out the experience of great trials and encounters with deep suffering as a path to rejuvenation. As he wrote to Suvorin on 9 March 1890,

> Sakhalin is a place of unbearable sufferings, the sort only man, free or subjugated, is capable of. The people who worked near it or on it were trying to solve problems of terrible responsibility, and they are still trying now. I'm sorry I'm not sentimental or I would say that we ought to make pilgrimages to places like Sakhalin the way Turks go to Mecca, and sailors and prison officials in particular ought to look upon Sakhalin as soldiers do Sevastopol.

Chekhov, it appears, understood before Mircea Eliade that in the modern, desacralized world, we can still find the pattern of descent and ordeals "in the spiritual crises, the solitude and despair through which every human being must pass in order to attain to a responsible, genuine, and creative life." According to Eliade, "If we look closely, we see that every human life is made up of a series of ordeals, of 'deaths,' and of 'resurrections.'"[22] This was no new idea in nineteenth-century Russian literature, and Chekhov would have gathered a prominent version of it from reading Dostoevsky.

Thus, although Chekhov frequently structured his works of fiction and drama as arrivals and departures, the real journeys of his neurotic heroes are most often inward, and their most important confrontations (and failures) are with the self. This is especially the case in stories with a rather explicit initiatory pattern—another typical descent motif[23]—the central events of which deserve to be called existential crises.[24] Here the epigraph to Freud's *The Interpretation of Dreams* should be recalled: "Flectere si nequeo superos, Acheronta movebo." The metaphoric association between the unconscious and the mythological underworld is one to which Freud and psychoanalysts since have frequently returned.[25]

One of the most distinctive features of Chekhov's poetics is his treatment of time and memory. The structure of a story by Chekhov is apt to foreground the tension between change and repetition that can be found in any narrative, and intimations of timelessness are often experienced by characters or suggested by outbursts of lyricism in the narration. Chekhov's much-vaunted tendency toward plotlessness and a restraint in vocabulary that lends itself to the repetition of lexical motifs are two formal factors contributing to this effect. His tendency toward what can be loosely called literary impressionism (let us ignore for now arguments over a precise definition) subjectivizes the handling of time in works.[26] And his habitual use of holidays as settings—derived, it has been suggested, from his formative years as a writer of short, occasional pieces for the popular press—underlines the role of cyclical, ritual time in the everyday life of his poetic world. As we shall see, all these aspects of Chekhov's handling of time are profoundly relevant to the descent motif.

Chekhov's characters often indulge in speculation about what will be in fifty, a hundred, or a thousand years, now with optimism, now with existential despair. This statement by the student in **"Lights"** (**"Ogni,"** 1888) is typical of the latter attitude:

At some time there lived in this world Philistines and Amalekites; they made war, played a certain role, and now there's no trace of them. And that's how it will be with us. Now we are building a railroad, we stand here and philosophize, but after two thousand or so years pass, there won't even be any dust left from this whole embankment and all these people now sleeping after their heavy labors. In essence, it's horrible!

(7:107)

But the same indifference of nature to man becomes a "pledge of our eternal salvation" in the lyrical passage describing Gurov's reflections on a bench overlooking the sea in **"The Lady with a Lapdog"** (1899; 10:133). Both the low and high points of **"The Student"** involve reflections on how the present is connected with the past. And the physician in **"A Doctor's Visit"** promises his patient a bright future—perhaps beyond their lifetimes—when the social ills entrapping them will have been overcome, while the medical man in *The Wood Demon* declares that "if in a thousand years man is happy, then to some small extent I shall be guilty of it" (12:141).

The theme of time and memory is no less vexed when elaborated within the bounds of an individual life. In **"Grisha"** (1886) and **"The Steppe"** (1888), both of which are in part assays in child psychology, the retention of impressions which surpass the child's ability to assimilate them causes illness. In **"Rothschild's Fiddle,"** the undertaker Iakov, a sullen and cruel man obsessed with financial losses, becomes human when he recalls a loss suppressed from consciousness, that of his child who died fifty years ago.[27]

The narrator of **"My Life,"** one of Chekhov's gloomiest works, opens the story's final chapter by saying that if he had a ring, he would etch on its inside the words: "Nothing passes," because "each of our tiniest steps has meaning for present and future life" (9:279). As in **"The Student,"** this linkage of temporalities holds as much anguish for the narrator as it does hope: he is oppressed by painful memories which recede only in the oblivion of menial labor, and it appears that he and others of his generation can free themselves from the social and psychological legacies of their fathers only at the cost of self-destruction. This assertion of absolute memory arises in contrast to one of forgetting, since the narrator proposes the ring in response to the one his wayward wife has had inscribed in Hebrew: "Everything passes." But even her notion that all is forgotten, that all links eventually rupture, is no less ambivalent than its antithesis: "When I'm sad," she writes him, "then these words cheer me up, and when I'm cheerful, they sadden me" (9:272).

One critic has been led by such motifs to speak of a "flight from time" in Chekhov's works.[28] In fact, the few examples above suffice to demonstrate the ambivalence of Chekhov's treatment of memory and forgetting: one can find both positive and negative valuations of the connectedness between past and present, both positive and negative values associated with the dissolution of such links. A systematic treatment of this topic would require closer attention to the characters and contexts involved in each instance. In **"My Life,"** for example, the opposing attitudes toward time expressed by the two mottos come to stand for opposing character types and ethical codes, much as in **"Rothschild's Fiddle."** The chief point here is that forgetting and remembering have traditionally been central events in katabatic journeys: although the poles of memory and forgetting are not uniformly located, respectively, in the other world or in this world, they nonetheless operate as a structuring semantic opposition. So it is in Plato's Myth of Er, where pasts are contemplated for a thousand years, futures are then chosen, and all of it is forgotten (due to a drink from the River of Heedlessness on the Plain of Forgetting) before reemergence in the upper world; so it is the underworlds of Virgil and Dante, where nothing has been forgotten, and where even the future can be glimpsed;[29] and so it is in Freud's underworld of the unconscious where, indeed, "nothing can be brought to an end, nothing is past or forgotten."[30] Chekhov's works underline precisely this sharp opposition between the position where "nothing passes" and the one where "everything passes." One of the most succinct expressions of this is found in **"Kashtanka,"** the story about a dog which is really about time and memory. Kashtanka's descent into the hellish circus ring and her ascent to her former masters in the audience at the story's end constitutes "a restoration of ruptured time."[31]

If the theme of chronological time in Chekhov can be associated with the descent pattern, the same is even more true of cyclical, seasonal time—time as measured, for instance, by the ritual translocations of Persephone, whose periodic descent was associated with the cycle of seasons and corresponding fertility rites. Here the themes of time and the underworld intersect with that of gender: Father Time, Mother Earth.

Jung read Persephone's abduction by Hades and Demeter's search for her as a katabatic myth told from the woman's point of view.[32] Recent treatments of this and associated myths have emphasized the significance of their reemergence in particular historical contexts: it has been argued, for example, that American women writers of the late nineteenth century transformed Pluto's kidnapping of Persephone into a popular metaphor for industrialization, the raping of the female countryside, a distancing from seasonal, cyclical time, and the co-opting of a distinctively feminine world of discourse.[33] Joanna Hubbs has theorized about a series of analogous moments, spanning Russian cultural history from the earliest times, where matrilocal customs and worldviews were challenged, suppressed, and covertly incorporated by patrilocal religious and political structures.[34] To be sure, in the Russian cultural context this aspect of the descent motif—the descent into hell as a descent into "Moist Mother Earth"—can only take on even greater significance. Once again, Chekhov could look to Dostoevsky for literary precedence (consider for instance "The Peasant Marei"). For contemporary relevance, he could look to the changing economic and ecological conditions around him, as we know he did.

Chekhov's underworlds are clearly marked by gender and gender conflict. Hell can be a distinctively masculine world, as in the professor's house in *The Wood Demon*; more often it is a woman's world—a world which, however, has fallen into thralldom. In **"A Doctor's Visit"** Korolev remarks that it seems there is not a single man in the house where his patient is held captive by her patrimony, and this is confirmed. The woman's kingdom of **"A Woman's Kingdom"** is the lower floor, the pagan underworld, while the lawyer Lyseich rules the upstairs. The women are masters in the kitchen garden where the student stops to warm himself and retell the story of Peter's denial in **"The Student,"** but the widow Vasilisa has a history of servitude and her daughter was oppressed (*zabitaia*) by her husband. Sasha's malicious grandmother dominates the family in **"Peasants,"** while she is in turn subservient to the swarthy (another underworld motif) village elder. But it is "The Cherry Orchard" that most closely echoes the model of a woman's world—the symbol of which is the annually blossoming orchard—falling to the axe of changing socioeconomic trends.

In name the underworld presents itself as a spatial dimension, but the very special temporal values it embodies are central to Chekhov's art.

For the nonbelieving Chekhov, a reader of Nietzsche, descent had a meaning quite different than for his Russian precursors, especially Gogol and Dostoevsky. As has been pointed out many times, in the desacralized modern world such myth-making tends to be a rather idiosyncratic affair.

In **"Easter Eve"** (**"Sviataia noch',"** 1886), crossing to the other world—in this case a monastery—is associated with artistic inspiration, indeed, becomes a lesson in writing. The genre is the *akafist,* church songs in praise of Christ, Mary, and certain saints; the artist is a monk who has died this Easter holiday. For the narrator, crossing becomes a lesson in the poetics of *akafisty* from the one monk who appreciated the song's artistry, the one monk who will not be able to hear them performed because he must serve as the ferryman. The devout attending the Easter eve service, on the other hand,

are deaf to the music's beauty—for believers, of all people, the descent is meaningless, and they return from it exhausted, in lower form than that in which they departed.

In the absence of a religious belief system underwriting the mythic journey, the traditional metaliterary implications of descent can become central. To the extent that this is true of Chekhov's descents, he would seem to anticipate the following generation of poets, and the katabatic theme indicates an essentially symbolic and modernist dimension to Chekhov's writings.

Notes

1. Thus, Laurence Senelick has observed that whenever Chekhov makes a classical allusion it is likely to be to an Offenbachian perversion of Virgil or Homer (paper delivered at Chekhov Symposium, Yale University, April 1990).

2. For a concise typology of the descent motif based on the purpose of descent see John G. Bishop, "The Hero's Descent to the Underworld," in *The Journey to the Other World,* ed. H. R. Davidson (Cambridge, Eng., 1975), 109-29.

3. Unless otherwise noted, all translations are mine, and all references to Chekhov's works will be made in the text and are to the first eighteen volumes of A. P. Chekhov, *Polnoe sobranie sochinenii i pisem v tridtsati tomakh* (Moscow: Nauka, 1974-83; hereafter *PSS*). Chekhov's letters are referenced by date.

4. This means that Chekhov was somewhat disingenuous when he wrote Suvorin, "While I was living on Sakhalin, I suffered only something of a sour stomach, as from rancid butter, but now, recollecting, Sakhalin appears to me a total hell" (9 December 1890). At some level, Chekhov apparently *sought* or *staged* the epistemological crisis that, Cathy Popkin has convincingly argued, he experienced during his visit to Sakhalin ("Chekhov as Ethnographer: Epistemological Crisis on Sakhalin Island," *Slavic Review* 51 [Spring 1992]: 36-51).

   Mircea Eliade's remarks on the "eschatological implications of colonization" are very interesting in this respect; see his *The Quest: History and Meaning in Religion* (Chicago, 1969), 89-111. See also Mikhail Bakhtin's discussion of connection between the descent in Rabelais and the exploration of the New World in *Rabelais and His World,* trans. Helene Iswolsky (Bloomington: Indiana University Press, 1984), 397-400.

5. For parallels between *Sakhalin Island* and Dante's *Inferno* in addition to those presented below see Kenneth John Atchity, "Chekhov's Infernal Is-

land," *Research Studies: A Quarterly Publication of Washington State University* 36 (December 1968): 335-40. Popkin notes that, in a significant contradistinction to the principle of "contrapasso" in Dante's hell, Chekhov finds no connection between the crime and the punishment on Sakhalin ("Chekhov as Ethnographer," 44).

6. Many features of the infirmary at Aleksandrovsk are repeated in the description of the hospital in "Ward Six" (1892; see editors' commentary, *PSS* 7:449). Although I do not take up "Ward Six" here, it deserves to be considered among Chekhov's hellish visions.

7. See Linda Ivanits, *Russian Folk Belief* (Armonk, NY: M. E. Sharpe, 1989), 64-70.

8. The play ends with allusions to the opera based on Pushkin's "Rusalka" (*PSS* 12:188, 394).

9. In his discussion of the theme of the apocalypse in nineteenth-century Russian literature, David Bethea mentions in passing the scene in "Peasants" depicting a black horse spooked by the fire running wild, and says that Chekhov uses this apocalyptic motif in order to describe "a popular world falling apart in an orgy of drunkenness and ignorance" (*The Shape of the Apocalypse in Modern Russian Fiction* [Princeton: Princeton University Press, 1989], 57). In a fine analysis of the setting of "Peasants," L. Michael O'Toole suggests that certain motifs of the story are taken from the apocryphal "Journey of the Mother of God through Hell," and he associates the character Fekla with the water-nymph. See his *Structure, Style and Interpretation in the Russian Short Story* (New Haven: Yale University Press, 1982), 215-16, 211.

10. O'Toole, *Structure,* 209.

11. See Bishop, "The Hero's Descent," 116-17.

12. See R. L. Jackson, "Chekhov's 'A Woman's Kingdom': A Drama of Character and Fate," in *Critical Essays on Anton Chekhov,* ed. Thomas A. Eekman (Boston: G. K. Hall & Co., 1989), 101-2.

13. See Lord Fitzroy Richard Somerset Raglan, Baron, *The Hero: A Study in Tradition, Myth, and Drama* (London, 1936); Joseph Campbell, *The Hero with a Thousand Faces* (New York, 1949); and Northrop Frye, *The Secular Scripture: A Study of the Structure of Romance* (Cambridge, MA, 1976), 102, passim. See also Ol'ga Freidenberg, who demonstrates the centrality of the descent episode in Homer's *Odyssey* in "The Plot Semantics of the *Odyssey,*" *Soviet Studies in Literature* 27 (Winter 1990-91): 22-32. On the treatment of the heroes of ancient Greek religion see Erwin Rohde, *Psyche: The Cult of Souls and Belief in Immortal-*

ity among the Greeks, translated from eighth edition by W. B. Hillis (New York, 1925), 115-55, passim. See also René Girard, *Deceit, Desire, and the Novel: Self and Other in Literary Structure,* trans. Yvonne Freccero (Baltimore, 1965), 253.

14. The paradigmatic opposition is between Prometheus and Orpheus. See Walter A. Strauss, *Descent and Return: The Orphic Theme in Modern Literature* (Cambridge, MA, 1971), 10-12; and Herbert Marcuse, *Eros and Civilization: A Philosophical Inquiry into Freud* (Boston, 1966), 161ff.

15. See Simon Karlinsky's criticism of this commonly held view in *Letters of Anton Chekhov,* trans. Michael H. Heim and Simon Karlinsky, ed., introd., and commentary by Simon Karlinsky (New York, 1973), 152-54; and the letter of 9 March 1890, where Chekhov tells Suvorin that his chief reason for going to Sakhalin is to do medical research.

16. Raglan, *The Hero,* 171.

17. Senderovich calls this motif the "key to a very important deep semantic formation" as well as a personal obsession in Chekhov. See his "Anton Chekhov and St. George the Dragonslayer (An Introduction to the Theme)," in *Anton Chekhov Rediscovered: A Collection of New Studies with a Comprehensive Bibliography,* ed. S. Senderovich and Munir Sendich (East Lansing: *Russian Language Journal,* 1987): 167-87. See also the longer version, "Chudo Georgiia o zmie: Istoriia oderzhimosti Chekhova odnim obrazom," in *Russian Language Journal,* vol. 39, nos. 132-4 (1985): 135-225.

18. See his letter to I. L. Leont'ev (Shcheglov), 10 December 1890.

19. Letter to Suvorin, 15 April 1890.

20. G. I. Rossolimo, "Vospominaniia o Chekhove," in *A. P. Chekhov v vospominaniiakh sovremennikov,* ed. N. I. Gitovich (Moscow: Khudozhestvennaia literatura, 1986), 436.

21. See S. Senderovich's treatment of this aspect of Chekhov in "The End of Carnival in Anton Chekhov," *Studies in Slavic Literatures and Culture in Honor of Zoya Yurieff,* ed. Munir Sendich (East Lansing: *Russian Language Journal,* 1988): 293-302.

22. Mircea Eliade, *Birth and Rebirth: The Religious Meaning of Initiation in Human Culture,* trans. Willard R. Trask (New York, 1958), 128. One might rather say that the *story* of every life is made up of a series of ordeals, and so on, and that the katabatic masterplot is a supremely attractive and powerful tool in the individual's aestheticization of his own life.

23. See Bishop, "The Hero's Descent," 117-18.

24. Some salient examples of such stories, all of which can be demonstrated to employ descent motifs, are "The Steppe" (1888), "An Attack of Nerves" ("Pripadok," 1889), and "Ward 6" ("Palata No. 6," 1892). On Chekhov and existentialism see Marena Senderovich, "Chekhov's Existential Trilogy," *Anton Chekhov Rediscovered,* 77-91.

25. See, for instance, James Hillman, *The Dream and the Underworld* (New York, 1979); Joseph L. Henderson and Maud Oaks, *The Wisdom of the Serpent: The Myths of Death, Rebirth, and Resurrection* (New York, 1963); and C. G. Jung, "The Psychological Aspects of the Kore," in C. G. Jung and C. Kerényi, *Essays on a Science of Mythology* (New York, 1949), 215-45.

26. See, for instance, the chapters on impressionism and time in "The Kiss" in Peter M. Bitsilli, *Chekhov's Art: A Stylistic Analysis,* trans. Toby Clyman and Edwina Cruise (Ann Arbor: Ardis, 1983), 44-73, 173-83.

27. See Robert Louis Jackson, "'If I Forget Thee, O Jerusalem': An Essay on Chekhov's 'Rothschild's Fiddle,'" *Anton Chekhov Rediscovered,* 35-49.

28. See Edgar L. Frost, "The Search for Eternity in Čexov's Fiction: The Flight from Time as a Source of Tension," *Russian Language Journal,* no. 108 (1977): 111-20.

29. Of the hell of Christianity generally speaking, Frye writes: "The notion of a world of pure memory, where everything forever continues to be as it has been, is the core of the religious conception of hell" (*The Secular Scripture,* 175).

30. Sigmund Freud, *The Interpretation of Dreams,* trans. James Strachey (New York, 1965), 617. Frye adds: "Hence many descent themes, from the Harrowing of Hell to the psychological quests of Freud and his successors, center on the theme of the release, revival, or reemergence of parental figures buried in a world of amnesia or suppressed memory" (*The Secular Scripture,* 121-22).

31. See M. Senderovich, "Chekhov's 'Kashtanka': Metamorphoses of Memory in the Labyrinth of Time (A Structural-Phenomenological Essay)," *Anton Chekhov Rediscovered,* 63-75.

32. Jung, "Psychological Aspects of the Kore," 220.

33. See Josephine Donovan, *After the Fall: The Demeter-Persephone Myth in Wharton, Cather, and Glasgow* (University Park: Pennsylvania State University Press, 1989). See also the pathbreaking work of Carolyn Merchant, *The Death of Nature: Women, Ecology, and the Scientific Revolution* (San Francisco, 1980).

34. Joanna Hubbs, *Mother Russia: The Feminine Myth in Russian Culture* (Bloomington: Indiana University Press, 1988).

Willa Chamberlain Axelrod (essay date 15 February 1994)

SOURCE: Axelrod, Willa Chamberlain. "The Biblical and Theological Context of Moral Reform in 'The Duel.'" *Russian Literature* 35, no. 2 (15 February 1994): 129-52.

[*In the following essay, Axelrod offers a comprehensive study of the extensive theological references in "The Duel," arguing that an understanding of these allusions is necessary to appreciate the story.*]

In **'The Duel'** (**'Duèl''**, 1891), one of A. P. Čechov's longest stories, there are numerous allusions to the Old and New Testaments and to the teachings of the Russian Orthodox Church. Without understanding the biblical and theological references, one cannot respect the genius and artistry of this masterpiece, which has been neglected because of its allegedly "artificial" and "absurd" ending.[1] Critics from Čechov's time and the present perceive the outcome of **'The Duel'**, that is Ivan Andreič Laevskij's reformed life, as unconvincing and unanticipated. A. M. Skabičevskij, for example, believes Laevskij's sudden change is impossible, and K. Medvedskij does not perceive any reason or impetus for his moral metamorphosis and thinks the story would be more convincing had he committed suicide.[2] Carolina de Maegd-Soëp claims that "the portrayal of both Laevsky and Nadezhda at the end of the novel seems rather artificial and even melodramatic".[3] Ronald Hingley considers the ending "perhaps the worst writing to be found in any of Chekhov's mature work".[4] Such common and unjust interpretations of **'The Duel'** illustrate that one cannot understand and appreciate the story while being ignorant of the extensive biblical allusions in **'The Duel'**.

The central issue of the story is the need for salvation and moral reform. Moral reform is discussed on two levels:

> 1) on an individual one, as it concerns the main protagonist, Ivan Andreič Laevskij, and, to a lesser extent, the zoologist Nikolaj Vasil'ič fon Koren; and,

> 2) on a general level, as it concerns a greater Russian population. Laevskij experiences a major change of heart and succeeds in reforming his life. His search for renewal and his eventual reform represent the need for salvation of the Russian population.

Čechov draws mainly from Psalm 79, the Books of Isaiah and Jeremiah, and from the Gospels to develop the theme of moral reform or salvation. Psalm 79 is a supplicatory prayer for the salvation or restoration of the Kingdoms of Israel and Judah, allegedly written during the Babylonian exile. The vine, a central metaphor in Psalm 79, which represents the Israelites, is a constant image associated with salvation throughout the Bible, and is a leitmotif in **'The Duel'**.

In the Books of Isaiah and Jeremiah, the prophets foretell of a new age to follow the Babylonian exile: eventually God will restore Israel and Judah and initiate a new, eternal covenant. This messianic promise of salvation and of a new covenant is an underlying biblical motif in **'The Duel'**. This new covenant, which the Christian Church interprets as inaugurated and fulfilled by Christ, will still require obedience to the Law, but three additional terms will be added:

> 1) spontaneous forgiveness of sins;
>
> 2) individual retribution for sins rather than collective punishment; and
>
> 3) interiorization of religion, that is, the Law will not only guide external behavior, but it will inspire the heart.

These three terms of the new covenant are associated with Laevskij's reform.

Fundamental signs from the Gospels, such as the eucharistic meal, the breath of the Holy Spirit, and the image of Christ as sacrifice in exchange for salvation, are central to Laevskij's conversion. The three virtues of Christianity, Faith, Hope, and Love, are focal to Laevskij's reform.

The central event in **'The Duel'** is Laevskij's drastic change from a superfluous ne'er-do-well and philanderer, who spends his days in slippers, drinking and playing vint, to a humble and devoted husband who works hard to pay off his debts. For most of the story's twenty-one chapters, Laevskij speaks of "saving" his life, of "renewal" and "rebirth", and for most of the story, he seeks salvation to no avail in material things and in man. Towards the end, in Chapter XVII, however, he experiences a spiritual rebirth initiated by himself and others around him but ultimately realized through divine grace. This sudden change occurs on the eve of the duel. The duel, which has extensive religious implications, occurs the morning after Laevskij's moral reform and thus emphasizes his rebirth in that it saves him physically.

The main characters, the army doctor Aleksandr Davidyč Samojlenko, the young deacon Pobedov, and fon Koren, are astounded by Laevskij's reformed life. The Darwinist fon Koren, who despises Laevskij, the "superfluous man", is especially surprised. He considers Laevskij's immoral behavior, that is, his excessive drinking, mindless card-playing, cohabitation with Na-

dežda Fedorovna, a married woman, and lack of respect for his administrative career, a menace to "the perfection of mankind". He is so morally sick, according to fon Koren, that reform is impossible. Thus, the zoologist thinks that to destroy this immoral and spineless person is a service to humanity (VII: 394).[5] In Chapter XV, when Laevskij, in a fit of anger, impulsively threatens Samojlenko and fon Koren with a fight, fon Koren eagerly takes this as a challenge to a duel and schedules one for the following morning.

Although the night before the duel the zoologist concludes that killing Laevskij is not worth three years in prison, during the duel he is so overcome by disgust for him, that he decides to kill Laevskij. The deacon, however, causes fon Koren to miss his aim, thus Laevskij is saved. Subsequently, a new man, he begins his humble life of virtue. The story closes with fon Koren, who himself is somewhat humbled by Laevskij's conversion, paying the hard working Laevskij a farewell visit. The two men shake hands and fon Koren departs on a journey.

1. THE PICNIC, PSALM 79, AND THE IMAGE OF THE VINE

In Chapter VI, a Sunday, the principal and secondary characters are seen together for the first time as they leave for a picnic dinner (Chapters VI-IX). This is the first event of the story and is thematically crucial in that it intensifies the need for renewal for Laevskij as well as for all the characters.

The picnic dinner unites the characters under the image of the biblical vine and is an allegory of the eucharistic meal. The picnic as eucharistic ritual is suggested by the food consumed, the location of the picnic, and, most importantly, the deacon's vision of himself as Bishop, blessing his congregation or "vine". The picnic dinner is consumed on Sunday evening with "religious solemnity" (VII: 391). The only food and drink mentioned are fish (in the form of fish soup), salt, bread, and wine, all biblical symbols of the eucharist or the new covenant initiated through Christ. Fish, a traditional symbol of Christ,[6] is associated in **'The Duel'** with the deacon Pobedov, hence underlining its religious value. On the way to the picnic spot, the deacon sits next to the basket of fish, and he picks up the fish after it is cleaned for the soup. "Deacon, where's the fish?" asks Samojlenko (VII: 389). Moreover, the deacon spends his days catching bullheads (VII: 389).

Along with wine and fish soup, salt is also associated with the picnic. "Where is the salt?" Samojlenko asks (VII: 388). Salt, a biblical synonym for essential life-giving forces, seasons all sacrifices in the Old Testament (Lev. 2: 13; Ezek. 43: 24) and it symbolizes the making of a covenant (The Book of Numbers, 18: 19).

In the Russian Liturgy, salt seasons the bread of the eucharist. Bread and wine represent the body and blood of Christ and call to mind his sacrifice and salvation.

Shortly before the picnic meal begins, the deacon imagines himself serving the Liturgy in a cathedral. Indeed the glorious natural setting for the picnic evokes the grandeur of a cathedral. The dark mountains, "piled together by nature out of huge rocks" (VII: 385), like walls of a basilica, emit "dampness and mystery". The many gorges or recesses in the cliffs are the alcoves which line the nave. Distant mountains are pink, lilac, smokey, or flooded with light, colors which suggest incense and sunlight pouring through stained glass. A melody drifts over from the other shore of the river. It sounds like a Lenten hymn. The deacon envisions himself dressed in a golden miter, carrying the "panagija", or bread honoring the Virgin.[7] In preparation for the Epistle reading, he blesses the congregation, holding two- and three-branched candelabra ('dikerion' and 'trikerion') and pronouncing,

> Призри с небесе Боже, и виждъ и посети виноград сей,
> его насади десница твоя!

> Look down from heaven, O God, behold and visit this vine
> which your right hand has planted.

(VII: 389)[8]

This fifteenth verse of Psalm 79 is recited only by a bishop when a bishop participates in serving the Liturgy. While the deacon envisions himself blessing the congregation and reciting the above-mentioned verse, he hears the choir sing the Trisagion (Trisvjatoe or Svjatyj Bože). This prayer, asking for God's mercy, reads:

> O Holy God, Holy Mighty, Holy Immortal
> One, have mercy upon us [three times].
> Glory be to the Father, and to the Son,
> and to the Holy Spirit, now and forever,
> and unto the ages of ages. Amen.

The vine mentioned in Pobedov's blessing, implicitly implies all present at the picnic. The picnickers are the vine to be visited by God and tended by the deacon. This association of the story's characters with the vine is also evoked in the final chapter. In response to Laevskij's reformed life and fon Koren's farewell visit to his former enemy, Pobedov paraphrases verse fifteen of Psalm 79, exclaiming,

> Боже мой, какие люди! Воистину десница
> Божия насадила виноград сей! Господи,
> господи!

(VII: 453)

> My God, what people! It's true the
> right hand of God has planted this vine!
> Lord! Lord!

The vine, a common metaphor for Israel in the Old Testament prophets, is a central image in Psalm 79. God initially bestows favor on his people: "You [God] brought a vine out of Egypt, you drove out the nations and planted it. You cleared the ground for it, and it took root and filled the land," sings Asaph, the putative author of Psalm 79.[9] After the vine flourishes, it is disloyal to God and thus God abandons it. The vine is sacked by Israel's enemies: "Boars from the forest ravage it, and the creatures from the field feed on it."[10] Asaph beseeches God to tend his vine once again and to save his people. Thrice he sings: "God Almighty, renew us; let your face shine upon us that we may be saved."[11] For church-going Russian Orthodox, this refrain comes to mind when Pobedov recites verse fifteen. The refrain epitomizes the theme of salvation in **'The Duel'.**

In the Old Testament, a flourishing vine or vineyard is thus a sign of divine blessing. The verse "everyone under his vine and his fig tree" (1 Kings 4: 25; Micaiah 4: 4) is a metaphor for prosperity and divine blessing. A sacked vineyard or the absence of one, represents devastation (Jeremiah 35: 7) and the need for restoration. In Isaiah, God's punishment of the wicked is likened to the treading of a winepress (Isaiah 63: 1-3).

In the New Testament, Christ adapts the image of the vine to describe his relationship with his disciples and his future Church. Christ is "the true vine" and his people are its branches (John 15: 1). Russian Orthodox priests commonly sign letters to each other with "May God bless you in your work in the vineyard of Christ". "The fruit of the vine" is the symbol of salvation or the new covenant, which is celebrated in the eucharistic sacrament. In **'The Duel'**, Čechov draws from the Old Testament image of the vine as a people in need of salvation and from the New Testament image of "the fruit of the vine" as a sign of salvation through sacrifice.

The main characters and all the 'Laevskijs', or superfluous people embodied by Ivan Andreič, are likened to the biblical image of the Israelites in need of salvation, by the fact that 1) they are an uprooted people living away from their homeland, and 2) they are associated with the image of the vine either through specific reference to a vineyard or to wine.

The theme of exile is subtly introduced in Chapter I: the setting is a small resort town on the Black Sea, inhabited by a transitory and nonnative population. At the end of the first chapter, the simple mentioning of a Jew points to the theme of exile. Samojlenko orders a drink of soda water from an elderly Jewish woman ("evrejka") who gives herself out to be a Georgian. In Chapter II, Laevskij speaks of his life on the Black Sea as "cursed slavery" ("prokljataja nevolja"; VII: 364). The picnic site is carefully described as a spot where two rivers flow into each other. This geographical detail skillfully hints at the city of Babylon, a place of Jewish exile, situated where the Euphrates River most closely approaches the Tigris. Samojlenko, who has not been to Russia in eighteen years, and forgets what the homeland looks like (VII: 359), is the son of "David" (Aleksandr Davidyč), an uncommon name among non-Jewish Russians. Fon Koren's physical appearance is semitic. He has a swarthy complexion and curly hair, and he wears a flowered shirt which looks like a "Persian carpet" (VII: 367). In the nineteenth century, ancient Semites were thought to have populated the area from Persia to Africa. Laevskij, using the pejorative Russian word "žid", denigratingly refers to fon Koren, who has an obviously German name, as one of those "Germans, Jewish by birth" (VII: 426).

All of the main characters are associated with the image of the vine. In Chapter I, the vineyard is mentioned by Laevskij three times. He tells how he and Nadežda came to the Caucasus two years before to escape the "pošlost' and emptiness of life" in the capital and to work by the sweat of their brow on their own plot of land, where they would plant a vineyard (VII: 355). While the desire for physical toil and a plot of land evoke Tolstoyan and Voltairian ethics, Laevskij's dream of his own vineyard especially signifies the Old Testament ideal of peace, prosperity, and divine blessing. Laevskij soon realizes, however, that his dream of "physical work and a vineyard are for the devil" (VII: 356). But he admits that someone like Samojlenko or fon Koren could, no doubt, leave their heirs "a rich vineyard and three thousand acres of corn" (VII: 356). Laevskij's failure to procure a vineyard, especially in the fertile land of Black Sea Georgia where viticulture flourishes, symbolizes the devastation of his existence and his need for salvation.

To illustrate Laevskij's perverted outlook on life, fon Koren claims that the former is not able to perceive the beauty in "a bunch of grapes", for he thinks only of their ugliness once they are chewed and digested. This image of chewed grapes, and also Laevskij's fantasy of trampling on his archenemy the zoologist (VII: 427), evoke the treading of grapes in the winepress, an image of divine disfavor. Thus Čechov suggests, once again, the ruined state of the metaphorical vine.

Late Sunday night, after returning from the picnic, Laevskij visits Samojlenko and twice begs him to save him. ("Save me, Vanja, save me [. . .] Aleksandr Davidyč, save me!"; VII: 396) The doctor offers Laevskij wine from his own vineyard. But his wine has a bitter taste. Nevertheless, according to Laevskij, the doctor's fruit of the vine has life-giving qualities. Over three bottles, Laevskij twice thanks Samojlenko for "re-

juvenating" him ("Ja ožil." "Ty oživil menja"; VII: 396, 399). This delusive rejuvenation prefigures his genuine rebirth. The bitterness of the wine suggests that Samojlenko's wine is not of the "true vine". Church regulations warn priests to take special care that the eucharistic wine is not bitter.[12] As we shall see shortly, bitter grapes and a bunch of grapes are specific references to the Books of Jeremiah and Isaiah respectively. Both Nikodim Aleksandryč Bitjugov and Egor Alekseič Kirilin, minor characters, speak of "their own" wine, implying that, like Samojlenko, they too have vineyards. At the picnic, there is an abundance of wine: thirty bottles for nine adults and two children, who even drink a little. Given the eucharistic suggestions of the picnic, these thirty bottles of wine evoke 1) the passion of Christ; the thirty bottles hint at the thirty silver pieces Judas receives for betraying Jesus; and 2) the blood of Christ, or "the cup of salvation", which the new covenant promises the Israelites.

2. LAEVSKIJ'S SEARCH FOR MORAL REFORM IN THE MATERIAL WORLD

From the beginning of the story, Laevskij is obsessed with the need "to save" or "renew" his life, and continually speaks of "salvation", of "saving" his life from "lies and deception" and from his "absurd" existence with a woman he does not love. In the third year of his relationship with Nadežda Fedorovna, he wants to abandon her and the Caucasus, and return to St. Petersburg to start a new life.

He perceives himself as "an empty, destroyed, fallen person" (VII: 399). Along with the rest of the Russian gentry, he is degenerating (VII: 355, 370) and therefore professes "to thirst for renewal" and hopes to be "resurrected and become a different person" (VII: 399). He confides in Samojlenko his disrespect for himself:

> The air I breathe, this wine, love, life in fact, for all that, I have given nothing in exchange so far but lying, idleness, and cowardice . . . I bow my back humbly before fon Koren's hatred because at times I hate and despise myself.
>
> (VII: 399)

Laevskij is a weak man, but he perceives his own weaknesses and wants help.

For most of the story, his search for new life is unsuccessful. He seeks, or thinks he seeks, salvation in a new locale, money, and, most significantly, in literature and ideas. That is, he seeks salvation in material things and in solely secular terms. To "renew" his life, he must have 300 rubles to run away to St. Petersburg, convinced he will die if he remains in the Caucasus with Nadežda. In Chapter IX, late Sunday night after the picnic, Laevskij asks Samojlenko for a 300 ruble loan. Like an addicted gambler, he is haunted by this sum which, allegedly, will save his life. On Wednesday of the same week, "with excitement", he asks the doctor if he has the money yet. His face expresses "fear, extreme uneasiness, and hope" (VII: 405). On Thursday, at Kostja Bitjugov's birthday party, Samojlenko promises Laevskij that he will have the money by Friday. But neither the 300 rubles nor his escape to the capital will save his life. Material and geographical change do not guarantee moral change.

Laevskij also believes salvation is found in literature and ideas. Before his reform, it is implied that he has no God. He admits this himself (VII: 436), and the deacon Pobedov refers to him as a non-believer. Laevskij turns to literature, not theology, to find a reason for living. He sees justification for his life and actions in the literary and social idea that the aristocracy is degenerating. This is an excuse for the weak Laevskij not to take action and reform his ways. In Chapter I, he admits to Samojlenko that

> [. . .] all salvation is in talking. I have to generalize each one of my actions; I have to find an explanation and justification for my absurd existence in someone else's theories, in literary types, in that we, the landowning class are degenerating. . . .
>
> (VII: 355)

Literary figures define Laevskij's moral standards and guide his thoughts. Always in slippers, like Oblomov, Laevskij lives in the shadow of past literary figures. He considers his behavior to be organically dependent on the natures of his "fathers of flesh and spirit", "Onegin, Pečorin, Byron's Cain, and Bazarov". He takes himself for Faust, and a "second Tolstoj" (VII: 374), and he ironically refers to himself as Wilhelm Tell (VII: 427). Through the epigraph of Chapter XVII, Laevskij is associated with Puškin's poetic persona who laments his past ('Vospominanie', 1828).

Laevskij thinks of his own existence in terms of Tolstoj's presentation of life. "How true is Tolstoj!" ("Kak prav Tolstoj!"; VII: 355), he thinks when reflecting on his own existence. He places personal experience in the context of literature. When he feels repulsed by Nadežda's white neck, for example, he thinks of Anna Karenina's hatred for Karenin expressed by her aversion for his ears. "How true it is, how true it is," exclaims Laevskij ("Kak èto verno, kak verno!"; VII: 362). In his indecision, Laevskij reminds himself of Hamlet: "How truly Shakespeare describes it! Ach, how truly!" (VII: 366). Laevskij's faith is in man and his literary creation. For Laevskij, man is truth, not God.

This emphasis on truth is starkly juxtaposed to Laevskij's frequent mention of lies and deception. The contrast of truth and falsehood is a significant theme running through the story, climaxing in the final scene

when the reformed Laevskij states "No one knows the real truth" (VII: 453). Before his conversion, however, Laevskij believes Tolstoj knows the truth. Tolstoj is the truth. Shakespeare is the truth. Truth for Laevskij before his reform is only man and his ideas. In the Bible, only God, not man, is Truth. According to the Russian Catechism, the image of God is defined by "righteousness and the holiness of truth" ("pravda i prepodobie istiny").[13]

In addition, while man is truth for Laevskij, man is also his source of hope. This is suggested in Chapter IX, when he declares to Samojlenko "all hope is in you", as preface to his request for 300 rubles. The Russian Catechism states that hope in man ("čelovekonadejanie") is one of the thirteen sins which defile the First Commandment, "I am your God, you shall not have any other god beside me".[14]

3. LAEVSKIJ'S MORAL REFORM

The material stimuli for Laevskij's conversion in Chapter XVII are many: the zoologist's hatred for him and the prospect of the duel, the doctor's suspicion of his plan to leave Nadežda behind in the Caucasus, and Nadežda's betrayal. In addition, Laevskij is by nature an introspective person. This is established already in Chapter I, when he remarks that his thoughts keep him awake at night. But introspection, acknowledgment of one's weaknesses, and outside material stimuli are not enough to save him. It does, however, set the stage for the insight or wisdom which he receives through grace at the beginning of Chapter XVII.

When it grows dark on Friday, the same day Laevskij and fon Koren agree to duel on Saturday, Laevskij suddenly loses interest in card-playing and the people he always plays with. As if he "suddenly fell ill", he has the urge to go home, "lie motionless in bed, and prepare his thoughts for the coming night" (VII: 427). He is frightened by the idea that something unprecedented in his life will occur the next morning. And he is frightened by the approaching night. The desire to lie motionless and make ready his mind is an unconscious preparation for the divine grace he receives in the following scene:

At home in his study (beginning of Chapter XVII), his thoughts focus on Nadežda and himself. He has just witnessed Nadežda secretly meeting with the police officer Kirilin at Mjuridov's place, and he is stunned by the sight. He perceives himself and Nadežda as "dead" (VII: 435). Nothing matters, including the outcome of the duel. Death is on his mind. Then suddenly the window blows open.

> Suddenly the window opened with a bang. A violent wind burst into the room, and the papers fluttered from the table. Laevskij closed the windows and bent down

to pick up the papers. He was aware of something new in his body, a sort of awkwardness he had not felt before, and his movements were strange to him. He moved timidly, jerking with his elbows and shrugging his shoulders; [. . .] His body had lost its suppleness.[15]

This strong wind clearly implies the Holy Spirit, as when, in The Acts of the Apostles (2: 2), that Spirit descends in the room of the disciples like a strong wind: "Suddenly a sound like the blowing of a violent wind came from the heaven and filled the whole house . . ."[16] This descent makes a loud noise, translated in 'The Duel' by the slamming of the window. The suddenness of the wind's descent in the biblical account is repeated in 'The Duel' and in both instances it is a "violent wind" ("sil'nyj veter"). The Holy Spirit, in the Old and New Testaments, bestows inspiration, power, and wisdom on all the prophets, Jesus, and the disciples. In 'The Duel', Laevskij is suddenly graced with wisdom. His physical change, that is, jerky, awkward movements and loss of suppleness, is a sudden onslaught of old age, or a metaphor for the mental maturity or wisdom received through the Holy Spirit. This wisdom is the "something new in his body". This wisdom is the essence of his reform or new life. His sudden maturation is noticed the following morning by the deacon: "'Strange,' thought the deacon, not recognizing Laevskij's walk. 'It's as if he's an old man'" (VII: 443). Nadežda also comments on Laevskij's "strange walk" (VII: 450). Literally overnight, Laevskij changes from a "defenseless child", as Samojlenko describes him in Chapter I, to "an old man", as the deacon perceives him in Chapter XVIII. Grace, according to Russian Orthodoxy, however, does not infringe upon man's free will. One must be willing to receive God's grace. This is an important point, for it implies that Laevskij the superfluous man is not all bad nor his situation hopeless, as fon Koren contends. From the start, there is the will in him to be virtuous, and he does recognize his weaknesses, feel pity for Nadežda, and, most importantly, he desires to amend his life. But he is weak. He becomes spiritually strong, however, through the third term of the new covenant foretold by the prophets: through the interiorization of religion, or God's grace, which gives spiritual knowledge or truth, thus strengthening one's faith.

The insight Laevskij receives through grace enables him to realize that he cannot renew his life through a new locale, through money, literature, or people. He comes to the conclusion that he must find salvation within himself, and if he does not find it there, then he must die (VII: 438).

> One must seek salvation only within one's self, and if one does not find it, why waste time? One must kill oneself, and that is all. . . .
>
> (VII: 438)

Orthodox theology places great emphasis on the doctrine of the image of God, which, based on Genesis 1: 26, asserts that the image and likeness of God is in every man and woman. "The best icon of God is man," states the priest during the Russian Orthodox Liturgy.[17] Thus, to find God, one must look within oneself. The Orthodox hero, St. Anthony of Egypt states: "Know yourself . . . He who knows himself knows God."[18] Another authority, St. Isaac the Syrian declares: "If you are pure, heaven is within you; within yourself you will see the angels and the Lord of the angels."[19] St. Luke states: "The Kingdom of God is within you" (17: 21). Thus, Laevskij's resolution at the end of his spiritual catharsis is that if he cannot find goodness, implicitly the divine image, hidden under the "pile of lies" which characterize his past life, then there is no reason to live. More vividly, at the end of Chapter XVII, Laevskij deduces that "if there is no God", then Nadežda may as well die, because then she "has no reason to live" either (VII: 439). Laevskij's insight acquired through grace enables him to understand the extent and meaning of Nadežda's suffering and, therefore, to love her, and it enables him to pray and ask forgiveness. Because of this grace, Laevskij's hatred changes to love, his pride to humility. His understanding of love and hope is no longer secular but approaches the Christian ideal of these virtues. It is also suggested that his faith is no longer in man but beginning to turn to God. During this stormy Friday night, Laevskij feels anguish, despair and loathing towards himself for having only "destroyed, ruined, and lied . . ." throughout his life. He realizes he has destroyed Nadežda, causing her great suffering, epitomized by her unwilling submission to Kirilin. He understands that Kirilin and the shopkeeper's son, Ačmianov, have learned their ignoble philandering from him: they take advantage of Nadežda as Laevskij took advantage of her when he stripped her of her husband, friends, and native city (VII: 437). Nadežda can only reflect "like a mirror, his idleness, viciousness, and lies—and that was all she had to fill her weak, listless, pitiable life" (VII: 437). Laevskij realizes that Nadežda is his "victim" or "sacrifice" ("žertva"), and that he, in effect, has caused her "death". Under the old law of Moses, sacrifices or offerings are the most prominent aspect of worship. Animal sacrifices are offered to God for atonement and thanksgiving. All sacrifices are sprinkled with salt. In the New Testament, Jesus Christ is the sacrificial offering who dies on the Cross for the atonement of humanity's sins. In 'The Duel', Nadežda is the sacrifice offered for the atonement of Laevskij's sins. She is referred to as a sacrifice: "but she was his sacrifice" ("no ona byla ego žertvoj"; VII: 438) and, at the end of the picnic, she is subtly associated with salt: "Ona ponjala čto peresolila, vela sebja sliškom razvjazno" (VII: 392). As sacrifice, Nadežda metaphorically dies for Laevskij. He "fears her as if she were dead" (VII: 438), and when departing for the duel, Laevskij approaches Nadežda, who is wrapped in a blanket, lying motionless like "an Egyptian mummy" (VII: 439). As sacrifice and expiation for Laevskij's past life of vice, it is not surprising, therefore, that Nadežda is called "Hope". The Russian Catechism defines Hope as the trust in salvation as promised by God.[20] Thus, Nadežda is Laevskij's hope in new life.

On Friday night, Laevskij has the urge to pray and ask forgiveness. He wishes he could replace "lies with truth, idleness with hard work, boredom with happiness, and he would return chastity to those from whom he took it, and would find God and justice" (VII: 438). His desire to pray is first suggested by his urge to write to his mother. He jots down "Matuška!" and later calls out "Matuška!". This invocation suggests the calling out to the Mother of God, the Divine Intercessor and Mother of Humanity. But he keeps thinking only of his literal, unsympathetic mother, and therefore his thoughts move on to the storm, his childhood, and back to Nadežda. As Laevskij calls out to his mother, so does he call out to the storm. "'The storm,' whispered Laevskij; he had a longing to pray to someone or to something, if only the lightning or storm clouds. 'Dear storm!'" (VII: 436). This invocation parallels "Matuška!" at the head of his letter. And although praying to lightning or the storm appears like pagan worship, in, especially, Exodus, Psalms, and the Gospels, God is often associated with such forces of nature.

Laevskij's desire to pray is an expression of his hope in new life. The Russian Catechism states that "the means for attaining saving hope" are "first prayer; secondly the true doctrine of blessedness and its applications".[21] Not only does Laevskij pray for the first time in Chapter XVII, but as of Friday night he begins to live by the majority of the nine beatitudes or doctrines of blessedness. The first four beatitudes are:

> 1) Blessed are the poor in spirit, for theirs is the Kingdom of Heaven.
>
> 2) Blessed are those who mourn, for they will be comforted.
>
> 3) Blessed are the meek, for they will inherit the earth.
>
> 4) Blessed are those who thirst and hunger for truth, for they will be satisfied.[22]

The first beatitude blesses spiritual poverty or humility. Through recognition of his shortcomings, his pleas for forgiveness, and his effort to pray, Laevskij shows humility. During the duel, Laevskij demonstrates humility by offering fon Koren his forgiveness. Thus, Laevskij is also a peacemaker, the person blessed in the seventh beatitude: "Blessed are the peacemakers, for they will be called children of God." On the eve of the duel, Laevskij manifests sorrow and contrition of heart, a virtue blessed in the second beatitude. After his reform, he adopts "a quiet disposition of spirit", a requirement for the third beatitude which blesses meekness. His new humble disposition is especially obvious in Chapter XXI, which takes place three months after the duel. He speaks little and meekly invites fon Koren, Samojlenko, and the deacon into his home: "I humbly beseech you . . ." he says ("Pokornejše prošu"; VII: 452). He bows to fon Koren when the latter takes leave. At the end of Chapter XXI, Laevskij speaks of "the thirst for truth" ("žažda pravdy") and strongly implies that he himself searches for truth. Thus he embodies also the fourth beatitude, "Blessed are they who hunger and thirst for truth, they shall be fulfilled." "Who are they who hunger and search for truth?" asks the Catechism.

> They who love to do good, but do not count themselves righteous, nor rest on their own good works, but acknowledge themselves sinners and guilty before God; and who, by the wish and prayer of faith, hunger and thirst after the justification of grace through Jesus Christ as after spiritual meat and drink.[23]

After his reform, Laevskij also manifests a new understanding of the third theological virtue, love. The last third of the Russian Catechism, the section on the virtue of love, discusses the Ten Commandments, the obligations required to fulfill them, and the sins which defile them. Love is manifested through "good works", which are distinguished from "bad works" by the Ten Commandments. The Commandments are divided into two kinds of love: 1) love for God, treated in the first four commandments, and 2) love for neighbor, treated in the last six. St. Paul says that the inclusive commandment is to love your neighbor, for this subsumes love for God. ("For the entire law is summed up in one command: 'Love your neighbor as yourself'"; Galatians 5: 14). The emphasis on neighborly love strongly distinguishes the old covenant from the new. Love for one's neighbor is a significant theme in **'The Duel'**, the meaning of which is debated in Chapters III, IV, and XVI, by the zoologist, doctor, and deacon. The last six commandments require love and honor for one's neighbor:

> 5) Honor your father and mother.
>
> 6) You shall not kill.
>
> 7) You shall not commit adultery.
>
> 8) You shall not steal.
>
> 9) You shall not bear false witness against your neighbor.
>
> 10) You shall not covet your neighbor's possessions.[24]

The Catechism paraphrases these laws: One is not to hurt one's neighbor's life, nor the purity of his morals, nor his property; one is not to hurt him by word, or to wish to hurt him. Before his reform, Laevskij shows little if any love for his neighbor. He commits adultery, thus contaminating the purity of Nadežda's morals, who was satisfied in her married life. He hurts his neighbor's life, in particular the lives of Nadežda and her husband. The latter grows sick and dies after Laevskij steals his wife. Laevskij even feels responsible for his death. In a rage, he slanders his neighbor, calling Samojlenko "a snooper" ("syščik"; VII: 425), which strongly offends him, and disparagingly refers to fon Koren as one of those "Germans born of Jews" ("nemeckie vychodcy iz židov"; VII: 425). He wishes to hurt his neighbor: he imagines trampling fon Koren underfoot. The sin of "eating the bread of idleness", of which Laevskij is obviously guilty before his reform, is one of the eight sins forbidden by the eighth commandment, "You shall not steal".

The love Laevskij acquires after his reform is similar to the ideal of Judeo-Christian love. He shows respect and honor for his neighbor, bears no malice towards his one-time archenemy fon Koren, who attempts to kill him. He lives in peaceful matrimony with Nadežda, and no longer "eats the bread of idleness". In addition, his love for Nadežda is associated with fear for her. This fear suggests a spiritual love. Although he wants to "fall at her feet and kiss her hands and feet", "he feared her as if she were dead" (VII: 438). One of the obligations in fulfilling the first commandment, "I am the Lord your God, you shall not have any other Gods", is "to fear God or stand in awe of him".[25]

At the end of Chapter XXI, it is also suggested that Laevskij's faith is redirected from man to God. Concerning scientific theories, fon Koren tells Laevskij: "No one knows the real truth." ("Nikto ne znaet nasto-jaščej pravdy"; VII: 453). Agreeing with the zoologist, Laevskij responds: "Yes, no one knows the real truth." He repeats this to himself later on as he sadly looks at the rough, dark sea (VII: 455). Laevskij's ambiguous statement for the first time shows lack of faith in man's knowledge. While before his reform he has faith in man's knowledge ("How true is Tolstoj!", "How truly Shakespeare noticed things!"), at the end of the story he shows a lack of faith in this knowledge. In addition, "No one knows the real truth" may be understood in a spiritual sense, referring to God. The Catechism states that the image of God consists of "righteousness and holiness of truth" ("pravda i prepodobie istiny"); thus, "pravda" and "istina". In the Old and New Testaments, God is both moral truth (pravda) and intellectual truth (istina). In **'The Duel'**, 'pravda' suggests both kinds of truth. While fon Koren's use of 'pravda' refers to man's acquired knowledge, Laevskij seems to pick up on this specified use of 'pravda' and attribute a more comprehensive, abstract, and spiritual meaning to 'truth'. Thus, to say "No one knows the truth", is to state a theological commonplace: one does not know or understand God.

Russian Orthodoxy, however, emphasizes the doctrine of 'deification' or the potential to be assimilated with God through virtue. The life of the Russian Orthodox Christian is to be a search for God. Through contemplation, prayer, and good deeds, one will "find God" and potentially unite with him, while remaining distinct. The full deification of the body will occur at the Last Judgment.[26] Laevskij's final words reveal faith as well as hope in the potential to find truth or God. He responds to his own statement "No one knows the real truth" with "Who knows? Maybe they [people] will find real truth . . ." ("I kto znaet? Byt' možet, doplyvut do nastojaščej pravdy . . ."; VII: 455).

In ecclesiastical writings, as in **'The Duel'**, the search for God or truth by man or woman is often represented as a boat sailing on a rough sea. Once one finds God, as the Church Father St. John Chrysostom writes, the waters become calm.[27] In the final scene of **'The Duel'**, as Laevskij, Samojlenko, and Pobedov accompany fon Koren to the boat, Laevskij compares mankind's life, which he perceives as a search for truth, to a boat on a rough sea. As a boat sails forward and backwards on restless water, so

> People, in search for truth take two steps forward and one step backwards, but the thirst for truth and a strong will chase one forward and forward. And who knows? Maybe they will sail to the real truth.
>
> (VII:455)

The storm at the end of the story, like the earlier wind in Chapter XVII, thus serves a major thematic and theological purpose.

4. FAITH VERSUS KNOWLEDGE

Laevskij's reformed attitude towards Faith, Hope, and Love is prefaced by a discussion between the zoologist and the priest on the relationship between love and faith and the distinction between faith and knowledge (Chapter XVI). The discussion occurs unexpectedly, on the eve of the duel, and rather unrealistically, thus implying a strong thematic purpose. Love is discussed in terms of love for neighbor, which subsumes love for God, as Saint Paul states (Galatians 5: 14). According to fon Koren, love is ultimately guided by reason, by "knowledge and evidence". The "moral law", organically inherent to all humanity, instinctively dictates love for neighbor. Common sense and rationality define love for neighbor as preservation of the strong by destruction of the weak. "The exact sciences", or "evidence and the logic of facts", distinguish the weak from the strong. The zoologist believes that this love reflects Christ's teaching, for he assumes that "Christ taught a love that is rational, intelligent, and practical" (VII: 432). That is, a love derived from reason and acquired knowledge, love born of the mind, not of the heart.

Obviously, this sharply opposes Orthodox teachings. The Catechism states that Love, i.e. good deeds shown to one's neighbor, is derived from Faith. Without Faith, there is no Love. "Faith without deeds is dead," states the deacon, quoting the Catechism and James 2: 20, 26, "but works without faith is still worse, mere waste of time and nothing more," he concludes (VII: 433). The deacon implies that fon Koren practices "works without faith". "Faith moves mountains," the deacon says, echoing Matthew 21: 21. And if fon Koren had faith, his work as zoologist would produce results (VII: 433). In other words, faith, not knowledge, makes things happen:

> Yes . . . here you are teaching all the time, fathoming the depths of the ocean, dividing the weak and the strong, writing books and challenging to duels, and everything remains as it is; but look, some feeble old man will mutter just one word through the holy spirit, or a new Mahomet with a sword will gallop from Arabia, and everything will be topsy turvy, and in Europe not one stone will be left standing on another.
>
> (VII: 433)

This last phrase, "not one stone will be left standing on another", is another use of Matthew (24: 2), in which Jesus speaks of the Second Coming when nothing will remain the same. Once again, faith is what makes things happen, not knowledge. The distinction between faith and knowledge is also discussed in the Catechism. God, "invisible and incomprehensible", cannot be understood by knowledge but only through faith. "Faith is the substance of things hoped for, the evidence of things not seen," states the Catechism, citing Hebrews 11: 1.[28]

This theological discussion in Chapter XVI serves two purposes. First, it reveals fon Koren's lack of faith, and second, strategically placed before Laevskij's conversion, it alerts the reader to the faith Laevskij acquires as a result of his spiritual rebirth. The discussion of love and faith, read with the Russian Catechism in mind, a tract which Russian Orthodox children of the nineteenth century learned by heart, implies that if one manifests love and hope, then, it goes without saying that one has faith: love is dependent on faith and faith is "the substance of things hoped for". And if one has faith, anything can happen: a superfluous Laevskij can even become a useful citizen overnight.

5. THE DUEL AS RELIGIOUS RITE

If Laevskij is spiritually resurrected on the stormy Friday night, he is bodily saved on Saturday morning during the duel. The priest saves his life by causing the zoologist to miss his aim. Therefore, after the duel, Laevskij is able to say that he feels as if he were returning from a funeral, "where they buried a wearisome, insufferable person" (VII: 450). Yes, he returns from his own funeral, but alive, in body and soul. He is

bodily resurrected during the duel. Before the duel begins, "for the first time in his life he sees the sunrise" (VII: 443). This sunrise symbolizes his renewed life. His natural and domestic surroundings, which previously generated scorn and frustration, now provoke "lively, child-like happiness" (VII: 450). Though his mind has acquired the wisdom of old age, his heart expresses child-like happiness and innocence. To be of such a spirit fulfills a Christian ideal. The New Testament teaches the wisdom of a child-like nature. Jesus says: "I tell you the truth, unless you change and become like little children, you will never enter the kingdom of heaven" (Matthew 18: 3).

The spiritual nature of the duel, that is the duel as a religious rite, is implied by its association with the picnic. Both take place in the same spot: in the cathedral of nature. If the picnic is an allegory of the eucharistic meal, the duel is also a memorial of the passion and redemption. Laevskij leaves the duel alive, but there are intimations of his death. When he arrives on the scene, he feels the exhaustion and weariness of a person who may soon die (VII: 443), and when he realizes fon Koren is aiming at him with the intention to kill, Laevskij thinks it's all over (VII: 447). An important but subtle detail are the 30 rubles which are to be paid to Dr. Ustimovič for the victim's dead body, that is for the sacrifice (VII: 444) of the duel. In the Gospels, Judas is paid 30 silver pieces for identifying Jesus, that is, 30 silver pieces for the body of Christ. In addition, these thirty rubles echo the thirty bottles of wine at the picnic and the 300 ruble loan. The duel, hence, is an allegorical celebration of the death and resurrection, as is the sacrament of the eucharist.

6. FON KOREN'S CHANGE OF HEART

Although fon Koren does not practice love for neighbor in the Christian sense, and values knowledge over faith, it is implied in the final chapter, that he has a spiritual change of heart, catalyzed by Laevskij's reform.

Although physically Laevskij and fon Koren are opposites: Laevskij is blond and frail, the zoologist dark and strong, they do have similar natures to the extent that both are in need of salvation. The deacon states this need when, as he walks to the site of the duel early Saturday morning, he assures himself that his "non-believing" friends, Laevskij and fon Koren, "will be saved" ("They are non-believers, but they are good people and will be saved . . . certainly they will be saved!"; VII: 440). The non-believers are also united through their association with evolutionism, a science which contradicts the beliefs of the Russian Church, as cited in a nineteenth century treatise on "teachings opposed to Christianity and Russian Orthodoxy".[29]

Fon Koren's views on the weak and strong of society, his definition of love, defined by destruction of the weak in order to protect society's strong, obviously affiliates him with Darwinism and distances him from the Church. Laevskij is united with fon Koren through his association with Spencerian philosophy. The Russian Church refutes Spencer's theory, derived from Darwinism, that morality also is a product of evolution, that one's moral nature is dependent on that of previous generations. This philosophical claim is opposed to Orthodoxy because it denies the likelihood of sudden moral change, inspired, for example, by divine grace.[30] Laevskij is initially attracted to Nadežda because she reads Spencer, and he brags of this detail. More significantly, however, his apathetic and hopeless attitude towards his own immoral and lazy character implies faith in the evolutionary theory of morality. According to fon Koren, Laevskij presents his own character as organically dependent on those of his "fathers of flesh and spirit", "Onegin, Pečorin, Byron's Cain, and Bazarov" (VII: 370). Fon Koren explains:

> We are to understand that . . . his [Laevskij's] dissoluteness, his lack of culture and moral purity, is a phenomenon of natural history, sanctified by inevitability, that the causes of it are worldwide, elemental.

> (VII: 370, 371)

Fon Koren inadvertently groups himself with Laevskij and those whom he represents, thus accentuating that he too, in biblical terms, is of the same vine in need of restoration, as is his weak neighbor. Paraphrasing Laevskij, he mocks, "it is not he [Laevskij] who is dissolute, false, disgusting, but we . . . 'we men of the eighties', 'we the spiritless, nervous offspring of the serf-owning class'" (VII: 370). And indeed, in Chapter XVIII the deacon points out that the two have similar upbringings: "if they had not been spoiled from childhood by the pleasant surroundings and the select circle of friends they lived in, [. . .]" they would not hate each other so strongly (VII: 442). They both are "of the serf-owning class". In addition, the deacon associates Laevskij with fon Koren by likening them to moles. As he surreptitiously watches the two prepare for the duel, the priest whispers "moles" ("kroty"; VII: 447), recalling how fon Koren in Chapter XI explains that when two moles meet underground, they instinctively fight each other until the weakest dies. In one of Isaiah's visions concerning everlasting peace for Jerusalem, the mole represents decadence and idolatry (Isaiah 2: 20). Isaiah groups the mole with the bat: two animals who live in darkness, a common metaphor for spiritual emptiness. Curiously enough, the zoologist also mentions the bat when speaking about the mole's great physical strength (VII: 407). Fon Koren is like the bat and mole: physically strong but spiritually weak, living in darkness.

Fon Koren's reform is suggested in Chapter XXI, mainly by his show of unprecedented humility, which is praised by the deacon. But first, fon Koren's reform is hinted at through the expedition which he plans to take in three years from the setting of the story. This expedition, significantly in the third year (as Laevskij's crisis occurs in the third year of his relationship with Nadežda), and mentioned at various points throughout the story, is first introduced during the picnic. After the picnic, Laevskij speaks to Samojlenko about this expedition, not as a trip to the Arctic, but as a trek across the desert. Laevskij calls fon Koren "the despot and czar of the desert" (VII: 397). In biblical terms, the desert, as in Exodus, is a symbol of conversion.

Fon Koren manifests considerable humility in his farewell visit to Laevskij before leaving the Black Sea resort-town. He is still too proud to admit that his theories of the strong and weak may be wrong, and he tells Laevskij that he does not stop by to excuse himself. Nevertheless, he admits that concerning Laevskij's allegedly "hopeless situation" he was wrong. His humility is further revealed by the subtle implication that he seeks Laevskij's forgiveness. The Russian verb 'proščat'sja/prostit'sja', 'to say good-bye', repeated four times in the context of fon Koren's farewell visit to Laevskij, is distinguished from the verb 'to forgive' only by the reflexive particle 'sja': 'proščat'/prostit''. As fon Koren rows off on the stormy sea, his last word is "Proščaj!" or "Good-bye". 'Proščaj', however, is also the imperfective command of the verb 'to forgive' ('proščat'). As Laevskij previously receives instantaneous forgiveness from Nadežda, so fon Koren obtains forgiveness from Laevskij, as symbolized in Laevskij's humble welcome and in the farewell handshakes of the two (VII: 453, 454). This forgiveness of sins evokes the first term of the new covenant foretold by the Old Testament prophets: God's spontaneous forgiveness of sins.

The deacon praises the zoologist for overcoming man's greatest vice, pride: "You conquered man's greatest enemy—pride" (VII: 453). Prior to this statement, the deacon paraphrases verse 14 of Psalm 79, exclaiming "My God, what people! It's true the right hand of God has planted this vine! Lord! Lord", and adds a verse from First Kings 18: 7 (1 Samuel 18: 7): "One man vanquishes thousands and another tens of thousands." In First Kings, these two vanquishers are Saul and David respectively. In **'The Duel'**, the two conquerors are fon Koren and Laevskij. While Laevskij has "conquered tens of thousands", that is vanquished many vices through his moral reform, fon Koren too has done great things by "conquering thousands", that is "pride". While Laevskij has accomplished more, fon Koren is also to be praised.

The ultimate victor, however, is neither of these two individuals, but Christian morality and the terms of the new covenant as presented by the Church; and the deacon embodies the teachings of the Church. The deacon's name, Pobedov, is derived from the word 'conquest' or 'pobeda'. The fisher-of-men, Pobedov, who spends his days catching bull-heads, is the ultimate victor of souls.

One may infer still more from the reference to First Kings. Through this allusion, Laevskij is very loosely paralleled with King David. In Christian doctrine, David is a prefiguration of Christ, which insinuates a parallel between Laevskij and Christ. As Christ is the sacrifice for humanity, so Laevskij is the sacrifice for "the men of the eighties", "the serf-owning class", the progeny of "Onegin, Pečorin, Byron's Cain, and Bazarov", and for all the 'Laevskijs' whom Ivan Andreič represents. Laevskij dies and is reborn for their sake. In Chapter XVII and during the duel, there are numerous intimations of death and rebirth. Laevskij as sacrifice is subtly suggested by the facts that he is referred to as "the sacrifice of the times" ("žertva vremeni"; VII: 374), and prior to his reform, Nadežda looks at Laevskij "as she would look at an icon" (VII: 415). But most importantly, his moral reform occurs on Friday night. This day, and the anguish and torment which Laevskij endures, evoke the Passion of Christ.

It is crucial to note, however, that in this story carefully chronicled by the days of the week, the duel takes place on Saturday, not Sunday, the day of the Resurrection. This detracts from the parallel between Christ and Laevskij. Thus, similar to David, Laevskij is a foreshadowing of Christ. His spiritual and physical rebirth is more reminiscent of the release of those in Hell on Holy Saturday, or the raising from the dead of Lazarus, celebrated on the Saturday before Holy Week. The Harrowing of Hell and Lazarus Saturday are signs of things to come. So is Laevskij's rebirth. It is a sign of the times. A sign of the times in Russia. The agitated sea in the last scene also suggests times yet to come. The time of the new covenant, initiated by the Resurrection, has not yet arrived; for as St. John Chrysostom writes, with Christ there is "peaceful sailing" on the sea of life. The sea is restless in the centuries before Christ as it is restless at the end of **'The Duel'**. As the prophets at the close of the sixth century B.C. foretell of ruin and new life to come, so Čechov, at the end of the nineteenth century, prophesies future times in Russia of passion and redemption, when "not one stone will be left on another".

Notes

1. Thomas Winner, *Chekhov and his Prose*. New York 1966, 103.

2. A. M. Skabičevskij, 'Duèl'-Žena'. *Novosti i Birževaja gazeta*, 41, Febr. 13, 1892.

   K. Medvedskij, 'Žertva bezvremen'ja'. *Russkij vestnik*, 7, 1896, 242.

3. Carolina de Maegd-Soëp, *Chekhov and Women*. Columbus, Ohio 1987, 307.

4. Ronald Hingley, *A New Life of Anton Chekhov*. New York 1976, 152.

5. All citations refer to Vol. VII of A. P. Čechov, *Polnoe sobranie sočinenij i pisem v tridcati tomach*. Moskva 1974-1982.

6. This symbolism is derived in part from the Greek word for fish, 'ichthys', which is the acronym of Jesus (i) Christ (ch), God's (th), Son (y), Savior (s).

7. The 'panagija' is the second of five loaves consecrated during the first part of the Liturgy ('Proskomidija'). It is blessed after the first loaf or lamb ('agnec'), which represents Christ. Reference to the bread honoring Mary foreshadows the eucharist or the covenant of salvation.

8. Psalm 79: 15-16. Russian:

   > Боже сил! обратисъ же призри с неба и воззри, и посети виноград сей; Охрани то, что насадила десница Твоя, и отрасли, которые Ты укрепил Себе.

   Church Slavonic:

   > Боже сил! Убратисе убо, и призри с небесе и вижд, и посети виноград сей: И соверши и, егоже насади десница твое, и на сына человеческаго, егоже укрепил еси себе.

9. Psalm 79: 9, 10. Russian:

   > Из Египта перенес Ты виноградную лозу, выгнал народы, и посадил ее. Очистил для нее место, и утвердил корни ее, и она наполнила землю.

   Church Slavonic:

   > Виноград из Египта пренесл еси: изгнал еси языки, и насадил еси и. Путесотворил еси пред ним, и насадил еси корение его, и исполни землю.

10. Psalm 79: 14. Russian: "Lesnoj vepr' podryvaet ee, i polevoj zver' ob''edaet ee." Church Slavonic: "Uzoba i vepr u dubravy, i uedinenyj divyj poede i."

11. Psalm 79: 4, 8, 20. Russian: "Bože sil! Vosstanovi nas; da vossijaet lice Tvoe, i spasemsja!" Church Slavonic: "Bože sil naverni nas i pokaži lice tvoe, i budemmo spaseni."

12. Konstantin Nikol'skij, *Ustav bogosluženija pravoslavnoj cerkvi*. Sankt-Peterburg 1900, 378.

13. Filaret, Metropolitan of Moscow, *Prostrannyj christianskij katichizis*. Moskva 1909, 23.

14. *Katichizis, ibid.*, 87.

15. Окно вдруг отворилосъ и хлопнуло, в комнату ворвался силъный ветер, и бумаги полетели со стола. Лаевский

запер окно и нагнулся, чтобы собрать с полу бумаги. Он чувствовал в своем теле что-то новое, какую-то неловкость которой раньше не было, и не узнавал своих движений; ходил он несмело, тыча в сторону локтями и подергивая плечами . . . Тело его потеряло гибкость.

('Дуэль'; VII: 435)

16. Деяние святых апостолов 2: 2: "И внезапно сделался шум с неба, как-бы от несущегося сильного ветра, и наполнил весь дом где они находились."

17. Paul Evdokimov, *L'Orthodoxie.* Paris 1959, 218.

18. Timothy Ware, *The Orthodox Church.* New York 1986, 226.

19. Evdokimov, *ibid.,* 88.

20. *Katichizis, ibid.,* 67.

21. *Katichizis, ibid.,* 67.

22. Блаженство Божие: 1) Блажени нищии духом, яко тех есть Царствие небесное. 2) Блажени плачущии, яко тии утешатся. 3) Блажени кротцыи, яко тии наследят землю. 4) Блажени алчущии и жаждущии правды, яко тии насытятся. 5) Блажени милостывии, яко тии помиловани будут. 6) Блажени чисти сердцем, яко тии Бога узрят. 7) Блажени миротворцы, яко тии сынове Божии нарекутся. 8) Блажени изгнани правды ради, яко тех есть Царствие небесное. 9) Блажени есте, егда поносят вам, и ижденут, и рекут всяк зол глагол, на вы лжуще Мене ради. Радуйтеся и веселитеся, яко мзда ваша многа на небесах.

23. *Katichizis, ibid.,* 77.

24. Десять заповедей Закона Божия: 1) Аз есмь Господ Бог твой: да не будут тебе Бози иний, азве Мене. 2) Не сотвори себе кумира, и всякаго подобия, елика на небеси горе, и елика на земли низу, и елика в водах под землею: да не поклонишися им, ни послужиши им. 3) Не восмеши имене Господа Бога твоего всуе. 4) Помни день субботный, еже святити его: шесть дней делай, и сотвориши (в них) вся дела твоя, в день же седмый суббота, Господу Богу твоему. 5) Чти отца твоего и матерь твою, да благо ти будет, и да долголетен будеши на земли. 6) Не убий. 7) Не прелюбы сотвори. 8) Не укради. 9) Не послушествуй на друга твоего свидетельства ложна. 10) Не пожелай жены искренняго твоего, не пожелай дому ближняго твоего, ни

села его, ни раба его, ни рабыни его, ни вола его, ни осла его, ни всякого скота его, ни всего, елика симъ ближняго твоего.

25. *Katichizis, ibid.,* 86.

26. Ware, *ibid.,* 236, 237.

27. Ioann Zlatoust, *Polnoe sobranie tvorenij svjatogo otca Ioanna Zlatoustogo,* IV. Sankt-Peterburg 1898, 903-905.

28. *Katichizis, ibid.,* 3.

29. Эволюоционизм. Преимущественно философския и некоторыя религиозныя и другия противныя христианству и православию учения, надравления и мнения.

(S. V. Bulgakov, *Nastol'naja kniga dlja svjaščenno-cerkovno-služitelej. Otdel istoriko-statističeskij.* Char'kov 1900, 209-211)

30. Bulgakov, *ibid.,* 211.

George S. Pahomov (essay date 15 February 1994)

SOURCE: Pahomov, George S. "Essential Perception: Čechov and Modern Art." *Russian Literature* 35, no. 2 (15 February 1994): 195-202.

[*In the following essay, Pahomov contends that Chekhov's minimalist narrative style "anticipates the intent of Russian Formalism and of modern art to defamiliarize the world around us and to see once more with an essential perception."*]

The history of literary criticism is marked by the borrowing of concepts from other disciplines. Thus, such terms as the baroque, neo-classicism, impressionism, and futurism have enriched literary discourse. It is the intention of this paper to adapt the recently coined term 'minimal art' (or minimalism) in a similar fashion and apply it to the case of Čechov. Čechov's description of landscape, character, or setting frequently focuses on a telling feature which remains vivid in the reader's memory while all else fades. Scenes are thus reduced to a single object's visual impact. The power of such a singular impression is also the goal of minimal art. Its primal colors, sharp lines, geometric patterns and geometric solids impress the viewer with an all-eliminating simplicity. The minimal is at once supremely meaningful. Such reduction to 'essential' irreducible form and to 'pure' experience is a central method of phenomenology as set forth by Husserl and his school. Further analysis of prose, art and philosophy suggests the existence of similarities at their very root.

Čechov's valuing of the effectiveness of such a reduced style has been noted. Maurice Valency quotes Čechov's letter:

> Do not give too much space to an overinsistent image . . . To emphasize the poverty of a beggar woman it is not necessary to speak of her miserable appearance, it is enough to remark in passing that she wore an old rusty cloak. . . .
>
> (Valency 1966: 61)

Valency himself feels that Čechov "[. . .] was chiefly concerned with the surface, and [. . .] made no obvious inference as to what, if anything, lay beneath it" (1966: 230). And it is specifically a concern "with the surface" or form, that marks the sphere of the psychology of perception. In a conversation with Bunin, Čechov is recorded as saying:

> It is very difficult to describe the sea. Do you know the description I read of it in the copybook of a schoolboy not long ago? "The sea was huge." *Only that.* I think it is beautiful.
>
> (Simmons 1962: 462; emphasis added)

Čechov's discovery of the salient feature is evident in this statement to Gor'kij:

> [. . .] it is not easily understood, and it is difficult for the mind if I write: "A tall, narrow-chested, middle-sized man, with a red beard, sat on the green grass trampled by passersby, sat silently, looking around him timidly and fearfully." This is not immediately grasped by the mind, whereas good writing should be grasped at once, in a second.
>
> (Simmons 1962: 464)

Čechov practiced what he preached, and his prose is marked by what interior decorators call 'accent pieces' which singularly 'fix' the scene in the mind of the reader. These are seemingly innocuous details which add nothing to characterization, promoting neither narrative nor advancing the plot. Yet the reader remembers Anna Sergeevna only when reminded that she is the woman with the white Pomeranian (**'Lady with the Dog'**). The dog and its whiteness that trails the mistress is reiterated five times in the first two pages of the story until it becomes an internalized visual tag. Even Gurov, her lover, much later thinks of Anna as "the lady with the dog", with the phrase purposely set in quotation marks by the narrator. (In the language of linguistics the phrase is composed of 'the lady', the 'theme', the unmarked, known, neutral member of the utterance; and the 'rheme', 'with the dog', the marked, charged, new member of the utterance—the tag.) The story is replete with other examples.

Hoping to meet Anna, Gurov goes to her town and takes a hotel room in which the floor is covered with a field-gray felt "and the desk has an inkwell, gray with dust, with a rider on horseback holding up a hat in his hand with his *head broken off*" (**'Dama s sobačkoj'**; VIII, 1956: 404; emphasis added). Gurov finds Anna's house. "Immediately opposite it there stretched a fence, gray, long, *with nails*" (404; emphasis added). When Gurov first meets Anna, the narrator provides a lengthy scene of the theater-going provincial gentry and ends with the governor's box in which "in front sat the governor's daughter in a feather boa with the governor meekly hiding behind a 'portiere', only *his hands* showing" (406; emphasis added). When Anna starts coming to Moscow, each time that she comes "she takes a room at the 'Slav-janskij bazar' and immediately sends to Gurov a man in a *red cap*" (408). (I have been rendering the original Russian word order, in which the telling, marked information comes at the end of the sentence.)

Other stories reveal the same device. In **'Peasants'** Nikolaj Čikil'deev, a waiter in the restaurant of the 'Slav-janskij bazar' Hotel falls ill. His legs go numb so that his gait changes and "once while negotiating a corridor he trips and falls along with the tray on which there was a plate of *ham and peas*" (**'Mužiki'**; VIII, 1956: 202). He is forced to quit his job. The story **'In the Ravine'** has the following:

> [. . .] after the funeral [of Lipa's child] the guests and priests ate a great deal and with such greed as though they had not eaten for a long time. Lipa waited at table, and the priest, pointing with his fork on which lay a *pickled mushroom,* told her: "Don't mourn for the child. For theirs is the kingdom of heaven."
>
> (**'V ovrage'**; VIII, 1956: 451; emphasis added)

The unexpectedness of the images, their non-sequitur quality, break all continuities and make us confront them as pure phenomena on the brink of absurdity stripped of all presuppositions and a priori systems.

The concreteness of these details indicates Čechov's underscoring of the importance of what is given in (visual) experience—a primary stance of the phenomenologist. A "room with dirty wallpaper" in **'Kaštanka'** (the story of a lost dog), the lady "with the dog", the waiter with a plate of "ham and peas", the narrator's brother always talking of or eating gooseberries in **'Gooseberries',** the house "with the raised porch" (in **'Dom s mezoninom'**) are all examples of the visual tag, and suggest that frequently the salient point of any experience is not a cosmology but a smell, or an image. Sensory memory, Čechov seems to say, is foremost. "You ask what is life? That is just the same as asking: What is a carrot? A carrot is a carrot, and nothing more is known about it" (Čechov in a letter to Ol'ga Knipper, 20 April 1904). The orangeness of the carrot, the whiteness of the Pomeranian. In the observation of an object, we apprehend among other things its color as a property, so that each time the dog is mentioned we see its whiteness. White as a color can be rigorously defined: white is white is white all the time to all observers (a particular wavelength). Čechov has brought the reader to an irreducible minimal unit, which exists in the only given reality—an empirical reality.

> The Minimal artist attempts to state point-blank in visual form what [modern] philosophies and [modern] writers have been saying verbally—phenomenology is the basis of experience; to deal with experience directly, we must stop misusing language to construct ambiguous meanings.
>
> (Leepa 1968: 205)

Leepa, writing some sixty years after Čechov, echoes him, as does the well-known artist Frank Stella in the following:

> I always get into arguments with people who want to retain the old values in painting . . . If you pin them down, they always end up asserting that there is something there besides the paint on the canvas. My painting is based on the fact that only what can be *seen* there *is* there [. . .] All I want anyone to get out of my paintings, and all I ever get out of them, is the fact that you can see the whole idea without any confusion . . . What you see is what you see.
>
> (Stella 1968: 157-158)

The minimalist view sees man as placed in a world in which there is no cosmology, no history, no secrets to be revealed, no linked discourse, no story to be told—only occurrences, the purely phenomenological. It is my belief that Čechov anticipated such a world and that this can be progressively demonstrated in his work. Čechov gradually removed encrustation from literature: fewer metaphors, less metonymy, less figuration, in favor of the work without signification, without message; the intentionality and the privileging of the author/sender is reduced, there is no context, only text and the apprehension of the reader/receiver. The code is that there is no code, which serves as a negative (-) code that denies the loaded-up literary inheritance of Russia: the politics of Černyševskij, Michajlovskij, Gleb Uspenskij; the refined emotionalism of Nadson, Mej and Apuchtin; the tendentiousness of Tolstoj and Dostoevskij. To all this encumbrance, this baggage of ideology and sensibility Čechov says "no". The questions "What does it mean?", "What am I supposed to feel?" (standard questions begging for a canon) remain intentionally unanswered in Čechov and are left to the perceiver. Čechov thus reinvigorates and legitimates *individual* perception. (And that may be a secret message: remove yourself from the herd, trust yourself, you are a free person, not a slave. Historically, if Čechov had a political stance, this was it. This movement through minimalism to 'freedom' may parallel the transmutation of phenomenology from Husserl through Heidegger to the existentialism of Sartre.)

The seeds of minimalism are already present in Čechov's widely-recognized impressionism, for in impressionism "it is no longer the object or the event in itself that is of interest, but its *appearance* to the observer" (Clarke 1977: 124; emphasis added). Moving the process of perception along, Joseph L. Conrad writes that "the natural setting in the later stories is generally seen through the prism of the hero's perception, e.g., in **'The Bishop'** (1902) and **'The Betrothed'** (1903). Thus refracted, nature becomes internalized . . ." (Conrad 1977: 95).

It may be seen that Čechov worked in the manner of the minimalists who make "works which are internal 'gestalts', [. . .] which demand to be seen all at once, as a single image" (Brook 1975: 23). So essential a perceptual core is achieved that it cannot be further resolved into available meanings. While seemingly a reductive working it is not "a process of diminution, but of intentional distillation aimed at more potent results" (Goossen 1968: 172). If the above word "distillation" is replaced with the philosopher's 'essentialization', the phrase becomes a virtual description of the central step in phenomenology, at least of Husserl's phenomenology in which 'transcendental reduction' leads to the apprehension of 'pure essence' (eidos) and which is an inquiry into the irreducible formal elements of any experience through a speculative effort to determine what is, wholly on the basis of the examination and analysis of what appears. As Čechov internalizes the object within the perceiver, he unknowingly (?) attacks the classic 'phenomenon-noumenon' dichotomy in a way similar to that of phenomenology, as it has the subject intentionally 'grasp' the object in a 'living dialogue' through a kind of subjectivist fusion: what appears must be and what is must appear. In this dialectic "the perceived world is the always presupposed foundation of all rationality, all value and all existence" (Merleau-Ponty 1964: 13).

Thus, all a priori suppositions, all tacit metaphysical premises are "stripped away" so that a radical suspension of all beliefs takes place and the perceiving self achieves unadulterated cognition, a kind of pure seeing. This is central because "direct observation is the primary concern of phenomenology; and [. . .] is held to be prior to all theory. Thus Husserl spoke of the finality of 'seeing'. That which is seen cannot be explained away, and is the final standard in all truly philosophical thought" (Farber 1966: 48).

Čechov seems to have been intuitively close to such sensibility. This is evident when he writes "I feel I'd like them [nature descriptions] to be shorter, more compact, only about two or three lines long" (Heim 1973: 333). Later he writes: "Color and expressivity in nature descriptions are achieved through simplicity alone, through simple phrases like 'the sun set', 'it grew dark', 'it began to rain', etc . . ." (Heim 1973: 338).

At times the radical stripping away to pure cognition is used at peak moments. In **'Poprygun'ja'** Ol'ga confronts her lover, the painter Rjabovskij, in an action that should precipitate a resolution of their affair. They have spent a summer on the Volga sharing a cottage in which a peasant woman cooks for them. In response to Ol'ga, Rjabovskij moves her aside:

> Он отстранил ее руками и отошел, и ей показалось, что лицо его выражало отвращение и досаду. В это время баба осторожно несла ему в обеих руках тарелку со щами, и Ольга Ивановна видела как она обмочила во щах свои большие пальцы.

(**'Poprygun'ja'**; VII, 1956: 64-65)

He begins to eat.

Minimalism. Ol'ga expects intense meaning at this culminating point of her affair with Rjabovskij. It is to be a turning point in her life but she gets only absurdity. Or rather, it is neither absurdity nor meaningfulness, it is just two thumbs in a bowl of cabbage soup. Further in the same story, as Ol'ga Ivanovna's husband, Dymov, lies dying of typhoid, she asks Korostelev, a doctor friend of her husband's, whether he had sent for the famous specialist Schreck. The response is classic minimalist understatement. "È, da čto Šrek! V suščnosti, ničego Šrek. On Šrek, ja Korostelev—i bol'še ničego" (**'Poprygun'ja'**; VII, 1956: 74). Later, while half-asleep, Ol'ga thinks of her dying husband and the famous specialist: "'Nature morte', port . . .—dumala ona, opjat' vpadaja v zabyt'e,—sport . . . kurort . . . A kak Šrek? Šrek, grek, vrek . . . krek" (**'Poprygun'ja'**; VII, 1956: 75).

In painting and in the visual arts the minimalist finds the essence of his art in a holistic irreducible structure, stripped of all reference. This may be pure geometric shape or pure color. In the above example a man's name, stripped of all reference, is reduced to an essential holistic structure that is pure sound. "Šrek, grek, vrek . . . krek". It is sound without nuance, connotation, without attributable value. If it were music it would be pure tone, without overtones, without the continuum of melody.

In another story, **'Gooseberries'** (**'Kryžovnik'**), the hero fantasizes about his dream estate:

> И рисовалисъ у него в голове дорожки в саду, цветы, фрукты, скворешни, караси в прудах . . . Эти воображаемые картины были различны, [. . .] но почему-то в каждой из них непременно был крыжовник. Ни одной усадьбы, ни одного поэтического угла он не мог себе представитъ без того, чтобы там не было крыжовника.

(**'Kryžovnik'**; VIII, 1956: 302)

The gooseberries are the distilled essence of the dream, the irreducible core. Through a process of elimination there is reduction to a holistic minimum. At these moments Čechov is not concerned with attributing value to things. He does not analyze experience, he just presents it. Minimalism tends toward presentation, not interpretation.

When presented with something, one perceives but may not understand because things can be named and described but ultimately never defined or explained. In the nineteenth century, Mendeleev's periodic table demonstrated that the universe was made up of irreducible components. These elemental components could not be ultimately defined, one could only name them: hydrogen was hydrogen, cobalt was cobalt. The minimalist sensibility brought this inference into art: a carrot is a carrot, is a carrot. The world was neither meaningful nor absurd. It simply was.

When the minimalist views art as an object he/she views it in opposition to the process of signification. Meaning flows from the presence of the work of art, not from its capacity to signify absent events or values. Čechov's "ham and peas", a sudden, concrete specific detail in a narrative stream to which it is unrelated and unconnected stops the gaze of the perceiver, distances him, isolates him, depriving him of the process of signification. (In the language of phenomenology and perception psychology this event is referred to as 'eidetic prehension', the grasping of the image: the arresting of the viewer's gaze and the singular, instantaneous 'internalization' of the image.) In the words of the art critic Mel Bochner:

> [If] we bracket out all questions that, due to the nature of language, are indiscussable (such as why did this or that come to exist, or what does it mean) it will then be possible to say that the entire being of an object, in this case an art object, is in its appearance. Things being whatever it is they happen to be, all we can know about them is derived directly from how they appear.

(Bochner 1968: 92-93)

One cannot help but feel that if the mature Čechov could have read formulations such as the above, he would have found them immediately meaningful and congenial. And it seems clear that in his attempt to surprise us into a radical mode of seeing Čechov anticipates the intent of Russian Formalism and of modern art to defamiliarize the world around us and to see once more with an essential perception.

Bibliography

Bochner, M. 1968. 'Serial Art, Systems, Solipsism'. *Minimal Art: A Critical Anthology* (Ed. G. Battcock). New York.

Brook, D. 1975. 'Flight From the Object'. *Concerning Contemporary Art* (Ed. B. Smith). Oxford.

Čechov, A. P. 1954-1956. *Sobranie sočinenij v dvenadcati tomach*. Moskva.

Clarke, C. C. 1977. 'Aspects of Impressionism in Chekhov's Prose'. *Chekhov's Art of Writing: A Collection of Critical Essays* (Eds. P. Debreczeny and T. Eekman). Columbus, Ohio.

Conrad, J. L. 1977. 'Anton Chekhov's Literary Landscapes'. *Chekhov's Art of Writing: A Collection of Critical Essays* (Eds. P. Debreczeny and T. Eekman). Columbus, Ohio.

Farber, M. 1966. *The Aims of Phenomenology: The Motives, Methods, and Impact of Husserl's Thought*. New York.

Goossen, E. C. 1968. 'Two Exhibitions'. *Minimal Art: A Critical Anthology* (Ed. G. Battcock). New York.

Heim, M. H., Karlinsky, S. (Eds.) 1973. *Anton Chekhov's Life and Thought: Selected Letters and Commentary*. Berkeley.

Leepa, A. 1968. 'Minimal Art and Primary Meanings'. *Minimal Art: A Critical Anthology* (Ed. G. Battcock). New York.

Merleau-Ponty, M. 1964. *The Primacy of Perception and Other Essays*. Evanston.

Simmons, E. J. 1962. *Chekhov: A Biography*. Boston.

Stella, F. 1968. 'Interview in *Art News*'. *Minimal Art: A Critical Anthology* (Ed. G. Battcock). New York.

Valency, M. 1966. *The Breaking String: The Plays of Anton Chekhov*. New York.

Carol A. Flath (essay date 15 November 1998)

SOURCE: Flath, Carol A. "Delineating the Territory of Čechov's 'A Woman's Kingdom.'"[1] *Russian Literature* 44, no. 4 (15 November 1998): 389-408.

[*In the following essay, Flath views "A Woman's Kingdom" as exemplifying Chekhov's tendency to occupy a philosophical and artistic "middle ground" in his short fiction.*]

For Čechov, a true artist must only pose, not solve, problems ("ne belletristy dolžny rešat' takie voprosy, kak bog, pessimizm, i t. d."; Pis'ma II, 289). Čechov's refusal to embed political, social or religious messages into his works, to offer answers to eternal questions (eternal, because unanswerable), is a function of his brutal honesty as an artist. For, as someone who makes a living manipulating language and making up stories, Čechov knows that words can lie; the truth we seek to delineate with words must be found beyond them.

Čechov's awareness and quiet acceptance of this paradox is his trademark as a writer, and it marks a shift away from the great didactic tradition of nineteenth-century Russian realism (see Popkin 1994: 218). It is indeed a significant moment in Russian literary history. For Čechov, confronted with the extremism that had characterized political, cultural, and religious life in Russia, took the radical step of occupying a middle ground, of not committing himself to either extreme. As he writes in his notebooks:

> Между "есть бог" и "нет бога" лежит целое громадное поле, которое проходит с большим трудом истинный мудрец. Русский [же] человек знает какую-либо одну из этих крайностей, середина же между ними не интересует его; и потому обыкновенно он не знает ничего или очень мало.
>
> (1974-1982, XXVII: 224)
>
> (Between "There is a God" and "There is no God" lies a whole huge field, which a true wise man crosses with great difficulty. The Russian knows only one of these two extremes; the middle ground between them does not interest him. This is why as a rule he knows nothing or very little.)

Čechov makes the conscious decision to turn against tradition, to enter the middle ground and make it the subject of his art. On the philosophical level, this middle ground represents a truth that cannot be expressed in language; on the thematic level, it can be seen as the wide variety of middle- and lower-class people who populate his stories; on the level of plot, it is Čechov's avoidance of improbable or extreme subjects. I would like to identify this territory as the one that is the subject of Svetlana Boym's *Common Places*. According to Boym, in the realm of everyday life, "byt", we find a truth that transcends and renders obsolete Lotman and Uspenskij's tenacious binary model for Russian culture (1994: 29-30). Boym's somewhat impressionistic discussion of manifestations of "pošlost'" in Čechov's stories does not do justice to the enormous potential of her model for a discussion of his art. For what might seem to be a retreat into passivity is rather a brave step forward into an acceptance of uncertainty as an inevitable condition of human life; what Čechov does is use language in this middle ground metaphorically, to *represent*, without *telling*, the truth. Čechov refuses to anchor his artistic truth in any specific model of the world; for him there is no "last word" (on the level of plots we might even take this literally, for he is famous for the "zero ending"). By his example, Čechov challenges a simplistic view of the world that is implied by the operation of traditional literary plots.

Čechov's truth is not, and cannot be, spoken; we should therefore study the how, rather than the what, of what he says. In his rich and complex mature stories, meaning is dependent on context and character and there are no absolutes. The words themselves are less important than what they reveal about the context in which they are spoken. This is perhaps best expressed by Svetlana Evdokimova:

Focusing on speech, Čechov gradually dispenses with plot and produces a new type of conflict: not so much the conflict between individual wills, but rather the clash of various cultural discourses. The alleged un-eventfulness of many of Čechov's short stories and dramas is motivated, in part at least, by Čechov's wish to expose the rhetorical nature of man's mentality and behavior.

(1994: 165)

Only by exploring the tension among the various rhetorics in a Čechov story can we discover its true meaning. The truth is located in the middle territory between the words.

In **'A Woman's Kingdom'** (**'Bab'e carstvo'**, 1894), Čechov demonstrates the falsity of a world defined by literary cliches and the dangers of giving in to the seductive action of literary plots. Stories, while providing their readers with relief from the cares and concerns of our everyday lives, at the same time have a powerful effect on the way we act. A naive acceptance of literature as a truthful model for the world can result in a denial of responsibility and an inability to act ethically.

Anna Akimovna Glagoleva, the protagonist of **'A Woman's Kingdom'**,—whose very name, from the Russian word for "verb", hints at the importance of her attitudes towards language—is a twenty-five year old unmarried woman of ordinary working-class origin, who has become wealthy by inheriting a factory from her uncle. It is Christmas eve, and Anna faces the yearly task of distributing charity to needy members of her community. To amuse herself, she decides to give the entire sum of 1500 rubles to a single individual, whom she chooses at random. When she goes to his house, she is disgusted by the squalor of his life—the sour smells, the pregnant wife and numerous small, dirty children, the man's evident drunkenness—and impulsively decides to give the family only a small amount after all. At the apartment she is struck by the cleanliness and modesty of the room of the absent lodger, a master worker in her own factory named Pimenov, whom she meets as she is about to leave.

Anna returns home, has a good sleep, and spends Christmas day receiving visitors. Towards evening she is joined for dinner by two men, Krylin, a senior civil servant, and the wealthy lawyer Lysevič. They eat a delicious meal, Krylin takes a nap, and Lysevič entertains Anna with a literary performance. On impulse Anna gives the lawyer the entire sum of money intended for charity and, after he leaves, spends the rest of the evening gossiping and playing cards in the kitchen in the company of servants, assorted relatives and hangers-on.

As Robert Louis Jackson shows in his study of the Christian symbolism of this story, whenever Anna is given the opportunity to make an ethical choice, she re-

jects it, thus renouncing her free will and turning herself over to the blind workings of fate. If we extend our analysis beyond the symbolic level explored by Jackson, we can see this renunciation as having consequences that reach to every level of human existence, extending from metaphysical abstractions to the most basic level of physical and sexual need. After all, in Čechov's work, every truth is anchored in the human body. As he says:

Мое святая святых—это человеческое тело, здоровъе, ум, талантъ, вдохновение, любовъ и абсолютнейшая свобода, свобода от силы и лжи.

(Letter to A. N. Pleščeev, Pis'ma III, 11)

(My holy of holies is the human body, health, intelligence, talent, inspiration, love and absolute freedom—freedom from force and falsehood. [. . .])

It is imperative that our reading should recognize the way all these "holy of holies" are inseparably linked in Čechov's poetics.[2]

The extraordinarily rich and complex text illustrates the fragmentation of consciousness and moral paralysis that can result from giving in to the seductive action of literary fictions. Our protagonist is rendered incapable of living a wholly integrated life in which spiritual, moral, social and physical demands are at harmony with each other. By thus metaphorizing the action of literature within this story, Čechov renders problematical the very nature and function of narrative fiction itself.[3]

We will focus on two scenes of the story. In the first of these, parody directs our attention to the content and form—the "what"—of the literary model; the second "mimes" a literary performance, thus exposing the "how" of a literary exchange—the way texts affect their readers.

Literary parody is a major building block in the first chapter of **'A Woman's Kingdom'**, as we watch Anna Akimovna attempt to act out a stock plot—one that we associate with melodramatic fiction or drama. To free herself from the drudgery and boredom of meting out charity in small amounts, Anna decides to give all the money to a single person chosen at random from among the petitioners:

А то, пожалуй, выбрать одного из просителей, писавших эти письма, какого-нибудь несчастного, давно уже потерявшего надежду на лучшую жизнь, и отдать ему полторы тысячи. Бедняка ошеломятъ эти деньги, как громъ, и, быть может, первый разъ въ жизни онъ почувствуетъ себя счастливымъ. Эта мысль показаласъ Анне Акимовне оригинальной и забавной и развлекла ее.

(259)

(Or maybe she could choose one of the petitioners who had written these letters, some unfortunate man who'd long ago lost hope for a better life, and give him the whole fifteen hundred. The poor man would be thunderstruck by the money, and perhaps for the first time in his life he would see himself as happy. This thought struck Anna as original and amusing, and it entertained her.)

Anna has scripted herself a fantasy of rescue; her goal in choosing this dramatic course of action is as much to amuse herself—as one amuses oneself in reading literature—as it is to help someone in need. As we look closely at the scene that follows, we should be aware of the two levels of perception that are in play. The first is Anna's, as her fantasy clashes with harsh reality, complete with poverty, vice and bad smells. The second is our own, as we savor Čechov's offering, a rich literary parody, infused with his own characteristic humor and irony.[4]

Anna's mission of charity takes her straight into a setting from Dostoevskij, to the apartment of the impoverished civil servant Čalikov. She knows it well from her own childhood, and we know it well from books as a scene inherited by Dostoevskij from the Natural School:

> И во дворе, и около крайней двери, даже на лестнице был тот же противный запах, что и под воротами [. . .] узкая каменная лестница с высокими ступенями, грязная, прерываемая в каждом этаже площадкою; засаленный фонарь в пролете; смрад, на площадках около дверей корыта, горшки, лохмотья—все это было знакомо ей уже давным-давно.
>
> (263)

(The courtyard, and the outer door, even the stairway had that same disgusting smell as the gate [. . .] the narrow stone stairway with high steps and a landing at each story; the greasy lamp in the stairwell, the stench, the bins outside the doors, the pots, the rags—she knew all of it intimately, from long ago.)

The characters amount to a lampoon of Dostoevskij's downtrodden, but noble "insulted and injured" underclass:

> В углу за столом сидел спиной к двери какой-то мужчина в черном сюртуке, должно быть, сам Чаликов, и с ним пять девочек. Старшей, широколицей и худенькой, с гребенкой в волосах, было на вид лет пятнадцать, а младшей, пухленькой, с волосами как у ежа,—не больше трех. Все шестеро ели. Около печи, с ухватом в руке, стояла маленькая, очень худая, с желтым лицом женщина в юбке и белой кофточке, беременная.
>
> (263)

(At the table in the corner sat a man in a black frock coat with his back to the door, most likely Čalikov himself, and five little girls. The oldest, broad-faced and thin, with a comb in her hair, looked about fifteen, and the youngest, plump, with hair like a hedgehog's, not over three. All six of them were eating. Next to the oven, holding a pair of tongs, stood a small, very thin, yellow-faced woman wearing a skirt and white blouse. She was pregnant.)

The gestures of the drunken Čalikov resemble those of a character of a cheap melodrama. When he sees Anna, he flings his arms out in a gesture of slavish amazement and gratitude, calling her his benefactress and an angel, orders his children to their knees, tells his wife to "die, unfortunate one!" ("umiraj, nesčastnaja"; 264) to illustrate how ill she is, hints that his daughters may have to enter on lives of sin (in an implied reference to Dostoevskij's Sonja), etc.

As a fantasy, Anna's plot was amusing; faced with the drunken Čalikov and the smelly, dirty apartment, she is disgusted. There is no place for her fantasy in *this* reality—which, after all, was once her own—, and she snaps out of it, interrupting the man's hysterical lamentations about his wife's illness to tell him to give up the melodrama: "Govorite so mnoj, požalujsta, po-čelovečeski, [. . .] ja komedij ne ljublju!" (264). She makes a perfectly realistic, reasonable decision—to give the family a small amount of money for medicine, making efforts to ensure it will not be spent on drink. This return to realism takes her deep inside the apartment, beyond the outer rooms of the Čalikov family into the room of the lodger where she can write a letter of referral to a doctor for Čalikov's wife.

In 'A Woman's Kingdom'—which is constructed, as Jackson notes, like a four-act drama—the carefully set scenes comprise symbolic spaces that reflect the predicaments and desires of the characters. The lodger's room, which, as we will see, represents Anna's dream of domestic happiness, is presented in contrast not only to Čalikov's apartment, but also to her own large, empty house and her factory. When Pimenov returns home, the black soot on his face and his greasy clothes clash with the whiteness and cleanliness of the room and remind us of the factory, which we have seen through Anna's recollections. Before looking closely into his room, then, we should recall the factory, which we must view as the "man's kingdom" of this story:

> Высокие потолки с железными балками, множество громадных, быстро вертящихся колес, приводных ремней и рычагов, пронзительное шипение, визг стали, дребезжание вагонеток, жесткое дыхание пара, бледные или багровые или черные от угольной пыли лица, мокрые от пота рубахи, блеск стали, меди и огня, запах масла и угля, и ветер, то очень горячий, то холодный, произвели на нее впечатление ада.
>
> (260)

(High ceilings with iron beams, a multitude of huge, whirling wheels, conveyor belts and levers, a piercing whine, the shriek of steel, the clattering of the trollies, the harsh breath of steam, faces, pale or scarlet or black with coal dust, shirts soaked with sweat, the gleam of steel, copper and fire, the smell of oil and coal, and the wind, now very hot, now cold, gave her the impression of being in hell.)

On her one and only visit there, Anna's senses had been assaulted by the blinding fires and the noise, and it seemed to her that the machines were trying to break loose and destroy the men working there, rather than serving them. She could understand none of the explanations she was given by, as she will realize later, that very Pimenov. Her lack of understanding is reflected in the theme of impaired senses—men "not hearing one another" ("ne slyša drug druga") and a one-eyed old man ("starik s odnim glazom")—that is introduced in this scene and will permeate the entire story. The way Anna perceives the factory is central to any interpretation of this story. For although everything about it is alien to her and completely out of her control, it is in fact the source of her wealth. Inheriting the factory has dislodged Anna from her working-class roots and caused the inner disharmony in her that drives the plot of the story.[5]

The cleanliness, neatness and order of the room where Anna finds herself presents such a sharp contrast to the squalor of the rest of Čalikov's apartment that it seems to represent a completely different dimension. Čechov seems to offer two differing ways of structuring life—one patently two-dimensional, cliché-ridden, melodramatic and false; the other firmly anchored in the territory of ordinary life, modest, comfortable, and apparently realizable. For Anna this room will come to represent a dream of a "real" life, one that is free both from the falsity and delusions of fiction and from the extremes of poverty and wealth represented by the story's other symbolic spaces.

In his studies of Russian writers, Gary Saul Morson identifies the literary presentation of such values—of an honest, ordinary life—as "prosaics". They can be contrasted to the extreme and unrealizable ideals of escapist literature, and in fact to any simplistic view of life as containable within traditional literary plots, limited as they are by rules of cause and effect. In this story we will see how Čechov undermines even such a moderate and apparently realistic dream as Anna's, showing it, paradoxically, to be unrealistic and unrealizable—at least within the boundaries of his fiction. For it is a vision in which *should* predominates over *is*. When we see the room through Anna's eyes, it seems too good to be true:

> В следующей затем комнате жильца, в самом деле, было чисто. Опрятная постель с красным шерстяным одеялом, подушка в белой наволочке, даже башмачок для часов, стол, покрытый пеньковою скатертью, а на нем чернильница молочного цвета, перья, бумага, фотографии в рамочках, все как следует.
>
> (265)

(The next room, that of the lodger, was indeed clean. *Everything was as it should be*—the neat bed with its red wool blanket, the pillow in a white pillow case, even the watch case, the table covered with a linen tablecloth and the milky-colored inkwell on it, the pens, paper, the framed photographs.)

The cleanliness, calm, neatness and order of Pimenov's room domesticate and tame the raw masculine brute force embodied in the factory: the huge roaring machines are replaced by the fine repair tools and little watches and clocks arranged neatly on the table and walls; instead of their deafening noise, Anna hears the clocks' docile ticking. And if the cleanliness and calm of the room offer a refuge from the sensory assaults of the factory, the clocks surely seem to offer Anna relief from the boredom and empty time that dominate her life in her large, empty house, devoid as it is of family and occupation. Surely this promise of relief is akin to that which we experience when we escape from the complexity of our lives into literary fictions.

Clearly Anna seeks to escape an excess of freedom and choice; given our focus, we can view the simple, linear and measurable time symbolized here as yet another aspect of her dream that life can be as simple and determined as a literary plot. When we see Anna's own framed photograph, together with her father's, on Pimenov's table, we are willing to dismiss the utter improbability of their presence there; the relief we share with her upon entering the room, together with our sympathy for her desire for domestic tranquility, is too great.

As we explore the action of Anna's dreams throughout this story it is important for us to remember that the room comes first. Her dream of domestic happiness is a holistic one, in which love will be inseparable from home and family. But Pimenov himself is the perfect man for her:

> Это был мужчина лет тридцати, среднего роста, черноволосый, плечистый и, по-видимому, очень сильный. Анна Акимовна [. . .] определила в нем старшего [. . .] строгого, крикливого, бъющего рабочих по зубам. [. . .]
>
> (267)

(He was a man of thirty, average height, black haired, broad-shouldered and obviously very strong. Anna Akimovna [. . .] identified him as a senior worker, [. . .] stern, loud-mouthed, the kind who would punch the workers in the teeth.)

Pimenov's most striking characteristic is physical strength of a purely masculine kind. His physicality will serve as the focus of Anna's desires as she strives to find a way to anchor herself firmly in the material world and gain some control over her life. Furthermore, for Anna, the crude violence of which Pimenov is capable seems to offer a counterbalance to her own help-lessness and passivity. In setting up Anna's dream of domestic happiness in this way, Čechov has achieved the goal of the fiction writer, to seduce us into sharing the desires of her character.

It will be important to recall this scene when we turn to the other striking literary paradigm of this story. Chapter 3—as in Act 3 of Čechov's plays—is where we find the real action of the story. After a long day of receiving holiday visits and greetings from the implied "subjects" of her kingdom, Anna spends the evening upstairs with an elderly state councillor and the younger, successful and utterly unscrupulous lawyer Lysevič. This scene is marked by an opposition between physicality and abstraction. Čechov sets it in the upper story of the house which, elevated as it is above the ground, represents formality, culture, Western—particularly French—values, and abstraction, in opposition to the informal, "down-to-earth", Russian, old-fashioned values suggested by the lower, the woman's ("bab'e" includes a strong connotation of lower class or peasant women) story. From the first words spoken by Lysevič in the scene—"you mustn't, just mustn't gain weight" ("ne nado . . . ne nado polnet'")—Anna finds herself sublimating her physical and sexual needs in the abstract pleasures of literature and culture. The rich sensual details of the scene—the smells and taste of the food, which is described in detail, the warmth of the fire, the seductive sounds of Lysevič's voice, the very physicality of the man and the woman—present a sharp contrast to Anna's self-denial.

During an elaborate, elegant French meal (during which Anna eats absolutely nothing while Lysevič displays a positive lust for food ["zametnoe vozbuždenie"], piggish greed and repulsive manners; 280-281), the conversation turns to love. Lysevič, Čechov's take-off on a typical fin-de-siècle decadent, tells Anna that she should let herself go and indulge in wild love affairs, accumulating a different man for every day of the week:

> Заройтесъ в цветы с одуряющим ароматом, задыхайтесь в мускусе, ешъте гашиш, а главное, любите, любите, любите. . . .
>
> (281)
>
> (Bury yourself in flowers with an intoxicating aroma, smother yourself in musk, take hashish, but most important, love, love, love. . . .)

Anna is "excited" ("volnovalo") by his talk, but with the image of Pimenov still fresh on her mind after her visit to Čalikov's apartment, she replies heatedly that she wants nothing more than an ordinary life, a good husband and family. Anna's passionate affirmation of a holistic view of love that integrates body and spirit conforms to a specifically Russian eros which, we read in Boym's gloss of an enigmatic statement by Zinaida Gippius linking sexuality and "pošlost'":

is a more spiritual approach that integrates flesh and spirit. Russian "eros", in the philosophical writings of the Symbolist writers and philosophers, is different from French eighteenth-century eroticism and from Freud's sexuality. It does not exist by itself but merges with spirituality and compassion, with *agape* and *caritas*. In this neo-Platonic philosophy, love has to be Christian and transcendent.

(303)

When the older man, exhausted by the excesses of the meal, goes off for a nap, Anna and Lysevič are left alone together. The scene is ripe for romance; Lysevič, successful, healthy, well-educated, handsome, would seem to be a good match for the marriage-ready and unchaperoned Anna. The man and the woman are in their prime. Anna has drunk some fine wine on an empty stomach and is surely quite tipsy. Lysevič is mellowed by the wonderful meal, he has been urging Anna to take lovers, and the two of them are alone. From his comfortable and relaxed position on the sofa, Lysevič (who has told his friend that Anna is the only woman he ever loved) looks down at her as she sits on the carpet near him gazing into the fire on Christmas night.

What ensues? Instead of the romantic scene we have been set up to expect, Lysevič (whose name, from the root for "bald", surely is suggestive of emasculation)—launches into a discussion about *literature,* specifically French literature. Let us follow the course of Lysevič's performance, noticing not the content of his speech, but the way in which he tells it. Lysevič is nearly asleep at the beginning:[6]

> Теперъ он начал как-то кисло, расслабленным голосом и закрывши глаза.
>
> (284)
>
> [. . .] сонно бормотал Лысевич и еще глубже забился в угол дивана. [. . .] Лысевич, казалосъ, уснул.
>
> (285)
>
> (Now he began speaking somewhat feebly and sourly, with his eyes closed. [. . .] mumbled Lysevič sleepily, snuggling deeper into the corner of the sofa [. . .] It seemed that Lysevič had fallen asleep.)

When he begins talking about Maupassant, he starts coming to life:

> Лысевич открыл глаза [. . .] Лысевич задвигался на диване [. . .] Лысевич встал с дивана и поднял кверху правую руку [. . .] "Мопассан!" сказал он в восторге [. . .] Лысевич замахал руками и в силъном волнении прошелся из угла в угол. . . .
>
> (285)
>
> (Lysevič opened his eyes. [. . .] Lysevič stirred on the sofa. [. . .] Lysevič got up from the sofa and raised his right hand into the air. [. . .] "Maupassant!" he said ecstatically. [. . .] Lysevič waved his arms and in great excitement paced from one corner to the other. . . .)

Lysevič's mental state has progressed gradually from half-sleep to great excitement as Čechov builds up an impressionistic and sensual catalogue of clichés taken straight from decadent art:

> Мягчайшие, нежнейшие движения души сменяются сильными, бурными ощущениями, ваша душа точно под давлением сорока тысяч атмосфер обращается в ничтожнейший кусочек какого-то вещества неопределенного, розоватого цвета, которое, как мне кажется, если бы можно было положитъ его на язык, дало бы терпкий, сладострастный вкус. Какое бешенство переходов, мотивов, мелодий! вы покоитесъ на ландышах и розах, и вдруг мыслъ, страшная, прекрасная, неотразимая мыслъ неожиданно налетает на вас, как локомотив, и обдает вас горячим паром и оглушает свистом. Читайте, читайте Мопассана!
>
> (285)

(The most tender and soft stirrings of the soul are replaced by powerful, stormy sensations, your soul, as though under the pressure of forty thousand atmospheres, turns into the most insignificant piece of some sort of substance of an indefinite, pinkish color, which, it seems to me, if you could put it on your tongue, would give an acrid, sensuous taste. What a frenzy of transitions, motifs, melodies! You are reclining on lilies-of-the-valley and roses, and suddenly a thought, a terrifying, beautiful, irresistable thought swoops down on you like a locomotive which engulfs you in its hot steam and deafens you with its whistle. Read, read Maupassant!)[7]

"Pinkish substance, tongue, acrid, sensuous taste, frenzy, railroad train, hot steam . . ." even a jaded reader of late twentieth-century Western popular fiction blushes. But so far Lysevič has only been talking *about* literature. He now tells Anna a story, or more precisely, re-tells a "novel" (etymologically, of course, both the French and Russian words for novel, roman, come from "romance"). Čechov chooses to focus our attention not on the plot of this novel, of which he quotes only a few key descriptive words, but rather on the way Lysevič tells the story, his mannerisms, physical movements, the tone of his voice and the way Anna listens. The performance is an extremely *sensual* experience, both for performer and for listener. Lysevič performs as an "actor", modulating his voice, throwing his arms around, clutching his head; Anna listens, imagining herself playing a part in the story:

> Рассказывал он уже не так вычурно, но очень подробно, приводя наизустъ целые описания и разговоры; действующие лица романа восхищали его, и, характеризуя их, он становился в позы, менял выражение лица и голос, как настоящий актер. От восторга он хохотал то басом, то очень тонким голоском, всплескивал руками или хватал себя за голову с таким выражением, как будто она собиралась у него лопнутъ. Анна Акимовна

> слушала с восхищением, хотя уже читала этот роман, и в передаче адвоката он казался ей во много раз красивее и сложнее, чем в книжке. Он обращал ее внимание на разные тонкости и подчеркивал счастливые выражения и глубокие мысли, но она видела только жизнь, жизнъ, жизнъ и самое себя, как будто была действующим лицом романа; у нее поднимало дух, и она сама, тоже хохоча и всплескивая руками, думала о том, что так житъ нелъзя, что нет надобности житъ дурно, если можно житъ прекрасно; она вспоминала свои слова и мысли за обедом и гордиласъ ими, и когда в воображении вдруг вырастал Пименов, то ей было весело и хотелосъ, чтобы он полюбил ее.
>
> (286)

(He was telling the story now with less embellishment, but in great detail, quoting from memory whole descriptions and conversations; the characters of the novel entranced him, and as he gave their characterizations, he posed and changed the expression of his face and voice, like a real actor. In ecstasy he laughed first in a bass, then a very thin voice, waved his arms or seized his head as though it was about to burst. Anna Akimovna listened, entranced, although she had already read that novel, and in the lawyer's rendition it seemed many times more beautiful and complex than in the book. He directed her attention to various subtleties and emphasized the happy expressions and deep thoughts, but she saw only life, life, life and herself, as though she was a character in the novel; her spirits rose and she herself, also laughing and waving her arms, thought about how this was no way to live, that there was no need to live badly if you can live a fine life; she recalled her words and thoughts at dinner and was proud of them, and when suddenly Pimenov appeared in her imagination, she felt happy and wanted him to love her.)

The desire to be loved by Pimenov that flashes through Anna's mind marks the climax, and the end of Lysevič's story; in the next moment

> Кончивши рассказыватъ, Лысевич, изнеможенный, сел на диван.
>
> —Какая вы славная! Какая хорошая!—начал он немного погодя слабым голосом.
>
> (286)

(Having finished his narration, Lysevič, exhausted, sat down on the sofa.

"How fine you are! How good!" he began shortly afterwards in a weak voice.)

The theme of marriage and love that permeates the entire text of the story, Lysevič's suggestive comments to Anna that she let herself go, the romantic setting, the sensual details of the surroundings and of Lysevič's story, the growing excitement of both performer and listener as the story builds tension, the image of the man of her dreams that flashes through Anna's mind at the end of the story and Lysevič's immediate physical exhaustion after that moment—all these elements combine inexorably to make this scene, which is in a very real sense the climax of the entire story, a literary substitute for sex.[8]

Keeping in mind Čechov's emphasis on the importance of the physical aspects of our being (the body as the "holy of holies"), we can read this episode as representing how literature deludes by leading away from the body. Language by its very essence abstracts from the basic physical needs of the body; as Peter Brooks says in his reading of Rousseau's *Julie,* "not need but passion presides at the creation of language itself" (1993: 46). Anna's primary concern throughout **'A Woman's Kingdom'** has been a search for a man who will solve all her problems, from the complex decision-making about the factory and household to the most basic needs of her body. This performance by Lysevič has temporarily distracted and relieved her from the pressures of this need. Accepting Peter Brooks' argument that desire, often reducible to sexual desire, is the driving force behind the action of narrative literature as a whole, what we find interesting about Čechov's story is that in this scene the pattern enacts itself purely on the *formal* level. We do not hear the plot or content of Lysevič's narrative; we have no idea what his story is about. It is the flow of language itself and the actions and attitudes of speaker and listener that model the contours of sexual arousal and consummation, not the content of the story itself. In that sense Lysevič's performance is in the truest possible sense *about* narrative. And this is our basic premise, that in order to understand Čechov we must concentrate not on the *what,* but on the *how* of his art.[9]

When the story ends, we hear no more of French literature or of Maupassant; instead it is Turgenev who is on Lysevič's mind—Turgenev, whose best stories—'First Love' and 'Asja', for example, are elegies for a love that was never consummated. And the poetry of the love scene that has just been enacted will yield its place to "stern prose" ("surovaja proza", which, as we learned when we first met him, is how Lysevič refers to his salary; 279). With his next words—reproaching Anna for not giving him a Christmas bonus, Lysevič induces her to hand over to him all the money that had been intended for charity. The literary act of seduction has corrupted Anna morally.

The sad moment in the fourth act of this drama when Anna reverses her request to the matchmaker to work out a marriage for her with Pimenov, is already determined at this point of the story. After her guests leave, Anna feels a tremendous sense of release; by giving the money to Lysevič she has relieved herself of the adult responsibilities of managing her money; the literary seduction has displaced her adult sexual need and she retreats into a world of childhood and innocence—the release is so complete she is likened to a little *boy:*

Она быстро сбросила платъе, которое уже наскучило ей, надела капот и побѣжала вниз. И когда бѣжала по лѣстницѣ, то смѣяласъ и стучала ногами, какъ малъчишка. Ей сильно хотѣлосъ шалитъ.

(288)

(She quickly shed her dress, already bored with it, put on her housecoat and ran downstairs. And as she ran down the stairs, she laughed and stamped her feet, like a little boy. She felt very mischievous.)

Upstairs, the literary exchange has isolated Anna's sexual nature from her physical being and sublimated it. Taken out of the context of a realistic, integrated and specifically Russian "commonplace" dream of marriage, family and home it becomes not only unreal (the stuff of fiction), but also treacherous to her well-being. Downstairs, it is Anna's physical self that dominates. It is downstairs, for example, that she finally sits down to a meal, after a whole day without food. Downstairs is where the women of the household discuss the practical details of marrying her off—not so she can enjoy her fantasy of family life, but so that she will gain the freedom to love whomever and whenever she wants to. Thus the problem of Anna's sexual need drives the plot, in spite of the differences between the two floors. Similarly, many of the symbolic details that represent the Christian moral values can be shown to signify this very basic physical need as well. For example, the references to the Mother of God (it IS Christmas, after all) inevitably remind us of the virginity that both Anna and her comic double, the "upstairs" maid Maša (from Marija, Mary), perceive as a burden. It is a great mystery, too—why is it that Anna has no suitors?[10] The Christian mystery of the virgin birth is blasphemed by pointed references to Anna's deceased uncle's mistress Varvara, who affects virtue but has had illegitimate children and turned them over to the foundling home. When Anna, playing "romances" on the piano alone upstairs, imagines herself appealing to Pimenov to "relieve me of this burden" ("snimite s menja ėtu tjažest'"; 294), although, as Jackson points out (1985: 102), she is indeed borrowing the famous phrase spoken by Jesus to his disciples ("remove this cup from me . . ."), the words also express the blunt and simple desire of a woman to be loved. The burden is, paradoxically, her emptiness, her sexual need, and the never-ending boredom she experiences in her empty house (in Čechov, we can often identify an association between boredom and sexual need). For that reason, at least given the focus of the present study, Pimenov is better seen not as a father figure (see Jackson 1985: 102, n. 7), but as a husband figure and an object of Anna's sexual fantasy, clearly anchored in the context of marriage and family—and after all, his name is Osip (Joseph). The many references throughout the text to cleanliness and purity ("čistota", which covers both meanings)—the cleanliness of Pimenov's room and the purity of the white snow on Christmas, for example—echo and strengthen this theme.

Ultimately Anna cannot act to secure her place either upstairs or downstairs—there is an equilibrium between them that she cannot disturb. Adrift from the usual supports of class and family, but unable to completely deny her physical self, she finds herself in an in-between place—that same "middle territory", in fact, that we identified at the outset as the focus and origin of Čechov's art. Anna's sense of moral propriety and her origin in the conservative values of her deeply Russian working class background will not let her indulge herself in the decadent, "French" love affairs urged upon her by Lysevič.[11] But as a product of culture and literature, she enjoys their pleasures too much to feel comfortable in the territory of ordinary, middle-class life that is the focus of her dream; and when her lackey Miša smirks at the prospect of Pimenov having dinner upstairs with the likes of Lysevič and Krylin, she realizes she cannot bring that kind of life upstairs into the realm of abstraction and literary delusion.

Paradoxically then, but most appropriately, given Čechov's message, the end of the story reveals that it is the most prosaic and realizable dream that turns out to be the wildest fantasy. As Anna begins to recede into sleep, thus leaving this story behind, she relinquishes her dream as well:

> Она думала теперъ, что если бы можно было только что прожитый длинный день изобразить на картине, то все дурное и пошлое, как, например, обед, слова адвоката, игра в короли, были бы правдой, мечты же и разговоры о Пименове выделялись бы из целого, как фальшивое место, как натяжка. И она думала также, что ей уже поздно мечтать о счастье.

(296)

> (She now thought, that if you could paint a picture of the long day she had just lived through, then everything bad and vulgar, like, for example, the dinner, the lawyer's words, and the card game, would be the truth, and the dreams and conversations about Pimenov would stand out of the overall picture as something false and strained. And she also thought that it was already too late for her to dream of happiness.)

The "middle territory" has in this way turned out to be the most difficult of all to delineate and domesticate. The picture Anna imagines, of course, is this story itself. The Pimenov segments—Anna's dream of "real life", an escape from the prison of literary plots—seem false and strained because the fullness and richness of true, real human life cannot be conveyed through the weak instruments of literary fiction (perhaps this is why Čechov is notoriously unable to grant his characters happiness in love).

Čechov's best art is built around an emptiness—the expected event that doesn't happen, the unfulfilled need. In Anna's case, her boredom, her sexual need, her lack of a man is the story. Placing her permanently in Pimenov's room, thereby satisfying that need, would reduce her story to yet another conventional fictional plot, and Čechov is too true an artist to allow that to happen. What is real is Anna's dream, which we have shared, and which has filled the elegant structure of Čechov's art with meaning.

Notes

1. All emphases, ellipses and translations are mine, except where noted.

2. The difficulty of locating absolutes (what V. Kataev, in studying this story, calls "trezvost' otnositel'nosti" ["the sobriety of relativity"; 1979: 147]) in Čechov is acknowledged by every serious scholar of his work. The most recent studies have moved away from vague truisms about Čechov's "impressionism", "humanism", "mood", etc., into deep analysis of the "how" of his art. I believe any discussion of physicality and the body in Čechov—which is a key focus of the present study—should reference Čudakov (1986), whose insightful *Mir Čechova* shows how tightly the physical and metaphysical are linked in Čechov's art.

3. In suggesting that this is a story about what literature does, I purposely avoid the term "metapoesis", as applied by Michael Finke to Čechov's use of self-referential literary metaphors in 'The Steppe'. Čechov's mature narrative technique is characterized by self-referentiality in the sense that his best stories—the Little Trilogy, as Freedman shows, is a particularly good example—call into question the ability of stories to tell the truth. In fact, I suspect that the best fiction—being by definition false—can be read as doing so, and therefore can be seen as "covertly metapoetic" (Finke 1995: 134); if this is the case, metapoesis becomes a word describing a critical perspective, rather than a characterization of a particular kind of literature. This is not to challenge the validity of the term as a way of reading what might be called "overtly" self-referential works.

4. Holquist's book offers an in-depth look at how an author can use parody metaphorically in a literary text to represent a character's retreat from real life. Naturally we readers can draw an analogy from the example given us in a literary text to our own strategies of reading and of living.

5. I cannot resist the temptation to speculate on a link between this story and Zola's *Nana* (1880— translated into Russian the same year), defending

the frivolity of the attempt by citing Čechov's own love for practical jokes and his consummate irony. Zola's heroine is probably the most famous courtesan in literary history—a polar opposite to our Anna, as her palindromic name suggests. But like Anna, she has risen from humble origins to control a vast empire of men and possessions. Čechov's striking description of Anna's factory—the material base on which her wealth is built, calls to mind the workmen and factories that strain to satisfy Nana's insatiable desires. In the factory of Steiner, one of Nana's rich lovers,

> workmen black with coal-dust and soaked with sweat strained their sinews and heard their bones crack day and night to satisfy Nana's pleasures. Like a huge fire, she devoured everything, the profits from financial swindles no less than the fruits of labour.

(1972: 435)

According to Peter Brooks, nearly all of Zola's novels are constructed around the image of a machine (1984: 45), and though I would certainly quarrel with his suggestion that Nana's sexual desire is a "machine", the economics of the two stories are quite similar. Furthermore, like 'A Woman's Kingdom', *Nana* is driven by the force of a woman's desires. And as the most scandalous example of French naturalism—granted, not French *decadence*—Zola's novel would certainly be on the mind of any Russian reader contemplating the issue of sex and French literature—the target of Čechov's irony in this story. In his stories and letters, Čechov occasionally refers ironically to Nana, as a kind of generic French courtesan (see, for example, the story 'Moja nana'; 1883).

6. Lysevič's sleepiness, both before and after his telling of the story, Čalikov's exclamation that he must be dreaming Anna's presence in his apartment, the sleepiness that Anna notices in Pimenov as she leaves his apartment (he looks at her as though he is dreaming her), the sleep that keeps Anna from attending church on Christmas morning, all place this story in the "sleep/talk economy" that Popkin identifies as a pattern in Čechov wherein stories are worthy as long as they keep sleep at bay (see 1993: 143). We can also see the ways stories emerge from sleep in 'A Woman's Kingdom' as a veiled hint of their fictionality, that is, their unreality.

7. My reading of Maupassant, by the way, does not yield a text, or even a style, that could serve as a basis for parody; rather, Čechov offers a generalized lampoon of the license, decadence and sensuality the average Russian would associate with French *decadent* literature of the time. There is

certainly at work here a touch of the comic Čechov, who constantly butchered French language for humorous effect (see Erofeev 1992). Lysevič's enraptured exhortation to "read, read Maupassant", according to the editors of the Academy Edition of the story, is most likely an inside joke on Čechov's part; apparently the literary critic and lawyer (!) A. I. Urusov inscribed a portrait of himself with the words (in French), "Read Flaubert!", and Čechov often joked about the inscription with his close friends. Vladimir Lakšin suggests that by the mid-1890s, when Čechov was working on 'A Woman's Kingdom', it was very likely that he was already tired of being constantly compared with Maupassant:

> [. . .] автор рассказа 'Бабье царство' уже испытывал, по-видимому, ощущение неприятного осадка от того, что его непрерывно сравнивают с Мопассаном [. . .] Иные недалекие читатели, будто обрадовавшисъ находке, твердили о "подражании" [Мопассана], и Чехов, по свидетельству В.А. Лазаревского, вынужден был защищаться: "Таланту подражатъ нелъзя, потому что каждый настоящий талант есть нечто совершенно своеобразное. Золота искусственным путемъ не сделаешъ. Поэтому никто и никогда не мог подражатъ Мопассану."

(68)

Although we cannot accept Maupassant's style as the target for Čechov's parody, it is nevertheless true that a great many of Maupassant's stories are premised on acts of deception between husband and wife; reading (or listening to) them would surely undermine Anna Akimovna's dream of a pure, modest, moral and loving family life.

8. Whereas it may be true that Čechov's most striking and naturalistic treatment of the sexual theme is found in stories from 1886-1890 (Conrad 1980: 103), the theme does not disappear in his mature work, but rather blends into the overall sensual richness of his texts and takes on deeper meaning.

9. It is here that my focus differs from Cathy Popkin's in her explorations of what used to be called Čechov's "understatement". Her studies find in Čechov's preoccupation with externally insignificant events a testing of the limits of what is "tellible". For example, in her excellent study of 'The Kiss', she suggests that

> Čechov is more drawn to investigate the other extreme of the forbidden, the less dramatic but nevertheless consistent power of veto over prospective subject matter; the inclination to exclude material that is not provocative *enough,* not "sexy" enough to engage the attention, arouse interest, and stimulate desire for more. No external

agency is required to enforce this exclusion; when a story falls below this threshold, the audience disperses quite on its own, as a deflated Ryabovich discovers.

(1993: 154)

Too often Čechov's focus is not on an apparently insignificant event, but rather on an extraordinarily significant event that does *not* happen (in the case of this story, a marriage and a seduction). It is because so many of his stories and plays are built around non-events that we have nowhere to turn but to their *how,* thus looking at Čechov's art primarily as art—there is nothing else there. It is possible that Čechov is attempting to make this point when he says, "podnimite podol našej muze, i Vy uvidite tam ploskoe mesto" (Pis'ma, V, 133), although in this statement Čechov is ostensibly commenting on the lack of political or philosophical absolutes among writers of his generation. See also Popkin (1993).

10. By the way, this part of the story has been misinterpreted. Anna has no suitors, pure and simple. When she is asked why someone as beautiful, strong and healthy as herself isn't getting married, she answers, "Что же делать, если никто не берет?" This doesn't mean she's worried no one will want her: "But suppose no one will have me" or that she "believes nobody will take her" (Jackson 1985: 7). The fact is that no one is even courting her, now. This is so improbable that even Žuželica, the prospective matchmaker, misinterprets her answer: "A, možet, dala obet ostat'sja v devach?—prodolžala, kak by ne slyša" (291).

11. The image of France in Čechov has been identified as representing the idea of freedom. We may prefer to call it, at least in our discussion of this particular story, as "license". See Erofeev (1992).

References

Boym, Svetlana. 1994. *Common Places: Mythologies of Everyday Life in Russia.* Cambridge, Mass.

Brooks, Peter. 1993. *Body Work: Objects of Desire in Modern Narrative.* Cambridge, Mass.

——1984. *Reading for the Plot: Design and Intention in Narrative.* Cambridge, Mass.

Čechov, A. P. 1974-1982. *Polnoe sobranie sočinenij i pisem,* 30 tt. Moskva (Letters volumes are identified in the references as "Pis'ma").

Chekhov, Anton. 1989. *A Woman's Kingdom and Other Stories* (Transl. Ronald Hingley). Oxford.

Conrad, Joseph. 1980. 'Sensuality in Čexov's Prose'. *Slavic and East European Journal,* Vol. 24, No. 2 (Summer, 1980), 103-117.

Čudakov, A. 1986. *Mir Čechova.* Moskva.

Erofeev, Viktor. 1992. 'Mif Čechova o Francii'. *Čechoviana. Čechov i Francija.* Moskva, 19-24.

Evdokimova, Svetlana. 1994. 'The Curse of Rhetoric and the Delusions of Sincerity: Čechov's Story "Misfortune"'. *Russian Literature,* XXXV, 153-170.

Finke, Michael C. 1995. *Metapoesis: The Russian Tradition from Pushkin to Chekhov.* Durham, N.C.

Freedman, John. 1988. 'Narrative Technique and the Art of Story-telling in Anton Chekhov's "Little Trilogy"'. *South Atlantic Review,* 53, No. 1 (January 1988) (Reprinted in *Critical Essays on Anton Chekhov*; Ed. Thomas A. Eekman, Boston, 1989).

Holquist, Michael. 1977. *Dostoevsky and the Novel.* Princeton.

Jackson, Robert Louis. 1985. 'Chekhov's "A Woman's Kingdom": A Drama of Character and Fate'. *Russian Language Journal,* 39, Nos. 34, 1-11.

Kataev, V. B. 1979. *Proza Čechova. Problemy interpretacii.* Moskva.

Lakšin, Vladimir. 1992. 'Čechov i Mopassan pered sudom L. Tolstogo'. *Čechoviana: Čechov i Francija.* Moskva.

Morson, Gary Saul. 1988. 'Prosaics and *Anna Karenina*'. *Tolstoy Studies,* 1, 1-12.

Popkin, Cathy. 1993. 'Kiss and Tell: Narrative Desire and Discretion'. *Sexuality and the Body in Russian Culture* (Ed. Jane T. Costlow, Stephanie Sandler, Judith Vowles). Stanford.

——1993. *The Pragmatics of Insignificance: Chekhov, Zoshchenko, Gogol.* Stanford.

——1994. 'Paying the Price: The Rhetoric of Reckoning in Čechov's "Peasant Women"'. *Russian Literature,* XXXV, 203-222.

Zola, Emile. 1972. *Nana* (Transl. George Holden). London.

Richard Ford (essay date 1998)

SOURCE: Ford, Richard. "Introduction: Why We Like Chekhov." In *The Essential Tales of Chekhov,* translated by Constance Garnett, edited by Richard Ford, pp. vii-xix. Hopewell, N.J.: Ecco Press, 1998.

[*In the following essay, Ford assesses Chekhov's achievement as a short fiction writer, praising the maturity, subtlety, and vitality of his stories.*]

Until I began the long and happy passage of reading all of Anton Chekhov's short stories for the purpose of selecting the twenty that follow, I had read very little of

Chekhov. It seems a terrible thing for a story writer to admit, and doubly worse for one whose own stories have been so thoroughly influenced by Chekhov through my relations with other writers who had been influenced by him directly: Sherwood Anderson. Isaac Babel. Hemingway. Cheever. Welty. Carver.

As is true of many American readers who encountered Chekhov first in college, my experience with his stories was both abrupt and brief, and came too early. When I read him at age twenty, I had no idea of his prestige and importance or why I should be reading him—one of those gaps of ignorance for which a liberal education tries to be a bridge. But typical of my attentiveness then, I remember no one telling me anything more than that Chekhov was great, and that he was Russian.

And for all of their surface plainness, their apparent accessibility and clarity, Chekhov's stories—especially the greatest ones—still do not seem so easily penetrable by the unexceptional young. Rather, Chekhov seems to me a writer for adults, his work becoming useful and also beautiful by attracting attention to mature feelings, to complicated human responses and small issues of moral choice within large, overarching dilemmas, any part of which, were we to encounter them in our complex, headlong life with others, might evade even sophisticated notice. Chekhov's wish is to complicate and compromise our view of characters we might mistakenly suppose we could understand with only a glance. He almost always approaches us with a great deal of focussed seriousness which he means to make irreducible and accessible, and by this concentration to insist that we take life to heart. Such instruction, of course, is not always easy to comply with when one is young.

My own college experience was to read the great anthology standard, **"The Lady with the Dog"** (published in 1899 and included here), and basically to be baffled by it, although the story's fundamental directness and authority made me highly respectful of something I can only describe as a profound-feeling gray light emanating from the story's austere interior.

"The Lady with the Dog" concerns the chance amorous meeting of two people married to two other people. One lover is a bored, middle-aged businessman from Moscow, and the other an idle young bride in her twenties—both on marital furlough in the Black Sea spa of Yalta. The two engage in a brief, fervid tryst that seems—at least to the story's principal character Dmitri Gurov, the Muscovite businessman—not very different from other trysts in his life. And after their short, breathless time together, their holiday predictably ends. The young wife, Anna Sergeyevna, departs for her home and husband in Petersburg, while Gurov, with no specific plans for Anna, travels back to his coolly intellectual wife and the tiresome business connections of Moscow.

But the effect of his affair and of Anna (the very lady with the dog—a Pomeranian) soon begin to infect and devil Gurov's daily life and torment him with desire, so that eventually he thinks up a lie, leaves home and travels to Petersburg where he reunites (more or less) with the pining Anna, whom he encounters between the acts of a play expressively titled *The Geisha*. In the weeks following this passionate lovers' meeting, Anna begins a routine of visiting Gurov in Moscow where, the omniscient narrator observes, they "loved each other like people very close and akin, like husband and wife, like tender friends; it seemed to them that fate itself had meant them for one another, and they could not understand why he had a wife and she a husband; and it was as though they were pair of birds of passage, caught and forced to live in different cages."

Their union, while hot-burning, soon seems to them destined to stay furtive and intermittent. And in their secret lovers' room in the Slaviansky Bazaar, Anna cries bitterly over the predicament, while Gurov troubles himself in a slightly imperious manner to console her. The story ends with the narrator concluding with something of a knowing poker face, that . . . "it seemed as though in a little while the solution would be found, and then a new and splendid life would begin; and it was clear to both of them that they had still a long, long road before them, and that the most complicated and difficult part of it was only just beginning."

What I didn't understand back in 1964, when I was twenty, was: what made this drab set of non-events a great short story—reputedly one of the greatest ever written. It was, I knew, a story about passion, and that passion was a capital subject; and that although Chekhov didn't describe any of it, sex took place, adulterous sex no less. I could also see that the effect of passion was calculated to be loss, loneliness and indeterminacy, and that the institution of marriage came in for a beating. Clearly these were important matters.

But it seemed to me at the story's end, when Gurov and Anna meet in the hotel, away from spousal eyes, that far too little happened, or at least too little that *I* could detect. They make love (albeit offstage); Anna weeps; Gurov fussily says "Don't cry, my darling . . . that's enough. . . . Let us talk now, let us think of some plan." And then the story is over, with Gurov and Anna wandering off to who knows where—probably, I thought, no place very exciting were we to accompany them. Which we don't.

Back in 1964, I didn't dare to say, "I don't like this," because in truth I didn't *not* like **"The Lady with the Dog."** I merely didn't sense what in it was *so* to be liked. In class, much was made of its opening paragraph, containing the famously brief, complex, yet direct setting out of significant information, issues and strategies of telling which the story would eventually develop. For this reason—economy—it was deemed good. The ending was also said to be admirable *because* it wasn't very dramatic and wasn't conclusive. But beyond that, if anybody said something more specific about how the story made itself excellent I don't remember it. Although I distinctly remember thinking the story was over my head, and that Gurov and Anna were adults (read: enigmatic, impenetrable) in a way I wasn't one, and what they did and said to each other must reveal heretofore unheard of truths about love and passion, only I wasn't a good enough reader or mature enough human to recognize these truths. I'm certain that I eventually advertised actually *liking* the story, though only because I thought I should. And not long afterward I began maintaining the position that Chekhov was a story writer of near mystical—and certainly mysterious—importance, one who seemed to tell rather ordinary stories but who was really unearthing the most subtle, and for that reason, unobvious and important truth. (It is of course still a useful habit of inquiry to wonder, when the surface of reputedly great literature—and life—seem plain and equable, if something important might not be revealed upon closer notice; and also to realize that a story's ending may not always be the place to locate that something.)

In 1998, what I would say is good about **"The Lady with the Dog"** (and maybe you should stop here, read the story, then come back and compare notes) and indeed why I like it is primarily that it concentrates its narrative attentions *not* on the conventional hot spots—sex, deceit and what happens at the end—but rather, by its precision, pacing and decisions about what to tell, it directs our interest toward those flatter terrains of a love affair where we, being conventional souls, might overlook something important. **"The Lady with the Dog"** demonstrates by its scrupulous notice and detail that ordinary goings-on contain moments of significant moral choice—willed human acts judgeable as good or bad—and as such they have consequences in life which we need to pay heed to, whereas before reading the story we might've supposed they didn't. I'm referring specifically to Gurov's rather prosaic feelings of "torment" at home in Moscow, followed by his decision to visit Anna; his wife's reasonable dismissal of his suffering, the repetitiveness of trysts, the relative brevity of desire's satiation, and the necessity for self-deception to keep a small passion inflamed. These are matters the story wants us *not* to skip over, but to believe are important and that paying attention to them is good.

In a purely writerly way, I also find interest and take pleasure in Chekhov's choosing *these* characters and this seemingly unspectacular liaison upon which to stake a claim of significance and to treat with intelligence, amusement and some compassion. And superintending all there is Chekhov's surgical deployment of

his probing narrator as inventor and mediator of Gurov's bland but still provocative interior life with women: "It seemed to him," the narrator says of the stolid Dmitri, "that he had been so schooled by bitter experience that he might call them [women, of course] what he liked, and yet he could not get on for two days together without 'the lower race.' In the society of men he was bored and not himself, with them he was cool and uncommunicative; but when he was in the company of women he felt free. . . ."

Finally, in **"The Lady with the Dog,"** what seems good is Chekhov the fastidious and amused ironist who finds the right exalted language to accompany staid Gurov and pliant Anna's most unexalted amours, and in so doing discloses their love's frothy mundaneness. High on a hill overlooking Yalta and the sea, the two lovers sit and moon off, while the narrator archly muses over the landscape.

> The leaves did not stir on the trees, grasshoppers chirruped, and the monotonous hollow sound of the sea rising up from below, spoke of peace, of the eternal sleep awaiting us. So it must have sounded when there was no Yalta, no Oreanda here; so it sounds now, and it will sound as indifferently and monotonously when we are all no more. And in this constancy, in this complete indifference to the life and death of each of us, there lies hid, perhaps, a pledge of our eternal salvation, of the unceasing movement of life upon earth, of unceasing progress towards perfection.

* * *

Over the years, **"The Lady with the Dog"** has come to stand high in my esteem as the story by whose subtleties I not only began to know how and why to like Chekhov, but also by its exemplary fullness I came to experience literature as F. R. Leavis portrays it in his famous essay on Lawrence, as the supreme means by which we "undergo a renewal of sensuous and emotional life, and learn a new awareness." Chekhov's representation of this minor-key love affair committed by respectable nonentities more than renewed, it helped give early form to my awareness of what the words "emotional life" might entail, but also conceal and importantly leave out.

Yet this one small masterpiece aside, what sort of awareness do we typically achieve when we read Chekhov's stories? (As though story writing were not a matter of beauty, felicity, restraint and implicitness but was an art harnessed only to Walter Benjamin's utilitarian injunction that "every real story . . . contains, openly and covertly something useful. . . ." and that "the storyteller is a man who has counsel for his readers.")

There is, of course, no *typical* Chekhov story, a fact that by itself should please us, and makes the pseudo-critical shorthand of "Chekhovian" essentially pointless.

For if there are plenty of stories in which the surface of everyday life seems unremarkable and dramatically unyielding except that Chekhov makes it the object of intense narrative inquiry the result of which is, say, the exposure of unexpected emotional cowardice or painful moral indecision (the famous **"Gooseberries"** is such a story), there are also stories of unquestionably high, even fulminant surface drama that rattle the windows, alarm or enrage us, move us to tears, and then roar off to their appointed endings like freight trains. In **"Enemies,"** a distraught young husband bursts into a physician's home late at night pleading that the doctor honor his oath by coming at once to the young man's expiring wife. (The doctor's own child has only moments before, and startlingly, breathed his last!) At pains, the doctor sets aside his private grief and complies. Yet when he arrives at the man's house, the wife, again startlingly, proves absent having gone off with another man. The story's title offers a sufficient hint of the furious night's outcome.

Likewise, if the standard Chekhov ending is thought to leave readers clutching at air for answers to the story's profound but ambiguous scruplings—answers the author may have been unwilling or found too intellectually reductive to provide—there is conversely the unqualifiedly *direct* Chekhov who routinely tells us exactly what he wishes us to know. In **"The Kiss,"** another anthology regular, a young Cossack officer has his life turned topsy-turvy by the misplaced kiss of a mysterious woman he quickly become obsessed by. Later, alone, at the story's end, the young officer realizes bitterly that his own sensuous and emotional hopes will not be renewed because the mysterious woman will never be found nor the kiss repeated. "And the whole world, the whole of life," the narrator tells us, "seemed to Ryabovitch an unintelligible, aimless jest. . . . And turning his eyes from the water and looking at the sky, he remembered again how fate in the person of an unknown woman had by chance caressed him, he remembered his summer dreams and fancies, and his life struck him as extraordinarily meagre, poverty-stricken, and colourless. . . ."

And finally, if all of Chekhov's stories are thought to radiate importance and severity like the gray light that momentarily shines on poor, unkissed Ryabovitch, there is yet the burlesquing Chekhov of **"A Blunder."** There, the eager parents of an overly marriageable daughter eavesdrop through the wall as she is wooed by the district school teacher and minor poet, Shchupkin. The parents' plan is, at some compromising moment, to burst into the room like police, holding an ikon (the father, old Poplov, believes, "A blessing with an ikon is sacred and binding"). But just as the daughter's hand is finally, hungrily kissed by the unsuspecting Shchupkin, and the parents spring across the threshold burbling their would-be contractual blessings, Poplov discovers

his wife (the too-eager Kleopatra) has brought with her not an ikon but an absurd portrait of an *author*—Lazhetchnikov—thereby scuttling the longed-for marriage. As the story's *envoi*, the narrator modestly informs us that in the catastrophe's excitement, "the writing master took advantage of the general confusion and slipped away."

Indeed, one regularly finds humor in Chekhov, often in surprising though never really mistakable moments. As in Shakespeare as in Faulkner as in Flannery O'Connor, the comic turn not only counterweighs and intensifies a serious story's gravity, it also humanizes our own fated intimacy with what's grave by permitting life's fullest, most actual context to be brought into view, even as it points us toward an approved method of acceptance: laughter. (Acceptance and life's dogged continuance being ever Chekhov's concerns.)

In the masterful long story **"An Anonymous Story,"** a saga of revenge, moral deception, outrage, absurdity and flight, Chekhov almost at the story's opening movement sets out one of his signature—and in this case astoundingly acid—character summaries (partly of course calculated to delight us). And with it, he observes the nearly unplumbable complexity and baseness of the human species, even as he strengthens our resilience to depravities in life we cannot control. So, it is Kukushkin, the classic Petersburger, civil councillor, cowardly cohort of the unscrupulous and reluctant husband Orlov, who becomes the special target of the author's venom:

> He [Kukushkin] was a man with the manners of a lizard. He did not walk, but, as it were, crept along with tiny steps, squirming and sniggering, and when he laughed he showed his teeth. He was a clerk on special commissions . . . [and a] man of personal ambition, not only to the marrow of his bones, but more fundamentally—to the last drop of his blood; but even in his ambitions he was petty and did not rely on himself, but was building his career on the chance favour flung him by his superiors. For the sake of obtaining some foreign decoration, or for the sake of having his name mentioned in the newspapers as having been present at some special service in the company of other great personages, he was ready to submit to any kind of humiliation, to beg, to flatter, to promise.

In dismantling the wretched Kukushkin's impoverished character, it is as if Chekhov were subscribing to the ancient and comic maxim governing life's basic duality: if nothing's funny, nothing's really ever serious.

Far from his stories' ever sinking to typicality or being knowable by a scheme, Chekhov seems so committed to life's multifariousness that the stories provoke in us the sensation Ford Madox Ford must have had in mind when he observed that the general effect of fiction "must be the effect life has on mankind"—by which I've always thought he meant that it be persuasively important, profuse, irreducible in its ambiguities, full of diverse pleasures, and always on the brink of being unknowable except that our ordering intelligence ardently urges us toward clarity. In Chekhov, there are no potted or predictable attitudes about *anything*: women, children, dogs, cats, the clergy, teachers, peasants, the military, businessmen, government officials, marriage, all Russia itself. And if anything can be termed "typical" it is that he insists we keep our notice close to life's nuance, its intimate gestures and small moral annotations. "To be unloved and unhappy—how interesting that was," sixteen-year-old Nadya Zelenin in **"After the Theatre"** thinks after seeing a performance of *Eugene Onyegen*. "There is something beautiful, touching, and poetical about it when one loves and the other is indifferent."

The entirety of Chekhov's stories, in fact, often seem—but for their formal, sturdy existence in language—not even *artful* (although that would be wrong) but rather to be assiduous in mapping out degree by precise degree an accurate, ground-level constellation of ordinary existence—each story representing a subtly-distinguished movement in a single sustained gesture of life confirmed.

* * *

It is worth noticing now what precisely strikes us about Chekhov's subtlety—since surely the apprehension of great subtlety is what most of us emerge with after reading **"Gooseberries"** or **"The Kiss,"** stories in which the surfaces of life seem routine and continuous while Chekhov goes about illuminating its benighted *other* terrains as a way of inventing what's new, sustaining or calamitous in human existence.

One exemplary subtlety is that what we readers finally learn about humankind—one of our new awarenesses—is often quite similar to what we might acknowledge about a person we know intimately. Indeed, our typical response to some signal moment of moral discovery in a Chekhov story—that whatever this character did is good, whatever that one thought is wrong—is almost always, consolingly enough, *recognition* rather than shock, as though we really knew in our hearts that people were like that, but until now hadn't needed to disclose it. Such is the case in **"Peasants."** There, a tubercular waiter Nikolay Tchikildyeev journeys home to his poor village perhaps to die, but also unfortunately to re-experience the grinding, battering, drunken poverty and debasement of his familial past. Tchikildyeev does indeed die, near the story's end, barely noticed by his preoccupied, disorderly kin. But before this can happen the narrator pronounces a sobering verdict we readers know to be true almost before we read it, although we might never have pronounced it for fear of what it might mean about us. (Chekhov, of course, means us to admit it, and makes that admission one of the story's shrewd ethical snares):

> Sasha and Motka and all the little girls in the hut huddled on the stove in the corner behind Nikolay's back, and from that refuge listened in silent terror, and the beating of their little hearts could be distinctly heard. Whenever there is someone in a family who has long been ill, and hopelessly ill, there come painful moments when all timidly, secretly, at the bottom of their hearts long for his death. . . .

Can we say, when we read this, that it's a complete surprise that life and long relation should culminate with such woeful news? But also can we say we have ever specifically *thought* that?

Or what of this disquisition on beauty from **"The Beauties"**:

> I felt this beauty [the narrator declares of a young woman] rather strangely. It was not desire, nor ecstacy, nor enjoyment that Masha excited in me, but a painful though pleasant sadness. It was a sadness vague and undefined as a dream. For some reason I felt sorry for myself . . . even for the girl herself, and I had a feeling as though we all . . . had lost something important and essential to life which we should never find again.

Exquisite beauty's perturbing consequence in everyday life: Loss. Pain. Regret. A rather unpromising view. But who hasn't glimpsed it among beauty's brighter allures, only to force it brusquely out of sight?

Not that these stories overflow with pithy observation. Chekhov is *not* famously aphoristic, and seems mostly to prefer stressing the way life struggles unheroically toward normalcy rather than serving up moments in which it is exceptional or by canny observation caused to seem so. And as absolutely full of life's experience as the stories are, Chekhov also seems to proportion and blend the *amount* of complexity they contain, as though there were limits to the literary significance we can accommodate. His stories rarely resolve in highly dramatic, epiphanic endings. And by largely eschewing this strategy they seem to refer us back to their own often unsensational, interior details. There, we are to reconsider moments of overlooked decisiveness and issue and possibly see mankind more clearly. Consequently, we are not only moved that poor Nikolay the waiter goes home to die and *does* die rather undramatically (not at the end), but we are also affected as we re-view the story that Chekhov, master of fine human distinctions, has elected exactly these people, these unlikely peasants to elevate to the condition of human exemplars.

One can say with some assurance that in settling upon the short story as his chosen narrative form, Chekhov elected in essence not to represent *all* of life, not to make a big splash, but to fashion discrete parts of life and focus our attentions and sharpest sensibilities there as a form of indispensable moral instruction; to *not* attempt what Walter Benjamin says the novel *always* attempts: "to carry the incommensurable to extremes in the representation of human life." Chekhov made his stories precisely *commensurate* with life and with a view of it we can accept in an almost homely way. He almost never suggests that life isn't worth living, or makes us feel at a loss or even feel over-indebted to his genius. But rather he measures his genius alongside our own and according to what we can understand as an act of empathy whose message is that life is much as we know it to be in our efforts to accept and go on.

* * *

All this may just be a way of saying that the reason we like Chekhov so much, now at our century's end, is because his stories from the last century's end feel so modern to us, are so much of our own time and mind. His meticulous anatomies of complicated human impulse and response, his view of what's funny and poignant, his clear-eyed observance of life as lived—all somehow matches our experience. His stories could, we feel, be written today, appear in *The New Yorker,* and be read for their insight with avidity and delight—no alterations or footnotes to account for periodicity or foreign provenance. To us, such fresh aptness confirms not only the continuity and saving vitality of the literary impulse, but it also assures us that we ourselves are part of a continuum and are sustainable. How we feel today about a dying wife, our married lover, our unsuitable suitor, our loyalties to our forsaken family, about the overmastering way in which life is too dense with subjectivity and too poor in objectifiable truth—all this was exactly how Russians felt far away in time, and when just as now a story was judged to be a saving response. Chekhov makes us feel corroborated, indemnified inside our human frailty, even smally hopeful of our ability to cope, to order and find clarity.

With Chekhov, we share the frankness of life's inalienable thereness; we share the conviction of how much we would profit if more of human sensation could be elevated into clear, expressive language; we share a view that life (particularly life with others) is a surface beneath which we must strive to construct a convincing subtext in order that more can be clung to less desperately; and we share a hopeful intuition that more of ourselves—especially those parts we feel only *we* know about—can be made susceptible to clear, useful exposition.

This last, indeed, is the case with the sad, wounded, forsaken Pyotr Mihalitch Ivashin of **"Neighbours,"** portrayed by Chekhov in full retreat from his botched effort to "rescue" his sister Zina from the arms of her

pompous, married seducer Vlassitch. Here, near the story's end, is one of the great, full Chekhov moments, when as readers we recognize that although we may not have been exactly here before, we still recognize a situation and a set of emotions which *should* surrender a lesson—reveal some keener sense of how we actually *are* as humans, a sense for which conventional language and inquiry offer little help. Thus the need for literary notice.

> Vlassitch walked by his right stirrup, and Zina by the left; both seemed to have forgotten that they had to go home. It was damp, and they had almost reached Koltovitch's copse. Pyotr Mihalitch felt that they were expecting something from him, though they hardly knew what it was, and he felt unbearably sorry for them. Now as they walked by the house with submissive faces, lost in thought, he had a deep conviction that they were unhappy, and could not be happy, and their love seemed to him a melancholy, irreparable mistake. Pity and the sense that he could do nothing to help them reduced him to that state of spiritual softening when he was ready to make any sacrifice to get rid of the painful feeling of sympathy.

Though shortly on and even more trenchantly, as Mihalitch enters the first bitter awareness that he has miscalculated love and passion and that such errors are to be the signature of his life, Chekhov's narrator notes:

> He was heavy at heart. When he got out of the copse he rode at a walk and then stopped his horse near the pond. He wanted to sit and think without moving. The moon was rising and was reflected in a streak of red on the other side of the pond. There were low rumbles of thunder in the distance. Pyotr Mihalitch looked steadily at the water and imagined his sister's despair, her martyr-like pallor, the tearless eyes with which she would conceal her humiliation from others. He imaged her with child, imagined the death of their mother, her funeral, Zina's horror. . . . Terrible pictures of the future rose before him on the background of smooth, dark water, and among pale feminine figures he saw himself, a weak, cowardly man with a guilty face. . . . And thinking about his life, he came to the conclusion that he had never said or acted upon what he really thought, and other people had repaid him in the same way. And so the whole of life seemed to him as dark as this water in which the night sky was reflected and waterweeds grew in a tangle. And it seemed to him that nothing could ever set it right.

* * *

As readers of imaginative literature, we are always seeking clues, warnings: where in life to search more assiduously; what not to overlook; what's the origin of this sort of human calamity, that sort of joy and pleasure; how can we live nearer to the latter, further off from the former? And to such seekers as we are, Chekhov is guide, perhaps *the* guide.

To twentieth-century writers, of course, his presence has affected all of our assumptions about what's a fit subject for imaginative writing; about which moments in life are too crucial or precious to relegate to conventional language; about how stories should begin, and the variety of ways a writer may choose to end them; and importantly about how final life is, and therefore how tenacious must be our representations of it.

More than anything else, though, it is Chekhov's great sufficiency that moves us and makes us admire; our reader's awareness that story to story, degree by degree around the sphere of observable human existence, Chekhov's measure is perfect. Given the subjects, the characters, the actions he brings into play, we routinely feel that everything of importance is always there in Chekhov. And our imaginations are for that reason ignited to know exactly what that great sufficiency is a reply to; what is the underlying urgency such that almost any story of Chekhov's can cause us to feel, either joyfully or pitifully, confirmed in life? As adults, we usually like what makes us want to know more, and are flattered by an assertive authority which makes us trust and then provides good counsel. It is indeed as though Chekhov knew us.

Finally, the stories found here are never difficult but often demanding; always dense but never turgid; sometimes dour, but rarely hopeless. Yet occasionally, reading through the great body of Chekhov's stories (220 plus), I have experienced secret relief when a story, here or there, seemed somehow *lesser,* was possibly tossed off in a way that allows me to imagine this most humane of writers in a new light—as a man agreeably unburdened by some demonic masterpiece-only obsession, a man I could've known, as a writer indeed willing to take us unblinkingly into the musing consciousness of kittens (!) and offer us assurance us that nothing very important goes on there: "The kitten lay awake thinking. Of what? . . . The soul of another is darkness, and a cat's soul more than most. . . . Fate had destined him to be the terror of cellars, store-rooms and corn bins, and had it not been for education . . . we will not anticipate, however." ("Who Was to Blame")

And so, no more anticipation. Just read these wonderful stories for pleasure, first, and do not read them fast. The more you linger, the more you reread, the more you'll experience and feel addressed by this great genius who, surprisingly, in spite of distance and time, shared a world we know and saw as his great privilege the chance to redeem it with language.

Carol A. Flath (essay date July 1999)

SOURCE: Flath, Carol A. "Art and Idleness: Chekhov's 'The House with a Mezzanine.'" *Russian Review* 58, no. 3 (July 1999): 456-66.

[*In the following essay, Flath delineates the contrast between work and idleness in "The House with a Mez-* zanine," *asserting that the theme may offer a "key to understanding Chekhov's creative process—the origins of his art."*]

> Естъ иволги в лесах, д гласных долгота
> В тонических стихах единственная мера.
> Но только разв году бывает разлита
> В природе длителъностъ, как в метрике Гомера.
>
> Как бы цезурою зияет этот денъ:
> Уже с утра покой и трудные длинноты;
> Волы на пастбище, и золотая ленъ
> Из тростника извлечъ богатство целой ноты.
>
> —Osip Mandelstam

Art . . . is a spirit seeking flesh but finding words.

> —Joseph Brodsky

Chekhov's best works often feature a contrast between work and idleness, a contrast that suggests an opposition between prosaic and poetic views of the world. This is perhaps best evident in the late plays—*Uncle Vania,* in which artistic sensibility (Elena) is opposed to a sober work ethic (Sonia), *The Three Sisters* (Andrei vs. Olga), and *The Cherry Orchard* (Ranevskaia vs. Lopakhin)—but it is a strong theme in his narratives as well.[1] Chekhov's intense interest in this issue suggests that it may have a significance beyond the merely thematic, and may in fact provide a key to understanding Chekhov's creative process—the origins of his art.

It is always dangerous to generalize when discussing Chekhov. For that reason, I would like to focus on a single story, **"The House With a Mezzanine: An Artist's Story" ("Dom s mezoninom: Rasskaz khudozhnika"** [1896]), which, as its subtitle suggests, foregrounds the theme of art. In this, one of Chekhov's best-known stories, the narrator, a landscape artist spending the summer in the Russian countryside, is briefly tempted romantically by the younger of two daughters of a local landowning family, the Volchaninovs, then goes back to the city (Petersburg). What interests us is the clear contrast between the tireless, selfless, socially active Lida, who is always working, and her dreamy, idle, and contemplative younger sister Zhenia, or Missy, who is always reading. As we will see, the narrator finds himself in a position between the two sisters.

A surface reading establishes the artist firmly in Zhenia's camp. They are both characterized by "idleness" (*prazdnost'*); the word serves as a leitmotif for both of them throughout the story. Even the time they spend together and Zhenia's dress bear the mark of this root, which, in addition to signifying idleness or emptiness, also carries the meaning of holiday, church holiday or Sunday (Zhenia bears the religious theme in this story). *Prazdnik* is opposed to *buden',* an ordinary working day.[2]

The center of gravity for the Zhenia/narrator story is a single long, lazy *prazdnik* the narrator spends at the Volchaninov estate. The time is midsummer (the end of July),[3] it is the day of rest, and no one (except Lida) feels like doing anything:

> When you think that all these healthy, well-fed, attractive people would spend the whole long day doing nothing, you wish that all life were like that. And I thought the same thing as I walked around in the garden, content to go on walking like that with nothing to do, aimlessly, all day long, for the whole summer.[4]

The narrator and Zhenia gather mushrooms, talk of religion and miracles, and of "eternal life" (p. 180). It is as if time has stood still: "It was hot, the wind had died down long ago, and it seemed as though the day would never end" (p. 181). Although nothing happens, this day is in a significant sense the center of the story. For it inevitably does end, and it is at that moment that the narrator experiences both a new awareness of his closeness to the Volchaninov family and, for the first time that summer, a desire to paint:

> As I left the Volchaninovs' house that evening, I took with me the impression of a long, long, idle day, with the sad awareness that everything in this world comes to an end, no matter how long it might last. Zhenia walked us to the gate, and perhaps because she had spent the whole day with me, from morning to night, I felt somehow bored without her; this whole dear family was close to me, and for the first time that whole summer I felt the desire to paint (*pisat'*).
>
> (p. 182)

In this way the beginnings of romantic love are linked with artistic inspiration (in this case, either painting or artistic literature can be suggested by the ambiguous verb "to paint/to write" [*pisat'*]), and both of them are associated with an awareness of the inevitable passage of time. The idle day must come to an end and be replaced by *buden'*—which is associated with the active, hard-working Lida. It is at this point that the narrator feels the desire and the energy necessary to transform his inspiration into a work of art.

It is appropriate that the narrator, a landscape artist, should find inspiration in a sense of timelessness and harmony. His is an art that denies plots.[5] In this sense we may identify the narrator/Zhenia story as lyrical in origin—representing that unique and timeless moment of inspiration and emotion from which all poetry originates. And it is in this joining of pastoral indolence with the lyrical impulse that we see in Chekhov the legacy of Pushkin, the father of both prose and poetic writing in Russia. Pushkin's poetic inspiration comes to him in moments of introspection, during the "free idleness" (*prazdnost' vol'nuiu*) of his time spent away from the bustle of the city.[6]

I quote Osip Mandelstam's beautiful poem about the caesura, "Orioles are in the Forest" (although there can be no question of influence) because it so precisely captures the mood of this part of Chekhov's story with its midsummer heat, its timelessness (duration suspended in the poetic caesura), its peace and "golden indolence" (Zhenia's languor, the sunlight in the treetops), and its lack of action.[7] Even Mandelstam's orioles echo the oriole in the orchard in the beginning of **"The House with a Mazzanine,"** who seems too lazy to produce "the wealth of a whole note": "On the right, in an old orchard, an oriole—most likely, an elderly one, too—sang reluctantly, in a weak voice" (pp. 174-75) These striking similarities reinforce the point that I am making here, that Chekhov's inspiration is lyrical, and that his story, like Mandelstam's poem, is about the creation of literary art.

For Joseph Brodsky, analyzing this Mandelstam poem, time is not a theme, but rather a tangible presence in poetry; "the words, even their letters—vowels especially—are almost palpable vessels of time."[8] It was this respect for the ability of poetry to transcend the passage of historical time that both led to Mandelstam's ultimate physical destruction and guaranteed the immortality of his verse: "For lyricism is the ethics of language and the superiority of this lyricism to anything that could be achieved within human interplay . . . is what makes for a work of art and lets it survive."[9] The plot of this story will illustrate this point, that the attempt to reconcile the lyric moment with the passage of time (the medium for narrative art) is doomed, though Chekhov's art proves the value of the attempt to do so.

Chekhov is among the most lyrical of prose writers. It is perhaps his superior ability to stay the flow of time in his narratives that has led to a suggestion among many readers that plot is not important for him.[10] Nevertheless, a close look at the narrator's interactions with the elder sister will reveal a strong story line that dominates the Zhenia plot and determines its ultimate outcome. For, however lyrical his works, Chekhov is ultimately a writer of narrative.

If Zhenia spends her time in idleness, Lida makes up for it with her constant activity. She is in charge of her entire household, works as a schoolteacher, distributes booklets, and participates in local political battles. In contrast to the mutual understanding and affection the narrator shares with Zhenia, his relations with Lida are marked by conflict, struggle and tension; the recurring word here—phonetically similar, in fact, both to Zhenia's *prazdnost'* and Lida's *pravda* (truth), to which it responds—is *razdrazhenie* (irritation): "Why are you irritated?" asks Zhenia (*Pochemu vy razdrazheny?*) "Because she [Lida] is *wrong*," he answers (*Potomu chto ona neprava*).[11]

The center of gravity of the narrator/Lida plot is the argument that erupts between them in chapter 3 over what the narrator sees as the futility of Lida's civic and charitable activities. To her attempts to improve her immediate environment within the political system he opposes a revolutionary philosophy which manages to combine a passionate affirmation of the spiritual value of art with a justification of abstraction, defeatism, and idleness. For the artist, human activity should be directed at solving philosophical issues, rather than curing individual ailments without eliminating their causes, and art and science must transcend practical needs. Naturally this amounts to a personal attack on Lida and everything she stands for.

A great deal has been written about the content of this debate; one line of Soviet criticism explored in this story the conflict between two "truths" of "great" vs. "small" deeds: *bol'shie dela* vs. *malen'kaia pol'za,* concluding that in spite of the difficulty of extracting a commitment to one or the other side of the argument on the basis of the text alone, Chekhov is making a statement for a protorevolutionary "greater" truth.[12] Nevertheless, Chekhov's political and ideological debates cannot be forced into resolution. Rather than attempting to do so, we should recognize the vital importance of the issue to Chekhov himself as an artist. Whenever he discussed his "artistic philosophy," like the narrator of this story he proclaimed the independence of the artist: "I am not a liberal, not a conservative, not a gradualist, not a monk, not an indifferentist. I would like to be a free artist—that is all."[13] At the same time he lived his life as Lida did, working tirelessly at a local level to improve the lot of the poor and needy.[14] We can suggest that Chekhov, in setting up this passionately argued debate in his story, was to at least some degree playing out for us an internal conflict of his own—one that it is tempting to set forth in terms of an irresolvable spirit (art)/body (practical life) split. To me it is enough to point out that Lida "received patients" to establish the autobiographical connection (p. 178). After all, what is Lida, a schoolteacher in her early twenties, doing examining sick people? Chekhov permeates the personality not only of Zhenia and the narrator, but Lida as well. A work of art is always to some degree an expression of its creator's soul. As Nadezhda Mandelstam says, discussing the poetic impulse that is my subject here, "any portrait is at the same time also a self-portrait of the painter, just as anything with any degree of abstraction is the same portrait, impression, imprint of the spirit and inner form of its creator. . . . A poem is a phenomenon created by a poet, and in this phenomenon the subject and the object are inseparable."[15]

And in his study of the interaction of prose and poetry in Chekhov, who in his view can be identified as a "synthetic" (as opposed to analytical) writer, Petr Bitsilli suggests that it is in part the entrance of Chekhov's personality into his prose work that gives the impression of poetry: "The poetic, intuitive perception of observable reality," Bitsilli remarks, "consists in an identification of the perceiving subject with the perceived object; the object of perception is thereby subjectivized, and creates its own poetic reality."[16] In our exploration of the genesis of Chekhov's art, we will inevitably discover the author's own tangible and complex presence in the text. It is not limited to one bearer of his views, as often seems to be the case in artistic literature, but rather is distributed among various characters.

What interests us in the plot of **"The House with a Mezzanine"** is the way the debate brings to a climax the conflict between the narrator and Lida. Zhenia and Lida are a pair; they are introduced to us together, and when we encounter one of them alone, we feel the absence of the other. Though both are described as slender and pale, it is the differences between them that we notice: at twenty-three, Lida is serious, businesslike and mature—maybe *too mature*: young as she is, she refers pejoratively to the "youth" of the district ("You see what our young people are like!" [p. 176]). Zhenia, still in her teens (seventeen or eighteen years old), is childlike, curious and receptive to impressions—maybe *too childish*.[17] B. F. Egorov astutely assigns Lida the "imperative" mood, with Zhenia's interrogative tendencies serving as the "negative antonym" to her "dominant."[18] The most marked contrast, and the one most important to the narrator, a painter, has to do with vision: Zhenia has large eyes and is always looking directly at the narrator, whereas Lida always looks away.

Clearly the plot of the story traces the development of a romance between the narrator and the younger sister. But if we are to accept the story as what it seems to be, we will have to explain away some disturbing facts. If the narrator is primarily interested in Zhenia, then why is she always presented in the narrative as an afterthought to her elder sister? "As for the other one . . ." (p. 175); "But her sister, Missy . . ." (p. 178); "Why haven't you fallen in love yet with Lida or Zhenia?" (p. 182) Why is he driven to *analyze* and *justify* his love for Zhenia?

> *Perhaps because* she had spent the whole day with me, from morning to night, I felt somehow bored without her.
>
> (p. 182)

> I loved Zhenia. *Most likely I loved her because* she had met me and seen me off, *because* of the tender and adoring way she looked at me. . . . I admired the breadth of her outlook, maybe *because she had a different way of thinking from stern, beautiful Lida, who did not love me.*
>
> (p. 188)

The whole depth and poignancy of Chekhov's art is expressed in this "*did not love me*" (*ne liubila menia*), the deeper meaning of which is lost is most translations, which naturally opt for "disliked." For the narrator is in fact attracted to both the active, inaccessible Lida and the passive, romantic Zhenia. He is rationalizing, trying to domesticate and project onto the younger sister the disturbing emotions he feels for the elder. He is caught between them, and ultimately will be unable to sustain a relationship with either.[19]

Criticism of the story has recognized the ambiguities in the artist's position between the two women. Egorov, for example, notes the complexity of Lida's reactions to the growing intimacy between him and her sister:

> Chekhov did not like to dot his "i"s; Lida's irritation can be interpreted any number of ways: *jealousy*, a desire to keep her sister away from a man with a different ideology, concern for an inexperienced girl, fear that her sister might slip from her control etc., but what is important is that she is *not indifferent to the growing intimacy* taking place before her very eyes between her sister and the artist.[20]

Joseph Conrad asks the question directly:

> Is this story an examination of the mystery of sexual attraction? In other words, are Lida and the narrator engaged in vehement denial of each other's position (utilitarian aid vs. art for art's sake) to hide, or deny, their mutual attraction?[21]

Our affirmative answer to this risky question allows us to reveal the workings of the creative principle underlying Chekhov's narrative art. **"The House with a Mezzanine"** dramatizes the way literary art emerges from erotic tension.

It is Lida who is described as "very beautiful" (p. 175). And in spite of her repeated statements to the narrator that what she is saying "cannot be interesting" to him, she is the one who keeps the narrator's attention and interest.[22] The word "interesting" recurs throughout the text in association with Lida. Chekhov's subject is so often boredom (*skuka*) that we should pay close attention when a character finds something or someone "interesting," especially when the idea is stressed and repeated. The narrator's interest in Lida, and her struggle against that interest, seem clearly to serve as the alternative to the emptiness and languor that mark his interactions with Zhenia. It is here that the plot "intrigue," as opposed to the lyrical impulse, is concentrated. For support we turn to Patricia Meyer Spacks' exploration of women's writing in the eighteenth and nineteenth centuries, which elucidates the "dialect of interest and boredom" that lies at the base of all fiction: "The act of writing implicitly claims interest (boredom's antithesis) for the assertions or questions or exclamations it generates. At the very least, any autonomous process of writing protects the writer for a time against the vacuity we call boredom."[23] Literary plots spring from interest and intrigue, and are driven forward by desire. As Peter Brooks puts it:

Narratives both tell of desire—typically present some story of desire—and arouse and make use of desire as dynamic of signification. Desire is in this view like Freud's notion of Eros, a force including sexual desire but larger and more polymorphous. . . . Desire as Eros, desire in its plastic and totalizing function, appears to me central to our experience of reading narrative.[24]

In **"The House with a Mezzanine,"** the narrator's battle with Lida over "interest" actually plays out a disguised drama of sexual desire.[25] This struggle is fundamental to the story, not because of its content, but because of the way it propels and determines the plot.[26] The development of the interest between them constitutes the plot.[27]

Given the visual focus of the artist-narrator, we must pay particularly close attention to the pointed contrast between Lida's willful blindness and Zhenia's wide-eyed curiosity. As her civic concern suggests, Lida is blind to the beauty of art and love; Zhenia is pure perception and lyricism but does not inspire a desire to work. The tendency to *denial* in Lida masks the workings of the sexual tension between her and the narrator. When we look from this perspective, everything falls into place. The mutual irritation (*razdrazhenie*) that marks the conversations between Lida and the narrator in fact masks an intense erotic friction.

Chekhov is not the first Russian writer to use the word in this sense. In Tolstoy's "Kreutzer Sonata" (1889), non-purposeful music acts as an irritant, leading to erotic stimulation:

> This music only excites, but does not satisfy (*razdrazhaet, a ne konchaet*). . . . Take a military march: the soldiers march in step to it, and the music has achieved its goal; they play a dance, I dance, and the music has achieved its goal; or, say, a liturgy is sung, I take communion, and that music has achieved its goal, but this—it's just irritation/stimulation (*razdrazhenie*), without an outlet for what you're supposed to do with this irritation.[28]

The "irritation" music arouses in "Kreutzer Sonata" leads to adultery and murder.[29] This would explain Lida's need to send Zhenia out of the room when the artist says he will not work to support the existing order (especially considering that "order" is one of Lida's leitmotifs), for the entertainment of "a predatory, slovenly animal":

> And I don't want to work, so I won't. . . . I don't have to do anything; the world can go to hell!

> "Leave the room, Missy," said Lida to her sister, evidently finding my words harmful to such a young girl.

> (p. 187)

It is a combination of the content of the argument and the passionate emotion that is flaring up between the artist and Lida that makes the atmosphere unsuitable for a young girl; and undoubtedly Lida recognizes the infectious erotic potentiality inherent in the languorous Zhenia. Both sisters function as a kind of catalyst for the emergence of love between the artist and the other. Chekhov's deep insight into the complexity of human psychology works here on all levels, transcending both the surface layer of the dialogue and the artist's half-truths and denial on the level of the narration. By banishing Zhenia from the room Lida may be protecting herself as much as her sister; at the same time she may be making a move to secure the artist for herself. Surely, then, when she puts a stop to the argument, saying that she and the narrator will never agree ("sing together" [*spoemsia*]), the flush on her face reflects not simply anger at the artist (as most translations imply), but a combination of anger, strong emotion, arousal, guilt and shame. This would explain Lida's need to "hide her agitation" (*volnenie*; p. 187). As in the third act of Chekhov's plays, this culminating scene of the third chapter of his story predetermines the ending, when Lida banishes Zhenia not only from the room but also from the house with the mezzanine—and from the story itself.[30]

"The House with a Mezzanine" dramatizes the incompatibility of two equally essential sides of love: the harmonic, lyrical feelings the narrator shares with Zhenia contrast starkly with the dramatic tension of his attraction to Lida, which thrives on contradiction and denial. Our assertion that this attraction is indeed sexual is also reinforced by a glance into literary tradition. During that long, lazy day the narrator and Zhenia have spent together, Lida has been conspicuously absent. Then she appears, and,

> standing at the porch with a riding crop in her hands, shapely and beautiful in the sunlight, she gave orders to a workman. She hurriedly received a couple of sick villagers, talking in a loud voice, then walked through the rooms with a businesslike, concerned look on her face, opening first one cupboard, then another, then went up into the mezzanine; it took a long time to find her and call her to dinner, and she came down only after we had finished our soup. For some reason I recall and love (*liubliu*) all these minor details, although nothing special took place.
>
> (180-81)

Chekhov was deeply influenced by Turgenev.[31] The otherwise incongruous[32] riding crop (*khlyst*) that Lida shows up with, interrupting the narrator's idyll with her sister, can be explained by a look at the powerful climactic moment in Turgenev's "First Love" (1860). In this scene the sixteen-year old narrator eavesdrops on a tryst between Zinaida, the young woman whom he has adored and idealized all summer, and her lover, his own father. The boy's father strikes Zinaida's arm through the window with his *khlyst,* she kisses the welt it leaves, and the father rushes inside the house to her. At this moment the boy suddenly realizes the power and pain

of mature sexual attraction, a passion infinitely deeper than the romantic crush that he has experienced as his first love.[33] The motif of beating and striking that has pervaded the entire text of Turgenev's story is distilled into a single word in **"The House with a Mezzanine,"** but it is enough to communicate Chekhov's message. In the Chekhov scene, Lida is a striking and attractive presence, and her beauty is inseparable from her power and dominance; Lida, after all, is associated with *action,* in direct opposition to the passivity and spiritual nature of her sister and the narrator. Furthermore, like Turgenev's Zinaida, she is inaccessible to the narrator. These are not "minor details," as the artist, in his own denial, says, but the very essence of Lida's attractiveness, and it is telling that the narrator remembers them so vividly and "loves" them.

Another glance into Chekhov's biography supports the assertion that argument and irritation serve as erotic stimulation. While composing **"The House with a Mezzanine,"** Chekhov wrote in a letter that he was "working on a short story: 'My Fiancée.' I had a fiancée once. . . . She was called Missy. That's what I'm writing about."[34] This fiancée would have to be Dunia Efros, to whom he seems to have been engaged briefly in 1886.[35] The history of this stormy relationship does not, as Carolina De Maegd-Soëp points out, allow us to see the temperamental Efros as a prototype for Zhenia. But if we continue our "denial-based" reading—an approach useful for interpreting Chekhov's irony-bound letters as well as his multilayered literary texts—we may suggest his relationship with her as a model, at least to some degree, for the artist's relationship with *Lida.* For by all accounts the engagement was a stormy one, complicated by clashes over religion (Efros was Jewish) and class as well as emotional issues. Elena Tolstaia provides the most interesting analysis of Chekhov's short-lived engagement. "From the very beginning," she writes, "it was obviously a conflict of two strong personalities, accompanied on his side by a class- and nationality-based ill-will; but all this against the background of a very strong attraction."[36] In general, as a reading of his letters or any biography will suggest, Chekhov seems to have been attracted not to waif types like Zhenia, but to boistrous, even "loud" women like Lida.[37]

A work of art is always to some degree a self-portrait. When we look beyond the content of the narrator's arguments with Lida, when we follow the flow of his language, when we watch what characters do, rather than simply what they say, and when we consider facts from the author's own biography, we discover the real profundity of **"The House with a Mezzanine."** This story illustrates metaphorically the author's own process of artistic creation, and by analogy, the principles underlying narrative art as a whole.[38] If we view the two sisters as representing two different poles of literary art, the lyrical and the narrative, with the narrator suspended between them, we can see the story itself as the fruit of their "triangular" interaction—Brodsky's "spirit seeking flesh but finding words." Zhenia represents an ideal harmony that cannot be sustained beyond a timeless moment (the "duration of vowels"); Lida represents the conflict that lies at the base of a good narrative. Chekhov's notorious elusiveness as an artist manifests itself in the narrator's inability to establish or sustain a commitment to either of them: the narrator's romance with Zhenia must not be consummated ("this day would never end" [p. 181]), and he will never attain harmony with Lida. As we have suggested here, this echoes a similar elusiveness in Chekhov's life, both as regards his artistic and political philosophies and in his own romantic relationships. And as in similar stories by Turgenev ("Asia" [1857] and "First Love," for example), the very beauty of this story depends on its lack of resolution; there is nothing compelling or "narratable" in a conflictless, harmonic love. But no art can be created without an interaction between both of these elements; inspiration (Zhenia) is meaningless unless it is crafted, by hard work (Lida), into a finished work of art. This is exactly what Chekhov has done in **"The House with a Mezzanine."**

Notes

The author would like to thank Professors Paul Debreczeny, Denis Mickiewicz, Kira Rogova, and Maia Turovskaia for their careful reading and insightful comments on drafts of this article.

1. Gary Saul Morson's theory of prosaics finds virtue in what I am calling here the "work" side of this opposition. Morson, analyzing *Uncle Vania*, finds that Sonia's "prosaic" work ethic is the source of value, directly opposed to idle Elena's ideal of work for "all humanity." See his "*Uncle Vanya* as Prosaic Metadrama," in *Reading Chekhov's Text,* ed. Robert Louis Jackson (Evanston, 1993), 223. The theme is developed further in Morson's "Sonya's Wisdom," in *A Plot of Her Own: The Female Protagonist in Russian Literature,* ed. Sona Stephan Hoisington (Evanston, 1995), 58-71. In this study I will be attempting in part to salvage artistic value from the idleness of characters like Elena.

2. Vladimir Dal', *Tolkovyi slovar' zhivago velikoruskago iazyka* (1882; reprint ed. Moscow, 1980), 3:380-81.

3. The significance of midsummer, especially in cold Russia, as the location of the poetic moment, is worth a thorough exploration in its own right. Such a study would explore the migration of the Russian landowning nobility to the country for the summer, pastoral myths in the Russian context, the religious theme of a fall from Edenic grace, and Western literary precedents such as Shakespeare's midsummer comedies.

4. A. P. Chekhov, *Polnoe sobranie sochinenii i pisem v tridtsati tomakh* (Moscow, 1977), 9:179. All citations to "The House with a Mezzanine" are from this volume of *Sochineniia*; quotations from letters are noted *Pis'ma*, with the volume number indicated. All translations from the Russian are my own. In-text parenthetical page references refer only to "The House with a Mezzanine."

5. In his study of the narrator's orientation in the visual arts, Paul Debreczeny suggests that the relevant distinction between narrative and landscape painting, given the political climate of the time, is that of social criticism. This illuminates the conflict between the narrator and Lida. See Paul Debreczeny, "Chekhov's Use of Impressionism in 'The House with the Mansard,'" in *Russian Narrative and Visual Art: Varieties of Seeing,* ed. Roger Anderson and Paul Debreczeny (Gainesville, 1994), esp. 101-4.

6. See, for example, "Derevnia" (1819), in Pushkin, *Polnoe sobranie sochinenii,* vol. 2, *Stikhotvoreniia, 1817-1825* (Moscow, 1994), 82-83. Monika Greenleaf builds a similar argument in her fascinating study of Pushkin's elegies. She suggests that Pushkin's historical narratives represent a struggle against the lyrical "indolence" (*len'*) of elegaic poetry; and that this is one reason why *Len*skii has to be killed off in *Eugene Onegin*. "Did not Pushkin's 'historical elegy' of 1825, 'Andre Chenier,' dramatize the duel between the private, elegaic impulse and the poet's public, odic responsibility?" (Monika Greenleaf, *Pushkin and Romantic Fashion: Fragment, Elegy, Orient, Irony* [Stanford, 1994], 87). The subject of Pushkin as a kindred spirit and source for Chekhov's art has not been sufficiently explored, although a new issue of *Chekhoviana* gives grounds for optimism. See *Chekhoviana: Chekhov i Pushkin* (Moscow, 1997).

7. Of the three verbs in the poem, two are existential (*est'* and *byvaet*) and one points to emptiness (*ziiaet*).

8. Joseph Brodsky, "The Child of Civilization," in his *Less Than One: Selected Essays* (New York, 1986), 125.

9. Ibid., 137.

10. See, among others, A. B. Derman, *O masterstve Chekhova* (Moscow, 1959), 63.

11. *Sochineniia* 9:180 (emphasis added here and throughout unless otherwise noted). Chekhov's lyricism extends to the level of sound play. For

example, женя reads книжки, лежа; the artist is а художник, пейиаздст; as for Lida, always раздраженная, her mother says: « Этак жа книжками и аптечками и не убидишъ, как жизнъ пройдет. . . . Замуз нузно » (p. 181). At the very least an awareness of this aspect of the text deepens our appreciation for Chekhov's poetic art. "Razdrazhenie," framed phonetically in this way, bears enormous significance in this story, and we will return to it later.

12. See, for example, G. P. Berdnikov, *A. P. Chekhov: Ideinye i tvorcheskie iskaniia,* 2d ed. (Leningrad, 1970), 367-68: "Chekhov opposed . . . liberal philanthropizing, the theory of 'small deeds' that was popular at that time, whose supporters consciously closed their eyes to the real state of things, sowing harmful illusions that indeed it was possible to change something in the lives of the people by means of these 'small deeds.'" For a description of the Soviet criticism on this issue see I. N. Sukhikh, *Problemy poetiki A. P. Chekhova* (Leningrad, 1987), 117.

13. Chekhov letter to Pleshcheev, 4 October 1888, *Pis'ma* 3:11.

14. Joseph Conrad makes the same point in his "Čechov's 'House with an Attic': Echoes of Turgenev," *Russian Literature* 26 (1989): 373-96: "What is puzzling about these two dramatically opposed views is that they each are representative of Čechov's own approach to the problems of his day" (p. 384).

15. Nadezhda Mandelstam, *Mozart and Salieri,* trans. Robert A. McLean (Ann Arbor, 1973), 28, 47.

16. Petr M. Bitsilli, *Chekhov's Art: A Stylistic Analysis,* trans. Toby W. Clyman and Edwina Jannie Cruise (Ann Arbor, 1983), 64.

17. As Conrad points out in "Čechov's 'House with an Attic'" (p. 380). Svetlana Evdokimova has explored the moral implications of childishness in Chekhov's works in "The Discreet Charms of a Nursery: Chekhov's *The Cherry Orchard*" (Paper presented at the National Convention of the AAASS, Boston, 1996).

18. B. F. Egorov, "Struktura rasskaza 'Dom s mezoninom,'" *Vtvorcheskoi laboratorii Chekhova* (Moscow, 1974), 259. Of course, the narrator's mode would be indicative (or subjunctive).

19. The configuration of artist with the two women in this story resonates with Chekhov's own oft-repeated statement of his predicament as an artist and doctor (or alternatively, playwright and short-story writer); he claims to be caught between a wife and a lover. For example, in a letter to his

brother Aleksandr, he notes, "In addition to my wife, medicine, I also have a lover, literature" (*Pis'ma* 2:15).

20. Egorov, "Struktura rasskaza," 261.

21. Conrad, "Čechov's 'House with an Attic,'" 382.

22. See, for example, *Sochineniia* 9:177, 183. The quote is from page 175.

23. Patricia Meyer Spacks, *Boredom: The Literary History of a State of Mind* (Chicago, 1996), 247, 1. Peter Brooks points out that "the adjective *interessante,* applied to young women, has a long history in both sentimental and erotic literature, and in both cases suggests that the signs of suffering, linked to erotic constraint, make the object of attention more appealing." See his *Body Work: Objects of Desire in Modern Narrative* (Cambridge, MA, 1993), 37.

24. Peter Brooks, *Reading for the Plot: Design and Intention in Narrative* (Cambridge, MA, 1984), 37.

25. The issue of the limits to the permissible in literary art concerned Chekhov more during the late 1880s than the period of "The House with a Mezzanine." I would suggest that in the later stories Chekhov has developed an art of sensual descriptiveness that implies the sexual without having to directly describe it. For more on the erotic in Chekhov see Joseph Conrad, "Sensuality in Čexov's Prose," *Slavic and East European Journal* 24 (Summer 1980): 103-17; Elena Tolstaia, "Evreiskaia tema v russkoi literature," *Novoe literatumoe obozrenie* 8 (1994): 221-49; and idem, *Poetika razdrazheniia: Chekhov v kontse 1880-kh—nachale 1890-kh godov* (Moscow, 1994), 35-36.

26. "Interest" sparks sexual passion elsewhere in Chekhov as well, perhaps most notably in *Uncle Vania,* which was completed in the same year as "The House with a Mezzanine":

ELENA ANDREEVNA:

And is it interesting?

ASTROV:

Yes, it is an interesting thing to do.

VOINITSKII:

(*sardonically*) Very! . . .

ELENA ANDREEVNA:

That doctor has a tired, nervous face. An interesting face.

(*Sochineniia* 13:72, 74)

The triangular relationships that move the plot in *Uncle Vania* differ from those in the story, however, for Sonia represents pure unreciprocated longing, whereas here the narrator's desire is truly suspended between the two sisters.

27. We are doubly convinced of this by the narrator's return to "boredom" at the end of the story, after Lida sends Zhenia away: "A sobor, everyday (*budnichnoe*) mood overcame me, and I was ashamed of everything that I had said at the Volchaninovs', and life became boring again, as before" (p. 191).

28. L. N. Tolstoi, "Kreitserova sonata," in his *Polnoe sobranie sochinenii v 91 tomakh* (Moscow-Leningrad, 1933), 27:61.

29. For further discussion of this aspect of Tolstoy's story see Charles Isenberg, *Telling Silence: Russian Frame Narratives of Renunciation* (Evanston, 1993), 92-93; and Richard Gustafson, *Leo Tolstoy: Resident and Stranger: A Study in Fiction and Theology* (Princeton, 1986), 354. We also find support for our position in dictionaries, for example, M. H. T. and V. L. Alford, *Russian-English Scientific and Technical Dictionary* (Oxford, 1974), 2:978 ("раздразение: irritation, stimulation"); and Dal, *Tolkovyi slovar'* 4:27 ("Раздражать, раздразить: to excite [arouse] . . . (people): to anger, arousing impatience, irritation, or in general a feeling of passion"). Making the association between irritation, stimulation and passion does not, naturally, deny the primary meaning of the verb.

30. It is ironic, though fitting, that Lida, whose energies are focused on sheltering homeless people (p. 175) should be the cause of her sister's ultimate homelessness in this story, the very title of which stresses the importance of the theme. It is also most fitting that the narrator—himself without a permanent address—seems to find himself more often in the entranceways to the house with a mezzanine (the gate to the estate, the steps of the front porch) than inside it. His place is truly *between* the territories of Zhenia (outside) and Lida (inside). Domesticity is both unattainable and deeply threatening to him, as it is to many other narrators in Chekhov's stories.

31. See, for example, Conrad, "Čechov's 'House with an Attic.'"

32. After all, Lida rides not on horseback, but in a carriage (*ressornaia koliaska,* p. 175), one with springs, no less—a fact significant to Soviet critics as evidence of Lida's hypocrisy. See I. N. Sukhikh, *Problemy poetiki A. P. Chekhova* (Leningrad, 1987), 124.

33. I. S. Turgenev. "Pervaia liubov'," in his *Polnoe sobranie sochinenii i pisem v dvadtsati vos'mi tomakh. Sochineniia* (Moscow-Leningrad, 1965), 9:70.

34. *Pis'ma* 6:103.

35. See Donald Rayfield, *Anton Chekhov: A Life* (New York, 1997), 123-27; Carolina De Maegd-Soëp, *Chekhov and Women: Women in the Life and Work of Chekhov* (Columbus, OH, 1987), 102-7; and Elena Tolstaia, "Evreiskaia tema." The evidence for the engagement is contained in a series of letters Chekhov wrote to Bilibin in 1886 (See *Literaturnoe nasledstvo,* vol. 68 (Moscow, 1960); and *Pis'ma* 1:190, 212-13).

36. Tolstaia, "Evreiskaia tema," 225.

37. For example, "We find a marked preference on his part for robust, outgoing, active girls. It is remarkable then that his fiction appears to idealize a type of woman who possesses none of these qualities" (Ronald Hingley, *A Life of Anton Chekhov* [Oxford, 1989], 199). For the facts of Chekhov's relationships with women, the indispensible source is Rayfield's definitive new biography, cited in note 35.

38. Isenberg's exploration of the frame narrative in Russian literature suggests that inserted tales "do not so much demonstrate a truth as narrativize a desire. . . . The act of framing of stories may equate with a rationalization of the narrator's unconscious desire" (*Telling Silence,* 17). In unframed or weakly framed narratives such as this one we may not notice an attempt at *rationalization* of desire, but the desire, as something basic to the narrative genre, is present nonetheless. The difficulty we face here has to do with our direct confrontation with the author, rather than a displaced author or narrator-surrogate.

Harvey Pitcher (essay date 1999)

SOURCE: Pitcher, Harvey. Introduction to *Chekhov: The Comic Stories,* translated by Harvey Pitcher, pp. 1-10. Chicago: Ivan R. Dee, 1999.

[*In the following entry, Pitcher discusses the defining characteristics of Chekhov's humorous stories.*]

There it was, on the theatre page of that highly respectable newspaper, the *Independent,* an advertisement for 'Britain's Biggest Bottled Beer' and above it, in eye-catching capitals, the words: HEAVIER THAN CHEKHOV.

Chekhov would have loved this. In Russia, he predicted, his work would not be read for more than a few years after his death, and he was sure it could never be understood in the West. How amazing, then, to be so well known in Britain almost a century later! An avid newspaper reader and not one to skip the adverts (they might give him an idea for a comic story), he would cheerfully have agreed to promote 'The One and Only Newcastle Brown Ale'. As for 'heavier than Chekhov', that would have amused him most of all: were my plays really so boring, he would have asked, throwing up his hands in mock despair.

They weren't, but that makes no difference. Labels stick and images lead a life of their own. Chekhov has been especially vulnerable to labelling. Beware of the ubiquitous adjective 'Chekhovian': the more confidently people use it, the profounder their ignorance. The present volume, the first substantial collection in English to be devoted solely to his comic stories, is intended to provide a counterbalance to the worn-out image of Chekhov as a heavy writer.

As a man, he was anything but heavy. His friend and fellow-writer, Ivan Bunin, described him figuratively as 'very light on his feet'. Easily bored, he was mistrustful of anyone solemn or pretentious, preferring the company of people who were lively and amusing, unpredictable and good fun; he loved comic banter and was forever inventing comic nicknames for himself and other people, assigning them comic roles and weaving comic fantasies around them; and he had his own laconic conversational style, with an offbeat, understated sense of humour. Few people were able to resist his infectious laughter. All this, however, was not simply a matter of temperament or disposition. Chekhov adopted the humorous stance deliberately, as a means of distancing himself from other people and avoiding unwanted intimacy. Often, he seems to conduct the relationships of real life as if they were comic fiction.

As a writer, too, Chekhov does not reveal himself. His great gift is to reveal others. It is no accident that **'The Chameleon'** (1884) is one of his best-known early stories, for he himself has a chameleon-like, mimetic gift. His lowly origins and social mobility meant that throughout his life he was constantly participating in different worlds, meeting different kinds of people. He seems to have developed an almost uncanny ability to absorb how other people behaved, how they viewed the world, how they talked, all of which he later reproduced imaginatively in his fiction. These acts of impersonation mean that readers of Chekhov, as William Gerhardie put it, may congratulate themselves when they die 'on having lived a hundred lives—but paid for one!'

From 1879 to 1884 he led a double life. 'I began contributing to the journals during my first year at university,' he wrote later, 'and as a student had hundreds of stories published under the pseudonym "A. Chekhonte", which, as you see, is very similar to my own name. And not one of my fellow students knew that I was "A. Chekhonte", none of them was interested.' That he successfully combined these contrasting lives—as a medical student (so unassuming that his contemporaries remembered only that he attended lectures regularly and sat somewhere near the window) and as a literary Bohemian—was a tribute to his remarkable energy, chameleon quality and a strength of character lacking in his elder brothers. When the father's grocery business in Taganrog, a port in the south of Russia, failed in 1876, the family decamped hurriedly to Moscow, all except Anton, who stayed on for three years, tutoring younger pupils to help pay for his own schooling and acquiring an independence of mind and action.

In Moscow the family were very dependent on his income from writing, and as a result he had a go at everything, 'except a novel, poetry and denunciations to the police'. He soon learned to be succinct (better to cut a story yourself than leave it to an editor) and never forgot the lesson: the mature Chekhov is the least flowery or self-indulgent of writers. He seemed not so much to invent stories as to find them everywhere in the life around him. All those flighty young girls and downtrodden civil servants step straight on to his pages from the streets of 1880s Moscow.

To the serious business of comic writing, for which there was a regular demand from the popular press, he applied himself assiduously, happy to turn his hand to anything in the humour line: captions to cartoons, comic advertisements and announcements, menus, questionnaires, mathematical problems ('My mother-in-law is 75 and my wife 42. What time is it?') and calendars of past and future events ('Sarah Bernhardt [who toured Russia in 1881] is about to marry an assistant secretary at the Chinese Embassy'). Most frequently, though, he contributed short stories, seldom more than a few pages long.

Certain conventions had to be followed. Merchants, priests and usually civil servants had to be given funny names. Chekhov fell in with this, but brought his own originality to bear. Only certain comic genres were acceptable. Here, too, he had to toe the line, but with distinctive variations of his own. His first published story was in the well-established genre of parody. **'The Swedish Match'** (1883), one of his best-known and longest early stories, he also refers to as a parody (of the crime stories so popular at the time), but it is more than that: the lively writing turns it into a comedy thriller, and in exploiting the interplay of character between the inspector and his bright young assistant ('That's enough of your fancy theories. Get on with your lunch.') Chekhov was anticipating every television crime series you can think of in the late twentieth century. In **'From the Diary of a Book-keeper's Assistant'** (1883) he takes another well-worn genre, the comic diary or memoir, and does something quite distinctive with it: this sketch with its 'zero ending', still unusual then, hovers precariously between humour and pathos. In the many stories that involve simple mistakes, errors of judgement, mistaken identity, jumping to false conclusions, misinterpreting other people's behaviour and so on, Chekhov is making use of seemingly universal sources of humour, which at its most basic level is all to do with expectations. In **'Overdoing It'** (1885) he goes a step further by showing how both protagonists build up a false picture of the other; mutual incomprehension, here happily resolved, will be a later, non-humorous Chekhov theme. Very often these error-based stories are resolved by means of a comic twist. Here Chekhov could be highly ingenious and produced some of his most wonderful comic effects. Especially unforgettable are the endings of stories like **'Revenge'** (1886) and **'No Comment'** (1888), where the reader is not only taken completely by surprise, but has to admit that the outcome is entirely plausible. **'The Burbot'** (1885) ends with a comic twist of a literal kind.

Far less inspired are those stories—over fifty of them—in which Chekhov takes a facetious look at (nearly always thwarted) romance. They are represented here by two comic memoir stories, where much of the fun derives from the use of a narrator's mask. **'Notes from the Memoirs of a Man of Ideals'** (1885) is a simple story with a cast of two and a comic twist, whereas **'Notes from the Journal of a Quick-tempered Man'** (1887) is full of invention, has an unusually large cast and reverses many a romantic cliché, whether that of romantic atmosphere—'The revolting moon was creeping up from behind the shrubbery. The air was still, with an unpleasant smell of fresh hay . . .'—or the delights of the first kiss: 'So there was nothing else for it—I got up and put my lips to her elongated face, experiencing the same sensation I had as a child when I was made to kiss my dead grandmother's face at her funeral.'

Almost as numerous, not so overtly comic, but more satirical and in their own way subversive, are those stories in which the central character is a 'little man', usually a minor civil servant, a literary descendant of Gogol's Akaky Akakiyevich in 'The Overcoat' (1842). His view of the world is imposed upon him by society's rules and regulations, by his place within a strict hierarchy in which social rank is all-important. All is well until some chance happening disrupts the fabric of his life. The humour of **'The Civil Service Exam'** (1884) and **'The Exclamation Mark'** (1885) is very gentle, but Chekhov also produces disturbingly original variations on the theme. In **'The Malefactor'** (1885), a story much admired by Tolstoy, no contact is ever made between the simple world of the uneducated peasant and the magistrate's world of civilized legal procedures.

In the famous **'Fat and Thin'** (1883) the natural world of friendship yields at once to the unnatural world of social hierarchy. The rank-conscious central character in **'The Chameleon'** (1884) can no longer 'see' the world properly: his inability to sort out who owns the dog makes it impossible for him to decide whether he should be looking up or down. As for **'Sergeant Prishibeyev'** (1885), he is the dangerous little man who identifies with the bosses and turns dictator, only to find that his view of the world has nothing in common with theirs, either.

Chekhov's distinctive mimetic gift shows up in stories where the humour derives from the highly individual way in which the central character construes the world. In **'Kashtanka'** (1887) the young dog 'divided the human race into two very unequal classes, masters and customers . . . the former had the right to beat her, whereas she herself had the right to seize the latter by the calves.' For the very young child, the sole purpose of the clock 'is to swing its pendulum and strike' (**'Grisha'**, 1886). The would-be runaways in **'Boys'** (1887) simplify the world: once they reach America, 'California's no distance'. These two boys are dreamers, constructing an ideal world of the imagination, youthful representatives of a type found elsewhere in Chekhov; the defiant ten-year-old at the end of the story has all the makings of a future revolutionary.

One other element in the comic stories peculiar to Chekhov is that of the absurd. This ranges from the incongruous and the ridiculous to the bizarre, the grotesque and even black humour. Here everyday expectations of the world are turned completely upside down. In **'The Daughter of Albion'** (1883) grotesque physical description of the English governess, with her nose that looks like a hook and her rotten smell, is combined with a bizarrely improbable situation. This absurd element takes over at the climaxes of **'The Death of a Civil Servant'** (1883), **'A Drama'** (1887) and **'Encased'** (1898). Like several of the more sophisticated comic stories, **'A Drama'** operates on different levels. It combines a parody of a cliché-ridden play, the potentially serious theme of the abyss that separates the two characters, and a bizarre climax that is immediately overtaken by a comic twist.

By March 1888 Chekhov had published an incredible 528 stories, about half of them comic. Critics in his lifetime were quick to distinguish what they regarded as the lightweight outpourings of Antosha Chekhonte from the serious work of Anton Chekhov, who published only 60 stories between 1888 and his death in 1904, and gave up comic writing altogether, apart from the one-act farce-vaudevilles of 1888-91. This contrast was inevitable, especially given the very variable quality of the early stories, but it had the unfortunate effect of making it seem as if Chekhonte and Chekhov were two different people, rather than different manifestations of one person. Most Russian critics in the Soviet era concentrated on the handful of comic stories that could be made to yield a strong socio-political message, and likewise failed to look for any deeper continuity. But in 1979 V. B. Kataev wrote that 'it was in the humorous stories of 1884-7 that Chekhov found himself as an artist. Their aim is no longer to make the reader laugh at all costs, but to formulate in comic terms Chekhov's central underlying theme.' That theme, he argues, is philosophical: Chekhov is preoccupied with how each person makes sense of the world differently, and with what happens when these different world-pictures are juxtaposed or come into conflict.

The comic twists of Chekhonte may disappear, but what stands out very clearly in the later Chekhov is a highly developed sense of irony. Story after story turns on some kind of ironic reversal (often that was how the plot suggested itself to him), as if his mind were always patterning the world in that kind of way. The heroine of **'The Grasshopper'** (1898) spends all her time collecting 'remarkable' people, only to discover, too late, that the one truly remarkable person in her life was her very 'ordinary' doctor-husband; Dr Ragin in **'Ward No. 6'** (1892) finds himself incarcerated in the very ward that he has presided over with such calm indifference for so many years; while Belikov in **'Encased'** finally discovers the ideal case that he has been searching for all his life—in his coffin. At the start of **'Lady with a Little Dog'** (1899) the womanizing Gurov is unattractive, but by the end he has become a sympathetic, even a pathetic, figure.

If Chekhonte is preoccupied with social rank and the unnatural attitudes and relationships it engenders, in Chekhov this theme has a much wider application. He rejects authoritarian attitudes of every kind. He deflates the pretensions of all those who are self-centred, self-satisfied or self-important, and is quick to see through their self-deceits and double standards. He is suspicious of all those who seek to interfere with other people's lives, even when, as in the case of Lida, the elder sister in **'The House with a Mezzanine'** (1896), they seem to be well intentioned. In **'Encased',** a late story full of comic details that might have been invented by Chekhonte, Chekhov makes a psychological link between Belikov's own insecurity and the role that he feels compelled to play in the outside world as a guardian of public morals. How many more Belikovs there are still to come, the narrator comments, giving the story the widest possible application.

The imaginative empathy that can lead to comic effects when applied by Chekhonte to children and animals is used seriously by Chekhov to depict other 'minority viewpoints', like that of the *déclassée* village schoolmistress in **'A Journey by Cart'** (1897) or the closed com-munity of the **'Horse Thieves'** (1890), and most effectively in **'Peasants'** (1897). To *see* accurately was of great importance to Chekhov, and in this story a whole marginalized class of Russian society is brought miraculously to life from within. No wonder it provoked such a furore.

As for the comic-absurd element in Chekhonte's writing, that surfaces again magnificently in Chekhov's major plays, especially *Three Sisters* (1901) and *The Cherry Orchard* (1904). Among the events and prophecies in the weekly comic *Calendar* that Chekhonte compiled in March-April 1882 we read: 'In Tambov [a well-known provincial railway junction, a place of extreme ordinariness] a volcano is going to erupt'; 'In Berdichev [an important commercial centre in the Ukraine] the refraction of light will take place'; 'On the island of Borneo [here the place is exotic, the event ordinary] there's an outbreak of diphtheria'. Anyone familiar with *Three Sisters* will be reminded at once of the old army doctor Chebutykin. When he first wanders on to the stage, he is copying down in his notebook a formula from the newspaper to prevent hair falling out. In Act II, still carrying his newspaper, he announces that 'Balzac was married in Berdichev', and follows this up soon after with the information that 'in Tsitsikar they've got a smallpox epidemic'.

Without his early experience of comic-absurd writing, it is unlikely that Chekhov would have made a character read out irrelevant scraps of information from a newspaper, although it needed a touch of genius to perceive how this would at once fix him in the audience's mind. The very incongruity of his remarks makes them stand out so sharply that we remember where Balzac was married long after more serious lines have been forgotten. Indeed, the unconventional (and highly influential) approach to stage dialogue that Chekhov perfected could probably *only* have occurred to someone with a taste for the comic-absurd. Faced by conventional dialogue, so neat and rational and orderly, Chekhov said: that's not what conversation is like, it's haphazard and unpredictable, people are having a serious discussion, then someone else reads out something totally irrelevant from a newspaper.

If Chekhonte appears only at odd moments in *Three Sisters,* in *The Cherry Orchard* he is seldom absent for long. The improbable name Simeonov-Pishchik is a combination of the ordinary Simeonov and the absurd Pishchik, 'Squeaker'. Squeaker describes himself as 'an old horse': his constitution and appetite are horse-like, and his father used to joke that the ancient stock of the Simeonov-Squeakers was descended from the horse that Caligula made into a senator. On his first appearance Yepikhodov drops the bunch of flowers he is carrying and is unable to stop his new boots from squeaking; when not dropping something, he is knocking something over or squashing something flat. Chekhonte creates the memorable image of the governess Charlotta, reminiscent of the strikingly visual portrait of the Daughter of Albion. He stage-manages her conjuring tricks and her ventriloquism. He is the instigator of lost galoshes and of sticks that come down over the wrong person's head.

Just as *The Cherry Orchard* resists all attempts to give it a simple comic or serious label, so not every story in this volume will be seen as purely comic. Often, however, critics look too hard for the undercurrent of sadness or the serious implication. It is difficult to accept Gorky's view that in **'The Daughter of Albion'** Chekhov wanted to show up the abominable behaviour of the Russian landowner 'towards a lonely, alienated human being', while to comment on **'Vint'** (1884) that the little men's obsession with their ridiculous card game only shows up the futility of their lives seems to miss the point: what makes the story delightful is that for once distinctions of rank break down, and the head of department becomes even more enthusiastic about the game than his subordinates ('Sit down, gentlemen, let's have one more rubber!') With **'The Darling'** (1899), the last story in this collection, the comic or serious question is especially delicate. Chekhov in a letter describes it as 'a humorous story'. The heroine perfectly illustrates the thesis that we are nothing more than how we view the world. Because she has no view of her own, she can only make sense of the world through other people; without them she collapses. Tolstoy found Olenka's selfless love very moving, but the story is told in a comically deadpan style that makes such an emotional response seem inappropriate; it is equally possible to see in 'the darling' a sinister figure, who feeds on other people and buries two husbands. I prefer to accept Chekhov's own description and to see the story as a light-hearted exploration of what happens when the idea of the chameleon figure is taken to an absurd extreme.

Who is to say what will make a person laugh, or what will make people laugh in one society and not another?

Chekhov's humour has always seemed to me very accessible to people in the English-speaking world. It is not slick or contrived, does not depend on verbal or logical gymnastics, does not shout or show off. It is very much person-oriented. That his characters are Russian is irrelevant: they are immediately recognizable people in easily understood situations.

Why, then, are his comic stories not better known? Partly it is a matter of translation. It is much harder to translate the short comic stories than the serious long ones. The former are often full of dialogue, which is difficult to translate at the best of times and especially so if the speakers are not very literate; in the latter there

is less dialogue and the speakers are more educated. Translating the long stories with their smooth narrative flow gives you the feeling of driving along in top gear, with only occasional interruptions to negotiate a roundabout or check the map. Not so the short ones: with them it is a matter of constant stops and starts, of jumping out to look under the bonnet, of being endlessly patient and resourceful. Few translators can be bothered. Such translations as exist are often painfully inadequate. Small wonder that Chekhov's numerous commentators in the West who manage to function without a knowledge of Russian conclude that the comic stories deserve no more than a passing glance.

Then there are publishers. In the 1970s, trying to interest a publisher in Chekhov's comic stories, I took along a pile of translations to leave with her. On top was **'An Incident at Law'** (1883), at that time unknown in the West. Since it was so short, I suggested she might like to read it on the spot. The massed editions of Virginia Woolf lining her shelves looked down with interest. Two or three minutes passed in silence. Then she suddenly went very red in the face, her eyes filled with tears, and she began choking. A secretary was sent out for a glass of water. Had this been an example of Chekhov's black humour, she would have had a heart attack and died, but since it was real life, she soon recovered her composure. Surely, I thought, after a response like that she will not be able to turn the stories down? But she did. With a literary flourish now rare among publishers, she wrote of her fears of being 'hauled over the coals in offering them to the world'. In the background the voice of Belikov in **'Encased'** can be heard whining: 'Yes, it's a good idea, of course, but what will the critics say?' The Chekhov of the comic stories was not sufficiently 'literary', he was not the high culture figure whose short stories had influenced Virginia Woolf and Katherine Mansfield, and whose plays had changed the course of world drama. As if the author of **'Ward No. 6'** or *The Cherry Orchard* might in some way be diminished by being revealed as the author of **'The Complaints Book'** or **'A Horsy Name'**! No use protesting, though. Haven't I heard, Chekhov's been labelled, Chekhov's a *heavy* writer.

This introduction is becoming heavy, too. It might have been more effective to write: here are forty of Chekhov's comic stories, I've chosen the ones I like best, they cover a wide range, read them for their own sake and see how you enjoy them. They start from the simple and unsophisticated, and proceed to the more sophisticated and complex; the resulting order is roughly but not strictly chronological.

Nineteen of the stories appeared originally in *Chekhov: The Early Stories 1883-88,* a joint translation by Patrick Miles and myself, first published by John Murray in 1982, reprinted in 1984 by Sphere Books under their

Abacus imprint, and in 1994 by Oxford University Press in their World's Classics series. These stories are indicated by an asterisk in the Notes. I am very grateful to Patrick Miles and to Oxford University Press for granting me permission to include them in the present volume.

It is a pleasure to acknowledge my debt to Professor V. B. Kataev of Moscow University for responding with such patience and expertise to my tedious lists of queries; to Richard Davies of the Leeds Russian Archive, together with Tamara Kulikova and Kirill Degtiarenko, for answering queries and especially for making corrections and suggesting improvements to my original versions; and to Patrick Miles for helping a non-angler in his attempts to catch the elusive **'Burbot',** which was by far the most difficult story to translate.

Nadezhda Katyk-Lewis (essay date September 2000)

SOURCE: Katyk-Lewis, Nadezhda. "'Agaf'ia'—A Song about a Song." *Canadian Slavonic Papers* 42, no. 3 (September 2000): 331-42.

[*In the following essay, Katyk-Lewis considers the theme of technological progress and its impact on the Russian people as portrayed in Chekhov's story "Agaf'ia."*]

> За рекой на другой стороне, . . .
> да соловей-птица песню поет . . .
>
> Across the river, on the other side, . . .
> A nightingale sings his song. . . .
>
> —Russian folk song

> Я знаю, когда поезды ходят!
>
> I know when the trains come!
>
> —A. P. Chekhov

"We know Chekhov's drama, certainly, far better than we do his prose . . . and we are continually discovering new [masterpieces], even among the anecdotes, 'scenes,' and miniatures produced in the first years of his writing in the early 1880s."[1] This observation certainly applies to **"Agaf'ia,"** which possesses much deeper interest than merely as an early example of Chekhov's peasant stories, his lyricism or his incomplete form. Besides all of these features, **"Agaf'ia"** contains the seed of one of the main themes of Chekhov's entire work: the encroachment of progress and technology on the old, idyllic Russia. It is mainly for this reason that the story deserves attention.

After its initial publication in 1886, in *Novoe vremia,* **"Agaf'ia"** prompted divergent responses from contemporary critics, mainly regarding the psychology of the

characters and the story's open ending.[2] The nature descriptions were greatly admired and in general terms compared to those of Turgenev.[3] After the initial reaction died out, however, **"Agaf'ia"** attracted little or no attention from literary scholarship. There is no essay that focuses specifically on this story, though Nicholas G. Žekulin does devote some attention to it in his study of nature descriptions in various stories by Chekhov and Turgenev. Žekulin compares **"Agaf'ia"** specifically to Turgenev's "Ermolaj i mel'nichikha" and draws parallels not only between the nature descriptions in the two stories but also between their basic fabulas. He also points out the differences between the two female characters, Turgenev's Arina and Chekhov's Agaf'ia. As he correctly observes, "Turgenev provides us with the whole background story of Arina . . . [and] places the burden of Arina's story squarely on serfdom." Chekhov, in contrast, "has neatly shifted the burden away from the socio-political into the psychological."[4]

However, as so often with Chekhov's work, the meaning of the story does not lie on the surface of the text and is not limited to the basic fabula. As Jackson points out, "the multilayered meanings of Chekhov's text are inseparable from its poetic structure and dynamics. We read his prose as we would read a poem, seeking out its meaning in the complex interrelationship and interplay of language, image, structure, detail and device."[5] In fact, a close reading of **"Agaf'ia"** reveals not only that its structure, images and details are poetic but also that it strongly resembles a Russian folk song. This is not to suggest that Chekhov had any conscious intention of imitating folk lyrics, or that folklore elements generally pervade his writing. But folklore, as an element of collective memory, stimulated the consciousness and nourished the inspiration of Russian poets over the centuries, affecting literature in the most subtle ways and penetrating its very fiber. As A. Gorelov points out,

> The song taught (and still teaches) the language of metaphors and suggestions, nonnarrative development of siuzhet, devices of compositional gradation and symmetry. By its intonation it enriched not only poetry but also prose; it introduced the symbolism and phraseology of folklore . . . it revealed possibilities of the Russian language and disclosed the almost forgotten connotations of etymologically related words.[6]

This is certainly true of **"Agaf'ia,"** which resembles a folk song not only in its general mood but also in the character and function of the poetic images.

In accordance with the poetics of folklore, each thematic group displays a range of elements that repeatedly appear in the texts of different songs, creating a stock of somewhat stereotypical imagery. In folklore studies these constantly recurring features are most commonly referred to as "traditional formulas." Not connected exclusively with any particular song, they constitute the entire repertory of the traditional lyric. Thus the function of traditional formulas in folk lyrics is not only to express the meaning of the particular text but at the same time to enhance it with the rich associations which they carry.

> These permanent components of a traditional text—recurrent epithets, similes and tropes, standard themes, stylistic clichés, stereotypical images—provide the form for the situations, for the portraits of the characters, their emotions, actions, dialogues, for descriptions of nature, the passage of time, etc., even to the smallest stylistic details.[7]

Although the actual theme of a folk song is also of a stereotypical character, here the artist has freedom of choice. The selection of the elements through which the theme is conveyed, on the other hand, is limited to the formulas associated with that theme. Thus it is the theme that determines the elements of the composition: the place, time, action, etc.[8] Such is the aesthetic principle of the folk lyric. The formula carries both the form and the content of the text. It is a condensation of socio-cultural experience, and as such it endows the text with its own meaning. It projects the tradition onto the text.[9]

Chekhov's focus on contemporary life provided him, as the basis of his story, with the theme of a woman locked in an unhappy marriage. Unlike Turgenev, however, Chekhov gives us no information about Agaf'ia's life before her marriage or any reason that would justify or explain her infidelity. The missing background strips Agaf'ia of the individual features of her life and generalizes her story, just as a folk song represents general human experience rather than one particular destiny. This gives her a double function in the narrative. Agaf'ia, the wife of a railroad switchman, is also a traditional folklore character: the wife of the unloved "старый или грозный муж" ("old or fearsome husband"). This makes the story comparable to a particular type of folk lyric: the non-narrative song about marriage. In its basic siuzhet the story belongs in even more specific thematic groups, such as that of the young wife who loves another man or of the young wife who is secretly unfaithful.[10] But the similarity between **"Agaf'ia"** and traditional lyric is not limited to the story's theme. Writing on a traditional theme of folk song, Chekhov instinctively selected other folk elements to express and embody it. Once it was chosen, the theme itself guided his hand in solving the problems of style and composition in accordance with the aesthetic canon of the folk lyric. The basic elements in **"Agaf'ia,"** such as place, time, and action, are all identical with traditional folklore formulas, and hence they enhance Chekhov's text with traditional meaning.

In a folk song, understanding the conventions of the folk lyric and its traditional stock of symbolism enables the performer and the audience to focus not on the surface meaning of the text but instead on another, deeper meaning which is revealed, and to some extent created, at the time of the performance. The content of a folk song, according to Likhachev, is the very act of singing. The performer is singing not only the song itself: at the same time he is singing *about* what he sings. The song expresses what the performer *thinks* at the moment of singing. "It is a mirror, infinitely reflected in another mirror, so that a folk song in fact is a song about a song."[11] In order to grasp the meaning of a folk song, then, as expressed by a particular performer, we need to understand first of all the traditional symbolism of the folk lyric. In the same way, to perceive the true meaning of Chekhov's story, we need to expose the rich traditional allusions woven into his text.

Thus the traditional elements in **"Agaf'ia"** are not only interesting from the point of view of Chekhov's lyricism but also, and far more importantly, enable us to discover the story's real meaning. Contrary to Žekulin's view, the burden of the story is not only psychological; it also deals with social change. Although on the surface **"Agaf'ia"** appears to be a story about adultery, under its simple plot of the "eternal triangle" there runs an undercurrent theme of a woman torn between two worlds: a disappearing, slumberous rural Russia and a new, modern world of technology. While Turgenev's story openly denounced serfdom and portrayed Arina as its victim, Chekhov set himself a different task, for he wholeheartedly welcomed the progress that took place during his era but at the same time felt nostalgic for the disappearing world which he loved. Chekhov's artistic aim was also different from Turgenev's: not to deliver a message, a statement or a moral, but to inspire his readers to arrive at their own conclusions.

Even reading the story for the first time, we realize that there is a certain disproportion between the extensive description of the village gardens and the portrayal of their keeper, Savka, and the terse portraits of the remaining two characters, Agaf'ia and her husband Iakov. Such a concentration on landscape description, especially at the expense of the key character, cannot be without significance. Chekhov is giving location the same kind of importance it has in folk lyric, where it is connected with the particular mood of a song, such as sorrow, love, or happiness. It may seem that a character "chooses to go" to a field, a forest, or a river, but the choice is actually determined by his or her state of mind. Each location has a special symbolic value in the tradition of folk lyric: tell me where you are and I will tell you what is happening to you, and vice versa.[12] For example, in folk lyric, lovers always meet in some private, idyllic setting, usually a garden or an orchard. Hence, in **"Agaf'ia,"** the lovers' tryst takes place in a garden. Of course, Chekhov is writing about a specific, concrete locale, the "Dubovskie" gardens in the S district, but these gardens nonetheless function as metaphor and symbol, just as gardens do in many folk songs.

У Ивана Петровича во саду,
Сладки яблочки хорошие рвала,
Ой люли, ой люли, да лели,
Сладки яблочки хорошие рвала,
Сладки яблочки хорошие рвала,
Да Ивана Петровича кормила.

In Ivan Petrovich's orchard,
I picked the good sweet apples,
Hey, nonny, nonny no!
I picked the good sweet apples,
I picked the good sweet apples,
And I fed Ivan Petrovich.

This association with traditional folklore symbolism elevates Chekhov's vegetable garden from mere landscape to the Garden of Eden.

This symbolism is enhanced by the garden's isolation, since it is separated from the village by a river. In folk lyric, rivers are connected with sorrow. "The image of a river has, in itself, the power to dispose at once the singer and his hearers toward a definite emotional mood, since this image, in popular poetry, is known to be an established symbol of sorrow, longing, and separation."[13] It is the place where a young girl comes to mourn, to wash away her grief, longingly to await her lover.

Ой, разнеси ты, быстрая реченька,
Печаль мою, тоску . . .

Oh, quick-flowing river,
bear away my sadness and my grief . . .

On other occasions, the river, like a long road, a steep mountain, or a wide field, represents an obstacle that keeps the lovers apart.

Эа рекой, за реченькой,
Эа рекой на другой стороне,
Да на ракитовом кустышке,
Да на малиновом листышке,
Да соловей-птица песню поет . . .

Across the river, across the stream,
Across the river, on the other side
On one little broom-shrub,
On a leaf of a raspberry-bush,
A nightingale sings his song . . .

Again, the parallel with traditional folk lyric considerably enriches the meaning of the river in **"Agaf'ia."** It is not simply a body of water running between the village and the garden but a carrier of traditional meanings that envelop the story in a mood of sorrow and separation.

At the same time the river is an integral part of the portrait of Agaf'ia herself. "Devushka u reki" ("the girl at the river") is one of the basic traditional formulas of

folk poetry,[14] and Chekhov's Agaf'ia is related to it. Agaf'ia stands at the end of a long line of "devushki u reki" and shares with them their destiny, their sorrow and their longing for the lover on the other side of the river. It is the traditional meaning of this image that provides the missing background of Agaf'ia's story and her psychology. Since the river flows between the village and the garden, Agaf'ia must cross it twice in the course of the story. The first time is when she is coming to meet Savka:

В потемках глухо зазвучали робкие шаги, и из рощи показался силует женщины. Я узнал ее, несмотря даже на то, что было темно,—это была Агафъя Стрелъчиха. Она несмело подошла к нам, остановилась и тяжело перевела дыхание. Запыхалась она не столько от ходъбъы, сколько, вероятно, от страха и неприятного чувства, испытываемого всяким при переходе в ночное время через брод.

(5:29)

Light footsteps rustled in the night, and a woman's silhouette came out of the wood. I recognized her in spite of the darkness; it was Agaf'ia. She approached us timidly, stopped and drew a deep breath. She was out of breath, probably not so much from the walk as from the fear and the uneasy feeling experienced by anyone crossing a ford by night.

She crosses the river again on her way home:

Я взглянул и увидел Агафъю. Приподняв платье, растрепанная, со сползшим с головы платком, она переходила реку. Ноги ее ступали еле-еле. . . .

(5:34)

I looked and saw Agaf'ia. Disheveled, her kerchief slipping from her hair, she was holding up her skirts and wading across the river. Her feet scarcely moved . . .

The river is not only a physical obstacle challenging Agaf'ia; it symbolizes at the same time the psychological barrier of her fear and hesitation. Every time she crosses the water that separates the garden from the village, she has to conquer this inner barrier as well.

On both occasions, when she gets across the ford to the other bank, she "drew a deep breath"—in Russian, "perevela dykhanie" and then "perevela dukh." "Она пугливо обернуласъ, остановиласъ и перевела дух" (5:34). ("She turned around fearfully, stopped and took a deep breath.") Both "dukh" and "dykhanie" are translated into English as "breath," but as Jackson points out in another connection, "dukh" also means "spirit." "Perevesti" means to transfer, move or shift, so that the phrase "perevesti dukh" or "perevesti dykhanie," besides its idiomatic meaning, also means "transfer of the spirit."[15] Thus, Agaf'ia undergoes a spiritual transformation every time she passes from one to the other of the spheres between which her life oscillates. The appearance of the river at the beginning and the end of the story frames the main motif like a refrain in a song. The repetition enhances the connotations both of Agaf'ia's sorrow and longing and of the isolation of the garden idyll. The same device of repetitiveness is used in folk song as a basic principle of organization with the same purpose of "deepening" the image.[16]

Chekhov applies the same technique in regard to the time of the story. There is no passage devoted to the description of the night itself; instead, we are given descriptions of the evening and morning twilight, which appear, like the river, at the beginning and the end of the story, enhancing the pattern of repetition and creating a certain symmetry. Chekhov pays considerable attention to the changing evening light as a process of gradual transition from daily reality to the idyll of the night. "За бугром догорала вечерняя заря. Осталась одна только бледно-багровая полоска, да и та стала подергиваться мелкими облачками, как уголья пеплом" (5:26). ("The evening light was fading behind the hill; only a pale strip of crimson remained, and across this little clouds were gathering, as ashes gather on dying embers.") "Заря еще не совсем погасла, а летняя ночь уж охватывала своей нежащей, усыпляющей лаской природу" (5:26). ("The glow had not yet quite died away, but the summer night was already enfolding nature in its caressing, lulling embrace.") "Потемки, между тем, все более сгущались, и предметы теряли свои контуры. Полоска за бугром совсем уже потухла, а звезды становились все ярче, лучистее . . ." (5:28). ("Meanwhile the darkness was growing thicker and thicker, and objects began to lose their contours. The streak behind the hill had completely died away, and the stars were growing brighter and more luminous . . .")

Toward the end of the story Chekhov uses the dawn to signal the end of the idyll. It is traditionally the dawn, "zaria-zoriushka," often personified in folk song, that brings an end to a nighttime romance, often finding the girl unprepared. So it is with Agaf'ia: the dawn finds her still laughing in the orchard, while her husband, Iakov, begins to look for her. This time, instead of a gradual change, Chekhov makes an abrupt cut and directly juxtaposes the lyrical dawn to Iakov's call.

> Я видел, как звезды стали туманиться и терять свою лучистость, как легким вздохом пронеслась по земле похлада и тронула листья просыпавшихся ив . . .—А-га-фья . . . ! донесся из деревни чей-то глухой голос.—Агафья!
>
> (5:33)

I saw the stars begin to grow misty and lose their brightness; a cool breath passed over the earth like a faint sigh and touched the leaves of the slumbering willows . . . "A-ga-f'a!" a hollow voice called from the village. "Agaf'ia!"

This is not only the most dramatic moment of the story but also a direct collision between the two realities with which the story deals: the poetry of the secluded garden as opposed to the harsh prose of daily life.

The contrast and antagonism between these worlds are embodied not only in the two locations but in the two male characters and their ways of life. The main focus is on Savka. The entire first page of this ten-page story is devoted to a description of him: his healthy, handsome physique; the soft, expressive features of his face; his innate idleness and careless way of life, which have earned him the somewhat demeaning post of keeper of the village garden. Further on, Chekhov devotes an additional four or five passages to Savka's character. All this effort seems to be directed to solving the question of Savka's attractiveness to the local women, who pamper him, spoil him, and compete for his attention. His good looks and the touching role of a failure can only partly explain Savka's irresistible charm, which even his contemptuous attitude toward the women cannot taint.

Perhaps, besides his beauty and soft-heartedness, the women appreciate the kindness and tenderness reflected in his eyes. "Он был красив и строен, в глазах его всегда, даже при взгляде на презираемых женщин, светилась тихая ласковость . . ." (5:32). ("He was handsome and well-built; his eyes always shone with quiet tenderness, even when he was looking at the women he so despised . . .") Perhaps they sense Savka's deep humanity: "—Любопытно!—потянулся Савка.—Про что ни говори, все любопытно. Птица таперя, человек ли . . . камешек ли этот взять—во всем своя умственность! . . ." (5:27). ("It's interesting," said Savka. "Whatever one talks about, it is always interesting. Take a bird now, or a man . . . or take this little stone; all of them have their hidden meaning! . . .") Perhaps the women simply crave the aura of serenity and poetry that surrounds this half Pan, half Ivan the Fool. "От всей его фигуры так и веяло безмятежностью, врожденной, почти артистической страстью к Житью зря, спустя рукава" (5:25). ("His whole figure suggested unruffled serenity, an innate, almost artistic passion for living carelessly, never with his sleeves tucked up.")

The story as originally published contained a passage in which the narrator commented further on Savka's way of life.

> . . . мне стало казаться, что я понимаю неподвижность молодого Савки . . . К чему, в самом деле, двигаться, желать, искать? Не лучше ли раз навсегда замереть в этом благоухании ночи под взглядом бесконечно великого числа небесных скромно мерцающих светил, стать частью всеобщего, величаво торжественного покоя и дышать, дышать без конца? Не в слиянии ли с этой веч-

ной, много говорящей, но непонятной красотой цель и наслаждение жизни?

(5:493)

> . . . it began to appear to me that I understood the immobility of young Savka. . . . Indeed, for what should one move, wish, search? Is it not better to freeze once, for ever, in the fragrance of the night, under the gaze of the infinite number of modestly shimmering luminaries of the sky, to become part of the majestically solemn universal peace and to breathe, breathe endlessly? Do not the purpose and the delight of life rest in merging with this eternal, so eloquent but incomprehensible, beauty?

The next time the story appeared—in the collection *V sumerkakh,* published in 1887—Chekhov omitted this passage. But even without it, we see clearly that what brings the narrator to the garden is the serenity and peace, the poetic atmosphere of the place: "Собственно говоря, меня не так занимала рыбная ловля, как безмятежное шатание, еда не вовремя, беседа с Савкой и продолжительные очные ставки с тихими летними ночами" (5:25). ("To tell the truth, it was not so much the fishing that attracted me as the serene roaming, the meals at no set time, the talk with Savka, and being for such long stretches of time face to face with the calm summer nights.") This sentence, which appears in the opening paragraph of the story, explains from the outset the double motive of the narrator's visit. The fishing gives him a practical reason for frequenting the gardens, but he also admits to a more important emotional one: the need to come in contact with nature and the simple life. After setting his lines, he enjoys the beauty of the summer night, his conversation with Savka, and their improvised meal. "Мы выпили из кривого, не умевшего стоять стаканчика и принялись за еду . . . Серая, крупная соль, грязные, сальные лепешки, упругие, как резина, яйца, но зато как все это вкусно!" (5:28). ("We drank from a crooked little glass that could not stand up, and began to eat. . . . Gray, coarse salt, dirty greasy flat cakes, eggs hard like rubber, but how delicious all of it was!") This experience on the part of the narrator takes place before Agaf'ia appears on the scene. However, the function of the passage is not merely to set the mood. Rather, it parallels the main theme of the story, echoing it in a subdued manner. Savka and his garden are, above all, a refuge from the world, which in its pursuit of practical values excludes the intangible qualities of peace and beauty as unnecessary burdens. It is this world that Agaf'ia shares with her husband.

Agaf'ia and Iakov are described only in few short strokes.

> Стрельчиху Агафью я знал . . . Это была совсем еще молодая бабенка, лет девятнадцати—двадцати, не далее как год тому назад вышедшая замуж за железнодорожного стрелочника, молодого

и бравого парня. Жила она на деревне, а муж ходил ночевать к ней с линии каждую ночь.

(5:28)

> I knew Agaf'ia Strelchikha. . . . She was quite a young peasant woman of nineteen or twenty, who had been married not more than a year earlier to a railroad switchman, a young and vigorous lad. She lived in the village, and her husband came home there from the line every night.

The gift of potatoes that Agaf'ia brings to Savka proves that she and her husband live better than most villagers: Iakov is a good provider—the exact opposite of Savka, who ". . . жил как птица небесная: утром не знал, что будет есть в полдень" (5:25). (". . . lived like a bird in the sky: he did not know in the morning what he would eat at noon.")

Iakov's relationship with Agaf'ia is demonstrated only by his commanding call to her and by his stern look, under which she cowers in fear. But Chekhov really has no need to draw a more detailed portrait of this man; instead, he can again rely on an established association with a traditional figure of folk lyric: the well-to-do man who does not love his wife. However, Chekhov gives this traditional image a new twist. Iakov is not just another crude peasant: he is a modern man with a modern profession. His life, running as it does on a precise schedule, could not be more distant from that of his rival, who spends his time imitating bird calls with his whistle and catching nightingales in the bushes. It is this profession of railroad switchman that gives the story a new dimension.

Chekhov was nine years old when the Kursk-Kharkov-Azov railroad reached Taganrog. Freight cars filled with grain soon replaced the traditional ox-carts driven by "muzhik-chumaks."[17] The appearance of the railroad had an enormous impact not only on the economy but on human behavior and culture as well. This, of course, was a universal phenomenon at the time, one of whose most striking features was well expressed by Henry David Thoreau:

> The startings and arrivals of the cars are now the epoch in the village day. They go and come with such regularity and precision, and their whistle can be heard so far, that the farmers set their clocks by them, and so one well-conducted institution regulates a whole country. Have not men improved somewhat in punctuality since the railroad was invented? Do they not talk and think faster in the depot than they did in the stage-office?[18]

Railroads and trains are common in Chekhov's work, generally as an integral part of the overall scenery. They are far from playing the kind of dramatic, indeed tragic, role that the train plays in Tolstoy's *Anna Karenina*. Nevertheless, in Chekhov's **"Anna na shee"**

("**Anna on the Neck,**" 1895), Anna compares the school principal, of whom she is childishly afraid, to a locomotive ready to crush someone. In "**Agaf'ia**" the train is real, not a figure of speech, and Agaf'ia's fear of the train and her fear of her husband are closely linked. The man and the train are interchangeable, both threatening Agaf'ia. "—Мне уходить пора!—проговорила она волнующимся голосом.—Сейчас поезд придет. Я знаю, когда поезды ходят!" (5:31). ("It's time I was going!" she said in an agitated voice. "The train will come any minute! I know when the trains come!") And indeed, the train and Iakov will arrive on schedule.

Events in the garden, on the other hand, are not so predictable. First Savka leaves Agaf'ia waiting while he tries to catch a nightingale. Then Agaf'ia, prolonging her stay, ignores both the narrator and Savka when they urge her to return home. "Агаша, а ведь поезд давно уж пришел!—сказал я.—Пора, пора тебе,—подхватил мою мысль Савка . . ." (5:32). ("'Agasha, the train has been in a long time,' I said. 'It's time—it's time you were gone,' Savka, tossing his head, took up my thought.") But try as she may, Agaf'ia is not able to follow a schedule and tear herself away from Savka. Fully aware of the consequences, she chooses to overstep the limits of time and to pay the price. "А ну его!—сказала она с диким грудным смехом, и в этом смехе слышалась безрассудная решимость, бессилие, боль" (5:32). ("'Bother him!' she said, with a wild, guttural laugh, and reckless determination, impotence and pain could be heard in that laugh.") Although Agaf'ia's life is tied to Iakov and the village, she cannot resist the lure of the free, poetic and spontaneous world of Savka.

Agaf'ia is torn between two men: one organized and efficient, the other a free spirit. Her dilemma is also Chekhov's dilemma, between the poetic garden—Paradise Lost—and the train, the symbol of the sweeping power of progress, with all its positive and negative aspects. It is this theme that finally culminates in *The Cherry Orchard* (1903-1904). As Stephen L. Baehr points out, "Chekhov's play is in large part structured on a 'battle' between two master images—those of the garden and the machine—to symbolically represent the transition occurring in his contemporary Russia."[19] But as Baehr also observes, "one axis of the play stresses—at least on the surface—the idea of a Russian 'paradise lost,' depicting the 'Fall' of the nobility from their Edenic existence in the Garden of Cherries."[20] In "**Agaf'ia**" Chekhov did not draw any line between the classes: Savka's cabbage garden represents Russia itself, adjusting to the radical changes of modern times and losing in the process some of its old qualities and values.

Thus Chekhov has written a song about a romantic love and a loveless marriage, in which all elements perform a role determined by tradition, and each contributes to the total harmony. Chekhov writes about a woman and two men in her life. What he is thinking about, however, are two worlds—one at its sunset, the other at its dawn. And he sings of an Arcadian world where "the summer night is enfolding nature in its caressing, lulling embrace," and of a world where the train whistle shatters the freshness and peace of the dawn.

Notes

References in the text are to A. P. Chekhov, *Sobranie sochinenii i pisem v tridtsati tomakh* (Moscow: Izdatel'stvo Nauka, 1974-1982). All translations from Russian-language works are my own.

1. Robert Louis Jackson, *Reading Chekhov's Text* (Evanston: Northwestern University Press, 1993) 2.

2. For praise of the striking truthfulness both of the individual images and of the story as a whole, see D. V. Grigorovich's letter to Chekhov of December 30, 1887 (see N. I. Gitovich, *Letopis' zhizni i tvorchestva A. P. Chekhova* [Moscow, 1955] 217); on the other hand, Korolenko complained that the story was completely lacking in psychological analysis. Likewise, an anonymous critic in *Severnyi vestnik* attacked the open ending, while K. Arsen'ev wrote that the reader could easily complete the story by using his imagination (5:614, 615).

3. Nicholas G. Žekulin, "Chekhov and Turgenev: The Case of Nature Description," in *Anton P. Čechov: Werk und Wirkung,* ed. Regine Nohejl, vol. 2 (Wiesbaden: Otto Harrassowitz, 1990): 697.

4. Žekulin 699.

5. Jackson 3.

6. A. Gorelov, *Russkaia narodnaia poeziia* (Leningrad: Khudozhestvennaia literatura, 1984) 16.

7. G. I. Mal'tsev, *Traditsionnye formuly russkoi narodnoi neobriadovoi liriki* (Leningrad: Nauka, 1989) 3.

8. Mal'tsev 145.

9. Mal'tsev 72.

10. N. P. Kolpakova, *Pesni i liudi* (Leningrad: Nauka, 1977) 92.

11. D. S. Likhachev, *Poetika drevnerusskoi literatury* (Leningrad, 1971) 222, 223.

12. Mal'tsev 139.

13. Y. M. Sokolov, *Russian Folklore,* trans. C. R. Smith (New York: Macmillan, 1950) 521.

14. Mal'tsev 144.

15. Jackson 131.

16. Mal'tsev 162.

17. L. A. Bodik et al., *Taganrog* (Rostov: Rostovskoe knizhnoe izdatel'stvo, 1971) 60.

18. Henry David Thoreau, *Walden; or, Life in the Woods* (1854; reprint New York, 1960) 82-83.

19. Stephen L. Baehr, "The Machine in Chekhov's Garden: Progress and Pastoral in *The Cherry Orchard*," *Slavic and East European Journal* 43.1 (1999): 99.

20. Baehr 102.

Carol A. Flath (essay date autumn 2000)

SOURCE: Flath, Carol A. "Chekhov's Underground Man: 'An Attack of Nerves.'" *Slavic and East European Journal* 44, no. 3 (autumn 2000): 375-92.

[*In the following excerpt, Flath perceives "An Attack of Nerves" to be a response to Fyodor Dostoevsky's "On Account of the Wet Snow" from his* Notes from Underground.]

> "Why am I not Dostoevsky?! No! Why am I not even, say, Garshin?! It would even be good to be Chekhov! O, just think how much I would be paid per line then!"
>
> Anonymous sketch by a contributor to *Razvlechenie*
> 27 (15 June 1893)

Dostoevsky's works are characterized by extremes: "the beauty of Sodom and the beauty of the Madonna"; passionate verbal clashes with apocalyptic impact; melodramatic plots of suicide or homicide culminating in sublime visions of redemption. Chekhov is a master of moderation, restraint and understatement. On the surface, it is hard to imagine two Russian writers less alike. And yet, striking patterns and motifs in Chekhov's best works can be shown to reflect Dostoevskian prototypes. A close look at Chekhov's 1888 story **"An Attack of Nerves"** (**"Pripadok"**) as a response to Dostoevsky's "On Account of the Wet Snow" from *Notes from Underground* (*"Po povodu mokrogo snega,"* *Zapiski iz podpol'ia,* 1864), will reveal a relationship that is deeper than previously suspected.[1]

Chekhov's references to Dostoevsky—in his letters, conversations, and works—are relatively meager and laconic.[2] Unsurprisingly, criticism has generally avoided in-depth study of the connections between the two writers. Implying that the two are so different as to make analysis difficult, scholars briefly contrast them in sweeping terms. Dostoevsky and Chekhov tend to be perceived as polar opposites.[3] This general critical silence is broken by the insightful short studies of such scholars as E. A. Polotskaia, Mikhail Gromov, Robert Louis Jackson, E. M. Rumiantseva, and Andrew Durkin, who probe beneath the surface to find hidden connections.[4]

The complexity of Chekhov's attitude to literary tradition makes it difficult to reduce his use of predecessors' work to a simple matter of parody, although parody is obvious in many of his works, particularly in the early comic stories.[5] The seminal discussions of parody in the context of Russian literary history use the language of struggle and opposition. Yuri Tynianov, for example, analyzing Gogol's influence on Dostoevsky, argues that authors use parody to struggle against preceding models within artistic traditions. In his discussion of Dostoevsky's "polyphonic novel" Mikhail Bakhtin suggests that "parody introduces into [the original discourse] a semantic intention that is directly opposed to it" (193). In discussing Chekhov's complex and subtle poetics, it may be wiser to speak of irony than of parody. Polotskaia offers a more moderate characterization of the literary process:

> The stages of literary development proceed through calm, rather than extreme new forms of expression, through reform generalizing on the basis of the entirety of past experience, rather than blatant rebellion. . . .
>
> (217)
>
> Literature does not progress along a spiral moving upward and forward; it follows more complex paths, rejecting, but at the same time accepting old forms.
>
> (244)

Identifying similarities between the two writers, Polotskaia describes Dostoevsky's characters as "both . . . and," whereas Chekhov's are "neither . . . nor" (211). Victor Terras' seemingly very different formula, that Dostoevsky's poetics are "marked" (31), in fact harmonizes neatly with Polotskaia's perspective and allows us in our turn to suggest *"unmarkedness"* as a defining characteristic of Chekhov's art. Paradoxically, the works of both writers give an impression of authorial objectivity and detachment. In Dostoevsky, as Bakhtin famously asserts, the author seems to be just another voice; in Chekhov, he seems to be missing altogether.[6]

Even critics who point out similarities between the two writers agree on a basic opposition between Dostoevsky as a writer of ideas and Chekhov as a realist describing the material world. But here as well they both address a basic disharmony between the spirit and the flesh. In "On Account of the Wet Snow" and **"An Attack of Nerves,"** Dostoevsky and Chekhov depict a thinking man's encounter with a physical reality that is at variance with his ideals and preconceptions, offering a strikingly similar, and fundamentally tragic, vision.

Although links between "On Account of the Wet Snow" and **"An Attack of Nerves"** have been identified—most notably by Joseph Conrad in his 1967 study of Chekhov's story—to my knowledge they have not been subjected to an in-depth comparative analysis. Critical attention has been distracted by a number of factors: the absence of direct references to Dostoevsky in discussions of **"An Attack of Nerves"** by critics during Chekhov's lifetime, and in fact by Chekhov himself; the presence of another, more obvious connection—the compelling and explicit link between this story and the biography and works of another writer, Chekhov's contemporary Vsevolod Garshin;[7] and the overall theme of the "fallen woman" in Russian literature.

Like **"An Attack of Nerves,"** two of Garshin's stories ("An Incident" ["Proisshestvie," 1878] and "Nadezhda Nikolaevna" [1885]) treat the theme of a sensitive man's encounter with a prostitute. Both stories end violently, with suicide or murder/suicide. Chekhov responds to some details in Garshin's story (Conrad 430-32), but I find the links to Garshin's own personality and mental illness move convincing than any stylistic connections.[8]

All of Russia's major nineteenth-century writers before Chekhov—Pushkin, Gogol, Chernyshevsky, Dostoevsky, Turgenev, Goncharov, and Tolstoy—address the theme of the fallen woman and her potential for salvation.[9] By the second half of the nineteenth century the theme could not be treated sentimentally, and in fact, most of the canonical post-Karamzinian Russian realists ironize or deflate received romantic myths of rescue.[10] A typical plot leads an intelligent and sensitive man to an encounter with a prostitute, with whom he falls in love; whether or not he succeeds in rescuing her, or she redeems his sin, depends on the author's purpose. The fallen woman tradition in mid-nineteenth-century Russian literature provides a high level of "white noise" that can make it difficult to isolate a specifically Dostoevskian influence on Chekhov. This is why it is necessary to establish links on many levels: setting, character, language, symbolic detail, and overall theme, as well as on the level of wording—what Gromov calls "hidden quotations." Taken together, the many similarities between the two texts cannot be explained merely on the basis of a shared tradition; they suggest a deeper relationship.

Hints of such a relationship can be discerned in one of Chekhov's early stories, **"Words, Words, and Words"** (**"Slova, slova, i slova,"** 1883). In this story, which has unsurprisingly escaped critical attention, a prostitute, Katia, is questioned by her client, a telegraph operator, about her personal history. Outside, "dim street lights barely illuminated the dirty, slushy snow. Everything was wet, dirty, and gray . . . (*tusklye fonarnye ogni edva osveshchali griaznyi, razzhizhennyi sneg. Vse bylo mokro, griazno, sero . . .*)" (2: 113). The young man

expresses indignation at Katia's tale of seduction and betrayal, and urges her to reform. Ultimately his questioning leads her into hysterics. Her glimmer of hope that he might, like "the eloquent hero of a novel that she had read somewhere," raise her out of her fallen state, "fade[s] away" (*stushevalsia*[11]) as the "hero" looks at his watch and realizes his time is nearly up. The inevitable ellipses (. . .) ensue, and the wind whistling through the ventilation ducts bemoans the "violence that a crust of bread can cause" (115). As this short synopsis suggests, Chekhov's modest little sketch contains many textual echoes of "On Account of the Wet Snow" and shares Dostoevsky's focus on the emotional cruelty of its male protagonist. There is no question that when treating the theme of the fallen woman, Chekhov has Dostoevsky on his mind.

The similarities between "On Account of the Wet Snow" and **"An Attack of Nerves"** begin on the level of very fine detail. The opera theme that pervades Chekhov's story echoes a reference to the "Italian arias" that the underground narrator sings after his triumph in the "bumping duel" at the end of Chapter I of "On Account of the Wet Snow." Sullen lackeys figure in both texts, and both protagonists spend hours lying on their sofas in anguish. The main plots of both works feature a "unity of time" (they last about three days). Both authors mention "stupid faces" and "toothache." As Joseph Conrad points out, the "guilty smile" mentioned in Chekhov's story comes from *Notes from Underground,* and both stories take place against a background of falling snow (Conrad 442, n. 9). Given the importance of the snow imagery, it is worth taking a closer look.

In Dostoevsky's story, snow continues to fall throughout the evening of the underground man's encounter with the prostitute Liza; wet and unpleasant from the beginning, it reflects his emotions:

> В невыразимой тоске я подходил к окну, отворял форточку и вглядывался в мутную мглу густо падающего снега.
>
> (Dostoevskii 5: 141)

In inexpressible anguish I went over to the window, opened the vent pane and looked out into the dull haze of the thickly falling snow.

> Мокрый снег валил хлопьями; я раскрылся, мне было не до него . . . Пустынные фонари угрюмо мелькали в снежной мгле, как факелы на похоронах.
>
> (151)

The wet snow fell in large flakes; I opened my coat, I was beyond caring . . . The desolate streetlamps flickered in the snowy haze, like torches at a funeral.

> Было тихо, валил снег и падал почти перпендикулярно, настилая подушку на тротуар и на пустынную улицу. Никого не было прохожих, никакого звука не слышалось. Уныло и бесполезно мерцали фонари.
>
> (177)

It was quiet; the snow came down, falling almost perpendicularly, blanketing the sidewalk and the deserted street. There was no one in sight, and not a sound was heard. The streetlamps flickered fruitlessly and despondently.

In Chekhov's story, the protagonist is taken by two friends for a night on the town. The naive Vasiliev expects to encounter mystery, sin, and guilt; instead, on S—Alley (Moscow's red light district) he finds only indifference, routine, cynicism, and banality. It is the shock of this encounter with "reality" that triggers his attack.[12] Throughout the story, the falling snow reflects the emotions of the protagonist:[13]

Хлопъя [снега], попав в свет, лениво кружились в воздухе, как пух, и еще ленивее падали на землю. Снежинки кружилисъ толпой около Василъева и висли на его бороде, ресницах, бровях. Извозчики, лошади и прохожие были белы.

(Chekhov PSSiP, 7: 211)

The [snow]flakes, coming into the light, lazily circled in the air like fluff, and fell even more lazily to the ground. The snowflakes circled and crowded around Vasiliev and stuck to his beard, eyelashes, eyebrows. The coachmen, horses, and passers-by were white.

Ему было страшно потемок, страшно снега, который хлопъями валил на землю и, казалосъ, хотел засыпать весь мир; страшно было фонарных огней, бледно мерцавших сквозь снеговые облака.

(214)

He was frightened by the darkness, by the snow that came down in big flakes onto the ground and seemed about to blanket the entire world; he was frightened by the pale flickering of the street lamps through the clouds of snow.

The snow in Chekhov's story in general reflects Vasiliev's emotions and the overall theme of loss of innocence (his disillusionment, as well as, by implication, the prostitutes').[14] Here, and as we will demonstrate below, Dostoevsky's images, in some cases their exact wording, infuse Chekhov's language, transcending the purely thematic or symbolic echo commonly noted.[15]

It is against this shared background that Dostoevsky and Chekhov build their psychological dramas. Unlike "On Account of the Wet Snow," Chekhov's story is told in the third person; still, the narration reflects almost exclusively Vasiliev's point of view. Although Vasiliev lacks the wounded vanity and spite that characterize Dostoevsky's famous underground narrator, there are striking similarities between the two protagonists, which render them both susceptible to allegorization as forms of pure consciousness. Both Vasiliev and the underground man are excruciatingly sensitive intellectuals, introverted, periodically alienated from their fellow men, irresponsible with money, idealistic, excitable, emotionally unstable, prone to illness, and bookish. At

the time of the events of "On Account of the Wet Snow," Dostoevsky's narrator is twenty-four; Chekhov's protagonist must be just about the same age, since, although he is still a university student, he has already earned one degree (in natural sciences). Both of them begin their night out in a group, but do not feel comfortable with their companions. Their separation from the group is emphasized, as is their emotional instability. The situation itself is similar: it is snowing, and the men begin their evening with drinking and conversation.

Even the differences suggest a close relationship between the two texts. Vasiliev, *initially unwilling, is persuaded* to go out to the brothels by two school friends; the underground man *forces his presence* on a party of *unwelcoming* ex-school friends; the *six rubles* Vasiliev *foolishly wastes* on port for a prostitute are reflected in the *six rubles* the underground man *abjectly begs* from his friend so he can tag along to the brothel. Both of them experience feelings of envy for the unselfconsciousness and physical health of their comrades. In both cases, the protagonist's hypertrophied self-consciousness results in a deep sense of alienation from his physical body, metonymically implying an isolation from the body social as well.

The motivations of Chekhov's characters are never simple. Still, the complexity of Vasiliev's motives should not distract the reader from what in any other context would be obvious: the goal of a visit to a brothel is a sexual encounter. Naturally, then, the act itself would seem to be a key moment in the plot of these stories. Here the two writers display their most characteristic features: for Dostoevsky, action; for Chekhov, non-action. The underground man winds up in the arms of the prostitute Liza within minutes of entering the first (and only) brothel.[16] As for Vasiliev, although he and his friends make the rounds of countless houses, he ends the evening without the anticipated sexual encounter.[17] This reflects the overall dynamic of Chekhov's reworking of Dostoevsky, but in both stories the relation of the psychological drama to the action—or, to put it another way, the opposition between mind and body—is key.

An examination of the initial goals and expectations of the protagonists in the context of the overall development of the plot reveals the workings of this dynamic. The motives of both are complex; at the beginning of "On Account of the Wet Snow," the underground man fantasizes about encountering "reality" (*deistvitel'nost'*) and saving humanity. These ambitious and grandiose dreams culminate in a deeply personal and sexual encounter. Vasiliev also fantasizes about saving humanity (fallen women), and he, too, cannot separate these ideals from his own personal and physical desires. The kinship between the two is reflected in unmistakable "hidden quotations." Here is Vasiliev's dream:

And he wanted, if just for one night, to live *as his companions did,* to come out of his shell, to free himself from his own control. Was there vodka to be drunk? He would drink it, even if it meant that tomorrow *his head would be splitting with pain.* Would he be taken to see women? He would go. He would laugh, play the fool, and *respond light-heartedly to the jostling of passers-by.*

(Chekhov 7: 200-202 [here and in the following quotations: emphasis added])

Vasiliev's modest dream resonates with the underground man's mood the day after his encounter with Liza, when he borrows money to pay back his debt to his friend. The underground man thanks his new creditor in tones that imply his complete integration into the society of his companions; he is indeed "one of the boys" now:

As he signed the receipt he *carelessly* [*Dostoevsky's emphasis*], with a rakish look, informed him that yesterday he "*had caroused with some fellows* at the Hôtel de Paris; a farewell party for one of us, one might even say, a childhood friend, and—he really likes to have a good time, he's spoiled—, well, of course he's from a good family, with a considerable fortune, a brilliant career, clever, kind, has intrigues going with the ladies, you understand: we had a few too many and . . . [. . .]." *My head was still aching and spinning from last night.*

(Dostoevskii 5: 164-5)

In other words, the underground man's mood on the "day after," his sense of normalcy and belonging, are what Vasiliev dreamed of as he set out into the streets of Moscow. The underground man's brief interlude of "sanity" will soon be followed, when Liza visits him, by a nervous attack that in many ways parallels Vasiliev's (The underground man reports: "I suddenly burst into tears. It was an attack of nerves [*pripadok*]" [172]).

Gromov astutely writes that "Chekhov's characters keep Dostoevsky's novels on their tables" (52). While it is possible that Vasiliev had read *Notes from Underground,* it is more likely that Chekhov had; no reader of Dostoevsky's work is likely to want to emulate his protagonist. Thus Vasiliev and the underground man are better seen as variants of the same basic paradigm, with Chekhov offering his own version of Dostoevskian psychology. Both writers are merciless in their exploration of the dark sides of human psychology. Polotskaia's commentary on their shared approach to the "little man" tradition in Russian literature is apropos: "Like Dostoevsky, Chekhov dredged up the dark residue from the bottom of the soul of the 'little man,' exposing it to view" (207). Dostoevsky's protagonist feels both love and hatred for the prostitute Liza. And although Vasiliev's deep sympathy and concern for fallen women are real, the text supports an interpretation that he anticipates a sexual encounter as well.[18] His romantic preconceptions and delusive fantasies of rescue feed his desire. The very sinfulness of the prostitutes is what attracts his interest:

Their mothers and sisters mourn for them as for the dead; science treats them as an evil; men address them disrespectfully. But in spite of all that, they do not lose *the image and likeness of God.* They are all aware of their sin and hope for salvation. . . . [H]e recalled a story he had read once somewhere: a certain young man, pure and selfless, had fallen in love with a fallen woman and had asked her to be his wife; but, considering herself unworthy of such happiness, she had poisoned herself.

(Chekhov 7: 199)

Vasiliev's actions and thoughts during the evening reflect a covert desire to live one of these stories himself. From this point of view, an ideal outcome for his night out would be a sexual encounter, spiced with a sense of danger and evil, piquant but unthreatening; a brief experience of true love would be followed by the girl's convenient suicide, freeing him, like that other "pure and self-denying" young man, from the obligation actually to *live* with a sinful woman. In addition to providing him with a way out of whatever entanglements he might incur during the evening, those same romantic stereotypes would serve as a catalyst for the physical encounter that otherwise would be no more than an economic transaction; they would spark his desire:

In his imagination Vasiliev saw himself and his friends ten minutes from now, knocking at the door; they would steal their way to the women *through dark corridors and through dark rooms; taking advantage of the darkness, he would strike a match and suddenly illuminate a suffering face and guilty smile.* The mysterious blond or brunette would most likely have her hair down and would be wearing a white nightgown; she would be frightened of the light, would be terribly embarrassed and would say: "For God's sake, what are you doing! Put it out!" All of this was terrible, but curious and novel.[19]

(202)

As Vasiliev proceeds through the different houses of prostitution, each moment of disillusionment is inextricably bound up with the frustration of not finding the kind of woman who would attract his sexual interest by just the right combination of sinfulness, mystery, and shame:

As for the darkness, the silence, the guilty smile—everything that he had expected to encounter here and that had frightened him—he saw not a trace of it.

Everything was ordinary, prosaic and uninteresting . . . "How poor and stupid it all is!" thought Vasiliev. "What is there in all this nonsense that I see now that could tempt a normal man, lead him to commit a terrible sin—to buy a human being for a ruble? I could understand any sin for the sake of brilliance, beauty, grace, passion, or taste, but what is this? What is it here that causes people to sin?"

(204)

"How inept they are at selling themselves!" he thought, "can it be that they don't understand that sin is only seductive when it is beautiful and conceals itself, when it bears a shell of virtue? *Modest black dresses, pale faces, sad smiles and darkness* are more effective than these tawdry trappings. They are stupid! If themselves don't understand this, you'd think that at least their clients would teach them."[20]

(206)

Vasiliev responds to stereotypes presented by Dostoevsky:

I passed with quick steps through *the darkened shop* into a room familiar to me, where *a single candle burned.* . . . Before me flashed a fresh, young, somewhat *pale face*, with straight dark eyebrows and wearing a serious and somewhat startled expression.

(5: 152)

It was almost completely dark in the narrow, cramped and low-ceilinged room. *A candle-end* on the table at the other end of the room had nearly burned itself out and was sputtering feebly. In a few minutes *it would be completely dark.*

(152)

In addition to reflecting the combination of saintliness and sinfulness in fallen women so characteristic of Dostoevsky (in *Crime and Punishment* as well as *Notes from Underground* and other works), Vasiliev's strange language ("*the image and likeness of God*"[21]) echoes the underground man's use of the same phrase as he cruelly creates a dream of family life for Liza:

[Your children] will bear your thoughts and feelings their whole lives through, since they got them from you, they will take on your *image and likeness.*

(Dostoevskii 5: 158)

Vasiliev's failure to connect sexually with another human being is only one symptom of a greater failure: a disharmony between the intellectual, moral, emotional, and physical aspects of his character. Vasiliev's three fantasies at the beginning of his night out (1. to have a sexual encounter, as we deduced above; 2. to take action to save a prostitute; and 3. to learn the story of one of the prostitutes) are inextricably bound together. Without attempting to determine the level of Vasiliev's conscious awareness of his desire, it is easy to interpret his attempts to "get a story"—*to gain knowledge*—as the beginnings of a seduction:[22]

Vasiliev had a lot he wanted to talk about with the girl. He felt *a strong desire to learn* where she was from, whether her parents were alive and whether they knew that she was here, how she had ended up in this house, whether she was happy and satisfied or sad and oppressed with gloomy thoughts, whether she had any hopes of getting out of her current situation . . . But he could not think of *a way to begin and what words to use for his question so that he would not come across as immodest.*

(207)

"*I have to begin with something superficial,*" he thought, "*and then gradually move into something more serious.*" "What a pretty dress you're wearing!" *he said and touched the gold fringe on her scarf with his finger.*

(210)

Vasiliev's fantasies lead nowhere. Meanwhile, his friends succeed where he fails. Not only do they get the anticipated sexual encounter, but the medical student *learns the story* of his dance partner in one of the houses (208), and it is the art student who *takes physical action* to protect a prostitute who is being abused. Vasiliev recoils and flees, repelled by the girl's drunkenness, and it is his companion, the art student, who gets into a fight with her abuser and is thrown down the stairs:

"I will not allow you to beat the women!" the piercing voice of the artist came from upstairs.

Something heavy and cumbersome clattered down the stairway. It was the artist tumbling down head over heels. He had obviously *been pushed.*

(213)

The physicality of the art student ("something heavy and cumbersome") is striking, and presents a clear contrast to Vasiliev's disconnection with his body. It also links Vasiliev directly with the underground man, who himself dreamt of being able to take physical action, to be "thrown out the window" of a billiard room (128), and to bump into an officer on the street (129-32). This desperate need for physical contact of any kind is echoed in Vasiliev's desire to bump into people on the street. And in both cases the spiritual pain of the young men translates into metaphors of physical exposure, initially to the touch of the falling snow, and later to a more brutal and painful contact with the elements. The underground man's exposure of his chest to the snow reflects a spiritual anguish:

The snow piled up under my overcoat, under my frock-coat, under my tie and melted there. I did not button it up; what did it matter, since all was lost anyway.

(151)

I am vain, *as though my skin had been peeled away and the very touch of the air caused me pain.*

(174)

Chekhov unmistakably builds on Dostoevsky's motif when Vasiliev exposes his bare chest to the falling snow in an attempt to substitute physical for spiritual and psychological pain:

In order to distract from his *spiritual pain* with some new sensation or with a different form of pain, not knowing what to do, sobbing and trembling, Vasiliev *unfastened his coat and frock coat and exposed his bare chest to the damp snow and wind.*

(218)

The moral and spiritual pain of both characters prevents them from fitting comfortably into the physical world, and it is associated with a heightened knowledge and self-consciousness.[23]

As the plot of Chekhov's story illustrates, the abstract nature of Vasiliev's ideals, thoughts, theories, and desires, and their complete detachment from physical reality are the cause of his illness. For a healthy life, body and spirit must be in harmony; this is one of the most prevalent themes of Chekhov's stories from the late eighties and early nineties.[24] During this period in particular, Chekhov's ruthless examination of the moral implications of an imbalance between body and soul leads to what his contemporaries considered to be nihilistic conclusions. Although Vasiliev's retreat from the prostitute in **"An Attack of Nerves"** reveals him to be morally upright, sensitive and altruistic, at the same time we cannot easily dismiss his exasperated comrade's accusation at the end of the evening:

> You think that now you have grand thoughts and ideas in your head? No, the devil knows what, but it's not ideas! You are now looking at me with hatred and *disgust,* but I think you would be better off building twenty houses like that than looking that way. There is more sin in that look of yours than in this entire alley!
>
> (214)

This is the deepest link between the two stories. The "illness" of both protagonists, which is clearly associated with their nature as "thinkers," is the root of evil, cruelty and pain. If for Chekhov health and the human body are "the holy of holies," then illness must be close to the opposite. And certainly the underground man's characterization of himself as "a sick man, an evil [translated variously as "nasty," "mean," "bad-tempered," etc.] man (*chelovek bol'noi . . . zloi chelovek* [99]) is saying something similar. The balance of evil and illness differs—Dostoevsky emphasizes cruelty, Chekhov emphasizes pain—but their ways of presenting the issue are surprisingly similar. The anguish of their heroes is due to excessive self-consciousness; body and mind are out of harmony. Both writers present a similar scene—the hero's confrontation with his own image in a mirror—to make this point. Just before his encounter with Liza, the underground man

> *chanced to see myself in the mirror.* My excited face seemed *extremely disgusting* to me: pale, mean, nasty, with my hair all in disarray. "So be it, I'm glad of it," thought I. "I'm particularly glad that I will seem *disgusting* to her; I like that."
>
> (151)

Certainly the disgust (*otvratitel'nym*) the underground man feels when he looks at his own face in the mirror leads to the disgust (*s otvrasheniem*) the art student notes in Vasiliev's face, a face we see through Vasiliev's own eyes as he confronts his reflection:

> *He caught a glimpse of himself in the mirror. His face was pale* and pinched, and his temples were sunken; his eyes were bigger, darker, motionless, as though they belonged to someone else, *and expressed unbearable spiritual suffering.*
>
> (218)

As the mirror imagery suggests, Vasiliev's suffering, like that of the underground man, comes from his acute isolation from others and the destructive self-consciousness that results from that solitude. The narrator presents an acquaintance's characterization of Vasiliev as an altruistic, empathetic human being:

> He has a fine, marvelous sensitivity to pain in general. As a good actor expresses other people's movements and voice, so Vasiliev has the ability to reflect other people's pain in his soul. When he sees tears, he cries; when he's near a sick person he himself becomes ill and moans; if he sees violence, it seems to him that the violence is being inflicted on him; he is as cowardly as a boy, and when frightened, he runs to help. *Other people's pain irritates him, excites him, brings him to the point of ecstasy, etc.*
>
> (217)

This ostensibly positive description of Vasiliev's character is undermined, however, both by "hidden quotations" reminding us of the underground man's cruelty and by Vasiliev's own actions in the text of the story. Chekhov's language here is curiously ambiguous for such a careful writer. Vasiliev "is cowardly" but "runs to help"? The plot of the story shows that in spite of his general "helpfulness," Vasiliev runs in the *opposite direction*—away from meaningful engagement with other people, into himself. Furthermore, this passage allows us to link the very sympathy Vasiliev feels for those who suffer with the attraction to sin and guilt that I have shown to be so integral a part of his sexual desire. This attraction emerges from those very stereotypes of romantic literature that are Dostoevsky's subject. Unrealistic sexual expectations may very well be linked with the infliction and suffering of pain, as the words "irritate, [stimulate], excite, bring to a state of ecstasy" here imply.[25] Nothing else seems to stir Vasiliev as much as "other people's suffering," though, as the plot of the story shows, he is powerless to act on these impulses—for good *or* evil. Like the underground man, he inevitably turns them against himself.

It is hard to accept that Chekhov finds evil in Vasiliev's failure to have sex with a prostitute! Indeed the author spoke out many times against the institution of prostitution, as in a letter to Suvorin on November 11, 1888: "Why do you never have anything in your newspaper about prostitution? It's a terrible evil, you know. Our Sobolev Alley is a slave market" (*Pis'ma,* 3: 67). And of course there is more to the story than this. Indeed Chekhov is condemning the institution of prostitution.

But, ever true to his ruthless artistic program—to provide only an unblinking view of reality as he sees it—he refuses to allow his protagonist a refuge in pure righteousness. Vasiliev is a man living in human flesh, and moral precepts, like ideas in general in Chekhov's work, cannot fully encompass the realities and challenges of human life. A comment made by Robert Jackson in discussing Garshin's attitude toward Dostoevsky may be equally relevant to *Chekhov*: "[Garshin's] conscious rejection of the 'underground' elements in Dostoevsky's writings may have been part of a struggle against such elements in himself" (*Dostoevsky's Underground Man*, 73-4). Beyond the often-mentioned expedition made ostensibly for "research" (Popkin 8), Chekhov had spent a fair amount of time in brothels (as documented recently by Rayfield). Such information should serve to deepen, rather than hinder, our understanding of Chekhov's genius—as Ronald Hingley in his own time suggested (316-19). The fact that Chekhov's own personal, physical experience may have been at variance with his moral convictions seems to prove our point as to the message of his work.

The commonality of Dostoevsky's and Chekhov's vision is reinforced by the conclusions of their stories. The precedents of Gogol's Piskarev, of Garshin (the person and the writing), and the romantic tradition clearly offer the solipsistic protagonist the option of suicide. Both Dostoevsky and Chekhov are keenly aware of this as an easy way to resolve their plots; Dostoevsky's other works abound in suicides and other forms of violence,[26] and Garshin's suicide weighed heavily on Chekhov's mind as he wrote his story. Nevertheless, both authors reject this solution. Instead, their characters choose life, though for both of them "life" amounts to a retreat into a cerebral world. The underground man enters the underground of writing, and after turning away from the "black, turbulent Iauza," (218-19), Vasiliev ultimately heads back to the university. Thus at a key moment both writers present a "realistic," non-poetic solution consistent with their overall attack on romantic myths.[27] Although Vasiliev and the underground man are often considered as exceptional or pathological cases, it is more true to the art of these profound works to suggest that they present a common tragic vision of the human condition.[28]

Notes

I am grateful to Andrei Stepanov for his valuable help, and would also like to thank the anonymous readers for their excellent comments.

1. I have chosen to focus on the second part of *Notes from Underground*, as it tells a *story* similar to Chekhov's. The underground man's monologue of Part I is too dissimilar to "An Attack of Nerves" to allow rigorous textual comparison, though it is relevant to any discussion of Chekhov's exploration of his protagonist's character, in particular his hints at a connection between illness and evil.

2. The index to the twelve-volume Academy edition of Chekhov's letters offers only forty-seven references to Dostoevsky (1¼ inches of text); the index to the eighteen volumes of literary works contains only 106 references (3 inches)—a total of 4¼ inches. By contrast, Turgenev merits a total of 10½ inches worth of references (4¼ in letters and 6½ in works); Gogol—12 inches (5¼ in letters; 6¾ in works); Pushkin—15½ inches (7½ in letters; 8 in works); Tolstoy is mentioned most: 19¼ inches (11 in letters; 8¼ in works). Among these great writers of nineteenth-century Russian literature, Dostoevsky is a distant last, mentioned less than half the times Turgenev is, and just over one fifth of Tolstoy's total. Nowhere does Chekhov offer a sustained discussion of Dostoevsky or of his works.

3. "Of the important Russian writers of the nineteenth century, Dostoevsky interested Chekhov least of all" (Karlinsky/Heim 331); "None of his figures emerges with the almost demonic vitality of a Dostoevsky character [. . .] Chekhov is not a metaphysical writer in Tolstoy's or Dostoevsky's sense" (Hahn 8, 57); "Significantly, Chekhov wrote not a single word [*sic*] about Dostoevsky; with the possible exception of one oblique criticism, it is as if Dostoevsky did not exist for him" (Bitsilli 5); ". . . the metaphysical striving of [Dostoevsky], his consuming desire to put stock in Christian certainties, remained forever alien to Chekhov" (De Sherbinin 40). Chudakov's comment that Chekhov's and Dostoevsky's ways of presenting human psychology are "fundamentally different phenomena" (*Chekhov's Poetics*, 178) is representative of his contrastive treatment of all aspects of the two writers' works; the volumes available to me of the excellent new *Chekhoviana* series do not contain any in-depth comparative study of the two writers, nor does the enormous 1997 Badenweiler collection on religion and philosophy in Chekhov's life and works (*Anton P. Čehov*).

4. Polotskaia builds on the insights of Bakhtin to identify surprising, but convincing similarities based on authorial "objectivity" and artistic principles of balance. Gromov offers an apt formula, "hidden quotations" (*skrytye tsitaty*), to describe the covert way Chekhov borrows from Dostoevsky. In a close reading of an 1880 Chekhov story "Because of Little Apples" ("Za iablochki"), Jackson proves that at the very beginning of his career, Chekhov was responding to his predecessor's most important themes: childhood innocence

and the immorality of violence. Rumiantseva explores Dostoevskian echoes in Chekhov's 1890 *Gloomy People* (*Khmurye liudi*) collection. Durkin offers a multilayered and probing analysis of Chekhov's response to Dostoevsky in the mature story "Ward Six."

5. See Kramer 29-49.

6. I use the word "seems" consciously. The question of authorial objectivity in Dostoevsky and Chekhov cannot be addressed adequately in a study of this length.

7. Chekhov's story was written for a volume commemorating Garshin, who had committed suicide in March, 1888. For details, see the editors' notes in *PSSiP, Sochineniia* 7: 659-65; Rayfield 181; and Berdnikov. As Semanova points out, Chekhov's protagonist Vasiliev shares personality traits with Garshin. Gleb Uspenskii tells of a nervous attack (*pripadok*) Garshin had suffered; the circumstances and details in his account resemble details Chekhov was to include in his story. See Berdnikov 155.

8. See Chekhov's comments quoted in the editors' notes in *Sochineniia* 7: 661. It is interesting that one of the most perceptive readers of both Chekhov and Dostoevsky, Robert Louis Jackson, chose to focus on *Garshin's,* not Chekhov's, story in his book on the Underground Man in Russian literature. Jackson analyzes Garshin's "An Incident" as reflecting Dostoevsky's influence. In his reading, it is the *prostitute* who speaks from the underground, not the "lover" (77-81).

9. See Siegel and Matich for discussions of this tradition.

10. Matich explores the ways this is done by identifying four basic patterns of victimization and rescue in these works.

11. This word *stushevat'sia* is associated with Dostoevsky in the Russian literary consciousness, thanks to Dostoevsky's note in the *Writer's Diary* for November 1877 entitled "The Origin of the Verb 'Stushevatsia,'" in which he proudly claims that it was he who introduced it into Russian literature. In a piece of quaint hyperbole, Dostoevsky writes: ". . . in the course of my literary career, what I've liked most is the fact that I managed to introduce an entirely new word into the Russian language; and whenever I encounter that word in print I'm always very pleased . . ." (*A Writer's Diary* 1186).

12. A link between Vasiliev's reaction and that of Gogol's Piskarev in the story "Nevskii Prospect" (1835) is pointed out both by Joseph Conrad (442,

n. 10) and by the editors of the Academy edition (*Sochineniia* 7: 662). Piskarev discovers that the object of his idealized desire is a prostitute and undergoes a fit that closely resembles Vasiliev's in many details. Significantly for us, Piskarev's fit ends in suicide—a fate shared by both Garshin and his protagonists, but not by Dostoevsky's or Chekhov's.

13. The most thorough treatment of the snow symbolism in Chekhov's story is Marena Senderovich's "The Symbolic Structure of Chekhov's Story 'An Attack of Nerves.'" Senderovich does not draw the link to Dostoevsky.

14. Many readers note the symbolic significance of the motif of "falling" in Chekhov's story. Senderovich lucidly discusses the symbolic relationship between the snow and Vasiliev's inner drama. Most provocative, given our focus on the clash between ideals and reality, is Senderovich's implication that the black-and-white tonality of the story reflects the limited dimensionality of Vasiliev's purely "literary" views on morality.

15. See Conrad 443, n. 14. It is also worth noting that although Rumiantseva quotes at length a reminiscence of Dostoevsky that demonstrates the author's disgust at the behavior of three young men of lofty and romantic pretension who insult a prostitute, she does not draw a textual link between Dostoevsky's *literary* work (*Notes from Underground*) and "An Attack of Nerves" (92-3).

16. Oddly enough, Leo Tolstoy could have been speaking for *Dostoevsky* when, commenting on the Chekhov story, he said "The hero should have used her first, and waited until later to agonize about it!" (quoted in the editors' notes, 7: 664).

17. Failure of an expected event to occur is a key constructive plot element in Chekhov. Usually the expected event has to do with human interaction—in many cases, a marriage or marriage proposal ("A Woman's Kingdom," 1894; "The House with a Mezzanine," 1896; *Uncle Vania,* 1896; "A Visit to Friends," 1898; *The Cherry Orchard,* 1903; and many others). "An Attack of Nerves," which also is built around an anticipated, but not consummated, encounter between a man and a woman, operates on the same dynamic principle.

18. Conrad notes this possibility in passing: "[Is] Vasiliev [. . .] more attracted to 'vice' than he would like to admit?" (432).

19. Loose-flowing hair is one of Chekhov's markers for sexual desire. See de Sherbinin 122. The words "curiosity" and "interest" in Chekhov's works also build sexual tension.

20. It is tantalizing to speculate on the aesthetic roots of Vasiliev's disillusionment. What would have

happened if he had encountered the prostitute of his fantasies? In Chekhov's world, however, where dreams and reality do not coincide, such a turn of events is unimaginable. In this story, the beauty and seductiveness of his vision, as opposed to the reality he encounters, renders Vasiliev unable to take action. The moral implications of Chekhov's presentation of the problem are serious, as we shall see below.

21. This of course is a not-so-hidden quotation from *Genesis* 26: "И сказал Бог: сотворим человека по образу Нашему, по подобию Нашему . . . (And God said, Let us make man in our image, after our likeness . . .)". Although this phrase was a cliché for humanistic ideas among the nineteenth-century Russian *raznochintsy,* Chekhov's use of it in this context specifically recalls Dostoevsky's famous text.

22. Cathy Popkin's fascinating essay illuminates the many kinds of dangers accompanying the search for cognition in this rich text. I focus here on "carnal knowledge."

23. As Schopenhauer puts it, ". . . in this world the capacity to feel pain increases with knowledge and therefore reaches its highest degree in man, a degree that is higher, the more intelligent the man" (quoted in Kelly 328-29). Kelly's discussion of Turgenev's presentation of this issue is surely relevant to Chekhov and Dostoevsky as well: "Like Schopenhauer, [Turgenev] sees consciousness as an illness, a pathological deviation from the universal order of things; hence all those aspects of culture in which humanity has enshrined its highest goods—philosophy, science, *morality* [*emphasis added*], art, poetry—are nothing other than sedatives, *'des palliatifs,'* against the pain of unfiltered reality and the horror of final extinction" (Kelly 109).

24. The doctor and the writer are inseparable in Chekhov. His "holy of holies" is health and the human body (*Pis'ma,* 3: 11). Many stories of this period deal with illness. Chekhov insists that this story is firmly based in his medical knowledge: "It seems to me that as a medical man I gave a correct depiction of his psychological pain, following all the rules of psychiatric science" (*Pis'ma,* 3: 68). He makes similar assertions about stories of human illness and stress from this and other periods, such as "Oysters" (1884), "The Name-Day Party" (1888) and "The Black Monk" (1894). A soul that fits well in the body is a metonym for an individual who fits well in society and in the material world. The best discussion of the embededness of Chekhov's characters in the material world is A. Chudakov's *Mir Chekhova.*

25. Inevitably here the Marquis de Sade comes to mind. His notorious cruelty seems to have stemmed from a sexual inadequacy. In his brilliant discussion of the moral implications of the recent scholarly infatuation with the sadistic Marquis, Roger Shattuck allows Camus the last word: "Prometheus ends up as Onan" (284). Might this insight contribute to our understanding of Dostoevsky's and Chekhov's protagonists' retreat from human contact? See Shattuck's Chapter VII, especially 233, 263-4, and 283-4.

26. For a thorough exploration of Dostoevsky's attitudes toward suicide, as well as Russian attitudes in general toward the issue during the nineteenth century, see 123-84 of Irina Paperno's excellent book.

27. Each new generation of writers strives to present an image of the world that seems more "real" than that offered by its predecessors. But this does not have to be a hostile, polemical process. Both "On Account of the Wet Snow" and "An Attack of Nerves" build heavily on a distinction between fantasies and literary preconceptions and life itself. Both protagonists discover that excessive reliance on ideological cliché renders meaningful action impossible. Paradoxically, the message of "Ward 6," "People are not equivalent to their ideas and cannot and must not live by them" (Durkin 59), is applicable to Dostoevsky's message as well.

28. In the works for which they are most famous, both writers allow their protagonists—Chekhov's lovers in "The Lady with the Dog" (1899) and Dostoevsky's Dmitry in *The Brothers Karamazov,* 1880—to achieve the elusive harmony between body and soul. In both cases, the text is infused with an atmosphere of mystery approaching the sacred, and the characters so blessed are free of any tendency to abstract thinking and analysis.

Works Cited

Anton P. Čechov—Philosophie und Religion in Leben und Werk. Ed. Vladimir V. Kataev, Rolf-Dieter Kluge, and Regine Nohejl. Munich: Verlag Otto Sagner, 1997.

Bakhtin, Mikhail. *Problems of Dostoevsky's Poetics.* Ed., and trans. Caryl Emerson. Minneapolis: U of Minnesota P, 1984.

Berdnikov, G. P. *Chekhov: Ideinye i tvorcheskie iskaniia.* Leningrad: "Khudozhestvennaia literatura," 1970.

Bibliia. Knigi sviashchennogo pisaniia Vetkhogo i Novogo zaveta kanonicheskie. UBS, 1989.

Bitsilli, Peter M. *Chekhov's Art: A Stylistic Analysis.* Trans. Toby W. Clyman and Edwina Jannie Cruise. Ann Arbor: Ardis, 1983.

Chekhov, Anton P. *Anton Chekhov's Life and Thought: Selected Letters and Commentary.* Trans. Michael Henry Heim. Ed. and annot. Simon Karlinsky. Evanston, Ill.: Northwestern UP, 1997.

———. *Polnoe sobranie sochinenii i pisem v tridtsati tomakh* [PSSiP]. Ed. I. F. Bel'chikov et al. Moskva: "Nauka," 1974-83.

Chudakov, A. P. *Chekhov's Poetics.* Trans. Edwina Jannie Cruise and Donald Dragt. Ann Arbor: Ardis, 1983.

———. *Mir Chekhova: Vozniknovenie i utverzhdenie.* Moscow: Sovetskii pisatel', 1986.

Conrad, Joseph. "Čexov's 'An Attack of Nerves.'" *Slavic and East European Journal* 13.4 (1969): 429-43.

De Sherbinin, Julie. *Chekhov and Russian Religious Culture: The Poetics of the Marian Paradigm.* Evanston, Ill.: Northwestern UP, 1997.

Dostoevskii, F. M. "Zapiski iz podpol'ia." *Polnoe sobranie sochinenii v tridtsati tomakh,* 5. Leningrad: "Nauka," 1973. 99-179.

Dostoevsky, F. M. *A Writer's Diary.* Volume Two. Trans. and annot. Kenneth Lantz. Evanston, Ill.: Northwestern UP, 1997.

Durkin, Andrew R. "Chekhov's Response to Dostoevsky: The Case of 'Ward Six.'" *Slavic Review* 40.1 (1981): 49-59.

Garshin, V. M. *Sochineniia.* Moscow: Gosudarstvennoe izdatel'stvo khudozhestvennoi literatury, 1955.

Gromov, M. N. "Skrytye tsitaty (Chekhov i Dostoevskii)." *Chekhov i ego vremia.* Moscow: "Nauka," 1977. 39-52.

Hahn, Beverly. *Chekhov: A Study of the Major Stories and Plays.* Cambridge: Cambridge UP, 1977.

Hingley, Ronald. *A Life of Anton Chekhov.* Oxford: Oxford UP, 1989.

The Holy Bible (King James Version). New York: American Bible Society, 1974.

Jackson, Robert Louis. "Dostoevsky in Chekhov's Garden of Eden: 'Because of Little Apples.'" *Dialogues with Dostoevsky: The Overwhelming Questions.* Stanford: Stanford UP, 1993. 83-103.

———. *Dostoevsky's Underground Man in Russian Literature.* The Hague: Mouton, 1958.

Kelly, Aileen. *Toward Another Shore: Russian Thinkers Between Necessity and Chance.* New Haven: Yale UP, 1998.

Matich, Olga. "A Typology of Fallen Women in Nineteenth Century Russian Literature." *American Contributions to the Ninth International Congress of Slavists, II: Literature, Poetics, History.* Ed. Paul Debreczeny. Columbus, Ohio: Slavica, 1983. 325-43.

Paperno, Irina. *Suicide as a Cultural Institution in Dostoevsky's Russia.* Ithaca and London: Cornell UP, 1997.

Polotskaia, E. A. "Chelovek v khudozhestvennom mire Dostoevskogo i Chekhova." *Dostoevskii i russkie pisateli: traditsii, novatorstvo, masterstvo. Sbornik statei.* Comp. V. Ia. Kirpotin. Moscow: Sovetskii pisatel', 1971. 184-245.

Popkin, Cathy. "Humpty Dumpty Had a Great Fall: Cognition and Collapse in Chekhov's 'Pripadok.'" Unpublished paper.

Rayfield, Donald. *Anton Chekhov: A Life.* London: HarperCollins, 1997.

Rumiantseva, E. M. "Dostoevskii i rasskazy Chekhova kontsa 80-kh godov." *F. M. Dostoevskii, N. A. Nekrasov (Sbornik nauchnykh trudov).* Ed. N. N. Skatov. Leningrad, 1974. 87-102.

Semanova, M. L. "Rasskaz o 'cheloveke garshinskoi zakvaski.'" *Chekhov i ego vremia.* Ed. L. D. Opul'skaia, Z. S. Papernyi, and S. E. Shatalov. Moscow: "Nauka," 1977. 62-84.

Senderovich, Marena. "The Symbolic Structure of Chekhov's Story 'An Attack of Nerves.'" Trans. Lois Strunk in *Chekhov's Art of Writing: A Collection of Critical Essays.* Ed. Paul Debreczeny and Thomas Eekman. Columbus, OH: Slavica, 1977. 11-26.

Shattuck, Roger. *Forbidden Knowledge: From Prometheus to Pornography.* San Diego, N.Y., London: Harcourt Brace & Co., 1996.

Siegel, George. "The Fallen Woman in Nineteenth-Century Russian Literature." *Harvard Slavic Studies* 5 (1970): 81-107.

Terras, Victor. *Reading Dostoevsky.* Madison: U of Wisconsin P, 1999.

Tynianov, Iu. *Arkhaisty i novatory.* Priboi, 1929; reprint Ann Arbor: Ardis, 1985.

Nadezhda Katyk-Lewis (essay date 15 November 2000)

SOURCE: Katyk-Lewis, Nadezhda. "Sketch as Impressionist Technique in the Prose of Čechov." *Russian Literature* 48, no. 4 (15 November 2000): 351-65.

[*In the following essay, Katyk-Lewis finds parallels between the nature of Impressionist art and Chekhov's narrative style.*]

> Not a single secondary detail,
> not a single superfluous line.
>
> (Evgenij Zamjatin)

Čechov's art is traditionally defined as the final stage in the development of nineteenth-century Russian Realism. Within this historical context the unique quality of his work is generally identified as his individual "Chekhovian" style. Occasionally, in searching for a more precise definition of the individuality of this style, critics have described it also in terms of the analogy with Impressionist painting. In doing so, they have focused mainly on the general "vagueness" of Čechov's images, which they perceive as the dominant feature of Impressionism in art.

It is indeed true that "vagueness" is the most immediately striking quality of Impressionist painting, and therefore it is certainly important to establish its counterpart in Čechov's text. Critics who have attempted to analyze the Impressionism of Čechov have taken as the most striking examples of "vagueness" those of his stories in which reality and dreams are mixed in the minds of the characters, such as **'Archierej'** and **'Spat' chočetsja'.**[1] However, Var'ka's dreams of her family mixed with the waving shadows of hanging laundry, or the blurred faces in the crowded church as seen through the teary eyes of the sick and exhausted bishop, are actually in direct contrast with what Impressionist paintings convey.

The substance of the "vagueness" in Impressionist painting is the result of the painter's first brief glance at the object, the instant impression it evokes in him, captured immediately on canvas. The style of this "vagueness" consists in a specially developed technique of broken, fleeting brushstrokes fixing and conveying this freshness of perception. In order to compare Čechov's art to Impressionist painting and establish the presence of analogous qualities in it, we need to demonstrate a parallel artistic manner in his text.

Čechov started to write in the 1880s, when Russian Realism had reached its peak. The philosophy and style of Realism were the ultimate measure of artistic quality, and the names of Turgenev, Dostoevskij, and Tolstoj were almost sacred in the eyes of public and critics alike. At this time, when Realist art was striving to create a lifelike, concrete image, based on the thorough knowledge and observation of reality, Čechov began to form his own aesthetic ideal. The elliptic, concise style dominating Čechov's prose from the early to the late works was a disturbing novelty at a time when the effect and beauty of Realist images was achieved by the accumulation of numerous, although of course carefully selected, fine details. This contrast is particularly clear in the different styles of landscape description found in Čechov, as opposed to a Realist writer such as Tolstoj, whether it is the whole image, or a single element, for example a tree.

In **'Skripka Rotšil'da'** Čechov has a description of a willow-tree which is associated with Jakov's memories of Marfa. When she and Jakov were young, they used to sit with their baby under the willow and sing songs. Now, fifty years later, after Marfa is gone, Jakov comes to the river and finds the tree, and his forgotten memories revive. This moment of recognition is no doubt an opportunity to endow the tree with an abundance of traces of longevity with which Jakov could identify. This concrete realistic tree is at the same time imbued with a symbolic meaning like another tree-portrait: the famous oak-tree in *Vojna i mir* which Tolstoj displayed so splendidly.

> На краю дороги стоял дуб. Вероятно, в десять раз старше берез, составлявших лес, он был в десять раз толще и в два раза выше каждой березы. Это был огромный, в два охвата дуб, с обломанными, давно видно, суками и с обломанной корой, заросшей старыми болячками. С огромными своими, неуклюже, несимметрично растопыренными корявыми руками и пальцами, он старым, сердитым и презрительным уродом стоял между улыбающимися березами.
>
> (Tolstoj 1974: 528)

By the roadside stood an oak. It was evidently ten times as old as the birches of which the forest was mainly composed; it was ten times as large round and twice as high as any of the birches. It was enormous, two spans around in girth, and with ancient scars where huge limbs, evidently long ago lopped off, had been, and with bark stripped away. With monstrous, disproportioned, unsymmetrically spreading arms and fingers, it stood like an ancient giant, stern and scornful, among the smiling birches.[2]

In an earlier version of the manuscript the oak-tree has a different appearance—it is forked. Here is evidence of how important and toilsome it was for Tolstoj to achieve the precise, satisfying image.

Čechov portrayed his willow-tree like this:

> А вот широкая старая верба с громадным дуплом, а на ней вороньи гнезда . . . Да, это и есть та самая верба—зеленая, тихая, грустная . . . Как она постарела, бедная!
>
> (**'Skripka Rotšil'da'**, Čechov 1985, 8: 250)[3]

Here is the ancient spreading willow-tree with a huge hollow, and crows' nests among its branches . . . Yes, this is the same tree, so green, quiet, sad . . . How old it had grown, poor thing!

Čechov, too, worked meticulously on his manuscripts. His idea of polishing the text was, however, somewhat different. In a letter of February 1899 he writes about preparing his material for publication: "Čerkaju bezžalostno . . . Čto ja ni čitaju—svoe i čužoe, vse predstavljaetsja mne nedostatočno korotkim" ("I am mercilessly crossing out . . . Whatever I read, my own work or anyone else's, everything appears to me insufficiently short"; Gitovič 1955: 222).

Čechov sets down only the most essential traces of the long fifty years, as they strike Jakov on seeing them: the enormous hole in the wide trunk and the crows' nests. Neither are the three following adjectives— "green", "quiet", "sad"—products of any meticulous observation; they convey no more than the global impression and mood of the perceiver of the tree. This is no solid object observed from near and far, nor does the reader get any feeling of the rough, cracked bark. Čechov, like the Impressionists, does not try to feel the object, but only lightly touches it. Any additional details, which could illuminate or emphasize the image, are missing. It is only what Jakov's eye scans. What Čechov records here is the first impact of the object on the observer—which is the fundamental principle of Impressionist painting.

It is well known that the Impressionists were trying to eliminate or suppress their knowledge of the objects they painted, to separate knowledge from pure observation. Monet supposedly wished that he had been born blind and would suddenly gain his sight (Gordon, Forge 1989: 56). That would enable him to paint a green blob in the distance just as he saw it, without the danger of giving it any characteristics of a bush, which, as he knew, it really was.

In the beginning of **'Step''**, Egoruška is passing by the churchyard on his way out of town. Čechov describes it as observed by the little boy:

> [. . .] из-за ограды весело выглядывали белые кресты и памятники, которые прячутся в зелени вишневых деревъев и издали кажутся белыми пятнами. Егорушка вспомнил, что когда цветет вишня, эти белые пятна мешаются с вишневыми цветами в белое море; а когда она спеет, белые памятники и кресты бывают усыпаны багряными, как кровъ, точками.

> (**'Step''**, 1985, 6: 316)

> [. . .] white crosses and tombstones, nestling among green cherry-trees and looking in the distance like patches of white, peeped out gaily from behind the wall. Egorushka remembered that when the cherries were in blossom those white patches melted with the flowers into a sea of white; and that when the cherries were ripe the white tombstones and crosses were dotted with splashes of red like bloodstains.

The world as a complex fabric of color is presented to Egoruška's unspoiled, naive eye—the eye of the Impressionist. By recording the appearance of an object without preconception of any kind, Čechov added to the concrete, contemporary subject of the Realist a new, crucial quality of immediacy.

In painting, an important role in this development was played by the discovery of photography. The technical process could produce an exact copy of reality with ev-

ery detail. The value of verisimilitude was suddenly shattered, and art was shifted in a new direction. The role of the painter was not to compete with the photographic lens in imitation of the real. His challenge was to grasp the freshness of immediate perception, and to capture it in a few fleeting strokes, which could be instantly perceived. The aim was to monumentalize the instant itself.

In one of his letters Čechov gave Gor'kij a piece of advice:

> Понятно, когда я пишу: "человек сел на траву"; это понятно, потому что ясно и не эадерживает внимания. Наоборот, неудобопонятно и тяжеловато для мозгов, если я пишу: "высокий, узкогрудый, среднего роста человек с рыжей бородкой сел на зеленую, уже измятую пешеходами траву, сел бесшумно, робко и пугливо оглядываясъ." Это не сразу укладывается в мозгу, а беллетристика должна укладыватъся сразу, в секунду.[4]

> (1974-1983, VIII: 258)

> It is easy to understand when I write: "A man sat on the grass"; it is easy because it is clear and does not distract the reader's attention. On the other hand it is clumsy and difficult for the brain to grasp, if I write: "A tall narrow-chested man of medium height with a red beard sat on the green trampled grass, he sat down quietly, timidly and fearfully looked back." It does not settle in the brain at once, and fiction has to settle at once, in a second.

Čechov wrote this letter in 1899, when his style was already fully developed and his work was no longer limited by publishing constraints. It is further evidence of Čechov's striving for a brief, spare description, with the clear goal that it would be grasped instantly. It was not concern for the editor, but concern for the reader, which led him to strip his descriptions to bare necessities.

The first critics of Čechov did not fail to notice this novelty of his style. In 1888 a critic wrote in *Nedelja*:

> Он просто вышел гулятъ в жизнъ. Во время прогулки он встречает иногда интересные лица, характерные сценки, хорошенъкие пейзажи. Тогда он останавливается на минуту, достает карандаш и легкими штрихами набрасывает свой рисунок. Кончен рисунок, и он идет далъше.

> [. . .] Теперъ ему встречается уже другой предмет, он так же легко набрасывает его, так же легко его забывает и ждет новых впечатлений прогулки.

> (quoted in Čudakov 1971: 178)

> He simply took a walk into life. During his walk he sometimes meets interesting faces, characteristic scenes, pretty landscapes. He stops for a minute, takes out a pencil, and with light strokes sketches his picture. The picture is done and he walks on.

[. . .] Now he comes across another object, he sketches it just as easily, just as easily forgets it and waits for the next impression of his walk.

The critic may not have appreciated such an approach, but he certainly made a correct observation: for reproducing an impression Čechov used the only possible technique—the sketch. The problem at the time, however, was in accepting the sketch as a form of art. Čechov's lightly sketched landscapes or portraits could have served in earlier literature only as preliminary studies, eventually to be rewritten into more elaborate images (Čudakov 1971: 167).

In painting, the unfinished form of Impressionist works became a target of severe criticism. Although sketches had been done before and had been valued for their freshness and charm, they were no more than preparatory studies for more ambitious compositions, for detailed paintings with a smooth surface, which alone could be considered works of art. The sketch, then, was an outline, an annotation for the final pieces. For a Realist painter a sketch was the beginning of a creative process while for an Impressionist it became its final result.

At the first Impressionist exhibition there were no "finished" pieces. Mere sketches were presented to the public as works of art. There was outrage and laughter at both the paintings and the artists. "It was said that they did not carry the execution of their work beyond a first glance, that their landscapes had been viewed through the window of a train" (Courthion 1977: 28). These "sketches" were certainly different from the previous finished paintings as well as from the new photography. Photography, although reproducing every detail, at the same time froze the moment so completely and suddenly that it rendered the object or figure inert. Contrary to this, the Impressionists strove to capture the throb of life in each instant (Cogniat n.d.: 26).

This was a serious deviation from Realism and the beginning of a new era in art. Quite symbolically, it was heralded by a painting titled "Impression: Sunrise". This banner picture of the entire Impressionist movement was a conglomerate of its principles and features. This was no traditional view of a seaport. In this piece Monet was searching for something other than a mere landscape.

> He fixed the movement of light and water between the morning sun, dulled by fog, and the small dark skiff in the foreground. Jotting as though taking notes, he set down essentials, not details, yet his skill at translating vision into paint managed to register a complex reality: distance, atmosphere, light, time of day, place are all convincingly portrayed. This is a moment of transition, which in a few minutes would disappear.
>
> (Wood et al. 1989: 245)

For the Impressionists things do not simply exist, but they constantly evolve, so that the world does not contain completed objects. Instead, everything is in constant transition. Translated into painting, this leads to fusion of objects, destruction of contours, to "blurred" images.

The idea of the cycle of existence, of the motion of life, became a part of the consciousness of the late nineteenth century. It was proclaimed as part of the modern scientific worldview by widely read authors such as Ludwig Büchner, whose *Kraft und Stoff* Čechov studied in the course of his medical training:

> There is no repose of any kind in nature; its whole existence is a constant cycle, in which every motion, the consequence of preceding motion, becomes immediately the cause of an equivalent succeeding one.
>
> (Büchner 1864: 169)

The flux of life became the subject both of the Impressionist painters and of Čechov. They still insisted on fidelity to reality, but it was a reality of only the fleeting moment. This became part of Čechov's brief and concise style. Thus, when describing a morning or an evening, Čechov mostly chooses dawn or sunset—the moment of transition. Moreover, the individual descriptions themselves are imbued with actual motion:

> Над травой носился легкий туман, а на небе мимо луны куда-то без огдядки бежали облака. [. . .] Лунный свет сколъзил по релъсам. Болъшие тени от облаков то и дело пробегали по насыпи.
>
> (**'Strachi',** 1985, 5: 42)

Light fog floated over the grass, and in the sky the clouds were running past the moon without looking back. [. . .] The moonlight was sliding over the rails. The big shadows of the clouds were now and then running over the embankment.

This characteristic has been noted by Čudakov:

> Природа у Чехова—это не ландшафт, флора, фауна, зависящие толъко от смены сезонов и времени суток. Географическая его непременностъ колеблется подвижными сиюминутными предметами. Это—природа в ее непредвидимых, постоянно новых состояниях, которые она сама ежесекундно творит [. . .] Пейзаж Чехова запечатлевает [. . .] трепетный, меняющийся облик мира.
>
> (Čudakov 1986: 158)

Nature in Čechov is not a landscape in which the flora and fauna depend only on the change of seasons and the time of day. Its geographic invariability is constantly altered by momentary, moving objects. It is nature, with its unforeseeable, constantly new conditions, which creates itself every second. [. . .] Čechov's landscape projects [. . .] the trembling, changing appearance of the world.

However, apart from the aspect of objects revealed in motion, there is a sensation of movement created by the aesthetic material of the work. This compositional movement is in fact a movement of the beholder's attention (Rothschild 1960: 86). The Impressionist technique of applying brushstrokes of different colors partially fusing in the eyes of the beholder creates an effect of shimmering, vibrating color. Also, the effort to capture the character of the illuminating atmospheric effects and reflections, as well as of the separate light patches spread all over the painting, creates the sensation of movement.

The same kind of sensation is created also by Čechov's landscapes.

> Солнце беззаботно улыбалосъ на звездочках поручика, на белых стволах берез, на кучах битого стекла, разбросанныхъ там и сям по двору. На всем лежала светлая здоровая красота летнего дня, и ничто не мешало сочной молодой зелени весело трепетатъ и перемигиватъся с ясным голубым небом.

> (**'Tina'**, 1985, 5: 162)

The sun smiled carelessly on the lieutenant's little stars, on the white trunks of the birch-trees, on the heaps of broken glass scattered here and there in the yard. The radiant, vigorous beauty of a summer day lay over everything, and nothing hindered the sappy young green leaves from quivering gaily and winking at the clear blue sky.

> Красные пятна от костра, вместе с тенями ходили по земле около темных человеческих фигур, дрожали на горе, на деревъях, на мосту, на сушилъне; на другой стороне обрывистый, изрытый бережок весъ был освещен, мигал и отражался в речке, и быстро бегущая бурливая вода рвала на части его отражение.

> (**'Duèl'**, 1985. 7: 242)

Shadows and red patches thrown by the bonfire flickered on the ground near the dark shapes of people and quivered on mountain, trees, bridge and barn. The precipitous, rutted opposite bank was brightly lit, its glimmering reflected in the water, but torn to shreds by the churning torrent.

It is striking that Čechov does not observe the landscape in any organized way—from ground to sky or from left to right—but his attention and that of the reader is drawn at the same time in different directions to the points of light scattered as if at random all over the picture. The winking between the verdure and the sky, or in the language of the palette, the reflecting of blues in greens, the fusing of the two main parts of the scenery, coincide with their blurred outline, their sketchiness, and contribute at the same time to the restless sensation of compositional movement.

In the same way, the motion of the human figures in **'Duèl'** is subdued, and the general movement of the scenery is emphasized by the shimmering red patches of light from the bonfire. Moreover, the riverbank and its reflection in the water are not solid but ripped to pieces like the trembling reflections chopped by the slashing Impressionist brushstrokes. Compare also:

> Река бежала быстро и едва слышно журчала около сваен купалъни. Красная луна отражаласъ у левого берега; маленькие волны бежали по ее отражению, растягивали его, разрывали на части и, казалосъ, хотели унести. . . .

> (**'Poceluj'**, 1985, 6: 275)

The river was running past swiftly, murmuring almost inaudibly against the bathing-box piles. Near the left bank glowed the moon's ruddy reflection; tiny waves were running over the reflection, stretching it, tearing it to pieces, and, it seemed, trying to carry it away . . .

Although projection of the trembling, changing appearance of the world is considered a feature unique to Čechov's style, unprecedented in Russian Realism, it is not an isolated phenomenon in the art of his era. The same perception of the world is reflected in the trembling quality of Impressionist painting.

While the motion in Čechov's landscapes has received some attention, how much space he grants to and what a role he bestows upon air, with all its many fragrances, seems to have passed completely unnoticed. This feature persists from the earliest to the last of his landscape descriptions. Of course, air also plays a role in the landscapes of earlier writers like Turgenev. But in these, the air is no more than one of many elements of detailed description. Not so with Čechov:

> По дачной платформе взад и вперед прогуливаласъ парочка недавно поженившихся супругов. [. . .] Из-за облачных обрывков глядела на них луна и хмуриласъ. [. . .] Неподвижный воздух был густо насыщен запахом сирени и черемухи. Где-то, по ту сторону релъсов кричал коростелъ. . . .

> (**'Dačniki'**, 1985, 3: 53)

Two young people who had not long been married were walking up and down the platform of a little country station. [. . .] The moon peeped up from the drifting cloudlets and frowned. [. . .] The still air was heavy with the fragrance of lilac and wild cherry. Somewhere in the distance beyond the railway a corncrake was calling . . .

This landscape is not visual; we do not see any lilac or wild cherry, nor what is beyond the railway. What we perceive is the air filled with the scents of the flowers and the sound of the corncrake. One might object that this is an evening scene, lit only by the moon. But the same thing happens also at midday:

> А солнце печет и печет. Тени становятся короче и уходят в самих себя, как рога улитки . . . Высокая трава, пригретая солнцем, начинает испускатъ из себя густой, приторно-медовый запах. Уж скоро полденъ. [. . .]

> (**'Nalim'**, 1985, 3: 58)

And the sun is burning and burning. The shadows are growing shorter and are retracting into themselves, like the horns of a snail . . . The tall grass, heated by the sun, is beginning to exhale the thick, sickly sweet smell of honey. It is almost noon [. . .]

There is hardly anything of substance in this landscape. Although the sense of heat is created immediately, the sun itself does not receive any attention. This is not a Turgenev sun described with every nuance not only of what it is like, but even of what it is not like:

Солнце—не огнистое, не раскаленное, как во время знойной засухи, не тускло багровое, как перед бурей, но светлое и приветно лучезарное. [. . .]

(Turgenev 1991: 61)

The sun, not fiery, not red-hot, as in the season of sultry drought, not of a dull crimson, as before a tempest, but bright, and agreeably radiant [. . .]

Čechov's sun is not imbued with a single attribute. It is set down with an absolute minimum of description—a bare noun, like a simple spot of paint. Čechov's focus is on its effect, its activity. By repeating the verb, he creates a feeling of crescendo; nevertheless it is the same verb, void of any accompaniment. Čechov depicts the entire image literally in three words, as in three energetic, visible strokes: "A solnce pečet i pečet" ("And the sun is burning and burning"). In the same way the tall grass is mentioned only as source of what we perceive—the fragrance. It is the fragrance which is the most specific part of the landscape, the main bulk of it. It dominates all other sensations.

Čechov's air, saturated with fragrances, fills his landscapes, which we perceive through its volume. It is a tangible, substantial part of them. It is the motif itself, just as the atmosphere was the motif of Monet. Monet no longer saw an object separated from its environment and the light. Instead he saw a union, a confluence of the mass and the void. He saw atmosphere as an envelope within which everything visible is located and which cannot be separated from the form of the objects. This envelope at the same time affects the degree to which these forms are realized in themselves. Fog, smoke, hot hazy air, falling snow along with fragrances, all mediate the envelope, which is an omnipresent feature of Čechov's art:

Травы в цвету—зеленые, желтые, лиловые, белые, и от них, и от нагретой земли идет аромат. . . .

('V rodnom uglu', 1985, 9: 203)

The grasses are flowering—green, yellow, mauve, white, and from them as from the warm earth is coming the scent . . .

[. . .] когда в неподвижном, застоявшемся воздухе начинало пахнуть сеном, и медом, и слышалось короткое жужжание пчел, маленький человечек совсем овладел Ольгой Михайловной.

('Imeniny', 1985, 7: 31)

[. . .] when the motionless, stagnant air became filled with the scent of hay and honey and she could hear the gentle buzzing of bees, the tiny creature would take complete possession of her.

Был седьмой час вечера—время, когда белая акация и сиренъ пахнут так сильно, что кажется, воздух и сами деревъя стынут от своего запаха. В городском саду уже играла музыка. Лошади звонко стучали по мостовой; со всех сторон слышалисъ смех, говор, хлопание калиток . . .

[. . .]

Выехали за город и побежали рысью по болъшой дороге. Здесь уже не пахло акацией и сиренъю, не слышно было музыки, но зато пахло полем, зеленели молодые рожъ и пшеница, пищали суслики, каркали грачи.

('Učitel' slovesnosti', 1985, 8: 266-267)

It was seven o'clock in the evening—the time when the scent of white acacia and lilac is so strong that the air and the very trees seem heavy with the fragrance. The band was already playing in the town gardens. The horses made a resounding thud on the pavement, on all sides there were sounds of laughter, talk, and banging gates . . .

[. . .]

They rode on out of the town and set off at a trot along the highroad. Here there was no scent of lilac and acacia, no music of the band, but there was the fragrance of the fields, there was the green of young rye and wheat, the marmots were squeaking, the rooks were cawing.

Air constantly surrounds Čechov's scenery, it is an integral part of it. We are constantly confronted with vapors, scents, different sounds of insects or of a town. The flowers of the blooming steppe, which Čechov knew very well, are of no specific kind, no shape—only spots of pure color scattered around, submerged in the vapors of its own fragrance.

Čechov does not even state that there "was" hay and honey, or rye, dill and so forth; he does not say that there "were fields", or that "the fields started to spread". It only "smelled of fields". He describes location not by describing the facts of landscape from which we can deduce the atmosphere of the place. Instead, he describes the atmosphere, the envelope, through which the realities are only lightly sketched. The difference between two different places for Čechov lies in the fact that one smells of acacia and the other does not. The substance itself is of much less importance.

Čechov applied the same approach to his interiors. It is useful to compare these with a similar description, for instance in Bunin's 'Temnye allei':

В горнице было тепло, сухо и опрятно: новый золотистый образ в левом углу, под ним покрытый чистой суровой скатертъю стол, за столом чисто вымытые лавки; кухонная печъ, занимавшая дальний правый угол, ново белела мелом; ближе стояло нечто вроде тахты, покрытой пегими погонами, упиравшейся отвалом в бок печи; изза печной заслонки сладко пахло щами—разварившейся капустой, говядиной и лавровым листом.

(Bunin 1946: 10)

The room was warm, dry and neat: a new golden icon in the left corner, under it a table covered with a clean unbleached cloth, behind the table thoroughly washed benches; the kitchen stove, occupying the far right corner, had been newly whitened with chalk; closer to the table was something like an ottoman covered with a piebald spread, and leaning to the side of the stove; from behind the oven door was coming a sweet smell of soup—boiled cabbage, beef and a bay-leaf.

Here are some interiors of Čechov:

Мы вошли в чистую комнату, где сильно пахло скатертями.

(**'Žena'**, 1985, 7: 349)

We entered a clean room, where it smelled strongly of tablecloths.

В первой комнате, куда он вошел, было просторно, жарко натоплено и пахло недавно вымытыми полами.

(**'Vory'**, 1985, 7: 168)

The first room he entered was spacious, heated, and smelled of recently washed floors.

В номере стоял удушливый запах гвоздики, креозота, йода, карболки и других вонючих веществ, которые Софъя Саввишна употребляла против своей зубной боли.

(**'Žitejskie nevzgody'**, 1985, 6: 55)

The room was filled with a suffocating smell of cloves, creosote, iodine, carbolic, and other strong-smelling substances, which Sof'ja Savvišna used for her toothache.

Пахло в комнате чем-то затхлым и кислым.

(**'Step''**, 1985, 6: 333)

The room smelled of something mouldy and sour.

Both Bunin's and Čechov's descriptions are metonymic: they are extensions of the characters. The neatness of Bunin's room refers to the neatness of the hostess. All the following details confirm and emphasize this basic quality. The smell of the soup with the list of ingredients only adds another detail to this scene, which is described in a concrete, realistic manner: the table covered with a clean cloth, the thoroughly washed benches, and so on.

Čechov does not describe a tablecloth itself. For him the smell is evocative. He does not see the freshly washed floor, but the room smells of it. In **'Step''** he does not even say what it was; just "something" smelled

unpleasant. Analysis of Monet's art once again fully applies to that of Čechov: "Empty volume becomes tangible, and solid masses insubstantial" (Seitz 1982: 40).

The aroma arising from the warm earth and grass, the stiff air smelling of hay and honey, the hot sticky air pouring over the woman's body, the smell of acacia so strong that the trees themselves stiffen in it, just like the room smelling of a clean tablecloth or of a washed floor, present Čechov's way of feeling and let us feel the envelope. This focus on the air, on atmosphere rather than on substance, constitutes the essence of Impressionism. The sketch is then the medium through which all of these qualities are conveyed.

The sketch, with its "unfinished" quality proclaimed as a completed work of art in its own right, constituted a serious challenge to traditional values. It was a statement of contemporary reality embodying a forceful, innovative viewpoint toward it. The whole question of what constituted a sketch and when a painting was finished or completed had to be redefined. The very notion of what constituted a work of art was itself challenged. For Monet it became a dominant concern, almost an obsession. Debate on whether his works were completed or not continued for years, until in 1885 a critic, Alfred de Lostalot, made a clear statement: "His [Monet's] pictures are not sketches: neither he nor anyone else could add anything to them" (Gordon, Forge 1989: 55).

Čechov himself was aware of the impact of his innovative writing on literature. What he wrote he expected to be forgotten. But he believed that the new ways and means that he laid down would remain. He fulfilled his role of bringing Russian prose onto the path of Modernism. His style, often puzzling to his contemporaries, was not the end of nineteenth-century Realism; it was already the "sunrise" of the new era. Gor'kij intuitively sensed this when he wrote to his wife: "On rodilsja nemnožko rano" ("He [Čechov] was born a bit too early"; Gitovič 1955: 557).

Twenty years after Čechov's death, however, Zamjatin wrote, in the course of formulating new principles of prose for young writers: "Not a single secondary detail, not a single superfluous line: nothing but the essence, the extract, the synthesis, revealed to the eye within one-hundredth of a second . . ." Perhaps without realizing it, Zamjatin repeatedly proclaimed the principles of Čechov: "[. . .] today the rule is brevity—but every word must be supercharged, high voltage. [. . .] And hence, syntax becomes elliptic, volatile. [. . .] The image is sharp, synthetic, with a single salient feature— the one feature you will glimpse from a speeding car" (Zamyatin 1970: 111).

The voice of Zamjatin sounds more assertive and demanding than the voice of Čechov. For him the "old, slow, creaking descriptions are a thing of the past".

Čechov still had to struggle with them. Zamjatin with bursting energy dismantles, as he puts it, the pyramids of complex syntax stone by stone, and with enthusiasm observes life from his speeding car.

However, the road on which he and twentieth-century prose are running is paved with the cobblestones of Čechov's art. It was Čechov who opened and cleared that road by the soft and gentle touch of his Impressionist pen. He created a new kind of story—a sketch that was complete in itself, since neither he nor anyone else could add anything to it.

Notes

1. Clarke (1977: 125); Stowell (1980: 96).

   The concept of "vagueness" also influences the somewhat different approaches to Čechov's Impressionism found in Chizhevsky (1967); Bitsilli (1983); Senderovich (1977).

2. All translations are my own.

3. References in the text with an Arabic volume number are referring to Čechov (1985).

4. References in the text with a Roman volume number are referring to Čechov (1974-1983, *Pis'ma*).

References

Bitsilli, P. M. 1983. *Chekhov's Art: A Stylistic Analysis* (Trans. T. W. Clyman and E. J. Cruise). Ann Arbor.

Büchner, L. 1864. *Force and Matter*. London.

Bunin, I. 1946. *Temnye allei*. Paris.

Čechov, A. P. 1974-1983. *Polnoe sobranie sočinenij i pisem v tridcati tomach*. Moskva.

———. 1985. *Sobranie sočinenij v dvenadcati tomach* (Ed. M. Eremin). Moskva.

Chizhevsky, Dmitri. 1967. 'Chekhov in the Development of Russian Literature'. In: *Chekhov: A Collection of Critical Essays* (Ed. Robert Louis Jackson). Englewood Cliffs, N.J.

Clarke, Charanne C. 1977. 'Aspects of Impressionism'. In: *Chekhov's Art of Writing: A Collection of Critical Essays* (Eds. Paul Debreczeny and Thomas Eekman). Columbus, Ohio.

Cogniat, R. n.d. *The Century of Impressionists*. New York.

Courthion, P. 1977. *Impressionism*. New York.

Čudakov, A. P. 1971. *Poėtika Čechova*. Moskva.

———. 1986. *Mir Čechova*. Moskva.

Gitovič, N. I. 1955. *Letopis' žizni i tvorčestva A. P. Čechova*. Moskva.

Gordon, R., Forge, A. 1989. *Monet*. New York.

Rothschild, L. 1960. *Style in Art: The Dynamics of Art as Cultural Expression*. New York.

Seitz, W. C. 1982. *Monet: 25 Masterworks*. New York.

Senderovich, Savely. 1977. 'Chekhov and Impressionism: An Attempt at a Systematic Approach to the Problem'. In: *Chekhov's Art of Writing: A Collection of Critical Essays* (Eds. Paul Debreczeny and Thomas Eekman). Columbus, Ohio.

Stowell, H. Peter. 1980. *Literary Impressionism: James and Chekhov*. Athens, Ga.

Tolstoj, L. N. 1974. *Vojna i mir*. Moskva.

Turgenev, I. S. 1991. *Zapiski ochotnika*. Moskva.

Wood, M., Cole, B., Gealt, A. 1989. *Art of the Western World*. New York.

Zamyatin, Y. 1970. *A Soviet Heretic: Essays by Yevgeny Zamyatin* (Ed. and Trans. M. Ginsburg). Chicago.

Philip Hensher (essay date January 2002)

SOURCE: Hensher, Philip. "Incomparable Naturalism." *Atlantic Monthly* 289, no. 1 (January 2002): 126-31.

[*In the following essay, a critique of Janet Malcolm's* Reading Chekhov: A Critical Journey, *Hensher focuses on Chekhov's skill for creating "the powerful illusion of real life."*]

Even the greatest of writers can boast a distinguished posthumous detractor: Shakespeare had Tolstoy and Shaw, and Jane Austen had Charlotte Brontë. The statements these detractors made are so important and interesting that in the end they actually contribute to the sense of their subjects' worth and complexity. Indeed, one might ask whether a writer can ever be regarded as of the first rank if he or she has never attracted intelligent, passionate rejection. Regarding minor talents we don't trouble to disagree, and no one has ever thought it worth being extensively rude about Surtees, whereas Dostoyevsky, Thomas Mann, and Marcel Proust stand at the summit of literary achievement partly because we are never finished arguing about them.

But Chekhov has never attracted anything but admiration. As far as I know, no one has ever tried to mount a general case against him. Since his death very few practitioners of the art have regarded him as anything but the supreme artist of the short story. It is true that Hemingway, in a combative mood, once pretended not to care for him; but even Hemingway was obliged to exempt half a dozen stories from condemnation. Chekhov's influence has been enormous, and always benevolent; even those writers closest to him in manner, such as Katherine Mansfield and V. S. Pritchett, strike us not as imitators but as writers who found in his characteristic manner ways in which they could discover their own characteristic manners. Writers find their own classics; but sooner or later everyone must reckon with Chekhov.

The reason for this supremacy among writers is often said to be Chekhov's incomparable naturalism. Put in a naive way, the usual claim is that Chekhov was not really a writer, with all the artifice and manipulation that implies, but someone who simply set down "life." His stories, like life, have no beginnings, middles, or ends; they do not deal in crises and happy endings; they are simply glimpses of ordinary lives in their untidiness and irresolution. (How radical an approach that remains may be attested by any writer, even now: like many serious writers of short stories, I've experienced having a story turned down on the grounds that it had "no beginning, middle, or end." I wish I'd had the wit to say, "Few episodes in life do, apart from this telephone call.")

It's certainly true that Chekhov always wanted to give the impression that life continued outside the boundaries of his narrative, and many of his stories end by telling us that his characters' lives go on beyond the last page. "The day after this meeting I left Yalta and how Shamokhin's story ended I do not know" (**"Ariadne"**). The child Sonya sits, at the end of **"An Anonymous Story,"** looking at the narrator "as if she knew that her fate was being decided," but what that fate is, the story does not explore. "There is no more to be said about him" dismisses the eponymous hero of **"Doctor Startsev,"** but his life goes on. Many stories end with unanswered questions—"What kind of life would it be?" (**"The Steppe"**)—or with the initiation of some new action. Many, like **"Terror"** and **"A Marriageable Girl,"** end with a departure for some new place, or, like **"The Russian Master,"** with the promise to run away. Almost all of them contain, like the beautiful last paragraph of **"A Lady with a Dog,"** the contemplation of "a wonderful new life." At the simplest level a remarkable number of Chekhov's stories end with a change in the weather: "It began to drizzle" (**"The Duel"**); "All night long rain drummed on the windows" (**"Gooseberries"**); "The sun began to rise" (**"Lights"**); the extravagant and, for once, rather overdone transformation of the seascape at the end of **"Gusev."**

All these endings, focusing on a new beginning rather than concluding something, emphasize what many people have most admired in Chekhov: a sense that life has been glimpsed here, and not glimpsed fully. At its grandest and most mysterious that conviction homes in on the famous unexplained noise that interrupts and concludes the action of *The Cherry Orchard*—a great

string breaking in the distance. Plenty of productions have tried to turn that into a symbol, but it is rather more than that: it is a convulsive acknowledgment that there are things in the world, and in these lives, that neither the artist nor the audience can understand. But to describe Chekhov as purely a chronicler of life, as naive critics have done, is quite wrong. Rather, these expressions of incompleteness are supremely effective artistic conventions, designed to give the powerful illusion of real life. The inconclusive ending may be thought of as something that springs from Chekhov's observations of life; on the other hand, just as plausibly, one could say that Chekhov was imitating one of the most effective devices of his great master, Pushkin. Many of Chekhov's endings are variations on the beautiful and startling conclusion of Pushkin's *Tales of the Late Belkin*: "My readers will excuse me from the unnecessary chore of relating the denouement." (It's always worth remembering what a huge international reputation Laurence Sterne's *Tristram Shandy* acquired—in the unlikeliest places—in the decades after the initial craze for it in England.) Chekhov's characteristic untidiness is, surely, drawn directly from the very deliberate narrative shape of *Eugene Onegin*. The illusion of reality in Chekhov is dazzlingly effective; only an artificer of the highest skill could have produced so seamless an illusion. And, viewed coldly, Chekhov's plots can be as sensational and melodramatic as anything to be found in Dostoyevsky. The fantastic farrago of the immense dramatic torso which posthumous editors have titled *Platonov* is customarily written off as an early aberration, but a distinct taste for the extreme persisted to the end of Chekhov's life. Men, women, and infants are brutally murdered; coincidences abound; passionate declarations and terrible confessions come thick and fast. We don't normally think of Chekhov as a gothic writer, but we shouldn't neglect the ghost in **"The Black Monk"** or the frightful escalations of **"Murder"** and **"In the Hollow."** The extraordinary sadistic sequence of **"Ward Number Six,"** with the brutal payoff of the doctor's being confined to the asylum, is one from which even O. Henry might have shrunk; and it is one of Chekhov's very best things.

The standard reading of Chekhov's career is that having started as a writer of comic sketches, he turned away from those brilliant but artificial jokes toward a much looser, more naturalistic style. This is basically accurate, of course, but it neglects a fundamental continuity. What is apparent from those sketches is his genius for formal variation; a story may be no more than entries in the complaints book of a provincial railway station; it may, like **"The Death of a Civil Servant,"** that brilliant imitation of Gogol, conclude with startling inappropriateness. A story may be about nothing very much, as children play cards inconclusively and ineptly, or a huntsman and his wife meet by chance in the woods; a dramatic explosion may erupt without warning, or a furiously exciting crescendo may be manufactured out of nothing more than increasing numbers of people standing and staring up into the sky. It is a mistake to think that he abandoned that keen awareness of literary form in favor of the shapeless sequences of life. The slow escalation of **"A Dreary Story,"** the profoundly moving and unconventional last section of **"Murder,"** are the work of a supreme manipulator of form; and Chekhov perfected his craft in the zany puppet dramas of his first stories.

The idea that Chekhov's stories trace the disorganized, untidy shape of real-life events is a powerful one, but to see how false it is, one might look at the structure of **"Doctor Startsev."** Startsev is a young physician in a provincial town. He is taken up by a rather vulgar but charming family, the Turkins, who give "artistic" soirees. Their daughter, Catherine, who dreams of going to Moscow to study the piano, attracts his attention, and he proposes to her. She refuses, saying that she wants to devote herself to her art. Some years pass, and Startsev attends another soiree. Catherine tries to get him to propose again, but he has grown cold and bored with her. The story ends with Startsev, fat, unfeeling, and rich, and Catherine, older and suffering from poor health, living their sad separate lives.

In one sense this is a beautifully naturalistic performance with an unremarkably unhappy ending, but in another it could hardly be more formal. The structure is as artificial as a Bach fugue; the first soiree at the Turkins' is recapitulated in every detail, but the recapitulation is in a minor key. The only difference—it is one of Chekhov's grandest coups—is that what once delighted Startsev now bores and irritates him. The illusion of life is, as ever, overpowering—and immensely skillful. In reality Chekhov's art is as calculated as Swinburne's. So where does that illusion come from? Why do we feel that here we are being shown "real life" in a way we are not in, say, the first book of *The Idiot*? **"In the Hollow,"** perhaps Chekhov's greatest story, has much of the same quality of steadily mounting fury, but at no point do we have the sense, which Dostoyevsky was at some pains to instill, of being caught in the workings of a gigantic, relentless machine. **"Doctor Startsev,"** once examined, is as mechanical a morality tale in its awesomely literal recapitulations as Tolstoy's "How Much Land Does a Man Need?" But always one feels the illusion of real life, and never the organizing hand of the creative imagination. In part this is owing to Chekhov's addiction to unfinished actions; even **"In the Hollow,"** which has as shatteringly final a narrative as can be imagined, ends with a fade-out, as Lipa and Praskovya go on crossing themselves, over and over. And in part it is down to Chekhov's refusal ever to intrude himself with a judgmental adverb. I reflected, when I read Janet Malcolm's description in *Reading Chekhov* of "an almost satirically long empty corridor" in a hotel, that that was an indulgence Chekhov would never have permitted himself. Chekhov's judgments were sure and final and terrible; but he did not make them with adverbs.

Overwhelmingly, that sense of life arises from the astonishing, unelaborated concreteness of Chekhov's evocations of the world. He was the son of a grocer, and in a sense one could say that he never lost the attention a grocer pays to trivial domestic objects. Chekhov's world is, supremely, a world of things. To list those things is an instructive exercise. From the first four paragraphs of **"In the Hollow"**: belfry, chimney, factory, road, railway station, unpressed caviar, jar, mud, fences, willows, waste, acetic acid, cotton, calico, tannery, cattle, stonebuilt house, church, vodka, skins, grain, pigs, peasant bonnet, timber. (A deliberately random stretch of prose). The properties of objects are always specified: always "Ukrainian" rugs, for instance. The objects of actions are always delineated; if people eat or drink, we are always told what they are eating or drinking. (There is a slightly odd limit to Chekhov's specificity: we are hardly ever told about financial facts—something that Jane Austen never neglected—for a reason I don't pretend to be able to explain.) Many, perhaps most, novelists direct their attention toward the facts of the world only when those facts reflect some psychological truth. This is not so with Chekhov; it is not particularly necessary that when Olga takes a walk in **"The Party,"** we are told she walks through "a thicket of wild pears, wood-sorrel, young oaks and hops." The landscapes are hardly ever illustrative backdrops to an emotional crisis; food and clothes—two things Chekhov was evidently fascinated by—may demonstrate a character's social status, but no more than that. It is impossible to imagine Chekhov's using a dress to prove a moral point in the way Proust used the Duchesse de Guermantes's red ball gown in "The Guermantes Way."

That throughout Chekhov the physical details are lavish and specific is one of the reasons that many of his readers have come to prefer the stories to the plays, where this aspect of his genius could not be fully expressed. These details very rarely attain the status of descriptions, however. More characteristically they are simply lists of objects: "pickled sturgeon, button mushrooms, Malaga wine and plain honey cakes which left a tang of cypress in the mouth" (**"The Princess"**); "fringes, ribbons, braid, knitting material, buttons" (**"Three Years"**). Each object appears unnecessary and even surprising in so frugal a writer; cumulatively, though, they create not just a world of unprecedented solidity but the sensation of human lives lived in that world. And every so often we do get a glimpse of what Chekhov surely felt—a sort of ecstasy induced by the simplest objects and self-effacingly ascribed to his characters: "The timid novices, the stillness, the low ceilings, the smell of cypress-wood, the modest fare, the cheap curtains on the windows—these things all touched her, moved her, disposing her to contemplation and good thoughts" ("**The Princess**").

I said the appearance of life was an illusion, but perhaps it would be truer to say that Chekhov's manner reflects a conviction that there is nothing for the writer to talk about but the physical world and people's lives within it; the means by which the conviction is conveyed are not naive ones, and are clearly identifiable by analysis. But the effectiveness and subtlety of Chekhov's conventions do not mean that his supreme artifice is, in any sense, a conjuring trick, or meretricious.

Many writers have attempted to capture Chekhov, but very few have succeeded. If the list of his imitators is long, fascinating, and rewarding, the secondary literature proper is not an inviting prospect. It is not quite as depressing as, say, Pushkin criticism (my idea of hell would be confinement in a library containing nothing but the Pushkin secondary literature), but still, hardly any of his many biographers have succeeded in conveying our inexhaustible fascination with him. Janet Malcolm's *Reading Chekhov* is a great improvement on the usual standard, and has the merit of being imbued with Malcolm's loving engagement with her subject on every page. The route she has taken is an honest one, but one that seems peculiarly inappropriate as an approach to Chekhov. It is largely an account of a journey through the former Soviet Union, a pilgrimage to the Chekhovian holy places, and is filled with the small irritations of such a journey: the needling and officious guides one knows so well; the loss of luggage; the sullen, greasy hotels. The memoir is a predominant literary form of our time, and perhaps inescapable, but one very remote from Chekhov's aesthetic. Chekhov described himself as suffering from "autobiographophobia," and when he resorted to the form of a first-person narrative, in "**An Anonymous Story**" and "**A Dreary Story**," the narrator was pointedly unsympathetic, remote from the interests and values of both author and reader. Of all authors, Chekhov is the one least easy to imagine trying to charm the reader in propria persona.

Nevertheless, if Malcolm's book is not Chekhovian in tone or manner, that is not a requirement in a biography—one wouldn't want a biography of Milton to be in blank verse, after all. Her project, one slowly realizes, is to travel to Chekhov's territory in the hope of coming across some plausibly Chekhovian stories and lives. Applied to most writers, that would be a terrible idea: it would be a foolhardy biographer of Proust who wangled invitations to the luncheon parties of modern French duchesses. But Chekhov's subjects are mundane, and it is not obviously embarrassing for an investigator like Malcolm to explore ordinary Russian lives, to try to set out the wishes and disappointments of her guides and acquaintances in the course of her Russian journey.

Well, no one expects her to fall in love and conduct an affair with an aimless waster encountered at a shabby spa, but there are plenty of lives in our own world as disappointed and blocked as anything in Chekhov; Chekhov's great subject is the most ordinary thing in the world. In the end, it must be said, Malcolm doesn't produce anything as rich as the slightest of Chekhov's stories on these subjects, but who, truly, could have?

Other aspects of Malcolm's study can only be put down to an incompatibility of cultures. Malcolm is an intensely metropolitan figure, of course, and her journey from her milieu to the ramshackle provinces of the former Soviet Union is, to a striking degree, the reverse of the journey the sisters dream of in *Three Sisters*. And her interests, I think, are not exactly Chekhov's. Some valuable work has been done recently on Chekhov's relations with formal religion, but it is perverse to pay attention to such issues in so short a study: Chekhov was, surely, the most worldly and secular of Russian writers. He very rarely even troubled to attack religion and its human manifestations. An exception is the assault on faith in "**In the Hollow**"—a story Malcolm rather startlingly misreads on this score, failing to see how thoroughly Chekhov damned the consolations offered by a belief in the afterlife. Quite simply, Chekhov wasn't particularly interested. The Jewish question, which emerges in Malcolm's attempts to visit a Moscow synagogue, is certainly a big one in contemporary Russia, but is not one that seems to have engaged Chekhov very extensively.

When Malcolm writes about Chekhov's relations with his family, there is a distinct and rather damaging mismatch of cultures. She quotes two splendid letters to his brothers. In one he told Nikolai, "You have only one failing . . . your utter lack of culture," and set out what he saw as the virtues and dignity of the cultured outlook. In the other he berated Alexander for treatment of his common-law wife that was "unworthy of a decent, loving human being." Malcolm reads this in a contemporary Freudian manner:

> Not being an actual firstborn, Chekhov evidently never felt comfortable in the firstborn's posture of superiority, and expressed his dislike of the censorious side of himself by stacking the deck against his fictional representations of it: von Koren and Lvov [characters in "**The Duel**" and *Ivanov*] are "right," but there is something the matter with them; they are cold fish. Chekhov, in his relationship with his older brothers, brings to mind the biblical Joseph. Chekhov's "sourceless maturity"— like Joseph's—may well have developed during *his* enforced separation from the family . . . Chekhov's love for his big brothers transcended his anger with them; he evidently never entirely shed his little brother's idealization of them.

There is a troubling sense here that Malcolm thinks that European culture, then and since, placed the same value on intimate and open family relations that contemporary American culture does; like many American commentators on European writers, she fails to see the extremely high value other cultures place on the notion of personal dignity. The subject of *The Cherry Orchard,* **"My Life," "In the Hollow," "The Princess,"** and dozens of other unsparing examinations of domestic conduct is not primarily emotional failure but impropriety. Worryingly, Malcolm seems to think that Chekhov was deploring a failure to talk, a failure to be sufficiently loving and sharing.

Chekhov is a notoriously difficult writer from whom to draw general conclusions—that is at the heart of his greatness. But it seems to me that on the whole he thought unhappy families would often be better off if their members stopped talking to one another altogether. What often raised Chekhov to a point of fury was people who behaved without dignity and did not fulfill the obligations of their social position. Curious as this may be in a man whose social ascent was so vertiginous, he rarely conceded the possibility that marriages between unequal partners could work. The vicious portrayal of the sister-in-law in *Three Sisters* is repeated again and again in the stories, and the message is quite unambiguous: if—like Modeste Alekseyevich, in **"The Order of St. Anne,"** or the hero of **"My Life"**—one seeks to abandon social position through marriage or behavior, disaster and a terrible loss of dignity inevitably follow. Really, Chekhov was as snobbish as Ouida. The few times he seemed to imagine a happy marriage on unequal terms, in, for instance, **"A Woman's Kingdom"** and that magnificent vignette **"At a Country House,"** he was content to leave the envisaged marriage as a hopeless dream. Of course, like many of the greatest Russian writers, he could also be fascinated and excited when a character helplessly disobeyed the demands of propriety: the sublime moment in *War and Peace* when the Princess Bolkonsky declares her love, and the social abdication at the heart of *The Idiot,* are rivaled by Chekhov at the climax of **"The Princess"** and in the beautiful abandonment of **"A Lady with a Dog."** But he saw no happiness proceeding from such moments. Good and curious as Malcolm's study is, one feels throughout that it is a period piece in a way Chekhov would not have appreciated and might not even have understood.

Chekhov will survive the adulation of his admirers, and the limitations inadvertently placed on him by such homage direct our attention to the gigantic range of his intelligence. Even a genius like Mansfield or Pritchett or Raymond Carver strikes us now as starting from a particular moment in the indefinite history of our engagement with Chekhov; with every re-reading the most careful reader of the master will see more, and become more painfully aware that his mind, his powers of observation, were larger than ours to an inconceivable degree. His subjects were confined and specific, and he

was the great poet of the provincial. But when an observer as sophisticated and open as Janet Malcolm looks at him, the conclusion is painful and inescapable: our limitations are rigid and proximate; to Chekhov's genius no limits have yet been plausibly proposed.

Jefferson J. A. Gatrall (essay date summer 2003)

SOURCE: Gatrall, Jefferson J. A. "The Paradox of Melancholy Insight: Reading the Medical Subtext in Chekhov's 'A Boring Story.'" *Slavic Review* 62, no. 2 (summer 2003): 258-77.

[*In the following essay, Gatrall renders a medical diagnosis of Nikolai's physical condition in "A Boring Story," focusing on the character's self-examination and analysis of his symptoms.*]

> Why is it that all men who are outstanding in philosophy or politics or poetry or the arts are melancholic, and some to such an extent that they are infected by the diseases arising from black bile, as the story of Heracles among the heroes tells?
>
> —Aristotle, Problem XXX.1

Throughout his "notes," Nikolai Stepanovich, the renowned professor of physiology and fictional author of Anton Chekhov's novella **"A Boring Story,"** describes the symptoms and signs of a disease that he believes will kill him within half a year. Psychological symptoms figure prominently in his self-examination. He complains that since the onset of his illness he has undergone a change in his personality, his moods, and his "worldview" (*mirovozzrenie*). It is his search for the origins of a new and uncharacteristic pessimism that initiates the crisis of identity around which the plot of the novella is largely structured. In a conversation with his adopted daughter Katia, Nikolai Stepanovich describes how his life has changed before asking a series of probing questions:

> day and night evil thoughts fester in my head, and feelings I've never known before have built a nest in my soul. I hate, I despise, I'm indignant, I'm exasperated, and I'm afraid. I've become excessively strict, demanding, irritable, unobliging, and suspicious. Even things that would have once given me occasion to make an unnecessary pun and laugh amiably now only produce a sense of weariness in me. My sense of logic has also changed. . . .

> What does this mean? If these new thoughts and new feelings have arisen from a change in my convictions, then where could this change have come from? Has the world really grown worse, and me better, or was I just blind and indifferent before? If this change has arisen from a general decline in my physical and mental powers—I'm sick, after all, I'm losing weight every day—then my situation is pitiful; it means that my new thoughts are abnormal, morbid, that I should be ashamed of them and consider them worthless.[1]

In this passage and elsewhere in the novella, several possible reasons for the change in Nikolai Stepanovich's view of life are evoked: illness, the world around him, new insight. Of particular importance for an understanding of the professor's crisis is that he establishes a mutually exclusive choice between illness and insight in a search for the origin of his pessimism. Either his new thoughts are "abnormal" (*nenormal'ny*) and "morbid" (*nezdorovy*) or he has only now ceased to be "blind and indifferent" (*slep i ravnodushen*). Interrupting Nikolai Stepanovich's speech, Katia repeats this opposition even as she seeks to answer his questions: "Sickness hasn't got anything to do with it. . . . Your eyes have simply been opened, that's all." As a physician treating himself, however, Nikolai Stepanovich seriously weighs the merits of the opposing, psychopathological explanation. If his new pessimistic thoughts are symptoms of his illness, then they must be, as he suggests in another passage, "accidental, fleeting, and not deeply rooted within me." If these new thoughts are not just symptoms, on the other hand, but the result of a deeper penetration into the general lack of meaning in his life, then "the sixty-two years I've lived through must be considered wasted."[2]

Literary critics, following the lead of the novella's two main characters, have weighed in on both sides of this debate. Among those who stress the importance of illness for an understanding of Nikolai Stepanovich's predicament, M. M. Smirnov argues, "it is useless to analyze the judgments of the hero-narrator, because they are only a symptom of his disposition [*mirooshchushenie*]."[3] Carol A. Flath, in a recent article, defends Nikolai Stepanovich against those critics who would "condemn [his] behavior in the present": "For all of the professor's perceptions are colored by his pain and suffering. . . . I would like to suggest [his disease] is primarily physical in the sense that the crisis is provoked by the illness, not the reverse."[4] On the opposing side, several critics have emphasized how penetrating, if not always reliable, Nikolai Stepanovich's insights can be. Lev Shestov leans heavily on the "originality" of the professor's pessimism in **"A Boring Story"** to justify his famous claim that Chekhov is the "poet of hopelessness," and Marina Senderovich considers Nikolai Stepanovich "an existential thinker" who faces his existence "as a vital necessity of his own being."[5] In a statement that contradicts Smirnov's and Flath's views almost point by point, Leonid Gromov writes: "The hero of the novella, having understood the [futility] of his work and not having found the meaning of life, loses the ground under his feet, loses the mark of a 'living person,' and senses the approach of death. Precisely in this lies the terrible tragedy of the old scientist— whose life changes into a 'boring story'—and not in his physical illness."[6]

What has not yet been undertaken in the critical literature on **"A Boring Story,"** despite some steps in this direction by Flath and Evgenii Meve, is a thorough examination of the novella's medical subtext.[7] Cribbing the cryptic title Nikolai Stepanovich gives to his own romance with his wife, it can be said that the novella depicts, among many other parallel and often loosely connected plot lines, a "Historia morbi."[8] Significantly, Nikolai Stepanovich informs neither the reader nor Katia what disease he believes himself to be suffering from. He does not even consult other physicians to confirm his own, unnamed diagnosis. This omission provides the impetus for the present article. From the few offhand comments he makes concerning the symptoms and signs of his disease, I have attempted not so much to render a scientifically precise diagnosis as to historically reconstruct, by drawing on contemporary medical intertexts, the diagnosis he himself seems to have made.[9] Nikolai Stepanovich scatters many symptoms and signs of an unnamed disease throughout **"A Boring Story."** If the conceptual leap that he himself makes from these signs and symptoms to his own self-diagnosis entails a movement from the surface of the body to deep organic structures, then an examination of his condition on the part of a literary critic involves a similar movement from the body of the text to an underlying medical subtext. This medical subtext is not directly visible in **"A Boring Story,"** yet the novella does trace a network of signs that evoke the outline of a specific, contemporary disease concept. Since psychopathology plays an integral role in the novella's argument, determining the disease from which Nikolai Stepanovich believes himself to be suffering places the implications of his crisis in a new critical light.

At first glance, such a diagnostic undertaking might appear to be of little scholarly interest. A precise diagnosis of Nikolai Stepanovich's illness would demonstrate what is already a commonplace in Chekhov criticism, namely, that his medical portraiture is rigorously realistic. Conversely, an overreliance on the method of differential diagnosis would superficially resolve the philosophical problems that the novella presents.[10] These pitfalls aside, there nevertheless remains room for balanced comparative analysis of the intersection between medicine, poetics, and epistemology in Chekhov's **"A Boring Story."** As literary critics since Lev Tolstoi have noted, there is in Chekhov's prose an "impressionistic" quality; or, as Aleksandr Chudakov puts it, an "incidental wholeness."[11] In **"A Boring Story,"** symptoms and signs are abundant, but the professor's own self-diagnosis, which might unite them into a coherent clinical picture, is lacking. Instead, these symptoms and signs appear as disconnected and often incidental details in Nikolai Stepanovich's broader literary self-portrait. His notes are filled with many other "boring" matters ostensibly unrelated to his medical condition, ranging from his digressions on various topics in contemporary Russian society to his reflections on Katia's tragic life. This lack of a unifying diagnosis seems structurally strategic, for the novella not only withholds a disease whose name might have upset the balance between the two main, conflicting interpretations of its protagonist's crisis—illness and insight—but this omission also creates a certain affective ambivalence. Does not the professor's propensity for digression, ellipsis, and surface details, as well as his inability to draw on his life experience to say something meaningful to Katia in her despondency, reflect some of the speech patterns of melancholia? In an observation that has wider stylistic relevance for Chekhov's so often melancholy prose, Nikolai Stepanovich confesses of his thoughts that "I have lost the sense of their organic connection."[12]

Shifting from literary to clinical portraiture, it is nonetheless possible to provide a reasonably exhaustive list of the symptoms and signs to which Nikolai Stepanovich alludes. At the beginning of the novella, he complains of an "incurable tic" (*neizlechimyi* tic). This tic appears again in the last section: "There's a dull pain in my cheek—the tic has started" (*V shcheke tupaia bol'*—*eto nachinaetsia* tic).[13] He is also suffering from chronic insomnia, which he wryly claims has become the "chief and fundamental feature of my existence" (*glavnuiu i osnovnuiu chertu [moego] sushchestvovaniia*).[14] Elsewhere he notes that he loses weight daily, that he often feels chilled, and that his head and hands "shake from weakness" (*triasutsia ot slabosti*).[15] While lecturing he experiences an "unconquerable weakness in [his] legs and shoulders" (*nepobedimuiu slabost' v nogakh i v plechakh*), his "mouth becomes dry" (*vo rtu sokhnet*), his "voice grows hoarse" (*golos sipnet*), his "head spins" (*golova kruzhitsia*), and he "incessantly drinks water" (*to i delo p'iu vodu*).[16] At one point during the novella he faints; at another he wakes during the night in a sweat, tries to take his pulse, and begins to hyperventilate.[17] In a particularly revealing passage, he expresses the hope that he is mistaken "about the albumin and sugar I find, about my heart, and about the edema I've now twice seen in the morning" (*naschet belka i sakhara, kotorye nakhozhu u sebia, i naschet serdtsa, i naschet tekh otekov, kotorye uzhe dva raza videl u sebia po utram*).[18] Nikolai Stepanovich's psychological symptoms are more difficult to isolate and categorize than these physical ones. In broad terms, his psychological symptoms include withdrawal from family and friends, irritability, uncontrollable sadness and fear, weakness in memory, pessimistic thoughts, and paralyzing indifference, a condition he calls "premature death" (*prezhdevremennaia smert'*).[19]

Since the argument of the novella is based upon the very nature of these psychological symptoms, however, any attempt to summarize them is inherently problematic. Indeed, the search for a diagnosis of Nikolai Stepanovich's disease in **"A Boring Story,"** far from

resolving his crisis, opens onto an expanse of further problems, ranging from the reliability of self-analysis in mental disease to the lingering dualism in nineteenth-century materialist psychiatry. First, as the Russian psychiatrist Sergei Korsakov writes in the introduction to his *Course on Psychiatry* (1893), a textbook Chekhov owned, "the manifestations of mental diseases in separate cases are extremely varied, but what is common to all of them is that the 'personality' [*lichnost' cheloveka*] alters."[20] Yet, as is the case with several of Chekhov's medically inflected stories and plays, **"A Boring Story"** opens *after* a change in Nikolai Stepanovich's personality has apparently already taken place.[21] The reader is directly familiar only with the character of an altered, dying Nikolai Stepanovich. From a purely clinical perspective, his tendency for most of the novella to contrast his dreary present with a happier past might thus be seen as itself symptomatic of a pervasive melancholia. In a related manner, the reader is never able to step outside the shadow cast by Nikolai Stepanovich's melancholy prose, and thus it remains difficult to gauge the merit of his increasingly self-critical judgments on his own life, which he claims had earlier seemed to be "a beautiful and ably made composition" (*krasivoi, talantlivo sdelannoi kompozitsiei*) but whose "finale" (*final*) he now fears he is spoiling.[22]

Second, this question of the reliability of the narrator-protagonist's self-examination has an epistemological dimension arising from the superimposition of two central dualities in modern medicine; namely, those of mind and body and of physician and patient. Nikolai Stepanovich reveals to the reader his symptoms, which as a patient he experiences directly, as well as the clinical signs that he has gathered as a physician. In his hypochondriacal attention to medical textbooks, however, he seems troubled by more than just the clinical dimensions of his self-diagnosis: "Now, when I diagnose and treat myself, I have the hope every now and then that my ignorance is deceiving me . . . when, with the zeal of a hypochondriac, I reread my textbooks on therapy and daily change my medications, it always seems to me that I'll come across something comforting."[23] Nikolai Stepanovich's hypochondria would seem to result in part from the conflation of roles that arises, not only as his professional impartiality breaks down during the course of self-treatment, but also as his diseased body begins to infect the thought processes of his medically trained mind. In Chekhov's realist aesthetic, an aesthetic that is arguably more phenomenological than materialistic, it is not just the objective fact of a disease that is portrayed, but a character's subjective experience of illness.[24] The physiological processes that govern the progression of his disease acquire meaning inasmuch as Nikolai Stepanovich strives, as a physician, to understand their psychopathological consequences. Conversely, and more pressingly, Nikolai Stepanovich's "new" and "evil" thoughts—which have provoked a re-evaluation of his long and illustrious life—become an existential problem to the extent that he grapples, as a patient, with the question of whether they derive from recent illness or belated insight.[25]

Nikolai Stepanovich's role as a renowned physiologist during the rise of materialism in psychiatry further renders the crisis occasioned by his illness all the more acute. As the soul gradually disappeared as an explanatory principle in mental disease throughout the nineteenth century, the humanist attributes of the soul—the immaterial intellect and free moral agency—began to lose their epistemological footing. Nikolai Stepanovich's anxiety about the origin of his pessimism can be interpreted against the background of the tendency in materialist psychiatry to dissolve the mind into physiological processes as well as the philosophical and ethical problems that this reduction—which preceded Freud and now, in the "Age of Prozac," seems to be outliving him—has long engendered. Caught between the options of illness and insight, which had become mutually exclusive in mainstream psychiatry by the end of the nineteenth century, Nikolai Stepanovich follows the course of his own spiraling thoughts, which seem to grow more penetrating the more his marasmus advances, yet unearth less meaning from his life the deeper they penetrate.

DIABETES

One of the clinical signs that Nikolai Stepanovich mentions in passing in his notes is glycosuria. Glycosuria, or sugar in the urine, was the definitive sign of diabetes in the second half of the nineteenth century. Yet, as the celebrated French physiologist Claude Bernard suggests in one of his seminal midcentury studies on diabetes, "the existence of sugar in the urine does not constitute diabetes. It is the proportion of this material that is important." Indeed, the difficulty in distinguishing between a glycosuria that is "in a certain sense normal" and the glycosuria of diabetes presents a diagnostic dilemma: "the majority of physicians do not render a diagnosis of diabetes until glycosuria becomes permanent."[26] In **"A Boring Story,"** Nikolai Stepanovich mentions the sugar he "finds" (*nakhozhu*), presumably in his urine, using an imperfective verb in the present tense. This would seem to indicate a recurring clinical result, but he does not mention for how long or how many times this sign has presented itself. Moreover, in the same passage, he even compares himself to a hypochondriac, a comparison it would be at least possible to take at face value. If on the one hand hypochondria (as a subtype of melancholia) was often cited as a concomitant condition of diabetes, then on the other hand, as the British pathologist William Dickinson notes in his 1877 monograph on diabetes, "in acute mania and in melancholia a trace of sugar is the rule rather than the exception."[27] While a diagnosis of hypochondriacal

melancholia would not necessarily preclude one of diabetes, it is nevertheless typical of the clinical portrait that follows that a single clinical sign evokes both physical and psychological conditions.

In terms of differential diagnosis, however, the evidence in favor of diabetes is much more substantial than simply glycosuria. A second clinical sign especially indicative of the terminal stages of diabetes, and which Nikolai Stepanovich mentions alongside glycosuria, is albuminuria, or albumin in the urine. Dickinson explains that this "later complication" is often the only visible sign of an underlying "renal change": "When sugar and albumen are together, the sugar as a rule is primary, the albumen consequent. The kidneys, goaded by the diuretic action of the sugar, after a time show signs of irritation and allow a little albumen to escape as the result of congestion or tubal disturbance."[28] The presence of albuminuria suggests that one of the sequelae of Nikolai Stepanovich's diabetes may be what was known as "Bright's disease." In the second half of the nineteenth century, Bright's disease was a common diagnosis that covered a variety of forms of nephritis (inflammation of the kidneys) and that was often noted alongside diabetes. In his 1872 treatise *Des terminaisons du diabète sucré,* Pierre Costes, for example, describes how in many cases the patient dies as a "result of Bright's disease, which comes to complicate the preexisting diabetes. . . . The two ailments march in tandem and precipitate the *dénouement . . .* in such cases it is difficult to determine precisely what should be attributed to Bright's disease and what to diabetes." In terms of diet, furthermore, Nikolai Stepanovich mentions not only that he drinks water "incessantly" (polydipsia), a characteristic symptom of diabetes, but also that he suffers from "daily" weight loss (autophagia), indicating that his illness has likely reached an advanced stage. As Costes writes, after the commencement of "the stage of autophagia" further complications arise and "the patient is lost": "In the midst of diverse impairments, the marasmus particular to the diabetic [*le marasme particulier au diabétique*] imperceptibly prepares itself."[29]

Nikolai Stepanovich's cardiovascular complications can also be situated in this clinical portrait of diabetes. The edema that he has twice seen (likely in his extremities) further suggests the onset of the serious heart congestion typical of Bright's disease. Even more ominously, Nikolai Stepanovich seems to suffer from what Flath calls a "panic attack" and Meve "angina pectoris" (*grudnaia zhaba*) when he awakes during a "sparrow's night" (*vorob'inaia noch'*) in section five.[30] As Nikolai Stepanovich writes, "in my body there was not one sensation that might indicate that the end was near, but my soul was oppressed by horror, as if I had suddenly seen a vast, ominous glow." Having awakened, the professor becomes immediately concerned with such bodily functions as his breathing and heart rate: "I feel for my pulse and, not finding it in my wrist, search for it in my temples, then under my chin, then again in my wrist. . . . My breathing becomes more and more rapid" (*shchupaiu u sebia pul's i, ne naidia na ruke, ishchu ego v viskakh, potom v podborodke i opiat' na ruke. . . . Dykhanie stanovitsia vse chashche i chashche*).[31]

In terms of etiology, the relationship between heart congestion and Bright's disease, although clinically evident to nineteenth-century researchers, had not received a commonly accepted explanation. Taken in the context of the history of medicine, however, Nikolai Stepanovich's nervous symptoms do suggest a possible, if speculative, origin for his illness. The tic and pain in his cheek, which he mentions three times, mostly likely represent trigeminal neuralgia or, as it is commonly known, "tic douloureux." If glycosuria is the sign that most supports a diagnosis of diabetes, then trigeminal neuralgia is perhaps the most important clue in determining the historical form of diabetes from which Nikolai Stepanovich suffers. In the second half of the nineteenth century, the pathology of diabetes was a matter of considerable controversy. One of the main theories postulated what would become commonplace in the twentieth century, namely, that the anatomical anomaly responsible for diabetes lies in the pancreas. In 1889, the same year that **"A Boring Story"** was published, Joseph von Mering and Oskar Minkowski were able to induce permanent diabetes in a dog by removing its pancreas. The French clinician Apollinaire Bouchardat, who gained renown for his dietary treatment of the disease, argued instead that diabetes has its source in the stomach.[32] In contrast to these theories based on localized organ failures, Nikolai Stepanovich's trigeminal neuralgia tentatively evokes the then widespread theory that diabetes is a disease of the nervous system. This "angioneurotic" theory of diabetes originated with Bernard's famous (and retrospectively notorious) *piqûre* of the fourth ventricle of a dog's brain. In an influential 1857 article, Bernard argued that excess secretion of glucose by the liver into the bloodstream (hyperglycemia) can be caused by a lesion in this supposed "sugar center" in the brain, by a lesion in the nerves from this sugar center to blood vessels in the liver, or by stimulation of the nerves that dilate these vessels. In other words, as Bernard concluded, "one can thus consider diabetes to be a nervous disease."[33] As late as 1892, the French pathologist J. Thiroloix could still argue that "the grand varieties of diabetes that have been established . . . are all 'functions of an impairment of the central nervous system.'"[34] While not all contemporary researchers and clinicians would have been comfortable with the scope of Thiroloix's generalization, many sought and found evidence of lesions in the fourth ventricle of the brain during autopsies of patients who had died of diabetes. As Horst and Joseph

Schumacher write concerning the angioneurotic theory of diabetes: "The clinician saw in numerous phenomena—disturbances of sensation and motility, reflex anomalies, occipital and *trigeminal neuralgias, physical and mental fatigue, frequent depression,* etc.—genuine manifestations of a disorder of the nervous system in line with the theory."[35] This level of physiological and clinical detail, of course, extends beyond the range of **"A Boring Story."** Nikolai Stepanovich's tic is directly present in the text, yet the move from this symptom to a particular etiology, from text to subtext, remains a speculative one. Nikolai Stepanovich's tic might instead represent a symptom only incidentally related to his diabetic condition. Francis Anstie, for example, in a contemporary monograph on neuralgia, observed that late onset trigeminal neuralgias "are almost invariably connected with a strong family taint of insanity, and very often with strong melancholy."[36] Once again, a single symptom evokes the possibility of an ailment of either body or mind.

Without insisting that a single disease concept accounts for all of Nikolai Stepanovich's symptoms, it is nevertheless significant that trigeminal neuralgia suggests that he may be suffering from a diabetes of nervous origin. There is evidence that Nikolai Stepanovich himself supports a nervous explanation for his general condition. In a passage that provides a link—one typical of diabetes—between his diet and his moods, he writes, "it is especially after dinner, in the early evening, that my nervous excitation [*moe nervnoe vozbuzhdenie*] attains its highest pitch"; at a later point in the novella he also alludes to his "violent nervous tension" (*sil'noe nervnoe napriazhenie*).[37] In the context of nervous disease, trigeminal neuralgia represents a possible bridge between Nikolai Stepanovich's physical symptoms and signs—glycosuria, albuminuria, polydipsia, autophagia, heart congestion, and edema—and the psychological symptoms so crucial to the story's argument. In the late nineteenth century, symptoms of a psychological nature were situated in a complex, dual relationship with the physical symptoms of diabetes. On the one hand, sadness, apathy, and despondency were commonly observed during the terminal stages of diabetes. Costes's psychologically nuanced depiction of "le malheureux diabétique" resembles Nikolai Stepanovich's self-portrait in several suggestive ways: "The patient complains of various problems, which are no more than precursory or concomitant phenomena, such as a loss of strength, a certain general malaise, a greater sensitivity to external cold, apathy, and an aversion to movement. . . . [A] nonchalance he finds hard to overcome sentences the unfortunate diabetic to rest. Despondency and sadness take hold of him."[38] On the other hand, the angioneurotic theory made it possible to include diabetes among the many ailments thought to be influenced by what was known as the "neurotic diathesis" (that is, neurosis as predisposing cause). In a popular contemporary Anglo-American medical textbook, for example, William Osler notes of diabetes that "persons of a neurotic temperament are often affected."[39] And although Dickinson insists that diabetes "clearly belong[s] to the body and not its surroundings," he, too, suggests, "Of all the causes of diabetes mental emotion is the one which we can most often trace and which we must believe to be the most frequent. . . . Grief, anxiety, protracted intellectual toil, violent anger and mental shock, might all be shown to be directly productive of this disease."[40]

It is precisely at this pathological threshold between physical and psychological symptoms that the question of whether Nikolai Stepanovich's pessimism is symptomatic or insightful becomes meaningful. His symptoms and signs can be placed, without undue strain, into this historically reconstructed portrait of diabetes. Moreover, his own bleak prognosis would seem to be warranted: his heart and kidneys are failing; his body is wasting away. What is at stake in the novella's argument, however, is whether his pessimism results from this decline in his health. Reflecting on the relationship between the medical evidence in **"A Boring Story"** and Nikolai Stepanovich's crisis of identity, I would like to suggest that certain features of diabetes, as it was understood in the nineteenth century, make it an artistically nuanced and epistemologically unsteady source for the professor's pessimism. First, Bernard's work on diabetes belonged to his broader effort to establish the legitimacy of a physiological approach to the study of disease (his term for this approach, *la médecine expérimentale,* came to live a fortuitous existence in literary criticism after Émile Zola). In particular, Bernard's interest in the pathology of diabetes was closely related to his groundbreaking research on the metabolism of the liver and helped illustrate his contention that "physiology and pathology now march in an ever more intimate union." As Bernard writes, diabetes presents a problem for those "doctor-nosologists" who would consider all diseases as "morbid entities" and classify them "as objects of natural history, as if they were living beings like plants or animals." Diabetes does not exist as an independent entity within the body, as if it were a microbe, but results from "a simple functional disruption that, from our point of view, represents nothing beyond the realm of physiology."[41]

In **"A Boring Story,"** Nikolai Stepanovich, a famous physiologist in his own right, neither names his disease nor burdens it, as something foreign to himself, with responsibility for his pessimism; instead, he faults the "general decline in my mental and physical powers" (*obshchii upadok fizicheskikh i umstvennykh sil*).[42] His loss of health is not sudden and localized, like the blow to Ivan Il'ich's side in Tolstoi, but insidious and multifaceted. Accordingly, Nikolai Stepanovich, rather than being haunted by the name of a particular disease, feels compelled to read and reread, across a range of different body functions, his disparate symptoms and signs. Such clinical diligence, moreover, reflects the scientific reserve typical of the ethos of experimental medicine. In advising the practitioner to be "an observing physician," Bernard writes, "if we take advantage . . . of a few possible connections between pathology and physiology, to try to explain the whole disease at a single stroke, then we lose sight of the patient, we distort the disease";[43] or, as Nikolai Stepanovich suggests, the physician should "individualize each separate case."[44] Far from making hasty or reifying judgments, Nikolai Stepanovich reads his body as thoroughly as his textbooks and reads both to the point of hypochondria, in a perpetual medical hermeneutic—literally, a *sémiologie,* which in the nineteenth century referred solely to the interpretation of clinical signs.[45]

Lastly, in his search for the cause of his pessimism, Nikolai Stepanovich struggles physically, intellectually, and spiritually with a disease whose etiology remained elusive throughout the nineteenth century. Even were it granted that he is suffering from diabetes—which I would conclude is what the professor himself suspects, given the clinical signs he selectively presents to the reader—the question of whether his pessimism has been caused by illness or insight would remain unresolvable. If the change in his moods and thoughts can be regarded as part of the marasmus wrought by diabetes, then it is nevertheless possible to take this causal regress one step further by attributing diabetes itself to an underlying neurotic diathesis. Yet if his pessimism derives from a diabetes of nervous origin, then what, in turn, causes neurosis? While the causal relationships between neurosis and diabetes cannot be resolved diagnostically in **"A Boring Story,"** an epistemological exploration of Nikolai Stepanovich's crisis of identity in the context of a nineteenth-century understanding of nervous disease is nevertheless fruitful. It is important not only to assess the question of whether Nikolai Stepanovich's pessimism is symptomatic in light of the novella's medical evidence but to consider what such a question means within the context of nineteenth-century medical thought. In short, how could the professor's question have taken the historical form that it does?

THE ANATOMY OF THOUGHT

The gradual shift in the locus of mental disease from the soul to the body over much of the nineteenth century proved crucial to the formation of modern psychiatry. At the risk of oversimplifying this history, it can be argued that the writings of the German "somaticists," active especially in the 1830s and 1840s, provide the first clear traces of the question that will later haunt Nikolai Stepanovich; namely, whether his thoughts are insights or symptoms. While the "psychicists" considered the soul to be the seat of mental illness, their opponents the somaticists argued that, by definition, only the body could ever become diseased. The somaticism of the German psychiatrist Maximilian Jacobi can serve here as a representative example: "all morbid psychical phenomena can only be considered as symptomatic, as concomitant to states of disease formed and developed elsewhere in the organism."[46] Later in this somaticist tradition, Wilhelm Griesinger, aware of the successes of physiology in neurology, transferred the site of mental disease from the organism as a whole to the brain in particular. For Griesinger, the "father of modern psychiatry," the study of cerebral pathology is largely confined to insanity, which is "only a complication of symptoms of various morbid states of the brain."[47]

In the closing pages of **"A Boring Story,"** Nikolai Stepanovich echoes this somaticist tradition: "When nothing within a person rises higher and stronger than all the external influences around him, then, it is true, a good head-cold is enough to make him lose his equilibrium . . . all his pessimism or optimism, all his thoughts, big or small, have in that case the meaning of a mere symptom and nothing more [*imeiut znachenie tol'ko simptoma i bol'she nichego*]."[48] The relegation of mental phenomena to a secondary order of being with respect to their primary material causes has had profound epistemological and ethical implications for modern psychiatry. As a result of the reduction of soul to body in mental disease, thought does not disappear but is instead rendered passive and silent. The psychiatrist interprets a patient's morbid thoughts as pathological effects, not as insights requiring a response in their own terms. Near the end of **"A Boring Story,"** Nikolai Stepanovich similarly regards his pessimism as a mere symptom, yet he avoids a naive materialism by holding out the possibility that a person's thoughts can rise above "external influences." In this he differs from his colleague Ivan Sechenov, the most famous Russian physiologist of the second half of the nineteenth century. In his 1867 essay "Reflexes of the Brain," Sechenov argues that all thought—diseased or otherwise—is the result of external processes: "A psychological act . . . cannot appear in consciousness without external sensory excitement. It follows that thought [*smysl'*] is subordinate to this law. With thought there is the beginning of a reflex, its continuation, but not, evidently, its end result—movement. *Thought is the first two-thirds of a psychological reflex.*"[49] By contrast, Nikolai Stepanovich, who has a fondness for such Stoic philosophers as Marcus Aurelius and Epictetus, considers his pessimistic thoughts in physiological terms only inasmuch as he is ill. Instead of the thoroughgoing monism of Sechenov, Nikolai Stepanovich maintains a dualism between sickness and health on the one hand and, on the other, between those who are governed by a "general idea" (*obshchaia ideia*) and those who are not.[50] For the latter group, in which he includes himself by the end of his notes, the onset of disease initiates a

descent into the impersonal laws of nature. Nikolai Stepanovich claims his thoughts are "stinging [his] brain, like mosquitoes" (*zhalit' moi mozg, kak moskity*). Elsewhere he calls them "Arakcheev thoughts" (*arakcheevskie mysli*), alluding to the brutal war minister under Alexander I.[51] In as intimate a manner as Nikolai Stepanovich responds to his own deteriorating body, he tends throughout his notes to treat his thoughts as if they were foreign objects. Even in their most lucid forms, such thoughts are incapable of being vehicles of genuine insight.

Nikolai Stepanovich's habit of deflecting responsibility for his thoughts away from himself toward his illness reflects not just the norms of modern psychiatry in general but a popular fin-de-siècle understanding of nervous disease in particular. Among contemporary disease concepts, it is perhaps neurasthenia, which its American "discoverer" George Beard defined as a "deficiency or lack of nerve-force," that best exemplifies the pervasive élan of "nervosity" among the European middle class near the turn of the twentieth century.[52] After a German translation of Beard's *A Practical Treatise on Nervous Exhaustion (Neurasthenia)* appeared in 1881, neurasthenia rapidly spread across Europe, reaching Chekhov's plays and short stories by the end of the decade.[53] While Nikolai Stepanovich suffers from a condition grounded much less contentiously in the body than the disease concept neurasthenia would ever manage to become, the professor's facial tic, his irritability, his appeals to his "nervous tension" and "nervous excitability," as well as the broader evidence suggesting that he is suffering from a diabetes of nervous origin, all make it possible to situate **"A Boring Story"** alongside other works by Chekhov involving nervous disorders, such as **"An Attack of the Nerves,"** *Ivanov,* **"The Duel,"** and **"The Black Monk."**[54]

In terms of what might be called the "poetics of nervosity," nervous disease in the late nineteenth century not only served as an artistic means for reworking, along materialist lines, the traditional thematics of the mind-body divide but also enabled writers and critics to transform social commentary into an extended symptomology in which the nervous system acted, literally or metaphorically, as an interface between society and the individual. Concerning neurasthenia, for instance, Beard argues that its many forms "are diseases of civilization, and of modern civilization, and mainly of the nineteenth century, and of the United States."[55] Chekhov expresses a somewhat more circumspect view on the social pathology of neurasthenia in a letter to Aleksei Suvorin, whose son appears to have been diagnosed with the trendy disease: "[He] has a disease that is mental, socioeconomical, and psychological, which perhaps does not exist at all, or, if it does exist, then perhaps does not have to be considered a disease."[56] In **"A Boring Story,"** Nikolai Stepanovich generally rejects the arguments that Katia and her suitor, Mikhail Fedorovich, put forward to support their bleak assessment of contemporary society. In a remarkable passage near the beginning of the novella, however, Nikolai Stepanovich implicitly raises the possibility that one of the causes of his pessimism, its "diathesis," may lie in the decay of Russian society around him: "On the whole, the decrepit condition of the university buildings, the gloom of its corridors, the soot on its walls, its lack of lights, the dejected appearance of its steps, coat hooks, and benches, in the history of Russian pessimism, occupy one of the first places in the many rows of the diathesis [*prichin predraspolagaiushchikh*]."[57]

Throughout his notes, Nikolai Stepanovich fears that illness may have brought about a change in his view of life. At the end of the novella, however, Nikolai Stepanovich develops a more subtle dialectic on the relationship between mind, body, and society in disease. In these concluding pages, Nikolai Stepanovich no longer seeks to absolve himself of responsibility for his pessimism by appealing to his illness or to his environs. It is not that free will does not exist for Nikolai Stepanovich, but that he himself, Katia, and those around him have not the strength of character to rise above the sway of "external influences." He evokes the possibility of free moral agency—"of a god of the living man" (*bog zhivogo cheloveka*)—only to note its general absence in his life. It is his lack of a "general idea," a lack whose implications are more ethical than psychopathological, that paradoxically provides Nikolai Stepanovich with his final justification for reducing his own thoughts to the level of a mere "symptom."[58]

Melancholia and Insight

As opposed to attributing his pessimism to pathology, Nikolai Stepanovich and Katia both consider the possibility that he has only now attained full insight into the nature of his own existence and of the world around him. In Katia's view, the professor has at last come to see long-standing problems in his family and his career: "You see now what for some reason you did not want to notice before. In my opinion, you must first of all make a final break with your family and leave them. . . . Do they still remember you exist? . . . And the university, too. What do you want it for? . . . You have been lecturing for thirty years, and where are your pupils? Are there many famous scientists among them? . . . You are superfluous."[59] Although Katia and Nikolai Stepanovich ultimately resolve the question of the latter's pessimism in different ways, what remains consistent in their conversations and the professor's monologues is the mutual exclusion of illness and insight. In a letter to Suvorin, Chekhov himself reinforces this mutual exclusion by arguing that Nikolai Stepanovich's opinions should be considered as "things" (*veshchi*): "For me, as an author, all these opinions do not in themselves have any value. The main thing is not their substance; their substance is interchangeable and not new. The whole thing lies in the nature of these opinions, in their dependence on external influences and such. One should regard them as things, as symptoms, completely in an objective manner, not trying to agree or disagree with them."[60] In *The Skepticism and Belief of Chekhov*, Vladimir Linkov criticizes Chekhov's one-sided interpretation of his own character in this letter. Although Chekhov enumerates many of Nikolai Stepanovich's flawed personality traits, Linkov argues that the author "is silent about his self-criticism, about his capacity for merciless self-analysis." Rather than falling entirely on the side of either illness or insight, as Nikolai Stepanovich, Katia, Chekhov, and so many literary critics since have done, Linkov proposes that the professor's judgments be divided into two groups whose artistic functions differ. The first type, those in which Nikolai Stepanovich "understands the truth, no matter how terrible it is," represents real, substantial thoughts. The second type, in which he "flees from the truth," reflects "only symptoms of [his] diseased condition."[61]

Linkov's proposal breaks with a long critical tradition of "either-or," but his sorting of the professor's thoughts into groups leaves intact the mutual exclusivity of illness and insight. In contrast to this functional division, I have attempted to argue that within the context of mainstream nineteenth-century psychiatry a pessimism that is symptomatic is by definition devoid of insight. Yet there remains at least one more way to modulate the alternatives of illness and insight in **"A Boring Story."** Neither Nikolai Stepanovich nor his main interlocutor Katia consider the possibility, so common to the romantic cult of melancholia, that his pessimistic thoughts about himself and the world might be both pathological and insightful. Indeed, the tight and meticulously "realistic" connection between Nikolai Stepanovich's deteriorating body and his deteriorating mind serves throughout the novella as a check to any valorization of his pessimism. His habit of denigrating his own thoughts can nonetheless be seen to sharpen what I would like to call "the paradox of melancholy insight." Nikolai Stepanovich's thoughts become all the more melancholy in that they perpetually erase their own value. Instead of having thoughts that are "as bright and as deep as the sky" (*gluboki, kak nebo, iarki*),[62] as would be fitting for a man of his station in life, he is overcome by a pessimism that he thoroughly belittles. At the novella's close, nothing has meaning in his life, neither past nor present, not even the insights that could express such an annihilating self-judgment.

While the opposition between illness and insight remains mutually exclusive throughout **"A Boring Story,"** Chekhov does make a connection between nervous disease and nobility of character in an 1899 letter to a young Vsevolod Meierkhol'd about a character in a play: "Now about [this character's] nervousness [*nervnost'*]. This nervousness should not be emphasized, or else the neuropathological nature will obscure and overwhelm what is more important, namely, his loneliness, the kind of loneliness experienced only by great and otherwise healthy organisms ('healthy' in the highest sense)."[63] By placing the neuroses of noble organisms beyond the realm of pathology, Chekhov is here echoing a tradition begun by Aristotle, rediscovered by humanists in the Renaissance, and epitomized by Hamlet—namely, the tradition of the melancholy great being. Nikolai Stepanovich's status as a renowned Russian physiologist, one afflicted with pessimism near the end of his life, places him within this humoral tradition. As he tells Katia, "I always felt myself to be a king. . . . But I'm a king no longer" (*ia vsegda chuvstvoval sebia korolem. . . . No teper' uzh ia ne korol'*). The tragic fall of this king of Russian science coincides with the appearance of "evil thoughts" that he considers "tolerable only to slaves" (*prilichno tol'ko rabam*). Although he once availed himself of the "most sacred right of kings—the right to pardon" (*samoe sviatoe pravo korolei-eto pravo pomilovaniia*), he has come to react with hate, spite, indignation, exasperation, and fear to all that is wrong around him.[64]

Nikolai Stepanovich's tragic fall occurs before the opening lines of his notes. These notes are not devoted to the events that lead to this fall, however, but to his present experience of loss. While the often tortuous paths of psychoanalysis are foreign in spirit to Chekhov's fictional world, not to mention to the author's views as a physician, Sigmund Freud's understanding of melancholia as loss is relevant to **"A Boring Story."** In his essay "Mourning and Melancholia," Freud writes that "mourning is regularly the reaction to the loss of a loved person, or to the loss of some abstraction which has taken the place of one, such as fatherland, liberty, an ideal, and so on." Melancholia is "an effect of the same influences," but mourning differs from melancholia in one important way: "the fall in self-esteem is absent in grief."[65] It is not difficult to find instances of loss in Nikolai Stepanovich's life. Not only is he facing death, but he is facing it alone. His family is preoccupied with its own drama—to which he feels entirely indifferent—as his daughter elopes with her fiancé. Even Katia, his "treasure" (*sokrovishche*), leaves him at the end of the story, and likely will not even attend his funeral. In addition to this loneliness, he is afraid that if he were to approach his medical colleagues about his condition he would be advised to give up his work: "And that would deprive me of my last hope."[66] If work is his last hope, however, then it is a bitter one, for he has already lost all the joy he once experienced while lecturing. Nikolai Stepanovich has even become divorced from his illustrious name, which lives its own independent existence in journals and newspapers.[67] This estrangement from his own name epitomizes a

general erosion of his former identity. His grief at the approach of death might be considered the work of mourning, but this alteration in his self-image gives rise to a deprecatory self-analysis that is more suggestive of melancholia. If near the beginning of the novella he fears that he is spoiling the end of a life that has otherwise been beautiful and productive, he eventually comes to regard his entire life as having been wasted.

Nikolai Stepanovich has lost not only all sense of the meaning that his life once held for him but also his former nobility of thought. During his trip to Khar'kov he finds himself no longer able to stay above such "external influences" as "family troubles, merciless creditors, the rudeness of the railroad staff, the inconvenience of the passport system, the expensive and unhealthy food in the buffets, the universal ignorance and coarseness in attitudes." Yet the pessimism that has come to supplant his former nobility of thought provides him with insights, however unreliable or pathological they might be, that are self-examining, penetrating, and uncompromising, and that thus partake of a different, yet no less ancient or distinguished, ethos than the Stoicism he would wish to emulate; as he caustically puts it, he has nothing better to do in Khar'kov than to sit on a "strange bed," "[clasp his] knees," and heed the fabled oracle of Delphi: "Know thyself."[68] Freud similarly writes of the insights of the melancholic patient in terms of a greater tendency toward self-analysis: "In certain other self-accusations he also seems to us justified, only that he has a keener eye for the truth than others who are not melancholic . . . for all we know it may be that he has come very near to self-knowledge; we only wonder why a man must become ill before he can discover truth of this kind."[69]

While Nikolai Stepanovich's "boring story" is devoted at least as much to digressions and to the quotidian as to his pessimism and to his failing health, those passages in which he directly confronts his condition illuminate, with short bursts of insight, a crisis of meaning. This crisis follows its own plot development: Nikolai Stepanovich first alludes to his "new thoughts" near the end of the first section; he poses the question of whether he is ill or insightful in the third; and he returns to this question at the end of the fourth. It is only in the sixth and final section of **"A Boring Story"** that Nikolai Stepanovich at last puts this question to rest. In his final summation of his predicament, he does not climactically resolve the question of whether he is ill or insightful. On the contrary, in an anticlimax permeated in equal measure with pathos and bathos, he dissolves its original meaning. Succumbing to the very pessimism he dismisses, he writes, "in my passion for science, in my desire to live, in my sitting on a foreign bed and my striving to come to know myself, in all these thoughts, feelings, and notions that I form about everything, there is nothing general that might bind them into a single whole." Nikolai Stepanovich concludes that he has lacked a "general idea," not as a result of illness, but all his life, and thus the antithesis between illness and insight no longer preserves the dramatic potential for meaning that it had earlier held for him.[70]

It is this loss of meaning—in the very question from which his crisis of identity arose—that is so characteristic of melancholy insight. Nevertheless, if Nikolai Stepanovich dissolves the original opposition between insight and illness, then his final meditation conceals a self-referential paradox. This paradox of melancholy insight can be expressed in the terms he uses in his argument. If his pessimism is only a symptom of disease, then is his current pessimism about the merit of his life and career likewise only a symptom? If his self-analysis has revealed the absence of a ruling idea in his thoughts, then has not this symptomatic pessimism brought him insight, no matter how bitter, into the true nature of his own existence? Whatever the value of such objections, no further questions along these lines generate conflict in the novella. The paradox in this passage is therefore better articulated in terms of the form of Nikolai Stepanovich's final meditation. Nikolai Stepanovich's writing is never more lyrical than in the very passage where he reduces his thoughts to the level of pathological phenomena. As his own self-analysis becomes more lucid and insightful, as his writing style attains an organic coherence and a sense of conviction that it had previously lacked, he concludes that his view of the world is subject to the whim of external influences, rejects calmly and categorically the value of his long and illustrious life, and perceives, with unflinching clarity, that he has always lacked a ruling idea that might have connected his thoughts and feelings into a meaningful whole. It is the lyrical movement of his self-analysis that seems so discordant with the endpoint to which this self-analysis leads—the dismissal of his thoughts as a symptom.

Notes

Financial support for this project was initially provided by the Hannah Institute for the History of Medicine at the University of Toronto. I presented portions of this article at the annual conference of the Royal College of Physicians and Surgeons, Toronto, 1998, as well as at the annual convention of the American Association for the Advancement of Slavic Studies, Denver, Colorado, 2000. The source for the epigraph is Aristotle, *Problems,* ed. T. E. Page (Cambridge, Mass., 1937), 2:154-55.

1. A. P. Chekhov, "Skuchnaia istoriia (iz zapisok starogo cheloveka)," *Polnoe sobranie sochinenii i pisem v tridtsati tomakh,* ed. N. Bel'chikov et al. (Moscow, 1974-1983), *Sochineniia,* 7:282, 307 (hereafter *Sochineniia,* 1-18, or *Pis'ma,* 1-12).

2. Ibid., 7:282, 291.

3. M. M. Smirnov, "Geroi i avtor v 'Skuchnoi istorii,'" *V tvorcheskoi laboratorii Chekhova* (Moscow, 1974), 219.

4. Carol A. Flath, "The Limits to the Flesh: Searching for the Soul in Chekhov's 'A Boring Story,'" *Slavic and East European Journal* 41, no. 2 (Summer 1997): 279, 281.

5. Lev Shestov, "Anton Chekhov (Creation from the Void)," in Thomas A. Eekman, ed., *Critical Essays on Anton Chekhov* (Boston, 1989), 11; Marina Senderovich, "Chekhov's Existential Trilogy," in Savely Senderovich and Munir Sendich, eds., *Anton Chekhov Rediscovered: A Collection of New Studies with a Comprehensive Bibliography* (East Lansing, Mich., 1987), 84.

6. Leonid Gromov, *Realizm A. P. Chekhova vtoroi poloviny 80-kh godov* (Rostov-on-Don, 1958), 186. In contrast to these two main lines of interpreting Nikolai Stepanovich's pessimism, several critics have transferred the novella's emphasis on lack and deficiency from his thoughts themselves to character flaws that his self-analysis fails to address. Beverly Hahn, for example, commenting on Nikolai Stepanovich's indifference toward a despondent Katia in her own home, argues that he "fulfills the pattern of unconscious compromise, of which, one way or another, he has been guilty throughout his adult life." See Hahn's *Chekhov: A Study of the Major Stories and Plays* (Cambridge, Eng., 1977), 164.

7. See E. Meve, *Meditsina v tvorchestve i zhizni A. P. Chekhova* (Kiev, 1989), 92-103.

8. *Sochineniia,* 7:257.

9. Such an exercise in differential diagnosis is not foreign to Chekhov's own scholarly endeavors. Having studied forensic medicine in his fourth year of medical school, he assisted forensic experts several times during autopsies in criminal investigations. Furthermore, during his preparation for an eventually abandoned dissertation on the history of medicine in Russia, Chekhov argued that it was theoretically possible, as the official tsarist version attested, that the tsarevich Dmitrii killed himself with a knife during an epileptic fit in 1591. His investigation of whether the False Dmitrii ever suffered seizures similarly led him to conclude "that the pretender was in fact a pretender, because he did not have epilepsy." See A. V. Maslov, "A. P. Chekhov—sudebno-meditsinskii ekspert," *Sudebno-meditsinskaia ekspertiza* 34, no. 4 (1991): 59-60. Commenting on *War and Peace,* moreover, Chekhov writes that it is "strange that the wound of Prince [Andrei] . . .

gave off a cadaverous odor . . . if I had been nearby, I would have cured Prince Andrei." See his letter to A. S. Suvorin, 25 October 1891, *Pis'ma*, 4:291. As Leonid Grossman suggests, "even in letters to young writers, as he indulgently and gently examines their purely artistic short-comings, Chekhov mercilessly chides them for the slightest defect in medical matters in their stories." See Grossman's "The Naturalism of Chekhov," in Robert Louis Jackson, ed., *Chekhov: A Collection of Critical Essays* (Englewood Cliffs, N.J., 1967), 33.

10. Indeed, such a reductionism has at times occurred in Russian criticism on Chekhov. Meve, for example, in his highly informative study *Meditsina v tvorchestve i zhizni A. P. Chekhova,* diagnoses the character Kovrin in "Chernyi monakh" ("The Black Monk") with dysnoia or, "in the modern understanding," schizophrenia. Dysnoia is a diagnosis with which Chekhov would likely have been familiar from his copy of S. S. Korsakov's 1893 *Kurs psikhiatrii.* Meve suggests that it was not Chekhov's intention to use the "mystical and decadent ideas of [Fedor] Dostoevskii . . . to uncover the theme of the story" but precisely to "condemn" these ideas (162). Nevertheless, if mysticism falls under Chekhov's pervasive critical gaze, then this is no less true of psychiatry. When Kovrin is treated for "megalomania" (*maniia velichiia, Sochineniia*, 8:251), partly against his will, his academic career decidedly suffers. If he is not a divinely chosen one, as the black monk suggests, then is he not, as he himself argues during a period of remission, a greater man when he is manic? Meve's diagnosis of dysnoia does not resolve this philosophical question on the relationship between genius and mania. Moreover, this question itself extends to the problem of differential diagnosis. Korsakov writes that it "is often difficult" to distinguish between pure mania and the "maniacal form of dysnoia." The criteria for distinguishing mania from dysnoia include the manic's "accelerated flow of representations" and "ease of associations," two characteristics that might arguably have facilitated Kovrin's academic work. See Korsakov's *Kurs psikhiatrii*, 2d ed. (Moscow, 1901), 2:826, 909. Even when drawing on a contemporary psychiatric text, it is not possible to determine categorically the full implications of Kovrin's mental illness in "The Black Monk." Korsakov's diagnostic dilemma between dysnoia and mania could even be considered a restatement of the story's central philosophical question.

11. A. P. Chudakov, *Chekhov's Poetics,* trans. Edwina Jannie Cruise and Donald Dragt (Ann Arbor, Mich., 1983), 141.

12. *Sochineniia,* 7:252.

13. Ibid., 7:252, 305.

14. Ibid., 7:252.

15. Ibid., 7:252, 282.

16. Ibid., 7:263.

17. Ibid., 7:301.

18. Ibid., 7:290.

19. Ibid., 7:306.

20. Korsakov, *Kurs psikhiatrii,* 1:1.

21. For example, Chekhov's *Ivanov* opens a little less than a year after the play's eponymous protagonist first begins to struggle with "psychopathy" (*psikhopatiia, Sochineniia,* 12:58), and in the first paragraph of "The Black Monk," Kovrin, already unwell, is advised by a "physician friend" to retire to the countryside for the spring and summer (*Sochineniia,* 8:226).

22. *Sochineniia,* 7:284.

23. Ibid., 7:290.

24. In the history of medicine, this conceptual distinction between "disease" and "illness," at least in English, belongs to the nineteenth century. See Stanley W. Jackson, *Melancholia and Depression: From Hippocratic Times to Modern Times* (New Haven, 1986), 12, 13. In a related manner, Chekhov's former classmate, the neurologist Grigorii Rossolimo, records the author as having said, "If I were an instructor, I would try as much as possible to involve students in the domain of the patient's subjective experience." See G. I. Rossolimo, "Vospominaniia o Chekhove," in A. K. Kotov, ed., *A. P. Chekhov v vospominaniiakh sovremennikov* (Moscow, 1960), 670.

25. *Sochineniia,* 7:282.

26. Claude Bernard, *Leçons sur le diabète et la glycogenèse animale* (Paris, 1877), 70-72.

27. W. Howship Dickinson, *Diabetes* (London, 1877), 64.

28. Ibid., 95.

29. Pierre Alexandre Costes, *Des terminaisons du diabète sucré* (Paris, 1872), 8, 9.

30. Flath, "Limits to the Flesh," 273; Meve, *Meditsina v tvorchestve i zhizni A. P. Chekhova,* 93. Focusing on this episode, Meve draws a suggestive clinical parallel between Nikolai Stepanovich's condition and that of one of his acknowledged prototypes, the embryologist A. I. Babukhin: "In the last years of his life A. I. Babukhin suffered

terribly from angina pectoris or, in modern terms, stenocardia. His sufferings and those of the hero of 'A Boring Story' were extremely similar." Unfortunately, Meve does not develop this clinical parallel, nor does he address symptoms beyond those that appear in the "sparrow's night" episode.

31. *Sochineniia,* 7:301.

32. See Jean-Jacques Peumery, *Histoire illustrée du diabète: De l'antiquité à nos jours* (Paris, 1987), 109.

33. Bernard, "Leçons sur le diabète," *Leçons de pathologie expérimentale* (Paris, 1872), 338.

34. J. Thiroloix, *Le Diabète pancréatique: Expérimentation, clinique, anatomie pathologique* (Paris, 1892), 5.

35. Horst and Joseph Schumacher, "Then and Now: 100 Years of Diabetes Mellitus," in Dietrich von Engelhardt, ed., *Diabetes: Its Medical and Cultural History* (Berlin, 1989), 251 (my emphasis).

36. Francis E. Anstie, *Neuralgia and the Diseases That Resemble It* (New York, 1882), 31.

37. *Sochineniia,* 7:280, 302.

38. Costes, *Des terminaisons du diabète sucré,* 9, 10. Compare, for instance, Nikolai Stepanovich's description of his condition during his stay in a hotel in Khar'kov in the final section: "I felt sick on the train, chilled by the drafts passing through, and now I'm sitting on the bed. . . . I should really go to see some fellow professors today, but there's no strength or desire" (*Sochineniia,* 7:304).

39. William Osler, *The Principles and Practice of Medicine: Designed for the Use of Practitioners and Students of Medicine* (New York, 1892), 295.

40. Dickinson, *Diabetes,* 2, 20, 75.

41. Bernard, *Leçons sur le diabète et la glycogenèse animale,* 46, 475.

42. *Sochineniia,* 7:282.

43. Claude Bernard, *An Introduction to the Study of Experimental Medicine,* trans. Henry Copley Greene (New York, 1927), 198-99. In an article on Chekhov's realism, the literary critic Aleksandr Roskin draws an intriguing parallel between the author's aesthetic of "accidentalness" (*sluchainost'*) and Bernard's emphasis on the importance of the accidental in medical observation. See A. Roskin, *A. P. Chekhov: Stat'i i ocherki* (Moscow, 1959), 193-201.

44. Nikolai Stepanovich is here quoting a maxim of one of Chekhov's own teachers, G. A. Zakhar'in, who sought to impart to his students a patient-oriented clinical methodology. For a discussion of Chekhov's relationship to the "school of Zakhar'in," see Vladimir B. Kataev, "Ob"iasnit' kazhdyi sluchai v otdel'nosti," *Proza Chekhova: Problemy interpretatsii* (Moscow, 1979), 87-97.

45. In Émile Littré's *Dictionnaire de la langue française* (Paris, 1873-74), 4:1889, "sémiologie" is defined as: "Terme de médecine. Partie de la médecine qui traite des signes des maladies."

46. Quoted in Gerlof Verwey, *Psychiatry in an Anthropological and Biomedical Context* (Dordrecht, 1985), 27.

47. Wilhelm Griesinger, *Mental Pathology and Therapeutics* (New York, 1965), 9.

48. *Sochineniia,* 7:307.

49. I. M. Sechenov, "Refleksy golovnogo mozga," in M. G. Iaroshevskii, ed., *Psikhologiia povedeniia: Izbrannye psikhologicheskie trudy* (Moscow, 1995), 107 (emphasis in the original). It is interesting to note that Nikolai Stepanovich's eclectic list of "famous friends" (*Sochineniia,* 7:251) includes the historian and psychologist Konstantin Kavelin, who defended the duality of body and soul in a public polemic with Sechenov during the 1870s.

50. *Sochineniia,* 7:307.

51. Ibid., 7:264, 291.

52. George M. Beard, *American Nervousness, Its Causes and Consequences* (New York, 1881), vi.

53. Edward Shorter, *From Paralysis to Fatigue: A History of Psychosomatic Illness in the Modern Era* (New York, 1992), 221. Daniel Gillès has suggested that Chekhov's first encounter with neurasthenia occurred in 1885, when his acquaintance, the artist Isaak Levitan, happened to be diagnosed with the new disease. See Daniel Gillès, *Chekhov: Observer without Illusion,* trans. Charles Lam Markmann (New York, 1968), 70.

54. The term *neurasthenic (nevrastenik)* appears, for instance, in "Duel'" ("The Duel"), which Chekhov began writing before the completion of "A Boring Story" (*Sochineniia,* 7:374). Ivanov, in the play of the same name, complains about his "weakness" (*slabost'*) and "nerves" (*nervy, Sochineniia,* 12:53). And in "Pripadok" (An attack of the nerves), the doctor's use of the catchword *exhaustion (pereutomlenie)* during his examination of Vasil'ev, as well as his testing of reflexes (*refleksy*) and skin sensitivity (*chuvstvitel'nost' ego kozhi*), all suggest that he fears his patient may be suffering from neurasthenia (*Sochineniia,* 7:220, 221). "The Black Monk" focuses mostly on

Kovrin's megalomania, but the narrator opens the story with a clear, and lightly parodic, allusion to neurasthenia: "Andrei Vasil'ich Kovrin, Master [of Sciences], became exhausted and upset his nerves [*utomilsia i rasstroil sebe nervy*]" (*Sochineniia*, 8:226). Kovrin's progression from neurasthenia to megalomania follows a pattern outlined by Korsakov in *Kurs psikhiiatrii*, 2:1015.

55. George M. Beard. *A Practical Treatise on Nervous Exhaustion (Neurasthenia), Its Symptoms, Nature, Sequences, Treatment* (New York, 1880), 3. In a popular tract on neurasthenia, Bernard goes so far as to suggest that the five major precipitating causes of neurasthenia are steam power, the periodical press, the telegraph, the sciences, and the mental activity of women: "when civilization, plus these five factors, invades any nation, it must carry nervousness and nervous disease along with it." See Beard, *American Nervousness: Its Causes and Consequences*, 96.

56. Letter to Suvorin, 29 March 1890, *Pis'ma*, 4:50. Regarding Chekhov's interest in the new discipline of social pathology, see G. V. Arkhangel'skii, "A. P. Chekhov i zemskie vrachi," *Sovetskoe zdravookhranenie*, 1986, no. 3:61-64.

57. *Sochineniia*, 7:257, 258.

58. Ibid., 7:307.

59. Ibid., 7:282, 283.

60. Letter to Suvorin, 17 October 1889, *Pis'ma*, 3:266.

61. V. Ia. Linkov, *Skeptitsizm i vera Chekhova* (Moscow, 1995), 50.

62. *Sochineniia*, 7:291.

63. Letter to V. E. Meierkhol'd, October 1899, *Pis'ma*, 8:274.

64. *Sochineniia*, 7:281, 282.

65. Sigmund Freud, "Mourning and Melancholia," in Philip Rieff, ed., *General Psychological Theory* (New York, 1997), 164, 165.

66. *Sochineniia*, 7:290, 310.

67. Ibid., 7:251, 305, 306.

68. Ibid., 7:305, 306.

69. Freud, "Mourning and Melancholia," 167.

70. *Sochineniia*, 7:307.

Jack Coulehan (essay date 2003)

SOURCE: Coulehan, Jack. Introduction to *Chekhov's Doctors: A Collection of Chekhov's Medical Tales*, edited by Jack Coulehan, pp. xiii-xxv. Kent, Ohio: Kent State University Press, 2003.

[*In the following essay, Coulehan provides an overview of Chekhov's career as a physician and maintains that the author "thrived on the effective, if not always seamless, integration of the arts of medicine and writing, which reinforced one another throughout his creative life."*]

1.

The postcard is a reproduction of an oil painting, a familiar and sentimental late-nineteenth-century scene—a darkened sick room with a narrow shaft of light, a doctor sitting at the foot of a child's bed, a second child playing on the floor. The doctor appears to be reassuring the anxious mother, who stands beside him, hanging on every word. The sick child stares longingly from the shadows. The barefoot woman wears crumpled clothes and a babushka. Is the news good or bad? Will the child survive? Whatever the outcome, this doctor embodies the ideals of fidelity and compassion. It is a familiar domestic scene in popular art of the time, if not in reality. What makes this particular painting so unusual is the identity of the doctor—Anton Pavlovitch Chekhov, one of great masters of world literature.

The reverse side of the postcard, which I purchased at the entrance kiosk to Chekhov's estate at Melikhovo, contains a quotation from a letter to Alexei Suvorin, Chekhov's friend and editor, in which the author explains, "While you have been inviting me to Vienna . . . I have been busy being sole doctor of the Serpehovskovo district, and trying to catch cholera by the tail and organize health services. I have in my district 25 villages, 4 factories, and 1 monastery. In the morning I receive patients and in the afternoon go on house calls" (to Suvorin, August 16, 1892).

At the time he wrote the letter to Suvorin the author had recently purchased the small, dilapidated estate and moved with his family from Moscow. He was energetically renovating—planting trees, putting in a garden, and remodeling the house. However, no sooner had the Chekhovs settled at Melikhovo than a cholera epidemic threatened the region. And then there were so many sick peasants. Soon Chekhov was up and running, practicing medicine and public health by day and writing masterpieces like **"The Grasshopper"** and **"Ward No. 6"** by night.

How did he find the time and energy to pursue two such demanding careers? Several years earlier, at the height of Chekhov's early literary success, the same Alexei Suvorin had urged the young writer to give up medicine. Medicine is a waste of your time and energy, he said. Take my advice, you'd better learn to play the game. Become more focused. You'll never reach your potential unless you concentrate on writing. In response, Chekhov wrote, "You advise me not to chase after two hares at once and to forget about practicing medicine. Well, I don't see what's so impossible about chasing two hares at once. . . . Medicine is my lawful wedded wife and literature my mistress. When one gets on my nerves, I spend the night with the other. This may be somewhat disorganized, but then again it's not boring, and anyway, neither loses anything by my duplicity." In this famous passage the twenty-eight-year-old writer dances lightly over a fundamental truth of his life and identity. In fact Chekhov's career wasn't so much a matter of jumping back and forth from one bedroom to another, as was the case later perhaps with the poet Wallace Stevens or the composer Charles Ives. Rather, Chekhov thrived on the effective, if not always seamless, integration of the arts of medicine and writing, which reinforced one another throughout his creative life.

By the time young Anton graduated from the University of Moscow School of Medicine in 1884 he was already a professional writer. His affair with the muse had started innocently enough. The grandson of serfs, Anton was the third of six children in a poor merchant family from Taganrog, a provincial town deep in the south of Russia on the shore of the Sea of Azov. His stern, moralistic father fared poorly in the retail business and went bankrupt when the boy was sixteen years old. While the rest of the family moved to Moscow to seek a better future, Anton remained behind in Taganrog to finish high school. Though even then he was amusing himself by writing plays and sketches, the adolescent Chekhov decided to become a physician, perhaps influenced by the positive image projected by a Dr. Schrempf, who had treated him for peritonitis when he was fifteen. Thus in 1879 the nineteen-year-old arrived in Moscow, scholarship in hand, and began his medical studies. He also discovered his family living in squalor. His father's job paid poorly. His older brothers were irresponsible. The apartment was appalling. Anton soon discovered that he could help ameliorate the situation by selling his stories and sketches to local papers for eight kopecks per line. He wrote obsessively on nights and weekends, often knocking off a story or two in a day, ultimately publishing more than two hundred during this period, all under pseudonyms like Mr. Balastov, the Man without a Spleen, or (his preferred) Antosha Chekhonte.

These proved so successful that by the time he graduated in 1884, Anton was the acknowledged family breadwinner. However, although the student Chekhov viewed his writing pragmatically, the young physician soon came to view literature as integral to his identity. The writing appeared to come effortlessly. Whatever he saw or heard in life bubbled up into a tale. Thus, it wasn't surprising that the newly minted Doctor Chekhov continued to write after he had hung up a shingle at his rented house in Moscow, and the patients began to arrive. "Continued to write" doesn't exactly do justice to Chekhov's productivity—he published fifty-four stories in 1885, seventy-six in 1886, and fifty-seven in 1887. During this period he garnered the notice of well-known authors and editors, especially Alexei Suvorin, the editor-owner of *New Times,* an influential St. Petersburg periodical. Soon the young writer graduated from pulp fiction into the literary elite; his advancement capped in 1888 by receiving the Pushkin Prize, one of Russia's most prestigious literary honors.

Yet Chekhov never turned away from medicine, which remained an integral part of his self-consciousness, though writing increasingly demanded the lion's share of his time. In 1889 Chekhov did, in fact, retire from "normal" practice; he never again charged for his medical services, even though he never became a wealthy man and frequently found himself strapped for money. Nonetheless, he pursued his medical identity at the expense of his writing career—by providing free care to the country folk near Melikhovo (as depicted in the painting), by donating his services to the government as a district physician, and by engaging regularly in public health initiatives. In less than five months in 1891, Chekhov reported seeing 453 patients at a district health center and making 576 house calls, in addition to his home practice. Throughout his life, Chekhov also was heavily involved in "grassroots" activism, building schools for peasants, raising funds to help famine victims, and, later, near the end of his life, supporting the establishment of a sanitarium for tuberculosis victims at Yalta.

One of the most well known of these public health efforts was his epidemiological survey of health and social conditions in the prison colonies on Sakhalin Island in 1890. Traveling by himself, Chekhov left Moscow in April 1890 and journeyed six weeks by train, steamboat, and horse-drawn carriage across Siberia to reach the 1000-kilometer-long island. There he embarked on a one-man, three-month survey of the population, tenaciously picking his way from settlement to settlement and from house to house, often by foot. Biographers have long tried to pinpoint his motivation for this perilous journey. During the year prior to the trip to Sakhalin, Chekhov had undergone a crisis of confidence. Was he a good enough writer? Was he an adequate doctor? Did he really have what it takes? What direction should he pursue in the future? In a letter to Suvorin he opined, "I don't love money enough for medicine, and I lack the necessary passion—and therefore talent—for literature. The fire in me burns with an even, lethargic flame; it never flares up or roars . . . I have very little passion. Add to that the following psychopathic trait: for two years now, seeing my works in print has for some reason given me no pleasure" (to Suvorin, May 4, 1889). These reported experiences—lack of passion and loss of pleasure—suggest that he may have had an episode of clinical depression, perhaps in part precipitated by the recent death of his brother Nicholas from tuberculosis. There were also literary issues. He had promised himself and his friends that he would turn his attention to a novel, a big book that would establish him as a truly serious writer. But he couldn't do it; the novel didn't come.

However, the overt reason for Sakhalin—as opposed to embarking on some other major project or life change—was Chekhov's desire to pay his debt to medicine. He had developed a scientific interest in penology and became aware of the Russian government's establishment of penal colonies on the distant Pacific island, which had recently been wrested from Japanese control. Although Chekhov had graduated as a medical doctor, he had never completed the research thesis (the equivalent of a Ph.D.) that would make him eligible to become a professor. Hence, his debt to medicine—he would document health status and living conditions in the prison colonies.

Ultimately, Chekhov visited every settlement and aimed to survey every household on Sakhalin, using a twelve-item data collection form for demographic and medical information. He later claimed to have completed over ten thousand of these forms in three months, a feat that (if true) qualifies Chekhov as the speediest shoe-leather epidemiologist of all time. The author found it difficult to write of his work on Sakhalin Island. What form should the writing take? He had planned to make it a scientific monograph, but the creative artist struggled with the limitations of data and inference. What about his personal experience? And what about the interesting stories he heard some of the prisoners tell? After struggling with the material for years, Chekhov published *The Island of Sakhalin* (1895), a curious (but often engrossing) mixture of geography, history, medicine, statistics, and travelogue. Unfortunately, the University of Moscow was not impressed.

In early 1892 Chekhov purchased the rundown Melikhovo estate. He and his family lived there for the next six years, his "middle period," during which he matured as a writer as well as a humanitarian. This is also the period depicted in the painting of Dr. Chekhov visiting a sick child. The thirty-something landowner of Melikhovo wrote fewer stories than he had in his youth. However, the majority of these are masterpieces, including most of his great novellas (**"The Duel," "An Anonymous Story," "A Woman's Kingdom," "Three Years,"** and **"My Life"**). Here, too, he wrote his groundbreaking plays *The Seagull* and *Uncle Vanya*.

But what was this 1890s Chekhov like? Picture a middle-aged bachelor, longish face, rather neatly trimmed beard, a pince-nez clipped to the bridge of his nose. The man is a paterfamilias whose household consists of his parents and his sister Masha, a teacher who has become his confidant and secretary. His three surviving brothers look to him for guidance and sometimes for financial help. He is popular in literary circles, witty, and generous with his time and energy. Yet, too, he enjoys the solitude of his garden. The Chekhovs often entertain guests at Melikhovo, and quite commonly numbered among the guests are Anton's women admirers. His encounters with women are flirtatious and obviously enjoyable. Over the years he conducts teasing, sexually charged relationships (largely by letter) with several women, especially Lika Mizinova, a teacher-friend of Masha's. Whether any of these liaisons are "affairs" is uncertain. Most biographers conclude that Chekhov's emotional reserve and ambivalence about commitment kept these friendships from being consummated. Hence, the teasing and tension remained nonphysical. More recently, Donald Rayfield in his massive biography *Anton Chekhov* suggests that the author's "stringing along" was doubly cruel because it concealed a series of true sexual relationships. Nonetheless, the Chekhov of Melikhovo remains a bachelor.

The doctor in the painting already suffers from the tuberculosis that will kill him at the age of forty-four years. In fact he had first coughed blood when he was still a medical student. Yet Chekhov dismissed that episode and each subsequent episode over many years as "influenza" or "bronchitis," steadfastly refusing to give himself the diagnosis of consumption. As a physician Chekhov surely must have been aware of the meaning of his symptoms, especially during the period when he spent weeks nursing his brother Nicholas, who died of tuberculosis in 1889. Was Chekhov aware that he suffered from tuberculosis, but simply chose to deny it to others? Or was this a case of such massive denial that the man did not understand his own condition? The cat was finally let out of the bag in early 1897. While dining at a restaurant in Moscow, Chekhov suddenly experienced a violent spell of hemoptysis (coughing blood) that left him critically ill. He was admitted for the first time to a medical clinic, in fact, a clinic run by Dr. Ostropov, one of his medical school professors. After this episode, Chekhov's illness resulted in progressive physical limitation, and he was no longer able to deny its nature. Weakness, coughing, and shortness of breath defined his life. At the insistence of his doctors Chekhov left his beloved Melikhovo and spent much of the year at his new home in the sunny Black Sea resort of Yalta.

It was also during these last years that the bachelor writer courted and married Olga Knipper, an actress with the Moscow Theater Arts Company. Even after their marriage in 1901 Olga remained at work in Moscow during much of the year, while the invalid Chekhov lived in Yalta. He found himself able to devote less and less of his waning energy to writing, especially because he refused to give up his many social and philanthropic activities. Nonetheless, between 1898 and his death in 1904 Chekhov completed some of his greatest work, including several stories, two novellas (**"Peasants"** [1897] and **"In the Ravine"** [1900]), and his last plays, *The Three Sisters* (1900) and *The Cherry Orchard* (1903).

2.

In Chekhov's story **"About Love"** (1898), the narrator speculates on the nature of love. What is its essence? What are universal characteristics that identify love wherever it occurs? "What seems to fit one instance doesn't fit a dozen others," the narrator concludes. "It's best to interpret each instance separately in my view, without trying to generalize. We must isolate each individual case, as doctors say." Indeed, Chekhov's stories and plays rigorously follow this dictum. While many of his Russian contemporaries used fiction to advance their moral or social theories, Dr. Chekhov focused on the complexities of human interaction. In Chekhov's world, biology and circumstance constrain human freedom. People don't listen to one another. Communication often fails. Acts performed with good intentions frequently result in hurtful outcomes. Yet occasionally and in unexpected places, one finds a glimmer of love, courage, spirituality, or healing. "Never generalize," Chekhov tells his readers. "Never theorize. Pay attention to the particulars. Focus on the concrete." In this respect, the nineteenth-century physician-storyteller presages the twentieth-century physician-poet, William Carlos Williams, who coined the aphorism, "No ideas but in things."

Chekhov experienced no conflict between art and science, or art and medicine. He believed that knowledge of one complements the other. He explained this to Suvorin: "If a man knows the theory of the circulatory system, he is rich. If he learns the history of religion and the song 'I Remember a Marvelous Moment' in addition, he is the richer, not the poorer for it. We are consequently dealing entirely in pluses" (to Suvorin, May 15, 1890). In an 1899 autobiographical statement prepared for his medical school classmate the neurologist Dr. Grigory Rossolimo, Chekhov confirmed that his clinical "eye" and medical knowledge are important characteristics of his writing: "My knowledge of natural sciences and scientific methods has made me careful and I have always tried, when possible, to take into consideration the scientific data. When it was not possible, I preferred not to write at all" (to Rossolimo, Oct. 11, 1899).

Chekhov brought medical knowledge and sensitivity to his creative writing. Several characteristics of his work reveal the influence of medical training. For example,

he used his medical knowledge to lend accuracy to descriptions of diseases and medical situations. This characteristic is perhaps most clearly seen in Chekhov's description of mental disorders. For example, the title character in *Ivanov*, Chekhov's first full-length play, is a subtle portrait of a man suffering from clinical depression, who eventually commits suicide. The young heiress in **"A Doctor's Visit"** (included in this collection) presents symptoms we would now label generalized anxiety or panic disorder. The title character in *Uncle Vanya* appears to have characterologic or constitutional depression, which today we would likely call "dysthymia." In the peculiar story called **"The Black Monk,"** Chekhov describes a psychotic condition, presumably schizophrenia. As we see, the author's intimate knowledge of medicine and medical practice also allowed him to create numerous physician characters at work in clinical or public health environments.

However, medical attitudes and methodology play a far larger role in Chekhov's work than does specific medical knowledge. He believed that his duty as a writer was to present his observations clearly and accurately; in other words, to lay out the data in an objective fashion and allow readers to reach their own conclusions, rather than provide an author's interpretation. He wrote, "The artist should not be a judge of his characters and what they say, but only an objective observer" (to Suvorin, May 30, 1888).

Chekhov's commitment to introducing the objectivity of science into his writing was a source of conflict with Tolstoy, at that time Russia's most beloved writer, widely revered as a living saint. The two men enjoyed a close personal bond despite the great difference in their ages, but they approached writing (and living) with radically different philosophies. After his midlife religious conversion, Tolstoy viewed literature as a way to communicate his moral vision. He preached the gospel of a radical Christianity, in which all men (but certainly not women—Tolstoy was a thoroughgoing misogynist) would achieve economic and social equality. However, Tolstoy rejected material progress. He did not believe that the fruits of science could benefit mankind; in particular, he was skeptical of medicine and doctors. He said that Chekhov would be a better writer if he gave up medicine. Chekhov, on the other hand, complained, "Tolstoy calls doctors scoundrels and flaunts his ignorance of important matters because he is a second Diogenes. . . . So to hell with the philosophy of the great men of the world" (to Suvorin, Dec. 17, 1890).

The older man could not comprehend why Chekhov did not advocate a particular moral point of view in his writing. Chekhov, on the other hand, had a different conception of the writer's role. He strove to be objective, to present people as they are, to present the world as it is. His medical training taught him to be a careful observer; his medical attitude made him leery of judging others. Chekhov presented his negative responses to Tolstoy's ideas in several of his mature stories, especially **"The Duel"** (1891), **"An Artist's Story"** (1896), and **"My Life"** (1896). Nonetheless, despite their differences, Chekhov revered the aged master.

Although Tolstoy focused on a morality of radical communalism, many other writers and intellectuals of the time spoke out against Russia's repressive social and political institutions. Much of this protest was disguised in various ways to satisfy the omnipresent state censors, but late-nineteenth-century Russians (like their twentieth-century counterparts) learned to speak and understand a subtle code of protest. The intellectuals addressed "big issues"—democracy, education, and social revolution. They wrote articles and organized meetings and gave speeches. Here again, Chekhov seemed to be on a different wavelength. He rarely engaged in theoretical discussion of these issues (at least publicly), and he did not advocate radical social change. Rather, as we have seen, he preferred a pragmatic, case-based approach. His goals were relatively limited, but achievable. Treat the sick patient. Document and publicize the abysmal condition of prisoners on Sakhalin Island. Contain the cholera epidemic. Provide financial assistance to keep farmers afloat during the famine. Raise money for a new school. It goes on and on but is always specific and personal.

In the long run Chekhov's objectivity and aversion to theory played a major role in the development of modern literature. Twentieth-century writers followed Chekhov in attempting to describe the world of human character and relationship objectively, and allowing that world to speak for itself. Contrary to the beliefs of critics who argued that Chekhov's work had no moral center, the moral dimension of Chekhov's writing is firmly rooted in the individual. The moral stories of Chekhov's world arise from the relationships among weak, vulnerable people who have difficulty communicating with one another. They represent grassroots morality, not a moral or social theory imposed from above. Similarly, Chekhov's doctors are individuals, not representatives. Yet in the aggregate they reveal the author's deep understanding of human nature as it applies to the complex and often overwhelming profession of medicine.

3.

Chekhov also drew from his medical experience in creating a multitude of physician characters. Doctors play significant roles in thirty or so of Chekhov's stories and in every one of his major plays, except *The Cherry Orchard*. In most cases they function in specific medical situations or are the principal protagonists. In other cases the doctor is an observer or subsidiary character. The author's sensibility as a medical insider gives spe-

cial insight and poignancy to these characters. These doctors demonstrate a wide spectrum of behavior, personality, and character. Some are committed, some are lazy, and some suffer from burnout. Many are pompous, several are drunks, and very few are heroes. Chekhov knew too much about medicine to think that his doctors could actually heal many people, or make the world a better place. Thus, his medical men and women often appear impotent. Yet their impotence provides an arena in which a moral drama takes place. They define themselves as moral beings by the manner in which they respond to the overwhelming nature of their task.

Chekhov's doctors provide an especially interesting vantage point from which to view their author's project. For one thing, their world is Chekhov's world. At their best they convey the seamless fabric of tenderness (compassion) and steadiness (detachment) that lies at the heart of good medical practice. In fact, some of them demonstrate the same imaginative attention that Dr. Chekhov himself gave to his patients and to his characters. Dr. Pavel Archangelsky, who supervised Chekhov's first job as a physician, captured the author's ability to listen carefully when he later commented on the young doctor's performance: "he did everything with attention and a manifest love of what he was doing, especially toward the patients who passed through his hands. He listened quietly to them, never raising his voice however tired he was and even if the patient was talking about things quite irrelevant to his illness" (as quoted in John Coope, *Doctor Chekhov: A Study in Literature and Medicine* [Chale, Isle of Wight: Cross Publishing, 1997], 27).

At their best, Chekhov's doctors also demonstrate courage, altruism, and self-effacement. Dr. Dymov in **"The Grasshopper"** (1892) dies as a result of his work taking care of diphtheria patients, and Dr. Thompson, an almost Christ-like figure in **"The Head Gardener's Story"** (1894), is murdered. Dr. Kirilov in **"Enemies"** (1887) demonstrates extraordinary devotion to duty by leaving his distraught wife and the body of his son to make what appears to be an emergency house call.

Perhaps Chekhov's most textured and realistic portrait of a good physician appears in the late story called **"A Doctor's Visit"** (1898). Interestingly, the protagonist, Korolyov, is a young doctor substituting for his boss, the professor of medicine. During the course of the story he moves from being a sensitive and careful observer (with detached concern) who ascertains that his patient has no organic problem to making an imaginative leap that leads him to connect more deeply with his patient and her story. This imaginative connection allows him to relieve some of her suffering by reframing her illness. He is unable to solve the existential problems that press heavily on her, but his demonstration of solidarity leads her to trust him and develop a better understanding of her problems. Korolyov's transformation is not only characteristic of good medical practice, it is also emblematic of Chekhov's approach to literature—a "privileging" of the individual in which the moral dimension arises from the case itself, rather than the case being used to illustrate an aspect of morality.

From what we know of Korolyov, it is reasonable to believe that his empathy and openness may protect him from the emotional slings and arrows that might damage others in a medical career. Although he displays a similar sense of social injustice, unlike the highly theoretical Dr. Blagovo in **"My Life"** (1896), Korolyov looks like he might avoid the mistake of championing revolutionary theories in lieu of doing constructive work. Korolyov appears too well grounded in the particular and too interested in individual human narratives to become a theorist. Likewise, I suspect that Korolyov would be comfortable acknowledging and using the power of the doctor-patient relationship to promote his patients' welfare, as does his fictional colleague, Marfa Petrovna Petchonkin (**"Malingerers,"** 1885). I can imagine this young doctor in middle age, having become a well-liked and respected local physician like Samoylenko in **"The Duel"** (1891), a man who empathizes with them, respects them, and attempts to mediate their conflicts.

Other physician characters present us with surprising contradictions. In **"Excellent People"** (1886) Vera suffers from what today we might call an "existential crisis." After surviving a suicide attempt she appears to have given up medicine completely but then all of a sudden reactivates herself and goes off to become a public-health worker in the provinces. Dr. Tsvyetkov (**"The Doctor,"** 1886) displays admirable compassion as he keeps vigil over the dying child of an unmarried woman, but at the same time we learn that he may well be the child's father. The doctor is desperate for the boy's mother to tell him the "truth"; he wants to hear that someone else is the father so that he can regain his professional reserve and need not experience the anguish of attending his own son's death. Another doctor who loses his cool is Mikhail Ivanovitch (**"The Princess,"** 1889), who is working part time at a monastery. He and his former employer, the princess, meet at the monastery, and as they talk she implores the mild-mannered doctor to tell her about her faults. He responds with a full-fledged diatribe—the woman is a vain and heartless hypocrite. But almost as soon as these words are out of his mouth, the doctor backs off, expresses his humility, and tries to make amends.

At the other end of the spectrum, many of Chekhov's doctors are insensitive, incompetent, or impaired. Klotchkov, the callous medical student in **"Anyuta"** (1886), and Mayer, one of the students in **"A Nervous Breakdown"** (1889), are youthful versions of this pro-

fessional type. Perhaps a few more years of experience will help these young men to become more empathic and compassionate, but that seems doubtful. Take Mayer, for example. He can quote accurate statistics on the numbers of whores in London and Moscow, but he is unable to "see" (empathize with) the suffering of the living-and-breathing whores he actually encounters. Or consider Klotchkov, who conceives of his mistress as an object to be discarded at the drop of a hat. Shelestov in **"Intrigues"** (1883) and the public health doctor in **"Darkness"** (1887) are examples of self-centered physicians a little further along in their professional lives. The former is superficial and pompous; the latter is narrow-minded and detached. Neither presents the face of healing.

Chekhov's most complete imagining of the doctor as an insensitive, acquisitive social climber is found in **"Ionitch"** (1898). Startsev, when the reader first meets him, is a young physician setting up practice in a provincial town. He appears earnest and energetic, albeit a bit self-important. After surviving an unrequited infatuation with Ykaterina, the daughter of a wealthy townsman, Startsev gets down to the business of medicine. His practice prospers, and he branches out into the real estate business. He grows corpulent and wealthy:

> Probably because his throat is covered with rolls of fat, his voice has changed; it has become thin and sharp. His temper has changed, too; he has become ill humored and irritable. When he sees his patients, he is usually out of temper; he impatiently taps the floor with his stick, and shouts in his disagreeable voice: "Be so good as to confine yourself to answering my questions! Don't talk so much!"

"Ionitch" traces the progressive change that may occur in a medical practitioner who finds that medical affluence is more to his liking than the emotionally and physically difficult path of medical virtue. The story begins when Startsev is young and relatively "unformed." His abortive romance with Ykaterina results in a conscious decision to harden himself and turn away from the world of emotional commitments. To avoid getting hurt a second time, Startsev will simply never again become emotionally involved. He becomes detached to the point that he cannot "see" the suffering of others. Although **"Ionitch"** places this change in a romantic context, the outcome parallels that of "clinical distance" or "detached concern," in which the vulnerable doctor gradually comes to look on emotion as his enemy in the quest for objectivity in medical practice.

Some of Chekhov's most interesting doctors are those whose hearts are tortured by existential or spiritual conflict. At one level, this conflict might deserve a clinical description. Chekhov accurately depicted many of the symptoms of "burnout," the syndrome of depletion, detachment, depersonalization, denial, and depression that plagues some physicians. Emotional detachment from family and friends is a relatively early phase. Dr. Kirilov, who chooses to "go to the office" instead of mourning with his wife, may illustrate this condition. Dr. Ovchinnikov in **"An Awkward Business"** (1888) presents the more advanced symptom of depersonalization when he slugs his assistant because of frustration over the man's incompetence. Clearly, Ovchinnikov is overworked, the hospital resources are inadequate, and the doctor feels impotent. However, he responds by objectifying and dehumanizing his assistant, a response that threatens to compromise the work that he was trying to protect. Dr. Chebutykin in *The Three Sisters* (1900) illustrates the extreme end of the burnout spectrum, where the process has resulted in chemical dependency. Though still employed as a military physician, Chebutykin makes no claim to be a "real" doctor. In fact, he convincingly asserts that he has forgotten all he ever learned about medicine. All that remains of him is an alcoholic husk.

Ragin (**"Ward No. 6,"** 1892) and Nikolai Stepanovich (**"A Dreary Story,"** 1889) are complex characters in whom depression and burnout are superimposed on (or accentuate) their deep sense of having been failures in life. Chekhov's characters typically suffer from a lack of self-knowledge, wandering through their lives relying on one form of self-deception or another, and often causing pain and miscommunication in their wake. Ragin and Stepanovich fill that bill. When they were younger, they apparently meant well. They committed themselves to useful enterprises—Stepanovich to academic medicine and Ragin to a life of service in provincial medical practice. However, in the long run the center didn't hold and they failed. They never "found" themselves. Professor Stepanovich experiences this failure as a yearning for a unifying moral principle that would meld together the fragments of his life. Dr. Ragin experiences the failure as emotional numbness, an inability to feel. He yearns to experience suffering, because at least if he felt physical or emotional pain, he would be freed from the prison of dullness or numbness in which he dwells. Thus, the academic physician pines for cognitive salvation; the practitioner pines for emotional redemption. In both cases they remain wedded to themselves rather than to a concern for others, in whom salvation might actually be found.

Ragin and Stepanovich are physicians, of course, and they perhaps at one level illustrate the perils of clinical detachment taken too far, but their spiritual crisis is common to all of us—the search for meaning in our lives. This was a quest that Chekhov himself faced soberly, with a cold eye and a warm heart.

An anthology that included all of Chekhov's doctors would be cumbersome indeed, roughly the size of a medical textbook. I intended this collection to be considerably lighter (at least in weight), as well as more enjoyable to read than *Harrison's Textbook of Internal Medicine*. Many of the doctors had to be left out, but which were they? To a large extent, the nature of the texts dictated my exclusion criteria. First, I was unable to present doctors that appear in Chekhov's plays. This is unfortunate because physicians play major roles in four of Chekhov's five full-length dramas—Drs. Lvov in *Ivanov*, Dorn in *The Seagull*, Astrov in *Uncle Vanya*, and Chebutykin in *The Three Sisters*. However, it would be difficult to characterize any of these individuals without including the entire text. Even if I could identify a single scene that captured the "essence" of the character, the benefits of including that scene would likely be outweighed by the burdens. This collection is meant to be thoroughly readable and enjoyable, and I doubt whether a single scene or part of a scene from one or more of the plays, even if preceded by a summary of the story, would be attractive on its own merits. Likewise, I had to exclude the doctors portrayed in **"The Duel"** (Samoylenko) and **"My Life"** (Blagovo). To include one or both of these novellas would severely compromise the space available for their colleagues in shorter stories.

The inclusion criteria for the remaining pieces were far less quantitative. I wanted to include stories in which the doctor character played a major role and in which medicine itself makes more than a cameo appearance. The fact that Sobol in **"The Wife"** (1892) is a physician may represent a feature of his character that Chekhov wishes to communicate to the reader. Nonetheless, **"The Wife"** is neither Sobol's story, nor medicine's story. Likewise, the doctor makes a fine narrator in **"The Lights"** (1888), but the tale would do just as well if he were a young lawyer or landowner. I also wanted to avoid repetition, so I would not have included more than one of the three stories, **"Perpetuum Mobile"** (1884), **"The Examining Magistrate"** (1887), and **"On Official Business"** (1899), each of which depicts a magistrate and a physician on their way to an inquest. In the end I elected to use **"The Examining Magistrate"** in response to my final inclusion criterion—personal preference. I wanted to share with you the stories that I like most. I hope you enjoy them, too.

Selected Bibliography

Callow, Phillip. *Chekhov: The Hidden Ground*. Chicago: Ivan R. Dee, 1998.

Chekhov, Anton. *A Journey to Sakhalin*. Trans. Brian Reeve. Cambridge: Ian Faulkner, 1993.

———. *Letters of Anton Chekhov*. Ed. Simon Karlinsky. Trans. Michael Henry Heim. New York: Harper & Row, 1973.

Coope, John. *Doctor Chekhov. A Study in Literature and Medicine*. Chale, Isle of Wight: Cross, 1997.

Jackson, Robert Louis, ed. *Reading Chekhov's Text.* Evanston, Ill.: Northwestern Univ. Press, 1993

Johnson, Ronald L. *Anton Chekhov: A Study of the Short Fiction,* New York: Twayne, 1993.

Kataev. Vladimir. *If Only We Could Know. An Interpretation of Chekhov.* Chicago, Ill.: Ivan R. Dee, 2002

Malcolm, Janet. *Reading Chekhov. A Critical Journey.* New York: Random House, 2001.

Pritchett, V. S. *Chekhov: A Spirit Set Free.* New York: Random House, 1988

Rayfield, Donald. *Anton Chekhov. A Life.* New York: Henry Holt, 1997.

————. *Understanding Chekhov. A Critical Study of Chekhov's Prose and Drama.* Madison: Univ. of Wisconsin Press, 1999.

Simmons, Ernest R. *Chekhov. A Biography.* Boston: Little, Brown, & Co., 1962.

Troyat, Henri. *Chekhov.* New York: E. P. Dutton, 1986.

Nikita Nankov (essay date 2006)

SOURCE: Nankov, Nikita. "Narrative Realms/Narrative Limits: Chekhov's Story 'At Home' in the Context of Modernity." *Slavic and East European Journal* 47, no. 3 (fall 2003): 441-69.

[*In the following essay, which originally appeared in* the Slavic and East European Journal *in 2003 and has been revised by the author for its publication here, Nankov explores notions of modernity in "At Home," viewing the story as "a literary representation of some fundamental contradictions of modern civilization as it was formed after the end of the eighteenth century."*]

> The child creates as he borrows.
>
> —Roman Jakobson (1972, 14)

This paper explores the narrative realms and the narrative limits in Anton Chekhov's short story **"At Home"** (**"Doma"** 1887; Chekhov 6: 97-106; hereafter only page numbers will be given parenthetically)[1] concerning some general issues of modernity. "Realms of the narrative" and "limits of the narrative" are the literary notions correlative to two philosophical concepts, "expressivism" and "objectification," respectively. These four notions are explained below. I view **"At Home"** as a literary representation of some fundamental contradictions of modern civilization as it was formed after the end of the eighteenth century. The presumption of this interpretation is that the work of art and the real world are structurally homologous, which means that the work represents reality not through *what* it says but by *how* it

says it. My reading of **"At Home"** examines certain features of modernity by investigating some aspects of Chekhov's poetics and vice versa.

"At Home" is about a father, the prosecuting attorney Evgeny Petrovich Bykovsky, who tries to convince his seven-year-old son Serezha that he must quit smoking because smoking is socially and medically bad. After unsuccessfully applying different pedagogical tactics based on logic and coercion, Bykovsky finally succeeds by telling Serezha an improvised naïve didactic fairy tale about an old king whose little son also smoked and, due to this, died young without inheriting the kingdom.

"Expressivism" and "objectification" are philosophical conceptions describing a major tension in modern industrial civilization after the eighteenth century (see Taylor 537-71, esp. 539-47). After the seventeenth century, men define themselves no longer with respect to a cosmic order but as subjects with their own purposes. This new notion of subjectivity goes together with objectification of the world: the world is no longer perceived as a reflection of a cosmic order to which man is related, but as a domain to be manipulated for human goals. Mastery over nature becomes a confirmation of the new human identity. Objectification includes, besides nature, human life and society as well. Industrial and rationalized civilization acts upon men's lives, nature, and society in the name of higher efficiency. In this civilization driven by utilitarianism, social practices, nature, and individual existences are objectified through social institutions which target external purposes. This trend is the fundament of modern civilization, and, historically, its major tenets were formulated in the Enlightenment mainstream but they go beyond that era.

Expressivism is in part a reaction to the objectivism of modern technological civilization. For expressivism, human actions and lives are intrinsically valuable; they are expressions of what we authentically are. This trend of thought affirms that each person's fulfillment is unique, and this fulfillment cannot be dictated. This belief is an essential element of the contemporary belief in individual liberty. In historical terms, expressivism is connected with the Romantic mainstream (see Todorov 1982b, 184-94), but its forms, as with those of objectivism, are multifarious and transcend the historical framework of Romanticism per se.

European civilization in the second part of the nineteenth century affirms the priority of objectivism by entrenching the Enlightenment idea of man in its social structures and in science. Yet the objectivist and expressivist trends of thought and sensibility coexist and complement one another. The former encapsulates the latter in the private sphere, thus allotting to expressivism a subordinate place. "Modern society [. . .] is Romantic in its private and imaginative life and utilitarian or instrumentalist in its public, effective life" (Taylor 541). The important thing for the objectivistic structures is what they *do,* whereas for expressivist ones it is what they *express.* This division of domains partially resolves the expressivist or Romantic crisis which occurred at the dawn of modern technological society and which keeps resurfacing in the modernist aesthetic and political avant-garde, the social unrest in Western Europe in the late 1960s, or, twenty-some years later, the unrest in Eastern Europe with the collapse of communism. However, the expressivist or Romantic spirit is—if not openly then at least potentially—a protest against instrumentalist and expressively dead industrial civilization as defined by the Enlightenment and developed later.

Before delving into Chekhov, it is necessary to define the central terms and method of my study. "Narrative realm" means an artistic structural and thematic unity manifesting expressivism. The nexus between the philosophic notion of expressivisim and the literary concept of narrative is that they both stand for something hidden, for a potential that unfolds and tries to reach its fulfillment. Both expressivism and the narrative realm are a gradual deciphering of experience, which leads to increasingly adequate comprehension.[2] Historically and semiotically, both these philosophic and literary spheres are forms of Hermetism. This is why further I use the notion of "hermetic."[3] In this paper, "hermetic" means that certain messages need to be approached as hiding a secret that must be uncovered through interpretation. Conversely, the "limit of a narrative" means that the first, narrative realm in **"At Home"** is in conflict with the representations of objectification where a hermetic or expressivist narrative is no longer possible. The link between objectification and the non-narrative can be explained negatively: they are not hermetic; they do not stand for something which must be revealed. The methodological premise of my research on Chekhov in the context of modernity is one that presupposes unveiling of meaning or, conversely, the lack of such meaning. I elaborate this overarching hermetic and non-hermetic method by other, more restricted methods.

Initially, my interpretation will predominantly emphasize the text of **"At Home"** and then its context. Analyzing the text, I expect to show that the non-narrative domain dominates the narrative. Dealing with the context, I will find arguments in support of the opposite assertion. The resolution of these interpretive oscillations is left for the conclusion of the essay. Preliminarily, it can be sketched like this: the homology of the tension between objectivism and expressivism, on the one hand, and the contrast between the non-narrative and the narrative, on the other, allows us to read **"At Home"** as a representation of the lacerated identity of the modern subject in whom these two tendencies coexist in conflict but also in balance.

In **"At Home"** the switching between the narrative and the non-narrative realm starts with the clash between the title (designating a private sphere) and the business-like report of the governess (suggesting the official domain) about the house events during the day to Bykovsky upon his arrival home (97). This principle of contrast and alternation of the narrative and the non-narrative zones structures the whole work—from the self-evident contrariety between and within the characters to almost imperceptible artistic details. Serezha embodies expressivity and is opposed to the realm of non-narrativity represented by the governess and the father. Bykovsky participates in two conflicts between the narrative and the non-narrative domains: first, he is opposed to his son Serezha and, second, he is split within himself into a father and a state official. The contrast/alternation rule is valid for the details as well. The governess is official with both Bykovsky and Serezha, yet the words she directs to the boy are a combination (with a comic tint owing to the polarity of the two spheres) of detachment and care. To Serezha she speaks first in French, a sign of official aloofness, and then in Russian, a mark of domestic closeness (99). In its turn, the Russian part "Vam govoriat!" (6: 99; in a free translation that underscores the stylistic nuances: "I'm speaking to you, Mr. Bykovskii Jr.!") is a semantic fusion of the colloquial and threatening "Tebe govoriat!" ("I'm speaking to you, Serezha!"—the motherly figure to the naughty orphan boy) and the officially polite "Poslushaite, pozhaluista!" ("Please, Mr. Bykovskii Jr., could you listen to me?"—the humble employee to her employer's son).

Traditionally, the relation between the father and the son in **"At Home"** is seen only as an antagonism between either the adult and the child, or between reality and art. However, things are far richer than this. The broadest opposition between Bykovsky and Serezha is the difference between their use of language. The most characteristic language functions for the father (and the governess) are the referential, the conative, and the metalingual, while the son prefers the referential (but in a sense different from the father's), the emotive, and the poetic (for the six functions see Jakobson *SW* [Roman Jakobson, *Selected Writings*] 3: 21-27). Nevertheless the main contrast is not the asymmetry of the language aspects but their relation to one another. Bykovsky's dominant function tends to be the referential one, and the other aspects are subordinate to it. Conversely, for Serezha the functions are equivalent, and functionally synonymous. Bykovsky's use of language is vertically structured, that is, it is based on a hierarchy, whereas Serezha's is horizontally organized, and in it there are no hierarchies. Read through the prism of the language functions, **"At Home"** portrays how the father (or the objectifying and the non-narrative) tries to impose his referential dominance over the son (or the expressivist and the narrative) by adjusting this dominance to the son's language use. This imposition through adjustment takes place in four spheres: the referential, the emotive, the poetic, and the metalingual.

Before exploring these four fields, I must clarify two matters. (1) Why does the father adapt his language usage to the son's and not vice versa? The referential aspect is "minimally dependent on the grammatical pattern" and "directly requires recoding interpretation, i.e., translation," whereas in the poetic function "the grammatical categories carry a high semantic import" (Jakobson *SW* 2: 265; also 3: 63-86). To put it differently, the verbal signs of Bykovsky's leading referential function can be easily interpreted by means of other signs of the same language, while Serezha's poetic function (and its equivalent emotive one) is more difficult to translate. Consequently, for Bykovsky, the referential aspect is at the top of the hierarchy of language functions and all other functions operate as its interpretations. For Serezha, however, the referential, emotive, and poetic functions are autonomous and interchangeable. Thus, modern objectification and its respective nonnarrative realm are represented through Bykovsky's referentially guided language, whereas expressivism and the narrative sphere related to it are modeled by Serezha's horizontally placed referential, emotive, and poetic aspects. The connection between philosophy (the opposition of objectivism versus expressivism), narratology (the opposition of narrative realms versus the narrative limits), and literary semiotics (the opposition of language use based on the dominance of the referential aspect versus language use based on horizontal relations between the language functions) is a crucial methodological presupposition in my analysis of the story. (2) Language is not solely verbal language but also the other communication systems based on it. The six cardinal functions of verbal language as defined by Jakobson and their hierarchies in the different types of messages can be applied in the study of other semiotic systems.[4]

The referential aspect is "an orientation toward the CONTEXT" (Jakobson *SW* 3: 22). For Bykovsky, the context is social and is defined by pedagogy and law. Serezha's context is domestic. The father refers to the world as a systematic hierarchy, the son refers to it as autonomous particulars.[5] For this reason, the basis for the misunderstanding between the father and the son is their different contexts of reference or universes of discourse. The meeting between Bykovsky and Serezha is a tripartite comparison between the general and systematic universe of discourse of the former and the singularity-driven and non-systematic universe of discourse of the latter:

(1) The father commences by trying to explain what "possession" is, but the son retorts by asking "what is glue made of?" (100; 31)[6]; Bykovsky's most abstract basis for social cohesion collides with the son's most idiosyncratic segment of the system. The father attempts a deduction to bridge his and his son's discursive universes. He quotes a legal principle and then applies it to the concrete family case: "A man has a right to enjoy only his own property, and if he takes another's then . . . he is a wicked man! [. . .] You have your little horses and pictures . . . I don't take them, do I?" (100; 97-98; 30-31).[7] However, Serezha does not make the expected reciprocal induction but remains on the level of the particular. To the deduction of the father concerning the little horses the son answers: "You can take them if you want to!" (100; 31). The son fails to perceive the law of private property behind the father's example.

(2) The father, adjusting to the son, shifts from social relations to personal health. Although the topic is closer to the son's thinking, it is still within the father's systematic reasoning that he attempts a second deductive move: tobacco is harmful, and he who smokes dies before his time; therefore, if Serezha smokes, he will die young as did his Uncle Ignaty (100-1). The son responds with an association comprising only particulars: Uncle Ignaty played the violin well; now his violin is with the Grigorievs (101). The difference between the universes of discourse is underscored in two ways. (a) The story suggests Serezha's inductive transition from the particular to the general: from Uncle Ignaty he passes to death in general (101). Yet this induction is conjectural because it is introduced by "veroiatno": *probably* Serezha thinks about death, but we, the readers, do not know with certainty; and if he does not, he remains in the zone of the particular. (b) Even if he makes the induction, it is not reciprocal to his father's deduction as the father hopes, and Serezha does not reach the conclusion that tobacco is harmful but that death separates people.

(3) Finally, when Serezha comes up with another two segments of his world—the cut finger of the cook and the girl who sang and danced during the dinner (102)—the father remains silent, and this suggests the father's fiasco in trying to make his and his son's discursive universes compatible.

The conative function or the "orientation toward the ADDRESSEE," whose purest grammatical expression is the vocative and the imperative (Jakobson *SW* 3: 23), is used by the father when the referential one fails to communicate. After Bykovsky's silence marks his referential surrender, he says to his son: "Listen, give me your word of honour that you won't smoke again" (102; 34). Imperative sentences cannot be put to a truth test as can the declarative because they do not have a reference.

Because the reference of a declarative sentence is its truth value, a sentence without a reference has no truth value (Frege 68; for Frege's concepts of "reference" and "sense," see note 20). At this point the father's situation can be understood in two ways. First, he gives orders not because he is necessarily right but because he is undoubtedly stronger. In this way Bykovsky is implicitly equated with the other male pedagogues in the story, whose main characteristic is coercion. Bykovsky's efforts to avoid the systematic field of pedagogy and law lead him, by a different path, to the coalescence of these two spheres. Second, since there is no reference in the imperative, the communication—in relation to reference—is over and it can be resumed only on a new level. The resumption requires a transition from the conative aspect of the father to the emotive and poetic aspects of the son.

The emotive function is "focused on the ADDRESSER, [and] aims a direct expression of the speaker's attitude toward what he is speaking about" (Jakobson *SW* 3: 22). In the story, it is necessary to distinguish between two forms of this function: verbal and body language. For Serezha, this aspect is autonomous; it is related to the referential and the poetic functions horizontally, and is their synonym or equivalent: the cut finger of the cook (102) is emotionally as meaningful as the death of his Uncle Ignaty and his mother (101); his affection for his father is as strong as his grief about the ruined kingdom in the fairy tale that Bykovsky tells him (105). In contrast, for Bykovsky the expression of feelings (real or feigned) is always subordinate to certain social principles voiced through his referential aspect. The most detailed verbal statement of Bykovsky's feelings for Serezha is in his internal monologues. In them, as we will see in discussing Bykovsky's metalingual aspect, the emotive side is again subordinate to the referential one. The body language of the characters reiterates their emotive verbal behavior—the father is restraint incarnate, while the son is all affection (99).

Now let us analyze the poetic function, the "focus on the message for its own sake" (Jakobson *SW* 3: 25), as employed by the father and the son. As with the emotive aspect, I detail only Serezha's case, leaving Bykovsky's for the time when I turn to the metalingual function. Serezha's poetic aspect is represented by a variety of instances:

(1) The son modifies the father's conative aspect into poetic; the father's order is turned into a song:

> "Listen, give me your word of honour that you won't smoke again," he said. "Wo-ord of honour!" sang Serezha [. . .]. "Wo-ord of ho-nour! Nour! Nour!"
>
> (102; 34-35)

(2) Serezha's artistic use of signs—verbal, auditory, and visual—is synaesthetic: "In his mind, sound was closely connected with form and color, so that in painting let-

ters he invariably colored the sound L, yellow; M, red; A, black; and so forth" (103; 36).[8] Synaesthesia, or the identity of all arts based on the fact that they make beautiful objects through the operation of the same principle—the autonomous totality—is a Romantic (and Modernist) postulate (Todorov 1982b, 159-61). Associating language sounds with colors is a concrete case within that mental framework (Genette 1994, 314-22).[9] In this way, Serezha is implicitly connected with Modernism, an intellectual trend contemporary to Chekhov, which tends to replace reality (believed to be unexpressive) with an artistic reality (thought of as an individual expression). Traditionally only the vowels are "colored" (424 n. 17), but Serezha raises the expressivity a notch higher: he colors both the consonants and the vowels.[10] Mimophony is hermetic because it deals with the symbolic relevance of language sounds: "The symbolic capacity of the sounds of the language system is a matter of fact, or more precisely an a priori certainty" (323).[11]

Moreover, a European tradition exists which perceives the vowels as feminine, expressing sensations, and introvert, while perceiving the consonants as masculine, expressing ideas, and extrovert (310). In a parallel tradition, the vowels are also seen as the most primitive phonic elements; thus the emerging languages consist mainly of vowels (310-12). Serezha colors two sonorous consonants (*l* and *m*), in other words, those standing closest to the vowels (*l* is also traditionally associated with smoothness and femininity (321-22), but so is *m* (Jakobson *SW* 1: 542)). By means of his synaesthetic use of language Serezha is related explicitly to the expressivist Romantic-Modernist line and implicitly to his feminine and "primitivist" features; the latter two features are analyzed below.

(3) Serezha sings or is attentive to singing (98, 102). He stands for music and, through it, for the domination of the poetic function in the semiotic systems of art because "music appears to be *un langage qui se signifie soimême*" (Jakobson *SW* 2: 704; also 704-5).[12] Historically, music is a facet of expressivism.[13] Music is also another connection between Serezha and the "primitive" because "vocal music seems to be more widespread than instrumental music. Thus syncretism of poetry and music is perhaps primordial as compared to poetry independent of music and to music independent of poetry" (*SW* 2: 705).

(4) Serezha's drawings suggest another feature of his use of the poetic function of different semiotic systems. Because many of the characteristics of these drawings have already been discussed by other scholars, here I point out only two details. (a) His drawing—a house and a soldier next to it (103)—is a *mise en abyme* of **"At Home."** The house stands for the private values and the domain of narrativity and expressivism, whereas

the soldier symbolizes the social system or the lack of narrativity and objectification. These meanings are detailed in Birgit Wetzler's notes (67-68) on Chekhov's story **"The Kiss"** [**"Potselui,"** 1887]. (b) Serezha's understanding and treatment of artistic space connects him with the "primitive," whereas his father is connected with the "civilized." According to Bykovsky, the soldier cannot be taller than the house; for Serezha, however, if the man is not taller, one will not see his eyes. In historical terms, the father advocates Renaissance and post-Renaissance perspective as an optical geometry that originates in "civilized" modern Europe.[14] Conversely, Serezha draws using the pre-Renaissance and non-Western tradition where the size of the depicted objects depends not on their proximity to the viewer but on their importance in the represented world. But Serezha's artistic handling of space is also similar to the Modernist subversion of (post-)Renaissance perspective. The latter was thought of as academic and expressively dead, while the Modernist doctrine and practice were, among other things, nurtured by "primitive" art.

(5) Bykovsky and Serezha are opposed by their phonemic emblems (for the artistic significance of the phonemic level in prose fiction see Kolarov). Some key words associated with the father contain the consonantal combination /pr/ or /p . . . r/ and more rarely /br/ or /b . . . r/, usually in an initial position. As a rule, these words are social, scientific, and abstract notions, such as "*pr*okuror [prosecuting attorney]," "*por*oli [flogged]" (97; 27), "*por*okom [vice]," "*pr*igovarival [sentenced]," "*pr*estuplenie [crime]," "*pr*isposobliat'sia, *pr*ivykat' i *pr*iniukhivat'sia [adapting, accustoming itself to, and getting used to]," "*pr*avdy [justice]" (98; 27-28), "*pr*avo [a right]," "*pr*avda [truth]" (100; 30; 97), "*pr*ostupkov [faults]" (101; 100), "*pr*avoved, polzhizni u*pr*azhnia-vshiisia vo vsiakogo roda *pr*esecheniiakh, *pr*edu*pr*ezh-deniiakh [a legal scholar, who had spent half a lifetime exercised in all kinds of sanctions and preventions]" (102; 101; 34), "*b*orodoi [beard]" (103; 36), "*pr*opove-dei [sermons]," "*pr*irode [nature]" (106; 107), and so on. On the other hand, many of the important words characterizing the son begin with /pl/ or /bl/ or include the cluster /p . . . l/ or /b . . . l/ (in some cases /l'/), and they express body parts or states, and emotions, such as "*p*ol [sex]," "*b*elolitsy [pale-faced]," "*p*olezaia [climbing onto]," "*pl*okhim [bad]" (99; 29-30; 96), "ob-*l*okotilsia [set his elbows on]," "*bl*izorukie glaza [near-sighted eyes]," "vzgliad ego po*bl*uzhdal [his glance wandered around]" (100; 98; 31), "po*gl*iadel [looked at]," "*p*al'tsem [with a finger]," "*p*echal' [sadness]," "*b*ol'shikh [. . .] glazakh [big [. . .] eyes]" (101; 32), "*p*ela i *pl*iasala [sang and danced]," "*pl*akat' [weep]" (102; 101; 34), and so on.

(6) Serezha's referential, emotive, and poetic aspects are interchangeable and neither dominates the other: "Pa-pa has come!" sang the boy. "Papa has come! Pa!

Pa! Pa! [Pa-pa priekhal!—zapel mal'chik.—Papa pri-ekhal! Pa! pa! pa!]" (98; 29). The bond of equivalence between the referential aspect (the father's homecoming as the context of the message) and the poetic one (the son's song as a form of the poetic function) is underlined by an implicit equation of the two verbs based on a cluster of the consonant /p/ plus a group of a liquid consonant /r/ or /l/ and a front vowel /i/ or /e/: "*pr*iekhal [has come]"—"za*pel* [sang]"—"*pr*iekhal" or /pri . . . pel . . . pri/. The sameness of the referential and the poetic aspect is suggested by a second phonemic figure—a triple repetition of /papap/ which covers and unites the referential and the poetic: "*Pa-pa p*riekhal! [. . .] *Papa p*ri-e-khal! *Pa! p*a! *p*a!" or /papap . . . papap . . . papap/. The symmetry within the combination as a whole and within each of its parts additionally emphasizes the harmony between the two language aspects. Nevertheless, in this meaningful embroidery of sound and semantics the son and the father are at the same time contrasted through their emblematic phonemes: "*pr*iekhal"—"za*pel*" or /pr/ versus /p.l/; /pr/ and /p.l/ occupy the initial and the final position of the key words, which suggests the distance separating the father and the son from the very beginning of the story when Bykovsky and Serezha have not yet met in the fictional world of the work.

In a similar way, Serezha perceives the referential, the emotive, and the poetic functions as interchangeable: "He found it possible and reasonable [. . .] to render with the pencil [drawing as the poetic function] not only objects [the referential aspect] but also his own sentiments [the emotive function]" (103; 103). The son's emotive body language, his affectionate actions are as artistic as his use of verbal language; by reshaping his father's beard Serezha theatrically, as it were, changes Bykovsky's identity: the father first resembles one Ivan Stepanovich and then the concierge (103).

(7) Finally, Serezha's child language can be viewed as bordering on glossolalia, a discourse that, compared to language, strengthens syntax (the relationship of constituent elements among themselves) at the expense of semantics (the interconnection of the elements with what they designate). This is traditionally considered an atavistic or a poetic feature (Todorov 1982b, 264-65).

Only the father is aware of the miscommunication that results from the different universes of discourse. That is why time and again he employs the metalingual function in which "speech is focused on the CODE" (Jakobson *SW* 3: 25). The metalingual aspect operates as a series of dialogues (mostly internal) in which Bykovsky checks the code: "You don't understand me" (100; 31); "I'm not explaining it to him right!" (100; 31); and so on. In stricter narratological vocabulary, the father's internal focalization is composed of all these dialogues. Internal focalization of a narrative is the perceptual or conceptual position in terms of which the narrated events are presented; it is located in a character and entails certain restrictions on what is rendered (Prince 31-32; for a classification of focalizations see Genette 1988, 72-78). Since the referential aspect requires interpretation, it presupposes metalinguistic operations (Jakobson *SW* 2: 265). The omniscient narrator mentions this very early: Bykovsky explains what private property is, "counterfeiting the speech of a child" (100; 31). Later, the father spells out the same need to translate in the following way: "He [Serezha] would have understood me perfectly had I really regretted the tobacco, and been offended and burst into tears. [. . .] Nothing can be accomplished by logic and moralizing. Well, what shall I say to him? What?" (102; 34). In the first sentence, Bykovsky points out the new, emotive aspect that is understandable for Serezha, the code in which he, the father, should speak. In the second, he acknowledges that the referential function needs interpretation. Finally, the last two sentences are formulae for checking the non-working referential code. This is the model that suggests the need to translate the referential into other—emotive and poetic—aspects. This model is employed twice before the end of the story (102-3, 105-6).

Read in the semiotic framework of language functions and the possibility of translating the father's referential function into emotive and poetic ones, the story ends with the triumph of Bykovsky's referential systematic function, which uses the emotive and the poetic functions to its advantage. Though this conclusion runs against the traditional interpretations of **"At Home"** that indulge in the victory of the child principle (the unsystematic referential, emotive, and poetic aspects) over the adult principle (the systematic referential function), it is homologous to the model of modernity in which the private or expressivist domain is encapsulated by the social or objectifying one.

The manipulation of the emotive and poetic functions by the referential is at the same time the limit of the hermetic narrative. Bykovsky's final thoughts about the practical success of his tale are: "Medicine must be sweet, truth must be beautiful . . . And man has come up with this foolish reverie since the time of Adam . . . After all . . . maybe it is natural thus, and cannot be otherwise . . . Aren't there in nature many expedient deceits and illusions . . ." (106; 40, 107). The assertion that narratives are valuable not for what they are but for what they achieve cannot be interpreted further, because in **"At Home,"** as in modernity, this is a natural and social axiom: "must be," "since the time of Adam," "it is natural thus, and cannot be otherwise," "in nature."

The juxtaposition of Bykovsky and Serezha is not confined to the dominant aspects of language. A complete analysis requires the consideration of three more oppositions: first, in terms of the adult's versus the child's

architectural space; second, of the "male" versus the "female" principle; and, third, of pediatric, psychoanalytic, and "primitivist" utterances of the father and the implied silence of the son. An utterance designates the meaning of a text in a context of enunciation (see Todorov 1984, 41-74; and 1982a, 9-11, 149).

Architectural space is artistically meaningful because architecture is one of the "applied semiotic structures" (Jakobson *SW* 2:703). In **"At Home"** the spaces of the father and the son are distinguished and contrasted. Serezha is initially in the nursery (98), but when summoned to explain his smoking, he goes to his father's study (99) where the rest of the action takes place. The area of the study, however, is not entirely official but is subdivided into an official or father's and a private or son's sphere: Serezha has his own corner for drawing on the father's desk (101-2).

Bykovsky and Serezha are also differentiated as two philosophical and cultural paradigms related to (but not identical with) gender. Let us examine two conflicts between the masculine (Bykovsky) and the feminine (Serezha).

(1) The opposition between the father and the son as a contrast between the masculine and feminine should be understood within the framework of what Wetzler (63-65) defines as the "male" and the "female" principle in Chekhov. Wetzler's "male" principle overlaps with what I term the "objectivist," and the "female" with the "expressivist" trends of modernity (Wetzler does not deal with **"At Home"**). **"At Home"** implicitly equates the father (with his masculine attributes: both state and domestic power, smoking, beard), the state (Bykovsky personifies jurisdiction), and pedagogy (at home, Bykovsky is a pedagogue; moreover, pedagogy in the story is a male profession (98, 101)). This masculine domestic and institutional power is placed side by side with Serezha's femininity: "This was a person whose sex could only be divined from his clothes [. . .] everything about him looked unusually dainty and soft" (99; 29).

For Bykovsky, his son stands for the father's beloved women—his mother and deceased wife—and love in general (103-4). The masculine attributes of the son make the father see him in his imagination as an amusing caricature: Serezha has a gigantic cigarette a yard long, and is surrounded by clouds of tobacco smoke (97).

The male institutionalized pedagogy of power and constraint is opposed to the female domestic pedagogy of love and empathy. Bykovsky remembers that while the other boys who smoked were beaten, he was kept away from sin by his mother's presents (101). The father also feels the limits of male pedagogy based on force as compared with the female based on empathy: "That is why nothing can replace the mothers in bringing up children, for they are able to feel and weep and laugh with the children . . . Nothing can be accomplished by logic and moralizing" (102; 34, 101).

(2) The association of Bykovsky with the masculine and of Serezha with the feminine comes also from the history of rhetoric (see Todorov 1982b, 65-79; and 1982a, 123-26, 129-30). For almost two millennia, from Quintilian in the first century A.D. to Pierre Fontanier in the early nineteenth century, rhetoric existed as a discipline of ornamented, beautiful, figurative speech whose object coincides with literature. Rhetoric is "the theory of language admired in and for itself" (Todorov 1982b, 68). But in that period rhetoric lives through an internal contradiction: in agreement with imperial Roman and later Christian ideology, the rhetoricians claim that they value only unadorned discourse that conveys pure thought; yet at the same time they deal only with tropes that embellish. The conflict is illustrated by the place of tropes in the opposition outside/inside. Tropes are seen only as an embellishment of thought; the thought is "the inside," whereas the tropes are "the outside." Moreover, "the inside" is perceived as the body, while "the outside" is its apparel. To speak in tropes is to dress the body; to understand embellished speech is to undress the body. The moral values connected with the dressing and undressing of the body lead to the devalorization of rhetoric. "Rhetorical ornamentation changes the sex of discourse" (1982b, 75). Ornamental discourse is viewed as feminine and goes with dressing/undressing, whereas direct discourse is masculine. Christian morality looks down on rhetoric (and on beautiful speech and the feminine) because it values thought (the signified, the body, the substance, "the inside," the spirit) above words (the signifier, apparel, ornament, "the outside," the carnal). Now when Bykovsky asks himself, "Why is it that morals and truth must not be presented in their raw state but mixed with something else, by all means sugar-coated and gilded, like pills?" (105; 40), he echoes unawares the Christian condemnation of rhetoric, embellished speech, and fictional literature, which in **"At Home"** are personified by Serezha. In the Christian ideological tradition, the combination "truth must be beautiful [istina krasivaia]" (106; 40) is contradictory or at best a compromise: "truth" is pure thought, "the inside," the body, the masculine, whereas "beautiful" is just an ornament attached to thought, "the outside," the apparel, the feminine. Because Bykovsky strives to convey an important message about private property and health, he stands for the only possible truth and thus for the masculine; conversely, Serezha, who grasps this truth solely through a fairy tale, not directly, represents the feminine.

The opposition between the father and the son also rests on three utterances (or motifs of the theme of a narra-

tive versus lack of it) which I call pediatric, "primitivist," and neuro-pathological, respectively. The utterances are intertwined and synonymous: "From daily observations of his son the prosecuting attorney had become convinced that *children* [u detei, the pediatric utterance], like *savages* [u dikarei, the "primitivist" one], have their own artistic outlook and their own idiosyncratic requirements, inaccessible to the understanding of adults [vzroslykh]. Under close observation Serezha to an adult [vzroslomu] seemed *abnormal* [nenormal'nym, the neuro-pathological utterance]" (103; 36, 102-3; emphasis added). The father differentiates between his son as a child, savage, and mentally ill person, on the one hand, and himself as an adult, civilized and mentally normal, on the other. Only the first of these features (adulthood versus childhood) is explicitly stated, and that one has been the focus of critical attention, but the other two are no less important not only for Chekhov's œuvre as a whole[15] but also for its connection with modernity. At this point I am passing from the predominantly textual to the prevalently contextual analysis of **"At Home."**

The simultaneous use of the pediatric, "primitivist," and neuro-pathological utterances illustrates in what sense **"At Home"** is part and parcel of modern reasoning and sensibility. The overlapping of these utterances in the story is a literary analogue to certain trends in neuropathology at the end of the nineteenth and the beginning of the twentieth century. In Freud, the same three types of utterances are also intertwined and bear a hermetic mark: neither the child, nor the savage, nor the mentally ill person can clearly state his or her ideas; these ideas belong to the unconscious, which only the therapist can formulate logically by interpreting certain somatic and psychic symptoms. The therapist (who is adult, civilized, and mentally healthy), through a complex professional methodology and vocabulary, uncovers the covered and translates the unconscious into the conscious. Psychoanalysis is a doctrine that supposes that everything is to be interpreted, and therefore a text does not need internal indices to call for interpretation; everything has an indirect meaning (Todorov 1982a, 36). In this regard, Freud is one of the great expressivist thinkers from the second half of the nineteenth and the first half of the twentieth century.

However, here we face the methodological inconvenience of thinking of late nineteenth-century science as an archetype and **"At Home"** as its variant (which is a sort of neo-Cartesianism or extreme rationalism and idealism). This predicament can be avoided when we postulate that, if the story repeats Freud's ideas, for instance, it is only to the extent to which Freud repeats the ideas in the story. In other words, the nexus between works of art and scientific ideas is circular, neither being the matrix that precedes the other but rather its transposition.[16] If I turn to Freud, it is not to look for influences on or mastermodels of certain utterances in the story, but, first, to interpret the story by referring to some well-defined paradigms in Freud, and, second, to shed light on Chekhov as a writer and thinker opposed to rational doctrines. Bykovsky opts for a hermetic or expressivist move opposite to that of the Viennese doctor. Instead of uncovering the covered (making the unconscious conscious or the primitive civilized), our hero covers the uncovered or transforms the conscious into the unconscious. To borrow a formula, we can describe the second possible direction in the relation between the "civilized" and the "primitive" in the modern age by saying that Bykovsky, by telling the fairy tale to Serezha, "goes primitive" (see Torgovnick 34-37). If we follow the critical tradition regarding this fairy tale as a specimen of high narrative art, Bykovsky's choice is not surprising, because it is parallel to the process in European art in the nineteenth and early twentieth centuries when "primitive" objects became involved in what was considered high art (75-104). In other words, on this level of the work where the father as a non-narrative or objectifying realm is opposed to the son as a narrative or expressivist realm, Bykovsky adopts the narrative stance of his son by improvising a fairy tale for him.

The didactic fable that Bykovsky tells to Serezha at the end of the story is the apex of the narrative domain as represented in the opposition between the father and the son. The fairy tale is an ultimate expressivist experience because it interprets itself. To narrate is already to uncover a hidden meaning; narrating is simultaneously a hermetic and hermeneutic act that does not require the interpretive mediation of the father as a narrator: "The scenes, the characters, and the situations all came at hazard, as luck would have it, and the plot and the moral somehow flowed out by themselves independent of the will of the storyteller" (104; 38, 104-5).

For Bykovsky, the narrative (not only the fairy tale but any narrative in principle) as a hermetic act has two poetic forms. First is the fictional one which is aesthetically marked: "It will be said that beauty and artistic form were the influences in this case" (105; 39). From prose fiction thought of as a traditional narrative mode, the father takes a second step and brings under the common denominator of the hermetic narrative not only fictional prose (his didactic tale) but also historiography, sermons, and legal discourse: "He remembered the jurymen who invariably had to be addressed in a 'speech' [rech']; the public who could only assimilate history [istoriiu] by means of epics and historical novels [po bylinam i istoricheskim romanam]; and of himself drawing a philosophy of life [zhiteiskii smysl] not from sermons and laws [ne iz propovedei i zakonov], but from fables, novels, poetry [iz basen, romanov, stikhov] . . ." (105-6; 40, 107). Bykovsky considers historical texts to be not signs referring to events but

signs referring to other signs, and, consequently, narratives (see White 1973, 1987, 1989). For the protagonist, the realm of the narrative includes the two traditional narrative modes: prose fiction and historiography (Aristotle 55, 62-63; and Ricoeur, 1984-1988), but to it he adds other discourses as well, most notably, legal debating. In narratological terms, Bykovsky's two "theoretical" moves, as regards the innate hermetic character of every narrative, cover both essentialist and conditionalist poetics, to use Gérard Genette's terms (1993).

The relation between these two poetics leads us, in a new way, to our issue of the narrative and non-narrative realms. The aesthetic character of literature can be described either through essentialist theories of literariness or conditionalist theories of literariness. In the former, the literariness of certain texts is taken for granted as universally perceptible. In the latter, some texts are not inherently aesthetic but could become works of art under certain circumstances. Essentialist poetics is closed; conditionalist poetics is open. Conditionalist poetics is not theoretical but intuitive. For it, every text is literary if it gives the reader aesthetic satisfaction. Conditionalist poetics traces the transition in European thinking during the last two centuries from universality toward cultural relativism, toward an overt subjective interpretation. Conditionalist poetics is a poetics of modernity. We are then justified in concluding that Bykovsky's inclusion not only of canonical but also non-canonical texts in the sphere of literariness, his siding with the conditionalist poetic trends of modernity, makes him a champion of the expressivist and narrative tendencies in **"At Home."** This is the highest degree of affirmation of the hermetic or expressivist character of every narrative, as we will now discuss.

But now we encounter the problem of why, for Bykovsky, every narrative is hermetic, or, to rephrase the question, what every narrative expresses. To resolve it we must switch to the second level of the juxtaposition of the narrative and the non-narrative, namely, the conflict between these two domains in the father himself, in his internal focalization.

The conflict in Bykovsky is a disagreement between what can be explained but not expressed/narrated (logic, reason, institutions, utilitarianism) and what can be expressed/narrated but not explained (emotions, pleasures, fantasies, leisure, self-fulfillment). The antagonism is formulated twice. The omniscient narrator says: "For men [Dlia liudei] who are obliged for whole hours, even for whole days, *to think official thoughts [dumat' kazenno]* all in the same direction, *such free, domestic speculations [takie vol'nye, domashnye mysli]* are a sort of comfort and a pleasant restfulness" (98; 95, 28; emphasis added). In the internal focalization of the protagonist, a voice reiterates the following: "But the fact is that all these confounded questions [kanal'skie voprosy] are settled so much more easily *at school or in court* [*v shkole i sude*] than *at home* [*doma*]; here, at home, one has to do with people whom one unreasoningly loves, and love is exacting and complicates things" (102; 35; emphasis added).

In the light of this internal conflict, Bykovsky tries to solve the problem of why smoking is bad and must be punished or, which is the practical outcome of the resolution, why Serezha must quit this allegedly sinful and harmful habit. The protagonist tries two approaches. The first is deductive: smoking is always socially persecuted and unhealthy; Serezha smokes; therefore, Serezha is in trouble. The second is abductive: Serezha smokes; if we suppose that smoking in all cases is bad, then Serezha may be in trouble.[17] Deduction is the least dialogical inference; more dialogical is induction; and the most dialogical is abduction (Petrilli, esp. 134-35). The gist of abduction is that its hypothesized rule is not cast in stone but can be reformulated. The adjustments result from the meeting of the interpretation with the objective reality that is interpreted. This leads to changes in the actions of the interpreting subject (in our case, Bykovsky), and these changes are the pragmatic result of his interpretive labor. The dialectic between semiosis (or interpretation) and action consists in the fact that semiosis ends and starts at every moment: action is the end of a semiosis, but it is also the beginning of a new one.[18] In the deductive instance leading to a communicative impasse, Serezha's smoking is tackled as an example of legal *subtilitas applicandi,* whereas in the abductive his smoking is represented as a hermetic narrative. Let us consider these two options.

The first, deductive case is subdivided into two parts—one that envelops the whole story and another that pertains directly to the split in Bykovsky.

(1) Above, I postulated that the referential aspect can be translated, and, with this in mind, I reached the conclusion that this language function dominates all others, and this dominance is a literary representation of the subordinate role of expressivism/narrativity to the objectivism/non-narrativity in modernity. However, in this part of my rumination, for methodological convenience, I skipped one crucial circumstance, namely, that **"At Home"** uses the translatability of the systematic referential aspect *ironically.* It seems as if the systematic referential aspect in this work can be fully translated into the emotive and poetic aspects but, in reality, there is always an untranslatable residue, certain referential meanings that remain opaque. Therefore, it is not only Serezha who does not understand the references of the father; the reader, before the son, undergoes a similar interpretive confusion. The governess's report opening the story starts *ex abrupto* and the reader is unaware who is talking, to whom, and about what. As the first and second paragraphs unfold, the reader figures

out all these issues except the one stated in the story's very first sentence: "They sent over from Grigorievs for some book, but I said that you were not at home" (97; 93). Who are the Grigorievs? Later in the story, Serezha mentions the same name saying that the violin of his dead uncle is with them (101). But if they are not allowed to borrow (or take back?) a book from Bykovsky while he is not at home, why are they able to keep the undoubtedly more financially and sentimentally valuable violin of the beloved dead uncle? The reader never learns whether this family is Bykovsky's neighbors, relatives or something else, or if the governess's Grigorievs are the same as Serezha's Grigorievs. The unresolvable gap (Wolfgang Iser's term denoting a structural locus in the literary work whose meanings the reader has to create by him- or herself) in the referential language of the governess signaled most disturbingly by the enigmatic Grigorievs is taken over by Bykovsky's internal focalization: the struggle against smoking is guided by irrational horror.

(2) Bykovsky is aware of the old pedagogical practice of persecuting smoking. Nevertheless, he and those who mistreat youngsters for smoking do not know why this must be so:

> [S]moking at school and in the nursery aroused in masters and parents a *strange, almost incomprehensible horror* [*strannyi, ne sovsem poniatnyi uzhas*]. It really was horror. Children were unmercifully flogged, and expelled from school, and their lives were blighted, although *not one of the teachers nor fathers knew exactly* [*ni odin iz pedagogov i ottsov ne znal, v chem imenno*] what constituted the harm and offense of smoking. Even very intelligent people did not hesitate to combat the vice they *did not understand* [*ne ponimali*]. [. . .] Probably that is one of the laws of society—*the less an evil is understood* [*chem neponiatnee zlo*] the more bitterly and rudely is it attacked. [. . .] The living organism possesses the faculty of quickly adapting, accustoming itself to, and getting used to every condition; if it were not so, man would be conscious every moment of *the unreasonable foundations on which his reasonable actions often rest and of how little of conscious justice and assurance* [*kakuiu nerazumnuiu podkladku neredko imeet ego razumnaia deiatel'nost' i kak malo osmyslennoi pravdy i uverennosti*] are to be found even in those activities which are fraught with so much responsibility and which are so appalling in their consequences, such as education, the law, literature. . . .
>
> (97-98; 27-28; emphasis added)

This is the very core of modern objectification, the result of which is the alienation of the modern individual from his or her own activity and institutions. Utilitarian performativity and its institutions, in the final analysis, are estranged from and hostile to the people who have created them. Paradoxically, extreme rationalism is irrational (see, for instance, Ritzer, esp. 134-58). If the domain of objectification limits narrativity, it is precisely because the former does not make personal sense any more; it is not hermetic; it does not express the qualitative aspect of the modern subject. Hence, objectification is not only expressively dead but narratively barren as well. Alienation, the severed link between modern man and his activities, is the source of the non-hermetic character of institutional discourses.

In this context, the institutionalized struggle against smoking is oppressive for individuals, while smoking is an act of personal choice, of heretical, anarchistic, even suicidal expression of one's own self: "Every boy caught smoking was flogged. The faint-hearted and cowards, indeed, gave up smoking; *the braver and smarter one* [*kto zhe pokhrabree i umnee*], after the whipping, would carry the tobacco in the leg of his boot and smoke in the barn. When he was caught in the barn and whipped again, he would go and smoke by the river . . . and so on until the lad was grown up" (101; 33, 100; emphasis added).

But in **"At Home"** smoking as self-fulfillment is only one case of the singularity of every human being. The issue is much broader (and this is why the work is both about the child's psyche and, through it, about modern man in general). The father thinks of his son in the following way: "He has *a little world of his own* [*svoi mirok*] in his head, and knows what, according to him, is important and what is not. To gain his attention and conscience it is not enough to imitate his language but it's also necessary *to be able to reason in his manner* [*umet' i myslit' na ego maner*]" (102; 34, 101; emphasis added). The recognition of each person's uniqueness is the first step toward Bykovsky's second chance to solve his pedagogic predicament.

Bykovsky's second option is entering the pedagogic case of smoking from the opposite direction, namely, as something that does make concrete personal sense. This is achieved in three steps:

(1) The protagonist logically formulates the self-tortures of a split (or self-alienated) person to his son: "I smoke, and know that it is not clever, and I scold myself, and do not love myself on account of that . . ." (100; 98-99). At this point, Bykovsky is still halfway between the logic of his first, deductive option ("it is not clever") and the practical action characteristic, as we will see, of his second, abductive one ("I scold myself, and do not love myself").

(2) The next step is the reciprocal development of one motif expressing the antagonism between the non-narrative and the narrative realm. Above, I have connected the explanation of the domain of objectification with a quote ending in the following way: "how little of conscious justice and assurance are to be found even in those activities which are fraught with so much responsibility and which are so appalling in their conse-

quences, such as *education, the law, literature* [*pedagogicheskaia, iuridicheskaia, literaturnaia*] . . ." (98; 27-28; emphasis added). Just before Bykovsky starts his tale, the motif of the alienated and irrational character of pedagogy, law, and literature is presented in a reversed way, as spheres of the highest individual involvement and responsibility: "And, indeed, if one considers it seriously, what a lot of courage and faith in oneself one must have *to undertake teaching, or judging, or writing a big book* [*brat'sia uchit', sudit', sochiniat' tolstuiu knigu*] . . ." (104; 37, 104; emphasis added).

(3) The last and decisive step in the direction of solving the case is Bykovsky's artless fairy tale about the prince who smoked and thus failed to inherit the kingdom of his old father because he died too young. Two moments in the tale deserve attention. First, the tale is connected with Serezha himself; it speaks of the child's experience: "The old king had only one son, who was heir to the kingdom, a little boy, just as little as you are" (105; 39). And second, the tale produces an immediate practical effect—Serezha decides to quit smoking: "I won't smoke any more . . ." (105; 39).

Here I refer to the notion of narrative identity (see Ricoeur, 1984-1988 3: 186-89, 246-49) that is a component of the hermetic layer of **"At Home."** Personal narrative identity means that an individual builds his or her identity by accepting the story that he or she has invented or, in our case, the story contrived by someone else on his or her behalf. Bykovsky, by means of the fairy tale, bestows an identity upon Serezha that the son readily embraces as his own. Applying to modernity the notion of narrative identity as represented in **"At Home,"** we may add: the modern individual accepts this narrative because it expresses what, for him or her, constitutes personal uniqueness. In this sense, a narrative identity is the realm where the individual finds his or her own self, becomes one with him- or herself. Yet the narrative identity becomes a true self-constancy only when the narrative transcends the level of its own verbal structuration, and becomes human practice, i.e., acting and taking responsibility for it. The seemingly unsophisticated didactic tale, if perceived in the context of modernity and certain narrative and semiotic theories, is a specimen of a hermetic narrative but also a practical fulfillment of the modern individual.[19]

Above, I have touched upon the similarities and the differences between Freud and Chekhov in dealing with hermetic and expressivist issues. Taking this comparison a step further, I will better explain the narrative domain in **"At Home"** as the practical self-fulfillment of modern man. In the Post-script to *Dora*, his famous case study of hysteria, Freud explains why his eighteen-year-old patient, whom he names Dora, interrupts their therapeutic meetings after only three months, and thus prevents the complete treatment of her neurosis. Freud's answer to this question is framed within the notion of transference (Freud 106-10). Transference means that some earlier fantasies of the patient made conscious during the analysis "replace some earlier person by the person of the physician" (106). Freud concludes about Dora's breaking of her treatment, "she took her revenge on me as she wanted to take her revenge on him [Herr K., an older man whom she unconsciously loves, though she thinks that she hates him], and deserted me as she believed herself to have been deceived and deserted by him" (109; for further clarification of Dora's vengeance, see 100, 110-12).

In the context of my analysis of Chekhov, I would respectfully disagree with Freud's account of Dora's motives. Nevertheless, in parting company with Freud, I would like to draw on one of his observations about transference, upon which he himself does not elaborate as regards Dora's disappearance:

> Psychoanalytic treatment does not create transferences, it merely brings them to light, like so many other hidden psychical factors. The only difference is this—that *spontaneously a patient will only call up affectionate and friendly transferences to help towards his recovery; if they cannot be called up, he feels the physician is "antipathetic" to him, and breaks away from him as fast as possible and without having been influenced by him.* In psychoanalysis, on the other hand, since the play of motifs is different, all the patient's tendencies, including hostile ones, are aroused; they are then turned to account for the purposes of the analysis by being made *conscious,* and in this way the transference is constantly being destroyed. Transference, which seems ordained to be the greatest obstacle to psychoanalysis, becomes its most powerful ally, if its presence can be detected each time and explained to the patient.

> (108; emphasis added)

Two points are important here; first, the patient *spontaneously* accepts the positive and rejects the negative transferences; and, second, the transferences are destroyed by reformulating them *rationally.* In my opinion, Freud loses his patient not because she unconsciously takes revenge on him but because she spontaneously spurns the identity that Freud imposes on her in the name of the final triumph of reason. Dora rebuffs the rationalized narrative identity offered to her by the therapist, whereas Serezha heartily embraces the fictionalized narrative identity bestowed upon him by Bykovsky. Once again, the difference between Freud and Bykovsky in the case of the fairy tale is the direction of the hermetic proceeding. For Freud, it is from the unconscious to the conscious, and the practical result is failure. For Bykovsky, the direction is opposite— from the conscious to the unconscious (to use Freud's terms, standing here for the objectivist/non-narrative

and the expressivist/narrative), and the outcome is success. The important similarity, however, is that in both cases the synonymous chains—the unconscious/ expressivist/narrative/hermetic and the conscious/objectivist/non-narrative/non-hermetic—are inseparable. But this very alliance is exactly the conflict of modern civilization. Freud tries to square the hermetic expressivist circle at the expense of the unconscious by assuming *a priori* that the conscious or the rational is the ideal to be achieved. Freud, the stentorian champion of the unique quality of the modern subject, raises his voice only to rationalize and, in the final analysis, to objectify this uniqueness. Expressivism in Freud, as a tendency, serves the purposes of objectification. Drawing on Karl Jaspers (185-89), one may view Freud as an example of how Western philosophical rationalism analyzes the nonrational by converting it into the rational, and thus fails to explain human existence. Chekhov, in **"At Home"** as well as in his work in general, follows the opposite direction.

Had I ended my analysis on a high and beautiful note praising the triumph of the narrative in **"At Home,"** I would have only refuted the rational or performative pole in modernity in relation to **"At Home."** Certainly I would have fallen short in going beyond the traditional interpretations of the story, which view it only as a eulogy to the power of narrative art. My essay would have been plausible owing not so much to the essay's interpretive but to its aesthetic and teleological qualities, because "most literary histories close where they do for formal, narrative reasons—usually for climax" (Perkins 37). And this climax, in the case of **"At Home,"** is when the critic reaches the pole of expressivism or hermetic narrativity personified by the child. Before going beyond the objectivist/non-narrative and the expressivist/narrative poles (two antagonistic yet equally one-sided interpretive options for **"At Home"** and for Chekhov as a whole), let us scrutinize the second one in greater historical detail.

A traditional formulation of the expressivist pole in relation to **"At Home"** can be found, for instance, in Zinovy Samoilovich Paperny: "The movement of the story's plot as a whole is linked not only with the clash between the adult's and child's point of view, but also with the approbation of the moral superiority of the child over the pedagogical logic and all things official" (68; my translation). Vladimir Golstein's analysis of **"At Home"** stresses the emotive function of language in Freud-flavored dicta (see esp. 77-81): Bykovsky's fairy tale "discloses such elements of the prosecutor's psyche that he prefers to overlook" (78); the tale reveals the father's unconscious, his fears of remaining unprotected like the old king in the tale. Golstein's interpretation emphasizes the hermetic side of **"At Home"** by excluding the rationalistic rationale of psychoanalysis. Though Golstein focuses on the expressivism of the father, not of the child as in the tradition prior to him, his analysis is still within the frame of expressivism alone.

The expressivist/hermetic/narrative pole in Chekhov is proclaimed in its purest form by the Russian Symbolists. In 1904-1907, Andrei Bely holds that Chekhov is both the last Realist and the first Symbolist in Russian literature. The Symbolist/symbolic trend in Chekhov (of which, as Bely holds, Chekhov is not aware) is explained by defining the Symbolist symbolism in him. Bely conveys the hermetic essence of this symbolism by metaphors of transparency and glass: Chekhov's realistic representations are like a glass prison house through whose walls the reader perceives deeper meanings (399, 403-4).

The extreme hermetic line of Symbolism is taken over, for example, by Boris Eikhenbaum in 1944. Eikhenbaum's own hermetic thesis unfolds in four steps. (1) Chekhov effaces a series of traditional oppositions in Russian literature: between the social and the personal, the historical and the intimate, the general and the particular, and the big and the small (360-61, 364). (2) This obliteration is achieved by a hermetic shift on the part of Chekhov, the result of which is that the small starts to express the big or, to refer to stage one, the second members of the oppositions begin to designate the first. (3) Medicine in Chekhov's life and œuvre is viewed as a hermeneutic operation, the reading of symptoms leading to a diagnosis. Medical diagnosis is the same as the artistic asking of (but not answering) the right social questions (363-64); Eikhenbaum speaks of the "artistic diagnoses of Chekhov" (369; my translation). Medicine and literature are hermeneutically similar. (4) Chekhov's expressivism culminates in the lyrical principle of his prose fiction and dramas, that is, the presence of a subtext and hidden meanings in his works (367).

For both Bely and Eikhenbaum, Chekhov's dominant language aspect is the poetic, in Jakobson's sense (music or lyric); historically, both critics think of Chekhov as a Modernist. Read side by side, Bely's and Eikhenbaum's articles are a cultural paradox displaying the intellectual continuity beneath the mutable jargons of two different eras. In hermetic and hermeneutic terms, Bely's mysticism and Eikhenbaum's medical materialistic positivism, which look so antagonistic, are actually similar: they both uncover something covered and present Chekhov as an expressivist artist *par excellence*. This apotheosis of Chekhov's hermetic narrativity encompasses the interpretations of **"At Home"** only as an opposition between the child and the adult and/or between art and reality, glamorizing the first member of the oppositions at the expense of the second.

After seeing the two poles of modernity and the preference of some Chekhov critics for the expressivist one, it is time to demonstrate in **"At Home"** how the two sides are represented not only as antagonistic but also as coexistent. On a thematic level, Bykovsky is in a pedagogic quandary only because Serezha is his flesh and blood (102-3). Without the contiguity and continuity of the generations there would be no need to translate the father's referential language into the son's referential, emotive, and poetic languages. The father and the son are, in fact, one larger, Siamese-twin type of representation of the human condition in modernity. (Paired characters—among whom Cervantes's Don Quixote and Sancho Panza or Dickens's Mr. Pickwick and Sam Weller are among the most famous—portray the human with astounding sophistication (see Georgiev).)

The linguistic and semiotic expression of the thematic Siamese-twin bond is the character of child language as "a kind of pidgin, a typical mixed language, where the addressers try to adjust themselves to the verbal habits of their addressee and to establish a common code suitable for both interlocutors in a child-adult dialogue" (Jakobson *SW* 1: 538). We have seen that it is not only Bykovsky who translates his referential functions into Serezha's emotive and poetic ones, but the son who also reshapes the father's conative function into his own poetic function (an order is turned into a song) and travesties the high social status and image of the prosecuting attorney through emotive body language (Bykovsky is travestied like the concierge). The father's metalanguage and his internal focalization result from his acting on the son and the son's acting on him; if the active part were solely Bykovsky, there would be no need of metalanguage, no internal focalization, and **"At Home"** would not be what it is. The Bykovsky-Serezha relation is "an interaction between both worlds" (Jakobson *SW* 1: 538).

The tradition of stressing the child's or the poetic/emotive aspect in **"At Home"** overlooks the fact that the child-adult verbal intercourse is an interlanguage. Golstein, for instance, by placing the famous Wordsworth line "The child is the father of the man" from the poem "My Heart Leaps Up When I Behold" as the first epigraph to his analysis of **"At Home,"** signals a Romantic-expressivist approach. Jakobson, facing similar attitudes in dealing with child language creativity, speaks of the balance between the Romantic (or expressivist) and the realistic (or objectifying) views: "The child creates as he borrows" (Jakobson 1972, 14; see also 13-14).

The interaction between Bykovsky and Serezha is also suggested by means of their phonemic highlights. Bykovsky's cluster /pr/ or /br/ is different but also similar to Serezha's /pl/ or /bl/: a labial plosive voiceless or voiced consonant is followed by a liquid consonant. Moreover, the /pr/ or /br/ group is not restricted to the father but, on several key occasions when Bykovsky emphasizes the family bond between his son and himself by addressing the boy as "*br*atets [little brother]," it becomes the son's phonemic emblem as well.

There are two groups of designations for Bykovsky. The omniscient narrator refers to him either as "Evgeny Petrovich" or "Bykovsky" (without a significant distinction between the two) or as "prosecuting attorney [prokuror]." Serezha calls his father "papa [papa]," the nursery version of "father [otets]" which is adopted in adult language. Gottlob Frege's classical distinction between "reference [Bedeutung]" and "sense [Sinn]"[20] allows us to say that Bykovsky as the reference of all these appellations is the mediator between them, that they are his "senses." The theory of reference and sense helps us to understand better the split in Bykovsky, his belonging simultaneously to the objectivist/non-narrative realm (as "prosecuting attorney") and the expressivist/narrative realm (as "papa"), or, as Golstein nicely puts it, his being "both at home and not at home" (81). The phonemic parallels between the two senses (an initial /p/ plus a double repetition in both words /ro.. ro/ and /papa/) also suggest the link between them.

I have spoken of three levels of the conflict between the narrative and the non-narrative realms which encircle each other: Bykovsky's apartment, the opposition between the father and the son, and the inner split of the protagonist. These three spaces are placed within a broader fourth one that I have not mentioned yet, namely, the building where Bykovsky's apartment is. While the father is in his study waiting for his son, the space of the building is introduced in this way:

> It was nine o'clock in the evening. Overhead, over the ceiling, on the second floor, someone was pacing from corner to corner, and still higher up, on the third floor, four hands were playing scales. The pacing of the person, who, as it seemed from his nervous strides, was thinking tormentedly of something or was suffering from toothache, and the monotonous scales added to the quiet of the evening something somnolent that predisposed to idle thoughts.
>
> (98; 28, 95)

This space, like the other three, is endowed with both private and public characteristics. The former include the affectionate and artistically colored connection of the four hands on the third floor and the second-floor inhabitant's probable suffering from toothache. But what happens on the second and the third floor can also be understood as a productive effort. The four hands designate not solely an intimate bond but also a practical activity: the hands are a synecdoche for two persons and emphasize the performative aspect of the action, while playing the scales suggests not real music but rather exercising or warming up. Moreover, the inhabitant on the second floor may not be suffering from a bad tooth but may be torn by tortuous thoughts. The fourth and broadest space in the fictional world of "At Home" is as torn between the domestic and the productive or the narrative and the non-narrative as the other three. This again confirms that in the story's artistic world the rule is the contrast and alternation but also the coexistence of the non-narrative and the narrative. "At Home" ends with a modified representation of the fourth space: "He [Bykovsky] sat down to his work, and the idle, domestic thoughts long wandered in his head. The scales could no longer be heard overhead, but the dweller on the second floor still continued to walk from corner to corner . . ." (106; 40, 107). Thus, the story's two most important compositional points—the opening and the closure—reiterate the same principle of sharp distinction, alternation, and simultaneity of the narrative and the non-narrative domains.

Finally, the rule of dividing the fictional space—and world—into two counteractive and coexistent areas is suggested by Bykovsky's being associated with the person on the second floor through the motif of pacing the room. The motif consists of the following elements: "The prosecuting attorney rose and walked about the study" (101; 33); "While he was walking and meditating, Serezha climbed up and was standing with his feet on a chair by the side of the table and began to draw" (101; 33, 100); "When he had said good night and gone to bed, his father walked softly from corner to corner and smiled" (105; 39). The most palpable connection is the similar predicate of both subjects: "was walking/ pacing from corner to corner [khodil/shagal iz ugla v ugol]." This is the last phrase of the story and it emphasizes the general rule that in the broadest fictional space of the building all the inhabitants are at the same time at home and not at home, and neither the expressivist/ narrative nor the objectivist/non-narrative can provide the final solution to the tension between the two realms.

The ambiguity of "At Home" as regards the question of which is the winner—the objectivist or the expressivist, the non-narrative or the narrative—is an adequate artistic representation of the modern civilization that exists through this very tension. Returning to my parallel between Freud and Chekhov and the strong expressivist trends in Chekhov criticism, I can conclude that "At Home," by modeling but not solving the antagonism between the narrative and the non-narrative at the expense of one of them, offers a portrayal of modernity which we today accept more readily than Freud's rationalistic approach, though more reluctantly than our expressivist craving. And accept it we must, because this is also our world and our art.[21]

Notes

1. I traced only one article dedicated solely to this short story, that of Golstein. Paperny (66-69) does

one of the very few more detailed brief analyses of "At Home." Chekhov bibliographies do not contain titles dealing specially with this story. In both Russian/Soviet and Western criticism, "At Home" is mentioned *en passant* and usually as an illustration of the opposition between the child and the adult and/or art or narrative and reality; often the work is discussed in the context of Chekhov's so called "children" stories. See Toumanova 142-43; Bruford, 193, 195-96; Kramer 77-78; Rayfield 63; Berdnikov, for the "children" stories see 89-92, 96-100; Johnson 21-22, 37. For a summary of four general opinions on "At Home" from English-writing scholars, see Meister 60. For recent references to "At Home"—not necessarily connected with the father-child or/and reality-art relationship—see Tulloch 137; Popkin 125; Broide 531; Dieckmann 717; Polotskaia 990; and Jackson 7-8.

2. For some philosophical aspects of understanding as the revealing of some hidden meaning or of meaning as the expression of something covered see Heidegger; Ricoeur 1979, 35; Jaspers 191-92; and Jameson 69-71. For the linguistic characteristics of this question see Genette 1994, 326; and Todorov 1982b, 170-72, 178-79, and 286-87.

3. For Hermetism, Gnosticism, and their semiotic tradition see Eco 1976, 192-200; 1984b, 147-57; 1990, 8-22; and 1992, 26-38, 45-53.

4. See Jakobson *SW* 2: 703-4; for the philosophical aspect of the same problem, see also Ricoeur, 1984-1988 1: 54-64, esp. 57; and 1991, 140-43.

5. The opposition between a vertical system and horizontal particulars has historical meaning pointing to the conflict between objectification and expressivism. For instance, in Romanticism there is a strong tendency toward fragmentation (see McFarland). Nietzsche, one of the philosophical fathers of Modernism, is an atomistic, not systematic thinker (see Stern, esp. 126-38). The Modernist aesthetic and political avant-garde are disruptive in relation to the cultural and social tradition (see Calinescu 95-148; and Eco 1984c, 66-67). These philosophical and artistic trends are based on the principle of the particular, and are opposed to the systematic.

6. The English translations are taken from *Stories of Russian Life* and *The Black Monk and Other Stories*. Often I use collages of the two translations—neither of which is satisfactory—which I have reshaped to better render the original; I give credit to each translation used by listing its page number after the page of the original. Where page numbers are missing, this means that the translation is mine.

7. The hermeneutic term for the father's legal procedure is *subtilitas applicandi*: an ability to apply an interpretation to the present case (see Palmer 186–91). Yet this is not hermetic expressivism of the type I discuss for two reasons. First, in "At Home" law belongs to the non-narrative domain. Second, *subtilitas applicandi* is an application, not an interpretation in the sense of uncovering something covered.

8. Arthur Rimbaud is one of the very few who associate—like Serezha—*a* and black (Genette 1994, 318). For the agreement between the systems of color and sound see Jakobson 1972, 82-84.

9. For connections of Chekhov's plays with Modernism in its Modern Style/New Art version consult Kšicová. Szilard researches why Chekhov was considered to be one of the harbingers of Russian Symbolism. Gracheva (9, see also 6-11) observes that in "At Home" the passage "the sounds of an orchestra he represented as spherical, smoky spots; whistling as a spiral thread . . ." (103; 103) is an artistic equivalent of the scientific theories about associative perception.

10. For the more restricted mimophony of the consonants in comparison with the vowels see Genette 1994, 321-22.

11. Polakiewicz's article is one of the few studies on color in Chekhov and deals with twenty-three of his works, mainly short stories; "At Home" is not discussed, however.

12. For the musicality of Chekhov's works, see Kšicová 778, 788 n. 8.

13. For instance, Mallarmé (230, 233-34, 238) repeatedly refers to the musicality of Edgar Allan Poe's poetry which he interprets in accordance with his own ideas about the kinship between music and poetry. In this way, Mallarmé establishes the tradition of thinking of Poe as one of the fathers of French Symbolism. For Mallarmé's ideas on the relation between music and poetry see Wellek 4: 455-56.

14. For perspective as a geometry not of logic but of the eye see Losev 263-74.

15. The neuro-pathological and the medical utterances in Chekhov are well researched. Meve (42-112) studies the neuro-pathological in his work—the issue closest to my project. Tulloch maintains that "Chekhov's world view as an environmentalist doctor profoundly determined the thematic structure of his literary works. [. . .] his literary aesthetic was profoundly influenced by his positivism, inculcated as a medical student" (ix).

16. For the connections among symbolic activities as based on translation see Peirce 5: 284; Jakobson *SW* 2: 261; Ricoeur 1991, 151; and Eco 1984a, 24, 175-99.

17. For deduction, induction, and abduction see Eco qtd. in Bondanella 85; Eco 1976, 131-33, 148 n. 24; 1984a, 26; 1984c 54-58; and 1990, 29, 59, 148-49, 152-62.

18. See Eco 1984a, 193-98; 1990, 29, 37-43, 59-60, 148, 203-21; and 1992, 52, 65, 144-46, 148-51.

19. Booth, advocating "the ethics of narrative" (x) and "the validity and importance of ethical criticism" (xi), refers to "At Home" by underscoring the connection between narrative and real action (483-84), i.e., he comes close to Ricoeur's last feature of narrative identity—narrative self-constancy as applied in my analysis. Booth writes: "we all are equipped, by a nature (a 'second nature') that has created us out of story, with a rich experience in choosing which life stories, fictional or 'real,' we will embrace wholeheartedly" (484).

20. The reference of the sign is that to which the sign refers, whereas its sense is the mode of designation. Frege's famous example is: "The reference of 'evening star' would be the same as that of 'morning star' [i. e., the planet Venus], but not the sense" (57). For Frege's theory of sense and reference within his philosophy see Carl; for the reference and sense of names—which interests us here—see Carl 161-85.

21. The reader may raise objections to this finale: my initial presumption that the work of art and the real world are structurally homologous is Romantic (and neo-Platonic; see Todorov 1982b 153-54), and thus to refute Romanticism by building upon a Romantic axiom is a logical inconsistency. In reality, there is no violation of logic here because the assertion of structural homology is only an element of the Romantic aesthetics, but for us today it has a different meaning because its context is no longer Romantic. No matter how Romantic we still are, we can grasp the Romantic doctrine as a whole, which means that we are no longer part of it.

References

Aristotle. *Poetics. Critical Theory Since Plato.* Ed. Hazard Adams. Revised Edition. Fort Worth, TX: Harcourt Brace Jovanovich, 1992. 50-66.

Belyi, Andrei. "Chekhov." *Arabeski.* Moskva: Musaget, 1911. 395-408.

Berdnikov, G[eorgii] P[etrovich]. *A. P. Chekhov: Ideinye i tvorcheskie iskaniia.* Moskva, Leningrad: GIKhL, 1961.

Bondanella, Peter. *Umberto Eco and the Open Text: Semiotics, Fiction, Popular Culture.* Cambridge: Cambridge UP, 1997.

Booth, Wayne C. *The Company We Keep: An Ethics of Fiction.* Berkeley and Los Angeles; London: U of California P, 1988.

Broide, Edgar. "K problematike khristianskogo polifonizma v tvorchestve Chekhova. Mnogoglasie i edino-glasie." In Nohejl 1: 531-41.

Bruford, W[alter] H[orace]. *Chekhov and His Russia: A Sociological Study.* New York: Oxford UP, 1947.

Calinescu, Matei. *The Five Faces of Modernity: Modernism, Avant Garde, Decadence, Kitsch, Postmodernism.* Durham, NC: Duke UP, 1987.

Carl, Wolfgang. *Frege's Theory of Sense and Reference: Its Origins and Scope.* Cambridge: Cambridge UP, 1994.

Chekhov, A[nton] P[avlovich]. *Polnoe sobranie sochinenii i pisem v tridtsati tomakh.* 30 vols. Moskva: Nauka, 1974-1983.

———. [Tchekhoff, Anton]. "At Home." *Stories of Russian Life.* Trans. Marian Fell. New York: Charles Scribner's Sons, 1915. 26-40.

———. [Tchekhoff, Anton]. "At Home." *The Black Monk and Other Stories.* Trans. R. E. Long. New York: Frederick A. Stokes, 1916. 93-107. (The book is reprinted without the name of the translator as Anton Chekhov. *The Black Monk and Other Stories.* Gloucester, UK: Alan Sutton, 1985; "At Home" is on pp. 64-74.)

Dieckmann, Eberhard. "Das Čechov-Bild L. N. Tolstojs." In Nohejl 2: 714-22.

Eco, Umberto. *A Theory of Semiotics.* Bloomington: Indiana UP, 1976.

———. *The Role of the Reader: Explorations in the Semiotics of Texts.* Bloomington: Indiana UP, 1984a.

———. *Semiotics and the Philosophy of Language.* Bloomington: Indiana UP, 1984b.

———. *Postscript to* The Name of the Rose. Trans. William Weaver. San Diego, New York, London: Harcourt Brace Jovanovich, 1984c.

———. *The Limits of Interpretation.* Bloomington and Indianapolis: Indiana UP, 1990.

———, with Richard Rorty, Jonathan Culler, Christine Brooke-Rose. *Interpretation and Overinterpretation.* Ed. Stefan Collini. Cambridge: Cambridge UP, 1992.

Eikhenbaum, B[oris]. "O Chekhove." *O proze: Sbornik statei.* Leningrad: Izdatel'stvo "Khudozhestvennaia literatura," 1969. 357-70.

Frege, Gottlob. "On Sense and Reference." *Translations from the Philosophical Writings of Gottlob Frege.* Eds. Peter Geach and Max Black. Oxford: Basil Blackwell, 1966. 56-78.

Freud, Sigmund. *Dora: An Analysis of a Case of Hysteria.* Ed. Philip Rief. New York: Simon and Schuster, 1963.

Genette, Gérard. *Narrative Discourse Revisited.* Trans. Jane E. Lewin. Ithaca, NY: Cornell UP, 1988.

———. "Fiction and Diction." *Fiction and Diction.* Trans. Catherine Porter. Ithaca, NY and London: Cornell UP, 1993. 1-29.

———. *Mimologics.* Trans. Thaïs E. Morgan. Lincoln, NE and London: U of Nebraska P, 1994.

Georgiev, Nikola. "Tsitirashtiiat chovek v khudozhestvenata literatura." *Tsitirashtiiat chovek v khudozhestvenata literatura.* Sofiia [Sofia]: Universitetsko izdatelstvo "Sv. Kliment Okhridski," 1992. 5-83.

Golstein, Vladimir. "'At Home': At Home and Not at Home." *Reading Chekhov's Text.* Ed. Robert Louis Jackson. Evanston, IL: Northwestern UP, 1993. 74-81.

Gracheva, I. V. "A. P. Chekhov—estestvennik i khudozhnik." *O poetike Chekhova: Sbornik nauchnykh trudov.* [n. p.]: Izdatel'stvo Irkutskogo universiteta, 1993. 4-22.

Heidegger, Martin. "What Is Metaphysics?" In Kaufmann, 242-64.

Iser, Wolfgang. *The Implied Reader: Patterns of Communication in Prose Fiction from Bunyan to Beckett.* Baltimore, MD and London: Johns Hopkins UP, 1974.

Jackson, Robert Louis, ed. Introduction. *Reading Chekhov's Text.* Evanston, IL: Northwestern UP, 1993. 1-16.

Jakobson, Roman. *Child Language, Aphasia and Phonological Universals.* The Hague, Paris: Mouton, 1972.

———. *Selected Writings* [=*SW*]. 8 vols. The Hague, Paris: Mouton, 1971-1988.

Jameson, Frederic. "Postmodernism, or the Cultural Logic of Late Capitalism." *Postmodernism: A Reader.* Ed. Thomas Docherty. New York: Columbia UP, 1993. 62-92.

Jaspers, Karl. "Kierkegaard and Nietzsche." In Kaufmann, 185-211.

Johnson, Ronald L. *Anton Chekhov: A Study of the Short Fiction.* New York: Twayne, 1993.

Kaufmann, Walter, ed. *Existentialism from Dostoevsky to Sartre.* Revised and expanded. [n.p.]: A Meridian Book, 1975.

Kolarov, Radosvet. *Zvuk i smisŭl: Nabliudeniia nad fonichnata organizatsiia na khudozhestvenata proza.* Sofiia [Sofia]: Izdatelstvo na Bŭlgarskata akademiia na naukite, 1983.

Kramer, Karl D. *The Chameleon and the Dream: The Image of Reality in Čexov's Stories.* The Hague and Paris: Mouton, 1970.

Kšicová, Danuše. "Stil' Modern v dramaturgii Chekhova." In Nohejl 2: 777-89.

Losev, A[leksei] F[edorovich]. *Estetika Vozrozhdeniia.* Moskva: Mysl', 1982.

Mallarmé, Stéphane. *Oeuvres completes.* Eds. Henri Mondor et G. Jean-Aubry. Paris: Gallimard, 1945.

McFarland, Thomas. *Romanticism and the Forms of the Ruin: Wordsworth, Coleridge, and the Modality of Fragmentation.* Princeton: Princeton UP, 1981.

Meister, Charles W. *Chekhov Criticism: 1880 through 1986.* Jefferson, NC and London: McFarland, 1988.

Meve, E[vgenii] B[orisovich]. *Meditsina v tvorchestve i zhizni A. P. Chekhova.* Kiev: Gosudarstvennoe meditsinskoe izdatel'stvo SSSR, 1961.

Nohejl, Regine, ed. *Anton P. Čechov: Werk und Wirkung. Vorträge und Diskussionen eines internationalen Symposiums in Badenweiler im Oktober 1985.* Opera Slavica, Neue Folge, Band 18. 2 vols. Wiesbaden: Otto Harrassowitz, 1990.

Palmer, Richard E. *Hermeneutics.* Northwestern University Studies in Phenomenology and Existential Philosophy. Evanston: Northwestern UP, 1969.

Papernyi, Z[inovii] S[amoilovich]. *A. P. Chekhov: Ocherk tvorchestva,* 2nd ed. Moskva: GIKhL, 1960.

Peirce, Charles Sanders. *The Collected Papers of Charles S. Peirce,* 8 vols. Vols. 1-6, edited by Charles Hartshorne and Paul Weiss; vols. 7-8, edited by Arthur Burks. Cambridge, MA: Harvard UP, 1980.

Perkins, David. *Is Literary History Possible?* Baltimore, MD and London: Johns Hopkins UP, 1992.

Petrilli, Susan. "Toward Interpretation Semiotics." *Reading Eco: An Anthology,* Ed. Rocco Capozzi. Bloomington: Indiana UP, 1997. 121-36.

Polakiewicz, Leonard A. "Color in the Works of Anton Chekhov." In Nohejl 1: 147-81.

Polotskaia, E. A. "Rannii etap mirovoi izvestnosti Chekhova (1886-nach. 1923)." In Nohejl 2: 987-1000.

Popkin, Cathy. "Chekhov and the Pragmatics of Insignificance." In Nohejl 1: 123-45.

Prince, Gerald. *A Dictionary of Narratology.* Aldershot, UK: Scolar P, 1988.

Rayfield, Donald. *Chekhov: The Evolution of His Art.* New York: Barnes and Noble, 1975.

Ricoeur, Paul. *Main Trends in Philosophy.* New York and London: Holmes and Meier, 1979.

———. *Time and Narrative.* Trans. Kathleen McLaughlin and David Pellauer (vols. 1 and 2), Kathleen Blamey and David Pellauer (vol. 3). 3 vols. Chicago and London: U of Chicago P, 1984-1988.

———. "Mimesis and Representation." *A Ricoeur Reader: Reflections and Imagination.* Ed. Mario J. Valdés. Toronto and Buffalo, NY: U of Toronto P, 1991. 137-55.

Ritzer, George. *The McDonaldization of Society.* Revised New Century Edition. Thousand Oaks, California; London; New Delhi: Pine George Press, 2004.

Stern, J[oseph] P[eter]. *A Study of Nietzsche.* Cambridge, London, New York, Melbourne: Cambridge UP, 1979.

Szilard, Lena. "Chekhov i proza russkikh simvolistov." In Nohejl. 2: 791-804.

Taylor, Charles. *Hegel.* Cambridge, London, New York, Melbourne: Cambridge UP, 1974.

Todorov, Tzvetan. *Symbolism and Interpretation.* Trans. Catherine Porter. Ithaca, NY: Cornell UP, 1982a.

———. *Theories of the Symbol.* Trans. Catherine Porter. Ithaca, NY: Cornell UP, 1982b.

———. *Mikhail Bakhtin: The Dialogical Principle.* Trans. Wlad Godzich. Theory and History of Literature. Vol. 13. Minneapolis: U of Minnesota P, 1984.

Torgovnick, Marianna. *Gone Primitive: Savage Intellects, Modern Lives.* Chicago: U of Chicago P, 1990.

Toumanova, Nina Andronikova. *Anton Chekhov: The Voice of Twilight Russia.* New York: Columbia UP, 1937.

Tulloch, John. *Chekhov: A Structuralist Study.* New York: Barnes and Noble, 1980.

Wellek, René. *A History of Modern Criticism 1750-1950.* 8 vols. New Haven, CT: Yale UP, 1955-1992.

Wetzler, Birgit. *Die Überwindung des traditionellen Frauenbildes im Werk Anton Čechovs (1886-1903).* Europäische Hochschulschriften, Reihe XVI Slawische Sprachen und Literaturen Bd. 40. Frankfurt am Main, Bern, New York, Paris: Peter Lang, 1992.

White, Hayden. *Metahistory: The Historical Imagination in Nineteenth-Century Europe.* Baltimore, MD: Johns Hopkins UP, 1973.

———. *The Content of the Form: Narrative Discourse and Historical Representation.* Baltimore, MD and London: Johns Hopkins UP, 1987.

———. "'Figuring the Nature of the Times Deceased': Literary Theory and Historical Writing." *The Future of Literary Theory.* Ed. Ralph Cohen. New York: Routledge, 1989. 19-43.

FURTHER READING

Criticism

Blaisdell, Bob. "A Few Words of Advice from . . . Anton Chekhov." *The Writer* 117, no. 9 (September 2004): 26-30.

> Elucidates Chekhov's creative process and literary philosophy through an analysis of a letter to his older brother, Alexander.

Eekman, Thomas A., ed. *Critical Essays on Anton Chekhov.* Boston: G. K. Hall & Co., 1989, 208 p.

> Collection of essays focusing on Chekhov's short stories and plays.

Evdokimova, Svetlana. "The Curse of Rhetoric and the Delusions of Sincerity: Čechov's Story 'Misfortune.'" *Russian Literature* 35, no. 2 (15 February 1994): 153-69.

> Maintains that "Misfortune" was influenced by Tolstoy's *Anna Karenina* on the subjects of social constraints and sexual morality.

Flath, Carol A. "The Limits to the Flesh: Searching for the Soul in Chekhov's 'A Boring Story.'" *Slavic and East European Journal* 41, no. 2 (summer 1997): 271-86.

> Views "A Boring Story" as a tale about life and death.

Hardwick, Elizabeth. "The Disabused." *The New Republic* 223, no. 22 (27 November 2000): 24-7.

> Review of *Anton Chekhov: Stories,* translated by Richard Pevear and Larissa Volokhonsky, underscoring the ephemeral nature of several of the stories.

Kataev, Vladimir. *If Only We Could Know!: An Interpretation of Chekhov,* translated and edited by Harvey Pitcher. Chicago: Ivan R. Dee, 2002, 301 p.

Collection of essays written by a prominent twentieth-century Chekhov scholar.

Malcolm, Janet. *Reading Chekhov: A Critical Journey.* New York: Random House, 2001, 201 p.

Explores Chekhov's writing through encounters with modern Russians.

Polotskaya, Emma. "Chekhov and His Russia." In *The Cambridge Companion to Chekhov*, edited by Vera Gott-lieb and Paul Allain, pp. 17-28. Cambridge: Cambridge University Press, 2000.

Discusses Chekhov's portrayal of Russia.

Popkin, Cathy. "Paying the Price: The Rhetoric of Reckoning in Čechov's 'Peasant Women.'" *Russian Literature* 35, no. 2 (15 February 1994): 203-22.

Illuminates moral ambiguities in a Chekhov story.

Additional coverage of Chekhov's life and career is contained in the following sources published by Thomson Gale: *Beacham's Guide to Literature for Young Adults,* **Vol. 14;** *Contemporary Authors,* **Vols. 104, 124;** *Dictionary of Literary Biography,* **Vol. 277;** *DISCovering Authors*; *DISCovering Authors: British Edition*; *DISCovering Authors: Canadian Edition*; *DISCovering Authors Modules: Dramatists* **and** *Most-studied Authors*; *DISCovering Authors 3.0*; *Drama Criticism,* **Vol. 9;** *Drama for Students,* **Vols. 1, 5, 10, 12;** *Encyclopedia of World Literature in the 20th Century,* **Ed. 3;** *European Writers,* **Vol. 7;** *Exploring Short Stories*; *Literature and Its Times,* **Vol. 3;** *Literature and Its Times Supplement,* **Ed. 1;** *Literature Resource Center*; *Reference Guide to Short Fiction,* **Ed. 2;** *Reference Guide to World Literature,* **Eds. 2, 3;** *Short Stories for Students,* **Vols. 5, 13, 14;** *Short Story Criticism,* **Vols. 2, 28, 41, 51;** *Something About the Author,* **Vol. 90;** *Twayne's World Authors*; *Twentieth-Century Literary Criticism,* **Vols. 3, 10, 31, 55, 96; and** *World Literature Criticism.*

Marguerite de Navarre
1492-1549

(Born Marguerite d'Angoulême; also known as Marguerite d'Alençon) French short fiction writer, poet, and playwright.

INTRODUCTION

Although Marguerite wrote devotional poetry and several plays, she is best remembered for her collection of short fiction, *L'Heptaméron des Nouvelles* (1559; the *Heptaméron*). Modeled after Giovanni Boccaccio's celebrated short story cycle the *Decameron,* the *Heptaméron* is a series of seventy-two stories (alternately termed novellas, numbers, nouvelles, and tales) that were completed before Marguerite's death in 1549 but not published under her name until 1559. Narrated by a group of five ladies and five gentlemen staying in a French monastery for seven days, the stories explore themes of love, sexuality, morality, spirituality, and sixteenth-century gender roles. Critics regard the psychological, spiritual, and sexual complexity of the stories in the volume as a precedent for the nuanced approach of modern short fiction and maintain that the stories credit women with greater virtue and intelligence than fiction written by men during the same period.

BIOGRAPHICAL INFORMATION

The daughter of Charles d'Orleans, Marguerite was born into the royal family of France and raised with her brother, François, by her widowed mother in Angoulême. She was married to Charles, Duke of Alençon, at the age of seventeen. François became king in 1515, and Marguerite became involved in church reform, often meeting and corresponding with fellow reformers, such as John Calvin. In 1525 her husband was killed in a battle against Emperor Charles V of Spain, and her brother was captured during the same conflict. She subsequently traveled to Madrid and negotiated her brother's release. Two years later she married Henri d'Albret, King of Navarre—an independent kingdom situated between France and Spain. This union produced a daughter, Jeanne d'Albret, and a son who died shortly after his birth. Though Marguerite had been composing devotional poetry for a number of years, it was not until after the death of her son in 1530 that she allowed her work to be published. *Le Miroir de l'âme pécheresse* (1531; *The Glass of the Sinful Soul*) was condemned by church officials for its Protestant overtones. The poem would later be translated by the eleven-year-old future Queen Elizabeth I of England in 1544. Throughout the following decade Marguerite wrote and staged several plays. In 1547, following her brother François's death, Marguerite published a collection of poetry entitled *Les Marguerites de la Marguerite des princesses* (1547). She died on December 21, 1549 at her castle in Turbes, France. Her most famous work, the *Heptaméron,* was published posthumously.

MAJOR WORKS OF SHORT FICTION

Often compared to Boccaccio's *Decameron,* the *Heptaméron* contains seventy-two tales told over seven days; although Marguerite had intended to write ten tales for ten days—following the form of Boccaccio's book—she was only able to get as far as the second tale of the eighth day. The framework of the collection involves ten travelers—five men and five women of various ages and social roles—who become stranded at an abbey in the Pyrenees during a massive flood. To pass the time, they take turns telling stories; each day's stories revolve around a specific theme, such as "A Collection of Low Tricks Played by Women on Men and by Men on Women," which is the topic of the first day's tales. Each story concludes with a group discussion concerning the morality and contradictions inherent in the story. One of most frequently discussed tales, "Novella 21," chronicles a young woman's love for a man of noble heritage who was born out of wedlock. Her father's disapproval prevents the two from marrying, so she remains unwed until after her beloved's death. In this manner, the girl observes social custom and authority while simultaneously honoring her private passions. In another popular tale, "Novella 10," the widowed Lady Floride rejects the advances of a potential suitor, Amador, and devotes herself to the religious life. When Amador is captured in battle, he kills himself rather than denounce Christianity and Lady Floride. Marguerite explores gender norms in "Novella 69," which features an unfaithful husband who wears his mistress' smock to please her. The mistress then summons the man's wife so that they may ridicule him. In "Novella 59," a husband rebukes his wife for flirting with other men, but he is having an affair with the chambermaid. Bawdy humor is another aspect of the stories in the *Heptaméron.* In "Novella 11," Madame de Roncex soils her beautiful dress in the convent's filthy toilets, screaming so loudly that everyone present thinks a monk is raping her. When they break in to rescue her, they find Madame with her skirts hitched up and have a good laugh at her expense. "Novella 70" is often studied for its extreme depiction of the consequences of acting contrary to one's duty. The Duchess of Burgundy has a young nobleman and his lover killed after he rejects her advances. When the Duke learns of his wife's actions, he becomes so outraged that he stabs her.

Commentators agree that the stories in the *Heptaméron* touch on themes of love, marital fidelity, friendship, human weakness, and the conflict between the spiritual and the earthly life, particularly as it pertains to marriage. Both comic and tragic in tone, the stories also highlight the allure of sexual pleasure for women as well as men, the pitfalls of greed and vengeance, the sin of incest, and fidelity to Christian principles. Critics consider the stories to be a reflection of aristocratic, monastic, and lower-class life in the sixteenth century, and explore the inequities that arise from gender and socioeconomic differences. The dark side of the religious life is a prominent theme in the stories; church officials often betray their vows of chastity and poverty and are portrayed as crooked, lecherous, and duplicitous. Attempts to control women's sexuality through religious conventions, rigid social mores, rape, and seduction is a central and recurring motif in the *Heptaméron.* Several of the stories are viewed as autobiographical in nature, and critics have found parallels between the characters in the collection and figures from Marguerite's life: Marguerite' life is thought to inform both characters Floride and Parlamente; her husband, Henri, is regarded as the model for Hircan; and her mother, Louise of Savoy, has been compared to Oisille. Furthermore, a number of the stories in the collection incorporate political themes, such as the repercussions of treason and dishonor, the value of class and socioeconomic position, and revenge against tyrannical leaders.

CRITICAL RECEPTION

Acknowledged as Marguerite's best-known work, the *Heptaméron* is viewed as an insightful look at the attitudes, concerns, ideas, and language of the sixteenth century. After its initial appearance in a pirated and bowdlerized 1558 version entitled *Histoires des Amans Fortunez,* the tales were denounced as risqué and lacking in morality and literary merit. A year later, Marguerite's daughter published another version of the collection and named her mother as author; it wasn't until 1853 that the original manuscript was published with all seventy-two stories and the prologues. For several years, critics debated the authorship of the stories, with many arguing that the stories in the *Heptaméron* were not written by Marguerite, but by male authors of the period. They contended that Marguerite should be regarded as the editor of the collection, not the author. Yet most scholars now conclude that Marguerite is the author of the stories, citing the similarity of style and concerns from her poetry and plays. Modern criticism of the *Heptaméron* has focused on its treatment of gender differences, and the variations of sexual conflicts and resolutions in the stories. Many scholars have pointed out Marguerite's tendency to leave room for ambiguities in her moral lessons, as well as her sparing use of sensual description in her tales. Other critics have analyzed the narrative structure of the book, finding similarities to the *Decameron,* the anonymously composed *Cent nouvelles nouvelles,* and the thirteenth-century poem *Chastelaine de Vergi.* Marguerite's use of motifs from ancient mythology has also been acknowledged, specifically in regard to her utilization of the heroic archetype. Feminist critics often focus on Marguerite's portrayal of women as capable, intelligent, and calculating individuals. Her depiction of self-determining women is frequently viewed in light of Marguerite's belief in church reform, while the depiction of the stifling of such independence is interpreted as an early form of social criticism, prompting many scholars to cite Marguerite as a pioneer of feminist literature.

PRINCIPAL WORKS

Short Fiction

L'Heptaméron des Nouvelles [*Heptaméron*] 1559

Other Major Works

Le Dialogue en forme de vision nocturne (poetry) c. 1524-26
Le Miroir de l'âme pécheresse [*The Glass of the Sinful Soul*] (poetry) 1531
Le Mallade (play) c. 1535
L'Inquisiteur (play) 1536
Comédie des quatre femmes (play) 1542
Trop, Prou, Peu, Moins (play) 1544
Comédie sur le trespas du roy, (play) 1547
Les Dernières poèsies de Marguerite de Navarre (poetry) 1547
Les Marguerites de la Marguerite des princesses (poetry) 1547
La Navire (poetry) c. 1547-49
Les Prisons [*The Prisons of Marguerite de Navarre*] (poetry) c. 1547-49

CRITICISM

H. P. Clive (essay date 1970)

SOURCE: Clive, H. P. Introduction to *Tales from the* Heptaméron, by Marguerite de Navarre, edited by H. P. Clive, pp. 1-14. London: Athlone Press, 1970.

[*In the following excerpt, Clive describes the basic themes and structure of the* Heptaméron, *emphasizing its similarity to Boccaccio's* Decameron.]

THE *HEPTAMÉRON*

Marguerite de Navarre, who is celebrated for her generous patronage of many contemporary writers, was herself a prolific author. Her literary output comprises, notably, several long religious poems (e.g. *Le Miroir de l'âme pécheresse* and *Le Triomphe de l'Agneau*); some shorter spiritual pieces (e.g. the *Chansons religieuses*); a vast allegorical poem, *Les Prisons,* on the spiritual evolution of man; an important secular poem, *La Coche,* in the tradition of medieval debates on love; four biblical and seven non-biblical plays; and the collection of tales known as the **Heptaméron,** from the title chosen by Claude Gruget for the posthumous edition of 1559.[1]

Whilst the origin of the French *nouvelle* can be traced back to earlier medieval literature—e.g. the *lais* of Marie de France, the numerous moral tales associated with the Virgin Mary and with different saints, the *fabliaux,* and various stories written during the thirteenth and fourteenth centuries—its spectacular rise as an important prose genre in the fifteenth and sixteenth centuries is due primarily to the influence of the Italian *novella* and in particular of Boccaccio's *Decameron.* The great success of the latter work, of which a French version was completed by Laurent de Premierfait in 1414, inspired the composition, in or before 1462, of the *Cent Nouvelles Nouvelles,* the first major collection of French prose tales. The continuing popularity of the *Decameron* is attested by the publication, between 1485 and 1541, of at least eight editions of Laurent de Premierfait's version; but being based on a Latin text, it was often

faulty, and whatever merit it had possessed was destroyed by the many arbitrary alterations made in the printed editions. It is therefore not surprising that Marguerite should have commissioned a new translation, this time from the original Italian. The person she entrusted with this task was Antoine Le Maçon, a high government official[2] who had an excellent knowledge of Italian and considerable literary skill. His translation, published in 1545, evidently enjoyed a considerable success, for it was reissued at least ten times during the following fifteen years. A distinguished modern scholar, Henri Hauvette, considered it 'un des meilleurs ouvrages que le XVIe siècle nous ait légués dans le genre de la traduction'.[3]

It is not known when Marguerite began to compile her own collection—perhaps around the year 1540, although some critics have suggested earlier dates. What is certain, however, is that she was still engaged on her task shortly before her death, for **'Nouvelle LXVI'** describes an incident which occurred after her daughter's marriage to Antoine de Bourbon in October 1548. Brantôme relates that she worked on her stories during her travels: 'Elle composa toutes ses Nouvelles, la pluspart dans sa lityère en allant par pays. . . . Je l'ay ouy ainsin conter à ma grand'mère [Louise de Daillon], qui alloyt tousjours avecq' elle dans sa lityère, comme sa dame d'honneur, et luy tenoit l'escritoyre dont elle escrivoit. . . .'[4] The Prologue (ll. 324-5) shows clearly that, like Boccaccio, Marguerite proposed to write a hundred stories, arranged in ten sections or days. However, the various manuscripts as well as Gruget's edition of 1559 contain only seventy-two stories which can with certainty be attributed to Marguerite;[5] and while it is, of course, possible that others may still come to light, all the available evidence suggests that Marguerite failed to complete her collection. Gruget had presumably reached the same conclusion when he coined the title **L'Heptaméron des Nouvelles** . . . for his edition of 1559.

The general setting of Marguerite's tales recalls that of the *Decameron.* In both works ten men and women spend several days cut off from the outside world—in the *Decameron* because they wish to escape the plague raging in Florence, in the **Heptaméron** because the flooded mountain streams have made the roads impassable; they decide to while away their enforced seclusion by taking turns at narrating stories. Marguerite indicates that her collection, unlike Boccaccio's, contains no tale 'qui ne soit veritable histoire', and she takes great pains to convince the reader of the truthfulness of the stories: partly by giving them precise geographical locations and linking them with well-known contemporary persons; partly by stressing the speakers' personal acquaintance with the heroes of the *nouvelles* or their relatives ('il n'y a nul de vous qui ne connoisce les parens d'un coté et d'autre'[6]; 'qui auroit connu le personnage comme moy'"); and partly by repeated insistence on the factual basis of the stories ('asseurez vous que la chose est veritable'[8]; 'nous avons tant juré de dire verité, que je suis contraint . . . de ne la celer'[9]). However, despite Marguerite's claim that all the incidents are founded on fact, some are almost certainly based on existing stories; nevertheless the *Heptaméron* tales are by no means as derivative as some editors have suggested. In the first place, many supposed analogies with earlier literature turn out, on closer examination, to be far too slight to constitute proof of imitation. Furthermore, when Marguerite on occasion incorporates in her narrative details from earlier stories (e.g. in **'Nouvelle** xxxvi'), this does not necessarily disprove the authenticity of the events she describes. And even when she does appear to be adapting existing stories, she is as a rule not content simply to retell them, but considerably modifies them. The most important analogues which Marguerite can be expected to have known and which she seems to have followed are cited in the notes (pp. 160 ff.). The latter contain, however, no reference to Matteo Bandello's *novelle* which used to be considered one of the most prominent sources of the *Heptaméron*; it is now widely held that of the two writers Bandello, and not Marguerite, was the imitator.

The principal subject of the *Heptaméron* is love, in all its countless manifestations, from lechery and the ruthless gratification of sexual desire to romantic passion and selfless devotion. Marguerite is not concerned with describing the spiritual or psychological transformation which lovers may undergo as a result of their passion. Indeed, one speaker asserts that 'Amour ne change point le cueur, mais le montre tel qu'il est, fol aus folz, et sage aus sages'.[10] Many stories derive their interest from the clash of contrasting moral qualities: virtue combats depravity, continence joins battle with promiscuity, faithfulness opposes infidelity, chaste love is set beside wanton passion. In a wider sense, the *Heptaméron* presents different concepts of love which it illustrates in a variety of situations placed within the context of contemporary society. For the book is not a theoretical treatise on love, but a realistic portrayal of its various aspects set against the background of public morality; indeed, more than one story is concerned with lovers who infringe social conventions.

The *Heptaméron* is essentially a didactic work (there may well be a link between its didacticism and the author's emphasis on its complete truthfulness). The didactic purpose is most clearly reflected in the discussions in the course of which Parlamante and her friends[11] examine the moral implications of the stories. These conversations constitute one of the most interesting features of the book, for they offer the reader many a fascinating glimpse of the intellectual and social life of the period. Moreover, Marguerite has a marked flair for writing natural and lively dialogue; and the great variety of tone, which ranges from the light-hearted to the profoundly serious, ensures that the reader's interest is constantly engaged. Furthermore, Marguerite succeeds admirably in endowing each member of the group with a well-defined character which is skillfully developed in the discussions and convincingly sustained by the stories he or she chooses to relate. This individuality of character is most sharply delineated in the attitude adopted towards love. The two extreme positions are occupied by Dagoncin (or Dagoucin), a dreamily romantic idealist, inclined to turn women into spiritual abstractions, and Hircain (or Hircan), a cynical sensualist who regards continence as a violation of natural law, and dismisses a woman's preoccupation with her 'honour' as pure humbug and hypocrisy. If love for Hircain is a game which only two can play (though preferably with a frequent change of partners), it becomes essentially a solitary experience for Dagoncin whose primary concern is to love, irrespective of whether the affection is returned or not. The lover must refrain from any action which could tarnish his lady's honour, and this profound regard for her reputation may lead him to keep his passion a secret even from her, so as to protect her from any suspicions, however ill-founded, of improper conduct. Indeed, the desire to conceal one's love is, according to Dagoncin, evidence of its intensity; and the supreme proof of the lover's devotion is his readiness to die rather than disclose it. The fullest exposition of Dagoncin's ideal of *fin amor* will be found in the discussions of nouvelles 'viii' and 'liii.' Also of particular interest in this connection is **'Nouvelle ix'** in which Dagoncin tells of a young man who died as a result of his 'perfette amour' for a lady of higher birth.

If this latter story clearly illustrates Dagoncin's attitude to love, Hircain's reaction is no less characteristic: 'Voyla le plus grand fol dont j'oÿ jamais parler. Est il raisonnable, par ma foy, que nous mourons pour les femmes, qui ne sont faites que pour nous, et que nous craindons leur demander ce que Dieu leur commande nous donner?' Hircain's standpoint is thus diametrically opposed to that of Dagoncin. The latter approaches women with a chaste reverence in which one recognizes the courtly love ideal, refined and spiritualized by the admixture of a potent dose of neoplatonism. Hircain, for his part, views woman as a highly imperfect being, and he would have agreed with Rabelais's doctor Rondibilis that in creating her, Nature 'a eu esguard à la sociale delectation de l'homme et à la perpetuité de l'espece humaine plus qu'à la perfection de l'individuale muliebrité'.[12] Since it is woman's function to gratify man's sexual urges, he who fails to ask of her what is no more than his due acts not only foolishly, but also contrary to natural law. In any case, Nature has endowed woman with the same desire and capacity for sexual enjoyment as man. If, therefore, she refuses to accede to his wishes, her conduct is not virtuous but hypocritical, and motivated by a misguided regard for social conventions or by false pride;[13] most of the time, though, she is only too ready to be conquered by the male aggressor. The relationship between the sexes is frequently depicted by Hircain and the other men (with the exception of Dagoncin) as literally a battle, and effective use is made of military metaphors. 'Oncques place ne fut bien assaillie qu'elle ne fut prise', affirms Saffredan.[14] And Géburon, during a discussion of 'tactics' employed by men, remarks: 'J'ai autresfois veu assieger des places et prendre par force, pour ce qu'il n'etoit possible, ne par argent ne par menaces, faire parler ceus qui les gardoient. Car on dit que place qui parlamante est demy gangnée'.[15] All is fair in love and war!

The third main concept of love is expressed by Parlamante; and since it is quite probable that she represents Marguerite herself, her attitude is of particular interest. At first glance, Parlamante's views might appear to be very similar to Dagoncin's. Certainly, she closely echoes his own words in her famous platonic definition of lovers as persons 'qui cerchent en ce qu'ilz ayment quelque perfection, soit beauté, bonté, ou bonne grace, tousjours tendans à la vertu; et qui ont le cueur si haut et si honnette qu'ilz ne voudroient, pour mourir, le mettre aus choses basses, que l'honneur et la conscience repreuvent'.[16] However, despite certain obvious points of contact, Parlamante's attitude is essentially different from that of Dagoncin, whose rather sterile idealism she replaces with the realistic outlook of a devout Christian, conscious of living in an imperfect world. The fact is that Dagoncin's notion of a love, the object of which is the contentment of the lover rather than the creation of a spiritually enriching human relationship, is at once socially destructive and difficult to reconcile with Christian ethics. For Marguerite human love is not an end in itself, but a means to an end: the first necessary step in man's ascent towards communion with God: 'Encores ai je une opinion, que jamais homme n'aymera perfettement Dieu, qu'il n'ait perfettement aymé quelque creature en ce monde'.[17] Clearly there is no place on this Neoplatonic 'ladder of love' for a passion which in its most perfect form leads to the lover's death. Unlike Dagoncin, Marguerite views love as an essentially reciprocal relationship, and one, moreover, which has a physical as well as a spiritual aspect: 'L'ame au corps jointe et unie, c'est l'homme', declares La Sage in Marguerite's *Comédie jouée au Mont de Marsan*.[18] Marguerite is no ascetic who would deny the demands of the flesh. At the same time, it is understandable that she particularly stresses the spiritual side—if only in reaction to Hircain's views; for what she condemns above all is the concept of a love which has for its sole object the brutish gratification of physical desires. The *Heptaméron*, in its stories as well as in the discussions, repeatedly gives prominence to the tragic consequences of unbridled passion, just as it demonstrates more than once the destructive effect of romantic idealism.

It is characteristic of Marguerite's outlook that she should lay special stress on the happiness attainable in marriage. This idea contradicts the assumption underlying much medieval literature,[19] and in particular the courtly romances, that true love exists only outside marriage. The *Heptaméron* extols the delights of conjugal bliss—all the more pleasurable for being enjoyed with an untroubled conscience.[20] Parlamante defines the conditions for a happy marriage as follows: 'il faut que les personnes se soumettent à la volonté de Dieu, ne regardans ny à la gloire, ny à l'avarice, ny à la volupté, mais par une amour vertueuse et d'un consentement desirent vivre en l'etat de maryage, comme Dieu et nature l'ordonnent'.[21] Marriage is thus regarded as an institution established by divine and natural law; its object is the perfect union of two bodies and two souls. The *Heptaméron* contains several examples of married couples bound together by ties of deep affection and devotion.[22] The strongest praise of Christian marriage is offered by the pious Oysille: 'Dieu a mis si bon ordre, tant à l'homme qu'à la femme, que si l'on n'en abuse, je tien le mariage le plus bel et plus seur etat qui soit en ce monde.'[23] To appreciate fully the importance of Marguerite's eulogy of marriage, it must be set in the wider context of contemporary religious controversy. The Christian humanists had coupled their condemnation of ecclesiastical celibacy with praise of marriage; and the argument that it is an institution established by God and sanctioned by natural law is commonly encountered in anti-monastic treatises such as the *Encomium matrimonii* of Erasmus (1518).

Of the remaining men, Symontaut and Saffredan share in large measure Hircain's cynical views of women. It is true that Symontaut's outlook is tinged with a certain romanticism and that Saffredan professes some fine sentiments; however, Parlamante is clearly right in taking the former's fervent remarks with a grain of salt, and Saffredan blandly admits that his courtly manners are merely a stratagem, for 'nous couvrons notre Diable du plus bel Ange que nous pouvons'.[24] Géburon, on the other hand, does adopt a more genuinely sympathetic attitude towards women, but he acknowledges rather ruefully that it is mainly the result of his advancing years and failing powers.[25]

Among the ladies, Ennasuyte and Longarine are staunch feminists who delight in provoking the male interlocutors by their unfavourable comments on masculine behaviour. Nommerfide, the youngest, is also the gayest and her stories are invariably short and amusing. Though skilfully presented and carefully differentiated, these three women make a less forceful impression on the reader than Parlamante. Finally, the old and venerable Oysille, to whom the others look up as to a mother,[26] is of particular interest for her contribution to the other main theme of the *Heptaméron,* religion.

Although this subject is not as fully developed in this work as in Marguerite's spiritual poetry, the book does bring out at least two important aspects of Christian humanist thought: anti-clericalism and evangelism; the two are, of course, closely linked. Many of the stories expose the hypocrisy, avarice and sexual depravity of monks and friars. In this respect, the *Heptaméron* might be said to be merely continuing a well-established tradition, for satire of the clergy had become a stock feature of later medieval literature. This satire assumed, however, a fierce new topicality in the sixteenth century, which is strikingly reflected in the violent attacks made by the pious Oysille and other speakers on the clergy, and especially the mendicants. Equally significant is the fact that some of the most outspoken passages were toned down in Gruget's edition.

Parallel with the criticism of the morals of the clergy runs the theme of evangelism. The singular importance of the Bible, both as an inexhaustible source of spiritual nourishment and delight[27] and as the ultimate authority in matters of doctrine and belief,[28] is stressed throughout the *Heptaméron.* Each morning Oysille reads a passage from the Scriptures to the rest of the company. No less characteristic than the preeminent place accorded to the Bible are the references to private meditation and prayer,[29] and the emphasis on the supreme importance of faith which alone 'peut montrer et faire recevoir le bien que l'homme charnel et animal ne peut entendre'.[30] The fundamental aim of evangelism was to intensify the spiritual aspects of the Christian's life. Attention was accordingly focused on personal piety and private devotions rather than on formal public rituals, the edifying content of which was frequently obscured by pomp and ceremonial. Similarly, it was often felt that the hierarchical structure of the Church interposed too many intermediaries between man and God, thus making it more difficult for the believer to achieve direct communion with the divine. It should be added that Marguerite's writings displayed from the outset a marked inclination towards mysticism, which became increasingly stronger during the final years of her life.

At the same time, there is, of course, no suggestion in the *Heptaméron* or in Marguerite's other works of doing away with public worship, which in fact regulates the daily life of the company, for everyone attends mass and vespers. In the same way, Marguerite's anti-clericalism reflects her hostility towards contemporary abuses rather than any desire to abolish the monastic orders; at any rate, she is known to have given generous support to convents and to have spent religious re-

treats in them, notably a lengthy one at Tusson after the death of Francis I. In December 1549, at Odos, she was to receive the last rites from a Franciscan, Gilles Caillau.

It will be seen from this Introduction that the *Heptaméron,* in addition to its intrinsic literary merit, offers a fascinating insight into the intellectual trends and social mores of the period. It is a most entertaining work; it is also, and above all, a profoundly moral one.

Notes

1. For a representative anthology of Marguerite's writings, see H. P. Clive (ed.), *Marguerite de Navarre: Œuvres choisies* (New York, 1968). 2 vols.

2. Among other appointments, he held those of Receiver General of Finances in Burgundy and Royal Councillor.

3. H. Hauvette and J. Chouzet, 'Antoine Le Maçon et sa traduction du «Décaméron» (1545)', *Bulletin Italien,* viii (1908), 311.

4. L. Lalanne (ed.), *Œuvres complètes de Pierre de Bourdeille, seigneur de Brantôme* (Paris, 1864-82), viii, 126.

5. At least four others have been attributed to her: a story transcribed in BN Mss 1513 and Dupuy 736, as well as in Pierpont Morgan Library, New York, Ms 242; and the three stories substituted in Gruget's 1559 edition for Nouvelles 'XI,' 'XLIV' and 'XLVI' of the manuscripts. The authenticity of the first is uncertain, that of the other three very doubtful. The four tales are printed in the appendix to M. François's edition of the *Heptaméron* (Paris, 1943), together with a variant version of 'Nouvelle LII.'

6. 'Nouvelle IX.'

7. N'ouvelle XXVI.'

8. 'Nouvelle IX.'

9. 'Nouvelle XXXI.'

10. 'Nouvelle XXVI.'

11. Parlamante probably represents Marguerite herself. For the possible identity of the other characters, see the notes to the Prologue.

12. *Tiers Livre* xxxii.

13. See, for instance, 'Nouvelle XXVI.'

14. 'Nouvelle IX.'

15. 'Nouvelle XVIII.'

16. 'Nouvelle XIX.'

17. Ibid.

18. ll. 321-2.

19. Notably the stories illustrating the *mal mariée* theme.

20. 'Nouvelle XL.'

21. Ibid.

22. E.g. in Nouvelles 'XXVI,' 'LXIII,' 'LXVII.'

23. 'Nouvelle XXXVII.'

24. 'Nouvelle XII.'

25. 'Nouvelle XVI' (not included in this anthology).

26. Prologue, ll. 207-8.

27. In this connection, see especially Oysille's speech in the Prologue.

28. It constitutes 'la vraye touche pour sçavoir les paroles vrayes ou mensongieres' ('Nouvelle XLIV').

29. E.g. Prologue, ll. 237-48, 336-7.

30. 'Nouvelle XIX.'

Betty J. Davis (essay date 1978)

SOURCE: Davis, Betty J. "Part 1: The Storytellers." In *The Storytellers in Marguerite de Navarre's* Heptaméron, pp. 14-54. Lexington, Ky.: French Forum, 1978.

[*In the following essay, Davis details the individual characteristics of the ten storytellers in the* Heptaméron, *as well as their methods of intellectual inquiry.*]

«Ces personnages, nous voulons les connaître de plus près parce qu'éminemment vrais, éminemment vivants,» writes James Andon concerning the storytellers of the **Heptaméron** (p. 294). The most important aspect of the reality of the *devisants,* he feels, is their individuality (p. 294), the definitive proof of which he sees in «le maintien pendant plus de quatre cents pages de la personnalité propre de chaque devisant» (p. 301). Andon attributes their consistent nature to «la clarté de la conception artistique de l'auteur» (p. 294). Another factor which contributes to their consistency is the fact that they were based, most commentators agree, on real persons who were Marguerite's friends and members of her court.[1] «Marguerite,» says Yves Delègue, «a mis tous ses soins à déguiser sous des anagrammes plus ou moins transparentes des personnes réelles prises dans son entourage, et dont elle a fait ses Devisants. Aussi bien, ne cherchait-elle pas à les dissimuler vraiment, pour rendre plus vraisemblables encore ses récits; et si le doute subsiste de nos jours sur l'identité de tel ou tel d'entre eux, il ne devait sûrement en être de même à l'époque» (p. 34).

While Marguerite has given us few concrete details about the *devisants,* the personality of each storyteller is conveyed by his or her own words and actions and by the reactions of the other members of the group. Before turning to the *devisants* individually, however, let us consider certain characteristics common to all. They are independent, determined, and individualistic, as shown both in their actions in the Prologue and in their reactions to the stories they tell each day. It was because of their «diverses opinions» on how best to proceed that they separated after leaving Cauterets. They continue to express their «diverses opinions» in the debates following the stories, allowing us to consider from many vantage points opposing and contrasting views on love, honor, marriage, fidelity, religion, and virtue.

The *devisants* have a common basis for discussing these questions, for all have read the Scriptures (Prol., p. 8), probably indicating an evangelical or reform bias within the group, and Boccaccio's *Decameron* (Prol., p. 9), which had recently been translated from Italian into French by Antoine Le Maçon. They also seem to be familiar with various Neoplatonic theories in vogue at that time, and there are several references to Plato's *Republic* and to concepts found elsewhere in Plato's writings, such as the myth of the Androgyne.

The *devisants* have a common social background as well. They are described as «seigneurs et dames francoys» (Prol., p. 1), members of the upper classes, or, as Oisille says, «Nous qui sommes de bonnes maisons» (I, **"Novella 2,"** p. 21). They have powerful connections. The abbot of Notre-Dame de Serrance, for instance, dared not refuse them lodging «pour la craincte du seigneur de Bearn, dont il sçavoit qu'ilz estoient bien aimez» (Prol., p. 6).

The *devisants* approach life in an active, confident manner. When confronted with difficulties, danger, or natural disasters, they do not passively accept the situation and let nature take its course. They set out to find solutions to their problems and, if necessary, to alter their environment. They make their way through treacherous mountain roads and attempt to fight their way through violent and deadly currents. When they reach Notre-Dame de Serrance and learn that they will not be able to proceed until the waters subside, they decide to build a bridge. Fortunately, they possess the financial resources necessary, for the abbot of Notre-Dame de Serrance, although he supplied workmen, «n'y meist pas ung denier, car son avarice ne le permectoit» (Prol., p. 6).

Once the *devisants* have made arrangements to have a bridge built, they are confronted with another problem—what to do with themselves in the meantime. Accustomed to active and amusing pastimes in their daily lives—«la chasse et la vollerye» for the men and «leur mesnaige, leur ouvraige et quelquesfois les dances où elles prennent honneste exercice» for the women (Prol., p. 8)—they are easily bored. Some even say that without pleasant activities and diversion, they would fall ill or die. Once again, they consider the problem and come up with a solution: the devotional exercises and story-telling sessions of the framework narrative of the *Heptaméron.*

OISILLE

Oisille is the first of the ten to whom we are introduced as she makes her way over difficult roads to the pilgrimage station of Notre-Dame de Serrance.[2] «Mais une dame vefve, de longue experience, nommée Oisille, se delibera d'oblier toute craincte par les mauvais chemins jusques ad ce qu'elle fut venue à Nostre-Dame de Serrance» (Prol., p. 2). This introductory sentence contains several important details about Oisille: her social class («une dame»), her marital status («vefve»), her age («de longue experience»), and her name («nommée Oisille»). The words «de longue experience» imply not only age, but wisdom accumulated over a long period of time. The sentence also shows us something of her character. Her willingness to put fear aside indicates that she is intrepid, despite her age, and determined to reach a goal once set, no matter what the difficulty.

In the following sentence, we see that Oisille retains a lively curiosity in the world about her and that she possesses a practical turn of mind. She has resolved to make her way to Notre-Dame de Serrance, not because of any superstitious beliefs, but as a tourist eager to visit a famous site. She is also convinced that the monks would know how to escape from danger, if anyone would:

> Non qu'elle fut si supersticieuse qu'elle pensast que la glorieuse Vierge laissast la dextre de son filz où elle est assise pour venir demorer en terre deserte, mais seullement pour envye de veoir le devot lieu dont elle avoit tant oy parler; aussy qu'elle estoit seure que s'il y avoit moyen d'eschapper d'un dangier, les moynes le debvoient trouver.
>
> (Prol., p. 2)

This sentence also gives an indication of Oisille's views on religion, which are stated by the narrator in a positive, factual manner. There is no doubt that Oisille believes that the Virgin Mary, «la glorieuse Vierge,» is seated in the place of honor at the right hand of her son. While the Virgin is respected and honored, she apparently remains remote from the lives of men. Oisille, or at least the narrator, equates the views of those who believe otherwise with superstition. The comment on the monks' ability to find a method of extricating themselves from danger, while possibly an expression of admiration for their resourcefulness, may also be regarded

as an anticlerical statement. Although Oisille does not believe that we should judge all priests by the transgressions of some of their number (III, **"[Novella] 22,"** p. 185), she severely condemns corrupt practices of the clergy, particularly in matters of sexual license. She goes so far as to say that those who make a mockery of their vows should be burned alive (III, **"23,"** p. 193).

Oisille is then further characterized physically and morally; although old and heavy, she is determined and persistent in the face of great difficulty: «Et feit tant qu'elle y arriva, passant de si estranges lieux et si difficilles à monter et descendre que son aage et pesanteur ne la garderent poinct d'aller la pluspart du chemin à pied» (Prol., p. 2). The extent of the difficulty is shown by the heavy toll it takes of her servants and horses. «Mais la pitié fut que la pluspart de ses gens et chevaulx demorerent mortz par les chemins et arriva à Serrance avecq ung homme et une femme seullement, où elle fut charitablement receue des religieux» (Prol., p. 2). The impression of hardship is reinforced by the report of an aged monk who shared her adventure and who had made the same journey annually for many years. He said that he had come through «les plus mauvais chemins qu'il avoit jamais faict» (Prol., p. 5).

Oisille, described by the monk as «une antienne vefve» (Prol., p. 5), is respected by those at Notre-Dame de Serrance not only for her age, but for her wisdom and her experience. In answer to Parlamente's request for advice on how to pass their days of enforced confinement, Oisille proposes Scripture reading, to which she attributes her own joy, health, and tranquillity. Her choice of active Scripture reading and spiritual contemplation may be seen as enthusiastic and joyful, a positive choice made, not from a lack of other experience, but after having tried and rejected the other distractions which the world has to offer: «le passetemps auquel me suis arrestée long temps après avoir cherché en tous autres, et non trouvé contentement de mon esprit» (Prol., p. 8). It may also be seen as a last resort to which she has turned after all else has failed. In any case, Oisille's lifelong search for a remedy for her troubles has led her to the Scriptures, which she recommends with evangelical fervor to those around her.

Oisille's religious beliefs combine adherence to the traditional doctrines and practices of the Catholic Church with attitudes strongly indicative of sympathy for the reform movement. Traditional elements include a belief in the Trinity (VII, **"70,"** p. 418), formal worship, and the sacraments, including communion and confession. Her sympathy for the reform movement is evident in her belief in the right of the laity to read and interpret the Scriptures without reference to canonical authority and in her belief in a personal Savior accessible to believers without any intermediary (Prol., p. 7). She not only considers the Bible the ultimate source of truth, but advocates frequent Bible reading as a defense against priestly misinterpretations (V, "**44**," p. 304). Although many advocates of reform stressed faith to the exclusion of works, Oisille acknowledges the importance of both. She finds such practices as lighting candles in God's honor acceptable provided they are an expression of faith (VII, "**5**," p. 389). She does not, however, approve of sumptuous displays in houses of worship meant to buy pardon for one's sins. Rather, she believes that we should honor God with a contrite heart, true repentance, and a virtuous life as Christ has taught us (VI, "**55**," p. 347).

Since Oisille often refers to God by one of His attributes, usually accompanied by elaborate descriptions of His relationship with the faithful, we are able to form a well-rounded picture of her conception of God. She sees God as perfect (V, "**48**," p. 317), omnipotent (III, "**22**," p. 186), full of goodness (Prol., p. 7; IV, "**32**," p. 345), love (Prol., p. 8; VII, "**70**," p. 418), and mercy (VII, "**55**," p. 389). He is our Creator (III, "**22**," p. 186; IV, "**34**," p. 253), our Redeemer (III, "**22**," p. 186), and the source of all virtue (VII, "**67**," p. 394). He is our consolation in this life and our Savior in the life hereafter (III, "**22**," p. 186). Oisille considers grace a gift of God, «laquelle n'est jamais refusée à ceulx qui en foy la requierent» (Prol. VII, p. 370), a gift which God freely bestows upon the faithful without regard to wealth or station (I, "**2**," p. 21).

On religious matters, Oisille speaks with the authority of a lay preacher in a manner strongly influenced by her frequent reading of the Scriptures. She takes her responsibility for the morning's Bible reading and commentary very seriously, rising early day after day to prepare her lessons. She acquits herself quite well of the task according to the narrator's glowing descriptions of the company's favorable reactions to her lessons (Prol. III, p. 157; Prol. IV, p. 282; Prol. VI, p. 328; Prol. VII, p. 370; Prol. VIII, p. 421). Oisille, for her part, is an enthusiastic participant in the afternoon's diversions. On the first day, she even fails to inform the others that the bell for vespers has rung, «car la devotion d'oyr la fin du compte estoit plus grande que celle d'oyr vespres» (I, "**10**," p. 85).

Oisille's attitudes on love, sex, and marriage are in keeping with her religious beliefs and the teachings of the Church. She warns that sin leads to death (VIII, "**72**," p. 427) and feels that there can be no true pleasure if the conscience is not at peace (IV, "**39**," p. 247). She attributes sins of the flesh, such as homosexuality (IV, "**34**," pp. 253-54),[3] incest (IV, "**33**," p. 249), and promiscuity (V, "**49**," p. 322), to spiritual separation from God, rejection of His teachings, or possession by the devil: «la personne delaissée de Dieu se rend pareille à celluy avecq lequel elle est joincte; car, puis que ceulx qui adherent à Dieu ont son esperit avec eulx,

aussi sont ceulx qui adherent à son contraire; et n'est rien si bestial que la personne destituée de l'esperit de Dieu» (V, "**49**," p. 322). Yet, in some cases, her views are more practical than moral. She is more tolerant of faults than of scandal and considers maintaining the proprieties more important than avoiding sin (III, "**25**," p. 207). Her moral judgments are also colored by class prejudice. She describes the case of a highborn lady who took a mule driver for a lover as a «grande villenye» (II, "**20**," p. 155), not because the lady transgressed the moral law, but because she took a lover so far below her on the social scale.

Oisille's conception of marriage is far removed from the medieval view of marriage as a condition inferior to celibacy. She considers marriage an honorable estate instituted by God, «le plus beau et le plus seur estat qui soit au monde» (IV, "**37**," p. 269). As did most men and women of her day, she favors arranged marriages and heartily disapproves of persons so lacking in respect for their parents as to marry «à leur volunté» (IV, "**40**," p. 277). On the other hand, she does not consider marriage a simple business transaction, but a sharing of the good and evil fortune life has to offer (VI, "**54**," p. 343). Nevertheless, she warns against great passion in marriage or attaching too much importance to earthly love, which might distract us from seeking the eternal love of God (VII, "**70**," p. 418).

Although Oisille praises chastity and urges women to remain faithful to their husbands no matter what the provocation, she believes that infidelity is common among women as well as men (IV, "**32**," p. 245). She is well aware of the force of sexual attraction and the overpowering nature of sexual desire: «trouver chasteté en ung cueur amoureux,» she remarks, «c'est chose plus divine que humaine» (I, "**9**," p. 53). She admires those whose spirits control their physical desires and considers those who are lustful no better and sometimes worse than animals. Still, in spite of human frailty, she believes that God will protect and strengthen those who in humility turn to Him.

Three main possibilities have been proposed for the identity of Oisille—Marguerite de Navarre; Marguerite's mother, Louise de Savoie; and Louise de Daillon, the sénéschale de Poitou and Marguerite's *dame d'honneur*. Génin noted the important part Oisille plays in organizing and directing each day's activities and concluded that Marguerite had cast herself in that role.[4] Le Roux de Lincy, observing that the name Oisille is almost an anagram of Louise, proposed Louise de Savoie.[5] Félix Frank suggested another possibility, Louise de Daillon.[6]

Those who identified Oisille with Marguerite had to account for the fact that Marguerite was not a widow when she wrote the ***Heptaméron*** and was not of an extremely advanced age. Those who opted for Louise de Savoie had to justify the divergence between the character of Oisille as presented in the **Heptaméron** and that of the historical Louise de Savoie. Nevertheless, the identification of Oisille with Louise de Savoie prevailed and stood essentially unchallenged from the time Jourda's thesis (*Marguerite d'Angoulême*) was published in 1930 until the question was reopened by A. J. Krailsheimer and Joseph Palermo in articles published in 1968 and 1969, respectively. Palermo returned to the identification of Oisille with Marguerite, Krailsheimer to that of Louise de Daillon, for whom he builds a strong case. Although he considers the anagram sound, Louise de Savoie, who died in 1531, was most likely not the original of Oisille. The *devisants,* he feels, were actually part of the same circle at the time Marguerite composed her collection of stories (probably around 1546). Louise de Daillon, whose character seems to be in keeping with that of Oisille, was Marguerite's «constant companion from about 1535 to the end» (p. 87). Indeed, according to Brantôme, it was his grandmother, Louise de Daillon, who held Marguerite's writing table as she worked on her collection of tales.[7] From the evidence available, Louise de Daillon seems the best choice for the original of Oisille.

HIRCAN AND HIS GROUP

We meet the next group of characters under very romantic circumstances, including a daring midnight rescue in the wilds of the Pyrénées. Two young Frenchmen had been among those at the baths of Cauterets, not so much because they needed to take the waters, but rather «pour accompaigner les dames dont ils estoient serviteurs» (Prol., p. 2). When the ladies and their husbands (for the ladies were married) left Cauterets, the two young men followed secretly. One might they were awakened by a great commotion. Upon learning that their lady loves are under attack by a brigand and his companions, they take up their arms and rush off to save their ladies or die in the attempt. In true romantic fashion, «ilz estimoient la mort plus heureuse que la vie après elles» (Prol., p. 3). They find the two married gentlemen and their servants outnumbered by the evildoers and fighting a losing battle. The sight of their ladies «cryans et plorans,» however, inspires them with such courage that in epic fury they descend on the brigands and rout the wicked aggressors: «comme deux ours enraigés descendans des montaignes, frapperent sur ces bandoulliers tant furieusement qu'il y en eut si grand nombre de mortz que le demourant ne voulut plus actendre leurs coups mais s'enfouyrent où ilz sçavoient bien leur retraicte» (Prol., p. 3).

Not only did many servants die fighting the bandits (servants were considered expendable), but the husband of one of the ladies died of his wounds. After the slain gentleman has been buried, the names of the survivors are revealed. «Et s'il vous plaist sçavoir le nom des trois gentilz hommes, le maryé avoit nom Hircan et sa femme Parlamente et la damoiselle vefve Longarine et le nom des deux gentilz hommes, l'un estoit Dagoucin et l'autre Saffredent» (Prol., p. 3). The surviving husband, who came through the battle relatively unscathed, invited the two young Frenchmen to join his party, and they were only too happy to oblige. We are not told the reactions of the ladies or whether they were even aware that the two young gentlemen were their devoted admirers. Nor are we told which gentleman is the *serviteur* of which lady.

Before engaging in extramarital matchmaking, it would be advisable to define the word *serviteur.* As used by Marguerite de Navarre, the word seems to denote a gentleman who has dedicated himself to the service of a lady. The lady, however, is not necessarily aware of his devotion. In most cases, the favors accorded by the lady do not extend beyond allowing her *serviteur* to enjoy the pleasure of her company and her conversation. The relationship, in any case, is a less intimate one than implied by the word *ami,* which meant much more than friend and often meant lover. The relationship of a *serviteur* to his *dame* is in many ways like that of a servant to his mistress, subservient and respectful, but the possibility is not excluded that the relationship may one day become more intimate. No matter how sublimated the desire may be, a *serviteur,* consciously or unconsciously, espouses the proverb cited by Saffredent: «De bien servir et loyal estre, / De serviteur l'on devient maistre» (I, **"10,"** p. 84). Even Dagoucin, whose conception of love seems detached and spiritual, acknowledges the existence of hope as an element in sustaining the *serviteur*'s interest and inspiring him to valor and virtue.

PARLAMENTE

Intelligent, well-read, and thoughtful, Parlamente is a determined defender of the honor of her sex and a staunch champion of virtue and morality. Her name is perhaps a reference to her reputation for speaking at length or to the high court, the Parlement, where matters of importance were discussed and decided. It may be that Parlamente speaks for Marguerite, for most critics agree in naming Marguerite herself as the original of Parlamente.[8]

Parlamente, «la directrice en second de cette petite société» (Darmesteter, p. 224), shares with Oisille the responsibility for organizing the activities at Notre-Dame de Serrance. «Jamays oisifve ne melencolicque» (Prol., p. 6), she formulates the company's need for diversion and turns to Oisille for advice. She is then herself designated to select the afternoon's more secular pastime, for, says Hircan, «elle sçaura mieulx que nul autre dire celluy où chascun prendra plaisir» (Prol., p. 9). Parlamente's suggestion that they take up a proposal once made by the Dauphin, the Dauphine, and Madame Marguerite to create a French version of Boccaccio's *Decameron* reveals an intimate knowledge of the French court and a familiarity with the literary favorites of her day.

From the Prologue we learn that Parlamente is married to Hircan. She is also the recipient of the attentions of either Dagoucin or Saffredent, and Simontault is a longtime admirer as well (Prol., pp. 2-3, 5). Although at the center of several romantic relationships in the *Heptaméron,* Parlamente is not in the first blush of youth, for she speaks of «jeunes dames» as though she were somewhat older (V, **"56,"** p. 352), just as Hircan speaks of «jeunes gens» (VI, **"57,"** p. 356).

Parlamente sets high standards of conduct for herself and other women. For all her admirers, she is in many ways the incarnation of *La Belle Dame sans mercy,* whom she quotes on two occasions as an excellent example for women to follow (II, **"12,"** p. 95; VI, **"56,"** p. 352). Rigid and uncompromising in her sense of morality, Parlamente refuses to forgive or even tolerate sin, especially sexual transgressions. She would see sin severely punished and is even vindictive in her attitude. She heartily approves of the husband who forced his faithless wife to drink from the skull of her dead lover and keep his bones in her armoire. «Je trouve,» says Parlamente, «ceste punition autant raisonnable qu'il est possible; car, tout ainsy que l'offense est pire que la mort, aussy est la pugnition pire que la mort» (IV, **"32,"** p. 245). Death, in her opinion, is a suitable punishment as well. She applauds a betrayed husband who poisoned his unfaithful wife and asserts that «ceste pauvre femme-là porta la peyne que plusieurs meritent» (IV, **"36,"** p. 264). She suggests that women should punish men who hold unfavorable opinions of their sex by depriving them of their company (II, **"20,"** p. 156; III, **"24,"** p. 201) and would punish severely priests who violate their vows (V, **"41,"** p. 286). Words which appear frequently in her vocabulary are «justice,» «juger,» «juges,» «loy,» and «avocats.» Others recognize her tendency to be judgmental and legalistic in her thinking, and Ennasuitte and Hircan, at least, do not like it (IV, **"35,"** p. 261; IV, **"36,"** p. 264). Although she is not materialistic, Parlamente's vision of life is often expressed in financial terms, in terms of profit and loss.

Parlamente possesses a philosophical turn of mind which is evident in her long and detailed analysis of the Neoplatonic theory of human love as a God-given means of awakening in man a longing for the beauty, virtue, and perfection of his Creator (II, **"19,"** p. 151). Her philosophical inquiries, however, are strongly influenced by Christian ethics. She has no sympathy for agnostic or secular philosophical speculation. She maintains that faith is necessary for attaining knowledge of life's mysteries and warns against the danger of inquiry without faith (II, **"19,"** p. 152). She sees the Word of God as «la vraye touche pour sçavoir les parolles vraies ou mensongeres» (V, **"44,"** p. 304) and is totally opposed to those who would consider the Scriptures in the same way they consider other ancient writings (V, **"44,"** pp. 303-04).

Although Parlamente admits that there are some good men in the priesthood, she stands with the advocates of reform in her disapproval of the immorality, hypocrisy, and worldliness of many clergymen and in her stress on the Word of God as revealed in the Scriptures as the ultimate source of truth. She feels that those priests whose lives do not conform to the teachings of the Scriptures should be exposed to public shame. «Je croy . . . que envers chascun se doibt user le conseil de l'Evangile, sinon envers ceulx qui scandalisent tout le monde. Et me semble que c'est grand merite de les faire congnoistre telz qu'ilz sont, afin que nous ne prenons pas ung doublet pour ung bon rubis» (V, **"41,"** p. 286). The Le Hir edition continues with a warning about the sexual abuses of the clergy: «et nous donnons garde de leurs séductions à l'endroit des filles, qui ne sont pas tousiours bien avuisées» (p. 245). This warning accurately reflects Parlamente's views on the dangers women face in associating with the clergy. «Il me semble,» she says elsewhere, «que une femme estant dans le lict, si ce n'est pour luy administrer les sacremens de l'Eglise, ne doibt jamais faire entrer prebstre en sa chambre; et quant je les y appelleray, on me pourra bien juger en danger de mort» (III, **"23,"** p. 193).

Women should be extremely prudent in their dealings with men in any case, Parlamente warns, and should be on guard against their wickedness and lies. While the love of women is founded on God and honor, she says, the love of men is based on pleasure. Furthermore, the honor of men is fundamentally in opposition to the laws of God. «Votre plaisir,» she says of men, «gist à deshonorer les femmes, et vostre honneur à tuer les hommes en guerre: qui sont deux poinctz formellement contraires à la loy de Dieu» (III, **"26,"** p. 221). Although certain women, like men, may seek pleasure in love, Parlamente reasons that by so doing they have betrayed the essential nature of their sex:

> . . . celles qui sont vaincues en plaisir ne se doibvent plus nommer femmes, mais hommes, desquelz la fureur et la concupiscence augmente leur honneur; car ung homme qui se venge de son ennemy et le tue pour ung desmentir en est estimé plus gentil compagnon; aussy est-il quant il en ayme une douzaine avec sa femme. Mais l'honneur des femmes a autre fondement: c'est doulceur, patience et chasteté.
>
> (V, **"43,"** p. 301)

Even though Parlamente at times lauds submissiveness and patience in women, at others, she finds these characteristics offensive (IV, **"38,"** p. 271). She asserts that men have responsibilities in marriage as well as women. The husband should be the head of the household, she believes, but he should neither abandon his wife nor treat her ill (IV, **"37,"** p. 269). She feels that marriage is most likely to be successful if those involved «se submectent à la volunté de Dieu ne regardent ny à la gloire, ni à l'avarice, ny à la volupté, mais par une amour vertueuse et du consentement des parens, desirent de vivre en l'estat de mariage, comme Dieu et Nature l'ordonnent» (IV, **"40,"** p. 280).

Parlamente, described as «une femme de bien» and «une femme qui n'est poinct scandaleuse» (III, **"26,"** p. 220), is extremely concerned with questions of honor, conscience, virtue, and reputation. She herself is called «la plus saige de la compaignye» (Prol. IV, p. 237) and claims that she is not even interested in knowing any other kind of woman (V, **"43,"** p. 301). Although she does not feel that a woman can be considered virtuous if she does not hold firm until the very end (VII, **"62,"** p. 379), she is adamant in upholding the honor of her sex and does not allow men to generalize from the misdeeds of one woman. Nevertheless, she recognizes the weakness of the creature and warns against pride and overconfidence in one's own ability to resist evil, for she fears the power of the passions and feels that they must be controlled. She, who is praised for her own «bon sens» (Prol. III, p. 157), admires those whose reason, good sense, and self-control dominate their desires.

Hircan

Hircan has been described as a «grand seigneur sensuel et sarcastique» (Darmesteter, p. 212), «brillant, mais volage,»[9] «brutal, sensuel et grossier,»[10] «un homme de morale très relâchée, aimant fort le plaisir & les dames qui répondent à ses avances» (Dillaye, I, 265). He has also been called «the second most attractive person in the *Heptaméron*» (after Parlamente).[11] The others consider Hircan full of «malice» and «finesses» (I, **"6,"** p. 47), a reputation which he accepts with good humor and even pride.

Hircan admires those who are clever, brave, and audacious in the pursuit of their goals and condemns those who are stupid, timid, and fearful. One of the company's most forceful advocates of the pleasures of the flesh, he feels that a man's honor depends on sexual successes. Women, he believes, were made for man's pleasure; if women are not cooperative, men should not hesitate to use «finesses et forces» (II, **"14,"** p. 115).

Although Hircan sees no differences in the desires of men and women, he espouses the double standard, feeling that infidelity is the greatest injury a woman can inflict on a man (IV, **"36,"** p. 264), but maintaining that men who no longer love their wives need not remain faithful (VI, **"59,"** p. 365); nor does he repent of his own infidelities, about which he comes very close to boasting (III, **"25,"** p. 207). He does try to conduct his affairs discreetly and without scandal and hopes that his wife would do the same (III, **"26,"** pp. 220-21).

Hircan sees no harm in sharing physical pleasure with people of any social class and readily excuses the upper class lady who took a mule driver as her lover (II, **"20,"** p. 155). He draws the line at marriage, however. Believing that class distinctions should be preserved, he condemns even those of the minor nobility who dare to marry above their station and refuses to condone the actions of a handsome and virtuous gentleman who married a lady of a more important family than his own, «chose qui en rien ne luy apartenoit» (III, **"22,"** p. 278).

Hircan's indulgence for sexual activity outside the bonds of marriage extends to those in religious orders. He is tolerant of priests who violate their vows of celibacy since he believes that they are no different from other men in their sexual needs and desires (V, **"41,"** p. 285; VI, **"55,"** p. 347). He, nonetheless, has harsh words for priests on many scores and, in particular, condemns them for their hypocrisy, avarice, and lies (IV, **"33,"** p. 249; VI, **"55,"** p. 347; VI, **"56,"** p. 351). They are, he says, «ceux qu'on ne doibt jamais veoir que en l'eglise» (V, **"46,"** p. 310). Those who invite them into their homes and fall victim to their lustful desires are duly punished for their own stupidity (III, **"23,"** pp. 192-93; V, **"46,"** p. 310).

Although Hircan expresses deep veneration for the Holy Communion (VII, **"61,"** p. 376), he is rather nonchalant about confession. «Il est bien difficile,» he says of love-making, «de se repentir d'une chose si plaisante. Quant est de moy, je m'en suys souventesfois confessé, mais non pas gueres repenty» (III, **"25,"** p. 207). Hircan, whose conception of the Almighty is essentially feudal (IV, **"33,"** p. 249; IV, **"34,"** p. 254; IV, **"35,"** p. 260), nevertheless thinks of God as a man like any other who would understand and easily forgive sins of the flesh: «je vouldrois que Dieu,» he says, «print aussi grand plaisir à mes plaisirs, comme je faictz, car je luy donnerois souvent matiere de se resjouir» (III, **"25,"** p. 207). Hircan, in fact, frequently refers to God in a context relating to sexuality or desire, for example: «Est-il raisonnable, par vostre foy, que nous morions pour les femmes, qui ne sont faictes que pour nous, et que nous craignions leur demander ce que Dieu leur commande de nous donner?» (I, **"9,"** p. 53).

Hircan can be depended upon for an unsentimental appraisal of stories others find touching or edifying and usually finds a base motive for any apparently virtuous action. If a woman resists a lover, he hints that she probably had another lover already (IV, **"42,"** p. 294). If a wife treats her unfaithful husband with kindness, he suggests that she was in love with someone else (IV, **"38,"** p. 271). If a woman resists temptation, he says that she must have done so out of pride, a worse vice in his opinion, for «toujours ung pire diable mect l'autre dehors» (III, **"26,"** p. 220).

Hircan is one of the leaders of the company and takes precedence over the other men in the group. When Hircan, Saffredent, and Dagoucin rush to the aid of the man (Geburon) pursued by two others, the narrator speaks of «Hircan et les autres gentils hommes» and «Hircan et ses compaignons» (Prol., p. 4), emphasizing Hircan's role and subordinating that of the other men. Furthermore, when Oisille proposes that the company pass their time in religious pursuits, Hircan acts as spokesman for the men in agreeing to her proposal for the morning's activity, but suggests something more physical for the afternoon's diversion (Prol., p. 8). When Hircan stresses on the first day that they are all equal in the game of storytelling (Prol., p. 10), he seems to imply that they are not equal in their day-to-day lives and that he outranks the others.

Le Roux de Lincy proposed the Duc d'Alençon, Marguerite's first husband, as the original of Hircan (pp. cxxxj-cxxxij). Jacob, however, believed that Marguerite meant instead to depict her second husband, Henri de Navarre. The name, he thought, might be the synonym of «*sauvage,* comme si ce cynique personnage était né dans les forêts d'Hyrcanie, *Hyrcanus.* L'étymologie qu'on tirerait du latin *hircus,* qui signifie *bouc,* conviendrait également au mari de Parlamente . . . » (pp. xxvj-xxvij). Dillaye observed that Hircan was the anagram of the name Henri (I, 265). The identification of Henri de Navarre as Hircan was adopted by Frank[12] and Jourda (*Marguerite d'Angoulême,* II, 763), among others, and seems to be the best choice for Hircan, just as Marguerite seems the best choice for Parlamente.[13]

LONGARINE

When we first meet Longarine, she is in the company of her husband and another married couple, Parlamente and Hircan. She is also accompanied by a *serviteur,* either Dagoucin or Saffredent. Since her husband is killed by bandits in the Prologue, she is a widow throughout the rest of the book and is called «la damoiselle vefve Longarine» (Prol., p. 3) and «la jeune vefve Longarine» (Prol., p. 7).

«Longarine is discreetly unhappy for her dead husband,» wrote George Saintsbury, «but appears decidedly consolable. . . . »[14] While she may seem to be somewhat insensitive to her husband's death since she joins in the storytelling and merriment with no apparent reservations, we can sense that she is not unmoved, but feels that it would be a mistake to give in to her sadness. In seconding Parlamente's suggestion that the

company find a pleasant way to spend their days at Notre-Dame de Serrance, she says: «Mais, qui pis est, nous deviendrons fascheuses, qui est une maladie incurable; car il n'y a nul ne nulle de nous, si regarde à sa perte, qu'il n'ayt occasion d'extreme tristesse» (Prol., p. 7). Although expressed in general terms, we may well interpret Longarine's statement as an indication that she finds her own loss a cause for extreme sorrow. This supposition seems to be borne out in a passage in which she speaks of her dead husband in passionate terms, claiming that she loved him so much that she would have killed him and herself if she had known him to be unfaithful, but that he had never given her cause for anything but to regret him all her life (IV, **"37,"** p. 269).

In any event, Emile Telle's description of Longarine as «cette jeune veuve qui aime tant rire» (p. 140) is appropriate. She often laughs at the stories others tell and at amusing remarks or situations which arise during the discussions, and she is known as well for her ability to make others laugh (I, **"7,"** p. 43). Longarine also has a reputation for telling the truth and for not sparing men or women (II, **"14,"** p. 116; III, **"24,"** p. 202).

One of Longarine's major preoccupations is shame, as shown by her responses during the discussions: «Comment sçauriezvous amender la honte?» (V, **"32,"** p. 245). «Ne faictes-vous poinct cas de la honte qu'elle receut . . . et de sa prison?» (IV, **"40,"** p. 279). «Je m'esbahys . . . que ceste pauvre femme ne moroit de honte devant ses prisonniers» (V, **"49,"** p. 323). She herself would be ashamed if she knew that she had done wrong even if no one else knew of her misdeeds (I, **"10,"** p. 84).

Although Longarine acknowledges the sinful nature of man (IV, **"34,"** p. 254), she makes a clear distinction between sinful desires and sinful actions. God will love us, she feels, if we do not put our sinful desires into action (III, **"26,"** p. 221). Apparently more concerned with this world than the next, however, Longarine stresses reputation, conduct, and the appearance of our actions to others. She considers virtue preferable to hypocrisy, but feels that we should take pains to cover our imperfections (VI, **"52,"** p. 335). God will not hold us accountable for our faults if we do not give men reason to judge us by commiting visible offenses (III, **"26,"** p. 221). Indeed, she believes, God in His mercy will cover the sins of those who for the love of Him show true repentance (VII, **"61,"** p. 337).

Although Longarine advocates the traditional feminine virtues of «chasteté, doulceur, patience et longanimité» (II, **"15,"** p. 128), her position is not entirely consistent. On the one hand, she says: «il y a bien peu de mariz que patience et amour de la femme ne puisse gaingner à la longue, ou ilz sont plus durs qu'une pierre que l'eau foible et molle, par longueur de temps, vient à caver» (IV, **"38,"** p. 271). On the other, she reacts strongly on several occasions against unfaithful husbands, of whom she says, «de telz marys que ceulx là, les cendres en seroient bonnes à faire la buée» (IV, **"37,"** p. 269). She believes, nonetheless, that women would do anything to regain the love of their husbands (VII, **"68,"** p. 397). Virtuous women, according to Longarine, seek their husbands' love, but are not driven by excessive sexual desires. A chaste woman, she continues, values perfect love over physical gratification (VII, **"69,"** p. 399). This does not mean that Longarine denies the force of sexual desire. On the contrary, she warns against its dangers no matter what the circumstances (III, **"30,"** p. 234).

There is no stronger passion than that of love, Longarine declares (V, **"49,"** p. 323). Amour, «ce glorieux dieu,» seeks to bring all under his power. Love enslaves great princes (III, **"24,"** p. 202). Love is stronger than priests or lawyers, who are accustomed to deceive everyone else (III, **"24,"** p. 203; III, **"25,"** p. 206). Since love deceives the deceivers, the rest of us should fear love indeed (III, **"26,"** pp. 206-07). Love changes our very nature. Love has the power «d'affoiblir les fortz, fortifier les foibles, donner intelligence aux ignorans, oster les sens aux plus sçavans, favoriser aux passions et destruire raison» (III, **"24,"** p. 202). Love is not an unmixed blessing. «Mais, tout ainsy qu'elle faict entreprendre choses quasi impossibles, pour acquerir quelque contentement en ceste vie, aussy mene-elle, plus que autre passion, à desespoir celluy ou celle qui pert l'esperance de son desir . . . » (V, **"49,"** p. 323). The worst pain of love is to bear the burden alone: «car il n'y a faiz si pesant, que l'amour de deux personnes bien unyes ne puisse doulcement supporter; mais, quant l'un fault à son debvoir et laisse toute la charge sur l'autre, la pesanteur est importable» (III, **"21,"** p. 174). Although Longarine's final statement on love is pessimistic, «c'est le meilleur du tout de n'aymer poinct» (VII, **"70,"** p. 418), she believes that human love, despite all its difficulties, is necessary for our salvation. A person who does not love in this world will never experience the love of God, «car la terre de son cueur est sterile, froide et damnée» (II, **"19,"** p. 152).

Félix Frank identified Longarine as Aymée Motier de La Fayette, la baillive de Caen: «*Longarine* est la dame de *Longrai* ou *Longray* en Normandie, dite la baillive de Caen, de son nom Aymée Motier de La Fayette, une des femmes de l'intimité la plus étroite de la reine Marguerite, avec sa fille, Françoise. . . . Sur *Longarine* le doute n'est pas possible. Ce nom est formé par l'anagramme de Longrai (Longari), et la mention de ce lieu revient plusieurs fois dans les lettres de la reine de Navarre.»[15] Aymée was one of Marguerite's ladies-in-waiting and accompanied her to Spain on her mission to negotiate the release of François Ier after the Battle of Pavia. She was governante to Marguerite's daughter Jeanne and later to Jeanne's children.[16] Jourda and most other critics have adopted Frank's identification.[17] Everything considered, Aymée Motier de La Fayette seems the best choice for Longarine.

DAGOUCIN

Dagoucin, a young gentleman and an admirer of either Parlamente or Longarine, has been called a «gentle, otherworldly semi-Platonist» (Ely, p. 8), a «philosophe délicat» (Darmesteter, p. 212), «le sentimental de la réunion, idéaliste impénitent, qui entretient sans affectation ni fausse pruderie la flamme robuste de ses illusions» (Lefranc, p. 42). According to one critic, «Le caractère de Dagoucin est certainement ce qu'il y a de plus délicat et de plus charmant dans l'*Heptaméron*» (Darmesteter, p. 228). Nomerfide describes him as «si saige, que, pour mourir, ne diroit une follye» (II, **"11,"** p. 89).

While generally silent, gentle, and mild-mannered during the discussions preceding and following the stories, speaking up only to defend the Neoplatonic conception of love (he does not utter a word on the first day until after the eighth story), Dagoucin is an active participant in the adventures leading to the company's assembly at Notre-Dame de Serrance. He and Saffredent embark on a romantic adventure in accompanying their *dames* to the baths of Cauterets and following them and their husbands after the others have gone their separate ways. When their ladies are in danger, Dagoucin takes up his sword along with Saffredent and goes to rescue Parlamente and Longarine. They fight so furiously that the bandits who are not killed are put to flight. He joins Saffredent in sending the wife of the host, who was killed in the fighting, after her husband, having heard that she was worse than he. Dagoucin also is an active participant in the fight against Geburon's pursuers, a fight which ends in the death of those two men.

By process of elimination we can deduce that Dagoucin is not married. After Parlamente outlines the requisites for a successful marriage, we read: «Hircan, Geburon, Simontault et Saffredent jurerent qu'ilz s'estoient mariez en pareille intention et que jamais ilz ne s'en estoient repentiz . . . » (IV, **"40,"** p. 280). Therefore, all the men in the company are married except Dagoucin. Although Dagoucin has no personal experience of marriage, he offers several comments about marriage as an institution. While he fully understands the sociological justification for the marriage customs of his day, he has his reservations about the emotional and spiritual benefits of unions concluded simply to maintain the established social and political order, disregarding questions of compatibility or love. Such marriages frequently lead to unhappiness for those involved, «en lieu de prendre ung estat pour mener à salut, ilz entrent aux faulxbourgs d'enfer» (IV, "**40**," p. 280). In spite of this, Dagoucin encourages women to make every effort to win the love and loyalty of their husbands through patience and devotion, no matter what their husbands' faults or misdeeds may be. A woman should consider herself more fortunate, he concludes, to have won her husband by patience and long-suffering than if fortune and her parents had given her one more perfect (IV, "**37**," p. 268). On the other hand, Dagoucin believes that men who falsely suspect their wives of infidelity should be punished by having their suspicions come true (V, "**47**," p. 314).

The topic to which Dagoucin returns again and again to the exclusion of almost everything else is love. His primary desire is to conform to his own conception of perfect love, which he envisions as a solitary, constant sentiment not dependent upon reciprocity or even the knowledge of the beloved. As a matter of fact, Dagoucin often affirms his belief in the importance of keeping love secret (I, "**9**," p. 48; II, "**19**," p. 152; III, "**23**," p. 193; III, "**24**," p. 200; IV, "**32**," p. 246; V, "**42**," p. 295; VI, "**53**," p. 341). Love, in Dagoucin's view, should not be dependent upon the beauty or virtues of the object of one's affection. The most important element is the lover's own desire to love perfectly. Rather than abandon the love in his heart, he would abandon his soul to death (I, "**8**," p. 48).

The theme of love is often associated in Dagoucin's mind with death (I, "**9**," pp. 48, 49, 54; II, "**12**," pp. 94, 95; II, "**14**," p. 115; II, "**19**," p. 152; IV, "**32**," p. 246; VI, "**53**," p. 341; VII, "**70**," pp. 418, 419). In many cases, this is allied with his belief that the perfect lover would rather die than reveal his love or ask his lady to do anything contrary to her conscience or her honor. Even Dagoucin, with his high conception of love, is aware of love's dangers. We should fear «ce petit dieu,» he warns, «qui prent plaisir à tormenter autant les princes que les pauvres, et les fortz que les foibles, et qui les aveuglit jusque là d'oblier Dieu et leur conscience, et à la fin leur propre vie» (II, "**12**," p. 94).

The text does not give any evidence concerning Dagoucin's profession. As Krailsheimer points out: «there is no hint that Dagoucin is in orders» (p. 79). As a matter of fact, a case could be made for the opposite conclusion. Dagoucin does not take offense at the numerous anticlerical remarks made by various members of the company. Nor does he seem to be offended or touched by remarks that priests should not frequent the company of women or take part in society. The few times that Dagoucin does mention the Church or men of the cloth can be interpreted in various ways. In a discussion about why the Church does not choose women as confessors, Oisille remarks that women would be too severe. Dagoucin replies: «Si elles l'estoient autant . . . qu'elles sont en leurs responces, elles feroient deses-

perer plus de pecheurs qu'elles n'en attireroient à salut; parquoy l'Eglise, en toute sorte, y a bien pourveu» (V, "**49**," p. 322). Since this is a general discussion, Dagoucin's reply cannot be taken as any privileged pronouncement. As a matter of fact, it probably tells more about his attitude toward women than toward the Church.

In another passage, Dagoucin outlines his theory of love. «Je sçay bien . . . que les hommes sont hommes et subjectz à toutes passions; mais si est-ce qu'il y en y a qui aymeroient myeulx mourir, que pour leur plaisir leur dame feist chose contre sa conscience.» Geburon's reply is open to various interpretations. «C'est beaucoup que mourir, dist Geburon; je ne croiray ceste parolle, quant elle seroit dictes de la bouche du plus austere religieux qui soit» (VI, "**53**," p. 341). Geburon might mean that he would not believe Dagoucin's statement even if Dagoucin were a man of the Church, implying that he is not. He might mean that he would not believe it even if an extremely austere churchman made the statement, implying that even though Dagoucin is in orders, he is not especially austere. On the other hand, since Geburon obviously would not believe these words under any circumstances, Dagoucin could both be in orders and live an austere life, and Geburon still would not believe him.

Elsewhere, Dagoucin says: «Mais qui penseroit que les dames n'aymassent point, il fauldroit, en lieu d'hommes d'armes, faire des marchans; et, en lieu d'acquerir honneur, ne penser que à amasser du bien» (VII, "**70**," p. 419). This passage would seem to be a strong argument against considering Dagoucin as a man of the Church. Why, otherwise, would he make such a point about acquiring honor as a man of arms? It seems clear that Dagoucin (whatever he is) is not an «austere religieux.»

Various possibilities have been proposed for the original of Dagoucin. Jacob, no doubt because of the similarity of names, thought he might be a «comte d'Angoust» (p. xxvij). Dillaye, basing his conjecture on Dagoucin's affinity for the philosophy of Plato, suggested J. de la Haye, a member of Marguerite's household and translator of Marsilio Ficino's *Commentaries* on the *Symposium* of Plato (I, 263). Both these hypotheses were rejected by Frank. He dismissed Jacob's suggestion rather quickly. «Je n'aperçois de ce côté aucune référence applicable ici» (***L'Heptaméron***, I, CLVIII). Although the rule against men of letters set down in the Prologue would not necessarily have excluded Symon Silvius, called de La Haye, Frank did not consider him of a sufficiently high station in life to be counted among the *devisants* (***L'Heptaméron***, III, 402-03).

Frank's candidate is Nicolas Dangu. Frank takes the anagram from the first three letters of Dangu's first name combined with his last name. «Le nom de *Dangu* et les premières lettres du prénom (*Nic*) fournissent d'ailleurs les formes *Danguncin* et *Daguncin,* aisément converties en Dagoncin ou Dagoucin.»[18] One of the intimate circle of Marguerite de Navarre, it was Nicolas Dangu who announced to Marguerite in 1539 or 1540 that her daughter, to whose bedside she was rushing, was out of danger (Frank, *L'Heptaméron,* I, CLXI-CLXIII). A natural son of Cardinal Du Prat, Dangu was bishop of Séez in 1539, head of Saint-Savin of Tarbes around 1540, bishop of Mende in 1545 (Febvre, p. 186). According to Abel Lefranc, «Marguerite aimait à s'entretenir avec lui de questions philosophiques et littéraires.»[19]

In spite of the question about whether or not Dagoucin is a man of the Church, Nicolas Dangu still seems a reasonable choice for Dagoucin.

SAFFREDENT

Dagoucin's companion in the romantically inspired visit to the baths of Cauterets and in the daring rescue of Longarine, Parlamente, and Hircan has been characterized as a «brillant mauvais sujet, violent et sans scrupules, mais non dénué de charme» (Darmesteter, p. 212). Although a *serviteur* of either Longarine or Parlamente, Saffredent is married (IV, "**40,**" p. 280). Saffredent himself mentions being married in one passage (VI, "**44,**" p. 344); in another, Longarine accuses Saffredent and Hircan of having made love to the chambermaids of their wives (I, "**8,**" p. 47).

Saffredent is rather casual in his attitude toward marriage. Unfaithful himself, he advises women to deceive their mates if they are not faithful (I, "**3,**" p. 27). Marriage, in Saffredent's view, is merely a legal bond which ends with death (VIII, "**71,**" p. 424). At best, his comments about marriage are unfavorable; at worst, they border on the sacrilegious. Men do indeed maintain the same relationship to their wives as Christ to His Church, he claims, and more than that, «si possible estoit nous le passerions, car Christ ne morut que une foys pour son Eglise; nous morons tous les jours pour noz femmes» (VI, "**54,**" p. 344). He even says that nothing encourages a man more to leave home for wars in foreign lands than to be married (VII, "**70,**" p. 419).

Saffredent's belief in male supremacy colors his view of marriage as it does his thinking in other areas. «Je m'esbahys,» he says, «pourquoy l'on trouve mauvais que ung simple gentil homme, ne usant d'autre force que de service et non de suppositions, vienne à espouser une femme de grande maison, veu que les saiges philosophes tiennent que le moindre homme de tous vault myeulx que la plus grande et vertueuse femme qui soyt?» (IV, "**40,**" p. 280). Like Hircan, he believes that a man should use any means necessary, to get his way with a woman. A man can pay a woman no greater

compliment, he declares, than to take her by force (II, "**18,**" p. 142). The fun-loving Saffredent not only takes pleasure in the company of women, but also likes to eat and drink (V, "**50,**" p. 326) and is accustomed to haunting taverns (VI, "**57,**" p. 355). He also delights in amusing the other members of the group (I, "**2,**" p. 22; VI, "**53,**" p. 342).

Saffredent seems to be one of the more literate and widely read members of the company, if we are to judge by his ability to find a literary, philosophical, or Biblical precedent to support his points. His quotations are in Latin on three occasions (I, "**9,**" p. 49; II, "**18,**" p. 141; III, "**23,**" p. 193). He mentions the *Roman de la Rose* of Jean de Meung twice (I, "**9,**" p. 54; III, "**29,**" p. 228). He quotes a proverb (I, "**10,**" p. 84), cites philosophers or Plato (IV, "**34,**" p. 253; IV, "**36,**" p. 265; IV, "**40,**" p. 280), and refers on many occasions to the Bible, Christ, saints, God, or theologians. These references to Biblical tradition or Platonic philosophy should not be taken to indicate a religious or Platonic bent, however, for Saffredent uses them for his own purposes, which are usually worldly and pleasure-oriented. What they do indicate is a great familiarity with some of the more commonly discussed topics of the day.

Saffredent prizes audacity and intelligence and despises timidity and stupidity. Indeed, he finds stupidity the one unpardonable sin:

> . . . je ne veiz oncques meffaict pugny, sinon la sottise; car il n'y a meurtrier, larron, ny adultere, mais qu'il soyt aussy fin que maulvais, qui jamais soit reprins par justice, ny blasmé entre les hommes. Mais souvent la malice est si grande, qu'elle les aveugle; de sorte qu'ilz deviennent sotz et comme j'ay dict. Seulement les sotz sont punis, et non les vicieux.
>
> (II, "**13,**" pp. 108-09)

Saffredent believes that God shares his attitude toward stupidity, and wisdom is the one attribute of God which he values above all others. «Si ne croy-je pas . . . que Dieu, qui est souveraine sapience, sceut avoir agreable la sottise des femmes; car, nonobstant que la simplicité luy plaist, je voy, par l'Escripture, qu'il desprise l'ignorant; et, s'il commande d'estre simple comme la coulombe, il ne commande moins d'estre prudent comme le serpent» (VII, "**65,**" p. 389).

Saffredent, who is extremely tolerant of sins of the flesh, thinks that God shares his opinion in this area as well. No matter what he does, a man in love, he feels, can be guilty of no more than a venial sin (IV, "**36,**" p. 264). He believes that such a sin is not only easily pardoned, but does not even anger God (IV, "**36,**" p. 265).

While Saffredent may at times seem tolerant of the sexual failings of priests and nuns, he basically distrusts those in religious orders. No one is safe from their lustful desires: «si en une maison si honorable ilz n'ont poinct de paour de declarer leurs follies, qu'ilz peuvent faire aux pauvres lieux où ordinairement ilz vont faire leurs questes, où les occasions leur sont presentées si faciles, que c'est miracle quant ilz eschappent sans scandalle» (V, "**41,**" p. 285). He believes, however, that there is some danger in exposing their evil ways (III, "**23,**" p. 193).

Somewhat contradictory statements have been made concerning Saffredent's age. In the Prologue, Dagoucin and Saffredent are called «deux jeunes gentilz hommes» (Prol., p. 2). When Saffredent is chosen to tell the third story, he says that there are others older than he who should precede him. Since Simontault is the only man who has spoken at that point, Saffredent is younger than one or more of the remaining three men, Hircan, Dagoucin, and Geburon, and than some of the women if the phrase «de plus antiens experimentez que luy» (I, "**2,**" p. 22) refers to women as well. (Oisille, the oldest member of the group, has already taken her turn.) Saffredent, thus, seems to be one of the younger members of the company. However, Ennasuitte says to him: «maintenant que les cheveulx vous blanchissent, il est temps de donner treves à voz desirs.» In the absence of contrary evidence, Saffredent's reply might indicate that he is no longer young. «Ma damoiselle, dist Saffredent, combien que l'esperance m'en soit ostée par celle que j'ayme, et la fureur par l'aage, si n'en sçaurois diminuer la volunté» (I, "**3,**" p. 27).

Le Roux de Lincy proposed Admiral Bonnivet, whose amorous adventures are the subject of several stories in the *Heptaméron,* as the original of Saffredent (Le Roux de Lincy and Montaiglon, IV, 202-03). Frank's candidate was Jean de Montpezat or Montpesat. Montpesat combined with the last syllables of Montferrand, a fief belonging to his family—Montpe*sat-ferrant*—gives Sarfredant or Saffredant (*L'Heptaméron,* I, CXLVII-CLI). Mary Robinson theorized that Saffredent was not an anagram at all, but a nickname: «As to the name . . . Saffredent is obviously Safre-dent, greedy-tooth or sweet-tooth, as we say in English.» Her choice is the vicomte de Rohan, extravagant, but amusing husband of Henri de Navarre's sister, Isabeau d'Albret.[20] Krailsheimer notes that Montpesat was not closely linked with Marguerite. He proposes Jean (or Gensane) de Bourbon, vicomte de Lavedan, head of Marguerite's household and *gouverneur* to her daughter Jeanne from 1542. He, too, sees Saffredent as a nickname, «from 'safre,' which meant variously 'greedy, lively,' together with 'dent.'» He suggests: «There may be a play on the sound as well as the sense of Lavedan, for heavy drinking is one way of washing one's teeth, but it is prudent to keep one's imagination in check» (pp. 89-90). Krailsheimer's arguments seem convincing, both with respect to Jean de Bourbon's relationship with Marguerite and to the origin of the name.

Ennasuitte

Ennasuitte's adventures before arriving at the Abbey of Saint-Savyn are described in the Prologue by the abbot himself. She first appears as an as-yet-unnamed «damoiselle,»[21] one of two who had escaped from a ferocious mountain bear. As the recital of their adventures continues, we learn that these ladies prefer to flee from danger rather than to stand and fight. They do so with little or no thought for their horses, which fall dead beneath them as they arrive at the abbey, or for their servants, who are left to fend for themselves. Ennasuitte and Nomerfide had a fairly large retinue, it would seem, for two of their ladies who arrive some time later tell them that the rest of their servants have all been killed.

The ladies are far from stoical in the face of difficulty. In our first face-to-face view of them, we see Ennasuitte and her companion crying and carrying on and much in need of comfort by the abbot and the new arrivals, including, presumably, the recently widowed Longarine. It is unlikely, however, that Ennasuitte was especially upset about losing her servants. As she so clearly puts it: «pour perte des serviteurs ne se fault desesperer, car l'on en recouvre assez» (Prol., p. 7). Her attitude toward the lower classes is also revealed in her comment about an old woman who tried to affix a candle to the forehead of a sleeping soldier. «Ce n'est pas chose estrange que d'avoir faict paour à ung varlet qui dormoit, car aussy basses femmes qu'elles ont bien faict paour à de bien grands princes, sans leur mectre le feu au front» (VII, "**65,**" p. 389). These remarks probably account for Saintsbury's description of Ennasuitte as «a haughty damsel, disdainful of poor folk» (p. lxiv).

Though upset by her run-in with the bear, Ennasuitte is quite resilient. By the time the group reaches Notre-Dame de Serrance, she is cheerful, in good spirits, and heartily agrees that the company should find some «plaisant exercice» for passing the time (Prol., p. 7). She herself enjoys telling merry stories, and the author mentions her laughter several times (Prol., p. 7; I, "**3,**" p. 27; III, "**26,**" p. 221; VII, "**65,**" p. 389). Her emotions, whether amusement, unhappiness, embarrassment, or anger, are very close to the surface and are often reflected in her face. On the third day, for instance, she decides to tell a funny story she had just heard instead of the serious one she originally had in mind. She was afraid she would not be able to keep a straight face if she told a serious story and would thereby spoil the effect of her words (III, "**26,**" p. 221). We read elsewhere that she blushes under Saffredent's gaze when he turns toward her while speaking of the cruelty of his lady (Prol. VII, p. 371). We also see Ennasuitte change color when angry, for example, as a reaction to a comment by Parlamente: «Ennasuitte, qui par ce mot ce sentyt touchée, en changeant de couleur, luy dist . . . » (IV, "**36,**" p. 261). Quick-tempered and sensitive to criticism, when she feels herself attacked, Ennasuitte tends to react quite strongly, either physically, by changing color, or verbally by an angry or cutting reply. She has a sharp tongue and is given to remarks of a personal nature (I, "**3**," p. 27; IV, "**36**," p. 261; VI, "**57**," p. 355).

We learn from the text that Ennasuitte is married. She herself makes two direct references to her husband. «Je ne me soulcie . . . quel nom les hommes me donnent, mais que Dieu me pardonne et mon mary aussy» (IV, "**32**," p. 246). «Mais je suyvrai mon propos, que, si mon mary estoit en tel dangier, je ne l'habandonnerois, pour morir» (VII, "**67**," p. 395). Hircan also refers to Ennasuitte's husband (VI, "**44**," p. 343).

Ennasuitte's experiences with marriage may not have been altogether happy. She takes personally Parlamente's comment that «il y a des mariz qui sont si bestes, que celles qui vivent avecq eulx ne doibvent poinct trouver estrange de vivre avecq leurs semblables» (VII, "**67**," p. 394). Whatever her relationship with her husband, Ennasuitte has probably found consolation elsewhere, for she also takes personally a remark that women should content themselves with their husbands (IV, "**35**," p. 261). Perhaps because of her own experiences, Ennasuitte is somewhat cynical and at times sarcastic in her attitude toward men. She even suggests that there is probably very little good that can be said about them (II, "**17**," p. 137).

Ennasuitte is sufficiently well educated to possess a knowledge of Latin. «Mais,» she says, «*quis est ille et laudabimus eum,* ainsy parfaict que vous le dictes?» Her use of Latin at that moment is an additional reflection of her character. She wants to show off her own education at the expense of Simontault, who has just said that he is not well versed in Latin (II, "**19**," p. 152).

Compared to the independent and well developed thoughts on religion of Oisille or Parlamente, Ennasuitte's views seem rather naïve. While Oisille and Parlamente judge preachers by the conformity of their words with the Scriptures, Ennasuitte is willing to accept their authority without question. «Mais qui se garderoit de croire à eulx,» she asks, «veu qu'ils sont ordonnez de noz prelatz pour nous prescher l'Evangille et pour nous reprendre de noz vices?» Even after Parlamente's exposé of her belief that those who preach the Word of God are to be believed only if their words and their lives are in accord with the teachings of the Scriptures, Ennasuitte persists in her appeal to authority. «En bonne foy, je pensois,» she says, «que nous fussions tenuz, sur peyne de peché mortel, de croire tout ce qu'ilz nous dient en chaire de verité . . . » (V, "**44**," p. 303).

Although she recognizes the authority of the Church with regard to doctrine, Ennasuitte is strongly anticlerical and anti-monastic. She believes that priests «ont quelque chose diabolicque en eulx contre la commune malice des hommes» (V, "**47**," p. 315) and attributes their wickedness to the unnaturalness of monastic life (V, "**48**," p. 317). Priests are so completely useless, she thinks, that were it not for their wicked deeds, we would never speak of them at all (V, "**48**," p. 317). The less we see of them, the better it is for their reputation (III, "**22**," p. 185). Ennasuitte sums up her own concept of religion in these terms: «Et, quant à moy, je me arreste à la religion que dict sainct Jacques: avoir le cueur envers Dieu, pur et nect, et se exercer de tout son povoir à faire charité à son prochain» (V, "**48**," p. 317).

As to possible identifications, most critics agree that Anne de Vivonne was the original of Ennasuitte. Married at the age of thirteen to François de Bourdeille, Anne de Vivonne was the daughter of Louise de Daillon and André de Vivonne (Le Roux de Lincy and Montaiglon, IV, 196). She was also the mother of Brantôme, who specifically says that his mother was one of the *devisantes*: «à ce que j'ay ouy dire à ma mère, qui estoit à la reine de Navarre et qui en sçavoit quelques secrets de ses *Nouvelles,* et qu'elle en estoit l'une des devisantes. . . . »[22] Frank explains the name Ennasuitte as follows: «Le nom d'*Ennasuicte,* en se décomposant, nous fournit d'ailleurs une preuve supplémentaire.—Il renferme d'abord le nom même d'*Anne*; mais celui de *suicte* ou *suite,* qui rappelle la situation de dame *suivante* d'Anne de Vivonne auprès de la reine Marguerite» (*L'Heptaméron,* I, CXXXIX). Given Anne de Vivonne's relationship to Marguerite, Brantôme's declaration that his mother was one of the *devisantes,* and the possibility of explaining the name with reference to Anne de Vivonne, it seems reasonable to conclude that she was the original of Ennasuitte.

NOMERFIDE

Nomerfide is twice singled out as the youngest in the group (Prol. II, p. 87; Prol. VII, p. 370). Along with her youth comes an intolerance of age, as seen in her remark to Geburon: «c'est la gloire des vielles gens qui cuydent tousjours avoir esté plus saiges que ceulx qui viennent après eulx» (II, "**16**," p. 133).

Her companions expect Nomerfide to tell short and amusing stories, and she does not disappoint them as shown by many comments by Nomerfide or her companions throughout the *Heptaméron,* for example:

> Il me semble, mes dames, que ce compte n'a esté ne long, ne melencolique, et que vous avez eu de moy ce que vous en avez esperé?
>
> (II, "**11**," p. 89)

> Ne sçavois-je pas bien, dist Simontault, que Nomerfide ne nous feroit poinct pleurer, mais bien fort rire. . . .
>
> (IV, "**34**," p. 252)

Or doncques, dist Nomerfide, selon ma coustume, je
vous le diray court et joieulx.

(VII, "**67**," p. 395)

Even though many of her stories deal in an amusing
way with the antics of those in religious orders, Nomerfide is strongly anticlerical and is revolted by the
thought of any personal or intimate contact with the
clergy (I, "**5**," p. 37; III, "**22**," p. 185).

Nomerfide affects an extremely modest view of her intellectual ability (IV, "**51**," p. 322). She likes to appear
innocent and naïve and cultivates an empty-headed,
scatterbrained image. Her innocence is partly real, partly
a role she is playing and one that suits her well. She often uses her naïveté to engage others in discussion. Her
position as the youngest in the company makes it easy
for her to ask a seemingly innocent question, giving the
others a chance to show their superior wisdom and experience.

Although Nomerfide rarely expresses any opinions on
most of the subjects under discussion, on love, to which
she has apparently given considerable thought, she ex-
patiates at length and with confidence. She views love
and marriage with the romanticism of youth, valuing
present happiness over future consequences, and would
willingly disregard social conventions for love matches
because of the pleasure such unions can afford. Realisti-
cally, she realizes that it is an unaccustomed pleasure
«d'espouser l'homme du monde que l'on ayme le
mieulx,» especially among the higher nobility (IV, "**40**,"
p. 278). Nevertheless, she advocates sharing physical
pleasure within the bonds of marriage in accordance
with the laws of God. In such love, there can be no
shame or dishonor except in betrayal of that love itself
(IV, "**40**," pp. 278-79). From a practical point of view,
Nomerfide does not think either husbands or wives
should inquire too closely into the actions of their partners (VI, "**59**," p. 365).

Nomerfide is openly enthusiastic when it comes to this
world's goods. She loves luxury and presents as shown
by her reaction to the story about the lady who gave a
diamond to the wife of her *serviteur*. «Voulez-vous dire,
ce dist Nomerfide, que ung beau dyamant de deux cens
escuz ne vault riens? Je vous asseure que, s'il fust tumbé
entre mes mains, sa femme ne ses parens n'en eussent
riens veu. Il n'est rien mieulx à soy, que ce qui est
donné» (II, "**13**," p. 108).

Nomerfide is flirtatious and a tease, with an appealing
personality. She has the confidence of a woman who
has been admired and found attractive without having
suffered any serious disappointments, though Geburon
warns that she may change her attitude after she has
been betrayed by her *serviteurs* (II, "**16**," p. 133). She
is a great supporter of sexual pleasure, «la felicité qui

se peult seule nommer en ce monde *felicité*» (IV, "**40**,"
p. 278), but Hircan suggests that she may not be capable of any really deep involvement (VII, "**70**," p.
420).

Jacob thought that Nomerfide might be «Françoise de
Foix, la belle comtesse de Châteaubriant» (p. xxviij).
Dillaye pointed out that the countess, born in 1475, was
older than Marguerite herself and, therefore, not a suitable candidate for the youngest member of the company. His choice was Marguerite's niece, Marguerite de
France (later Marguerite de Savoie) (I, 266-67). Frank
sees in Nomerfide the wife of Jean de Montpesat, a
daughter of the house of Fimarcon, from which he derives the name.[23] Mary Robinson thought that Nomerfide was the sister of Henri de Navarre, «'ceste fine
mouche,' la folâtre Isabeau d'Albert, vicomtesse de Rohan,»[24] whose personality as seen in Marguerite's letters
and the poems of Clément Marot was very much like
that of Nomerfide in the *Heptaméron*. Krailsheimer rejects the identifications of Nomerfide and Saffredent
with Françoise de Fimarcon and her husband Jean Car-
bon de Montpesat on the grounds that they were not
closely linked with Marguerite and that the title of Fimarcon did not belong to the wife of Jean de Montpesat, but to Anne, wife of Aimery de Narbonne. Krailsheimer favors Françoise de Silly, daughter of the baillive
de Caen, widow of Frédéric de Foix, and wife of the vicomte de Lavedan, whom he proposed as the original
of Saffredent (pp. 89-91). If Nomerfide is meant to be
married to Saffredent, then Françoise de Silly seems the
best choice for Nomerfide.

GEBURON

Geburon is or has been a military man. He alludes to
his military background in describing Cordeliers as
«aussy beaulx, aussi fortz et plus reposez que nous autres, qui sommes tous cassez du harnoys . . . » (I, "**5**,"
p. 37) and speaks of his experiences with places under
siege (II, "**18**," p. 142). He apparently took part in the
Italian campaigns of Charles XII, for he describes
atrocities which took place after the capture of Rivolta
by the French in 1509 (VI, "**51**," pp. 331-32).

Geburon is one of the older members of the company.
He mentions his «viellesse» when contrasting his current attitudes with the actions of his youth:

> Il est bien vray . . . que j'ay parlé maintenant contre
> ce que j'ay toute ma vie dict, mais pour ce que j'ay les
> dentz si foibles que je ne puis plus mascher la venai-
> son, je advertiz les pauvres bisches de se garder des
> veneurs, pour satisfaire sur ma viellesse aux maulx que
> j'ay desiré en ma jeunesse.

(II, "**16**," p. 133)

The expressions «de mon temps» (III, "**21**," p. 175)
and «toute ma vie» (II, "**16**," p. 133; III, "**24**," p. 200)
also indicate that Geburon is well past his prime.

Despite his age, Geburon still possesses presence of mind in an emergency, skill with a sword, a sense of tactics, and agility. When we first meet him, he is in a state of almost complete undress, running as though pursued, and calling for help. After Hircan, Dagoucin, and Saffredent have dispatched his pursuers, we learn of Geburon's adventure:

> . . . estant en une borde auprès de Peyrehitte, arriverent trois hommes, luy estant au lict; mais, tout en chemise, avecq son espée seullement, en blessa si bien ung qu'il demora sur la place. Et, tandis que les deux autres s'amuserent à recueillir leur compaignon, voyant qu'il estoit nud et eulx armez, pensa qu'il ne les povoit gaingner sinon à fuyr, comme le moins chargé d'habillement, dont il louoit Dieu et eulx qui en avoient faict la vengeance.
>
> (Prol., p. 4)

It is a tribute not only to Geburon's quick thinking, but also to his physical condition that he was able to outrun his attackers and find help. While the fact that Geburon does not refer to any servants in describing his adventure may not be a reflection of his social standing, at the very least, he is the only member of the company for whom no servants are mentioned.

Geburon, who frequently quotes «les antiens,» the Bible, or proverbs to make his points, is considered more sensible than the other men in the company. When Hircan cannot choose Parlamente to begin the fourth day (she had spoken first on the previous day), his choice falls to Geburon. «Puisque je ne la puys bailler à la plus saige de la compaignye,» he says, «je la bailleray au plus saige d'entre nous, qui est Geburon» (Prol. IV, p. 237). It is interesting to note, however, that the other members of the group usually refer to Geburon's «bon sens» or his customary good behavior when his opinions are contrary to their expectations. Since Geburon himself admits that his current pronouncements contradict the desires of his youth, his «bon sens» may not be a true reflection of his personality.

Although Andon describes Geburon as «le grand raccommodeur du groupe» (p. 297), very often Geburon's remarks seem more likely to prolong a dispute rather than to put an end to it. He also seems to enjoy teasing the other members of the company. He makes fun of Dagoucin's declarations about love (IV, "**32,**" p. 246). He teases Longarine about her *serviteurs* (I, "**5,**" p. 246) and for making Hircan and Saffredent angry (I, "**8,**" p. 47), Simontault about not deserving a virtuous wife (II, "**12,**" p. 96), Saffredent about preferring pleasure to virtue (II, "**12,**" p. 96) and about his confession aggravating his sin (II, "**20,**" p. 156).

On a personal level, Geburon, who is married (II, "**12,**" p. 96; IV, "**40,**" p. 280), says that he once loved a virtuous woman so much that he would rather have died than have had her do anything for him for which he would have admired her less (VI, "**53,**" p. 341). In contrast, he says that if he endured much for a lady, he would expect to be well rewarded, or he would give her up (VII, "**63,**" p. 382).

Geburon's view of love is generally pessimistic. He now warns women to beware of the lustful desires of men and to guard their chastity, which he considers their greatest treasure (I, "**5,**" p. 37; II, "**16,**" p. 133). Love, «la passion la plus aveuglante» (VII, "**68,**" p. 397), does not last (II, "**16,**" pp. 132-33). Love is a battle in which the woman is under siege (II, "**18,**" p. 142) or an animal pursued by a hunter (II, "**16,**" p. 133). Men do not take great pains for the love of their ladies, but only for their own pleasure and gratification (II, "**14,**" pp. 114-15; II, "**16,**" p. 133). Even marriages based on love often turn bad (IV, "**40,**" p. 280).

Geburon shows strong anticlerical feelings in several of his stories and in his comments during the discussions. «J'ay veu le temps,» he says of priests, «que en nostre pays il n'y avoit maison où il n'y eust chambre dediée pour les beaux peres; mais maintenant ilz sont tant congneuz, qu'on les craint plus que advanturiers» (III, "**23,**" p. 193). His first story concerns two Cordeliers, «deux si malitieux hommes» (I, "**5,**" p. 37), who try to take a ferrywoman by force. Sister Marie Heroët's resistance to the unwelcome attentions of the Prior of Saint-Martin des Champs, «un meschant religieux» (III, "**21,**" p. 175), is the subject of his story on the third day. He tells of a woman who ran off with a *chantre* on the sixth day and, on the seventh, describes how the priests at the Church of Saint-Jean de Lyon tried to create a false miracle.

Geburon's story on the fourth day concerns a Cordelier who murdered three people and kidnapped a young wife. In his list of variants, Adrien de Thou included a long anticlerical diatribe in Geburon's introduction to the story:

> Geburon donc' commença ainsi. Mes Dames, j'avoi délibéré de ne vous raconter plus nulle histoire des fautes commises par les gens de Religïon, sachant que ceus qui ayment leur honneur en ce monde, doivent plus craindre de les offensér, que tous les Princes de la chretïanté, pour le pouvoir qu'ils ont de mal dire et de mal fé comme il est trop mieùs déclaré, que ne le vous sçauroye dire, par see Jan de Meun, au Chapitre de faus semblant, où il leur donne tant de puissance de la faire qu'apres avoir véu le Rommant de la Rose j'ay autant de desir d'avoir leur amytïe et bonne grace, que la gloire de ce monde. Si ést ce que maintenant je vien de voir racontér à Monsieur de Saint Vincent Ambassadeur de l'empereur, un cas si merveilleus, qu'il ne se doit oublyér. C'est qu'aux terres, etc.[25]

Even without this variant, Geburon's comment at the conclusion of the story is sufficiently damning:

Je suis bien marry, mes dames, de quoy la verité ne nous amene des comptes autant à l'advantaige des Cordeliers, comme elle faict à leur desadvantaige, car ce me seroit grand plaisir, pour l'amour que je porte à leur ordre, d'en sçavoir quelcun où je les puisse bien louer; mais nous avons tant juré de dire verité, que je suis contrainct, après le rapport de gens si dignes de foy, de ne la celer, vous asseurant, quant les religieux feront acte de memoire à leur gloire, que je mectray grand peyne à leur faire trouver beaucoup meilleur que je n'ay faict à dire la verité de ceste-cy.

(IV, **"31,"** p. 241)

Notwithstanding his stories about the evil deeds of those in religious orders, Geburon still seems to believe in contributing to their cause and in the efficacity of their prayers for putting things right with God (VI, **"55,"** pp. 346-47).

Dillaye's candidate for Geburon was Nicolas Bourbon, «bon pédagogue & précepteur de Jeanne d'Albret, fille de Marguerite d'Angoulême» (I, 264). Frank suggested the seigneur de Burye, «un des Capitaines des guerres d'Italie dont a parlé Brantôme, son cousin-germain par alliance.»[26] Krailsheimer feels it better to accept Frank's conclusions rather than spending a great deal of time on other possibilities. At the same time, he suggests other areas for investigation, such as «some connection with the important Norman fief of Neubourg, near Evreux, held by the families of Harcourt and Coëme» (p. 88).

SIMONTAULT

The adventures of Simontault are recounted in the Prologue by the old monk who had shared Oisille's difficult journey to the Abbey of Notre-Dame de Serrance. Simontault, an impatient sort, tired of waiting for the waters to go down and allow him to cross the river safely. Therefore, as the monk tells us, Simontault «s'estoit deliberé de la forcer, se confiant à la bonté de son cheval, et avoit mis tous ses serviteurs à l'entour de luy pour rompre l'eau.» Unfortunately, all his servants were carried away, and Simontault, weak and half drowned, barely made it back to the riverbank. Unlike Ennasuitte, however, Simontault was concerned about the loss of his servants, for a shepherd who arrived on the scene found him «tout moillé et non moins triste de ses gens qu'il avoit veu perdre devant luy» (Prol., p. 5).

Simontault, like Geburon, is a military man. Whether or not we can draw any conclusions from the fact that he is called «le gentil chevalier Symontault» (Prol., p. 5), his reference to horses and the accountrements of war indicates not only that he is personally involved in military pursuits, but that they are not limited for him to time of war. «S'il estoit ainsy, dist Simontault, que les dames fussent sans mercy, nous pourrions bien faire reposer nos chevaulx et faire rouller noz harnoys jusques à la premiere guerre, et ne faire que penser du me-

snaige» (VI, **"56,"** p. 352). Simontault has probably taken part in the Italian campaigns as well, for he speaks of the cruelty of the Italians as though he had witnessed it himself. «Ne vous esbahissez, dist Simontault, de cette cruauté: car ceulx qui ont passé par Italie en ont vu de si très incroyables, que ceste-cy n'est au pris qu'un petit pecadille» (VI, **"51,"** p. 331).

Most commentators consider Simontault of a lower rank than the other men in the company, or at least lower on the social scale than Hircan. They base this conclusion on Hircan's reply when Simontault asks who will begin the storytelling. Simontault himself will be in command, Hircan says, because «au jeu nous sommes tous esgaulx» (Prol., p. 10), implying an inequality in the ranks of the two at other times. Whatever the case may be, Simontault holds a respectable position in life, for he is several times referred to as a gentleman. A «chevalier» was not necessarily of the highest nobility, however, for Amadour, also described as a «chevalier» (I, **"10,"** p. 84), was lower in rank than Floride. At any rate, Simontault was well provided with servants and had a good horse (Prol., p. 5), an indication that he was fairly well off.

According to the Prologue, Simontault is a long-time *serviteur* of Parlamente (Prol., p. 5). We also know that he is married. In addition to the general reference to Hircan, Geburon, Simontault, and Saffredent (IV, **"40,"** p. 280), Simontault's wife is mentioned on more than one occasion—by Simontault himself and by Geburon (II, **"12,"** p. 96) and by Parlamente, who comments on Simontault's reputation for not being the most faithful of husbands. In a rather rude reply, Simontault tells Parlamente to mind her own business. He then denies her allegation by stressing his success in satisfying his wife's physical desires (VII, **"69,"** p. 399).

Although Frank says that Simontault speaks of his «vieilz ans» (*L'Heptaméron,* I, CXXIV), he gives no reference for these words. Oisille, in fact, is the only person to use the expression (I, **"1,"** p. 18). Simontault does speak of his «longs services» (I, **"1,"** p. 11), but that is in reference to love, not to his age. If Simontault were not a fairly vigorous specimen, it is doubtful that he would boast of his sexual prowess.

Simontault, the misanthrope of the group, has little use for men or women:

. . . pour faire conclusion du cueur de l'homme et de la femme, la meilleur des deux n'en vault riens.

(III, **"21,"** p. 175)

. . . sans faire tort à nul, pour bien louer à la verité l'homme et la femme, l'on ne peult faillir de dire que le meilleur n'en vault rien.

(V, **"45,"** p. 307)

He is especially bitter against women and constantly threatens to avenge himself against all women because of the cruelty of one of their sex. As Parlamente points out, however, he does not appear to have suffered any lasting harm (VI, **"56,"** p. 352).

Simontault thinks differences in the sexual attitudes of men and women are innate. «J'ai tousjours oy dire,» he says, «que les hommes ne doibvent poinct estre reprins de pourchasser les femmes, car Dieu a mis au cueur de l'homme l'amour et la hardiesse pour demander, et en celluy de la femme la crainte et la chasteté pour refuser» (IV, **"40,"** p. 279). Simontault admits that he has often wished «toutes les femmes meschantes, hormis la sienne» (II, **"12,"** p. 96) and would prefer that women not be concerned about their consciences (VI, **"54,"** p. 344). He considers woman a creature full of faults, the weaker sex in every sense of the word. Women are excessively jealous (V, **"49,"** pp. 319, 320). Their emotions overcome their reason (VII, **"70,"** p. 420). Many, if not most, women are hypocrites and feign a virtue which they do not actually possess (II, **"13,"** p. 109; II, **"14,"** p. 114; II, **"18,"** p. 141; II, **"20,"** p. 155). Woman is the source of original sin and man's torment ever since (I, **"1,"** p. 18). Men, on the other hand, are prudent, sensible, and great-hearted (VII, **"70,"** p. 419). When a woman does something Simontault admires, he believes it is contrary to the normal behavior of her sex (II, **"16,"** p. 128; VII, 66, p. 392).

Simontault is very touchy and easily angered. Often he reacts as though he were being attacked or criticized when another person would consider the same words a compliment, Longarine, Nomerfide, and Saffredent are pleased to be chosen for their ability to make the company laugh. Simontault reacts by becoming angry and saying that he will avenge himself by telling a story unfavorable to women (II, **"13,"** p. 109). Longarine is pleased when the other members of the group refer to her reputation for telling the truth and not sparing men or women. When Oisille chooses Simontault, «lequel je sçay bien qu'il n'espargnera personne,» he seems to consider her words a veiled insult. «Autant vault, dist-il, que vous mectez à sus que je suis un peu medisant? Si ne lairray-je à vous monstrer que ceulx que l'on disoit mesdisans ont dict verité» (IV, **"32,"** p. 246). Even when Nomerfide speaks about the conduct of men in general, Simontault suspects that he is being attacked:

> Il semble, à vous oyr parler, dist Simontault, que les hommes prennent plaisir à oyr mal dire des femmes, et suis seur que vous me tenez de ce nombre-là? Parquoy, j'ay grande envye d'en dire bien d'une, afin de n'estre de tous les autres tenu pour mesdisant.
>
> (VII, **"66,"** pp. 391-92)

Religion is not one of Simontault's major preoccupations. He considers philosophy and theology the domain of dreamers (IV, **"34,"** p. 254) and thinks that there is great cause for doubt in most supposed miracles (IV, **"32,"** p. 246; IV, **"33,"** p. 249). He does express a belief, however, that happiness and virtue are given to man by the grace of God (VI, **"56,"** p. 352; VII, **"67,"** p. 394) and that man attains the love of God through earthly love: «Car, par les choses visibles, on est tiré à l'amour des invisibles» (II, **"19,"** p. 152).

Simontault comments occasionally on priests, with only mild disapproval, if any, of immorality on their part. He seems somewhat surprised that priests do not respect the marriage vows of others since they themselves administer such vows (III, **"23,"** p. 193). Elsewhere, however, he says, «J'ay ouy dire . . . que l'on auroit plus tost faict rompre deux marriages, que separer l'amour d'un prebstre et de sa chamberiere» (VI, **"60,"** p. 368). He excuses a priest for trying to seduce a young girl since the time and the circumstances were so tempting (V, **"41,"** p. 285). He does not even discuss the moral question involved in the story of the murderous monk who abducted a young wife, wondering rather «comment il eut la patience, la voyant en chemise et ou lieu où il en povoit estre maistre, qu'il ne la print par force» (IV, **"31,"** p. 241).

Frank, who rejected Le Roux de Lincy's identification of Henri de Navarre, Marguerite's second husband (Le Roux de Lincy, pp. cxxij-cxxiij), proposed instead François de Bourdeille, the father of Brantôme and the husband of Anne de Vivonne.[27] Montaiglon finds it «un peu étonnant» that Brantôme did not mention his father as one of the *devisants* (Le Roux de Lincy and Montaiglon, IV, 202). Brantôme's silence on this point is not sufficient cause, however, to eliminate him from consideration. In fact, one statement by Brantôme seems to correspond to Simontault's pride in his sexual abilities. His father, Brantôme tells us, was so well endowed that his future wife's parents were concerned. Anne de Vivonne was only thirteen at the time and «il avoit un advitaillement si grand et advantageux, qu'il eust faict peur et appréhension à une femme d'un plus grand aage.»[28]

Notes

1. The identification of the historical personages upon whom the *devisants* are thought to be based was of great interest to such nineteenth-century critics and editors as Le Roux de Lincy, Frédéric Dillaye, Paul Lacroix (le bibliophile Jacob), Félix Frank, and Mary Robinson. The identifications of the *devisants* by Félix Frank in his 1879 edition of the *Heptaméron* (Paris: Isidore Liseux) have generally been followed by later scholars, including Pierre Jourda (*Marguerite d'Angoulême*, II, 761-66). Two more recent studies have challenged these identifications: A. Krailsheimer, «The *Heptaméron* Reconsidered,» in *The French Renais-*

sance and Its Heritage: Essays Presented to Alan M. Boase by Colleagues, Pupils and Friends (London: Methuen, 1968), pp. 75-92, and Joseph Palmero, «L'Historicité des devisants de l'*Heptaméron*,» *Revue d'Histoire Littéraire de la France*, 69 (1969), 193-202. After reviewing the identifications proposed by nineteenth- and twentieth-century scholars, I have found Krailsheimer's arguments the most convincing.

2. The storytellers will be studied in the order in which they are introduced by the author in the Prologue.

3. Referring to a passage in Romans (Ch. 1) in which Saint Paul says: «For this cause God gave them up unto vile affections: for even their women did change the natural use into that which is against nature: And likewise also the men, leaving the natural use of the woman, burned in their lust one toward another; men with men working that which is unseemly, and receiving in themselves that recompense of their error which was meet.»

4. *Lettres de Marguerite d'Angoulême, sœur de François Ier, Reine de Navarre*, ed. F. Génin (Paris: Renouard, 1841), pp. 100-01. Mary James Darmesteter (also known as Agnes Mary Francis Robinson, A. Mary F. Robinson, A. M. F. Robinson, Mrs. James Darmesteter, and Madame Duclaux) also favored the identification of Oisille with Marguerite. See *La Reine de Navarre: Marguerite d'Angoulême,* trans. Pierre Mercieux (Paris: Calmann Lévy, 1900), pp. 214 and 229. This is a translation of *Margaret of Angoulême, Queen of Navarre* (London: Allen, 1886).

5. Marguerite de Navarre, *L'Heptaméron des nouvelles de très haute & très illustre princesse Marguerite d'Angoulême, Reine de Navarre,* ed. A.-J.-V. Le Roux de Lincy (Paris: La Société des Bibliophiles François, 1853), pp. cxxx-xccj.

6. *Les Comptes du Monde adventureux,* ed. Félix Frank (Paris: Alphonse Lemerre, 1878), pp. xcix-c. Frédéric Dillaye also favored Louise de Daillon as the original of Oisille. See Marguerite de Navarre, *L'Heptaméron des nouvelles de Marguerite d'Angoulesme, Royne de Navarre,* ed. Frédéric Dillaye (Paris: Alphonse Lemerre, 1879), I, 267-68. By the time Frank made his own edition of the *Heptaméron,* he had firmly decided in favor of Louise de Savoie, rather than Louise de Daillon, having concluded that the sénéschale de Poitou was not a person of sufficient consequence to command the deferential treatment accorded her by the other members of the group. See *L'Heptaméron de la Reine Marguerite de Navarre,* ed. Félix Frank (Paris: Isidore Liseux, 1879), I, lxxv-lxxxii.

7. Brantôme (Pierre de Bourdeille), *Vies des dames illustres françaises et étrangères* (Paris: Garnier, 1939), p. 287.

8. Although Palermo sees in Parlamente the representation of Catherine de Médicis (p. 199), the identification will not stand up in the context of the relationship of Parlamente and Hircan in the *Heptaméron.*

9. Marguerite de Navarre, *La Coche,* ed. F. Ed. Schneegans (Strasbourg: Heitz, 1936), p. xi.

10. Marguerite de Navarre, *L'Heptaméron des nouvelles de très-haute et très-illustre princesse, Marguerite d'Angoulême, royne de Navarre,* ed. P. L. Jacob (Paris: Adolphe Delahaye, 1858), p. xxvj.

11. Gladys Ely, «The Limits of Realism in the *Heptaméron* of Marguerite de Navarre,» *Romanic Review,* 43 (1952), 9.

12. Frank, *L'Heptaméron,* I, lxxxvi-lxxxviii. Frank noted that Hircan was the anagram of *Hanric,* abbreviation of *Hanricus* (for *Henricus*), p. lxxxviii.

13. Palermo (p. 200) proposed the husband of Catherine de Médicis, the future Henri II, as the original of Hircan. The character of Henri II, however, does not correspond to that of Hircan. Henri was taciturn and rather gloomy, quite unlike the good-natured Hircan. There also seems to be little in common between Catherine's relationship with her husband and Parlamente's with Hircan. Though probably unfaithful, Hircan shows both admiration and respect for his wife. Henri was ashamed of his wife's background since she was not of royal blood (Darmesteter, p. 167). Unlike Hircan, who would not tie himself down even to one mistress, Henri II was quite faithful in his way to Diane de Poitiers.

14. Marguerite de Navarre, *The Heptameron of the Tales of Margaret, Queen of Navarre,* trans. from the authentic text, with an essay upon the *Heptameron* by George Saintsbury, M.A. (London: Privately Printed for Members of the Aldus Society, 1903), p. lxiv.

15. Frank, *L'Heptaméron,* I, clxv. Le Roux de Lincy had identified Longarine as Blanche de Tournon, «veuve en secondes noces de Jacques de Coligny, seigneur de Châtillon, dame d'honneur de la Reine de Navarre» (p. cxxxij). Frank remarked: «Elle ne devait guère être jeune au moment où se reporte Marguerite, si tant est qu'elle fût vivante!» (*L'Heptaméron,* I, clxv).

16. Nancy Lymann Roelker, *Queen of Navarre, Jeanne d'Albret, 1528-1572* (Cambridge: The Belknap Press of Harvard University Press, 1968), pp. 21-25.

17. Jourda, *Marguerite d'Angoulême,* II, 765. Frank suggested that the identification of Longarine as the «dame de Longrai» might apply as well to the daughter of the baillive de Caen, who would have been even younger. Aymée's daughter Françoise, both during her first marriage and during her second, «demeura toujours avec sa mère auprès de la princesse Jeanne» (*L'Heptaméron,* I, clxvii-clxviii). Palermo proposed «la jeune duchesse de Montpensier, première femme de Louis II de Bourbon, dont le nom Jacqueline de Longwy, comporte en ordre inverse deux des trois syllabes du nom de Longarine» (p. 201).

18. Frank, *L'Heptaméron,* I, clxv. This might explain Adrien de Thou's preference for the form *Dagoncin* (FR 1524).

19. «Le Platonisme et la littérature en France à l'époque de la Renaissance (1500-1550),» in *Grands Ecrivains français de la Renaissance* (Paris: Champion, 1914), pp. 127-28.

20. *The Fortunate Lovers,* ed. A. Mary F. Robinson (London: Allen, 1887), p. 30.

21. Although Montaigne wrote: «Les femmes de qualité, on les nomme Dames; les moyennes, Damoiselles; et Dames encore, celles de la plus basse marche» («Des vaines subtilitez,» I, 54), the word «damoiselle» cannot be used as the basis for speculation about either the marital status or the social standing of these two ladies. This title was used for women who were married as well as for those who were not. In the *Heptaméron,* «damoiselle» is often used interchangeably with «dame.» Nomerfide and Ennasuitte, referred to as «deux damoiselles,» are described in the very next sentence as «les pauvres dames» (Prol., p. 4). Longarine and Parlamente are called «les dames» in the Prologue. Very shortly thereafter, Longarine is described as a «damoiselle vefve» (Prol., p. 3). Both Parlamente and Longarine are referred to as «Damoyselles» in the Le Hir edition (p. 13). Rolandine, from a very high ranking family (III, 21, p. 158), was called «ceste damoiselle» (III, 21, p. 174).

22. *Les Dames gallantes,* ed. Maurice Rat (Paris: Garnier, 1947), pp. 146-47.

23. «Le nom de *Fimarcon, Fiémarcon* ou *Fiedmarcon* (en latin *Feudimarco*) est une première indication, car il donne le nom de *Nomarcfide* ou *Nomercfida,* par anagramme des mots Fiedmarcon ou de Fimarcon, soit, par simplification: *Nomerfide*» (*L'Heptaméron,* I, cxlvii). Jourda, who systematically follows Frank's identifications, opts for Françoise de Fiedmarcon as well (*Marguerite d'Angoulême,* II, 764).

24. Darmesteter, p. 227. Nomerfide's anticlericalism seems to correspond to Isabeau's attitude. During the celebration of her marriage on August 16, 1534, she took part in a *mommerie* written by Marot in which three young girls representing Faith, Hope, and Charity, Isabeau among them, brought from Hell a letter to Marguerite congratulating her on her victory over the theologians (Jourda, *Marguerite d'Angoulême,* I, 183-84).

25. Adrien de Thou, «La Table Contenant le Répertoire, ou Indice des Omissions, Inversions de sens, & Diversité de Lectures de ce présent Livre» (FR 1524), columns 12-13. Essentially the same passage appears in manuscripts Fonds FR 1513, fol. 22; FR 1514, fol. 175 verso; FR 1525 fol. 174; and Pierpont Morgan Library MS. M 242 fol. 24.

26. Le Roux de Lincy and Montaiglon, IV, 203. Frank explains the name as follows: «il est forgé par l'anagramme du mot *Burye,* ou *Yebur,* avec la finale *on* et le changement facile de l'Y en G qui transforme Yeburon en Geburon» (*L'Heptaméron,* I, cxxiii-cxxiv). Jourda accepted Frank's identification, though he did not find the anagram entirely convincing (*Marguerite d'Angoulême,* II, 764).

27. *L'Heptaméron,* I, cxxxi. He accounts for the anagram in the following manner: «Quant au motif qui aura présidé au choix du pseudonyme de *Simontault*: il me semble fondé sur une double allusion au fief de *Montauris* possédé par la famille avec celle de *Montaut,* ce qui fournit les formes *Simontau, Simontaur,* par anagramme, d'où *Simontaut*» (*L'Heptaméron,* I, cxxxvii). Mary Robinson tentatively suggested another possibility: Clément Marot (*The Fortunate Lovers,* p. 33). As a man of letters, however, Marot would have been excluded by the terms of the Prologue. Palermo's choice is Anne de Montmorency, grand connétable de France (pp. 201-02). Considering the ill will that existed between them in her later years, it is unlikely that Marguerite would have included Montmorency among the *devisants.* See Jourda, *Marguerite d'Angoulême,* I, 182, 241-42, 254-57, 265-66, 320.

28. *Oeuvres complètes de Pierre de Bourdeille, Seigneur de Brantôme,* ed. Ludovic Lalanne (Paris: Renouard, 1876-81), X, 46.

Mary J. Baker (essay date August 1992)

SOURCE: Baker, Mary J. "Rape, Attempted Rape, and Seduction in the *Heptaméron.*" *Romance Quarterly* 39, no. 3 (August 1992): 271-81.

[*In the following essay, Baker explores the complexity of the sexual dynamics in the* Heptaméron *as viewed from a feminist standpoint.*]

In her important book *Renaissance Feminism,*[1] Constance Jordan writes that although feminist positions vary, the arguments all share "a pervasive concern with questions of authority and subordination, that is, with the origins of the control of man over woman" (p. 3). Such a concern is clearly manifested in Marguerite de Navarre's **Heptaméron,** and is conveyed with particular acuity in a number of stories in which there are occurrences of rape or attempted rape (classified by Nicole Cazauran under the broad heading of *amour meschant*),[2] and seduction.[3] It is on several of these stories that I propose to focus here, with special emphasis on their similar imagery,[4] imagery which both enhances our understanding of the depiction of the relative power of men and women in the **Heptaméron,** and also attests to the complexity of the work's insights into the relations between the sexes.

Close examination of rape, attempted rape, and seduction stories reveals that several of them contain imagery pertaining to openings and access, including doors and staircases, and imagery suggesting barriers and denial or difficulty of access, including walls and coverings. Freud has pointed out that narrow spaces and doors are common sexual symbols.[5] More recently, Andrea Dworkin has claimed: "Physically, the woman in intercourse is a space inhabited, a literal territory operated literally. . . ."[6] But not only does Marguerite's imagery of space show a surprising pertinence to Freud and to current discussions of male aggression and rape,[7] it also reflects positions taken in medieval as well as Renaissance debates about the difference between rape and seduction, and about the importance of divining intention in order to determine innocence or guilt.[8]

Three stories listed by Nicole Cazauran as examples of an *amour meschant* in which there is an effort to take a recalcitrant woman by force are Numbers **"2," "10,"** and **"22"** (p. 225). Another story that should be added to this category is **"Number 4."** A fifth story, **"Number 62,"** initially appears to fit into this category, but should be excluded from it, because doubts are cast on the genuine recalcitrance of the woman. In three other stories, numbers **"23," "46,"** and **"48,"** rape is recognized *after* the fact. Out of these eight stories, five contain significant spatial imagery of the sort mentioned above. In a group of four other stories (nos. **"14," "16," "18,"** and **"50"**), cited by Cazauran as exemplifying exceptions to the rule that "toute tentative pour satisfaire cet appétit de jouissance paraît condamné" (p. 225), three have either door, or door and staircase imagery. It is worth noting, however, that stories that do not contain this imagery are consistent with those that do.

Tale **"Number 2"** is one of the rare tales in the **Heptaméron** in which there is no disagreement among the *devisants* about the virtue of the conduct of one of the characters, in this case a mule-driver's wife, who dies resisting the advances of her husband's servant. The use of imagery of openings and barriers supports the unambiguous character portrayal in the story. The *muletière* rejects the servant's overtures *aigrement,* and he decides as a result "qu'il pourroit avoir par force ce que par nulle priere ne service n'avoit peu acquerir."[9] He *breaks through* a wooden partition that separates his room from that of his mistress. His entry into the bedroom, just as his subsequent rape of the *muletière,* is a violent invasion of private space. The hidden character of this space and the secretive nature of the entry are also suggested: ". . . le rideau, tant du lict de son maistre et d'elle que des serviteurs de l'autre cousté, couvroit les murailles si bien que l'on ne povoit veoir l'ouverture qu'il avoit faicte . . ." (p. 19). As the scene progresses, Marguerite uses additional sexual imagery: "entra le varlet, par l'ais qu'il avoit rompu, dedans son lit, l'espée nue en sa main" (p. 19). Literally, his repeated stabbing of her with his sword results in her death; the language in the sentence quoted above also suggests, however, that at another level Marguerite is equating rape with murder.

Just as the violence of the attack is uncontestable, so also are the evil intentions of the servant, who is described as committing an act of "meschante concupiscence" (p. 20). An examination of intentions is not new in the Renaissance. Beginning in the twelfth century, both the degree of violence and the intentions of the perpetrator were critical factors in determining whether or not rape occurred. In his *Decretum* (c. 1140) Gratian distinguished between rape, where violence was a necessary condition, and seduction, where guile might be applied and promises made. If a man's intentions were only to seduce, then his actions could not be condemned as a sexual offense.[10] The idea that beguiling speeches did not constitute violence was upheld into the sixteenth century. Given the prevailing views, then, it is not surprising to find the rape deplored; the valet is condemned and the *muletière* is praised for her "belle vertu de chasteté" (p. 21).

The attempted rape in the fourth tale is less violent than the successful rape in **"Number 2,"** and the intent of the perpetrator is less unequivocally wicked. The story is correspondingly more ambiguous. Further complicating the moral issue is the introduction of a new factor: the possible public perception of the woman. That an attempted rape took place is not disputed; what becomes a major issue in the story is whether or not the woman should openly accuse the man of attempted rape and demand his death, because if she does accuse him, people might then say that she encouraged him (thereby facilitating a defense on the basis of seduction rather than rape). In raising this question, Marguerite exposes what Frances Ferguson has described as the peculiar status of rape as a crime, "where the mental states of *two* persons are crucial" (emphasis mine).[11]

The two main characters in **"Number 4"** belong to a higher social class than the *muletière* and the servant; the woman is a well-born widow, sister to a prince, and the man is a *gentil homme*. Marguerite appears to suggest that conventions of *politesse* and also attractiveness of members of this social group encourage alliances and contribute to difficulty in emphatically rejecting a suitor. An early overture made by the gentleman is politely turned down by the widow, who "le voyant tant beau et honneste comme il estoit, . . . luy pardonna aisement sa grande audace" (p. 28). But the gentleman forgets his promise not to pursue his courtship, and "se pensa que, s'il la povoit trouver en lieu à son advantaige, elle qui estoit vefve, jeune, et en bon poinct, et de fort bonne complexion, prandroit peult-estre pitié de luy et d'elle ensemble" (p. 29).[12]

The more ambiguous attitude toward the attempted rape is conveyed by the opening/barrier imagery, which, though reminiscent of the imagery in **"Number 2,"** is subtly different. Significantly, the attempted rape takes place at the *gentleman's* house. The widow may perhaps have placed herself in a more vulnerable position by agreeing to be his guest. Unlike the *muletière,* she defends a territory that is no longer entirely her own. Her accommodations are opulent, and, as in **"Number 2,"** the imagery suggests the private nature of the space the gentleman is soon to invade; however, here there is not a wall to be penetrated, but a trap door. In the bedroom, "tapissée par le hault, et si bien nattée, . . . il estoit impossible de s'apercevoir d'une trappe que estoit en la ruelle de son lict, laquelle descendoit en celle ou logeoit sa mere . . ." (p. 29). This trap door provides relatively simple and natural access to the widow; it is an opening that is part of the architecture of the room, and one that can be manipulated without great difficulty. Furthermore, the tapestry hiding the trap door is a covering that suggests pleasure and comfort. Both door and tapestry, then, assure relative ease of entry.

The gentleman, whose passion has been further aggravated by attending the widow's "habiller et deshabiller" (p. 29), changes rooms with his mother in order to reach the widow with facility. He dismisses his attendants, and when all is quiet "il voulut commencer son doulx traveil, et peu à peu abbatit la trappe qui estoit si bien faicte et accoustré de drap, qu'il ne feit ung seul bruit . . ." (p. 30). The greater tolerance in the story of the gentleman relative to the servant in **"Number 2"** is suggested by this entry, which is much gentler than that of the servant; it is in fact the widow's reaction that is violent. She scratches and bites, and the gentleman, fearful that he will be recognized, beats a hasty retreat back down through the trap door, thereby abandoning consummation.[13]

Although the gentleman's actions are not condoned—he did, after all, attempt to take the lady by force, and he came from a room *below,* a detail that could be interpreted as establishing his dishonorable intentions[14]—the character portrayal and the commentary of a third character confirm the more forgiving attitude toward his conduct suggested by the opening/barrier imagery. The widow's lady-in-waiting discreetly hints at her mistress's role in determining the turn of events. She advises her *not* to demand the gentleman's death: "laissez faire à l'amour et à la honte, qui le sçauront mieulx tormenter que vous" (p. 31), reasoning that if the event became public people might say that the gentleman got what he came for, and that she encouraged him. She then pointedly states: "il n'y a nul en ceste court, qu'il ne voye la bonne chere que vous faictes au gentil homme dont vous avez soupson . . ." (p. 32).[15]

The widow's leniency appears to be partially justified by the gentleman's contrition. He acquires a new understanding of himself, one facilitated by the use of a mirror. Before his attempted possession of the widow, he admires himself in the mirror: "luy sembla bien, en soy mirant, qu'il n'y avoit dame en ce monde qui sceut refuser sa beaulté et bonne grace" (p. 29). Here the mirror reflects the image of the person he thinks he is and wants others to see.[16] After the unsuccessful attack, the gentleman picks up his mirror again and gazes at his reflection. He sees his "visaige tout sanglant d'esgratineures et morsures" (p. 30) and recognizes the image of his true self, a vain, flawed creature. His good looks have been a "vaine promésse," and he has committed a "follie" (p. 30). Now the image of the mirror could be said to convey the new awareness of the unconscious self by the conscious self.[17]

The apparent indulgence toward the gentleman, and the recommendation to the widow to acquiesce to social pressures, do not betray an insensitivity on Marguerite's part to the plight of a woman threatened by rape as much as they reveal her confidence in the capacity of human beings, aided by God's grace, to repent of their sins, and reform their lives. Marguerite's optimistic attitude is compatible with the view of Guillaume Briçonnet, the bishop of Meaux with whom she corresponded between 1521 and 1524, who saw the possibility of good subsisting in evil.[18]

Finally, in the discussion, Ennasuite praises the widow for her virtue and good sense, but Hircan criticizes the gentleman for lacking *cueur* in not accomplishing his original purpose. Hircan's recommendation that the gentleman could have made his task easier by murdering the older lady-in-waiting is not really taken seriously by the other *devisants*; however, the fact that such a point of view is expressed at all indicates that this story is less clearly exemplary than **"Number Two."**

A door figures importantly in several rape and attempted rape stories, and one of its major functions is to suggest whether or not a man is behaving responsibly toward a woman by adequately protecting her against assaults. In tale **"Number 23,"** the wicked intentions of the Franciscan, who burns with lust, are made amply clear, and there is no question that he is guilty of committing a vicious rape. But Marguerite introduces a new element into the discussion of rape, namely, that a husband bears a responsibility to assure his wife's safety.

In this tale, a Franciscan rapes the wife of a gentleman, a young woman who has recently given birth to a son. When she learns after the fact what has occurred, she hangs herself, and inadvertently smothers her baby at the same time. Although the Franciscan is condemned for the rape, the husband is also blamed for facilitating it. Sexually impatient, he has asked the Franciscan earlier in the evening for permission to resume relations with his wife. The Franciscan instructed him to go to her bedroom at two in the morning. The eager husband told his wife to leave her door *open* for him, which she did. But the Franciscan went to the bedroom first, and was able to enter with no difficulty because, thanks to the husband, the door had been left open and unattended. That the husband must bear some responsibility for what occurred is confirmed in the discussion. Hircan describes him as a "bon sot" (pp. 192-93) who never should have invited the Franciscan to dine with his beautiful, upright wife.

The responsibility to deny illicit sexual access and to protect the female body extends at times to adult women as well—wives who must look after themselves intelligently, and mothers who should guard their young daughters. In this connection, we find one remarkable story, **"Number 46,"** in which staircase imagery is exploited.[19] There are two examples of sexual aggression in this story involving the lecherous Franciscan De Vale: in the first episode, the friar is not successful, in the second, he is. In both cases, his intentions are dishonorable. First, he lusts after the wife of a judge. One day he follows her to the attic, on the pretext that he has a secret to tell her. She warns him not to climb the staircase—"'si vous montez plus avant en ce degré, vous vous en repentirez'" (p. 309). He ignores the warning, and she kicks him in the stomach causing him to fall down the stairs. The humiliated friar flees and joins another household. The judge's wife is successful in repulsing the friar in part because she exercises her rational faculties. (It is perhaps no accident that she is the wife of a *judge*.) She is aware of the friar's passion for her and finds it ridiculous. Appropriately, she is in the *attic* when she kicks the friar down the stairs; this is a room in the house associated with the capacity to think rationally.[20]

In the second household, the friar desires the young daughter of a woman "qui aymoit les Cordeliers sur toutes gens" (p. 309). The mother, annoyed that her daughter does not like to get out of bed in the morning and therefore misses the friar's sermons, expresses the wish to De Vale that her daughter "'eust ung peu tasté des disciplines que entre vous religieux prenez!'" (p. 309). The friar promises to remedy the situation, and he gains access to the girl's room with no difficulty at all, climbing a wooden staircase aptly described as a *little* staircase. The girl is asleep when he rapes her, a fact that underscores her innocence and suggests her lack of sexual awakening.[21] The friar escapes without ever being found. Unlike the judge's wife, the girl is too young and naive to defend herself; she needed her mother to think intelligently and rationally on her behalf. It is not coincidental that the *devisants* condemn the mother; Hircan describes her as a "'sotte et folle mere'" (p. 310), and Parlamente adds: "'si elle eut esté aussi saige que la jugesse, elle luy eust plustost faict descendre le degré que de monter'" (p. 310). The mother thus clearly bears the responsibility for allowing access to the daughter's staircase.

Not all of Marguerite's women, then, are equally perceptive in discerning male intent to rape. They do not all defy male aggression with equal vigor either. Sometimes, as in the case of **"Number 62,"** the intentions of the perpetrator are not clearly malevolent, and, in the final analysis, the woman herself may not regret the attack. Here again we enter a nebulous area, where the question of the woman's actual mental state is raised. Further complicating the characterization of this story as an unequivocal example of rape is the fact that there is no forced entry, and no effort to hide the entry.[22] A nobleman long in love with a married woman thinks that if he can surprise her when he has the advantage she may not be so *rigoureuse*.[23] He jumps into her bed with his clothes on, including boots and spurs, "sans avoir le sens de fermer la porte" (p. 378), and takes her by force. The fact that the door is left open suggests not only his haste, but also his lack of concern about the need to be discreet, possibly because he has an inkling that ultimately the woman may not be too hard on him (and this turns out to be true), and possibly because his intentions are not malevolent (he is actually in love with her). His impetuosity has one unexpected result. Just when the chambermaids return to the bedroom, his spur catches on the top sheet, pulling it away. The lady is left naked for all to see through the open door. Her reaction is principally one of surprise, not shame or anger: "'Jamais femme ne fust si estonnée que moy, quant je me trouvay toute nue'" (p. 378), she says to her audience. The royal lady listening to the story laughs. This reaction, along with the open door and the fact that the narrator herself characterizes her story as a "beau compte," suggest that in this case at least, the sexual aggression should not be viewed as a malicious rape, but as a calculated (though misguided) act designed to win over the lady, to complete seduction of her. Such an interpretation is further supported by Longarine, who hints in the discussion that the nobleman's action may not have been entirely distasteful to the woman.

The complicity of the woman in **"Number 14"** clearly situates this story in the category of seduction rather than rape. The woman here has made herself accessible by leaving the door open and a staircase free. She is a consenting adult who has made it possible for *any* man to take her. Bonnivet becomes infatuated with her, but she is in love with an Italian. He insinuates himself into the good graces of the latter, and then takes his place in bed to avenge himself, for the lady has disdained him. In this case, the woman has sanctioned the entry of the male.[24] She left the front door of her house open for the Italian, who had been told not to go up the main steps, but to take a staircase on the right, a detail that suggests the unconventional nature of the relationship. He was to continue along a gallery to another door[25]; if that door was closed, he was to leave, if it was open, he was to enter quietly and lock it behind him. Bonnivet follows the directions intended for the Italian, and takes his revenge. Although the woman is initially distressed to discover that Bonnivet has taken the place of the Italian, she ultimately accepts his suit when he professes his love and promises to be discreet. When the Italian arrives, Bonnivet watches from the top of the staircase; it is now his staircase to dominate.[26]

As mentioned previously, this tale belongs to a group of four stories ("[Number] 14," "16," "18," "50") cited by Cazauran as exceptions to the rule of condemnation of the *appétit de jouissance*. Tale **"Number 62"** belongs in this category as well. Examination of the other stories in this group reveals that most of them express indulgence toward male passion when it can be presumed that seduction has occurred rather than rape. The situation in tale **"Number 18"** is anomalous, however, in that neither rape nor seduction takes place. Both tales **"16"** and **"18"** also contain significant door imagery.

The Italian widow in **"Number 16"** clearly assents to a seduction, granting the wish of her suitor (again Bonnivet) after three years, a time period that indicates a long courtship.[27] First, though, she tests his mettle by having two chambermaids pretend to be her brothers rattling their swords outside her bedroom. His legitimacy is conveyed when he grabs his *espée nue* and proclaims his determination to "garder ceste porte" (p. 131).

An indulgence toward male passion also occurs when seduction is actually desired by a woman, but is thwarted by her. The cautious lady in **"Number 18"** "qui estoit vaincue d'amour, [et] n'avoit poinct besoing de force" (p. 138) nevertheless imposes difficult tests on her timid suitor. Marguerite shows here that a woman's refusal to permit seduction to take place may be less

natural and recommendable than allowing it. In this case, unhappiness results from the man's subordination to the woman: the woman, controlling all moves, denies him the right to seduce. She sets out to thwart seduction first by insisting that he share her bed without exchanging any more than chaste kisses with her. When he obeys, she is more surprised than pleased. She then leads the gentleman to believe that she will welcome him into her bed, but puts a pretty girl in her entourage in her place, thereby challenging him once again not to seduce.

The woman leaves the door to her bedroom *half* open, a detail which indicates the incomplete access she is allowing him. In turn, he reveals his superior discretion by closing the door behind him. When he notices the substitution, however, he leaves the room in a rage at both the girl and his mistress. The woman, who has seen and heard everything, is surprised by her suitor's restraint, a reaction that suggests that she did not act in good faith, and that she expected him to succumb. But because she does not want to lose him, she asks his forgiveness, and the two are eventually reconciled. Interestingly, in the discussion, even though there is no agreement on the virtue of the gentleman's behavior (Saffredent thinks he should have taken the woman by force; Nomerfide does not), no one disagrees that the woman was less virtuous than the man. We have seen in other stories that seduction is more forgivable than rape; in this story we see that under certain circumstances seduction may even be preferable to continence.[28]

In sum, Marguerite's depiction of sexual encounters between the sexes is complex but not incoherent. She recognizes and condemns male aggression when it is directed against an unwilling victim. At the same time, perhaps in part reflecting a prevailing view that there was a difference between rape and seduction, she attempts to differentiate between the two, examines motives and intentions on the part of both men and women, and suggests greater indulgence for male aggression in cases where women do not appear unwilling.

From the point of view of the history of feminist thought, Marguerite can best be described as rejecting individualistic arguments in favor of relational ones.[29] She does suggest admiration for a woman like the judge's wife in **"Number 46,"** who is alert, rational, and capable of guarding her own virtue, but responsibility toward others is of critical importance: husbands should take proper care of their wives, mothers should protect their daughters, and women should try to reform aggressive suitors. Finally, Marguerite's remarkable use of imagery pertaining to openings and barriers helps clarify the issues, and constitutes a significant artistic contribution to an important topic.

Notes

1. Constance Jordan, *Renaissance Feminism: Literary Texts and Political Models* (Cornell University Press, 1990).

2. Nicole Cazauran, *L'Heptaméron de Marguerite de Navarre* (Paris: Société d'Enseignement Supérieur, 1976), p. 225. These stories stand in opposition to those tales dealing with *la parfaicte amour,* in which lovers escape consummation by sublimating or denying their passion—among other actions, they write poetry, flee to a monastery, or even die. For a perspective on these stories, see my article, "Aspects of the Psychology of Love in the *Heptaméron*," *The Sixteenth Century Journal* 19 (Spring 1988): 81-87.

3. Some feminist critics might object to the inclusion of the category of seduction in a discussion that also treats rape, but my aim is to be faithful to Marguerite's depiction of sexual encounters between the sexes. Just what exactly constitutes rape is a debated issue today; for example, Linda Brookover Bourque writes: "Even at the extremes, there is much disagreement in evaluating a particular instance as a rape or not a rape" (*Defining Rape* [Duke University Press, 1989], p. xv). John Forrester ("Rape, Seduction and Psychoanalysis," in *Rape,* ed. Sylvana Tomaselli and Roy Porter, [Oxford: Basil Blackwell, 1986], pp. 57-83) notes that the "interminable ambiguities of seduction" (p. 57) are antithetical to "certainties" of feminist critics who yield to a "hasty temptation to regard seduction as just rape under another name" (p. 58). As will be seen in this essay, some of the stories in the *Heptaméron* tackle a few of the "interminable ambiguities of seduction."

4. For a broad and useful discussion of imagery in the *Heptaméron* see Marcel Tetel, *Marguerite de Navarre's* Heptaméron: *Themes, Language, and Structure* (Duke University Press, 1973), especially chapters 2 and 3.

5. Freud has written that "penetrating into narrow spaces and opening closed doors are among the commonest of sexual symbols" (*The Interpretation of Dreams,* translated from the German and edited by James Strachey [New York, 1965], p. 433).

6. Andrea Dworkin, *Intercourse* (New York: The Free Press, 1987), p. 133.

7. To name just a few often cited studies, Susan Brownmiller, *Against Our Will: Men, Women and Rape* (New York: Bantam, 1975); Diana E. H. Russell, *The Politics of Rape: The Victim's Perspective* (New York: Stein & Day, 1975); Susan Griffin, *Rape: The Politics of Consciousness,* 3rd rev. and updated ed. (New York: Harper & Row, 1986); Sue Bessmer, *The Laws of Rape* (New York: Praeger, 1984); Susan Estrich, *Real Rape* (Harvard University Press, 1987).

8. For a significant study of rape in medieval French literature and law, and an excellent bibliography on that topic, see Kathryn Gravdal, *Ravishing Maidens: Writing Rape in Medieval French Literature and Law* (University of Pennsylvania Press, 1991). Shortly before this issue of *Romance Quarterly* was due to go to press, a new book relevant to the subject of this essay appeared, Patricia Francis Cholakian's *Rape and Writing in the* Heptaméron *of Marguerite de Navarre* (Southern Illinois University Press, 1991). It was too late to incorporate a discussion of this work into the body of this essay (I treat some, but not all of the same stories), but I will refer in the notes to a few of the author's points, particularly those that differ from my own. In her book, Cholakian expresses dismay that critics "mute and cover over [Marguerite's] gender, as well as her preoccupation with issues that today we would call feminist" (p. xii). Cholakian aims "to demonstrate a way of reading that is both flexible and penetrating" (p. xiii). To that end, she has "in addition to feminist criticism, . . . had recourse to semiotics, narratology, deconstruction, film theory, anthropology, and psychoanalysis" (p. xiii). One of Cholakian's central claims is that "there is every reason to believe that it was the autobiographical experience narrated in the fourth novella that eventually led to the creation of the *Heptaméron* and that the variations of the rape scenario form the work's nucleus" (p. 18).

9. Marguerite de Navarre, *L'Heptaméron,* ed. Michel François, (Paris: Garnier, 1967), p. 19. All references will be to this edition, and will be indicated parenthetically in the text.

10. For a discussion of Gratian's views, see James A. Brundage, *Law, Sex, and Christian Society* (University of Chicago Press, 1987), esp. pp. 229-55.

11. Frances Ferguson, "Rape and the Rise of the Novel," *Misogyny, Misandry, and Misanthropy,* eds. R. Howard Bloch and Frances Ferguson (University of California Press, 1989), p. 88.

12. Here the gentleman's attitude suggests his belief that the widow might consent, thereby exonerating him. This point of view toward rape is discussed by Estrich in chapter 6, "New Answers" (*Real Rape,* pp. 92-104), in the context of the 1975 decision in the British House of Lords in *Director of*

Public Prosecutions v. Morgan according to which a man's *belief* in the woman's consent, even if unreasonable, was enough to prevent a conviction of rape.

13. Cholakian interprets the marks made by the widow on the gentleman's face as "the sign of the princess's transformation from object to subject. They are, in fact, a kind of feminine writing, inscribing onto the man's body the inviolability of the woman's" (p. 25).

14. C. G. Jung gives this description of the descent into lower regions of the house: ". . . the deeper we descend into the house the narrower the horizon becomes, and the more we find ourselves in the darkness, till finally we reach the naked bedrock, and with it that prehistoric time when reindeer hunters fought for a bare and wretched existence against the elemental forces of wild nature. The men of that age were still in full possession of their animal instincts, without which life would have been impossible. The free sway of instinct is not compatible with a strongly developed consciousness" (*Civilization in Transition,* trans. R. F. C. Hull, Bollingen Series XX, vol. 10, 2nd edition, Princeton, 1966, p. 32).

15. The argument of the lady-in-waiting is based on what Susan Griffin ("Rape: The All-American Crime," in *Forcible Rape: The Crime, the Victim, and the Offender,* eds. Duncan Chappell, Robley Geis, and Gilbert Geis [Columbia University Press, 1977], pp. 47-66) would term a "rape myth," here, "that most or much of rape is provoked by the victim" (p. 51). Marguerite's slant is that myth or not, the woman should conduct herself with circumspection. Cholakian's view here is that the widow, by not fulfilling her desire to punish the rapist, has abandoned her "plot," and accepted "a patriarchal definition of her place in the sexual economy" (p. 29).

16. In Lacanian terms, his action might be interpreted as being similar to the "mirror stage," where the child finds a pleasing image of itself reflected back from the mirror, but an image that is nevertheless fictitious. Cholakian asserts that "by attributing to him this fatuous posturing, the writer communicates not his ideas but hers. . . . Her fictionalized version of what he did and thought before he tried to rape her is really a feminine discourse on male vanity" (p. 24). This interpretation seems to suggest that men might not be capable of having insights into male vanity.

17. See Jung, "The Structure of the Unconscious," Bollingen Series, vol. 7, p. 298: "The individual stands, as it were, between the conscious part of the collective psyche and the unconscious part. He

is the reflecting surface in which the world of consciousness can perceive its own unconscious, historical image, even as Schopenhauer says that the intellect holds up a mirror to the universal Will."

18. On February 5, 1522, Briçonnet wrote this to Marguerite: ". . . combien qu'il semble que en la creature que l'on cuide maulvaise il n'y ayt point de bien, il est certain qu'il y en a, qui faict subsister le mal, car dès l'heure que tout le bien seroit estainct, aussi seroit la creature" (Guillaume Briçonnet-Marguerite d'Angoulême, *Correspondance, 1521-1524,* eds. Christine Martineau and Michel Veissière with the help of Henry Heller, Genève, 1975, tome I, p. 149). Henry Heller has pointed out Briçonnet's debt to Pseudo-Dionysius here, and has documented Briçonnet's decisive influence on Marguerite's religious and artistic development ("Marguerite de Navarre and the Reformers of Meaux," *Bibliothèque d'Humanisme et Renaissance* 33 [1971]: 271-310).

19. Freud writes: "Steps, ladders or staircases, or, as the case may be, walking up or down them, are representations of the sexual act" (*The Interpretation of Dreams,* p. 390). Jung takes issue with Freud, arguing that staircase imagery does not necessarily have a sexual connotation ("General Aspects of Psychoanalysis," Bollingen Series, vol. 4, p. 238). Given the context in which this imagery is found in the stories under discussion, however, a sexual interpretation seems fully justified.

20. Jung describes a dream in which a patient rummaged in his attic trying to find something. In the course of his analysis, Jung equates the attic with the head, and therefore the rational faculties (*Civilization in Transition,* p. 354). The judge's widow is not the only female in the *Heptaméron* who uses her head to guard her virtue. The *batelière* in "Number 5" and Françoise in "Number 42" are two more examples. On the other hand, in "Number 72," the nun who is taken advantage of by the monk is described as a "sotte religieuse"; she recognizes too late that she lost her virginity "sans force ny amour, mais par une sotte craincte" (p. 425).

21. In this episode, as in "Number 23," there is no question of the victim needing to defend herself against a possible accusation of encouraging male aggression. In the Renaissance, as now, certain situations are more favorable to a woman's defense. Sue Bessmer lists cases in which the law speaks for the woman (*The Laws of Rape,* pp. 301-43). These include statutory rape, rape of a sleeping or unconscious woman, and impersonation of the husband.

22. Cholakian finds this story less ambiguous than I do, writing that "This assault is clearly and unequivocally rape" (p. 208).

23. We find again a belief that the woman will consent.

24. I read this story differently from Cholakian, who insists on the woman's virtue: "The proof that rape is not seduction is the rape itself, for before she was doubly deceived by Bonnivet, the Milanese lady had been virtuous. In other words, a woman's dishonesty is proved by a man's lie . . . it makes no difference that the Milanese lady was faithful to her husband" (p. 121). In point of fact, though, the woman was evidently willing to be unfaithful to her husband with the Italian.

25. The presence of more than one door, and also a gallery, is suggestive of a brothel, and consistent with the fact that the woman in question welcomed more than one lover into her bed. See Freud, *The Interpretation of Dreams*, p. 390: "A dream of going through a suite of rooms is a brothel or harem dream."

26. In another story (no. 25), the staircase to a woman is unwittingly conceded by the husband to the lover. The woman has left the door open for her suitor, a prince (possibly the future François Ier). He arrives at her home, and her husband, an aged lawyer, leads him up the staircase to her, lighting the way with his candle.

27. In this story, as in "Number 4" and 62, prior time spent in the company of the desired woman seems crucial for establishing a distinction between seduction and rape. Forrester points out that seduction "takes time" (p. 81). On the other hand, rape is "punctual, instantaneous" (p. 82).

28. It appears that in a case in which neither rape nor seduction takes place, the woman exercises greater power than the man. This is a reversal of what some feminist critics would view as the standard situation, one in which men have power and women do not.

29. Jordan writes: "Renaissance feminism can fairly be analyzed in individualist and relational terms" (p. 8).

Carla Freccero (essay date 1993)

SOURCE: Freccero, Carla. "Unwriting Lucretia: 'Heroic Virtue' in the *Heptaméron*." In *Heroic Virtue, Comic Infidelity: Reassessing Marguerite de Navarre's* Heptaméron, edited by Dora E. Polachek, pp. 77-89. Amherst, Mass.: Hestia Press, 1993.

[*In the following essay, Freccero examines the mythic notion of heroism in the* Heptaméron, *particularly in relation to class and gender differences.*]

Every encounter with a representation of the rape of Lucretia is an encounter with a literary topos of Western civilization. And, as topos, the meaning of this rape is constructed as universal, transcending historical conditions: in every age and place, Lucretia had to be raped so that Rome could be liberated from tyranny. A topos, however, can also be understood in its "literal" meaning as a concrete place, a particular reproduction of the universal meaning of the rape of Lucretia at a local site. From this perspective, a description of the details of textual experience enables the scholar to challenge (or at least dilute) the ahistorical meaning of the rape of Lucretia with the experience of other historical messages.

Stephanie Jed[1]

At the end of **"Novella 42,"** Parlamente concludes her tale in characteristic exemplary moralistic fashion with the words, "Je vous prie que, à son exemple, nous demorions victorieuses de nous-mesmes, car c'est la plus louable victoire que nous puissions avoir" (294; 389).[2] Oisille, the surprisingly feisty grandmother of the group, remarks,

—Je ne voy que ung mal, . . . que les actes vertueux de ceste fille n'ont esté du temps des historiens, car ceulx qui ont tant loué leur Lucresse l'eussent laissé au bout de la plume, pour escripre bien au long les vertuz de ceste-cy.

(294; 389)

The name of Lucretia in such a context reminds us, as Stephanie Jed points out, of "the meaning of Lucretia's rape in the history of ideas: a prologue to republican freedom" (54), and presents feminist scholars with a peculiar political (and ethical) dilemma:

To retell the story of the rape of Lucretia . . . is to enter into some sort of binding relationship with all of those readers and writers who somehow found the narrative of this rape edifying, pleasurable, or even titillating, and to be bound by the vision of those readers and writers to look at the rape as they did (and do)—as a paradigmatic component of all narratives of liberation.

(Jed, *Chaste Thinking* 49)

Thus it is with trepidation (and grief) that I confront the apotropaic power of this name as memorial to and icon of my entry into and complicity with humanism. But like Hélène Cixous, who argues the phallogocentricity of horrifying myths of femininity and says, "You only have to look at the Medusa straight on to see her. And she's not deadly. She's beautiful and she's laughing," Oisille takes a skeptical view.[3] For what is already (and strikingly) apparent in Oisille's invocation of the *topos* of the rape of Lucretia is the way she first un-topics Lucretia by referring to the work of historians—thus historicizing the tale and its exemplary function—then dismisses "her," this emblem, this proper name, as "their" creation, "leur Lucresse". Lucretia lived, and should have been left, she says, at the tip of their pens, the point of contact or penetration that constitutes the humanist philological impulse to contaminate and violate in order, subsequently, to castigate and purge. To leave Lucretia there, "au bout de la plume," is to name her a patriarchal fantasm, the ventriloquizing automaton that permits what Alice Jardine has called gynesis.[4]

Jed argues that "only the description of textual experience can interrupt this tradition of imagining freedom in the context of sexual violence" (52), and her work examines the relations between (masculinist) philology, the production of meaning, and the political ideologies of humanism. However, in this study she does not discuss what might arise from a textual encounter less clearly conceived of as adversarial, that is the potentially sororal filiation that might arise in the encounter between a feminist scholar and a woman writer of the past. While I cannot here propose to study the conditions of production of the **Heptaméron,** I would like to describe disturbances produced by the intercalation of some of the castigated manuscripts and editions of this text as they relate, in part, to the question of authorial agency and (perhaps) to the interplay between the woman writer and the apparatus through which we read "her" text.

"Novella 42" is a novella that, editors argue, deals with a family romance starring Marguerite's brother, the young prince François. Patricia Cholakian concurs, and devotes a chapter to it, aptly entitled "My Brother, My Hero."[5] In at least three places in the narrative and discussion of **"Novella 42,"** the definitive edition A (*ms. français* 1512) reproduced by Michel François, and Adrien de Thou's 1553 manuscript (*ms. français* 1524), seem at war with Marguerite's first recognized and accredited editor, Claude Gruget's 1559 edition, which was commissioned by Marguerite's daughter Jeanne after her death.[6]

The struggle, what Bakhtin has called the dialogics of discourse, competing voices unharmoniously coexisting on different registers in a text, turns around, predictably, the person of the king, here described in terms that the editors and Cholakian attribute to Marguerite's enscripting of her sibling worship:

[Parlamante:]—Des perfections, grace, beaulté et grandes vertuz de ce jeune prince, ne vous en diray aultre chose, sinon que en son temps ne trouva jamays son pareil.

(*L'Heptaméron,* 286; 381)

[Longarine:]—Et, voiant les occasions que ceste fille avoit d'oblier sa conscience et son honneur, et la vertu qu'elle eut de vaincre son cueur [;voyant les occasions et moyens qu'elle avoit, je dy qu'elle se povoit nommer la forte femme.] et *sa volunté et celluy qu'elle aymoit plus qu'elle-mesmes avecq toutes perfections* des occasions et moiens qu'elle en avoit, je dictz qu'elle se povoit nommer la forte femme.

(295, with intercalated variant from Gruget; *ms.* A "addition" in italics; 390)

In Longarine's speech praising the self-control of the female protagonist Françoise, manuscript A includes the passage "et celluy qu'elle aymoit plus qu'elle-mesmes avecq toutes perfections," referring to the young prince, thus "adding" the flattery that Adrien de Thou's summary of the story also provides:

Un jeune prince meit son affection en une fille, de laquelle (combien qu'elle fut de bas et pauvre lieu) ne peut jamais obtenir ce qu'il en avoit esperé, quelque poursuyte qu'il en feit. Parquoy, le prince, congnoissant sa vertu et honnesteté, laissa son entreprinse, l'eut toute sa vie en bonne estime, et luy feit de grands biens, la maryant avec un sien serviteur.

(286)

The Gruget edition is far more terse, relegating the narrative to the genre of medieval *pastourelle* with its predictable, class-conditioned, rape scenario that, in this case, has a happy ending:

Continence d'une jeune fille contre l'opiniastre poursuitte amoureuse d'un des grands seigneurs de France et l'heureux succez qu'en eut la damoiselle.

(481)

As these variants and others suggest, what tears at the narrative is a gendering of heroic virtue at the site of nationalism, at the site of what also might be called a conflict between the people and their prince. Lucretia meets Marianne.[7]

Jed's study of the relation between the rape of Lucretia and the philological birth of humanism shows, in part, how a certain relation to "liberty" is established via a chastizing or castigating of a violated body, which is in turn associated with the excessive passions of tyranny (27-28). She retells the narrative of Brutus the castigator, Lucretia's brother, who admonishes the Romans not to cry for the death of Lucretia but to take up arms against the Tarquins in order to found Republican Rome (15-17). When she points out that "Brutus finds in Lucretia's chastity the female version of his self-castigation" (15), Jed rightly marks Brutus' relation to Lucretia as a projective displacement. But she does not explain why this narrative of masculine initiation into nationhood (into a being-for-the-state) should require passage through the violated and castigated female body in order to erect itself. This narrative of masculine accession to impassivity, to chaste thinking, to objectivity, literally passes through the body of a woman; it thus founds itself upon the bloody remains of a violated and excised femininity.[8]

Jean-Joseph Goux discusses masculine initiatory transitions in terms of loss and compensation:

In this transition it is, among other things, the sacrifice (the bloody loss necessary for the establishment of the phallus) that is recovered, forgotten, or rather changed

in meaning to the point of becoming quite unrecogniz-
able, . . . That which the exercise of philosophy ne-
cessitates, is it not the cutting off of, the break with,
sensible nature, the immediate, those things which
alone allow elevation, ascension? It is in this movement of death to the sensible, indeed of the execration
of bad matter, source of all evil, for the purpose of attaining the enjoyment of the idea, that the sacrificial
motion would continue by interiorizing and sublimating itself. This restoration, this liberation, were archaically called phallic.

(52)[9]

The sacrifice of initiation is a symbolic castration, a
movement from the penis (corruptible materiality, the
body) to the phallus (incorruptible ideality, the mind), a
movement from the realm of the mother (matter) to the
father (idea), negotiated by and through the masculine
initiate himself (56-61). As anthropological/mythic antecedent to modern phallocentricity, the symbolic initiatory process haunts, as Jed's narrative of the birth of
humanism helps to show, the valorization of a chaste
impassivity, an adult masculine heroics (of citizenship),
won or restored at the cost of a violent and "bloody renunciation," a cutting off:

> Access to the phallus is thus, in the initiation, the com-
> pensation, the symbolic reward for the loss that the
> masculine subject must suffer by the bloody renuncia-
> tion of maternal ties, the sign of the torturous emanci-
> pation from an anterior bond, sealed by the first birth.
> The phallus has thus the role of a detachable value (it
> is detachment itself) which arises from the bloody cut-
> ting of a vital bond ("symbolic castration") and which
> rewards (by a second birth) the metaphoric joining of
> the paternal ancestors, even if they are only evoked by
> a name which continues the lineage and allows admis-
> sion to the society of males.

("The Phallus" 61)

In the symbolic order that constitutes phallocratic modernity, this process inhabits, as representational remnant, the constitution of the citizen subject, and thus a
splitting off occurs whereby instead of the penis (body)
of the masculine subject himself, the bloody matter that
is excised, destroyed, castigated, is figured as *the body,*
the mother, woman. In the narrative of the rape and
death of Lucretia as the prelude to republican freedom,
in the narrative whereby, mythically and eternally, "in
every age and place, Lucretia had to be raped so that
Rome could be liberated from tyranny," the (meaning
of the) constitution of the masculine citizen-subject is
thus re-enacted.

Cholakian makes the point that **"Novella 42"** "develops
the theme of the sentimental education [. . .]. The question is how the hero will make the transition from boy
to man (and from prince to king)" (*Rape and Writing,*
168), and thus is, in some sense, an initiatory narrative.
But, as she also notes, the narrative shifts in point of

view between a masculine perspective and a feminine
one, for the moment the prince catches sight of the girl,
a genealogy and a name, Françoise, is conferred upon
her. If this is an encrypting of the hero's name, François,
in its feminine form, (and for the purposes of my argument it will suit me well to go along with the editors
and critics in believing that this is a story about Marguerite's brother, the king), then it is also a narrative
about, at its simplest figural level, an accession to royal
heroic virtue that passes through the (middle-class)
body, person, of a woman. For what the story is designed in part to demonstrate is how the prince develops from a boy into a (worthy) king. From penis to
phallus. From François, through Françoise, to France.
Françoise, as the feminine form of the nation for which
François is the nominal icon, is thus somehow also
France or French matter, and the French are, indeed, the
people, the members of the body politic whose head is
their king. French matter, in its encounter with the royal
imprint, is also, and not incidentally, the text.

This story is about Françoise too; indeed it is her heroic
virtue which Parlamente and the other women praise at
the end of the novella, heroic virtue defined in classic
consonance with chaste thinking. Says Parlamente: "Je
vous prie que, à son exemple, nous demorions victorieuses de nous-mesmes, car c'est la plus louable victoire que nous puissions avoir . . ." (294; 389). And
Longarine: "il fault estimer la vertu dont la plus grande
est à vaincre son cueur" (295; 390).

Or is it? Chilton's English translation supplies the name
of Saffredent as speaker in the passage that follows
Longarine's remark. In manuscript A (*ms. 1512*), however, it is Longarine who goes on to contradict herself
by saying: "Puisque vous estimez la grandeur de la
vertu par la mortification de soy-mesmes, je dictz que
ce seigneur estoit plus louable qu'elle, veu l'amour
qu'il luy portoit, la puissance, occasion et moien qu'il
en avoit . . ." (295; 390). Thus she nearly echoes the
words (she) used to praise Françoise.[10] Once again, textual variants produce or manifest the symptoms of what
Cholakian calls the problematic perspectival shifts between masculine and feminine points of view in these
narratives and suggest the possibility that what is occurring is, indeed, a splitting of the same (subject) into
masculine and feminine subjects of heroic virtue. Whose
story is this anyway?[11] Elements of the tale suggest that
remnants of symbolic masculine initiatory transitions
mythically haunt the accession to sovereign masculinity. There is, in **"Novella 42,"** what has been called an
"excessive" reference to kinship ties, most notably
around Françoise:

> Ung jour, estant en une eglise, regarda une jeune fille,
> laquelle avoit aultresfois en son enffance esté nourrye
> au chasteau où il demeuroit. Et, après la mort de sa
> mere, son pere se remaria; parquoy, elle se retira en

Poictou, avecq son frere. Ceste fille, qui avoit nom Françoise, avoit une suer bastarde, que son pere aymoit très fort; et la maria en ung sommelier d'eschansonnerye de ce jeune prince, dont elle tint aussi grand estat que nul de sa maison. Le pere vint à morir et laissa pour le partage de Françoise ce qu'il tenoit auprès de ceste bonne ville; parquoy, après qu'il fut mort, elle se retira où estoit son bien. Et, à cause qu'elle estoit à marier et jeune de seize ans, ne se vouloit tenir seule en sa maison, mais se mist en pension chez sa suer la sommeliere . . . elle sembloit mieulx gentil femme ou princesse, que bourgeoise. . . . Et quant il fut retourné en sa chambre, s'enquist de celle qu'il avoit veu en l'eglise, et recongneut que aultresfois en sa jeunesse estoit-elle allée au chasteau jouer aux poupines avecq sa suer, à laquelle il la feit recongnoistre.

(287; 381)[12]

The continuous reminder, throughout the narrative, that Françoise was raised in the household of the prince, serves to impose the incest taboo on their relationship (Cholakian, *Rape and Writing* 173). The kinship references in the tale are thus specific and overdetermined, for they function to mark the sororal relation of Françoise to the prince.

Françoise, in the tale, both is and is not the prince's sister. The resemblance prevaricates so that she can be simultaneously circulating goods and prohibited sister. The narrative makes clear the dysfunctionality of her kin relative to the responsibility they have to circulate her properly (and to prohibit incest): her sister begs her to meet with the prince, while her brother-in-law arranges a tryst at his behest. The agent of accession to heroic virtue in the tale is thus also Françoise herself, for herself as much as for the prince. Another element that marks the narrative as initiatory remnant is the determining presence of the prince's mother in the tale, she who recalls him to the household, or detains him there, who is his treasurer, and whose disapproval places constraints upon his actions; in short, she who controls his circulation. The family romance thus entails not the relation of the son and his desired, passive, and prohibited mother, to the father (or the law), but rather a relation of the son to his closest female kin.

If the mother succeeds in keeping her son within the household, how does this young prince then accede to phallic sovereignty? Does the mother embody both maternal and paternal positions in the way that Françoise acts both as the prince's split subject (his abjected bodily self) and as resistance to the ideology of chaste thinking that would have her body as the castigated cost of its achievement?[13] Here the narrative seems to militate against phallocratic teleology by strengthening and rendering efficacious the maternal-filial relation and by installing the law as a maternal, rather than a paternal prohibition (291; 386; and 292; 387). The place of sovereign phallic privilege is conserved, as we might expect it to be, with an interesting twist: the phallic feminine—she who keeps her phallus and her son—rules. And yet, is this maternal (writer, queen) not herself a split subject, both sovereign and sororal (both Louise and Marguerite)?[14]

Female agency in Marguerite's tales frequently coincides with class difference, that is, with a non-aristocratic subject-position, and while this is a commonplace of more comic narratives of female agency (clever and/or lusty lower-class women) and a stereotype of the lower born in Marguerite as elsewhere, it also works in this tale as a recognition of bourgeois resistance to aristocratic abrogation of privilege, where the Christian and courtly ideologies of "vraye amitié," equalize, as Longarine/Saffredent points out, "le prince et le pauvre" (295; 390). Françoise is French, after all, and a bourgeoise. Thus her resistance to inscription in the narrative of abjection (that is as bloody mutilated corpse that is defiled, reviled, and castigated) makes of her a revolutionary force. However, this resistance is performed in the name of chaste thinking, that is in the name of a self-castigation, a cutting off from desire and pleasure, for the good of . . . the prince, the nation, honor. She is victorious in the tale, victorious over herself, as Parlamente points out, adding that this is the lesson that "nous," the female addressees of the moral exemplarity of the tale, must learn. Then our accession to honor, like Lucretia's, would be achieved through the self-castigating gesture of overcoming our emotions and desires, like Lucretia, for the good of the state.

Lucretia's self-castigation was, however, suicidal, and the rebirth it produced was in her brother-citizens. Marguerite's narrative, with its split agency, its double rebirth into honor of both masculine prince and feminine "pauper," suggests a more modern path toward the narrative of republican "freedom," one where the woman may live. The life into which one is reborn in this narrative is, as Goux notes, a phallic order; it is, indeed, phallocracy.[15] Marguerite's tale thus indicates one direction in which female subject-citizenry will be constituted, attested by the advent of bourgeois nationalism in Europe and the documents of nineteenth century liberal political philosophy.[16]

Goux argues that "In Western society, the masculine agent must consent to a sacrifice to which the returns (his entitled returns) correspond only virtually and abstractly," and that

> What remains is subjection to a universal law, a symbolic order which is the same for all, and to which the subject must submit. This symbolic order arises from the interiorization of certain demands which are no longer experienced as social demands, and above all not as the demands of a social exchange.

("The Phallus" 67)

His concern in this essay is to historicize and culturally delineate the phallus or symbolic order of contemporary (Lacanian) psychoanalysis and to show how an archaic and mythic initiatory configuration inhabits the unconscious of modern philosophical phallocentrism. In modernity, he argues,

> We see that the phallus must thus take on a new meaning. Rather than appearing as the immediately negotiable restitution of a loss, it becomes pure mediation, the mark of an integrity rediscovered after the sacrifice of the mother. With the phallus, the masculine subject affirms himself, but without any nuptial counterpart being necessary to ratify the function of renunciation. The phallus becomes a mediation in itself, an abstract opening which attests to the subject's accession to an order and a unity conceived of in their metaphysical elevation. Obtaining a woman surrendered by the group and thus the function of communication, is no longer the point. Erected for itself, the phallus is a monastic, celibate attestation of the detachment of "matter" and "nature" which guarantees integrity, identity, unity.
>
> (68)

The result is that

> that which had been thought of as a procedure of gift-exchange, of giving and receiving between present and living partners maintaining a reciprocal relationship, is now broken into two acts which not only may be unaware of each other, but which no longer have any necessary relationship, either in social space or in social time, save the abstract subjection to a constraint which becomes law.
>
> (70)

In his concern with the phallus as the "general equivalent for the objects of the drives," and thus for the inscription of the phallus within a Marxian economic logic, Goux overlooks or does not concern himself with what might be thought of as the intermediary historical stage of the symbolic or, to work against the notion of a progressive historical evolution of the phallus, what might be called another moment in the genealogy of phallocentrism, a moment that might also be said to mark Marguerite de Navarre's text as both early and modern. For in this text, it is true that the demands one must interiorize, the constraint to which one must submit, are not experienced as concretely (and entirely) social, as part of an immediate exchange, and do indeed become law. The order and unity to which the subject accedes are conceived of in their metaphysical elevation, as honor and virtue. Yet the biographical aura of the novella and the absent place of its paternal prohibition (and the present place of its maternal, royal, and phallic prohibition) suggest not quite a "pure" mediation; indeed, they suggest the presence of a nuptial counterpart, albeit of a potentially queerer sort. Nor is this symbolic order the same for all, though we might want to argue that the erection of the phallic sovereign

subject of the nation-state produces the appearance of the godhead as guarantor of the universality of that symbolic order. Rather, what **"Novella 42"** delineates, in its tortured and (more or less) unconscious way, is the subject's submission to a law that is the nation-state, a place of phallocracy that is not quite yet phallocentrism. Both François and Françoise, in the self-castigating movement that leaves behind emotion and desire, are reborn into honor and virtue, into France.

And it is here that we can witness one of the peculiarly modern inflections of Marguerite's text, in that it designates a future site not only for the masculine citizen-subject of the nation, but for the feminine one as well. In its most nationalistic version, we might read a rallying cry to the nation's women to let their honor, virtue, and self-restraint be the civilizing force behind the nation's barbaric, appetite-driven, but nevertheless noble, virtuous, and heroic men, even as those men learn that women, as citizen-subjects, have the right (and the duty) to accede to honor and virtue, to be themselves citizens, *Françoises*. What of, then, the revolutionary and feminine force of the tale, its disdain for Lucretia? And what of, on the other hand, the maternal phallus, the phallic feminine placed and displaced throughout the *Heptaméron*'s conspicuously absented paternal/royal spaces? An alternative heroic figure haunts this narrative, haunts it because she appears only in the Gruget variant of the manuscript and substitutes for the name of Jambicque, whose story follows that of Françoise and the young prince. Jambicque is a woman who acts upon her desire, her pleasure, and gets away with it, as do many of the women in the tales of the fifth day (stories that deal with successful female agency).[17] Gruget replaces the name of Jambicque with Camilla throughout his edition, as Michel François notes (482 n. 609). Camilla, amazon-like servant of Diana, chaste (lesbian?) warrior of Vergil's *Aeneid* and Aeneas' intra-textual twin, assists Turnus against the ancestors of those whose historians will later celebrate the rape and death of Lucretia. Can we speak then of another archaic remnant in this text, the remains of what myth and anthropology, as well as contemporary radical lesbian feminism, might call matriarchy? A dream of another social order, a feudal one nevertheless, where women rule, where, in Luce Irigaray's formulation, the goods get together, where the traffic is among but not in women?

> . . . She is a warrior;
> her woman's hands have never grown accustomed
> to distaffs or the baskets of Minerva;
> a virgin, she was trained to face hard battle
> and to outrace the wind with speeding feet.
> Across the tallest blades of standing grain
> she flies—and never mars the tender ears;
> or poised upon the swelling wave, she skims
> the sea—her swift soles never touch the water.
> And as Camilla passes, all the young

pour out from the field and house; the matrons crowd
and marvel, staring, in astonishment
at how proud royal purple veils Camilla's
smooth shoulders, how a clasp of gold entwines
her hair, at how she bears her Lycian quiver,
her shepherd's pike of myrtle tipped with steel.[18]

A guerrilla girl and not a Roman matron. And what if Turnus, and not Rome? Is it a ruse of modern and western phallocentrism, of the nation-state that France will become, that passion, emotion, lust, desire, cluster on the side of tyranny, to become the rapist designs of Tarquin? That, to be enfranchised citizens we women must excise these emotions from ourselves and ally with a Brute who would kill his own for the sake of the nation? Marguerite seems to suggest that yes, indeed, we must. And yet, in the disturbances of her text, the text we read as hers, shadows of a (utopian) doubt remain.

Notes

1. *Chaste Thinking: The Rape of Lucretia and the Birth of Humanism* (Bloomington: Indiana UP, 1989) 51. I would like to thank John Freccero, Beth Pittenger, Lyn Staack, and Scott Straus for the discussions that have assisted me in thinking through this paper.

2. Marguerite de Navarre, *L'Heptaméron,* ed. Michel François (Paris: Garnier, 1967); Marguerite de Navarre, *The Heptaméron,* trans. P. A. Chilton (London: Penguin, 1984, repr. 1986). All citations refer to these editions; page numbers to the French edition are given first.

3. "The Laugh of the Medusa," in *New French Feminisms: An Anthology,* ed. E. Marks & I. de Courtivron (New York: Schocken, 1980): 245-264; 255.

4. *Gynesis: Configurations of Woman and Modernity* (Ithaca: Cornell UP, 1985).

5. See Michel François, *L'Heptaméron,* 481: "Il n'est pas de doute que Marguerite veuille ainsi désigner son propre frère, le futur François Ier; on se souvient qu'elle a déjà usé de la même périphrase dans la vingt-cinquième nouvelle. La ville de Touraine est donc Amboise où résidait Louise de Savoie." Patricia Cholakian, *Rape and Writing in the* Heptaméron *of Marguerite de Navarre* (Carbondale: Southern Illinois UP, 1991), 167-8: ". . . all the evidence points to Marguerite's brother François as the hero/villain. The author's close emotional involvement with her male protagonist causes this tale to be split in focus between the heroine's and the hero's perspectives."

6. Pierre Boaistuau's 1558 edition is banished by François as corrupt because it "défigure par trop le texte de la Reine," (*L'Heptaméron* xviii) and because "Le texte est incomplet; il ne compte que 67 nouvelles qui ne sont pas divisées en journées et ont été distribuées dans un ordre arbitraire" (xxv).

7. See Neil Hertz, "Medusa's Head: Male Hysteria under Political Pressure" and the responses from C. Gallagher and J. Fineman, in *The End of the Line: Essays on Psychoanalysis and the Sublime* (New York: Columbia UP, 1985): 161-217; also Kaja Silverman, "Liberty, Maternity, Commodification," *New Formations* 5 (summer 1988): 69-89.

8. See Elizabeth Pittenger's discussion, via Luce Irigaray and Gayatri Spivak, of a similar phenomenon as it relates to textuality, in "Dispatch Quickly: The Mechanical Reproduction of Pages," 395: "The female body serves as symbolic site in which social meaning is concretized at the same time that any concrete, material specificity is emptied out of 'the female body' in order to insure its service as a pure and proper vehicle. The power of Irigaray's argument is the link she makes between sexuality and textuality. The formulation 'female as bearer of imprints' exposes the implications of a textuality figured as female." *Shakespeare Quarterly* 42: 4 (winter 1991): 389-408. See also "Women on the Market," in *This Sex Which Is Not One,* trans. C. Porter and C. Burke (Ithaca: Cornell UP, 1985): 170-91; and Gayatri Spivak, "Displacement and the Discourse of Woman," in *Displacement: Derrida and After,* ed. M. Krupnick (Bloomington: Indiana UP, 1983): 169-95.

9. "The Phallus: Masculine Identity and the 'Exchange of Women,'" in *differences* 4: *The Phallus Issue* (spring 1992): 40-75.

10. The differences are that *puissance* appears in this phrase, whereas desire and love appear in the first; honor and virtue are mentioned in the first but not the second, which takes a distance from chaste thinking by disparagingly calling it self-mortification.

11. Using the notion of split focalization, Cholakian argues that Marguerite deliberately encodes a "view from elsewhere" (20) to insert female agency and perspective into the conventional narrative plot of male desire. My argument differs in that I attribute the shifts in "Novella 42" to a phenomenon of twinning or splitting, whereby what is at work in the text is a (gendered) splitting or doubling of the subject of heroic virtue. Thus I am concerned less with authorial intentionality and agency and more with a psychoanalytics of the text.

12. Cholakian says of Françoise's genealogy that "Although it does provide a kind of garrulous verisimilitude, this explanation seems at first glance to supply more information than the reader can possibly want or need" (*Rape and Writing,* 169).

13. See Goux's discussion here, "The Phallus" 63-64.

14. This is another instance of the way in which the *Heptaméron* can be called a maternal text, and Marguerite's praxis that of maternal sovereignty. See my "Marguerite de Navarre and the Politics of Maternal Sovereignty," in *Cosmos* 7 (1992), Special Issue: *Women and Sovereignty,* ed. L. Fradenburg (132-149). See also Goux, "The Phallus," 63: "The phallus would thus be the more or less cryptic symbolic attestation that the masculine subject (and it is this which makes him a subject) is entitled to enter as a taker into the circuit of the exchange of women: the sign, more precisely, that he has satisfied the differentiated requirements of a double sacrifice—maternal and sororal."

15. "The Phallus," 64: "It would be archaically, as a *male subject,* and in a close relationship to the phallic simulacrum, that the subject would constitute itself."

16. See Cora Kaplan's discussion of Mary Wollstonecraft's "reply" to Rousseau in "Wild Nights: Pleasure/Sexuality/Feminism," in *Sea Changes: Essays on Culture and Feminism* (London: Verso, 1986): 31-56; see also Carla Freccero, "Notes of a Post-Sex Wars Theorizer," in *Conflicts in Feminism,* ed. M. Hirsch & E. Fox Keller (New York: Routledge, 1990): 305-25.

17. I disagree with Colette Winn's view that "L'appellatif Jambicque dénonce ainsi la hardiesse de la femme qui affirme son désir d'aimer." To argue that Jambicque is denounced for her desire is to accept only the moralizing judgments of some of the *devisants.* The narrative, in this case, contradicts their judgments, so that the question of Jambicque's desire is, at the very least, problematized. See "La Dynamique appellative des femmes dans l'*Heptaméron* de Marguerite de Navarre," *Romanic Review* 77 (1986): 209-218, 217.

18. *The* Aeneid *of Vergil,* trans. A. Mandelbaum (New York: Bantam, 1971): 189 (vii: 1057-1072).

Dora E. Polachek (essay date 1993)

SOURCE: Polachek, Dora E. "Save the Last Laugh for Me: Revamping the Script of Infidelity in Novella 69." In *Heroic Virtue, Comic Infidelity: Reassessing Marguerite de Navarre's* Heptaméron, edited by Dora E. Polachek, pp. 155-70. Amherst, Mass.: Hestia Press, 1993.

[*In the following essay, Polachek compares the use of transvestism, humor, and gender conflict in "Novella 69" of the* Heptaméron *and novella 17 of the fifteenth-century* Cent nouvelles nouvelles.]

If I give the same title to two different texts, are they not all the more opposites for the arbitrary, circumstantial unity imposed on them?

The conflict is internal.

Edmond Jabès (180)

OF SMILES, SMIRKS, AND LITERARY CRITICISM

The nineteenth century played a crucial role in disseminating the work of Marguerite de Navarre. Not only were her poems and letters published (Sainte-Beuve 1), but by 1880 eight different French editions of the *Heptaméron* were in circulation (*Heptaméron*; François xxvi).[1] Such notoriety, however, did exact its price. Perhaps the unease engendered by a woman writing—and prolifically at that—played itself out under the guise of literary criticism. As we approach the twenty-first century, Sainte-Beuve's pronouncement on Marguerite de Navarre's literary undertaking still resonates:

Et puis, quand une femme écrit, on est tenté toujours de demander, en souriant, qui est là derrière.

(327 n.30)

If, for a moment, one were willing to bracket that smile and engage in an academic exercise of lending credence to Sainte-Beuve's evaluation, a cursory reading of the *Heptaméron*'s **"Novella 69"** could be cited. Indeed, there is a man standing behind it. The sixteenth-century tale takes as its intertext novella 17 of the fifteenth-century *Cent nouvelles nouvelles.* Critics identify the author of the novella (someone the text calls "Monseigneur") as either Louis XI or Philippe le Bon.[2] "Monseigneur" and the 35 other tellers of the 100 tales are linked by one essential quality—their maleness: "tout le personnel de la cour . . . mais pas de femmes!" remarks Pierre Jourda. He also notes the antifeminist thrust of their tales, characteristic of the kinds of stories that unite men after a good dinner as they relax around a hearty fire (xix).

But such a clearly misogynistic vantage point should put on the alert anyone familiar with the *Heptaméron,* for if there is anything clear about the work, it is its ambiguity.[3] Furthermore, to dismiss any one of its novellas as a mere rehashing of an original tale is to beg the question, for what in fact does "original" mean in a genre characterized by its extensive borrowing from both an oral and written tradition?[4] How, then, are we to take Sainte-Beuve's round condemnation of Marguerite de Navarre's artistic endeavor? In his review of Le Roux de Lincy's magisterial three-volume 1853 edition of **L'Heptaméron des Nouvelles de très haute et très illustre princesse Marguerite d'Angoulême,** he puts it this way:

Comme poète et comme écrivain, son originalité est peu de chose, ou, pour parler plus nettement, elle n'en a aucune.

(3)

Coupled with his previous remark we see the two premises informing Sainte-Beuve's logic: Since the work
cannot give what it does not have, it would be a waste
of time to look for anything "new" there. Secondly,
anything "creative" that a reader might find in the work
certainly could not be attributed to Marguerite de Navarre's hand. What Sainte-Beuve is hinting at is that the
power to create lies with those who "have it where it
counts" (to borrow Roland Barthes' expression [75]);
and Marguerite de Navarre is sorely lacking.

Putting definitively to rest the complex question of authorship lies beyond the scope of this paper. What I offer is a strategy of reading which strongly supports the
presence of Marguerite de Navarre's hand in the writing of **"Novella 69."** The red herring of "originality"
has led me to uncover at least three subsequent versions
of *CNN* [*Cent nouvelles nouvelles*] 17: the earliest by
Nicolas de Troyes (c. 1535-1537), the next by Giovan-
battista Giraldi (1565) and the third by Celio Malespini
(c. 1583-4).[5] All three are male-penned and virtually
identical to the medieval source. The subtle modifications wrought in **"Novella 69"** stand out because they
are unique. Sainte-Beuve may have been smiling, but I
propose to show that the last laugh may very well be on
him.

By comparing *CNN* 17 with the ***Heptaméron***'s **"Novella 69,"** I shall demonstrate that the author of the
Heptaméron transforms a male-authored misogynistic
medieval intertext so that it embodies a distinctly feminist vision. I shall focus upon the new version's radical
change in tonality and emphasis.[6] What specific modifications does the Renaissance version make in order to
create a story which differs so markedly from its source?
To answer this question I shall examine the following
four aspects of the two versions: center of orientation
(i.e., which protagonist is perceived as the dominant
one)[7], plot, peripety (the moment of surprise reversal),
and denouement (how the story ends).

CENTER OF ORIENTATION: WHO COUNTS

There is no doubt that **"Novella 69"** maintains the identical schema found in its medieval source: the protagonists are the same (an old married couple and a young,
female servant) as is the plot (the husband tries repeatedly to seduce the servant); so is its comic reversal of
the husband's expectations (he is outwitted in a ruse
where his wife discovers him wearing the female servant's clothes and performing her work).

As similar as these two versions may appear they nevertheless tell two different stories. When we compare
the beginning of each tale, we find each version privileging the position of a different protagonist. With its
first sentence, the *Cent nouvelles nouvelles* version
clearly places in the foreground both the social and
physical presence of the husband:

N'agueres que a Paris presidoit en la chambre des
comptes ung grand clerc chevalier assez sur eage, mais
tres joyeux et plaisant homme estoit, tant en sa maniere
d'estre comme en ses devises, ou qu'il les adressast, ou
aux hommes ou aux femmes.

(76)

These opening four lines of text stress the magnitude of
the husband's position in this society (a great nobleman
who presides over the court of accounts). By his demeanor ("sa maniere d'estre") and verbal prowess ("ses
devises"), he exerts the same type of force in his social
encounters. His being old ("assez sur eage") becomes,
then, a virtual anomaly. What remains with the reader is
the accumulation of adjectives which function as eras-
ers of any of the negative markers of old age in the
man.

The second sentence presents the salient features of the
wife and emphasizes the marked contrast between the
two:

Ce bon seigneur avait femme espousée desja ancienne
et maladive, dont il avoit belle lignée.

(76)

This sentence devoted to the wife is remarkable in at
least four respects: It constitutes barely two lines of
text; not only is its subject the man, but it adds yet another laudatory adjective to his list ("bon"), this time
appended to a new noun ("seigneur") which, in the
manner of the introductory "chevalier" stresses his sovereignty. On the side of the sentence's object, the wife,
we find two adjectives: old and sickly. Her lack of
power in the story is also prefigured by her other marking trait: that she has already provided her husband
with a fine lineage. Having done that, she is both literally and figuratively spent.[8] St. Augustine's commentary
on women in his *De Genesi ad Litteram* is particularly
apt here, for it describes well what constitutes woman's
value:

Now, if the woman was not made for the man to be his
helper in begetting children, in what way was she to
help him? How much more agreeably could two male
friends enjoy companionship and conversation in a life
shared together . . . consequently, I do not see in what
sense the woman was made as a helper for the man if
not for the sake of bearing children.

(79)

In *CNN* 17, once the wife has fulfilled her procreative
function she becomes, at best, superfluous. At worst,
she is a disturbing signifier of impotence from which
the male will do his utmost to distance himself. Fittingly, she has no voice in the tale. As we shall see, her
one moment of speech paradoxically thwarts her will to
agency and casts her even more definitively into a position of powerlessness. The core of the medieval ver-

sion, then, revolves around the man and the maid and his progressively more vigorous attempts to verbally woo and, all else failing, physically pursue and undo her.

The *Heptaméron*'s "Nouvella 69" opens as follows:

> Au chateau d'Odoz en Bigorre, demoroit ung escuier d'escuyrie du Roy, nommé Charles, Italien, lequel avoit espousé une damoiselle, fort femme de bien et honneste; mais elle estoit devenue vielle, après luy avoir porté plusieurs enfans. Luy aussi n'estoit pas jeune; et vivoit avecq elle en bonne paix et amityé.
>
> (398)

In rewriting the intertext, Marguerite de Navarre also begins with a description of the husband, but gives us only the bare facts: his profession (an equerry), his name (Charles) and his nationality (Italian). Instead of devoting the first sentence solely to him (and in this manner centralizing his position), she allots twice the amount of space to the wife as she does to the husband. She also saves all her laudatory adjectives to describe the wife. What the medieval narrative obfuscates in its overcharged first sentence "Novella 69" chooses to highlight in a second sentence marked by its brevity and bipartite structure: that the husband is far from being young. Further, instead of creating a topos of marital strife, the sentence emphasizes the harmony and companionship of the couple's conjugal life.

Even though she has grown old and has produced heirs, the wife remains active and effective, as the rest of the tale makes clear. The two live "en bonne paix et amityé" not because of an inherent equality in their relationship but because the wife is relentlessly watchful. Whereas in *CNN* 17 the husband's verbal prowess is metonymic of his virility, here it is precisely through his speech that his virility is thwarted. For whenever he "speaks" to a maid, that is, verbally attempts to seduce her, the wife discretely fires her, should she show any proclivity towards being seduced. When she hires this maid, she reveals to her the husband's penchants and the rules—established by the wife—that govern the household. Should the maid violate these rules, she will pay with her livelihood. Because she can wield this kind of economic power, the wife becomes the counterpart of the lord in the medieval intertext: whereas the lord rules over the chamber of accounts, the wife here holds a similar position within the household.

Marguerite de Navarre creates a female alliance in order to further modify the dynamics of the tale's power struggle. By the adjectives used to describe her, the maid becomes a veritable double of the wife. Like the wife, she is virtuous and good-humored. In order to keep her job, she chooses to be a "femme de bien" (398), a term which we saw used to describe the wife.

In this alliance the maid has the role of expanding the reach of the wife's power. Specifically, whenever the old husband speaks in order to seduce her, the maid recounts all to the wife. She thus allows the wife to be an everpresent spectator of her husband's attempts at potency. Thus, the wife always maintains the position of subject, and the husband that of the disempowered object of amusement.

Because of this female alliance, the husband's attempts at seduction are amusing, and not threatening. As the text tells us, "toutes deux passoient le temps de la follye de lui" (398). The topos illustrates well a point made by Laurent Joubert, in his 1579 *Traité du ris*: something is facetious when it is the opposite of what is expected, "toute autre de ce qu'on s'imaginoit" (35). By extension, the disjunction between the husband's libidinal drive and his old age becomes a laughing matter. From a narrative point of view, the reaction of amusement (which is the response of the two women to every sexual foray of the male) makes it unnecessary to recount each one of his ploys. By summing up all of his discourse indirectly and in one line ("Et, combien que souvent son maistre luy tint quelques propos . . . n'en voulut tenir compte, et le racompta tout à sa maistresse" [398]) Marguerite de Navarre emphasizes what unifies his repeated efforts: they are all stymied, not worthy of narration.

In the medieval version, instead of a female alliance we find an attempt at self-reliance. The maid, for fear of bringing discord into the household ("mettre male paix entre monseigneur et madame" [76]), keeps the husband's advances hidden from the wife and acts on her own behalf. Consequently, instead of the one-line summation we find in "Novella 69," in *CNN* 17 a full third of the story is allotted to the interactions between the master and the servant. The master's linguistic game of seduction is both humorous and serious—humorous because it offers a parody of the language of courtly love (typical of the fabliau tradition), serious because of what the euphemisms belie. Even though the narrator indicates that the servant felt no fear ("ne s'en effraya gueres" [76]), the reader quickly notices the progressive escalation in this "pourchaz de la bouche" (76). From "gracieux motz" (76) to "gracieux adieu" (76) to "cent mille sermens et autant de promesses" (77) the discursive interchanges seem to arrive at a stalemate when in reality they culminate in a verbal ultimatum. In reluctantly taking leave of the unwilling maid, the master warns that should he ever find her alone again, she will have to obey or fare the worse for it (77).

FLESHING OUT THE PLOT: WHAT COUNTS

If the language in the verbal seduction section seems veiled, what is at stake becomes clear in the section leading up to the moment of surprise reversal. In both versions, the maid is sifting grain early one morning (whereas *CNN* 17 uses the verb "tamiser" **"Novella 69"** uses the synonymous "beluter"), wearing a special hooded smock (known as a "sarot"). The master surprises her. Marguerite de Navarre's narrative summarizes his actions in five words: "la vint bien fort presser" (398). It moves on immediately to describe how the maid, in order to trick the master, agrees without hesitation to his demands but with the proviso that she be allowed to leave for a moment to make sure the wife will not interrupt their encounter. So that the wife will continue to hear the sifting sounds of the maid's work, the maid convinces the master to don her garment and continue the sifting. In **"Novella 69"** the allusion to a possible rape occupies a minimal amount of space, indicative once again of the comical powerlessness of the old seducer. In *CNN* 17 the sequence accounts for a full third of the story, depicting diegetically the progressive stages of the rape, and concluding with the maid's futile verbal pleas (related in direct discourse) for mercy: "Helas! monseigneur, je vous crie mercie . . . ma vie et mon honneur sont en vostre main, aiés pitié de moy!" (76-77). The maid's decision to employ the cross-dressing ruse is figured as her last resort. How she describes what motivated her is significant: she talks about "comment monseigneur . . . l'avoit assaillie" and asks the wife to come see "comment j'en suis eschappée" (78).[9] Thus, the preparation for the scene of reversal adds yet another defeat suffered at the hands of the master. In order to save herself the maid is forced to involve the wife.

In **"Novella 69"** mobilizing the cross-dressing ruse increases the already strong power base of the females, and is understood as such by the maid. She "acquiesces" to the master's demands in the sifting room because she sees it as a better than usual opportunity to fashion a one-man dumb show for the benefit of the females, with the husband-turned-transvestite as the center of attraction. She transforms the private space of violation into an open space of performance by adding the woman's touch to the fantasy script of the seducer. Outfitted by the maid for the maximum comedic effect—his body sheathed in the hooded smock, his hands busy with the sifter—he will be able to demonstrate his "skills" on center stage. In **"Novella 69,"** as in the medieval intertext, the maid hastens to get her mistress. Here, however, delight replaces fear ("[elle] n'estoit poinct melencolicque" [399]). Instead of assault and escape, the maid emphasizes the fun and surprises of the show that is about to begin: "Venez veioir vostre bon mary, que j'ay aprins à beluter pour me deffaire de luy" (399).

The pivotal point in each version will involve a moment of transvestism. In order to invade the female body, each male is required to become that body, at least in outward appearance. Casting a man as female by his dress brings not only gender into question but also destabilizes the concomitant markers of status and rank.[10] But staged sexual inversion can paradoxically clarify and thus buttress what is being temporarily destabilized. As Natalie Davis points out, such performances "are ultimately sources of order and stability in a hierarchical society" (130). Literally the most dramatic difference between the two versions of our tale occurs at this point, where each puts cross-dressing to different use.

PERIPETY: UNVEILING THE TRUTH

In both versions the men have their reality revealed to them during this moment of both physical and mental illusion. In each case, peripety depends upon the physical and verbal presence of the wife. When he sees his wife each knows that he has been tricked. But it is the words of the wife that determine whether the male has really been disempowered. In *CNN* 17, upon discovering her husband dressed in the maid's clothes, the wife scornfully remarks,

> Ha! monseigneur, et qu'est cecy? et ou sont vos lectres, voz grands honeurs, voz sciences et discrecions?
>
> (78)

Her goal is to belittle her husband, but her question has the opposite effect. Not only does she still see him as "monseigneur," but she highlights, by her naming of them, all the things that define his power and concomitant masculinity. Her words have the paradoxical effect of undressing the cross-dresser, for they emphasize precisely what is hidden by the garb, but remains firmly intact under it. Instead of robbing him of his power, she actually restores it.

Her moment of speech further disempowers her because her question offers the possibility of a retort. To his wife's query as to where his letters, titles, honors, have gone, the lord snaps back:

> Au bout de mon vit, dame, la ay je tout amassé aujourd'uy.[11]
>
> (79)

The force of this obscenity ("Lady, I've got it all right here, at the end of my dick") can best be understood if we turn to Freud. In *Jokes and Their Relation to the Unconscious* his analysis of the smutty joke applies well to the issues involved in the power play being enacted:

> Smut is like an exposure of the sexually different person to whom it is directed. By the utterance of the obscene words it compels the person who is assailed to imagine the part of the body . . . in question and shows her that the assailant is himself imagining it.
>
> (98)

This moment of cross-dressing spotlights the husband's potency. It allows the husband not only to verbally reconstitute the hidden penis but, thanks to the wife's words, to conflate it with all the other markers of sovereignty. It becomes the Lacanian phallus (*avant la lettre*), supreme signifier of power.

Recovering the penis and consequently transforming it into the transcendent phallus involves a linguistic uncovering. It is therefore not surprising that in Marguerite de Navarre's version the husband never regains it. As she looks upon what the "performer" is up to, his "sarot en la teste et le belluteau entre ses mains" (399), the wife announces the moment of surprise reversal by bursting into a fit of laughter and clapping her hands. If each of these two non-verbal signs serves to extend the trope of performance, laughter also signals agency. In Nicole Cazauran's words, "le rire sépare des couples ou des groupes opposés, les uns marquant leur triomphe par leurs paroles et se faisant spectateurs . . . de ceux qu'ils ont réduits à une position ridicule" (113).

With her ensuing words—"Goujate, combien veulx-tu par moys de ton labeur?" (399)—the wife further forecloses the possibility of her husband's assuming a position of dominance. Unlike the case in the medieval scenario, these words ("How much do you want per month for your work, wench?") offer no opportunity for a comeback. Equally important, the temporal element in her question—monthly wages—inscribes the husband into the effeminized role indefinitely, so well does being a serving girl suit him. The cross-dressing incident not only undercuts his masculinity but it demotes him socially and economically.

But what about the obscenity that marked the turning point in the medieval version? Although not as outright, its trace remains in **"Novella 69,"** in the form of the double entendre of "beluter," whose primary meaning refers to the sifting process but which also belongs to another linguistic register, that of "la langue verte," where it alludes to sexual intercourse (Huguet 547).[12] In a story barely longer than a page, forms of "beluter" or "bulleteau" appear five times. Here, though, they figure as part of the private joke between the two women, a joke which the Renaissance reader fully understood. It is the maid who has gotten the master to "sift" in her absence (398), and it is this sifting scene that inspires the wife's belly laugh as she gazes upon her smocked husband, his hands manipulating the sifter (399).[13] The fantasy of sexual consummation which drives the old seducer is realized here, but in a grotesque parody of what union with the other involves. Dressed as a woman, the phallic sifter in his hands, he is engaging in an act of copulation—with himself.[14]

PREPARING THE ENDING: PATHS TO POWER

Given the pronounced differences at each tale's moment of reversal, the movement toward denouement must

also inscribe difference. In *CNN* 17 the husband's retort signals the first part of an extended trope of ascendancy. As we have seen, his quick repartee enables him to verbally extricate himself from a position of potential humiliation and begin the trajectory towards his definitive reinstatement into sovereignty. In essence he has turned his wife's "Ha!" of derision into an aggressive joke at her expense. His vigorous recovery of power on the linguistic plane is followed immediately by a literal uncovering (and therefore recovering) of his identity as he divests himself of the feminine garb. With his next step he physically removes himself from the feminine space in which he unwittingly has become the object of a gaze mobilized to disempower him. Fittingly, it is a step marked not only by moving away, but moving up— "et en sa chambre remonte" (79). The relentless and uninterrupted nature of this movement is underscored by the narratological strategies employed to reposition the wife into her original subordinate role. Obliterated from the sensorial field of the husband, who has consistently remained the text's center of orientation, she is well on her way to being textually expunged. As she trails behind, she becomes faceless and worse than voiceless, for she speaks without being heard. As the narrative tells us, "Et madame le suyt, qui son preschement recommence, don't monseigneur ne tient gueres de compte" (79).

The culmination of the husband's ascendancy is reserved for a space marked by its maleness, for the true sphere of magnitude is the one he had occupied at the beginning of the story: in the palace, as head of "la chambre des comptes" (76). Because he finally regains that place as the story approaches its end, *CNN* 17 stages a scenario where the tricked male closes the door on the scene of the momentary status reversal. The narrative gives him the prerogative to escape to a more favorable terrain: that of phallocracy.

No such narratological option exists in the **Heptaméron**'s **"Novella 69."** As we have seen, at the point of peripety, the wife's words demote the man by gender and social and economic status. Whereas *CNN* 17 stages the progressive reascent of the male protagonist, here he is never allowed to get up. The choice of equerry as the husband's profession may therefore be a sly reworking of *CNN* 17's realistic detail concerning how the master got out of a space of defeat into a space of power: "il manda sa mule, et au palais s'en va" (79). Equerry, keeper of the horse, moves from picturesque detail to paradoxical signifier of powerlessness, for flight, as much as the husband may desire it, is made textually impossible.

For him the road to denouement is paved with impediments both physical and linguistic. As in the medieval version, he casts off the female garb, but instead of affirming his masculinity, he uncovers a lack. Every attempt to undo humiliation underscores his impotence. When he tries to take physical action against the maid ("Pour courir sus à la chamberiere" [399]), the wife literally steps in. His attempt to wrest economic control from the wife by firing the maid also fails ("et si sa femme ne se fut mise au devant, il l'eut payée de son quartier" [399]). Linguistically he is reduced to name-calling ("l'appelant mille fois meschante" [399]), comparable in its inefficacy to the wife's "preschement" (79) in the medieval version. Speaking, then, becomes dangerous for the man, for within the context of this female-scripted scenario, it renders him ridiculous. Imprisoned in this female space, his words fall on unsympathetic ears. Branded as linguistically inferior from start to finish, his words thwart his desire to dominate, for they can only provoke laughter—at his expense.

If we turn to the medieval version, we see to what extent Marguerite de Navarre has revised the original equation. The male who speaks and provokes laughter at his own expense is the wry subversion of *CNN* 17's model of the male who speaks and provokes laughter for his own benefit. At the story's end, the medieval novella caps the master's reascension by further extending his linguistic superiority. At the palace, instead of delivering a one-liner, he gets the opportunity to recount the entire story:

> il compta son adventure a pluseurs gens de bien qui en risirent bien fort.
>
> (79)

The text plays with the polysemy of "compter"—to count, to recount (i.e., to narrate). For the one who recounts is the one who determines what counts. The "raconteur" can also even the score, settling past accounts to his or her liking.[15] As the above quotation shows, the storytelling lord first of all appropriates the incident: because of its modifier it is textually marked as his. By becoming the teller of the tale he transforms "aventure" into "conte." The movement from reality to the narration of that reality carries with it a linguistic mediation, a mediation made possible only through a shift in perspective. A victim recounting his story recasts himself into a position of agency by becoming not only the "voice" of that experience, but its observer. By becoming a spectator of the incident, he dissociates himself further from a humiliating moment where, unwittingly cast as an object of derision, his will to power had been thwarted. As storyteller he enters into an alliance with the "gens de bien" who as a group support his agency by laughing at his tale. By transforming defeat into a funny story the master is not really creating a joke at his own expense, for he has discarded his former self, a former self that he can now laugh at along with his cronies. Ernst Kris makes a profound observation when he points out that one must feel totally secure from danger in order to enjoy the comic potential of a situation (209).

Laughter, though not devoid of anxiety, reorients that anxiety by allowing the laughter to take pleasure in the feeling of having mastered a former stumbling block. The pleasure is based on being able to look back "at the harmlessness of what has once been dangerous" (Kris 210).[16]

DENOUEMENT: A CALL TO ORDER

In *CNN* 17 the therapeutic nature of this laughter is emphasized in the final scene, where it serves as the glue of male bonding. The master's anger vanishes and gives way to the magnanimity of his final act: "si l'ayda il depuis de sa parolle et de sa chevance a marier" [79]). He thus succeeds in bringing the source of disorder (the maid) under patriarchal rule. On yet another level, by marrying off the maid he eliminates the obstacle to his amatory pursuits, and opens up again a position which will now have to be filled by another maid. The medieval version thus closes with the potential of the tale being reenacted—surely with a more satisfying ending for the master the next time.

Order is something which Marguerite de Navarre's version also restores, but it is of an entirely different nature. Whereas *CNN* 17 ends by opening a window for a sequel, **"Novella 69"**'s last scene forecloses the possibility of a new script. As the final impediment to his will to power, the wife assures that the maid retains her job. In this way she guarantees that they—i.e., the *three* of them—will live "ensemble sans querelles" (399).

Creative revisions can be effected only by someone who has a voice. In Marguerite de Navarre's version, the male protagonist is denied even one moment of direct discourse. While **"Novella 69"** also plays with the polysemy of "compter" the signifier shifts to the side of the women, for the females decide what counts and what to recount. As we saw at the beginning of the novella, the old man's words of seduction are reduced to "propos" (398), an amorphous trace which can be reformed and deformed according to the desires of the females. The maid first discounts these "propos" ("n'en voulut tenir compte"); then she recounts them ("et le racompta tout à sa maistresse") but in a way to transform them into laughter-provoking jokes, enabling the pleasant passing of time by the storyteller and her listener ("et toutes deux passoient le temps de la follye de luy" [398]). In the next to the last sentence, through indirect discourse, we are allowed to hear what, in fact, the old husband's speaking self is capable of formulating: "meschante" is the best retort he can muster. As readers we become as convinced as the women that he is not worth listening to.

BACK TO THE MAN BEHIND

To return to Sainte-Beuve and borrow his metaphor, we see what Marguerite de Navarre does with the man behind her. She takes his story, subverts it, and marks it as her story. Her modifications change every dimension of the original tale. Because she moves the center of orientation from the husband to the wife, her narrative develops the wife and maid scenes at the expense of those involving the husband and maid. At the point of peripety, she replaces fear (on the part of the servant) and anger (on the part of the wife) with female amusement. She eliminates any signs of male fraternity in favor of a female alliance. Concomitantly, laughter and storytelling, signifiers of agency, are shifted from the mouths of the males to the mouths of the females. By these narratological strategies Marguerite de Navarre transforms a misogynistic intertext into a story where the cause of the females predominates.

Her story wreaks humorous havoc upon everything that denotes male sovereignty. Whereas *CNN* 17 ends by opening a space for the male's reinstatement into a position of dominance and control, in Marguerite de Navarre's rewriting, the female, from beginning to end, keeps male power in check. By displacing and reorienting the markers of male power, Marguerite de Navarre puts an uncanny spin on the medieval tale's signifiers. With her version comes a new vision. No longer a story of a seducer temporarily disarmed, her skillful and subtle hand has created a story of a seducer permanently unmanned.[17]

Notes

1. All my citations are from the Michel François edition of the *Heptaméron*. For the most recent English translation see Chilton's *The Heptameron*.

2. For details concerning the theories of authorship of the *Cent nouvelles nouvelles,* see Pierre Jourda's preface to *Conteurs français du XVIe siècle* (xix-xx); all my citations are taken from this edition of the *Cent nouvelles nouvelles*. For a recent English translation see Judith Diner's *The One Hundred New Tales*. In this paper I shall frequently use the abbreviation *CNN* 17 instead of *Cent nouvelles nouvelles* 17. All translations from *CNN* 17 and from the *Heptaméron* are my own.

3. For one of the most cogent expositions of this idea see Marcel Tetel's chapter on "Ambiguity or the Splintering of Truth" (104- 49).

4. On the relationship between originality and the evolution of the novella, see Patricia and Rouben Cholakian's introduction (17- 73).

5. For Nicolas de Troyes, it is "Novella 139," available in manuscript form (Bibliothèque Nationale, cote fr. 1510); see also the Kasprzyk edition reference to the tale (25); for Giraldi, see "Novella 9" (79-84); for Malespini, see "Novella 97" (267-69).

6. I follow in the methodological footsteps of Janet Ferrier whose *Forerunners of the French Novel* continues to afford a valuable foundation upon

which to build. To my knowledge her 1954 analysis constitutes the only other study of the novellas in question here; see 92-103 and 117-19.

7. The term derives from Stanzel's theory of narrative. For a masterful application of the concept to *CNN* 19, see Mary J. Baker.

8. The spent woman as expendable is not just a literary topos. For an historical parallel, see recent archival work on European witchcraft, which demonstrates that postmenopausal women—those who were spent—were the most likely victims of witchcraft hysteria. E. William Monter calculates the median age as 60 (123). For the situation in England, see Marianne Hester's chapter, "The accused and the accusations against them" (160-96, especially 161-65).

9. In *Rape and Writing* Patricia Cholakian argues that "the variations of the rape scenario form the work's nucleus" (18). Although Cholakian does not analyze "Novella 69," the tale's semiotic richness increases if we read it within this framework. Specifically, in a collection of stories where recounting rape figures so prominently, "Novella 69" is even more remarkable because Marguerite de Navarre chooses to virtually eliminate the rape that lies at the heart of her intertext. To my knowledge critical work on the topos of rape in the *Heptaméron* (see also Baker's article on rape imagery) has never included "Novella 69" in its corpus of tales.

10. Among the many recent books on this subject, see Marjorie Garber's *Vested Interests* for an illustrated analysis of the historical preoccupation with transvestism.

11. For a discussion of the word "vit" and other frequently used obscenities in the fabliau tradition, see Charles Muscatine's chapter on "Sexuality and Obscenity" (105-51, especially 112-13).

12. For the sexual meaning's survival into the nineteenth century, see Delvau's 1864 dictionary (551).

13. Because of the "sight gag" dimension of this scene, I offer Richelet's 1680 definition of "bluteau": "instrument d'étamine blanche en forme de manche fort large, dont on se sert pour passer de la farine" (81).

14. The masturbatory potential of this sifting scene is pushed to its limit by Guillaume Bouchet in his sixteenth-century *Serées* (113); to my knowledge Bouchet is the only writer to have used Marguerite de Navarre's version as his intertext.

15. To explain why it is Hircan, the most politically incorrect of the five male storytellers, who tells this story of women triumphant involves an issue

beyond the scope of this paper, what I have described elsewhere as the tension in the *Heptaméron* between two competing realms, the secular and the spiritual. Hircan introduces "Novella 69" as illustrative of what characterizes wives who are truly wise: they are those "qui prennent autant de passetemps à se mocquer des oeuvres de leurs mariz, comme les mariz de les tromper secretement" (397). The word "passetemps" is a semantically charged term in the *Heptaméron*. For a discussion of how the prologue mobilizes "passetemps" in the service of ideological exposition, see Polachek (304).

16. In this paper I extend to the sphere of adult laughter Kris's theory of laughter as a function of ego development in children.

17. I am grateful to Marcel Tetel and Marcel Gutwirth for their guidance, scholarship and administrative flair in facilitating the lively interchange of ideas as directors of NEH summer programs in which I participated. For thoughtful discussions and comments, I also thank Mary Webster, Paul Finkelman, Byrgen Finkelman, and Joanna Banquier.

Works Cited

Baker, Mary J. "Authorial Bias in Tale No. 19 of the *Cent nouvelles nouvelles.*" *Romance Notes* 27.3 (Spring 1987): 272-74.

———. "Rape, Attempted Rape, and Seduction in the *Heptaméron.*" *Romance Quarterly* 39.3 (August 1992): 271-81.

Barthes, Roland. "Le vin et le lait." *Mythologies.* Paris: Seuil, 1957. 74-77.

Bouchet, Guillaume. *Les Serées.* 1st ed. 1584-98. Ed. C. E. Roybet. Vol. 2. Paris: Alphonse Lemerre, 1873. 6 vols. 1873-1882.

Cazauran, Nicole. *L'Heptaméron de Marguerite de Navarre.* Paris: Société d'Édition d'Enseignement Supérieur, 1976.

Les Cent nouvelles nouvelles. Conteurs français du XVIᵉ siècle. Ed. Pierre Jourda. Paris: Pléiade-Gallimard, 1965. xix-xxi; 1-358; 1317-54.

Cholakian, Patricia Francis. *Rape and Writing in the* Heptaméron *of Marguerite de Navarre.* Carbondale: Southern Illinois UP, 1991.

Cholakian, Patricia Francis and Rouben Charles Cholakian, trans. and eds. *The Early French Novella: An Anthology of Fifteenth-and Sixteenth-Century Tales.* Albany: State U of New York P, 1972.

Davis, Natalie Z. *Society and Culture in Early Modern France.* Stanford: Stanford UP, 1965.

Delvau, Alfred. *Dictionnaire érotique moderne.* 1st ed. 1864. Geneva: Slatkine Reprints, 1968.

Ferrier, Janet M. *Forerunners of the French Novel. An Essay on the Development of the* Nouvelle *in the Late Middle Ages.* Manchester: Manchester UP, 1954.

Freud, Sigmund. *Jokes and Their Relation to the Unconscious.* Trans. and Ed. James Strachey. New York: Norton, 1963.

Garber, Marjorie. *Vested Interests: Cross-Dressing and Cultural Anxiety.* New York: Routledge, 1992.

Giraldi, Gio. Battista Cintio. *Gli Ecatommiti.* Vol. 2. Turin: Cugini Pomba, 1609. 2 vols.

Hester, Marianne. *Lewd Women and Wicked Witches: A Study of the Dynamics of Male Domination.* London and New York: Routledge, 1992.

Huguet, Edmond. *Dictionnaire de la langue française du seizième siècle.* Paris: Champion, 1925-1973.

Jabès, Edmond. *From the Book to the Book: An Edmond Jabès Reader.* Trans. Rosmarie Waldrop. Hanover: Wesleyan/University P of New England, 1991.

Joubert, Laurent. *Traité du ris.* 1st ed. 1579. Geneva: Slatkine Reprints, 1973.

Kris, Ernst. *Psychoanalytic Explorations in Art.* New York: International Universities P, 1962.

Malespini, Celio. *Ducento Novelle.* Vol. 2. Venice: Al Segno dell'Italia, 1853.

Marguerite de Navarre. *L'Heptaméron.* Ed. Michel François. 1st ed. 1943. Paris: Garnier, 1967.

———. *The Heptameron.* Trans. Paul A Chilton. London: Penguin, 1984.

Monter, E. William. *Witchcraft in France and Switzerland: The Borderlands During the Reformation.* Ithaca: Cornell UP, 1976.

Muscatine, Charles. *The Old French Fabliaux.* New Haven: Yale UP, 1986.

Nicolas de Troyes. *Le grand parangon des nouvelles nouvelles (choix).* Ed. Krystyna Kasprzyk. Paris: Marcel Didier, 1970.

The One Hundred New Tales. Trans. Judith Bruskin Diner. New York: Garland, 1990.

Polachek, Dora E. "Narrating the 'Truth': the Problematics of Verisimilitude in the *Heptaméron* Prologue." *Romance Languages Annual* I (1989): 301-5.

Richelet, Pierre. *Dictionnaire françois contenant les mots et les choses.* 1st ed. 1860. Geneva: Slatkine Reprints, 1970.

St. Augustine. *De Genesi ad Litteram.* Trans. John Hammond Taylor. *Woman Defamed and Woman Defended: An Anthology of Medieval Texts.* Ed. Alcuin Blamires. Oxford: Clarendon, 1992.

Sainte-Beuve, Charles Augustin. "Marguerite de Na-varre." *Les grands écrivains français. XVIᵉ siècle: les prosateurs.* Ed. Maurice Allem. Paris: Garnier, 1926. 1-22; 325-32.

Stanzel, F. K. *A Theory of Narrative.* Trans. Charlotte Goedsche. Cambridge, England: Cambridge UP, 1984.

Tetel, Marcel. *Marguerite de Navarre's* Heptaméron: *Themes, Language, and Structure.* Durham, N.C.: Duke UP, 1973.

Carla Freccero (essay date March 1995)

SOURCE: Freccero, Carla. "Bodies and Pleasures: Early Modern Interrogations." *Romanic Review* 86, no. 2 (March 1995): 379-90.

[*In the following essay, Freccero notes the lack of representations of female sexual pleasure in the* Heptaméron.]

Julia Epstein and Kristina Straub, in their introduction to *Body Guards: The Cultural Politics of Gender Ambiguity,* note the prevalence of academic criticism's recent focus on the body as a "subject" of culture and of embodiedness as a paradigm of subjectivity. They trace an interesting recent history of this focus on the body (in culture, in history) as related, on the one hand, to feminist inquiry and politics, with its focus on gender and sexual difference as important operative distinctions in culture that carry political implications; and, on the other, to recent political and social developments: "the current containment and control of bodies by technologies and right-wing political discourses," (10) and to the catastrophe of AIDS:

> Academic critical theory has focused on paradigms of the body and embodiedness, then, just at the moment that the AIDS epidemic and HIV infection have focused social concerns on the human body as a carrier of culture, values, and morality. . . . This is not a co-incidence. AIDS discourses have in many ways catalyzed the operations of cultural analysis. . . .
>
> (12-13)

One of the effects of attempts to contain or control the HIV virus by "policing desire" (to use Simon Watney's phrase), is to make strikingly clear, according to Epstein and Straub, the extent to which the cultural production of identity and subjectivity is conducted through the terms of sexuality (13). Thus, the attention to both gender and sexuality as constitutive constructing agents of identity and subjectivity—and here we might stress as well the discourses of identity construction that focus on racial marking—that is, an attention to the ways in which subjectivities and identities are organized and categorized according to bodily designations, has brought academic criticism to focus on embodiment.

The presentism of this suggestion—that what turns us to the body are recent social, political, cultural developments that produce the body as a site of representational and discursive struggle—both illuminates and runs the risk of obscuring thoughts about historical moments in the past as well as the present when the body as subject of culture becomes an "urgent" or "necessary" theoretical concern—for example, times of famine or of plague, of war or of witch-burning.[1] To counter such a discourse of present urgency, Linda Lomperis and Sarah Stanbury, editors of *Feminist Approaches to the Body in Medieval Literature,* argue for the particular salience of analyses of embodiment in relation to the Middle Ages:

> As the writings of historians Jacques Le Goff, Peter Brown, and Caroline Bynum have demonstrated, the Middle Ages was anything but a purely metaphysical time period. It was, on the contrary, a moment of history governed by what we might call an incarnational aesthetic. . . . Indeed, everyday life in the Middle Ages was what we in the late twentieth century might see as supremely, if not unrelievedly, 'bodily.'
>
> (viii-ix)

Both approaches tend to obscure somewhat the relation between the body and culture at work in moments when no such "thematic" focus is present. This is the argument Harry Berger makes in "From Body to Cosmos," drawing on the work of anthropologist Mary Douglas:

> 'The social body constrains the way the physical body is perceived. The physical experience of the body, always modified by the social categories through which it is known, sustains a particular view of society.' Thus the body is a representation as well as a presence . . . the body naturalizes or detextualizes 'the social categories through which it is known.' It lends them its immediacy and reality as an organism, something humans did not fabricate and therefore cannot change. And in many cultures, 'nature'—in exchange for the naturalness it bestows—borrows logocentric forms which the human body signifies: person, consciousness, presence, and self-presence. Then the signifying body tends to expand into all available spaces until it permeates society, nature, the cosmos, and the gods with the resonance of its categories, imagery, and voice.
>
> (557-558)

Here the body is posited as always bearing a relationship to the social, conceived of as textual; its "disappearance," then, from academic discourse in the time "before" the present, could be said to constitute precisely the body's signifying function in culture as that which "confers the appearance of inevitability, inalienability, and transcendent reality inscribed in it by 'nature'" (Berger 1987, 147). Thus when critics argue for a return to the body and to embodiment, they risk reinstating the opposition between text and body, reifying the body's role as purveyor of "nature": "Representing socially constructed interpretations of gender, generation, and genealogy in the body rather than in nonbodily media of textualization confers on them the inalienable aura of natural difference" (Berger 1987, 151). Nature, as Jonathan Dollimore (*Sexual Dissidence*) points out, has been one of the most difficult ideological concepts to eradicate in its oppositional (and sometimes complementary) relationship to culture (113-116), although Donna Haraway and others involved in the current critique of science have contributed in large part to the current understanding of nature as cultural, and thus ideological (*Simians, Cyborgs, and Women*).

Toward the end of the *History of Sexuality,* vol. 1, Michel Foucault writes:

> We are often reminded of the countless procedures which Christianity once employed to make us detest the body; but let us ponder all the ruses that were employed for centuries to make us love sex, to make the knowledge of it desirable and everything said about it precious. Let us consider the stratagems by which we were induced to apply all our skills to discovering its secrets, by which we were attached to the obligation to draw out its truth, and made guilty for having failed to recognize it for so long. These devices are what ought to make us wonder today. Moreover, we need to consider the possibility that one day, perhaps, in a different economy of bodies and pleasures, people will no longer quite understand how the ruses of sexuality, and the power that sustains its organization, were able to subject us to that austere monarchy of sex, so that we became dedicated to the endless task of forcing its secret, of exacting the truest of confessions from a shadow.
>
> (159)

Foucault's work on the historicity of the body and its pleasures has spawned an era of academic criticism in the U.S. focused on embodiment, in particular recent efforts to theorize sexuality as a historical phenomenon. What Foucault's focus on the body—in and as history, in and as culture—and its relation to questions of power, knowledge, discipline, seems to have made possible is precisely a materialist means of interrogating historical formations and historical change, one that charts the microstructuring, not of individuals, but of bodies in space, text, discourse, representation, through agents of history we call institutions:

> The body is directly involved in a political field; power relations have an immediate hold upon it: they invest it, train it, torture it, force it to carry out tasks, to perform ceremonies and emit signs. The political investment of the body is bound up, in accordance with complex, reciprocal relations, with its economic use; it is largely as a force of production that the body is invested with power and domination; but, on the other hand, its constitution as a labor power is possible only if it is caught up in a system of subjection . . . the body becomes a useful force only if it is both a productive body and a subjugated body.
>
> (Foucault, *Discipline and Punish,* 25-26)

While it might be argued that feminist and race studies have similarly, and for a long time, drawn attention to the importance of the production of "marked" bodies in history, and reread history through such attention, each has often focused on a particular "ascription" (see Berger, "From Body to Cosmos," 561) or characteristic belonging to the body, attributes of the body rather than the ways in which bodies are materialized, and thus these studies have often foundered in their efforts to analyze the interstructuredness of gender, race, and sexuality as modes of embodiment that produce subjects and subjectivity itself. The attention to the body in cultural and historical analyses of sex and gender has been both salutary and necessary in marking the (clearly ideological) naturalization at work in prior analyses whose denials or repressions of embodiment produced the appearance of an abstracted subject as the subject of history, using this abstraction as a means of class, gender, race and sex promotion. But it is equally important to continually acknowledge the body as a textualization, not only as that which produces, manifests itself in the social, but as that which is already contained within the social, produced, in other words, by culture.

Once the body, as a non-naturalized, constructed and produced subject of history enters the field of theoretical analysis as one of the available categories through which to rethink culture and history, it becomes possible to re-materialize textuality (in the ways that some of the New Philologists have done, by focusing on the material aspects of manuscript and text production, the technological dimensions of extensions of the body) and to textualize that which has been regarded as "matter," the bodily outside of texts.[2] We might seek a historically specific moment when the category came into being in such a way as to produce a recognizable entity we might call by that name; but also we might look at other places and times with these (our modern) categories to see what the juxtaposition of such categories and other places and times produces as new knowledge.[3] Thus in the work of historical cultural analysis there are at least these two challenges: to historicize the category (in this case, of the body) in order to construct a genealogy of our own deployment of that category; and, simultaneously, to deploy our own categories of analysis in such a way as to "draw partly on [these] differences for their interrogative power" (Fradenburg, "Criticism, Anti-Semitism," 74), their power to conduct ideological critiques in languages that do not simply mirror the self-representations of the period in question.

For the purpose of this issue, with its specific focus on sex and gender, I want to ask what is produced by a feminist literary criticism that re-reads the question of female authorship through the (post-Foucaultian) body, that is through subjectivity as embodiment in texts as well as through constructions of the body or imaginary morphologies, and discourses of the body in texts. If bodies are repeatedly, continually, and normatively materialized as sexed, gendered, and racialized in social orders (in culture), then the specificities of these materializations will constitute, in part, how we are to understand the relation of textuality to embodiment. Judith Butler's recent work moves in this direction by interrogating the ways in which matter is produced through the regulatory power of norms which delineate what counts as a body, and thus as a subject, in the first place; her work both suggests a way to begin to historicize the notion of the body and a way to understand how determinants such as sex constitute part of the very process of materialization that produces "bodies that matter."

> Hence, it will be as important to think about how and to what end bodies are constructed as is it will be to think about how and to what end bodies are not constructed and, further, to ask after how bodies which fail to materialize provide the necessary "outside," if not the necessary support, for the bodies which, in materializing the norm, qualify as bodies that matter.
>
> (*Bodies that Matter,* 16)

One dimension of Butler's work is the psychoanalytic argument that such regulatory norms form a sexed subject "in terms that establish the indistinguishability between psychic and bodily formation" (22). If psychoanalysis asserts that subjectivity is in some sense a bodily relation, a relation to the body in other words, then we might argue that subjectivity is itself material and textual. It will not, of course, be given in advance what such a subjectivity might be: subjectivity will be constituted by the reiterated, that is citational, temporal practices of specific historical and cultural formations.[4]

Feminist literary criticism of pre- and early modern periods has focused primarily on an interrogation of the category of gender as it applies to periods other than the modern and has set about analyzing how gender is historically as well as culturally constituted. Since the critique of feminism's cultural hegemony by women of color critics, which produced the imperative to (culturally) specify generalizations regarding gender, and the critical movement referred to as New Historicism, it has become important to specify what is meant by gender and how it operates in specifically situated moments and places.[5] Pre- and early modernists have moved in similar directions in recent studies of racial formations.[6] Indeed such work has already begun to question the relation between the category "race" and its purported referent—so assumed in modernity—the body. The recent "detachment" of sexuality from gender as a category of analysis in queer theory and sexuality studies, suggests also that historical formations of sexuality must be interrogated with the same attentive specificity as has been applied to gender.[7] Yet, as Butler has argued with regard to the sex/gender divide as the conceptual distinction between "nature" or the body

and "culture" or the social, "sex" is already gendered, insofar as "gender is also the discursive/cultural means by which 'sexed nature' or a 'natural sex' is produced and established as 'pre-discursive,' prior to culture, a politically neutral surface on which culture acts" (Gender Trouble, 7). Thus the link between gender and heteronormativized sexuality might be usefully uncoupled or "troubled."

Such studies have usefully made explicit those "regulatory norms" governing the conceptual categories through which to theorize subjectivities in all their historical and cultural specificities; indeed they offer a denaturalizing corrective to approaches that elide what has been assigned to the body as the "natural," and thus non-signifying or "given" in culture, according to Berger's analysis. Historical studies, however, successful as they may be in articulating the norms that produce embodied subjects, cannot suffice in studying the subjectivities constituted or realized through such norms, for they focus on these categories as "objects" in their field of study. As objects, they can be separated; in the complex of subjectivity, they are not separable. Furthermore, to analyze subjectivity in the past, we must have recourse to "literary" reading, to the places where embodiment means, that is constitutes itself as desiring, agential, expressive. Embodied subjectivity occurs, that is, in "text" as active, technological extension of, and active abstraction from, the body.[8]

Subjectivity will thus require an analysis attentive to the ways in which gender, race, and sexuality are discursively materialized; for literary studies this means the elimination of transcendence as a pertinent factor in the relationality between authorial embodiment and textual product. Transcendence, in this view, would no longer be an operative and desirable category of literary "art"; rather the connection between body and text is made from within a materialist framework, from within the notion that there is no unconnected place, no place above, outside of embodiment.

These theoretical interrogations are motivated in part as a response to challenges by male colleagues in Renaissance Studies who have once again raised the question of the authorship of the ***Heptaméron*** (the earlier debate having been about whether she or a more illustrious male colleague in fact composed the text), and added, no doubt with a hint of glee, that feminist critics would be much perplexed by the revelation of male authorship.[9] How might this question be approached using some of the frameworks I have outlined, such that we might be able to begin to answer this challenge in our readings of texts? What happens when we look for traces of matter called bodies in a text in a way that does not automatically make the leap to the regulatory norms that govern those bodies? How can we approach the question of subjectivity as bodies materialized in textuality? And, to return to Foucault's formulation, how might we begin to understand regimes of "bodies and pleasures" in times and places other than our own? While it would be impossible to answer these questions in the space remaining, I want to speculate about the possibilities, particularly with regard to the question of materializations of bodily pleasures in this early modern text.

Traditional literary history has constructed female authorship as saturated in embodiment. The most familiar version argues that female authored texts are non-universal (particularized, marked, bodily) because they address feminine (social) concerns, and they treat the narrow purview of women's connections to the Real (a return to the view that women's desires are not sublimated therefore female authorship will display to excess the signs of female embodiment). According to this way of thinking, female authored texts are gendered embodiment itself. The feminist version of this argument is that women write the body, though at least in its French feminist version, this is understood in symbolic terms, not as an argument about women but as an argument about the place occupied by "woman" in the organizing ideological scheme of binary oppositions under western phallogocentrism.[10]

Either way, if we look at this body of prose compared to some other sixteenth-century bodies of prose we find a surprising thing: the absence of the body, the absence of bodies, of discourses of the body, of bodily sensation. Not as referent of course; Marguerite names bodies, refers to bodily activities and states: the pregnant body, the laughing body, the dirty body, the wounded body. But if we are to understand subjectivity as embodiment, as formed through bodily sensations and as such, at times, indistinguishable from them, then we find in this text a significant silence. The irony of literary history is that it has so deeply linked women's texts to their identities, or their embodiments as women, that it has often failed to notice such absences as these.

Patricia Cholakian cites Nancy Miller's essay, "Emphasis Added" (in *Subject to Change*) to say of Marguerite that; "In Miller's analysis, therefore, under patriarchy, male desire is erotic, whereas female desire is political. A woman desires the power that will elevate her to the status of subject." (*Rape and Writing in the* Heptameron, 3) Miller writes that "the repressed content" of women's fiction would be "not erotic impulses but an impulse to power: a fantasy of power that would revise the social grammar in which women are never defined as subjects; a fantasy of power that disdains a sexual exchange in which women can participate only as objects of circulation." (*Subject to Change,* 35) Here she reads the "bypassing of the dialectics of desire" as "a peculiarly feminine act of victory" in female-authored fictional texts of the French tradition (31-32). "To the

extent that we can speak of a triumph of her Majesty the Ego in France, it lies in being beyond vulnerability, indeed beyond it all." (33)

This might be a way of thinking about what might seem to be the frustrating absence of female pleasure(s) in Marguerite de Navarre's stories, if we look for pleasures in the place where we traditionally expect to find them, that is, the domain of the conventional erotic: the sexual. Or rather, if we seek to discern pleasure as a material affect of embodiment, that is if we link pleasure to bodies in the **Heptaméron,** then we are met with an extraordinary silence. Unlike the exuberant (if allegorical and highly symbolic) bodily pleasures celebrated, ridiculed, parodied, etc. in Rabelais's text, or the perverse pleasures of bodily indulgence that accompany descriptions of illness in Montaigne, Marguerite de Navarre's text remains curiously resistant to attempts to read embodiment and its material affect, pleasure.[11] One question might be then, what is made possible by her refusal of that (overdetermined) interpellation? Could we argue for the elision of embodiment as a discursive politics with designs upon another kind of accession to subjectivity, as Miller and Cholakian suggest, and as Cora Kaplan has so interestingly documented with regard to the discourses of female bodily pleasure in nineteenth century women's bids for political citizenship?[12] Indeed, the one certain domain of female bodily pleasure discernible in this period is in the discourse of mysticism, as though the domain of the absolute spiritual or transcendent were the only one where female pleasure might find safe and ready voice, the secular being overly fraught with accusations of saturated embodiment.[13]

We know some of the ways in which bodies are "directly involved in a political field" for Marguerite: the political investment of the body with kingship, thus the importance of François I's rescue from captivity and the substitution of other bodies for his; we also know to some extent how that investment (of bodies) is bound up with their dynastic use, as in Marguerite's "trafficking" in the circulation of the body of her daughter, and of aristocratic female subjects generally; but what do we know about the body's pleasures, about pleasure as a material affect of embodied subjectivity?[14]

Might we instead look for furtive embodied pleasures, as furtive as the textual slippage between Jambicque (the lusty woman of **"Story 43"**) and Camilla that introduces a kind of queer desire into the text? Or that which doubles and confuses François and Françoise in **"Story 42,"** a prince and a pauper, so that both become the embodiments of the just nation?[15] Or perhaps even the furtive but uncontrollable laughter of the lady in **"Story 13,"** as she witnesses the triumph of her ruse?

I am thinking, of course, about the pleasures of prose, the disembodied embodiment of textual production.

Writing as a locus of pleasure has a long history, but its pertinence to a sixteenth-century female author is suggested by the love poet Louise Labé's famous lines: "le plus grand plaisir qui soit après amour, c'est d'en parler" (The greatest pleasure that comes after love is talking about it.)[16] perhaps we might say instead: "le plus grand plaisir—le seul?—c'est d'en parler/écrire." This would not be, however, a model of sublimation that might suggest a transcendence of embodiment, nor a pornographic model that would suggest the supreme importance either of the addressee of the text, or of a thematically pertinent erotic trajectory (such as the one Peter Brooks has described in his studies of prose narrative and plot), but perhaps a model of perversity, including auto-eroticism, whereby pleasure is fetishistically derived as in tranvestism, or voyeurism, or ventriloquism (all places and positions in Marguerite's text).[17] Pleasure of the sort found in virtual reality perhaps, the taking on and playing out of other bodies, voices, modes of address to equally fantasmatic others. And perhaps, with Foucault, we would have to look for an altogether different sort of economy of bodies and pleasures—and certainly it would be one less fully capitalized, where the body is not wholly given over to laborious regimes of productivity and discipline—to understand the regimes materializing these manifestations of embodied subjectivity.

Notes

1. I wish to thank Louise Fradenburg for drawing my attention to the "presentism" of the discourse of cultural studies and other academic discourses seeking to theorize the importance of their subject matter.

2. See Stephen Nichols, ed., The New Philology; Nichols and Lee Patterson, eds., *Commentary as Cultural Artifact*; Stephanie Jed, *Chaste Thinking: The Rape of Lucretia and the Birth of Humanism*; Jonathan Goldberg, *Writing Matter: From the Hand of the English Renaissance*.

3. As Louise Fradenburg has argued in "Criticism, Anti-Semitism, and the *Prioress's Tale*," it does not suffice merely to argue that such categories have no meaning for a past moment or another place because they are not the terms through which those moments and those places theorize themselves. To construct another time or place as "other," as alterity itself in other words, renders impossible the analysis of internal differences, of the alterities within, in particular those that are ideological, those that are precisely about a culture's (a cultural elite's) own mis-recognition of itself, its own idealized self-representation to itself. Thus Fradenburg asks, "even if the later Middle Ages would have preferred to discuss the *Prioress's Tale* in terms of injustice rather than in terms of anti-semitism, does this mean, in fine, that the tale is not anti-semitic? That analysis of its possible anti-semitic qualities would produce nothing of interest in a reading of the tale?" (76) Indeed, medievalists have conducted a salutary critique of the field of Renaissance Studies in these terms, that is for the way in which the Renaissance and its modern scholars construct their own continuity with modernity through an absolute othering of the Middle Ages, thus externalizing alterity from itself and from modernity as well, an important ideological move within the strategy of self-representation.

4. Berger makes a similar observation when he writes, "Performance communities cite and recite these 'texts' not merely in the reproduction of speech and custom but also in the reproduction of bodies" ("Bodies and Texts," 151).

5. See Lomperis and Stanbury (*Feminist Approaches to the Body*, vii-viii): ". . . just as medievalists have been engaging with the materials of contemporary feminist theory, so have feminist theorists been turning their attention increasingly to questions of history. This move toward history has come about largely in response to feminists of color in the United States who have criticized mainstream (i.e., white, Western, middle-class) feminist theory for unacknowledged models of racist and totalizing thought. . . . Acknowledging these pitfalls and at the same time working to avoid them, a number of contemporary feminist theorists have made explicit their resistance to the homogenous and the monolithic."

6. See, for example, the essays in Margo Hendricks and Patricia Parker, eds., *Women, "Race," and Writing in the Early Modern Period*.

7. See, for example, Thomas Laqueur, *Making Sex: Body and Gender from the Greeks to Freud*. For arguments about the separation between sexuality and gender as objects of study, see the introduction to *The Gay and Lesbian Studies Reader*, edited by Abelove, Barale, and Halperin. Heather Findlay, in her review of Jonathan Goldberg's *Sodometries*, praises the separation between sexuality studies and gender studies ("Queerying the English Renaissance"). Gayle Rubin's "Thinking Sex," has often been considered the first feminist argument concerning the inadequacy of feminism to a theory of sexuality. For a critique of the pitfalls of such a separation, see Judith Butler, "Against Proper Objects."

8. See the work of Teresa de Lauretis, among others, for the use of psychoanalysis as methodology for "reading" subjectivity: *Alice Doesn't*; *Technologies of Gender*; and *The Practice of Love*.

9. For the extensive literary history of this debate, see Dora Polachek, "Save the Last Laugh for Me: Revamping the Script of Infidelity in Novella 69."

10. Butler's "Against Proper Objects" has an excellent discussion of French feminist thinking about sexual difference relative to US feminist focuses on gender.

11. My recent work focuses on these dimensions of male-authored texts as well; see "Cannibalism, Homophobia, Women: Montaigne's 'Des cannibales' and 'De L'amitié.'"

12. *Sea Changes: Culture and Feminism*; see in particular "Wild Nights: Pleasure/Sexuality/ Feminism," 31-56.

13. This latter argument might well put a new spin on *jouissance* as the place where the repressed of women's pleasure finds ecstatic outlet and thus approximates the Bakhtinian grotesque as that which is both "recuperative, a sort of safety valve in the service of dominant ideology, and as subversive, that which exceeds and refuses that ideology." (Epstein and Straub, eds., *Body Guards,* 9) for a discussion of female pleasure in a religious context, see Caroline Walker Bynum, *Holy Feast and Holy Fast* and *Fragmentation and Redemption*; also Kathy Lavezzo, "Sobs and Sighs Between Women: Female Homosocial Bonding and *The Book of Margery Kempe*."

14. Carla Freccero, "Marguerite de Navarre and the Politics of Maternal Sovereignty."

15. Freccero, "Practicing Queer Philology with Marguerite de Navarre: Nationalism and the Castigation of Desire." De Lauretis suggests that lesbian subjectivity be read through the lens of Freud's theories of perverse desire in *The Practice of Love.* I take up her suggestion here in my reference to "furtive embodied pleasures." Indeed, Jonathan Dollimore, in *Sexual Dissidence,* suggests that perversion is the "proper" category through which to think desire and pleasures in early modernity.

16. Louise Labé, *Oeuvres complètes,* 7. On a more sinister—and popular—note, Don Johnson, the diabolical womanizer and (literal) ladykiller in the film "Guilty as Sin," delivers the following line to his lawyer (the modern day secular priest who occupies the role of recipient of our confessional truths, à la Foucault): "The only problem with the perfect murder is that you can't tell anybody about it" (this after having explained that he removes his gloves to kill his victims, because "strangling someone with gloves is like having sex with a condom").

17. The use of these terms again suggests the pertinence of psychoanalysis in the study of subjectivity, particularly in relation to sexuality (psychoanalysis' usefulness in analyzing racialization has proved more challenging, as Freud did not posit racial difference and racialization as constitutive as sexual difference and sexuality in the formation of subjectivity). With regard to the well-worn debate about the anachronism of such terms and methodologies, see note 4.

Works Cited

Abelove, Henry; Barale, Michèle Aina; Halperin, David M., eds. *The Gay and Lesbian Studies Reader.* New York & London: Routledge, 1993.

Berger, Harry, Jr., "From Body to Cosmos: The Dynamics of Representation in Pre-capitalist Society," *The South Atlantic Quarterly* 91: 3 (summer 1992): 557-602.

———. "Bodies and Texts," *Representations* 17 (winter 1987): 144-166.

Butler, Judith, "Against Proper Objects," in *differences* 6.2 + 3 (1994): 1-26.

———. *Bodies that Matter: On the Discursive Limits of "Sex".* New York & London: Routledge, 1993.

———. *Gender Trouble: Feminism and the Subversion of Identity.* New York & London: 1990.

Bynum, Caroline Walker. *Fragmentation and Redemption: Essays on Gender and the Human Body in Medieval Religion.* New York: Zone, 1991.

———. *Holy Feast and Holy Fast: The Religious Significance of Food to Medieval Women.* Berkeley: University of California Press, 1987.

Cholakian, Patricia Francis. *Rape and Writing in the* Heptaméron *of Marguerite de Navarre.* Carbondale: Southern Illinois University Press, 1991.

De Lauretis, Teresa. *The Practice of Love: Lesbian Sexuality and Perverse Desire.* Bloomington, In.: Indiana University Press, 1994.

———. *Technologies of Gender: Essays on Theory, Film, and Fiction.* Bloomington, In.: Indiana University Press, 1987.

———. *Alice Doesn't: Feminism, Semiotics, Cinema.* Bloomington, In.: Indiana University Press, 1984.

Dollimore, Jonathan. *Sexual Dissidence: Augustine to Wilde, Freud to Foucault.* Oxford: Oxford University Press, 1991.

Epstein, Julia and Straub, Kristina, eds., *Body Guards: The Cultural Politics of Gender Ambiguity.* New York & London: Routledge, 1991.

Findlay, Heather, "Queerying the English Renaissance," in *diacritics* 24: 2-3 (summer-fall 1994): 227-237. Special Issue: *Critical Crossings,* ed. Judith Butler and Biddy Martin.

Foucault, Michel. *The History of Sexuality, Volume I: An Introduction.* New York: Random House, 1978.

———. *Discipline and Punish: The Birth of the Prison.* New York: Random House, 1979.

Fradenburg, Louise, "Criticism, Anti-Semitism, and the *Prioress's Tale,*" *Exemplaria* 1.1 (spring 1989): 69-115.

Freccero, Carla, "Practicing Queer Philology with Marguerite de Navarre: Nationalism and the Castigation of Desire," in Jonathan Goldberg, ed., *Queering the Renaissance.* Durham, NC: Duke University Press, 1994.

———. "Cannibalism, Homophobia, Women: Montaigne's 'Des cannibales' and 'De l'amitié,'" in Margo Hendricks and Patricia Parker, eds., *Women, "Race," and Writing in the Early Modern Period.* London & New York: Routledge, 1994: 73-83.

———. "Marguerite de Navarre and the Politics of Maternal Sovereignty," Special Issue: *Women and Sovereignty,* ed. Louise Fradenburg. *Cosmos* 7: 132-149.

Goldberg, Jonathan. *Sodometries: Renaissance Texts, Modern Sexualities.* Stanford, Ca.: Stanford University Press, 1992.

———. *Writing Matter: From the Hands of the English Renaissance.* Stanford, Ca.: Stanford University Press, 1990.

Haraway, Donna. *Simians, Cyborgs, and Women: The Reinvention of Nature.* New York: Routledge, 1991.

Hendricks, Margo, and Parker, Patricia, eds., *Women, "Race," and Writing in the Early Modern Period.* London & New York: Routledge, 1994.

Jed, Stephanie H. *Chaste Thinking: The Rape of Lucretia and the Birth of Humanism.* Bloomington, In.: Indiana University Press, 1989.

Kaplan, Cora. *Sea Changes: Culture and Feminism.* London: Verso, 1986.

Labé, Louise. *Oeuvres complètes.* Ed. François Rigolot. Paris: Garnier Flammarion, 1986.

Laqueur, Thomas. *Making Sex: Body and Gender from the Greeks to Freud.* Cambridge, Ma.: Harvard University Press, 1990.

Lavezzo, Kathy, "Sobs and Sighs Between Women: Female Homosocial Desire and *The Book of Margery Kempe,*" in Louise Fradenburg and Carla Freccero, eds., *The Pleasures of History: Reading Sexualities in Premodern Europe.* New York & London: Routledge, 1995: forthcoming.

Lomperis, Linda and Stanbury, Sarah, eds. *Feminist Approaches to the Body in Medieval Literature.* Philadelphia: University of Pennsylvania Press, 1993.

Miller, Nancy K. *Subject to Change: Reading Feminist Writing.* New York: Columbia University Press, 1988.

———. "Arachnologies: The Woman, The Text, and the Critic," in Nancy K. Miller, ed., *The Poetics of Gender.* New York: Columbia University Press, 1986: 270-295.

Nichols, Stephen G., and Patterson, Lee, eds. *Commentary as Cultural Artifact.* Special Issue, *South Atlantic Quarterly* 91: 4 (Fall 1992).

Nichols, Stephen G., ed. *The New Philology.* Special Issue, *Speculum* 65 (January 1990).

Polachek, Dora, "Save the Last Laugh for Me: Revamping the Script of Infidelity in Novella 69," in Dora Polachek, ed., *Heroic Virtue, Comic Infidelity: Reassessing Marguerite de Navarre's* Heptaméron. Amherst, Ma.: Hestia Press, 1993: 155-170.

Rubin, Gayle S., "Thinking Sex: Notes for a Radical Theory of the Politics of Sexuality," in Abelove, Barale, Halperin, eds., *The Lesbian and Gay Studies Reader.* New York & London: Routledge, 1993: 3-44.

Gary Godfrey (essay date 1999)

SOURCE: Godfrey, Gary. "Animal Symbolism and the Language of Transformation in *Heptaméron* 70." *Journal of the Utah Academy of Sciences, Arts, and Letters* 76 (1999): 213-24.

[*In the following essay, Godfrey considers the use of animal imagery and metaphors in "Novella 70" of the* Heptaméron *and determines the novella's indebtedness to the thirteenth-century love story* Chastelaine de Vergi.]

Marguerite de Navarre's **"Seventieth Novella"** from the **Heptaméron** retells the well-known story of the *Chastelaine de Vergi,* a thirteenth-century love poem. In the original story, a beautiful duchess falls in love with a chevalier of the court, and believing her charms to be irresistible, tries to seduce him. But the chevalier secretly loves another and spurns the duchess's advances, thus incurring her wrath. Through a two-fold manipulation of her husband, the duchess discovers the identity of the secret lady whom she subsequently humiliates in public, and the tragic death of the lovers and the duchess ensues.

By Marguerite's time the poem had enjoyed a great deal of popularity, so much so that decorative panels depicting various key scenes from the story were carved in wood and ivory and were displayed in homes and on various articles of furniture. Moreover, twenty extant copies of the poem make up its manuscript tradition and demonstrate that a number of versions were in circulation, including a prose rendition of the story and a play known as *La Chastellene du Vergier.* These latter two versions, both lost, are known to have existed in the fifteenth century.

Critical interest in **Heptaméron "[Novella] 70"** stems largely from three central concerns: the question of Marguerite's possible sources, the extent and the nature of her innovations,[1] and the thematic and aesthetic aspects of the story. Our main interest in the present discussion focuses on the latter two questions, especially as they involve aesthetic qualities of the tale resulting directly from Marguerite's own stylistic formulation of her narrative.

Jean Frappier's well-known 1946 study of Marguerite's source for **Heptaméron "70"** and of Bandello, her translator, clearly shows that a number of elements in Marguerite's narrative are original with her. He points out that her version is more modern in tone, especially concerning its psychological and intellectual content, and he examines the stylistic effects of Marguerite's use of past and present verb tenses (425-463). One aspect of Marguerite's transposition of the novella that Frappier only mentions briefly, and largely from the perspective of semantics, however, is her pervasive reliance on animal imagery and animal metaphors. This type of imagery proliferates throughout the **Heptaméron,** and falls along largely predictable line for the period.

As Marcel Tetel has pointed out, it becomes a "quite important category in the language of love" (57), and revolves around hunting, reversed biblical concepts and the animality of man (see chapter 2). Medieval tradition provides a source for many of these stylistic devices as does the folk wisdom of the day. A stock catalogue of symbols found in literature, some of which derive from biblical, ancient or other literary sources, give many commonplace examples.[2] So while Marguerite's additions to **Heptaméron "70"** in this respect show a marked deviation from her medieval model, other traditions seem to provide ample inspiration from which these images may have been derived. However, an examination of these and related features in the light of Julia Kristeva's model of transformation theory will reveal an intricate relationship between such images and Marguerite's story as a signifying practice.

According to Kristeva's theory, a semiotic transformation consists of an inversion or a reversal of two opposite terms existing in a disjunctive relationship, disjunctive being defined negatively or as the absence of a quality (427-29). In the case of the duchess in **Heptaméron "70,"** then, the first reference to her, coming in the prologue, characterizes her a "beautiful and well married" 'belle et bien maryée' (512; 340). But failing to find satisfaction in "what is honourable for women in matters of love" 'l'honneste amour des femmes' (512; 339), she becomes "more carnal in her desires than

swine and more cruel than the lions" 'plus charnelle que les porceaus, et plus cruelle que les lyons' (512; 340). This initial description of the duchess's transformation from beautiful to beastly introduces a major theme of the novella—the animalistic tendencies of human nature—and provides a key for its interpretation.

As Oysille, the narrator of the novella, introduces the duchess to us, she emphasizes her unusual beauty and relates that because of it the duchess has great sway over her husband. And although her elegance and charm are important, her social influence is mostly due to her high rank. Indeed, she commands the loyalty of the ladies of the court and is their leader and their idol. But as the level of the narration, this seeming perfection is disturbed by the presence of signifiers which betray the duchess's baseness. When she falls in love with a nobleman who is in the service of the duke, she loves him "beyond all reason" 'outre reaison' (513; 340), becomes a "poor impassioned creature" 'pauure fole' (513; 340), and even abandons the social graces of her rank by openly attempting to seduce the nobleman, "forgetting that she was a wife whose duty was to receive advances and reject them" 'oublyant qu'elle étoit femme qui deuoit ettre priée, et refusé' (513; 340). She abandons the code of honest friendship, *honnette amytié,* commencing her descent into animality and destruction. To love beyond all reason, *outré raison* already places her actions beyond human rationality, leaving her prey to her own madness.

But this first phase of the transformation is a mere beginning. A pivotal figure in the signifying chain is the niece's little dog. In the *Chastelaine de Vergi* he is described as "afetier" (I.718), and Marguerite retains the adjective (affété), adding the expression "trained" 'fait à la main' (526; 350) as a further indication, from the duchess's point of view, of the dog's discipline. Frappier discusses the evolution and meaning of both terms (141-42), concluding that affètè implies "well dressed, formed, styled, cunning" 'bien dresse, forme, style' as well as "cunning" 'rusè' (141), and that hand trained, fait à la main, derived from the vocabulary of horsemen, suggests that the dog's training is so polished as to permit him to obey his mistress's orders almost instinctively. Frappier calls this "training that testifies of a singular professional skill" 'un dressage qui temoigne d'une singulière habileté professionnelle' (143). In Huguet's dictionary, the range of definitions for the entry "fait à la main" further amplifies the term's meaning to include "pretty, graceful, and skilled at speaking" 'joli, gracieux, et habile à parler,' which buttress Marguerite's own modification of the original story on which the dog's signal was purely visual. He would run out into the garden when the chevalier could safely approach, but in **Heptaméron "70"** the dog barks out his signal from the niece's garden, demonstrating that he is indeed "skilled at speaking" 'habile à parler.'[3]

The overall effect of the dog's role is that he begins to assume certain qualities of his mistress. He is well trained, or rather, well mannered, gracious and above all, his "speech" reflects the conventions of his society. He offends no one. In other words, the dog begins to take on human qualities, even as the duchess assumes the traits of the lowest of beasts—a pig.

This reversal of roles is most clearly revealed by the duchess's sarcastic reply when the niece tries to dodge questions about her amorous life. "'Fair niece, fair niece,' answered the Duchess, with terrible bitterness in her voice, 'There is no love so secret that is not known, and no little dog so tame, so trained that his yapping is not heard!'" 'Belle niéce, belle niéce . . . dit la Duchesse, par un extéme dépit. Il n'y a amour si secrete, qui ne soit sceue, ny petit chien si afété, ne si fait à la main, duquel lon n'entende le japer' (526; 349-350) To which the niece replies that she "did not understand the language of the beasts" 'ne s'entendoit point au langage des bestes' (526; 350). The obvious double play on the duchess's comment heightens the dramatic tension of the story at the level of the content while widening the distance separating the signifiers and the signifieds. When the duchess uses "terrible bitterness" 'extréme dépit' (526; 350) in putting the niece on public display, she again transgresses the code of her society, further reinforcing Oysille's statement that she is "more cruel than the lions" 'plus cruelle que les lyons' (512; 340). The niece responds with "virtuous dissimulation" 'sage dissimulation' (526; 350), that she does not understand the language of animals, and we immediately grasp the ironic dimension of her rejoinder. The duchess is the beast whose language she does not understand. Of course, it was not the dog at all who revealed the niece's secret, but rather the duchess herself who has become the signified of the signifier dog. The transformation is now complete; the duchess has begun to yap like some ill-mannered cur who will in the end have provoked the demise of all. So it would appear that having changed the silent dog of the *Chastelaine de Vergi* into a barking dog in **Heptaméron "70"** serves the theme of human bestiality well.

A similar transformation occurs with regard to the nobleman. He is initially portrayed as "endowed with all the perfections a man should have, and greatly loved by all around him" 'tant accomply en toutes les perfections que lon pourrait demander en l'homme, qu'il était de tous aymé' (513; 340). But his personal resolve is ultimately undone and his promise to the niece broken as the duchess becomes more and more crafty in her manipulating of the duke. When he finally realizes that his loose tongue has led to his mistress's death, he laments that he would have been better off as her dog. "My God, why did you create me a man, whose heart knows nothing and whose love is light? Why was I not created to be her little dog, who served his mistress

faithfully?" 'O mon Dieu pour quoy me créates vous homme ayant l'amour si légére et le Coeur si ignorant? Pour quoy ne me créates vous le petit chien qui fidélement serui sa maitresse?' (529; 352).

The nobleman, unlike the duchess, has not become carnal and therefore bestial. Rather, he has not emulated the "best" qualities of the little dog—faithfulness. He has placed a mixed sentiment of loyalty and fear of the duke above the promise of fidelity and secrecy he had made to his mistress. So he now longs to be the steadfast dog whose bark once was a sign of joy and who knows that he has never betrayed the trust of his mistress.

The niece herself asks whether or not the nobleman hasn't become like the duchess, of whom she speaks in these terms just before dying: "Has she changed you from virtue to vice, from goodness to evil, from a man into a ferocious beast?" 'Vous a elle fait venir de vertueus, vicious; de bon, mauais; et d'homme, beste cruelle?' (527; 350-351). The answer seems to be clear "yes" from the niece's perspective, but the nobleman finds himself in the most ambiguous situation of any of the novella's characters. In the niece's eyes he undergoes a transformation from man to cruel beast, but for the duke, he proves himself revealing the name of his mistress.

In still another way, the niece herself becomes the subject of a transformation. She has, of course, remained completely faithful to the nobleman, nor has she broken any other code of behavior. Her crime is that she allowed her earthly love of the nobleman to occupy her so completely that she has forgotten the divine love of the Creator whom she now apostrophizes as "true and perfect love" 'la vraye et perfette amour' (528; 351). There has been no vice in her love of the nobleman, she says, "other than loving him too much" 'si non de trop aymer' (528; 351).

Again the nobleman is identified with the bestial, carnal side of human love in that he becomes the creature and has now been replaced in the niece's eyes by God himself, who is the only true and perfect love. The nobleman was only an earthly detractor from true devotion.[4]

When the niece apostrophizes her soul we see a working out of a highly significant division of the self. Unlike the duchess and the nobleman, also fallen characters, the niece culls out, through her use of language, that aspect of her person that loves the flesh, and she commends her soul to her maker. This split in her being is an exemplary instance of disjunctive opposition which now comes to signify and prefigure her impending death as the soul moves toward spiritual realms.

A highly imaginative metaphor also characterizes the duke. When he arrives at the scene of his niece's death, he has only a brief instant before the nobleman's death to ask what has happened. Suddenly, and angry duke becomes as agitated as a wounded wild boar (sanglier), but his is a spiritual wound: "Then in a frenzied rage he rose, drew the dagger from the young man's body, and like the wild boar which, wounded by a spear, runs headlong at the hunter who has thrown it, he ran from the room in pursuit of the woman who had wounded him to the depths of his soul" 'Tout furieus il se leua tyrant le poignal du cors du gentilhomme. Et tout ainsi qu'un sanglier étant nauré di'un épieu, court . . . contre celuy qui a fait le coup, ainsi le Duc s'en ala chercher celle qui l'avait nauré jusques au fond do son ame' (531; 354). He seeks her out at the dance and kills her.

Once so taken with his wife's beauty that it "gave him such great happiness that he was blind to her true character" 'elle luy faisoit ignorer ses conditions, tant qu'il ne regardoit qu'àluy complaire' (513; 340), the duke resolutely keeps the only promise he has not broken to this point by killing the duchess. So, within the framework of the transformation he goes from breaking his promise to the nobleman to honoring is threat to kill the duchess for betraying a trust. And though once a handsome prince, he becomes like unto a wounded wild boar seeking revenge. But in the final phase of the transformation, he, like his niece, turns toward heaven for repentance. He founds an abbey as partial remission for his crime, and then undertakes a crusade against the Turks where God recognizes and repays his efforts: "God granted him such success that he returned a wealthy and much honored man" 'Dieu le fauorisa tant, qu'il en rapporta honneur et profit' (531; 354). The transformation of the duke has now come full circle: "once a Duke and a virtuous and handsome prince" 'un Duc treshonnete et beau Prince' (513; 340) at the first of the novella, his beastly traits inspired the brutal slaying of the duchess, and he now returns from his crusade to live out a pious life near his abbey, "And there, in the sight of God, he peacefully passes away his old age" 'Et là passa sa vieillesse heuresusement auec Dieu' (532; 354).

The thematic axis of **Heptaméron "70,"** based as it is on the opposition of human and bestial traits, draws on a literary tradition at least as old as the Greeks. The symbols of a carnal pig and a cruel lion belong to a well-established canon of symbols, and in other novellas Marguerite used folklore and medieval literary conventions as sources for her animal symbols. (See Le Hyr xx) But in **"Novella 70,"** these symbols assume a semiotic function within a signifying narrative practice. In the first place, animal symbols have lost all but their most basic referentiality. The pig, the dog, and the wild boar become signifiers operating within a hierarchical relationship of dynamic concentric dualism. As discussed above, then, the transformations are in a vertical, or paradigmatic relationship, the paradigm being characterized by its substitutability. The carnal pig re-

places the charming duchess, and is assimilated to the dog. Hence, the duchess replaced by pig, displaced by dog, becomes a hierarchical metaphor functioning in descending order, and is characterized by its dynamism. In a dyadic structure of diametrical opposition, the spiritual and the carnal would exist in a mutually exclusive and therefore irreducible relationship. The duchess could never represent any quality other than the one with which she is associated in the first instance, in this case honest love.

In a structure of concentric dualism, by contrast, the duchess is a faithful friend (amie fidele) and a perfidious friend (amie perfide), but the dynamics of this dualism allow her to evolve away from ambiguity as the transformation progressively confirms her bestiality. Each transformation of a character occurs within a similar paradigmatic, or metaphoric relationship, but with dissimilar results. Even as the beauty/beast (belle/bête) opposition characterizing the duches becomes ultimately completely negative, the nobleman retains positive and negative traits. He honors his obligations to the duke, but betrays the niece. The niece aspires to honor, but dishonors herself through carnal love. So within these vertical relationships, the concentric circles representing various signifieds can move about in limited, but complex asymmetrical orbits, which gives them an implicit triadic quality (Kristeva 14).

There is, however, another dimension to the process of transformation within **"Novella 70"** which bears examination—the syntagmatic relationship. Each character progresses through a series of events within a narrative segment, establishing a precise relationship with the other characters. The narrative's linear movement, therefore, gives rise to further transformations. From the duke's perspective the nobleman is twice transformed, once through the duchess's denegration of him, and finally through his own proofs of faithfulness. Likewise, the duke, once suspicious of the nobleman, becomes his spokesman and avenger, but the most significant transformation occurs between the duchess and the dog. Even as the duchess becomes more and more animal-like in her behavior, the dog assumes the traits of the most worthy courtier. In fact, no member of the court so well exemplifies the ideal code of courtly conduct as does the dog. He is faithful, loyal, and the envy of the nobleman who wished he too had "served his mistress faithfully" 'fidélement serui sa maitresse' (529; 352). Furthermore, the niece refuses to blame the dog. She sees him as being perfectly trained and sums up her feelings thus: "Alas! my little dog, so obedient, you who were my only messenger throughout this long and virtuous love of mine, it was not you who betrayed me! It was this man, whose voice has carried farther than the bark of any dog!" 'Hélas mon petit chien tant bien appris, le seul moyen de ma longue et vertueuse amytié, ce n'a 'as été vous qui m'auex décelée, mais celuy qui a la voys plus éclantante que le chien abboyant, et le cueur plus ingrat que nulle beste' (527; 350). So, just as the duchess succumbs to a negative state of complete animality, the dog sheds his referential traits to become the only unequivocally positive participant in the drama. They remain in an irreducible disjunctive relationship incapable of further transformations.

As we have seen, the dog's syntagmatic transformation places him at a pivotal point in the novella. He becomes a dual symbol, but he also functions in one additional way. As mentioned earlier, in **"Novella 70"** he has been given a "voice." In the *Chastelaine de Vergi* his signal was purely visual, but now he barks, and his bark provides the duchess with her comment that there is no dog so well trained that his bark cannot be heard, which merits the niece's ironic retort. Later, in her chamber, she laments her situation saying: "'O unhappy woman, what are these words that assail my ears? What is this sentence of death that I have heard pronounced?'" 'O malheureuse, quelle parole est ce que j'ai oye? Quel arrest de ma mor ai je entendu?' (527; 350). This has become a drama of language,[5] with the little dog once again occupying a symbolic position of central importance.[6] In fact, the "acts" in the novella acquire their greatest importance when seen in relationship to the speech "act." The duchess's attempts to seduce the nobleman are essentially verbal with promises of great joy and perfect contentment ("'grand' joye, et . . . perfet contentement'" 341). But the greatest of ironies, the lady who was to have been the source of this perfection instead delivers only heartache and death, again as a result of a verbal act—the betrayal of a secret. The duke wavers in his opinion of the nobleman only because of what his wife tells him. He has no cause to suspect the man's devotion.

Furthermore, he fluctuates between anger and esteem for his wife and the nobleman, threatening and making promises to both, breaking promises and renewing threats. His final act of indignation comes when he marches off to the ball having left his niece and the nobleman dead. He finds the duchess, but rather then silently killing her as the duke does in the *Chastelaine de Vergi,* he first says to her, "You swore on your life to keep the secret, and with your life you shall pay for what you have done" 'Vous auez pris le secret sur votre vie, et sur votre vie tombera la punition' (531; 354). Nor does it stop there. The duke assembles his court "to recount the piteous and noble story of his niece, and the cruel action of his wife" 'et leurraconta l'honnete et piteuse histoire de sa niéce, et le méchant tour que luy avait fait sa femme' (531; 354). It is this retelling of the story that establishes the proper perspective among the court.

Marguerite further enhances her version of the *Dame du Verger* placing great importance on the niece's lament at the moment of death. It is here that she devel-

ops the psychological analysis of the niece and shortly thereafter of the nobleman. The niece's words summarize the movement of the entire novella as she crystallizes the earlier transformations into verbal parings— "virtue/vice, goodness/evil, man/beast, Creator/creature" 'vertueus/vicious; bon/mauuais; homme/beste cruelle; la vie/la mor; le Créateur/la créature' (527-28; 350-51).[7] When the duke arrives, the nobleman, near death of self-inflicted wounds, is embracing the corpse of his beloved. In his dismay the duke asks: "'Alas! Who is the cause of all this?'" 'Hélas, et qui est cause de cecy?' (531; 353), to which the nobleman responds with his last breath: "'The cause, my Lord, is my tongue (my emphasis), and yours!'" 'Votre langue et las miéne, Monsieur' (531; 353). Marguerite has made her novella into a tragedy of language, one of broken promises and betrayed secrets.

"Novella 70" is clearly conceptualized and constructed within the Renaissance framework of a hierarchically structured cosmos which places God at the pinnacle of creation both physically and morally, with the animals occupying the bottom rung. From a spiritual point of view then, "animality is in effect the privation of God since the beast does not see the divine being [. . .]" 'l'animalité est en effet privation de Dieu, puisque la bête ne voit pas l'être divin . . .' (Joukovsky 90). The duchess and the niece perfectly typify this opposition as they pass to the next realm, one having succumbed to the instincts of pure animality and the other having renounced all human sensuality, even her "chaste, noble and most virtuous love" 'chaste, honnette et vertueuse amour' (527; 350) in her desire to replace it with a more "perfect love" 'perfette amour' (528; 351)—her only desire.[8]

The narrative frame of the storytellers (devisants) further enhances the spiritual dimension of the novella. Dagoncin introduces the idea leading Oysille to recount the niece's story by saying of women unable to content themselves with a single husband, "if she does [not] live in accordance with what is honourable for women in matters of love, then she is bound to be tempted by infernal animal concupiscence" 'Car ne viuant de l'honneste amour des femmes, faut qu'elle soit toute de l'insatiable cupidité des bestes' (512; 339). And Oysille concludes with a similar admonition: "I should think you should let it stand as an example to you not to fix your affections on men, for, however pure and virtuous your affections may be, it will always lead to some disastrous conclusion. [. . .] For the more one fixes one's affections on earthly things, the further one is from heavenly affection" 'll me semble que deuez tirez exemple de cecy, pour vous garder de mettre votre affection aus homes. . . . Car d'autant que notre cueur est affectionné à quelque chose terriéne, d'autant s'éloigne il de l'affection céleste' (532; 354).

There can be little question that her contemporary read-ers grasped the symbolic implications of Marguerite's lesson: There is no greater moral degradation or de-structiveness in matters of the heart than to become "more carnal in her desires than swine" 'plus charnel que les porceaus' (512; 340), and no greater spiritual purity than the transformation of beastly passions into a rarified affection for the only perfect friend (parfait ami)—God himself.

Notes

1. A recent study by Suarez compares Marguerite's version with its source, concluding that the stories are not radically different from each other, since only some of the details differ. It would be diffi-cult, however, to overlook the Renaissance char-acter of "Novella 70."

2. Two such sources are *Master Richard's Bestiary of Love and Response,* and the Ashmole Bestiary, published in French by Philippe Lebaud as *Le Be-staire.* Cooper sees dogs as embodying "the quali-ties of fidelity, watchfulness and nobility" (74) as in Marguerite's tale, and in her "Duel of Bestia-ries," Beer details the medieval context of animal symbolism in relationship to love in ways that provide a literary tradition for this element in "No-vella 70."

3. An additional discussion of Marguerite's use of the term "fait à la main" may be found in the Bensi study. He discusses the phrase in relation-ship to Bandello's translation of "Novella 70" and sheds new light on Frappier's arguments.

4. Gelernt provides the best study of the varieties of love in the *Heptaméron.*

5. Further discussions on the role of language in "Novella 70" may be found in the studies by Per-rigaud and Cholakian. Giardiana's discussion of other novellas points out the fact that the rights of speech were tied to rank and wealth (3), which appears to be the case in "Novella 70" as well. The duchess's social ascendancy allows her a de-gree of verbal freedom that is denied to the niece. But in time the duchess pays dearly for exercising that prerogative. On the topic of the proscription of women's speech during the Renaissance see Kelso (50-51). Wiley discusses the ambiguity of speech in the *Heptaméron,* specifically, and states that direct communication, that is unveiled mes-sages, can have tragic results (135), as they do in this novella. O'Brien gives additional details on the theme of silence in Renaissance literature in France.

6. Dogs have enjoyed the widespread use as sym-bols. In a central position in the late fifteenth-century tapestry "To My Only Desire" 'A mon seul désir,' (from the series "La Dame à la Licorne," Musée national du Moyen Age de Cluny), one notices a small dog seated on a table near the lady, as a lion and a unicorn hold up the corners of her cloak. Kenneth Clark sees emblems of lust and ferocity in these animals while the dog represents the domestication of desire (61), the taming of the beast within, as he seemingly does in Marguerite's tale as well.

7. For a discussion of the "éloquence appretée des deux lamentations," see Frappier (455-57).

8. Joukovsky discusses the Renaissance use of ani-mal symbolism in the most comprehensive article of its kind to date, while Laurence Mal exten-sively treats aspects of animal and divine desires within the context of Renaissance concepts of love in "Novella 10." He sees the question which is central to *Heptaméron* "70," "how to love the creature without betraying the creator" 'comment aimer la créature sans trahir le créateur' (188) as running through the entire *Heptaméron.*

Works Cited

Beer, Heanett. "Duel of Bestiaries." *Beats and Birds of the Middle Ages: The Bestiary and Its Legacy.* Ed. Wil-lene B. Clark and Meradith T. McMunn. Philadelphia: Univ. Pennsylvania Press, 1989: 96-105.

Le Bestaire. Trans. Marie-France Dupuis and Sylvie Louis. n.p. Philippe Lebaud, 1988.

La Chatelaine de Vergi. Ed. Gaston Rynaud and Lucien Foulet. Les Classiques Français du Moyen Age. 1. Paris: Honoré Champion, 1921.

Cholakian, Patricia Francis. "Sublimation as Subver-sion. Novella 70." *Rape and Writing in the* Heptaméron *of Marguerite de Navarre.* Carbondale and Edwards-ville: Southern Illinois Univ. Press, 1991. 182-206.

Clark, Kenneth. *Civilisation.* New York: Harper and Row, 1969.

Cooper, J. C. *Symbolic and Mythological Animals.* Lon-don: Aquarian Press, 1992.

Frappier, Jean. *"La Chastelaine de Vergi,* Marguerite de Navarre et Bandello." *Du Moyen Age à la Renaissance: Etudes d'histoire et de Critique Littéraire.* Paris: Hon-oré Champion, 1976. 393-473.

Gelernt, Jules. *World of Many Loves: The* Heptaméron *of Marguerite de Navarre.* Chapel Hill: The Univ. of North Carolina Press, 1966.

Giardiana, C. "La Parole dans l'*Heptaméron* de Mar-guerite de Navarre." *L'Information Littéraire: Revue Parissant cinq Fois par an.* 43.1 (1991): 3-6.

Huguet, E. *Dictionnaire de la langue française du XVIe siècle.* Paris: Honoré Champion, 1925-46.

Joukovsky, Françoise. "Del'animal métaphysique à l'animal nu (Bovelles, Belon et Montaigne)." *L'Animalité. Hommes et animaux dans la Littérature française*. Ed. Alain Niderst. Tübingen: Gunter Narr Verlag, 1994. 87-101.

Kelso, Ruth. *Doctrine for the Renaissance*. Urbana: Univ. of Illinois Press, 1956.

Kristeva, Julia. "Narration et transformation." *Semiotica*. 1 (1969): 422-48.

Mall, Laurence. "'Pierre ou bestes': le corps dans las dixiéme nouvelle de l'*Heptaméron* de Marguerite de Navarre." *French Forum*. 171992: 169-90.

Master Richard's Bestiary of Love and Response. Trans. Jeanette Beer. Berkeley: Univ. of California Press, 1986.

Navarre, Marguerite de. *Marguerite de Navarre: Nouvelles*. Ed. Yves Le Hir. Publications de la Faculté des Lettres et Sciences Humaines, Univ. de Grenoble, 44. Paris: PUF, 1967.

———. *The Heptameron*. Trans. P. A. Chilton. London: Penguin, 1984.

O'Brien, John "*Vox Faucibus Haesit*." *Symposium*. 49 (Winter, 1996): 297-306.

Perrigaud, Martha C. "Oisille's Tale of the Duchesse de Bourgogne: The Power of the Word." *Degré Second: Studies in French Literature*. D Section. 6 July 1982: 25-40.

Suarex, Ramon M. "Dos Textos para una Historia." *Rivista Chilena de Literatura*. 40 (1992): 73-81.

Tetel, Marcel. *Marguerite de Navarre's* Heptameron: *Themes, Language, and Structure*. Durham, N.C.: Duke Univ. Press, 1973.

Wiley, Karen. "Communication Short-Circuited: Ambiguity and Motivation in the *Heptaméron*." *Ambigious Realities: Women in the Middle Ages and Renaissance*. Ed. Carol Levin and Jeanie Watson. Detroit: Wayne State Univ. Press, 1987. 137-44.

Richard Regosin (essay date 1999)

SOURCE: Regosin, Richard. "Leaky Vessels: Secrets of Narrative in the *Heptaméron* and the Châtelaine's Lament." *Mediaevalia* 22 (1999): 181-200.

[*In the following essay, Regosin investigates the political, religious, and social implications of sexual passion and desire as represented in "Novella 70" of the* Heptaméron.]

In his narrative of the complex relationship of sexuality, concealment, and discourse in *Histoire de la sexualité: La volonté de savoir* Foucault makes the disclosure of transgressive desire a defining trait of modern western culture.[1] Arguing against the thesis that characterizes the period since the 17th century as an age that repressed and silenced sexual discourse, he contends that in the last three centuries sexuality has burst forth in a veritable discursive explosion that has not only been sanctioned by the institutions of power themselves but incited, proliferated, and disseminated by them: "Mais l'essentiel, c'est la multiplication des discours sur le sexe, dans le champ d'exercice du pouvoir lui-même" (26) [But more important was the multiplication of discourses concerning sex in the field of exercise of power itself (18)]. For Foucault the prohibitions that allegedly forbid frank sexual discourse, the taboos that purportedly exclude its open expression, the common perception that the expression of sexuality and desire are enjoined to secrecy are nothing more, or less, than a theme that is part of the mechanism of incitement, a fable that is indispensable to the endlessly proliferating economy of sexual discourse. Secrets and secrecy are necessary, indeed essential, to the production of these discourses, even if, or especially if, in this case, they constitute for him a theme or a fable, not "real" secrets but what I would call generative fictions: "Ce qui est propre aux sociétés modernes, ce n'est pas qu'elles aient voué le sexe à rester dans l'ombre, c'est qu'elles se soient vouées à en parler toujours, en le faisant valoir comme *le* secret" (Foucault, 48-49) [What is peculiar to modern societies, in fact, is not that they consigned sex to a shadow existence, but that they dedicated themselves to speaking of it *ad infinitum,* while exploiting it as *the* secret (35)]. The secrets and the secrecy of sexuality engender discourse, including Foucault's own narrative of the history of sexuality.

Foucault's emphasis on the proliferation of sexual discourses through institutional incitement and the instigation of secrecy makes a persuasive argument, but it is important to stress as well that the verbalizing of sexuality existed long before the classical age that for many inaugurates the "modern" and before it received official sanction and encouragement. The frank sexual idiom had, for example, traditionally enlivened the languages of medieval and Renaissance carnival, languages both authorized by the political and religious institutions and simultaneously contained as elements of festive ritual. In Rabelais's *Pantagruel* (1532) the character of Panurge embodies the carnival spirit in the explosive celebration of explicit sexual and verbal energy. But even where the same political and religious powers, and social and cultural forces as well, forbade their articulation and sought to suppress, muffle, and to silence their voices, sexuality and desire also spoke incessantly. What was repressed and driven into hiding by the laws of state or the dictates of the Church, what was bound and obliged to secrecy by the codes of chivalry or courtly love, was precisely what surfaced ceaselessly, irresistibly, however veiled its form. In his essay "On some verses of Virgil" (circa 1586), Montaigne represents his own effort to speak frankly of his sexual experience in the face of severe cultural constraints but he is well aware, as Foucault will later be, that by relegating sexuality to silence and to secrecy these same constraints paradoxically ensure its expression. "Is it not the same as in the matter of books," he asks, "which become all the more marketable and public by being suppressed?"[2] *The* secret is not formalized in the early modern period, as in Foucault's narrative of the succeeding age, but we might say that inadvertently it also produces distinctive discursive effects, effects that in this case are strikingly more oblique but equally as ubiquitous.

This is the lesson of Marguerite de Navarre's ***Heptaméron*** (written 1546-49 and first published posthumously in 1558) where desire cannot be admitted but passion cannot be denied. Because sexual expression challenges political and paternal authority, violates religious dictates, and contravenes social decorum, its voices must be stilled. Because it places virtue in jeopardy, compromises honor, and invites moral condemnation, its expression must be stifled. But in spite of this, or because of it, sexuality informs endless discourse and occasions countless narratives. The repression of desire is not its suppression but the paradoxical incitement to speak, and secret desire does not long remain secret. In the Prologue the sublimation of sexual impulse founds the community of storytellers; the not entirely facetious suggestion that the ten travelers isolated by a flood relieve the boredom of their idle hours by making love is rejected in favor of the pastime of telling tales. Libidinous instincts may be refused a direct outlet, but they lurk constantly beneath the surface, seeking and finding voice surreptitiously, clandestinely, indirectly. The narrative tales of the ***Heptaméron*** are replete with secrets of sexual longing, and secret relationships and desires inform the narratives constituted by the exchanges of the storytellers themselves both in the Prologue and in the discussions and debates that frame their tales. Narratives in Marguerite's text are generated by secrets but we might also say that secrets are in turn characterized by their narratability.[3] Only the possibility of disclosure makes a secret a secret, and in its paradoxical and seemingly inevitable exposition what is produced is not an unmediated truth but a narrative, a verbal structure that itself could be said to contain "secrets" and latent meanings, and that invites further reading, interpretation, discussion. In the ***Heptaméron*** secrets open to produce narratives of disclosure and disclosures in turn appear to enfold their own productive secrets.[4]

One of the most pregnant examples of the complex and mutually generative relation between narrative and secrecy occurs near the end of the ***Heptaméron*** (**"Novella 70"**) in the reprise of the medieval poem, "La Châtelaine de Vergy."[5] In the dynamic interplay of enclosure and disclosure within this tale, secrets and secrecy inaugurate narrative, they circulate within to give it shape, they propel its movement, cause its dilation, and affect its denouement.[6] Marguerite de Navarre's novella reaches its tragic apex in the betrayed lady's heartrending lament when she discovers that the secret of her relationship is out, but we will see that from the opening of the story, when neither the Châtelaine nor her secret was known or even in question, the lament is already inscribed in the narrative as the secret of her secret. And we will see as well that what is also inscribed as the secret of that secret is the birth and operation of narrative itself.

In order for the tale to be told, exception has to be made to the clause in the narrative contract established in the Prologue that requires that the tale be true, and new(s), and that the teller have actually witnessed the events of the tale or heard it from a trustworthy source. Madame Oisille only proceeds when assured that because this previously written story appears in an old, and therefore unfamiliar, language it surely is not known to more than one or two of the group: "parquoy sera tenu pour nouveau" (400) [So it can be regarded as a new one (512)].[7] We might say that the old story itself functions like a secret. Concealed as it were in a remote and inaccessible code that is there for all to see and yet, in this case, is not seen, the manuscript beckons to those curious to know and at the same time resists penetration to safeguard its secret. And like all secrets, especially those contained in enigmatic or cryptic writing, it can be known only by those already in the know ("hors mis nous deux, il n'y a icy homme ne femme qui en ayt ouy parler" [400]) [apart from you and me, there's no one here who will have heard it (512)]. Secrecy operates on a principle of inclusion and exclusion that always creates "insiders" and "outsiders" and confers privilege and power on those "in" on the secret.[8] It is not coincidental that Madame Oisille and Parlamente alone know this secret, given their roles as the leading inflections of authorial voice in the ***Heptaméron,*** but it is also not coincidental that the secret, like all secrets, is eventually divulged. Here it is the spirit of equality regulating the discourse of the "passetemps" in which the characters are engaged ("au jeu nous sommes tous esgaulx" [10]) that justifies disclosure of the "secret" of the Châtelaine de Vergy as the last narrative of the seventh day.

The narrative secreted in a manuscript written in Old French thus gives rise to the "oral" narration of the ***Heptaméron***; the enclosed and impenetrable poetic discourse generates the open narration that is the novella. The secret is translated from an old to a modern language, carried over to another genre that is appropriately called "nouvelle," and from one expressive mode to another (even though the "oral" is a fiction of Marguerite's written text); in this carriage the secret is disclosed as "news."⁹ But to divulge the secret of the Châtelaine de Vergy in this way—the secret of the poem as well as that of the woman—is not to bring everything to light once and for all and to render further discourse superfluous. Because the novella itself contains obscure folds and enigmatic turns, and because (as always) it exceeds the intentions of its narrator, the tale generates further discourse. In the debate among the storytellers that follows, it produces multiple interpretations and judgments that give different values to secrecy and to the secret itself.

The narrators' discussion constitutes a narrative in its own right, but we might add that this narrative also proliferates because each of the commentaries of the interlocutors is an implicit narrative that would recast or retell the tale from a distinct point of view, however briefly or allusively the specific comment or judgment is made. The members of the group are both listeners and producers of discourse; they hear different stories, draw different moral lessons, and in the course of the discussion project what would be different narratives, even if only in the form of a suggestive remark or two. In the interlocking sequence of stories and debates in the *Heptaméron,* and in the mutually generating relation of secrets and narrative, these "implied narratives" represent the seeds of further storytelling. The simple story of a woman who gets the last laugh on her silly husband (**"Novella 69"**) elicits serious discussion about honor, carnal desire, and the needs of women and jogs Oisille's memory about the Châtelaine de Vergy, as if this second, tragic narrative were in some way already contained in the humorous tale that precedes as an implicit, and anamorphic version. As narrative dilates, themes and forms are worked and reworked by the narrators in their tales and their debates over the course of the seven days of storytelling.

The earlier account on which Oisille draws, written in Old French, had made no secret of the fact that the story of the Châtelaine was about secrecy itself. As the poet states in the opening lines of the medieval poem, there are certain people who pretend to be faithful and worthy of secrets and in whom one is led to confide. But these people betray the avowal of love and mock the covenant of secrecy they had promised to honor, so that love founders in despair and shame. The poem announces at the outset that it will tell what happened in Burgundy to a valiant chevalier and to la dame de Vergy and it makes the exemplary value of their story explicit in the coda that completes the didactic frame: love should be carefully hidden; nothing is gained in its disclosure; secrecy is absolutely preferable.¹⁰ Marguerite de Navarre, and her narrator, Oisille, proceed otherwise in the *Heptaméron.* The secret covenant and the covenant of secrecy at the beginning of the narrative are deftly concealed and attention is deflected from what will come to occupy the thematic and structural center

of the tale. As if this were, in fact, another tale, the novella opens as a variation on the story of Joseph and Potiphar's wife (*Genesis,* 39), where the Duchess falsely accuses the young courtier of making improper sexual advances to cover up her own unsuccessful seduction. In the first part of the novella the Duchess's erotic desire drives the plot, staged as a series of confrontations with the gentleman whose refusal to acknowledge her meaning and acquiesce serves only to enflame her passion. The unbearable secret of desire must be divulged ("ceste pauvre folle . . . print le cueur d'un homme transporté pour descharger le feu qui estoit importable" [401]) [the poor madwoman . . . acted with the emotion of a man beside himself in order to quench the unbearable flames (my translation)], but because it is also an unspeakable secret, one that cannot be said and must not be heard, it must surface cautiously, obliquely, each time with increased daring until it finally discloses its naked intent.

One consequence of telling the story in this way is that we see how the unspeakable secret of desire provides the impetus for building narrative. These opening pages devoted to the leakage of the secret and the confrontations it occasions may allow for both characters involved to appear more psychologically complex as the Duchess struggles both to reveal and to mask her feelings and the young courtier seeks for his part to mask his own understanding of these feelings. This opening may as well develop a narrative of secrecy itself. What we might call the burden of the secret—and this seemingly applies to any secret, whether its content is profoundly transgressive or simply trivial—causes it inevitably to be divulged. Just as inevitably and always before the final revelation the bearer of the secret advertently or inadvertently draws attention to the fact that something is hidden, and even teasingly lets slip signs of what is hidden itself. That the Duchess is characterized by the narrator as "ceste pauvre folle," described as prey to "ung furieux desespoir" [wild desperation], and portrayed as having literally, as I read it, become a mad *man* ("[elle] print le cueur d'un homme transporté" [401]) certainly marks the folly of her passion and her conduct but it marks as well the folly of secrecy itself, the impossibility of its carriage, the necessity of its circulation and communication. The madness of desire—the flame that is irresistible but unbearable, rapturous but intolerable, life-giving but consuming—thus cannot be contained or cured by secrecy. Secrets are themselves always oxymorons (from Greek, *moros,* foolish); they are the height of folly because by definition contradictory and incongruous, simultaneously concealed and revealed. They are also the height of madness because they lie beyond reason's capacity to negotiate meaningfully between the pressure to withhold and the impulse to divulge, and beyond the capacity of will to master them. Like the fire they are meant to contain, secrets spread; because they are oxymoronic in this regard, secrets always unfold as narrative.

This infectious madness motivates the Duchess's frenzied effort to safeguard the unspeakable secret even after it has been spoken, as if it could be recovered by being covered up again, hidden behind something else, in this case the false accusation. The "real" secret thus propels the narrative by unfolding a false one—the alleged advances of the gentleman—that the Duchess pretends to have been keeping and that she now discloses to her husband. Interestingly, bogus secrets function just like real ones (how can one ever be certain that what is disclosed as a secret is in fact true or that what one claims is secret is in fact secret?). They too circulate upon disclosure, they too contain recesses and folds that invite elucidation and elaboration and that amplify narrative. Here the purported secret precipitates and conditions a ducal response that ironically will lead to the very real, and still deferred, secret of the gentleman, from which all parties, including the reader, continue to be excluded. Torn between love for his wife and for his subject, uncertain of the truth of the secret of misconduct, the Duke temporarily banishes the courtier, generating further narratives within the overall narrative, this time in defense of the young man. Accused secretly of a crime that remains for him a secret, the courtier counters a story he does not know—the Duchess's secret disguised as a narrative of seduction that he refers to as a "mauvais rapport" [405]) [some ill report (518)]—with his own story of faithful service, first told by a friend sent to the Duke and then reiterated in a letter that he himself writes. In this dizzying proliferation and alternance of secret and narrative the Duke initiates another secret by meeting clandestinely with the courtier ("et secretement l'envoia querir en sa chambre" [405]) [and sent for the young man to come secretly to see him in his room (518)] where he admits that only his doubts keep him from inflicting a secret punishment for harm done in secret ("pour vous rendre en secret la pugnition du mal que en secret m'avez pourchassé" [405]) [to punish you in secret for the dishonour you have in secret sought to bring on me! (518)]. And although the Duke divulges another secret by revealing that his wife is the accuser, the gentleman does not in turn disclose the secret of her illicit passion.

At this point we might ask about this insistent recurrence of secrets and secrecy, of counterfeit, real, and potential secrets (like the threatened punishment), all of which have leaked or are leaking as the content of the novella. We might wonder what imperative of the narrative calls for the courtier to be summoned secretly or for the Duke to project a secret punishment (besides the thematic balance of crime and punishment or the rhetorical balance of his phrase). Every encounter of two

characters seems to disclose another secret and every disclosure seems to create a new secret. The story, we might say, is leaking what could be called its obsessions, teasingly pointing in the process to the very mechanism that both produces and constitutes its unfolding. Secrets are shared, new secrets are produced and divulged, new thematic and structural recesses form in and as the generation of the narrative. And new interpretive issues, secreted in these recesses, emerge: psychological issues of personal identity and being defined by the characters' relation to the secrets they hold and to those they share; social issues where interpersonal relations are shaped in reference to secrets; political issues defined as the competing demands of the duties of love and of chivalric obligation, as in the situation of the gentleman or the Duke; issues of the rhythm and organization of the plot; and rhetorical issues concerning the figure of the secret, its operation, its status.

In her effort to preserve the apparent integrity of the counterfeit secret, to prove the "truth" of the false accusation, the Duchess unwittingly moves the narrative toward the opening of the secret at its core, that of the gentleman and the Châtelaine de Vergy. As the Duchess's libidinal drive turns into an equally powerful craving for vengeance, as her jealousy fuels her relentless pursuit of the gentleman, she happens by chance upon the clandestine relationship. Up to this point in the novella, the narrator has not made any mention of this secret. Except for the gentleman, no one—neither the Duke nor the Duchess, nor for that matter, the reader—even knows that it exists. The Châtelaine de Vergy herself has been kept secret by the narrator; she has not yet appeared as a character nor has her name been mentioned. The narrative will move irresistibly toward this disclosure, it will draw its impetus from the repeated deferral of the name and will extend itself through the progressive escape and circulation of elements of the secret until it has unfolded the full implications of this disclosure for all the characters.

The first leak occurs when the courtier is pressed to admit to the Duke that he does in fact love another woman; to have denied this love would have been to admit that he was capable of seducing the Duchess. "L'on esbahit que, vous estant si honneste et jeune, n'avez jamais aymé, que l'on ayt sceu: qui me faict penser que vous avez l'opinion qu'elle (the Duchess) dict, de laquelle esperance vous rend si content, que vous ne pouvez penser en une autre femme" (407) [It is rather astonishing that a man like you, young, and noble in every respect, should not, as far as anyone knows, have ever had an affair of the heart. This leads me to suspect that what she says about your feelings is true—that your hope that one day they may be fulfilled gives you such satisfaction that you cannot bear to think about other women (520)]. Constrained by the absolute obedience demanded of the vassal by the chivalric code ("[je]

vous commande, comme maistre, que vous aiez à me dire, si vous estes serviteur de nulle dame de ce monde"; [(I) order you as your master, to tell me whether you are devoted to the service of any lady at all (520)], the gentleman betrays the absolute loyalty and discretion demanded of the courtier by the code of courtly love and gives up the secret. Not the whole secret; what leaks out is the admission that there is another woman. What remains hidden is the name of the woman, which the Duke promises to respect. The integrity of the relationship between the gentleman and the unnamed lady depends on this secret: "l'accord de luy et de s'amye estoit de telle sorte qu'il ne se povoit rompre, sinon par celluy qui premier le declareroit. Le duc luy promit de ne l'en presser poinct" [there was a bond between them and an understanding that it would be broken if one of them were to make it known. The Duke promised not to press him further. . . . (520)].

The "accord" consecrates the secret, what the medieval poem had earlier called a "couvenant" and what the narrator will call most often a "promesse." A secret, we might say, is a compact that etymologically brings the parties "heart to heart" (Latin *ad + cor*) to hide a certain knowledge by their silence. But a secret is not to be entered into lightly nor is its integrity to be taken lightly. The compact is most significantly a contract, formalized and sealed by an oath or vow, what the narrative will refer to repeatedly as a "serment," or by the verb "jurer," to swear. Throughout the **Heptaméron** secrets are treated as if ritualized, that is, marked by a prescribed act that formally binds the participants and imposes duty and responsibility. Even if the "sacramentum" (from Latin *sacer,* sacred) that obligates one to silence is not articulated, it founds the secret and functions just as meaningfully as its sacred law. When the Duchess insists that her husband pressure the gentleman for the truth, she invokes the sanctity of the chivalric oath as a way of trapping her victim: "mectez-le à serment de son amour" (407) [put him on his oath to tell you where his heart does lie (520)]. The vassal, as we said, cannot violate the oath without risking dire consequences.

The lover cannot violate the oath to his lady either without risking dire consequences. Within the code of courtly love functioning in this novella, the vow of secrecy and the promise that seals it serve as a trial of faithfulness and discretion (the etymological link of discretion and secret is operative here). To break the vow or the promise, to break one's word (the verb is always "rompre"), is to commit a "fault" (from Old French *faulte,* from Latin *fallere*), to default on a formal obligation where honor, integrity, and life itself are at stake. When once again the gentleman is obliged to submit to ducal power and authority and to reveal the secret of the name, the Châtelaine de Vergy reproaches him for having brought her dishonor, but she is more distraught

that he has broken his promise to her: "l'honneur, si soingneusement gardé et si malheureusement perdu, la tourmentoit, mais encore plus le soupson qu'elle avoit que son amy luy eust failly de promesse" (412) [Her honor, so carefully guarded, yet now so ignominiously lost, tortured her; but even more tortured was she by the suspicion that her lover had broken his promise (526)]. She deplores an action taken contrary to his oath and his promise ("contre son serment et sa promesse" [413]) and tells him as she sees him in her mind's eye, "vous me faillez de promesse" (413) [you have broken your promise to me (527)]. But while faithfulness to the promise of secrecy might measure the mettle of the man, it is also true that secrecy bound by the promise enhances the value of the love relationship. As the secret accelerates toward disclosure, the narrator states that what the Châtelaine de Vergy appreciates most in their virtuous love is secrecy itself: "la chose que plus elle estimoit en leur honneste amityé estoit qu'elle estoit secrette devant tous les hommes" (410) [the thing that she prized most about this noble love of theirs was that it should remain secret before all men (524)].

Because the narrator does not elaborate, we can only speculate on the value accorded to secrecy, or its attraction. Although the Châtelaine seems unmotivated by worldly concerns, secret love does create a privileged society (even a society of the two lovers)—just as secrecy has functioned traditionally to initiate and maintain community—and it provides a sense of social power and distinction—just as secrecy has operated on a larger scale historically as a source of political power and distinction for those in the know. And in ways that are not entirely unrelated to the enjoyment of power and distinction, a secret—even a shameful one—can also function on a personal level as something proprietary, a private and individual possession that is intimately bound up with one's sense of self. Hidden from the eyes, and the judgment, of others, and undefiled by them, the Châtelaine's secret love belongs only to herself (and to her lover), it depends solely on herself, and is in all ways an extension of herself or of her image of herself as innocent and pure. Thus it is that she experiences the public disclosure of her secret love as a kind of dispossession, as the tragic loss not only of trust and of love, but of virtue, honor, and most importantly, of herself. Secrecy ennobles her love, as she says, but it also enables her to be "herself."

Earlier in the **Heptaméron,** the most platonically inclined storyteller in the group of ten, Dagoucin, had unwittingly exposed the personal dimension of secret love in its striking narcissism. Misconstruing platonic love in the discussion that precedes the **"Ninth Novella,"** he described his own fear that the expression of love necessarily betrays its perfection ("j'ay grand paour que la demonstration face tort à la perfection de mon amour"

[48]) [my love is a perfect love, and I fear lest showing it openly should betray it (113)]. To ensure love's purity, Dagoucin hides his feelings from his beloved, and in a reduction *ad absurdum,* seeks even to hide them from himself ("mesmes je n'ose penser ma pensée") [I scarcely dare think my own thoughts]. Love's intensity heightens in relation to its secrecy: "tant plus je tiens ce feu celé et couvert, et plus en moy croist le plaisir de sçavoir que j'ayme parfaictement" [the longer I conceal the fire of my love, the stronger grows the pleasure in knowing that it is indeed a perfect love]. At the center of a narcissistic circle Dagoucin loves entirely within himself and for himself, the object of his desire is his own love, the source of his pleasure his own conviction of love's perfection. While the Châtelaine appears less self-centered than Dagoucin, our discussion suggests that her "self" is also at the center of her love. It might be that pleasure and self-satisfaction irresistibly accompany her secret as well, and enhance its value and its attraction.

If Dagoucin, and for that matter the Châtelaine de Vergy, had their way, secrecy would stifle and even eliminate narrative. But the desire to keep a secret, and the will to do so, are pressured from *within* by the equally strong and paradoxical inclination to betray secrecy, to share and to tell stories, as we have seen. This is true even of the Châtelaine who only yields the secret of her love—recklessly, as it happens—to the courtier. And secrets are pressured just as intensely from *without* by those who are not yet privy to them, and whether or not they even know that a secret exists. In this regard, secrets are double-edged, because if there is satisfaction in keeping a secret, some sense of domination and gratification that resembles sexual fulfillment, it is also true that penetrating a secret appears equally to be a source of power and of pleasure. In the world of courtly love everyone knows that secrets exist everywhere, and the urge to find and enter or expose them is constantly stimulated by the assumption that there is always some forbidden knowledge masked beneath the denial and dissimulation that characterize the formal or public practice of courtship and of life at the court. Curiosity and suspicion (legitimate or not) are aroused like passion itself, and their deception or satisfaction are felt just as keenly.[11] Like love, or the desire for revenge, these passions motivate the characters of the novellas and the interlocutors themselves. The Duchess's burning desire to learn the gentleman's secret substitutes for and expresses all the fire of her unrequited libidinal energy.

The forbidden knowledge that characterizes secrets in the *Heptaméron* and forms their content represents an initial transgression that is variously political, social, or moral. What risks being a challenge to authority, or that violates its law, what affronts norms of decorum at the risk of one's good name, what constitutes a sin at the expense of one's virtue, all this has to be concealed to preserve reputation and even life itself. What is most often at stake in the novellas, and in the discussions, is honor, woman's honor, imperiled by desire or the imputation of desire, since an alleged trespass carries the same consequences as a real one. It is therefore not only imperative to hide or to dissimulate desire but to mask any sign that might be misread as desire, even signs of the most innocent or purest kind. And yet, as the *Heptaméron* strikingly demonstrates, the signs of desire—real or alleged—are constantly read, the secrets of desire constantly divulged, and narratives of desire endlessly recounted.[12] The dictate to hide, and to hide behind one's speech—both verbal and body language—appears to call forth its converse, to speak of that which one hides.

The Duchess thus speaks of hidden desire precisely because it should remain hidden, the gentleman discloses secret love precisely because it should remain secret. An initial transgression calls for secrecy, but secrecy appears in turn to call for the subsequent transgression of the secret itself. A promise is exacted to honor the secret at the very moment a promise is being betrayed, an oath is sworn at the very site where an oath is being forsworn. I'll tell you a secret if you promise not to tell. This contradiction at the heart of secrecy assures that secrets will always be told and that they will circulate endlessly not in spite of the promise but because of it. It is not coincidental that the Duke, the character who most often promises not to reveal a secret, is precisely the one who most often reveals secrets and betrays his promise, as if betrayal inevitably accompanied the promise and resided not outside as its opposite but paradoxically within as its other and necessary face. The Duke promises not to press the gentleman further when he learns the secret of the "accord" with the Châtelaine de Vergy and he subsequently presses further. He promises in a hyperbolic oath not to reveal the lady's name and he ultimately reveals it: "le duc luy jura tous les sermens qu'il se peut adviser, de jamais à creature du monde n'en reveler riens, ne par parolles, ne par escript, ne par contenance" (408-9) [The Duke then swore by all the oaths he knew that he would never divulge the secret to anyone in the world, either in speech, in writing or in manner (522)]. When accompanying the gentleman to the assignation with the Châtelaine, the Duke insistently reiterates a promise he is destined to break: "le duc juroit incessamment au gentil homme myeulx aymer morir que de reveler son secret" (410) [the Duke swore again and again that he would die sooner than reveal the secret (524)].

One could argue, of course, that in this novella political power or the personal seductiveness of others force characters to break their promises, that promises are in fact challenged from outside and not subverted from within. The gentleman repeatedly invokes his obligation to the Duke and his love for him to justify his disclosures ("l'obligation que j'ay à vous et le grand amour que je vous porte" [408]) and the narrator attributes the Duke's disclosures to his fear of losing his wife and the child he believes she is carrying (411). But the fact that there are always reasons for explaining or justifying the breach of faith, or that one can always find reasons for disclosing a secret, compellingly suggests that it is the vulnerability of the promise of secrecy itself that makes it susceptible to betrayal rather than the degree of pressure applied from outside. The wisdom of common knowledge reminds us that promises are made to be broken. When the Duke insists that he would rather die than breach the confidence of the courtier, he echoes a choice that suitors bearing the heavy burden of secret love face more than once in the **Heptaméron,** "parler ou mourir" (62) [speak or die (129)]. But secrets in Marguerite de Navarre's text are not carried to the grave, either by lovers or by the Duke, nor are oaths ratified by death. "Mourir," we might say, is never a real option because "parler" already inhabits both secrecy and the promise meant to be its seal.

In thematic terms, the Duke's broken promises appear to be the most unfortunate element of the tale because they eventuate in the deaths of the other characters. If only he had kept his word, and the secret, the tragedy would not have occurred. But the narrative would not have occurred either. In terms of narrative structure, his broken promises are thus the most fortunate and the most necessary element because they are the essential links that connect and extend the narrative chain. The Duke, we might say, represents the broken promise of secrecy that is both the content of the novella itself and that constitutes its form: as he shares in and betrays secrets, he advances the narrative and embodies the movement by which it unfolds. Circulating between the gentleman who wants to say nothing (and who therefore inhibits narrative) and the Duchess who wants to know everything (and who thus provides the opening for narrative), the Duke promises absolute secrecy (the obstacle to narrative) and then breaks his word. At each interaction prior secrets are revealed and new secrets are formed, earlier promises broken and new promises made; only by looking backward does the narrative move forward. The Duke functions literally as a leaky vessel, charged with a secret that he transports from one place to another and where it seeps out; what breaches the vessel and causes the leak is the breach of faith that is the broken promise. When he does, finally, keep his word, and kill the Duchess for having broken her own promise to respect the hidden identity of the Châtelaine ("Vous avez prins le secret sur vostre vie, et sur vostre vie tombera la pugnition" [417]) [You swore on your life to keep the secret, and with your life you shall pay for what you have done! (531)], he effectively brings the novella to a close as if, in this context, keeping promises were antithetical to narrative.

Before this promise is kept, however, the chain of secrets unsealed by broken promises results in an astonishing dilation and proliferation of narrative. No longer a secret herself, the Châtelaine de Vergy emerges from the shadows of silence to enter into the narrative and to give utterance to her long and plaintive lament (413-14). Now present, and in her own voice, she performs the narratability of the secret made possible by broken promises. She speaks *of* her secret and she speaks *to* her secret; she speaks about the secret and the gentleman's broken promise, about its meaning and the motives for its betrayal. In turn she reproaches herself for having chosen a lover unworthy of the secret (this was the lesson of the medieval poem), the lover for having violated "son serment et sa promesse" (413) ["his vow and promise" (527)], cruel Fortune for having imposed this undeserved fate. Her thoughts move from the mocking image of the Duchess to the consolation of God's love, from the faithlessness of the lover who has broken confidence to the true and perfect love of God in whom she can have full confidence ("O mon Dieu . . . en vous seul j'ay ma parfaicte confiance" [414]). And because she remains faithful to her vow never to see the gentleman again if their secret is betrayed, she dies from the painful consequence of their separation: "O mon amy, combien que vous me faillez de promesse, si vous tiendray de la myenne" (413) [O my love, you have broken your promise to me, but I shall not break mine (527)]. Honoring the secret and the promise closes off the lament, and in the silence that death imposes, it begins to close the narrative as well.

But closure does not occur before one more convulsive expansion of narrative. The Châtelaine intended to lament her fate alone, and in secret, and to carry her sorrow with her to the silence of the grave. Otherwise she would not have spoken. Her words, however, are overheard and reported to the gentleman by a witness who is unaware of their significance: "Elle (the servant) luy compta du long les parolles qu'elle luy avoit oy dire" (415) [Every word that she had overheard she retold to him (528-29)]. Once again a secret is shared, this time by someone who does not even know she shares in it (secrets, we said earlier, are only secrets to those "insiders" who already know how to hear them). Once again secrecy generates a lengthy narrative ("du long") although the reiteration of the lament that the reader has already heard is only alluded to—for the purposes of effective storytelling—and remains absent from the text. And once again from the recesses of narrative a secret unfolds, the heretofore secret betrayal of the gentleman's confidence by the Duke: "il congneut que le duc avoit revelé son secret à sa femme" (415) [Now he knew that the Duke had revealed his secret to his wife (529)]. This circulation of secrets, and the doubling or dilation of narrative that occurs without actually increasing its length, will take place a second time when the servant recounts to the Duke the gentleman's own lament and his death: "Le duc . . . contraignit la damoiselle de luy dire ce qu'elle en avoit veu et entendu; ce qu'elle feit tout du long, sans en espargner rien" (417) [The Duke . . . ordered the young woman to tell him everything that she had heard and seen, and she told her tale from start to finish, leaving nothing out (531)]. No detail is spared in this full account although those listening to Madame Oisille's tale, and those reading the novella, are spared the actual repetition.

The accelerating disclosure of secrets and the increasing repetition of narrative is thus what characterizes the denouement of the novella. The Châtelaine's lament becomes a narrative, the gentleman's lament becomes one too, and so does the whole occurrence itself, even before it is told as Madame Oisille's final contribution to the seventh day of storytelling. After killing his wife in full view of the Court, the Duke tells the story in its entirety to all those present: "assembla en la salle tous ses serviteurs et leur compta l'honneste et piteuse histoire de sa niece et le meschant tour que luy avoit faict sa femme, qui ne fut, sans faire pleurer les assistans" (417) [the Duke called all his liegemen round him in the hall to recount the piteous and noble story of his niece and the cruel action of his wife. It was a tale that did not fail to call forth the tears of those who listened to it (531)]. The "Châtelaine de Vergy" comes into being as a tale (henceforth the name must be bracketed) at this very moment when the Duke gives narrative coherence and significance to the events that have just transpired. What has occurred is related as an "honneste et piteuse histoire" [piteous and noble story], and because it is intended as such the narrative appropriately touches its audience and elicits their tears, just as Madame Oisille's own narrative will ("je congnois bien à voz oeilz n'avoir esté entendue sans compassion" [418]) [I can tell from your eyes that it hasn't left you unmoved (my translation)]. We understand here at the end of the narrative that what Madame Oisille's tale tells besides "what happened," what it also narrates, is the birth of narrative itself and most significantly its own birth. The end, we might say, is the beginning. Just as death unites the lovers for the first time and forever—in the embrace of his beloved's corpse that accompanies the gentleman's own death and in the tomb where their bodies lie together—so the death that encompasses the protagonists inaugurates their storied life, so the stillness of death opens to the endless voice of narrative. The tragic story of the Châtelaine de Vergy is also inscribed as an epitaph on the tombstone of the lady and her lover ("une épitaphe déclarant la tragédie de leur histoire" [418]) where from beyond the grave it forever breaks the silence of secrecy and of death itself.

The narrative is thus born (paradoxically) in what was already a narrative. What is true of the Châtelaine's lament also holds for the narrative itself: it too is inscribed in (the) "histoire" from the beginning, in a sense it too is always already born. In a *mise en abîme* without origin and without end the narrative tells of secrets and secrets tell of narrative. Each retelling bears witness to the death and life of both the Châtelaine and her narrative. And while each narrative discloses its secrets as it tells its story, the narratability of secrets ensures that the secrets of narrative are never entirely disclosed. In each of these rebirths, the voice of narrative endlessly repeats its complex, enigmatic tale, just as it is repeated endlessly through the many avatars of the story, from its uncertain beginnings even before the anonymous thirteenth-century poem to the novellas of Madame Oisille and of Marguerite de Navarre and beyond to my own retelling.

Notes

1. Michel Foucault, *Histoire de la sexualité. La volonté de savoir* (Paris, 1976), esp. pp. 9-49. [*The History of Sexuality,* trans. Robert Hurley, pp. 3-49].

2. *The Complete Essays of Montaigne,* trans. Donald Frame, p. 644.

3. For a discussion of the narratability of secrets, see Gordon Hutner.

4. For the implications of latent meanings and textual secrecy in the interpretation of narrative, see Frank Kermode.

5. *Heptaméron* 62, where the narrator of the tale inadvertently reveals a scandalous secret about herself in the course of a purported story about another, represents the most straightforward example of the way secrets generate narrative in the *Heptaméron.* François Cornilliat and Ullrich Langer choose to examine the social, sexual, and theological issues raised by this novella precisely because it performs "the obvious mise en abyme of narration" (124). I have chosen the longer and more complex story of the Châtelaine de Vergy precisely because there the relationship between secret and narrative is less obvious and for this reason more representative of the way this textual and interpretive issue is embedded in the very fabric of the *Heptaméron.*

6. For narrative and secrets in the *Heptaméron* see Cornilliat and Langer, and Mary McKinley. In her analysis of gender boundaries in *Heptaméron,* 43, Hope Glidden discusses secrecy and dissimulation in the narrative of female subjectivity and their significance for both fictional character and female author. On the centrality of dissimulation and secrecy see Gisèle Mathieu-Castellani, *La conversation conteuse,* esp. pp. 231-42. On silence and secrecy see Lawrence Kritzman, "Verba erotica" and "Changing places"; see also Colette Winn.

7. All French citations from the *Heptaméron* are taken from the Michel François edition (1960, where "Novella 70" can be found on pp. 400-422; unless otherwise noted, the English translations are from the P. A. Chilton translation of *The Heptameron* (1984), where the novella can be found on pp. 512-36. Quotations will cite the French text and corresponding page numbers, followed by the English translation and page numbers.

8. Kermode shows how the disclosure of narrative secrets always depends on the interpreter being "inside." For studies of various aspects of secrets and secrecy—aspects that are psychological, literary, etymological, semantic, structural—see the special issue of the *Nouvelle Revue de Psychanalyse,* No. 14 (automne, 1976) entitled "Du secret." See also articles devoted to secrets in *Versants.*

9. On the multiple meanings of "nouvelle," see Duval.

10. The text of *La Châtelaine de Vergy* is presented in a bilingual edition (old/modern French) by Jean Dufournet and Liliane Dulac. André Maraud analyzes the secret in the poem from a comparative viewpoint.

11. See Mathieu-Castellani, "l'*Heptaméron*: l'ère du soupçon."

12. For desire in the *Heptaméron* see Mathieu-Castellani, *La conversation conteuse* esp. pp. 41-55.

Works Cited

La Châtelaine de Vergy, eds. Jean Dufournet and Liliane Dulac. Paris, 1994.

Cornilliat, François and Ullrich Langer. "Naked Narrator: *Heptameron,* 62," *Critical Tales. New Studies of the* Heptameron *and Early Modern Culture.* Eds. John D. Lyons and Mary B. McKinley. (Philadelphia, 1993), 123-45.

Duval, Edwin. "Et puis, quelles nouvelles?: The Project of Marguerite's Unfinished Decameron," *Critical Tales. New Studies of the* Heptameron *and Early Modern Culture.* Eds John D. Lyons and Mary B. McKinley. (Philadelphia, 1993), 241-62.

Glidden, Hope. "Gender, Essence, and the Feminine (*Heptaméron,* 43)," *Critical Tales. New Studies of the* Heptameron *and Early Modern Culture.* Eds. John D. Lyons and Mary B. McKinley. (Philadelphia, 1993), 25-40.

Foucault, Michel. *Histoire de la sexualité. I. La volonté de savoir.* Paris, 1976.

———. *The History of Sexuality: An Introduction.* Trans. Robert Hurley. New York, 1978, rpt. 1990.

Hutner, Gordon. *Secrets and Sympathy. Forms of Disclosure in Hawthorne's Novels.* Athens, GA, 1988.

Kermode, Frank. *The Genesis of Secrecy: On the Interpretation of Narrative.* Cambridge, MA, 1979.

Kritzman, Lawrence. "*Verba Erotica*: Marguerite de Navarre and the Rhetoric of Silence," *The Rhetoric of Sexuality and the Literature of the French Renaissance.* (Cambridge, 1991), 45-56.

———. "Changing Places: Marguerite de Navarre and the rhetoric of the gaze (l'*Heptaméron*: 70)". *Les Visages et les Voix de Marguerite de Navarre: Actes du Colloque International sur Marguerite de Navarre.* Ed. Marcel Tetel. (Paris, 1995), 67-78.

Maraud, André. "Le Lai de *Lanval* et *La Chastelaine de Vergi*," *Romania,* t. 93 (1972): 433-59.

Marguerite de Navarre. *Heptaméron.* Ed. Michel François. Paris, 1960.

———. *The Heptameron.* Trans. P. A. Chilton. New York, 1984.

Mathieu-Castellani, Gisèle. *La conversation conteuse. Les Nouvelles de Marguerite de Navarre.* Paris, 1992.

———. "*L'Heptaméron*: l'ère du soupçon," *Les visages et les voix de Marguerite de Navarre: Actes du Colloque International sur Marguerite de Navarrre.* Ed. Marcel Tetel. (Paris, 1995), 123-34.

McKinley, Mary B. "Telling Secrets: Sacramental Confession and Narrative Authority in the *Heptameron,*" *Critical Tales. New Studies of the* Heptameron *and Early Modern Culture.* Eds. John D. Lyons and Mary B. McKinley. (Philadelphia, 1993), 146-71.

Montaigne, Michel de. *The Complete Essays of Montaigne.* Trans. Donald M. Frame. Stanford, CA. 1958.

La Nouvelle Revue de Psychanalyse. No. 14 (automne, 1976).

Versants. Revue Suisse de Littératures Romanes. Nos. II (hiver, 1981) and III (1982).

Winn, Colette. "'La loi du non-parler dans' l'*Heptaméron* de Marguerite de Navarre," *Romance Quarterly* 33, 2 (1986): 157-68.

Marc-André Wiesmann (essay date summer 2000)

SOURCE: Wiesmann, Marc-André. "Rolandine's *lict de reseul*: An Arachnological Reading of a Tale by Marguerite de Navarre." *Sixteenth Century Journal* 31, no. 2 (summer 2000): 433-52.

[*In the following essay, Wiesmann stresses the connection between the myth of Arachne and Minerva and "Novella 21" of the* Heptaméron.]

The **"Twenty-First Tale"** of Marguerite de Navarre's *Heptaméron* recounts the tribulations of Rolandine, a young noblewoman who, although very virtuous, lacks the advantages of beauty and worldly skills. Rolandine's father and the queen she serves have slighted her by not actively pursuing her marriage.[1] At the age of thirty, Rolandine is still a spinster, and her desire for affection leads her into a chaste but fervent commerce with a courtier who shares her marginalization because of his bastardy. With God as their only witness, these two protagonists defy the paternal and royal instances by contracting a marriage which, as Rolandine insists, must remain unconsummated until societally sanctioned. In the middle of the tale, a pivotal episode shows the "bastard de bonne maison" and Rolandine engaging in a forbidden and eroticized conversation from opposite windows of the king's castle. At his window, the "bastard" has opened a ponderous "Livre des Chevaliers de la Table Ronde" that he feigns to read as a pretext for his loitering. At her window, Rolandine works on her own pretext, namely a work of embroidery termed "un lict tout de reseul de soye cramoysie" [an open-work bedcover in crimson silk] (164). This feminine "textum" thus enters in a dialogical commerce with its male textual counterpart, a book of chivalric adventures enacting the heroics of exemplary manhood while developing the fiction of the subservience of the "Chevalier" to his "Dame." The inscription of knightly ideology at this key moment of the novella onomastically energizes the surname "Rolandine," a feminized form of the archetypal French epic hero's name, Roland—protoknight with historical as well as legendary credentials. In a thematic situation that evokes her own heroism and her mutiny against the cruel dictates of the established order, the ornate bedspread or coverlet Rolandine is actively crafting thus serves as a gendered emblem which captivates the reader's attention.

The following pages will examine the narratological, semantic, and topical dimensions of the "lict de reseul" (openwork bedcover) site upon which Rolandine weaves her contestatory self-assertion. Rolandine's textual work singles her out as a figure reminiscent of Ovid's Arachne in the famous weaving contest which pits this mortal woman against Minerva, goddess of war but also of intellectual pursuits and of technically demanding crafts such as spinning, weaving, and embroidering.[2] Nancy Miller, who introduces the term "arachnology" in literary critical parlance, has posited in a seminal article that Arachne represents the woman writer whose textual production, no matter how successful, is remembered only as a hubristic challenge to the Minervan or male-sanctioned symbolic order.[3] In her conflict with Arachne, Minerva's tapestry/writing wins the day because it stages a justification of the rule of Jupiter, a rule Arachne had challenged by exposing in her own weaving the sexual crimes of the male divinities. Arachne's hubristic depiction of pantheonic ex-

cesses, especially the rape of mortal women, makes use of all the cunning intelligence—a dangerous quality the Greeks call "mêtis"—which is the irreducibly feminine hallmark of weaving itself.[4] Rolandine, as this article shall argue, exhibits such a "mêtis" for she plies, like Arachne, a textile/textual activity that opposes the strictures imposed upon her by the dominant order. To bring out fully the arachnological implications of the bedcover or "lict" in the story of Rolandine, it will be necessary to analyze how the preceding tale, **"Novella 20,"** prepares the reader's response to **"Novella 21."** As a conclusion to the arachnological reading of **"[Novella] 20"** and **"21,"** I shall examine how the public persona of Marguerite de Navarre—whose "porte parole" Parlamente narrates **"21"**—is itself entangled in the gendered dimensions of the weaving/writing complex that Rolandine promulgates through her crafting of the "lict de reseul."[5]

The "arachno-logoi" pertinent to the elaboration of Rolandine's story originate in **"Novella 20,"** told by Saffredent, a sophisticated misogynist who seldom misses an occasion to insult the opposite sex. The "propos des devisants," the commentaries of the various storytellers following the tale, rehearse his biased views on women. Furthermore, as we will see, these responses display a metaphor, "et plus ces bons seigneurs drapperont sur la tissure de Simontault" [and the more these fine gentlemen will embroider on Simontault's weavings] (155), which equates storytelling with weaving and subtly alludes to the rivalry between Minerva and Arachne. **"Story 20"** recounts "an honneste amityé" [respectable friendship] (153) between a perfect gentilhomme, the Seigneur de Riant, woeful martyr ("ce pauvre martir") of his unconsummated love, and an attractive widow.[6] One day, de Riant, urgently seeking to contemplate and entreat the object of his affections, hurries to the lady's house. There he fulfills his calling as martyr (from the Greek "martureo," "to testify") when he witnesses what, from Saffredent's point of view, is the true nature of women: the lady is taking her sexual pleasure, "couchée dessus l'herbe" [stretched out on the grass] in the arms of one of her stable-boys who, "laid, ord et infame" [ugly, dirty and despicable] is the exact opposite of the "beau, fort, honneste et aimable" [handsome, strong, gallant and lovable] gentilhomme. This scene of sexual abandonment finds its particular "piquant" in the details the text gives about the "lieu" or place of the lady's telling excesses. Upon its initial mention, this setting takes on a religious signification which ironically amplifies the thematic note introduced by "martir." When the gentleman asks questions about the whereabouts of the widow, "on luy dist qu'elle ne faisoit que venir de vespres et estoit entrée en sa garenne pour parachever son service" [he was told that she had only just come from vespers, and that she had gone into the game park to finish off her devotions] (154). The game park or "garenne" refers to the innermost recess of a vast private garden ("a planted and enclosed space, a park," as Michel François glosses), although it already has, in the sixteenth century, a special connection with rabbits, whose sexual promiscuities are proverbial, and whose French name ("conin") connotes the female genitalia.[7] At first, however, the sexual hint is muted and superseded by an aura of superior piety, as we picture the lady devoting herself to the most personal and culminant part of her religious observances or "service," and displaying an almost protestant insistence upon being alone with the divinity.

The "garenne," an intimate place of apparent religious worship, possesses compelling esthetic dimensions, especially at its center where de Riant suddenly beholds "un pavillon faict d'arbres pliez, lieu tant beau et plaisant qu'il n'estoit possible de plus" [a garden pavilion made of folded trees, in the most delightful spot you ever did see] (154). The hyperbolic praise of this "lieu," underlined by the rhetorical gesture admitting the weakness of rhetoric when faced with its description ("il n'étoit possible . . ."), recalls the several instances in the *Heptaméron* where the "locus amoenus" in which the tales are told undergoes a similar esthetic valorization. In a passage of the general prologue, the "pré si beau et plaisant" [this so beautiful and pleasant meadow] finds the narrator similarly faced with the impossibility to describe the meadow and humbling herself by admitting that only Boccaccio's rhetorical mastery could handle the description: ". . . il avoit besoin d'un Boccace pour le depaindre à la vérité" [it (the meadow) was in need of a Boccaccio to describe it as it really was] (10). The "lieu" of the frame, where the storytellers or "devisants" fictionally generate the entire text of the book, and the "pavillon faict d'arbres pliez" of **"Novella 20,"** have in common the foregrounding of the trees which provide a hiding place from the light of the sun and from the gaze of inquisitive others. In the prologue's expression, "ce beau pré . . . où les arbres sont si foeillez que le soleil ne sçauroit percer l'ombre . . ." [this lovely meadow, where the trees are so leafy that the hot sun cannot penetrate the shade] (10), Tom Conley has discerned how the graphic peculiarity of "foeillez" (leafy) visually rhymes with "oeil" (eye) in the next sentence.[8] This rhyme installs in the collection the thematic of the "couverture," with its dichotomies visibility/invisibility, light/shade, and confession/concealment which punctuate the "recueil" from beginning to end and come into special focus in de Riant's mishap.

In **"Novella 20,"** the trees shaping the "pavillon" are "pliez" (folded), a detail underscoring the artificial facture of the bower, a structure invading the order of nature with the wiles of rhetoric, bending the means of natural language to its own dubious purposes, hiding while revealing. The folding of the trees, a type of rudimentary weaving, functions as a central arachnological

feature of the episode, and the possessive adjective associated with the game park or "garenne" (*"sa* garenne") commemorates the active role of the lady in the cultural assault upon nature. Directly or indirectly, she has been the skillful craftswoman of the "pavillon." Her need to hide the truth of her sexual desires has dictated her engagement (using branches to weave walls) in the shaping of the protective edifice within the edenic, exemplary meadow.[9] The forceful closure of **"Tale 20"** accuses the illicit nature of this female desire by using paternalistic biblical language: "puisqu'elle ne povoit couvrir sa honte, couvrit-elle ses oeilz, pour ne voir celuy qui la voyoit trop clairement, nobostant sa disimullation" [as she could not hide her shame, she covered up her eyes, so as not to see the man who, in spite of her long dissimulation, could now see her all too clearly] (154). The rhyme "foeilles/oeils," underlined by Conley as a "lenticular property" of the prologue, continues to exercise its spell, since the expression "couvrir sa honte" brings to mind the leaves of Genesis, the archetypal topos of "couverture" in the religious problematics of the *Heptaméron.*[10] "Ses oeils" gains prominence as the second term of the zeugma which yokes it to "sa honte," a euphemism for the female sexual parts open to the violent appropriation of the male gaze. Furthermore, "sa dissimullation" is the active synonym of "sa garenne," and refers to the process of crafting the "pavillon," a female enterprise which, like Arachne's weaving, incurs the radical opprobrium of men and finds itself threatened and soon destroyed when read from a male perspective.

The licentiousness of Saffredent's brief tale provokes among the "devisants" a heated debate, serving as the conclusion of the second day and thereby marking a major compositional fold of the *Heptaméron.* In the tale, the lady's sexual sport occurs at Vespers, a liturgical detail which chimes with the storytellers' hurrying to Vespers in the frame narrative. Simontault perversely exploits the tacit link between religion and sexuality by commenting that some women use men as "evangelistes pour prescher leur vertu et leur chasteté" ["evangelists" to preach abroad their virtue and chastity] (155) and hinting that a so-called "religious" devotion to women, such as de Riant's, rests upon the frustrated sexual desire women encourage but do not reward. Stung by this politically flavored use of "evangelistes," Parlamente cuts short the debate with language which has crucial consequences for an arachnological interpretation: "Or, tant plus avant entrons en ce propos, et plus ces bons seigneurs icy *drapperont sur la tissure* de Simontault et tout à nos despens. Parquoy, vault myeulx aller oyr vespres . . ." [The more we pursue this subject, the more these fine gentlemen will embroider on Simontault's weavings at the expense of us ladies. It's therefore better for us to go hear Vespers . . .] (155). The expression I underline uses the literal fabrication of cloth ("tissure") and its ornamentation ("drapper") to convey how the literary "textum" under our eyes is operating. According to Parlamente, Simontault and Saffredent—whom in **"Novella 37"** Oisille will pointedly call "the spider" ("l'araignée")—weave and embroider upon each other's tales in a "one-upmanship" designed to heighten progressively the level of verbal abuse of women.[11] Furthermore, the term "drapper," the spreading of additional sheets ("draps") of mendacious elaboration, evokes an initial "lit" or "bed," the promiscuous "garenne."

At this fold of the text, Parlamente's irritated accusation establishes **"Novella 21"** as a "counter yarn" to Saffredent's efforts. With the workwomanship of her own "tissure" and "draperie," she, like some aggressive Penelope, must now labor to undo the efficient workmanship of the male opponent. It is in these terms that, in the prologue shared by the third day and Rolandine's story, the male offender, the ill-meaning and therefore, from Oisille's perspective, the Arachnean Saffredent ("l'araignée"), solicits Parlamente to inaugurate the proceedings: "Je dois donner ma voix à Parlamente, laquelle, pour son bon sens, sçaura si bien louer les dames, qu'elle fera mectre en obly la verité que je vous ay dicte" [I must call upon Parlamente who, being a woman with plenty of good sense, will be able to praise ladies in such a way as to make everyone forget the truth I have told you] (157). Playing with the ambiguous onomastic resonances of "Parlamente," which can suggest both a respect for the truth (Parler/"mens," "to speak one's mind") and a propensity to lie ("Parler/mentir"), Saffredent maintains his claim upon "verité."[12] He very diplomatically advances that she, too, can play the game of cover-up and create a fustian capable of veiling, and even of eradicating the truth. The expression "mectre en obly" (make forget) is salient in this context for it refers to a "mêtis" subtending a particular "technê," a skill of rhetorical (cf. "louer . . . to praise") obfuscation or erasure whose locus is the threads of the text as they interact with the reader's eyes to form the fictions he or she enjoys. Etymologically, the French "oubli" comes from the Latin "oblivio" and "obliterare," and involves "a metaphor borrowed from the act of erasing something written."[13] This compelling semantic feature contributes to the definition of a narrative dynamic which pits male tale against its female counterpart in a contest refiguring that between Minerva and Arachne. Furthermore, "oubli" echoes "p*liez*" and sets up the first "maille" or stitch of a visual rhyme which, when we add "*lict*" to the paradigm, will have determinant repercussions in the graphic aspects of the texture of **"Novella 21,"** its visual play with the shape of words and with the insistent recurrence of certain syllables, such as "li".

When we read **"21"** as an active erasure, a hostile disentanglement or unraveling of the threads of the preceding novella, we soon realize that the entire first half

of the tale (159-67) depicts the impossibility for Rolandine and the "bastard de bonne maison" she will soon choose for a clandestine husband to establish a stable space or "lieu" (another term sponsoring the syllable "li") for truly fulfilling encounters. Whereas **"Novella 20"** voyeuristically exhibits the "lieu si beau et plaisant" of the general prologue, negatively rewritten, from a male perspective, as the excessive "garenne," the relations between Rolandine and the "bastard" now move along a sequence of "lieus." Each time, these "lieus" are pulled away from them and, under the spell of bastardy, delegitimized. The two lovers start their encounters in "tous lieus" (159), which they exchange for the "chambre" of Rolandine (160-61). After a valet denounces them, they must abandon this bedroom, and the next setting for their trysts is "l'esg*lis*e ou chappelle du chasteau" [the church or chapel of the castle] (161-62), where they secretly marry, with God as the only witness of a union which Rolandine insists must remain unconsummated until her father dies or until she finds "moyen de le y faire consentir" [means to make him consent to it] (162). Unlike the widowed lady of the preceding tale, who weaves the "garenne" as a cover for her sexual sport, the dissimulative strategies of the two lovers use prewoven artifacts, namely the clothes of "Cordelier ou Jacobin" [Franciscans and Dominicans] (161) and, as their hidden sentimental commerce ("honneste amytié") blooms, "l'habit de toutes les re*li*gions qu'ils se peurent penser" [all the monastic habits they could think of] (163). This convocation of "tissure," of the woven construct to their rendezvous, underscores the propensity of humans—ever since Adam and Eve—to hide under crafty textualities. The insistence on the "habit," the "cloth" metonymical of religion, thus installs the conceptual rime "foeille/oeil" into the heart of Rolandine's story and heightens the lenticular properties of the narrative through the significant repetition of the syllable "li."

The relentless consumption of new locations by the protagonists culminates in the elaborate description of the central, most momentous "lieu," which both the textual and the textile heavily invest. This space is the last possible site for the clandestine spouses to meet and, once it is discovered, their irritated superiors effectively prevent them from ever seeing each other again. Whereas the queen has heretofore alone been present as the representative of supreme power, the final locus of illicit interaction is ushered in by a reference to the king. The monarch's travels force the court to inhabit lodgings which do not afford the sentimentally beneficial church settings previously providing a haven for Rolandine and her mate:

> et . . . ils continuaient leur honneste amityé jusques à ce que le Roy s'en alla en une maison de plaisance près de Tours, non tant près que les dames pussent aller

à pied à aultre eg*li*se que à celle du chasteau, qui estoit si mal bastye à propos, qu'il n'y avoit *li*eu à se cacher, où le confesseur eust esté clairement congneu.

(163)

[and . . . they continued their noble love until the king moved to a country seat near Tours. It was not, however, close enough to Tours for the ladies to walk to church there, and they had to use the chapel in the château, which was so inconveniently constructed that there was nowhere to hide without the confessor being clearly in view.]

The influence of the king, bolstered by the phallic "Tours," imposes its male sanction upon those who seek hypocritically to use religious observances to hide other, more carnal purposes. In opposition to the central "lieu" of the preceding tale, heavily marked, in men's eyes, by a transgressive feminine instance, we now have a situation where maleness rules. In other words, Parlamente unweaves **"Novella 20"** and inverts its axiological markers in her own narrative construction.

The upsurge of a gendered terminology finds support in the description of the alternate site for trysting to which love leads Rolandine and the "bastard," a description which impedes the reader's eyes by its laboriousness, its obsessive and somewhat unsatisfactory attempt at clearly establishing the topography of the key episode of the tale:

Car il arriva à la court une dame de laquelle le bastard estoit proche parent. Ceste dame avecq son filz furent logez en la maison du Roy; et estoit la chambre de ce jeune prince advancée toute entiere oultre le corps de la maison où le Roy estoit, tellement que de sa fenestre povoit voir et parler à Rolandine, car les deux fenestres estoient proprement à l'angle des deux corps d'une maison. En ceste chambre, qui estoit sur la salle du Roy, là estoient logées toutes les damoiselles de bonne maison en la compaignie de Rolandine.

(163-64)

[For there arrived at the court a lady to whom the bastard was closely related. This lady and her son were accommodated in the part of the building occupied by the king; and the room of this son, a young prince, was thrust forward in its entirety from the body of the building where the king was, so much so that from his window he could see and talk to Rolandine, because the two windows were exactly at the angle of the bodies of a house. In this chamber, which was above the king's hall, were lodged all the young noblewomen, including Rolandine.]

In this context ruled by the king's aura, the "bastard," for the first time in the novella, acquires something of a face recognizable in patriarchal terms, a possible malehood in his otherwise castrated existence. His blood connections with the highest nobility of the kingdom are converted into spatial privileges, namely his ability to circulate freely into the private apartment of the "je-

une prince." These genealogical hints (one wonders if the "bastard" is not, in effect, the son of the "dame") obliquely hearken to the very scene of "illegitimate" procreation.[14] The architectural setting captures this sexual undertone through its uncanny corporeal activity: the catachrestic "corps de la maison où le Roy estoit" [body of the house where the king was] achieves a phallic extension ("chambre advancée toute entiere oultre le corps" [room thrust out in its entirety from the body]) and projects it towards another architectural body or "corps" whose inhabitants are females. The repetition of the term "corps," the de-doubling of the king's "maison" into two distinctly gendered bodies engaged in close intercourse, is especially telling in view of the persuasive speech of courtship the "bastard" has recently proffered to Rolandine. As a prologue to their clandestine wedding, he expressed his fear that another man could claim her, a man who "vouldra estre maistre et regardera plus à vos biens que à votre personne" [will want to be master and will gaze more upon your worldly possessions than upon your person], and who "traictera autrement votre corps qu'il ne le merite" [will treat your body otherwise than it deserves] (161-62). The description of the topographical situation of the two "fenestres" thus reflects the repressed scenario of mastery the "bastard" had heretofore carefully condemned. Furthermore, the topographical setting insists on the visual dimensions of possession: "povoit voir" [was able to see] replaces the "regardera" [will gaze upon] of the courtship ploy, and announces that Rolandine is in great peril from a usurping, domineering, violating male gaze. This elaboration of the scopic dimensions of the encounter encourages the reader to be aware of the lenticular "mailles" of the text.

In his book on the *Heptaméron,* Marcel Tetel makes perceptive observations about the phenomenology of windows in the collection. One of his remarks can be adduced to refine the analysis of the central scene of **"Novella 21"**: "In essence then, Marguerite proposes that the window actually impairs the real view; she considers it just another screen, a subterfuge, the very antithesis of truth."[15] In **"21,"** what is at stake in the active space delimited by the two windows is the very fact of textuality, its production, its uses, and its abuses seen from the irreconcilable perspectives of male and female. Poised at their strategic location for an interactive, eroticized visual and/or spoken transaction, each sex deploys a stratagem one could aptly name a dissimulative "pre-text" which actually annuls the possibility of an honest exchange or view. At his window, the "bastard," phallically enabled by the male protrusions of the architecture, "feyt semblant de prendre fort grand plaisir de *li*re ung *Li*vre des Cheva*li*ers de la Table Ronde" [feigned he was greatly delighted in reading a book about the Knights of the Round Table] (164), a tome whose narratives exemplify both the chivalric declarations he has recently made during courtship and the particularly difficult obstacles which exist between him and his object of desire.[16] But the stratagem is unmasked by the "dame" whose son occupies the chamber, and she initially levels against the antiquated literary monument to courtly love this terse accusation: "Je m'esbahy comme les jeunes gens perdent le temps à li*re* tant de fol*lyes*" [It amazes me that young people waste their time reading so many crazy things] (164). In the early sixteenth century this moral qualm reveals, in pious circles, a pervasive indictment of overly imaginative and erotic "romans de Chevalerie" which detract the young from more spiritually nourishing sorts of reading.[17] The reinscription of "lire" in "follyes" heightens the semantic and visual importance of the syllable "li," and stresses that "lire" amounts to a central issue in the unfolding relations between Rolandine and the "bastard": "le varlet de chambre . . . trouva que le *li*vre où il *li*soit estoit la fenestre où Rolandine venoit parler à *luy*" [the valet de chambre . . . found out that the book in which he (the bastard) was reading was the window at which Rolandine came to speak to him] (165). The text thus projects the pretextual "lecture" of the Roman of the Knights of the Round Table onto the man's actual gaze, his visual desire embracing Rolandine's window.

This other window, feminine pole of the (non-)interaction, functions as a counterpart to the "garenne" and its pavilion of "arbres p*ly*ez" we found so negatively branded by males in **"Novella 20."** Similar to the cunning architectural weaving of the widow, Rolandine's stratagem for forbidden contact with her lover is a patterned display of textual material she is actively producing for that crucial topographical occasion: "Elle se mist à faire ung *li*ct tout de reseul de soye cramoisie, et l'atachoit à la fenestre où elle vouloit demorer seulle" [She set about making an openwork bedcover in crimson silk, and this she would hang up in the window where she wanted to be left alone] (164). Whereas the "livre des Chevaliers de la Table Ronde" is only horizontally accessible to the gaze occupying the opposite window, the weaving of Rolandine disseminates its truth for all to see: it frontally occupies the field of vision of all concerned, including the readers of the tale and, of course, the "bastard," who reads "la fenestre où Rolandine estoit" as a book. Her engagement with textiles allows her to escape through a type of communication with the outside and to express—within the possibilities of the hiding/revealing dichotomy associated with all cloths and texts—the truth of her condition. Archetypally, she is, of course, Arachne, but also Philomela, who embroiders the awful truth on a coverlet, and the Lady in Marie de France's lai "Laostic," who wraps the dead nightingale, token of her crushed love, "En une piece de samit / A or brusdè et tout escrit" [In a heavy silk fabric, with gold embroidery and writing].[18]

Importantly, Rolandine's exertions on the "lict de reseul" strengthen her association with the works of thread or "ouvrage" which characterizes her at the very beginning of the tale, where Parlamente indicates that, sorely vexed by the impediments of the queen and the father thwarting her chances to marry, Rolandine "du tout . . . se retira à Dieu, laissant les mondanitez et les gorgiasetez de la court; son passetemps fut à prier Dieu ou à faire quelques ouvraiges" [turned herself entirely to God, abandoning the elegant and worldly play of the court; she passed the time by praying to God and by embarking on some pieces of needlework] (158-59). "Ouvrage," and especially the adjective "ouvragé" it elicits, conjures up, at a primary level in its semantic field, "the work of the needle."[19] Rolandine's retirement into God, a kind of protective custody she seeks as solace, is paired with the "ouverture" implicit in "ouvraige," the sole outlet or freedom left to women in her predicament. Her needlework remains the only opening for her, the only space onto which to exercise her desires and aspirations. The term "gorgiasetez," pointing to the worldly pleasures Rolandine is forced to reject, contributes richly to the arachnological tenor of this statement, for it has a vestmental dimension, the "gorgias," "from the fifteenth to the seventeenth century, a part of women's clothing covering the neck and the breasts and so transparent at first that its name was given to any provocative outfit."[20] The "gorgeous" or even "gorgianic" material of this garment participates in the slippery characteristics of dangerous textualities which play an essential role in human "couverture."[21] Rolandine's spurning of "gorgiasetez" therefore valorizes her own "ouvraige," a cloth whose function is to reveal stubbornly both her licit social and sexual needs and her chastity, prudence, obedience, and devotion to God.

From this perspective, the "lict tout de reseul," which Michel François glosses as "réseau, lingerie à jour," exemplifies the only open space available to Rolandine for the feminine fulfillment she is seeking in a court where she is a virtual prisoner of the caprices and ill will of those superior to her. Her virtual incarceration determines her solitude: "reseul" rhymes with "seule" (cf. "où elle voulait demeurer seule"), a juxtaposition proleptically announcing that the "bastard" will betray her at the end of the tale, at which point he will convert her solitude into unrequited love: "en son coeur seul estoit l'amour entier" [in her heart alone was all the love that once had dwelt in two] (173). The semantic facture of "reseul" contributes to the sense of imprisonment invested in the characterization of Rolandine, since "reseul" can also mean "rets" or "filet," nets designed to entrap animals.[22] However, "reseul" also denotes a special type of fabric quite similar to the "gorgias" just mentioned, cloth which hides to reveal and seduce better.[23] Rolandine's "ouvraige" thus achieves an ambiguity that both manifests her entrapment and conveys a sense of the urgency of her own quest for the consummation of her marriage, of her longing for the erotic experience inscribed in "lict de reseul" and heightened by the exotic nature of the "soye" [silk] and of its carnate hue, "cramoysie." The "lict" corresponds, on one level, to the "garenne" or "pavillon faict d'arbres pliez" of the previous tale. On the other hand, it can also be perceived as a defensive apotropaïc ploy designed to counter the chivalric theses of the "Livre des Chevaliers de la Table Ronde," the pretext the "bastard" uses to advance his own schemes against Rolandine's virginity. In this perspective, the active openness of her "ouvraige" questions the chivalric code's seductive but fictionalized reversal of gender roles, whereby the dominated ladies become the domineering masters of the knights. In Ovid, Arachne's weaving similarly uncovers the duplicities of Minerva's tapestry, a text which tries to authorize politically the abuses that male gods perpetrate against mortal women.

The key term "lict" arrests the flow of reading, forcing the reader to puzzle over the expression "un lict de reseul," a visual counter prominently displayed at Rolandine's window. One can construe "lict" as either "couvre-lit" (bed) or "ciel de lit" (canopy) in order logically to overcome the obstacle, but it is the fact of obstacle which endows "lict" with its peculiar power. We have noted that the verb "lire" (to read) and its complement "livre" (book) saturate the context. We thus seem to stumble, in our readings and re-readings, upon our own activity, and we are compelled to read ourselves reading. The orthograph the text predilects, "l-i-c-t," reminds us that "lit," the center piece of a bedroom, comes from the Latin "lectus," which is also the passive past participle of "legere" (to read). In addition, the French "lire" is close to "lier"—etymologically and historically, "lire" encapsulates both "lego" (to select, to choose) and "ligo" (to unite). As a modern definition has it, "lire," before anything else, is "to be familiar with the letters of the alphabet and to know how to assemble them," a qualification which underlines the importance of linkage, of grouping and unifying disparate pieces in order to make them accede to signification.[24] These observations establish that the episode at the window privileges, in the reader's consciousness, the meaningful juxtaposition between "*lict*," "*lier*," and "*lire*" in order that we consider the act of reading/ writing according to its phenomenological aspects and that we infuse in this semantic network the dimension of desire and sexual union implicit in "lict" and, earlier, in "es*lire* pour mary" [elect as a husband] (161). As we go on reading, the insistence on the connection between "lire" and "lier" becomes more and more evident and the narrative itself, as we are about to see, brings out this conjunction.

The temporary union that the clandestine couple achieves at their respective windows is interrupted by the "dame," whose apartments the "bastard" occupies, and who, upon discovering the illicit trysts, threatens Rolandine with informing the queen. The important confrontation between Rolandine and her royal mistress is nevertheless deferred by a long narrative sequence depicting the many unsuccessful attempts the "bastard" makes to keep communicating with his wife (164-66). In order to prolong their exchanges, he sends to Rolandine letters by "subtils moyens" [subtle means] (165), thereby trying to weave ("subtil" = "sub" + "tela," "underneath" + "web") his own messages underneath the webs of censure which are proliferating in the court.[25] But, under the pressure of their enemies, these "lettres" or "lectres" meet repeated destruction, once by fire and finally when a faithful servant of the "bastard," hounded by spies, tears up a "lectre" and attempts to hide the pieces behind a door.[26] This to no avail, since the fragments are recovered:

> trouva l'on ce que l'on cerchoit: c'estoient les pieces de la lectre. On envoya querir le confesseur du Roy, lequel, après les avoir assemblées sur une table, leut la lectre tout du long, où la vérité du marriage tant dissimulé se trouva clairement; car le bastard ne l'appeloit que sa *femme*.

(166)

> [they found what they were looking for: it was the fragments of the letter. They sent for the king's confessor, who, after having assembled the pieces on a table, read the letter in its entirety. The truth about the marriage, so long kept secret, stood revealed, for throughout the letter, the bastard had addressed her only as his *wife*.]

Femme (in French, both "wife" and "woman") is in italic characters in the text in order graphically to mime the reassembly of the pieces of the "l-e-c-t-r-e," a rememberment that shows how reading is, to use Lucien Dällenbach's expression, "une activité isiaque," a collection and a re-collection, a putting back together of the disparate fragments of a former unity, rent by violence.[27] The narrative thus endorses the affiliation the text has crafted between "lict," "lier," and "lire," and suggests that the linkage or bridging the last two terms presuppose is, in the human world, predicated upon an original tear in the fabric, a severance that always threatens to reassert itself. The graphic slant of "femme" shows that, in the syntax of the dominant discourse, the union or "lyen" which Rolandine had contracted with the "bastard" is ungrammatical. This remarking of "femme" is all the more poignant since it makes Rolandine finally readable to the eyes of the institutions that have victimized her. She gains this readability not through the only means available to her for self-assertion (i.e. the crafting of the "lict de reseul" emblematic of an impossible union or "election" on her own terms), but through the bastard's letter, a type of writing sharing a male signature with the "Livre des Chevaliers de la Table Ronde."

The parable of the tearing up and reconstitution of the "lectre" makes us aware that we process the word "femme" as the product of a male code, deciphered first by a very distinctive male reader operating inside the narrative. Indeed, the salient introduction of the "confesseur du Roy" reinforces the sway of the male monarch in the text and, from Rolandine's perspective, denounces the collusion between the political and the religious, an alliance which tarnishes the presumably impartial nature of the churchman's responsibilities.[28] The etymological and graphic logic which the favoring of the syllable "li" develops draws the word "religion" itself into its orbit, along with "lire," "lict," "lieu," "eglise," and all other terms catching the reader's eye through this common linguistic trait. Etymologically, "religio" comes from the verb "ligare" (to bind, to tie to). In its Christian and Augustinian acceptance, religion is thus the bond or "lien" between us and the divinity, a concept of which Rolandine shows a keen awareness.[29] In her lengthy defense (167-69), she imputes to her father and to the queen a telling disrespect for the sanctity of the religious bond, and she uses the term "religion" and "religieuse" to express her own unswerving understanding of the religious responsibilities that bind her to God.

The distorted views of her guardians, she implies, forced her to accept the love of the "bastard" and, therefore, to subvert the official "religion" in order to dissemble and make her life more livable, to pluralize and disfigure the religious into "l'habit de toutes les religions" (163), the different types of clothes religious orders chose as cover. In arachnological terms, we could say that the initial engine of Rolandine's plight is, on the queen's part, a cruel refusal to recognize what the proper linkage or "*ly*ens," what the right re*lig*ion, should be for her protégée. Indeed, before Rolandine is finally rehabilitated into the structures of the male hierarchies, Parlamente once more belabors the point of the proper reading religion presupposes, the rule of the vertical "liens" or "bonds" with God: ". . . car si amour et bonne volonté fondée sur la craincte de Dieu sont les vrays et seurs lyens de mariage, elle [Rolandine] estoit si bien lyée, que fer, ne feu, ne eaue, ne pouvoient rompre son lien . . ." [for if love and honest intent founded on the fear of God were the true and sure bonds of marriage, then she was so firmly bound that nothing, neither fire, nor steel nor water, could loose her bonds] (171). Along with the queen's "desdain" and the confessor's warped sense of "religion," "la négligence du père" counts as the most momentous cause of Rolandine's plight. "Negligence" (158, 170) comes from the Latin "nec" + "lego," "not" + "to read," thereby implicating the father in the novella's thematic insistence upon reading, and extending the cluster of words marked by "li."

In the vicinity of the second appearance of "negligence" (170), one finds, in notable contrast, the "diligence" (171) of the "bastard" who tries once more to convince the king that he has indeed lawfully married Rolandine. The opposition "negligence/diligence" spotlights the father's fault and the temporary virtue of the clandestine husband. However, in Parlamente's own assessment of the tale in the "propos des devisants" (174-75), this "diligence" of the "bastard" weighs nothing against his "malice" (175), the evil disposition he betrays by pursuing other women and spurning Rolandine's fierce respect for the "lyens de marriage." On the other hand, Parlamente describes Rolandine's predilection for the "bastard" as one of women's "courtes follies," and thus embroils her in the difficulties of the "mauvaise lecture" ("faux/lire") we have seen as initially tainting the motives of the "bastard" towards the wife who has denied him the satisfaction of sexual consummation.[30]

In the concluding discussion of the tale by the storytellers, the "lict de reseul" as arachnological statement, along with the "negligence du père," are therefore "oubliés" or erased by Parlamente in favor of an alternative and radicalizing schema pitting against each other two modes of reading and their dangerous interpretive consequences: "follies" or "false, mistaken reading" vs. "malice," "evil or Satan-inspired reading." "Follies" rewrites the earlier criticism of chivalric novels ("les jeunes gens perdent le temps à lire tant de follies!" 164), and, in Parlamente's gloss, the male ideology of "fin' amor" seems a redeemable and lesser sin. The blackness of the deeds of the "bastard," on the other hand, takes over as the "telos" of evil.[31] His ultimate "malice" and "desloyauté" as a "mary" (Parlamente's words, 174) justify the condemnation we should all level against him. Conveniently, his illegitimacy—ironically the direct result of the liberties that males take with religiously sanctioned "liens" of marriage—alone remains a threat to the established male order. This scapegoating of the "bastard" makes us forget the abusive readings and willful victimization of Rolandine by the queen, father, king, and confessor. Although Parlamente defends Rolandine and recognizes the holiness and courage of her marriage, her interpretation of the events concurs with the female rebel's reabsorption into the status quo. As John Lyons has observed, Rolandine's recuperation by the established order coincides with her loss of voice after her final encounter with the queen (170).[32] This silencing of Rolandine's dissenting voice, corresponding to Arachne's demise in Ovid's story, leaves only, as witnesses of her failed "mêtis," the visually and semantically active "mailles" of the "lict" which, as we have demonstrated, mark the text of the novella as loci of resistance. These marks now function proleptically by questioning the resolution of the story, namely the total disempowerment of Rolandine and the restoration of the dominant discourse.

Taking a certain distance from the "micro-lecture" of the texts of **"20"** and **"21,"** we can now better assess the relevance of the arachnological procedures we have applied to these two novellas. Of special significance is the complex narratological role played by Parlamente, the narrator of **"Novella 21."** Parlamente, of course, entertains a close relationship with the authorial instance of the whole collection, Marguerite de Navarre. In the interpretation she gives of the tale she has just recounted, Parlamente carefully glosses over the ideological implications of Rolandine's oppositional stance, thereby validating the preeminence of Marguerite, who is the sister of the king and who has an important stake in the maintenance of the power structure. The narrative itinerary of **"Novella 21"** thus negates its initial move as an Arachnean "counter-yarn" to the male slander of **"Novella 20"** and establishes a position which, while not embracing this slander, nevertheless shuns direct antagonism to it and blunts the eristic lines by paying certain dues to a male-dominated world. As in Ovid, Minerva wins the day, and this triumph can be ascribed to both the ideological propensities of the narrator Parlamente and to those of her "double," the queen of Navarre. Strikingly, we can find, in the panegyric discourse which surrounded this queen in the sixteenth century, confirmation of the Minervan characteristics which redound to her through an arachnological reading of **"20"** and **"21."** A discussion of a few aspects of the contemporary application of the Minervan topos to Marguerite by her admirers and courtiers illuminates the manner in which her peers envisaged the phenomenon of the woman writer and how writing, especially when women are involved, is closely bound to the traditionally female avocation to textiles.

References to the queen of Navarre as a French Minerva have often been noted, and it is perhaps Clément Marot who did the most to impose the comparison.[33] Marot, in a pre-1542 translation of a colloquy of Erasmus condemned by the archconservative Sorbonne in 1527, associates Marguerite with a type of feminist activism he ascribes to Minerva.[34] This short dialogue, which stages as interlocutors an "ignorant friar" and the "erudita" Ysabeau, staunchly defends the literary pursuits of women, especially their mastery of Greek and Latin. To the friar's remark that "la quenoille et le fuseau / Sont armes des femmes" [the distaff and the spindle / are women's weapons] (vv. 155-56), Ysabeau counters that the books she cherishes develop in her the "prudence" to "gouverner sa maison à poinct" [punctiliously to govern her house] (vv. 158-60), where the expression "à poinct" is in fact a pun on the "poinct" of needlecraft, a play on words indicating the compatibility existing between the work of thread and women's intellectual ambitions.[35] Ysabeau later celebrates Marguerite as a bright exemplar of the learned woman: "En France tenons pour Minerve / La seur du roy, que Dieu conserve" [In France we equate Minerva / With the king's sister, whom God preserve] (vv. 335-36), a canonization that designates the queen, wise weaver, as a spokesperson for women while maintaining the manly privileges which her blood relations to the king, the male God's representative on earth, insure.

Banking perhaps on the notoriety of Marot's censored translation, the official eulogy delivered at Marguerite's funeral stresses her involvement with, on the one hand, distaff, spindle, and needle, and, on the other, reading and writing. The "Oraison funebre de la Royne de Navarre" of Charles de Sainte-Marthe notes the queen's frequent replacement of spinning and embroidering with literary occupations: "tenait souvent un livre au lieu de quenouille, une plume au lieu de fuseau, et la touche de ses tablettes au lieu d'aiguilles" [she often held a book instead of a distaff, a quill instead of a spindle, and she handled her writing pad instead of her sewing needles].[36] The "panégyriste" then dwells upon the relationship existing between Marguerite's exertions on fabrics and her literary endeavors:

> Et si elle s'appliquoit ou aux tappis ou à d'aultres ouvrages de l'eguille (qui lui estoit une tres delectable occupation) elle avoit près d'elle quelcun qui luy lisoit ou un historiographe ou un poëte, ou un aultre notable et utile auteur, ou elle luy dictoit quelque méditation qu'il mettoit par escrit. Je diray davantage un acte d'elle qui pourra possible emerveiller . . . c'est que bien souvent elle entendoit à son ouvrage et de deux costés, autour d'elle, deux de ses secretaires ou aultres, estoient soubs elle occupés, l'un à recevoir des vers françois qu'elle composeoit promptement, mais avec une erudition et gravité admirable, l'aultre à escrire des lettres qu'elle envoioit à quelcun.[37]

> [While she was exerting herself either upon a tapestry or upon other tasks of needlework—a very pleasurable occupation for her—she had someone nearby who read to her a historian or a poet, or some other famous and useful writer; otherwise she dictated to that person some meditation that he took down in writing. I will even recount one of her actions which is liable to amaze . . . it is that quite often she was tending to her needlework while, around her, two of her secretaries were busy with her orders, the one taking down French verses she was composing rapidly, albeit with a remarkable erudition and seriousness, the other penning a letter she was sending to someone.]

In this encomium, Sainte-Marthe's "émerveillement" concerns Marguerite's capacities to attend to two activities at once: the crafting or ornamentation of a literal text (e.g. "tappis") and the reception or creation of a literary text. He finds himself amazed at how she combines seamlessly the feminine "delectable occupation" with pursuits that, in a sixteenth-century context, rather belong to men: an interest in listening to serious poetry, history, or other didactic subjects, and the expenditure of intellectual work in the production of philosophical and literary constructs ("meditation," "vers françois," "lettres"). Furthermore, Sainte-Marthe's focus on the queen's affinity for textiles projects the work of thread onto the reading and writing she so forcefully cultivates, and creates a significant overlap between the literal textuality of "ouvrage" and the composition of erudite verses and letters.

These contemporary assessments of the queen's activities valorize the close attention we have paid to the nexus of references to the literally textual in novellas **"20"** and **"21"**. They establish the close identification with the fabrication of "textum" that Marguerite de Navarre felt as she was crafting the **Heptaméron** and her awareness that she was transferring the textual enterprise from its literal acceptance to its metaphorical counterpart. In turn, they privilege the mention of Rolandine's "lict de reseul" as a self-reflexive moment of particular interest. This "lict" becomes a "mise en abyme" of the activity of women writers in the sixteenth century, and also of our own efforts ("lire" / "lict") at reading and interpreting their literary products. By staging a confrontation between the "lict de reseul" and the "Livre des Chevaliers de la Table Ronde," **"Novella 21"** self-consciously inscribes itself into the diachronic aspects of literary history, hinting at the constant rewritings which motivate this history along ideological and gendered lines. Macroscopically, Marguerite de Navarre is putting to the question the effects that the reading of "roman courtois" has upon readers' hermeneutic grasp of her own work. Furthermore, several critics have noted that the scenario at the windows of the king's castle in Tours mirrors and distorts the famous episode of Dante's *Inferno* (5.82-142) in which Paolo and Francesca describe how they were seduced into adultery through a reading of *Lancelot du Lac,* an exemplary "gros livre de la Table Ronde."[38] Dante brands this book a "Galeotto," a "go-between," "pander," or "pimp" which lands the two lovers into hell. Significantly for Marguerite, who acknowledges the *Decameron* as a primordial literary model, Boccaccio chooses "Galeotto" as the subtitle of his monumental collections of stories. The "lict de reseul" therefore participates in this vertiginous display of intertextual self-consciousness, and posits itself as a member of this sequence of distinguished texts. Avatar of the established paradigm, it both benefits from its literary ancestry and also reacts against it and articulates new possibilities whereby traditionally excluded subject-positions can generate loci for dialogic exchange and self-assertion. Although the arachnological reading we have undertaken demonstrates how the Minervan voice still controls its suppressed partner in the dialogue, the deployment of Rolandine's "lict" undermines the tale's resolution, and provides a "discreet encouragement" for women seeking an untrammeled or Arachnean voice in sixteenth-century France.[39]

Notes

1. Marguerite de Navarre, *L'Heptaméron,* ed. Michel François (Paris: Garnier, 1966). The Michel François edition of the *Heptaméron* preserves graphic and orthographic details central to my arguments. For the English translations of the citations, I used Marguerite de Navarre, *The Heptaméron,* trans. P. A. Chilton (London: Penguin Books, 1984). Occasionally, I lightly modify Chilton's very adequate English renderings. All other translations from the French are mine.

2. Ovid, *Metamorphoses* (Leipzig: Teubner, 1977), 6.1-145. For expert readings of this episode, increasingly considered as fundamental for an understanding of Ovid's poetic "programme," see E. W. Leach, "Ekphrasis and the Theme of Artistic Failure in Ovid's *Metamorphoses,*" *Ramus* 3 (1974): 102-42; Byron Harries, "The Spinner and the Poet: Arachne in Ovid's *Metamorphoses,*" *Proceedings of the Cambridge Philological Society* 39 (1990): 64-82.

3. Nancy K. Miller, "Arachnologies: The Woman, the Text, and the Critic," in *The Poetics of Gender,* ed. Nancy K. Miller (New York: Columbia University Press, 1986), 270-95; see also François Rigolot, *Louise Labé Lyonnaise ou la Renaissance au féminin* (Paris: Champion, 1997), esp. chap. 3, "Faire taire Pallas et parler Arachné," 117-51. Rigolot cites Miller's notion of "arachnology," underlines, in the Renaissance, the prevalence of the equation "weaving=writing," and skillfully discusses how Louise Labé identifies herself with Arachne in order to promulgate militantly the endeavors of women writers.

4. The Greek myth of Minerva's birth recounts in fact how Zeus attempts to eradicate the fundamental threat "mêtis" presents for a patriarchy by swallowing a divinized Mêtis and mimicking women's bodily privileges in order to give birth himself to Minerva, the male domestication of singular forms of female powers. The myth is told by Hesiod, *Theogony* (vv. 886-900); see Hésiode, *Théogonie: Les Travaux et les Jours: Le bouclier* (Paris: Les Belles Lettres, 1951). For a very pertinent treatment of "mêtis" and weaving in Greek thought, see Ann Bergren, "The (re)marriage of Penelope and Odysseus: Architecture, Gender, Philosophy: A Homeric Dialogue," in *The Ages of Homer: A Tribute to Emily Townsend Vermeule,* ed. Jane B. Carter and Sarah P. Morris (Austin: University of Texas Press, 1995), 205-20.

5. For very perceptive treatments of the gendered dimensions of the tale of Rolandine, see Carla Freccero, "Rewriting the Rhetoric of Desire in the

Heptaméron," in *Contending Kingdoms: Historical, Psychological, and Feminist Approaches to the Literature of Sixteenth-Century England and France,* ed. Marie-Rose Logan and Peter L. Rudnytsky (Detroit: Wayne State University Press, 1991), 298-312. Frecero's approach, however, is purely "macroscopic" and generalizing, and does not explore the semantic complexities of the novella. See also Carla Freccero, "Rape's Disfiguring Figures: Marguerite de Navarre's *Heptaméron,* Day 1: 10," in *Rape and Representation,* ed. Lynn A. Higgins and Brenda R. Silver (New York: Columbia University Press, 1991), 227-47. In this article, Freccero endorses Nancy Miller's notion of "arachnologies" and elaborates upon it.

6. The "Deuxième Journée" of the *Heptaméron* can profitably be read under the sign of Laughter, as heralded by its first story (Mlle. de Roncex falls into the latrine). It is therefore significant that the protagonist of the last story is called "de Riant."

7. For "garenne," see Randle Cotgrave, *A Dictionarie of the French and English Tongues: Reproduced from the First Edition, London 1611* (Columbia, S.C.: University of South Carolina Press, 1950). Cotgrave glosses "garenne" as "a warren of connies." For the sexual connotations, see Edmond Huguet, *Dictionnaire de la langue française du seizième siècle* (Paris: Champion and Didier, 1925-67).

8. Tom Conley, "The Graphics of Dissimulation: Between *Heptaméron* 10 and 'l'histoire tragique,'" in *Critical Tales: New Studies of the* Heptaméron *and Early Modern Culture,* ed. John Lyons and Mary McKinley (Philadelphia: University of Philadelphia Press, 1993), 63-81.

9. Bergren, "The (re)marriage of Penelope," 210-11, points out that "the beginning of building coincides with the beginning of textiles" and that, immemorially, walls are weavings.

10. As Hircan's expressions make clear in the "propos" following "Novella 26": "enfans d'Adam et d'Eve . . . couvrir notre nudité de feulles . . ." [children of Adam and Eve . . . cover our nakedness with leaves] (221).

11. Oisille, whose persona is generally accepted to reflect the character of Marguerite's mother Louise de Savoie, is the most "evangelistic" of all the storytellers. It is important to note that Oisille narrates the seventieth story, a rewriting of the popular medieval tale *La Chastelaine de Vergi.* In this tale, we find once more the "locus amoenus" harboring the love of the protagonists. Tellingly, Oisille emphasizes the lady's connection with her bower by calling her "la dame du Vergier," where

"vergier" means "orchard" or "bower." See Nancy Virtue, "*Le Sainct Esperit . . . parlast par sa bouche*: Marguerite de Navarre's Evangelical Revision of the *Chastelaine de Vergi,*" *Sixteenth Century Journal* 28 (1997): 811-24.

12. See Freccero, "Rewriting the Rhetoric of Desire," 302.

13. See A. Ernout and E. Meillet, *Dictionnaire étymologigue de la langue latine: Histoire des Mots* (Paris: Klincksieck, 1985), 455: "*Oblivio* is a metaphor borrowed from the act of erasing something written. It is a word belonging to the family of *oblinere,* 'to erase,' 'to cross out.'" I checked all etymologies in this dictionary.

14. Later, Rolandine reminds the queen that the father of the "bastard" is of a rank even higher than Jossebelin's: "car vous savez que son pere passeroit devant le myen" [for you know that his father would stand before mine] (168).

15. Marcel Tetel, *Marguerite de Navarre's* Heptaméron: *Themes, Language, and Structure* (Durham: Duke University Press, 1973), 92-94. The phenomenology of windows has, of course, a very long cultural and literary history we cannot evoke here. See, for example, H. Scolnicov, *Women's Theatrical Space* (Cambridge: Cambridge University Press, 1994), esp. "The Woman in the Window," 49-68. See also Conley, "The Graphics of Dissimulation," 77: "Windows provide a frame for confined opening, a momentarily closed perspective, an area in which the other appears as an absence . . . the *fenestre* is also an inscription of appearance invested into the scenography and the verbal matter. The staging draws attention to the art of concealment."

16. He called himself his lady's "mary, amy et serviteur" [husband, friend and servant] for the rest of his life (161).

17. See Nicole Cazauran, "Les Romans de Chevalerie en France: Entre 'exemple' et 'récréation,'" in *Le Roman de Chevalerie au temps de la renaissance,* ed. M. T. Jones-Davies (Paris: Jean Touzot, 1987), 29-48.

18. The story of Philomela is also in Ovid, *Metamorphoses,* 6.424-674. For a treatment of weaving as the revelatory instrument of raped women, see Patricia Klindienst-Joplin, "The Voice of the Shuttle Is Ours," in *Rape and Representation,* 35-64. For "Laostic," see Marie de France, *Lais* (Oxford: Basil Blackwell, 1969), 97-101.

19. See Cotgrave, *A Dictionarie*: "Ouvrager: To worke needle-worke, to sow."

20. *Grand Larousse Encyclopédique* (Paris: Librairie Larousse, 1962).

21. Ernest Klein, *Comprehensive Etymological Dictionary of the English Language* (Amsterdam: Elsevier, 1966), gives this etymology for the English "gorgeous," a term related to the French "gorgiaseté": "From Old French 'gorgias,' 'finely dressed, luxurious,' formed from the name of Gorgias, a Greek sophist and rhetorician (about 483-375), who took pleasure in showing off his luxury." Gorgias is the archetypal sophist and protagonist of Plato's dialogue *Gorgias,* which exposes how rhetoric radically relativizes Truth. In the world of the *Heptaméron,* such duplicity or "gorgianic" sophistry is not at all reserved to women since, as exemplified in the "Fourth Novella," the "gentilhomme" rapist banks much on his "chemise gorgiase" (29) to operate its seduction upon the unwilling lady (anecdotally, Marguerite de Navarre herself). As Michel François notes (453), the anecdote linking Marguerite with the "Fourth Novella" is in Brantôme's *Vies des Hommes illustres et grands Capitaines français* and *Les Dames galantes.* The Amiral de Bonnivet is the presumed aggressor.

22. See Frédéric Godefroy's entry for "reseuil" in his *Dictionnaire de l'ancienne langue française et de tous les dialectes du IXè au XVè siècle* (Paris: F. Vieweg, 1880-1902). As examples of netted animals, rabbits ("connins," "lievre," with a mention of the related "garenne") are prominently featured in Godefroy's illustrative citations. The essential property of such nets is their close approximation of invisibility, their abilities to deceive the eyes. Godefroy's entry goes on to list the acceptances of "reseuil" which indicate woven material imitating the deceptive (lack of) appearance of such hunting meshes: "Tissu en forme de rets, réseau" [material in the form of nets, network].

23. See Michel de Montaigne, *Les Essais* (Paris: Presses Universitaires de France, 1988), 880, for this use of "reseul": "Les vers de ces deux poetes [i.e. Virgil and Lucretius], traitant aussi reservéement et discrettement de la lascivité comme ils font, me semblent la descouvrir et esclairer de plus pres. Les dames couvrent leur sein d'un reseu, les prestres plusieurs choses sacrées; les peintres ombragent leur ouvrage, pour lui donner plus de lustre; et dict-on que le coup du Soleil est plus poisant par reflexion qu'à droit fil" [The verses of these two poets, in their handling of lascivious matters in such a discreet and reserved manner, seem to me thereby to unveil and to illuminate them much more blatantly. Ladies cover their breasts with a "reseuil," and, with a similar cloth, priests veil their sacred objects; painters shadow their work to give it more lustre and it is said that the power of the Sun is stronger by reflection than directly]. The conjunction of "reseuil" with Art (verse and painting), Eros, and religion in this citation is also present in Rolandine's tale. Huguet's dictionary gives a citation from D'Urfé's *L'Astrée* accentuating the erotic aspects of the term: "Elle . . . n'avoit rien sur le sein qu'un mouchoir de reseul" [She wore nothing on her bosom but a "reseuil" handkerchief].

24. For the recent definition, see the *Grand Larousse Encyclopédique.* Ernout and Meillet trace in detail the semantic development of "legere" from its initial sense "to pick," "to select," to, much later, "to read."

25. This etymology of "subtil" is emphasized by François Rigolot in "Les 'sutils' ouvrages de Louise Labé, ou: quand Pallas devient Arachné," *Etudes Littéraires* 20 (1987): 43-60. The textual tenor of "subtils moyens" is reinforced by the expression "il n'estoit sepmaine qu'elle n'eust deux fois de ses nouvelles" [not a week passed without her twice getting news from him] (165), where "nouvelles" obliquely hearkens to the type of text we are processing, namely "nouvelles."

26. An uncanny remark engraves the tearing up of the letter in the reader's mind: the faithful servant simulates urinating against a wall in order to destroy the letter without being seen. This detail gives a phallic twist to the episode. The orthographic variant "lectre" is significant: it uses the "c-t" combination we find in "l-i-c-t" to remind us of the past participle "lectus."

27. Lucien Dallenbach, "Reading as Suture: Problems of Reception of the Fragmentary Text: Balzac and Claude Simon," *Style* 18 (1984): 195-206. "Activité isiaque," referring to Isis's collecting the fragments of the body of a dismembered Osiris, appears on 204.

28. The question of confession and its gendered implications in the *Heptaméron* recently has been addressed remarkably by Mary B. McKinley, "Telling Secrets: Sacramental Confession and the Narrative Authority in the *Heptaméron*," in *Critical Tales,* 146-72.

29. For the history of the term "religio," see Italo Ronca, "What's in Two Names: Old and New Thoughts on the History and Etymology of *religio* and *superstitio*," *Res Publica Literarum* 15 (1992): 43-60. Following Lactantius, Augustine prefers the etymology "ligare" to Cicero's "legere." He also plays, as does Marguerite de Navarre, with the etymology of "legere" by connecting the verb with "diligent" and "negligent" (*De Civitate Dei,* 10.3).

30. "Mais l'amour de la plupart des hommes de bien est tant fondée sur le plaisir, que les femmes, ignorant leurs mauvaises volontez, se y mectent au-

cunes fois bien avant; et quand Dieu leur faict congnoistre la malice du coeur de celluy qu'elles estimoient bon, s'en peuvent departir avecq leur honneur et bonne reputation, car les plus courtes follies sont toujours les meilleures" [But the love of most respectable men is based on pleasure, so much so that women, not being aware of men's evil intentions, sometimes allow themselves to be drawn too far. But when God makes them understand the wickedness (malice) in the heart of the man whom they previously thought good, they can still break it off with their honour and reputation intact, for the shortest follies are always the best!] [my emphasis] (175).

31. The black/white dichotomy is announced in the text by the term "lustre," a light made more striking by the bastard's evil deeds: "mais ce qui donne autant de lustre à sa [i.e Rolandine's] fermeté, c'est la desloyauté de son mary" [but what gives so much luster to her determination is the disloyalty of her husband] (174).

32. John Lyons, "The *Heptaméron* and the Foundation of Critical Narrative," *Yale French Studies* 70 (1986): 150-63.

33. See C. A. Mayer, "Clément Marot et Marguerite d'Angoulême," *Revue d'Histoire Littéraire de la France* 86 (1986): 819-30. Mayer, 821, cites Marot's *L'Enfer* (1526) in a passage where the poet calls Marguerite Pallas.

34. Clément Marot, *Trois Colloques d'Erasme traduictz de Latin en François par Clement Marot, Colloque Intitulé Abbatis & Eruditae*, in *Oeuvres Poétiques Complètes*, vol. 2, ed. Gérard Defaux (Paris: Bordas, 1993), 517-29.

35. The term "poinct," of course, puns on the fact that "faire des points" describes the fundamental nature of stitching, knitting, and weaving. The wordplay of this colloquy is very similar to the type of semantic work we find occurring in Rolandine's tale. See especially verses 86-95, which concatenate the terms "delecter . . . alecter," "delivres," "livres," "livré," "religieux," "livres," to provoke a reflection upon the etymology of "legere," "to read."

36. From the citation of Sainte-Marthe's "Oraison Funebre" by Le Roux de Lincy in his preface to *L'Heptaméron des Nouvelles, Tome premier* (Paris: Société des Bibliophiles françois, 1853), 43.

37. Le Roux de Lincy, preface to *L'Heptaméron des Nouvelles*, 44. For "entendre à" in "elle entendoit à son ouvrage," Cotgrave gives "to heed, to mind, to attend to."

38. Dante Alighieri, *Inferno*, trans. John D. Sinclair (Oxford: Oxford University Press, 1961). For Mar-

guerite's allusion to Dante, see Tetel, *Marguerite de Navarre's* Heptaméron, 75, and Freccero, "Rewriting the Rhetoric of Desire," 307.

39. "Encouragement discret" is Colette Winn's expression in her brief assessment of "Novella 21." See Colette Winn, *L'esthétique du jeu dans l'*Heptaméron *de Marguerite de Navarre* (Paris: Vrin, 1993), 130-31.

Mary J. Baker (essay date winter 2001)

SOURCE: Baker, Mary J. "Friendship Revisited: *Heptaméron* Tales 10, 21, 15, and 70." *Romance Quarterly* 48, no. 1 (winter 2001): 3-14.

[*In the following essay, Baker considers the importance placed on conversation and platonic friendship in the* Heptaméron.]

In his thoughtful book on friendship, Ullrich Langer devotes most of one chapter to a study of tale **"Number 10"** of Marguerite de Navarre's **Heptaméron** and several paragraphs to her tale **"Number 21,"** arguing in both cases that de Navarre contributes "female figures of friendship to the line of male exemplars, although her heroines' male choices are not up to the demands of the relationship" (Langer 117). The failure of the relationship between Floride and Amadour in **"Number 10"** is attributed to Amadour's "choice of an economy of desire incompatible with true friendship." Amadour is viewed as a dissimulator whose desire is unavowed, and Floride as honest and nondissimulating. Rolandine, the main character in **"Number 21,"** is perceived as providing "a model for a description of a voluntary, rational, and virtuous relationship aristocratic women were mostly prevented from considering" (Langer 125). Langer argues that Rolandine justifies her choice of a male friend (*le Bâtard*) in one critical speech in a way that "tightly reproduces the rhetoric of classical friendship" (126). The fact that the *Bâtard* is not up to the demands of the relationship is apparent when he pursues other women once "it is clear that he cannot have his marriage to Rolandine recognized" (Langer 126).

Langer gives an excellent overview of earlier writings on friendship, including those of Aristotle, Cicero, and Seneca. He describes "true friendship" in the classical sense as existing when both parties are virtuous and have complete confidence in the "other" and when there is absence of hope for gain. Importantly, he points out the multivalence of *ami, amant, amour,* and *amitié* in the French vernacular, words that "often seem interchangeable, signifying relationships whose degree is determined by the context of their use" (118). This multivalence contributes to the difficulty of generalizing about the **Heptaméron.**

The sample of stories examined in the book is small, and in the case of **"Number 21,"** the discussion is brief. I would like to suggest respects in which the two stories can be considered ambiguous in their portrayal of the women as exemplary female figures of friendship, and then broaden the study of friendship to include two more stories—numbers **"15"** and **"70."** The additional stories will provide supporting evidence for my contention that to understand the failure of friendship we must also look carefully at other factors, including the difference between male and female satisfaction with, and commitment to, conversational companionship, and the divergence between men and women in their inclination or disinclination to assign or accept responsibility for a "failure event."

The term *failure event* is used by Peter Schönbach in his article on responses to reproach. I rely on his taxonomy in this essay. He describes four categories of response: concessions, excuses, justifications, and refusals, referring to these as a "taxonomy of accounts for failure events." In his taxonomy, Schönbach is careful to note gray areas where categories overlap. For instance, an appeal to a specific external circumstance might contain both justificatory and exculpatory elements. Perusing the ***Heptaméron*** as a whole, readers will discover both women and men making excuses for their behavior in response to a reproach. The men refuse (or ignore) a reproach and/or justify their behavior more often than the women, however. The women concede defeat more often than the men and commonly weep when reproached. As will be seen, Amadour's response conforms to the more typical male patterns of justification and refusal as defined by Schönbach.

In tale **"Number 10,"** Amadour, a handsome and brave Spanish nobleman, falls in love with Floride, the twelve-year-old daughter of the comtesse d'Arande.[1] He has no hope of marrying her, as she outranks him socially. Since he wants to continue to see her, he marries Avanturade, a woman in whose company Floride has grown up, and who can provide access to Floride. Years pass, and Amadour's frustration at separations from Floride, and at the loss of opportunities to establish himself first as Floride's *serviteur* and then as her *ami* (*ami* here in the sense of sexual lover), lead him to attempt on one occasion to seduce her and on another to take her by force. Not long after the second attempt, he commits suicide on the battlefield rather than allow himself to be captured by the enemy. Floride, whose husband has also died, enters a convent.

The reasons for the failure of a "true friendship" between Amadour and Floride are complex. Amadour's desire, though significant, is not always unavowed, and Floride is herself not without desire and dissimulation. When in the discussion following **"Number 10"** the *devisant* Saffredent suggests that there is comparable sexual desire in men and women ("[O]ù amour seul est juge de noz contenances, nous sçavons très bien qu'elles sont femmes et nous homes."), he is confirming information given in the story itself about Floride's desire. The relationship between Floride and Amadour fails partly because chance and timing interfere with the synchronization of Floride's desire with that of Amadour, and partly because of temperamental differences between Floride and Amadour. Floride values conversational companionship; Amadour is basically indifferent to it and is ultimately discontented with conversation alone. Further complicating their relationship is Amadour's unwillingness to take personal responsibility for his error in attempting to take Floride by force. The mystified Floride never seems to quite understand the reasons for the change in her relationship with Amadour.

At the beginning of their relationship, Floride's interest in Amadour is not sexual; she is lonely. Early in the narrative Avanturade explains to Amadour that because of Spanish custom, few people speak to Floride (58). Amadour then proceeds to relieve Floride's loneliness by conversing with her. In the first phase of their conversational relationship, Amadour is essentially uninterested in the content of their exchange. He is nevertheless happy to have a means to be in her company. His role is similar to one that might be played by a close female friend:[2]

> [E]lle estoit si privée de luy, qu'elle ne luy dissimuloit chose qu'elle pensast; et eut cest heur qu'elle luy declaira toute l'amour qu'elle portoit au filz de l'Infant Fortuné. Et luy, qui ne tashoit que à la gaingner entierement, luy en parloit incessamment; car il ne luy chailloit quel propos il luy tint, mais qu'il eut moyen de l'entretenir longuement.
>
> (60)

Floride, a simple, unsophisticated woman, is differentiated from another female character, Poline, a woman of the world who "fine, experimentée en amour, ne se contenta de parolles" (62).

The story depicts Floride losing some of her simplicity over time and growing to love Amadour. After a conversation with him in which he offers her his *honnête amitié* (here *amitié*, coupled with *honnête*, has a nonsexual sense), Floride "commencea en son cueur à sentir quelque chose plus qu'elle n'avoit accoustumé" (65). Later, jealous of Poline, on whom Amadour has been bestowing attention, her affective state is described in this way: "Et commencea l'amour, poulcée de son contraire, à monstrer sa très grande force, tellement que elle, congnoissant son tort, escripvoit incessamment à Amadour, la priant de vouloir retourner" (66). The words *congnoissant son tort* are noteworthy, as they imply that Floride—not an exemplary female figure of friendship here—is aware that she is inappropriately encouraging Amadour's affections. When Amadour is taken prisoner, Floride, "qui sçavoit bien dissimuller, luy dist que c'estoit grande perte pour toute leur maison, et que surtout elle avoit pitié de sa pauvre femme [. . . et] laissa aller quelques larmes [. . .] afin que, par trop faindre, sa faincte ne fust descouverte" (68). Subsequently, when Avanturade gives Floride the news that Amadour's return is imminent, Floride "s'en resjouyt comme pour l'amour d'elle" and flees into a dark stairway so that the change in her color will not be observed (70). When she finally speaks to Amadour, she "se delibera de prendre sa consolation en l'amour et seurté qu'elle portoit à Amadour, ce que toutesfois elle ne luy osoit déclairer" (71). Amadour, however, suspects that she loves him: "[il] s'en doubtoit bien" (71). But before he can act, he is called away. At this point, Floride is described as "presque toute gaingnée de le recepvoir non à serviteur, mais à seur et parfaict amy" (71).

The evolution from *serviteur* to *ami* is described by Saffredent in the discussion: "[Q]uant nous sommes à part, où amour seul est juge de noz contenances, nous sçavons très bien qu'elles sont femmes et nous hommes; et à l'heure, le nom de *maistresse* est convertie en *amye,* et le nom de *serviteur* en *amy*" (84). The use of *ami* in this last declaration is aptly characterized by Langer as meaning "sexual lover" and as a word that constitutes the sexual counterpoint to *serviteur* (119). It is not inconsistent to read a similar sexual connotation into those words when they are used in the story itself to describe Floride's sentiments. Notably, Floride's apparent new readiness to accept Amadour as a lover, as well as her own previously unavowed desire and her capacity to dissimulate, suggest that she is not an exemplary female figure of friendship.

The conversation following Amadour's failed first seduction attempt underscores an impediment to friendship in addition to desire: Amadour's inability to take responsibility for his behavior, a characteristic that is exposed in his response to reproach. A puzzled Floride reproaches him with questions: "Amadour, quelle follye est montée en vostre entendement? et qu'est-ce qu'avez pensé et voulu faire?" (73). By virtue of formulating her criticism as questions, she allows Amadour some latitude of response.

In turn, Amadour counters with a rhetorical question that implicates cruelty on Floride's part, and simultaneously refuses the imputation of guilt and justifies his conduct. His reply is formulated in such a way as to imply a general rule of behavior that validates his conduct. He asks: "Ung si long service mérite-il recompense de telle cruauté?" (73). Floride then reproaches him with a third politely formulated, open-ended question, thereby again giving Amadour an opportunity to

tailor a response to suit his own purpose. She alludes to past conversations, and raises an ethical issue: "Et où est l'honneur [. . .] que tant de foys vous m'avez presché?" (73). In two more rhetorical questions, categorical in their claims, Amadour again refuses to admit any guilt and justifies his behavior by minimizing its potential damage and asserting his right to satisfy himself. In his first question he shifts the focus of the discussion from the abstract category of honor (*l'honneur*) to the practical category of Floride's honor (*votre honneur*) and his right to her. Now that you are married, he argues, and "vostre honneur peult estre couvert, quel tort vous tiens-je de demander ce qui est mien?" (73). Then, several sentences later, in a demonstration of the "economy of desire" pointed out by Langer, Amadour fabricates another rule that underscores his unequivocal interest in pursuing his own pleasure: "Et, si la passion d'amour est la plus importable de tous les autres, et celle qui plus aveugle tous les sens, quel peché vouldriez-vous attribuer à celluy qui se laisse conduire par une invincible puissance?" (73).

Floride's continued bafflement is conveyed in three more polite but reproachful questions. Again, her questions open up the discussion rather than close it off. They include additional references to past conversations. Floride returns to the abstract notion of *honneur* and introduces new, ethically charged vocabulary. The nature of her questions suggests that in past conversations with Amadour she sought some kind of moral guidance:

> Hélas! Amadour, sont-ce icy les *vertueux* propos que devant ma jeunesse m'avez tenuz? Est-ce cy *l'honneur* et la *conscience* que vous m'avez maintes foys conseillé plutost mourir que de perdre mon ame? Avez-vous oblyé les *bons exemples* que vous m'avez donnéz des *vertueuses dames* qui ont resisté à la folle amour, et le despris que vous avez tousjours faict des folles?
>
> (74, my emphasis)

Amadour's response to these last reproaches supports the utilitarian, self-justifying arguments formulated in their prior formal question-reproach exchange. He moves from the general to the particular, from the broad notion of *vertueuses dames* to his special case. He asserts that he had always wanted to love a *femme de bien,* and so therefore conducted a test to see if she was indeed such a woman. This justification for his behavior is accompanied by what at first sounds like a concession: Amadour begs Floride to "pardonner ceste follye et audatieuse entreprise." The true concessionary intent of the remark is doubtful, however, as Amadour proceeds to articulate still another justification, one that affirms his right to self-fulfillment: "la fin en tourne à vostre honneur et à mon grand contentement" (75). Significantly, it is Amadour's *avowed* desire that is inimical to true friendship here, since at this point it is unwelcome. But his self-justifying stance and refusal to accept personal responsibility after being rightfully reproached for his behavior are inimical to true friendship as well.

Although it is largely true that Rolandine in tale **"Number 21"** enters into a "voluntary, rational and virtuous relationship" with the *Bâtard* (Langer 125), this unhappy woman is not a clear exemplar of friendship. Rolandine, an unmarried "fille de grande maison" approaching her thirtieth birthday, secretly marries a bastard "d'une grande et bonne maison," but vows not to consummate the marriage unless her father is dead or has been persuaded to accept the union. The unconsummated relationship, or *amitié* as it is referred to, is entered into voluntarily, and is also virtuous, from a sexual point of view. There is no compelling evidence, however, that she is drawn to any specific virtuous qualities the bastard may possess. If she did think he was virtuous, she was mistaken.[3] The beginning of their friendship is described in this way: "Et, se complaignans l'un à l'autre de leurs infortunes, prindrent une très grande amitié; et, se trouvans tous deux compaignons de malheur, se cerchoient en tous lieux pour se consoler l'un l'autre" (159). Rolandine fails in part as a model for "true friendship" because she seeks the *Bâtard* primarily out of misery and the need for consolation.

The rationality of Rolandine's decision to marry the *Bâtard* is also questionable because at the time the risks of clandestine marriage would have been well known. The marriage is indeed ultimately discovered and vigorously objected to by both her father and the queen. The father imprisons Rolandine in a château, and the *Bâtard* flees to Germany, eventually dying in pursuit of another woman. Rolandine's father finally relents and frees his daughter, who then marries a gentleman who is her social equal.

The *Bâtard* does, however, provide Rolandine with valued conversational companionship. The story is replete with references to the frequency and importance of her conversations with the *Bâtard*. Indeed, the frequency so irks the queen that she explicitly forbids Rolandine from talking to the *Bâtard* in public. Rolandine finds other opportunities to talk to him, however—the two of them "desroboient le temps, comme faict ung larron une chose pretieuse" (161).[4]

The importance of conversational companionship for a woman and its relevance to friendship between husband and wife are dramatically illustrated in tale **"Number 15."** Here, one reason for the absence of friendship is the husband's failure to meet his wife's need for conversational companionship. The husband, a gentleman of no means who has married a wealthy younger woman, is described as neglectful: "[il] tenoit si peu de compte de sa femme, que à peyne en ung an couchoit-il une nuict avecq elle. *Et ce qui plus luy estoit importable,* c'est que jamais il ne parloit à elle, ni luy faisoit signe d'amityé" (116, my emphasis).

Like Floride, the wife is lonely. A *grand seigneur* takes pity on her ("il se voulut essayer à la consoler," 117), and she takes pleasure in talking to him, although she is mindful of preserving her honor. The narrator writes that "ceste amityé dura quelque temps" (118). Although it should be noted that the wife derives satisfaction from seeing herself "aymée et estimée," her friendship with the *grand seigneur* is nonsexual and leaves her counterpart wishing for more than he gets: "[il] desira beaucoup d'estre en sa bonne grâce, que de luy parler de son mary, sinon pour luy monstrer le peu d'occasion qu'elle avoit de l'aymer" (117-18). As in the case of Amadour, the male is more interested in the pursuit of pleasure than in the pursuit of conversation.

After the *grand seigneur* accedes to pressure brought by the king to cease communicating with her, the wife replaces him with a *jeune gentilhomme* who also has taken pity on her. The new relationship is again conversational. The wife is eager to "finement conduire" the second friendship, but her husband nevertheless discovers them together. When she realizes that he has noticed her "avecq cellui auquel devant luy elle n'avoit jamais parlé" (119), she jumps over a table and flees. That night her husband first reproaches her with silence, a treatment that evokes tears. Both her flight and her tears are concessions and constitute an implicit acknowledgment of guilt.

After her tears, the wife expresses to her husband her fear of his anger. His reaction is ambiguous. He claims that he saw nothing wrong with her talking to a man ("jamais il ne luy avoit defendu de parler à homme, et qu'il n'avoit trouvé mauvais qu'elle y parlast," 120), but that he objected to her guilty flight after she saw him observing her with the *jeune gentilhomme*. Yet, her conversational relationship obviously troubles him as he threatens her with death if she speaks to the gentleman again ("il la tueroit sans pitié ne compassion," 120). The fact that the husband feels threatened by the conversational relationship suggests suspicion of its erotic potential.

When the husband discovers his wife meeting the gentleman again on the evening of that same day, he threatens her: "c'est la main qui vous tiendra promesse; parquoy, ne faillez à venir, quand je vous manderay" (121). When she responds to his summons, she begins by justifying her behavior: no damage occurred. She maintains that her relationship with the gentleman was in fact an *amour honnête* and primarily conversational (with a few harmless embraces thrown in). Her next argument is longer and more significant: It is an extended excuse. Her husband is no better than she is because he has not set a proper moral example: "Et vous, monsieur, qui estes seul la cause de mon malheur, vouldriezvous prendre vengeance d'un oeuvre, dont, si, long temps a, vous m'avez donné exemple, sinon que la vostre estoit sans honneur et conscience?" (123). It is worth noting that the wife frames her reproach as a question, thus maintaining a semblance of deference and courtesy. She then elaborates, with rhetorical flourish, numerous differences between her and her husband, none of which are to his credit, with the exception of the contrast between his wisdom and experience and her youth and ignorance—an opposition undoubtedly relevant to his obligation to set a good example.[5] Her closing salvo is framed as another question, one that blunts the virulence of the reproach.[6]

The husband concedes defeat in one area when he agrees that "l'honneur d'un homme et d'une femme n'estoient pas semblables" (124), but this concession has no practical effect, as the interdiction against speaking to the gentleman stays in place. And when he makes the "concession," he does not relate it to the particular situation in which he and his wife find themselves.

In this story, there is ultimately no friendship of any sort either inside or outside marriage. By the end of the story the fickle wife has replaced the young gentleman with someone else. Denied conversational companionship with her husband, and longing for love, she is transformed from virtuous wife into trollop.[7] Her husband's inability to accept ultimate responsibility for his wife's initial need to turn to other men for conversational companionship also contributes to the failure of the relationship.

A successful conversational friendship does exist in tale **"Number 70."** A significant difference between this tale and its source, the medieval poem *La Chastelaine de Vergi,* is the emphasis in the later narrative on the nonphysical nature of the relationship between the gentleman and the *dame.*[8] When the gentleman describes to the duke how he regularly met his lady, he says that as soon as he heard her little dog bark, "il s'en alloit *parler* à elle toute la nuyct" (409, my emphasis). This flourishing conversational friendship ends when the gentleman reveals the identity of the dame de Vergi to the duke, who has been pressured by his wife, herself smitten by the gentleman, to secure that information. After the duke reveals the secret to his wife, the duchess publicly leads the dame de Vergi to infer that she knows about the late night visits because she is herself the object of the gentleman's affections.

Although the gentleman does appear to have an interest in enjoying a conversational relationship with the dame de Vergi, that interest is not strong enough to give such a friendship precedence over his loyalty to the duke. The bond of allegiance to a more powerful male overrides the bond of friendship with a female companion. In his subordinate role as *serviteur,* he obeys the command of his *maître,* and reveals the identity of the woman who expected him to keep their alliance secret.

The dame de Vergi and the gentleman do not reproach each other, but they do reproach themselves. The way in which they reproach themselves points to a fundamental incompatibility between them similar (though not identical) to that revealed in the reproach conversations in tales **"Number 10"** and **"[Number] 15."** When the gentleman and the dame de Vergi express personal anguish and self-reproach in a monologue, they do not lament the same occurrence. The gentleman's monologue begins after he discovers the moribund dame de Vergi, and her monologue begins when she believes that she has a rival and has lost her honor (that is, her reputation). The dame de Vergi initially refuses any imputation of sin or guilt, but finally concedes responsibility for what she assumes to have been a loss of honor; and the gentleman initially concedes responsibility for the death of the dame de Vergi, but diminishes the force of the concession with various evasive excuses. In fact, close inspection reveals his excuses to be tantamount to a refusal of responsibility for the outcome.

The dame de Vergi speaks first. Her monologue opens with a series of questions betraying bewilderment and distress at the turn of events. She then underscores the fact of her "longue et vertueuse amityé" (nonsexual friendship) and mourns the loss of her friend, her honor, and her happiness. Her first impulse is to refuse personal responsibility; she asserts that "mon peché ne ma couple ne m'ont pas osté mon honneur; ma faulte et mon demerite ne m'ont poinct fait perdre mon contentement" (413-14). Responsibility is attributed to "l'Infortune cruelle, qui rendant ingrat le plus obligé de tous les hommes, me faict recevoir le contraire de ce que j'ay desservy" (414). A subtle shift occurs toward the close of the monologue, however, when she reproaches herself and effectively admits her personal responsibility. She confesses to having forgotten the Creator "par trop avoir adoré la creature." Her vice was to "trop aimer." She repents of having failed to obey God's first commandment and asks for God's mercy: "excusez la faulte que trop d'amour m'a faict faire" (414).

The gentleman begins his monologue with a self-reproach that is a concession: "O moy, traistre, meschant et malheureux amy, pourquoy est-ce que la pugnition de ma trahison n'est tumbée sur moy et non sur elle, qui est innocente?" (415). He explicitly targets himself as the responsible party: "Je n'accuse que moy seul de la plus grande meschanceté qui oncques fut commise entre amys" (415). But subsequently, he makes excuses that distance him from direct culpability. He reproaches God—"O mon Dieu! Pourquoi me creastes-vos homme, aiant l'amour si legiere et le cueur tant ignorant?" (416)—and excuses himself by appealing to his own shortcomings and insufficient knowledge, saying "ignorance m'a vaincu" and "par ignoramment aymer, je vous ay offensé" (416). Although his avowals of ignorance are mingled with admissions of responsibility and regret, the final picture is blurred, and the gentleman's attitude toward the extent of his own personal responsibility is ambivalent. The excuses blunt the concessions and appear as evasions allowing him to disavow at least some responsibility. Clearly, the gentleman *tempers* his concessions.

The fact that the gentleman's allegiance to his *maître* ultimately takes precedence over the value he places on conversational friendship differentiates him from the dame de Vergi, whose commitment to friendship does not waver, that is, not until she learns of the gentleman's betrayal. At this point, persuaded of the imperfection of human love, she turns to God. The gentleman does not make a comparable move, a fact that underscores the magnitude of the difference separating the two characters from each other. The monologue of the dame de Vergi conveys faith in a loving, merciful God:

> Helas! ma pauvre ame, qui, par trop avoir adoré la creature, avez oblié le Createur, il fault retourner entre les mains de Celluy duquel l'amour vaine vous avoit ravie. Prenez confiance, mon ame, de le trouver meilleur pere que vous n'avez trouvé amy celluy pour lequel l'avez souvent oblyé. O mon Dieu, mon createur, qui estes le vray et parfaict amour, par la grace duquel l'amour que j'ay portée à mon amy n'a esté tachée de nul vice, sinon de trop aymer, je suplye vostre misericorde de recepvoir l'ame et l'esperit de celle qui se repent avoir failly à vostre premier et très juste commandement; et, par le merite de Celluy duquel l'amour est incomprehensible, excusez la faulte que trop d'amour m'a faict faire; car en vous seul j'ay ma parfaicte confiance.
>
> (414)

In contrast, in his monologue, the gentleman reproaches God in two short questions. His questions convey the image of a powerful God against whom a mutinous son rebels: "O mon Dieu! pourquoy me creastes-vous homme, aiant l'amour si legiere et cueur tant ignorant? Pourquoy ne me creastes-vous le petit chien qui a fidellement servy sa maistresse?" (416).[9] Mixed in with the gentleman's reproach of God and his self-reproach is his expression of unhappiness with himself as a non-heroic male. This preoccupation demonstrates a concern that is basically peripheral to the issue of friendship. The gentleman would welcome a spectacular death: "O mon cueur, trop crainctif de mort et de banissement, deschiré soys-tu des aigles perpetuellement comme celluy d'Ixion!" (415). He claims that he should have allowed himself to be thrown into the river, which the duke had earlier threatened to do; under those circumstances he would at least have been "glorieusement mort" (415). Finally, he contends that if someone else had dared to

kill the dame de Vergi, he would have taken his sword and avenged her. In contrast, the dame de Vergi reaches a conclusion that has no connection to heroic ideals, but is relational in nature, and clearly pertinent to the issue of friendship—she should have loved God more than any human creature.

Friendship between the sexes in the *Heptaméron* stories fails for a variety of reasons. Neither female protagonist in tales "**10**" and "**21**" is an exemplary female figure of friendship. In tale "**Number 10**," in addition to the male "economy of desire," factors including the timing of events and the woman's early overriding need for conversational companionship explain the failure of friendship. A woman's loneliness, and therefore her vulnerability, may be so acute, or her judgment of a man's character so flawed, that true friendship in the classical sense cannot develop ("**Number 21**"). Potential friendship is also negatively affected by a woman's need for ethical and moral guidance from the man (numbers "**10**" and "**15**"), a need that men do not always meet, and also by a man's failure to value friendship with a woman above allegiance to a man ("**Number 70**").

Another explanation of the failure of friendship is the temperamental chasm existing between men and women that is revealed by the way they reproach each other, or themselves, and respond to reproaches. When issuing a reproach, men resort more often than women to threats, commands, or categorical assertions, and women to indirection or attenuation.[10] In responding to a reproach, men more often tend to justify their behavior and/or to refuse responsibility, and women more often tend to concede. In "**Number 70**" an additional difference between the sexes is the divergent attitude toward the Deity. This may reflect in part the larger phenomenon of the sexes' different style of moral reasoning, a difference that can contribute to misunderstandings and rifts: The gentleman reasons in hierarchical terms, and the dame de Vergi in relational terms.[11]

In the *Heptaméron,* enduring friendship of any kind between the sexes is unlikely. At the close of "**Number 16**," the narrator places more blame on men than on women for failed relationships:

> Et, comme si la volunté de l'homme estoit immuable, se jurerent et promirent ce qui n'estoit en leur puissance: c'est une amityé perpetuelle, qui ne se peult naistre ne demorer au cueur de l'homme; et celles seulles le sçavent, qui ont experimenté combien durent telles opinions.
>
> (132-33)

But although men often appear more at fault than women, women are not totally exonerated, as three out of the four stories demonstrate. With the exception of

Rolandine (unless one faults her for her poor taste in men), the women bear some responsibility for failed relationships as well, and in most cases it is risky to speak of the women as exemplars. Floride, who has her own capacity for dissimulation, shares some blame with Amadour for the failure of their friendship.[12] The wife in **"Number 15,"** though not to blame for failing at the onset to forge a friendship with her husband, is criticized for her regrettable turn to deceit and promiscuity, which dims the prospects for reconciliation with her husband.[13] The dame de Vergi, although wronged by the gentleman, admits responsibility for having loved the *créature* more than the *Créateur*. In three of the four stories, social and/or economic inequality also appear to put special strains on relationships: Floride is more wealthy and highborn than Amadour; Rolandine is more wealthy than the *Bâtard*; and the wife in **"Number 15"** is more wealthy than her husband. The most significant element pertaining to friendship that links all four stories, however, is the importance the women place on conversational companionship with men. Later in the century, Montaigne also considers the value of honest conversational relationships. He mentions three contexts for "honest" conversation, without ranking any of the options. Open, honest talk ("parler ouvert"), which is desirable, can be evoked by "un autre parler," by *vin,* or by *amour* (Montaigne 794). In the **Heptaméron** stories that I have discussed, the avenue of honest intimacy initially most sought by women eager for friendship with men is undoubtedly un *autre parler.*

Notes

1. All textual page references to Marguerite de Navarre's tales, indicated parenthetically, come from l'*Heptaméron,* ed. Michel François (Paris: Garnier, 1967).

2. Langer has pointed out the "sibling-like and feminine status of Amadour" in connection with Amadour's "innocuous and familiar" insinuation into the household (135).

3. The bastard's calculating nature is revealed early on when he decides to try to marry Rolandine in part because of "l'honneur que ce luy seroit s'il la povoit avoir" (160). Later in the story he is described as being guilty of avarice and ambition (172).

4. In "Désir et parole dans les devis de l'*Heptaméron,*" *Les Visages et les voix de Marguerite de Navarre,* comp. Marcel Tetel (Paris: Klincksieck, 1995) 41-49, Françoise Charpentier observes that speech in the *Heptaméron* can be a "substitut érotique" and take the place of "une sexualité impossible" (41).

5. The wife's declarations about her husband's obligation to set a moral example recall Rabelais's reworking of Erasmian thought in the *Tiers livre* in

the character of the evangelical Hippothadée, who tells Panurge that if a husband wants a moral wife, he must himself be moral. For an excellent discussion of this topic, see M. A. Screech, *The Rabelaisian Marriage* (London: Edward Arnold, 1958) 68-83.

6. "Or, jugez sans faveur lequel de nous deux est le plus punissable ou excusable, ou vous, estimé homme saige et experimenté, qui, sans occasion donnée de mon costé, avez, non seullement à moy, mais au Roy auquel vous estes tant obligé, faict ung si meschant tour; ou moy, jeune et ignorante, desprisée et contennée de vous, aymée du plus beau et du plus honneste gentil homme de France, lequel j'ay aymé, par le desespoir, de ne povoir jamais estre aymée de vous?" (123-24). The wife in "Number 15" does make categorical assertions about her husband's behavior, but by virtue of ending her diatribe with a question, she leaves the ultimate assessment to her husband. In this way she attenuates the reproaches.

7. For a more sympathetic view of the wife, see Patricia Francis Cholakian, "Heroic Infidelity: Novella 15," *Heroic Virtue, Comic Infidelity: Reassessing Marguerite de Navarre's* Heptaméron, ed. Dora E. Polachek (Amherst: Hestia Press, 1993) 62-76.

8. Jean Frappier made this point many years ago in his essay "La Chastelaine de Vergi, Marguerite de Navarre et Bandello," *Publications de la Faculté de Lettres de l'Université de Strasbourg: Mélanges 1945, 2: Etudes littéraires* (Paris: Les Belles Lettres, 1946) 89-150.

9. This response to God is consistent with the Freudian view that God is a "magnified father." See Ernest Jones, *The Life and Work of Sigmund Freud,* vol. 3 (New York: Basic Books, 1957) 354.

10. In *Bridging Separate Worlds: Why Men and Women Clash and How Therapists Can Bring Them Together* (Washington: American Psychological Association, 1997), the authors (Carol L. Philpot, Gary R. Brooks, Don-David Lusterman, and Roberta L. Nutt) note that "women are often tentative and indirect in their speech patterns" (115).

11. See my essay "Mapping the Moral Domain in the *Heptaméron,*" *Les Visages et les voix de Marguerite de Navarre,* comp. Marcel Tetel (Paris: Klincksieck, 1995) 9-18. I argue that men and women are generally portrayed as differing in the ways in which they reason morally.

12. I examined some of the same aspects of the nonexemplary nature of Floride in an essay published many years ago ("Didacticism and the *Hep-*

taméron: The Misinterpretation of the Tenth Tale as an Exemplum," *The French Review* 45.3 [1971]: 84-90). I did not study Floride in the specific context of friendship, however.

13. Longarine's remarks opening the discussion following the story include the declaration that "nulle femme de bien [. . .] en quelque sorte que ce soit, ne sçauroit trouver excuse à mal faire" (128).

Works Cited

Langer, Ullrich. *Perfect Friendship: Studies in Literature and Moral Philosophy from Boccaccio to Corneille.* Genève: Droz, 1994.

de Montaigne, Michel. "De l'utile et de l'honneste." *Les Essais.* Livre 3. Ed Pierre Villey. Paris: Quadrige/PUF.

Schönbach, Peter. "A Category System for Account Phases." *European Journal of Social Psychology* 10 (1980): 195-200.

Nancy Frelick (essay date fall 2001)

SOURCE: Frelick, Nancy. "Female Infidelity: Ideology, Subversion, and Feminist Practice in Marguerite de Navarre's *Heptaméron.*" *Dalhousie French Studies* 56 (fall 2001): 17-26.

[*In the following essay, Frelick examines the portrayal of marriage throughout the* Heptaméron, *maintaining that Marguerite offers no absolute judgment on marital relations.*]

> Literature has been given diametrically opposed functions. Is literature an ideological instrument: a set of stories that seduce readers into accepting the hierarchical arrangements of society? If stories take it for granted that women must find their happiness, if at all, in marriage; if they accept class divisions as natural and explore how the virtuous serving-girl may marry a lord, they work to legitimate contingent historical arguments. Or is literature the place where ideology is exposed, revealed as something that can be questioned? Literature represents, for example, in a potentially intense and affecting way, the narrow range of options historically offered to women, and, in making this visible, raises the possibility of *not* taking it for granted. Both claims are thoroughly plausible: that literature is the vehicle of ideology and that literature is an instrument for its undoing.
>
> (Culler 39)

Although Jonathan Culler uses the depiction of women and marriage as an instance among others in his introduction to literary theory, the example above might just as well be describing the debates surrounding Marguerite de Navarre's **Heptaméron,** for the sixteenth-century

text appears to oscillate between these two propositions. Is Marguerite a (proto-)feminist, eager to expose the condition of women and question the *status quo*? Or does she espouse traditional views on marriage and on the subordination of the wife to her husband? As is often the case, arguments supporting both sides can be found in the 72 *nouvelles* and surrounding discussions, as well as in the overarching story that frames the tales of the **Heptaméron.**

Indeed, much has been written on the subject of love and marriage in Marguerite de Navarre's **Heptaméron,** yet it is difficult to resolve the sorts of questions posed above without feeling that one has somehow oversimplified the issues raised in the text. In this article, I shall not pretend to resolve these questions, or discuss all the studies on the subject, nor shall I make an inventory of the kinds of matrimonial union in the work or summarize all the views on marriage expressed by characters and discussants of the tales. Instead, I would like to take a different tack: I plan to explore the ways in which psychoanalysis and feminism can inform the complications in the text without, I hope, oversimplifying them. In particular, I shall explore some of the ways in which Jane Gallop's theories about female infidelity as a kind of feminist practice can help us reframe, and thus shed new light on, the debates about love and marriage in the **Heptaméron.**

The characters in the frame of the **Heptaméron** that emblematize marriage—Parlamente and Hircan, the only married couple present at Notre Dame de Serrance—do not offer a progressive image of matrimony. On the contrary, they are quite conventional in their spousal roles and in their polarized views of masculine and feminine honour and virtue. Indeed, as Guild reminds us, although the characters are supposed to be equal in the story-telling game they use to pass the time and to avoid the perils of *ennui* while they await the (no doubt significant) rebuilding of bridges, Parlamente still defers to her husband (79).

This image of spousal compliance seems to be in perfect accord with the dominant ideology. Indeed, the **Heptaméron,** which portrays the unequal relationship between men and women, can be said to reproduce the discourses of patriarchy and hence help to preserve the *status quo.* Yet, there are stories in the work in which female characters appear to subvert the system. If one looks at those stories, the sixteenth-century text can seem quite revolutionary. I am thinking, in particular, of the stories of female infidelity, such as *nouvelles* **"15"** and **"49,"** in which women are presented as claiming the same rights to extra-marital liaisons as men.

In her *Daughter's Seduction,* Jane Gallop describes female infidelity as a feminist practice undermining the patriarchal order (48). According to her, infidelity emphasizes the use value rather than the exchange value of women, creating an opposition between acquisition (possession and exchange) and enjoyment (use, usufruct) that destabilizes traditional phallic modes of circulation (49). Gallop's argument springs from her Lacanian reading of the work of Claude Lévi-Strauss who describes marriage as a symbolic system of exchange, much like language, wherein women are circulated, as signs and values, to strengthen kinship ties between men. In this patriarchal order, women are expected to produce heirs to ensure the continuation of the patrilineal line. As objects of exchange, women are not treated as fully-functioning beings of equal status to men, but as possessions whose value and circulation are governed by what Lacan names the *Nom/Non du Père*.

One might wish to argue that there are other modes of subversion to the system. For example, in other contexts, homosexuality (especially lesbianism) could be seen as a challenge to traditional practices. However, this option does not appear to exist in Marguerite de Navarre's text. The only other possibility (aside from infidelity) open to women that might be read as challenging the system involves choosing chastity. One can argue that in sixteenth-century Europe, monasteries provided women with ways of subverting the conjugal system under patriarchy. By refusing to function as reproductive agents for men, women who choose chastity over marriage can be seen as subverting the phallic order. As Cottrell points out, discussing Peter Brown's account of virginity in early Christianity:

> From the pagan point of view, sexuality was (in theory, at least) a desire that led to a *social* act. Marriage was an investment in the future of the social order. By refusing marriage, and more drastically, sexuality, Christians claimed for themselves a "freedom" that loosened the bonds of community. The body that was maintained in a virgin state was kept out of circulation and could not be recruited by society for its own benefit. It resisted the demands that society made on it and thus represented a threat to the sexual social contract that held society together. As the pagan elite recognized, the Christian advocacy of virginity implied a new social order that was radically different from the old.
>
> (18)

While it might be argued that over time this subversive practice was incorporated into a larger symbolic economy through the increasingly masculinist institution of the Church (to be sure, a system ruled by/in the Name of the Father) and naturalized as a kind of marriage (to the deity), it is nevertheless true that it opened up a space for many women writers to devote themselves to the life of the mind and spirit, a space beyond the rudimentary system of exchange represented by worldly marriage.[1]

Although the *Heptaméron* explores aspects of monastic life[2] and examples of women choosing chastity, I will leave this line of inquiry to others in order to focus on

the question of female infidelity in Marguerite de Navarre's work, limiting my inquiry to two of the more subversive *nouvelles* in the *Heptaméron* in light of Gallop's theories.

As Gisèle Mathieu-Castellani explains, the relationships between men and women in Marguerite de Navarre's tales are governed by the rules of exchange outlined by Lévi-Strauss: "La loi archaïque de l'échange, qui règle dans les sociétés dites primitives les modalités du don et du contre-don, et contrôle la circulation (des produits, des femmes, de la parole), soutient tout l'édifice de l'*Heptaméron*" (1992:71-72). Marguerite de Navarre's work is quite typical in this respect, for many of the images of women and relationships between men and women in the early modern period reflect this economy. Yet, lest we forget the conundrum with which we began this study, the question is: does the *Heptaméron* merely reproduce the dominant ideology? Is it an ideological instrument, a set of stories that seduce readers into accepting the hierarchical arrangements of society? Or does it make it possible to question the ways in which reality has been constructed and in so doing offer possibilities for change?

While there are a number of stories of female infidelity in the *Heptaméron*, interpreted differently by the various *devisants*, *nouvelles* "**15**" and "**49**" stand out as particularly assertive challenges to the patriarchal order. The main character in the fifteenth story is a rich young lady much neglected by a poorer husband who squanders money and affections elsewhere, particularly on the king's mistress. After years of trying everything in her power to win him over, and after much grief and torment, the wife, who has become quite beautiful, attracts a handsome admirer. When the king notices this friendship, he asks the suitor to break off the relationship, which he does. However, the lady, who now has a better appreciation of her worth, finds a new lover to replace him. When her husband admonishes her for her behaviour, she upbraids him for his and points out that she is no more at fault than he is. The lady's lover, who does not want to alienate her husband, eventually leaves because of his suspicions. This lover is also replaced: we are told at the end of the story that the young man returns hoping to marry the lady after her husband's death but is devastated when he discovers she has "acquired another companion whom she now prefer[s]" (201 in Chilton's translation).

In her reading of "*Nouvelle 15*," Mathieu-Castellani would appear to concur with Gallop's argument about the subversiveness of female infidelity, for she describes it as "une subtile variation sur le thème du *donnant donnant* et sur les transgressions de la loi d'échange" (1998:89). Madeleine Lazard seems to be going in the same direction for she reminds us that Hircan states that infidelity is "la plus grande injure que la femme peut

faire à l'homme" (101). There is, however, a big difference between Gallop's point and Mathieu-Castellani's
reading, which implies a nostalgic view of ancient history by suggesting that there was a time (presumably in
classical Rome) when the symbolic system of exchange
was reciprocal:

> La dame de la quinzième nouvelle, cette primitive,
> héroïne d'une autre modernité, apprend à ses contem-
> porains la nécessaire égalité qui régnait dans les so-
> ciétés archaïques soumises à la loi d'échange. Les nar-
> ratrices et les devisantes semblent ainsi se rallier aux
> vues traditionnelles, où se conjuguent les traces de la
> culture romaine classique (le *pater familias* toutpuis-
> sant, la mère gardienne de la «race») [. . .], l'héritage
> chrétien et la lecture de saint Paul, et *l'aggiornamento*
> humaniste dans sa nouvelle conception du mariage.
> [. . .]

(1998:89-91)

It is difficult to justify Mathieu-Castellani's reconstruction of ancient history (though it may be said that in
many ways women did lose ground over time[3]), but it is
true that the female character in *"Nouvelle 15"* does
question the inequality of the system, which requires fidelity of women but not of men. Her subversive act is
to propose that she should submit to the same rules as
her husband, and that she is modeling her behaviour on
his. As Nancy Bouzrara points out, traditional gender
roles are reversed as the woman turns men into objects
of exchange: "The wife repeatedly exchanges men as
objects, transforming the novella from a simplistic story
of a *trompeur trompé* into a more complex tale of multiple deceptions more characteristic in Renaissance literature of men's behavior than of women's" (182).

In *"Nouvelle 49"* the libidinal economy undergoes a
similar reversal. In this story, a foreign countess, whose
husband was sent away on business by the king so that
he could enjoy her favours, becomes the object of desire of several gentlemen. Each of these gentlemen,
who believe she is fierce and proud, cannot believe his
luck when he succeeds in his advances and eagerly
agrees to be shut up in her dressing room for days at a
time in order to be with her. Each is later stunned to
discover, during a boastful conversation, that they have
been her successive "prisoners." What is subversive
about *"Nouvelle 49"* is that the foreign countess claims
the right to desire in a typically "masculine" way: she
not only becomes a subject rather than just an object of
desire, but she allows herself to focus her attentions on
several objects of desire, her so-called "prisoners." The
carceral image elaborated from the lovers' servitude to
the lady is an ironic play on the language of courtly
love and on the lovers' willingness to submit to being
locked up in the lady's *garderobe* in order to enjoy
her favours. Their submission, however, is far from
complete—either to the courtly code or to the lady—for
they break the injunction to silence required of courtly

lovers because they cannot resist boasting of their exploits in a conversation that might be compared to
locker-room bravado. In addition, once they discover
that they have all been duped by the lady, and that she
has therefore stepped beyond the bounds reserved for
women in patriarchy, they work together to return her
to her rightful place as an object to be circulated in a
system regulated by men.

The homosocial bond between men—particularly when
their mastery is in jeopardy—proves stronger than the
bond between men and women. As Eve Sedgwick points
out: "In any male-dominated society, there is a special
relationship between male homosocial (including
homosexual) desire and the structures for maintaining
and transmitting patriarchal power" (25).

Yet, despite the efforts of her erstwhile "servants" to
shame her into submission, the lady in *"Nouvelle 49"*
refuses to be "circulated" as an object of exchange. By
refusing the value (or lack thereof) they attempt to con-
fer on her by turning her both into an object of the public gaze and of ridicule, she refuses not only the shame
and humiliation the men wish to heap on her, but also
reintegration into the system of exchange traditionally
reserved for women:

> Le matin venu, tous six, habillez de noir, leurs chaynes
> de fer tournées à l'entour de leur col en façon de col-
> lier, vindrent trouver la contesse, qui alloit à l'église.
> Et, si tost qu'elle les vid ainsi habillez, se print à rire et
> leur dist: «Où vont ces gens si douloureux?» «Ma-
> dame, dist Astillon, nous vous venons acompaigner
> comme voz pouvres esclaves et prisonniers, qui som-
> mes tenuz à vous faire service». La contesse, faisant
> semblant de n'y entendre rien, leur dist: «Vous n'estes
> point mes prisonniers, ny je n'entendz point que vous
> ayez occasion de me faire service plus que les autres».
> Valnebon s'avança et luy dist: «Si nous avons mengé
> vostre pain si longuement, nous serions bien ingratz, si
> nous ne vous faisions service». Elle fist si bonne myne
> de n'y entendre rien qu'elle cuydoit, par ceste gravité,
> les estonner. Mais ilz poursuyvirent si bien leur propoz
> qu'elle entendit que la chose estoit descouverte. Mais
> elle les trompa bien, car elle, qui avoit perdu l'honneur
> et la conscience, ne voulut point recevoir la honte qu'ilz
> luy cuydoient faire, mais, comme celle qui preferoit
> son plaisir à tout l'honneur du monde, ne leur en fist
> pire visaige, ny n'en changea de contenance: dont ilz
> furent tant estonnez qu'ilz rapporterent en leur sain la
> honte qu'ilz luy avoient voulu faire.

(387)

The Lady appears to take on a specular function: like a
mirror whose surface reflects rather than absorbs light,
her refusal to absorb the servile image the men project
on her means that the shame destined for her ultimately
reflects back on them. Thus, their game turns against
them, reconfirming (rather than refuting) their servile
role as mere subject positions (subject to infinite
substitutions) in a chain of signifiers over which they

have no power. The foreign countess (and here one can enjoy the irony of her designation and its homophonic association with counting and systems of exchange) remains in the dominant position, confused with the Symbolic Phallus that governs the laws of circulation and exchange.

Yet, it might be argued that even though *nouvelles* "15" and "49" seem to offer a subversive perspective on the patriarchal system, they offer no definitive solution. While reversing the roles of men and women may allow for a critique of men's infidelity, it does not get rid of inequalities between men and women. Instead of resolving age-old questions, these tales raise new ones. Indeed, that generally seems to be the case in the work, as every example seems to have at least one counter-example.

While it is true that the women in these two tales seem to suffer no grave consequences as a result of their illicit behaviour, other stories about female infidelity offer examples of cruel punishment inflicted on women who commit adultery. As Lazard reminds us, women paid a much higher price for infidelity than men, and it is no wonder that most women in the **Heptaméron** take great pains to keep such relationships secret:

> On comprend la crainte des femmes de l'**Heptaméron** à l'idée de voir leurs liaisons découvertes et les précautions qu'elles prennent pour les tenir secrètes. Les punitions des épouses infidèles sont terribles. La nouvelle 32 montre la demoiselle d'Allemagne rencontrée par Bernage, la tête rasée, vêtue de noir, contrainte à boire dans le crâne de son amant, tué par le mari, et séquestrée dans sa chambre avec son squelette, vivant avec humilité en «grande repentance». Le Président de Grenoble de la nouvelle 36 attend quinze jours avant de faire manger une mortelle «saladde d'herbes» à sa femme qui l'a trompé avec un jeune clerc. La traîtresse duchesse de Bourgogne de la nouvelle 70 est poignardée par son mari.

(99)

Judy Kem explains that the reasons for such severe punishment of adulterous women have to do with the threats female infidelity pose to the male line: "[A]dulterous wives may give birth to bastards and therefore cast doubt on their husbands' legitimate children, presenting a biological, social, and legal problem that does not arise in the case of adulterous husbands. If the wife's good name is lost, so is the descendants'" (52). Indeed, far from presenting an ideal world of possibilities for women, "*Nouvelle* 15" includes reminders of the inequities between husbands and wives. As Patricia Cholakian notes:

> When this neglected lady decides to find happiness outside marriage, she comes into direct conflict with the truth about how things operate at a Renaissance court. The "old-boy network" prevents her from bringing dis-

honor on her husband; and after the king's warning, her admirer's ardor is immediately quenched. Far from worrying about her feelings, his main concern is to assure her husband, who has been watching him from the window, that he is complying with the king's orders. For these men, ties to other men take precedence over romantic entanglements, and they all work together to control female sexuality.

> Her second attempt to find a substitute for her husband calls attention to another cruel reality: Although a wife had to suffer her husband's infidelity in impotent silence, he had the right to kill her if she was unfaithful to him. Furthermore, there is no indication that his jealousy stems from his love for her. It is based solely on his right as her husband to have exclusive possession of her body.

(69)

In what has sometimes been described as one of the clearest feminist indictments of the inequalities of marriage in the **Heptaméron,** the wife in *"Nouvelle* 15" admonishes her husband, listing the inequities between them as if she were reading from a balance sheet:

> [. . .] combien que la loy des hommes donne grant deshonneur aux femmes qui ayment autres que leurs mariz, sy esse que la loy de Dieu n'exempte point les mariz qui ayment autres que leurs femmes. Et, s'il fault mectre à la balance l'offence de vous et de moy, vous estes homme saige, experimenté et d'aage pour congnoistre à éviter le mal, moy jeune et sans experience nulle de la force et puissance d'amour. Vous avez une femme qui vous cherche, estime et ayme plus que sa vye propre, et j'ay ung mary qui me fuyt, qui me hayt et me desprise plus que une chambriere. Vous aymez une femme desja d'aage, et en mauvais poinct, et moings belle que moy; et j'ayme ung gentilhomme plus jeune que vous, plus beau que vous et plus aymable que vous. Vous aymez la femme d'un des plus grans amys que vous ayez en ce monde, et l'amye de vostre maistre, offensant d'un cousté l'amytié et de l'autre la reverance que vous debvez à tous deux; et j'ayme ung gentilhomme qui n'est à riens lyé, sinon à l'amour qu'il me porte. Or, jugez, Monsieur, sans faveur, lequel de nous deux est le plus pugnissable ou excusable: ou vous, estimé homme saige, experimenté, qui, sans occasion donnée de mon cousté, avez non seullement à moy, mais au roy auquel vous estes tant obligé, faict ung si meschant tour; ou moy, jeune et ignorante, desprisée et contempnée de vous, aymée du plus beau et du plus honneste gentilhomme de France, lequel j'ay aymé par le desespoir de ne jamais pouvoir estre aymée de vous.

(152-53)

The lady's critique of her husband does not exonerate her; it reminds readers that both parties are at fault. A simple inversion of roles in a system of exchange is as unjust whether dominated by men or women. The *devisants'* comments seem to concur: simply reversing the system does not get rid of injustice, it creates new injustices. Vengeance is also criticized in all cases where men or women are treated badly as a result of infidelity. Human beings must reserve judgment. It is not for them to mete out punishments. Only God may judge human hearts.

That is no doubt why, although, as some have suggested, the **Heptaméron** often seems to be structured like a legal debate, in the end, it is difficult to say whether its author is advocating for any particular side of the case.[4] Ultimately Marguerite's work exposes men and women as equals (equal in number, in their humanity, in their weakness of flesh and spirit) before God (Mathieu-Castellani 1998:96-97). In Lacanian terms, no character (male or female) can do more than occupy shifting subject positions. No matter what their position, they cannot achieve a truly transcendent perspective, for they are subject to the Imaginary and Symbolic regimes that structure their realities. This is also true of the *devisants* who act as storytellers in the work. While characters in the stories and frame may create essentialized discourses on the nature of *man* and *woman,* the author avoids doing so by reminding us that men and women are ultimately subject to the gaze of God, who alone can truly see and judge. No human perspective can serve as a stable vantage point. All emanate from the Imaginary, the site of *méconnaissance,* and are subject to the laws of the Symbolic that structure their interaction. Only God's perspective, which transcends these bounds, is located in the Real. As Robert Cottrell reminds us:

> [T]he **Heptameron** [. . .] is powerfully informed by "the sacred," by the Logos, by a Real that is situated eternally beyond the world of phenomena but that is simultaneously always inscribed in it. That Real is, of course, Christ, the Word made flesh, which, from the Christian perspective that shapes Marguerite's views as well as those of all the protagonists in the **Heptameron,** operates in the *hic et nunc* of phenomena, in the fleshy, sinful, suffering world of the desiring body.
>
> (4)

From the godly perspective both men and women are subject to sin in equal measure, and humankind is nothing without God's grace. Thus, neither gender can posit itself as superior. In practical terms this means that while the reversal of gender roles in *nouvelles* **"15"** and **"49"** presents a challenge to the dominant ideology and thus compels one to question the Imaginary realm that constitutes our vision of the world, it fails to change the Symbolic structures that govern the relationships between the sexes. In order to solve the problems of gender inequity and create a better system for both men and women, another system altogether has to be imagined wherein the binary subject/object categories no longer apply. This logic can be found in the very structure of the **Heptaméron.** One could suggest that the dialogic structure of the work, its *heteroglossia* (to use Bakhtin's terminology) subtly undermines any authori-

tarian system of signification or system of exchange ruled by the laws of the Symbolic. The alternation of male and female voices in equal numbers suggests an equality between the sexes that is essential to the economy of the work (Mathieu-Castellani 1998:80-81).[5]

As Gallop suggests elsewhere (125-26), the notion of marriage may be redefined, not as a fusion (which is, in any case, impossible according to Lacan) but as a union of differences. Marriage, like language, can become a system of differences without positive terms. The endless repositing of possibilities in the text of the **Heptaméron** shows that marriage need not be scripted according to old binaries (wherein men and women are opposed) but may be rewritten as a dialogue without end.

One might also look for subtle kinds of resistance at the level of the signifier that could give us clues about Marguerite de Navarre's world view. For example, Gallop suggests that a kind of subversive feminist writing may find its expression in texts in a manner analogous to female infidelity by undermining (not being faithful to) phallic authority (125-26). One way this is done, Gallop seems to suggest, is by overusing certain terms, so that they literally seem to wear out. Another strategy, close to that suggested by Gallop, might be the repetition of terms, not to the point of erosion so much as explosion, multiplying meanings exponentially so that signifiers become so plurivocal and indeterminate in their meaning and usage that they lose their air of vigour and certainty, pointing to the slippage of signs and to the imaginary nature of the Symbolic Phallus. An example of such a slippage in terminology may be seen in Marguerite's use of *vertu*. The use of this word in the **Heptaméron** is a perfect illustration not only of the constitution of the patriarchal symbolic system according to unequal binaries, but also of the ways in which the system may be subtly undermined by calling attention to its problematic construction of meaning (double standards) according to gender. *Vertu,* which has its etymological roots in the Latin *virtus* and therefore manly (*vir*) goodness, is particularly significant because of its reference to the masculinist values that dominated early modern discourse. As can be seen in the tenth tale, for example, masculine virtue is associated with strength and conquest (Amadour, the warrior who will stop at nothing to obtain his prize, is described as an exemplar of manly virtues), whereas feminine virtue is a superior moral quality that allows women to ensure that they remain chaste (Floride, who resists Amadour to the bitter end, exemplifies female virtue). As can be seen in **"Nouvelle 10,"** the two semantic codes are necessarily in conflict, as male *vertu* can only be proved at the cost of female *vertu*.[6] This all too cruel irony illustrates the double standard (and double-bind) present in relationships between men and women and underscores the slippage of terms that can, and often do, mean both one thing and its opposite.

In conclusion, while it is difficult to find an *ultima verba* regarding marriage in Marguerite's text, perhaps we can find suggestive clues to her inclinations in the very form of her writing. While all the *devisants* may not act as equals, it is nevertheless true that their utterances are given equal value in the text. Although the text does not offer a utopian vision of human relations, even in the privileged space of Serrance, the dialogic equality it presents does show a way in which spaces may be opened up so that women may enter the debate, and it does suggest a direction to follow in relations between men and women. Love and marriage need not be a fusion, nor a structure wherein women (or men) function as mere objects of exchange. Marguerite's text suggests a different kind of *commerce*: an exchange based not on the circulation of women (or men) as commodities, but on the free circulation of the signifier, a verbal economy, a dialogue without end wherein each participant may have his or her own distinct voice.

The fact that the **Heptaméron** offers no final solutions either in the content of its stories or in the perspectives offered by the storytellers—as example gives way to counter-example in a never-ending play of signification—need not be a problem. Undecidability need not mean negativity: on the contrary, it means, rather optimistically I think, that the dialogue need never end. Reaching the end of the conversation implies the end of desire, a kind of death for the relationship. The fact that there is no "sexual relation" (in the Lacanian scheme) means that there is no end to the attempts to relate. It is, no doubt, fitting that Marguerite's work was never finished, suggesting that the dialogues remain incomplete, forever tantalizing us with lines of flight that can be followed, if only in our imaginations, drawing us in and compelling us to engage in other dialogues about possible itineraries and thus creating ever more intricate and infinite webs of possibilities for the circulation of meaning and for building sites of exchange for human communication and relationships.

Notes

1. See King, Jordan, and Wiesner for discussions of the situation of women in convents in early modern Europe.

2. Telle argues that, far from recommending monastic life, Marguerite, like many other humanist reformers, criticizes the incontinence of monks and priests who are incapable of keeping their vows and sees marriage as preferable to an impossible system (celibacy) that often puts women in danger (329-30). For an extensive discussion of the negative examples of monastic life presented in the *Heptaméron,* see Lyons, chapter 2.

3. See Kelly's landmark article.

4. Mathieu-Castellani 1998:93. See Bideaux for more on the debate structure in the work.

5. Mathieu-Castellani emphasizes the difference between the *Heptaméron,* wherein there are 5 male and 5 female discussants in the frame, all commenting on the stories told, and the *Decameron* in which the storytellers comprise 7 women and 3 men. She points out that the debates in the frame allow one to see the ways in which some stories provoke different gendered readings. Mathieu-Castellani also reminds us that the equality given male and female voices in Marguerite's text is not a reflection of any reality, but of a game in which all have agreed to participate in a time and place beyond the participants' normal spatio-temporal realm, as their lives have literally been bracketed by floods that have washed away all links (bridges) to civilization. The society they erect in the midst of the abbey is in a sense a privileged one that is at two removes from the one they are presumed to inhabit normally (that is, if there were an extratextual world the characters did inhabit), as the discussants are surrounded by, but quite separate from, the cloistered brotherhood of the monks, who themselves live in a realm designed to separate them from the world. See Winn for a discussion of the dialogic aspects of the work.

6. See Kritzman for an excellent discussion of "*Nouvelle* 10."

Works Cited

Bideaux, Michel. L'Heptaméron *de l'enquête au débat.* Mont-de-Marsan: Éditions InterUniversitaires, 1992.

Bouzrara, Nancy Erickson. "A Fall from Thélème: Patterns of Infidelity in *L'Heptaméron.*" *The World and Its Rivals: Essays on Literary Imagination in Honor of Per Nykrog.* Eds. Kathryn Karczewska and Tom Conley. Amsterdam: Rodopi, 1999. 171-92.

Cholakian, Patricia Francis. "Heroic Infidelity: Novella 15." *Heroic Virtue, Comic Infidelity: Reassessing Marguerite de Navarre's* Heptaméron. Ed. Dora E. Polachek. Amherst, MA: Hestia, 1993. 62-76.

Cottrell, Robert D. "Inmost Cravings: The Logic of Desire in the *Heptameron.*" *Critical Tales: New Studies of the* Heptaméron *and Early Modern Culture.* Eds. John D. Lyons and Mary B. McKinley. Philadelphia: University of Pennsylvania Press, 1993. 3-24.

Culler, Jonathan. *Literary Theory: A Very Short Introduction.* Oxford: Oxford University Press, 1997.

Gallop, Jane. *The Daughter's Seduction: Feminism and Psychoanalysis.* Ithaca: Cornell University Press, 1982.

Guild, Liz. "'Au commencement était l'amour'. . . ." *Women's Writing in the French Renaissance: Proceedings of the Fifth Cambridge French Renaissance Colloquium 7-9 July, 1997*. Cambridge: Cambridge French Colloquia, 1999. 75-90.

Jordan, Constance. *Renaissance Feminism: Literary Texts and Political Models*. Ithaca: Cornell University Press, 1990.

Kelly, Joan. "Did Women Have a Renaissance?" *Women, History, and Theory: The Essays of Joan Kelly*. Chicago: University of Chicago Press, 1986. 19-50.

Kem, Judy. "Sins of the Mother: Adultery, Lineage, and the Law in the *Heptaméron*." *Heroic Virtue, Comic Infidelity: Reassessing Marguerite de Navarre's* Heptaméron. Ed. Dora E. Polachek. Amherst, MA: Hestia, 1993. 51-59.

King, Margaret L. "Book-Lined Cells: Women and Humanism in the Early Italian Renaissance." *Beyond Their Sex: Learned Women of the European Past*. Ed. Patricia E. Labalme. New York: New York University Press, 1980. 66-90.

———. *Women of the Renaissance*. Chicago: University of Chicago Press, 1991.

Kritzman, Lawrence D. "*Verba erotica*: Marguerite de Navarre and the Rhetoric of Silence." *The Rhetoric of Sexuality and the Literature of the French Renaissance*. Cambridge: Cambridge University Press, 1991. 45-56.

Lazard, Madeleine. "L'infidélité féminine dans l'*Heptaméron*." *Les visages et les voix de Marguerite de Navarre: actes du Colloque international sur Marguerite de Navarre (Duke University) 10-11 avril 1992*. Ed. Marcel Tetel. Paris: Klincksieck, 1995. 97-106.

Lebègue, Raymond. "La fidélité conjugale dans l'*Heptaméron*." *La nouvelle française à la Renaissance*. Eds. Lionello Sozzi and V. L. Saulnier. Geneva: Slatkine, 1981. 425-33.

Lyons, John D. *Exemplum: The Rhetoric of Example in Early Modern France and Italy*. Princeton: Princeton University Press, 1989.

Marguerite de Navarre. 1984. *The Heptameron*. Trans. P. A. Chilton. Middlesex: Penguin.

———. 1999. *Heptaméron*. Ed. Renja Salminen. Geneva: Droz.

Mathieu-Castellani, Gisèle. 1992. *La conversation conteuse: les nouvelles de Marguerite de Navarre*. Paris: Presses universitaires de France.

———. 1998. *La quenouille et la lyre*. Paris: José Corti.

———, ed. 1999. *L'Heptaméron*. Paris: Livre de Poche.

Sedgwick, Eve Kosofsky. *Between Men: English Literature and Male Homosocial Desire*. New York: Columbia University Press, 1985.

Telle, Émile. *L'œuvre de Marguerite d'Angoulême, reine de Navarre, et la querelle des femmes*. Toulouse: Lion, 1937.

Wiesner, Merry E. *Women and Gender in Early Modern Europe*. Cambridge: Cambridge University Press, 1993.

Winn, Colette H. "Toward a Dialectic of Reconciliation: The *Navire* and the *Heptameron* of Marguerite de Navarre." *The Dialogue in Early Modern France, 1547-1630: Art and Argument*. Ed. Colette H. Winn. Washington: Catholic University of America Press, 1993.

Cathleen M. Bauschatz (essay date summer 2003)

SOURCE: Bauschatz, Cathleen M. "Rabelais and Marguerite de Navarre on Sixteenth-Century Views of Clandestine Marriage." *Sixteenth Century Journal* 34, no. 2 (summer 2003): 395-408.

[*In the following essay, Bauschatz observes similar attitudes toward church reform, especially on the subject of clandestine marriage, in the works of Marguerite and François Rabelais.*]

When Rabelais dedicated his *Tiers Livre* to Marguerite de Navarre in 1546, he invited her to come down from her "manoir divin, perpetuel," and to pay attention to more earthly things:

> Esprit abstraict, ravy, et ecstatic,
> Qui frequentant *les cieulx, ton origine*,
> As delaissé ton hoste et domestic,
> Ton corps concords, qui tant se morigine
> A tes edictz, en vie peregrine,
> *Sans sentement, et comme en Apathie*;
> Voudrois tu poinct faire quelque sortie
> De *ton manoir divin, perpetuel?*
> Et ca bas veoir une tierce partie
> Des faictz *joyeux* du bon Pantagruel?[1]

> [François Rabelais to the spirit of the Queen of Navarre:
> Abstracted soul, ravished in ecstasy,
> Returned now to thy home, the Firmament,
> Leaving thy body, formed in harmony,
> Thy host and servant, once obedient
> To thy commands in this life transient,
> Wouldst thou not care to quit, just fleetingly,
> Thy heavenly mansion and perpetual,
> And here below for the third time to see
> The jovial deeds of good Pantagruel?][2]

This essay will take seriously the question of why Rabelais addressed his book to Marguerite as well as whether she responded to his invitation to leave, in Bakhtin's terminology, the domain of the "upper body" and return to that of the "lower body" as she read the *Tiers Livre* and also began to assemble the tales for the **Heptaméron** the same year (1546).[3]

Rabelais had gotten permission from François I in September 1545 to republish *Gargantua and Pantagruel* and the *Tiers Livre*.[4] The fact that he then, in his own name, dedicated the *Tiers Livre* to the king's sister in 1546 adds to our sense that during 1545-46 relations between Rabelais and the royal family must have been quite cordial.[5]

Marguerite herself spent the winter of 1545-46 at the French court in Paris.[6] During this time, conversations may have taken place between Rabelais and Marguerite, possibly regarding the *Tiers Livre* and her plans for the **Heptaméron** as well as current literary debates such as the "Querelle des Femmes."[7] Rabelais had been named Maître des Requêtes in 1543, and his relations with the court were good until March 1546, when he left for Metz.[8]

Beyond exploring the political circumstances surrounding the privilege and dedication, we need to consider the meaning of the dedication itself, which has baffled most commentators. There are various interpretations, French and American, and from specialists on both authors. Marguerite scholars tend to take the dedication more seriously; the increasing attention to Marguerite over the past twenty years, typical of greater interest in women writers in general, has brought the dedication into the limelight. More attention to the reception of literary works pushes us to ask as well what Marguerite's reaction to the dedication may have been. We need to consider her possible point of view as well as that of Rabelais.

Most earlier Rabelais and Marguerite scholars commented on the dedication. Abel Lefranc (1931) and Emile Telle (1937) both stressed difference and disagreement between the two authors, since both scholars saw the *Tiers Livre* and the **Heptaméron** as clearly on opposite sides of the "Querelle des Femmes." Lefranc asks "Faut-il s'étonner?" (xx), and Telle exclaims, "on s'est demandé pourquoi" (187). Both essentially throw up their hands at the mystery of the dedication.

In the 1970s and 1980s, interest in women writers and readers led scholars to try again to answer the question of the dedication. Marcel Tetel (1973) saw Rabelais as paying homage to Marguerite,[9] while Robert Cottrell (1986) wondered whether Rabelais really understood her work very well.[10] Cottrell was the only scholar to suggest this lack of comprehension, perhaps because his primary focus was Marguerite's religious poetry, which Rabelais appeared to ridicule in the dedication. Finally, in the 1990s, scholars continued to wonder about the unexpected dedication: Carla Freccero sees it as part of the problematizing of gender relations in the two books,[11] while Edwin Duval comes back to the earlier sense that Rabelais makes an "unflattering portrait" of the queen in his dedication.[12]

This survey of French Renaissance scholarly opinion suggests that there is at present no consensus on the question of why Rabelais dedicated the *Third Book* to Marguerite de Navarre or what he meant by the dedication. Certainly political factors, such as her help in obtaining the *privilège* from her brother, cannot be ruled out, but it is tempting to speculate that there is more at work besides a simple nod in her direction. We know very little about the relationship between the two "Evangéliques," and the dedication offers a tantalizing glimpse at what may have been an ongoing conversation. Many scholars seem to agree, however, that the dedication appears to be ironic, and that it may actually point to difference and disagreement between the two writers rather than to similarity or agreement. In contrast, for example, Antoine Le Maçon's dedication of his translation of the *Decameron* to the queen, in the previous year, is simply polite and respectful.[13]

By moving on to ask what Marguerite's response to the dedication might have been, perhaps we may shed more light on the dedication itself. We will evaluate Marguerite's potential point of view on the relationship between the two writers as well as that of Rabelais, which has been more frequently explored.

It was customary in the early modern period to give a copy of a book to its dedicatee. Writers frequently dedicated and gave books to aristocratic women patrons, and the books were generally found in their collections after their deaths.[14] This did not mean, necessarily, that the books had actually been read, and we must assume that frequently they had not been, or if they were, these women left no written evidence of their reactions. Félix Frank and others have suggested that Marguerite did read the *Tiers Livre,* based on a comment she makes in an epistle to her husband, printed with the *Suyte des Marguerites* of 1547.[15]

The "Epistre de la Royne de Navarre au Roy de Navarre Malade" is a sort of get-well card for the absent Henri, in which Marguerite offers him condolences on an illness and expresses the hope that he will soon be able to rejoin her. She imagines someone running in to tell her that the king is on his way, recognized on the horizon by the *Muletz* of his train:

> *Pantagruel a bien prophetisé*
> *Car j'ay desja les Muletz advisé*
> *De cestuy là qui vous avoit promis*
> *D'estre en trois jours en sa santé remis.*
>
> (*Les Marguerites,* 3:237)
> [Pantagruel prophesied well
> For I have already spied the mules
> Coming from the one who promised you
> To be back in good health in three days.]
>
> (Trans. author)

Félix Frank and several commentators after him have suggested that this passage contains an allusion to a minor incident in chapter 35 of the *Tiers Livre*. There, Pantagruel sees Gargantua's dog approaching and deduces that Gargantua is not far away: "Nostre roy n'est pas loing d'icy, levons nous" [Our king is not far away. Let us stand up (*Tiers Livre*, trans. Cohen, 385)]. This reference marks the first appearance in the *Tiers Livre* of Gargantua, who had been transported to the realm of the fairies in chapter 23 of *Pantagruel*.[16]

Whether or not we can see this reference as a direct allusion to the *Tiers Livre,* it is worth spending a little more time on it since it may open up some of the general affinities between Rabelais and Marguerite, instead of their differences. The whole passage from chapter 35 of the *Tiers Livre* follows:

> En cestuy instant, Pantagruel aperceut vers la porte de la salle le petit chien de Gargantua, lequel il nommoit Kyne, *pource que tel fut le nom du chien de Thobie.* Adoncques dist à toute la compaignie: "Nostre Roy n'est pas loing d'icy: levons nous." Ce mot ne feut achevé que Gargantua entra dedans la salle du banc- quet: chacun se leva pour luy faire révérence.[17]
>
> (*Tiers Livre,* ed. Jourda, 550)

> [At this moment Pantagruel saw at the door of the hall Gargantua's little dog, which he had called Kyne, after Tobias's dog in the Bible. So he said to the assembled company: "Our king is not far away. Let us stand up." And no sooner had he spoken than Gargantua entered the banqueting hall. Everyone then arose to make him a bow. . . .
>
> (*Tiers Livre,* trans. Cohen, 385)]

The reverence shown here toward the king, Gargantua, would also be flattering to François I or to Henri de Navarre, each of whom could have read in it a comparison of himself with the patriarch of Rabelais's series. While Marguerite in the "Epistre" mentions the *mulets* that announce her husband's return, the animal in the *Tiers Livre* passage is actually a dog. Both animals, however, are significant as we look at their common source, the apocryphal book of Tobit.

The use of dogs by Rabelais is fascinating, but there is not space to develop it here. They range from philosophical to vicious (as in the "Dame de Paris" episode), and, in the preface to the *Tiers Livre,* hover about the character Diogenes, since the cynics were themselves named for dogs. Marguerite's dog is small, domesticated, and seems to function as a symbol of fidelity, much like the dog in the well-known Van Eyck painting of the Arnolfini marriage, or like the lapdogs in the François Clouet and Dumoutier portraits of Marguerite herself.

Rabelais refers here to the book of Tobit, in which a dog runs ahead, letting Tobias's mother know that her son is on his way home from a mission on which his father has sent him. Rabelais apparently read the Tobit in the Latin Vulgate, for the treatment of the dog is much more extensive there than in earlier Hebrew or later Protestant versions.[18] The Vulgate pays special attention to the dog (Tob. 11:9):

> Tunc praecucurrit canis, qui simul fuerat in via: et quasi nuntius adveniens, blandimento suae caudae gaudebat.[19]

> [Then the dog, which had been with them in the way, ran before, and coming as if he had brought the news ("quasi nuntius adveniens"), shewed his joy by fawning and wagging his tail.][20]

Like Rabelais in the *Tiers Livre,* and like Marguerite in the "Epistre," St. Jerome (who apparently translated the book of Tobit himself) shows an animal as a messenger, bringing the good news of the return of a family member.

The status of the book of Tobit was in question at the same time that Rabelais and Marguerite were writing their texts. One concern of the Council of Trent, convened in 1546, was to determine the validity of the Apocrypha. These books were retained in the Catholic Bible as inspirational, although not canonical. During the seventeenth century, they disappeared from most Protestant Bibles, including the Authorized, or King James, version.

The book of Tobit, however, was a favorite of the sixteenth-century Reformers. Erasmus and Luther both wrote commentaries on it. The reason for this interest was not simply the presence of the family dog, although that certainly may have contributed to the sense of affinity which northern Europeans felt for the story. The real interest of the book of Tobit lay in a more significant matter, also debated at the Council of Trent, and which preoccupied both Rabelais and Marguerite de Navarre intensely. This was the issue of parental consent for marriage, and in particular, the implicit and explicit criticism of clandestine marriage, permitted by canon law but criticized by reformers such as Calvin in 1541, strongly discouraged by Henri II in 1556, condemned by the Council of Trent in 1563, and finally outlawed by French law under Henri III in 1579.[21]

The book of Tobit appeared to give a biblical source for the condemnation of clandestine marriage, especially in the Vulgate. There, the angel Raphael had earlier explained to Tobias the bad results of entering into marriage hastily, from lust, and the recommended procedure for remaining continent for the first three nights after his wedding:

> Hi namque qui coniugium ita suscipiunt, ut Deum a se et a sua mente excludant, et suae libidini ita vacent, sicut equus et mulus, quibus non est intellectus: habet potestatem daemonium super eos.
>
> (Tob. 6:17)

[For they who in such manner receive matrimony, as to shut out God from themselves, and from their mind, and to give themselves to their lust, *as the horse and mule,* which have not understanding, over them the devil hath power.][22]

The book of Tobit seemed, in the 1540s, to be emblematic of filial piety with respect to marriage. The topic of marriage had been rehabilitated by humanists and reformers, in contrast to the praise of celibacy and condemnation of women in the medieval monastic tradition.[23] Tobit seemed relevant because it showed a young couple who entered into a marriage arranged by their parents, an arrangement in which the father played a prominent role.

Rabelais (like Marguerite) obviously knew the book of Tobit well and followed its sentiments. Rabelais's agreement with the book of Tobit on the subject of marriage is even more evident in chapter 48 of the *Tiers Livre,* where Gargantua appears yet again to talk with Pantagruel and to suggest that it is time that he, as well as Panurge, think about marriage. Pantagruel apparently has not yet considered this possibility, but places himself completely in his father's hands on the question:

> Père très debonnaire (respondit Pantagruel), encores n'y avois je pensé, de tout ce négoce; je m'en deportoys *sus votre bonne volunté et paternel commendement.* Plus tost prie Dieu estre à vos pieds veu roydde mort en vostre desplaisir *que sans vostre plaisir estre veu vif marié.* Je n'ay jamais entendu que par loy aulcune, feust sacré, feust prophane et barbare, ayt esté en arbitre des enfans soy marier, non consentans, voulens, et promovens leurs peres, mères et parens prochains. Tous legislateurs *ont es enfans ceste liberté tollue. es parens l'ont reservée.*

> (*Tiers Livre,* ed. Jourda, 597)[24]

["Most gracious father," replied Pantagruel, "till now I had not given the subject a thought. In this whole matter I have deferred to your desires and your paternal authority. I would rather lie stark dead at your feet and under your displeasure than be found living and married without your consent. That I swear to God. By no laws, sacred or profane and barbarous, that I have ever heard of have the children ever been free to marry, unless their fathers, mothers, and nearest relatives deign to desire and promote the match. No lawgiver has vested this right in the children. Every one of them has reserved it for the parents."

(*Tiers Livre,* trans. Cohen, 418)]

Rabelais here shows Pantagruel siding with Roman civil law, which placed responsibility for marrying children in the hands of their fathers. Rabelais knows perfectly well that canon law did permit clandestine marriage, but chooses to disregard that fact here.[25] The use of the word "legislateur" shows Rabelais in agreement with the humanist legal community on the subject of marriage, rather than with ecclesiastical custom.[26]

Gargantua gives Pantagruel credit for this conservative opinion, focusing again on secular law and on the role of fathers, which belief also inspires the title of chapter 48, "Comment Gargantua remonstre n'estre licite es enfans soy marier sans le sceu et adveu de leurs peres et mères":

> Car *(comme tresbien avez dict)* loy on monde n'estoit, qui es enfans liberté de soy marier donnast *sans le sceu, l'adveu et consentement de leurs peres.*

> (*Tiers Livre,* ed. Jourda, 598)[27]

[For, as you very well said, there never has been a law in the world that gave children permission to marry without their fathers' knowledge, will and consent.

(*Tiers Livre,* trans. Cohen, 419)]

Gargantua then launches into a long tirade that attacks clandestine marriage, comparing it to rape, and blaming the monks ("taulpetiers") who will perform such marriages. He depicts the grief of parents whose daughters are abducted or lured away for clandestine marriages, in contrast to their normal expectations:

> . . . esperans en temps oportun les colloquer par mariage *avecques les enfans de leurs voisins et antiques amis,* nourris et instituez de mesmes soing, pour parvenir *à ceste felicité de mariage,* que d'eux ilz veissent naistre *lignaige raportant et haereditant,* non moins *aux meurs* de leurs peres et mères que *à leurs biens meubles et haeritaiges.* . . .

> (*Tiers Livre,* ed. Jourda, 599)

[. . . hoping in due course to marry them to the sons of their neighbors and old friends, who had been brought up and schooled with the same care. They had looked forward to the birth of children from these happy marriages, who would inherit and preserve not only the morals of their fathers and mothers, but also their goods and lands. . . .

(*Tiers Livre,* trans. Cohen, 419)]

Rabelais goes so far as to excuse the father who may kill his daughter's abductor, and shows sympathy for the feelings of such a father, whose daughter, in his view, might as well be dead.[28] This extreme view would be valid even if the girl were consenting.

Most readers are struck by the extremity of Rabelais's views in this chapter, which appears to stand out from the lighter banter found in much of the *Tiers Livre.*[29] Gargantua's tirade is also surprisingly in favor of the woman, as he describes the love of fathers for their daughters, in contrast to the misogynistic rhetoric found elsewhere in the book.[30] Finally, the last description quoted has Old Testament overtones in its emphasis on lineage and inheritance, going so far as to mention "biens meubles" as well as "meurs."

* * *

If we are to speculate about Marguerite's possible reaction or response to the *Tiers Livre* and to its dedication, this is a chapter with which we might start. It is the most positive toward women of all the chapters in the book, and it treats a matter close to Marguerite's heart: that of marriage, and in particular, how marriage should be entered into, and who should be responsible for arranging and performing marriages. We know that Marguerite herself (as well as her daughter Jeanne) had been married twice, both times in arranged marriages, and that the second (for each woman) was happier than the first.[31] But marriage is not only a theme running through Marguerite's life—it is a major preoccupation of the **Heptaméron,** and concerns story characters as well as storytellers. Marguerite's position on this matter is not so extreme as Rabelais's, but she is obviously concerned with the problem, particularly with that of clandestine marriage, as a woman, a parent, and a writer.

Two tales, "[Tale] 21" and "40," both told by Parlamente, begin by seeming to promote clandestine marriage, but end by showing its failure.[32] Both are based on events occurring in the Rohan family, who made a practice of clandestine marriage.[33] The fact that Marguerite eventually condemns the practice in both cases gives credence to Rothstein's thesis that French society gradually was turning away from its late medieval acceptance of these marriages.[34]

"**Tale 21,**" that of Rolandine, is the first place to look for Marguerite's opinion on clandestine marriage, and, therefore, to ask whether she agreed or disagreed with Rabelais's views on it in the *Tiers Livre*. Like Rabelais, she seems to feel that it is the responsibility of parents or guardians to marry off their children. But her views are somewhat more nuanced than those of Rabelais, particularly when she comes to the discussion by the "devisants." The apportionment of blame is also more complex than in Gargantua's tirade, which targets only the "ravisseur."

From the start of "**Tale 21,**" Rolandine's father is to blame for his daughter's having become a spinster: "*car le pere aymoit tant son argent,* qu'il obloyoit l'advancement de sa fille."[35] [The reason was that Rolandine's father was so fond of his money that he neglected the interests of his daughter.[36]] The father and the girl's mistress are responsible in part for the situation which then develops. At thirty, she meets and becomes friendly with the "bastard de bonne maison," whom she can't marry officially because of his illegitimacy. One might note that his parents are partly to blame for the situation as well, for if he were legitimated, he could inherit and would be from as good a family as hers. Rolandine's "gouvernante" allows her to meet with the "bastard," stressing several times, as an excuse, the lack of responsible action on the part of her father. This theme is repeated by the "bastard" himself, when he suggests that they marry secretly.[37]

When Rolandine agrees to marry the "bastard," she has obviously thought through the pros and cons of the situation, knows her legal rights (she is over twenty-five), and is fairly sure that her father cannot disinherit her (as he could have if she had been younger). Rolandine asks that they not consummate the marriage right away, until her father dies or agrees to it. They exchange rings in church and kiss before God, which makes them husband and wife, according to canon law.

When the queen discovers the marriage, she remonstrates with Rolandine, stressing the shame she has brought on her father as well as on her other relatives. Rolandine responds astutely that her family has not carried out their obligations, and she defends her actions on the grounds of her age, her husband's good family, and the fact that the marriage has not been consummated. The discussion goes on at length, with Rolandine finally referring to the authority of her Father in heaven, who will exonerate her.[38]

Up to this point in the story, the narrator, Parlamente, seems to side with Rolandine and thus to defend clandestine marriage under certain circumstances (especially a marriage which has not been consummated). Her views so far contrast with Rabelais's in that she finds some ground for clandestine marriage, that is, when the father has not fulfilled his obligations. This possibility did not occur to Rabelais, who saw the problem entirely from the point of view of a father, Gargantua. The end of Marguerite's tale takes a curious turn, as the "bastard" goes to Germany and marries a rich woman. He thus technically becomes a bigamist (one of the concerns about clandestine marriage for Calvin and other reformers), and is found out as having been a fortune hunter all along.

After the death of the "bastard," Rolandine's father finally does shoulder his responsibility, finding her a husband who is a distant relative. This marriage, surprisingly, turns out well, and the story ends with an almost biblical flavor, stating that they lived to a ripe old age, inheriting her father's wealth, and raising two children.[39] The marriage seems strikingly similar to the picture of conventional marriage described in chapter 48 of the *Tiers Livre,* seen above. At this point in the story of Rolandine, the narrator has shifted away from the partial defense of clandestine marriage, back to the more usual (for Marguerite as well as for Rabelais) portrayal of the values of family, class, and monarchy.

Parlamente, interestingly, begins the discussion with a sentence which could be viewed as a response to the overall misogyny of the *Tiers Livre*:

> Or, mes dames, je vous prie que les hommes, *qui nous veullent peindre tant inconstantes,* viennent maintenant icy et me monstrent l'exemple d'un aussy bon mari, *que ceste-cy fut bonne femme, et d'une telle foy et persévérance. . . .*
>
> (*Tiers Livre,* ed. François, 174)

[Well, Ladies, let the men, who are so fond of representing us women as lacking in constancy, produce an example of a husband who was as good, as faithful and as constant as the woman in this story.

(*Tiers Livre*, ed. Chilton, 253)]

Rolandine is portrayed as a female example of filial piety, similar to well-known male examples such as Tobit. This discussion then turns away from marriage to an exploration of the differences between men and women in love.

Marguerite has not forgotten the issue of clandestine marriage, however, and takes it up again in **"Tale 40,"** that of Rolandine's aunt, which many commentators have seen as forming a sort of diptych to **"Tale 21."**[40] In this tale, we learn that Rolandine's father had earlier forbidden his sister to marry, again because of his love of money ("par trop aymer son argent"). Like Rolandine, the aunt falls in love with a man beneath her in class and wealth, and marries clandestinely, with only "ung prebstre et quelques femmes" as witnesses.[41] This time Jossebelin (her brother and Rolandine's father) kills the would-be "husband," who was his best "serviteur" and a good friend. Jossebelin obviously would have agreed with Gargantua (in chapter 48 of the *Tiers Livre*) on the equivalence between clandestine marriage and rape, and on the right of male relatives to kill the "ravisseur," if the opportunity presents itself.

During the lengthy discussion after this tale (also told by Parlamente), the narrator comes out even more strongly on the necessity to get permission for marriage from parents or "ceulx à qui on doibt porter obeissance" ["those to whom you owe obedience"].[42] In addition, Oisille stresses the lesson in this exemplum, for young girls: "cest exemple est suffisant pour leur donner plus de reverence à leurs parens, que de s'adresser à se marier à leur volunté." [Parlamente's example would be enough to make them show more respect for their parents and relatives than to take it into their heads to make marriages of their own choosing.][43] In case there was any doubt, the reader is given a strong defense of arranged marriage (despite contrary opinions expressed by some of the men in the group, such as Dagoucin). Parlamente concludes by explaining the need to follow the decision of parents, whose role parallels the wills of God and of Nature:

Il me semble, dist Parlamente, que l'une ne l'autre n'est louable, mais que les personnes qui se submectent à la volunté de Dieu ne regardent ny à la gloire, ni à l'avarice, ny à la volupté, *mais par une amour vertueuse et du consentement des parens,* desirent de vivre en l'estat de mariage, comme Dieu et Nature l'ordonnent.

(*L'Heptaméron,* ed. François, 280)

[In my opinion, said Parlamente, neither of these kinds of marriages is praiseworthy. If people submit to the will of God, they are concerned neither with glory, greed, nor sensual enjoyment, but wish only to live in the state of matrimony as God and Nature ordain.

(*L'Heptaméron,* trans. Chilton, 374)]

The tale ends with a sort of hymn to "legitimate" marriage by the married couples and particularly the men who are present.[44] God and Nature are now seen to be on the side of "legitimate" marriage, not on that of clandestine marriage, as canon law might have suggested earlier.

* * *

Although Rabelais and Marguerite de Navarre differ on many issues, and particularly in their attitudes toward and value for women, still there are some questions on which they are in surprising agreement. The issue of clandestine marriage appears to be one of these. As evangelical sympathizers, both Rabelais and Marguerite are opposed to the role of monks in clandestine marriage (see also Marguerite's **"Tale 56"**), and both writers participate in the rehabilitation of legitimate marriage typical of humanists and reformers. Both appear to be familiar with the book of Tobit: they echo its championing of filial piety, its praise for the role of fathers in arranging marriage, and its representation of domestic animals as emblems of fidelity and family unity.

As we explore the importance of the dedication to the *Tiers Livre* from Marguerite's point of view, we may examine her feminism as well as her evangelical leanings. Generally, the two work together to create a sort of spiritual feminism. Rabelais may be referring to this tendency of Marguerite's in the dedication. The issue of clandestine versus arranged marriage creates a conflict within this spiritual feminism, which should by rights champion the "Father in heaven" at the expense of the earthly father, and the "marriage made in heaven" over that put together by family and friends.

Marguerite's common sense, and her own personal experience, pull her back from espousing the position we might expect her to take here. In this way she may respond to Rabelais's invitation to come down from "les cieulx, ton origine." In writing the *Heptaméron,* she does at times move close to "le bon Pantagruel" and to his father, Gargantua, as well as to the tail-wagging of their faithful dog, Kyne. The question of clandestine marriage forces Marguerite to make a choice between a spiritual, other-worldly definition of marriage as belonging only to God, and a quite this-worldly, practical concern for class, family, and inheritance. Surprisingly, in almost every case, she chooses the latter.

Perhaps it is no accident that, in the "Epistre" quoted earlier, she recognizes the approach of her husband by the arrival of the humble but stubborn mule, which was the emblem of the physical side of marriage in the book of Tobit. She promises to rejoice at her husband's return: "Autant *aura de joye et de plaisir* / A vous revoir . . . ,"[45] in words that echo Rabelais's invitation to "*les faictz joyeux* du bon Pantagruel" [the jovial deeds of the good Pantagruel], and which remind us of the welcome by the dog in the book of Tobit, who "shewed his joy by fawning and wagging his tail."

Although Rabelais and Marguerite generally are seen to differ in their emphases on the lower versus the upper body and on physicality versus spirituality, when discussing the topic of marriage they reach consensus on the necessity for involvement of the entire person, as well as his or her family, friends, furniture, and domestic animals. Marriage seems to represent the union of the physical with the spiritual, and thus, for Marguerite, it borders on being itself an exemplum of the mystical union between humans and God.[46] While Rabelais does not go so far, his anger at the idea of clandestine marriage shows his desire to see spiritual and worldly authorities work together.

At my first reading of the dedication, it seemed that the poem pointed to differences between the two writers, and perhaps it did before the composition of the **Heptaméron,** when Marguerite was mostly known for her spiritual poetry. By writing the **Heptaméron,** however, Marguerite does, at least in some tales, appear to respond positively to Rabelais, and even to move closer to him. On the other hand, Rabelais's exploration in the *Tiers Livre* of the philosophical aspects of the decision about whether to marry shows that, for him too, marriage is not just a question of convenience and practicality. By dedicating his book to Marguerite, he does more than make a simple bow to courtesy. He may also be acknowledging an intellectual and spiritual affinity with her while admitting their shared adherence to reformist views on clandestine marriage.

Notes

1. François Rabelais, *Oeuvres Complètes,* ed. Pierre Jourda (Paris: Garnier, 1962), 391. Emphasis mine, as will be the case throughout this study, unless otherwise indicated.

2. François Rabelais, *The Histories of Gargantua and Pantagruel,* trans. J. M. Cohen (Hammondsworth: Penguin, 1955), *Third Book,* 280.

3. See Mikhail Bakhtin, *Rabelais and His World,* trans. Hélène Iswolsky (1968; repr., Bloomington: Indiana University Press, 1984). Abel Lefranc believed that the *Tiers Livre* was published in January or February of 1546, although the "Privilège" dates from September 1545; see *Oeuvres de François Rabelais,* ed. Abel Lefranc (Paris: Champion, 1931), vol. 5, *Le tiers livre,* xvi.

4. See Lefranc, *Le tiers livre,* xxi, and M. A. Screech, *Rabelais* (Ithaca: Cornell University Press, 1979), 211.

5. Jean Céard comments, "Cette dédicace, qui n'a pas pu être écrite et publiée sans son consentement, prouve que la reine soutient ouvertement Rabelais"; see *Le Tiers Livre,* ed. Jean Céard (Paris: Livre de Poche, 1995), 4 n. 1.

6. See Marguerite de Navarre, *L'Heptaméron,* ed. Renja Salminen (Geneva: Droz, 1999), xxxiv.

7. See Emile Telle, *L'Oeuvre de Marguerite d'Angoulême, Reine de Navarre et la Querelle des Femmes* (Toulouse: Lion et Fils, 1937).

8. See Pierre Jourda, *Marguerite d'Angoulême . . . Etude biographique et littéraire,* 2 vols. (1930; repr., Geneva: Slatkine, 1978), 1:303. Elizabeth Chesney-Zegura notes: "In his *Discours de la Court,* published in 1543, Claude Chappuys listed Rabelais among the Masters of the King's Requests, an honorary title accorded to scholars and poets in the monarch's entourage"; Elizabeth Chesney-Zegura and Marcel Tetel, *Rabelais Revisited* (New York: Twayne, 1993), 20.

9. The *Third Book* (1546) obviously was published before the *Heptaméron* (1558), but the dedication would indicate that Rabelais was quite familiar with Marguerite's works, some still in manuscript form, such as the "novellas"; Marcel Tetel, *Marguerite de Navarre's* Heptaméron: *Themes, Language and Structure* (Durham, N.C.: Duke University Press, 1973), 106 n. 7.

10. Robert D. Cottrell, *The Grammar of Silence: A Reading of Marguerite de Navarre's Poetry* (Washington, D.C.: Catholic University of America Press, 1986), 136.

11. "More work needs to be done to uncover the relation between the question of women addressed in this book (*Tiers Livre*) and Marguerite's own problematizing of gender relations"; Carla Freccero, *Father Figures: Genealogy and Narrative Structure in Rabelais* (Ithaca: Cornell University Press, 1991), 150 n. 22.

12. Edwin M. Duval, *The Design of Rabelais's* Tiers Livre de Pantagruel (Geneva: Droz, 1997), 130-31.

13. Giovanni Boccaccio, *Le Decameron de Messire Jehan Bocace Florentin,* nouvellement traduict d'Italien en Francoys par Maistre Anthoine Le Macon . . . (Paris: Estienne Rosset, 1545), sig. A2.

14. See recent work on women, books, and gifts, such as Cynthia J. Brown, *Poets, Patrons, and Printers: Crisis of Authority in Late Medieval France*

(Ithaca: Cornell University Press, 1995). Marian Rothstein has suggested how hard it is to document women readers in sixteenth-century France, since "they have disappointingly left no traces of their response"; Marian Rothstein, *Reading in the Renaissance: Amadis de Gaule and the Lessons of Memory* (Newark: University of Delaware Press, 1999), 115. See also Natalie Zemon Davis, *The Gift in Sixteenth-Century France* (Madison: University of Wisconsin Press, 2000).

15. See *Les Marguerites de la Marguerite des princesses,* and *Suyte des Marguerites, texte de l'édition de 1547,* ed. Félix Frank (Paris: Librairie des Bibliophiles, 1873); Abel Lefranc, "Les plus anciennes mentions du 'Pantagruel' et du 'Gargantua,'" *Revue des Etudes Rabelaisiennes* 3 (1905), and Marcel De Grève, "L'Interprétation de Rabelais au XVIe siècle," *Etudes Rabelaisiennes* 3: *L'interprétation de Rabelais au XVIe siècle* (Geneva: Droz, 1961).

16. *Les Marguerites,* ed. Frank, 248 (n. to 237.1.14), stated in 1873, "Allusion à un endroit de Rabelais, passé en proverbe. . . . Marguerite veut dire que la vue des mulets du roi de Navarre lui annonça l'arrivée de celui-ci, comme la vue du chien de Gargantua avertit Pantagruel de l'arrivée de son père." Lefranc, ed., *Tiers Livre,* n. 9 to dedication, picked up this theme in 1931, stating that the "Epistre" contains "une mention de Pantagruel, qui est vraisemblablement un souvenir du ch. xxxv du Tiers Livre." De Grève, "L'Interprétation de Rabelais," 62-63, agreed: "Marguerite de Navarre a lu *Pantagruel,* et elle s'est plu à cette lecture. Une allusion au chien de Gargantua, dans une épître à son mari malade, qui semble devoir être datée de 1546, montre que le livre de Rabelais leur était familier."

17. *Tiers Livre,* ed. Jourda, 550. The word "kyne" (1.2) is actually just the word for "dog," in Greek, as Lefranc (among others) notes. Marguerite's poem also contains a reference to standing up in order to greet the king: "Si je seray preste de me lever / Pour vous aller, où que soyez, trouver" [So I will be ready to stand up / To go to find you, wherever you are]; *Les Marguerites,* ed. Frank, 237.

18. See Céard's statement that this is the only pet dog in the entire Bible; *Tiers Livre,* ed. Céard, 332 n. 5. See also several biblical scholars on the frequently negative image of dogs in the Old Testament: Charles Cutler Torrey, *The Apocryphal Literature: A Brief Introduction* (New Haven: Yale University Press, 1945), 84, comments on the surprise with which the dog would have been greeted by most early readers: "This last clause is heard with a certain shock, for it is opposed to the uni-

form Hebrew tradition, which excludes the dog from good society . . ."; see also Bruce M. Metzger, *An Introduction to the Apocrypha* (New York: Oxford University Press, 1957), 37: "[T]he Jews generally regarded dogs as useless and unclean beasts."

19. *Bibliorum Sacrorum iuxta Vulgatam Clementinam,* ed. Aloisius Gramatica (Mediolani: R. Ghirlanda, 1922), Tob. 11:9.

20. Holy Bible, trans. from the Latin Vulgate, based on the Douay (1609) and Rheims (1582) English translations (Baltimore, Md.: John Murphy, 1914), Tob. 11:9.

21. I am indebted to M. A. Screech for much of this information: in his *Rabelaisian Marriage* (London: Arnold, 1958); in his edition of the Tiers Livre (Geneva: Droz, 1964); and in his *Rabelais.* For example, in Screech's edition of the *Tiers Livre,* he comments at 243, note to chap. 35, line 25: "Or, l'exemplum de Thobie, qui est rappelé au lecteur par la présence de ce chien, évoquait deux choses pour les gens de l'époque: la fidélité canine, et, surtout chez les évangéliques, la plus importante autorité biblique s'opposant aux mariages clandestins." More recently, Marian Rothstein has devoted attention to the issue of clandestine marriage and in particular to the increasingly negative attitude of French society toward it, from the 1540s to the 1560s; Marian Rothstein "Clandestine Marriage and *Amadis de Gaule*: The Text, the World, and the Reader," *Sixteenth Century Journal* 25 (1994): 873-86.

Earlier sources on this topic include Telle, *L'Oeuvre de Marguerite,* "La Question des Mariages 'Clandestins,'" chap. 9B, pp. 344-54. See also A. Esmein, *Le Mariage en Droit Canonique,* vol. 2 (1891; repr., New York: Burt Franklin, 1968). Esmein shows that the major issue dividing Catholics from Protestants in the sixteenth century was the question of whether marriage was a sacrament (122ff.). Catholics, especially during the Council of Trent, believed that it was a sacrament, whereas Protestants like Calvin maintained that it was not. See *L'Institution de la Religion Chrestienne* (1541), ed. Jean-Daniel Benoit (Paris: Vrin, 1961), bk. 4, chap. 19.

22. The fact that Marguerite refers to the mule, in the "Epistre" quoted above, may be a reference to the presence of that animal in the book of Tobit.

23. See Telle, *L'Oeuvre de Marguerite,* "Marguerite de Navarre et la Réhabilitation du Mariage par le Mouvement Réformiste," chap. 9A, pp. 313-43.

The Counter-Reformation would later rehabilitate marriage ideology for Catholics, however. See Charlene Villasenor Black, "Love and Marriage in the Spanish Empire: Depictions of Holy Matrimony and Gender Discourses in the Seventeenth Century," *Sixteenth Century Journal* 32 (2001): 637-67.

24. Several commentators have noticed the contrast between Panurge's agonized self-questioning in the *Tiers Livre* about whether to marry at all, and the simplicity of Pantagruel's acceptance of his father's decision on the matter. Screech, *Rabelais,* 281, sees this as showing the importance of family ties to Rabelais.

25. Screech, *Rabelais,* 282.

26. In the 1964 edition of the *Tiers Livre,* Screech commented: "Rabelais va s'attaquer au scandale des mariages clandestins. Ses hardiesses dans ce chapitre dépassent de loin celles d'Erasme et de Vives. Il semble, sur ce point, faire cause commune avec les luthériens et autres évangéliques schismatiques"; 318 n. to line 24. Donald Frame also pointed out that Rabelais's opposition to clandestine marriage was stronger than that of Erasmus, and closer to that of Luther, "favoring imperial over canon law"; Donald A. Frame, *François Rabelais: A Study* (New York: Harcourt Brace Jovanovich, 1977), 61.

27. Much has been written on this chapter, including Jean Plattard, "L'Invective de Gargantua contre les mariages contractés 'sans le sceu et adveu' des parents," *Revue du Seizième Siècle,* 14 (1927): 381-88.

28. *Tiers Livre,* "car homme vertueux on monde n'est qui naturellement et par raison plus ne soit en son sens perturbé, oyant les nouvelles du rapt, diffame et deshonneur de sa fille, que de sa mort" (*Tiers Livre,* ed. Jourda, 600) [For there is no virtuous man in the world who would not, naturally and reasonably, be more perturbed by the news of his daughter's rape, shame, and dishonour than by her death (*Tiers Livre,* trans. Cohen, 420)].

29. Max Gauna, for example, comments on the lack of irony, authorial ambivalence, humor, or jokes, in chap. 48; idem, *The Rabelaisian Mythologies* (Teaneck, N.Y.: Fairleigh Dickinson University Press, 1996), 190-91.

30. See *Tiers Livre,* ed. Screech, 322 n. to line 94: "Notez les sentiments nettement philogamiques de ce passage."

31. At the time of composition of the early tales of the *Heptaméron,* Jeanne was recently divorced, and Marguerite was involved in negotiations to arrange a second marriage for her daughter; *L'Heptaméron,* ed. Salminen, xxxvi. See also Laurent Ripart, "Les Mariages de Marguerite," in

Marguerite de Navarre: 1492-1992: Actes du Colloque international de Pau (1992), ed. Nicole Cazauran and James Dauphiné (Mont-de-Marsan: Editions Interuniversitaires, 1995).

32. According to *L'Heptaméron,* ed. Salminen, 111, these two tales were part of the original group written in 1545-46, while Marguerite stayed in Paris at the court of her brother. They can be found in MS-C, a copy of the "première rédaction," and the two tales are found next to each other, there. Also viewable on a Bibliothèque nationale de France website; see http://gallica.bnf.fr/scripts/ConsultationTout.exe?O=28121& T=0 (accessed 1 May 2003).

33. See Telle, *L'Oeuvre de Marguerite,* 351: "Cest à croire que de tels mariages étaient une tradition de famille chez les Rohan."

34. See Rothstein, "Clandestine Marriage." It is interesting to compare Marguerite's treatment of clandestine marriage with that of her earlier model, Boccaccio, who was much more favorable to it. See Mihoko Suzuki, "Gender, Power, and the Female Reader: Boccaccio's *Decameron* and Marguerite de Navarre's *Heptaméron,*" *Comparative Literature Studies* 30 (1993): 231-52. Day 2, story no. 3 of the *Decameron* illustrates this difference.

35. Marguerite de Navarre, *L'Heptaméron,* ed. Michel François (Paris: Garnier, 1967), 158.

36. Marguerite de Navarre, *The Heptameron,* trans. Paul A. Chilton (Hammondsworth: Penguin, 1984), 236.

37. *L'Heptaméron,* ed. François, 159; "Vous voyez, d'autre part, quel pere vous avez, qui ne pense, en quelque façon que ce soit, de vous marier. Il a tant refusé de bons partiz, que je n'en sçache plus, ny près ny loing de luy, qui soit pour vous avoir" (ibid., 161) [What is more, you know what your father is like, and that nothing could be farther from his thoughts than arranging for you to marry. He has turned down so many good matches that I can think of no one, however far and wide he looked, whom he would accept as your husband (*Heptameron,* trans. Chilton, 239)].

38. "Je sçay qu'en vous espousant, je n'offenseroye poinct Dieu, mais je faictz ce qu'il commande" (*L'Heptaméron,* ed. François, 162) [I know that in marrying you, I would be doing no offence to God but would be carrying out His commands (*Heptameron,* trans. Chilton, 240)].

39. *L'Heptaméron,* ed. François, 174.

40. See John Lyons, *Exemplum: The Rhetoric of Example in Early Modern France and Italy* (Princeton, N.J.: Princeton University Press,

1989), chap. 2, "The *Heptaméron* and Unlearning from Example," and especially "Rolandine and Her Aunt," pp. 93-103.

41. *L'Heptaméron,* ed. Frank, 275.

42. *L'Heptaméron,* ed. Frank, 275; trans. Chilton, 370-71. *L'Heptaméron,* ed. Salminen, 752, comments that Marguerite may have been thinking of conversations with her daughter on the subject of marriage around the time that she composed this tale.

43. *L'Heptaméron,* ed. Frank, 277; trans. Chilon, 371.

44. "Hircan, Geburon, Simontault et Saffredent jurerent qu'ilz s'estoient mariez en pareille intention et que jamais ilz ne s'en estoient repentiz . . ." (*L'Heptaméron,* ed. François, 280) [Hircan, Geburon, Simontault, and Saffredent affirmed that they had all been married in this way, and swore that they had never regretted it (*Heptameron,* trans. Chilton, 374)].

45. *Les Marguerites,* ed. Frank, 237.

46. Telle, *L'Oeuvre de Marguerite,* 337: "Dans ses effusions mystiques, elle fait souvent usage du symbole, employé aussi par Luther, qui compare l'union de l'âme avec Dieu à un marriage."

Todd W. Reeser (essay date winter 2004)

SOURCE: Reeser, Todd W. "Fracturing the Male Androgyne in the *Heptaméron*." *Romance Quarterly* 51, no. 1 (winter 2004): 15-28.

[*In the following essay, Reeser argues that the* Heptaméron *"represents a move away from a relationship reminiscent of a Neoplatonic male-male androgyne toward heterosexuality."*]

It is well known among Renaissance scholars that Ficinian Neoplatonism factors into the intertextual fabric of Marguerite de Navarre's **Heptaméron** (1558), particularly through the storyteller Dagoucin. But whereas Ficino is generally interested in ideal love, the **Heptaméron** as a whole focuses more on the obstacles to ideal love between men and women.[1] Few are the examples of a lover finding perfect love. Robert Bernard, for example, argues that "we find in the **Heptaméron** an accurate account of the demise of the Platonic ideal and in its place not only an apology for marriage but also a witty and malicious parody of Platonic love" (4). Philippe de Lajarte discusses "le dagoucinisme" as "un ficinisme laïcisé, paganisé, qui élimine toute transendance et réduit la mystique surnaturelle de Ficin à un système de valeurs purement immanent" (364).[2]

Almost every critical discussion of Neoplatonism deals with relations between the sexes. Strikingly, however, some of the most classic representations of Neoplatonic

physical and psychological union in the **Heptaméron** portray two men. *"Nouvelle 47"* begins: "Auprès du pays du Perche, y avoit deux gentilzhommes" (376), who as childhood friends, "avoient vescu en si grande et parfaicte amytié que ce n'estoit que ung cueur, une maison, ung lict, une table et une bourse" (376). They lived in this "parfaicte amytié" for many years "sans que jamais il y eust entre eulx une seulle volunté ne parolle où l'on peust veoir difference de personnes, tant que, non seulement ilz vivoient comme deux freres, mais comme ung homme tout seul" (376). Similarly, the opening of *"Nouvelle 12,"* better known as the Lorenzaccio story, introduces two intimate male friends—"ung duc de la maison de Medeci" (110) and "un gentilhome que le duc aymoit comme luy mesmes" (110). The duke gives him the same authority as he has such that "sa parolle estoit obeye et craincte comme celle du duc." In addition, "n'y avoit secret en sa maison ny en son cueur qu'il ne declairast à ce gentilhomme, en sorte que l'on le pouvoit nommer le second luy mesmes" (110). During one of their later conversations, the *gentilhomme* tells him: "Vous pouvez parler à moy comme à vostre ame" (111).

Yet by the end of both of those *nouvelles,* each relationship is clearly split in two, as if Plato's original male-male androgyne had been spliced.[3] In *"Nouvelle 47,"* after a jealousy crisis on the part of one friend, the other friend concludes: "j'ay tousjours pensé qu'il n'y eust entre vostre cueur et le myen ung seul moyen ny obstacle. Mais, à mon tresgand regret [. . .] je veoy le contraire" (378). He concludes his speech with an image not of union but of separation: friend A suspects friend B of sleeping with his wife. It is this suspicion that, he says to his former friend, "vous a separé de mon amytié" (379). In the final lines of the *nouvelle,* the separation is carried out in the passive voice, as if by some divine agent: "Et furent avecq leurs cueurs autant separez qu'ilz avoient esté unyz" (379). In the Lorenzaccio story, a similar fracture takes place. The duke wants to sleep with the *gentilhomme*'s sister, but the *gentilhomme* refuses. The duke cries out in his anger: "Or bien, bien, puis que je ne treuve en vous nulle amytié, je sçay que j'ay affaire" (112). Suddenly, the *cueur,* the previous locus of corporeal unity between the two men, becomes his own as the duke asks for something considered so cruel "que son cueur ne son honneur ne se povoient accorder à luy faire ce service" (112). In the end, the *gentilhomme* kills the duke and leaves Italy for Turkey, the friendship so destroyed that it is not even mentioned in the conclusion of the *nouvelle.*

On one level, what appears to be an impossibility of male-male "parfayte amytié" in the two tales might be one aspect of Marguerite's view of Neoplatonic near impossibility, which would simply be gender blind. This type of relationship is rarely found between two men or between a man and a woman, and its absence is indicative of human beings' fallen, imperfect state (see Tetel 10-11). Yet the reason for the impossibility is the same in both of these cases: Misplaced heterosexual desire disrupts and in the end destroys both *parfaytes amytiés*. As a result of what appears to be a pattern, I will argue, at certain points in the text, the **Heptaméron** represents a move away from a relationship reminiscent of a Neoplatonic male-male androgyne toward heterosexuality. Masculine oneness must be fractured to make room for, or to create, heterosexuality in the text. This heterosexuality is, however, rarely an idealized replacement for the broken Neoplatonic bond, nor does it take its place without a certain sense of loss for what once was. But though imperfect, heterosexuality can and does exist when all is said and done. I am not claiming that any homoerotics inherent or suggested in these relationships must be disbanded or read out, but that male-male intimacy—be it homosocial or homoerotic—must be pushed out and that the process of so doing must be explicitly represented.[4] A Renaissance brand of heterosexuality—as one of the bases of the **Heptaméron** project that is taken for granted—thus is "invented" out of a relationship to which it is juxtaposed. My use of the term *heterosexuality* thus should not suggest its modern opposite *homosexuality*. In my reading, heterosexuality and intimate male-male *amytié* are orthogonal to each other—in this context taking the place of a heterosexual/homosexual binary opposition that subtends modernism (see *Epistemology*). Although often considered an anachronistic term, *heterosexuality* will designate sexual desire for, and the sexual act with, members of the opposite sex. It also will be distinguished from marriage, though not considered necessarily antithetical to it.

Although I am suggesting that heterosexuality must be invented in the **Heptaméron,** it may be more accurate to say that it is reinvented in certain *nouvelles* after an original invention in the prologue. The opening of the work establishes the narrative's assumption of reproductive heterosexuality so that the **Heptaméron** can explore issues of gender and gender relations (Reeser). But even if a type of heterosexuality is created in the prologue, it remains an unstable fabrication and must be reaffirmed, reinvented, and reified in the *nouvelles* themselves so as to attempt to stabilize itself.[5] In part, this reaffirmation maintains the focus of the work as not *une affaire entre hommes,* as in Rabelais, for example, but as about love and desire between the two sexes. For male and female voices to be heard in equal amounts and for marriage to become the undisputed ideal form of union between two human beings, the importance accorded to male-male intimacy in Renaissance culture (most famously represented in Montaigne's "De l'amitié") must be discounted and a counter-discourse of separation established.

This reinvention of heterosexuality might also be necessary in the face of Renaissance Neoplatonism and a cultural anxiety about Platonic sexuality. Although the homoeroticism of Plato's oeuvre often was read out or recast in heterosexual terms, it was too well known to be simply denied (see Kraye). As a devout Christian, Marguerite may have wanted to insure that no homoerotic intention be attributed to the Neoplatonic elements of the work. Although Ficino's *Commentary on Plato's Symposium on Love* (*De Amore*) explicitly discounts Platonic homosexuality and pederasty as "against the order of nature" (54), it still considers chaste male-male love the prime genre of love.[6] Like Castiglione, Leone Ebreo, and others in Italy, Marguerite goes a step further than Ficino and presents Neoplatonic love as a heterosexual *fait accompli* as she pulls male-male intimacy apart. Unlike the Italians, however, Marguerite illustrates the process of movement from male-male to male-female love, positioning herself within the strand of Renaissance humanism that must "set Plato straight."

In the discussion that follows, I will examine the specific ways in which *nouvelles* "**47**" and "**12**" display this reinvention. I will then read "**Nouvelle 63**" as a contrasting case to the two stories, for in it, the possibility of privileging male-male intimacy over male-female love is rejected before it can take place. Unlike *nouvelles* "**47**" and "**12**," in which things go awry for the men involved, "**Nouvelle 63**" ends happily, in large part because the heterosexuality portrayed in it is considered the dominant type of relationship. It is as if the lesson has been learned in the two earlier *nouvelles* that male-male intimacy does not last, and the later story responds to and corrects the earlier ones.

The three *nouvelles* are connected not only by their subject matter but also by the fact that Dagoucin recounts them. The prologue already allegorized the fracturing of his own relationship with Saffredent. Presented at first as inseparable (they repeatedly are referred to only as "les gentilzhommes"), as the text moves along, the two men increasingly are individualized both linguistically and ideologically, as if to put Dagoucin through the split he will later recount to his fellow storytellers. As the archetype of the courtier and a naive Neoplatonist, Dagoucin has a major investment in a certain purity of male/female relations, thus in the necessity of fracturing a male-male union. His proclamation after the end of "**Nouvelle 8,**" in which he defines ideal love and which Simontault considers Platonic (57-58), unquestionably refers only to love between men and women because in his theoretical framework, perfect love only can be heterosexual. In fact, in other tales Dagoucin tells love between man and woman is not impossible. "**Nouvelle 37**" concludes with the couple living "en si grande et bonne amityé que mesmes les faultes passées, par le bien qui en estoit venu, leur estoient augmentation de contantement" (326). For Dagoucin, only ideal love between men must be destroyed.

HETEROSEXUALITY IMAGINED

"*Nouvelle* 47" makes it clear that marriage has no effect on the two male friends' intimacy. The terse sentence following the opening "ung cueur, une maison, ung lict, une table et une bourse" paragraph at first might suggest rupture: "L'un des deux se maria" (376). But it does not matter which of the two men married, for: "Toutesfoiz, pour cella ne laissa il à continuer sa bonne amytié et de tousjours vivre avecques son compaignon, comme il avoit acoustumé" (376). Nothing has changed—as the ambiguity of the pronoun referents indicates—and it might be assumed that the two men still share "ung lict." Indeed, when they find themselves "en quelque logis estroict," the husband has his best friend sleep with his wife and himself, even if "il est vray qu'il estoit au milieu" (376). They continue their material unity as well: "Leurs bien estoient tousjours en commun, en sorte que le marriage, ne cas qui peust advenir, ne sceut empescher ceste parfaicte amytié" (376).[7] Strikingly, the *nouvelle* up until this point is devoid not only of rupture, but of representations of sexual desire of any type.

This happy stasis cannot last because jealousy brings change with it: "Mais, au bout de quelque temps, la felicité de ce monde, qui avecques soy porte une mutabilité, ne peut durer en la maison qui estoit trop heureuse" (376). Instead of marriage, jealousy causes the separation, as the husband "oubliant la seuretté qu'il avoit à son amy, sans nulle occasion, print ung tresgrant souspeson de luy et de sa femme" (376-37). This imagined desire is the moment when heterosexuality is mentioned first in the text. The inevitability of the jealousy is reinforced by its proclaimed naturalness. Despite his anger, the best friend tells the husband: "Je sçay bien que la jalousie est une passion aussi veritable comme l'amour" (377), and in their second confrontation scene, the friend becomes angry and tells him: "Si vous estes jaloux, mon compaignon, ce n'est que chose naturelle" (378). With jealousy as the disruptive force, the end of male-male intimacy and imagined heterosexuality also become coded as "chose naturelle."

From the moment of the jealousy, all discussions about the suspected affair take place between the husband and wife. It is his wife "à laquelle il ne le peut dissimuler" (377) and with whom "luy en tint quelques fascheux propoz" (377). When the best friend attempts to find out if this is all true—having been informed of it by the wife—"luy dist ce qu'il avoit entendu, le priant de ne luy en celler la verité, car il ne vouldroit, en cella ny en autre chose, luy donner occasion de romper l'amytié

qu'ilz avoient si long temps entretenue" (377). Still, the husband lies to the friend, telling him that all is fine, but then, predictably, "le gentilhomme marié rentra en son souspeson plus que jamais" (378). Again he lies to his friend and tells the truth to his wife. The husband also orders his wife not to speak to the friend: "luy deffendoit la parolle, si ce n'estoit en grande compaignye" (377). But he in effect cuts off *parolle*—and the intimacy it implies—with his friend as well, for unlike in the opening paragraph, no longer do they have "entre eulx une seulle volunté ne parolle où l'on peust veoir difference de personnes" (376). Two scenes between the men follow when the friend tries to get the husband to admit his jealousy (a "passion aussi veritable comme l'amour"), but the husband will not engage in honest *parolle,* continuing to express his *parolle* only to his wife. The best friend, however, figures out that jealousy has reared its ugly head "par la parolle d'elle et par quelques contenances qu'il voyoit faire à son compaignon" (377). In this tale, truth, then, can only circulate between man and woman—whether married or not—and honest male-female verbal exchange is closely tied to the end of male-male *amytié.*

Although the opening of the *nouvelle* focuses on male-male intimacy, its conclusion has more to do with the consummation of heterosexuality. The final spoken line of the story consists of the friend's curse: "Et dorénavant gardez vous de moy, car, puis que le souspeçon vous a separé de mon amytié, le dépit me separera de la vostre" (379). In the final lines of the tale, the best friend does in fact sleep with the husband's wife. The friends' physical and psychological split accompanies the sexual act and appears indistinguishable from it:

> [son compaignon] retira sa part de ses meubles et biens, qui étaient tous en commun. Et furent avec leurs coeurs aussi séparés qu'ils avaient été unis, en sorte que le gentilhomme qui n'était point marié ne cessa jamais qu'il n'eût fait son compagnon cocu comme il lui avait promis.
>
> (379)

As the second and final step in the separation process (and in the narrative), the imagined heterosexuality in the form of jealous *souspeson* is replaced with the heterosexual act itself, functioning as the final nail in the coffin of the *amytié.* Imagined heterosexuality leads to—and even produces—its reality. This new state is in no way as ideal as the original relationship; in fact, it has undertones of a kind of fallen state where ideal love no longer exists.

In addition to the conclusion of the *nouvelle,* the ensuing discussion among the *devisants* assumes heterosexuality, implying its successful reinvention. Before the tale, Dagoucin had introduced his story as about male-male *amytié*: "vous diray que ce qui plus facilement rompt une bonne amytié, Mesdames, c'est quant la seureté de l'amytié commance à donner lieu au souspeson" (376). Suspicion can destroy "beaucoup de bonnes amytiez" and "rendre les amys ennemys" (376), he warns. The discussion after the tale, however, centers largely on the relation between the husband and wife and the question of whether the wife acted appropriately. Dagoucin himself immediately comments:

> Ainsi en puisse il prandre, Mesdames, à tous ceulx qui à tort souspesonnent mal de leurs femmes, car plusieurs sont cause de les faire telles qu'ilz les souspeçonnent, pource que une femme de bien est plustost vaincue par ung desespoir que par tous les plaisirs du monde.
>
> (379)

Those who say that "le souspeson est amour" are wrong, Dagoucin adds, as jealousy destroys love. His commentary is odd because love in marriage was never the focus or even the implication of the story. The wife was never "vaincue par ung desespoir," and she literally does not figure in the text in the description of the cuckoldry: "le gentilhomme qui n'était point marié" is the agent and "son compagnon" the receiver of the action (379). Although Hircan alone makes a commentary on male-male friendships, he positions male-male and female-male relationships on an equal footing: "Je ne pense point [. . .] qu'il soit ung plus grant desplaisir à homme ou à femme que d'estre souspesonné du contraire de la verité" (379). A short debate subsequently takes place between three of the *devisantes* over whether the wife acted virtuously. Oisille's view claims a woman should not "se venger du souspeson de son mary à la honte d'elle mesmes" and that instead she ought to "ne parler jamais à luy, pour monstrer à son mary le tort qu'il avoit de la souspeçonner" (379). Ennasuite, on the other hand, believes that "si beaucoup de femmes faisoient ainsi, leurs mariz ne seroient pas si umbrageux qu'ilz sont" (380). Longarine adds that, in any event, "la pascience rend en fin la femme victorieuse et la chasteté louable" (380), and there puts an end to the debate as the commentary transitions into the next tale. Like the story itself, the interpretation of the *nouvelle* has shifted its focus from *entre hommes* to *entre homme et femme,* foreclosing other interpretive possibilities. How the masculine friendship is read becomes as integral to the gendered transition as what actually transpires in the tale.

TYRANNICAL HETEROSEXUALITY

In **"*Nouvelle* 12"** tyranny plays a central role in the end of male-male intimacy.[8] This time, heterosexual desire is not first imagined. The duke's desire for the *gentilhomme*'s sister creates the rupture as the latter must decide between family and friendship. In the end, he chooses what he says is family honor and decides to kill the "tyrant": "Print conclusion de ce differend, qu'il

aymoit myeulx mourir que de faire ung sy meschant tour à sa seur [. . .] mais que plustost debvoit delivrer sa patrye d'un tel tyran, qui par force vouloit mectre une telle tache en sa maison" (112). The duke can be assumed to have performed other "tyrannical" acts as well, for the *gentilhomme* "congnoissant la cruaulté de son maistre, eut crainte" (112). As this story indicates, tyranny and friendship often were related topics in the period. As Eric MacPhail states in his study of friendship as a political ideal in Montaigne and La Boétie, "[tyrants] have no equals and thus no friends" (179).[9] La Boétie, for instance, writes that the tyrant "estant au dessus de tous et n'aiant point de compaignon, il est desja au delà des bornes de l'amitié" (74).[10] In this case, the duke is not "desja au delà des bornes de l'amitié." Rather the *nouvelle* represents his move from inside to outside these "bornes" as a result of destructive heterosexual desire. On one level, the problem is one of sovereignty: the *duc* and the *gentilhomme a priori* simply cannot be equals and thus cannot be true friends. But on another level, tyranny was considered to fracture metaphorically the original male-male androgyne of the *Symposium*. As Ficino explains in his reading of the Platonic split, "pride was clearly the cause of the soul, which was born whole [. . .] being split [. . .] and it is seized by the senses and lust as though by police and a tyrant" (76). The tyranny here is the imagined sexual act that leads to the necessity of murder.

The way the *gentilhomme* carries out the murder of the tyrant re-evokes the harmony the two men once had, representing the murder as the very moment of rupture. The *gentilhomme* invites the duke into a bedroom, luring him with the thought that his sister is waiting for him: "Le gentilhomme le despoilla de sa robbe de nuyct et le mist dedans le lict" (113). He then invites one of his men to accompany him into the bedroom: "Auroys tu bien le cueur de me suyvre en ung lieu où je me veulx venger du plus grant enemy que je aye en ce monde?" (113). The two of them enter the room, and the duke is surprised to see them. As the murder attempt begins, the defenseless duke bites the *gentilhomme*'s finger and attempts to defend himself as best he can. The *gentilhomme* calls his *serviteur,* who "trouvant le duc et son maistre sy liez ensemble qu'il ne sçavoit lequel choisir, les tira tous deux par les piedz au milieu de la place" (114). This moment, when the two men are indistinguishable "dedans le lict," with the duke "tout en chemise," harkens back to the opening of the *nouvelle,* where the *gentilhomme* was a second self of the duke. Yet here, that moment of oneness is evoked to allegorize its destruction. The two men put the duke back in bed and finish him off "fermans le rideau, s'en alla, enfermant ce corps mort en la chambre" (114). The separation is completed when the *gentilhomme* leaves for Turkey.

The commentary on the *nouvelle* "engendra diverses oppinions" (116), which are split along gender lines.[11] The women "disoient qu'il estoit bon frere et vertueulx citoyen, les hommes, au contraire, qu'il estoit traistre et meschant serviteur" (116). The two-part epilogue describing the reactions and results of the murder within the *nouvelle* (115-16) already set up the possibility of the two interpretations that split the *devisants*. The first description (115) highlights the sadness of those who loved the duke, such as "la pouvre duchesse fut en grant peine." The *serviteurs* find "le pouvre corps endormy, en son lict, du dormir sans fin," and the narrator adds, "Vous pouvez penser quel dueil menerent ces pouvres serviteurs qui emporterent le corps en son palais" (115). Their mourning in the story corresponds to the desire of the male storytellers who would maintain friendship in its masculine configuration in the face of its textual demise (especially in this case, where it is beneficial in terms of class). For them, the real crime of the tale is the end of this kind of relationship. Like the "pouvres serviteurs," the voice of the male *devisant* regrets and mourns the loss of the institution of male-male intimacy in the tale, leaving a certain ambiguity as to the "justice" of the textual move away from male-male intimacy and perhaps even implying its criminality.[12]

The second interpretation—that of the *devisantes*—highlights the virtue of the *gentilhomme* and corresponds to the end of the tale, when marriage takes center stage and represents a rebirth from the wreckage of the murder and the mourning of the duke's subjects. It is first proved that the *gentilhomme*'s sister knew nothing of the assassination: "jamais sa pouvre seur n'en avoit ouy parler, laquelle, combien qu'elle feust estonnée du cas advenu, sy esse qu'elle en ayma davantaige son frere, qui n'avoit pas espargné le hazard de sa vye pour la delivrer d'un sy cruel prince enemy" (116). She thus continues her "vye honneste et ses vertuz, tellement que, combien qu'elle feust pouvre, pour ce que toute leur maison fut confisquée, sy trouverent sa seur et elle des mariz autant honnestes homes et riches qu'il y en eust poinct en Italie" (116). The two sisters' rise in class stature becomes the reward, their own as well as their brother's, for his assumed good deed. The sisters' upward move also parallels the earlier presumed rise in class stature of the *gentilhomme* when he became the close friend of the duke. The women each find *un homme riche*, much as the *gentilhomme* established his relationship with the more noble duke. The similarities between the relationships of the *duc/gentilhomme* and the sisters/*honnestes hommes et riches* implies, then, that male-male friendship has been replaced with male-female marriage. The tyranny of "pride" and "lust" that Ficino condemns gives way to what he calls "the natural light" that "shines forth and searches out the order of natural things" or "true love" (77), but in this case "true love" must be contained in marriage. Bernard's

"demise of the Platonic ideal" in favor of "an apology for marriage" (4) rings true here, although the "ideal" in question is a strictly masculine one.

In addition to this explicit establishment of heterosexuality through marriage, the ending of the *nouvelle* implies that "un sy cruel prince ennemy" has been killed to "delivrer sa patrye d'un tyrant" and that justice has been served. On one level, justice in the state leads to the justice of the sisters who marry, become rich, and live "en bonne et grande reputacion" (116)—the events that close the tale. Yet in the Neoplatonic framework, justice is also linked to heterosexuality. When he comments on the split hermaphrodite in Plato in *De Amore* 4: 2, Ficino follows Plato's "three sexes" (male, female, and mixed), but he assigns each "sex" one virtue, the virtue of the male-male courage, of the female-female temperance, and of the "mixed" sex "justice" (77). Justice is incarnated by the true hermaphrodite, the being that becomes the heterosexual couple after Jupiter splits the three sexes. The marriages of the "mixed" sexes at the end of the *nouvelle* imply justice, and justice implies the marriages.

Like the end of the story, the contentious commentary among the storytellers moves away from a focus on the men to efface the original male-male intimacy. As the debate over the crime becomes a bit too heated for his taste, Dagoucin changes the subject, warning the women present not to commit such a "murder": "Pour Dieu, Mesdames, ne prenez poinct querelle d'une chose desja passée, mais gardez que voz beaultez ne facent poinct de plus cruel meudre que celluy que j'ay compté" (117). The dangers of male-male friendship are transformed into those of heterosexual love, with the woman in the role of the murderer and the man in the role of the murdered. The lengthy discussion that follows appropriates the motifs and themes of the relationship between the two men of the *nouvelle,* recasting them in heterosexual terms. In particular, Dagoucin argues that "celluy qui ayme parfaictement craindroit plus de blesser l'honneur de sa dame que elle mesmes" (117), an ideal that could have been applied to the duke if "sa dame" were substituted with "son amy."

MASCULINITY RECAST

If Dagoucin recounts the destruction of male-male intimacy in the two tales I have examined, in **"Nouvelle 63"** he presents a "ung seigneur beau et honneste" (454), who privileges a heterosexual relationship while at the same time maintaining a relationship with a man. This husband already has made the appropriate choices about male-male friendship and heterosexuality, and the unreliability of male-male friendship presented in the two earlier tales has been taken to heart whereas the stability of male-female relationships in marriage is taken for granted. Unlike the *gentilhomme* of **"Nouvelle**

12," the main character successfully juggles a relationship with a political superior (in this case the king) and his wife. In fact, many of the details of the tale are reminiscent of the previous tales, as if to contrast the tales directly. The man of **"Nouvelle 63"** is invited to join a group of four men who will meet four women "de si grande beaulté et jeunesse et frescheur qu'elles avoient la presse de tous les amoureux" (454). Because the king offers him the invitation and he wants to appear to be a loyal subject, he feels an obligation to attend the banquet, so he "l'accepta de bon visaige, combien que en son cueur il n'en eust eu nulle voullunté" (454-55). The reasons given for his lack of *voullunté* evoke a kind of Platonic harmony not with the king but with his wife and his lover:

> Car, d'ung costé, il avoit une femme qui luy portoit de beaux enfans, dont il se contentoit tresfort: vivoient en telle paix que pour riens il n'euse voullu qu'elle eust prins mauvais soupson de luy. D'aultre part, estoit serviteur de l'une des plus belles dames qui fust de son temps en France, laquelle il aymoit et estimoit tant que toutes les aultres luy sembloient laides au pris d'elle, en sorte que, au commencement de sa jeunesse et avant qu'il fust marié, n'estoit possible luy faire veoir ne hanter autres femmes, quelque beaulté qu'elles eussent; et prenoit plus de plaisir à veoir s'amye et de l'aymer parfaictement que de tout ce qu'il eust sceu avoir d'ung aultre.
>
> (455)

The two women (his "femme" and his "dame") together hold the same place that the childhood best friend in **"Nouvelle 47"** held before the rupture caused by the *souspeson*. The man and his wife have a harmony ("paix") between them, and the issue of "mauvais soupson" is here explicitly discounted from the beginning. In addition, the man's desire for intimacy with his "dame" has lasted for many years ("au commencement de sa jeunesse et avant qu'il fust marié"). In short, whereas **"Nouvelle 47"** began as an ideal relationship and disintegrated because of dissimulation, the man's two combined relationships are the real example of "perfect friendship" ("aymer parfaictement"), one that will remain unchanged throughout the story. The honesty of husband and wife is a key element of the story: the man returns home one day to tell his wife about the king's plan for him to meet another woman, but instead of hiding truth or "parolle," "[c]e seigneur icy s'en vint à sa femme et luy dist en secret l'entreprise que son maistre faisoit" (455). Finally, the man finds a solution to the problem of simultaneously fulfilling the king's wishes and doing what he wants. He explains to his wife: "J'ay tousjours ouy dire que le saige a le voiaige ou une malladie sur la manche, pour s'en ayder à sa necessité. Parquoy, j'ay deliberé de faindre, quatre ou cinq jours devant, d'estre bien fort mallade: à quoy vostre contenance me pourra bien fort servir" (455). Whereas

the man of **"Nouvelle 47"** was possessed and controlled by the "maladie" of jealousy (377, 378)—an emotion he repeatedly hid from his friend—this husband plans to feign a disease to successfully dissimulate and maintain the peace of his relationship with the king. As a result of the feigned sickness, the king is duped: "et fust le roy fort marry d'entendre, par la femme, la malladie de son mary" (456). The "contenance" of the wife here aids in this act, unlike that of the wife of **"Nouvelle 47."** The husband believed her facial expressions betrayed him because she seduced the best friend with them (as he ordered "qu'elle ne luy fist plus le visaige qu'elle luy faisoit" [378]). The same images previously used to separate man and wife are used here to affirm their harmony.

Although it shares many of the details of **"Nouvelle 47,"** **"Nouvelle 63"** follows a plotline more similar to **"Nouvelle 12."** Both main characters are caught between personal desire on the one hand and the desires of an unfair ruler on the other. But here, the protagonist does not have the same interest in masculine intimacy as the *gentilhomme* and so is able to find a way out of the dilemma. Focused on two key aspects of heterosexuality—the "paix" of marriage with his wife and the perfect love of his "dame"—he escapes the precarious situation, and the disasters of the previous tales are avoided when heterosexuality begins as and remains stable. Here, the man is the subject not of the king or his anger, but rather, as cited above, "estoit serviteur de l'une des plus belles dames qui fust de son temps en France." In the end, however, it makes no difference that he was able to avoid the problem in the first place because the king's desire—indicative of the instability of male desire in male-male friendship—changes anyway: "pour quelques affaires qu'ilz vindrent, le roy oublia son plaisir pour regarder à son debvoir, et partit de Paris" (456). He later tells his subject that they were "bien sotz d'estre ainsi partiz soudain, sans avoir veu les quatre filles que l'on nous avoit promis estre les plus belles de mon royaulme" (456). The husband pretends to regret his inability to carry out the adulterous plan as he reminds the king of his "malladie." The tale thus concludes: "A ces parolles ne s'apperceut jamais le roy de la dissimulation de ce jeune seigneur, lequel depuis fut plus aymé de sa femme qu'il n'avoit jamais esté" (456). The man once again successfully employs "parolles" and "dissimulation" in a deceptive way—unlike the man of **"Nouvelle 47"**—to maintain his relationship with the king at the same time as he strengthens the love of his wife. In a larger sense, the choices of the husband are divinely sanctioned as the success is cast in religious terms. The wife calls the ruse "saincte" (455) and on the subject of their dissimulation concludes, "qui peult eviter l'offence de Dieu et le ire du prince est bien heureux" (456).

Conclusion: Interpretive Process

I have argued that *nouvelles* "12" and "47" represent a process within the narratives in which heterosexuality is established. The larger-scale move from *nouvelles* "12" and "47" to "*Nouvelle* 63," however, reveals a process over the course of Dagoucin's tales in which the fracture subsequently is made to seem final, permanent, and normalized. Potentially dangerous situations are avoided when heterosexuality and marriage are placed at the fore. Likewise, the commentary of the storytellers, which leaves some room for a critique of the loss of masculine intimacy, more generally contributes to its disappearance by ignoring the loss. Yet the commentary of the *devisants* in the **Heptaméron** can be seen as parallel to Renaissance exegesis in a larger sense (see Jeanneret). The storytellers interpret the stories in various and contradictory ways much as humanists interpreted the ancients. In this case, the commentaries of the ten characters take an approach to male-male "parfaicte amytié" that is similar to Louis Le Roy's 1582 translation and commentary of the *Symposium*. Although desexualized, male-male intimacy is left intact in his translation of Plato's *Symposium*. As in Ficino, men can seek out their other half in a chaste way.[13] In his commentary on the translation, male-male "love" of any type is erased as Le Roy transposes Plato's emphasis on this type of love to one based on heterosexuality. With ten pages of commentary on the *androgyne*, Le Roy ignores the fact that the male-male (and female-female) being also was split. He focuses instead on how men search out their female *moytié* and on how Plato's allegory should be read as the Fall. During his travels in Egypt, Plato read "Les livres de Moyse, et des Prophetes," Le Roy explains, and so was influenced by them that "Platon n'estoit autre qu'un Moyse, parlant le langage Attique" (451). To make the Fall the center of the Platonic split, of course, is not to allow the possibility of male-male intimacy, as there were not two men in Eden. But to focus on a failed Eden is also to associate heterosexuality with mankind's fallen state—the one in which the world of the **Heptaméron** operates. Like in the first two *nouvelles* of the **Heptaméron**—but unlike in Ficino—Le Roy goes through a process that discounts masculine *amytié* from original text to translation to commentary. Similarly, the **Heptaméron** does not evoke a static image but a process-oriented approach—which takes place on several levels—as if in parallel with this brand of Platonic exegesis.

Notes

1. On Neoplatonism and Marguerite de Navarre, see Bernard; Cottrell 9-10; Festugière 124-28; Gelernt; Lajarte; Lefranc; Martineau; Sage; Schmidt; Sommers; Telle; Tetel. A related issue is the possible influence of Castiglione. See Reynolds.

2. See, also, Tetel, who writes, "The myth of a Platonic Marguerite de Navarre becomes difficult to substantiate even from a reading of all her works" (7). Cottrell argues that Marguerite's "positioning of human love within the arena of sinful flesh is a mark of her profound rejection of Ficinian 'Neoplatonism'" (10).

3. The passage in question is Aristophanes's famous speech in the *Symposium* (Plato 188-94). On the Platonic androgyne/hermaphrodite in Renaissance France, see Freccero; Rothstein; Sommers.

4. One of the reasons I do not treat the question of the relation between this intimacy and homoeroticism is the difficulty of distinguishing "sodomy" and male-male friendship in the Renaissance. On this issue, see Bray's well-known article. For the idea of a continuum between the "homosocial" and the "homoerotic," see Sedgwick's *Between Men*. On the issue of categories of homosexuality in the pre-modern period, see Halperin.

5. For this approach to gender, see Butler.

6. On *pederasty*, see Ficino 163-64 (7: 6). On the Italians and homoerotics more generally, see Kraye.

7. Jerry Nash sees this "parfaicte amityé" as "a parody of Renaissance literary notions on male friendship, on brotherhood [. . .], when it comes to the opposite sex" (147). This mocking of friendship could be considered another technique to fracture male-male intimacy.

8. For historical background on the tale, see Rally; Bromfield 31-36.

9. On the difficulties of cross-class friendship in the Renaissance, see Shannon.

10. Ctd. in MacPhail 179.

11. On the ambiguity of this *nouvelle,* see Tetel 120-21 and 128-29.

12. I am grateful to Christopher Braider for this idea. For a reading of the tale that argues for the criminality of the murder, see Morrison, who writes that "[l]a nouvelle 12 propose donc, à l'arrière-plan, une critique extrêmement discrète du despotisme avec une condamnation plus nette de la trahison, et au premier plan, un conseil de prudence politique" (65). To mourn the loss of male-male intimacy could be a way to produce heterosexuality. For the relation between the birth of heterosexuality and mourning, see Butler 57-65. This mourning also could correspond to the recurrent link between a "poetics of loss" and Renaissance homoerotics. See Guy-Bray.

13. For instance, instead of Plato's men who find their male half and "take pleasure in physical contact with men" (62), Le Roy has these men "prennent plaisir à converser avec eux." On Le Roy's translation techniques, see Lloyd-Jones.

Works Cited

Bernard, Robert W. "Platonism—Myth or Reality in the *Heptaméron?*" *Sixteenth Century Journal* 5.1 (Apr. 1974): 3-14.

Bray, Alan. "Homosexuality and the Signs of Male Friendship in Elizabethan England." *History Workshop: A Journal of Socialist and Feminist Historians* 29 (1990): 1-19.

Bromfield, Joyce G. *De Lorenzino de Médicis à Lorenzaccio: Etude d'un thème historique.* Paris: Marcel Didier, 1972.

Butler, Judith. *Gender Trouble: Feminism and the Subversion of Identity.* New York: Routledge, 1990.

Cottrell, Robert D. "Inmost Cravings: The Logic of Desire in the *Heptameron.*" Lyons and McKinley. 3-24.

Festugière, Jean. *La Philosophie de l'amour de Marsile Ficin et son influence sur la littérature française au XVIe siècle.* Paris: Vrin, 1941.

Ficino, Marsilio. *Commentary on Plato's Symposium on Love.* Trans. and ed. Sears Jayne. Woodstock, CT: Spring Publications, 1985.

Freccero, Carla. "The Other and the Same: The Image of the Hermaphrodite in Rabelais." *Rewriting the Renaissance: The Discourses of Sexual Difference in Early Modern Europe.* Ed. Margaret W. Ferguson, Maureen Quilligan, and Nancy J. Vickers. Chicago: U of Chicago P, 1986. 145-58.

Gelernt, Jules. *World of Many Loves: The* Heptameron *of Marguerite de Navare.* Chapel Hill: U of North Carolina P, 1966.

Guy-Bray, Stephen. *Homoerotic Space: The Poetics of Loss in Renaissance Literature.* Toronto: U of Toronto P, 2002.

Halperin, David M. *How to Do the History of Homosexuality.* Chicago: U of Chicago P, 2002.

Jeanneret, Michel. "Renaissance Exegesis." *The Cambridge History of Literary Criticism.* Vol. 3: The Renaissance. Ed. Glyn P. Norton. Cambridge: Cambridge UP, 1999. 36-43.

Kraye, Jill. "The Transformation of Platonic Love in the Italian Renaissance." *Platonism and the English Imagination.* Ed. Anna Baldwin and Sarah Hutton. Cambridge: Cambridge UP, 1994. 76-85.

La Boëtie, Estienne de. *De la servitude volontaire ou contr'un.* Ed. Malcolm Smith. Geneva: Droz, 1987.

Lajarte, Philippe de. "*L'Heptaméron* et le ficinisme: Rapports d'un texte et d'une idéologie." *Revue des sciences humaines* 37.147 (July-Sept. 1972): 339-71.

Lefranc, Abel. "Marguerite de Navarre et le platonisme de la Renaissance." *Grands Ecrivains de la Renaissance.* Paris: Champion, 1914. 139-249.

Le Roy, Louis dit Regius, ed. and trans. *Le Timee de Platon.* Paris, 1582.

Lloyd-Jones, Kenneth. "'*Cest exercice de traduire . . .*': Humanist Hermeneutic in Louis Le Roy's Translations of Plato." *Recapturing the Renaissance: New Perspectives on Humanism, Dialogue and Texts.* Ed. Diane S. Wood and Paul A. Miller. Knoxville: New Paradigm P, 1996. 85-106.

Lyons, John D., and Mary B. McKinley, ed. *Critical Tales: New Studies of the* Heptameron *and Early Modern Culture.* Philadelphia: U of Pennsylvania P, 1993.

MacPhail, Eric. "Friendship as a Political Ideal in Montaigne's *Essais.*" *Montaigne Studies* 1 (1989): 177-87.

Marguerite de Navarre. *Heptaméron.* Ed. Renja Salminen. Geneva: Droz, 1999.

Martineau, Christine. "Le Platonisme de Marguerite de Navarre?" *Réforme, Humanisme, Renaissance* 2.4 (1976): 12-35.

Morrison, Ian R. "La nouvelle 12 de l'*Heptaméron* de Marguerite de Navarre." *Studia Neophilologica* 67 (1995): 61-66.

Nash, Jerry C. "The Male Butt of Comic Infidelity: Men Outwitting Men in Marguerite de Navarre's *Heptaméron.*" *Heroic Virtue, Comic Infidelity: Reassessing Marguerite de Navarre's* Heptaméron. Ed. Dora E. Polachek. Amherst: Hestia Press, 1993. 142-54.

Plato. *Lysis, Symposium, Gorgias.* Trans. W. R. M. Lamb. Cambridge: Harvard UP, 1925.

Rally, Alexandre. "Commentaire de la XIIe nouvelle de l'*Heptaméron.*" *Revue du seizième siècle* 11 (1924): 208-21.

Reeser, Todd W. "The Assumption and Reorganization of Sex in the Prologue to the *Heptaméron.*" *Women in French Studies* 10 (2002): 60-76.

Reynolds, Régine. "*L'Heptaméron* de Marguerite de Navarre: Influence de Castiglione." *Studi di Letteratura Francese* 5.154 (1979): 25-39.

Rothstein, Marian. "Mutations of the Androgyne: Its Functions in Early Modern French Literature." *The Sixteenth Century Journal* 34.2 (2003): 409-37.

Sage, Pierre. "Le Platonisme de Marguerite de Navarre." *Travaux de linguistique et de littérature* 7.2 (1969): 65-82.

Schmidt, Albert-Marie. "Traducteurs français de Platon (1536-1550)." *Etudes sur le XVIe siècle.* Paris: Albin Michel, 1967. 17-44.

Sedgwick, Eve Kosofsky. *Between Men: English Literature and Male Homosocial Desire.* New York: Columbia UP, 1985.

———. *The Epistemology of the Closet.* Berkeley: U of California P, 1990.

Shannon, Laurie J. "Monarchs, Minions, and 'Soveraigne' Friendship." *The South Atlantic Quarterly* 97.1 (winter 1998): 91-112.

Sommers, Paula. "Writing the Body: Androgynous Strategies in the *Heptameron*." Lyons and McKinley. 232-40.

Telle, Emile. *L'Oeuvre de Marguerite d'Angoulême, Reine de Navarre, et la querelle des femmes.* Toulouse: Imprimerie Toulousaine, 1937. 253-98.

Tetel, Marcel. *Marguerite de Navarre's* Heptameron: *Themes, Language, and Structure.* Durham: Duke UP, 1973.

FURTHER READING

Criticism

Baker, Mary J. "Shame in the *Heptaméron*." In *Medievalia et Humanistica: Studies in Medieval and Renaissance Culture,* edited by Paul Maurice Clogan, pp. 53-65. Lanham, Md.: Rowman & Littlefield Publishers, Inc., 1996.
    Chronicles the revelation and concealment of shameful acts in the *Heptaméron.*

LaGuardia, David. "The Voice of the Patriarch in the *Heptaméron* I: 10." *Neophilologus* 81, no. 4 (October 1997): 501-13.

Treats the discourse of female sexual desire and male dominance in "Novella 10."

Pensom, Roger. "Form and Meaning in the Eighteenth Nouvelle of Marguerite de Navarre's *Heptaméron*." *Orbis Litterarum* 47, no. 6 (1992): 288-302.
    Illustrates the linguistic complexity of "Novella 18."

Richards, Sylvie L. F. "The Burning Bed: Infidelity and the Virtuous Woman in *Heptaméron* XXXVII." *Romance Notes* 34, no. 3 (spring 1994): 307-15.
    Views Marguerite's portrayal of obedience and fidelity in "Novella 37" as an exploration of female subservience.

Sewall, Shelley. "The God of Love and the Love of God in a *Heptaméron* Tale." *Romance Notes* 36, no. 1 (fall 1995): 47-54.
    Explores the relationship between divine and earthly love in the *Heptaméron.*

Thysell, Carol. "Gendered Virtue, Vernacular Theology, and the Nature of Authority in the *Heptaméron*." *Sixteenth Century Journal* 29, no. 1 (spring 1998): 39-53.
    Elucidates the social debates held by the *devisants* in the *Heptaméron.*

Virtue, Nancy. "*Le Sainct Esperit . . . parlast par sa bouche*: Marguerite de Navarre's Evangelical Revision of the *Chastelaine de Vergi.*" *Sixteenth Century Journal* 28, no. 3 (fall 1997): 811-24.
    Questions the influence of Marguerite's evangelical beliefs on the spiritual revisionism of "Novella 70."

Additional coverage of Marguerite's life and career is contained in the following sources published by Thomson Gale: *Literature Criticism from 1400-1800,* Vol. 61; *Literature Resource Center*; and *Reference Guide to World Literature,* Ed. 2.

How to Use This Index

The main references

> **Calvino, Italo**
> 1923-1985 .... CLC 5, 8, 11, 22, 33, 39,
> 73; SSC 3, 48

list all author entries in the following Gale Literary Criticism series:

AAL = *Asian American Literature*
BG = *The Beat Generation: A Gale Critical Companion*
BLC = *Black Literature Criticism*
BLCS = *Black Literature Criticism Supplement*
CLC = *Contemporary Literary Criticism*
CLR = *Children's Literature Review*
CMLC = *Classical and Medieval Literature Criticism*
DC = *Drama Criticism*
HLC = *Hispanic Literature Criticism*
HLCS = *Hispanic Literature Criticism Supplement*
HR = *Harlem Renaissance: A Gale Critical Companion*
LC = *Literature Criticism from 1400 to 1800*
NCLC = *Nineteenth-Century Literature Criticism*
NNAL = *Native North American Literature*
PC = *Poetry Criticism*
SSC = *Short Story Criticism*
TCLC = *Twentieth-Century Literary Criticism*
WLC = *World Literature Criticism, 1500 to the Present*
WLCS = *World Literature Criticism Supplement*

The cross-references

> See also CA 85-88, 116; CANR 23, 61;
> DAM NOV; DLB 196; EW 13; MTCW 1, 2;
> RGSF 2; RGWL 2; SFW 4; SSFS 12

list all author entries in the following Gale biographical and literary sources:

AAYA = *Authors & Artists for Young Adults*
AFAW = *African American Writers*
AFW = *African Writers*
AITN = *Authors in the News*
AMW = *American Writers*
AMWR = *American Writers Retrospective Supplement*
AMWS = *American Writers Supplement*
ANW = *American Nature Writers*
AW = *Ancient Writers*
BEST = *Bestsellers*
BPFB = *Beacham's Encyclopedia of Popular Fiction: Biography and Resources*
BRW = *British Writers*
BRWS = *British Writers Supplement*
BW = *Black Writers*
BYA = *Beacham's Guide to Literature for Young Adults*
CA = *Contemporary Authors*
CAAS = *Contemporary Authors Autobiography Series*
CABS = *Contemporary Authors Bibliographical Series*
CAD = *Contemporary American Dramatists*
CANR = *Contemporary Authors New Revision Series*
CAP = *Contemporary Authors Permanent Series*
CBD = *Contemporary British Dramatists*
CCA = *Contemporary Canadian Authors*
CD = *Contemporary Dramatists*
CDALB = *Concise Dictionary of American Literary Biography*
CDALBS = *Concise Dictionary of American Literary Biography Supplement*
CDBLB = *Concise Dictionary of British Literary Biography*

CMW = *St. James Guide to Crime & Mystery Writers*
CN = *Contemporary Novelists*
CP = *Contemporary Poets*
CPW = *Contemporary Popular Writers*
CSW = *Contemporary Southern Writers*
CWD = *Contemporary Women Dramatists*
CWP = *Contemporary Women Poets*
CWRI = *St. James Guide to Children's Writers*
CWW = *Contemporary World Writers*
DA = *DISCovering Authors*
DA3 = *DISCovering Authors 3.0*
DAB = *DISCovering Authors: British Edition*
DAC = *DISCovering Authors: Canadian Edition*
DAM = *DISCovering Authors: Modules*
    DRAM: *Dramatists Module;* **MST:** *Most-studied Authors Module;*
    MULT: *Multicultural Authors Module;* **NOV:** *Novelists Module;*
    POET: *Poets Module;* **POP:** *Popular Fiction and Genre Authors Module*
DFS = *Drama for Students*
DLB = *Dictionary of Literary Biography*
DLBD = *Dictionary of Literary Biography Documentary Series*
DLBY = *Dictionary of Literary Biography Yearbook*
DNFS = *Literature of Developing Nations for Students*
EFS = *Epics for Students*
EXPN = *Exploring Novels*
EXPP = *Exploring Poetry*
EXPS = *Exploring Short Stories*
EW = *European Writers*
FANT = *St. James Guide to Fantasy Writers*
FW = *Feminist Writers*
GFL = *Guide to French Literature,* Beginnings to 1789, 1798 to the Present
GLL = *Gay and Lesbian Literature*
HGG = *St. James Guide to Horror, Ghost & Gothic Writers*
HW = *Hispanic Writers*
IDFW = *International Dictionary of Films and Filmmakers: Writers and Production Artists*
IDTP = *International Dictionary of Theatre: Playwrights*
LAIT = *Literature and Its Times*
LAW = *Latin American Writers*
JRDA = *Junior DISCovering Authors*
MAICYA = *Major Authors and Illustrators for Children and Young Adults*
MAICYAS = *Major Authors and Illustrators for Children and Young Adults Supplement*
MAWW = *Modern American Women Writers*
MJW = *Modern Japanese Writers*
MTCW = *Major 20th-Century Writers*
NCFS = *Nonfiction Classics for Students*
NFS = *Novels for Students*
PAB = *Poets: American and British*
PFS = *Poetry for Students*
RGAL = *Reference Guide to American Literature*
RGEL = *Reference Guide to English Literature*
RGSF = *Reference Guide to Short Fiction*
RGWL = *Reference Guide to World Literature*
RHW = *Twentieth-Century Romance and Historical Writers*
SAAS = *Something about the Author Autobiography Series*
SATA = *Something about the Author*
SFW = *St. James Guide to Science Fiction Writers*
SSFS = *Short Stories for Students*
TCWW = *Twentieth-Century Western Writers*
WLIT = *World Literature and Its Times*
WP = *World Poets*
YABC = *Yesterday's Authors of Books for Children*
YAW = *St. James Guide to Young Adult Writers*

Literary Criticism Series
Cumulative Author Index

al-Hariri, al-Qasim ibn 'Ali Abu Muhammad al-Basri
1054-1122 .... **CMLC 63**
See also RGWL 3

Ali, Ahmed 1908-1998 .... **CLC 69**
See also CA 25-28R; CANR 15, 34; EWL 3

Ali, Tariq 1943- .... **CLC 173**
See also CA 25-28R; CANR 10, 99

Alighieri, Dante
See Dante

Allan, John B.
See Westlake, Donald E(dwin)

Allan, Sidney
See Hartmann, Sadakichi

Allan, Sydney
See Hartmann, Sadakichi

Allard, Janet .... **CLC 59**

Allen, Edward 1948- .... **CLC 59**

Allen, Fred 1894-1956 .... **TCLC 87**

Allen, Paula Gunn 1939- .... **CLC 84, 202; NNAL**
See also AMWS 4; CA 112; 143; CANR 63, 130; CWP; DA3; DAM MULT; DLB 175; FW; MTCW 1; RGAL 4

Allen, Roland
See Ayckbourn, Alan

Allen, Sarah A.
See Hopkins, Pauline Elizabeth

Allen, Sidney H.
See Hartmann, Sadakichi

Allen, Woody 1935- .... **CLC 16, 52, 195**
See also AAYA 10, 51; CA 33-36R; CANR 27, 38, 63, 128; DAM POP; DLB 44; MTCW 1

Allende, Isabel 1942- ... **CLC 39, 57, 97, 170; HLC 1; SSC 65; WLCS**
See also AAYA 18; CA 125; 130; CANR 51, 74, 129; CDWLB 3; CLR 99; CWW 2; DA3; DAM MULT, NOV; DLB 145; DNFS 1; EWL 3; FW; HW 1, 2; INT CA-130; LAIT 5; LAWS 1; LMFS 2; MTCW 1, 2; NCFS 1; NFS 6, 18; RGSF 2; RGWL 3; SSFS 11, 16; WLIT 1

Alleyn, Ellen
See Rossetti, Christina (Georgina)

Alleyne, Carla D. .... **CLC 65**

Allingham, Margery (Louise)
1904-1966 .... **CLC 19**
See also CA 5-8R; 25-28R; CANR 4, 58; CMW 4; DLB 77; MSW; MTCW 1, 2

Allingham, William 1824-1889 ...... **NCLC 25**
See also DLB 35; RGEL 2

Allison, Dorothy E. 1949- .... **CLC 78, 153**
See also AAYA 53; CA 140; CANR 66, 107; CSW; DA3; FW; MTCW 1; NFS 11; RGAL 4

Alloula, Malek .... **CLC 65**

Allston, Washington 1779-1843 .... **NCLC 2**
See also DLB 1, 235

Almedingen, E. M. .... **CLC 12**
See Almedingen, Martha Edith von
See also SATA 3

Almedingen, Martha Edith von 1898-1971
See Almedingen, E. M.
See also CA 1-4R; CANR 1

Almodovar, Pedro 1949(?)- .... **CLC 114; HLCS 1**
See also CA 133; CANR 72; HW 2

Almqvist, Carl Jonas Love
1793-1866 .... **NCLC 42**

al-Mutanabbi, Ahmad ibn al-Husayn Abu al-Tayyib al-Jufi al-Kindi
915-965 .... **CMLC 66**
See also RGWL 3

Alonso, Damaso 1898-1990 .... **CLC 14**
See also CA 110; 131; 130; CANR 72; DLB 108; EWL 3; HW 1, 2

Alov
See Gogol, Nikolai (Vasilyevich)

al'Sadaawi, Nawal
See El Saadawi, Nawal
See also FW

Al Siddik
See Rolfe, Frederick (William Serafino Austin Lewis Mary)
See also GLL 1; RGEL 2

Alta 1942- .... **CLC 19**
See also CA 57-60

Alter, Robert B(ernard) 1935- .... **CLC 34**
See also CA 49-52; CANR 1, 47, 100

Alther, Lisa 1944- .... **CLC 7, 41**
See also BPFB 1; CA 65-68; CAAS 30; CANR 12, 30, 51; CN 7; CSW; GLL 2; MTCW 1

Althusser, L.
See Althusser, Louis

Althusser, Louis 1918-1990 .... **CLC 106**
See also CA 131; 132; CANR 102; DLB 242

Altman, Robert 1925- .... **CLC 16, 116**
See also CA 73-76; CANR 43

Alurista .... **HLCS 1**
See Urista (Heredia), Alberto (Baltazar)
See also DLB 82; LLW 1

Alvarez, A(lfred) 1929- .... **CLC 5, 13**
See also CA 1-4R; CANR 3, 33, 63, 101, 134; CN 7; CP 7; DLB 14, 40

Alvarez, Alejandro Rodriguez 1903-1965
See Casona, Alejandro
See also CA 131; 93-96; HW 1

Alvarez, Julia 1950- .... **CLC 93; HLCS 1**
See also AAYA 25; AMWS 7; CA 147; CANR 69, 101, 133; DA3; DLB 282; LATS 1:2; LLW 1; MTCW 1; NFS 5, 9; SATA 129; WLIT 1

Alvaro, Corrado 1896-1956 .... **TCLC 60**
See also CA 163; DLB 264; EWL 3

Amado, Jorge 1912-2001 ... **CLC 13, 40, 106; HLC 1**
See also CA 77-80; 201; CANR 35, 74; CWW 2; DAM MULT, NOV; DLB 113, 307; EWL 3; HW 2; LAW; LAWS 1; MTCW 1, 2; RGWL 2, 3; TWA; WLIT 1

Ambler, Eric 1909-1998 .... **CLC 4, 6, 9**
See also BRWS 4; CA 9-12R; 171; CANR 7, 38, 74; CMW 4; CN 7; DLB 77; MSW; MTCW 1, 2; TEA

Ambrose, Stephen E(dward)
1936-2002 .... **CLC 145**
See also AAYA 44; CA 1-4R; 209; CANR 3, 43, 57, 83, 105; NCFS 2; SATA 40, 138

Amichai, Yehuda 1924-2000 .. **CLC 9, 22, 57, 116; PC 38**
See also CA 85-88; 189; CANR 46, 60, 99, 132; CWW 2; EWL 3; MTCW 1

Amichai, Yehudah
See Amichai, Yehuda

Amiel, Henri Frederic 1821-1881 .... **NCLC 4**
See also DLB 217

Amis, Kingsley (William)
1922-1995 ...... **CLC 1, 2, 3, 5, 8, 13, 40, 44, 129**
See also AITN 2; BPFB 1; BRWS 2; CA 9-12R; 150; CANR 8, 28, 54; CDBLB 1945-1960; CN 7; CP 7; DA; DA3; DAB; DAC; DAM MST, NOV; DLB 15, 27, 100, 139; DLBY 1996; EWL 3; HGG; INT CANR-8; MTCW 1, 2; RGEL 2; RGSF 2; SFW 4

Amis, Martin (Louis) 1949- .... **CLC 4, 9, 38, 62, 101**
See also BEST 90:3; BRWS 4; CA 65-68; CANR 8, 27, 54, 73, 95, 132; CN 7; DA3; DLB 14, 194; EWL 3; INT CANR-27; MTCW 1

Ammianus Marcellinus c. 330-c. 395 .... **CMLC 60**
See also AW 2; DLB 211

Ammons, A(rchie) R(andolph)
1926-2001 ...... **CLC 2, 3, 5, 8, 9, 25, 57, 108; PC 16**
See also AITN 1; AMWS 7; CA 9-12R; 193; CANR 6, 36, 51, 73, 107; CP 7; CSW; DAM POET; DLB 5, 165; EWL 3; MTCW 1, 2; PFS 19; RGAL 4

Amo, Tauraatua i
See Adams, Henry (Brooks)

Amory, Thomas 1691(?)-1788 .... **LC 48**
See also DLB 39

Anand, Mulk Raj 1905-2004 ...... **CLC 23, 93**
See also CA 65-68; CANR 32, 64; CN 7; DAM NOV; EWL 3; MTCW 1, 2; RGSF 2

Anatol
See Schnitzler, Arthur

Anaximander c. 611B.C.-c. 546B.C. .... **CMLC 22**

Anaya, Rudolfo A(lfonso) 1937- ...... **CLC 23, 148; HLC 1**
See also AAYA 20; BYA 13; CA 45-48; CAAS 4; CANR 1, 32, 51, 124; CN 7; DAM MULT, NOV; DLB 82, 206, 278; HW 1; LAIT 4; LLW 1; MTCW 1, 2; NFS 12; RGAL 4; RGSF 2; WLIT 1

Andersen, Hans Christian
1805-1875 .... **NCLC 7, 79; SSC 6, 56; WLC**
See also AAYA 57; CLR 6; DA; DA3; DAB; DAC; DAM MST, POP; EW 6; MAICYA 1, 2; RGSF 2; RGWL 2, 3; SATA 100; TWA; WCH; YABC 1

Andersen, C. Farley
See Mencken, H(enry) L(ouis); Nathan, George Jean

Anderson, Jessica (Margaret) Queale
1916- .... **CLC 37**
See also CA 9-12R; CANR 4, 62; CN 7

Anderson, Jon (Victor) 1940- .... **CLC 9**
See also CA 25-28R; CANR 20; DAM POET

Anderson, Lindsay (Gordon)
1923-1994 .... **CLC 20**
See also CA 125; 128; 146; CANR 77

Anderson, Maxwell 1888-1959 .... **TCLC 2, 144**
See also CA 105; 152; DAM DRAM; DFS 16, 20; DLB 7, 228; MTCW 2; RGAL 4

Anderson, Poul (William)
1926-2001 .... **CLC 15**
See also AAYA 5, 34; BPFB 1; BYA 6, 8, 9; CA 1-4R; 181; 199; CAAE 181; CAAS 2; CANR 2, 15, 34, 64, 110; CLR 58; DLB 8; FANT; INT CANR-15; MTCW 1, 2; SATA 90; SATA-Brief 39; SATA-Essay 106; SCFW 2; SFW 4; SUFW 1, 2

Anderson, Robert (Woodruff)
1917- .... **CLC 23**
See also AITN 1; CA 21-24R; CANR 32; DAM DRAM; DLB 7; LAIT 5

Anderson, Roberta Joan
See Mitchell, Joni

Anderson, Sherwood 1876-1941 .. **SSC 1, 46; TCLC 1, 10, 24, 123; WLC**
See also AAYA 30; AMW; AMWC 2; BPFB 1; CA 104; 121; CANR 61; CDALB 1917-1929; DA; DA3; DAB; DAC; DAM MST, NOV; DLB 4, 9, 86; DLBD 1; EWL 3; EXPS; GLL 2; MTCW 1, 2; NFS 4; RGAL 4; RGSF 2; SSFS 4, 10, 11; TUS

Andier, Pierre
See Desnos, Robert

Andouard
See Giraudoux, Jean(-Hippolyte)

Baraka, Amiri 1934- .... **BLC 1; CLC 1, 2, 3, 5, 10, 14, 33, 115; DC 6; PC 4; WLCS**
See Jones, LeRoi
See also AFAW 1, 2; AMWS 2; BW 2, 3; CA 21-24R; CABS 3; CAD; CANR 27, 38, 61, 133; CD 5; CDALB 1941-1968; CP 7; CPW; DA; DA3; DAC; DAM MST, MULT, POET, POP; DFS 3, 11, 16; DLB 5, 7, 16, 38; DLBD 8; EWL 3; MTCW 1, 2; PFS 9; RGAL 4; TUS; WP

Baratynsky, Evgenii Abramovich 1800-1844 .... **NCLC 103**
See also DLB 205

Barbauld, Anna Laetitia 1743-1825 .... **NCLC 50**
See also DLB 107, 109, 142, 158; RGEL 2

Barbellion, W. N. P. .... **TCLC 24**
See Cummings, Bruce F(rederick)

Barber, Benjamin R. 1939- .... **CLC 141**
See also CA 29-32R; CANR 12, 32, 64, 119

Barbera, Jack (Vincent) 1945- .... **CLC 44**
See also CA 110; CANR 45

Barbey d'Aurevilly, Jules-Amedee 1808-1889 .... **NCLC 1; SSC 17**
See also DLB 119; GFL 1789 to the Present

Barbour, John c. 1316-1395 .... **CMLC 33**
See also DLB 146

Barbusse, Henri 1873-1935 .... **TCLC 5**
See also CA 105; 154; DLB 65; EWL 3; RGWL 2, 3

Barclay, Alexander c. 1475-1552 .... **LC 109**
See also DLB 132

Barclay, Bill
See Moorcock, Michael (John)

Barclay, William Ewert
See Moorcock, Michael (John)

Barea, Arturo 1897-1957 .... **TCLC 14**
See also CA 111; 201

Barfoot, Joan 1946- .... **CLC 18**
See also CA 105

Barham, Richard Harris 1788-1845 .... **NCLC 77**
See also DLB 159

Baring, Maurice 1874-1945 .... **TCLC 8**
See also CA 105; 168; DLB 34; HGG

Baring-Gould, Sabine 1834-1924 ... **TCLC 88**
See also DLB 156, 190

Barker, Clive 1952- .... **CLC 52, 205; SSC 53**
See also AAYA 10, 54; BEST 90:3; BPFB 1; CA 121; 129; CANR 71, 111, 133; CPW; DA3; DAM POP; DLB 261; HGG; INT CA-129; MTCW 1, 2; SUFW 2

Barker, George Granville 1913-1991 .... **CLC 8, 48**
See also CA 9-12R; 135; CANR 7, 38; DAM POET; DLB 20; EWL 3; MTCW 1

Barker, Harley Granville
See Granville-Barker, Harley
See also DLB 10

Barker, Howard 1946- .... **CLC 37**
See also CA 102; CBD; CD 5; DLB 13, 233

Barker, Jane 1652-1732 .... **LC 42, 82**
See also DLB 39, 131

Barker, Pat(ricia) 1943- ...... **CLC 32, 94, 146**
See also BRWS 4; CA 117; 122; CANR 50, 101; CN 7; DLB 271; INT CA-122

Barlach, Ernst (Heinrich) 1870-1938 .... **TCLC 84**
See also CA 178; DLB 56, 118; EWL 3

Barlow, Joel 1754-1812 .... **NCLC 23**
See also AMWS 2; DLB 37; RGAL 4

Barnard, Mary (Ethel) 1909- .... **CLC 48**
See also CA 21-22; CAP 2

Barnes, Djuna 1892-1982 .... **CLC 3, 4, 8, 11, 29, 127; SSC 3**
See Steptoe, Lydia
See also AMWS 3; CA 9-12R; 107; CAD; CANR 16, 55; CWD; DLB 4, 9, 45; EWL 3; GLL 1; MTCW 1, 2; RGAL 4; TUS

Barnes, Jim 1933- .... **NNAL**
See also CA 108, 175; CAAE 175; CAAS 28; DLB 175

Barnes, Julian (Patrick) 1946- . **CLC 42, 141**
See also BRWS 4; CA 102; CANR 19, 54, 115; CN 7; DAB; DLB 194; DLBY 1993; EWL 3; MTCW 1

Barnes, Peter 1931-2004 .... **CLC 5, 56**
See also CA 65-68; CAAS 12; CANR 33, 34, 64, 113; CBD; CD 5; DFS 6; DLB 13, 233; MTCW 1

Barnes, William 1801-1886 .... **NCLC 75**
See also DLB 32

Baroja (y Nessi), Pio 1872-1956 .... **HLC 1; TCLC 8**
See also CA 104; EW 9

Baron, David
See Pinter, Harold

Baron Corvo
See Rolfe, Frederick (William Serafino Austin Lewis Mary)

Barondess, Sue K(aufman) 1926-1977 .... **CLC 8**
See Kaufman, Sue
See also CA 1-4R; 69-72; CANR 1

Baron de Teive
See Pessoa, Fernando (Antonio Nogueira)

Baroness Von S.
See Zangwill, Israel

Barres, (Auguste-)Maurice 1862-1923 .... **TCLC 47**
See also CA 164; DLB 123; GFL 1789 to the Present

Barreto, Afonso Henrique de Lima
See Lima Barreto, Afonso Henrique de

Barrett, Andrea 1954- .... **CLC 150**
See also CA 156; CANR 92

Barrett, Michele .... **CLC 65**

Barrett, (Roger) Syd 1946- .... **CLC 35**

Barrett, William (Christopher) 1913-1992 .... **CLC 27**
See also CA 13-16R; 139; CANR 11, 67; INT CANR-11

Barrett Browning, Elizabeth 1806-1861 ... **NCLC 1, 16, 61, 66; PC 6, 62; WLC**
See also BRW 4; CDBLB 1832-1890; DA; DA3; DAB; DAC; DAM MST, POET; DLB 32, 199; EXPP; PAB; PFS 2, 16; TEA; WLIT 4; WP

Barrie, J(ames) M(atthew) 1860-1937 .... **TCLC 2, 164**
See also BRWS 3; BYA 4, 5; CA 104; 136; CANR 77; CDBLB 1890-1914; CLR 16; CWRI 5; DA3; DAB; DAM DRAM; DFS 7; DLB 10, 141, 156; EWL 3; FANT; MAICYA 1, 2; MTCW 1; SATA 100; SUFW; WCH; WLIT 4; YABC 1

Barrington, Michael
See Moorcock, Michael (John)

Barrol, Grady
See Bograd, Larry

Barry, Mike
See Malzberg, Barry N(athaniel)

Barry, Philip 1896-1949 .... **TCLC 11**
See also CA 109; 199; DFS 9; DLB 7, 228; RGAL 4

Bart, Andre Schwarz
See Schwarz-Bart, Andre

Barth, John (Simmons) 1930- ... **CLC 1, 2, 3, 5, 7, 9, 10, 14, 27, 51, 89; SSC 10**
See also AITN 1, 2; AMW; BPFB 1; CA 1-4R; CABS 1; CANR 5, 23, 49, 64, 113; CN 7; DAM NOV; DLB 2, 227; EWL 3; FANT; MTCW 1; RGAL 4; RGSF 2; RHW; SSFS 6; TUS

Barthelme, Donald 1931-1989 ... **CLC 1, 2, 3, 5, 6, 8, 13, 23, 46, 59, 115; SSC 2, 55**
See also AMWS 4; BPFB 1; CA 21-24R; 129; CANR 20, 58; DA3; DAM NOV; DLB 2, 234; DLBD 1980, 1989; EWL 3; FANT; LMFS 2; MTCW 1, 2; RGAL 4; RGSF 2; SATA 7; SATA-Obit 62; SSFS 17

Barthelme, Frederick 1943- ...... **CLC 36, 117**
See also AMWS 11; CA 114; 122; CANR 77; CN 7; CSW; DLB 244; DLBY 1985; EWL 3; INT CA-122

Barthes, Roland (Gerard) 1915-1980 .... **CLC 24, 83; TCLC 135**
See also CA 130; 97-100; CANR 66; DLB 296; EW 13; EWL 3; GFL 1789 to the Present; MTCW 1, 2; TWA

Bartram, William 1739-1823 .... **NCLC 145**
See also ANW; DLB 37

Barzun, Jacques (Martin) 1907- ..... **CLC 51, 145**
See also CA 61-64; CANR 22, 95

Bashevis, Isaac
See Singer, Isaac Bashevis

Bashkirtseff, Marie 1859-1884 .... **NCLC 27**

Basho, Matsuo
See Matsuo Basho
See also PFS 18; RGWL 2, 3; WP

Basil of Caesaria c. 330-379 .... **CMLC 35**

Basket, Raney
See Edgerton, Clyde (Carlyle)

Bass, Kingsley B., Jr.
See Bullins, Ed

Bass, Rick 1958- .... **CLC 79, 143; SSC 60**
See also ANW; CA 126; CANR 53, 93; CSW; DLB 212, 275

Bassani, Giorgio 1916-2000 .... **CLC 9**
See also CA 65-68; 190; CANR 33; CWW 2; DLB 128, 177, 299; EWL 3; MTCW 1; RGWL 2, 3

Bastian, Ann .... **CLC 70**

Bastos, Augusto (Antonio) Roa
See Roa Bastos, Augusto (Antonio)

Bataille, Georges 1897-1962 .... **CLC 29; TCLC 155**
See also CA 101; 89-92; EWL 3

Bates, H(erbert) E(rnest) 1905-1974 .... **CLC 46; SSC 10**
See also CA 93-96; 45-48; CANR 34; DA3; DAB; DAM POP; DLB 162, 191; EWL 3; EXPS; MTCW 1, 2; RGSF 2; SSFS 7

Bauchart
See Camus, Albert

Baudelaire, Charles 1821-1867 . **NCLC 6, 29, 55, 155; PC 1; SSC 18; WLC**
See also DA; DA3; DAB; DAC; DAM MST, POET; DLB 217; EW 7; GFL 1789 to the Present; LMFS 2; PFS 21; RGWL 2, 3; TWA

Baudouin, Marcel
See Peguy, Charles (Pierre)

Baudouin, Pierre
See Peguy, Charles (Pierre)

Baudrillard, Jean 1929- .... **CLC 60**
See also DLB 296

Baum, L(yman) Frank 1856-1919 .. **TCLC 7, 132**
See also AAYA 46; BYA 16; CA 108; 133; CLR 15; CWRI 5; DLB 22; FANT; JRDA; MAICYA 1, 2; MTCW 1, 2; NFS 13; RGAL 4; SATA 18, 100; WCH

Baum, Louis F.
See Baum, L(yman) Frank
Baumbach, Jonathan 1933- .... **CLC 6, 23**
See also CA 13-16R; CAAS 5; CANR 12, 66; CN 7; DLBY 1980; INT CANR-12; MTCW 1
Bausch, Richard (Carl) 1945- .... **CLC 51**
See also AMWS 7; CA 101; CAAS 14; CANR 43, 61, 87; CSW; DLB 130
Baxter, Charles (Morley) 1947- . **CLC 45, 78**
See also CA 57-60; CANR 40, 64, 104, 133; CPW; DAM POP; DLB 130; MTCW 2
Baxter, George Owen
See Faust, Frederick (Schiller)
Baxter, James K(eir) 1926-1972 .... **CLC 14**
See also CA 77-80; EWL 3
Baxter, John
See Hunt, E(verette) Howard, (Jr.)
Bayer, Sylvia
See Glassco, John
Baynton, Barbara 1857-1929 .... **TCLC 57**
See also DLB 230; RGSF 2
Beagle, Peter S(oyer) 1939- .... **CLC 7, 104**
See also AAYA 47; BPFB 1; BYA 9, 10, 16; CA 9-12R; CANR 4, 51, 73, 110; DA3; DLBY 1980; FANT; INT CANR-4; MTCW 1; SATA 60, 130; SUFW 1, 2; YAW
Bean, Normal
See Burroughs, Edgar Rice
Beard, Charles A(ustin)
1874-1948 .... **TCLC 15**
See also CA 115; 189; DLB 17; SATA 18
Beardsley, Aubrey 1872-1898 .... **NCLC 6**
Beattie, Ann 1947- ..... **CLC 8, 13, 18, 40, 63, 146; SSC 11**
See also AMWS 5; BEST 90:2; BPFB 1; CA 81-84; CANR 53, 73, 128; CN 7; CPW; DA3; DAM NOV, POP; DLB 218, 278; DLBY 1982; EWL 3; MTCW 1, 2; RGAL 4; RGSF 2; SSFS 9; TUS
Beattie, James 1735-1803 .... **NCLC 25**
See also DLB 109
Beauchamp, Kathleen Mansfield 1888-1923
See Mansfield, Katherine
See also CA 104; 134; DA; DA3; DAC; DAM MST; MTCW 2; TEA
Beaumarchais, Pierre-Augustin Caron de
1732-1799 .... **DC 4; LC 61**
See also DAM DRAM; DFS 14, 16; EW 4; GFL Beginnings to 1789; RGWL 2, 3
Beaumont, Francis 1584(?)-1616 .. **DC 6; LC 33**
See also BRW 2; CDBLB Before 1660; DLB 58; TEA
Beauvoir, Simone (Lucie Ernestine Marie Bertrand) de 1908-1986 .... **CLC 1, 2, 4, 8, 14, 31, 44, 50, 71, 124; SSC 35; WLC**
See also BPFB 1; CA 9-12R; 118; CANR 28, 61; DA; DA3; DAB; DAC; DAM MST, NOV; DLB 72; DLBY 1986; EW 12; EWL 3; FW; GFL 1789 to the Present; LMFS 2; MTCW 1, 2; RGSF 2; RGWL 2, 3; TWA
Becker, Carl (Lotus) 1873-1945 ..... **TCLC 63**
See also CA 157; DLB 17
Becker, Jurek 1937-1997 .... **CLC 7, 19**
See also CA 85-88; 157; CANR 60, 117; CWW 2; DLB 75, 299; EWL 3
Becker, Walter 1950- .... **CLC 26**
Beckett, Samuel (Barclay)
1906-1989 .. **CLC 1, 2, 3, 4, 6, 9, 10, 11, 14, 18, 29, 57, 59, 83; DC 22; SSC 16, 74; TCLC 145; WLC**
See also BRWC 2; BRWR 1; BRWS 1; CA 5-8R; 130; CANR 33, 61; CBD; CDBLB 1945-1960; DA; DA3; DAB; DAC; DAM DRAM, MST, NOV; DFS 2, 7, 18; DLB

13, 15, 233; DLBY 1990; EWL 3; GFL 1789 to the Present; LATS 1:2; LMFS 2; MTCW 1, 2; RGSF 2; RGWL 2, 3; SSFS 15; TEA; WLIT 4
Beckford, William 1760-1844 .... **NCLC 16**
See also BRW 3; DLB 39, 213; HGG; LMFS 1; SUFW
Beckham, Barry (Earl) 1944- .... **BLC 1**
See also BW 1; CA 29-32R; CANR 26, 62; CN 7; DAM MULT; DLB 33
Beckman, Gunnel 1910- .... **CLC 26**
See also CA 33-36R; CANR 15; CLR 25; MAICYA 1, 2; SAAS 9; SATA 6
Becque, Henri 1837-1899 .... **DC 21; NCLC 3**
See also DLB 192; GFL 1789 to the Present
Becquer, Gustavo Adolfo
1836-1870 .... **HLCS 1; NCLC 106**
See also DAM MULT
Beddoes, Thomas Lovell 1803-1849 .. **DC 15; NCLC 3, 154**
See also DLB 96
Bede c. 673-735 .... **CMLC 20**
See also DLB 146; TEA
Bedford, Denton R. 1907-(?) .... **NNAL**
Bedford, Donald F.
See Fearing, Kenneth (Flexner)
Beecher, Catharine Esther
1800-1878 .... **NCLC 30**
See also DLB 1, 243
Beecher, John 1904-1980 .... **CLC 6**
See also AITN 1; CA 5-8R; 105; CANR 8
Beer, Johann 1655-1700 .... **LC 5**
See also DLB 168
Beer, Patricia 1924- .... **CLC 58**
See also CA 61-64; 183; CANR 13, 46; CP 7; CWP; DLB 40; FW
Beerbohm, Max
See Beerbohm, (Henry) Max(imilian)
Beerbohm, (Henry) Max(imilian)
1872-1956 .... **TCLC 1, 24**
See also BRWS 2; CA 104; 154; CANR 79; DLB 34, 100; FANT
Beer-Hofmann, Richard
1866-1945 .... **TCLC 60**
See also CA 160; DLB 81
Beg, Shemus
See Stephens, James
Begiebing, Robert J(ohn) 1946- .... **CLC 70**
See also CA 122; CANR 40, 88
Begley, Louis 1933- .... **CLC 197**
See also CA 140; CANR 98; DLB 299
Behan, Brendan (Francis)
1923-1964 .... **CLC 1, 8, 11, 15, 79**
See also BRWS 2; CA 73-76; CANR 33, 121; CBD; CDBLB 1945-1960; DAM DRAM; DFS 7; DLB 13, 233; EWL 3; MTCW 1, 2
Behn, Aphra 1640(?)-1689 .. **DC 4; LC 1, 30, 42; PC 13; WLC**
See also BRWS 3; DA; DA3; DAB; DAC; DAM DRAM, MST, NOV, POET; DFS 16; DLB 39, 80, 131; FW; TEA; WLIT 3
Behrman, S(amuel) N(athaniel)
1893-1973 .... **CLC 40**
See also CA 13-16; 45-48; CAD; CAP 1; DLB 7, 44; IDFW 3; RGAL 4
Belasco, David 1853-1931 .... **TCLC 3**
See also CA 104; 168; DLB 7; RGAL 4
Belcheva, Elisaveta Lyubomirova
1893-1991 .... **CLC 10**
See Bagryana, Elisaveta
Beldone, Phil "Cheech"
See Ellison, Harlan (Jay)
Beleno
See Azuela, Mariano
Belinski, Vissarion Grigoryevich
1811-1848 .... **NCLC 5**
See also DLB 198

Belitt, Ben 1911- .... **CLC 22**
See also CA 13-16R; CAAS 4; CANR 7, 77; CP 7; DLB 5
Belknap, Jeremy 1744-1798 .... **LC 115**
See also DLB 30, 37
Bell, Gertrude (Margaret Lowthian)
1868-1926 .... **TCLC 67**
See also CA 167; CANR 110; DLB 174
Bell, J. Freeman
See Zangwill, Israel
Bell, James Madison 1826-1902 .... **BLC 1; TCLC 43**
See also BW 1; CA 122; 124; DAM MULT; DLB 50
Bell, Madison Smartt 1957- ...... **CLC 41, 102**
See also AMWS 10; BPFB 1; CA 111, 183; CAAE 183; CANR 28, 54, 73, 134; CN 7; CSW; DLB 218, 278; MTCW 1
Bell, Marvin (Hartley) 1937- .... **CLC 8, 31**
See also CA 21-24R; CAAS 14; CANR 59, 102; CP 7; DAM POET; DLB 5; MTCW 1
Bell, W. L. D.
See Mencken, H(enry) L(ouis)
Bellamy, Atwood C.
See Mencken, H(enry) L(ouis)
Bellamy, Edward 1850-1898 ..... **NCLC 4, 86, 147**
See also DLB 12; NFS 15; RGAL 4; SFW 4
Belli, Gioconda 1948- .... **HLCS 1**
See also CA 152; CWW 2; DLB 290; EWL 3; RGWL 3
Bellin, Edward J.
See Kuttner, Henry
Bello, Andres 1781-1865 .... **NCLC 131**
See also LAW
Belloc, (Joseph) Hilaire (Pierre Sebastien Rene Swanton) 1870-1953 .... **PC 24; TCLC 7, 18**
See also CA 106; 152; CLR 102; CWRI 5; DAM POET; DLB 19, 100, 141, 174; EWL 3; MTCW 1; SATA 112; WCH; YABC 1
Belloc, Joseph Peter Rene Hilaire
See Belloc, (Joseph) Hilaire (Pierre Sebastien Rene Swanton)
Belloc, Joseph Pierre Hilaire
See Belloc, (Joseph) Hilaire (Pierre Sebastien Rene Swanton)
Belloc, M. A.
See Lowndes, Marie Adelaide (Belloc)
Belloc-Lowndes, Mrs.
See Lowndes, Marie Adelaide (Belloc)
Bellow, Saul 1915- . **CLC 1, 2, 3, 6, 8, 10, 13, 15, 25, 33, 34, 63, 79, 190, 200; SSC 14; WLC**
See also AITN 2; AMW; AMWC 2; AMWR 2; BEST 89:3; BPFB 1; CA 5-8R; CABS 1; CANR 29, 53, 95, 132; CDALB 1941-1968; CN 7; DA; DA3; DAB; DAC; DAM MST, NOV, POP; DLB 2, 28, 299; DLBD 3; DLBY 1982; EWL 3; MTCW 1, 2; NFS 4, 14; RGAL 4; RGSF 2; SSFS 12; TUS
Belser, Reimond Karel Maria de 1929-
See Ruyslinck, Ward
See also CA 152
Bely, Andrey .... **PC 11; TCLC 7**
See Bugayev, Boris Nikolayevich
See also DLB 295; EW 9; EWL 3; MTCW 1
Belyi, Andrei
See Bugayev, Boris Nikolayevich
See also RGWL 2, 3
Bembo, Pietro 1470-1547 .... **LC 79**
See also RGWL 2, 3
Benary, Margot
See Benary-Isbert, Margot

Benary-Isbert, Margot 1889-1979 .... **CLC 12**
See also CA 5-8R; 89-92; CANR 4, 72; CLR 12; MAICYA 1, 2; SATA 2; SATA-Obit 21

Benavente (y Martinez), Jacinto 1866-1954 .... **DC 26; HLCS 1; TCLC 3**
See also CA 106; 131; CANR 81; DAM DRAM, MULT; EWL 3; GLL 2; HW 1, 2; MTCW 1, 2

Benchley, Peter (Bradford) 1940- .. **CLC 4, 8**
See also AAYA 14; AITN 2; BPFB 1; CA 17-20R; CANR 12, 35, 66, 115; CPW; DAM NOV, POP; HGG; MTCW 1, 2; SATA 3, 89

Benchley, Robert (Charles) 1889-1945 .... **TCLC 1, 55**
See also CA 105; 153; DLB 11; RGAL 4

Benda, Julien 1867-1956 .... **TCLC 60**
See also CA 120; 154; GFL 1789 to the Present

Benedict, Ruth (Fulton) 1887-1948 .... **TCLC 60**
See also CA 158; DLB 246

Benedikt, Michael 1935- .... **CLC 4, 14**
See also CA 13-16R; CANR 7; CP 7; DLB 5

Benet, Juan 1927-1993 .... **CLC 28**
See also CA 143; EWL 3

Benet, Stephen Vincent 1898-1943 ..... **PC 64; SSC 10; TCLC 7**
See also AMWS 11; CA 104; 152; DA3; DAM POET; DLB 4, 48, 102, 249, 284; DLBY 1997; EWL 3; HGG; MTCW 1; RGAL 4; RGSF 2; SUFW; WP; YABC 1

Benet, William Rose 1886-1950 ..... **TCLC 28**
See also CA 118; 152; DAM POET; DLB 45; RGAL 4

Benford, Gregory (Albert) 1941- ..... **CLC 52**
See also BPFB 1; CA 69-72, 175; CAAE 175; CAAS 27; CANR 12, 24, 49, 95, 134; CSW; DLBY 1982; SCFW 2; SFW 4

Bengtsson, Frans (Gunnar) 1894-1954 .... **TCLC 48**
See also CA 170; EWL 3

Benjamin, David
See Slavitt, David R(ytman)

Benjamin, Lois
See Gould, Lois

Benjamin, Walter 1892-1940 .... **TCLC 39**
See also CA 164; DLB 242; EW 11; EWL 3

Ben Jelloun, Tahar 1944-
See Jelloun, Tahar ben
See also CA 135; CWW 2; EWL 3; RGWL 3; WLIT 2

Benn, Gottfried 1886-1956 .. **PC 35; TCLC 3**
See also CA 106; 153; DLB 56; EWL 3; RGWL 2, 3

Bennett, Alan 1934- .... **CLC 45, 77**
See also BRWS 8; CA 103; CANR 35, 55, 106; CBD; CD 5; DAB; DAM MST; MTCW 1, 2

Bennett, (Enoch) Arnold 1867-1931 .... **TCLC 5, 20**
See also BRW 6; CA 106; 155; CDBLB 1890-1914; DLB 10, 34, 98, 135; EWL 3; MTCW 2

Bennett, Elizabeth
See Mitchell, Margaret (Munnerlyn)

Bennett, George Harold 1930-
See Bennett, Hal
See also BW 1; CA 97-100; CANR 87

Bennett, Gwendolyn B. 1902-1981 .... **HR 2**
See also BW 1; CA 125; DLB 51; WP

Bennett, Hal .... **CLC 5**
See Bennett, George Harold
See also DLB 33

Bennett, Jay 1912- .... **CLC 35**
See also AAYA 10; CA 69-72; CANR 11, 42, 79; JRDA; SAAS 4; SATA 41, 87; SATA-Brief 27; WYA; YAW

Bennett, Louise (Simone) 1919- .... **BLC 1; CLC 28**
See also BW 2, 3; CA 151; CDWLB 3; CP 7; DAM MULT; DLB 117; EWL 3

Benson, A. C. 1862-1925 .... **TCLC 123**
See also DLB 98

Benson, E(dward) F(rederic) 1867-1940 .... **TCLC 27**
See also CA 114; 157; DLB 135, 153; HGG; SUFW 1

Benson, Jackson J. 1930- .... **CLC 34**
See also CA 25-28R; DLB 111

Benson, Sally 1900-1972 .... **CLC 17**
See also CA 19-20; 37-40R; CAP 1; SATA 1, 35; SATA-Obit 27

Benson, Stella 1892-1933 .... **TCLC 17**
See also CA 117; 154, 155; DLB 36, 162; FANT; TEA

Bentham, Jeremy 1748-1832 .... **NCLC 38**
See also DLB 107, 158, 252

Bentley, E(dmund) C(lerihew) 1875-1956 .... **TCLC 12**
See also CA 108; DLB 70; MSW

Bentley, Eric (Russell) 1916- .... **CLC 24**
See also CA 5-8R; CAD; CANR 6, 67; CBD; CD 5; INT CANR-6

ben Uzair, Salem
See Horne, Richard Henry Hengist

Beranger, Pierre Jean de 1780-1857 .... **NCLC 34**

Berdyaev, Nicolas
See Berdyaev, Nikolai (Aleksandrovich)

Berdyaev, Nikolai (Aleksandrovich) 1874-1948 .... **TCLC 67**
See also CA 120; 157

Berdyayev, Nikolai (Aleksandrovich)
See Berdyaev, Nikolai (Aleksandrovich)

Berendt, John (Lawrence) 1939- ...... **CLC 86**
See also CA 146; CANR 75, 93; DA3; MTCW 1

Beresford, J(ohn) D(avys) 1873-1947 .... **TCLC 81**
See also CA 112; 155; DLB 162, 178, 197; SFW 4; SUFW 1

Bergelson, David (Rafailovich) 1884-1952 .... **TCLC 81**
See Bergelson, Dovid
See also CA 220

Bergelson, Dovid
See Bergelson, David (Rafailovich)
See also EWL 3

Berger, Colonel
See Malraux, (Georges-)Andre

Berger, John (Peter) 1926- .... **CLC 2, 19**
See also BRWS 4; CA 81-84; CANR 51, 78, 117; CN 7; DLB 14, 207

Berger, Melvin H. 1927- .... **CLC 12**
See also CA 5-8R; CANR 4; CLR 32; SAAS 2; SATA 5, 88; SATA-Essay 124

Berger, Thomas (Louis) 1924- .. **CLC 3, 5, 8, 11, 18, 38**
See also BPFB 1; CA 1-4R; CANR 5, 28, 51, 128; CN 7; DAM NOV; DLB 2; DLBY 1980; EWL 3; FANT; INT CANR-28; MTCW 1, 2; RHW; TCWW 2

Bergman, (Ernst) Ingmar 1918- ...... **CLC 16, 72, 219**
See also CA 81-84; CANR 33, 70; CWW 2; DLB 257; MTCW 2

Bergson, Henri(-Louis) 1859-1941 . **TCLC 32**
See also CA 164; EW 8; EWL 3; GFL 1789 to the Present

Bergstein, Eleanor 1938- .... **CLC 4**
See also CA 53-56; CANR 5

Berkeley, George 1685-1753 .... **LC 65**
See also DLB 31, 101, 252

Berkoff, Steven 1937- .... **CLC 56**
See also CA 104; CANR 72; CBD; CD 5

Berlin, Isaiah 1909-1997 .... **TCLC 105**
See also CA 85-88; 162

Bermant, Chaim (Icyk) 1929-1998 ... **CLC 40**
See also CA 57-60; CANR 6, 31, 57, 105; CN 7

Bern, Victoria
See Fisher, M(ary) F(rances) K(ennedy)

Bernanos, (Paul Louis) Georges 1888-1948 .... **TCLC 3**
See also CA 104; 130; CANR 94; DLB 72; EWL 3; GFL 1789 to the Present; RGWL 2, 3

Bernard, April 1956- .... **CLC 59**
See also CA 131

Bernard of Clairvaux 1090-1153 .. **CMLC 71**
See also DLB 208

Berne, Victoria
See Fisher, M(ary) F(rances) K(ennedy)

Bernhard, Thomas 1931-1989 ..... **CLC 3, 32, 61; DC 14; TCLC 165**
See also CA 85-88; 127; CANR 32, 57; CDWLB 2; DLB 85, 124; EWL 3; MTCW 1; RGWL 2, 3

Bernhardt, Sarah (Henriette Rosine) 1844-1923 .... **TCLC 75**
See also CA 157

Bernstein, Charles 1950- .... **CLC 142**
See also CA 129; CAAS 24; CANR 90; CP 7; DLB 169

Bernstein, Ingrid
See Kirsch, Sarah

Beroul fl. c. 1150- .... **CMLC 75**

Berriault, Gina 1926-1999 .... **CLC 54, 109; SSC 30**
See also CA 116; 129; 185; CANR 66; DLB 130; SSFS 7,11

Berrigan, Daniel 1921- .... **CLC 4**
See also CA 33-36R; CAAE 187; CAAS 1; CANR 11, 43, 78; CP 7; DLB 5

Berrigan, Edmund Joseph Michael, Jr. 1934-1983
See Berrigan, Ted
See also CA 61-64; 110; CANR 14, 102

Berrigan, Ted .... **CLC 37**
See Berrigan, Edmund Joseph Michael, Jr.
See also DLB 5, 169; WP

Berry, Charles Edward Anderson 1931-
See Berry, Chuck
See also CA 115

Berry, Chuck .... **CLC 17**
See Berry, Charles Edward Anderson

Berry, Jonas
See Ashbery, John (Lawrence)
See also GLL 1

Berry, Wendell (Erdman) 1934- ... **CLC 4, 6, 8, 27, 46; PC 28**
See also AITN 1; AMWS 10; ANW; CA 73-76; CANR 50, 73, 101, 132; CP 7; CSW; DAM POET; DLB 5, 6, 234, 275; MTCW 1

Berryman, John 1914-1972 ... **CLC 1, 2, 3, 4, 6, 8, 10, 13, 25, 62; PC 64**
See also AMW; CA 13-16; 33-36R; CABS 2; CANR 35; CAP 1; CDALB 1941-1968; DAM POET; DLB 48; EWL 3; MTCW 1, 2; PAB; RGAL 4; WP

Bertolucci, Bernardo 1940- ...... **CLC 16, 157**
See also CA 106; CANR 125

Berton, Pierre (Francis Demarigny) 1920-2004 .... **CLC 104**
See also CA 1-4R; CANR 2, 56; CPW; DLB 68; SATA 99

Bertrand, Aloysius 1807-1841 .... **NCLC 31**
See Bertrand, Louis oAloysiusc

Blom, Jan
 See Breytenbach, Breyten
Bloom, Harold 1930- .... **CLC 24, 103**
 See also CA 13-16R; CANR 39, 75, 92,
 133; DLB 67; EWL 3; MTCW 1; RGAL
 4
Bloomfield, Aurelius
 See Bourne, Randolph S(illiman)
Bloomfield, Robert 1766-1823 ..... **NCLC 145**
 See also DLB 93
Blount, Roy (Alton), Jr. 1941- .... **CLC 38**
 See also CA 53-56; CANR 10, 28, 61, 125;
 CSW; INT CANR-28; MTCW 1, 2
Blowsnake, Sam 1875-(?) .... **NNAL**
Bloy, Leon 1846-1917 .... **TCLC 22**
 See also CA 121; 183; DLB 123; GFL 1789
 to the Present
Blue Cloud, Peter (Aroniawenrate)
 1933- .... **NNAL**
 See also CA 117; CANR 40; DAM MULT
Bluggage, Oranthy
 See Alcott, Louisa May
Blume, Judy (Sussman) 1938- .... **CLC 12, 30**
 See also AAYA 3, 26; BYA 1, 8, 12; CA 29-
 32R; CANR 13, 37, 66, 124; CLR 2, 15,
 69; CPW; DA3; DAM NOV, POP; DLB
 52; JRDA; MAICYA 1, 2; MAICYAS 1;
 MTCW 1, 2; SATA 2, 31, 79, 142; WYA;
 YAW
Blunden, Edmund (Charles)
 1896-1974 .... **CLC 2, 56; PC 66**
 See also BRW 6; CA 17-18; 45-48; CANR
 54; CAP 2; DLB 20, 100, 155; MTCW 1;
 PAB
Bly, Robert (Elwood) 1926- .... **CLC 1, 2, 5,**
 10, 15, 38, 128; PC 39
 See also AMWS 4; CA 5-8R; CANR 41,
 73, 125; CP 7; DA3; DAM POET; DLB
 5; EWL 3; MTCW 1, 2; PFS 6, 17; RGAL
 4
Boas, Franz 1858-1942 .... **TCLC 56**
 See also CA 115; 181
Bobette
 See Simenon, Georges (Jacques Christian)
Boccaccio, Giovanni 1313-1375 ... **CMLC 13,**
 57; SSC 10
 See also EW 2; RGSF 2; RGWL 2, 3; TWA
Bochco, Steven 1943- .... **CLC 35**
 See also AAYA 11; CA 124; 138
Bode, Sigmund
 See O'Doherty, Brian
Bodel, Jean 1167(?)-1210 .... **CMLC 28**
Bodenheim, Maxwell 1892-1954 .... **TCLC 44**
 See also CA 110; 187; DLB 9, 45; RGAL 4
Bodenheimer, Maxwell
 See Bodenheim, Maxwell
Bodker, Cecil 1927-
 See Bodker, Cecil
Bodker, Cecil 1927- .... **CLC 21**
 See also CA 73-76; CANR 13, 44, 111;
 CLR 23; MAICYA 1, 2; SATA 14, 133
Boell, Heinrich (Theodor)
 1917-1985 ..... **CLC 2, 3, 6, 9, 11, 15, 27,**
 32, 72; SSC 23; WLC
 See Boll, Heinrich
 See also CA 21-24R; 116; CANR 24; DA;
 DA3; DAB; DAC; DAM MST, NOV;
 DLB 69; DLBY 1985; MTCW 1, 2; SSFS
 20; TWA
Boerne, Alfred
 See Doeblin, Alfred
Boethius c. 480-c. 524 .... **CMLC 15**
 See also DLB 115; RGWL 2, 3
Boff, Leonardo (Genezio Darci)
 1938- .... **CLC 70; HLC 1**
 See also CA 150; DAM MULT; HW 2

Bogan, Louise 1897-1970 .... **CLC 4, 39, 46,**
 93; PC 12
 See also AMWS 3; CA 73-76; 25-28R;
 CANR 33, 82; DAM POET; DLB 45, 169;
 EWL 3; MAWW; MTCW 1, 2; PFS 21;
 RGAL 4
Bogarde, Dirk
 See Van Den Bogarde, Derek Jules Gaspard
 Ulric Niven
 See also DLB 14
Bogosian, Eric 1953- .... **CLC 45, 141**
 See also CA 138; CAD; CANR 102; CD 5
Bograd, Larry 1953- .... **CLC 35**
 See also CA 93-96; CANR 57; SAAS 21;
 SATA 33, 89; WYA
Boiardo, Matteo Maria 1441-1494 .... **LC 6**
Boileau-Despreaux, Nicolas 1636-1711 . **LC 3**
 See also DLB 268; EW 3; GFL Beginnings
 to 1789; RGWL 2, 3
Boissard, Maurice
 See Leautaud, Paul
Bojer, Johan 1872-1959 .... **TCLC 64**
 See also CA 189; EWL 3
Bok, Edward W(illiam)
 1863-1930 .... **TCLC 101**
 See also CA 217; DLB 91; DLBD 16
Boker, George Henry 1823-1890 . **NCLC 125**
 See also RGAL 4
Boland, Eavan (Aisling) 1944- .. **CLC 40, 67,**
 113; PC 58
 See also BRWS 5; CA 143, 207; CAAE
 207; CANR 61; CP 7; CWP; DAM POET;
 DLB 40; FW; MTCW 2; PFS 12
Boll, Heinrich
 See Boell, Heinrich (Theodor)
 See also BPFB 1; CDWLB 2; EW 13; EWL
 3; RGSF 2; RGWL 2, 3
Bolt, Lee
 See Faust, Frederick (Schiller)
Bolt, Robert (Oxton) 1924-1995 .... **CLC 14**
 See also CA 17-20R; 147; CANR 35, 67;
 CBD; DAM DRAM; DFS 2; DLB 13,
 233; EWL 3; LAIT 1; MTCW 1
Bombal, Maria Luisa 1910-1980 .... **HLCS 1;**
 SSC 37
 See also CA 127; CANR 72; EWL 3; HW
 1; LAW; RGSF 2
Bombet, Louis-Alexandre-Cesar
 See Stendhal
Bomkauf
 See Kaufman, Bob (Garnell)
Bonaventura .... **NCLC 35**
 See also DLB 90
Bond, Edward 1934- .... **CLC 4, 6, 13, 23**
 See also AAYA 50; BRWS 1; CA 25-28R;
 CANR 38, 67, 106; CBD; CD 5; DAM
 DRAM; DFS 3, 8; DLB 13; EWL 3;
 MTCW 1
Bonham, Frank 1914-1989 .... **CLC 12**
 See also AAYA 1; BYA 1, 3; CA 9-12R;
 CANR 4, 36; JRDA; MAICYA 1, 2;
 SAAS 3; SATA 1, 49; SATA-Obit 62;
 TCWW 2; YAW
Bonnefoy, Yves 1923- . **CLC 9, 15, 58; PC 58**
 See also CA 85-88; CANR 33, 75, 97;
 CWW 2; DAM MST, POET; DLB 258;
 EWL 3; GFL 1789 to the Present; MTCW
 1, 2
Bonner, Marita .... **HR 2**
 See Occomy, Marita (Odette) Bonner
Bonnin, Gertrude 1876-1938 .... **NNAL**
 See Zitkala-Sa
 See also CA 150; DAM MULT
Bontemps, Arna(ud Wendell)
 1902-1973 .... **BLC 1; CLC 1, 18; HR 2**
 See also BW 1; CA 1-4R; 41-44R; CANR
 4, 35; CLR 6; CWRI 5; DA3; DAM
 MULT, NOV, POET; DLB 48, 51; JRDA;
 MAICYA 1, 2; MTCW 1, 2; SATA 2, 44;
 SATA-Obit 24; WCH; WP

Boot, William
 See Stoppard, Tom
Booth, Martin 1944-2004 .... **CLC 13**
 See also CA 93-96, 188; 223; CAAE 188;
 CAAS 2; CANR 92
Booth, Philip 1925- .... **CLC 23**
 See also CA 5-8R; CANR 5, 88; CP 7;
 DLBY 1982
Booth, Wayne C(layson) 1921- .... **CLC 24**
 See also CA 1-4R; CAAS 5; CANR 3, 43,
 117; DLB 67
Borchert, Wolfgang 1921-1947 .... **TCLC 5**
 See also CA 104; 188; DLB 69, 124; EWL
 3
Borel, Petrus 1809-1859 .... **NCLC 41**
 See also DLB 119; GFL 1789 to the Present
Borges, Jorge Luis 1899-1986 ... **CLC 1, 2, 3,**
 4, 6, 8, 9, 10, 13, 19, 44, 48, 83; HLC 1;
 PC 22, 32; SSC 4, 41; TCLC 109;
 WLC
 See also AAYA 26; BPFB 1; CA 21-24R;
 CANR 19, 33, 75, 105, 133; CDWLB 3;
 DA; DA3; DAB; DAC; DAM MST,
 MULT; DLB 113, 283; DLBY 1986;
 DNFS 1, 2; EWL 3; HW 1, 2; LAW;
 LMFS 2; MSW; MTCW 1, 2; RGSF 2;
 RGWL 2, 3; SFW 4; SSFS 17; TWA;
 WLIT 1
Borowski, Tadeusz 1922-1951 .... **SSC 48;**
 TCLC 9
 See also CA 106; 154; CDWLB 4; DLB
 215; EWL 3; RGSF 2; RGWL 3; SSFS
 13
Borrow, George (Henry)
 1803-1881 .... **NCLC 9**
 See also DLB 21, 55, 166
Bosch (Gavino), Juan 1909-2001 ..... **HLCS 1**
 See also CA 151; 204; DAM MST, MULT;
 DLB 145; HW 1, 2
Bosman, Herman Charles
 1905-1951 .... **TCLC 49**
 See Malan, Herman
 See also CA 160; DLB 225; RGSF 2
Bosschere, Jean de 1878(?)-1953 ... **TCLC 19**
 See also CA 115; 186
Boswell, James 1740-1795 ... **LC 4, 50; WLC**
 See also BRW 3; CDBLB 1660-1789; DA;
 DAB; DAC; DAM MST; DLB 104, 142;
 TEA; WLIT 3
Bottomley, Gordon 1874-1948 ..... **TCLC 107**
 See also CA 120; 192; DLB 10
Bottoms, David 1949- .... **CLC 53**
 See also CA 105; CANR 22; CSW; DLB
 120; DLBY 1983
Boucicault, Dion 1820-1890 .... **NCLC 41**
Boucolon, Maryse
 See Conde, Maryse
Bourdieu, Pierre 1930-2002 .... **CLC 198**
 See also CA 130; 204
Bourget, Paul (Charles Joseph)
 1852-1935 .... **TCLC 12**
 See also CA 107; 196; DLB 123; GFL 1789
 to the Present
Bourjaily, Vance (Nye) 1922- .... **CLC 8, 62**
 See also CA 1-4R; CAAS 1; CANR 2, 72;
 CN 7; DLB 2, 143
Bourne, Randolph S(illiman)
 1886-1918 .... **TCLC 16**
 See also AMW; CA 117; 155; DLB 63
Bova, Ben(jamin William) 1932- ...... **CLC 45**
 See also AAYA 16; CA 5-8R; CAAS 18;
 CANR 11, 56, 94, 111; CLR 3, 96; DLBY
 1981; INT CANR-11; MAICYA 1, 2;
 MTCW 1; SATA 6, 68, 133; SFW 4
Bowen, Elizabeth (Dorothea Cole)
 1899-1973 . **CLC 1, 3, 6, 11, 15, 22, 118;**
 SSC 3, 28, 66; TCLC 148
 See also BRWS 2; CA 17-18; 41-44R;
 CANR 35, 105; CAP 2; CDBLB 1945-

Breton, Andre 1896-1966 .. **CLC 2, 9, 15, 54; PC 15**
See also CA 19-20; 25-28R; CANR 40, 60; CAP 2; DLB 65, 258; EW 11; EWL 3; GFL 1789 to the Present; LMFS 2; MTCW 1, 2; RGWL 2, 3; TWA; WP

Breytenbach, Breyten 1939(?)- .. **CLC 23, 37, 126**
See also CA 113; 129; CANR 61, 122; CWW 2; DAM POET; DLB 225; EWL 3

Bridgers, Sue Ellen 1942- .... **CLC 26**
See also AAYA 8, 49; BYA 7, 8; CA 65-68; CANR 11, 36; CLR 18; DLB 52; JRDA; MAICYA 1, 2; SAAS 1; SATA 22, 90; SATA-Essay 109; WYA; YAW

Bridges, Robert (Seymour)
1844-1930 .... **PC 28; TCLC 1**
See also BRW 6; CA 104; 152; CDBLB 1890-1914; DAM POET; DLB 19, 98

Bridie, James .... **TCLC 3**
See Mavor, Osborne Henry
See also DLB 10; EWL 3

Brin, David 1950- .... **CLC 34**
See also AAYA 21; CA 102; CANR 24, 70, 125, 127; INT CANR-24; SATA 65; SCFW 2; SFW 4

Brink, Andre (Philippus) 1935- . **CLC 18, 36, 106**
See also AFW; BRWS 6; CA 104; CANR 39, 62, 109, 133; CN 7; DLB 225; EWL 3; INT CA-103; LATS 1:2; MTCW 1, 2; WLIT 2

Brinsmead, H. F(ay)
See Brinsmead, H(esba) F(ay)

Brinsmead, H. F.
See Brinsmead, H(esba) F(ay)

Brinsmead, H(esba) F(ay) 1922- ...... **CLC 21**
See also CA 21-24R; CANR 10; CLR 47; CWRI 5; MAICYA 1, 2; SAAS 5; SATA 18, 78

Brittain, Vera (Mary) 1893(?)-1970 . **CLC 23**
See also BRWS 10; CA 13-16; 25-28R; CANR 58; CAP 1; DLB 191; FW; MTCW 1, 2

Broch, Hermann 1886-1951 .... **TCLC 20**
See also CA 117; 211; CDWLB 2; DLB 85, 124; EW 10; EWL 3; RGWL 2, 3

Brock, Rose
See Hansen, Joseph
See also GLL 1

Brod, Max 1884-1968 .... **TCLC 115**
See also CA 5-8R; 25-28R; CANR 7; DLB 81; EWL 3

Brodkey, Harold (Roy) 1930-1996 .. **CLC 56; TCLC 123**
See also CA 111; 151; CANR 71; CN 7; DLB 130

Brodsky, Iosif Alexandrovich 1940-1996
See Brodsky, Joseph
See also AITN 1; CA 41-44R; 151; CANR 37, 106; DA3; DAM POET; MTCW 1, 2; RGWL 2, 3

Brodsky, Joseph . **CLC 4, 6, 13, 36, 100; PC 9**
See Brodsky, Iosif Alexandrovich
See also AMWS 8; CWW 2; DLB 285; EWL 3; MTCW 1

Brodsky, Michael (Mark) 1948- .... **CLC 19**
See also CA 102; CANR 18, 41, 58; DLB 244

Brodzki, Bella ed. .... **CLC 65**

Brome, Richard 1590(?)-1652 .... **LC 61**
See also BRWS 10; DLB 58

Bromell, Henry 1947- .... **CLC 5**
See also CA 53-56; CANR 9, 115, 116

Bromfield, Louis (Brucker)
1896-1956 .... **TCLC 11**
See also CA 107; 155; DLB 4, 9, 86; RGAL 4; RHW

Broner, E(sther) M(asserman)
1930- .... **CLC 19**
See also CA 17-20R; CANR 8, 25, 72; CN 7; DLB 28

Bronk, William (M.) 1918-1999 .... **CLC 10**
See also CA 89-92; 177; CANR 23; CP 7; DLB 165

Bronstein, Lev Davidovich
See Trotsky, Leon

Bronte, Anne 1820-1849 ..... **NCLC 4, 71, 102**
See also BRW 5; BRWR 1; DA3; DLB 21, 199; TEA

Bronte, (Patrick) Branwell
1817-1848 .... **NCLC 109**

Bronte, Charlotte 1816-1855 ...... **NCLC 3, 8, 33, 58, 105, 155; WLC**
See also AAYA 17; BRW 5; BRWC 2; BRWR 1; BYA 2; CDBLB 1832-1890; DA; DA3; DAB; DAC; DAM MST, NOV; DLB 21, 159, 199; EXPN; LAIT 2; NFS 4; TEA; WLIT 4

Bronte, Emily (Jane) 1818-1848 ... **NCLC 16, 35; PC 8; WLC**
See also AAYA 17; BPFB 1; BRW 5; BRWC 1; BRWR 1; BYA 3; CDBLB 1832-1890; DA; DA3; DAB; DAC; DAM MST, NOV, POET; DLB 21, 32, 199; EXPN; LAIT 1; TEA; WLIT 3

Brontes
See Bronte, Anne; Bronte, Charlotte; Bronte, Emily (Jane)

Brooke, Frances 1724-1789 .... **LC 6, 48**
See also DLB 39, 99

Brooke, Henry 1703(?)-1783 .... **LC 1**
See also DLB 39

Brooke, Rupert (Chawner)
1887-1915 ...... **PC 24; TCLC 2, 7; WLC**
See also BRWS 3; CA 104; 132; CANR 61; CDBLB 1914-1945; DA; DAB; DAC; DAM MST, POET; DLB 19, 216; EXPP; GLL 2; MTCW 1, 2; PFS 7; TEA

Brooke-Haven, P.
See Wodehouse, P(elham) G(renville)

Brooke-Rose, Christine 1926(?)- ..... **CLC 40, 184**
See also BRWS 4; CA 13-16R; CANR 58, 118; CN 7; DLB 14, 231; EWL 3; SFW 4

Brookner, Anita 1928- .. **CLC 32, 34, 51, 136**
See also BRWS 4; CA 114; 120; CANR 37, 56, 87, 130; CN 7; CPW; DA3; DAB; DAM POP; DLB 194; DLBY 1987; EWL 3; MTCW 1, 2; TEA

Brooks, Cleanth 1906-1994 . **CLC 24, 86, 110**
See also AMWS 14; CA 17-20R; 145; CANR 33, 35; CSW; DLB 63; DLBY 1994; EWL 3; INT CANR-35; MTCW 1, 2

Brooks, George
See Baum, L(yman) Frank

Brooks, Gwendolyn (Elizabeth)
1917-2000 ... **BLC 1; CLC 1, 2, 4, 5, 15, 49, 125; PC 7; WLC**
See also AAYA 20; AFAW 1, 2; AITN 1; AMWS 3; BW 2, 3; CA 1-4R; 190; CANR 1, 27, 52, 75, 132; CDALB 1941-1968; CLR 27; CP 7; CWP; DA; DA3; DAC; DAM MST, MULT, POET; DLB 5, 76, 165; EWL 3; EXPP; MAWW; MTCW 1, 2; PFS 1, 2, 4, 6; RGAL 4; SATA 6; SATA-Obit 123; TUS; WP

Brooks, Mel .... **CLC 12**
See Kaminsky, Melvin
See also AAYA 13, 48; DLB 26

Brooks, Peter (Preston) 1938- .... **CLC 34**
See also CA 45-48; CANR 1, 107

Brooks, Van Wyck 1886-1963 .... **CLC 29**
See also AMW; CA 1-4R; CANR 6; DLB 45, 63, 103; TUS

Brophy, Brigid (Antonia)
1929-1995 .... **CLC 6, 11, 29, 105**
See also CA 5-8R; 149; CAAS 4; CANR 25, 53; CBD; CN 7; CWD; DA3; DLB 14, 271; EWL 3; MTCW 1, 2

Brosman, Catharine Savage 1934- ..... **CLC 9**
See also CA 61-64; CANR 21, 46

Brossard, Nicole 1943- .... **CLC 115, 169**
See also CA 122; CAAS 16; CCA 1; CWP; CWW 2; DLB 53; EWL 3; FW; GLL 2; RGWL 3

Brother Antoninus
See Everson, William (Oliver)

The Brothers Quay
See Quay, Stephen; Quay, Timothy

Broughton, T(homas) Alan 1936- ..... **CLC 19**
See also CA 45-48; CANR 2, 23, 48, 111

Broumas, Olga 1949- .... **CLC 10, 73**
See also CA 85-88; CANR 20, 69, 110; CP 7; CWP; GLL 2

Broun, Heywood 1888-1939 .... **TCLC 104**
See also DLB 29, 171

Brown, Alan 1950- .... **CLC 99**
See also CA 156

Brown, Charles Brockden
1771-1810 .... **NCLC 22, 74, 122**
See also AMWS 1; CDALB 1640-1865; DLB 37, 59, 73; FW; HGG; LMFS 1; RGAL 4; TUS

Brown, Christy 1932-1981 .... **CLC 63**
See also BYA 13; CA 105; 104; CANR 72; DLB 14

Brown, Claude 1937-2002 ... **BLC 1; CLC 30**
See also AAYA 7; BW 1, 3; CA 73-76; 205; CANR 81; DAM MULT

Brown, Dan .... **CLC 209**
See also AAYA 55; CA 217; MTFW

Brown, Dee (Alexander)
1908-2002 .... **CLC 18, 47**
See also AAYA 30; CA 13-16R; 212; CAAS 6; CANR 11, 45, 60; CPW; CSW; DA3; DAM POP; DLBY 1980; LAIT 2; MTCW 1, 2; NCFS 5; SATA 5, 110; SATA-Obit 141; TCWW 2

Brown, George
See Wertmueller, Lina

Brown, George Douglas
1869-1902 .... **TCLC 28**
See Douglas, George
See also CA 162

Brown, George Mackay 1921-1996 ... **CLC 5, 48, 100**
See also BRWS 6; CA 21-24R; 151; CAAS 6; CANR 12, 37, 67; CN 7; CP 7; DLB 14, 27, 139, 271; MTCW 1; RGSF 2; SATA 35

Brown, (William) Larry 1951-2004 . **CLC 73**
See also CA 130; 134; CANR 117; CSW; DLB 234; INT CA-134

Brown, Moses
See Barrett, William (Christopher)

Brown, Rita Mae 1944- .... **CLC 18, 43, 79**
See also BPFB 1; CA 45-48; CANR 2, 11, 35, 62, 95; CN 7; CPW; CSW; DA3; DAM NOV, POP; FW; INT CANR-11; MTCW 1, 2; NFS 9; RGAL 4; TUS

Brown, Roderick (Langmere) Haig-
See Haig-Brown, Roderick (Langmere)

Brown, Rosellen 1939- .... **CLC 32, 170**
See also CA 77-80; CAAS 10; CANR 14, 44, 98; CN 7

Brown, Sterling Allen 1901-1989 ...... **BLC 1; CLC 1, 23, 59; HR 2; PC 55**
See also AFAW 1, 2; BW 1, 3; CA 85-88; 127; CANR 26; DA3; DAM MULT, POET; DLB 48, 51, 63; MTCW 1, 2; RGAL 4; WP

Brown, Will
See Ainsworth, William Harrison

Casas, Bartolome de las 1474-1566
See Las Casas, Bartolome de
See also WLIT 1

Casely-Hayford, J(oseph) E(phraim)
1866-1903 .... **BLC 1; TCLC 24**
See also BW 2; CA 123; 152; DAM MULT

Casey, John (Dudley) 1939- .... **CLC 59**
See also BEST 90:2; CA 69-72; CANR 23,
100

Casey, Michael 1947- .... **CLC 2**
See also CA 65-68; CANR 109; DLB 5

Casey, Patrick
See Thurman, Wallace (Henry)

Casey, Warren (Peter) 1935-1988 .... **CLC 12**
See also CA 101; 127; INT CA-101

Casona, Alejandro .... **CLC 49**
See Alvarez, Alejandro Rodriguez
See also EWL 3

Cassavetes, John 1929-1989 .... **CLC 20**
See also CA 85-88; 127; CANR 82

Cassian, Nina 1924- .... **PC 17**
See also CWP; CWW 2

Cassill, R(onald) V(erlin)
1919-2002 .... **CLC 4, 23**
See also CA 9-12R; 208; CAAS 1; CANR
7, 45; CN 7; DLB 6, 218; DLBY 2002

Cassiodorus, Flavius Magnus c. 490(?)-c.
583(?) .... **CMLC 43**

Cassirer, Ernst 1874-1945 .... **TCLC 61**
See also CA 157

Cassity, (Allen) Turner 1929- .... **CLC 6, 42**
See also CA 17-20R; 223; CAAE 223;
CAAS 8; CANR 11; CSW; DLB 105

Castaneda, Carlos (Cesar Aranha)
1931(?)-1998 .... **CLC 12, 119**
See also CA 25-28R; CANR 32, 66, 105;
DNFS 1; HW 1; MTCW 1

Castedo, Elena 1937- .... **CLC 65**
See also CA 132

Castedo-Ellerman, Elena
See Castedo, Elena

Castellanos, Rosario 1925-1974 .... **CLC 66;
HLC 1; SSC 39, 68**
See also CA 131; 53-56; CANR 58; CD-
WLB 3; DAM MULT; DLB 113, 290;
EWL 3; FW; HW 1; LAW; MTCW 1;
RGSF 2; RGWL 2, 3

Castelvetro, Lodovico 1505-1571 .... **LC 12**

Castiglione, Baldassare 1478-1529 ...... **LC 12**
See Castiglione, Baldesar
See also LMFS 1; RGWL 2, 3

Castiglione, Baldesar
See Castiglione, Baldassare
See also EW 2

Castillo, Ana (Hernandez Del)
1953- .... **CLC 151**
See also AAYA 42; CA 131; CANR 51, 86,
128; CWP; DLB 122, 227; DNFS 2; FW;
HW 1; LLW 1; PFS 21

Castle, Robert
See Hamilton, Edmond

Castro (Ruz), Fidel 1926(?)- .... **HLC 1**
See also CA 110; 129; CANR 81; DAM
MULT; HW 2

Castro, Guillen de 1569-1631 .... **LC 19**

Castro, Rosalia de 1837-1885 ... **NCLC 3, 78;
PC 41**
See also DAM MULT

Cather, Willa (Sibert) 1873-1947 . **SSC 2, 50;
TCLC 1, 11, 31, 99, 132, 152; WLC**
See also AAYA 24; AMW; AMWC 1;
AMWR 1; BPFB 1; CA 104; 128; CDALB
1865-1917; CLR 98; DA; DA3; DAB;
DAC; DAM MST, NOV; DLB 9, 54, 78,
256; DLBD 1; EWL 3; EXPN; EXPS;
LAIT 3; LATS 1:1; MAWW; MTCW 1,
2; NFS 2, 19; RGAL 4; RGSF 2; RHW;
SATA 30; SSFS 2, 7, 16; TCWW 2; TUS

Catherine II
See Catherine the Great
See also DLB 150

Catherine the Great 1729-1796 .... **LC 69**
See Catherine II

Cato, Marcus Porcius
234B.C.-149B.C. .... **CMLC 21**
See Cato the Elder

Cato, Marcus Porcius, the Elder
See Cato, Marcus Porcius

Cato the Elder
See Cato, Marcus Porcius
See also DLB 211

Catton, (Charles) Bruce 1899-1978 . **CLC 35**
See also AITN 1; CA 5-8R; 81-84; CANR
7, 74; DLB 17; SATA 2; SATA-Obit 24

Catullus c. 84B.C.-54B.C. .... **CMLC 18**
See also AW 2; CDWLB 1; DLB 211;
RGWL 2, 3

Cauldwell, Frank
See King, Francis (Henry)

Caunitz, William J. 1933-1996 .... **CLC 34**
See also BEST 89:3; CA 125; 130; 152;
CANR 73; INT CA-130

Causley, Charles (Stanley)
1917-2003 .... **CLC 7**
See also CA 9-12R; 223; CANR 5, 35, 94;
CLR 30; CWRI 5; DLB 27; MTCW 1;
SATA 3, 66; SATA-Obit 149

Caute, (John) David 1936- .... **CLC 29**
See also CA 1-4R; CAAS 4; CANR 1, 33,
64, 120; CBD; CD 5; CN 7; DAM NOV;
DLB 14, 231

Cavafy, C(onstantine) P(eter) .... **PC 36;
TCLC 2, 7**
See Kavafis, Konstantinos Petrou
See also CA 148; DA3; DAM POET; EW
8; EWL 3; MTCW 1; PFS 19; RGWL 2,
3; WP

Cavalcanti, Guido c. 1250-c.
1300 .... **CMLC 54**
See also RGWL 2, 3

Cavallo, Evelyn
See Spark, Muriel (Sarah)

Cavanna, Betty .... **CLC 12**
See Harrison, Elizabeth (Allen) Cavanna
See also JRDA; MAICYA 1; SAAS 4;
SATA 1, 30

Cavendish, Margaret Lucas
1623-1673 .... **LC 30**
See also DLB 131, 252, 281; RGEL 2

Caxton, William 1421(?)-1491(?) .... **LC 17**
See also DLB 170

Cayer, D. M.
See Duffy, Maureen

Cayrol, Jean 1911- .... **CLC 11**
See also CA 89-92; DLB 83; EWL 3

Cela (y Trulock), Camilo Jose
See Cela, Camilo Jose
See also CWW 2

Cela, Camilo Jose 1916-2002 .... **CLC 4, 13,
59, 122; HLC 1; SSC 71**
See Cela (y Trulock), Camilo Jose
See also BEST 90:2; CA 21-24R; 206;
CAAS 10; CANR 21, 32, 76; DAM
MULT; DLBY 1989; EW 13; EWL 3; HW
1; MTCW 1, 2; RGSF 2; RGWL 2, 3

Celan, Paul .... **CLC 10, 19, 53, 82; PC 10**
See Antschel, Paul
See also CDWLB 2; DLB 69; EWL 3;
RGWL 2, 3

Celine, Louis-Ferdinand .. **CLC 1, 3, 4, 7, 9,
15, 47, 124**
See Destouches, Louis-Ferdinand
See also DLB 72; EW 11; EWL 3; GFL
1789 to the Present; RGWL 2, 3

Cellini, Benvenuto 1500-1571 .... **LC 7**

Cendrars, Blaise .... **CLC 18, 106**
See Sauser-Hall, Frederic
See also DLB 258; EWL 3; GFL 1789 to
the Present; RGWL 2, 3; WP

Centlivre, Susanna 1669(?)-1723 .... **DC 25;
LC 65**
See also DLB 84; RGEL 2

Cernuda (y Bidon), Luis
1902-1963 .... **CLC 54; PC 62**
See also CA 131; 89-92; DAM POET; DLB
134; EWL 3; GLL 1; HW 1; RGWL 2, 3

Cervantes, Lorna Dee 1954- ..... **HLCS 1; PC
35**
See also CA 131; CANR 80; CWP; DLB
82; EXPP; HW 1; LLW 1

Cervantes (Saavedra), Miguel de
1547-1616 .... **HLCS; LC 6, 23, 93; SSC
12; WLC**
See also AAYA 56; BYA 1, 14; DA; DAB;
DAC; DAM MST, NOV; EW 2; LAIT 1;
LATS 1:1; LMFS 1; NFS 8; RGSF 2;
RGWL 2, 3; TWA

Cesaire, Aime (Fernand) 1913- .... **BLC 1;
CLC 19, 32, 112; DC 22; PC 25**
See also BW 2, 3; CA 65-68; CANR 24,
43, 81; CWW 2; DA3; DAM MULT,
POET; EWL 3; GFL 1789 to the Present;
MTCW 1, 2; WP

Chabon, Michael 1963- ... **CLC 55, 149; SSC
59**
See also AAYA 45; AMWS 11; CA 139;
CANR 57, 96, 127; DLB 278; SATA 145

Chabrol, Claude 1930- .... **CLC 16**
See also CA 110

Chairil Anwar
See Anwar, Chairil
See also EWL 3

Challans, Mary 1905-1983
See Renault, Mary
See also CA 81-84; 111; CANR 74; DA3;
MTCW 2; SATA 23; SATA-Obit 36; TEA

Challis, George
See Faust, Frederick (Schiller)
See also TCWW 2

Chambers, Aidan 1934- .... **CLC 35**
See also AAYA 27; CA 25-28R; CANR 12,
31, 58, 116; JRDA; MAICYA 1, 2; SAAS
12; SATA 1, 69, 108; WYA; YAW

Chambers, James 1948-
See Cliff, Jimmy
See also CA 124

Chambers, Jessie
See Lawrence, D(avid) H(erbert Richards)
See also GLL 1

Chambers, Robert W(illiam)
1865-1933 .... **TCLC 41**
See also CA 165; DLB 202; HGG; SATA
107; SUFW 1

Chambers, (David) Whittaker
1901-1961 .... **TCLC 129**
See also CA 89-92; DLB 303

Chamisso, Adelbert von
1781-1838 .... **NCLC 82**
See also DLB 90; RGWL 2, 3; SUFW 1

Chance, James T.
See Carpenter, John (Howard)

Chance, John T.
See Carpenter, John (Howard)

Chandler, Raymond (Thornton)
1888-1959 .... **SSC 23; TCLC 1, 7**
See also AAYA 25; AMWC 2; AMWS 4;
BPFB 1; CA 104; 129; CANR 60, 107;
CDALB 1929-1941; CMW 4; DA3; DLB
226, 253; DLBD 6; EWL 3; MSW;
MTCW 1, 2; NFS 17; RGAL 4; TUS

Chang, Diana 1934- .... **AAL**
See also CA 228; CWP; EXPP

Chomsky, (Avram) Noam 1928- ..... **CLC 132**
See also CA 17-20R; CANR 28, 62, 110, 132; DA3; DLB 246; MTCW 1, 2

Chona, Maria 1845(?)-1936 .... **NNAL**
See also CA 144

Chopin, Kate .... **SSC 8, 68; TCLC 127; WLCS**
See Chopin, Katherine
See also AAYA 33; AMWR 2; AMWS 1; BYA 11, 15; CDALB 1865-1917; DA; DAB; DLB 12, 78; EXPN; EXPS; FW; LAIT 3; MAWW; NFS 3; RGAL 4; RGSF 2; SSFS 17; TUS

Chopin, Katherine 1851-1904
See Chopin, Kate
See also CA 104; 122; DA3; DAC; DAM MST, NOV

Chretien de Troyes c. 12th cent. - . **CMLC 10**
See also DLB 208; EW 1; RGWL 2, 3; TWA

Christie
See Ichikawa, Kon

Christie, Agatha (Mary Clarissa)
1890-1976 .. **CLC 1, 6, 8, 12, 39, 48, 110**
See also AAYA 9; AITN 1, 2; BPFB 1; BRWS 2; CA 17-20R; 61-64; CANR 10, 37, 108; CBD; CDBLB 1914-1945; CMW 4; CPW; CWD; DA3; DAB; DAC; DAM NOV; DFS 2; DLB 13, 77, 245; MSW; MTCW 1, 2; NFS 8; RGEL 2; RHW; SATA 36; TEA; YAW

Christie, Philippa .... **CLC 21**
See Pearce, Philippa
See also BYA 5; CANR 109; CLR 9; DLB 161; MAICYA 1; SATA 1, 67, 129

Christine de Pizan 1365(?)-1431(?) .... **LC 9**
See also DLB 208; RGWL 2, 3

Chuang Tzu c. 369B.C.-c.
286B.C. .... **CMLC 57**

Chubb, Elmer
See Masters, Edgar Lee

Chulkov, Mikhail Dmitrievich
1743-1792 .... **LC 2**
See also DLB 150

Churchill, Caryl 1938- .... **CLC 31, 55, 157; DC 5**
See Churchill, Chick
See also BRWS 4; CA 102; CANR 22, 46, 108; CBD; CWD; DFS 12, 16; DLB 13; EWL 3; FW; MTCW 1; RGEL 2

Churchill, Charles 1731-1764 .... **LC 3**
See also DLB 109; RGEL 2

Churchill, Chick
See Churchill, Caryl
See also CD 5

Churchill, Sir Winston (Leonard Spencer)
1874-1965 .... **TCLC 113**
See also BRW 6; CA 97-100; CDBLB 1890-1914; DA3; DLB 100; DLBD 16; LAIT 4; MTCW 1, 2

Chute, Carolyn 1947- .... **CLC 39**
See also CA 123; CANR 135

Ciardi, John (Anthony) 1916-1986 . **CLC 10, 40, 44, 129**
See also CA 5-8R; 118; CAAS 2; CANR 5, 33; CLR 19; CWRI 5; DAM POET; DLB 5; DLBY 1986; INT CANR-5; MAICYA 1, 2; MTCW 1, 2; RGAL 4; SAAS 26; SATA 1, 65; SATA-Obit 46

Cibber, Colley 1671-1757 .... **LC 66**
See also DLB 84; RGEL 2

Cicero, Marcus Tullius
106B.C.-43B.C. .... **CMLC 3**
See also AW 1; CDWLB 1; DLB 211; RGWL 2, 3

Cimino, Michael 1943- .... **CLC 16**
See also CA 105

Cioran, E(mil) M. 1911-1995 .... **CLC 64**
See also CA 25-28R; 149; CANR 91; DLB 220; EWL 3

Cisneros, Sandra 1954- .... **CLC 69, 118, 193; HLC 1; PC 52; SSC 32, 72**
See also AAYA 9, 53; AMWS 7; CA 131; CANR 64, 118; CWP; DA3; DAM MULT; DLB 122, 152; EWL 3; EXPN; FW; HW 1, 2; LAIT 5; LATS 1:2; LLW 1; MAI-CYA 2; MTCW 2; NFS 2; PFS 19; RGAL 4; RGSF 2; SSFS 3, 13; WLIT 1; YAW

Cixous, Helene 1937- .... **CLC 92**
See also CA 126; CANR 55, 123; CWW 2; DLB 83, 242; EWL 3; FW; GLL 2; MTCW 1, 2; TWA

Clair, Rene .... **CLC 20**
See Chomette, Rene Lucien

Clampitt, Amy 1920-1994 .... **CLC 32; PC 19**
See also AMWS 9; CA 110; 146; CANR 29, 79; DLB 105

Clancy, Thomas L., Jr. 1947-
See Clancy, Tom
See also CA 125; 131; CANR 62, 105; DA3; INT CA-131; MTCW 1, 2

Clancy, Tom .... **CLC 45, 112**
See Clancy, Thomas L., Jr.
See also AAYA 9, 51; BEST 89:1, 90:1; BPFB 1; BYA 10, 11; CANR 132; CMW 4; CPW; DAM NOV, POP; DLB 227

Clare, John 1793-1864 .. **NCLC 9, 86; PC 23**
See also DAB; DAM POET; DLB 55, 96; RGEL 2

Clarin
See Alas (y Urena), Leopoldo (Enrique Garcia)

Clark, Al C.
See Goines, Donald

Clark, (Robert) Brian 1932- .... **CLC 29**
See also CA 41-44R; CANR 67; CBD; CD 5

Clark, Curt
See Westlake, Donald E(dwin)

Clark, Eleanor 1913-1996 .... **CLC 5, 19**
See also CA 9-12R; 151; CANR 41; CN 7; DLB 6

Clark, J. P.
See Clark Bekederemo, J(ohnson) P(epper)
See also CDWLB 3; DLB 117

Clark, John Pepper
See Clark Bekederemo, J(ohnson) P(epper)
See also AFW; CD 5; CP 7; RGEL 2

Clark, Kenneth (Mackenzie)
1903-1983 .... **TCLC 147**
See also CA 93-96; 109; CANR 36; MTCW 1, 2

Clark, M. R.
See Clark, Mavis Thorpe

Clark, Mavis Thorpe 1909-1999 ...... **CLC 12**
See also CA 57-60; CANR 8, 37, 107; CLR 30; CWRI 5; MAICYA 1, 2; SAAS 5; SATA 8, 74

Clark, Walter Van Tilburg
1909-1971 .... **CLC 28**
See also CA 9-12R; 33-36R; CANR 63, 113; DLB 9, 206; LAIT 2; RGAL 4; SATA 8

Clark Bekederemo, J(ohnson) P(epper)
1935- .... **BLC 1; CLC 38; DC 5**
See Clark, J. P.; Clark, John Pepper
See also BW 1; CA 65-68; CANR 16, 72; DAM DRAM, MULT; DFS 13; EWL 3; MTCW 1

Clarke, Arthur C(harles) 1917- .... **CLC 1, 4, 13, 18, 35, 136; SSC 3**
See also AAYA 4, 33; BPFB 1; BYA 13; CA 1-4R; CANR 2, 28, 55, 74, 130; CN 7; CPW; DA3; DAM POP; DLB 261; JRDA; LAIT 5; MAICYA 1, 2; MTCW 1, 2; SATA 13, 70, 115; SCFW; SFW 4; SSFS 4, 18; YAW

Clarke, Austin 1896-1974 .... **CLC 6, 9**
See also CA 29-32; 49-52; CAP 2; DAM POET; DLB 10, 20; EWL 3; RGEL 2

Clarke, Austin C(hesterfield) 1934- .. **BLC 1; CLC 8, 53; SSC 45**
See also BW 1; CA 25-28R; CAAS 16; CANR 14, 32, 68; CN 7; DAC; DAM MULT; DLB 53, 125; DNFS 2; RGSF 2

Clarke, Gillian 1937- .... **CLC 61**
See also CA 106; CP 7; CWP; DLB 40

Clarke, Marcus (Andrew Hislop)
1846-1881 .... **NCLC 19**
See also DLB 230; RGEL 2; RGSF 2

Clarke, Shirley 1925-1997 .... **CLC 16**
See also CA 189

Clash, The
See Headon, (Nicky) Topper; Jones, Mick; Simonon, Paul; Strummer, Joe

Claudel, Paul (Louis Charles Marie)
1868-1955 .... **TCLC 2, 10**
See also CA 104; 165; DLB 192, 258; EW 8; EWL 3; GFL 1789 to the Present; RGWL 2, 3; TWA

Claudian 370(?)-404(?) .... **CMLC 46**
See also RGWL 2, 3

Claudius, Matthias 1740-1815 .... **NCLC 75**
See also DLB 97

Clavell, James (duMaresq)
1925-1994 .... **CLC 6, 25, 87**
See also BPFB 1; CA 25-28R; 146; CANR 26, 48; CPW; DA3; DAM NOV, POP; MTCW 1, 2; NFS 10; RHW

Clayman, Gregory .... **CLC 65**

Cleaver, (Leroy) Eldridge
1935-1998 .... **BLC 1; CLC 30, 119**
See also BW 1, 3; CA 21-24R; 167; CANR 16, 75; DA3; DAM MULT; MTCW 2; YAW

Cleese, John (Marwood) 1939- .... **CLC 21**
See Monty Python
See also CA 112; 116; CANR 35; MTCW 1

Cleishbotham, Jebediah
See Scott, Sir Walter

Cleland, John 1710-1789 .... **LC 2, 48**
See also DLB 39; RGEL 2

Clemens, Samuel Langhorne 1835-1910
See Twain, Mark
See also CA 104; 135; CDALB 1865-1917; DA; DA3; DAB; DAC; DAM MST, NOV; DLB 12, 23, 64, 74, 186, 189; JRDA; LMFS 1; MAICYA 1, 2; NCFS 4; NFS 20; SATA 100; SSFS 16; YABC 2

Clement of Alexandria
150(?)-215(?) .... **CMLC 41**

Cleophil
See Congreve, William

Clerihew, E.
See Bentley, E(dmund) C(lerihew)

Clerk, N. W.
See Lewis, C(live) S(taples)

Cleveland, John 1613-1658 .... **LC 106**
See also DLB 126; RGEL 2

Cliff, Jimmy .... **CLC 21**
See Chambers, James
See also CA 193

Cliff, Michelle 1946- .... **BLCS; CLC 120**
See also BW 2; CA 116; CANR 39, 72; CD-WLB 3; DLB 157; FW; GLL 2

Clifford, Lady Anne 1590-1676 .... **LC 76**
See also DLB 151

Clifton, (Thelma) Lucille 1936- .... **BLC 1; CLC 19, 66, 162; PC 17**
See also AFAW 2; BW 2, 3; CA 49-52; CANR 2, 24, 42, 76, 97; CLR 5; CP 7; CSW; CWP; CWRI 5; DA3; DAM MULT, POET; DLB 5, 41; EXPP; MAICYA 1, 2; MTCW 1, 2; PFS 1, 14; SATA 20, 69, 128; WP

Conrad, Robert Arnold
See Hart, Moss

Conroy, (Donald) Pat(rick) 1945- ... **CLC 30, 74**
See also AAYA 8, 52; AITN 1; BPFB 1; CA 85-88; CANR 24, 53, 129; CPW; CSW; DA3; DAM NOV, POP; DLB 6; LAIT 5; MTCW 1, 2

Constant (de Rebecque), (Henri) Benjamin 1767-1830 .... **NCLC 6**
See also DLB 119; EW 4; GFL 1789 to the Present

Conway, Jill K(er) 1934- .... **CLC 152**
See also CA 130; CANR 94

Conybeare, Charles Augustus
See Eliot, T(homas) S(tearns)

Cook, Michael 1933-1994 .... **CLC 58**
See also CA 93-96; CANR 68; DLB 53

Cook, Robin 1940- .... **CLC 14**
See also AAYA 32; BEST 90:2; BPFB 1; CA 108; 111; CANR 41, 90, 109; CPW; DA3; DAM POP; HGG; INT CA-111

Cook, Roy
See Silverberg, Robert

Cooke, Elizabeth 1948- .... **CLC 55**
See also CA 129

Cooke, John Esten 1830-1886 .... **NCLC 5**
See also DLB 3, 248; RGAL 4

Cooke, John Estes
See Baum, L(yman) Frank

Cooke, M. E.
See Creasey, John

Cooke, Margaret
See Creasey, John

Cooke, Rose Terry 1827-1892 ...... **NCLC 110**
See also DLB 12, 74

Cook-Lynn, Elizabeth 1930- .... **CLC 93; NNAL**
See also CA 133; DAM MULT; DLB 175

Cooney, Ray .... **CLC 62**
See also CBD

Cooper, Anthony Ashley 1671-1713 .. **LC 107**
See also DLB 101

Cooper, Dennis 1953- .... **CLC 203**
See also CA 133; CANR 72, 86; GLL 1; St. James Guide to Horror, Ghost, and Gothic Writers.

Cooper, Douglas 1960- .... **CLC 86**

Cooper, Henry St. John
See Creasey, John

Cooper, J(oan) California (?)- .... **CLC 56**
See also AAYA 12; BW 1; CA 125; CANR 55; DAM MULT; DLB 212

Cooper, James Fenimore 1789-1851 .... **NCLC 1, 27, 54**
See also AAYA 22; AMW; BPFB 1; CDALB 1640-1865; DA3; DLB 3, 183, 250, 254; LAIT 1; NFS 9; RGAL 4; SATA 19; TUS; WCH

Cooper, Susan Fenimore 1813-1894 .... **NCLC 129**
See also ANW; DLB 239, 254

Coover, Robert (Lowell) 1932- ...... **CLC 3, 7, 15, 32, 46, 87, 161; SSC 15**
See also AMWS 5; BPFB 1; CA 45-48; CANR 3, 37, 58, 115; CN 7; DAM NOV; DLB 2, 227; DLBY 1981; EWL 3; MTCW 1, 2; RGAL 4; RGSF 2

Copeland, Stewart (Armstrong) 1952- .... **CLC 26**

Copernicus, Nicolaus 1473-1543 .... **LC 45**

Coppard, A(lfred) E(dgar) 1878-1957 .... **SSC 21; TCLC 5**
See also BRWS 8; CA 114; 167; DLB 162; EWL 3; HGG; RGEL 2; RGSF 2; SUFW 1; YABC 1

Coppee, Francois 1842-1908 .... **TCLC 25**
See also CA 170; DLB 217

Coppola, Francis Ford 1939- ... **CLC 16, 126**
See also AAYA 39; CA 77-80; CANR 40, 78; DLB 44

Copway, George 1818-1869 .... **NNAL**
See also DAM MULT; DLB 175, 183

Corbiere, Tristan 1845-1875 .... **NCLC 43**
See also DLB 217; GFL 1789 to the Present

Corcoran, Barbara (Asenath) 1911- .... **CLC 17**
See also AAYA 14; CA 21-24R, 191; CAAE 191; CAAS 2; CANR 11, 28, 48; CLR 50; DLB 52; JRDA; MAICYA 2; MAICYAS 1; RHW; SAAS 20; SATA 3, 77; SATA-Essay 125

Cordelier, Maurice
See Giraudoux, Jean(-Hippolyte)

Corelli, Marie .... **TCLC 51**
See Mackay, Mary
See also DLB 34, 156; RGEL 2; SUFW 1

Corinna c. 225B.C.-c. 305B.C. ...... **CMLC 72**

Corman, Cid .... **CLC 9**
See Corman, Sidney
See also CAAS 2; DLB 5, 193

Corman, Sidney 1924-2004
See Corman, Cid
See also CA 85-88; 225; CANR 44; CP 7; DAM POET

Cormier, Robert (Edmund) 1925-2000 .... **CLC 12, 30**
See also AAYA 3, 19; BYA 1, 2, 6, 8, 9; CA 1-4R; CANR 5, 23, 76, 93; CDALB 1968-1988; CLR 12, 55; DA; DAB; DAC; DAM MST, NOV; DLB 52; EXPN; INT CANR-23; JRDA; LAIT 5; MAICYA 1, 2; MTCW 1, 2; NFS 2, 18; SATA 10, 45, 83; SATA-Obit 122; WYA; YAW

Corn, Alfred (DeWitt III) 1943- .... **CLC 33**
See also CA 179; CAAE 179; CAAS 25; CANR 44; CP 7; CSW; DLB 120, 282; DLBY 1980

Corneille, Pierre 1606-1684 ... **DC 21; LC 28**
See also DAB; DAM MST; DLB 268; EW 3; GFL Beginnings to 1789; RGWL 2, 3; TWA

Cornwell, David (John Moore) 1931- .... **CLC 9, 15**
See le Carre, John
See also CA 5-8R; CANR 13, 33, 59, 107, 132; DA3; DAM POP; MTCW 1, 2

Cornwell, Patricia (Daniels) 1956- . **CLC 155**
See also AAYA 16, 56; BPFB 1; CA 134; CANR 53, 131; CMW 4; CPW; CSW; DAM POP; DLB 306; MSW; MTCW 1

Corso, (Nunzio) Gregory 1930-2001 . **CLC 1, 11; PC 33**
See also AMWS 12; BG 2; CA 5-8R; 193; CANR 41, 76, 132; CP 7; DA3; DLB 5, 16, 237; LMFS 2; MTCW 1, 2; WP

Cortazar, Julio 1914-1984 ... **CLC 2, 3, 5, 10, 13, 15, 33, 34, 92; HLC 1; SSC 7, 76**
See also BPFB 1; CA 21-24R; CANR 12, 32, 81; CDWLB 3; DA3; DAM MULT, NOV; DLB 113; EWL 3; EXPS; HW 1, 2; LAW; MTCW 1, 2; RGSF 2; RGWL 2, 3; SSFS 3, 20; TWA; WLIT 1

Cortes, Hernan 1485-1547 .... **LC 31**

Corvinus, Jakob
See Raabe, Wilhelm (Karl)

Corwin, Cecil
See Kornbluth, C(yril) M.

Cosic, Dobrica 1921- .... **CLC 14**
See also CA 122; 138; CDWLB 4; CWW 2; DLB 181; EWL 3

Costain, Thomas B(ertram) 1885-1965 .... **CLC 30**
See also BYA 3; CA 5-8R; 25-28R; DLB 9; RHW

Costantini, Humberto 1924(?)-1987 . **CLC 49**
See also CA 131; 122; EWL 3; HW 1

Costello, Elvis 1954- .... **CLC 21**
See also CA 204

Costenoble, Philostene
See Ghelderode, Michel de

Cotes, Cecil V.
See Duncan, Sara Jeannette

Cotter, Joseph Seamon Sr. 1861-1949 .... **BLC 1; TCLC 28**
See also BW 1; CA 124; DAM MULT; DLB 50

Couch, Arthur Thomas Quiller
See Quiller-Couch, Sir Arthur (Thomas)

Coulton, James
See Hansen, Joseph

Couperus, Louis (Marie Anne) 1863-1923 .... **TCLC 15**
See also CA 115; EWL 3; RGWL 2, 3

Coupland, Douglas 1961- .... **CLC 85, 133**
See also AAYA 34; CA 142; CANR 57, 90, 130; CCA 1; CPW; DAC; DAM POP

Court, Wesli
See Turco, Lewis (Putnam)

Courtenay, Bryce 1933- .... **CLC 59**
See also CA 138; CPW

Courtney, Robert
See Ellison, Harlan (Jay)

Cousteau, Jacques-Yves 1910-1997 .. **CLC 30**
See also CA 65-68; 159; CANR 15, 67; MTCW 1; SATA 38, 98

Coventry, Francis 1725-1754 .... **LC 46**

Coverdale, Miles c. 1487-1569 .... **LC 77**
See also DLB 167

Cowan, Peter (Walkinshaw) 1914-2002 .... **SSC 28**
See also CA 21-24R; CANR 9, 25, 50, 83; CN 7; DLB 260; RGSF 2

Coward, Noel (Peirce) 1899-1973 . **CLC 1, 9, 29, 51**
See also AITN 1; BRWS 2; CA 17-18; 41-44R; CANR 35, 132; CAP 2; CDBLB 1914-1945; DA3; DAM DRAM; DFS 3, 6; DLB 10, 245; EWL 3; IDFW 3, 4; MTCW 1, 2; RGEL 2; TEA

Cowley, Abraham 1618-1667 .... **LC 43**
See also BRW 2; DLB 131, 151; PAB; RGEL 2

Cowley, Malcolm 1898-1989 .... **CLC 39**
See also AMWS 2; CA 5-8R; 128; CANR 3, 55; DLB 4, 48; DLBY 1981, 1989; EWL 3; MTCW 1, 2

Cowper, William 1731-1800 ..... **NCLC 8, 94; PC 40**
See also BRW 3; DA3; DAM POET; DLB 104, 109; RGEL 2

Cox, William Trevor 1928-
See Trevor, William
See also CA 9-12R; CANR 4, 37, 55, 76, 102; DAM NOV; INT CANR-37; MTCW 1, 2; TEA

Coyne, P. J.
See Masters, Hilary

Cozzens, James Gould 1903-1978 . **CLC 1, 4, 11, 92**
See also AMW; BPFB 1; CA 9-12R; 81-84; CANR 19; CDALB 1941-1968; DLB 9, 294; DLBD 2; DLBY 1984, 1997; EWL 3; MTCW 1, 2; RGAL 4

Crabbe, George 1754-1832 .... **NCLC 26, 121**
See also BRW 3; DLB 93; RGEL 2

Crace, Jim 1946- .... **CLC 157; SSC 61**
See also CA 128; 135; CANR 55, 70, 123; CN 7; DLB 231; INT CA-135

Craddock, Charles Egbert
See Murfree, Mary Noailles

Craig, A. A.
See Anderson, Poul (William)

Craik, Mrs.
See Craik, Dinah Maria (Mulock)
See also RGEL 2

Day, Thomas 1748-1789 .... **LC 1**
See also DLB 39; YABC 1

Day Lewis, C(ecil) 1904-1972 . **CLC 1, 6, 10; PC 11**
See Blake, Nicholas
See also BRWS 3; CA 13-16; 33-36R; CANR 34; CAP 1; CWRI 5; DAM POET; DLB 15, 20; EWL 3; MTCW 1, 2; RGEL 2

Dazai Osamu .... **SSC 41; TCLC 11**
See Tsushima, Shuji
See also CA 164; DLB 182; EWL 3; MJW; RGSF 2; RGWL 2, 3; TWA

de Andrade, Carlos Drummond
See Drummond de Andrade, Carlos

de Andrade, Mario 1892(?)-1945
See Andrade, Mario de
See also CA 178; HW 2

Deane, Norman
See Creasey, John

Deane, Seamus (Francis) 1940- ...... **CLC 122**
See also CA 118; CANR 42

de Beauvoir, Simone (Lucie Ernestine Marie Bertrand)
See Beauvoir, Simone (Lucie Ernestine Marie Bertrand) de

de Beer, P.
See Bosman, Herman Charles

de Botton, Alain 1969- .... **CLC 203**
See also CA 159; CANR 96

de Brissac, Malcolm
See Dickinson, Peter (Malcolm de Brissac)

de Campos, Alvaro
See Pessoa, Fernando (Antonio Nogueira)

de Chardin, Pierre Teilhard
See Teilhard de Chardin, (Marie Joseph) Pierre

de Crenne, Hélisenne c. 1510-c. 1560 .... **LC 113**

Dee, John 1527-1608 .... **LC 20**
See also DLB 136, 213

Deer, Sandra 1940- .... **CLC 45**
See also CA 186

De Ferrari, Gabriella 1941- .... **CLC 65**
See also CA 146

de Filippo, Eduardo 1900-1984 ... **TCLC 127**
See also CA 132; 114; EWL 3; MTCW 1; RGWL 2, 3

Defoe, Daniel 1660(?)-1731 .... **LC 1, 42, 108; WLC**
See also AAYA 27; BRW 3; BRWR 1; BYA 4; CDBLB 1660-1789; CLR 61; DA; DA3; DAB; DAC; DAM MST, NOV; DLB 39, 95, 101; JRDA; LAIT 1; LMFS 1; MAICYA 1, 2; NFS 9, 13; RGEL 2; SATA 22; TEA; WCH; WLIT 3

de Gourmont, Remy(-Marie-Charles)
See Gourmont, Remy(-Marie-Charles) de

de Gournay, Marie le Jars 1566-1645 .... **LC 98**
See also FW

de Hartog, Jan 1914-2002 .... **CLC 19**
See also CA 1-4R; 210; CANR 1; DFS 12

de Hostos, E. M.
See Hostos (y Bonilla), Eugenio Maria de

de Hostos, Eugenio M.
See Hostos (y Bonilla), Eugenio Maria de

Deighton, Len .... **CLC 4, 7, 22, 46**
See Deighton, Leonard Cyril
See also AAYA 6; BEST 89:2; BPFB 1; CD-BLB 1960 to Present; CMW 4; CN 7; CPW; DLB 87

Deighton, Leonard Cyril 1929-
See Deighton, Len
See also AAYA 57; CA 9-12R; CANR 19, 33, 68; DA3; DAM NOV, POP; MTCW 1, 2

Dekker, Thomas 1572(?)-1632 ..... **DC 12; LC 22**
See also CDBLB Before 1660; DAM DRAM; DLB 62, 172; LMFS 1; RGEL 2

de Laclos, Pierre Ambroise Franois
See Laclos, Pierre Ambroise Francois

Delacroix, (Ferdinand-Victor-)Eugene 1798-1863 .... **NCLC 133**
See also EW 5

Delafield, E. M. .... **TCLC 61**
See Dashwood, Edmee Elizabeth Monica de la Pasture
See also DLB 34; RHW

de la Mare, Walter (John) 1873-1956 . **SSC 14; TCLC 4, 53; WLC**
See also CA 163; CDBLB 1914-1945; CLR 23; CWRI 5; DA3; DAB; DAC; DAM MST, POET; DLB 19, 153, 162, 255, 284; EWL 3; EXPP; HGG; MAICYA 1, 2; MTCW 1; RGEL 2; RGSF 2; SATA 16; SUFW 1; TEA; WCH

de Lamartine, Alphonse (Marie Louis Prat)
See Lamartine, Alphonse (Marie Louis Prat) de

Delaney, Franey
See O'Hara, John (Henry)

Delaney, Shelagh 1939- .... **CLC 29**
See also CA 17-20R; CANR 30, 67; CBD; CD 5; CDBLB 1960 to Present; CWD; DAM DRAM; DFS 7; DLB 13; MTCW 1

Delany, Martin Robison 1812-1885 .... **NCLC 93**
See also DLB 50; RGAL 4

Delany, Mary (Granville Pendarves) 1700-1788 .... **LC 12**

Delany, Samuel R(ay), Jr. 1942- .... **BLC 1; CLC 8, 14, 38, 141**
See also AAYA 24; AFAW 2; BPFB 1; BW 2, 3; CA 81-84; CANR 27, 43, 115, 116; CN 7; DAM MULT; DLB 8, 33; FANT; MTCW 1, 2; RGAL 4; SATA 92; SCFW; SFW 4; SUFW 2

De la Ramee, Marie Louise (Ouida) 1839-1908
See Ouida
See also CA 204; SATA 20

de la Roche, Mazo 1879-1961 .... **CLC 14**
See also CA 85-88; CANR 30; DLB 68; RGEL 2; RHW; SATA 64

De La Salle, Innocent
See Hartmann, Sadakichi

de Laureamont, Comte
See Lautreamont

Delbanco, Nicholas (Franklin) 1942- .... **CLC 6, 13, 167**
See also CA 17-20R, 189; CAAE 189; CAAS 2; CANR 29, 55, 116; DLB 6, 234

del Castillo, Michel 1933- .... **CLC 38**
See also CA 109; CANR 77

Deledda, Grazia (Cosima) 1875(?)-1936 .... **TCLC 23**
See also CA 123; 205; DLB 264; EWL 3; RGWL 2, 3

Deleuze, Gilles 1925-1995 .... **TCLC 116**
See also DLB 296

Delgado, Abelardo (Lalo) B(arrientos) 1930-2004 .... **HLC 1**
See also CA 131; CAAS 15; CANR 90; DAM MST, MULT; DLB 82; HW 1, 2

Delibes, Miguel .... **CLC 8, 18**
See Delibes Setien, Miguel
See also EWL 3

Delibes Setien, Miguel 1920-
See Delibes, Miguel
See also CA 45-48; CANR 1, 32; CWW 2; HW 1; MTCW 1

DeLillo, Don 1936- ..... **CLC 8, 10, 13, 27, 39, 54, 76, 143, 210**
See also AMWC 2; AMWS 6; BEST 89:1; BPFB 1; CA 81-84; CANR 21, 76, 92, 133; CN 7; CPW; DA3; DAM NOV, POP; DLB 6, 173; EWL 3; MTCW 1, 2; RGAL 4; TUS

de Lisser, H. G.
See De Lisser, H(erbert) G(eorge)
See also DLB 117

De Lisser, H(erbert) G(eorge) 1878-1944 .... **TCLC 12**
See de Lisser, H. G.
See also BW 2; CA 109; 152

Deloire, Pierre
See Peguy, Charles (Pierre)

Deloney, Thomas 1543(?)-1600 .... **LC 41**
See also DLB 167; RGEL 2

Deloria, Ella (Cara) 1889-1971(?) ..... **NNAL**
See also CA 152; DAM MULT; DLB 175

Deloria, Vine (Victor), Jr. 1933- ...... **CLC 21, 122; NNAL**
See also CA 53-56; CANR 5, 20, 48, 98; DAM MULT; DLB 175; MTCW 1; SATA 21

del Valle-Inclan, Ramon (Maria)
See Valle-Inclan, Ramon (Maria) del

Del Vecchio, John M(ichael) 1947- .. **CLC 29**
See also CA 110; DLBD 9

de Man, Paul (Adolph Michel) 1919-1983 .... **CLC 55**
See also CA 128; 111; CANR 61; DLB 67; MTCW 1, 2

DeMarinis, Rick 1934- .... **CLC 54**
See also CA 57-60, 184; CAAE 184; CAAS 24; CANR 9, 25, 50; DLB 218

de Maupassant, (Henri Rene Albert) Guy
See Maupassant, (Henri Rene Albert) Guy de

Dembry, R. Emmet
See Murfree, Mary Noailles

Demby, William 1922- .... **BLC 1; CLC 53**
See also BW 1, 3; CA 81-84; CANR 81; DAM MULT; DLB 33

de Menton, Francisco
See Chin, Frank (Chew, Jr.)

Demetrius of Phalerum c. 307B.C.- .... **CMLC 34**

Demijohn, Thom
See Disch, Thomas M(ichael)

De Mille, James 1833-1880 .... **NCLC 123**
See also DLB 99, 251

Deming, Richard 1915-1983
See Queen, Ellery
See also CA 9-12R; CANR 3, 94; SATA 24

Democritus c. 460B.C.-c. 370B.C. .. **CMLC 47**

de Montaigne, Michel (Eyquem)
See Montaigne, Michel (Eyquem) de

de Montherlant, Henry (Milon)
See Montherlant, Henry (Milon) de

Demosthenes 384B.C.-322B.C. ...... **CMLC 13**
See also AW 1; DLB 176; RGWL 2, 3

de Musset, (Louis Charles) Alfred
See Musset, (Louis Charles) Alfred de

de Natale, Francine
See Malzberg, Barry N(athaniel)

de Navarre, Marguerite 1492-1549 ... **LC 61; SSC 85**
See Marguerite d'Angouleme; Marguerite de Navarre

Denby, Edwin (Orr) 1903-1983 .... **CLC 48**
See also CA 138; 110

de Nerval, Gerard
See Nerval, Gerard de

Denham, John 1615-1669 .... **LC 73**
See also DLB 58, 126; RGEL 2

Denis, Julio
See Cortazar, Julio

Denmark, Harrison
See Zelazny, Roger (Joseph)

Dennis, John 1658-1734 .... **LC 11**
See also DLB 101; RGEL 2

Dennis, Nigel (Forbes) 1912-1989 ...... **CLC 8**
See also CA 25-28R; 129; DLB 13, 15, 233; EWL 3; MTCW 1

Dent, Lester 1904-1959 .... **TCLC 72**
See also CA 112; 161; CMW 4; DLB 306; SFW 4

De Palma, Brian (Russell) 1940- ...... **CLC 20**
See also CA 109

De Quincey, Thomas 1785-1859 ..... **NCLC 4, 87**
See also BRW 4; CDBLB 1789-1832; DLB 110, 144; RGEL 2

Deren, Eleanora 1908(?)-1961
See Deren, Maya
See also CA 192; 111

Deren, Maya .... **CLC 16, 102**
See Deren, Eleanora

Derleth, August (William)
1909-1971 .... **CLC 31**
See also BPFB 1; BYA 9, 10; CA 1-4R; 29-32R; CANR 4; CMW 4; DLB 9; DLBD 17; HGG; SATA 5; SUFW 1

Der Nister 1884-1950 .... **TCLC 56**
See Nister, Der

Der Stricker c. 1190-c. 1250 .... **CMLC 75**

de Routisie, Albert
See Aragon, Louis

Derrida, Jacques 1930-2004 .... **CLC 24, 87**
See also CA 124; 127; CANR 76, 98, 133; DLB 242; EWL 3; LMFS 2; MTCW 1; TWA

Derry Down Derry
See Lear, Edward

Dersonnes, Jacques
See Simenon, Georges (Jacques Christian)

Desai, Anita 1937- .... **CLC 19, 37, 97, 175**
See also BRWS 5; CA 81-84; CANR 33, 53, 95, 133; CN 7; CWRI 5; DA3; DAB; DAM NOV; DLB 271; DNFS 2; EWL 3; FW; MTCW 1, 2; SATA 63, 126

Desai, Kiran 1971- .... **CLC 119**
See also BYA 16; CA 171; CANR 127

de Saint-Luc, Jean
See Glassco, John

de Saint Roman, Arnaud
See Aragon, Louis

Desbordes-Valmore, Marceline
1786-1859 .... **NCLC 97**
See also DLB 217

Descartes, Rene 1596-1650 .... **LC 20, 35**
See also DLB 268; EW 3; GFL Beginnings to 1789

Deschamps, Eustache 1340(?)-1404 .. **LC 103**
See also DLB 208

De Sica, Vittorio 1901(?)-1974 .... **CLC 20**
See also CA 117

Desnos, Robert 1900-1945 .... **TCLC 22**
See also CA 121; 151; CANR 107; DLB 258; EWL 3; LMFS 2

Des Roches, Catherine 1542-1587 ..... **LC 117**

Destouches, Louis-Ferdinand
1894-1961 .... **CLC 9, 15**
See Celine, Louis-Ferdinand
See also CA 85-88; CANR 28; MTCW 1

de Tolignac, Gaston
See Griffith, D(avid Lewelyn) W(ark)

Deutsch, Babette 1895-1982 .... **CLC 18**
See also BYA 3; CA 1-4R; 108; CANR 4, 79; DLB 45; SATA 1; SATA-Obit 33

Devenant, William 1606-1649 .... **LC 13**

Devkota, Laxmiprasad 1909-1959 . **TCLC 23**
See also CA 123

De Voto, Bernard (Augustine)
1897-1955 .... **TCLC 29**
See also CA 113; 160; DLB 9, 256

De Vries, Peter 1910-1993 ..... **CLC 1, 2, 3, 7, 10, 28, 46**
See also CA 17-20R; 142; CANR 41; DAM NOV; DLB 6; DLBY 1982; MTCW 1, 2

Dewey, John 1859-1952 .... **TCLC 95**
See also CA 114; 170; DLB 246, 270; RGAL 4

Dexter, John
See Bradley, Marion Zimmer
See also GLL 1

Dexter, Martin
See Faust, Frederick (Schiller)
See also TCWW 2

Dexter, Pete 1943- .... **CLC 34, 55**
See also BEST 89:2; CA 127; 131; CANR 129; CPW; DAM POP; INT CA-131; MTCW 1

Diamano, Silmang
See Senghor, Leopold Sedar

Diamond, Neil 1941- .... **CLC 30**
See also CA 108

Diaz del Castillo, Bernal
1496-1584 .... **HLCS 1; LC 31**
See also LAW

di Bassetto, Corno
See Shaw, George Bernard

Dick, Philip K(indred) 1928-1982 ... **CLC 10, 30, 72; SSC 57**
See also AAYA 24; BPFB 1; BYA 11; CA 49-52; 106; CANR 2, 16, 132; CPW; DA3; DAM NOV, POP; DLB 8; MTCW 1, 2; NFS 5; SCFW 4; SFW 4

Dickens, Charles (John Huffam)
1812-1870 .... **NCLC 3, 8, 18, 26, 37, 50, 86, 105, 113; SSC 17, 49; WLC**
See also AAYA 23; BRW 5; BRWC 1, 2; BYA 1, 2, 3, 13, 14; CDBLB 1832-1890; CLR 95; CMW 4; DA; DA3; DAB; DAC; DAM MST, NOV; DLB 21, 55, 70, 159, 166; EXPN; HGG; JRDA; LAIT 1, 2; LATS 1:1; LMFS 1; MAICYA 1, 2; NFS 4, 5, 10, 14, 20; RGEL 2; RGSF 2; SATA 15; SUFW 1; TEA; WCH; WLIT 4; WYA

Dickey, James (Lafayette)
1923-1997 .... **CLC 1, 2, 4, 7, 10, 15, 47, 109; PC 40; TCLC 151**
See also AAYA 50; AITN 1, 2; AMWS 4; BPFB 1; CA 9-12R; 156; CABS 2; CANR 10, 48, 61, 105; CDALB 1968-1988; CP 7; CPW; CSW; DA3; DAM NOV, POET, POP; DLB 5, 193; DLBD 7; DLBY 1982, 1993, 1996, 1997, 1998; EWL 3; INT CANR-10; MTCW 1, 2; NFS 9; PFS 6, 11; RGAL 4; TUS

Dickey, William 1928-1994 .... **CLC 3, 28**
See also CA 9-12R; 145; CANR 24, 79; DLB 5

Dickinson, Charles 1951- .... **CLC 49**
See also CA 128

Dickinson, Emily (Elizabeth)
1830-1886 ... **NCLC 21, 77; PC 1; WLC**
See also AAYA 22; AMW; AMWR 1; CDALB 1865-1917; DA; DA3; DAB; DAC; DAM MST, POET; DLB 1, 243; EXPP; MAWW; PAB; PFS 1, 2, 3, 4, 5, 6, 8, 10, 11, 13, 16; RGAL 4; SATA 29; TUS; WP; WYA

Dickinson, Mrs. Herbert Ward
See Phelps, Elizabeth Stuart

Dickinson, Peter (Malcolm de Brissac)
1927- .... **CLC 12, 35**
See also AAYA 9, 49; BYA 5; CA 41-44R; CANR 31, 58, 88, 134; CLR 29; CMW 4; DLB 87, 161, 276; JRDA; MAICYA 1, 2; SATA 5, 62, 95, 150; SFW 4; WYA; YAW

Dickson, Carr
See Carr, John Dickson

Dickson, Carter
See Carr, John Dickson

Diderot, Denis 1713-1784 .... **LC 26**
See also EW 4; GFL Beginnings to 1789; LMFS 1; RGWL 2, 3

Didion, Joan 1934- . **CLC 1, 3, 8, 14, 32, 129**
See also AITN 1; AMWS 4; CA 5-8R; CANR 14, 52, 76, 125; CDALB 1968-1988; CN 7; DA3; DAM NOV; DLB 2, 173, 185; DLBY 1981, 1986; EWL 3; MAWW; MTCW 1, 2; NFS 3; RGAL 4; TCWW 2; TUS

di Donato, Pietro 1911-1992 .... **TCLC 159**
See also CA 101; 136; DLB 9

Dietrich, Robert
See Hunt, E(verette) Howard, (Jr.)

Difusa, Pati
See Almodovar, Pedro

Dillard, Annie 1945- .... **CLC 9, 60, 115**
See also AAYA 6, 43; AMWS 6; ANW; CA 49-52; CANR 3, 43, 62, 90, 125; DA3; DAM NOV; DLB 275, 278; DLBY 1980; LAIT 4, 5; MTCW 1, 2; NCFS 1; RGAL 4; SATA 10, 140; TUS

Dillard, R(ichard) H(enry) W(ilde)
1937- .... **CLC 5**
See also CA 21-24R; CAAS 7; CANR 10; CP 7; CSW; DLB 5, 244

Dillon, Eilis 1920-1994 .... **CLC 17**
See also CA 9-12R; 182; 147; CAAE 182; CAAS 3; CANR 4, 38, 78; CLR 26; MAICYA 1, 2; MAICYAS 1; SATA 2, 74; SATA-Essay 105; SATA-Obit 83; YAW

Dimont, Penelope
See Mortimer, Penelope (Ruth)

Dinesen, Isak ..... **CLC 10, 29, 95; SSC 7, 75**
See Blixen, Karen (Christentze Dinesen)
See also EW 10; EWL 3; EXPS; FW; HGG; LAIT 3; MTCW 1; NCFS 2; NFS 9; RGSF 2; RGWL 2, 3; SSFS 3, 6, 13; WLIT 2

Ding Ling .... **CLC 68**
See Chiang, Pin-chin
See also RGWL 3

Diphusa, Patty
See Almodovar, Pedro

Disch, Thomas M(ichael) 1940- ... **CLC 7, 36**
See Disch, Tom
See also AAYA 17; BPFB 1; CA 21-24R; CAAS 4; CANR 17, 36, 54, 89; CLR 18; CP 7; DA3; DLB 8; HGG; MAICYA 1, 2; MTCW 1, 2; SAAS 15; SATA 92; SCFW; SFW 4; SUFW 2

Disch, Tom
See Disch, Thomas M(ichael)
See also DLB 282

d'Isly, Georges
See Simenon, Georges (Jacques Christian)

Disraeli, Benjamin 1804-1881 ... **NCLC 2, 39, 79**
See also BRW 4; DLB 21, 55; RGEL 2

Ditcum, Steve
See Crumb, R(obert)

Dixon, Paige
See Corcoran, Barbara (Asenath)

Dixon, Stephen 1936- .... **CLC 52; SSC 16**
See also AMWS 12; CA 89-92; CANR 17, 40, 54, 91; CN 7; DLB 130

Dixon, Thomas 1864-1946 .... **TCLC 163**
See also RHW

Djebar, Assia 1936- .... **CLC 182**
See also CA 188; EWL 3; RGWL 3; WLIT 2

Doak, Annie
See Dillard, Annie

Dobell, Sydney Thompson
1824-1874 .... **NCLC 43**
See also DLB 32; RGEL 2

Doblin, Alfred .... **TCLC 13**
See Doeblin, Alfred
See also CDWLB 2; EWL 3; RGWL 2, 3

Dobroliubov, Nikolai Aleksandrovich
See Dobrolyubov, Nikolai Alexandrovich
See also DLB 277

Dobrolyubov, Nikolai Alexandrovich
1836-1861 .... **NCLC 5**
See Dobroliubov, Nikolai Aleksandrovich

Dobson, Austin 1840-1921 .... **TCLC 79**
See also DLB 35, 144

Dobyns, Stephen 1941- .... **CLC 37**
See also AMWS 13; CA 45-48; CANR 2,
18, 99; CMW 4; CP 7

Doctorow, E(dgar) L(aurence)
1931- .... **CLC 6, 11, 15, 18, 37, 44, 65,
113**
See also AAYA 22; AITN 2; AMWS 4;
BEST 89:3; BPFB 1; CA 45-48; CANR
2, 33, 51, 76, 97, 133; CDALB 1968-
1988; CN 7; CPW; DA3; DAM NOV,
POP; DLB 2, 28, 173; DLBY 1980; EWL
3; LAIT 3; MTCW 1, 2; NFS 6; RGAL 4;
RHW; TUS

Dodgson, Charles L(utwidge) 1832-1898
See Carroll, Lewis
See also CLR 2; DA; DA3; DAB; DAC;
DAM MST, NOV, POET; MAICYA 1, 2;
SATA 100; YABC 2

Dodsley, Robert 1703-1764 .... **LC 97**
See also DLB 95; RGEL 2

Dodson, Owen (Vincent) 1914-1983 .. **BLC 1;
CLC 79**
See also BW 1; CA 65-68; 110; CANR 24;
DAM MULT; DLB 76

Doeblin, Alfred 1878-1957 .... **TCLC 13**
See Doblin, Alfred
See also CA 110; 141; DLB 66

Doerr, Harriet 1910-2002 .... **CLC 34**
See also CA 117; 122; 213; CANR 47; INT
CA-122; LATS 1:2

Domecq, H(onorio Bustos)
See Bioy Casares, Adolfo

Domecq, H(onorio) Bustos
See Bioy Casares, Adolfo; Borges, Jorge
Luis

Domini, Rey
See Lorde, Audre (Geraldine)
See also GLL 1

Dominique
See Proust, (Valentin-Louis-George-Eugene)
Marcel

Don, A
See Stephen, Sir Leslie

Donaldson, Stephen R(eeder)
1947- .... **CLC 46, 138**
See also AAYA 36; BPFB 1; CA 89-92;
CANR 13, 55, 99; CPW; DAM POP;
FANT; INT CANR-13; SATA 121; SFW
4; SUFW 1, 2

Donleavy, J(ames) P(atrick) 1926- .... **CLC 1,
4, 6, 10, 45**
See also AITN 2; BPFB 1; CA 9-12R;
CANR 24, 49, 62, 80, 124; CBD; CD 5;
CN 7; DLB 6, 173; INT CANR-24;
MTCW 1, 2; RGAL 4

Donnadieu, Marguerite
See Duras, Marguerite

Donne, John 1572-1631 ... **LC 10, 24, 91; PC
1, 43; WLC**
See also BRW 1; BRWC 1; BRWR 2; CD-
BLB Before 1660; DA; DAB; DAC;
DAM MST, POET; DLB 121, 151; EXPP;
PAB; PFS 2, 11; RGEL 3; TEA; WLIT 3;
WP

Donnell, David 1939(?)- .... **CLC 34**
See also CA 197

Donoghue, Denis 1928- .... **CLC 209**
See also CA 17-20R; CANR 16, 102

Donoghue, P. S.
See Hunt, E(verette) Howard, (Jr.)

Donoso (Yanez), Jose 1924-1996 ... **CLC 4, 8,
11, 32, 99; HLC 1; SSC 34; TCLC 133**
See also CA 81-84; 155; CANR 32, 73; CD-
WLB 3; CWW 2; DAM MULT; DLB 113;
EWL 3; HW 1, 2; LAW; LAWS 1; MTCW
1, 2; RGSF 2; WLIT 1

Donovan, John 1928-1992 .... **CLC 35**
See also AAYA 20; CA 97-100; 137; CLR
3; MAICYA 1, 2; SATA 72; SATA-Brief
29; YAW

Don Roberto
See Cunninghame Graham, Robert
(Gallnigad) Bontine

Doolittle, Hilda 1886-1961 . **CLC 3, 8, 14, 31,
34, 73; PC 5; WLC**
See H. D.
See also AMWS 1; CA 97-100; CANR 35,
131; DA; DAC; DAM MST, POET; DLB
4, 45; EWL 3; FW; GLL 1; LMFS 2;
MAWW; MTCW 1, 2; PFS 6; RGAL 4

Doppo, Kunikida .... **TCLC 99**
See Kunikida Doppo

Dorfman, Ariel 1942- .... **CLC 48, 77, 189;
HLC 1**
See also CA 124; 130; CANR 67, 70, 135;
CWW 2; DAM MULT; DFS 4; EWL 3;
HW 1, 2; INT CA-130; WLIT 1

Dorn, Edward (Merton)
1929-1999 .... **CLC 10, 18**
See also CA 93-96; 187; CANR 42, 79; CP
7; DLB 5; INT CA-93-96; WP

Dor-Ner, Zvi .... **CLC 70**

Dorris, Michael (Anthony)
1945-1997 .... **CLC 109; NNAL**
See also AAYA 20; BEST 90:1; BYA 12;
CA 102; 157; CANR 19, 46, 75; CLR 58;
DA3; DAM MULT, NOV; DLB 175;
LAIT 5; MTCW 2; NFS 3; RGAL 4;
SATA 75; SATA-Obit 94; TCWW 2; YAW

Dorris, Michael A.
See Dorris, Michael (Anthony)

Dorsan, Luc
See Simenon, Georges (Jacques Christian)

Dorsange, Jean
See Simenon, Georges (Jacques Christian)

Dorset
See Sackville, Thomas

Dos Passos, John (Roderigo)
1896-1970 ... **CLC 1, 4, 8, 11, 15, 25, 34,
82; WLC**
See also AMW; BPFB 1; CA 1-4R; 29-32R;
CANR 3; CDALB 1929-1941; DA; DA3;
DAB; DAC; DAM MST, NOV; DLB 4,
9, 274; DLBD 1, 15; DLBY 1996; EWL
3; MTCW 1, 2; NFS 14; RGAL 4; TUS

Dossage, Jean
See Simenon, Georges (Jacques Christian)

Dostoevsky, Fedor Mikhailovich
1821-1881 .. **NCLC 2, 7, 21, 33, 43, 119;
SSC 2, 33, 44; WLC**
See Dostoevsky, Fyodor
See also AAYA 40; DA; DA3; DAB; DAC;
DAM MST, NOV; EW 7; EXPN; NFS 3,
8; RGSF 2; RGWL 2, 3; SSFS 8; TWA

Dostoevsky, Fyodor
See Dostoevsky, Fedor Mikhailovich
See also DLB 238; LATS 1:1; LMFS 1, 2

Doty, M. R.
See Doty, Mark (Alan)

Doty, Mark
See Doty, Mark (Alan)

Doty, Mark (Alan) 1953(?)- .... **CLC 176; PC
53**
See also AMWS 11; CA 161, 183; CAAE
183; CANR 110

Doty, Mark A.
See Doty, Mark (Alan)

Doughty, Charles M(ontagu)
1843-1926 .... **TCLC 27**
See also CA 115; 178; DLB 19, 57, 174

Douglas, Ellen .... **CLC 73**
See Haxton, Josephine Ayres; Williamson,
Ellen Douglas
See also CN 7; CSW; DLB 292

Douglas, Gavin 1475(?)-1522 .... **LC 20**
See also DLB 132; RGEL 2

Douglas, George
See Brown, George Douglas
See also RGEL 2

Douglas, Keith (Castellain)
1920-1944 .... **TCLC 40**
See also BRW 7; CA 160; DLB 27; EWL
3; PAB; RGEL 2

Douglas, Leonard
See Bradbury, Ray (Douglas)

Douglas, Michael
See Crichton, (John) Michael

Douglas, (George) Norman
1868-1952 .... **TCLC 68**
See also BRW 6; CA 119; 157; DLB 34,
195; RGEL 2

Douglas, William
See Brown, George Douglas

Douglass, Frederick 1817(?)-1895 ..... **BLC 1;
NCLC 7, 55, 141; WLC**
See also AAYA 48; AFAW 1, 2; AMWC 1;
AMWS 3; CDALB 1640-1865; DA; DA3;
DAC; DAM MST, MULT; DLB 1, 43, 50,
79, 243; FW; LAIT 2; NCFS 2; RGAL 4;
SATA 29

Dourado, (Waldomiro Freitas) Autran
1926- .... **CLC 23, 60**
See also CA 25-28R; 179; CANR 34, 81;
DLB 145, 307; HW 2

Dourado, Waldomiro Freitas Autran
See Dourado, (Waldomiro Freitas) Autran

Dove, Rita (Frances) 1952- . **BLCS; CLC 50,
81; PC 6**
See also AAYA 46; AMWS 4; BW 2; CA
109; CAAS 19; CANR 27, 42, 68, 76, 97,
132; CDALBS; CP 7; CSW; CWP; DA3;
DAM MULT, POET; DLB 120; EWL 3;
EXPP; MTCW 1; PFS 1, 15; RGAL 4

Doveglion
See Villa, Jose Garcia

Dowell, Coleman 1925-1985 .... **CLC 60**
See also CA 25-28R; 117; CANR 10; DLB
130; GLL 2

Dowson, Ernest (Christopher)
1867-1900 .... **TCLC 4**
See also CA 105; 150; DLB 19, 135; RGEL
2

Doyle, A. Conan
See Doyle, Sir Arthur Conan

Doyle, Sir Arthur Conan
1859-1930 . **SSC 12, 83; TCLC 7; WLC**
See Conan Doyle, Arthur
See also AAYA 14; BRWS 2; CA 104; 122;
CANR 131; CDBLB 1890-1914; CMW
4; DA; DA3; DAB; DAC; DAM MST,
NOV; DLB 18, 70, 156, 178; EXPS;
HGG; LAIT 2; MSW; MTCW 1, 2; RGEL
2; RGSF 2; RHW; SATA 24; SCFW 2;
SFW 4; SSFS 2; TEA; WCH; WLIT 4;
WYA; YAW

Doyle, Conan
See Doyle, Sir Arthur Conan

Doyle, John
See Graves, Robert (von Ranke)

Doyle, Roddy 1958(?)- .... **CLC 81, 178**
See also AAYA 14; BRWS 5; CA 143;
CANR 73, 128; CN 7; DA3; DLB 194

Doyle, Sir A. Conan
See Doyle, Sir Arthur Conan

Duras, Claire de 1777-1828 .... **NCLC 154**
Duras, Marguerite 1914-1996 . **CLC 3, 6, 11, 20, 34, 40, 68, 100; SSC 40**
See also BPFB 1; CA 25-28R; 151; CANR 50; CWW 2; DLB 83; EWL 3; GFL 1789 to the Present; IDFW 4; MTCW 1, 2; RGWL 2, 3; TWA
Durban, (Rosa) Pam 1947- .... **CLC 39**
See also CA 123; CANR 98; CSW
Durcan, Paul 1944- .... **CLC 43, 70**
See also CA 134; CANR 123; CP 7; DAM POET; EWL 3
Durfey, Thomas 1653-1723 .... **LC 94**
See also DLB 80; RGEL 2
Durkheim, Emile 1858-1917 .... **TCLC 55**
Durrell, Lawrence (George) 1912-1990 ..... **CLC 1, 4, 6, 8, 13, 27, 41**
See also BPFB 1; BRWS 1; CA 9-12R; 132; CANR 40, 77; CDBLB 1945-1960; DAM NOV; DLB 15, 27, 204; DLBY 1990; EWL 3; MTCW 1, 2; RGEL 2; SFW 4; TEA
Durrenmatt, Friedrich
See Duerrenmatt, Friedrich
See also CDWLB 2; EW 13; EWL 3; RGWL 2, 3
Dutt, Michael Madhusudan 1824-1873 .... **NCLC 118**
Dutt, Toru 1856-1877 .... **NCLC 29**
See also DLB 240
Dwight, Timothy 1752-1817 .... **NCLC 13**
See also DLB 37; RGAL 4
Dworkin, Andrea 1946- .... **CLC 43, 123**
See also CA 77-80; CAAS 21; CANR 16, 39, 76, 96; FW; GLL 1; INT CANR-16; MTCW 1, 2
Dwyer, Deanna
See Koontz, Dean R(ay)
Dwyer, K. R.
See Koontz, Dean R(ay)
Dybek, Stuart 1942- .... **CLC 114; SSC 55**
See also CA 97-100; CANR 39; DLB 130
Dye, Richard
See De Voto, Bernard (Augustine)
Dyer, Geoff 1958- .... **CLC 149**
See also CA 125; CANR 88
Dyer, George 1755-1841 .... **NCLC 129**
See also DLB 93
Dylan, Bob 1941- .... **CLC 3, 4, 6, 12, 77; PC 37**
See also CA 41-44R; CANR 108; CP 7; DLB 16
Dyson, John 1943- .... **CLC 70**
See also CA 144
Dzyubin, Eduard Georgievich 1895-1934
See Bagritsky, Eduard
See also CA 170
E. V. L.
See Lucas, E(dward) V(errall)
Eagleton, Terence (Francis) 1943- .. **CLC 63, 132**
See also CA 57-60; CANR 7, 23, 68, 115; DLB 242; LMFS 2; MTCW 1, 2
Eagleton, Terry
See Eagleton, Terence (Francis)
Early, Jack
See Scoppettone, Sandra
See also GLL 1
East, Michael
See West, Morris L(anglo)
Eastaway, Edward
See Thomas, (Philip) Edward
Eastlake, William (Derry) 1917-1997 .... **CLC 8**
See also CA 5-8R; 158; CAAS 1; CANR 5, 63; CN 7; DLB 6, 206; INT CANR-5; TCWW 2

Eastman, Charles A(lexander) 1858-1939 .... **NNAL; TCLC 55**
See also CA 179; CANR 91; DAM MULT; DLB 175; YABC 1
Eaton, Edith Maude 1865-1914 .... **AAL**
See Far, Sui Sin
See also CA 154; DLB 221; FW
Eaton, (Lillie) Winnifred 1875-1954 .... **AAL**
See also CA 217; DLB 221; RGAL 4
Eberhart, Richard (Ghormley) 1904- .... **CLC 3, 11, 19, 56**
See also AMW; CA 1-4R; CANR 2, 125; CDALB 1941-1968; CP 7; DAM POET; DLB 48; MTCW 1; RGAL 4
Eberstadt, Fernanda 1960- .... **CLC 39**
See also CA 136; CANR 69, 128
Echegaray (y Eizaguirre), Jose (Maria Waldo) 1832-1916 .... **HLCS 1; TCLC 4**
See also CA 104; CANR 32; EWL 3; HW 1; MTCW 1
Echeverria, (Jose) Esteban (Antonino) 1805-1851 .... **NCLC 18**
See also LAW
Echo
See Proust, (Valentin-Louis-George-Eugene) Marcel
Eckert, Allan W. 1931- .... **CLC 17**
See also AAYA 18; BYA 2; CA 13-16R; CANR 14, 45; INT CANR-14; MAICYA 2; MAICYAS 1; SAAS 21; SATA 29, 91; SATA-Brief 27
Eckhart, Meister 1260(?)-1327(?) ... **CMLC 9**
See also DLB 115; LMFS 1
Eckmar, F. R.
See de Hartog, Jan
Eco, Umberto 1932- .... **CLC 28, 60, 142**
See also BEST 90:1; BPFB 1; CA 77-80; CANR 12, 33, 55, 110, 131; CPW; CWW 2; DA3; DAM NOV, POP; DLB 196, 242; EWL 3; MSW; MTCW 1, 2; RGWL 3
Eddison, E(ric) R(ucker) 1882-1945 .... **TCLC 15**
See also CA 109; 156; DLB 255; FANT; SFW 4; SUFW 1
Eddy, Mary (Ann Morse) Baker 1821-1910 .... **TCLC 71**
See also CA 113; 174
Edel, (Joseph) Leon 1907-1997 .. **CLC 29, 34**
See also CA 1-4R; 161; CANR 1, 22, 112; DLB 103; INT CANR-22
Eden, Emily 1797-1869 .... **NCLC 10**
Edgar, David 1948- .... **CLC 42**
See also CA 57-60; CANR 12, 61, 112; CBD; CD 5; DAM DRAM; DFS 15; DLB 13, 233; MTCW 1
Edgerton, Clyde (Carlyle) 1944- ...... **CLC 39**
See also AAYA 17; CA 118; 134; CANR 64, 125; CSW; DLB 278; INT CA-134; YAW
Edgeworth, Maria 1768-1849 ... **NCLC 1, 51, 158**
See also BRWS 3; DLB 116, 159, 163; FW; RGEL 2; SATA 21; TEA; WLIT 3
Edmonds, Paul
See Kuttner, Henry
Edmonds, Walter D(umaux) 1903-1998 .... **CLC 35**
See also BYA 2; CA 5-8R; CANR 2; CWRI 5; DLB 9; LAIT 1; MAICYA 1, 2; RHW; SAAS 4; SATA 1, 27; SATA-Obit 99
Edmondson, Wallace
See Ellison, Harlan (Jay)
Edson, Margaret 1961- ...... **CLC 199; DC 24**
See also CA 190; DFS 13; DLB 266
Edson, Russell 1935- .... **CLC 13**
See also CA 33-36R; CANR 115; DLB 244; WP
Edwards, Bronwen Elizabeth
See Rose, Wendy

Edwards, G(erald) B(asil) 1899-1976 .... **CLC 25**
See also CA 201; 110
Edwards, Gus 1939- .... **CLC 43**
See also CA 108; INT CA-108
Edwards, Jonathan 1703-1758 .... **LC 7, 54**
See also AMW; DA; DAC; DAM MST; DLB 24, 270; RGAL 4; TUS
Edwards, Sarah Pierpont 1710-1758 .. **LC 87**
See also DLB 200
Efron, Marina Ivanovna Tsvetaeva
See Tsvetaeva (Efron), Marina (Ivanovna)
Egeria fl. 4th cent. - .... **CMLC 70**
Egoyan, Atom 1960- .... **CLC 151**
See also CA 157
Ehle, John (Marsden, Jr.) 1925- ...... **CLC 27**
See also CA 9-12R; CSW
Ehrenbourg, Ilya (Grigoryevich)
See Ehrenburg, Ilya (Grigoryevich)
Ehrenburg, Ilya (Grigoryevich) 1891-1967 .... **CLC 18, 34, 62**
See Erenburg, Il'ia Grigor'evich
See also CA 102; 25-28R; EWL 3
Ehrenburg, Ilyo (Grigoryevich)
See Ehrenburg, Ilya (Grigoryevich)
Ehrenreich, Barbara 1941- .... **CLC 110**
See also BEST 90:4; CA 73-76; CANR 16, 37, 62, 117; DLB 246; FW; MTCW 1, 2
Eich, Gunter
See Eich, Gunter
See also RGWL 2, 3
Eich, Gunter 1907-1972 .... **CLC 15**
See Eich, Gunter
See also CA 111; 93-96; DLB 69, 124; EWL 3
Eichendorff, Joseph 1788-1857 .... **NCLC 8**
See also DLB 90; RGWL 2, 3
Eigner, Larry .... **CLC 9**
See Eigner, Laurence (Joel)
See also CAAS 23; DLB 5; WP
Eigner, Laurence (Joel) 1927-1996
See Eigner, Larry
See also CA 9-12R; 151; CANR 6, 84; CP 7; DLB 193
Eilhart von Oberge c. 1140-c. 1195 .... **CMLC 67**
See also DLB 148
Einhard c. 770-840 .... **CMLC 50**
See also DLB 148
Einstein, Albert 1879-1955 .... **TCLC 65**
See also CA 121; 133; MTCW 1, 2
Eiseley, Loren
See Eiseley, Loren Corey
See also DLB 275
Eiseley, Loren Corey 1907-1977 .... **CLC 7**
See Eiseley, Loren
See also AAYA 5; ANW; CA 1-4R; 73-76; CANR 6; DLBD 17
Eisenstadt, Jill 1963- .... **CLC 50**
See also CA 140
Eisenstein, Sergei (Mikhailovich) 1898-1948 .... **TCLC 57**
See also CA 114; 149
Eisner, Simon
See Kornbluth, C(yril) M.
Ekeloef, (Bengt) Gunnar 1907-1968 .... **CLC 27; PC 23**
See Ekelof, (Bengt) Gunnar
See also CA 123; 25-28R; DAM POET
Ekelof, (Bengt) Gunnar 1907-1968
See Ekeloef, (Bengt) Gunnar
See also DLB 259; EW 12; EWL 3
Ekelund, Vilhelm 1880-1949 .... **TCLC 75**
See also CA 189; EWL 3
Ekwensi, C. O. D.
See Ekwensi, Cyprian (Odiatu Duaka)

102; DLBD 2; DLBY 1986, 1997; EWL 3; EXPN; EXPS; LAIT 2; LATS 1:1; LMFS 2; MTCW 1, 2; NFS 4, 8, 13; RGAL 4; RGSF 2; SSFS 2, 5, 6, 12; TUS

Fauset, Jessie Redmon 1882(?)-1961 .. **BLC 2; CLC 19, 54; HR 2**
See also AFAW 2; BW 1; CA 109; CANR 83; DAM MULT; DLB 51; FW; LMFS 2; MAWW

Faust, Frederick (Schiller) 1892-1944(?) .... **TCLC 49**
See Austin, Frank; Brand, Max; Challis, George; Dawson, Peter; Dexter, Martin; Evans, Evan; Frederick, John; Frost, Frederick; Manning, David; Silver, Nicholas
See also CA 108; 152; DAM POP; DLB 256; TUS

Faust, Irvin 1924- .... **CLC 8**
See also CA 33-36R; CANR 28, 67; CN 7; DLB 2, 28, 218, 278; DLBY 1980

Faustino, Domingo 1811-1888 ...... **NCLC 123**

Fawkes, Guy
See Benchley, Robert (Charles)

Fearing, Kenneth (Flexner) 1902-1961 .... **CLC 51**
See also CA 93-96; CANR 59; CMW 4; DLB 9; RGAL 4

Fecamps, Elise
See Creasey, John

Federman, Raymond 1928- .... **CLC 6, 47**
See also CA 17-20R, 208; CAAE 208; CAAS 8; CANR 10, 43, 83, 108; CN 7; DLBY 1980

Federspiel, J(uerg) F. 1931- .... **CLC 42**
See also CA 146

Feiffer, Jules (Ralph) 1929- ...... **CLC 2, 8, 64**
See also AAYA 3; CA 17-20R; CAD; CANR 30, 59, 129; CD 5; DAM DRAM; DLB 7, 44; INT CANR-30; MTCW 1; SATA 8, 61, 111

Feige, Hermann Albert Otto Maximilian
See Traven, B.

Feinberg, David B. 1956-1994 .... **CLC 59**
See also CA 135; 147

Feinstein, Elaine 1930- .... **CLC 36**
See also CA 69-72; CAAS 1; CANR 31, 68, 121; CN 7; CP 7; CWP; DLB 14, 40; MTCW 1

Feke, Gilbert David .... **CLC 65**

Feldman, Irving (Mordecai) 1928- ..... **CLC 7**
See also CA 1-4R; CANR 1; CP 7; DLB 169

Felix-Tchicaya, Gerald
See Tchicaya, Gerald Felix

Fellini, Federico 1920-1993 .... **CLC 16, 85**
See also CA 65-68; 143; CANR 33

Felltham, Owen 1602(?)-1668 .... **LC 92**
See also DLB 126, 151

Felsen, Henry Gregor 1916-1995 ..... **CLC 17**
See also CA 1-4R; 180; CANR 1; SAAS 2; SATA 1

Felski, Rita .... **CLC 65**

Fenno, Jack
See Calisher, Hortense

Fenollosa, Ernest (Francisco) 1853-1908 .... **TCLC 91**

Fenton, James Martin 1949- .... **CLC 32, 209**
See also CA 102; CANR 108; CP 7; DLB 40; PFS 11

Ferber, Edna 1887-1968 .... **CLC 18, 93**
See also AITN 1; CA 5-8R; 25-28R; CANR 68, 105; DLB 9, 28, 86, 266; MTCW 1, 2; RGAL 4; RHW; SATA 7; TCWW 2

Ferdowsi, Abu'l Qasem 940-1020 . **CMLC 43**
See also RGWL 2, 3

Ferguson, Helen
See Kavan, Anna

Ferguson, Niall 1964- .... **CLC 134**
See also CA 190

Ferguson, Samuel 1810-1886 .... **NCLC 33**
See also DLB 32; RGEL 2

Fergusson, Robert 1750-1774 .... **LC 29**
See also DLB 109; RGEL 2

Ferling, Lawrence
See Ferlinghetti, Lawrence (Monsanto)

Ferlinghetti, Lawrence (Monsanto) 1919(?)- ..... **CLC 2, 6, 10, 27, 111; PC 1**
See also CA 5-8R; CANR 3, 41, 73, 125; CDALB 1941-1968; CP 7; DA3; DAM POET; DLB 5, 16; MTCW 1, 2; RGAL 4; WP

Fern, Fanny
See Parton, Sara Payson Willis

Fernandez, Vicente Garcia Huidobro
See Huidobro Fernandez, Vicente Garcia

Fernandez-Armesto, Felipe .... **CLC 70**

Fernandez de Lizardi, Jose Joaquin
See Lizardi, Jose Joaquin Fernandez de

Ferre, Rosario 1938- ...... **CLC 139; HLCS 1; SSC 36**
See also CA 131; CANR 55, 81, 134; CWW 2; DLB 145; EWL 3; HW 1, 2; LAWS 1; MTCW 1; WLIT 1

Ferrer, Gabriel (Francisco Victor) Miro
See Miro (Ferrer), Gabriel (Francisco Victor)

Ferrier, Susan (Edmonstone) 1782-1854 .... **NCLC 8**
See also DLB 116; RGEL 2

Ferrigno, Robert 1948(?)- .... **CLC 65**
See also CA 140; CANR 125

Ferron, Jacques 1921-1985 .... **CLC 94**
See also CA 117; 129; CCA 1; DAC; DLB 60; EWL 3

Feuchtwanger, Lion 1884-1958 .... **TCLC 3**
See also CA 104; 187; DLB 66; EWL 3

Feuerbach, Ludwig 1804-1872 ..... **NCLC 139**
See also DLB 133

Feuillet, Octave 1821-1890 .... **NCLC 45**
See also DLB 192

Feydeau, Georges (Leon Jules Marie) 1862-1921 .... **TCLC 22**
See also CA 113; 152; CANR 84; DAM DRAM; DLB 192; EWL 3; GFL 1789 to the Present; RGWL 2, 3

Fichte, Johann Gottlieb 1762-1814 .... **NCLC 62**
See also DLB 90

Ficino, Marsilio 1433-1499 .... **LC 12**
See also LMFS 1

Fiedeler, Hans
See Doeblin, Alfred

Fiedler, Leslie A(aron) 1917-2003 ..... **CLC 4, 13, 24**
See also AMWS 13; CA 9-12R; 212; CANR 7, 63; CN 7; DLB 28, 67; EWL 3; MTCW 1, 2; RGAL 4; TUS

Field, Andrew 1938- .... **CLC 44**
See also CA 97-100; CANR 25

Field, Eugene 1850-1895 .... **NCLC 3**
See also DLB 23, 42, 140; DLBD 13; MAICYA 1, 2; RGAL 4; SATA 16

Field, Gans T.
See Wellman, Manly Wade

Field, Michael 1915-1971 .... **TCLC 43**
See also CA 29-32R

Field, Peter
See Hobson, Laura Z(ametkin)
See also TCWW 2

Fielding, Helen 1958- .... **CLC 146**
See also CA 172; CANR 127; DLB 231

Fielding, Henry 1707-1754 .... **LC 1, 46, 85; WLC**
See also BRW 3; BRWR 1; CDBLB 1660-1789; DA; DA3; DAB; DAC; DAM DRAM, MST, NOV; DLB 39, 84, 101; NFS 18; RGEL 2; TEA; WLIT 3

Fielding, Sarah 1710-1768 .... **LC 1, 44**
See also DLB 39; RGEL 2; TEA

Fields, W. C. 1880-1946 .... **TCLC 80**
See also DLB 44

Fierstein, Harvey (Forbes) 1954- ..... **CLC 33**
See also CA 123; 129; CAD; CD 5; CPW; DA3; DAM DRAM, POP; DFS 6; DLB 266; GLL

Figes, Eva 1932- .... **CLC 31**
See also CA 53-56; CANR 4, 44, 83; CN 7; DLB 14, 271; FW

Filippo, Eduardo de
See de Filippo, Eduardo

Finch, Anne 1661-1720 .... **LC 3; PC 21**
See also BRWS 9; DLB 95

Finch, Robert (Duer Claydon) 1900-1995 .... **CLC 18**
See also CA 57-60; CANR 9, 24, 49; CP 7; DLB 88

Findley, Timothy (Irving Frederick) 1930-2002 .... **CLC 27, 102**
See also CA 25-28R; 206; CANR 12, 42, 69, 109; CCA 1; CN 7; DAC; DAM MST; DLB 53; FANT; RHW

Fink, William
See Mencken, H(enry) L(ouis)

Firbank, Louis 1942-
See Reed, Lou
See also CA 117

Firbank, (Arthur Annesley) Ronald 1886-1926 .... **TCLC 1**
See also BRWS 2; CA 104; 177; DLB 36; EWL 3; RGEL 2

Fish, Stanley
See Fish, Stanley Eugene

Fish, Stanley E.
See Fish, Stanley Eugene

Fish, Stanley Eugene 1938- .... **CLC 142**
See also CA 112; 132; CANR 90; DLB 67

Fisher, Dorothy (Frances) Canfield 1879-1958 .... **TCLC 87**
See also CA 114; 136; CANR 80; CLR 71,; CWRI 5; DLB 9, 102, 284; MAICYA 1, 2; YABC 1

Fisher, M(ary) F(rances) K(ennedy) 1908-1992 .... **CLC 76, 87**
See also CA 77-80; 138; CANR 44; MTCW 1

Fisher, Roy 1930- .... **CLC 25**
See also CA 81-84; CAAS 10; CANR 16; CP 7; DLB 40

Fisher, Rudolph 1897-1934 .... **BLC 2; HR 2; SSC 25; TCLC 11**
See also BW 1, 3; CA 107; 124; CANR 80; DAM MULT; DLB 51, 102

Fisher, Vardis (Alvero) 1895-1968 .... **CLC 7; TCLC 140**
See also CA 5-8R; 25-28R; CANR 68; DLB 9, 206; RGAL 4; TCWW 2

Fiske, Tarleton
See Bloch, Robert (Albert)

Fitch, Clarke
See Sinclair, Upton (Beall)

Fitch, John IV
See Cormier, Robert (Edmund)

Fitzgerald, Captain Hugh
See Baum, L(yman) Frank

FitzGerald, Edward 1809-1883 ...... **NCLC 9, 153**
See also BRW 4; DLB 32; RGEL 2

Garrigue, Jean 1914-1972 .... **CLC 2, 8**
See also CA 5-8R; 37-40R; CANR 20

Garrison, Frederick
See Sinclair, Upton (Beall)

Garrison, William Lloyd
1805-1879 .... **NCLC 149**
See also CDALB 1640-1865; DLB 1, 43, 235

Garro, Elena 1920(?)-1998 .. **HLCS 1; TCLC 153**
See also CA 131; 169; CWW 2; DLB 145; EWL 3; HW 1; LAWS 1; WLIT 1

Garth, Will
See Hamilton, Edmond; Kuttner, Henry

Garvey, Marcus (Moziah, Jr.)
1887-1940 .... **BLC 2; HR 2; TCLC 41**
See also BW 1; CA 120; 124; CANR 79; DAM MULT

Gary, Romain .... **CLC 25**
See Kacew, Romain
See also DLB 83, 299

Gascar, Pierre .... **CLC 11**
See Fournier, Pierre
See also EWL 3

Gascoigne, George 1539-1577 .... **LC 108**
See also DLB 136; RGEL 2

Gascoyne, David (Emery)
1916-2001 .... **CLC 45**
See also CA 65-68; 200; CANR 10, 28, 54; CP 7; DLB 20; MTCW 1; RGEL 2

Gaskell, Elizabeth Cleghorn
1810-1865 .... **NCLC 5, 70, 97, 137; SSC 25**
See also BRW 5; CDBLB 1832-1890; DAB; DAM MST; DLB 21, 144, 159; RGEL 2; RGSF 2; TEA

Gass, William H(oward) 1924- . **CLC 1, 2, 8, 11, 15, 39, 132; SSC 12**
See also AMWS 6; CA 17-20R; CANR 30, 71, 100; CN 7; DLB 2, 227; EWL 3; MTCW 1, 2; RGAL 4

Gassendi, Pierre 1592-1655 .... **LC 54**
See also GFL Beginnings to 1789

Gasset, Jose Ortega y
See Ortega y Gasset, Jose

Gates, Henry Louis, Jr. 1950- ... **BLCS; CLC 65**
See also BW 2, 3; CA 109; CANR 25, 53, 75, 125; CSW; DA3; DAM MULT; DLB 67; EWL 3; MTCW 1; RGAL 4

Gautier, Theophile 1811-1872 .. **NCLC 1, 59; PC 18; SSC 20**
See also DAM POET; DLB 119; EW 6; GFL 1789 to the Present; RGWL 2, 3; SUFW; TWA

Gawsworth, John
See Bates, H(erbert) E(rnest)

Gay, John 1685-1732 .... **LC 49**
See also BRW 3; DAM DRAM; DLB 84, 95; RGEL 2; WLIT 3

Gay, Oliver
See Gogarty, Oliver St. John

Gay, Peter (Jack) 1923- .... **CLC 158**
See also CA 13-16R; CANR 18, 41, 77; INT CANR-18

Gaye, Marvin (Pentz, Jr.)
1939-1984 .... **CLC 26**
See also CA 195; 112

Gebler, Carlo (Ernest) 1954- .... **CLC 39**
See also CA 119; 133; CANR 96; DLB 271

Gee, Maggie (Mary) 1948- .... **CLC 57**
See also CA 130; CANR 125; CN 7; DLB 207

Gee, Maurice (Gough) 1931- .... **CLC 29**
See also AAYA 42; CA 97-100; CANR 67, 123; CLR 56; CN 7; CWRI 5; EWL 3; MAICYA 2; RGSF 2; SATA 46, 101

Geiogamah, Hanay 1945- .... **NNAL**
See also CA 153; DAM MULT; DLB 175

Gelbart, Larry (Simon) 1928- .... **CLC 21, 61**
See Gelbart, Larry
See also CA 73-76; CANR 45, 94

Gelbart, Larry 1928-
See Gelbart, Larry (Simon)
See also CAD; CD 5

Gelber, Jack 1932-2003 ...... **CLC 1, 6, 14, 79**
See also CA 1-4R; 216; CAD; CANR 2; DLB 7, 228

Gellhorn, Martha (Ellis)
1908-1998 .... **CLC 14, 60**
See also CA 77-80; 164; CANR 44; CN 7; DLBY 1982, 1998

Genet, Jean 1910-1986 . **DC 25; CLC 1, 2, 5, 10, 14, 44, 46; TCLC 128**
See also CA 13-16R; CANR 18; DA3; DAM DRAM; DFS 10; DLB 72; DLBY 1986; EW 13; EWL 3; GFL 1789 to the Present; GLL 1; LMFS 2; MTCW 1, 2; RGWL 2, 3; TWA

Gent, Peter 1942- .... **CLC 29**
See also AITN 1; CA 89-92; DLBY 1982

Gentile, Giovanni 1875-1944 .... **TCLC 96**
See also CA 119

Gentlewoman in New England, A
See Bradstreet, Anne

Gentlewoman in Those Parts, A
See Bradstreet, Anne

Geoffrey of Monmouth c.
1100-1155 .... **CMLC 44**
See also DLB 146; TEA

George, Jean
See George, Jean Craighead

George, Jean Craighead 1919- .... **CLC 35**
See also AAYA 8; BYA 2, 4; CA 5-8R; CANR 25; CLR 1; 80; DLB 52; JRDA; MAICYA 1, 2; SATA 2, 68, 124; WYA; YAW

George, Stefan (Anton) 1868-1933 . **TCLC 2, 14**
See also CA 104; 193; EW 8; EWL 3

Georges, Georges Martin
See Simenon, Georges (Jacques Christian)

Gerald of Wales c. 1146-c. 1223 ... **CMLC 60**

Gerhardi, William Alexander
See Gerhardie, William Alexander

Gerhardie, William Alexander
1895-1977 .... **CLC 5**
See also CA 25-28R; 73-76; CANR 18; DLB 36; RGEL 2

Gerson, Jean 1363-1429 .... **LC 77**
See also DLB 208

Gersonides 1288-1344 .... **CMLC 49**
See also DLB 115

Gerstler, Amy 1956- .... **CLC 70**
See also CA 146; CANR 99

Gertler, T. .... **CLC 34**
See also CA 116; 121

Gertsen, Aleksandr Ivanovich
See Herzen, Aleksandr Ivanovich

Ghalib .... **NCLC 39, 78**
See Ghalib, Asadullah Khan

Ghalib, Asadullah Khan 1797-1869
See Ghalib
See also DAM POET; RGWL 2, 3

Ghelderode, Michel de 1898-1962 ..... **CLC 6, 11; DC 15**
See also CA 85-88; CANR 40, 77; DAM DRAM; EW 11; EWL 3; TWA

Ghiselin, Brewster 1903-2001 .... **CLC 23**
See also CA 13-16R; CAAS 10; CANR 13; CP 7

Ghose, Aurabinda 1872-1950 .... **TCLC 63**
See Ghose, Aurobindo
See also CA 163

Ghose, Aurobindo
See Ghose, Aurabinda
See also EWL 3

Ghose, Zulfikar 1935- .... **CLC 42, 200**
See also CA 65-68; CANR 67; CN 7; CP 7; EWL 3

Ghosh, Amitav 1956- .... **CLC 44, 153**
See also CA 147; CANR 80; CN 7; WWE 1

Giacosa, Giuseppe 1847-1906 .... **TCLC 7**
See also CA 104

Gibb, Lee
See Waterhouse, Keith (Spencer)

Gibbon, Edward 1737-1794 .... **LC 97**
See also BRW 3; DLB 104; RGEL 2

Gibbon, Lewis Grassic .... **TCLC 4**
See Mitchell, James Leslie
See also RGEL 2

Gibbons, Kaye 1960- .... **CLC 50, 88, 145**
See also AAYA 34; AMWS 10; CA 151; CANR 75, 127; CSW; DA3; DAM POP; DLB 292; MTCW 1; NFS 3; RGAL 4; SATA 117

Gibran, Kahlil 1883-1931 . **PC 9; TCLC 1, 9**
See also CA 104; 150; DA3; DAM POET, POP; EWL 3; MTCW 2

Gibran, Khalil
See Gibran, Kahlil

Gibson, William 1914- .... **CLC 23**
See also CA 9-12R; CAD 2; CANR 9, 42, 75, 125; CD 5; DA; DAB; DAC; DAM DRAM, MST; DFS 2; DLB 7; LAIT 2; MTCW 2; SATA 66; YAW

Gibson, William (Ford) 1948- ... **CLC 39, 63, 186, 192; SSC 52**
See also AAYA 12, 59; BPFB 2; CA 126; 133; CANR 52, 90, 106; CN 7; CPW; DA3; DAM POP; DLB 251; MTCW 2; SCFW 2; SFW 4

Gide, Andre (Paul Guillaume)
1869-1951 ..... **SSC 13; TCLC 5, 12, 36; WLC**
See also CA 104; 124; DA; DA3; DAB; DAC; DAM MST, NOV; DLB 65; EW 8; EWL 3; GFL 1789 to the Present; MTCW 1, 2; RGSF 2; RGWL 2, 3; TWA

Gifford, Barry (Colby) 1946- .... **CLC 34**
See also CA 65-68; CANR 9, 30, 40, 90

Gilbert, Frank
See De Voto, Bernard (Augustine)

Gilbert, W(illiam) S(chwenck)
1836-1911 .... **TCLC 3**
See also CA 104; 173; DAM DRAM, POET; RGEL 2; SATA 36

Gilbreth, Frank B(unker), Jr.
1911-2001 .... **CLC 17**
See also CA 9-12R; SATA 2

Gilchrist, Ellen (Louise) 1935- .. **CLC 34, 48, 143; SSC 14, 63**
See also BPFB 2; CA 113; 116; CANR 41, 61, 104; CN 7; CPW; CSW; DAM POP; DLB 130; EWL 3; EXPS; MTCW 1, 2; RGAL 4; RGSF 2; SSFS 9

Giles, Molly 1942- .... **CLC 39**
See also CA 126; CANR 98

Gill, Eric 1882-1940 .... **TCLC 85**
See Gill, (Arthur) Eric (Rowton Peter Joseph)

Gill, (Arthur) Eric (Rowton Peter Joseph)
1882-1940
See Gill, Eric
See also CA 120; DLB 98

Gill, Patrick
See Creasey, John

Gillette, Douglas .... **CLC 70**

Gilliam, Terry (Vance) 1940- .... **CLC 21, 141**
See Monty Python
See also AAYA 19, 59; CA 108; 113; CANR 35; INT CA-113

Gillian, Jerry
See Gilliam, Terry (Vance)

Grove, Frederick Philip .... **TCLC 4**
See Greve, Felix Paul (Berthold Friedrich)
See also DLB 92; RGEL 2

Grubb
See Crumb, R(obert)

Grumbach, Doris (Isaac) 1918- . **CLC 13, 22, 64**
See also CA 5-8R; CAAS 2; CANR 9, 42, 70, 127; CN 7; INT CANR-9; MTCW 2

Grundtvig, Nikolai Frederik Severin
1783-1872 .... **NCLC 1, 158**
See also DLB 300

Grunge
See Crumb, R(obert)

Grunwald, Lisa 1959- .... **CLC 44**
See also CA 120

Gryphius, Andreas 1616-1664 .... **LC 89**
See also CDWLB 2; DLB 164; RGWL 2, 3

Guare, John 1938- .... **CLC 8, 14, 29, 67; DC 20**
See also CA 73-76; CAD; CANR 21, 69, 118; CD 5; DAM DRAM; DFS 8, 13; DLB 7, 249; EWL 3; MTCW 1, 2; RGAL 4

Guarini, Battista 1537-1612 .... **LC 102**

Gubar, Susan (David) 1944- .... **CLC 145**
See also CA 108; CANR 45, 70; FW; MTCW 1; RGAL 4

Gudjonsson, Halldor Kiljan 1902-1998
See Halldor Laxness
See also CA 103; 164

Guenter, Erich
See Eich, Gunter

Guest, Barbara 1920- .... **CLC 34; PC 55**
See also BG 2; CA 25-28R; CANR 11, 44, 84; CP 7; CWP; DLB 5, 193

Guest, Edgar A(lbert) 1881-1959 ... **TCLC 95**
See also CA 112; 168

Guest, Judith (Ann) 1936- .... **CLC 8, 30**
See also AAYA 7; CA 77-80; CANR 15, 75; DA3; DAM NOV, POP; EXPN; INT CANR-15; LAIT 5; MTCW 1, 2; NFS 1

Guevara, Che .... **CLC 87; HLC 1**
See Guevara (Serna), Ernesto

Guevara (Serna), Ernesto
1928-1967 .... **CLC 87; HLC 1**
See Guevara, Che
See also CA 127; 111; CANR 56; DAM MULT; HW 1

Guicciardini, Francesco 1483-1540 ..... **LC 49**

Guild, Nicholas M. 1944- .... **CLC 33**
See also CA 93-96

Guillemin, Jacques
See Sartre, Jean-Paul

Guillen, Jorge 1893-1984 . **CLC 11; HLCS 1; PC 35**
See also CA 89-92; 112; DAM MULT, POET; DLB 108; EWL 3; HW 1; RGWL 2, 3

Guillen, Nicolas (Cristobal)
1902-1989 .... **BLC 2; CLC 48, 79; HLC 1; PC 23**
See also BW 2; CA 116; 125; 129; CANR 84; DAM MST, MULT, POET; DLB 283; EWL 3; HW 1; LAW; RGWL 2, 3; WP

Guillen y Alvarez, Jorge
See Guillen, Jorge

Guillevic, (Eugene) 1907-1997 .... **CLC 33**
See also CA 93-96; CWW 2

Guillois
See Desnos, Robert

Guillois, Valentin
See Desnos, Robert

Guimaraes Rosa, Joao 1908-1967 .... **HLCS 2**
See Rosa, Joao Guimaraes
See also CA 175; LAW; RGSF 2; RGWL 2, 3

Guiney, Louise Imogen
1861-1920 .... **TCLC 41**
See also CA 160; DLB 54; RGAL 4

Guinizelli, Guido c. 1230-1276 ...... **CMLC 49**

Guiraldes, Ricardo (Guillermo)
1886-1927 .... **TCLC 39**
See also CA 131; EWL 3; HW 1; LAW; MTCW 1

Gumilev, Nikolai (Stepanovich)
1886-1921 .... **TCLC 60**
See Gumilyov, Nikolay Stepanovich
See also CA 165; DLB 295

Gumilyov, Nikolay Stepanovich
See Gumilev, Nikolai (Stepanovich)
See also EWL 3

Gump, P. Q.
See Card, Orson Scott

Gunesekera, Romesh 1954- .... **CLC 91**
See also BRWS 10; CA 159; CN 7; DLB 267

Gunn, Bill .... **CLC 5**
See Gunn, William Harrison
See also DLB 38

Gunn, Thom(son William)
1929-2004 . **CLC 3, 6, 18, 32, 81; PC 26**
See also BRWS 4; CA 17-20R; 227; CANR 9, 33, 116; CDBLB 1960 to Present; CP 7; DAM POET; DLB 27; INT CANR-33; MTCW 1; PFS 9; RGEL 2

Gunn, William Harrison 1934(?)-1989
See Gunn, Bill
See also AITN 1; BW 1, 3; CA 13-16R; 128; CANR 12, 25, 76

Gunn Allen, Paula
See Allen, Paula Gunn

Gunnars, Kristjana 1948- .... **CLC 69**
See also CA 113; CCA 1; CP 7; CWP; DLB 60

Gunter, Erich
See Eich, Gunter

Gurdjieff, G(eorgei) I(vanovich)
1877(?)-1949 .... **TCLC 71**
See also CA 157

Gurganus, Allan 1947- .... **CLC 70**
See also BEST 90:1; CA 135; CANR 114; CN 7; CPW; CSW; DAM POP; GLL 1

Gurney, A. R.
See Gurney, A(lbert) R(amsdell), Jr.
See also DLB 266

Gurney, A(lbert) R(amsdell), Jr.
1930- .... **CLC 32, 50, 54**
See Gurney, A. R.
See also AMWS 5; CA 77-80; CAD; CANR 32, 64, 121; CD 5; DAM DRAM; EWL 3

Gurney, Ivor (Bertie) 1890-1937 ... **TCLC 33**
See also BRW 6; CA 167; DLBY 2002; PAB; RGEL 2

Gurney, Peter
See Gurney, A(lbert) R(amsdell), Jr.

Guro, Elena (Genrikhovna)
1877-1913 .... **TCLC 56**
See also DLB 295

Gustafson, James M(oody) 1925- ... **CLC 100**
See also CA 25-28R; CANR 37

Gustafson, Ralph (Barker)
1909-1995 .... **CLC 36**
See also CA 21-24R; CANR 8, 45, 84; CP 7; DLB 88; RGEL 2

Gut, Gom
See Simenon, Georges (Jacques Christian)

Guterson, David 1956- .... **CLC 91**
See also CA 132; CANR 73, 126; DLB 292; MTCW 2; NFS 13

Guthrie, A(lfred) B(ertram), Jr.
1901-1991 .... **CLC 23**
See also CA 57-60; 134; CANR 24; DLB 6, 212; SATA 62; SATA-Obit 67

Guthrie, Isobel
See Grieve, C(hristopher) M(urray)

Guthrie, Woodrow Wilson 1912-1967
See Guthrie, Woody
See also CA 113; 93-96

Guthrie, Woody .... **CLC 35**
See Guthrie, Woodrow Wilson
See also DLB 303; LAIT 3

Gutierrez Najera, Manuel
1859-1895 .... **HLCS 2; NCLC 133**
See also DLB 290; LAW

Guy, Rosa (Cuthbert) 1925- .... **CLC 26**
See also AAYA 4, 37; BW 2; CA 17-20R; CANR 14, 34, 83; CLR 13; DLB 33; DNFS 1; JRDA; MAICYA 1, 2; SATA 14, 62, 122; YAW

Gwendolyn
See Bennett, (Enoch) Arnold

H. D. .... **CLC 3, 8, 14, 31, 34, 73; PC 5**
See Doolittle, Hilda

H. de V.
See Buchan, John

Haavikko, Paavo Juhani 1931- .. **CLC 18, 34**
See also CA 106; CWW 2; EWL 3

Habbema, Koos
See Heijermans, Herman

Habermas, Juergen 1929- .... **CLC 104**
See also CA 109; CANR 85; DLB 242

Habermas, Jurgen
See Habermas, Juergen

Hacker, Marilyn 1942- ...... **CLC 5, 9, 23, 72, 91; PC 47**
See also CA 77-80; CANR 68, 129; CP 7; CWP; DAM POET; DLB 120, 282; FW; GLL 2; PFS 19

Hadewijch of Antwerp fl. 1250- ... **CMLC 61**
See also RGWL 3

Hadrian 76-138 .... **CMLC 52**

Haeckel, Ernst Heinrich (Philipp August)
1834-1919 .... **TCLC 83**
See also CA 157

Hafiz c. 1326-1389(?) .... **CMLC 34**
See also RGWL 2, 3

Hagedorn, Jessica T(arahata)
1949- .... **CLC 185**
See also CA 139; CANR 69; CWP; RGAL 4

Haggard, H(enry) Rider
1856-1925 .... **TCLC 11**
See also BRWS 3; BYA 4, 5; CA 108; 148; CANR 112; DLB 70, 156, 174, 178; FANT; LMFS 1; MTCW 2; RGEL 2; RHW; SATA 16; SCFW 4; SFW 4; SUFW 1; WLIT 4

Hagiosy, L.
See Larbaud, Valery (Nicolas)

Hagiwara, Sakutaro 1886-1942 .... **PC 18; TCLC 60**
See Hagiwara Sakutaro
See also CA 154; RGWL 3

Hagiwara Sakutaro
See Hagiwara, Sakutaro
See also EWL 3

Haig, Fenil
See Ford, Ford Madox

Haig-Brown, Roderick (Langmere)
1908-1976 .... **CLC 21**
See also CA 5-8R; 69-72; CANR 4, 38, 83; CLR 31; CWRI 5; DLB 88; MAICYA 1, 2; SATA 12

Haight, Rip
See Carpenter, John (Howard)

Hailey, Arthur 1920- .... **CLC 5**
See also AITN 2; BEST 90:3; BPFB 2; CA 1-4R; CANR 2, 36, 75; CCA 1; CN 7; CPW; DAM NOV, POP; DLB 88; DLBY 1982; MTCW 1, 2

Hailey, Elizabeth Forsythe 1938- ..... **CLC 40**
See also CA 93-96; 188; CAAE 188; CAAS 1; CANR 15, 48; INT CANR-15

Harris, George Washington
1814-1869 .... **NCLC 23**
See also DLB 3, 11, 248; RGAL 4
Harris, Joel Chandler 1848-1908 ..... **SSC 19;**
TCLC 2
See also CA 104; 137; CANR 80; CLR 49;
DLB 11, 23, 42, 78, 91; LAIT 2; MAI-
CYA 1, 2; RGSF 2; SATA 100; WCH;
YABC 1
Harris, John (Wyndham Parkes Lucas)
Beynon 1903-1969
See Wyndham, John
See also CA 102; 89-92; CANR 84; SATA
118; SFW 4
Harris, MacDonald .... **CLC 9**
See Heiney, Donald (William)
Harris, Mark 1922- .... **CLC 19**
See also CA 5-8R; CAAS 3; CANR 2, 55,
83; CN 7; DLB 2; DLBY 1980
Harris, Norman .... **CLC 65**
Harris, (Theodore) Wilson 1921- .... **CLC 25,**
159
See also BRWS 5; BW 2, 3; CA 65-68;
CAAS 16; CANR 11, 27, 69, 114; CD-
WLB 3; CN 7; CP 7; DLB 117; EWL 3;
MTCW 1; RGEL 2
Harrison, Barbara Grizzuti
1934-2002 .... **CLC 144**
See also CA 77-80; 205; CANR 15, 48; INT
CANR-15
Harrison, Elizabeth (Allen) Cavanna
1909-2001
See Cavanna, Betty
See also CA 9-12R; 200; CANR 6, 27, 85,
104, 121; MAICYA 2; SATA 142; YAW
Harrison, Harry (Max) 1925- .... **CLC 42**
See also CA 1-4R; CANR 5, 21, 84; DLB
8; SATA 4; SCFW 2; SFW 4
Harrison, James (Thomas) 1937- ...... **CLC 6,**
14, 33, 66, 143; SSC 19
See Harrison, Jim
See also CA 13-16R; CANR 8, 51, 79; CN
7; CP 7; DLBY 1982; INT CANR-8
Harrison, Jim
See Harrison, James (Thomas)
See also AMWS 8; RGAL 4; TCWW 2;
TUS
Harrison, Kathryn 1961- .... **CLC 70, 151**
See also CA 144; CANR 68, 122
Harrison, Tony 1937- .... **CLC 43, 129**
See also BRWS 5; CA 65-68; CANR 44,
98; CBD; CD 5; CP 7; DLB 40, 245;
MTCW 1; RGEL 2
Harriss, Will(ard Irvin) 1922- .... **CLC 34**
See also CA 111
Hart, Ellis
See Ellison, Harlan (Jay)
Hart, Josephine 1942(?)- .... **CLC 70**
See also CA 138; CANR 70; CPW; DAM
POP
Hart, Moss 1904-1961 .... **CLC 66**
See also CA 109; 89-92; CANR 84; DAM
DRAM; DFS 1; DLB 7, 266; RGAL 4
Harte, (Francis) Bret(t)
1836(?)-1902 .... **SSC 8, 59; TCLC 1, 25;**
WLC
See also AMWS 2; CA 104; 140; CANR
80; CDALB 1865-1917; DA; DA3; DAC;
DAM MST; DLB 12, 64, 74, 79, 186;
EXPS; LAIT 2; RGAL 4; RGSF 2; SATA
26; SSFS 3; TUS
Hartley, L(eslie) P(oles) 1895-1972 ... **CLC 2,**
22
See also BRWS 7; CA 45-48; 37-40R;
CANR 33; DLB 15, 139; EWL 3; HGG;
MTCW 1, 2; RGEL 2; RGSF 2; SUFW 1
Hartman, Geoffrey H. 1929- .... **CLC 27**
See also CA 117; 125; CANR 79; DLB 67

Hartmann, Sadakichi 1869-1944 ... **TCLC 73**
See also CA 157; DLB 54
Hartmann von Aue c. 1170-c.
1210 .... **CMLC 15**
See also CDWLB 2; DLB 138; RGWL 2, 3
Hartog, Jan de
See de Hartog, Jan
Haruf, Kent 1943- .... **CLC 34**
See also AAYA 44; CA 149; CANR 91, 131
Harvey, Caroline
See Trollope, Joanna
Harvey, Gabriel 1550(?)-1631 .... **LC 88**
See also DLB 167, 213, 281
Harwood, Ronald 1934- .... **CLC 32**
See also CA 1-4R; CANR 4, 55; CBD; CD
5; DAM DRAM, MST; DLB 13
Hasegawa Tatsunosuke
See Futabatei, Shimei
Hasek, Jaroslav (Matej Frantisek)
1883-1923 .... **SSC 69; TCLC 4**
See also CA 104; 129; CDWLB 4; DLB
215; EW 9; EWL 3; MTCW 1, 2; RGSF
2; RGWL 2, 3
Hass, Robert 1941- ... **CLC 18, 39, 99; PC 16**
See also AMWS 6; CA 111; CANR 30, 50,
71; CP 7; DLB 105, 206; EWL 3; RGAL
4; SATA 94
Hastings, Hudson
See Kuttner, Henry
Hastings, Selina .... **CLC 44**
Hathorne, John 1641-1717 .... **LC 38**
Hatteras, Amelia
See Mencken, H(enry) L(ouis)
Hatteras, Owen .... **TCLC 18**
See Mencken, H(enry) L(ouis); Nathan,
George Jean
Hauptmann, Gerhart (Johann Robert)
1862-1946 .... **SSC 37; TCLC 4**
See also CA 104; 153; CDWLB 2; DAM
DRAM; DLB 66, 118; EW 8; EWL 3;
RGSF 2; RGWL 2, 3; TWA
Havel, Vaclav 1936- ..... **CLC 25, 58, 65, 123;**
DC 6
See also CA 104; CANR 36, 63, 124; CD-
WLB 4; CWW 2; DA3; DAM DRAM;
DFS 10; DLB 232; EWL 3; LMFS 2;
MTCW 1, 2; RGWL 3
Haviaras, Stratis .... **CLC 33**
See Chaviaras, Strates
Hawes, Stephen 1475(?)-1529(?) .... **LC 17**
See also DLB 132; RGEL 2
Hawkes, John (Clendennin Burne, Jr.)
1925-1998 .. **CLC 1, 2, 3, 4, 7, 9, 14, 15,**
27, 49
See also BPFB 2; CA 1-4R; 167; CANR 2,
47, 64; CN 7; DLB 2, 7, 227; DLBY
1980, 1998; EWL 3; MTCW 1, 2; RGAL
4
Hawking, S. W.
See Hawking, Stephen W(illiam)
Hawking, Stephen W(illiam) 1942- . **CLC 63,**
105
See also AAYA 13; BEST 89:1; CA 126;
129; CANR 48, 115; CPW; DA3; MTCW
2
Hawkins, Anthony Hope
See Hope, Anthony
Hawthorne, Julian 1846-1934 .... **TCLC 25**
See also CA 165; HGG
Hawthorne, Nathaniel 1804-1864 ... **NCLC 2,**
10, 17, 23, 39, 79, 95, 158; SSC 3, 29,
39; WLC
See also AAYA 18; AMW; AMWC 1;
AMWR 1; BPFB 2; BYA 3; CDALB
1640-1865; DA; DA3; DAB; DAC; DAM
MST, NOV; DLB 1, 74, 183, 223, 269;
EXPN; EXPS; HGG; LAIT 1; NFS 1, 20;
RGAL 4; RGSF 2; SSFS 1, 7, 11, 15;
SUFW 1; TUS; WCH; YABC 2

Hawthorne, Sophia Peabody
1809-1871 .... **NCLC 150**
See also DLB 183, 239
Haxton, Josephine Ayres 1921-
See Douglas, Ellen
See also CA 115; CANR 41, 83
Hayaseca y Eizaguirre, Jorge
See Echegaray (y Eizaguirre), Jose (Maria
Waldo)
Hayashi, Fumiko 1904-1951 .... **TCLC 27**
See Hayashi Fumiko
See also CA 161
Hayashi Fumiko
See Hayashi, Fumiko
See also DLB 180; EWL 3
Haycraft, Anna (Margaret) 1932-
See Ellis, Alice Thomas
See also CA 122; CANR 85, 90; MTCW 2
Hayden, Robert E(arl) 1913-1980 ..... **BLC 2;**
CLC 5, 9, 14, 37; PC 6
See also AFAW 1, 2; AMWS 2; BW 1, 3;
CA 69-72; 97-100; CABS 2; CANR 24,
75, 82; CDALB 1941-1968; DA; DAC;
DAM MST, MULT; DLB 5, 76;
EWL 3; EXPP; MTCW 1, 2; PFS 1;
RGAL 4; SATA 19; SATA-Obit 26; WP
Haydon, Benjamin Robert
1786-1846 .... **NCLC 146**
See also DLB 110
Hayek, F(riedrich) A(ugust von)
1899-1992 .... **TCLC 109**
See also CA 93-96; 137; CANR 20; MTCW
1, 2
Hayford, J(oseph) E(phraim) Casely
See Casely-Hayford, J(oseph) E(phraim)
Hayman, Ronald 1932- .... **CLC 44**
See also CA 25-28R; CANR 18, 50, 88; CD
5; DLB 155
Hayne, Paul Hamilton 1830-1886 . **NCLC 94**
See also DLB 3, 64, 79, 248; RGAL 4
Hays, Mary 1760-1843 .... **NCLC 114**
See also DLB 142, 158; RGEL 2
Haywood, Eliza (Fowler)
1693(?)-1756 .... **LC 1, 44**
See also DLB 39; RGEL 2
Hazlitt, William 1778-1830 ...... **NCLC 29, 82**
See also BRW 4; DLB 110, 158; RGEL 2;
TEA
Hazzard, Shirley 1931- .... **CLC 18**
See also CA 9-12R; CANR 4, 70, 127; CN
7; DLB 289; DLBY 1982; MTCW 1
Head, Bessie 1937-1986 ...... **BLC 2; CLC 25,**
67; SSC 52
See also AFW; BW 2, 3; CA 29-32R; 119;
CANR 25, 82; CDWLB 3; DA3; DAM
MULT; DLB 117, 225; EWL 3; EXPS;
FW; MTCW 1, 2; RGSF 2; SSFS 5, 13;
WLIT 2; WWE 1
Headon, (Nicky) Topper 1956(?)- ..... **CLC 30**
Heaney, Seamus (Justin) 1939- ..... **CLC 5, 7,**
14, 25, 37, 74, 91, 171; PC 18; WLCS
See also BRWR 1; BRWS 2; CA 85-88;
CANR 25, 48, 75, 91, 128; CDBLB 1960
to Present; CP 7; DA3; DAB; DAM
POET; DLB 40; DLBY 1995; EWL 3;
EXPP; MTCW 1, 2; PAB; PFS 2, 5, 8,
17; RGEL 2; TEA; WLIT 4
Hearn, (Patricio) Lafcadio (Tessima Carlos)
1850-1904 .... **TCLC 9**
See also CA 105; 166; DLB 12, 78, 189;
HGG; RGAL 4
Hearne, Samuel 1745-1792 .... **LC 95**
See also DLB 99
Hearne, Vicki 1946-2001 .... **CLC 56**
See also CA 139; 201
Hearon, Shelby 1931- .... **CLC 63**
See also AITN 2; AMWS 8; CA 25-28R;
CANR 18, 48, 103; CSW

Housman, Laurence 1865-1959 .... **TCLC 7**
See also CA 106; 155; DLB 10; FANT; RGEL 2; SATA 25

Houston, Jeanne (Toyo) Wakatsuki 1934- .... **AAL**
See also AAYA 49; CA 103; CAAS 16; CANR 29, 123; LAIT 4; SATA 78

Howard, Elizabeth Jane 1923- ..... **CLC 7, 29**
See also CA 5-8R; CANR 8, 62; CN 7

Howard, Maureen 1930- .... **CLC 5, 14, 46, 151**
See also CA 53-56; CANR 31, 75; CN 7; DLBY 1983; INT CANR-31; MTCW 1, 2

Howard, Richard 1929- .... **CLC 7, 10, 47**
See also AITN 1; CA 85-88; CANR 25, 80; CP 7; DLB 5; INT CANR-25

Howard, Robert E(rvin) 1906-1936 .... **TCLC 8**
See also BPFB 2; BYA 5; CA 105; 157; FANT; SUFW 1

Howard, Warren F.
See Pohl, Frederik

Howe, Fanny (Quincy) 1940- .... **CLC 47**
See also CA 117, 187; CAAE 187; CAAS 27; CANR 70, 116; CP 7; CWP; SATA-Brief 52

Howe, Irving 1920-1993 .... **CLC 85**
See also AMWS 6; CA 9-12R; 141; CANR 21, 50; DLB 67; EWL 3; MTCW 1, 2

Howe, Julia Ward 1819-1910 .... **TCLC 21**
See also CA 117; 191; DLB 1, 189, 235; FW

Howe, Susan 1937- .... **CLC 72, 152; PC 54**
See also AMWS 4; CA 160; CP 7; CWP; DLB 120; FW; RGAL 4

Howe, Tina 1937- .... **CLC 48**
See also CA 109; CAD; CANR 125; CD 5; CWD

Howell, James 1594(?)-1666 .... **LC 13**
See also DLB 151

Howells, W. D.
See Howells, William Dean

Howells, William D.
See Howells, William Dean

Howells, William Dean 1837-1920 ... **SSC 36; TCLC 7, 17, 41**
See also AMW; CA 104; 134; CDALB 1865-1917; DLB 12, 64, 74, 79, 189; LMFS 1; MTCW 2; RGAL 4; TUS

Howes, Barbara 1914-1996 .... **CLC 15**
See also CA 9-12R; 151; CAAS 3; CANR 53; CP 7; SATA 5

Hrabal, Bohumil 1914-1997 ...... **CLC 13, 67; TCLC 155**
See also CA 106; 156; CAAS 12; CANR 57; CWW 2; DLB 232; EWL 3; RGSF 2

Hrabanus Maurus c. 776-856 .... **CMLC 78**
See also DLB 148

Hrotsvit of Gandersheim c. 935-c. 1000 .... **CMLC 29**
See also DLB 148

Hsi, Chu 1130-1200 .... **CMLC 42**

Hsun, Lu
See Lu Hsun

Hubbard, L(afayette) Ron(ald) 1911-1986 .... **CLC 43**
See also CA 77-80; 118; CANR 52; CPW; DA3; DAM POP; FANT; MTCW 2; SFW 4

Huch, Ricarda (Octavia) 1864-1947 .... **TCLC 13**
See also CA 111; 189; DLB 66; EWL 3

Huddle, David 1942- .... **CLC 49**
See also CA 57-60; CAAS 20; CANR 89; DLB 130

Hudson, Jeffrey
See Crichton, (John) Michael

Hudson, W(illiam) H(enry) 1841-1922 .... **TCLC 29**
See also CA 115; 190; DLB 98, 153, 174; RGEL 2; SATA 35

Hueffer, Ford Madox
See Ford, Ford Madox

Hughart, Barry 1934- .... **CLC 39**
See also CA 137; FANT; SFW 4; SUFW 2

Hughes, Colin
See Creasey, John

Hughes, David (John) 1930- .... **CLC 48**
See also CA 116; 129; CN 7; DLB 14

Hughes, Edward James
See Hughes, Ted
See also DA3; DAM MST, POET

Hughes, (James Mercer) Langston 1902-1967 ..... **BLC 2; CLC 1, 5, 10, 15, 35, 44, 108; DC 3; HR 2; PC 1, 53; SSC 6; WLC**
See also AAYA 12; AFAW 1, 2; AMWR 1; AMWS 1; BW 1, 3; CA 1-4R; 25-28R; CANR 1, 34, 82; CDALB 1929-1941; CLR 17; DA; DA3; DAB; DAC; DAM DRAM, MST, MULT, POET; DFS 6, 18; DLB 4, 7, 48, 51, 86, 228; EWL 3; EXPP; EXPS; JRDA; LAIT 3; LMFS 2; MAI-CYA 1, 2; MTCW 1, 2; PAB; PFS 1, 3, 6, 10, 15; RGAL 4; RGSF 2; SATA 4, 33; SSFS 4, 7; TUS; WCH; WP; YAW

Hughes, Richard (Arthur Warren) 1900-1976 .... **CLC 1, 11**
See also CA 5-8R; 65-68; CANR 4; DAM NOV; DLB 15, 161; EWL 3; MTCW 1; RGEL 2; SATA 8; SATA-Obit 25

Hughes, Ted 1930-1998 . **CLC 2, 4, 9, 14, 37, 119; PC 7**
See Hughes, Edward James
See also BRWC 2; BRWR 2; BRWS 1; CA 1-4R; 171; CANR 1, 33, 66, 108; CLR 3; CP 7; DAB; DAC; DLB 40, 161; EWL 3; EXPP; MAICYA 1, 2; MTCW 1, 2; PAB; PFS 4, 19; RGEL 2; SATA 49; SATA-Brief 27; SATA-Obit 107; TEA; YAW

Hugo, Richard
See Huch, Ricarda (Octavia)

Hugo, Richard F(ranklin) 1923-1982 .... **CLC 6, 18, 32**
See also AMWS 6; CA 49-52; 108; CANR 3; DAM POET; DLB 5, 206; EWL 3; PFS 17; RGAL 4

Hugo, Victor (Marie) 1802-1885 .... **NCLC 3, 10, 21; PC 17; WLC**
See also AAYA 28; DA; DA3; DAB; DAC; DAM DRAM, MST, NOV, POET; DLB 119, 192, 217; EFS 2; EW 6; EXPN; GFL 1789 to the Present; LAIT 1, 2; NFS 5, 20; RGWL 2, 3; SATA 47; TWA

Huidobro, Vicente
See Huidobro Fernandez, Vicente Garcia
See also DLB 283; EWL 3; LAW

Huidobro Fernandez, Vicente Garcia 1893-1948 .... **TCLC 31**
See Huidobro, Vicente
See also CA 131; HW 1

Hulme, Keri 1947- .... **CLC 39, 130**
See also CA 125; CANR 69; CN 7; CP 7; CWP; EWL 3; FW; INT CA-125

Hulme, T(homas) E(rnest) 1883-1917 .... **TCLC 21**
See also BRWS 6; CA 117; 203; DLB 19

Humboldt, Wilhelm von 1767-1835 .... **NCLC 134**
See also DLB 90

Hume, David 1711-1776 .... **LC 7, 56**
See also BRWS 3; DLB 104, 252; LMFS 1; TEA

Humphrey, William 1924-1997 .... **CLC 45**
See also AMWS 9; CA 77-80; 160; CANR 68; CN 7; CSW; DLB 6, 212, 234, 278; TCWW 2

Humphreys, Emyr Owen 1919- .... **CLC 47**
See also CA 5-8R; CANR 3, 24; CN 7; DLB 15

Humphreys, Josephine 1945- ..... **CLC 34, 57**
See also CA 121; 127; CANR 97; CSW; DLB 292; INT CA-127

Huneker, James Gibbons 1860-1921 .... **TCLC 65**
See also CA 193; DLB 71; RGAL 4

Hungerford, Hesba Fay
See Brinsmead, H(esba) F(ay)

Hungerford, Pixie
See Brinsmead, H(esba) F(ay)

Hunt, E(verette) Howard, (Jr.) 1918- .... **CLC 3**
See also AITN 1; CA 45-48; CANR 2, 47, 103; CMW 4

Hunt, Francesca
See Holland, Isabelle (Christian)

Hunt, Howard
See Hunt, E(verette) Howard, (Jr.)

Hunt, Kyle
See Creasey, John

Hunt, (James Henry) Leigh 1784-1859 .... **NCLC 1, 70**
See also DAM POET; DLB 96, 110, 144; RGEL 2; TEA

Hunt, Marsha 1946- .... **CLC 70**
See also BW 2, 3; CA 143; CANR 79

Hunt, Violet 1866(?)-1942 .... **TCLC 53**
See also CA 184; DLB 162, 197

Hunter, E. Waldo
See Sturgeon, Theodore (Hamilton)

Hunter, Evan 1926- .... **CLC 11, 31**
See McBain, Ed
See also AAYA 39; BPFB 2; CA 5-8R; CANR 5, 38, 62, 97; CMW 4; CN 7; CPW; DAM POP; DLB 306; DLBY 1982; INT CANR-5; MSW; MTCW 1; SATA 25; SFW 4

Hunter, Kristin
See Lattany, Kristin (Elaine Eggleston) Hunter

Hunter, Mary
See Austin, Mary (Hunter)

Hunter, Mollie 1922- .... **CLC 21**
See McIlwraith, Maureen Mollie Hunter
See also AAYA 13; BYA 6; CANR 37, 78; CLR 25; DLB 161; JRDA; MAICYA 1, 2; SAAS 7; SATA 54, 106, 139; SATA-Essay 139; WYA; YAW

Hunter, Robert (?)-1734 .... **LC 7**

Hurston, Zora Neale 1891-1960 .... **BLC 2; CLC 7, 30, 61; DC 12; HR 2; SSC 4, 80; TCLC 121, 131; WLCS**
See also AAYA 15; AFAW 1, 2; AMWS 6; BW 1, 3; BYA 12; CA 85-88; CANR 61; CDALBS; DA; DA3; DAC; DAM MST, MULT, NOV; DFS 6; DLB 51, 86; EWL 3; EXPN; EXPS; FW; LAIT 3; LATS 1:1; LMFS 2; MAWW; MTCW 1, 2; NFS 3; RGAL 4; RGSF 2; SSFS 1, 6, 11, 19; TUS; YAW

Husserl, E. G.
See Husserl, Edmund (Gustav Albrecht)

Husserl, Edmund (Gustav Albrecht) 1859-1938 .... **TCLC 100**
See also CA 116; 133; DLB 296

Huston, John (Marcellus) 1906-1987 .... **CLC 20**
See also CA 73-76; 123; CANR 34; DLB 26

Hustvedt, Siri 1955- .... **CLC 76**
See also CA 137

Hutten, Ulrich von 1488-1523 .... **LC 16**
See also DLB 179

Jacob, (Cyprien-)Max 1876-1944 .... **TCLC 6**
See also CA 104; 193; DLB 258; EWL 3;
GFL 1789 to the Present; GLL 2; RGWL
2, 3

Jacobs, Harriet A(nn)
1813(?)-1897 .... **NCLC 67**
See also AFAW 1, 2; DLB 239; FW; LAIT
2; RGAL 4

Jacobs, Jim 1942- .... **CLC 12**
See also CA 97-100; INT CA-97-100

Jacobs, W(illiam) W(ymark)
1863-1943 .... **SSC 73; TCLC 22**
See also CA 121; 167; DLB 135; EXPS;
HGG; RGEL 2; RGSF 2; SSFS 2; SUFW
1

Jacobsen, Jens Peter 1847-1885 .... **NCLC 34**

Jacobsen, Josephine (Winder)
1908-2003 .... **CLC 48, 102; PC 62**
See also CA 33-36R; 218; CAAS 18; CANR
23, 48; CCA 1; CP 7; DLB 244

Jacobson, Dan 1929- .... **CLC 4, 14**
See also AFW; CA 1-4R; CANR 2, 25, 66;
CN 7; DLB 14, 207, 225; EWL 3; MTCW
1; RGSF 2

Jacqueline
See Carpentier (y Valmont), Alejo

Jacques de Vitry c. 1160-1240 ...... **CMLC 63**
See also DLB 208

Jagger, Mick 1944- .... **CLC 17**

Jahiz, al- c. 780-c. 869 .... **CMLC 25**

Jakes, John (William) 1932- .... **CLC 29**
See also AAYA 32; BEST 89:4; BPFB 2;
CA 57-60, 214; CAAE 214; CANR 10,
43, 66, 111; CPW; CSW; DA3; DAM
NOV, POP; DLB 278; DLBY 1983;
FANT; INT CANR-10; MTCW 1, 2;
RHW; SATA 62; SFW 4; TCWW 2

James I 1394-1437 .... **LC 20**
See also RGEL 2

James, Andrew
See Kirkup, James

James, C(yril) L(ionel) R(obert)
1901-1989 .... **BLCS; CLC 33**
See also BW 2; CA 117; 125; 128; CANR
62; DLB 125; MTCW 1

James, Daniel (Lewis) 1911-1988
See Santiago, Danny
See also CA 174; 125

James, Dynely
See Mayne, William (James Carter)

James, Henry Sr. 1811-1882 .... **NCLC 53**

James, Henry 1843-1916 .... **SSC 8, 32, 47;**
TCLC 2, 11, 24, 40, 47, 64; WLC
See also AMW; AMWC 1; AMWR 1; BPFB
2; BRW 6; CA 104; 132; CDALB 1865-
1917; DA; DA3; DAB; DAC; DAM MST,
NOV; DLB 12, 71, 74, 189; DLBD 13;
EWL 3; EXPS; HGG; LAIT 2; MTCW 1,
2; NFS 12, 16, 19; RGAL 4; RGEL 2;
RGSF 2; SSFS 9; SUFW 1; TUS

James, M. R.
See James, Montague (Rhodes)
See also DLB 156, 201

James, Montague (Rhodes)
1862-1936 .... **SSC 16; TCLC 6**
See James, M. R.
See also CA 104; 203; HGG; RGEL 2;
RGSF 2; SUFW 1

James, P. D. .... **CLC 18, 46, 122**
See White, Phyllis Dorothy James
See also BEST 90:2; BPFB 2; BRWS 4;
CDBLB 1960 to Present; DLB 87, 276;
DLBD 17; MSW

James, Philip
See Moorcock, Michael (John)

James, Samuel
See Stephens, James

James, Seumas
See Stephens, James

James, Stephen
See Stephens, James

James, William 1842-1910 .... **TCLC 15, 32**
See also AMW; CA 109; 193; DLB 270,
284; NCFS 5; RGAL 4

Jameson, Anna 1794-1860 .... **NCLC 43**
See also DLB 99, 166

Jameson, Fredric (R.) 1934- .... **CLC 142**
See also CA 196; DLB 67; LMFS 2

James VI of Scotland 1566-1625 .... **LC 109**
See also DLB 151, 172

Jami, Nur al-Din 'Abd al-Rahman
1414-1492 .... **LC 9**

Jammes, Francis 1868-1938 .... **TCLC 75**
See also CA 198; EWL 3; GFL 1789 to the
Present

Jandl, Ernst 1925-2000 .... **CLC 34**
See also CA 200; EWL 3

Janowitz, Tama 1957- .... **CLC 43, 145**
See also CA 106; CANR 52, 89, 129; CN
7; CPW; DAM POP; DLB 292

Japrisot, Sebastien 1931- .... **CLC 90**
See Rossi, Jean-Baptiste
See also CMW 4; NFS 18

Jarrell, Randall 1914-1965 .... **CLC 1, 2, 6, 9,**
13, 49; PC 41
See also AMW; BYA 5; CA 5-8R; 25-28R;
CABS 2; CANR 6, 34; CDALB 1941-
1968; CLR 6; CWRI 5; DAM POET;
DLB 48, 52; EWL 3; EXPP; MAICYA 1,
2; MTCW 1, 2; PAB; PFS 2; RGAL 4;
SATA 7

Jarry, Alfred 1873-1907 .... **SSC 20; TCLC 2,**
14, 147
See also CA 104; 153; DA3; DAM DRAM;
DFS 8; DLB 192, 258; EW 9; EWL 3;
GFL 1789 to the Present; RGWL 2, 3;
TWA

Jarvis, E. K.
See Ellison, Harlan (Jay)

Jawien, Andrzej
See John Paul II, Pope

Jaynes, Roderick
See Coen, Ethan

Jeake, Samuel, Jr.
See Aiken, Conrad (Potter)

Jean Paul 1763-1825 .... **NCLC 7**

Jefferies, (John) Richard
1848-1887 .... **NCLC 47**
See also DLB 98, 141; RGEL 2; SATA 16;
SFW 4

Jeffers, (John) Robinson 1887-1962 .. **CLC 2,**
3, 11, 15, 54; PC 17; WLC
See also AMWS 2; CA 85-88; CANR 35;
CDALB 1917-1929; DA; DAC; DAM
MST, POET; DLB 45, 212; EWL 3;
MTCW 1, 2; PAB; PFS 3, 4; RGAL 4

Jefferson, Janet
See Mencken, H(enry) L(ouis)

Jefferson, Thomas 1743-1826 . **NCLC 11, 103**
See also AAYA 54; ANW; CDALB 1640-
1865; DA3; DLB 31, 183; LAIT 1; RGAL
4

Jeffrey, Francis 1773-1850 .... **NCLC 33**
See Francis, Lord Jeffrey

Jelakowitch, Ivan
See Heijermans, Herman

Jelinek, Elfriede 1946- .... **CLC 169**
See also CA 154; DLB 85; FW

Jellicoe, (Patricia) Ann 1927- .... **CLC 27**
See also CA 85-88; CBD; CD 5; CWD;
CWRI 5; DLB 13, 233; FW

Jelloun, Tahar ben 1944- .... **CLC 180**
See Ben Jelloun, Tahar
See also CA 162; CANR 100

Jemyma
See Holley, Marietta

Jen, Gish .... **AAL; CLC 70, 198**
See Jen, Lillian
See also AMWC 2

Jen, Lillian 1956(?)-
See Jen, Gish
See also CA 135; CANR 89, 130

Jenkins, (John) Robin 1912- .... **CLC 52**
See also CA 1-4R; CANR 1, 135; CN 7;
DLB 14, 271

Jennings, Elizabeth (Joan)
1926-2001 .... **CLC 5, 14, 131**
See also BRWS 5; CA 61-64; 200; CAAS
5; CANR 8, 39, 66, 127; CP 7; CWP;
DLB 27; EWL 3; MTCW 1; SATA 66

Jennings, Waylon 1937- .... **CLC 21**

Jensen, Johannes V(ilhelm)
1873-1950 .... **TCLC 41**
See also CA 170; DLB 214; EWL 3; RGWL
3

Jensen, Laura (Linnea) 1948- .... **CLC 37**
See also CA 103

Jerome, Saint 345-420 .... **CMLC 30**
See also RGWL 3

Jerome, Jerome K(lapka)
1859-1927 .... **TCLC 23**
See also CA 119; 177; DLB 10, 34, 135;
RGEL 2

Jerrold, Douglas William
1803-1857 .... **NCLC 2**
See also DLB 158, 159; RGEL 2

Jewett, (Theodora) Sarah Orne
1849-1909 .... **SSC 6, 44; TCLC 1, 22**
See also AMW; AMWC 2; AMWR 2; CA
108; 127; CANR 71; DLB 12, 74, 221;
EXPS; FW; MAWW; NFS 15; RGAL 4;
RGSF 2; SATA 15; SSFS 4

Jewsbury, Geraldine (Endsor)
1812-1880 .... **NCLC 22**
See also DLB 21

Jhabvala, Ruth Prawer 1927- . **CLC 4, 8, 29,**
94, 138
See also BRWS 5; CA 1-4R; CANR 2, 29,
51, 74, 91, 128; CN 7; DAB; DAM NOV;
DLB 139, 194; EWL 3; IDFW 3, 4; INT
CANR-29; MTCW 1, 2; RGSF 2; RGWL
2; RHW; TEA

Jibran, Kahlil
See Gibran, Kahlil

Jibran, Khalil
See Gibran, Kahlil

Jiles, Paulette 1943- .... **CLC 13, 58**
See also CA 101; CANR 70, 124; CWP

Jimenez (Mantecon), Juan Ramon
1881-1958 .... **HLC 1; PC 7; TCLC 4**
See also CA 104; 131; CANR 74; DAM
MULT, POET; DLB 134; EW 9; EWL 3;
HW 1; MTCW 1, 2; RGWL 2, 3

Jimenez, Ramon
See Jimenez (Mantecon), Juan Ramon

Jimenez Mantecon, Juan
See Jimenez (Mantecon), Juan Ramon

Jin, Ha .... **CLC 109**
See Jin, Xuefei
See also CA 152; DLB 244, 292; SSFS 17

Jin, Xuefei 1956-
See Jin, Ha
See also CANR 91, 130; SSFS 17

Joel, Billy .... **CLC 26**
See Joel, William Martin

Joel, William Martin 1949-
See Joel, Billy
See also CA 108

John, Saint 10(?)-100 .... **CMLC 27, 63**

John of Salisbury c. 1115-1180 ..... **CMLC 63**

John of the Cross, St. 1542-1591 .... **LC 18**
See also RGWL 2, 3

John Paul II, Pope 1920- .... **CLC 128**
See also CA 106; 133

Kingman, Lee .... **CLC 17**
See Natti, (Mary) Lee
See also CWRI 5; SAAS 3; SATA 1, 67

Kingsley, Charles 1819-1875 .... **NCLC 35**
See also CLR 77; DLB 21, 32, 163, 178, 190; FANT; MAICYA 2; MAICYAS 1; RGEL 2; WCH; YABC 2

Kingsley, Henry 1830-1876 .... **NCLC 107**
See also DLB 21, 230; RGEL 2

Kingsley, Sidney 1906-1995 .... **CLC 44**
See also CA 85-88; 147; CAD; DFS 14, 19; DLB 7; RGAL 4

Kingsolver, Barbara 1955- . **CLC 55, 81, 130**
See also AAYA 15; AMWS 7; CA 129; 134; CANR 60, 96, 133; CDALBS; CPW; CSW; DA3; DAM POP; DLB 206; INT CA-134; LAIT 5; MTCW 2; NFS 5, 10, 12; RGAL 4

Kingston, Maxine (Ting Ting) Hong
1940- .... **AAL; CLC 12, 19, 58, 121; WLCS**
See also AAYA 8, 55; AMWS 5; BPFB 2; CA 69-72; CANR 13, 38, 74, 87, 128; CDALBS; CN 7; DA3; DAM MULT, NOV; DLB 173, 212; DLBY 1980; EWL 3; FW; INT CANR-13; LAIT 5; MAWW; MTCW 1, 2; NFS 6; RGAL 4; SATA 53; SSFS 3

Kinnell, Galway 1927- ..... **CLC 1, 2, 3, 5, 13, 29, 129; PC 26**
See also AMWS 3; CA 9-12R; CANR 10, 34, 66, 116; CP 7; DLB 5; DLBY 1987; EWL 3; INT CANR-34; MTCW 1, 2; PAB; PFS 9; RGAL 4; WP

Kinsella, Thomas 1928- .... **CLC 4, 19, 138**
See also BRWS 5; CA 17-20R; CANR 15, 122; CP 7; DLB 27; EWL 3; MTCW 1, 2; RGEL 2; TEA

Kinsella, W(illiam) P(atrick) 1935- . **CLC 27, 43, 166**
See also AAYA 7, 60; BPFB 2; CA 97-100, 222; CAAE 222; CAAS 7; CANR 21, 35, 66, 75, 129; CN 7; CPW; DAC; DAM NOV, POP; FANT; INT CANR-21; LAIT 5; MTCW 1, 2; NFS 15; RGSF 2

Kinsey, Alfred C(harles)
1894-1956 .... **TCLC 91**
See also CA 115; 170; MTCW 2

Kipling, (Joseph) Rudyard 1865-1936 . **PC 3; SSC 5, 54; TCLC 8, 17, 167; WLC**
See also AAYA 32; BRW 6; BRWC 1, 2; BYA 4; CA 105; 120; CANR 33; CDBLB 1890-1914; CLR 39, 65; CWRI 5; DA; DA3; DAB; DAC; DAM MST, POET; DLB 19, 34, 141, 156; EWL 3; EXPS; FANT; LAIT 3; LMFS 1; MAICYA 1, 2; MTCW 1, 2; RGEL 2; RGSF 2; SATA 100; SFW 4; SSFS 8; SUFW 1; TEA; WCH; WLIT 4; YABC 2

Kirk, Russell (Amos) 1918-1994 .. **TCLC 119**
See also AITN 1; CA 1-4R; 145; CAAS 9; CANR 1, 20, 60; HGG; INT CANR-20; MTCW 1, 2

Kirkham, Dinah
See Card, Orson Scott

Kirkland, Caroline M. 1801-1864 . **NCLC 85**
See also DLB 3, 73, 74, 250, 254; DLBD 13

Kirkup, James 1918- .... **CLC 1**
See also CA 1-4R; CAAS 4; CANR 2; CP 7; DLB 27; SATA 12

Kirkwood, James 1930(?)-1989 .... **CLC 9**
See also AITN 2; CA 1-4R; 128; CANR 6, 40; GLL 2

Kirsch, Sarah 1935- .... **CLC 176**
See also CA 178; CWW 2; DLB 75; EWL 3

Kirshner, Sidney
See Kingsley, Sidney

Kis, Danilo 1935-1989 .... **CLC 57**
See also CA 109; 118; 129; CANR 61; CD-WLB 4; DLB 181; EWL 3; MTCW 1; RGSF 2; RGWL 2, 3

Kissinger, Henry A(lfred) 1923- ..... **CLC 137**
See also CA 1-4R; CANR 2, 33, 66, 109; MTCW 1

Kivi, Aleksis 1834-1872 .... **NCLC 30**

Kizer, Carolyn (Ashley) 1925- ... **CLC 15, 39, 80; PC 66**
See also CA 65-68; CAAS 5; CANR 24, 70, 134; CP 7; CWP; DAM POET; DLB 5, 169; EWL 3; MTCW 2; PFS 18

Klabund 1890-1928 .... **TCLC 44**
See also CA 162; DLB 66

Klappert, Peter 1942- .... **CLC 57**
See also CA 33-36R; CSW; DLB 5

Klein, A(braham) M(oses)
1909-1972 .... **CLC 19**
See also CA 101; 37-40R; DAB; DAC; DAM MST; DLB 68; EWL 3; RGEL 2

Klein, Joe
See Klein, Joseph

Klein, Joseph 1946- .... **CLC 154**
See also CA 85-88; CANR 55

Klein, Norma 1938-1989 .... **CLC 30**
See also AAYA 2, 35; BPFB 2; BYA 6, 7, 8; CA 41-44R; 128; CANR 15, 37; CLR 2, 19; INT CANR-15; JRDA; MAICYA 1, 2; SAAS 1; SATA 7, 57; WYA; YAW

Klein, T(heodore) E(ibon) D(onald)
1947- .... **CLC 34**
See also CA 119; CANR 44, 75; HGG

Kleist, Heinrich von 1777-1811 ...... **NCLC 2, 37; SSC 22**
See also CDWLB 2; DAM DRAM; DLB 90; EW 5; RGSF 2; RGWL 2, 3

Klima, Ivan 1931- .... **CLC 56, 172**
See also CA 25-28R; CANR 17, 50, 91; CDWLB 4; CWW 2; DAM NOV; DLB 232; EWL 3; RGWL 3

Klimentev, Andrei Platonovich
See Klimentov, Andrei Platonovich

Klimentov, Andrei Platonovich
1899-1951 .... **SSC 42; TCLC 14**
See Platonov, Andrei Platonovich; Platonov, Andrey Platonovich
See also CA 108

Klinger, Friedrich Maximilian von
1752-1831 .... **NCLC 1**
See also DLB 94

Klingsor the Magician
See Hartmann, Sadakichi

Klopstock, Friedrich Gottlieb
1724-1803 .... **NCLC 11**
See also DLB 97; EW 4; RGWL 2, 3

Kluge, Alexander 1932- .... **SSC 61**
See also CA 81-84; DLB 75

Knapp, Caroline 1959-2002 .... **CLC 99**
See also CA 154; 207

Knebel, Fletcher 1911-1993 .... **CLC 14**
See also AITN 1; CA 1-4R; 140; CAAS 3; CANR 1, 36; SATA 36; SATA-Obit 75

Knickerbocker, Diedrich
See Irving, Washington

Knight, Etheridge 1931-1991 ... **BLC 2; CLC 40; PC 14**
See also BW 1, 3; CA 21-24R; 133; CANR 23, 82; DAM POET; DLB 41; MTCW 2; RGAL 4

Knight, Sarah Kemble 1666-1727 .... **LC 7**
See also DLB 24, 200

Knister, Raymond 1899-1932 .... **TCLC 56**
See also CA 186; DLB 68; RGEL 2

Knowles, John 1926-2001 ... **CLC 1, 4, 10, 26**
See also AAYA 10; AMWS 12; BPFB 2; BYA 3; CA 17-20R; 203; CANR 40, 74, 76, 132; CDALB 1968-1988; CLR 98; CN

7; DA; DAC; DAM MST, NOV; DLB 6; EXPN; MTCW 1, 2; NFS 2; RGAL 4; SATA 8, 89; SATA-Obit 134; YAW

Knox, Calvin M.
See Silverberg, Robert

Knox, John c. 1505-1572 .... **LC 37**
See also DLB 132

Knye, Cassandra
See Disch, Thomas M(ichael)

Koch, C(hristopher) J(ohn) 1932- .... **CLC 42**
See also CA 127; CANR 84; CN 7; DLB 289

Koch, Christopher
See Koch, C(hristopher) J(ohn)

Koch, Kenneth (Jay) 1925-2002 .... **CLC 5, 8, 44**
See also CA 1-4R; 207; CAD; CANR 6, 36, 57, 97, 131; CD 5; CP 7; DAM POET; DLB 5; INT CANR-36; MTCW 2; PFS 20; SATA 65; WP

Kochanowski, Jan 1530-1584 .... **LC 10**
See also RGWL 2, 3

Kock, Charles Paul de 1794-1871 . **NCLC 16**

Koda Rohan
See Koda Shigeyuki

Koda Rohan
See Koda Shigeyuki
See also DLB 180

Koda Shigeyuki 1867-1947 .... **TCLC 22**
See Koda Rohan
See also CA 121; 183

Koestler, Arthur 1905-1983 ... **CLC 1, 3, 6, 8, 15, 33**
See also BRWS 1; CA 1-4R; 109; CANR 1, 33; CDBLB 1945-1960; DLBY 1983; EWL 3; MTCW 1, 2; NFS 19; RGEL 2

Kogawa, Joy Nozomi 1935- ...... **CLC 78, 129**
See also AAYA 47; CA 101; CANR 19, 62, 126; CN 7; CWP; DAC; DAM MST, MULT; FW; MTCW 2; NFS 3; SATA 99

Kohout, Pavel 1928- .... **CLC 13**
See also CA 45-48; CANR 3

Koizumi, Yakumo
See Hearn, (Patricio) Lafcadio (Tessima Carlos)

Kolmar, Gertrud 1894-1943 .... **TCLC 40**
See also CA 167; EWL 3

Komunyakaa, Yusef 1947- .. **BLCS; CLC 86, 94, 207; PC 51**
See also AFAW 2; AMWS 13; CA 147; CANR 83; CP 7; CSW; DLB 120; EWL 3; PFS 5, 20; RGAL 4

Konrad, George
See Konrad, Gyorgy

Konrad, Gyorgy 1933- .... **CLC 4, 10, 73**
See also CA 85-88; CANR 97; CDWLB 4; CWW 2; DLB 232; EWL 3

Konwicki, Tadeusz 1926- .... **CLC 8, 28, 54, 117**
See also CA 101; CAAS 9; CANR 39, 59; CWW 2; DLB 232; EWL 3; IDFW 3; MTCW 1

Koontz, Dean R(ay) 1945- .... **CLC 78, 206**
See also AAYA 9, 31; BEST 89:3, 90:2; CA 108; CANR 19, 36, 52, 95; CMW 4; CPW; DA3; DAM NOV, POP; DLB 292; HGG; MTCW 1; SATA 92; SFW 4; SUFW 2; YAW

Kopernik, Mikolaj
See Copernicus, Nicolaus

Kopit, Arthur (Lee) 1937- ...... **CLC 1, 18, 33**
See also AITN 1; CA 81-84; CABS 3; CD 5; DAM DRAM; DFS 7, 14; DLB 7; MTCW 1; RGAL 4

Kopitar, Jernej (Bartholomaus)
1780-1844 .... **NCLC 117**

Kops, Bernard 1926- .... **CLC 4**
See also CA 5-8R; CANR 84; CBD; CN 7; CP 7; DLB 13

DAC; DAM MST, NOV, POP; DLB 2, 16, 28, 185, 278; DLBD 3; DLBY 1980, 1983; EWL 3; MTCW 1, 2; NFS 10; RGAL 4; TUS

Maillet, Antonine 1929- .... **CLC 54, 118**
See also CA 115; 120; CANR 46, 74, 77, 134; CCA 1; CWW 2; DAC; DLB 60; INT CA-120; MTCW 2

Maimonides 1135-1204 .... **CMLC 76**
See also DLB 115

Mais, Roger 1905-1955 .... **TCLC 8**
See also BW 1, 3; CA 105; 124; CANR 82; CDWLB 3; DLB 125; EWL 3; MTCW 1; RGEL 2

Maistre, Joseph 1753-1821 .... **NCLC 37**
See also GFL 1789 to the Present

Maitland, Frederic William
1850-1906 .... **TCLC 65**

Maitland, Sara (Louise) 1950- .... **CLC 49**
See also CA 69-72; CANR 13, 59; DLB 271; FW

Major, Clarence 1936- ... **BLC 2; CLC 3, 19, 48**
See also AFAW 2; BW 2, 3; CA 21-24R; CAAS 6; CANR 13, 25, 53, 82; CN 7; CP 7; CSW; DAM MULT; DLB 33; EWL 3; MSW

Major, Kevin (Gerald) 1949- .... **CLC 26**
See also AAYA 16; CA 97-100; CANR 21, 38, 112; CLR 11; DAC; DLB 60; INT CANR-21; JRDA; MAICYA 1, 2; MAICYAS 1; SATA 32, 82, 134; WYA; YAW

Maki, James
See Ozu, Yasujiro

Makine, Andrei 1957- .... **CLC 198**
See also CA 176; CANR 103

Malabaila, Damiano
See Levi, Primo

Malamud, Bernard 1914-1986 .. **CLC 1, 2, 3, 5, 8, 9, 11, 18, 27, 44, 78, 85; SSC 15; TCLC 129; WLC**
See also AAYA 16; AMWS 1; BPFB 2; BYA 15; CA 5-8R; 118; CABS 1; CANR 28, 62, 114; CDALB 1941-1968; CPW; DA; DA3; DAB; DAC; DAM MST, NOV, POP; DLB 2, 28, 152; DLBY 1980, 1986; EWL 3; EXPS; LAIT 4; LATS 1:1; MTCW 1, 2; NFS 4, 9; RGAL 4; RGSF 2; SSFS 8, 13, 16; TUS

Malan, Herman
See Bosman, Herman Charles; Bosman, Herman Charles

Malaparte, Curzio 1898-1957 .... **TCLC 52**
See also DLB 264

Malcolm, Dan
See Silverberg, Robert

Malcolm, Janet 1934- .... **CLC 201**
See also CA 123; CANR 89; NCFS 1

Malcolm X .... **BLC 2; CLC 82, 117; WLCS**
See Little, Malcolm
See also LAIT 5; NCFS 3

Malherbe, Francois de 1555-1628 .... **LC 5**
See also GFL Beginnings to 1789

Mallarme, Stephane 1842-1898 ...... **NCLC 4, 41; PC 4**
See also DAM POET; DLB 217; EW 7; GFL 1789 to the Present; LMFS 2; RGWL 2, 3; TWA

Mallet-Joris, Francoise 1930- .... **CLC 11**
See also CA 65-68; CANR 17; CWW 2; DLB 83; EWL 3; GFL 1789 to the Present

Malley, Ern
See McAuley, James Phillip

Mallon, Thomas 1951- .... **CLC 172**
See also CA 110; CANR 29, 57, 92

Mallowan, Agatha Christie
See Christie, Agatha (Mary Clarissa)

Maloff, Saul 1922- .... **CLC 5**
See also CA 33-36R

Malone, Louis
See MacNeice, (Frederick) Louis

Malone, Michael (Christopher)
1942- .... **CLC 43**
See also CA 77-80; CANR 14, 32, 57, 114

Malory, Sir Thomas 1410(?)-1471(?) . **LC 11, 88; WLCS**
See also BRW 1; BRWR 2; CDBLB Before 1660; DA; DAB; DAC; DAM MST; DLB 146; EFS 2; RGEL 2; SATA 59; SATA-Brief 33; TEA; WLIT 3

Malouf, (George Joseph) David
1934- .... **CLC 28, 86**
See also CA 124; CANR 50, 76; CN 7; CP 7; DLB 289; EWL 3; MTCW 2

Malraux, (Georges-)Andre
1901-1976 .... **CLC 1, 4, 9, 13, 15, 57**
See also BPFB 2; CA 21-22; 69-72; CANR 34, 58; CAP 2; DA3; DAM NOV; DLB 72; EW 12; EWL 3; GFL 1789 to the Present; MTCW 1, 2; RGWL 2, 3; TWA

Malthus, Thomas Robert
1766-1834 .... **NCLC 145**
See also DLB 107, 158; RGEL 2

Malzberg, Barry N(athaniel) 1939- ... **CLC 7**
See also CA 61-64; CAAS 4; CANR 16; CMW 4; DLB 8; SFW 4

Mamet, David (Alan) 1947- .. **CLC 9, 15, 34, 46, 91, 166; DC 4, 24**
See also AAYA 3, 60; AMWS 14; CA 81-84; CABS 3; CANR 15, 41, 67, 72, 129; CD 5; DA3; DAM DRAM; DFS 2, 3, 6, 12, 15; DLB 7; EWL 3; IDFW 4; MTCW 1, 2; RGAL 4

Mamoulian, Rouben (Zachary)
1897-1987 .... **CLC 16**
See also CA 25-28R; 124; CANR 85

Mandelshtam, Osip
See Mandelstam, Osip (Emilievich)
See also EW 10; EWL 3; RGWL 2, 3

Mandelstam, Osip (Emilievich)
1891(?)-1943(?) .... **PC 14; TCLC 2, 6**
See Mandelshtam, Osip
See also CA 104; 150; MTCW 2; TWA

Mander, (Mary) Jane 1877-1949 ... **TCLC 31**
See also CA 162; RGEL 2

Mandeville, Bernard 1670-1733 .... **LC 82**
See also DLB 101

Mandeville, Sir John fl. 1350- ...... **CMLC 19**
See also DLB 146

Mandiargues, Andre Pieyre de .... **CLC 41**
See Pieyre de Mandiargues, Andre
See also DLB 83

Mandrake, Ethel Belle
See Thurman, Wallace (Henry)

Mangan, James Clarence
1803-1849 .... **NCLC 27**
See also RGEL 2

Maniere, J.-E.
See Giraudoux, Jean(-Hippolyte)

Mankiewicz, Herman (Jacob)
1897-1953 .... **TCLC 85**
See also CA 120; 169; DLB 26; IDFW 3, 4

Manley, (Mary) Delariviere
1672(?)-1724 .... **LC 1, 42**
See also DLB 39, 80; RGEL 2

Mann, Abel
See Creasey, John

Mann, Emily 1952- .... **DC 7**
See also CA 130; CAD; CANR 55; CD 5; CWD; DLB 266

Mann, (Luiz) Heinrich 1871-1950 ... **TCLC 9**
See also CA 106; 164; 181; DLB 66; 118; EW 8; EWL 3; RGWL 2, 3

Mann, (Paul) Thomas 1875-1955 . **SSC 5, 80, 82; TCLC 2, 8, 14, 21, 35, 44, 60, 168; WLC**
See also BPFB 2; CA 104; 128; CANR 133; CDWLB 2; DA; DA3; DAB; DAC; DAM MST, NOV; DLB 66; EW 9; EWL 3; GLL 1; LATS 1:1; LMFS 1; MTCW 1, 2; NFS 17; RGSF 2; RGWL 2, 3; SSFS 4, 9; TWA

Mannheim, Karl 1893-1947 .... **TCLC 65**
See also CA 204

Manning, David
See Faust, Frederick (Schiller)
See also TCWW 2

Manning, Frederic 1882-1935 .... **TCLC 25**
See also CA 124; 216; DLB 260

Manning, Olivia 1915-1980 .... **CLC 5, 19**
See also CA 5-8R; 101; CANR 29; EWL 3; FW; MTCW 1; RGEL 2

Mano, D. Keith 1942- .... **CLC 2, 10**
See also CA 25-28R; CAAS 6; CANR 26, 57; DLB 6

Mansfield, Katherine .... **SSC 9, 23, 38, 81; TCLC 2, 8, 39, 164; WLC**
See Beauchamp, Kathleen Mansfield
See also BPFB 2; BRW 7; DAB; DLB 162; EWL 3; EXPS; FW; GLL 1; RGEL 2; RGSF 2; SSFS 2, 8, 10, 11; WWE 1

Manso, Peter 1940- .... **CLC 39**
See also CA 29-32R; CANR 44

Mantecon, Juan Jimenez
See Jimenez (Mantecon), Juan Ramon

Mantel, Hilary (Mary) 1952- .... **CLC 144**
See also CA 125; CANR 54, 101; CN 7; DLB 271; RHW

Manton, Peter
See Creasey, John

Man Without a Spleen, A
See Chekhov, Anton (Pavlovich)

Manzano, Juan Francisco
1797(?)-1854 .... **NCLC 155**

Manzoni, Alessandro 1785-1873 ... **NCLC 29, 98**
See also EW 5; RGWL 2, 3; TWA

Map, Walter 1140-1209 .... **CMLC 32**

Mapu, Abraham (ben Jekutiel)
1808-1867 .... **NCLC 18**

Mara, Sally
See Queneau, Raymond

Maracle, Lee 1950- .... **NNAL**
See also CA 149

Marat, Jean Paul 1743-1793 .... **LC 10**

Marcel, Gabriel Honore 1889-1973 . **CLC 15**
See also CA 102; 45-48; EWL 3; MTCW 1, 2

March, William 1893-1954 .... **TCLC 96**
See also CA 216

Marchbanks, Samuel
See Davies, (William) Robertson
See also CCA 1

Marchi, Giacomo
See Bassani, Giorgio

Marcus Aurelius
See Aurelius, Marcus
See also AW 2

Marguerite
See de Navarre, Marguerite

Marguerite d'Angouleme
See de Navarre, Marguerite
See also GFL Beginnings to 1789

Marguerite de Navarre
See de Navarre, Marguerite
See also RGWL 2, 3

Margulies, Donald 1954- .... **CLC 76**
See also AAYA 57; CA 200; DFS 13; DLB 228

Marie de France c. 12th cent. - ..... **CMLC 8; PC 22**
See also DLB 208; FW; RGWL 2, 3

Mather, Increase 1639-1723 .... **LC 38**
See also DLB 24

Matheson, Richard (Burton) 1926- .. **CLC 37**
See also AAYA 31; CA 97-100; CANR 88,
99; DLB 8, 44; HGG; INT CA-97-100;
SCFW 2; SFW 4; SUFW 2

Mathews, Harry 1930- .... **CLC 6, 52**
See also CA 21-24R; CAAS 6; CANR 18,
40, 98; CN 7

Mathews, John Joseph 1894-1979 .. **CLC 84;
NNAL**
See also CA 19-20; 142; CANR 45; CAP 2;
DAM MULT; DLB 175

Mathias, Roland (Glyn) 1915- .... **CLC 45**
See also CA 97-100; CANR 19, 41; CP 7;
DLB 27

Matsuo Basho 1644-1694 .... **LC 62; PC 3**
See Basho, Matsuo
See also DAM POET; PFS 2, 7

Mattheson, Rodney
See Creasey, John

Matthews, (James) Brander
1852-1929 .... **TCLC 95**
See also DLB 71, 78; DLBD 13

Matthews, (James) Brander
1852-1929 .... **TCLC 95**
See also CA 181; DLB 71, 78; DLBD 13

Matthews, Greg 1949- .... **CLC 45**
See also CA 135

Matthews, William (Procter III)
1942-1997 .... **CLC 40**
See also AMWS 9; CA 29-32R; 162; CAAS
18; CANR 12, 57; CP 7; DLB 5

Matthias, John (Edward) 1941- .... **CLC 9**
See also CA 33-36R; CANR 56; CP 7

Matthiessen, F(rancis) O(tto)
1902-1950 .... **TCLC 100**
See also CA 185; DLB 63

Matthiessen, Peter 1927- ... **CLC 5, 7, 11, 32,
64**
See also AAYA 6, 40; AMWS 5; ANW;
BEST 90:4; BPFB 2; CA 9-12R; CANR
21, 50, 73, 100; CN 7; DA3; DAM NOV;
DLB 6, 173, 275; MTCW 1, 2; SATA 27

Maturin, Charles Robert
1780(?)-1824 .... **NCLC 6**
See also BRWS 8; DLB 178; HGG; LMFS
1; RGEL 2; SUFW

Matute (Ausejo), Ana Maria 1925- .. **CLC 11**
See also CA 89-92; CANR 129; CWW 2;
EWL 3; MTCW 1; RGSF 2

Maugham, W. S.
See Maugham, W(illiam) Somerset

Maugham, W(illiam) Somerset
1874-1965 .. **CLC 1, 11, 15, 67, 93; SSC
8; WLC**
See also AAYA 55; BPFB 2; BRW 6; CA
5-8R; 25-28R; CANR 40, 127; CDBLB
1914-1945; CMW 4; DA; DA3; DAB;
DAC; DAM DRAM, MST, NOV; DLB
10, 36, 77, 100, 162, 195; EWL 3; LAIT
3; MTCW 1, 2; RGEL 2; RGSF 2; SATA
54; SSFS 17

Maugham, William Somerset
See Maugham, W(illiam) Somerset

Maupassant, (Henri Rene Albert) Guy de
1850-1893 . **NCLC 1, 42, 83; SSC 1, 64;
WLC**
See also BYA 14; DA; DA3; DAB; DAC;
DAM MST; DLB 123; EW 7; EXPS; GFL
1789 to the Present; LAIT 2; LMFS 1;
RGSF 2; RGWL 2, 3; SSFS 4; SUFW;
TWA

Maupin, Armistead (Jones, Jr.)
1944- .... **CLC 95**
See also CA 125; 130; CANR 58, 101;
CPW; DA3; DAM POP; DLB 278; GLL
1; INT CA-130; MTCW 2

Maurhut, Richard
See Traven, B.

Mauriac, Claude 1914-1996 .... **CLC 9**
See also CA 89-92; 152; CWW 2; DLB 83;
EWL 3; GFL 1789 to the Present

Mauriac, Francois (Charles)
1885-1970 .... **CLC 4, 9, 56; SSC 24**
See also CA 25-28; CAP 2; DLB 65; EW
10; EWL 3; GFL 1789 to the Present;
MTCW 1, 2; RGWL 2, 3; TWA

Mavor, Osborne Henry 1888-1951
See Bridie, James
See also CA 104

Maxwell, William (Keepers, Jr.)
1908-2000 .... **CLC 19**
See also AMWS 8; CA 93-96; 189; CANR
54, 95; CN 7; DLB 218, 278; DLBY
1980; INT CA-93-96; SATA-Obit 128

May, Elaine 1932- .... **CLC 16**
See also CA 124; 142; CAD; CWD; DLB
44

Mayakovski, Vladimir (Vladimirovich)
1893-1930 .... **TCLC 4, 18**
See Maiakovskii, Vladimir; Mayakovsky,
Vladimir
See also CA 104; 158; EWL 3; MTCW 2;
SFW 4; TWA

Mayakovsky, Vladimir
See Mayakovski, Vladimir (Vladimirovich)
See also EW 11; WP

Mayhew, Henry 1812-1887 .... **NCLC 31**
See also DLB 18, 55, 190

Mayle, Peter 1939(?)- .... **CLC 89**
See also CA 139; CANR 64, 109

Maynard, Joyce 1953- .... **CLC 23**
See also CA 111; 129; CANR 64

Mayne, William (James Carter)
1928- .... **CLC 12**
See also AAYA 20; CA 9-12R; CANR 37,
80, 100; CLR 25; FANT; JRDA; MAI-
CYA 1, 2; MAICYAS 1; SAAS 11; SATA
6, 68, 122; SUFW 2; YAW

Mayo, Jim
See L'Amour, Louis (Dearborn)
See also TCWW 2

Maysles, Albert 1926- .... **CLC 16**
See also CA 29-32R

Maysles, David 1932-1987 .... **CLC 16**
See also CA 191

Mazer, Norma Fox 1931- .... **CLC 26**
See also AAYA 5, 36; BYA 1, 8; CA 69-72;
CANR 12, 32, 66, 129; CLR 23; JRDA;
MAICYA 1, 2; SAAS 1; SATA 24, 67,
105; WYA; YAW

Mazzini, Guiseppe 1805-1872 .... **NCLC 34**

McAlmon, Robert (Menzies)
1895-1956 .... **TCLC 97**
See also CA 107; 168; DLB 4, 45; DLBD
15; GLL 1

McAuley, James Phillip 1917-1976 .. **CLC 45**
See also CA 97-100; DLB 260; RGEL 2

McBain, Ed
See Hunter, Evan
See also MSW

McBrien, William (Augustine)
1930- .... **CLC 44**
See also CA 107; CANR 90

McCabe, Patrick 1955- .... **CLC 133**
See also BRWS 9; CA 130; CANR 50, 90;
CN 7; DLB 194

McCaffrey, Anne (Inez) 1926- .... **CLC 17**
See also AAYA 6, 34; AITN 2; BEST 89:2;
BPFB 2; BYA 5; CA 25-28R; 227; CAAE
227; CANR 15, 35, 55, 96; CLR 49;
CPW; DA3; DAM NOV, POP; DLB 8;
JRDA; MAICYA 1, 2; MTCW 1, 2; SAAS
11; SATA 8, 70, 116, 152; SATA-Essay
152; SFW 4; SUFW 2; WYA; YAW

McCall, Nathan 1955(?)- .... **CLC 86**
See also AAYA 59; BW 3; CA 146; CANR
88

McCann, Arthur
See Campbell, John W(ood, Jr.)

McCann, Edson
See Pohl, Frederik

McCarthy, Charles, Jr. 1933-
See McCarthy, Cormac
See also CANR 42, 69, 101; CN 7; CPW;
CSW; DA3; DAM POP; MTCW 2

McCarthy, Cormac ...... **CLC 4, 57, 101, 204**
See McCarthy, Charles, Jr.
See also AAYA 41; AMWS 8; BPFB 2; CA
13-16R; CANR 10; DLB 6, 143, 256;
EWL 3; LATS 1:2; TCWW 2

McCarthy, Mary (Therese)
1912-1989 .. **CLC 1, 3, 5, 14, 24, 39, 59;
SSC 24**
See also AMW; BPFB 2; CA 5-8R; 129;
CANR 16, 50, 64; DA3; DLB 2; DLBY
1981; EWL 3; FW; INT CANR-16;
MAWW; MTCW 1, 2; RGAL 4; TUS

McCartney, (James) Paul 1942- . **CLC 12, 35**
See also CA 146; CANR 111

McCauley, Stephen (D.) 1955- .... **CLC 50**
See also CA 141

McClaren, Peter .... **CLC 70**

McClure, Michael (Thomas) 1932- ... **CLC 6,
10**
See also BG 3; CA 21-24R; CAD; CANR
17, 46, 77, 131; CD 5; CP 7; DLB 16;
WP

McCorkle, Jill (Collins) 1958- .... **CLC 51**
See also CA 121; CANR 113; CSW; DLB
234; DLBY 1987

McCourt, Frank 1930- .... **CLC 109**
See also AMWS 12; CA 157; CANR 97;
NCFS 1

McCourt, James 1941- .... **CLC 5**
See also CA 57-60; CANR 98

McCourt, Malachy 1931- .... **CLC 119**
See also SATA 126

McCoy, Horace (Stanley)
1897-1955 .... **TCLC 28**
See also AMWS 13; CA 108; 155; CMW 4;
DLB 9

McCrae, John 1872-1918 .... **TCLC 12**
See also CA 109; DLB 92; PFS 5

McCreigh, James
See Pohl, Frederik

McCullers, (Lula) Carson (Smith)
1917-1967 .... **CLC 1, 4, 10, 12, 48, 100;
SSC 9, 24; TCLC 155; WLC**
See also AAYA 21; AMW; AMWC 2; BPFB
2; CA 5-8R; 25-28R; CABS 1, 3; CANR
18, 132; CDALB 1941-1968; DA; DA3;
DAB; DAC; DAM MST, NOV; DFS 5,
18; DLB 2, 7, 173, 228; EWL 3; EXPS;
FW; GLL 1; LAIT 3, 4; MAWW; MTCW
1, 2; NFS 6, 13; RGAL 4; RGSF 2; SATA
27; SSFS 5; TUS; YAW

McCulloch, John Tyler
See Burroughs, Edgar Rice

McCullough, Colleen 1938(?)- .. **CLC 27, 107**
See also AAYA 36; BPFB 2; CA 81-84;
CANR 17, 46, 67, 98; CPW; DA3; DAM
NOV, POP; MTCW 1, 2; RHW

McCunn, Ruthanne Lum 1946- .... **AAL**
See also CA 119; CANR 43, 96; LAIT 2;
SATA 63

McDermott, Alice 1953- .... **CLC 90**
See also CA 109; CANR 40, 90, 126; DLB
292

McElroy, Joseph 1930- .... **CLC 5, 47**
See also CA 17-20R; CN 7

Mrozek, Slawomir 1930- .... **CLC 3, 13**
See also CA 13-16R; CAAS 10; CANR 29;
CDWLB 4; CWW 2; DLB 232; EWL 3;
MTCW 1

Mrs. Belloc-Lowndes
See Lowndes, Marie Adelaide (Belloc)

Mrs. Fairstar
See Horne, Richard Henry Hengist

M'Taggart, John M'Taggart Ellis
See McTaggart, John McTaggart Ellis

Mtwa, Percy (?)- .... **CLC 47**

Mueller, Lisel 1924- .... **CLC 13, 51; PC 33**
See also CA 93-96; CP 7; DLB 105; PFS 9,
13

Muggeridge, Malcolm (Thomas)
1903-1990 .... **TCLC 120**
See also AITN 1; CA 101; CANR 33, 63;
MTCW 1, 2

Muhammad 570-632 .... **WLCS**
See also DA; DAB; DAC; DAM MST

Muir, Edwin 1887-1959 . **PC 49; TCLC 2, 87**
See Moore, Edward
See also BRWS 6; CA 104; 193; DLB 20,
100, 191; EWL 3; RGEL 2

Muir, John 1838-1914 .... **TCLC 28**
See also AMWS 9; ANW; CA 165; DLB
186, 275

Mujica Lainez, Manuel 1910-1984 ... **CLC 31**
See Lainez, Manuel Mujica
See also CA 81-84; 112; CANR 32; EWL
3; HW 1

Mukherjee, Bharati 1940- ..... **AAL; CLC 53,**
115; SSC 38
See also AAYA 46; BEST 89:2; CA 107;
CANR 45, 72, 128; CN 7; DAM NOV;
DLB 60, 218; DNFS 1, 2; EWL 3; FW;
MTCW 1, 2; RGAL 4; RGSF 2; SSFS 7;
TUS; WWE 1

Muldoon, Paul 1951- .... **CLC 32, 72, 166**
See also BRWS 4; CA 113; 129; CANR 52,
91; CP 7; DAM POET; DLB 40; INT CA-
129; PFS 7

Mulisch, Harry (Kurt Victor)
1927- .... **CLC 42**
See also CA 9-12R; CANR 6, 26, 56, 110;
CWW 2; DLB 299; EWL 3

Mull, Martin 1943- .... **CLC 17**
See also CA 105

Muller, Wilhelm .... **NCLC 73**

Mulock, Dinah Maria
See Craik, Dinah Maria (Mulock)
See also RGEL 2

Munday, Anthony 1560-1633 .... **LC 87**
See also DLB 62, 172; RGEL 2

Munford, Robert 1737(?)-1783 .... **LC 5**
See also DLB 31

Mungo, Raymond 1946- .... **CLC 72**
See also CA 49-52; CANR 2

Munro, Alice 1931- .... **CLC 6, 10, 19, 50, 95;**
SSC 3; WLCS
See also AITN 2; BPFB 2; CA 33-36R;
CANR 33, 53, 75, 114; CCA 1; CN 7;
DA3; DAC; DAM MST, NOV; DLB 53;
EWL 3; MTCW 1, 2; RGEL 2; RGSF 2;
SATA 29; SSFS 5, 13, 19; WWE 1

Munro, H(ector) H(ugh) 1870-1916 .... **WLC**
See Saki
See also AAYA 56; CA 104; 130; CANR
104; CDBLB 1890-1914; DA; DA3;
DAB; DAC; DAM MST, NOV; DLB 34,
162; EXPS; MTCW 1, 2; RGEL 2; SSFS
15

Murakami, Haruki 1949- .... **CLC 150**
See Murakami Haruki
See also CA 165; CANR 102; MJW; RGWL
3; SFW 4

Murakami Haruki
See Murakami, Haruki
See also CWW 2; DLB 182; EWL 3

Murasaki, Lady
See Murasaki Shikibu

Murasaki Shikibu 978(?)-1026(?) ... **CMLC 1**
See also EFS 2; LATS 1:1; RGWL 2, 3

Murdoch, (Jean) Iris 1919-1999 ... **CLC 1, 2,**
3, 4, 6, 8, 11, 15, 22, 31, 51
See also BRWS 1; CA 13-16R; 179; CANR
8, 43, 68, 103; CDBLB 1960 to Present;
CN 7; CWD; DA3; DAB; DAC; DAM
MST, NOV; DLB 14, 194, 233; EWL 3;
INT CANR-8; MTCW 1, 2; NFS 18;
RGEL 2; TEA; WLIT 4

Murfree, Mary Noailles 1850-1922 .. **SSC 22;**
TCLC 135
See also CA 122; 176; DLB 12, 74; RGAL
4

Murnau, Friedrich Wilhelm
See Plumpe, Friedrich Wilhelm

Murphy, Richard 1927- .... **CLC 41**
See also BRWS 5; CA 29-32R; CP 7; DLB
40; EWL 3

Murphy, Sylvia 1937- .... **CLC 34**
See also CA 121

Murphy, Thomas (Bernard) 1935- ... **CLC 51**
See also CA 101

Murray, Albert L. 1916- .... **CLC 73**
See also BW 2; CA 49-52; CANR 26, 52,
78; CSW; DLB 38

Murray, James Augustus Henry
1837-1915 .... **TCLC 117**

Murray, Judith Sargent
1751-1820 .... **NCLC 63**
See also DLB 37, 200

Murray, Les(lie Allan) 1938- .... **CLC 40**
See also BRWS 7; CA 21-24R; CANR 11,
27, 56, 103; CP 7; DAM POET; DLB 289;
DLBY 2001; EWL 3; RGEL 2

Murry, J. Middleton
See Murry, John Middleton

Murry, John Middleton
1889-1957 .... **TCLC 16**
See also CA 118; 217; DLB 149

Musgrave, Susan 1951- .... **CLC 13, 54**
See also CA 69-72; CANR 45, 84; CCA 1;
CP 7; CWP

Musil, Robert (Edler von)
1880-1942 .... **SSC 18; TCLC 12, 68**
See also CA 109; CANR 55, 84; CDWLB
2; DLB 81, 124; EW 9; EWL 3; MTCW
2; RGSF 2; RGWL 2, 3

Muske, Carol .... **CLC 90**
See Muske-Dukes, Carol (Anne)

Muske-Dukes, Carol (Anne) 1945-
See Muske, Carol
See also CA 65-68, 203; CAAE 203; CANR
32, 70; CWP

Musset, (Louis Charles) Alfred de
1810-1857 .... **NCLC 7, 150**
See also DLB 192, 217; EW 6; GFL 1789
to the Present; RGWL 2, 3; TWA

Mussolini, Benito (Amilcare Andrea)
1883-1945 .... **TCLC 96**
See also CA 116

Mutanabbi, Al-
See al-Mutanabbi, Ahmad ibn al-Husayn
Abu al-Tayyib al-Jufi al-Kindi

My Brother's Brother
See Chekhov, Anton (Pavlovich)

Myers, L(eopold) H(amilton)
1881-1944 .... **TCLC 59**
See also CA 157; DLB 15; EWL 3; RGEL
2

Myers, Walter Dean 1937- .. **BLC 3; CLC 35**
See also AAYA 4, 23; BW 2; BYA 6, 8, 11;
CA 33-36R; CANR 20, 42, 67, 108; CLR
4, 16, 35; DAM MULT, NOV; DLB 33;
INT CANR-20; JRDA; LAIT 5; MAICYA
1, 2; MAICYAS 1; MTCW 2; SAAS 2;
SATA 41, 71, 109; SATA-Brief 27; WYA;
YAW

Myers, Walter M.
See Myers, Walter Dean

Myles, Symon
See Follett, Ken(neth Martin)

Nabokov, Vladimir (Vladimirovich)
1899-1977 .... **CLC 1, 2, 3, 6, 8, 11, 15,**
23, 44, 46, 64; SSC 11; TCLC 108;
WLC
See also AAYA 45; AMW; AMWC 1;
AMWR 1; BPFB 2; CA 5-8R; 69-72;
CANR 20, 102; CDALB 1941-1968; DA;
DA3; DAB; DAC; DAM MST, NOV;
DLB 2, 244, 278; DLBD 3; DLBY 1980,
1991; EWL 3; EXPS; LATS 1:2; MTCW
1, 2; NCFS 4; NFS 9; RGAL 4; RGSF 2;
SSFS 6, 15; TUS

Naevius c. 265B.C.-201B.C. .... **CMLC 37**
See also DLB 211

Nagai, Kafu .... **TCLC 51**
See Nagai, Sokichi
See also DLB 180

Nagai, Sokichi 1879-1959
See Nagai, Kafu
See also CA 117

Nagy, Laszlo 1925-1978 .... **CLC 7**
See also CA 129; 112

Naidu, Sarojini 1879-1949 .... **TCLC 80**
See also EWL 3; RGEL 2

Naipaul, Shiva(dhar Srinivasa)
1945-1985 ... **CLC 32, 39; TCLC 153**
See also CA 110; 112; 116; CANR 33;
DA3; DAM NOV; DLB 157; DLBY 1985;
EWL 3; MTCW 1, 2

Naipaul, V(idiadhar) S(urajprasad)
1932- .... **CLC 4, 7, 9, 13, 18, 37, 105,**
199; SSC 38
See also BPFB 2; BRWS 1; CA 1-4R;
CANR 1, 33, 51, 91, 126; CDBLB 1960
to Present; CDWLB 3; CN 7; DA3; DAB;
DAC; DAM MST, NOV; DLB 125, 204,
207; DLBY 1985, 2001; EWL 3; LATS
1:2; MTCW 1, 2; RGEL 2; RGSF 2;
TWA; WLIT 4; WWE 1

Nakos, Lilika 1903(?)-1989 .... **CLC 29**

Napoleon
See Yamamoto, Hisaye

Narayan, R(asipuram) K(rishnaswami)
1906-2001 .... **CLC 7, 28, 47, 121, 211;**
SSC 25
See also BPFB 2; CA 81-84; 196; CANR
33, 61, 112; CN 7; DA3; DAM NOV;
DNFS 1; EWL 3; MTCW 1, 2; RGEL 2;
RGSF 2; SATA 62; SSFS 5; WWE 1

Nash, (Frediric) Ogden 1902-1971 . **CLC 23;**
PC 21; TCLC 109
See also CA 13-14; 29-32R; CANR 34, 61;
CAP 1; DAM POET; DLB 11; MAICYA
1, 2; MTCW 1, 2; RGAL 4; SATA 2, 46;
WP

Nashe, Thomas 1567-1601(?) .... **LC 41, 89**
See also DLB 167; RGEL 2

Nathan, Daniel
See Dannay, Frederic

Nathan, George Jean 1882-1958 .... **TCLC 18**
See Hatteras, Owen
See also CA 114; 169; DLB 137

Natsume, Kinnosuke
See Natsume, Soseki

Natsume, Soseki 1867-1916 .... **TCLC 2, 10**
See Natsume Soseki; Soseki
See also CA 104; 195; RGWL 2, 3; TWA

Natsume Soseki
See Natsume, Soseki
See also DLB 180; EWL 3

Natti, (Mary) Lee 1919-
    See Kingman, Lee
    See also CA 5-8R; CANR 2

Navarre, Marguerite de
    See de Navarre, Marguerite

Naylor, Gloria 1950- ..... **BLC 3; CLC 28, 52, 156; WLCS**
    See also AAYA 6, 39; AFAW 1, 2; AMWS 8; BW 2, 3; CA 107; CANR 27, 51, 74, 130; CN 7; CPW; DA; DA3; DAC; DAM MST, MULT, NOV, POP; DLB 173; EWL 3; FW; MTCW 1, 2; NFS 4, 7; RGAL 4; TUS

Neff, Debra .... **CLC 59**

Neihardt, John Gneisenau 1881-1973 .... **CLC 32**
    See also CA 13-14; CANR 65; CAP 1; DLB 9, 54, 256; LAIT 2

Nekrasov, Nikolai Alekseevich 1821-1878 .... **NCLC 11**
    See also DLB 277

Nelligan, Emile 1879-1941 .... **TCLC 14**
    See also CA 114; 204; DLB 92; EWL 3

Nelson, Willie 1933- .... **CLC 17**
    See also CA 107; CANR 114

Nemerov, Howard (Stanley) 1920-1991 .... **CLC 2, 6, 9, 36; PC 24; TCLC 124**
    See also AMW; CA 1-4R; 134; CABS 2; CANR 1, 27, 53; DAM POET; DLB 5, 6; DLBY 1983; EWL 3; INT CANR-27; MTCW 1, 2; PFS 10, 14; RGAL 4

Neruda, Pablo 1904-1973 .. **CLC 1, 2, 5, 7, 9, 28, 62; HLC 2; PC 4, 64; WLC**
    See also CA 19-20; 45-48; CANR 131; CAP 2; DA; DA3; DAB; DAC; DAM MST, MULT, POET; DLB 283; DNFS 2; EWL 3; HW 1; LAW; MTCW 1, 2; PFS 11; RGWL 2, 3; TWA; WLIT 1; WP

Nerval, Gerard de 1808-1855 ... **NCLC 1, 67; PC 13; SSC 18**
    See also DLB 217; EW 6; GFL 1789 to the Present; RGSF 2; RGWL 2, 3

Nervo, (Jose) Amado (Ruiz de) 1870-1919 .... **HLCS 2; TCLC 11**
    See also CA 109; 131; DLB 290; EWL 3; HW 1; LAW

Nesbit, Malcolm
    See Chester, Alfred

Nessi, Pio Baroja y
    See Baroja (y Nessi), Pio

Nestroy, Johann 1801-1862 .... **NCLC 42**
    See also DLB 133; RGWL 2, 3

Netterville, Luke
    See O'Grady, Standish (James)

Neufeld, John (Arthur) 1938- .... **CLC 17**
    See also AAYA 11; CA 25-28R; CANR 11, 37, 56; CLR 52; MAICYA 1, 2; SAAS 3; SATA 6, 81, 131; SATA-Essay 131; YAW

Neumann, Alfred 1895-1952 .... **TCLC 100**
    See also CA 183; DLB 56

Neumann, Ferenc
    See Molnar, Ferenc

Neville, Emily Cheney 1919- .... **CLC 12**
    See also BYA 2; CA 5-8R; CANR 3, 37, 85; JRDA; MAICYA 1, 2; SAAS 2; SATA 1; YAW

Newbound, Bernard Slade 1930-
    See Slade, Bernard
    See also CA 81-84; CANR 49; CD 5; DAM DRAM

Newby, P(ercy) H(oward) 1918-1997 .... **CLC 2, 13**
    See also CA 5-8R; 161; CANR 32, 67; CN 7; DAM NOV; DLB 15; MTCW 1; RGEL 2

Newcastle
    See Cavendish, Margaret Lucas

Newlove, Donald 1928- .... **CLC 6**
    See also CA 29-32R; CANR 25

Newlove, John (Herbert) 1938- .... **CLC 14**
    See also CA 21-24R; CANR 9, 25; CP 7

Newman, Charles 1938- .... **CLC 2, 8**
    See also CA 21-24R; CANR 84; CN 7

Newman, Edwin (Harold) 1919- ...... **CLC 14**
    See also AITN 1; CA 69-72; CANR 5

Newman, John Henry 1801-1890 . **NCLC 38, 99**
    See also BRWS 7; DLB 18, 32, 55; RGEL 2

Newton, (Sir) Isaac 1642-1727 ...... **LC 35, 53**
    See also DLB 252

Newton, Suzanne 1936- .... **CLC 35**
    See also BYA 7; CA 41-44R; CANR 14; JRDA; SATA 5, 77

New York Dept. of Ed. .... **CLC 70**

Nexo, Martin Andersen 1869-1954 .... **TCLC 43**
    See also CA 202; DLB 214; EWL 3

Nezval, Vitezslav 1900-1958 .... **TCLC 44**
    See also CA 123; CDWLB 4; DLB 215; EWL 3

Ng, Fae Myenne 1957(?)- .... **CLC 81**
    See also BYA 11; CA 146

Ngema, Mbongeni 1955- .... **CLC 57**
    See also BW 2; CA 143; CANR 84; CD 5

Ngugi, James T(hiong'o) . **CLC 3, 7, 13, 182**
    See Ngugi wa Thiong'o

Ngugi wa Thiong'o
    See Ngugi wa Thiong'o
    See also DLB 125; EWL 3

Ngugi wa Thiong'o 1938- ... **BLC 3; CLC 36, 182**
    See Ngugi, James T(hiong'o); Ngugi wa Thiong'o
    See also AFW; BRWS 8; BW 2; CA 81-84; CANR 27, 58; CDWLB 3; DAM MULT, NOV; DNFS 2; MTCW 1, 2; RGEL 2; WWE 1

Niatum, Duane 1938- .... **NNAL**
    See also CA 41-44R; CANR 21, 45, 83; DLB 175

Nichol, B(arrie) P(hillip) 1944-1988 . **CLC 18**
    See also CA 53-56; DLB 53; SATA 66

Nicholas of Cusa 1401-1464 .... **LC 80**
    See also DLB 115

Nichols, John (Treadwell) 1940- .... **CLC 38**
    See also AMWS 13; CA 9-12R, 190; CAAE 190; CAAS 2; CANR 6, 70, 121; DLBY 1982; LATS 1:2; TCWW 2

Nichols, Leigh
    See Koontz, Dean R(ay)

Nichols, Peter (Richard) 1927- .... **CLC 5, 36, 65**
    See also CA 104; CANR 33, 86; CBD; CD 5; DLB 13, 245; MTCW 1

Nicholson, Linda ed. .... **CLC 65**

Ni Chuilleanain, Eilean 1942- .... **PC 34**
    See also CA 126; CANR 53, 83; CP 7; CWP; DLB 40

Nicolas, F. R. E.
    See Freeling, Nicolas

Niedecker, Lorine 1903-1970 ..... **CLC 10, 42; PC 42**
    See also CA 25-28; CAP 2; DAM POET; DLB 48

Nietzsche, Friedrich (Wilhelm) 1844-1900 .... **TCLC 10, 18, 55**
    See also CA 107; 121; CDWLB 2; DLB 129; EW 7; RGWL 2, 3; TWA

Nievo, Ippolito 1831-1861 .... **NCLC 22**

Nightingale, Anne Redmon 1943-
    See Redmon, Anne
    See also CA 103

Nightingale, Florence 1820-1910 ... **TCLC 85**
    See also CA 188; DLB 166

Nijo Yoshimoto 1320-1388 .... **CMLC 49**
    See also DLB 203

Nik. T. O.
    See Annensky, Innokenty (Fyodorovich)

Nin, Anais 1903-1977 ..... **CLC 1, 4, 8, 11, 14, 60, 127; SSC 10**
    See also AITN 2; AMWS 10; BPFB 2; CA 13-16R; 69-72; CANR 22, 53; DAM NOV, POP; DLB 2, 4, 152; EWL 3; GLL 2; MAWW; MTCW 1, 2; RGAL 4; RGSF 2

Nisbet, Robert A(lexander) 1913-1996 .... **TCLC 117**
    See also CA 25-28R; 153; CANR 17; INT CANR-17

Nishida, Kitaro 1870-1945 .... **TCLC 83**

Nishiwaki, Junzaburo
    See Nishiwaki, Junzaburo
    See also CA 194

Nishiwaki, Junzaburo 1894-1982 .... **PC 15**
    See Nishiwaki, Junzaburo; Nishiwaki Junzaburo
    See also CA 194; 107; MJW; RGWL 3

Nishiwaki Junzaburo
    See Nishiwaki, Junzaburo
    See also EWL 3

Nissenson, Hugh 1933- .... **CLC 4, 9**
    See also CA 17-20R; CANR 27, 108; CN 7; DLB 28

Nister, Der
    See Der Nister
    See also EWL 3

Niven, Larry .... **CLC 8**
    See Niven, Laurence Van Cott
    See also AAYA 27; BPFB 2; BYA 10; DLB 8; SCFW 2

Niven, Laurence Van Cott 1938-
    See Niven, Larry
    See also CA 21-24R, 207; CAAE 207; CAAS 12; CANR 14, 44, 66, 113; CPW; DAM POP; MTCW 1, 2; SATA 95; SFW 4

Nixon, Agnes Eckhardt 1927- .... **CLC 21**
    See also CA 110

Nizan, Paul 1905-1940 .... **TCLC 40**
    See also CA 161; DLB 72; EWL 3; GFL 1789 to the Present

Nkosi, Lewis 1936- .... **BLC 3; CLC 45**
    See also BW 1, 3; CA 65-68; CANR 27, 81; CBD; CD 5; DAM MULT; DLB 157, 225; WWE 1

Nodier, (Jean) Charles (Emmanuel) 1780-1844 .... **NCLC 19**
    See also DLB 119; GFL 1789 to the Present

Noguchi, Yone 1875-1947 .... **TCLC 80**

Nolan, Christopher 1965- .... **CLC 58**
    See also CA 111; CANR 88

Noon, Jeff 1957- .... **CLC 91**
    See also CA 148; CANR 83; DLB 267; SFW 4

Norden, Charles
    See Durrell, Lawrence (George)

Nordhoff, Charles Bernard 1887-1947 .... **TCLC 23**
    See also CA 108; 211; DLB 9; LAIT 1; RHW 1; SATA 23

Norfolk, Lawrence 1963- .... **CLC 76**
    See also CA 144; CANR 85; CN 7; DLB 267

Norman, Marsha 1947- . **CLC 28, 186; DC 8**
    See also CA 105; CABS 3; CAD; CANR 41, 131; CD 5; CSW; CWD; DAM DRAM; DFS 2; DLB 266; DLBY 1984; FW

Normyx
    See Douglas, (George) Norman

Okigbo, Christopher (Ifenayichukwu)
1932-1967 .... **BLC 3; CLC 25, 84; PC 7**
See also AFW; BW 1, 3; CA 77-80; CANR
74; CDWLB 3; DAM MULT, POET; DLB
125; EWL 3; MTCW 1, 2; RGEL 2

Okri, Ben 1959- .... **CLC 87**
See also AFW; BRWS 5; BW 2, 3; CA 130;
138; CANR 65, 128; CN 7; DLB 157,
231; EWL 3; INT CA-138; MTCW 2;
RGSF 2; SSFS 20; WLIT 2; WWE 1

Olds, Sharon 1942- .. **CLC 32, 39, 85; PC 22**
See also AMWS 10; CA 101; CANR 18,
41, 66, 98, 135; CP 7; CPW; CWP; DAM
POET; DLB 120; MTCW 2; PFS 17

Oldstyle, Jonathan
See Irving, Washington

Olesha, Iurii
See Olesha, Yuri (Karlovich)
See also RGWL 2

Olesha, Iurii Karlovich
See Olesha, Yuri (Karlovich)
See also DLB 272

Olesha, Yuri (Karlovich) 1899-1960 . **CLC 8;**
SSC 69; TCLC 136
See Olesha, Iurii; Olesha, Iurii Karlovich;
Olesha, Yury Karlovich
See also CA 85-88; EW 11; RGWL 3

Olesha, Yury Karlovich
See Olesha, Yuri (Karlovich)
See also EWL 3

Oliphant, Mrs.
See Oliphant, Margaret (Oliphant Wilson)
See also SUFW

Oliphant, Laurence 1829(?)-1888 .. **NCLC 47**
See also DLB 18, 166

Oliphant, Margaret (Oliphant Wilson)
1828-1897 .... **NCLC 11, 61; SSC 25**
See Oliphant, Mrs.
See also BRWS 10; DLB 18, 159, 190;
HGG; RGEL 2; RGSF 2

Oliver, Mary 1935- .... **CLC 19, 34, 98**
See also AMWS 7; CA 21-24R; CANR 9,
43, 84, 92; CP 7; CWP; DLB 5, 193;
EWL 3; PFS 15

Olivier, Laurence (Kerr) 1907-1989 . **CLC 20**
See also CA 111; 150; 129

Olsen, Tillie 1912- ... **CLC 4, 13, 114; SSC 11**
See also AAYA 51; AMWS 13; BYA 11;
CA 1-4R; CANR 1, 43, 74, 132;
CDALBS; CN 7; DA; DA3; DAB; DAC;
DAM MST; DLB 28, 206; DLBY 1980;
EWL 3; EXPS; FW; MTCW 1, 2; RGAL
4; RGSF 2; SSFS 1; TUS

Olson, Charles (John) 1910-1970 .. **CLC 1, 2,**
5, 6, 9, 11, 29; PC 19
See also AMWS 2; CA 13-16; 25-28R;
CABS 2; CANR 35, 61; CAP 1; DAM
POET; DLB 5, 16, 193; EWL 3; MTCW
1, 2; RGAL 4; WP

Olson, Toby 1937- .... **CLC 28**
See also CA 65-68; CANR 9, 31, 84; CP 7

Olyesha, Yuri
See Olesha, Yuri (Karlovich)

Olympiodorus of Thebes c. 375-c.
430 .... **CMLC 59**

Omar Khayyam
See Khayyam, Omar
See also RGWL 2, 3

Ondaatje, (Philip) Michael 1943- .... **CLC 14,**
29, 51, 76, 180; PC 28
See also CA 77-80; CANR 42, 74, 109, 133;
CN 7; CP 7; DA3; DAB; DAC; DAM
MST; DLB 60; EWL 3; LATS 1:2; LMFS
2; MTCW 2; PFS 8, 19; TWA; WWE 1

Oneal, Elizabeth 1934-
See Oneal, Zibby
See also CA 106; CANR 28, 84; MAICYA
1, 2; SATA 30, 82; YAW

Oneal, Zibby .... **CLC 30**
See Oneal, Elizabeth
See also AAYA 5, 41; BYA 13; CLR 13;
JRDA; WYA

O'Neill, Eugene (Gladstone)
1888-1953 ... **DC 20; TCLC 1, 6, 27, 49;**
WLC
See also AAYA 54; AITN 1; AMW; AMWC
1; CA 110; 132; CAD; CANR 131;
CDALB 1929-1941; DA; DA3; DAB;
DAC; DAM DRAM, MST; DFS 2, 4, 5,
6, 9, 11, 12, 16, 20; DLB 7; EWL 3; LAIT
3; LMFS 2; MTCW 1, 2; RGAL 4; TUS

Onetti, Juan Carlos 1909-1994 ... **CLC 7, 10;**
HLCS 2; SSC 23; TCLC 131
See also CA 85-88; 145; CANR 32, 63; CD-
WLB 3; CWW 2; DAM MULT, NOV;
DLB 113; EWL 3; HW 1, 2; LAW;
MTCW 1, 2; RGSF 2

O Nuallain, Brian 1911-1966
See O'Brien, Flann
See also CA 21-22; 25-28R; CAP 2; DLB
231; FANT; TEA

Ophuls, Max 1902-1957 .... **TCLC 79**
See also CA 113

Opie, Amelia 1769-1853 .... **NCLC 65**
See also DLB 116, 159; RGEL 2

Oppen, George 1908-1984 ..... **CLC 7, 13, 34;**
PC 35; TCLC 107
See also CA 13-16R; 113; CANR 8, 82;
DLB 5, 165

Oppenheim, E(dward) Phillips
1866-1946 .... **TCLC 45**
See also CA 111; 202; CMW 4; DLB 70

Opuls, Max
See Ophuls, Max

Orage, A(lfred) R(ichard)
1873-1934 .... **TCLC 157**
See also CA 122

Origen c. 185-c. 254 .... **CMLC 19**

Orlovitz, Gil 1918-1973 .... **CLC 22**
See also CA 77-80; 45-48; DLB 2, 5

O'Rourke, P(atrick) J(ake) 1947- .. **CLC 209**
See also CA 77-80; CANR 13, 41, 67, 111;
CPW; DLB 185; DAM POP

Orris
See Ingelow, Jean

Ortega y Gasset, Jose 1883-1955 ...... **HLC 2;**
TCLC 9
See also CA 106; 130; DAM MULT; EW 9;
EWL 3; HW 1, 2; MTCW 1, 2

Ortese, Anna Maria 1914-1998 .... **CLC 89**
See also DLB 177; EWL 3

Ortiz, Simon J(oseph) 1941- ... **CLC 45, 208;**
NNAL; PC 17
See also AMWS 4; CA 134; CANR 69, 118;
CP 7; DAM MULT, POET; DLB 120,
175, 256; EXPP; PFS 4, 16; RGAL 4

Orton, Joe ...... **CLC 4, 13, 43; DC 3; TCLC**
157
See Orton, John Kingsley
See also BRWS 5; CBD; CDBLB 1960 to
Present; DFS 3, 6; DLB 13; GLL 1;
MTCW 2; RGEL 2; TEA; WLIT 4

Orton, John Kingsley 1933-1967
See Orton, Joe
See also CA 85-88; CANR 35, 66; DAM
DRAM; MTCW 1, 2

Orwell, George ...... **SSC 68; TCLC 2, 6, 15,**
31, 51, 128, 129; WLC
See Blair, Eric (Arthur)
See also BPFB 3; BRW 7; BYA 5; CDBLB
1945-1960; CLR 68; DAB; DLB 15, 98,
195, 255; EWL 3; EXPN; LAIT 4, 5;
LATS 1:1; NFS 3, 7; RGEL 2; SCFW 2;
SFW 4; SSFS 4; TEA; WLIT 4; YAW

Osborne, David
See Silverberg, Robert

Osborne, George
See Silverberg, Robert

Osborne, John (James) 1929-1994 .... **CLC 1,**
2, 5, 11, 45; TCLC 153; WLC
See also BRWS 1; CA 13-16R; 147; CANR
21, 56; CDBLB 1945-1960; DA; DAB;
DAC; DAM DRAM, MST; DFS 4, 19;
DLB 13; EWL 3; MTCW 1, 2; RGEL 2

Osborne, Lawrence 1958- .... **CLC 50**
See also CA 189

Osbourne, Lloyd 1868-1947 .... **TCLC 93**

Osgood, Frances Sargent
1811-1850 .... **NCLC 141**
See also DLB 250

Oshima, Nagisa 1932- .... **CLC 20**
See also CA 116; 121; CANR 78

Oskison, John Milton
1874-1947 .... **NNAL; TCLC 35**
See also CA 144; CANR 84; DAM MULT;
DLB 175

Ossian c. 3rd cent. - .... **CMLC 28**
See Macpherson, James

Ossoli, Sarah Margaret (Fuller)
1810-1850 .... **NCLC 5, 50**
See Fuller, Margaret; Fuller, Sarah Margaret
See also CDALB 1640-1865; FW; LMFS 1;
SATA 25

Ostriker, Alicia (Suskin) 1937- .... **CLC 132**
See also CA 25-28R; CAAS 24; CANR 10,
30, 62, 99; CWP; DLB 120; EXPP; PFS
19

Ostrovsky, Aleksandr Nikolaevich
See Ostrovsky, Alexander
See also DLB 277

Ostrovsky, Alexander 1823-1886 .. **NCLC 30,**
57
See Ostrovsky, Aleksandr Nikolaevich

Otero, Blas de 1916-1979 .... **CLC 11**
See also CA 89-92; DLB 134; EWL 3

O'Trigger, Sir Lucius
See Horne, Richard Henry Hengist

Otto, Rudolf 1869-1937 .... **TCLC 85**

Otto, Whitney 1955- .... **CLC 70**
See also CA 140; CANR 120

Otway, Thomas 1652-1685 ... **DC 24; LC 106**
See also DAM DRAM; DLB 80; RGEL 2

Ouida .... **TCLC 43**
See De la Ramee, Marie Louise (Ouida)
See also DLB 18, 156; RGEL 2

Ouologuem, Yambo 1940- .... **CLC 146**
See also CA 111; 176

Ousmane, Sembene 1923- ... **BLC 3; CLC 66**
See Sembene, Ousmane
See also BW 1, 3; CA 117; 125; CANR 81;
CWW 2; MTCW 1

Ovid 43B.C.-17 .... **CMLC 7; PC 2**
See also AW 2; CDWLB 1; DA3; DAM
POET; DLB 211; RGWL 2, 3; WP

Owen, Hugh
See Faust, Frederick (Schiller)

Owen, Wilfred (Edward Salter)
1893-1918 ... **PC 19; TCLC 5, 27; WLC**
See also BRW 6; CA 104; 141; CDBLB
1914-1945; DA; DAB; DAC; DAM MST,
POET; DLB 20; EWL 3; EXPP; MTCW
2; PFS 10; RGEL 2; WLIT 4

Owens, Louis (Dean) 1948-2002 .... **NNAL**
See also CA 137, 179; 207; CAAE 179;
CAAS 24; CANR 71

Owens, Rochelle 1936- .... **CLC 8**
See also CA 17-20R; CAAS 2; CAD;
CANR 39; CD 5; CP 7; CWD; CWP

Oz, Amos 1939- ...... **CLC 5, 8, 11, 27, 33, 54;**
SSC 66
See also CA 53-56; CANR 27, 47, 65, 113;
CWW 2; DAM NOV; EWL 3; MTCW 1,
2; RGSF 2; RGWL 3

Paterson, A(ndrew) B(arton)
1864-1941 .... **TCLC 32**
See also CA 155; DLB 230; RGEL 2; SATA 97
Paterson, Banjo
See Paterson, A(ndrew) B(arton)
Paterson, Katherine (Womeldorf)
1932- .... **CLC 12, 30**
See also AAYA 1, 31; BYA 1, 2, 7; CA 21-24R; CANR 28, 59, 111; CLR 7, 50; CWRI 5; DLB 52; JRDA; LAIT 4; MAICYA 1, 2; MAICYAS 1; MTCW 1; SATA 13, 53, 92, 133; WYA; YAW
Patmore, Coventry Kersey Dighton
1823-1896 .... **NCLC 9; PC 59**
See also DLB 35, 98; RGEL 2; TEA
Paton, Alan (Stewart) 1903-1988 ...... **CLC 4, 10, 25, 55, 106; TCLC 165; WLC**
See also AAYA 26; AFW; BPFB 3; BRWS 2; BYA 1; CA 13-16; 125; CANR 22; CAP 1; DA; DA3; DAB; DAC; DAM MST, NOV; DLB 225; DLBD 17; EWL 3; EXPN; LAIT 4; MTCW 1, 2; NFS 3, 12; RGEL 2; SATA 11; SATA-Obit 56; TWA; WLIT 2; WWE 1
Paton Walsh, Gillian 1937- .... **CLC 35**
See Paton Walsh, Jill; Walsh, Jill Paton
See also AAYA 11; CANR 38, 83; CLR 2, 65; DLB 161; JRDA; MAICYA 1, 2; SAAS 3; SATA 4, 72, 109; YAW
Paton Walsh, Jill
See Paton Walsh, Gillian
See also AAYA 47; BYA 1, 8
Patterson, (Horace) Orlando (Lloyd)
1940- .... **BLCS**
See also BW 1; CA 65-68; CANR 27, 84; CN 7
Patton, George S(mith), Jr.
1885-1945 .... **TCLC 79**
See also CA 189
Paulding, James Kirke 1778-1860 ... **NCLC 2**
See also DLB 3, 59, 74, 250; RGAL 4
Paulin, Thomas Neilson 1949-
See Paulin, Tom
See also CA 123; 128; CANR 98; CP 7
Paulin, Tom .... **CLC 37, 177**
See Paulin, Thomas Neilson
See also DLB 40
Pausanias c. 1st cent. - .... **CMLC 36**
Paustovsky, Konstantin (Georgievich)
1892-1968 .... **CLC 40**
See also CA 93-96; 25-28R; DLB 272; EWL 3
Pavese, Cesare 1908-1950 .... **PC 13; SSC 19; TCLC 3**
See also CA 104; 169; DLB 128, 177; EW 12; EWL 3; PFS 20; RGSF 2; RGWL 2, 3; TWA
Pavic, Milorad 1929- .... **CLC 60**
See also CA 136; CDWLB 4; CWW 2; DLB 181; EWL 3; RGWL 3
Pavlov, Ivan Petrovich 1849-1936 . **TCLC 91**
See also CA 118; 180
Pavlova, Karolina Karlovna
1807-1893 .... **NCLC 138**
See also DLB 205
Payne, Alan
See Jakes, John (William)
Paz, Gil
See Lugones, Leopoldo
Paz, Octavio 1914-1998 . **CLC 3, 4, 6, 10, 19, 51, 65, 119; HLC 2; PC 1, 48; WLC**
See also AAYA 50; CA 73-76; 165; CANR 32, 65, 104; CWW 2; DA; DA3; DAB; DAC; DAM MST, MULT, POET; DLB 290; DLBY 1990, 1998; DNFS 1; EWL 3; HW 1, 2; LAW; LAWS 1; MTCW 1, 2; PFS 18; RGWL 2, 3; SSFS 13; TWA; WLIT 1

p'Bitek, Okot 1931-1982 .... **BLC 3; CLC 96; TCLC 149**
See also AFW; BW 2, 3; CA 124; 107; CANR 82; DAM MULT; DLB 125; EWL 3; MTCW 1, 2; RGEL 2; WLIT 2
Peacock, Molly 1947- .... **CLC 60**
See also CA 103; CAAS 21; CANR 52, 84; CP 7; CWP; DLB 120, 282
Peacock, Thomas Love
1785-1866 .... **NCLC 22**
See also BRW 4; DLB 96, 116; RGEL 2; RGSF 2
Peake, Mervyn 1911-1968 .... **CLC 7, 54**
See also CA 5-8R; 25-28R; CANR 3; DLB 15, 160, 255; FANT; MTCW 1; RGEL 2; SATA 23; SFW 4
Pearce, Philippa
See Christie, Philippa
See also CA 5-8R; CANR 4, 109; CWRI 5; FANT; MAICYA 2
Pearl, Eric
See Elman, Richard (Martin)
Pearson, T(homas) R(eid) 1956- .... **CLC 39**
See also CA 120; 130; CANR 97; CSW; INT CA-130
Peck, Dale 1967- .... **CLC 81**
See also CA 146; CANR 72, 127; GLL 2
Peck, John (Frederick) 1941- .... **CLC 3**
See also CA 49-52; CANR 3, 100; CP 7
Peck, Richard (Wayne) 1934- .... **CLC 21**
See also AAYA 1, 24; BYA 1, 6, 8, 11; CA 85-88; CANR 19, 38, 129; CLR 15; INT CANR-19; JRDA; MAICYA 1, 2; SAAS 2; SATA 18, 55, 97; SATA-Essay 110; WYA; YAW
Peck, Robert Newton 1928- .... **CLC 17**
See also AAYA 3, 43; BYA 1, 6; CA 81-84, 182; CAAE 182; CANR 31, 63, 127; CLR 45; DA; DAC; DAM MST; JRDA; LAIT 3; MAICYA 1, 2; SAAS 1; SATA 21, 62, 111; SATA-Essay 108; WYA; YAW
Peckinpah, (David) Sam(uel)
1925-1984 .... **CLC 20**
See also CA 109; 114; CANR 82
Pedersen, Knut 1859-1952
See Hamsun, Knut
See also CA 104; 119; CANR 63; MTCW 1, 2
Peele, George .... **LC 115**
See also BW 1; DLB 62, 167; RGEL 2
Peeslake, Gaffer
See Durrell, Lawrence (George)
Peguy, Charles (Pierre)
1873-1914 .... **TCLC 10**
See also CA 107; 193; DLB 258; EWL 3; GFL 1789 to the Present
Peirce, Charles Sanders
1839-1914 .... **TCLC 81**
See also CA 194; DLB 270
Pellicer, Carlos 1897(?)-1977 .... **HLCS 2**
See also CA 153; 69-72; DLB 290; EWL 3; HW 1
Pena, Ramon del Valle y
See Valle-Inclan, Ramon (Maria) del
Pendennis, Arthur Esquir
See Thackeray, William Makepeace
Penn, Arthur
See Matthews, (James) Brander
Penn, William 1644-1718 .... **LC 25**
See also DLB 24
PEPECE
See Prado (Calvo), Pedro
Pepys, Samuel 1633-1703 ... **LC 11, 58; WLC**
See also BRW 2; CDBLB 1660-1789; DA; DA3; DAB; DAC; DAM MST; DLB 101, 213; NCFS 4; RGEL 2; TEA; WLIT 3
Percy, Thomas 1729-1811 .... **NCLC 95**
See also DLB 104

Percy, Walker 1916-1990 .... **CLC 2, 3, 6, 8, 14, 18, 47, 65**
See also AMWS 3; BPFB 3; CA 1-4R; 131; CANR 1, 23, 64; CPW; CSW; DA3; DAM NOV, POP; DLB 2; DLBY 1980, 1990; EWL 3; MTCW 1, 2; RGAL 4; TUS
Percy, William Alexander
1885-1942 .... **TCLC 84**
See also CA 163; MTCW 2
Perec, Georges 1936-1982 .... **CLC 56, 116**
See also CA 141; DLB 83, 299; EWL 3; GFL 1789 to the Present; RGWL 3
Pereda (y Sanchez de Porrua), Jose Maria de 1833-1906 .... **TCLC 16**
See also CA 117
Pereda y Porrua, Jose Maria de
See Pereda (y Sanchez de Porrua), Jose Maria de
Peregoy, George Weems
See Mencken, H(enry) L(ouis)
Perelman, S(idney) J(oseph)
1904-1979 .. **CLC 3, 5, 9, 15, 23, 44, 49; SSC 32**
See also AITN 1, 2; BPFB 3; CA 73-76; 89-92; CANR 18; DAM DRAM; DLB 11, 44; MTCW 1, 2; RGAL 4
Peret, Benjamin 1899-1959 .... **PC 33; TCLC 20**
See also CA 117; 186; GFL 1789 to the Present
Peretz, Isaac Leib
See Peretz, Isaac Loeb
See also CA 201
Peretz, Isaac Loeb 1851(?)-1915 ...... **SSC 26; TCLC 16**
See Peretz, Isaac Leib
See also CA 109
Peretz, Yitzhok Leibush
See Peretz, Isaac Loeb
Perez Galdos, Benito 1843-1920 ..... **HLCS 2; TCLC 27**
See Galdos, Benito Perez
See also CA 125; 153; EWL 3; HW 1; RGWL 2, 3
Peri Rossi, Cristina 1941- .. **CLC 156; HLCS 2**
See also CA 131; CANR 59, 81; CWW 2; DLB 145, 290; EWL 3; HW 1, 2
Perlata
See Peret, Benjamin
Perloff, Marjorie G(abrielle)
1931- .... **CLC 137**
See also CA 57-60; CANR 7, 22, 49, 104
Perrault, Charles 1628-1703 .... **LC 2, 56**
See also BYA 4; CLR 79; DLB 268; GFL Beginnings to 1789; MAICYA 1, 2; RGWL 2, 3; SATA 25; WCH
Perry, Anne 1938- .... **CLC 126**
See also CA 101; CANR 22, 50, 84; CMW 4; CN 7; CPW; DLB 276
Perry, Brighton
See Sherwood, Robert E(mmet)
Perse, St.-John
See Leger, (Marie-Rene Auguste) Alexis Saint-Leger
Perse, Saint-John
See Leger, (Marie-Rene Auguste) Alexis Saint-Leger
See also DLB 258; RGWL 3
Persius 34-62 .... **CMLC 74**
See also AW 2; DLB 211; RGWL 2, 3
Perutz, Leo(pold) 1882-1957 .... **TCLC 60**
See also CA 147; DLB 81
Peseenz, Tulio F.
See Lopez y Fuentes, Gregorio
Pesetsky, Bette 1932- .... **CLC 28**
See also CA 133; DLB 130

Peshkov, Alexei Maximovich 1868-1936
　　See Gorky, Maxim
　　See also CA 105; 141; CANR 83; DA;
　　DAC; DAM DRAM, MST, NOV; MTCW
　　2

Pessoa, Fernando (Antonio Nogueira)
　　1888-1935 ..... **HLC 2; PC 20; TCLC 27**
　　See also CA 125; 183; DAM MULT; DLB
　　287; EW 10; EWL 3; RGWL 2, 3; WP

Peterkin, Julia Mood 1880-1961 ...... **CLC 31**
　　See also CA 102; DLB 9

Peters, Joan K(aren) 1945- .... **CLC 39**
　　See also CA 158; CANR 109

Peters, Robert L(ouis) 1924- .... **CLC 7**
　　See also CA 13-16R; CAAS 8; CP 7; DLB
　　105

Petofi, Sandor 1823-1849 .... **NCLC 21**
　　See also RGWL 2, 3

Petrakis, Harry Mark 1923- .... **CLC 3**
　　See also CA 9-12R; CANR 4, 30, 85; CN 7

Petrarch 1304-1374 .... **CMLC 20; PC 8**
　　See also DA3; DAM POET; EW 2; LMFS
　　1; RGWL 2. 3

Petronius c. 20-66 .... **CMLC 34**
　　See also AW 2; CDWLB 1; DLB 211;
　　RGWL 2, 3

Petrov, Evgeny .... **TCLC 21**
　　See Kataev, Evgeny Petrovich

Petry, Ann (Lane) 1908-1997 .. **CLC 1, 7, 18;**
　　TCLC 112
　　See also AFAW 1, 2; BPFB 3; BW 1, 3;
　　BYA 2; CA 5-8R; 157; CAAS 6; CANR
　　4, 46; CLR 12; CN 7; DLB 76; EWL 3;
　　JRDA; LAIT 1; MAICYA 1, 2; MAIC-
　　YAS 1; MTCW 1; RGAL 4; SATA 5;
　　SATA-Obit 94; TUS

Petursson, Halligrimur 1614-1674 .... **LC 8**

Peychinovich
　　See Vazov, Ivan (Minchov)

Phaedrus c. 15B.C.-c. 50 .... **CMLC 25**
　　See also DLB 211

Phelps (Ward), Elizabeth Stuart
　　See Phelps, Elizabeth Stuart
　　See also FW

Phelps, Elizabeth Stuart
　　1844-1911 .... **TCLC 113**
　　See Phelps (Ward), Elizabeth Stuart
　　See also DLB 74

Philips, Katherine 1632-1664 . **LC 30; PC 40**
　　See also DLB 131; RGEL 2

Philipson, Morris H. 1926- .... **CLC 53**
　　See also CA 1-4R; CANR 4

Phillips, Caryl 1958- .... **BLCS; CLC 96**
　　See also BRWS 5; BW 2; CA 141; CANR
　　63, 104; CBD; CD 5; CN 7; DA3; DAM
　　MULT; DLB 157; EWL 3; MTCW 2;
　　WLIT 4; WWE 1

Phillips, David Graham
　　1867-1911 .... **TCLC 44**
　　See also CA 108; 176; DLB 9, 12, 303;
　　RGAL 4

Phillips, Jack
　　See Sandburg, Carl (August)

Phillips, Jayne Anne 1952- .... **CLC 15, 33,**
　　139; SSC 16
　　See also AAYA 57; BPFB 3; CA 101;
　　CANR 24, 50, 96; CN 7; CSW; DLBY
　　1980; INT CANR-24; MTCW 1, 2; RGAL
　　4; RGSF 2; SSFS 4

Phillips, Richard
　　See Dick, Philip K(indred)

Phillips, Robert (Schaeffer) 1938- .... **CLC 28**
　　See also CA 17-20R; CAAS 13; CANR 8;
　　DLB 105

Phillips, Ward
　　See Lovecraft, H(oward) P(hillips)

Philostratus, Flavius c. 179-c.
　　244 .... **CMLC 62**

Piccolo, Lucio 1901-1969 .... **CLC 13**
　　See also CA 97-100; DLB 114; EWL 3

Pickthall, Marjorie L(owry) C(hristie)
　　1883-1922 .... **TCLC 21**
　　See also CA 107; DLB 92

Pico della Mirandola, Giovanni
　　1463-1494 .... **LC 15**
　　See also LMFS 1

Piercy, Marge 1936- .... **CLC 3, 6, 14, 18, 27,**
　　62, 128; PC 29
　　See also BPFB 3; CA 21-24R, 187; CAAE
　　187; CAAS 1; CANR 13, 43, 66, 111; CN
　　7; CP 7; CWP; DLB 120, 227; EXPP;
　　FW; MTCW 1, 2; PFS 9; SFW 4

Piers, Robert
　　See Anthony, Piers

Pieyre de Mandiargues, Andre 1909-1991
　　See Mandiargues, Andre Pieyre de
　　See also CA 103; 136; CANR 22, 82; EWL
　　3; GFL 1789 to the Present

Pilnyak, Boris 1894-1938 . **SSC 48; TCLC 23**
　　See Vogau, Boris Andreyevich
　　See also EWL 3

Pinchback, Eugene
　　See Toomer, Jean

Pincherle, Alberto 1907-1990 ...... **CLC 11, 18**
　　See Moravia, Alberto
　　See also CA 25-28R; 132; CANR 33, 63;
　　DAM NOV; MTCW 1

Pinckney, Darryl 1953- .... **CLC 76**
　　See also BW 2, 3; CA 143; CANR 79

Pindar 518(?)B.C.-438(?)B.C. .... **CMLC 12;**
　　PC 19
　　See also AW 1; CDWLB 1; DLB 176;
　　RGWL 2

Pineda, Cecile 1942- .... **CLC 39**
　　See also CA 118; DLB 209

Pinero, Arthur Wing 1855-1934 .... **TCLC 32**
　　See also CA 110; 153; DAM DRAM; DLB
　　10; RGEL 2

Pinero, Miguel (Antonio Gomez)
　　1946-1988 .... **CLC 4, 55**
　　See also CA 61-64; 125; CAD; CANR 29,
　　90; DLB 266; HW 1; LLW 1

Pinget, Robert 1919-1997 .... **CLC 7, 13, 37**
　　See also CA 85-88; 160; CWW 2; DLB 83;
　　EWL 3; GFL 1789 to the Present

Pink Floyd
　　See Barrett, (Roger) Syd; Gilmour, David;
　　Mason, Nick; Waters, Roger; Wright, Rick

Pinkney, Edward 1802-1828 .... **NCLC 31**
　　See also DLB 248

Pinkwater, Daniel
　　See Pinkwater, Daniel Manus

Pinkwater, Daniel Manus 1941- .... **CLC 35**
　　See also AAYA 1, 46; BYA 9; CA 29-32R;
　　CANR 12, 38, 89; CLR 4; CSW; FANT;
　　JRDA; MAICYA 1, 2; SAAS 3; SATA 8,
　　46, 76, 114; SFW 4; YAW

Pinkwater, Manus
　　See Pinkwater, Daniel Manus

Pinsky, Robert 1940- .... **CLC 9, 19, 38, 94,**
　　121; PC 27
　　See also AMWS 6; CA 29-32R; CAAS 4;
　　CANR 58, 97; CP 7; DA3; DAM POET;
　　DLBY 1982, 1998; MTCW 2; PFS 18;
　　RGAL 4

Pinta, Harold
　　See Pinter, Harold

Pinter, Harold 1930- .. **CLC 1, 3, 6, 9, 11, 15,**
　　27, 58, 73, 199; DC 15; WLC
　　See also BRWR 1; BRWS 1; CA 5-8R;
　　CANR 33, 65, 112; CBD; CD 5; CDBLB
　　1960 to Present; DA; DA3; DAB; DAC;
　　DAM DRAM, MST; DFS 3, 5, 7, 14;
　　DLB 13; EWL 3; IDFW 3, 4; LMFS 2;
　　MTCW 1, 2; RGEL 2; TEA

Piozzi, Hester Lynch (Thrale)
　　1741-1821 .... **NCLC 57**
　　See also DLB 104, 142

Pirandello, Luigi 1867-1936 .. **DC 5; SSC 22;**
　　TCLC 4, 29; WLC
　　See also CA 104; 153; CANR 103; DA;
　　DA3; DAB; DAC; DAM DRAM, MST;
　　DFS 4, 9; DLB 264; EW 8; EWL 3;
　　MTCW 2; RGSF 2; RGWL 2, 3

Pirsig, Robert M(aynard) 1928- ... **CLC 4, 6,**
　　73
　　See also CA 53-56; CANR 42, 74; CPW 1;
　　DA3; DAM POP; MTCW 1, 2; SATA 39

Pisarev, Dmitrii Ivanovich
　　See Pisarev, Dmitry Ivanovich
　　See also DLB 277

Pisarev, Dmitry Ivanovich
　　1840-1868 .... **NCLC 25**
　　See Pisarev, Dmitrii Ivanovich

Pix, Mary (Griffith) 1666-1709 .... **LC 8**
　　See also DLB 80

Pixerecourt, (Rene Charles) Guilbert de
　　1773-1844 .... **NCLC 39**
　　See also DLB 192; GFL 1789 to the Present

Plaatje, Sol(omon) T(shekisho)
　　1878-1932 .... **BLCS; TCLC 73**
　　See also BW 2, 3; CA 141; CANR 79; DLB
　　125, 225

Plaidy, Jean
　　See Hibbert, Eleanor Alice Burford

Planche, James Robinson
　　1796-1880 .... **NCLC 42**
　　See also RGEL 2

Plant, Robert 1948- .... **CLC 12**

Plante, David (Robert) 1940- . **CLC 7, 23, 38**
　　See also CA 37-40R; CANR 12, 36, 58, 82;
　　CN 7; DAM NOV; DLBY 1983; INT
　　CANR-12; MTCW 1

Plath, Sylvia 1932-1963 ..... **CLC 1, 2, 3, 5, 9,**
　　11, 14, 17, 50, 51, 62, 111; PC 1, 37;
　　WLC
　　See also AAYA 13; AMWR 2; AMWS 1;
　　BPFB 3; CA 19-20; CANR 34, 101; CAP
　　2; CDALB 1941-1968; DA; DA3; DAB;
　　DAC; DAM MST, POET; DLB 5, 6, 152;
　　EWL 3; EXPN; EXPP; FW; LAIT 4;
　　MAWW; MTCW 1, 2; NFS 1; PAB; PFS
　　1, 15; RGAL 4; SATA 96; TUS; WP;
　　YAW

Plato c. 428B.C.-347B.C. .... **CMLC 8, 75;**
　　WLCS
　　See also AW 1; CDWLB 1; DA; DA3;
　　DAB; DAC; DAM MST; DLB 176; LAIT
　　1; LATS 1:1; RGWL 2, 3

Platonov, Andrei
　　See Klimentov, Andrei Platonovich

Platonov, Andrei Platonovich
　　See Klimentov, Andrei Platonovich
　　See also DLB 272

Platonov, Andrey Platonovich
　　See Klimentov, Andrei Platonovich
　　See also EWL 3

Platt, Kin 1911- .... **CLC 26**
　　See also AAYA 11; CA 17-20R; CANR 11;
　　JRDA; SAAS 17; SATA 21, 86; WYA

Plautus c. 254B.C.-c. 184B.C. ...... **CMLC 24;**
　　DC 6
　　See also AW 1; CDWLB 1; DLB 211;
　　RGWL 2, 3

Plick et Plock
　　See Simenon, Georges (Jacques Christian)

Plieksans, Janis
　　See Rainis, Janis

Plimpton, George (Ames)
　　1927-2003 .... **CLC 36**
　　See also AITN 1; CA 21-24R; 224; CANR
　　32, 70, 103, 133; DLB 185, 241; MTCW
　　1, 2; SATA 10; SATA-Obit 150

Rulfo, Juan 1918-1986 .. **CLC 8, 80; HLC 2; SSC 25**
See also CA 85-88; 118; CANR 26; CD-WLB 3; DAM MULT; DLB 113; EWL 3; HW 1, 2; LAW; MTCW 1, 2; RGSF 2; RGWL 2, 3; WLIT 1

Rumi, Jalal al-Din 1207-1273 ...... **CMLC 20; PC 45**
See also RGWL 2, 3; WP

Runeberg, Johan 1804-1877 .... **NCLC 41**

Runyon, (Alfred) Damon
1884(?)-1946 .... **TCLC 10**
See also CA 107; 165; DLB 11, 86, 171; MTCW 2; RGAL 4

Rush, Norman 1933- .... **CLC 44**
See also CA 121; 126; CANR 130; INT CA-126

Rushdie, (Ahmed) Salman 1947- .... **CLC 23, 31, 55, 100, 191; SSC 83; WLCS**
See also BEST 89:3; BPFB 3; BRWS 4; CA 108; 111; CANR 33, 56, 108, 133; CN 7; CPW 1; DA3; DAB; DAC; DAM MST, NOV, POP; DLB 194; EWL 3; FANT; INT CA-111; LATS 1:2; LMFS 2; MTCW 1, 2; RGEL 2; RGSF 2; TEA; WLIT 4; WWE 1

Rushforth, Peter (Scott) 1945- .... **CLC 19**
See also CA 101

Ruskin, John 1819-1900 .... **TCLC 63**
See also BRW 5; BYA 5; CA 114; 129; CD-BLB 1832-1890; DLB 55, 163, 190; RGEL 2; SATA 24; TEA; WCH

Russ, Joanna 1937- .... **CLC 15**
See also BPFB 3; CA 5-28R; CANR 11, 31, 65; CN 7; DLB 8; FW; GLL 1; MTCW 1; SCFW 2; SFW 4

Russ, Richard Patrick
See O'Brian, Patrick

Russell, George William 1867-1935
See A.E.; Baker, Jean H.
See also BRWS 8; CA 104; 153; CDBLB 1890-1914; DAM POET; EWL 3; RGEL 2

Russell, Jeffrey Burton 1934- .... **CLC 70**
See also CA 25-28R; CANR 11, 28, 52

Russell, (Henry) Ken(neth Alfred)
1927- .... **CLC 16**
See also CA 105

Russell, William Martin 1947-
See Russell, Willy
See also CA 164; CANR 107

Russell, Willy .... **CLC 60**
See Russell, William Martin
See also CBD; CD 5; DLB 233

Russo, Richard 1949- .... **CLC 181**
See also AMWS 12; CA 127; 133; CANR 87, 114

Rutherford, Mark .... **TCLC 25**
See White, William Hale
See also DLB 18; RGEL 2

Ruyslinck, Ward .... **CLC 14**
See Belser, Reimond Karel Maria de

Ryan, Cornelius (John) 1920-1974 ..... **CLC 7**
See also CA 69-72; 53-56; CANR 38

Ryan, Michael 1946- .... **CLC 65**
See also CA 49-52; CANR 109; DLBY 1982

Ryan, Tim
See Dent, Lester

Rybakov, Anatoli (Naumovich)
1911-1998 .... **CLC 23, 53**
See Rybakov, Anatolii (Naumovich)
See also CA 126; 135; 172; SATA 79; SATA-Obit 108

Rybakov, Anatolii (Naumovich)
See Rybakov, Anatoli (Naumovich)
See also DLB 302

Ryder, Jonathan
See Ludlum, Robert

Ryga, George 1932-1987 .... **CLC 14**
See also CA 101; 124; CANR 43, 90; CCA 1; DAC; DAM MST; DLB 60

S. H.
See Hartmann, Sadakichi

S. S.
See Sassoon, Siegfried (Lorraine)

Sa'adawi, al- Nawal
See El Saadawi, Nawal
See also AFW; EWL 3

Saadawi, Nawal El
See El Saadawi, Nawal
See also WLIT 2

Saba, Umberto 1883-1957 .... **TCLC 33**
See also CA 144; CANR 79; DLB 114; EWL 3; RGWL 2, 3

Sabatini, Rafael 1875-1950 .... **TCLC 47**
See also BPFB 3; CA 162; RHW

Sabato, Ernesto (R.) 1911- .... **CLC 10, 23; HLC 2**
See also CA 97-100; CANR 32, 65; CD-WLB 3; CWW 2; DAM MULT; DLB 145; EWL 3; HW 1, 2; LAW; MTCW 1, 2

Sa-Carneiro, Mario de 1890-1916 . **TCLC 83**
See also DLB 287; EWL 3

Sacastru, Martin
See Bioy Casares, Adolfo
See also CWW 2

Sacher-Masoch, Leopold von
1836(?)-1895 .... **NCLC 31**

Sachs, Hans 1494-1576 .... **LC 95**
See also CDWLB 2; DLB 179; RGWL 2, 3

Sachs, Marilyn (Stickle) 1927- .... **CLC 35**
See also AAYA 2; BYA 6; CA 17-20R; CANR 13, 47; CLR 2; JRDA; MAICYA 1, 2; SAAS 2; SATA 3, 68; SATA-Essay 110; WYA; YAW

Sachs, Nelly 1891-1970 .... **CLC 14, 98**
See also CA 17-18; 25-28R; CANR 87; CAP 2; EWL 3; MTCW 2; PFS 20; RGWL 2, 3

Sackler, Howard (Oliver)
1929-1982 .... **CLC 14**
See also CA 61-64; 108; CAD; CANR 30; DFS 15; DLB 7

Sacks, Oliver (Wolf) 1933- .... **CLC 67, 202**
See also CA 53-56; CANR 28, 50, 76; CPW; DA3; INT CANR-28; MTCW 1, 2

Sackville, Thomas 1536-1608 .... **LC 98**
See also DAM DRAM; DLB 62, 132; RGEL 2

Sadakichi
See Hartmann, Sadakichi

Sa'dawi, Nawal al-
See El Saadawi, Nawal
See also CWW 2

Sade, Donatien Alphonse Francois
1740-1814 .... **NCLC 3, 47**
See also EW 4; GFL Beginnings to 1789; RGWL 2, 3

Sade, Marquis de
See Sade, Donatien Alphonse Francois

Sadoff, Ira 1945- .... **CLC 9**
See also CA 53-56; CANR 5, 21, 109; DLB 120

Saetone
See Camus, Albert

Safire, William 1929- .... **CLC 10**
See also CA 17-20R; CANR 31, 54, 91

Sagan, Carl (Edward) 1934-1996 .... **CLC 30, 112**
See also AAYA 2; CA 25-28R; 155; CANR 11, 36, 74; CPW; DA3; MTCW 1, 2; SATA 58; SATA-Obit 94

Sagan, Francoise .... **CLC 3, 6, 9, 17, 36**
See Quoirez, Francoise
See also CWW 2; DLB 83; EWL 3; GFL 1789 to the Present; MTCW 2

Sahgal, Nayantara (Pandit) 1927- .... **CLC 41**
See also CA 9-12R; CANR 11, 88; CN 7

Said, Edward W. 1935-2003 .... **CLC 123**
See also CA 21-24R; 220; CANR 45, 74, 107, 131; DLB 67; MTCW 2

Saigyō 1118-1190 .... **CMLC 77**
See also DLB 203; RGWL 3

Saint, H(arry) F. 1941- .... **CLC 50**
See also CA 127

St. Aubin de Teran, Lisa 1953-
See Teran, Lisa St. Aubin de
See also CA 118; 126; CN 7; INT CA-126

Saint Birgitta of Sweden c.
1303-1373 .... **CMLC 24**

Sainte-Beuve, Charles Augustin
1804-1869 .... **NCLC 5**
See also DLB 217; EW 6; GFL 1789 to the Present

Saint-Exupery, Antoine (Jean Baptiste Marie Roger) de 1900-1944 .... **TCLC 2, 56; WLC**
See also BPFB 3; BYA 3; CA 108; 132; CLR 10; DA3; DAM NOV; DLB 72; EW 12; EWL 3; GFL 1789 to the Present; LAIT 3; MAICYA 1, 2; MTCW 1, 2; RGWL 2, 3; SATA 20; TWA

St. John, David
See Hunt, E(verette) Howard, (Jr.)

St. John, J. Hector
See Crevecoeur, Michel Guillaume Jean de

Saint-John Perse
See Leger, (Marie-Rene Auguste) Alexis Saint-Leger
See also EW 10; EWL 3; GFL 1789 to the Present; RGWL 2

Saintsbury, George (Edward Bateman)
1845-1933 .... **TCLC 31**
See also CA 160; DLB 57, 149

Sait Faik .... **TCLC 23**
See Abasiyanik, Sait Faik

Saki .... **SSC 12; TCLC 3**
See Munro, H(ector) H(ugh)
See also BRWS 6; BYA 11; LAIT 2; MTCW 2; RGEL 2; SSFS 1; SUFW

Sala, George Augustus 1828-1895 . **NCLC 46**

Saladin 1138-1193 .... **CMLC 38**

Salama, Hannu 1936- .... **CLC 18**
See also EWL 3

Salamanca, J(ack) R(ichard) 1922- .. **CLC 4, 15**
See also CA 25-28R; 193; CAAE 193

Salas, Floyd Francis 1931- .... **HLC 2**
See also CA 119; CAAS 27; CANR 44, 75, 93; DAM MULT; DLB 82; HW 1, 2; MTCW 2

Sale, J. Kirkpatrick
See Sale, Kirkpatrick

Sale, Kirkpatrick 1937- .... **CLC 68**
See also CA 13-16R; CANR 10

Salinas, Luis Omar 1937- ... **CLC 90; HLC 2**
See also AMWS 13; CA 131; CANR 81; DAM MULT; DLB 82; HW 1, 2

Salinas (y Serrano), Pedro
1891(?)-1951 .... **TCLC 17**
See also CA 117; DLB 134; EWL 3

Salinger, J(erome) D(avid) 1919- .. **CLC 1, 3, 8, 12, 55, 56, 138; SSC 2, 28, 65; WLC**
See also AAYA 2, 36; AMW; AMWC 1; BPFB 3; CA 5-8R; CANR 39, 129; CDALB 1941-1968; CLR 18; CN 7; CPW 1; DA; DA3; DAB; DAC; DAM MST, NOV, POP; DLB 2, 102, 173; EWL 3; EXPN; LAIT 4; MAICYA 1, 2; MTCW 1, 2; NFS 1; RGAL 4; RGSF 2; SATA 67; SSFS 17; TUS; WYA; YAW

Salisbury, John
See Caute, (John) David

Schama, Simon (Michael) 1945- ..... **CLC 150**
  See also BEST 89:4; CA 105; CANR 39, 91

Schary, Jill
  See Robinson, Jill

Schell, Jonathan 1943- .... **CLC 35**
  See also CA 73-76; CANR 12, 117

Schelling, Friedrich Wilhelm Joseph von
  1775-1854 .... **NCLC 30**
  See also DLB 90

Scherer, Jean-Marie Maurice 1920-
  See Rohmer, Eric
  See also CA 110

Schevill, James (Erwin) 1920- .... **CLC 7**
  See also CA 5-8R; CAAS 12; CAD; CD 5

Schiller, Friedrich von 1759-1805 ...... **DC 12; NCLC 39, 69**
  See also CDWLB 2; DAM DRAM; DLB 94; EW 5; RGWL 2, 3; TWA

Schisgal, Murray (Joseph) 1926- .... **CLC 6**
  See also CA 21-24R; CAD; CANR 48, 86; CD 5

Schlee, Ann 1934- .... **CLC 35**
  See also CA 101; CANR 29, 88; SATA 44; SATA-Brief 36

Schlegel, August Wilhelm von
  1767-1845 .... **NCLC 15, 142**
  See also DLB 94; RGWL 2, 3

Schlegel, Friedrich 1772-1829 .... **NCLC 45**
  See also DLB 90; EW 5; RGWL 2, 3; TWA

Schlegel, Johann Elias (von)
  1719(?)-1749 .... **LC 5**

Schleiermacher, Friedrich
  1768-1834 .... **NCLC 107**
  See also DLB 90

Schlesinger, Arthur M(eier), Jr.
  1917- .... **CLC 84**
  See also AITN 1; CA 1-4R; CANR 1, 28, 58, 105; DLB 17; INT CANR-28; MTCW 1, 2; SATA 61

Schlink, Bernhard 1944- .... **CLC 174**
  See also CA 163; CANR 116

Schmidt, Arno (Otto) 1914-1979 ...... **CLC 56**
  See also CA 128; 109; DLB 69; EWL 3

Schmitz, Aron Hector 1861-1928
  See Svevo, Italo
  See also CA 104; 122; MTCW 1

Schnackenberg, Gjertrud (Cecelia)
  1953- .... **CLC 40; PC 45**
  See also CA 116; CANR 100; CP 7; CWP; DLB 120, 282; PFS 13

Schneider, Leonard Alfred 1925-1966
  See Bruce, Lenny
  See also CA 89-92

Schnitzler, Arthur 1862-1931 ..... **DC 17; SSC 15, 61; TCLC 4**
  See also CA 104; CDWLB 2; DLB 81, 118; EW 8; EWL 3; RGSF 2; RGWL 2, 3

Schoenberg, Arnold Franz Walter
  1874-1951 .... **TCLC 75**
  See also CA 109; 188

Schonberg, Arnold
  See Schoenberg, Arnold Franz Walter

Schopenhauer, Arthur 1788-1860 . **NCLC 51, 157**
  See also DLB 90; EW 5

Schor, Sandra (M.) 1932(?)-1990 ..... **CLC 65**
  See also CA 132

Schorer, Mark 1908-1977 .... **CLC 9**
  See also CA 5-8R; 73-76; CANR 7; DLB 103

Schrader, Paul (Joseph) 1946- .... **CLC 26**
  See also CA 37-40R; CANR 41; DLB 44

Schreber, Daniel 1842-1911 .... **TCLC 123**

Schreiner, Olive (Emilie Albertina)
  1855-1920 .... **TCLC 9**
  See also AFW; BRWS 2; CA 105; 154; DLB 18, 156, 190, 225; EWL 3; FW; RGEL 2; TWA; WLIT 2; WWE 1

Schulberg, Budd (Wilson) 1914- .. **CLC 7, 48**
  See also BPFB 3; CA 25-28R; CANR 19, 87; CN 7; DLB 6, 26, 28; DLBY 1981, 2001

Schulman, Arnold
  See Trumbo, Dalton

Schulz, Bruno 1892-1942 .. **SSC 13; TCLC 5, 51**
  See also CA 115; 123; CANR 86; CDWLB 4; DLB 215; EWL 3; MTCW 2; RGSF 2; RGWL 2, 3

Schulz, Charles M(onroe)
  1922-2000 .... **CLC 12**
  See also AAYA 39; CA 9-12R; 187; CANR 6, 132; INT CANR-6; SATA 10; SATA-Obit 118

Schumacher, E(rnst) F(riedrich)
  1911-1977 .... **CLC 80**
  See also CA 81-84; 73-76; CANR 34, 85

Schumann, Robert 1810-1856 ...... **NCLC 143**

Schuyler, George Samuel 1895-1977 .... **HR 3**
  See also BW 2; CA 81-84; 73-76; CANR 42; DLB 29, 51

Schuyler, James Marcus 1923-1991 .. **CLC 5, 23**
  See also CA 101; 134; DAM POET; DLB 5, 169; EWL 3; INT CA-101; WP

Schwartz, Delmore (David)
  1913-1966 ... **CLC 2, 4, 10, 45, 87; PC 8**
  See also AMWS 2; CA 17-18; 25-28R; CANR 35; CAP 2; DLB 28, 48; EWL 3; MTCW 1, 2; PAB; RGAL 4; TUS

Schwartz, Ernst
  See Ozu, Yasujiro

Schwartz, John Burnham 1965- .... **CLC 59**
  See also CA 132; CANR 116

Schwartz, Lynne Sharon 1939- .... **CLC 31**
  See also CA 103; CANR 44, 89; DLB 218; MTCW 2

Schwartz, Muriel A.
  See Eliot, T(homas) S(tearns)

Schwarz-Bart, Andre 1928- .... **CLC 2, 4**
  See also CA 89-92; CANR 109; DLB 299

Schwarz-Bart, Simone 1938- . **BLCS; CLC 7**
  See also BW 2; CA 97-100; CANR 117; EWL 3

Schwerner, Armand 1927-1999 .... **PC 42**
  See also CA 9-12R; 179; CANR 50, 85; CP 7; DLB 165

Schwitters, Kurt (Hermann Edward Karl Julius) 1887-1948 .... **TCLC 95**
  See also CA 158

Schwob, Marcel (Mayer Andre)
  1867-1905 .... **TCLC 20**
  See also CA 117; 168; DLB 123; GFL 1789 to the Present

Sciascia, Leonardo 1921-1989 .. **CLC 8, 9, 41**
  See also CA 85-88; 130; CANR 35; DLB 177; EWL 3; MTCW 1; RGWL 2, 3

Scoppettone, Sandra 1936- .... **CLC 26**
  See Early, Jack
  See also AAYA 11; BYA 8; CA 5-8R; CANR 41, 73; GLL 1; MAICYA 2; MAICYAS 1; SATA 9, 92; WYA; YAW

Scorsese, Martin 1942- .... **CLC 20, 89, 207**
  See also AAYA 38; CA 110, 114; CANR 46, 85

Scotland, Jay
  See Jakes, John (William)

Scott, Duncan Campbell
  1862-1947 .... **TCLC 6**
  See also CA 104; 153; DAC; DLB 92; RGEL 2

Scott, Evelyn 1893-1963 .... **CLC 43**
  See also CA 104; 112; CANR 64; DLB 9, 48; RHW

Scott, F(rancis) R(eginald)
  1899-1985 .... **CLC 22**
  See also CA 101; 114; CANR 87; DLB 88; INT CA-101; RGEL 2

Scott, Frank
  See Scott, F(rancis) R(eginald)

Scott, Joan .... **CLC 65**

Scott, Joanna 1960- .... **CLC 50**
  See also CA 126; CANR 53, 92

Scott, Paul (Mark) 1920-1978 ...... **CLC 9, 60**
  See also BRWS 1; CA 81-84; 77-80; CANR 33; DLB 14, 207; EWL 3; MTCW 1; RGEL 2; RHW; WWE 1

Scott, Ridley 1937- .... **CLC 183**
  See also AAYA 13, 43

Scott, Sarah 1723-1795 .... **LC 44**
  See also DLB 39

Scott, Sir Walter 1771-1832 .... **NCLC 15, 69, 110; PC 13; SSC 32; WLC**
  See also AAYA 22; BRW 4; BYA 2; CD-BLB 1789-1832; DA; DAB; DAC; DAM MST, NOV, POET; DLB 93, 107, 116, 144, 159; HGG; LAIT 1; RGEL 2; RGSF 2; SSFS 10; SUFW 1; TEA; WLIT 3; YABC 2

Scribe, (Augustin) Eugene 1791-1861 . **DC 5; NCLC 16**
  See also DAM DRAM; DLB 192; GFL 1789 to the Present; RGWL 2, 3

Scrum, R.
  See Crumb, R(obert)

Scudery, Georges de 1601-1667 .... **LC 75**
  See also GFL Beginnings to 1789

Scudery, Madeleine de 1607-1701 .. **LC 2, 58**
  See also DLB 268; GFL Beginnings to 1789

Scum
  See Crumb, R(obert)

Scumbag, Little Bobby
  See Crumb, R(obert)

Seabrook, John
  See Hubbard, L(afayette) Ron(ald)

Seacole, Mary Jane Grant
  1805-1881 .... **NCLC 147**
  See also DLB 166

Sealy, I(rwin) Allan 1951- .... **CLC 55**
  See also CA 136; CN 7

Search, Alexander
  See Pessoa, Fernando (Antonio Nogueira)

Sebald, W(infried) G(eorg)
  1944-2001 .... **CLC 194**
  See also BRWS 8; CA 159; 202; CANR 98

Sebastian, Lee
  See Silverberg, Robert

Sebastian Owl
  See Thompson, Hunter S(tockton)

Sebestyen, Igen
  See Sebestyen, Ouida

Sebestyen, Ouida 1924- .... **CLC 30**
  See also AAYA 8; BYA 7; CA 107; CANR 40, 114; CLR 17; JRDA; MAICYA 1, 2; SAAS 10; SATA 39, 140; WYA; YAW

Sebold, Alice 1963(?)- .... **CLC 193**
  See also AAYA 56; CA 203

Second Duke of Buckingham
  See Villiers, George

Secundus, H. Scriblerus
  See Fielding, Henry

Sedges, John
  See Buck, Pearl S(ydenstricker)

Sedgwick, Catharine Maria
  1789-1867 .... **NCLC 19, 98**
  See also DLB 1, 74, 183, 239, 243, 254; RGAL 4

Seelye, John (Douglas) 1931- .... **CLC 7**
  See also CA 97-100; CANR 70; INT CA-97-100; TCWW 2

Sheldon, Alice Hastings Bradley
1915(?)-1987
See Tiptree, James, Jr.
See also CA 108; 122; CANR 34; INT CA-108; MTCW 1

Sheldon, John
See Bloch, Robert (Albert)

Sheldon, Walter J(ames) 1917-1996
See Queen, Ellery
See also AITN 1; CA 25-28R; CANR 10

Shelley, Mary Wollstonecraft (Godwin)
1797-1851 ...... **NCLC 14, 59, 103; WLC**
See also AAYA 20; BPFB 3; BRW 3; BRWC 2; BRWS 3; BYA 5; CDBLB 1789-1832; DA; DA3; DAB; DAC; DAM MST, NOV; DLB 110, 116, 159, 178; EXPN; HGG; LAIT 1; LMFS 1, 2; NFS 1; RGEL 2; SATA 29; SCFW; SFW 4; TEA; WLIT 3

Shelley, Percy Bysshe 1792-1822 .. **NCLC 18, 93, 143; PC 14; WLC**
See also BRW 4; BRWR 1; CDBLB 1789-1832; DA; DA3; DAB; DAC; DAM MST, POET; DLB 96, 110, 158; EXPP; LMFS 1; PAB; PFS 2; RGEL 2; TEA; WLIT 3; WP

Shepard, Jim 1956- .... **CLC 36**
See also CA 137; CANR 59, 104; SATA 90

Shepard, Lucius 1947- .... **CLC 34**
See also CA 128; 141; CANR 81, 124; HGG; SCFW 2; SFW 4; SUFW 2

Shepard, Sam 1943- .... **CLC 4, 6, 17, 34, 41, 44, 169; DC 5**
See also AAYA 1, 58; AMWS 3; CA 69-72; CABS 3; CAD; CANR 22, 120; CD 5; DA3; DAM DRAM; DFS 3, 6, 7, 14; DLB 7, 212; EWL 3; IDFW 3, 4; MTCW 1, 2; RGAL 4

Shepherd, Michael
See Ludlum, Robert

Sherburne, Zoa (Lillian Morin)
1912-1995 .... **CLC 30**
See also AAYA 13; CA 1-4R; 176; CANR 3, 37; MAICYA 1, 2; SAAS 18; SATA 3; YAW

Sheridan, Frances 1724-1766 .... **LC 7**
See also DLB 39, 84

Sheridan, Richard Brinsley
1751-1816 .... **DC 1; NCLC 5, 91; WLC**
See also BRW 3; CDBLB 1660-1789; DA; DAB; DAC; DAM DRAM, MST; DFS 15; DLB 89; WLIT 3

Sherman, Jonathan Marc .... **CLC 55**

Sherman, Martin 1941(?)- .... **CLC 19**
See also CA 116; 123; CAD; CANR 86; CD 5; DFS 20; DLB 228; GLL 1; IDTP

Sherwin, Judith Johnson
See Johnson, Judith (Emlyn)
See also CANR 85; CP 7; CWP

Sherwood, Frances 1940- .... **CLC 81**
See also CA 146; 220; CAAE 220

Sherwood, Robert E(mmet)
1896-1955 .... **TCLC 3**
See also CA 104; 153; CANR 86; DAM DRAM; DFS 11, 15, 17; DLB 7, 26, 249; IDFW 3, 4; RGAL 4

Shestov, Lev 1866-1938 .... **TCLC 56**

Shevchenko, Taras 1814-1861 .... **NCLC 54**

Shiel, M(atthew) P(hipps)
1865-1947 .... **TCLC 8**
See Holmes, Gordon
See also CA 106; 160; DLB 153; HGG; MTCW 2; SFW 4; SUFW

Shields, Carol (Ann) 1935-2003 ...... **CLC 91, 113, 193**
See also AMWS 7; CA 81-84; 218; CANR 51, 74, 98, 133; CCA 1; CN 7; CPW; DA3; DAC; MTCW 2

Shields, David (Jonathan) 1956- ...... **CLC 97**
See also CA 124; CANR 48, 99, 112

Shiga, Naoya 1883-1971 ..... **CLC 33; SSC 23**
See Shiga Naoya
See also CA 101; 33-36R; MJW; RGWL 3

Shiga Naoya
See Shiga, Naoya
See also DLB 180; EWL 3; RGWL 3

Shilts, Randy 1951-1994 .... **CLC 85**
See also AAYA 19; CA 115; 127; 144; CANR 45; DA3; GLL 1; INT CA-127; MTCW 2

Shimazaki, Haruki 1872-1943
See Shimazaki Toson
See also CA 105; 134; CANR 84; RGWL 3

Shimazaki Toson .... **TCLC 5**
See Shimazaki, Haruki
See also DLB 180; EWL 3

Shirley, James 1596-1666 .... **DC 25; LC 96**
See also DLB 58; RGEL 2

Sholokhov, Mikhail (Aleksandrovich)
1905-1984 .... **CLC 7, 15**
See also CA 101; 112; DLB 272; EWL 3; MTCW 1, 2; RGWL 2, 3; SATA-Obit 36

Shone, Patric
See Hanley, James

Showalter, Elaine 1941- .... **CLC 169**
See also CA 57-60; CANR 58, 106; DLB 67; FW; GLL 2

Shreve, Susan
See Shreve, Susan Richards

Shreve, Susan Richards 1939- .... **CLC 23**
See also CA 49-52; CAAS 5; CANR 5, 38, 69, 100; MAICYA 1, 2; SATA 46, 95, 152; SATA-Brief 41

Shue, Larry 1946-1985 .... **CLC 52**
See also CA 145; 117; DAM DRAM; DFS 7

Shu-Jen, Chou 1881-1936
See Lu Hsun
See also CA 104

Shulman, Alix Kates 1932- .... **CLC 2, 10**
See also CA 29-32R; CANR 43; FW; SATA 7

Shuster, Joe 1914-1992 .... **CLC 21**
See also AAYA 50

Shute, Nevil .... **CLC 30**
See Norway, Nevil Shute
See also BPFB 3; DLB 255; NFS 9; RHW; SFW 4

Shuttle, Penelope (Diane) 1947- .... **CLC 7**
See also CA 93-96; CANR 39, 84, 92, 108; CP 7; CWP; DLB 14, 40

Shvarts, Elena 1948- .... **PC 50**
See also CA 147

Sidhwa, Bapsy (N.) 1938- .... **CLC 168**
See also CA 108; CANR 25, 57; CN 7; FW

Sidney, Mary 1561-1621 .... **LC 19, 39**
See Sidney Herbert, Mary

Sidney, Sir Philip 1554-1586 . **LC 19, 39; PC 32**
See also BRW 1; BRWR 2; CDBLB Before 1660; DA; DA3; DAB; DAC; DAM MST, POET; DLB 167; EXPP; PAB; RGEL 2; TEA; WP

Sidney Herbert, Mary
See Sidney, Mary
See also DLB 167

Siegel, Jerome 1914-1996 .... **CLC 21**
See Siegel, Jerry
See also CA 116; 169; 151

Siegel, Jerry
See Siegel, Jerome
See also AAYA 50

Sienkiewicz, Henryk (Adam Alexander Pius)
1846-1916 .... **TCLC 3**
See also CA 104; 134; CANR 84; EWL 3; RGSF 2; RGWL 2, 3

Sierra, Gregorio Martinez
See Martinez Sierra, Gregorio

Sierra, Maria (de la O'LeJarraga) Martinez
See Martinez Sierra, Maria (de la O'LeJarraga)

Sigal, Clancy 1926- .... **CLC 7**
See also CA 1-4R; CANR 85; CN 7

Siger of Brabant 1240(?)-1284(?) . **CMLC 69**
See also DLB 115

Sigourney, Lydia H.
See Sigourney, Lydia Howard (Huntley)
See also DLB 73, 183

Sigourney, Lydia Howard (Huntley)
1791-1865 .... **NCLC 21, 87**
See Sigourney, Lydia H.; Sigourney, Lydia Huntley
See also DLB 1

Sigourney, Lydia Huntley
See Sigourney, Lydia Howard (Huntley)
See also DLB 42, 239, 243

Siguenza y Gongora, Carlos de
1645-1700 .... **HLCS 2; LC 8**
See also LAW

Sigurjonsson, Johann
See Sigurjonsson, Johann

Sigurjonsson, Johann 1880-1919 ... **TCLC 27**
See also CA 170; DLB 293; EWL 3

Sikelianos, Angelos 1884-1951 .... **PC 29; TCLC 39**
See also EWL 3; RGWL 2, 3

Silkin, Jon 1930-1997 .... **CLC 2, 6, 43**
See also CA 5-8R; CAAS 5; CANR 89; CP 7; DLB 27

Silko, Leslie (Marmon) 1948- .... **CLC 23, 74, 114, 211; NNAL; SSC 37, 66; WLCS**
See also AAYA 14; AMWS 4; ANW; BYA 12; CA 115; 122; CANR 45, 65, 118; CN 7; CP 7; CPW 1; CWP; DA; DA3; DAC; DAM MST, MULT, POP; DLB 143, 175, 256, 275; EWL 3; EXPP; EXPS; LAIT 4; MTCW 2; NFS 4; PFS 9, 16; RGAL 4; RGSF 2; SSFS 4, 8, 10, 11

Sillanpaa, Frans Eemil 1888-1964 ... **CLC 19**
See also CA 129; 93-96; EWL 3; MTCW 1

Sillitoe, Alan 1928- .. **CLC 1, 3, 6, 10, 19, 57, 148**
See also AITN 1; BRWS 5; CA 9-12R; 191; CAAE 191; CAAS 2; CANR 8, 26, 55; CDBLB 1960 to Present; CN 7; DLB 14, 139; EWL 3; MTCW 1, 2; RGEL 2; RGSF 2; SATA 61

Silone, Ignazio 1900-1978 .... **CLC 4**
See also CA 25-28; 81-84; CANR 34; CAP 2; DLB 264; EW 12; EWL 3; MTCW 1; RGSF 2; RGWL 2, 3

Silone, Ignazione
See Silone, Ignazio

Silver, Joan Micklin 1935- .... **CLC 20**
See also CA 114; 121; INT CA-121

Silver, Nicholas
See Faust, Frederick (Schiller)
See also TCWW 2

Silverberg, Robert 1935- .... **CLC 7, 140**
See also AAYA 24; BPFB 3; BYA 7, 9; CA 1-4R; CAAE 186; CAAS 3; CANR 1, 20, 36, 85; CLR 59; CN 7; CPW; DAM POP; DLB 8; INT CANR-20; MAICYA 1, 2; MTCW 1, 2; SATA 13, 91; SATA-Essay 104; SCFW 4; SFW 4; SUFW 2

Silverstein, Alvin 1933- .... **CLC 17**
See also CA 49-52; CANR 2; CLR 25; JRDA; MAICYA 1, 2; SATA 8, 69, 124

Silverstein, Shel(don Allan)
1932-1999 .... **PC 49**
See also AAYA 40; BW 3; CA 107; 179; CANR 47, 74, 81; CLR 5, 96; CWRI 5; JRDA; MAICYA 1, 2; MTCW 2; SATA 33, 92; SATA-Brief 27; SATA-Obit 116

Smith, David (Jeddie) 1942-
See Smith, Dave
See also CA 49-52; CANR 1, 59, 120; CP 7; CSW; DAM POET

Smith, Florence Margaret 1902-1971
See Smith, Stevie
See also CA 17-18; 29-32R; CANR 35; CAP 2; DAM POET; MTCW 1, 2; TEA

Smith, Iain Crichton 1928-1998 .... **CLC 64**
See also BRWS 9; CA 21-24R; 171; CN 7; CP 7; DLB 40, 139; RGSF 2

Smith, John 1580(?)-1631 .... **LC 9**
See also DLB 24, 30; TUS

Smith, Johnston
See Crane, Stephen (Townley)

Smith, Joseph, Jr. 1805-1844 .... **NCLC 53**

Smith, Lee 1944- .... **CLC 25, 73**
See also CA 114; 119; CANR 46, 118; CSW; DLB 143; DLBY 1983; EWL 3; INT CA-119; RGAL 4

Smith, Martin
See Smith, Martin Cruz

Smith, Martin Cruz 1942- .. **CLC 25; NNAL**
See also BEST 89:4; BPFB 3; CA 85-88; CANR 6, 23, 43, 65, 119; CMW 4; CPW; DAM MULT, POP; HGG; INT CANR-23; MTCW 2; RGAL 4

Smith, Patti 1946- .... **CLC 12**
See also CA 93-96; CANR 63

Smith, Pauline (Urmson) 1882-1959 .... **TCLC 25**
See also DLB 225; EWL 3

Smith, Rosamond
See Oates, Joyce Carol

Smith, Sheila Kaye
See Kaye-Smith, Sheila

Smith, Stevie .... **CLC 3, 8, 25, 44; PC 12**
See Smith, Florence Margaret
See also BRWS 2; DLB 20; EWL 3; MTCW 2; PAB; PFS 3; RGEL 2

Smith, Wilbur (Addison) 1933- .... **CLC 33**
See also CA 13-16R; CANR 7, 46, 66, 134; CPW; MTCW 1, 2

Smith, William Jay 1918- .... **CLC 6**
See also AMWS 13; CA 5-8R; CANR 44, 106; CP 7; CSW; CWRI 5; DLB 5; MAICYA 1, 2; SAAS 22; SATA 2, 68, 154; SATA-Essay 154

Smith, Woodrow Wilson
See Kuttner, Henry

Smith, Zadie 1976- .... **CLC 158**
See also AAYA 50; CA 193

Smolenskin, Peretz 1842-1885 .... **NCLC 30**

Smollett, Tobias (George) 1721-1771 ... **LC 2, 46**
See also BRW 3; CDBLB 1660-1789; DLB 39, 104; RGEL 2; TEA

Snodgrass, W(illiam) D(e Witt) 1926- .... **CLC 2, 6, 10, 18, 68**
See also AMWS 6; CA 1-4R; CANR 6, 36, 65, 85; CP 7; DAM POET; DLB 5; MTCW 1, 2; RGAL 4

Snorri Sturluson 1179-1241 .... **CMLC 56**
See also RGWL 2, 3

Snow, C(harles) P(ercy) 1905-1980 ... **CLC 1, 4, 6, 9, 13, 19**
See also BRW 7; CA 5-8R; 101; CANR 28; CDBLB 1945-1960; DAM NOV; DLB 15, 77; DLBD 17; EWL 3; MTCW 1, 2; RGEL 2; TEA

Snow, Frances Compton
See Adams, Henry (Brooks)

Snyder, Gary (Sherman) 1930- . **CLC 1, 2, 5, 9, 32, 120; PC 21**
See also AMWS 8; ANW; BG 3; CA 17-20R; CANR 30, 60, 125; CP 7; DA3; DAM POET; DLB 5, 16, 165, 212, 237, 275; EWL 3; MTCW 2; PFS 9, 19; RGAL 4; WP

Snyder, Zilpha Keatley 1927- .... **CLC 17**
See also AAYA 15; BYA 1; CA 9-12R; CANR 38; CLR 31; JRDA; MAICYA 1, 2; SAAS 2; SATA 1, 28, 75, 110; SATA-Essay 112; YAW

Soares, Bernardo
See Pessoa, Fernando (Antonio Nogueira)

Sobh, A.
See Shamlu, Ahmad

Sobh, Alef
See Shamlu, Ahmad

Sobol, Joshua 1939- .... **CLC 60**
See Sobol, Yehoshua
See also CA 200

Sobol, Yehoshua 1939-
See Sobol, Joshua
See also CWW 2

Socrates 470B.C.-399B.C. .... **CMLC 27**

Soderberg, Hjalmar 1869-1941 ...... **TCLC 39**
See also DLB 259; EWL 3; RGSF 2

Soderbergh, Steven 1963- .... **CLC 154**
See also AAYA 43

Sodergran, Edith (Irene) 1892-1923
See Soedergran, Edith (Irene)
See also CA 202; DLB 259; EW 11; EWL 3; RGWL 2, 3

Soedergran, Edith (Irene) 1892-1923 .... **TCLC 31**
See Sodergran, Edith (Irene)

Softly, Edgar
See Lovecraft, H(oward) P(hillips)

Softly, Edward
See Lovecraft, H(oward) P(hillips)

Sokolov, Alexander V(sevolodovich) 1943-
See Sokolov, Sasha
See also CA 73-76

Sokolov, Raymond 1941- .... **CLC 7**
See also CA 85-88

Sokolov, Sasha .... **CLC 59**
See Sokolov, Alexander V(sevolodovich)
See also CWW 2; DLB 285; EWL 3; RGWL 2, 3

Solo, Jay
See Ellison, Harlan (Jay)

Sologub, Fyodor .... **TCLC 9**
See Teternikov, Fyodor Kuzmich
See also EWL 3

Solomons, Ikey Esquir
See Thackeray, William Makepeace

Solomos, Dionysios 1798-1857 .... **NCLC 15**

Solwoska, Mara
See French, Marilyn

Solzhenitsyn, Aleksandr I(sayevich) 1918- .. **CLC 1, 2, 4, 7, 9, 10, 18, 26, 34, 78, 134; SSC 32; WLC**
See Solzhenitsyn, Aleksandr Isaevich
See also AAYA 49; AITN 1; BPFB 3; CA 69-72; CANR 40, 65, 116; DA; DA3; DAB; DAC; DAM MST, NOV; DLB 302; EW 13; EXPS; LAIT 4; MTCW 1, 2; NFS 6; RGSF 2; RGWL 2, 3; SSFS 9; TWA

Solzhenitsyn, Aleksandr Isaevich
See Solzhenitsyn, Aleksandr I(sayevich)
See also CWW 2; EWL 3

Somers, Jane
See Lessing, Doris (May)

Somerville, Edith Oenone 1858-1949 .... **SSC 56; TCLC 51**
See also CA 196; DLB 135; RGEL 2; RGSF 2

Somerville & Ross
See Martin, Violet Florence; Somerville, Edith Oenone

Sommer, Scott 1951- .... **CLC 25**
See also CA 106

Sommers, Christina Hoff 1950- ...... **CLC 197**
See also CA 153; CANR 95

Sondheim, Stephen (Joshua) 1930- . **CLC 30, 39, 147; DC 22**
See also AAYA 11; CA 103; CANR 47, 67, 125; DAM DRAM; LAIT 4

Sone, Monica 1919- .... **AAL**

Song, Cathy 1955- .... **AAL; PC 21**
See also CA 154; CANR 118; CWP; DLB 169; EXPP; FW; PFS 5

Sontag, Susan 1933- ... **CLC 1, 2, 10, 13, 31, 105, 195**
See also AMWS 3; CA 17-20R; CANR 25, 51, 74, 97; CN 7; CPW; DA3; DAM POP; DLB 2, 67; EWL 3; MAWW; MTCW 1, 2; RGAL 4; RHW; SSFS 10

Sophocles 496(?)B.C.-406(?)B.C. .... **CMLC 2, 47, 51; DC 1; WLCS**
See also AW 1; CDWLB 1; DA; DA3; DAB; DAC; DAM DRAM, MST; DFS 1, 4, 8; DLB 176; LAIT 1; LATS 1:1; LMFS 1; RGWL 2, 3; TWA

Sordello 1189-1269 .... **CMLC 15**

Sorel, Georges 1847-1922 .... **TCLC 91**
See also CA 118; 188

Sorel, Julia
See Drexler, Rosalyn

Sorokin, Vladimir .... **CLC 59**
See Sorokin, Vladimir Georgievich

Sorokin, Vladimir Georgievich
See Sorokin, Vladimir
See also DLB 285

Sorrentino, Gilbert 1929- .. **CLC 3, 7, 14, 22, 40**
See also CA 77-80; CANR 14, 33, 115; CN 7; CP 7; DLB 5, 173; DLBY 1980; INT CANR-14

Soseki
See Natsume, Soseki
See also MJW

Soto, Gary 1952- ... **CLC 32, 80; HLC 2; PC 28**
See also AAYA 10, 37; BYA 11; CA 119; 125; CANR 50, 74, 107; CLR 38; CP 7; DAM MULT; DLB 82; EWL 3; EXPP; HW 1, 2; INT CA-125; JRDA; LLW 1; MAICYA 2; MAICYAS 1; MTCW 2; PFS 7; RGAL 4; SATA 80, 120; WYA; YAW

Soupault, Philippe 1897-1990 .... **CLC 68**
See also CA 116; 147; 131; EWL 3; GFL 1789 to the Present; LMFS 2

Souster, (Holmes) Raymond 1921- .... **CLC 5, 14**
See also CA 13-16R; CAAS 14; CANR 13, 29, 53; CP 7; DA3; DAC; DAM POET; DLB 88; RGEL 2; SATA 63

Southern, Terry 1924(?)-1995 .... **CLC 7**
See also AMWS 11; BPFB 3; CA 1-4R; 150; CANR 1, 55, 107; CN 7; DLB 2; IDFW 3, 4

Southerne, Thomas 1660-1746 .... **LC 99**
See also DLB 80; RGEL 2

Southey, Robert 1774-1843 .... **NCLC 8, 97**
See also BRW 4; DLB 93, 107, 142; RGEL 2; SATA 54

Southwell, Robert 1561(?)-1595 .... **LC 108**
See also DLB 167; RGEL 2; TEA

Southworth, Emma Dorothy Eliza Nevitte 1819-1899 .... **NCLC 26**
See also DLB 239

Souza, Ernest
See Scott, Evelyn

Soyinka, Wole 1934- .. **BLC 3; CLC 3, 5, 14, 36, 44, 179; DC 2; WLC**
See also AFW; BW 2, 3; CA 13-16R; CANR 27, 39, 82; CD 5; CDWLB 3; CN 7; CP 7; DA; DA3; DAB; DAC; DAM DRAM, MST, MULT; DFS 10; DLB 125; EWL 3; MTCW 1, 2; RGEL 2; TWA; WLIT 2; WWE 1

Stephens, James 1882(?)-1950 .... **SSC 50; TCLC 4**
See also CA 104; 192; DLB 19, 153, 162; EWL 3; FANT; RGEL 2; SUFW

Stephens, Reed
See Donaldson, Stephen R(eeder)

Steptoe, Lydia
See Barnes, Djuna
See also GLL 1

Sterchi, Beat 1949- .... **CLC 65**
See also CA 203

Sterling, Brett
See Bradbury, Ray (Douglas); Hamilton, Edmond

Sterling, Bruce 1954- .... **CLC 72**
See also CA 119; CANR 44, 135; SCFW 2; SFW 4

Sterling, George 1869-1926 .... **TCLC 20**
See also CA 117; 165; DLB 54

Stern, Gerald 1925- .... **CLC 40, 100**
See also AMWS 9; CA 81-84; CANR 28, 94; CP 7; DLB 105; RGAL 4

Stern, Richard (Gustave) 1928- ... **CLC 4, 39**
See also CA 1-4R; CANR 1, 25, 52, 120; CN 7; DLB 218; DLBY 1987; INT CANR-25

Sternberg, Josef von 1894-1969 .... **CLC 20**
See also CA 81-84

Sterne, Laurence 1713-1768 .... **LC 2, 48; WLC**
See also BRW 3; BRWC 1; CDBLB 1660-1789; DA; DAB; DAC; DAM MST, NOV; DLB 39; RGEL 2; TEA

Sternheim, (William Adolf) Carl 1878-1942 .... **TCLC 8**
See also CA 105; 193; DLB 56, 118; EWL 3; RGWL 2, 3

Stevens, Mark 1951- .... **CLC 34**
See also CA 122

Stevens, Wallace 1879-1955 . **PC 6; TCLC 3, 12, 45; WLC**
See also AMW; AMWR 1; CA 104; 124; CDALB 1929-1941; DA; DA3; DAB; DAC; DAM MST, POET; DLB 54; EWL 3; EXPP; MTCW 1, 2; PAB; PFS 13, 16; RGAL 4; TUS; WP

Stevenson, Anne (Katharine) 1933- .. **CLC 7, 33**
See also BRWS 6; CA 17-20R; CAAS 9; CANR 9, 33, 123; CP 7; CWP; DLB 40; MTCW 1; RHW

Stevenson, Robert Louis (Balfour) 1850-1894 ...... **NCLC 5, 14, 63; SSC 11, 51; WLC**
See also AAYA 24; BPFB 3; BRW 5; BRWC 1; BRWR 1; BYA 1, 2, 4, 13; CDBLB 1890-1914; CLR 10, 11; DA; DA3; DAB; DAC; DAM MST, NOV; DLB 18, 57, 141, 156, 174; DLBD 13; HGG; JRDA; LAIT 1, 3; MAICYA 1, 2; NFS 11, 20; RGEL 2; RGSF 2; SATA 100; SUFW; TEA; WCH; WLIT 4; WYA; YABC 2; YAW

Stewart, J(ohn) I(nnes) M(ackintosh) 1906-1994 .... **CLC 7, 14, 32**
See Innes, Michael
See also CA 85-88; 147; CAAS 3; CANR 47; CMW 4; MTCW 1, 2

Stewart, Mary (Florence Elinor) 1916- .... **CLC 7, 35, 117**
See also AAYA 29; BPFB 3; CA 1-4R; CANR 1, 59, 130; CMW 4; CPW; DAB; FANT; RHW; SATA 12; YAW

Stewart, Mary Rainbow
See Stewart, Mary (Florence Elinor)

Stifle, June
See Campbell, Maria

Stifter, Adalbert 1805-1868 .. **NCLC 41; SSC 28**
See also CDWLB 2; DLB 133; RGSF 2; RGWL 2, 3

Still, James 1906-2001 .... **CLC 49**
See also CA 65-68; 195; CAAS 17; CANR 10, 26; CSW; DLB 9; DLBY 01; SATA 29; SATA-Obit 127

Sting 1951-
See Sumner, Gordon Matthew
See also CA 167

Stirling, Arthur
See Sinclair, Upton (Beall)

Stitt, Milan 1941- .... **CLC 29**
See also CA 69-72

Stockton, Francis Richard 1834-1902
See Stockton, Frank R.
See also CA 108; 137; MAICYA 1, 2; SATA 44; SFW 4

Stockton, Frank R. .... **TCLC 47**
See Stockton, Francis Richard
See also BYA 4, 13; DLB 42, 74; DLBD 13; EXPS; SATA-Brief 32; SSFS 3; SUFW; WCH

Stoddard, Charles
See Kuttner, Henry

Stoker, Abraham 1847-1912
See Stoker, Bram
See also CA 105; 150; DA; DA3; DAC; DAM MST, NOV; HGG; SATA 29

Stoker, Bram . **SSC 62; TCLC 8, 144; WLC**
See Stoker, Abraham
See also AAYA 23; BPFB 3; BRWS 3; BYA 5; CDBLB 1890-1914; DAB; DLB 304; LATS 1:1; NFS 18; RGEL 2; SUFW; TEA; WLIT 4

Stolz, Mary (Slattery) 1920- .... **CLC 12**
See also AAYA 8; AITN 1; CA 5-8R; CANR 13, 41, 112; JRDA; MAICYA 1, 2; SAAS 3; SATA 10, 71, 133; YAW

Stone, Irving 1903-1989 .... **CLC 7**
See also AITN 1; BPFB 3; CA 1-4R; 129; CAAS 3; CANR 1, 23; CPW; DA3; DAM POP; INT CANR-23; MTCW 1, 2; RHW; SATA 3; SATA-Obit 64

Stone, Oliver (William) 1946- .... **CLC 73**
See also AAYA 15; CA 110; CANR 55, 125

Stone, Robert (Anthony) 1937- ... **CLC 5, 23, 42, 175**
See also AMWS 5; BPFB 3; CA 85-88; CANR 23, 66, 95; CN 7; DLB 152; EWL 3; INT CANR-23; MTCW 1

Stone, Ruth 1915- .... **PC 53**
See also CA 45-48; CANR 2, 91; CP 7; CSW; DLB 105; PFS 19

Stone, Zachary
See Follett, Ken(neth Martin)

Stoppard, Tom 1937- ... **CLC 1, 3, 4, 5, 8, 15, 29, 34, 63, 91; DC 6; WLC**
See also BRWC 1; BRWR 2; BRWS 1; CA 81-84; CANR 39, 67, 125; CBD; CD 5; CDBLB 1960 to Present; DA; DA3; DAB; DAC; DAM DRAM, MST; DFS 2, 5, 8, 11, 13, 16; DLB 13, 233; DLBY 1985; EWL 3; LATS 1:2; MTCW 1, 2; RGEL 2; TEA; WLIT 4

Storey, David (Malcolm) 1933- . **CLC 2, 4, 5, 8**
See also BRWS 1; CA 81-84; CANR 36; CBD; CD 5; CN 7; DAM DRAM; DLB 13, 14, 207, 245; EWL 3; MTCW 1; RGEL 2

Storm, Hyemeyohsts 1935- ... **CLC 3; NNAL**
See also CA 81-84; CANR 45; DAM MULT

Storm, (Hans) Theodor (Woldsen) 1817-1888 .... **NCLC 1; SSC 27**
See also CDWLB 2; DLB 129; EW; RGSF 2; RGWL 2, 3

Storni, Alfonsina 1892-1938 . **HLC 2; PC 33; TCLC 5**
See also CA 104; 131; DAM MULT; DLB 283; HW 1; LAW

Stoughton, William 1631-1701 .... **LC 38**
See also DLB 24

Stout, Rex (Todhunter) 1886-1975 ..... **CLC 3**
See also AITN 2; BPFB 3; CA 61-64; CANR 71; CMW 4; DLB 306; MSW; RGAL 4

Stow, (Julian) Randolph 1935- ... **CLC 23, 48**
See also CA 13-16R; CANR 33; CN 7; DLB 260; MTCW 1; RGEL 2

Stowe, Harriet (Elizabeth) Beecher 1811-1896 .... **NCLC 3, 50, 133; WLC**
See also AAYA 53; AMWS 1; CDALB 1865-1917; DA; DA3; DAB; DAC; DAM MST, NOV; DLB 1, 12, 42, 74, 189, 239, 243; EXPN; JRDA; LAIT 2; MAICYA 1, 2; NFS 6; RGAL 4; TUS; YABC 1

Strabo c. 64B.C.-c. 25 .... **CMLC 37**
See also DLB 176

Strachey, (Giles) Lytton 1880-1932 .... **TCLC 12**
See also BRWS 2; CA 110; 178; DLB 149; DLBD 10; EWL 3; MTCW 2; NCFS 4

Stramm, August 1874-1915 .... **PC 50**
See also CA 195; EWL 3

Strand, Mark 1934- .. **CLC 6, 18, 41, 71; PC 63**
See also AMWS 4; CA 21-24R; CANR 40, 65, 100; CP 7; DAM POET; DLB 5; EWL 3; PAB; PFS 9, 18; RGAL 4; SATA 41

Stratton-Porter, Gene(va Grace) 1863-1924
See Porter, Gene(va Grace) Stratton
See also ANW; CA 137; CLR 87; DLB 221; DLBD 14; MAICYA 1, 2; SATA 15

Straub, Peter (Francis) 1943- ... **CLC 28, 107**
See also BEST 89:1; BPFB 3; CA 85-88; CANR 28, 65, 109; CPW; DAM POP; DLBY 1984; HGG; MTCW 1, 2; SUFW 2

Strauss, Botho 1944- .... **CLC 22**
See also CA 157; CWW 2; DLB 124

Strauss, Leo 1899-1973 .... **TCLC 141**
See also CA 101; 45-48; CANR 122

Streatfeild, (Mary) Noel 1897(?)-1986 .... **CLC 21**
See also CA 81-84; 120; CANR 31; CLR 17, 83; CWRI 5; DLB 160; MAICYA 1, 2; SATA 20; SATA-Obit 48

Stribling, T(homas) S(igismund) 1881-1965 .... **CLC 23**
See also CA 189; 107; CMW 4; DLB 9; RGAL 4

Strindberg, (Johan) August 1849-1912 ... **DC 18; TCLC 1, 8, 21, 47; WLC**
See also CA 104; 135; DA; DA3; DAB; DAC; DAM DRAM, MST; DFS 4, 9; DLB 259; EW 7; EWL 3; IDTP; LMFS 2; MTCW 2; RGWL 2, 3; TWA

Stringer, Arthur 1874-1950 .... **TCLC 37**
See also CA 161; DLB 92

Stringer, David
See Roberts, Keith (John Kingston)

Stroheim, Erich von 1885-1957 ..... **TCLC 71**

Strugatskii, Arkadii (Natanovich) 1925-1991 .... **CLC 27**
See Strugatsky, Arkadii Natanovich
See also CA 106; 135; SFW 4

Strugatskii, Boris (Natanovich) 1933- .... **CLC 27**
See Strugatsky, Boris (Natanovich)
See also CA 106; SFW 4

Strugatsky, Arkadii Natanovich
See Strugatskii, Arkadii (Natanovich)
See also DLB 302

Strugatsky, Boris (Natanovich)
See Strugatskii, Boris (Natanovich)
See also DLB 302

Strummer, Joe 1953(?)- .... **CLC 30**

Strunk, William, Jr. 1869-1946 ...... **TCLC 92**
See also CA 118; 164; NCFS 5

Stryk, Lucien 1924- .... **PC 27**
See also CA 13-16R; CANR 10, 28, 55, 110; CP 7

Stuart, Don A.
See Campbell, John W(ood, Jr.)

Stuart, Ian
See MacLean, Alistair (Stuart)

Stuart, Jesse (Hilton) 1906-1984 ... **CLC 1, 8, 11, 14, 34; SSC 31**
See also CA 5-8R; 112; CANR 31; DLB 9, 48, 102; DLBY 1984; SATA 2; SATA-Obit 36

Stubblefield, Sally
See Trumbo, Dalton

Sturgeon, Theodore (Hamilton) 1918-1985 .... **CLC 22, 39**
See Queen, Ellery
See also AAYA 51; BPFB 3; BYA 9, 10; CA 81-84; 116; CANR 32, 103; DLB 8; DLBY 1985; HGG; MTCW 1, 2; SCFW; SFW 4; SUFW

Sturges, Preston 1898-1959 .... **TCLC 48**
See also CA 114; 149; DLB 26

Styron, William 1925- .... **CLC 1, 3, 5, 11, 15, 60; SSC 25**
See also AMW; AMWC 2; BEST 90:4; BPFB 3; CA 5-8R; CANR 6, 33, 74, 126; CDALB 1968-1988; CN 7; CPW; CSW; DA3; DAM NOV, POP; DLB 2, 143, 299; DLBY 1980; EWL 3; INT CANR-6; LAIT 2; MTCW 1, 2; NCFS 1; RGAL 4; RHW; TUS

Su, Chien 1884-1918
See Su Man-shu
See also CA 123

Suarez Lynch, B.
See Bioy Casares, Adolfo; Borges, Jorge Luis

Suassuna, Ariano Vilar 1927- .... **HLCS 1**
See also CA 178; DLB 307; HW 2; LAW

Suckert, Kurt Erich
See Malaparte, Curzio

Suckling, Sir John 1609-1642 . **LC 75; PC 30**
See also BRW 2; DAM POET; DLB 58, 126; EXPP; PAB; RGEL 2

Suckow, Ruth 1892-1960 .... **SSC 18**
See also CA 193; 113; DLB 9, 102; RGAL 4; TCWW 2

Sudermann, Hermann 1857-1928 .. **TCLC 15**
See also CA 107; 201; DLB 118

Sue, Eugene 1804-1857 .... **NCLC 1**
See also DLB 119

Sueskind, Patrick 1949- .... **CLC 44, 182**
See Suskind, Patrick

Suetonius c. 70-c. 130 .... **CMLC 60**
See also AW 2; DLB 211; RGWL 2, 3

Sukenick, Ronald 1932-2004 ..... **CLC 3, 4, 6, 48**
See also CA 25-28R, 209; 229; CAAE 209; CAAS 8; CANR 32, 89; CN 7; DLB 173; DLBY 1981

Suknaski, Andrew 1942- .... **CLC 19**
See also CA 101; CP 7; DLB 53

Sullivan, Vernon
See Vian, Boris

Sully Prudhomme, Rene-Francois-Armand 1839-1907 .... **TCLC 31**
See also GFL 1789 to the Present

Su Man-shu .... **TCLC 24**
See Su, Chien
See also EWL 3

Sumarokov, Aleksandr Petrovich 1717-1777 .... **LC 104**
See also DLB 150

Summerforest, Ivy B.
See Kirkup, James

Summers, Andrew James 1942- .... **CLC 26**

Summers, Andy
See Summers, Andrew James

Summers, Hollis (Spurgeon, Jr.) 1916- .... **CLC 10**
See also CA 5-8R; CANR 3; DLB 6

Summers, (Alphonsus Joseph-Mary Augustus) Montague 1880-1948 .... **TCLC 16**
See also CA 118; 163

Sumner, Gordon Matthew .... **CLC 26**
See Police, The; Sting

Sun Tzu c. 400B.C.-c. 320B.C. ...... **CMLC 56**

Surrey, Henry Howard 1517-1574 ...... **PC 59**
See also BRW 1; RGEL 2

Surtees, Robert Smith 1805-1864 .. **NCLC 14**
See also DLB 21; RGEL 2

Susann, Jacqueline 1921-1974 .... **CLC 3**
See also AITN 1; BPFB 3; CA 65-68; 53-56; MTCW 1, 2

Su Shi
See Su Shih
See also RGWL 2, 3

Su Shih 1036-1101 .... **CMLC 15**
See Su Shi

Suskind, Patrick .... **CLC 182**
See Sueskind, Patrick
See also BPFB 3; CA 145; CWW 2

Sutcliff, Rosemary 1920-1992 .... **CLC 26**
See also AAYA 10; BYA 1, 4; CA 5-8R; 139; CANR 37; CLR 1, 37; CPW; DAB; DAC; DAM MST, POP; JRDA; LATS 1:1; MAICYA 1, 2; MAICYAS 1; RHW; SATA 6, 44, 78; SATA-Obit 73; WYA; YAW

Sutro, Alfred 1863-1933 .... **TCLC 6**
See also CA 105; 185; DLB 10; RGEL 2

Sutton, Henry
See Slavitt, David R(ytman)

Suzuki, D. T.
See Suzuki, Daisetz Teitaro

Suzuki, Daisetz T.
See Suzuki, Daisetz Teitaro

Suzuki, Daisetz Teitaro 1870-1966 .... **TCLC 109**
See also CA 121; 111; MTCW 1, 2

Suzuki, Teitaro
See Suzuki, Daisetz Teitaro

Svevo, Italo .... **SSC 25; TCLC 2, 35**
See Schmitz, Aron Hector
See also DLB 264; EW 8; EWL 3; RGWL 2, 3

Swados, Elizabeth (A.) 1951- .... **CLC 12**
See also CA 97-100; CANR 49; INT CA-97-100

Swados, Harvey 1920-1972 .... **CLC 5**
See also CA 5-8R; 37-40R; CANR 6; DLB 2

Swan, Gladys 1934- .... **CLC 69**
See also CA 101; CANR 17, 39

Swanson, Logan
See Matheson, Richard (Burton)

Swarthout, Glendon (Fred) 1918-1992 .... **CLC 35**
See also AAYA 55; CA 1-4R; 139; CANR 1, 47; LAIT 5; SATA 26; TCWW 2; YAW

Swedenborg, Emanuel 1688-1772 ..... **LC 105**

Sweet, Sarah C.
See Jewett, (Theodora) Sarah Orne

Swenson, May 1919-1989 ...... **CLC 4, 14, 61, 106; PC 14**
See also AMWS 4; CA 5-8R; 130; CANR 36, 61, 131; DA; DAB; DAC; DAM MST, POET; DLB 5; EXPP; GLL 2; MTCW 1, 2; PFS 16; SATA 15; WP

Swift, Augustus
See Lovecraft, H(oward) P(hillips)

Swift, Graham (Colin) 1949- ...... **CLC 41, 88**
See also BRWC 2; BRWS 5; CA 117; 122; CANR 46, 71, 128; CN 7; DLB 194; MTCW 2; NFS 18; RGSF 2

Swift, Jonathan 1667-1745 ..... **LC 1, 42, 101; PC 9; WLC**
See also AAYA 41; BRW 3; BRWC 1; BRWR 1; BYA 5, 14; CDBLB 1660-1789; CLR 53; DA; DA3; DAB; DAC; DAM MST, NOV, POET; DLB 39, 95, 101; EXPN; LAIT 1; NFS 6; RGEL 2; SATA 19; TEA; WCH; WLIT 3

Swinburne, Algernon Charles 1837-1909 ... **PC 24; TCLC 8, 36; WLC**
See also BRW 5; CA 105; 140; CDBLB 1832-1890; DA; DA3; DAB; DAC; DAM MST, POET; DLB 35, 57; PAB; RGEL 2; TEA

Swinfen, Ann .... **CLC 34**
See also CA 202

Swinnerton, Frank Arthur 1884-1982 .... **CLC 31**
See also CA 108; DLB 34

Swithen, John
See King, Stephen (Edwin)

Sylvia
See Ashton-Warner, Sylvia (Constance)

Symmes, Robert Edward
See Duncan, Robert (Edward)

Symonds, John Addington 1840-1893 .... **NCLC 34**
See also DLB 57, 144

Symons, Arthur 1865-1945 .... **TCLC 11**
See also CA 107; 189; DLB 19, 57, 149; RGEL 2

Symons, Julian (Gustave) 1912-1994 .... **CLC 2, 14, 32**
See also CA 49-52; 147; CAAS 3; CANR 3, 33, 59; CMW 4; DLB 87, 155; DLBY 1992; MSW; MTCW 1

Synge, (Edmund) J(ohn) M(illington) 1871-1909 .... **DC 2; TCLC 6, 37**
See also BRW 6; BRWR 1; CA 104; 141; CDBLB 1890-1914; DAM DRAM; DFS 18; DLB 10, 19; EWL 3; RGEL 2; TEA; WLIT 4

Syruc, J.
See Milosz, Czeslaw

Szirtes, George 1948- .... **CLC 46; PC 51**
See also CA 109; CANR 27, 61, 117; CP 7

Szymborska, Wislawa 1923- ... **CLC 99, 190; PC 44**
See also CA 154; CANR 91, 133; CDWLB 4; CWP; CWW 2; DA3; DLB 232; DLBY 1996; EWL 3; MTCW 2; PFS 15; RGWL 3

T. O., Nik
See Annensky, Innokenty (Fyodorovich)

Tabori, George 1914- .... **CLC 19**
See also CA 49-52; CANR 4, 69; CBD; CD 5; DLB 245

Tacitus c. 55-c. 117 .... **CMLC 56**
See also AW 2; CDWLB 1; DLB 211; RGWL 2, 3

Tagore, Rabindranath 1861-1941 .... **PC 8; SSC 48; TCLC 3, 53**
See also CA 104; 120; DA3; DAM DRAM, POET; EWL 3; MTCW 1, 2; PFS 18; RGEL 2; RGSF 2; RGWL 2, 3; TWA

Taine, Hippolyte Adolphe
1828-1893 .... **NCLC 15**
See also EW 7; GFL 1789 to the Present

Talayesva, Don C. 1890-(?) .... **NNAL**

Talese, Gay 1932- .... **CLC 37**
See also AITN 1; CA 1-4R; CANR 9, 58;
DLB 185; INT CANR-9; MTCW 1, 2

Tallent, Elizabeth (Ann) 1954- .... **CLC 45**
See also CA 117; CANR 72; DLB 130

Tallmountain, Mary 1918-1997 .... **NNAL**
See also CA 146; 161; DLB 193

Tally, Ted 1952- .... **CLC 42**
See also CA 120; 124; CAD; CANR 125;
CD 5; INT CA-124

Talvik, Heiti 1904-1947 .... **TCLC 87**
See also EWL 3

Tamayo y Baus, Manuel
1829-1898 .... **NCLC 1**

Tammsaare, A(nton) H(ansen)
1878-1940 .... **TCLC 27**
See also CA 164; CDWLB 4; DLB 220;
EWL 3

Tam'si, Tchicaya U
See Tchicaya, Gerald Felix

Tan, Amy (Ruth) 1952- . **AAL; CLC 59, 120, 151**
See also AAYA 9, 48; AMWS 10; BEST
89:3; BPFB 3; CA 136; CANR 54, 105,
132; CDALBS; CN 7; CPW 1; DA3;
DAM MULT, NOV, POP; DLB 173;
EXPN; FW; LAIT 3, 5; MTCW 2; NFS
1, 13, 16; RGAL 4; SATA 75; SSFS 9;
YAW

Tandem, Felix
See Spitteler, Carl (Friedrich Georg)

Tanizaki, Jun'ichiro 1886-1965 ... **CLC 8, 14, 28; SSC 21**
See Tanizaki Jun'ichiro
See also CA 93-96; 25-28R; MJW; MTCW
2; RGSF 2; RGWL 2

Tanizaki Jun'ichiro
See Tanizaki, Jun'ichiro
See also DLB 180; EWL 3

Tannen, Deborah F. 1945- .... **CLC 206**
See also CA 118; CANR 95

Tanner, William
See Amis, Kingsley (William)

Tao Lao
See Storni, Alfonsina

Tapahonso, Luci 1953- .... **NNAL; PC 65**
See also CA 145; CANR 72, 127; DLB 175

Tarantino, Quentin (Jerome)
1963- .... **CLC 125**
See also AAYA 58; CA 171; CANR 125

Tarassoff, Lev
See Troyat, Henri

Tarbell, Ida M(inerva) 1857-1944 . **TCLC 40**
See also CA 122; 181; DLB 47

Tarkington, (Newton) Booth
1869-1946 .... **TCLC 9**
See also BPFB 3; BYA 3; CA 110; 143;
CWRI 5; DLB 9, 102; MTCW 2; RGAL
4; SATA 17

Tarkovskii, Andrei Arsen'evich
See Tarkovsky, Andrei (Arsenyevich)

Tarkovsky, Andrei (Arsenyevich)
1932-1986 .... **CLC 75**
See also CA 127

Tartt, Donna 1963- .... **CLC 76**
See also AAYA 56; CA 142

Tasso, Torquato 1544-1595 .... **LC 5, 94**
See also EFS 2; EW 2; RGWL 2, 3

Tate, (John Orley) Allen 1899-1979 .. **CLC 2, 4, 6, 9, 11, 14, 24; PC 50**
See also AMW; CA 5-8R; 85-88; CANR
32, 108; DLB 4, 45, 63; DLBD 17; EWL
3; MTCW 1, 2; RGAL 4; RHW

Tate, Ellalice
See Hibbert, Eleanor Alice Burford

Tate, James (Vincent) 1943- ..... **CLC 2, 6, 25**
See also CA 21-24R; CANR 29, 57, 114;
CP 7; DLB 5, 169; EWL 3; PFS 10, 15;
RGAL 4; WP

Tate, Nahum 1652(?)-1715 .... **LC 109**
See also DLB 80; RGEL 2

Tauler, Johannes c. 1300-1361 ...... **CMLC 37**
See also DLB 179; LMFS 1

Tavel, Ronald 1940- .... **CLC 6**
See also CA 21-24R; CAD; CANR 33; CD
5

Taviani, Paolo 1931- .... **CLC 70**
See also CA 153

Taylor, Bayard 1825-1878 .... **NCLC 89**
See also DLB 3, 189, 250, 254; RGAL 4

Taylor, C(ecil) P(hilip) 1929-1981 .... **CLC 27**
See also CA 25-28R; 105; CANR 47; CBD

Taylor, Edward 1642(?)-1729 . **LC 11; PC 63**
See also AMW; DA; DAB; DAC; DAM
MST, POET; DLB 24; EXPP; RGAL 4;
TUS

Taylor, Eleanor Ross 1920- .... **CLC 5**
See also CA 81-84; CANR 70

Taylor, Elizabeth 1932-1975 ..... **CLC 2, 4, 29**
See also CA 13-16R; CANR 9, 70; DLB
139; MTCW 1; RGEL 2; SATA 13

Taylor, Frederick Winslow
1856-1915 .... **TCLC 76**
See also CA 188

Taylor, Henry (Splawn) 1942- .... **CLC 44**
See also CA 33-36R; CAAS 7; CANR 31;
CP 7; DLB 5; PFS 10

Taylor, Kamala (Purnaiya) 1924-2004
See Markandaya, Kamala
See also CA 77-80; 227; NFS 13

Taylor, Mildred D(elois) 1943- .... **CLC 21**
See also AAYA 10, 47; BW 1; BYA 3, 8;
CA 85-88; CANR 25, 115; CLR 9, 59,
90; CSW; DLB 52; JRDA; LAIT 3; MAI-
CYA 1, 2; SAAS 5; SATA 135; WYA;
YAW

Taylor, Peter (Hillsman) 1917-1994 .. **CLC 1, 4, 18, 37, 44, 50, 71; SSC 10, 84**
See also AMWS 5; BPFB 3; CA 13-16R;
147; CANR 9, 50; CSW; DLB 218, 278;
DLBY 1981, 1994; EWL 3; EXPS; INT
CANR-9; MTCW 1, 2; RGSF 2; SSFS 9;
TUS

Taylor, Robert Lewis 1912-1998 .... **CLC 14**
See also CA 1-4R; 170; CANR 3, 64; SATA
10

Tchekhov, Anton
See Chekhov, Anton (Pavlovich)

Tchicaya, Gerald Felix 1931-1988 .. **CLC 101**
See Tchicaya U Tam'si
See also CA 129; 125; CANR 81

Tchicaya U Tam'si
See Tchicaya, Gerald Felix
See also EWL 3

Teasdale, Sara 1884-1933 .... **PC 31; TCLC 4**
See also CA 104; 163; DLB 45; GLL 1;
PFS 14; RGAL 4; SATA 32; TUS

Tecumseh 1768-1813 .... **NNAL**
See also DAM MULT

Tegner, Esaias 1782-1846 .... **NCLC 2**

Fujiwara no Teika 1162-1241 .... **CMLC 73**
See also DLB 203

Teilhard de Chardin, (Marie Joseph) Pierre
1881-1955 .... **TCLC 9**
See also CA 105; 210; GFL 1789 to the
Present

Temple, Ann
See Mortimer, Penelope (Ruth)

Tennant, Emma (Christina) 1937- .. **CLC 13, 52**
See also BRWS 9; CA 65-68; CAAS 9;
CANR 10, 38, 59, 88; CN 7; DLB 14;
EWL 3; SFW 4

Tenneshaw, S. M.
See Silverberg, Robert

Tenney, Tabitha Gilman
1762-1837 .... **NCLC 122**
See also DLB 37, 200

Tennyson, Alfred 1809-1892 ... **NCLC 30, 65, 115; PC 6; WLC**
See also AAYA 50; BRW 4; CDBLB 1832-
1890; DA; DA3; DAB; DAC; DAM MST,
POET; DLB 32; EXPP; PAB; PFS 1, 2, 4,
11, 15, 19; RGEL 2; TEA; WLIT 4; WP

Teran, Lisa St. Aubin de .... **CLC 36**
See St. Aubin de Teran, Lisa

Terence c. 184B.C.-c. 159B.C. ...... **CMLC 14; DC 7**
See also AW 1; CDWLB 1; DLB 211;
RGWL 2, 3; TWA

Teresa de Jesus, St. 1515-1582 .... **LC 18**

Terkel, Louis 1912-
See Terkel, Studs
See also CA 57-60; CANR 18, 45, 67, 132;
DA3; MTCW 1, 2

Terkel, Studs .... **CLC 38**
See Terkel, Louis
See also AAYA 32; AITN 1; MTCW 2; TUS

Terry, C. V.
See Slaughter, Frank G(ill)

Terry, Megan 1932- .... **CLC 19; DC 13**
See also CA 77-80; CABS 3; CAD; CANR
43; CD 5; CWD; DFS 18; DLB 7, 249;
GLL 2

Tertullian c. 155-c. 245 .... **CMLC 29**

Tertz, Abram
See Sinyavsky, Andrei (Donatevich)
See also RGSF 2

Tesich, Steve 1943(?)-1996 .... **CLC 40, 69**
See also CA 105; 152; CAD; DLBY 1983

Tesla, Nikola 1856-1943 .... **TCLC 88**

Teternikov, Fyodor Kuzmich 1863-1927
See Sologub, Fyodor
See also CA 104

Tevis, Walter 1928-1984 .... **CLC 42**
See also CA 113; SFW 4

Tey, Josephine .... **TCLC 14**
See Mackintosh, Elizabeth
See also DLB 77; MSW

Thackeray, William Makepeace
1811-1863 .... **NCLC 5, 14, 22, 43; WLC**
See also BRW 5; BRWC 2; CDBLB 1832-
1890; DA; DA3; DAB; DAC; DAM MST,
NOV; DLB 21, 55, 159, 163; NFS 13;
RGEL 2; SATA 23; TEA; WLIT 3

Thakura, Ravindranatha
See Tagore, Rabindranath

Thames, C. H.
See Marlowe, Stephen

Tharoor, Shashi 1956- .... **CLC 70**
See also CA 141; CANR 91; CN 7

Thelwell, Michael Miles 1939- .... **CLC 22**
See also BW 2; CA 101

Theobald, Lewis, Jr.
See Lovecraft, H(oward) P(hillips)

Theocritus c. 310B.C.- .... **CMLC 45**
See also AW 1; DLB 176; RGWL 2, 3

Theodorescu, Ion N. 1880-1967
See Arghezi, Tudor
See also CA 116

Theriault, Yves 1915-1983 .... **CLC 79**
See also CA 102; CCA 1; DAC; DAM
MST; DLB 88; EWL 3

Theroux, Alexander (Louis) 1939- .... **CLC 2, 25**
See also CA 85-88; CANR 20, 63; CN 7

Theroux, Paul (Edward) 1941- ..... **CLC 5, 8, 11, 15, 28, 46**
See also AAYA 28; AMWS 8; BEST 89:4; BPFB 3; CA 33-36R; CANR 20, 45, 74, 133; CDALBS; CN 7; CPW 1; DA3; DAM POP; DLB 2, 218; EWL 3; HGG; MTCW 1, 2; RGAL 4; SATA 44, 109; TUS

Thesen, Sharon 1946- .... **CLC 56**
See also CA 163; CANR 125; CP 7; CWP

Thespis fl. 6th cent. B.C.- .... **CMLC 51**
See also LMFS 1

Thevenin, Denis
See Duhamel, Georges

Thibault, Jacques Anatole Francois 1844-1924
See France, Anatole
See also CA 106; 127; DA3; DAM NOV; MTCW 1, 2; TWA

Thiele, Colin (Milton) 1920- .... **CLC 17**
See also CA 29-32R; CANR 12, 28, 53, 105; CLR 27; DLB 289; MAICYA 1, 2; SAAS 2; SATA 14, 72, 125; YAW

Thistlethwaite, Bel
See Wetherald, Agnes Ethelwyn

Thomas, Audrey (Callahan) 1935- .... **CLC 7, 13, 37, 107; SSC 20**
See also AITN 2; CA 21-24R; CAAS 19; CANR 36, 58; CN 7; DLB 60; MTCW 1; RGSF 2

Thomas, Augustus 1857-1934 .... **TCLC 97**

Thomas, D(onald) M(ichael) 1935- . **CLC 13, 22, 31, 132**
See also BPFB 3; BRWS 4; CA 61-64; CAAS 11; CANR 17, 45, 75; CDBLB 1960 to Present; CN 7; CP 7; DA3; DLB 40, 207, 299; HGG; INT CANR-17; MTCW 1; SFW 4

Thomas, Dylan (Marlais) 1914-1953 .... **PC 2, 52; SSC 3, 44; TCLC 1, 8, 45, 105; WLC**
See also AAYA 45; BRWS 1; CA 104; 120; CANR 65; CDBLB 1945-1960; DA; DA3; DAB; DAC; DAM DRAM, MST, POET; DLB 13, 20, 139; EWL 3; EXPP; LAIT 3; MTCW 1, 2; PAB; PFS 1, 3, 8; RGEL 2; RGSF 2; SATA 60; TEA; WLIT 4; WP

Thomas, (Philip) Edward 1878-1917 . **PC 53; TCLC 10**
See also BRW 6; BRWS 3; CA 106; 153; DAM POET; DLB 19, 98, 156, 216; EWL 3; PAB; RGEL 2

Thomas, Joyce Carol 1938- .... **CLC 35**
See also AAYA 12, 54; BW 2, 3; CA 113; 116; CANR 48, 114, 135; CLR 19; DLB 33; INT CA-116; JRDA; MAICYA 1, 2; MTCW 1, 2; SAAS 7; SATA 40, 78, 123, 137; SATA-Essay 137; WYA; YAW

Thomas, Lewis 1913-1993 .... **CLC 35**
See also ANW; CA 85-88; 143; CANR 38, 60; DLB 275; MTCW 1, 2

Thomas, M. Carey 1857-1935 .... **TCLC 89**
See also FW

Thomas, Paul
See Mann, (Paul) Thomas

Thomas, Piri 1928- .... **CLC 17; HLCS 2**
See also CA 73-76; HW 1; LLW 1

Thomas, R(onald) S(tuart) 1913-2000 .... **CLC 6, 13, 48**
See also CA 89-92; 189; CAAS 4; CANR 30; CDBLB 1960 to Present; CP 7; DAB; DAM POET; DLB 27; EWL 3; MTCW 1; RGEL 2

Thomas, Ross (Elmore) 1926-1995 .. **CLC 39**
See also CA 33-36R; 150; CANR 22, 63; CMW 4

Thompson, Francis (Joseph) 1859-1907 .... **TCLC 4**
See also BRW 5; CA 104; 189; CDBLB 1890-1914; DLB 19; RGEL 2; TEA

Thompson, Francis Clegg
See Mencken, H(enry) L(ouis)

Thompson, Hunter S(tockton) 1937(?)- .... **CLC 9, 17, 40, 104**
See also AAYA 45; BEST 89:1; BPFB 3; CA 17-20R; CANR 23, 46, 74, 77, 111, 133; CPW; CSW; DA3; DAM POP; DLB 185; MTCW 1, 2; TUS

Thompson, James Myers
See Thompson, Jim (Myers)

Thompson, Jim (Myers) 1906-1977(?) .... **CLC 69**
See also BPFB 3; CA 140; CMW 4; CPW; DLB 226; MSW

Thompson, Judith .... **CLC 39**
See also CWD

Thomson, James 1700-1748 .... **LC 16, 29, 40**
See also BRWS 3; DAM POET; DLB 95; RGEL 2

Thomson, James 1834-1882 .... **NCLC 18**
See also DAM POET; DLB 35; RGEL 2

Thoreau, Henry David 1817-1862 .. **NCLC 7, 21, 61, 138; PC 30; WLC**
See also AAYA 42; AMW; ANW; BYA 3; CDALB 1640-1865; DA; DA3; DAB; DAC; DAM MST; DLB 1, 183, 223, 270, 298; LAIT 2; LMFS 1; NCFS 3; RGAL 4; TUS

Thorndike, E. L.
See Thorndike, Edward L(ee)

Thorndike, Edward L(ee) 1874-1949 .... **TCLC 107**
See also CA 121

Thornton, Hall
See Silverberg, Robert

Thorpe, Adam 1956- .... **CLC 176**
See also CA 129; CANR 92; DLB 231

Thubron, Colin (Gerald Dryden) 1939- .... **CLC 163**
See also CA 25-28R; CANR 12, 29, 59, 95; CN 7; DLB 204, 231

Thucydides c. 455B.C.-c. 395B.C. . **CMLC 17**
See also AW 1; DLB 176; RGWL 2, 3

Thumboo, Edwin Nadason 1933- .... **PC 30**
See also CA 194

Thurber, James (Grover) 1894-1961 .. **CLC 5, 11, 25, 125; SSC 1, 47**
See also AAYA 56; AMWS 1; BPFB 3; BYA 5; CA 73-76; CANR 17, 39; CDALB 1929-1941; CWRI 5; DA; DA3; DAB; DAC; DAM DRAM, MST, NOV; DLB 4, 11, 22, 102; EWL 3; EXPS; FANT; LAIT 3; MAICYA 1, 2; MTCW 1, 2; RGAL 4; RGSF 2; SATA 13; SSFS 1, 10, 19; SUFW; TUS

Thurman, Wallace (Henry) 1902-1934 .... **BLC 3; HR 3; TCLC 6**
See also BW 1, 3; CA 104; 124; CANR 81; DAM MULT; DLB 51

Tibullus c. 54B.C.-c. 18B.C. .... **CMLC 36**
See also AW 2; DLB 211; RGWL 2, 3

Ticheburn, Cheviot
See Ainsworth, William Harrison

Tieck, (Johann) Ludwig 1773-1853 .... **NCLC 5, 46; SSC 31**
See also CDWLB 2; DLB 90; EW 5; IDTP; RGSF 2; RGWL 2, 3; SUFW

Tiger, Derry
See Ellison, Harlan (Jay)

Tilghman, Christopher 1946- .... **CLC 65**
See also CA 159; CANR 135; CSW; DLB 244

Tillich, Paul (Johannes) 1886-1965 .... **CLC 131**
See also CA 5-8R; 25-28R; CANR 33; MTCW 1, 2

Tillinghast, Richard (Williford) 1940- .... **CLC 29**
See also CA 29-32R; CAAS 23; CANR 26, 51, 96; CP 7; CSW

Timrod, Henry 1828-1867 .... **NCLC 25**
See also DLB 3, 248; RGAL 4

Tindall, Gillian (Elizabeth) 1938- ...... **CLC 7**
See also CA 21-24R; CANR 11, 65, 107; CN 7

Tiptree, James, Jr. .... **CLC 48, 50**
See Sheldon, Alice Hastings Bradley
See also DLB 8; SCFW 2; SFW 4

Tirone Smith, Mary-Ann 1944- .... **CLC 39**
See also CA 118; 136; CANR 113; SATA 143

Tirso de Molina 1580(?)-1648 .... **DC 13; HLCS 2; LC 73**
See also RGWL 2, 3

Titmarsh, Michael Angelo
See Thackeray, William Makepeace

Tocqueville, Alexis (Charles Henri Maurice Clerel Comte) de 1805-1859 .. **NCLC 7, 63**
See also EW 6; GFL 1789 to the Present; TWA

Toer, Pramoedya Ananta 1925- ...... **CLC 186**
See also CA 197; RGWL 3

Toffler, Alvin 1928- .... **CLC 168**
See also CA 13-16R; CANR 15, 46, 67; CPW; DAM POP; MTCW 1, 2

Toibin, Colm
See Toibin, Colm
See also DLB 271

Toibin, Colm 1955- .... **CLC 162**
See Toibin, Colm
See also CA 142; CANR 81

Tolkien, J(ohn) R(onald) R(euel) 1892-1973 .... **CLC 1, 2, 3, 8, 12, 38; TCLC 137; WLC**
See also AAYA 10; AITN 1; BPFB 3; BRWC 2; BRWS 2; CA 17-18; 45-48; CANR 36, 134; CAP 2; CDBLB 1914-1945; CLR 56; CPW 1; CWRI 5; DA; DA3; DAB; DAC; DAM MST, NOV, POP; DLB 15, 160, 255; EFS 2; EWL 3; FANT; JRDA; LAIT 1; LATS 1:2; LMFS 2; MAICYA 1, 2; MTCW 1, 2; NFS 8; RGEL 2; SATA 2, 32, 100; SATA-Obit 24; SFW 4; SUFW; TEA; WCH; WYA; YAW

Toller, Ernst 1893-1939 .... **TCLC 10**
See also CA 107; 186; DLB 124; EWL 3; RGWL 2, 3

Tolson, M. B.
See Tolson, Melvin B(eaunorus)

Tolson, Melvin B(eaunorus) 1898(?)-1966 .... **BLC 3; CLC 36, 105**
See also AFAW 1, 2; BW 1, 3; CA 124; 89-92; CANR 80; DAM MULT, POET; DLB 48, 76; RGAL 4

Tolstoi, Aleksei Nikolaevich
See Tolstoy, Alexey Nikolaevich

Tolstoi, Lev
See Tolstoy, Leo (Nikolaevich)
See also RGSF 2; RGWL 2, 3

Tolstoy, Aleksei Nikolaevich
See Tolstoy, Alexey Nikolaevich
See also DLB 272

Tolstoy, Alexey Nikolaevich 1882-1945 .... **TCLC 18**
See Tolstoy, Aleksei Nikolaevich
See also CA 107; 158; EWL 3; SFW 4

Tolstoy, Leo (Nikolaevich) 1828-1910 . **SSC 9, 30, 45, 54; TCLC 4, 11, 17, 28, 44, 79; WLC**
See Tolstoi, Lev
See also AAYA 56; CA 104; 123; DA; DA3; DAB; DAC; DAM MST, NOV; DLB 238; EFS 2; EW 7; EXPS; IDTP; LAIT 2; LATS 1:1; LMFS 1; NFS 10; SATA 26; SSFS 5; TWA

Tolstoy, Count Leo
   See Tolstoy, Leo (Nikolaevich)
Tomalin, Claire 1933- .... **CLC 166**
   See also CA 89-92; CANR 52, 88; DLB
   155
Tomasi di Lampedusa, Giuseppe 1896-1957
   See Lampedusa, Giuseppe (Tomasi) di
   See also CA 111; DLB 177; EWL 3
Tomlin, Lily .... **CLC 17**
   See Tomlin, Mary Jean
Tomlin, Mary Jean 1939(?)-
   See Tomlin, Lily
   See also CA 117
Tomline, F. Latour
   See Gilbert, W(illiam) S(chwenck)
Tomlinson, (Alfred) Charles 1927- .... **CLC 2,
   4, 6, 13, 45; PC 17**
   See also CA 5-8R; CANR 33; CP 7; DAM
   POET; DLB 40
Tomlinson, H(enry) M(ajor)
   1873-1958 .... **TCLC 71**
   See also CA 118; 161; DLB 36, 100, 195
Tonna, Charlotte Elizabeth
   1790-1846 .... **NCLC 135**
   See also DLB 163
Tonson, Jacob fl. 1655(?)-1736 .... **LC 86**
   See also DLB 170
Toole, John Kennedy 1937-1969 ..... **CLC 19,
   64**
   See also BPFB 3; CA 104; DLBY 1981;
   MTCW 2
Toomer, Eugene
   See Toomer, Jean
Toomer, Eugene Pinchback
   See Toomer, Jean
Toomer, Jean 1894-1967 .. **BLC 3; CLC 1, 4,
   13, 22; HR 3; PC 7; SSC 1, 45; WLCS**
   See also AFAW 1, 2; AMWS 3, 9; BW 1;
   CA 85-88; CDALB 1917-1929; DA3;
   DAM MULT; DLB 45, 51; EWL 3; EXPP;
   EXPS; LMFS 2; MTCW 1, 2; NFS 11;
   RGAL 4; RGSF 2; SSFS 5
Toomer, Nathan Jean
   See Toomer, Jean
Toomer, Nathan Pinchback
   See Toomer, Jean
Torley, Luke
   See Blish, James (Benjamin)
Tornimparte, Alessandra
   See Ginzburg, Natalia
Torre, Raoul della
   See Mencken, H(enry) L(ouis)
Torrence, Ridgely 1874-1950 .... **TCLC 97**
   See also CA 54, 249
Torrey, E(dwin) Fuller 1937- .... **CLC 34**
   See also CA 119; CANR 71
Torsvan, Ben Traven
   See Traven, B.
Torsvan, Benno Traven
   See Traven, B.
Torsvan, Berick Traven
   See Traven, B.
Torsvan, Berwick Traven
   See Traven, B.
Torsvan, Bruno Traven
   See Traven, B.
Torsvan, Traven
   See Traven, B.
Tourneur, Cyril 1575(?)-1626 .... **LC 66**
   See also BRW 2; DAM DRAM; DLB 58;
   RGEL 2
Tournier, Michel (Edouard) 1924- .... **CLC 6,
   23, 36, 95**
   See also CA 49-52; CANR 3, 36, 74; CWW
   2; DLB 83; EWL 3; GFL 1789 to the
   Present; MTCW 1, 2; SATA 23
Tournimparte, Alessandra
   See Ginzburg, Natalia

Towers, Ivar
   See Kornbluth, C(yril) M.
Towne, Robert (Burton) 1936(?)- ..... **CLC 87**
   See also CA 108; DLB 44; IDFW 3, 4
Townsend, Sue .... **CLC 61**
   See Townsend, Susan Lilian
   See also AAYA 28; CA 119; 127; CANR
   65, 107; CBD; CD 5; CPW; CWD; DAB;
   DAC; DAM MST; DLB 271; INT CA-
   127; SATA 55, 93; SATA-Brief 48; YAW
Townsend, Susan Lilian 1946-
   See Townsend, Sue
Townshend, Pete
   See Townshend, Peter (Dennis Blandford)
Townshend, Peter (Dennis Blandford)
   1945- .... **CLC 17, 42**
   See also CA 107
Tozzi, Federigo 1883-1920 .... **TCLC 31**
   See also CA 160; CANR 110; DLB 264;
   EWL 3
Tracy, Don(ald Fiske) 1905-1970(?)
   See Queen, Ellery
   See also CA 1-4R; 176; CANR 2
Trafford, F. G.
   See Riddell, Charlotte
Traherne, Thomas 1637(?)-1674 .... **LC 99**
   See also BRW 2; DLB 131; PAB; RGEL 2
Traill, Catharine Parr 1802-1899 .. **NCLC 31**
   See also DLB 99
Trakl, Georg 1887-1914 .... **PC 20; TCLC 5**
   See also CA 104; 165; EW 10; EWL 3;
   LMFS 2; MTCW 2; RGWL 2, 3
Tranquilli, Secondino
   See Silone, Ignazio
Transtroemer, Tomas Gosta
   See Transtromer, Tomas (Goesta)
Transtromer, Tomas (Goesta)
   See Transtromer, Tomas (Goesta)
   See also CWW 2
Transtromer, Tomas (Goesta)
   1931- .... **CLC 52, 65**
   See Transtromer, Tomas (Goesta)
   See also CA 117; 129; CAAS 17; CANR
   115; DAM POET; DLB 257; EWL 3; PFS
   21
Transtromer, Tomas Gosta
   See Transtromer, Tomas (Goesta)
Traven, B. 1882(?)-1969 .... **CLC 8, 11**
   See also CA 19-20; 25-28R; CAP 2; DLB
   9, 56; EWL 3; MTCW 1; RGAL 4
Trediakovsky, Vasilii Kirillovich
   1703-1769 .... **LC 68**
   See also DLB 150
Treitel, Jonathan 1959- .... **CLC 70**
   See also CA 210; DLB 267
Trelawny, Edward John
   1792-1881 .... **NCLC 85**
   See also DLB 110, 116, 144
Tremain, Rose 1943- .... **CLC 42**
   See also CA 97-100; CANR 44, 95; CN 7;
   DLB 14, 271; RGSF 2; RHW
Tremblay, Michel 1942- .... **CLC 29, 102**
   See also CA 116; 128; CCA 1; CWW 2;
   DAC; DAM MST; DLB 60; EWL 3; GLL
   1; MTCW 1, 2
Trevanian .... **CLC 29**
   See Whitaker, Rod(ney)
Trevor, Glen
   See Hilton, James
Trevor, William .. **CLC 7, 9, 14, 25, 71, 116;
   SSC 21, 58**
   See Cox, William Trevor
   See also BRWS 4; CBD; CD 5; CN 7; DLB
   14, 139; EWL 3; LATS 1:2; MTCW 2;
   RGEL 2; RGSF 2; SSFS 10
Trifonov, Iurii (Valentinovich)
   See Trifonov, Yuri (Valentinovich)
   See also DLB 302; RGWL 2, 3

Trifonov, Yuri (Valentinovich)
   1925-1981 .... **CLC 45**
   See Trifonov, Iurii (Valentinovich); Tri-
   fonov, Yury Valentinovich
   See also CA 126; 103; MTCW 1
Trifonov, Yury Valentinovich
   See Trifonov, Yuri (Valentinovich)
   See also EWL 3
Trilling, Diana (Rubin) 1905-1996 . **CLC 129**
   See also CA 5-8R; 154; CANR 10, 46; INT
   CANR-10; MTCW 1, 2
Trilling, Lionel 1905-1975 ..... **CLC 9, 11, 24;
   SSC 75**
   See also AMWS 3; CA 9-12R; 61-64;
   CANR 10, 105; DLB 28, 63; EWL 3; INT
   CANR-10; MTCW 1, 2; RGAL 4; TUS
Trimball, W. H.
   See Mencken, H(enry) L(ouis)
Tristan
   See Gomez de la Serna, Ramon
Tristram
   See Housman, A(lfred) E(dward)
Trogdon, William (Lewis) 1939-
   See Heat-Moon, William Least
   See also CA 115; 119; CANR 47, 89; CPW;
   INT CA-119
Trollope, Anthony 1815-1882 .... **NCLC 6, 33,
   101; SSC 28; WLC**
   See also BRW 5; CDBLB 1832-1890; DA;
   DA3; DAB; DAC; DAM MST, NOV;
   DLB 21, 57, 159; RGEL 2; RGSF 2;
   SATA 22
Trollope, Frances 1779-1863 .... **NCLC 30**
   See also DLB 21, 166
Trollope, Joanna 1943- .... **CLC 186**
   See also CA 101; CANR 58, 95; CPW;
   DLB 207; RHW
Trotsky, Leon 1879-1940 .... **TCLC 22**
   See also CA 118; 167
Trotter (Cockburn), Catharine
   1679-1749 .... **LC 8**
   See also DLB 84, 252
Trotter, Wilfred 1872-1939 .... **TCLC 97**
Trout, Kilgore
   See Farmer, Philip Jose
Trow, George W. S. 1943- .... **CLC 52**
   See also CA 126; CANR 91
Troyat, Henri 1911- .... **CLC 23**
   See also CA 45-48; CANR 2, 33, 67, 117;
   GFL 1789 to the Present; MTCW 1
Trudeau, G(arretson) B(eekman) 1948-
   See Trudeau, Garry B.
   See also AAYA 60; CA 81-84; CANR 31;
   SATA 35
Trudeau, Garry B. .... **CLC 12**
   See Trudeau, G(arretson) B(eekman)
   See also AAYA 10; AITN 2
Truffaut, Francois 1932-1984 ... **CLC 20, 101**
   See also CA 81-84; 113; CANR 34
Trumbo, Dalton 1905-1976 .... **CLC 19**
   See also CA 21-24R; 69-72; CANR 10;
   DLB 26; IDFW 3, 4; YAW
Trumbull, John 1750-1831 .... **NCLC 30**
   See also DLB 31; RGAL 4
Trundlett, Helen B.
   See Eliot, T(homas) S(tearns)
Truth, Sojourner 1797(?)-1883 ...... **NCLC 94**
   See also DLB 239; FW; LAIT 2
Tryon, Thomas 1926-1991 .... **CLC 3, 11**
   See also AITN 1; BPFB 3; CA 29-32R; 135;
   CANR 32, 77; CPW; DA3; DAM POP;
   HGG; MTCW 1
Tryon, Tom
   See Tryon, Thomas
Ts'ao Hsueh-ch'in 1715(?)-1763 .... **LC 1**
Tsushima, Shuji 1909-1948
   See Dazai Osamu
   See also CA 107

Weil, Simone (Adolphine)
1909-1943 .... **TCLC 23**
See also CA 117; 159; EW 12; EWL 3; FW;
GFL 1789 to the Present; MTCW 2

Weininger, Otto 1880-1903 .... **TCLC 84**

Weinstein, Nathan
See West, Nathanael

Weinstein, Nathan von Wallenstein
See West, Nathanael

Weir, Peter (Lindsay) 1944- .... **CLC 20**
See also CA 113; 123

Weiss, Peter (Ulrich) 1916-1982 .. **CLC 3, 15,
51; TCLC 152**
See also CA 45-48; 106; CANR 3; DAM
DRAM; DFS 3; DLB 69, 124; EWL 3;
RGWL 2, 3

Weiss, Theodore (Russell)
1916-2003 .... **CLC 3, 8, 14**
See also CA 9-12R, 189; 216; CAAE 189;
CAAS 2; CANR 46, 94; CP 7; DLB 5

Welch, (Maurice) Denton
1915-1948 .... **TCLC 22**
See also BRWS 8, 9; CA 121; 148; RGEL
2

Welch, James (Phillip) 1940-2003 ..... **CLC 6,
14, 52; NNAL; PC 62**
See also CA 85-88; 219; CANR 42, 66, 107;
CN 7; CP 7; CPW; DAM MULT, POP;
DLB 175, 256; LATS 1:1; RGAL 4;
TCWW 2

Weldon, Fay 1931- . **CLC 6, 9, 11, 19, 36, 59,
122**
See also BRWS 4; CA 21-24R; CANR 16,
46, 63, 97; CDBLB 1960 to Present; CN
7; CPW; DAM POP; DLB 14, 194; EWL
3; FW; HGG; INT CANR-16; MTCW 1,
2; RGEL 2; RGSF 2

Wellek, Rene 1903-1995 .... **CLC 28**
See also CA 5-8R; 150; CAAS 7; CANR 8;
DLB 63; EWL 3; INT CANR-8

Weller, Michael 1942- .... **CLC 10, 53**
See also CA 85-88; CAD; CD 5

Weller, Paul 1958- .... **CLC 26**

Wellershoff, Dieter 1925- .... **CLC 46**
See also CA 89-92; CANR 16, 37

Welles, (George) Orson 1915-1985 .. **CLC 20,
80**
See also AAYA 40; CA 93-96; 117

Wellman, John McDowell 1945-
See Wellman, Mac
See also CA 166; CD 5

Wellman, Mac .... **CLC 65**
See Wellman, John McDowell; Wellman,
John McDowell
See also CAD; RGAL 4

Wellman, Manly Wade 1903-1986 ... **CLC 49**
See also CA 1-4R; 118; CANR 6, 16, 44;
FANT; SATA 6; SATA-Obit 47; SFW 4;
SUFW

Wells, Carolyn 1869(?)-1942 .... **TCLC 35**
See also CA 113; 185; CMW 4; DLB 11

Wells, H(erbert) G(eorge) 1866-1946 . **SSC 6,
70; TCLC 6, 12, 19, 133; WLC**
See also AAYA 18; BPFB 3; BRW 6; CA
110; 121; CDBLB 1914-1945; CLR 64;
DA; DA3; DAB; DAC; DAM MST, NOV;
DLB 34, 70, 156, 178; EWL 3; EXPS;
HGG; LAIT 3; LMFS 2; MTCW 1, 2;
NFS 17, 20; RGEL 2; RGSF 2; SATA 20;
SCFW; SFW 4; SSFS 3; SUFW; TEA;
WCH; WLIT 4; YAW

Wells, Rosemary 1943- .... **CLC 12**
See also AAYA 13; BYA 7, 8; CA 85-88;
CANR 48, 120; CLR 16, 69; CWRI 5;
MAICYA 1, 2; SAAS 1; SATA 18, 69,
114; YAW

Wells-Barnett, Ida B(ell)
1862-1931 .... **TCLC 125**
See also CA 182; DLB 23, 221

Welsh, Irvine 1958- .... **CLC 144**
See also CA 173; DLB 271

Welty, Eudora (Alice) 1909-2001 .. **CLC 1, 2,
5, 14, 22, 33, 105; SSC 1, 27, 51; WLC**
See also AAYA 48; AMW; AMWR 1; BPFB
3; CA 9-12R; 199; CABS 1; CANR 32,
65, 128; CDALB 1941-1968; CN 7; CSW;
DA; DA3; DAB; DAC; DAM MST, NOV;
DLB 2, 102, 143; DLBD 12; DLBY 1987,
2001; EWL 3; EXPS; HGG; LAIT 3;
MAWW; MTCW 1, 2; NFS 13, 15; RGAL
4; RGSF 2; RHW; SSFS 2, 10; TUS

Wen I-to 1899-1946 .... **TCLC 28**
See also EWL 3

Wentworth, Robert
See Hamilton, Edmond

Werfel, Franz (Viktor) 1890-1945 ... **TCLC 8**
See also CA 104; 161; DLB 81, 124; EWL
3; RGWL 2, 3

Wergeland, Henrik Arnold
1808-1845 .... **NCLC 5**

Wersba, Barbara 1932- .... **CLC 30**
See also AAYA 2, 30; BYA 6, 12, 13; CA
29-32R, 182; CAAE 182; CANR 16, 38;
CLR 3, 78; DLB 52; JRDA; MAICYA 1,
2; SAAS 2; SATA 1, 58; SATA-Essay 103;
WYA; YAW

Wertmueller, Lina 1928- .... **CLC 16**
See also CA 97-100; CANR 39, 78

Wescott, Glenway 1901-1987 .. **CLC 13; SSC
35**
See also CA 13-16R; 121; CANR 23, 70;
DLB 4, 9, 102; RGAL 4

Wesker, Arnold 1932- .... **CLC 3, 5, 42**
See also CA 1-4R; CAAS 7; CANR 1, 33;
CBD; CD 5; CDBLB 1960 to Present;
DAB; DAM DRAM; DLB 13; EWL 3;
MTCW 1; RGEL 2; TEA

Wesley, John 1703-1791 .... **LC 88**
See also DLB 104

Wesley, Richard (Errol) 1945- .... **CLC 7**
See also BW 1; CA 57-60; CAD; CANR
27; CD 5; DLB 38

Wessel, Johan Herman 1742-1785 .... **LC 7**
See also DLB 300

West, Anthony (Panther)
1914-1987 .... **CLC 50**
See also CA 45-48; 124; CANR 3, 19; DLB
15

West, C. P.
See Wodehouse, P(elham) G(renville)

West, Cornel (Ronald) 1953- .... **BLCS; CLC
134**
See also CA 144; CANR 91; DLB 246

West, Delno C(loyde), Jr. 1936- .... **CLC 70**
See also CA 57-60

West, Dorothy 1907-1998 .. **HR 3; TCLC 108**
See also BW 2; CA 143; 169; DLB 76

West, (Mary) Jessamyn 1902-1984 ... **CLC 7,
17**
See also CA 9-12R; 112; CANR 27; DLB
6; DLBY 1984; MTCW 1, 2; RGAL 4;
RHW; SATA-Obit 37; TCWW 2; TUS;
YAW

West, Morris
See West, Morris L(anglo)
See also DLB 289

West, Morris L(anglo) 1916-1999 ..... **CLC 6,
33**
See West, Morris
See also BPFB 3; CA 5-8R; 187; CANR
24, 49, 64; CN 7; CPW; MTCW 1, 2

West, Nathanael 1903-1940 .. **SSC 16; TCLC
1, 14, 44**
See also AMW; AMWR 2; BPFB 3; CA
104; 125; CDALB 1929-1941; DA3; DLB
4, 9, 28; EWL 3; MTCW 1, 2; NFS 16;
RGAL 4; TUS

West, Owen
See Koontz, Dean R(ay)

West, Paul 1930- .... **CLC 7, 14, 96**
See also CA 13-16R; CAAS 7; CANR 22,
53, 76, 89; CN 7; DLB 14; INT CANR-
22; MTCW 2

West, Rebecca 1892-1983 ... **CLC 7, 9, 31, 50**
See also BPFB 3; BRWS 3; CA 5-8R; 109;
CANR 19; DLB 36; DLBY 1983; EWL
3; FW; MTCW 1, 2; NCFS 4; RGEL 2;
TEA

Westall, Robert (Atkinson)
1929-1993 .... **CLC 17**
See also AAYA 12; BYA 2, 6, 7, 8, 9, 15;
CA 69-72; 141; CANR 18, 68; CLR 13;
FANT; JRDA; MAICYA 1, 2; MAICYAS
1; SAAS 2; SATA 23, 69; SATA-Obit 75;
WYA; YAW

Westermarck, Edward 1862-1939 . **TCLC 87**

Westlake, Donald E(dwin) 1933- . **CLC 7, 33**
See also BPFB 3; CA 17-20R; CAAS 13;
CANR 16, 44, 65, 94; CMW 4; CPW;
DAM POP; INT CANR-16; MSW;
MTCW 2

Westmacott, Mary
See Christie, Agatha (Mary Clarissa)

Weston, Allen
See Norton, Andre

Wetcheek, J. L.
See Feuchtwanger, Lion

Wetering, Janwillem van de
See van de Wetering, Janwillem

Wetherald, Agnes Ethelwyn
1857-1940 .... **TCLC 81**
See also CA 202; DLB 99

Wetherell, Elizabeth
See Warner, Susan (Bogert)

Whale, James 1889-1957 .... **TCLC 63**

Whalen, Philip (Glenn) 1923-2002 .... **CLC 6,
29**
See also BG 3; CA 9-12R; 209; CANR 5,
39; CP 7; DLB 16; WP

Wharton, Edith (Newbold Jones)
1862-1937 ... **SSC 6, 84; TCLC 3, 9, 27,
53, 129, 149; WLC**
See also AAYA 25; AMW; AMWC 2;
AMWR 1; BPFB 3; CA 104; 132; CDALB
1865-1917; DA; DA3; DAB; DAC; DAM
MST, NOV; DLB 4, 9, 12, 78, 189; DLBD
13; EWL 3; EXPS; HGG; LAIT 2, 3;
LATS 1:1; MAWW; MTCW 1, 2; NFS 5,
11, 15, 20; RGAL 4; RGSF 2; RHW;
SSFS 6, 7; SUFW; TUS

Wharton, James
See Mencken, H(enry) L(ouis)

Wharton, William (a pseudonym) . **CLC 18,
37**
See also CA 93-96; DLBY 1980; INT CA-
93-96

Wheatley (Peters), Phillis
1753(?)-1784 ... **BLC 3; LC 3, 50; PC 3;
WLC**
See also AFAW 1, 2; CDALB 1640-1865;
DA; DA3; DAC; DAM MST, MULT,
POET; DLB 31, 50; EXPP; PFS 13;
RGAL 4

Wheelock, John Hall 1886-1978 .... **CLC 14**
See also CA 13-16R; 77-80; CANR 14;
DLB 45

Whim-Wham
See Curnow, (Thomas) Allen (Monro)

White, Babington
See Braddon, Mary Elizabeth

White, E(lwyn) B(rooks)
1899-1985 .... **CLC 10, 34, 39**
See also AITN 2; AMWS 1; CA 13-16R;
116; CANR 16, 37; CDALBS; CLR 1, 21;
CPW; DA3; DAM POP; DLB 11, 22;
EWL 3; FANT; MAICYA 1, 2; MTCW 1,
2; NCFS 5; RGAL 4; SATA 2, 29, 100;
SATA-Obit 44; TUS

Literary Criticism Series
Cumulative Topic Index

This index lists all topic entries in Gale's *Children's Literature Review* (CLR), *Classical and Medieval Literature Criticism* (CMLC), *Contemporary Literary Criticism* (CLC), *Drama Criticism* (DC), *Literature Criticism from 1400 to 1800* (LC), *Nineteenth-Century Literature Criticism* (NCLC), *Short Story Criticism* (SSC), and *Twentieth-Century Literary Criticism* (TCLC). The index also lists topic entries in the Gale Critical Companion Collection, which includes the following publications: *The Beat Generation* (BG), and *Harlem Renaissance* (HR).

SSC Cumulative Nationality Index

ALGERIAN

Camus, Albert **9**

AMERICAN

Abish, Walter **44**
Adams, Alice (Boyd) **24**
Aiken, Conrad (Potter) **9**
Alcott, Louisa May **27**
Algren, Nelson **33**
Anderson, Sherwood **1, 46**
Apple, Max (Isaac) **50**
Auchincloss, Louis (Stanton) **22**
Baldwin, James (Arthur) **10, 33**
Bambara, Toni Cade **35**
Banks, Russell **42**
Barnes, Djuna **3**
Barth, John (Simmons) **10**
Barthelme, Donald **2, 55**
Bass, Rick **60**
Beattie, Ann **11**
Bellow, Saul **14**
Benét, Stephen Vincent **10**
Berriault, Gina **30**
Betts, Doris (Waugh) **45**
Bierce, Ambrose (Gwinett) **9, 72**
Bowles, Paul (Frederick) **3**
Boyle, Kay **5**
Boyle, T(homas) Coraghessan **16**
Bradbury, Ray (Douglas) **29, 53**
Bradfield, Scott **65**
Bukowski, Charles **45**
Cable, George Washington **4**
Caldwell, Erskine (Preston) **19**
Calisher, Hortense **15**
Canin, Ethan **70**
Capote, Truman **2, 47**
Carver, Raymond **8, 51**
Cather, Willa (Sibert) **2, 50**
Chabon, Michael **59**
Chandler, Raymond (Thornton) **23**
Cheever, John **1, 38, 57**
Chesnutt, Charles W(addell) **7, 54**
Chopin, Kate **8, 68**
Cisneros, Sandra **32, 72**
Coover, Robert (Lowell) **15**
Cowan, Peter (Walkinshaw) **28**
Crane, Stephen (Townley) **7, 56, 70**
Davenport, Guy (Mattison Jr.) **16**
Davis, Rebecca (Blaine) Harding **38**
Dick, Philip K. **57**
Dixon, Stephen **16**
Dreiser, Theodore (Herman Albert) **30**
Dubus, André **15**
Dunbar, Paul Laurence **8**
Dybek, Stuart **55**
Elkin, Stanley L(awrence) **12**
Ellison, Harlan (Jay) **14**
Ellison, Ralph (Waldo) **26, 79**
Fante, John **65**
Farrell, James T(homas) **28**
Fisher, Rudolph **25**

Fitzgerald, F(rancis) Scott (Key) **6, 31, 75**
Ford, Richard **56**
Freeman, Mary E(leanor) Wilkins **1, 47**
Gaines, Ernest J. **68**
Gardner, John (Champlin) Jr. **7**
Garland, (Hannibal) Hamlin **18**
Garrett, George (Palmer) **30**
Gass, William H(oward) **12**
Gibson, William (Ford) **52**
Gilchrist, Ellen (Louise) **14, 63**
Gilman, Charlotte (Anna) Perkins (Stetson)
   13, 62
Glasgow, Ellen (Anderson Gholson) **34**
Glaspell, Susan **41**
Gordon, Caroline **15**
Gordon, Mary **59**
Grau, Shirley Ann **15**
Hammett, (Samuel) Dashiell **17**
Harris, Joel Chandler **19**
Harrison, James (Thomas) **19**
Harte, (Francis) Bret(t) **8, 59**
Hawthorne, Nathaniel **3, 29, 39**
Heinlein, Robert A(nson) **55**
Hemingway, Ernest (Miller) **1, 25, 36, 40, 63**
Henderson, Zenna (Chlarson) **29**
Henry, O. **5, 49**
Howells, William Dean **36**
Hughes, (James) Langston **6**
Hurston, Zora Neale **4, 80**
Huxley, Aldous (Leonard) **39**
Irving, Washington **2, 37**
Jackson, Shirley **9, 39**
James, Henry **8, 32, 47**
Jewett, (Theodora) Sarah Orne **6, 44**
Johnson, Denis **56**
Jones, Thom (Douglas) **56**
Kelly, Robert **50**
Kincaid, Jamaica **72**
King, Stephen (Edwin) **17, 55**
Lardner, Ring(gold) W(ilmer) **32**
Le Guin, Ursula K(roeber) **12, 69**
Ligotti, Thomas (Robert) **16**
Lish, Gordon (Jay) **18**
London, Jack **4, 49**
Lovecraft, H(oward) P(hillips) **3, 52**
Maclean, Norman (Fitzroy) **13**
Malamud, Bernard **15**
Marshall, Paule **3**
Mason, Bobbie Ann **4**
McCarthy, Mary (Therese) **24**
McCullers, (Lula) Carson (Smith) **9, 24**
Melville, Herman **1, 17, 46**
Michaels, Leonard **16**
Millhauser, Steven **57**
Mori, Toshio **83**
Murfree, Mary Noailles **22**
Nabokov, Vladimir (Vladimirovich) **11**
Nin, Anaïs **10**
Norris, (Benjamin) Frank(lin Jr.) **28**
Oates, Joyce Carol **6, 70**
O'Brien, Tim **74**
O'Connor, Frank **5**
O'Connor, (Mary) Flannery **1, 23, 61, 82**

O'Hara, John (Henry) **15**
Olsen, Tillie **11**
Ozick, Cynthia **15, 60**
Page, Thomas Nelson **23**
Paley, Grace **8**
Pancake, Breece D'J **61**
Parker, Dorothy (Rothschild) **2**
Perelman, S(idney) J(oseph) **32**
Phillips, Jayne Anne **16**
Poe, Edgar Allan **1, 22, 34, 35, 54**
Pohl, Frederik **25**
Porter, Katherine Anne **4, 31, 43**
Powers, J(ames) F(arl) **4**
Price, (Edward) Reynolds **22**
Pynchon, Thomas (Ruggles Jr.) **14, 84**
Roth, Philip (Milton) **26**
Salinger, J(erome) D(avid) **2, 28, 65**
Salter, James **58**
Saroyan, William **21**
Selby, Hubert Jr. **20**
Silko, Leslie (Marmon) **37, 66**
Singer, Isaac Bashevis **3, 53**
Spencer, Elizabeth **57**
Stafford, Jean **26**
Stegner, Wallace (Earle) **27**
Stein, Gertrude **42**
Steinbeck, John (Ernst) **11, 37, 77**
Stuart, Jesse (Hilton) **31**
Styron, William **25**
Suckow, Ruth **18**
Taylor, Peter (Hillsman) **10, 84**
Thomas, Audrey (Callahan) **20**
Thurber, James (Grover) **1, 47**
Toomer, Jean **1, 45**
Trilling, Lionel **75**
Twain, Mark (Clemens, Samuel) **6, 26, 34**
Updike, John (Hoyer) **13, 27**
Vinge, Joan (Carol) D(ennison) **24**
Vonnegut, Kurt Jr. **8**
Walker, Alice (Malsenior) **5**
Wallace, David Foster **68**
Warren, Robert Penn **4, 58**
Welty, Eudora **1, 27, 51**
Wescott, Glenway **35**
West, Nathanael **16**
Wharton, Edith (Newbold Jones) **6, 84**
Wideman, John Edgar **62**
Williams, William Carlos **31**
Williams, Tennessee **81**
Wodehouse, P(elham) G(renville) **2**
Wolfe, Thomas (Clayton) **33**
Wolff, Tobias **63**
Wright, Richard (Nathaniel) **2**
Yamamoto, Hisaye **34**

ARGENTINIAN

Bioy Casares, Adolfo **17**
Borges, Jorge Luis **4, 41**
Cortázar, Julio **7, 76**
Valenzuela, Luisa **14, 82**

SSC-85 Title Index